# Criminal Law and Procedure

# Criminal Law and Procedure

## EIGHTH EDITION

**JOHN M. SCHEB II, PH.D.**
*Professor of Political Science*
*University of Tennessee, Knoxville*

Australia • Brazil • Japan • Korea • Mexico • Singapore • Spain • United Kingdom • United States

*Criminal Law and Procedure,*
**Eighth Edition**
John M. Scheb II

Editor-in-Chief: Linda Ganster

Acquisitions Editor: Carolyn Henderson Meier

Assistant Editor: Rachel McDonald

Editorial Assistant: Casey Lozier

Associate Media Editor: Ting Jian Yap

Executive Brand Manager: Melissa Larmon

Market Development Manager: Michelle Williams

Manufacturing Planner: Judy Inouye

Rights Acquisition Specialist: Roberta Broyer

Art and Cover Direction, Production Services, Text Research, and Composition: PreMediaGlobal

Cover Images: Wooden judges gavel: © justasc/Shutterstock;
teen in handcuffs, young teen against wall with dirty hands and handcuffs: © Sascha Burkard/Shutterstock;
forensic analysis: © Alexandru-Radu Borzea/Shutterstock;
Forensic Science -place of shooting: © kilukilu/Shutterstock;
Day in Court: © Frances Twitty/iStockphoto;
Thumb Print: © Ana Abejon/iStockphoto

For product information and technology assistance, contact us at
**Cengage Learning Customer & Sales Support, 1-800-354-9706.**

For permission to use material from this text or product,
submit all requests online at **www.cengage.com/permissions.**
Further permissions questions can be e-mailed to
**permissionrequest@cengage.com.**

Library of Congress Control Number: 2012949691

Student Edition:
ISBN-13: 978-1-285-07011-7
ISBN-10: 1-285-07011-9

Loose-leaf Edition:
ISBN-13: 978-1-285-07023-0
ISBN-10: 1-285-07023-2

**Wadsworth**
20 Davis Drive
Belmont, CA 94002-3098
USA

Cengage Learning is a leading provider of customized learning solutions with office locations around the globe, including Singapore, the United Kingdom, Australia, Mexico, Brazil, and Japan. Locate your local office at **www.cengage.com/global.**

Cengage Learning products are represented in Canada by Nelson Education, Ltd.

To learn more about Wadsworth, visit **www.cengage.com/wadsworth**
Purchase any of our products at your local college store or at our preferred online store **www.cengagebrain.com.**

Printed in the United States of America
2 3 4 5 6 7 17 16 15 14 13

## DISCLAIMER

In this textbook, the author has attempted to present the general principles of substantive and procedural criminal law. However, because of the variance in statutes and court decisions from state to state, it is recommended that students and criminal justice professionals conduct their own research or consult with their legal advisors and not assume that principles of law discussed in the text are applicable in their jurisdictions or apply to specific situations.

## DEDICATION

This edition of *Criminal Law and Procedure* is dedicated to **Judge John M. Scheb**, the co-author of previous editions of this textbook, who passed away on November 17, 2010.

During his long and distinguished career, Judge Scheb served as a lawyer, a municipal judge, an appellate judge, a city attorney, a mediator, a law professor, and a reserve officer in the Judge Advocate General's Corps of the United States Air Force. He also was an exemplary husband and father. He is sorely missed by his family and many friends and colleagues.

# About the Author

**JOHN M. SCHEB II** was born in Sarasota, Florida in 1955. He attended the University of Florida from 1974 to 1982, receiving the B.A., M.A., and Ph.D. in political science. He is now Professor and Head of Political Science at the University of Tennessee, Knoxville, where he specializes in public law, courts, and the judicial process. Professor Scheb has authored numerous articles in professional journals and is coauthor of several other textbooks, including: *An Introduction to the American Legal System*, 3rd ed. (Wolters Kluwer 2013), *Law and the Administrative Process* (Thomson/Wadsworth 2005), and *American Constitutional Law*, 5th ed. (Wadsworth/Cengage 2012).

# Brief Contents

# Table of Contents

**PART THREE    Law Enforcement and Criminal Procedure   463**

# Preface

I am pleased to present the eighth edition of *Criminal Law and Procedure*. While students being exposed to this textbook for the first time will not know this, instructors who have used the book in the past know that previous editions were coauthored with my father, the late Judge John M. Scheb. While I am excited to offer a new edition of the book, doing so in the absence of my long-time coauthor is bittersweet.

Like the previous editions, the eighth edition provides a comprehensive introduction to substantive and procedural criminal law. It is designed primarily for students of criminal justice, legal studies, political science and paralegal studies. It is also an appropriate reference for the criminal justice professional who seeks a better understanding of the functioning of the criminal justice system in the United States.

Criminal law is among the most dynamic fields of American law. In preparing the eighth edition, I have endeavored to capture the most significant recent developments in the criminal law, including state and federal statutes, appellate court decisions, and trials. And yet I recognize that what students need to know most are the basic concepts of criminal law and procedure—concepts rooted in the English common law, the U.S. Constitution, and the fifty state constitutions. Thus I continue to emphasize the common-law background and constitutional foundations of criminal law and procedure.

## An Overview of the Text

In presenting the subject I have divided the text into three basic components. Part I furnishes an overview of the criminal law and the criminal justice system. Chapter 1 explains the origin and sources of the criminal law and introduces the reader to basic concepts, such as the legal definition of a crime, the statutory and judicial development of the criminal law, the distinction between substantive and procedural criminal law, constitutional limitations on the definitions of crimes, and the stages of the criminal process. Chapter 2 surveys the key agencies involved in the enactment and enforcement of the criminal law as well as the adjudication of criminal cases.

### Substantive Criminal Law

Part II surveys the substantive criminal law from its common-law sources to its modern statutory development. Chapter 3 provides an insight into the relevance of the U.S. Constitution and the fifty state constitutions to the enactment and enforcement of criminal prohibitions. Chapter 4 discusses elements of crimes and parties to crimes. Chapter 5 examines the inchoate offenses: attempt, solicitation, and conspiracy. Chapters 6 and 7, respectively, examine homicidal offenses and other crimes against persons. Chapter 8 surveys traditional property offenses, while Chapter 9 examines modern "white-collar" economic crimes. Some textbooks on criminal law designed for undergraduate students stop at this point, but this book goes on to examine crimes of vice, including drug and alcohol offenses (Chapter 10), offenses against public health and the environment (Chapter 11), crimes against public order, safety, and national security (Chapter 12), and offenses against justice and public administration (Chapter 13). The examination of the substantive criminal law concludes with a thorough treatment of criminal responsibility and defenses (Chapter 14).

## Law Enforcement and Criminal Procedure

Part III of the text examines law enforcement and criminal procedure and contains separate chapters on search and seizure (Chapter 15) and arrest, interrogation, and identification procedures (Chapter 16). The reader is then taken through the pretrial processes (Chapter 17), the criminal trial (Chapter 18), and sentencing and punishment (Chapter 19). The book concludes with an outline of the appeals process and postconviction relief (Chapter 20). Throughout Part III there are numerous examples of how procedures are regulated by federal and state statutes, court rules, and judicial decisions, as well as by the principles of the federal and state constitutions.

## What's New in the Eighth Edition?

In addition to thoroughly updating the book with respect to recent judicial decisions, statutes, and trials, I have attempted to streamline the text to make it more accessible to readers. I have also adopted four new pedagogical features: (1) each chapter now begins with a vignette designed to spark the reader's interest and provide a sense of what the chapter will cover; (2) throughout the book, shaded boxes labeled **Jurisprudence** provide summaries of important Supreme Court decisions pertaining to specific issues of criminal law and procedure; (3) key terms are now defined in marginal notes so that students do not have to turn to the end of the chapter or the glossary to find definitions; and (4) summaries placed at the end of each chapter are now keyed to the learning objectives that appear at the beginning of the chapter.

## Other Pedagogical Features

Other pedagogical features are included in the book to help students understand and retain the book's content:

- To enhance student comprehension, each chapter contains an **outline** delineating the major topics covered in the chapter.
- **Learning Objectives** highlight each chapter's key topics and themes.
- **Case-in-Point** boxes provide concise summaries of illustrative state court and lower federal court decisions.
- **Sidebars** highlight relevant information without disrupting the flow of the text.
- **Key terms** are identified in boldface type throughout each chapter and listed at the end of the chapter.

- A comprehensive **Glossary** includes definitions of all key terms.
- **Chapter Summaries** serve to reinforce key concepts.
- To test understanding and stimulate classroom dialogue, a set of **Questions for Thought and Discussion** is placed at the end of each chapter.
- Commencing with Chapter 3, hypothetical **Problems for Discussion and Solution** stimulate students' analytical skills.
- For students and instructors who wish to venture into the realm of **legal research**, Appendix A, "Access to the Law through Legal Research," includes guidance on researching law through the Internet and computerized services.

# Ancillaries

A number of supplements are provided by Wadsworth to help instructors use *Criminal Law and Procedure*, 8th edition, in their courses and to help students prepare for exams. These are available to qualified adopters. Please consult your local sales representative for details.

## For the Instructor

### Instructor's Manual with Test Bank

Revised by TBD of TBD, the manual includes learning objectives, key terms, a detailed chapter outline, a chapter summary, discussion topics, student activities, media tools and a newly expanded test bank. The learning objectives are correlated with the discussion topics, student activities, and media tools. Each chapter's test bank contains questions in multiple-choice, true/false, completion, essay formats, and critical thinking questions with a full answer key. The test bank is coded to the learning objectives that appear in the main text, and includes the page numbers in the main text where the answers can be found. Finally, each question in the test bank has been carefully reviewed by experienced criminal justice instructors for quality, accuracy, and content coverage. Our Instructor Approved seal, which appears on the front cover, is our assurance that you are working with an assessment and grading resource of the highest caliber.

The manual is available for download on the password-protected website and can also be obtained by e-mailing your local Cengage Learning representative.

### ExamView® Computerized Testing

The comprehensive Instructor's Manual is backed up by ExamView, a computerized test bank available for PC and Macintosh computers. With ExamView you can create, deliver, and customize tests and study guides (both print and online) in minutes. You can easily edit and import your own questions and graphics, change test layouts, and reorganize questions. And using ExamView's complete word-processing capabilities, you can enter an unlimited number of new questions or edit existing questions.

### Powerpoint Presentations

Helping you make your lectures more engaging while effectively reaching your visually oriented students, these handy Microsoft PowerPoint slides outline the chapters of the main text in a classroom-ready presentation. The PowerPoint slides were updated by TBD of TBD to reflect the content and organization of the new edition of the text and feature some additional examples and real world cases for application and discussion. Available for download on the password-protected instructor book companion website, the presentations can also be obtained by e-mailing your local Cengage Learning representative.

### Webtutor Toolbox™ on Blackboard® and WebCT®

A powerful combination: easy-to-use course management tools for whichever program you use—WebCT or Blackboard—and content from this text's rich companion as is, from the moment you log on—or, if you prefer, customize the program with web links, images, and other resources.

### The Wadsworth Criminal Justice Video Library

This engaging resource provides students with more than 300 ways to investigate current topics, career choices, and critical concepts.

## For the Student

### Companion Website

The book-specific website at www.cengage.com/criminaljustice/scheb offers students a variety of study tools and useful resources such as quizzing, Internet exercises, glossary, flashcards and more.

### CL eBook

CL eBook allows students to access Cengage Learning textbooks in an easy-to-use online format. Highlight, take notes, bookmark, search your text, and, in some titles, link directly into multimedia: CLeBook combines the best aspects of paper books and ebooks in one package.

### Careers in Criminal Justice Website

Featuring plenty of self-exploration and profiling activities, the interactive Careers in Criminal Justice Website helps students investigate and focus on the criminal justice career choices that are right for them. Includes interest assessment, video testimonials from career professionals, resume and interview tips, and links for reference.

### Course 360 Online Learning to the Next Degree

**Course 360** from Cengage Learning is a complete turnkey solution that teaches course outcomes through student interaction in a highly customizable online learning environment. **Course 360** blends relevant content with rich media and builds upon your course design, needs, and objectives. With a wide variety of media elements including audio, video, interactives, simulations, and more, **Course 360** is the way today's students learn.

## Acknowledgments

I wish to thank the team at Cengage—in particular, Carolyn Henderson Meier and Rachel McDonald, for their excellent assistance and constant support throughout this project. I also want to thank the reviewers of this and previous editions for their excellent guidance:

Richard Banahan, St. Louis Community College
Richard Barnhart, Dutchess Community College

John Boston, Austin Community College
Thomas Brennan, Lansing Community College
Stanley Brown, Webster University
Patrick Connolly, MiraCosta College
Christine Corken, Loras College
Jo-AnnDella Giustina, Bridgewater State University
Michael Ferrante, Keuka College
Paul Gormley, University of Massachusetts at Lowell
Thomas Gysegem, Kent State University
Ruth Harrison, Yavapai College
Dr. James Jengeleski, Argosy University Online
David Kirkland, Troy University, Dothan
Philip Lucas, The University of Findlay
Dyan McGuire, Saint Louis University
Nicholas Meier, Kalamazoo Valley Community College
Haley Slade, Delta Community College
Gary Todd, Virginia Intermont College
Jason Waller, Tyler Junior College

In preparing the 8th edition, I received particular assistance from Kristin Wagers, a recent graduate of the University of Tennessee College of Law, Hemant Sharma, a recent Ph.D. from and current lecturer in the University of Tennessee Political Science Department, and Sally Waters, a reference librarian at the Stetson University College of Law. Their assistance was invaluable. I must also acknowledge the many emails I have received over the years from students and instructors who have used previous editions of our book. Their questions, comments, and suggestions have been extremely useful. As always, I thank my wife, Sherilyn Claytor Scheb, for her steadfast support, without which the project could not have been completed.

I have endeavored to make the eighth edition of *Criminal Law and Procedure* the most complete, yet interesting, textbook in the field. I always welcome comments and suggestions from our readers. Of course, I assume responsibility for any errors contained herein.

**John M. Scheb II**
scheb@utk.edu
Knoxville, TN
December 1, 2012

# PART ONE

# Legal Foundations of Criminal Justice

# Fundamentals of Criminal Law and Procedure

## CHAPTER OUTLINE

## JURISPRUDENCE

*Brandenburg v. Ohio* (1969)

*Duncan v. Louisiana* (1968)

*Roper v. Simmons* (2005)

## LEARNING OBJECTIVES

After reading this chapter, you should be able to explain

1. the basic principles that underlie the American system of criminal justice

2. the essential elements of a crime and how crimes differ from other legal wrongs

3. the difference between substantive and procedural law

4. how American criminal law has developed from its medieval English origins

5. how various crimes protect different societal interests

6. the relevance of the U.S. Constitution, Bill of Rights, and the constitutions of the fifty states to the criminal justice system

7. the different roles of legislatures and courts of law in developing the criminal law and criminal procedure

8. how to read citations to statutes and cases and how to "brief" a case

9. basic procedural steps associated with criminal prosecutions

10. the variety of sanctions imposed on people convicted of crimes

## CHAPTER OPENING VIGNETTE

In what many in the media called the "trial of the century," former football and movie star O.J. Simpson was accused of murdering his ex-wife, Nicole Brown Simpson, and her companion, Ron Goldman. The trial began on January 24, 1995. The prosecution's case against Simpson appeared to be strong, but on October 3, 1995, the jury delivered a stunning verdict, declaring Simpson not guilty. A year later the families of the decedents initiated a civil suit against Simpson, alleging that he was liable for wrongful death. On February 4, 1997, a different jury in the civil trial found Simpson liable for the wrongful death of Nicole Brown Simpson and Ron Goldman and awarded the plaintiffs $8.5 million in damages.

The Simpson case illustrates dramatically how a defendant can be accused of a crime and a civil wrong based on the same alleged act. Many observers have wondered how the two cases could have come out differently. One answer is that they were independent legal actions resulting in separate trials before entirely different juries. Moreover, the standards of proof were different. In the criminal trial, the jury had to find Simpson guilty of murder beyond a reasonable doubt. In the civil case, the standard of proof was less demanding: the jury had only to find Simpson liable by a preponderance of the evidence. Why do we have these parallel systems of justice? How are crimes distinguished from civil wrongs? These are among the questions addressed in this chapter.

## Introduction

A fundamental problem facing every society is how to achieve social control—protecting people's lives and property and establishing socially desirable levels of order, harmony, safety, and decency. Societies have developed several informal means of achieving this control, including family structures, social norms, and religious precepts. In contrast, law is a formal means of social control. Law can be defined as *a body of rules prescribed and enforced by government for the regulation and protection of society*. Criminal law is *that branch of the law prohibiting certain forms of conduct and imposing penalties on those who engage in prohibited behavior*.

All modern societies have developed systems for administering criminal justice. What distinguishes democratic societies from authoritarian ones is a commitment to the **rule of law**. In democratic societies such as ours, a person cannot be convicted

**rule of law** The idea that law, not the discretion of officials, should govern public affairs.

*nullen crimen, nulla poena, sine lege* "There is no crime, there is no punishment, without law." Refers to the doctrine that one cannot be found guilty of a crime unless there is a violation of an existing provision of law defining the applicable criminal conduct.

**substantive criminal law** That branch of the criminal law that defines criminal offenses and defenses and specifies criminal punishments.

**procedural criminal law** The branch of the criminal law that deals with the processes by which crimes are investigated, prosecuted, and punished.

**constitutional supremacy** The doctrine that the Constitution is the supreme law of the land and that all actions and policies of government must be consistent with it.

**judicial review** The power of courts of law to review governmental acts and declare them null and void if they are found to be unconstitutional.

of a crime unless he or she has committed a specific offense against a law that provides for a penalty. This principle is expressed in the maxim ***nullen crimen, nulla poena, sine lege***, a Latin phrase meaning, "there is no crime, there is no punishment, without law." In the United States, formal law governs every aspect of criminal justice, from the enactment of criminal prohibitions to the imposition of punishment upon those who violate these prohibitions.

Our criminal law prescribes both substantive and procedural rules governing the everyday operation of the criminal justice system. **Substantive criminal law** prohibits certain forms of conduct by defining crimes and establishing the parameters of penalties. **Procedural criminal law** regulates the enforcement of the substantive law, the determination of guilt, and the punishment of those found guilty of crimes. For example, although substantive law makes the possession of heroin a crime, the procedural law regulates the police search and seizure that produce the incriminating evidence. The substantive law makes premeditated murder a crime and sets the penalty to be imposed for those convicted of the offense; the procedural law determines the procedures to be observed at trial and, if a conviction ensues, at sentencing.

Figure 1.1 provides an overview of the system of criminal law and procedure that exists in this country. The figure suggests three fundamental principles at work:

- **Constitutional supremacy.** In keeping with the ideal of the rule of law, the entire system of criminal law and procedure is subordinate to the principles and provisions of the U.S. Constitution. The Constitution sets forth the powers of government, the limits of those powers, and the rights of individuals. The Constitution thus limits government's power to make and enforce criminal sanctions in several important ways. These limitations are enforced by **judicial review**, which is the power of courts of law to

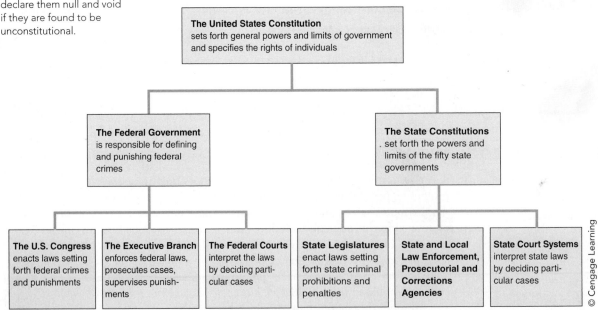

**FIGURE 1.1** Overview of the American system of criminal law and procedure.

invalidate substantive laws and procedures that are determined to be contrary to the Constitution.

- **Federalism.** There is a fundamental division of authority between the national government in Washington, D.C., and the fifty state governments. Although both levels of government have authority and responsibility in the realm of criminal justice, most of the day-to-day peacekeeping function is exercised by the states and their political subdivisions (primarily counties and cities). Each of the states has its own machinery of government as well as its own constitution that empowers and limits that government. Each state constitution imposes limits on the criminal justice system within that state. Of course, the provisions of the state constitutions, as well as the statutes adopted by the state legislatures, are subordinate to the provisions of the U.S. Constitution and the laws adopted by Congress.

- **Separation of powers.** The national government and each of the fifty state governments are constructed on the principle that legislative, executive, and judicial powers must be separated into independent branches of government. Thus, the federal government and the states have their own legislative branches, their own executive branches, and their own systems of courts. The legislative branch is responsible for enacting laws that specify crimes and punishments. The executive branch is responsible for enforcing those prohibitions and for carrying out the punishments imposed by the judicial branch, but it is the judicial branch that interprets the laws and ensures that persons charged with crimes receive fair treatment by the criminal justice system.

**federalism** The constitutional distribution of government power and responsibility between the national government and the states.

**separation of powers** Constitutional assignment of legislative, executive, and judicial powers to different branches of government.

# What Is a Crime?

**actus reus** A "wrongful act" which, combined with other necessary elements of crime, constitutes criminal liability.

Every crime involves a wrongful act (***actus reus***) specifically prohibited by the criminal law. For example, in the crime of battery, the *actus reus* is the striking or offensive touching of another person. Even the failure to take action can be considered a wrongful act if the law imposes a duty to take action in a certain situation. For example, a person who fails to file a federal income tax return may be guilty of a federal offense.

**mens rea** "Guilty mind"; criminal intent.

In most cases, the law requires that the wrongful act be accompanied by criminal intent (***mens rea***). Criminal intent does not refer to a person's motive or reason for acting, but merely refers to having formed a mental purpose to act. To convict a person of a crime, it is not necessary to know why that person committed the crime. It is only necessary to show that the individual intentionally committed a prohibited act. An unintentional act is usually not a crime, although, as we will discover, there are exceptions to this principle. Moreover, in certain instances, one may be held criminally responsible irrespective of intent. Crimes of this latter nature are classified as **strict liability offenses.** A good example of a strict liability offense is selling liquor to a minor. (Strict liability offenses and general elements of crimes are discussed in Chapter 4.)

**strict liability offenses** Crimes that do not require proof of the defendant's intent.

**felonies** Serious crimes for which a person may be imprisoned for more than one year.

## Felonies and Misdemeanors

**misdemeanors** Minor offenses, usually punishable by fine or imprisonment for less than one year.

Criminal law distinguishes between serious crimes, known as **felonies**, and less serious offenses, called **misdemeanors**. Generally speaking, felonies are offenses for which the offender can be imprisoned for more than one year; misdemeanors carry jail terms of less than one year. Common examples of felonies include murder, rape, robbery, burglary, aggravated assault, aggravated battery, and grand theft. Typical misdemeanors include petit theft, simple assault and battery, disorderly conduct, prostitution, and driving while intoxicated.

## Societal Interests Served by the Criminal Law

We can distinguish among types of crimes by the underlying societal interests that give rise to criminal prohibitions. Obviously, government has a duty to protect the lives and property of citizens—this is the essence of the social contract on which democratic government is based. Society also has an interest in protecting the public peace, order, and safety. Today, the protection of the national security from terrorism has become an important concern of the criminal law. Over the last several decades, the protection of the public health and the preservation of the natural environment have also come to be seen as interests that should be furthered by the criminal law. And, of course, society has an interest in efficient and honest public administration and, in particular, the administration of justice.

Table 1.1 lists the societal interests served by the criminal law and shows some particular crimes that relate to each interest. The table also indicates the chapters in this book that deal with the different types of crimes. Note that some of the crimes relate to more than one societal interest.

| TABLE 1.1 | An Overview of Types of Crimes and the Societal Interests Involved | |
|---|---|---|
| **Societal Interest Served** | **Examples of Crimes** | **Discussed in Chapter(s)** |
| Protection of Persons against Violence | Assault and Battery, Rape and Sexual Battery, Murder, Manslaughter, Spousal and Child Abuse, Kidnapping, Stalking | Chapter 6, Homicidal Offenses; Chapter 7, Other Offenses against Persons |
| Protection of Property and Economic Interests | Vandalism, Theft, Burglary, Arson, Robbery, Extortion, Forgery, Larceny, Embezzlement, Securities Fraud, Insider Trading, Mail Fraud | Chapter 8, Property Crimes; Chapter 9, White-Collar and Organized Crime |
| Maintenance of Standards of Decency | Prostitution, Obscenity, Bigamy, Indecent Exposure, Gambling, Alcohol and Drug Offenses | Chapter 10, Vice Crimes |
| Public Health and the Natural Environment | Fishing and Hunting Violations, Smoking Violations, Illegal Toxic Waste Disposal, Illegal Air Pollution | Chapter 11, Offenses against Public Health and the Environment |
| Public Peace, Order, and Safety | Disorderly Conduct, Incitement to Riot, Motor Vehicle Offenses, Loitering, Weapons Violations, Terrorism | Chapter 12, Offenses against Public Order, Safety, and Security |
| National Security | Treason, Espionage, Sabotage, Sedition, Terrorism | Chapter 12, Offenses against Public Order, Safety, and Security |
| Honest and Efficient Administration of Government and the Justice System | Resisting Arrest, Bribery, Perjury, Obstruction of Justice, Contempt, Escape | Chapter 13, Offenses against Justice and Public Administration |

© Cengage Learning

## Criminal Law, Morality, and Justice

Traditionally, the preservation of public morality has been regarded as an important function of the criminal law. Today this assumption is often questioned by those who believe that morality, like religion, is a personal matter. They argue that the state should be neutral in matters of morality, much as it is constitutionally required to be with respect to religion. Others, stressing the practical aspect of the problem, invoke the aphorism "you can't legislate morality." Over the last several decades, arguments over law and morality have focused on criminal prohibitions of consensual sexual conduct. Offenses such as adultery, fornication, and sodomy, which were inherited from the English common law, have become obsolete in modern America. In some cases, legislatures have abolished these offenses as they have modernized their criminal codes. In other instances, courts have declared unconstitutional the laws defining these crimes. See, e.g., *Lawrence v. Texas*, 539 U.S. 558, 123 S.Ct. 2472, 156 L.Ed.2d 508 (2003) (invalidating laws proscribing sodomy between consenting adults). However, students must realize that the moral basis of the law extends far beyond ancient prohibitions of sexual conduct. Many proscriptions of the criminal law, from animal cruelty to insider stock trading, are based on collective societal judgments about what is right and what is wrong.

In order to maintain its legitimacy, the criminal law must reflect the prevailing morality of the people. In a democratic society, laws that do not reflect broadly shared values will be challenged and eventually likely be changed. Of course, there is considerable inertia in the law, and someone has to lead the effort for change. Sometimes interest groups lead the way by lobbying elected officials and even filing lawsuits in the courts. In some instances, such as the civil rights movement of the 1950s and 1960s, grassroots social movements have resulted in profound changes in the law. In extreme situations, courageous people have resorted to **civil disobedience** in order to dramatize the injustice of a particular law. Such was the case when Dr. Martin Luther King, Jr. went to jail in Birmingham, Alabama rather than abide by racial segregation laws that he and many others deemed to be unjust. Today students read about the defunct Jim Crow laws in history books. It is hard to understand why such laws once were supported by political majorities in many states and communities. Ultimately, after many years of struggle, most Americans came to believe that the laws requiring racial segregation were unjust and needed to be done away with, a concept reflected in the Supreme Court's decision in *Brown v. Board of Education*, 347 U.S. 483, 74 S.Ct. 686, 98 L.Ed. 873 (1954). The idea that the law should not discriminate among people based on their race is a moral principle that has now become firmly established in our legal system. That is not to say that there is no racial discrimination in the criminal justice system. But the well-established principle of **equal protection of the laws** provides a moral and constitutional basis upon which to challenge any such discrimination.

**civil disobedience** Deliberate violation of a criminal law considered to be unjust or unconstitutional in order to dramatize one's objection to the law.

**equal protection of the laws** Constitutional principle enshrined in the Fourteenth Amendment by which law is supposed to apply equally to all persons without regard to race and other irrelevant characteristics.

## Crime: An Injury against Society

As suggested by the previous discussion of societal interests served by the criminal law, our legal system regards crimes not merely as wrongs against particular victims but as offenses against the entire society. Indeed, there does not have to be an individual victim in order for there to be a crime. For example, it is a crime to possess cocaine, even though it is unlikely that a particular individual will claim to have been victimized by another person's use of the drug. This is a crime because society, through its governing institutions, has made a collective judgment that cocaine use is inimical to the public welfare. Similarly, certain consensual sexual acts (e.g., incest) remain crimes in many jurisdictions because communities continue to regard such actions as contrary to public decency. Of course, as society evolves and its standards change, behaviors that were once defined as crimes (e.g., blasphemy) are no longer subject to criminal sanction. Over time, the particular prohibitions of the criminal law more or less reflect an evolving social consensus about both what is right and wrong and what is public and private. When a particular criminal prohibition (e.g., adultery) is no longer supported by societal consensus, it is apt to be unenforced or be stricken from the laws.

Because crime is an injury against society, the government, as society's legal representative, brings charges against persons accused of committing crimes. In the United States, we have a federal system—that is, a division of power and responsibility between the national and state governments. Both the national government and the states enact their own criminal laws. Thus, both the national government and the state governments may prosecute persons accused of crimes. The national government initiates a prosecution when a federal (national) law has been violated; a state brings charges against someone who is believed to have violated one of its laws.

## Criminal Responsibility

The criminal law—indeed, our entire legal system—rests on the idea that individuals are responsible for their actions and must be held accountable for them. This is the essential justification and rationale for imposing punishments on persons convicted of crimes. On the other hand, society recognizes that certain individuals (e.g., young children) lack the capacity to appreciate the wrongfulness of their conduct. Similarly, factors beyond individuals' control can lead them to commit criminal acts. In such instances the law exempts individuals from responsibility. Moreover, there are situations in which acts that would otherwise be crimes might be justified. The best example of this is committing a homicide in self-defense. Individuals can invoke a host of defenses beyond a simple denial of guilt. Indeed, a substantial body of law is devoted to the topic of criminal responsibility and defenses. We examine this topic in some detail in Chapter 14.

## The Role of the Crime Victim

**victim** A person who is the object of a crime or tort.

Because the government prosecutes criminals on behalf of society, the **victim** of a crime is not a party to the criminal prosecution. By filing a complaint with a law enforcement agency, a victim initiates the process that leads to prosecution, but once the prosecution begins, the victim's participation is primarily that of being a witness. Quite often, victims feel lost in the shuffle of the criminal process. They sometimes feel that the system is insensitive or even hostile to their interests in seeing justice done. Most states have taken steps to address victims' concerns, but despite these measures, crime victims remain secondary players in the criminal justice system. The principal parties in a criminal case are the prosecution (that is, the government) and the defendant (that is, the accused person). In some situations, however, the victim might have another remedy: a civil suit to recover damages for losses or injuries suffered.

## Criminal Law Distinguished from Civil Law

The criminal law is not the only body of law that regulates the conduct of persons. The civil law provides remedies for essentially private wrongs, offenses in which the state has a less direct interest. Most civil wrongs are classified as **torts** or **breaches of contract.** A breach of contract occurs when a party to a contract violates the terms of the agreement. A tort, on the other hand, is a wrongful act that does not violate any enforceable agreement but nevertheless violates a legal right of the injured party. Common examples of torts include wrongful death, intentional or negligent infliction of personal injury, wrongful destruction of property, trespass, and defamation of character. A crime normally entails intentional conduct; thus, a driver whose car accidentally hits and kills another person would not necessarily be guilty of a crime, depending on the circumstances (see discussions of manslaughter and vehicular homicide in Chapter 6). If the accident resulted from the driver's negligence, the driver would have committed the tort of wrongful death and would be subject to a civil suit for damages.

**torts** Noncriminal wrongs or injuries, other than breaches of contract, for which the remedy is a civil suit for damages.

**breaches of contract** Violations of provisions of legally enforceable agreements that give the damaged party the right to recourse in a court of law.

The criminal law and the civil law often overlap. Conduct that constitutes a crime can also involve a tort. For example, suppose Randy Wrecker intentionally damages a house belonging to Harvey Homeowner. Wrecker's act might well result in both criminal and civil actions being brought against him. Wrecker may be prosecuted by the state for the crime of willful destruction of property and may also be sued by Homeowner for the tort of wrongful destruction of property. The state would be seeking to punish Wrecker for his antisocial conduct, whereas Homeowner would be seeking compensation for the damage to his property. The criminal case would be designated *State v. Wrecker (or People v. Wrecker, or Commonwealth v. Wrecker*, depending on the state); the civil suit would be styled *Homeowner v. Wrecker.* A good real-world example is the O.J. Simpson case discussed at the outset of the chapter. Simpson was acquitted of murder after a criminal trial, yet he was found liable for wrongful death in a subsequent civil trial. Both the civil and criminal charges stemmed from the same alleged homicide.

# Origins and Sources of the Criminal Law

Many antisocial acts classified as crimes have their origin in the norms of primitive societies. Humanity has universally condemned certain types of behavior since ancient times. Acts such as murder, rape, robbery, and arson are considered ***mala in se***, or inherent wrongs. Many other acts that the modern law regards as criminal are merely ***mala prohibita***; they are offenses only because they are so defined by the law. Many so-called victimless crimes, such as gambling or possession of marijuana, are generally not regarded as offensive to universal principles of morality. Rather, they are wrong simply because the law declares them wrong. In the case of *mala prohibita* offenses, society has made a collective judgment that certain conduct, although not contrary to universal moral principles, is nevertheless incompatible with the public good.

*mala in se* "Evils in themselves." Refers to crimes such as murder, rape, arson, robbery, etc., which are universally condemned.

*mala prohibita* "Prohibited evils." Refers to crimes that are wrong primarily because the law declares them to be wrong.

## Development of Law in the Western World

The general consensus is that law developed in Western civilization as leaders began formalizing and enforcing customs that had evolved among their peoples. Eventually, informal norms and customs came to be formalized as codes of law. The Code of

Hammurabi regulated conduct in ancient Babylonia some two thousand years before Christ. In the seventh century B.C., Draco developed a strict code of laws for the Athenian city-states. Even today, one hears strict rules or penalties characterized as being "Draconian." These laws influenced the Romans in their development of the Twelve Tables in the fifth century B.C. And, of course, long before the time of Jesus, the Hebrews had developed elaborate substantive and procedural laws.

In the sixth century A.D., the Emperor Justinian presided over a codification of the Roman law that would prove to be very influential in the evolution of law on the European continent. The Napoleonic Code, promulgated under Napoleon Bonaparte in 1804 as a codification of all the civil and criminal laws of France, was based largely on the Code of Justinian and became a model for a uniform system of law for Western European nations. This is why the legal systems of Western Europe are often said to be "Roman law" systems. Roman law systems are based on the primacy of statutes enacted by the legislature. These statutes are integrated into a comprehensive code designed to be applied by the courts with a minimum of judicial interpretation.

## The English Common Law

**English common law** The body of decisional law based largely on custom as declared by English judges after the Norman Conquest of 1066.

American criminal law is derived largely from the **English common law**, which dates from the eleventh century. Before the Norman Conquest of 1066, English law was a patchwork of laws and customs applied by local courts. The new Norman kings appointed royal judges to settle disputes based on the customs of the people. By 1300, the decisions of the royal judges were being recorded to serve as precedents to guide judges in future similar cases. Eventually a common body of law emerged throughout the entire kingdom, hence the term *"common law."* As the centuries passed, coherent principles of law and definitions of crimes emerged from the judges' decisions. Thus, in contrast with Roman law systems, which are based on legal codes, the common law developed primarily through judicial decisions. The common-law doctrine of following precedent, known as ***stare decisis***, remains an important component of both the English and American legal systems today.

***stare decisis*** The doctrine of deciding cases based on precedent.

By 1600, the common-law judges had defined as felonies the crimes of murder, manslaughter, mayhem, robbery, burglary, arson, larceny, rape, suicide, and sodomy. They had also begun to define a number of lesser offenses as misdemeanors. In contrast with the criminal law that was developing on the continent, England developed trial by jury and trained barristers to argue cases on an adversarial basis. A barrister is a lawyer permitted to cross the "bar" in the courtroom that separates the bench from the spectators. Thus, in England, a barrister is a trial lawyer. Although we do not use the term "barrister" in the United States, we do refer to licensed attorneys as having been "admitted to the bar."

**statutes** Generally applicable laws enacted by a legislature.

As representative government emerged in England in the seventeenth century, the dominance of the common-law courts diminished. Parliament came to play a significant role in the formation of the criminal law by adopting **statutes** that revised and supplemented the common law. The adversarial system of justice continued, however, and most of the common-law felonies remain part of our criminal law today.

## Reception of the Common Law in America

Our criminal laws are rooted in the common law as it existed when America proclaimed its independence from England in 1776. After independence, the new

American states adopted the English common law to the extent that it did not conflict with the new state and federal constitutions. However, the federal government did not adopt the common law of crimes. From the outset, statutes passed by Congress defined federal crimes. Of the fifty states, Louisiana is the only one whose legal system is not based on the common law; rather, it is based primarily on the Napoleonic Code.

The new American judges and lawyers were greatly aided by Blackstone's *Commentaries on the Laws of England,* published in 1769, in which Sir William Blackstone, a professor at Oxford, codified the principles of the common law. Blackstone's seminal effort was a noble undertaking, but it demystified English law. Consequently, Blackstone's encyclopedic treatment of the law was less than popular among English barristers, who by this time had developed a close fraternity and took great pride in offering their services to "discover the law." In America, however, **Blackstone's Commentaries** became something of a "legal bible."

**Blackstone's *Commentaries*** A massive treatise on the English common law published in 1765–1769 by Sir William Blackstone, a professor at Oxford University.

## State and Local Authority to Enact Criminal Prohibitions

At the time of the American Revolution, the English common law constituted the criminal law of the new United States. As new states entered the Union, their legislatures usually enacted "reception statutes," adopting the common law to the extent that it did not conflict with the federal or their respective state constitutions. Eventually, most common-law definitions of crimes were superseded by legislatively defined offenses in the form of statutes adopted by the state legislatures. Today, the state legislatures are the principal actors in defining crimes and punishments. Persons who violate state criminal statutes are prosecuted in the state courts (see Chapter 2).

For the most part, modern state statutes retain the *mala in se* offenses defined by the common law, but many of the old common-law crime definitions have been modified to account for social and economic changes. For example, the offense of rape originated under English common law, but the offense is defined much differently under modern state statutes. Today, under most state laws, the offender and victim may be of either sex, and the offense encompasses anal and oral as well as vaginal penetrations by a sex organ or by another object. Indeed, the broader modern offense of sexual battery embraces all types of nonconsensual sexual impositions (see Chapter 7). As we shall see in subsequent chapters, modern criminal statutes often go far beyond the common law in prohibiting offenses that are *mala prohibita*. Drug and alcohol offenses, environmental crimes, offenses against public health, and traffic violations fall into this category.

When authorized by state constitutions or acts of state legislatures, cities and counties may adopt ordinances that define certain criminal violations. Local **ordinances** typically deal with traffic offenses, animal control, land use, building codes, licensing of businesses, and so forth. Usually these offenses are prosecuted in courts of limited jurisdiction, such as municipal or county courts (see Chapter 2).

**ordinances** Laws enacted by local governing bodies such as city councils and county commissions.

## Federal Authority to Define Crimes

As we have seen, the common law of crimes was more or less adopted by the various state legislatures. The U.S. Congress never adopted the common law, as there was no need for it to do so. The national government's responsibility in the criminal justice area has always been more limited than that of the states. Unlike the state

**police power** The power of government to legislate to protect public health, safety, welfare, and morality.

legislatures, Congress does not possess **police power**, which is the broad authority to enact prohibitions to protect public order, safety, decency, and welfare. Yet Congress does possess authority to enact criminal statutes that relate to Congress's particular legislative powers and responsibilities. Thus, there are federal criminal laws that relate to military service, immigration and naturalization, use of the mail, civil rights, and so forth. In particular, Congress has used its broad power to regulate interstate commerce to criminalize a wide range of offenses, including carjacking, loan sharking, kidnapping, illicit drug dealing, wire fraud, and a variety of environmental crimes (see Chapter 3). Of course, persons who commit federal crimes are subject to prosecution in the federal courts.

## The Model Penal Code

**Model Penal Code (MPC)** Published by the American Law Institute (ALI), the MPC consists of general provisions concerning criminal liability, sentences, defenses, and definitions of specific crimes.

The American Law Institute (ALI) is an organization of distinguished judges, lawyers, and academics that have a strong professional interest in drafting model codes of laws. In 1962, after a decade of work that produced several tentative drafts, the ALI published the **Model Penal Code** (MPC). A slightly revised version of the MPC with commentaries was issued in 1980. The MPC consists of general provisions concerning criminal liability, definitions of specific crimes, defenses, and sentences. The MPC is not law; rather, it is designed as a model code of criminal law for all states. It has had a significant impact on legislative drafting of criminal statutes, particularly during the 1970s, when the majority of the states accomplished substantial reforms in their criminal codes. In addition, the MPC has been influential in judicial interpretation of criminal statutes and doctrines, thereby making a contribution to the continuing development of the decisional law. In this text, we illustrate many principles of law by selected statutes from federal and state jurisdictions; however, in some instances where the MPC is particularly influential, the reader will find references to specific provisions of the MPC.

**rules of procedure** Rules promulgated by courts of law under constitutional or statutory authority governing procedures for trials and other judicial proceedings.

**treason** The crime of making war against one's own government or giving aid and comfort to its enemies.

## Sources of Procedural Law

**ex post facto laws** Retroactive laws that criminalize actions that were legal at the time they were performed or increase punishment for a criminal act after it was committed.

As we noted earlier, the criminal law has both substantive and procedural dimensions. The procedural criminal law is defined by legislative bodies through enactment of statutes and is promulgated by the courts through judicial decisions and the development of rules of court procedure. The U.S. Supreme Court prescribes **rules of procedure** for the federal courts. Generally, the highest court of each state, usually called the state supreme court, is empowered to promulgate rules of procedure for all the courts of that state.

# Constitutional Limitations

**bills of attainder** Legislative acts (prohibited by the U.S. Constitution) imposing punishment without trial upon persons deemed guilty of treason or felonies.

Substantive and procedural criminal laws are subject to limitations contained in the federal and state constitutions. For example, the U.S. Constitution defines the crime of **treason** in Article III, Section 3. In enacting the federal statute prohibiting treason against the United States, Congress must follow this constitutional definition. The Constitution (Article I, Sections 9 and 10) also prohibits Congress and the state legislatures from enacting *ex post facto* **laws** and **bills of attainder**. The prohibition of *ex post facto* laws means that an act cannot be made a crime retroactively. To be criminal, an act must be illegal at the time it was committed. A bill of attainder is a legislative act declaring someone guilty of a crime. The U.S. Constitution prohibits Congress and the state legislatures from doing this; only courts of law can convict people of criminal wrongdoing. (See Chapter 3 for more discussion of treason, *ex post facto* laws, and bills of attainder.)

## The Bill of Rights

**Bill of Rights**  A written enumeration of basic rights, usually part of a written constitution—for example, the first ten amendments to the U.S. Constitution.

Many of the most important constitutional provisions relative to criminal justice are found in the **Bill of Rights** (the first ten amendments to the Constitution, adopted by Congress in 1789 and ratified by the states in 1791). Among other things, the First Amendment to the U.S. Constitution prohibits government from using the civil or criminal law to abridge freedom of speech. The courts have said, for example, that people cannot be prosecuted merely for advocating violence; there must be "imminent lawless action" to justify a criminal sanction on public expression. *Brandenburg v. Ohio*, 395 U.S. 444, 89 S.Ct. 1827, 23 L.Ed.2d 430 (1969).

In addition to limitations on the enactment of criminal laws, the Bill of Rights has much to say about the enforcement of these laws. These provisions, which constitute much of the basis of criminal procedure, include the Fourth Amendment prohibition of unreasonable searches and seizures, the Fifth Amendment injunction against compulsory self-incrimination, and the Sixth Amendment right to trial by jury. Finally, the Eighth Amendment prohibition of "cruel and unusual punishments" protects citizens against criminal penalties that are barbaric or excessive.

Virtually all the provisions of the Bill of Rights have been held to apply with equal force to the states and to the national government. *Duncan v. Louisiana*, 391 U.S. 145, 88 S.Ct. 1444, 20 L.Ed.2d 491 (1968). Thus, the Bill of Rights limits the adoption of criminal laws, whether by Congress, the state legislatures, or the myriad city and county legislative bodies. The Bill of Rights also limits the actions of police, prosecutors, judges, and corrections officers at the local, state, and national levels.

State legislatures, courts, and law enforcement agencies must also be aware of the limitations contained in their own state constitutions. Although state constitutional provisions are subordinate to provisions of the federal constitution, state constitutions often go beyond the federal constitution in protecting citizens from governmental authorities. For example, in the area of search and seizure, a number of state courts have interpreted their respective state constitutions more stringently than the federal courts have interpreted the Fourth Amendment to the U.S. Constitution.

## JURISPRUDENCE

*Brandenburg v. Ohio*, 395 U.S. 444, 89 S.Ct. 1827, 23 L.Ed.2d 430 (1969).

Here the U.S. Supreme Court struck down a state statute prohibiting "criminal syndicalism," which was interpreted by the Ohio courts to mean the mere advocacy of violence to achieve political change. In reversing the conviction of a Ku Klux Klan leader who had conducted a televised rally characterized by threatening rhetoric, the Court held that "the constitutional guarantees of free speech and free press do not permit a State to forbid or proscribe advocacy of the use of force or of law violation except where such advocacy is directed to inciting or producing imminent lawless action and is likely to incite or produce such action." The Ohio statute purported to "punish mere advocacy and to forbid . . . assembly with others merely to advocate the described type of action." As such, it fell "within the condemnation of the First and Fourteenth Amendments."

## JURISPRUDENCE

*Duncan v. Louisiana*, 391 U.S. 145, 88 S.Ct. 1444, 20 L.Ed.2d 491 (1968).

Here the U.S. Supreme Court interpreted the Due Process Clause of the Fourteenth Amendment as incorporating the right to trial by jury recognized by the Sixth Amendment, thus making the right of trial by jury applicable to defendants in state criminal courts.

Gary Duncan was convicted of a misdemeanor (simple battery) and under Louisiana law at that time was not entitled to a jury trial. The Supreme Court reversed Duncan's conviction, holding that the right of trial by jury must apply to all serious offenses, including major misdemeanors.

# The Role of Courts in Developing the Criminal Law

**trial courts** Judicial tribunals, usually presided over by one judge, which conduct proceedings and trials in civil and criminal cases with or without a jury.

**appellate courts** Judicial tribunals that review decisions from lower tribunals.

Courts of law play a crucial role in the development of both the substantive and the procedural criminal law. **Trial courts** exist primarily to make factual determinations, apply settled law to established facts, and impose sanctions on those found guilty of criminal offenses. In so doing, trial courts are bound, as are all courts of law, by relevant constitutional provisions and principles. In reviewing the decisions of trial courts, **appellate courts** must interpret the federal and state constitutions and statutes. The federal and state constitutions are replete with majestic phrases, such as "equal protection of the laws" and "privileges and immunities," that require interpretation. That is, courts must define exactly what these grand phrases mean within the context of particular legal disputes. Likewise, federal and state statutes often use vague language like "affecting commerce" or "reasonable likelihood." Courts must assign meaning to these and a multitude of other terms. Although most states have abolished all, or nearly all, common-law crimes and replaced them with statutorily defined offenses, the common law remains a valuable source of statutory interpretation. This is because legislatures frequently use terms known to the common law without defining such terms. For example, in proscribing burglary, the legislature might use the term "curtilage" without defining it. In such an instance, a court would look to the common law, which defined the term to mean "an enclosed space surrounding a dwelling."

**lawmaking function** One of the principal functions of an appellate court; often referred to as the law development function.

**error correction function** The function of appellate courts in reviewing routine appeals and correcting the errors of trial courts.

**decisional law** Law declared by appellate courts in their written decisions and opinions.

In rendering interpretations of the law, appellate courts generally follow precedent, in keeping with the common-law doctrine of *stare decisis*. In our rapidly changing society, however, courts often encounter situations to which precedent arguably does not or should not apply. In such situations, courts will sometimes deviate from or even overturn precedent. Moreover, there are situations in which there is no applicable precedent. When this occurs, the appellate courts will have the opportunity to "make new law." Thus, appellate courts perform an important **lawmaking function** as well as an **error correction function**. Therefore, any serious student of criminal law must follow developments in the **decisional law**—that is, law as developed by courts in deciding cases.

## Legal Reasoning in Judicial Decisions

The English common-law judges originally arrived at decisions by applying community norms—the common customs of the English people. They then judged subsequent cases by analogizing issues to their previous decisions. In the United States we have written federal and state constitutions, but the process of reasoning by analogy continues, albeit on a more sophisticated basis. Students are prone to look upon these basic instruments of legal policy as a body of established rules that are applied by judges to determined facts. But the framers of our federal and state constitutions painted with a broad brush, leaving the courts to mold such concepts as "due process of law" to a dynamic society. Moreover, legislative rules are usually drafted with particular situations in mind and frequently are unclear when applied to situations the lawmakers did not contemplate or could not have contemplated. Legal reasoning develops rules to resolve ambiguities based on the presumed intent of the legislators, where necessary, "to fill in gaps," always subject to constitutional mandates. Thus, the use of analogy becomes an indispensable tool as lawyers and judges look for similarities to previously adjudicated cases. Finally, although reasoning by analogy preserves the experience of the past, increasingly it also requires a consideration of contemporary social, cultural, and economic norms when considering the importance given to the facts that resulted in decisions in analogous cases.

## References to Statutes and Judicial Decisions

Throughout this text the reader will find references to federal and state statutes and decisions of federal and state courts. Appendix A, "Access to the Law through Legal Research," explains how to find the law in statutes, court decisions, and other publications. But at this point we simply mention that statutes enacted by Congress are usually cited to the *United States Code Annotated* (U.S.C.A.), published by the West Group, while state criminal codes are cited to books published by state or commercial publishers. For example, a citation to 18 U.S.C.A. § 2101(a) defines "riot"; a citation to Ariz. Rev. Stat. § 13-2002 refers to a section of the Arizona Criminal Code that defines forgery. Court decisions cited in the text are almost always decisions of federal or state appellate courts. For example, *Brandenburg v. Ohio* indicates the name of the defendant petitioning for review and the state that prosecuted the defendant. Data under the name of the case indicates the name of the court and date of its decision, followed by numbers indicating the volume and page number of the Reporter, a compendium of judicial decisions, where the decision is found. To illustrate, in *Brandenburg v. Ohio*, the decision was made in 1969 by the U.S. Supreme Court and is found at 95 U.S. 444, 89 S.Ct. 1827, 23 L.Ed.2d 430 (1969). The U.S. citation refers to the volume and page number of an official set of reports; the remainder of the citation refers to commercial publications, the Supreme Court Reporter (S.Ct.) and Lawyers Edition (L.Ed.2d). *Whitner v. State*, 482 S.E.2d 777 (S.C. 1997) illustrates a state court decision—in this instance a 1997 decision of the Supreme Court of South Carolina—found in volume 482, page 777 of the second series of Reporters for the region encompassing South Carolina.

## The Criminal Process

**due process of law** Procedural and substantive rights of citizens against government actions that threaten the denial of life, liberty, or property.

By far the broadest and most important constitutional principle relating to criminal justice is found in the Due Process Clauses of the Fifth and Fourteenth Amendments to the Constitution. The same principle can be found in similar provisions of every state constitution. Reflecting a legacy that can be traced to the Magna Carta (1215), such provisions forbid the government from taking a person's life, liberty, or property, whether as punishment for a crime or any other reason, without **due process of law**.

## "BRIEFING CASES"

As noted earlier in the chapter, edited cases relevant to this book have been placed on a companion website. Reading these decisions can be useful to anyone seeking to understand the criminal law, and instructors may also ask their students to "brief" some or all of these cases. A case brief is simply a summary of a court decision, usually in outline format. Typically, a case brief contains the following elements:

- The name of the case and the date of the decision
- The essential facts of the case
- The key issue(s) of law involved (or those applicable to a point of law being considered)
- The holding of the court
- A brief summary of the court's opinion, especially as it relates to key issue(s) in the case
- Summaries of concurring and dissenting opinions, if any
- A statement commenting on the significance of the decision

Here is a sample case brief:

### Brandenburg v. Ohio
**U.S. SUPREME COURT**
*95 U.S. 444, 89 S.Ct. 1827, 23 L.Ed.2d 430 (1969)*

**FACTS:** Brandenburg, a member of the Ku Klux Klan, was convicted under Ohio law of "advocate[ing] . . . the duty, necessity, or propriety of crime, sabotage, violence, or unlawful methods of terrorism as a means of accomplishing industrial or political reform" and for "voluntarily assembling with any society, group, or assemblage of persons formed to teach or advocate the doctrines of criminal syndicalism." He was fined $1,000 and sentenced to 1–10 years in prison. His appeal was dismissed by the Ohio Supreme Court, and the U.S. Supreme Court granted review.

**ISSUE:** Does the First Amendment to the U.S. Constitution permit a state to criminalize the mere advocacy of violence?

**DECISION:** Conviction overturned; Ohio statute declared unconstitutional.

**OPINIONS:** Speaking through a *per curiam* opinion, the Court unanimously held that "the constitutional guarantees of free speech and free press do not permit a State to forbid or proscribe advocacy of the use of force or of law violation except where such advocacy is directed to inciting or producing imminent lawless action and is likely to incite or produce such action." Justices Black and Douglas wrote concurring opinions.

**COMMENT:** The Court narrowed the long-standing "clear and present danger" test to limit it to instances of expression involving "imminent lawless action." While recognizing that the protections of the First Amendment are not absolute, the Supreme Court in this decision afforded broad constitutional protection to speech, even that which is hateful, bigoted, or regarded by many in the community as dangerous.

*© Cengage Learning*

---

**fair notice** The requirement, stemming from due process, that government provide adequate notice to a person before it deprives that person of life, liberty, or property.

**fair hearing** A hearing in which both parties have a reasonable opportunity to be heard—to present evidence and make arguments to an impartial decision maker.

Due process refers to those procedural safeguards necessary to ensure the fundamental fairness of a legal proceeding. Daniel Webster defined due process to mean "a law which hears before it condemns, which proceeds on inquiry and renders judgment only after trial."

Most fundamentally, due process requires **fair notice** and a **fair hearing**. That is, persons accused of crimes must have ample opportunity to learn of the charges and evidence being brought against them as well as the opportunity to contest those charges and that evidence in open court.

One of the most basic tenets of due process in criminal cases is the **presumption of innocence.** Unless the defendant pleads guilty, the prosecution must establish the defendant's guilt by evidence produced in court. Everyone accused of a nonpetty offense has the right to a trial by jury (although, we shall see, trials are actually conducted in only a small minority of cases). In a criminal trial, the standard of proof is "beyond a reasonable doubt." The **reasonable doubt standard** differs

**presumption of innocence** In a criminal prosecution, a person accused of a crime is presumed innocent until proven guilty beyond a reasonable doubt.

**reasonable doubt standard** The standard of proof used by a judge or jury to determine whether criminal charges against a defendant have been proven. The term "beyond a reasonable doubt" is often defined as "moral certainty."

**indictment** A formal document handed down by a grand jury accusing one or more persons of the commission of a crime or crimes.

**grand jury** A group of citizens convened either to conduct an investigation or to determine whether there is sufficient evidence to warrant the prosecution of an accused.

**information** A document filed by a prosecutor under oath charging one or more persons with commission of a crime.

**arraignment** An appearance before a court of law for the purpose of pleading to a criminal charge.

**criminal trial** A trial in a court of law to determine the guilt or innocence of a person charged with a crime.

**rules of procedure** Rules promulgated by courts of law under constitutional or statutory authority governing procedures for trials and other judicial proceedings.

**rules of evidence** Legal rules governing the admissibility of evidence at trial.

**plea bargaining** Negotiations between a defendant and a prosecutor whereby the defendant agrees to plead guilty in exchange for some concession (such as a reduction in the number of charges brought).

markedly from the "preponderance of evidence" standard that applies to civil cases. In a civil trial, the judge or jury must find only that the weight of the evidence favors the plaintiff or the defendant. In a criminal case, the fact finder must achieve the "moral certainty" that arises from eliminating "reasonable doubt" as to the defendant's guilt. Of course, it is difficult to define with precision the term "reasonable." Ultimately, this is a judgment call left to the individual judge or juror.

## Basic Procedural Steps

Certain basic procedural steps are common to all criminal prosecutions, although specific procedures vary greatly among jurisdictions. (Figure 1.2 illustrates the major components of the criminal process.) In every jurisdiction law enforcement agencies make arrests, interrogate persons in custody, and conduct searches and seizures. All of these functions are regulated by the procedural law. In every jurisdiction there are procedures through which persons accused of crimes are formally notified of the charges against them and given an opportunity to answer these charges in court. There is a formal charging process which, depending on the jurisdiction, involves an **indictment** by a **grand jury** or an **information** filed by a prosecutor. In every jurisdiction there is a procedure known as an **arraignment**, in which the defendant enters a plea of guilty or not guilty, or in some instances a plea of *nolo contendere* (no contest). Only a plea of not guilty necessitates a **criminal trial.** The trial is the crown jewel of criminal procedure—an elaborate, highly formal process, governed by **rules of procedure** and **rules of evidence,** for determining guilt or innocence and imposing punishment on those found guilty.

The decisions of trial courts, with respect to pretrial matters as well as the conduct of criminal trials, are subject to review by appellate courts. All court procedures, from the initial appearance of an accused before a magistrate to the decision of an appellate court upholding a criminal conviction and/or sentence, are governed by an elaborate framework of laws, rules, and judicial decisions.

## The Sieve Effect

As cases move through the criminal justice system from arrest through adjudication and, in many instances, toward the imposition of punishment, there is considerable attrition. Of any one hundred felony arrests, perhaps as few as twenty-five will result in convictions. This "sieve effect" occurs for many reasons, including insufficient evidence, police misconduct, procedural errors, and the transfer of young offenders to juvenile courts.

Nationwide, less than 5 percent of criminal cases go to trial. Some cases are dropped by the prosecutor for lack of evidence or because of obvious police misconduct. Others are dismissed by judges at preliminary hearings, usually for similar reasons. In those cases that are not dismissed, defendants usually enter pleas of guilty, very frequently in exchange for concessions from the prosecution. To avoid trial, which is characterized by both delay and uncertainty, the prosecutor may attempt to persuade the defendant to plead guilty, either by reducing the number or severity of charges or by promising not to seek the maximum penalty allowed by law.

The U.S. Supreme Court has upheld the practice of **plea bargaining** against claims that it violates the Due Process Clauses of the Fifth and Fourteenth Amendments. *Brady v. United States*, 397 U.S. 742, 90 S.Ct. 1463, 25 L.Ed.2d 747 (1970);

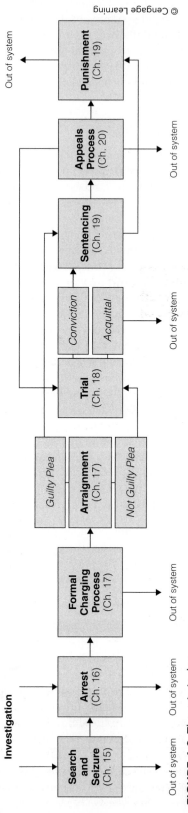

**FIGURE 1.2** The criminal process.

*North Carolina v. Alford*, 400 U.S. 25, 91 S.Ct. 160, 27 L.Ed.2d 162 (1970). However, because there is always a danger of coerced guilty pleas, especially when defendants are ignorant of the law, it is the judge's responsibility to ascertain whether the defendant's guilty plea is voluntarily and knowingly entered and that there is some factual basis for the offense charged. *Boykin v. Alabama*, 395 U.S. 238, 89 S.Ct. 1709, 23 L.Ed.2d 274 (1969).

## Criminal Sanctions

**death penalty** Capital punishment; a sentence to death for the commission of a crime.

**incarceration** Another term for imprisonment.

**monetary fines** Sums of money that offenders are required to pay as punishment for the commission of crimes.

**probation** Conditional release of a convicted criminal in lieu of incarceration.

**restitution** The act of compensating someone for losses suffered.

**pretrial diversion** A program in which a first-time offender is afforded the opportunity to avoid criminal prosecution by participating in some specified treatment, counseling, or community service.

**treatment programs** Programs designed to rehabilitate offenders. The term is most commonly used in connection with alcohol or drug abuse rehabilitation.

Courts have at their disposal a variety of sanctions to impose on persons convicted of crimes. During the colonial period of American history, and indeed well into the nineteenth century, the **death penalty** was often inflicted for a variety of felonies, including rape, arson, and horse theft. Today, the death penalty is reserved for only the most aggravated forms of murder and is infrequently carried out. **Incarceration** is the conventional mode of punishment prescribed for persons convicted of felonies, while **monetary fines** are by far the most common punishment for those convicted of misdemeanors. For first-time offenders, especially those convicted of nonviolent crimes, **probation** is a common alternative to incarceration, although probation usually entails a number of restrictions on the offender's freedom.

All criminal sanctions must comport with the Eighth Amendment's prohibition of "cruel and unusual punishments." The Supreme Court has said repeatedly that the Cruel and Unusual Punishments Clause must be interpreted in light of evolving standards of decency in the society. *Trop v. Dulles*, 356 U.S. 86, 78 S.Ct. 590, 2 L.Ed.2d 630 (1958). Thus, in *Roper v. Simmons*, 543 U.S. 551, 125 S.Ct. 1183, 161 L.Ed.2d 1 (2005), the Supreme Court held that the Eighth Amendment prohibits the execution of anyone who was under eighteen at the time of their offense.

As society becomes more cognizant of the rights of crime victims, courts are increasingly likely to require that persons convicted of crimes pay sums of money to their victims by way of **restitution**. Requiring offenders to make restitution and perform community service are common conditions of release on probation. Community service is often imposed as a condition as part of a **pretrial diversion** program in which first-time nonviolent offenders are offered the opportunity to avoid prosecution by completing a program of counseling or service. Increasingly, courts are requiring drug offenders to undergo **treatment programs** as conditions of probation.

## JURISPRUDENCE

*Roper v. Simmons*, 543 U.S. 551, 125 S.Ct. 1183, 161 L.Ed.2d 1 (2005)

Here the Supreme Court struck down capital punishment for juvenile offenders. The case involved Christopher Simmons, who was seventeen when he kidnapped and murdered a woman after burglarizing her home. Writing for the Court, Justice Anthony Kennedy noted the decreasing frequency with which juvenile offenders were being sentenced to death as evidence of an emerging national consensus against capital punishment for juveniles. Thus, the execution of juvenile offenders, even for the most atrocious crimes, was deemed to be cruel and unusual punishment in violation of the Eighth Amendment.

## Conclusion

The American system of criminal justice is deeply rooted in the English common law, but the specifics of criminal law and procedure have evolved substantially from their medieval English origins. Today, American criminal law is largely codified in statutes adopted by Congress and the state legislatures, as interpreted by the courts in specific cases.

One of the more tragic aspects of the crime problem is that many Americans are losing faith in the ability of their government to protect them from criminals. Indeed, in some areas of the country, victims are unlikely even to report crimes to the police. Some victims are unwilling to endure the ordeal of being a witness. Others simply believe that the perpetrator will not be apprehended or, if so, will not be punished. It also must be recognized that in many of the nation's inner cities, many people do not trust the police. Moreover, in certain communities cooperation with the police can be dangerous, as criminal gangs will often retaliate against those who cooperate with the authorities.

Our state and federal governments are severely constrained by both law and economic reality in their efforts to fight crime. Not only is the specter of "a cop on every corner" distasteful to most Americans, but it is also impossible to achieve, given the fiscal constraints on government. Local governments in particular often find it very difficult to provide adequate support to their law enforcement agencies.

Even though the nation's prison system is filled beyond capacity, the public is demanding that more convicted criminals be incarcerated and for longer periods of time. Yet the public appears unwilling to provide the revenues needed to build the additional prisons necessary to house these inmates. Increasingly courts are turning to alternatives to incarceration, especially for first-time and nonviolent offenders.

Finally, society must confront the problem of the constitutional limitations on crime definition and law enforcement. Judges do have considerable discretion in interpreting the state and federal constitutions. But if these documents are to be viable protections of our cherished liberties, we must accept that they place significant constraints on our efforts to control crime. For instance, to what degree is the public willing to allow erosion of the constitutional protection against unreasonable searches and seizures? To what degree are we willing to sacrifice our constitutionally protected privacy and liberty to aid the ferreting out of crime? Today the question is amplified by the threat of terrorism and the belief of many that government needs greater powers to address the terrorist threat. These are the fundamental questions of criminal law and procedure in a society that prides itself on preserving the rights of the individual.

## Chapter Summary

- Learning Objective 1

  - The American system of criminal justice is based on three fundamental constitutional principles: constitutional supremacy, which means that the U.S. Constitution is the supreme law of the land; federalism, the division of authority between the national government and the states; and separation of powers, the division of government into separate legislative, executive, and judicial branches.

- Learning Objective 2

  - Elements of crimes include a wrongful act (*actus reus*) and criminal intent (*mens rea*), yet certain offenses are strict liability crimes that do not require criminal intent.
  - More serious crimes are classified as felonies; less serious offenses are termed misdemeanors, This is somewhat related to the distinction between conduct that is *mala in se*, i.e., evil in itself, and *mala prohibita*, wrong only because it is prohibited by the law.
  - Crimes are punished by the state, whereas civil disputes such as torts and breaches of contract often are formally resolved in litigation between the disputants.

- Learning Objective 3

  - Substantive criminal law prohibits certain forms of conduct by defining crimes and establishing the parameters of penalties. Procedural criminal law regulates the enforcement of the substantive law, the determination of guilt, and the punishment of those found guilty of crimes.

- Learning Objective 4

  - We inherited our legal system from the common law of England, where judges, in 1066, began to record their decisions and adjudicate controversies based on rules developed in analogous situations. This led to development of the doctrine of *stare decisis*, largely followed by American courts.
  - As English Parliaments began defining crimes, a new America instituted legislative bodies that defined criminal conduct largely based on the English common law.
  - In the late 18th century Professor William Blackstone attempted to demystify the law in his famous treatise, Commentaries on the Laws of England.
  - Today the Model Penal Code (MPC) promulgated by the American Law Institute advocates uniformity in crime definitions. The MPC is not law, but a guide for courts and legislatures.

- Learning Objective 5

  - The criminal law serves a number of important societal interests. Obviously, government has a duty to protect the lives and property of citizens. Society also has an interest in protecting the public peace, order, and safety.
  - Today, the protection of the national security from terrorism has become an important concern of the criminal law.
  - Over the last several decades, the protection of the public health and the preservation of the natural environment have also come to be seen as interests that should be furthered by the criminal law.
  - Finally, society has an interest in efficient and honest public administration and the administration of justice.

- Learning Objective 6

  - The federal and state constitutions impose substantive and procedural limits on the criminal justice system.
  - Congress and the state legislatures are not free to enact any and all criminal prohibitions; they must respect constitutional limits on their powers and the constitutional rights of individuals.
  - Law enforcement agencies and courts must respect the procedural rules that flow from the basic constitutional principle of due process of law.

- Learning Objective 7

  - Legislatures enact criminal prohibitions in the form of statutes. Courts interpret these statutes on a case-by-case basis and thus play an important role in developing the criminal law.
  - Rules of criminal procedure are developed primarily by the courts in furtherance of due process and the various constitutional protections of persons suspected or accused of crimes.

- Learning Objective 8

  - Statutes enacted by Congress are usually cited to the *United States Code Annotated* (U.S.C.A.), while state criminal codes are cited to books published by state or commercial publishers.
  - Court decisions cited in the text are almost always decisions of federal or state appellate courts. Data under the name of the case indicates the name of the court and date of its decision, followed by numbers indicating the volume and page number of the Reporter, a compendium of judicial decisions, where the decision is found.
  - A case brief is simply a summary of a court decision, usually in outline format. Typically, a brief includes a summary of the facts and procedural history of the case, a statement of issue before the court, a statement of the court's decision, and summaries of any opinions produced by the court.

- Learning Objective 9

  - Before a person can be adjudicated guilty of a crime, the authorities prosecuting a defendant must follow strict guidelines set forth in the federal and state constitutions and the substantive and procedural law. There is a certain "sieve effect" in the criminal justice system as cases proceed from arrest through pretrial procedures, trial, and sentencing. Cases that do not merit prosecution are strained out. Others are dismissed after courts exclude key evidence. Negotiated guilty pleas remove the need for many criminal trials.

- Learning Objective 10

  - Criminal sanctions include the death penalty, incarceration, monetary fines, and probation. Requiring offenders to make restitution and perform community service are common conditions of release on probation.
  - Increasingly, courts are requiring drug offenders to undergo treatment programs as conditions of probation.
  - All criminal penalties are subject to the Eighth Amendment's prohibition against "cruel and unusual punishments."

## Key Terms

*actus reus*

appellate courts

arraignment

Bill of Rights

bills of attainder

Blackstone's *Commentaries*

breaches of contract

civil disobedience

constitutional supremacy

criminal trial

death penalty

decisional law

due process of law

English common law

equal protection of the laws

error correction function

*ex post facto* laws

fair hearing

fair notice

federalism

felonies

grand jury

incarceration

indictment

information

judicial review

lawmaking function

*mala in se*

*mala prohibita*

*mens rea*

misdemeanors

Model Penal Code (MPC)

monetary fines

*nullen crimen, nulla poena, sine lege*

ordinances

plea bargaining

police power

presumption of
    innocence

pretrial diversion

probation

procedural criminal law

reasonable doubt standard

restitution

rule of law

rules of evidence

rules of procedure

rules of procedure

separation of powers

*stare decisis*

statutes

strict liability offenses

substantive criminal law

torts

treason

treatment programs

trial courts

victim

## Questions for Thought and Discussion

1. Should morality, in and of itself, be considered a sufficient basis for defining particular conduct as criminal?
2. What are the chief distinctions between the civil law and the criminal law? Why do criminal and civil law sometimes overlap?
3. To what extent is the English common law significant in contemporary American criminal law?
4. What is the essential difference between substantive criminal law and procedural criminal law? Give examples of each.
5. What means of punishment for criminal offenses exist in your state? Is capital punishment available for persons convicted of first-degree murder? Which punishments, if any, do you think are most effective in controlling crime?
6. Was the Supreme Court right to prohibit the execution of juvenile offenders, regardless of the heinousness of their crimes?

# CHAPTER **2**

# Organization of the Criminal Justice System

## CHAPTER OUTLINE

## JURISPRUDENCE

*Gideon v. Wainwright* (1963)

*Hurtado v. California* (1884)

*Williams v. Florida* (1970)

*Solorio v. United States* (1987)

*Hamdan v. Rumsfeld* (2006)

*In re Gault* (1967)

## LEARNING OBJECTIVES

After reading this chapter, you should be able to explain

1. why federalism is such an important concept in understanding the American system of criminal justice

2. the different roles played by legislatures, courts, and law enforcement agencies at the federal, state, and local levels of government

3. the differences and similarities between Congress and the state legislatures with respect to their legislative powers

4. how modern American policing has evolved from its medieval English origins

5. the roles of prosecutor and defense counsel

6. how grand juries differ from trial juries

7. how the federal and state judicial systems are structured

8. how military tribunals differ from civilian criminal courts

9. how the juvenile justice system differs from the criminal justice system for adults

10. how the system of corrections is structured and how criminal punishment has evolved

# CHAPTER OPENING VIGNETTE

One of the basic organizing principles of the American system of criminal justice is *federalism*—the constitutional division of power and responsibility between the national government and the fifty states. Our federal system sometimes produces uncertainty and even conflict over what powers reside exclusively in the federal government, what powers are reserved to the states, and what powers may be exercised concurrently. The issue of illegal immigration provides a good example. Frustrated at what it perceived to be an inadequate effort by the federal government to control illegal immigration across the nation's southern border, the state of Arizona enacted a law allowing the state to enforce the federal law prohibiting unauthorized entry into the country. Senate Bill 1070 made it a crime to be in the state of Arizona illegally, banned undocumented immigrants from working in the state, and authorized warrantless arrest of persons believed to have committed deportable offenses. It also required state and local law enforcement agents who have made a lawful stop, detention, or arrest to verify a person's immigration status if they have "reasonable suspicion" that the person is in the United States illegally.

SB 1070 set off a firestorm of criticism from immigrants' rights and civil rights groups, who expressed fear that the law would lead to racial profiling. President Barack Obama called the Arizona law "ill-conceived" and said that it was an affront to civil rights to require people to produce proof of citizenship or lawful status based only on the suspicion of a police officer.

In July 2010 the U.S. Department of Justice filed suit in federal court against the state of Arizona, claiming that S.B. 1070 was a usurpation of federal authority. The complaint in *United States v. Arizona* asserted that "the federal government has preeminent authority to regulate immigration matters" and that "a state may not establish its own immigration policy or enforce state laws in a manner that interferes with the federal immigration laws." Several weeks later a federal district judge issued an injunction against enforcement of key provisions of the law and, later, that injunction was upheld by a federal appeals court.

In *Arizona v. United States*, 567 U.S. __, 132 S.Ct. 2492, 183 L.Ed.2d 351 (2012), the Supreme Court struck down the provisions of the Arizona law making illegal entry into the country a state offense, banning undocumented immigrants from working in the state, and allowing warrantless arrests of those suspected of deportable offenses. Noting that the U.S. Constitution grants authority over immigration solely to the federal government, the Court held that these provisions were preempted by federal law. However, the Court refused to strike down the most controversial provision of the bill, namely the one requiring police to verify immigration status if they have reasonable suspicion that someone is an illegal immigrant. The Court remanded this issue to the federal district court for a hearing on the constitutionality of the measure. The Court thus postponed to a later day a decision on the most controversial element of the Arizona law.

# Introduction

**federalism** The constitutional distribution of government power and responsibility between the national government and the states.

In every modern country, criminal justice is a complex process involving a plethora of agencies and officials. In the United States, criminal justice is particularly complex, largely because of **federalism,** the constitutional division of authority between the national and state governments. Under our federal scheme the national government operates one criminal justice system to enforce federal criminal laws; additionally, each state has a justice system to apply its own criminal laws. As a result of this structural complexity, it is difficult to provide a coherent overview of criminal justice in America. Each system is to some extent different in both substantive and procedural law.

**legislature** An elected lawmaking body such as the Congress of the United States or a state assembly.

**U.S. Congress** The national legislature of the United States, consisting of the Senate and the House of Representatives.

Despite the differences that exist between federal and state criminal justice systems, there are certain similarities. Like the federal system, all fifty states have legislative bodies, law enforcement agencies, prosecutors, defense attorneys, courts of law, and corrections agencies (see Table 2.1). All follow certain general procedures beginning with arrest and, in some cases, ending in punishment. Finally, all systems are subject to the limitations of the U.S. Constitution, as interpreted by the courts. In this chapter we present an overview of the roles played by the institutions that make up the criminal justice system in the United States.

# Legislatures

**statutes** Generally applicable laws enacted by legislatures.

The governmental institution with primary responsibility for enacting laws is the **legislature.** Because the United States is organized on the principle of federalism, there are fifty-one legislatures in this country—the **U.S. Congress** and the fifty state legislatures. Each of these bodies has the power to enact **statutes** that apply within its respective jurisdiction. The U.S. Congress adopts statutes that apply throughout the United States and its territories, whereas the Illinois General Assembly, for example, adopts laws that apply only within the state of Illinois. For the most part, federal and state statutes complement one another. When there is a conflict, the federal statute prevails.

| TABLE 2.1 | Criminal Justice Agencies and Their Functions |
|---|---|
| **Type of Agency** | **Functions** |
| Legislatures | Enacting Criminal Prohibitions |
| Law Enforcement Agencies | Enforcing Criminal Prohibitions<br>Maintaining Public Order and Security<br>Conducting Investigations of Crimes<br>Performing Searches and Seizures<br>Making Arrests of Persons Suspected of Crimes<br>Interrogating Suspects |
| Prosecutorial Agencies | Enforcing Criminal Prohibitions<br>Conducting Investigations<br>Gathering Evidence<br>Initiating Criminal Prosecutions<br>Representing the Government in Court |
| Public Defenders | Representing Indigent Persons Accused of Crimes |
| Grand Juries | Reviewing Evidence Obtained by Prosecutors<br>Indicting Persons Accused of Crimes<br>Granting Immunity to Witnesses |
| Courts of Law | Issuing Search Warrants<br>Issuing Arrest Warrants<br>Conducting Summary Trials in Minor Cases<br>Conducting Initial Appearances<br>Conducting Preliminary Hearings<br>Conducting Arraignments<br>Holding Hearings on Pretrial Motions<br>Conducting Trials<br>Sentencing Persons Convicted of Crimes<br>Conducting Posttrial Hearings<br>Hearing Appeals from Lower Court Rulings |
| Corrections Agencies | Incarceration of Persons Convicted of Crimes<br>Supervision of Persons on Probation or Parole<br>Carrying out Executions of Persons Sentenced to Death |

© Cengage Learning

## Legislative Powers of Congress

**enumerated powers** Powers explicitly granted to a government by its constitutions.

**implied powers** Powers not expressly granted to government by a constitution but fairly implied by the document.

Congress's legislative authority may be divided into two broad categories: **enumerated powers** and **implied powers.** Enumerated powers are those that are mentioned specifically in Article I, Section 8 of the Constitution, such as the power to tax and the power to borrow money on the credit of the United States. Among the constitutionally enumerated powers of Congress, there are only two direct references to criminal justice. Congress is explicitly authorized to "provide for the Punishment of counterfeiting the Securities and current Coin of the United States" and to "define and punish Piracies and Felonies committed on the high Seas, and Offenses against the Law of Nations." Of course, Congress's power to define federal crimes is much more extensive than these two clauses suggest.

The enumerated power to "regulate commerce among the states" has provided Congress with a vast reservoir of legislative power. Many of the criminal statutes enacted by Congress in recent decades have been justified on the basis of the Commerce Clause of Article I, Section 8 (see Chapter 3).

Congress's implied powers are those that are deemed to be "necessary and proper for carrying into Execution the foregoing Powers, and all other Powers vested . . . in the Government of the United States, or in any Department or Officer thereof." As long as Congress's policy goal is permissible, any legislative means that are "plainly adapted" to that goal are likewise permissible. *McCulloch v. Maryland,* 17 U.S. (4 Wheat.) 316, 4 L.Ed. 579 (1819). Under the doctrine of implied powers, scarcely any area exists over which Congress is absolutely barred from legislating, because most social and economic problems have a conceivable relationship to the broad powers and objectives contained in the Constitution.

As the nation expanded and evolved, Congress became more active in passing social and economic legislation. In the twentieth century, and especially the last several decades, Congress established a host of federal crimes. There is now an elaborate body of federal criminal law. Of course, Congress may not enact laws that violate constitutional limitations such as those found in the Bill of Rights (see Chapter 3).

### Publication of Federal Statutes

Federal statutes are published in *United States Statutes at Large,* an annual publication dating from 1789 in which federal statutes are arranged in order of their adoption. Statutes are not arranged by subject matter, nor is there any indication of how they affect existing laws. Because the body of federal statutes is quite voluminous, and because new statutes often repeal or amend their predecessors, it is essential that new statutes be merged into legal codes that systematically arrange the statutes by subject. To find federal law as it currently stands, arranged by subject matter, one must consult the latest edition of the *Official Code of the Laws of the United States,* generally known as the **U.S. Code.** The U.S. Code is broken down into fifty subjects, called "titles." Title 18, "Crimes and Criminal Procedure," contains many of the federal crimes established by Congress.

The most popular compilation of the federal law, used by lawyers, judges, and criminal justice professionals, is the **United States Code Annotated (U.S.C.A.).** Published by West Group, the U.S.C.A. contains the entire current U.S. Code, but each section of statutory law in U.S.C.A. is followed by a series of annotations consisting of court decisions interpreting the particular statute along with historical notes, cross-references, and other editorial features (for more discussion, see Appendix A).

**U.S. Code** The comprehensive and systematic collection of federal laws currently in effect.

**United States Code Annotated (U.S.C.A.)** An annotated version of the United States Code. The annotations include references to court decisions and other legal authorities.

## State Legislatures

Each state must have a democratically elected legislature because that is the most fundamental element of a "republican form of government" required by Article IV, Section 4 of the U.S. Constitution. State legislatures for the most part resemble the U.S. Congress. Each is composed of representatives chosen by the citizens of their respective states. All of them are bicameral (i.e., two-house) institutions, with the exception of Nebraska, which has a unicameral legislature. In adopting statutes, they all follow the same basic procedures. When state legislatures adopt statutes, they are published in volumes known as **session laws.** Then statutes are integrated into state codes. Lawyers make frequent use of annotated versions of state codes. These are available at law school libraries, and often at local law libraries, to those who wish to see how state statutes have been interpreted and applied by the state courts.

As we noted in Chapter 1, after the American Revolution, states adopted the English common law as their own state law to the extent that it did not conflict with their new state constitutions. (Congress, on the other hand, never did.) Eventually,

**session laws** Collection of laws enacted during a particular legislative session.

however, state legislatures codified much of the common law by enacting statutes, which in turn have been developed into comprehensive state codes. Periodically, states revise portions of their codes to make sure they remain relevant to a constantly changing society. For example, in 1989 the Tennessee General Assembly undertook a modernization of its criminal code. Old offenses that were no longer being enforced were repealed, other offenses were redefined, and sentencing laws were completely overhauled.

## Statutory Interpretation

Statutes are necessarily written in general language, so legislation often requires judicial interpretation. Because legislative bodies have enacted vast numbers of laws defining offenses that are *mala prohibita,* such interpretation assumes an importance largely unknown to the English common law. Courts have responded by developing certain techniques to apply when a statute appears unclear as related to a specific factual scenario. These techniques are generally referred to as **rules of statutory interpretation** and over the years have given rise to reference to legislative history and various maxims that courts apply in attempting to determine the legislature's intention in enacting a statute.

Courts recognize that it is the legislative bodies and not the courts that exercise the power to define crimes and penalties. It follows that the most frequent maxim applied by courts in determining legislative intention is the **plain meaning rule.** As the U.S. Supreme Court observed early in the twentieth century, "Where the language [of a statutory law] is plain and admits of no more than one meaning the duty of interpretation does not arise. . . ." *Caminetti v. United States,* 242 U.S. 470, 37 S.Ct. 192, 61 L.Ed. 442 (1917). The Court's dictum seems self-evident, yet even learned judges often disagree as to whether the language of a given statute is plain. This gives rise to certain **canons of construction** applied by courts to determine the **legislative intent** behind a statutory definition of a crime.

A primary canon of construction is that criminal statutes must be strictly construed. The rule originated at common law, when death was the penalty for committing a felony, but the rule has remained. However, it is now based on the rationale that every criminal statute should be sufficiently precise to give fair warning of its meaning. Today we see the rule applied most frequently in a constitutional context when courts determine a criminal statute to be **void for vagueness.** We address this aspect in more detail in the following chapter. Another canon of construction provides for an **implied exception** to a statute. For example, courts have ruled that there is an implied exception to a law imposing speed limits on the highway in instances where police or other emergency vehicles violate the literal text of the law. Would a court apply a statute that makes it an offense for any person to sleep in a bus terminal and thereby find a ticketed passenger guilty who fell asleep while waiting for a bus that was overdue? The implied exception doctrine seems to reflect a commonsense approach to determining the meaning of a statute.

Often a statute uses a term that has a definite meaning at common law. In general, courts interpret such terms according to their common-law meaning. Recall that in Chapter 1 we observed that in defining the crime of burglary a legislature might use the term "curtilage" without defining it. In such an instance, we noted that a court would ordinarily look to the common law, which defined the term to mean "an enclosed space surrounding a dwelling."

**rules of statutory interpretation** Rules developed by courts to determine the meaning of legislative acts.

**plain meaning rule** The judicial doctrine holding that if the meaning of a text is plain, a court may not interpret it but must simply apply it as written.

**canons of construction** Rules governing the judicial interpretation of constitutions, statutes, and other written instruments.

**legislative intent** The purpose the legislature sought to achieve in enacting a particular provision of law.

**void for vagueness** Doctrine of constitutional law holding unconstitutional (as a violation of due process) legislation that fails to clearly inform the person of what is required or proscribed.

**implied exception** An exclusion that can reasonably be inferred or assumed based on the purpose and intent of an ordinance, statute, or contract.

But this rule does not always apply when dealing with modern statutes, particularly at the federal level, where there is generally considerable legislative history in the form of committee reports and floor debates recorded in the *Congressional Record* that can aid in determining the true intent of a statute. Thus, in *Perrin v. United States,* 444 U.S. 37, 100 S.Ct. 311, 62 L.Ed.2d 199 (1979), the Supreme Court determined that the word "bribery" in a federal statute was not limited to its common-law definition because the legislative history revealed an intent to deal with bribery in organized crime beyond its common-law definition. In general, there is considerably less legislative history available at the state legislative level. However, at times state courts seek to determine legislative intent based on available resources.

# Law Enforcement Agencies

Law enforcement agencies are charged with enforcing the criminal law. They have the power to investigate suspected criminal activity, to arrest suspected criminals, and to detain arrested persons until their cases come before the appropriate courts of law. Society expects law enforcement agencies not only to arrest those suspected of crimes but also to take steps to prevent crimes from occurring.

## Historical Development

Before the Norman Conquest in 1066, there were no organized police in England, but by the thirteenth century constables and justices of the peace came to symbolize enforcement of the rule of law in England. Large communities, somewhat similar to counties in America, were called "shires." The king would send a royal officer called a "reeve" to each shire to keep order and to exercise broad powers within the shire. The onset of the Industrial Revolution led to the development of large cities. Industrialists and merchants began to establish patrols to protect their goods and buildings. But the need for more effective policing became evident. In 1829, Sir Robert Peel, the British Home Secretary, organized a uniformed but unarmed police force for London. The name "Bobbies" is still applied to police officers in England in honor of Peel. In later years, Parliament required counties and boroughs to establish police departments modeled along the lines of the London force.

Colonial America basically followed the English system, with local constables and county sheriffs following the English concept of constables and shire reeves. These early law officers were often aided by local vigilante groups of citizens known as "posses." Once America became a nation, states and local communities began to follow the Peel model, and by the mid-1800s, Boston, New York, and Philadelphia had developed professional police departments. By the twentieth century, police were aided by technological developments, and by the 1930s, many departments were equipped with motorcycles and patrol cars. Detectives were soon added to the force, police became equipped with modern communications equipment, and police were trained in ballistics and the scientific analysis of blood samples and handwriting.

## Policing in Modern America

**sworn officers** Law enforcement officers sworn to uphold the Constitution and laws of the United States and of their own states.

In the United States nearly 20,000 federal, state, and local agencies are involved in law enforcement and crime prevention. Collectively, these agencies employ nearly 800,000 **sworn officers.** Increasingly, law enforcement officers are trained professionals who must acquire a good working knowledge of the criminal law. At the local level, the typical police recruit now completes about 1,000 hours of training before being sworn in. Modern police forces are highly mobile and are equipped with computers, sophisticated communications technology, and scientific crime detection equipment.

## Policing at the National Level

**Federal Bureau of Investigation (FBI)** The primary federal agency charged with investigating violations of federal criminal laws.

At the national level, the **Federal Bureau of Investigation (FBI)** is the primary agency empowered to investigate violations of federal criminal laws. Located in the **Department of Justice (DOJ)**, the FBI is by far the most powerful of the federal law enforcement agencies, with broad powers to enforce the many criminal laws adopted by the Congress. On April 30, 2012, the FBI employed 13,851 **special agents** and 21,999 support professionals, such as intelligence analysts, language specialists, forensic scientists, information technology specialists, and other professionals. Its personnel are spread out over fifty-six field offices in major cities in the United States and more than sixty international offices in embassies worldwide. The FBI uses the most sophisticated methods in crime prevention and investigation. Its crime laboratory figures prominently in the investigation and prosecution of numerous state and federal crimes. In fiscal year 2012, the FBI's total budget was approximately $8.1 billion, including $119 million in program enhancements for intelligence, counterterrorism, laboratory, information technology, and **cybersecurity**. (See http://www.fbi.gov/quickfacts.htm.)

**Department of Justice (DOJ)** The department within the executive branch of the federal government that is headed by the Attorney General and staffed by U.S. Attorneys.

**special agents** Officers of the FBI with the power to make arrests and use force in the enforcement of federal law.

**cybersecurity** Security measures designed to protect computers and computer networks from unauthorized access.

The **U.S. Marshals Service** is the oldest unit of federal law enforcement, dating back to 1790. The agency employs nearly 4,000 deputy marshals and criminal investigators. Deputy Marshals provide security for the federal judiciary, execute federal court orders, apprehend federal fugitives, seize property under the federal forfeiture laws, provide security for federal witnesses, and serve as custodians for the transfer of federal prisoners.

**U.S. Marshals Service** Law enforcement officers of the U.S. Department of Justice who are responsible for enforcing federal laws, enforcing federal court decisions, and effecting the transfer of federal prisoners.

Nearly fifty other federal agencies have law enforcement authority in specific areas. Among them are the Bureau of Alcohol, Tobacco, and Firearms; the Internal Revenue Service; the Bureau of Indian Affairs; the Drug Enforcement Administration; the Bureau of Postal Inspection; the Tennessee Valley Authority; the National Park Service; the Forest Service; the U.S. Capitol Police; the U.S. Mint; the Secret Service; and Immigration and Customs Enforcement (ICE) within the Department of Homeland Security.

## State and Local Policing

All states have law enforcement agencies that patrol the highways, investigate crimes, and furnish skilled technical support to local law enforcement agencies. Similarly, every state has a number of state agencies responsible for enforcing specific areas of the law, ranging from agricultural importation to food processing and from casino gambling to dispensing alcoholic beverages. Probably among the best known to all citizens are the state highway patrol and the fish and game warden. Generally, cases developed by state officers are processed through local law enforcement and prosecution agencies.

**sheriff** The chief law enforcement officer of a county.

At the local level, we find both county and municipal law enforcement agencies. Nearly every county in America (more than three thousand of them) has a **sheriff**. In most states, sheriffs are elected to office and exercise broad powers as the chief law enforcement officers of their respective counties. They are usually dependent on funding provided by a local governing body, generally the county commission. In some areas, particularly the urban Northeast, many powers traditionally exercised by sheriffs have been assumed by state or metropolitan police forces. In the rest of the country, however, especially in the rural areas, sheriffs (and their deputies) are the principal law enforcement agents at the county level.

**police departments** Agencies, established by municipalities and sometimes states, whose function is to enforce the criminal laws within their respective jurisdictions.

Nearly 15,000 cities and towns have their own **police departments**. Local police are charged with enforcing the criminal laws of their states, as well as of their municipalities. Although the county sheriff usually has jurisdiction within the municipalities of the county, he or she generally concentrates enforcement efforts on those areas outside municipal boundaries.

In addition to city and county law enforcement agencies, there are numerous special districts and authorities that have their own police forces. Most state universities have their own police departments, as do many airports and seaports.

Besides providing law enforcement in the strictest sense of the term, local law enforcement agencies initiate the criminal justice process and assist prosecutors in preparation of cases. Sheriffs in many larger counties and many metropolitan police departments have developed SWAT (special weapons and tactics) teams to assist in the rescue of victims of catastrophes and persons taken hostage. They are also heavily involved in **order maintenance** or "keeping the peace," hence the term "peace officers." Often, keeping the peace involves more of a process of judgment and discretion rather than merely applying the criminal law.

**order maintenance** The police officer's function of keeping the peace, as distinct from enforcement of the law.

Some of the newer and more innovative policing responsibilities include community relations departments that seek to foster better relations among groups of citizens, especially minorities and juveniles, and to assist social agencies in efforts to rehabilitate drug and alcohol abusers. Finally, the public looks to the police to prevent crime through their presence in the community and through education of the public on crime prevention measures. Under the rubric of **community policing**, police agencies are making an effort to become actively involved in their communities in order to earn the trust and confidence of the citizens they serve. Most police departments in cities of 50,000 people or more now have specialized community policing divisions.

**community policing** Style of police work that stresses development of close ties between police officers and the communities they serve.

# Prosecutorial Agencies

**prosecutor** A public official empowered to initiate criminal charges and conduct prosecutions.

Although law enforcement agencies are the "gatekeepers" of the criminal justice system, prosecutors are central to the administration of criminal justice. It is the **prosecutor** who determines whether to bring charges against suspected criminals. Prosecutors have enormous discretion, not only in determining whether to prosecute but also in determining what charges to file. Moreover, prosecutors frequently set the tone for plea bargaining and have a powerful voice in determining the severity of sanctions imposed on persons convicted of crimes. Accordingly, prosecutors play a crucial role in the criminal justice system.

## Historical Background

The early English common law considered many crimes to be private matters between individuals; however, the role of the public prosecutor evolved as early as the thirteenth century, when the king's counsel would pursue crimes considered to be offenses against the Crown and, in some instances, when injured victims declined to prosecute. Today in England, a public prosecutor prosecutes crimes that have great significance to the government, but the majority of offenses are handled by police agencies that hire barristers to prosecute charges. Unlike American prosecutors, the English barrister may represent the police in one case and in the next case represent the defendant.

The office of public prosecutor in England became the prototype for the office of attorney general in this country at the national and state levels. In colonial days, an attorney general's assistants handled local prosecutions. However, as states became independent, the practice ceased. The state attorneys general assumed the role of chief legal officers, and local governments began electing their own prosecuting attorneys.

## Federal Prosecutors

**Attorney General** The highest legal officer of a state or of the United States.

**U.S. Attorneys** Lawyers appointed by the president with consent of the U.S. Senate to prosecute federal crimes in federal judicial districts.

**independent counsel** A special prosecutor appointed to investigate and, if warranted, prosecute official misconduct.

In the United States, the chief prosecutor at the federal level is the **Attorney General,** who is the head of the Department of Justice. Below the Attorney General are the **U.S. Attorneys**, each responsible for prosecuting crimes within a particular federal district. The U.S. Attorneys, in turn, have a number of assistants who handle most of the day-to-day criminal cases brought by the federal government. The president, subject to the consent of the Senate, appoints the Attorney General and the U.S. Attorneys. Assistant U.S. Attorneys are federal civil service employees.

In addition to the regular federal prosecutors, Congress has provided for the appointment of **independent counsel** (special prosecutors) in cases involving alleged misconduct by high government officials. By far, the most infamous such case was "Watergate," which resulted in the convictions of several high-ranking officials and led to the resignation of President Richard Nixon in 1974. But there have been numerous cases where, under congressional direction, a special prosecutor has been appointed. A more recent example of this was Kenneth Starr's appointment to investigate the Whitewater scandal, which involved close associates of President Bill Clinton and First Lady Hillary Rodham Clinton. This investigation eventually culminated in President Clinton's impeachment and his subsequent acquittal by the U.S. Senate in February 1999.

## State and Local Prosecutors

**state's attorneys** State prosecutors.

Each state likewise has its own attorney general, who acts as the state's chief legal officer, and a number of assistant attorneys general, plus a number of district or **state's attorneys** at the local level. Generally speaking, local prosecutors are elected for set terms of office and have the responsibility for the prosecution of crimes within the jurisdiction for which they are elected. In most states, local prosecutors act autonomously and possess broad discretionary powers. Many local prosecutors function on a part-time basis, but in the larger offices the trend is for the prosecutor and assistant prosecutors to serve on a full-time basis. Larger offices are establishing educational programs and developing specially trained assistants or units to handle specific categories of crime—for example, white-collar crime and governmental corruption, narcotics offenses, and consumer fraud.

Cities and counties also have their own attorneys. These attorneys, generally appointed by the governing bodies they represent, sometimes prosecute violations of city and county ordinances, but increasingly their function is limited to representing their cities or counties in civil suits and giving legal advice to local councils and officials.

## The Prosecutor's Broad Discretion

Federal and state prosecutors (whether known as district attorneys, state attorneys, or county prosecutors) play a vital role in the criminal justice system in the United States. As mentioned, a politically appointed U.S. Attorney supervises prosecutors at the federal level, whereas state and local prosecutors generally come into office by election in partisan contests. Thus, prosecutors become sensitive to community norms while exercising the broad discretion that the law vests in prosecutorial decision making.

Prosecutors not only determine the level of offense to be charged; in exercise of their very broad discretion they also exercise the power of **nolle prosequi**, usually called *nol pros*, which allows a prosecutor not to proceed in a given case, irrespective of the factual basis for prosecution. Prosecutors sometimes *nol pros* cases to secure cooperation of a defendant in furthering other prosecutions; in other instances, a prosecutor may allow a defendant to participate in some diversionary program of rehabilitation. In recent years, completion of a prescribed program in a drug court has often resulted in a case being *nol prossed* by a prosecutor. (See the discussion of drug courts in Chapter 10.)

*nolle prosequi* A formal entry by a prosecutor who declines to proceed further in the prosecution of an offense; commonly called a *nol pros*.

# Counsel for the Defense

In American criminal law, individuals accused of any crime, no matter how minor the offense, have the right to employ counsel for their defense. U.S. Const. Amend. VI. Indeed, the U.S. Supreme Court has held that a defendant has the right to be represented by an attorney at all criminal proceedings that may substantially affect the rights of the accused. *Mempa v. Rhay*, 389 U.S. 128, 88 S.Ct. 254, 19 L.Ed.2d 336 (1967).

In this country, many lawyers specialize in criminal defense work. Of course, defendants are free to employ an attorney of their choice at their own expense. Some well-known attorneys specialize in representing defendants in high-profile trials. However, most criminal defendants are not wealthy, and few people accused of crimes can afford to hire legal "dream teams" to represent them.

Many attorneys are highly skilled in handling criminal cases and are available for employment in federal and state criminal proceedings. In fact, it is not uncommon for attorneys who start their careers as prosecutors eventually to enter private practice in criminal matters. Today some state bar associations grant special recognition to lawyers who qualify by virtue of experience and examination as "certified criminal defense attorneys."

## Representation of Indigent Defendants

Beginning in the 1960s, the U.S. Supreme Court greatly expanded the right to counsel by requiring states to provide attorneys to **indigent defendants.** *Gideon v. Wainwright*, 372 U.S. 335, 83 S.Ct. 792, 9 L.Ed.2d 799 (1963); *Argersinger v. Hamlin*, 407 U.S. 25, 92 S.Ct. 2006, 32 L.Ed.2d 530 (1972). In some states, courts appoint attorneys from the private bar to represent indigent defendants. However, most states have chosen to handle the problem of indigent defense by establishing the office of the public defender. Like public prosecutors, **public defenders** are generally elected to set terms of office. Because of their constant contact with criminal cases, public defenders acquire considerable expertise in representing defendants. Moreover, because they are public officials who, like prosecutors, are provided with budgets, public defenders are often able to hire investigators to aid their staff of assistant public defenders in their representation of indigent defendants.

**indigent defendants** Persons accused of crimes who cannot afford to retain private legal counsel and are therefore entitled to be represented by a public defender or a court-appointed lawyer.

**public defenders** Public officials who are attorneys and are responsible for defending indigent persons charged with crimes.

## JURISPRUDENCE

*Gideon v. Wainwright,* 372 U.S. 335, 83 S.Ct. 792, 9 L.Ed.2d 799 (1963)

Clarence Earl Gideon, a fifty-one-year-old indigent drifter who had been in and out of jails all his adult life, was charged with felonious breaking and entering. At trial, he requested that the court appoint an attorney to represent him. The court refused, citing the Florida law that required appointment of counsel for indigent defendants only in capital cases. While serving his sentence in the Florida State Prison, Gideon unsuccessfully challenged his conviction in the Florida Supreme Court on a writ of habeas corpus. He then obtained review by the U.S. Supreme Court on a writ of certiorari. In a unanimous decision, the Court reversed Gideon's conviction. Writing for the Court, Hugo Black opined that "[t]he right of one charged with a crime to counsel may not be deemed fundamental and essential to fair trials in some countries, but it is in ours." Because *Gideon* was made retroactive, it allowed numerous persons serving time in state prisons to win their freedom by seeking writs of habeas corpus in the federal courts. Without question, *Gideon* was one of the most important decisions of the modern Supreme Court in the field of criminal justice.

## The Role of Defense Attorneys

**defense attorney** A lawyer who represents defendants in criminal cases.

The role of the **defense attorney** is perhaps the most misunderstood in the criminal justice system. First and foremost, a defense attorney is charged with zealously representing his or her client and ensuring that the defendant's constitutional rights are fully protected. To anyone who has watched *Law and Order* or a similar television program, the defense attorney's most visible role is that of vigorously cross-examining prosecution witnesses and passionately pleading for a client before a jury. However, the defense attorney's role is far greater than being a courtroom advocate. As a counselor, a defense attorney must evaluate the alternative courses of action that may be available to a defendant. The great majority of criminal cases are disposed of through plea bargaining. As part of this process, defense counsel must attempt to gauge the strength of the prosecution's case, advise the client on the feasibility of entering a plea of guilty, and attempt to negotiate a fair and constructive sentence. In instances where a defendant elects to plead not guilty, defense attorneys challenge the police and prosecution. Many observers point out that these efforts by defense attorneys "keep the system honest" by causing police and prosecuting authorities to be scrupulous in their adherence to constitutional standards.

Perhaps the most frequently voiced reservation concerning defense attorneys relates to representation of a defendant who, from all facts available, is believed to be guilty. Defense attorneys are quick to point out that it is not their function to make a judgment of the defendant's guilt or innocence; there are other functionaries in the system charged with that responsibility. The answer does not easily satisfy critics. Nevertheless, in our system of adversarial justice the defense attorney is required to represent a defendant with fidelity, to protect the defendant's constitutional rights, to assert all defenses available under the law of the land, and to make sure before a defendant is found guilty that the prosecution has sustained its burden of proving the defendant guilty beyond a reasonable doubt. A defense attorney must make sufficient objections and other tactical moves to preserve any contention of error for review by a higher court. If the defendant is convicted, the defense attorney's duty continues. He or she must seek a fair sentence, advise as to the right to appeal to a higher court, and, in some instances, seek postconviction relief if an appeal fails.

# Juries

**jury** A group of citizens convened for the purpose of deciding factual questions relevant to a civil or criminal case.

The **jury** is one of the great contributions of the English common law. By the twelfth century, juries had begun to function in England, but not as we know juries today. Rather, these early juries comprised men who had knowledge of the disputes they were to decide. However, eventually juries began to hear evidence and make their verdicts accordingly. By the eighteenth century, juries occupied a prominent role in the English common-law system and served as a buffer between the Crown and the citizenry. The colonists brought the concept to the New World. Today, juries composed of both men and women represent an important component of the American system of criminal justice.

There are two types of juries: the **grand jury** and the **petit (trial) jury.** The juries derive their names from the number of persons who serve, with the grand jury consisting of a larger number than the petit jury.

**grand jury** A group of citizens convened either to conduct an investigation or to determine whether there is sufficient evidence to warrant the prosecution of an accused.

**petit (trial) jury** A trial jury, usually composed of either six or twelve persons.

## Grand Juries

Grand juries essentially serve to consider whether there is sufficient evidence to bring charges against a person; petit or trial juries sit to hear evidence at a trial and render a verdict accordingly. The Fifth Amendment to the U.S. Constitution stipulates that "[n]o person shall be held to answer for a capital, or otherwise infamous crime, unless on a presentment or indictment of a grand jury." The constitutional requirement binds all federal courts; however, the Supreme Court has held that states are not bound to abide by the grand jury requirement. *Hurtado v. California,* 110 U.S. 516, 4 S.Ct. 111, 28 L.Ed.232 (1884).

**true bill** An indictment handed down by a grand jury in a criminal case.

**no bill** Decision of a grand jury not to return an indictment.

Sixteen to twenty-three persons serve on a federal grand jury. The number varies according to each state but usually consists of between twelve and twenty-three citizens. Grand jurors serve for a limited time to hear evidence and to determine whether to hand down an indictment, sometimes referred to as a **true bill,** or to refuse to indict when the jury determines there is insufficient evidence of a crime by returning a **no bill.** Twelve jurors must vote to return an indictment in federal court, and states usually require at least a majority of grand jurors to return an indictment. Courts have broad authority to call a grand jury into session, and grand juries are authorized to make wide-ranging inquiries and investigations into public matters. Grand juries may make accusations, called *presentments*, independently of a prosecutor.

---

### JURISPRUDENCE

*Hurtado v. California,* 110 U.S. 516, 4 S.Ct. 111, 28 L.Ed.232 (1884).

Joseph Hurtado was charged with murder by the state of California by way of an information rather than the traditional grand jury indictment. He was tried, convicted and sentenced to death. Hurtado claimed that the grand jury procedure required in federal criminal cases by the Fifth Amendment was an essential feature of "due process of law" and thus required in state criminal cases by the Fourteenth Amendment.

Dividing 7–1, the U.S. Supreme Court rejected that argument and sustained his conviction. The Court said that states should be free to design their own criminal justice systems without interference by the federal courts. Today, despite the application of most of the provisions of the Bill of Rights to the states via the Fourteenth Amendment, the *Hurtado* decision remains "good" law. States are not required by the federal constitution to use grand juries to bring criminal charges, although many still do.

## JURISPRUDENCE

*Williams v. Florida,* 399 U.S. 78, 90 S.Ct. 1893, 26 L.Ed.2d 446 (1970).

Johnny Williams was convicted of robbery by a Florida court and sentenced to life imprisonment. Under a Florida law amended in 1967, juries in noncapital criminal cases were reduced from twelve to six jurors. Williams claimed that this violated his constitutional right to trial by jury, which is protected by the Sixth Amendment and applicable to the states under the Fourteenth Amendment. The U.S. Supreme Court rejected Williams' argument, holding that the Sixth Amendment does not require a particular number of jurors. Writing for the Court, Justice Byron Whote observed that "the fact that the jury at common law was composed of precisely 12 is a historical accident, unnecessary to effect the purposes of the jury system and wholly without significance 'except to mystics'."

**indictment** A formal document handed down by a grand jury accusing one or more persons of the commission of a crime or crimes.

**information** An accusatorial document filed under oath by a prosecutor charging a person with one or more violations of the criminal law; similar to an indictment issued by a grand jury.

**speedy and public trial** An open and public criminal trial held without unreasonable delay as required by the Sixth Amendment to the U.S. Constitution.

Although the English common law system gave birth to the grand jury, England abolished grand juries in the 1930s, having found that the return of **indictments** was almost automatic and that the use of grand juries tended to delay the criminal process. Today, critics argue that grand juries are so dominated by the prosecutors who appear before them that they have ceased to serve as an independent body to evaluate evidence. Indeed, many states have eliminated the requirement that a grand jury hand down indictments and have substituted a prosecutor's **information,** an accusatorial document charging a crime. Yet many reformers would retain the grand jury as an institution for investigation of corruption in government.

## Trial Juries

Article III, Section 2 of the U.S. Constitution establishes the right to trial by jury in criminal cases. The Sixth Amendment guarantees "the right to a **speedy and public trial** by an impartial jury." The Seventh Amendment grants a right to a trial by jury in civil suits at common law. All state constitutions confer the right of trial by jury in criminal cases; however, the federal constitutional right to a jury trial applies to the states, thereby guaranteeing a defendant a right to a jury trial in a state criminal prosecution if such a right would exist in a federal prosecution. *Duncan v. Louisiana,* 391 U.S. 145, 88 S.Ct. 1444, 20 L.Ed.2d 491 (1968). However, as we note below, the right to trial by jury does not extend to juvenile delinquency proceedings.

A common-law trial jury consisted of "twelve men good and true." Today, twelve persons are required in federal juries; however, the number varies in states, although all states require twelve-person juries in capital cases. The Supreme Court has approved the use of six-person juries in noncapital felony prosecutions. *Williams v. Florida,* 399 U.S. 78, 90 S.Ct. 1893, 26 L.Ed.2d 446 (1970).

## The Courts

Courts of law are the centerpieces of the federal and state criminal justice systems. Courts of law are responsible for determining both the factual basis and legal sufficiency of criminal charges and for ensuring that criminal defendants are provided due process of law. Essentially, the federal courts adjudicate criminal cases where defendants are charged with violating federal criminal laws; state courts adjudicate alleged violations of state laws.

**trial courts** Judicial tribunals usually presided over by one judge who conducts proceedings and trials in civil and criminal cases with or without a jury.

**appellate courts** Judicial tribunals that review decisions from lower tribunals.

**jurisdiction** The authority of a court to hear and decide certain categories of legal disputes. Jurisdiction relates to the authority of a court over the person, subject matter, and geographical area.

Basically, there are two kinds of courts: trial and appellate courts. **Trial courts** conduct criminal trials and various pretrial and posttrial proceedings. **Appellate courts** hear appeals from the decisions of the trial courts. Trial courts are primarily concerned with ascertaining facts, determining guilt or innocence, and imposing punishments, whereas appellate courts are primarily concerned with matters of law. Appellate courts correct legal errors made by trial courts and develop law when new legal questions arise. In some instances appellate courts must determine whether there is legally sufficient evidence to uphold a conviction.

The first question facing a court in any criminal prosecution is that of **jurisdiction,** the legal authority to hear and decide the case. A court must have jurisdiction over both the subject matter of a case and the parties to a case before it may proceed to adjudicate that controversy. The jurisdiction of the federal courts is determined by both the language of Article III of the Constitution and the statutes enacted by Congress. The respective state constitutions and statutes determine the jurisdiction of the state courts.

## The Federal Court System

Article III of the U.S. Constitution provides that "[t]he judicial Power of the United States shall be vested in one supreme Court, and in such inferior Courts as the Congress may from time to time ordain and establish." Under this authority Congress enacted the Judiciary Act of 1789, creating the federal court system. After Congress passed the Judiciary Act of 1801, the Supreme Court justices were required to "ride circuit," a practice that had its roots in English legal history. The circuit courts then consisted of district court judges who heard appeals alongside "circuit-riding" Supreme Court justices. In 1891 Congress created separate appellate courts, and since then Supreme Court justices have remained as reviewing justices.

### U.S. District Courts

**U.S. District Courts** The principal trial courts in the federal judicial system, these courts sit in ninety-four geographical districts throughout the United States.

**U.S. District Courts** handle prosecutions for violations of federal statutes. In addition, federal courts sometimes review convictions from state courts when defendants raise issues arising under the U.S. Constitution. Appeals are heard by U.S. Courts of Appeals, and, of course, the Supreme Court is at the apex of the judicial system.

The principal trial court in the federal system is the U.S. District Court. There are district courts in ninety-four federal judicial districts around the country. A criminal trial in the district court is presided over by a judge appointed for life by the president with the consent of the Senate. Federal magistrate judges, who are appointed by federal district judges, often handle pretrial proceedings in the district courts and trials of misdemeanors.

Most of the cases filed in the federal district courts are civil, as distinct from criminal, cases. In 2011 nearly 290,000 civil cases were filed in the district courts. In that year 70,896 criminal cases were filed involving nearly 103,000 defendants. (Chief Justice's 2011 Year-End Report on the Federal Judiciary, December 31, 2011, p. 14.) The largest categories of criminal filings in the district courts tend to be drug crimes, weapons offenses, and immigration violations.

Congress created the district courts by the Judiciary Act of 1789. Since then, Congress has created specialized courts to handle specific kinds of cases (e.g., the U.S. Court of International Trade and the U.S. Claims Court).

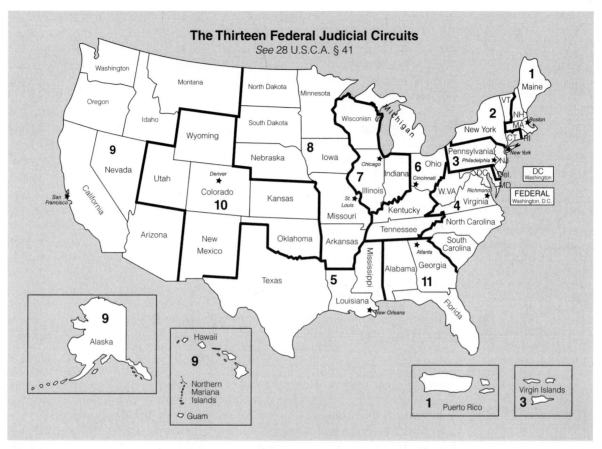

**FIGURE 2.1** The Federal Judicial Circuits. Source: *Federal Reporter,* 2nd series (West Publishing Company).

**intermediate appellate courts** Judicial tribunals consisting of three or more judges that review decisions of trial courts but that are subordinate to the final appellate tribunals.

**U.S. Courts of Appeals** The twelve intermediate appellate courts of appeals in the federal system that sit in specified geographical areas of the United States and in which panels of appellate judges hear appeals in civil and criminal cases, primarily from the U.S. District Courts.

**en banc hearing** A hearing in an appellate court in which all or a substantial number of the judges assigned to that court participate.

### The U.S. Courts of Appeals

The **intermediate appellate courts** in the federal system are the **U.S. Courts of Appeals** (also known as circuit courts). Twelve geographical circuits (and one "federal circuit") cover the United States and its possessions. Figure 2.1 indicates the geographical distribution of the circuit courts. The circuit courts hear criminal and civil appeals from the district courts and from quasi-judicial tribunals in the independent regulatory agencies. In 2011, 55,126 appeals were commenced in the federal circuit courts (Administrative Office of the U.S. Courts, *2011 Judicial Business,* online at http://www.uscourts.gov/uscourts/Statistics/JudicialBusiness/2011/JudicialBusiness2011_Summary.pdf).

Generally, decisions of the courts of appeals are rendered by panels of three judges who vote to affirm, reverse, or modify the lower-court decisions under review. There is a procedure by which the circuit courts provide an ***en banc* hearing,** where all judges assigned to the court (or a substantial number of them) participate in a decision. Like their counterparts in the district courts, federal appeals court judges are appointed to life terms by the president with the consent of the Senate.

### The U.S. Supreme Court

The highest appellate court in the federal judicial system is the **United States Supreme Court.** The Supreme Court has jurisdiction to review, either on appeal or by **writ of certiorari** (discretionary review), all the decisions of the lower federal courts and many decisions of the highest state courts. The Supreme Court comprises nine justices who, like district and circuit judges, are appointed for life by the president with the consent of the Senate. These nine individuals have the final word in determining what the U.S. Constitution requires, permits, and prohibits in the areas of law enforcement, prosecution, adjudication, and punishment. The Supreme Court also promulgates **rules of procedure** for the lower federal courts to follow in both criminal and civil cases.

As of June 1, 2011, John Roberts was the chief justice of the Supreme Court, and the associate justices were Antonin Scalia, Anthony Kennedy, Clarence Thomas, Ruth Bader Ginsburg, Stephen Breyer, Samuel Alito, Sonia Sotomayor, and Elena Kagan. During the October 2010 Term (which ended in June 2011), 7,857 cases were filed with the Court. The Court granted review in only 83 of these cases, which is just over 1 percent. During its 2010 Term, the Court issued only seventy-five signed opinions (Chief Justice's 2011 Year-End Report on the Federal Judiciary, December 31, 2011, p. 13). Of course, even a small number of Supreme Court opinions can have a major impact on the law, because they settle conflicts among lower courts and resolve salient issues of law and public policy.

**Military Tribunals**

Crimes committed by persons in military service are ordinarily prosecuted in proceedings before **courts-martial**. Article 1, Section 8 of the U.S. Constitution grants Congress the authority to regulate the armed forces. Under this authority, Congress has enacted the **Uniform Code of Military Justice (UCMJ)**, 10 U.S.C.A. §§ 801–940. The UCMJ gives courts-martial jurisdiction to try all offenses under the code committed by military personnel. Notwithstanding this grant of authority, the United States Supreme Court held in 1969 that military jurisdiction was limited to offenses that were service connected. *O'Callahan v. Parker*, 395 U.S. 258, 89 S.Ct. 1683, 23 L.Ed.2d 291 (1969). The *O'Callahan* decision greatly narrowed military jurisdiction over offenses committed by servicepersons. In 1987 the Court overturned *O'Callahan* and said that military jurisdiction depends solely on whether an accused is a military member. *Solorio v. United States*, 483 U.S. 435, 107 S.Ct. 2924, 97 L.Ed.2d 364 (1987). Thus, courts-martial may now try all offenses committed by servicepersons in violation of the UCMJ.

Commanders of various military units convene court-martial proceedings and appoint those who sit similar to a civilian jury. These commanders are called the convening authorities and are assisted by military lawyers designated as staff judge advocates. Military trial procedures and rules of evidence are similar to the rules applied in federal district courts.

---

## JURISPRUDENCE

*Solorio v. United States,* 483 U.S. 435, 107 S.Ct. 2924, 97 L.Ed.2d 364 (1987)

While serving in the Coast Guard, Richard Solorio was accused of sexually abusing children in his private residence. A general court-martial was convened to adjudicate the case. Solorio moved to dismiss the charges on the ground that they were not "service connected." The presiding judge granted the motion and dismissed the charges. The prosecution appealed to the Coast Guard

Court of Military Review, which reversed and reinstated the charges. After the Court of Military Appeals affirmed this ruling, Solorio obtained review by the U.S. Supreme Court. Dividing 5–4, the Court upheld the reinstatement of the charges and overturned its 1969 decision in *O'Callahan v. Parker.* Chief Justice William Rehnquist, writing for the Court, concluded that the "service connection approach" set forth in *O'Callahan* "has proven confusing and difficult for military courts to apply."

There are three classes of court-martial: summary, special, and general. The summary court-martial is composed of one military officer with jurisdiction to impose minor punishments over enlisted personnel. It is somewhat analogous to trial by a civilian magistrate, whereas special and general court-martial proceedings are formal military tribunals more analogous to civilian criminal courts of record.

A special court-martial must be composed of three or more members with or without a military judge, or a military judge alone, if requested by the accused. It can impose more serious punishments on both officers and enlisted personnel. A general court-martial tries the most serious offenses and must consist of five or more members and a military judge (or a military judge alone, if requested by the accused). A general court-martial may try any offense made punishable by the UCMJ and may impose any punishment authorized by law against officers and enlisted personnel, including death for a capital offense. Trial by a military judge alone is not permitted in capital cases.

A military judge presides at special and general courts-martial. A trial counsel serves as prosecutor, and a defendant is furnished legal counsel by the government unless the accused chooses to employ private defense counsel. The extent of punishment that may be imposed varies according to the offense and the authority of the type of court-martial convened.

Decisions of courts-martial are reviewed by military courts of review in each branch of the armed forces. In specified instances, appeals are heard by the **United States Court of Appeals for the Armed Forces.** This court is staffed by civilian judges who are appointed to fifteen-year terms by the president with the consent of the Senate.

**United States Court of Appeals for the Armed Forces** The court (formerly known as the Court of Military Appeals), consisting of five civilian judges, that reviews sentences affecting a general or flag officer or imposing the death penalty and cases certified for review by the judge advocate general of a branch of service. May grant review of convictions and sentences on petitions by service members.

Only under conditions of martial law do military tribunals have the authority to try American citizens in civilian life who are not connected with the military or naval services. *Ex parte Milligan*, 71 U.S. (4 Wall.) 2, 18 L.Ed. 281 (1866). Historically, the Supreme Court has permitted "enemy aliens" captured during wartime to be tried by military tribunals. See *Ex parte Quirin*, 317 U.S. 1, 63 S.Ct. 2, 87 L.Ed. 7 (1942). Under an executive order issued by President George W. Bush on November 13, 2001, the military established special tribunals to try foreign nationals accused of terrorism against the United States. Several accused terrorists detained at the U.S. Naval Base at Guantanamo Bay, Cuba were brought to trial, but the proceedings were interrupted by a dramatic decision from the nation's highest court. In *Hamdan v. Rumsfeld*, 548 U.S. 547, 126 S.Ct. 2749, 165 L.Ed.2d 723 (2006), the U.S. Supreme Court ruled that the military tribunals were neither authorized by federal law nor required by military necessity. Moreover, the Court held that they ran afoul of the Geneva Conventions governing the treatment of prisoners of war.

## JURISPRUDENCE

*Hamdan v. Rumsfeld*, 548 U.S. 547, 126 S.Ct. 2749, 165 L.Ed.2d 723 (2006)

Salim Ahmed Hamdan, a Yemeni national detained at the American naval base at Guantanamo Bay, Cuba, brought suit to challenge the legality of the military tribunal before which he was to be tried for conspiracy to commit terrorism. The Supreme Court held that the federal government's plan to try Guantanamo Bay detainees before military commissions was unauthorized by statute and violated international law. However, the Court indicated that Congress could, through appropriate legislation, provide for the use of military tribunals to try Guantanamo Bay detainees. In announcing the judgment of the Court, Justice John Paul Stevens noted that "in undertaking to try Hamdan and subject him to criminal punishment, the Executive is bound to comply with the Rule of Law that prevails in this jurisdiction."

In passing the Military Commissions Act of 2006, Pub. L. No. 109-366, 120 Stat. 2600 (Oct. 17, 2006), Congress provided for "the use of military commissions to try alien unlawful enemy combatants engaged in hostilities against the United States for violations of the law of war and other offenses triable by military commission." After a decade of delay and controversy, five foreign nationals accused of participating in the 9/11 terrorist attacks were arraigned before a military tribunal convened at Guantanamo Bay. When they were brought into the courtroom, Khalid Sheik Mohammed and his fellow defendants refused to speak, so the court entered pleas of not guilty on their behalf. It would be a year, however, before the trial would get underway.

### Tribal Courts

Article I, Section 8 of the U.S. Constitution mentions Indian tribes as being subject to Congressional legislation. Congress has provided that federal courts have jurisdiction over specified offenses committed by Native Americans on Indian reservations. 18 U.S.C.A. § 1153. At the same time, Congress has permitted certain states to exercise jurisdiction over such offenses. 18 U.S.C.A. § 1162. Furthermore, offenses committed by one Native American against another on a reservation are generally subject to the jurisdiction of tribal courts, unless the crime charged has been expressly made subject to federal jurisdiction. *Keeble v. United States,* 412 U.S. 205, 93 S.Ct. 1993, 36 L.Ed.2d 844 (1973). Courts of the state where a Native American reservation is located have jurisdiction over crimes on the reservation when the offense is perpetrated by a non-Indian against a non-Indian, but non-Indian defendants charged with committing a crime on a reservation are subject to federal jurisdiction if the victim is a member of the tribe. *United States v. Antelope,* 430 U.S. 641, 97 S.Ct. 1395, 51 L.Ed.2d 701 (1977).

## State Court Systems

**courts of general jurisdiction** Courts that conduct trials in felony and major misdemeanor cases. Also refers to courts that have jurisdiction to hear civil as well as criminal cases.

**courts of limited jurisdiction** Courts that handle pretrial matters and conduct trials in minor misdemeanor cases.

**state supreme court** The highest appellate court of a state.

**juvenile courts** Judicial tribunals having jurisdiction over minors defined as juveniles who are alleged to be status offenders or to have committed acts of delinquency.

Each state has its own independent judicial system. These courts handle more than 90 percent of criminal prosecutions in the United States. State judicial systems are characterized by variations in structure, jurisdiction, and procedure but have certain commonalities. Every state has one or more levels of trial courts and at least one appellate court. Most states have **courts of general jurisdiction**, which conduct trials in felony and major misdemeanor cases, and **courts of limited jurisdiction**, which handle pretrial matters and conduct trials in minor misdemeanor cases. Most states also have some form of intermediate appellate courts that relieve the **state supreme court** (known as the Court of Appeals in New York and Maryland) from hearing routine appeals. Many states also have separate **juvenile courts**, which operate in ways that differ significantly from the criminal courts for adults.

Some states, like North Carolina, have adopted tidy, streamlined court systems (see Figure 2.2). Other states' court systems are extremely complex, as is the case in Texas (see Figure 2.3). In structural complexity, most states' systems fall somewhere between the two extremes.

## Contrasting Judicial Functions and Environments

As we noted in Chapter 1, trial courts primarily make factual determinations, often assisted by juries; apply settled law to established facts; and impose sanctions. Appellate courts, on the other hand, interpret the federal and state constitutions and statutes, correct errors in law made by trial courts, and develop the law by "filling in the gaps" that often become apparent in the application of statutory laws.

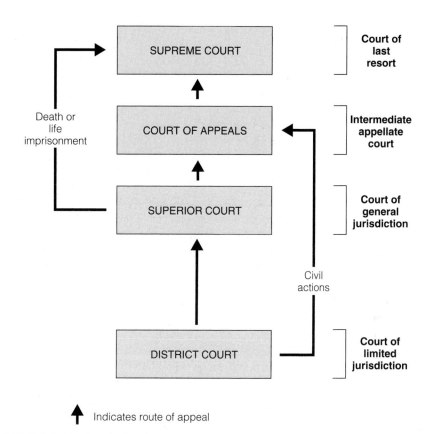

Indicates route of appeal

**FIGURE 2.2** The North Carolina court system. Source: U.S. Department of Justice/National Center for State Courts.

The difference in the roles of trial and appellate courts is also evident in the environment where trial and appellate judges perform their functions. A trial court usually sits in a county courthouse or other county judicial building. Trial judges preside over courtrooms where there is considerable daily activity with the impaneling of juries, testimony of witnesses, and attorneys making objections and pleas for their clients. At other times the judges are busy hearing arguments in their chambers. In short, the trial scene is one of high visibility and is often attended by numerous spectators and, where a high-profile case is being tried, by members of the print and television media. In short, the trial court setting is a venue of daily interaction between court personnel and the citizens of the community.

In contrast, appellate courts are often described as "invisible courts" because their public proceedings are generally limited to hearing legal arguments by attorneys on prescribed oral argument days. Few clients and even fewer spectators are generally in attendance. Media representatives usually attend only when some high-profile appeal is being argued. Many of the documents are delivered by mail to a staff of clerks. Proceedings are resolved primarily by review of records from the lower court or administrative agency, by study of the law briefs submitted by counsel, and by discussion among the panel of judges assigned a particular case, often supplemented by independent research by judges and their staff attorneys.

Unlike a trial court, which is normally surrounded by a busy atmosphere, an appellate court often sits in the state capitol building or in its own facility, usually with a complete law library. The décor in the buildings that house appellate courts is usually quite formal, and often features portraits of former judges regarded as oracles of the

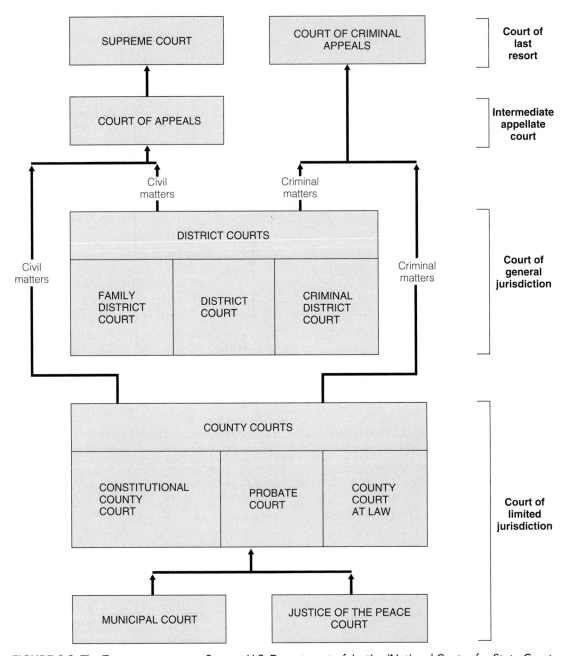

**FIGURE 2.3** The Texas court system. Source: U.S. Department of Justice/National Center for State Courts.

law. When a panel of judges sits to hear oral arguments, they normally emerge from behind a velvet curtain on a precise schedule and to the cry of the court's marshal. When not hearing oral arguments, appellate judges usually occupy a suite of offices with their secretaries and law clerks. It is in these individual chambers that appellate judges study and write their opinions on cases assigned to them.

The United States Supreme Court occupies a majestic building in Washington, D.C., with spacious office suites and impressive corridors and library facilities. With enhancements and attributes similar to those of appellate courts, the elegance and dignity of the facilities comport with the significant role of the Court as final arbiter in the nation's judicial system. There is a sparse crowd at most state and intermediate federal appellate courts; at the Supreme Court, by contrast, parties interested in the decisions that will result from arguments, a coterie of media persons, and many spectators fill the courtroom to hear arguments in cases that often significantly affect the economic, social, and political life of the nation. Photography is not allowed, and the arguments and dialogue between the counsel and the justices are observed silently and respectfully by those who attend. There is sometimes a contrasting scene outside the Supreme Court building, where demonstrators gather to give visibility to the causes they represent.

# The Juvenile Justice System

**juvenile delinquency** Actions of a juvenile in violation of the criminal law.

**status offenses** Noncriminal conduct on the part of juveniles that may subject them to the authority of a juvenile court.

The juvenile justice system includes specialized courts, law enforcement agencies, social services agencies, and corrections facilities designed to address problems of **juvenile delinquency** as well as child neglect and abuse. "Delinquency" refers to conduct that would be criminal if committed by an adult. In addition to being charged with delinquency, young people may be subjected to the jurisdiction of a juvenile court for engaging in conduct that is prohibited only for minors. Such behaviors, which include truancy (chronic absence from school) and incorrigibility, are often called **status offenses**, because they are peculiar to the status of children.

## Historical Basis

The common law treated all persons above the age of fourteen as adults for purposes of criminal responsibility (see Chapter 14). Because the American legal system was based on English common law, American courts followed the common-law rules for the treatment of juveniles. Young teenagers were treated essentially as adults for the purposes of criminal justice. During the colonial period of American history, it was not uncommon for teenagers to be hanged, flogged, or placed in the public pillory as punishment for their crimes. Later, as state penitentiaries were established, it was not unusual for 20 percent of prison populations to be juveniles.

In the late nineteenth century, public outcry against treating juveniles like adults led to the establishment of a separate juvenile justice system in the United States. Reformers were convinced that the existing system of criminal justice was inappropriate for young offenders who were more in need of guidance than punishment. Reformers proposed specialized courts to deal with young offenders not as hardened criminals, but as misguided youth in need of special care. This special treatment was justified legally by the concept of ***parens patriae,*** the power of the state to act to protect the interests of those who cannot protect themselves.

*parens patriae* "The parent of the country." Refers to the role of the state as the guardian of minors, mentally ill individuals, and other legally disabled persons.

The first state to act in this area was Illinois in 1899. By the 1920s, many states had followed suit, and by 1945, juvenile court legislation had been enacted by Congress and all state legislatures. The newly created juvenile courts were usually separate from the regular tribunals. Often, the judges or referees presiding over these courts did not have formal legal training. The proceedings were generally nonadversarial, and there was little in the way of procedural regularity or even the opportunity for the juvenile offender to confront his or her accusers. In fact, juvenile delinquency proceedings were conceived as civil, as opposed to criminal, proceedings. Dispositions of cases were usually nonpunitive in character; therefore, accused juvenile offenders were not afforded most of the rights of criminal defendants.

Because the juvenile justice system emphasized rehabilitation (rather than retribution, incapacitation, or deterrence), juveniles who were found delinquent were often placed in reformatories for indeterminate periods, sometimes until they reached the age of majority. Juvenile courts often suffered from lack of trained staff and adequate facilities, and by the 1960s, a system that was conceived by reformers was itself under attack by a new generation of reformers.

## The Constitutional Reform of Juvenile Justice

The abuses that came to be associated with juvenile courts were addressed by the Supreme Court in the landmark case of *In re Gault*, 387 U.S. 1, 87 S.Ct. 1428, 18 L.Ed.2d 527 (1967). In *Gault*, the Court essentially required that juvenile courts adhere to standards of due process, applying most of the basic procedural safeguards enjoyed by adults accused of crimes. Moreover, *Gault* held that juvenile courts must respect the right to counsel, the freedom from compulsory self-incrimination, and the right to confront (cross-examine) hostile witnesses. Writing for a nearly unanimous bench, Justice Fortas observed that "under our Constitution, the condition of being a boy does not justify a kangaroo court." 387 U.S. at 28, 87 S.Ct. at 1444, 18 L.Ed.2d at 546.

Four years later in *McKeiver v. Pennsylvania*, 403 U.S. 528, 91 S.Ct. 1976, 29 L.Ed.2d 647 (1971), the Court refused to extend the right to trial by jury to juvenile proceedings. In *Schall v. Martin*, 467 U.S. 253, 104 S.Ct. 2403, 81 L.Ed.2d 207 (1984), the Court upheld a pretrial detention program for juveniles that might well have been found violative of due process had it applied to adults. Writing for the Court, Justice Rehnquist stressed that "the Constitution does not mandate elimination of all differences in the treatment of juveniles." 467 U.S. at 263, 104 S.Ct. at 2409, 81 L.Ed.2d at 216.

In the wake of *Gault*, a number of states revised their juvenile codes to reflect the requirements of those decisions and to increase the qualifications of persons serving as juvenile judges and to transform juvenile courts into courts of record. Today it is common for the juvenile court to be simply a division of a court of general jurisdiction, such as a circuit or a superior court. Nevertheless, juvenile courts retain their distinctive character. For example, juvenile court proceedings are not subject to the constitutional "public trial" requirement. The Federal Juvenile Delinquency Act, 18 U.S.C.A. §§ 5031–5042, gives the court discretion on the issue of whether to close proceedings involving a child and whether to grant public access to the records of the proceedings.

### JURISPRUDENCE

*In re Gault*, 387 U.S. 1, 87 S.Ct. 1428, 18 L.Ed.2d 527 (1967)

After a neighbor complained of receiving an obscene phone call, fifteen-year-old Gerald Gault was taken into custody and brought before a juvenile court in Gila County, Arizona. As was normal at that time, the case against Gault proceeded without many of the constitutional protections afforded to adult defendants in criminal courts. In particular, Gault was denied the right to an attorney, was not formally notified of the charges against him, was not informed of his protection against self-incrimination, and was not given an opportunity to confront his accuser. After a brief hearing, Gault was judged to be delinquent and was ordered to serve six years in juvenile detention. Two years later, the U.S. Supreme Court held that the process leading to Gault's detention was constitutionally defective: juvenile proceedings must observe the rudiments of due process of law. Justice Abe Fortas, writing for the Court in *Gault*, observed, "Under our Constitution, the condition of being a boy does not justify a kangaroo court."

State laws vary, often allowing the presiding judge to exercise discretion in these matters. Despite reforms enacted after *Gault*, there remain significant differences in the adjudication of juvenile cases and adult criminal proceedings as well as the punishments imposed.

# The Corrections System

**corrections system** The system of prisons, jails, and other penal and correctional institutions.

The **corrections system** is designed to fulfill the criminal justice system's objective of providing punishment and rehabilitation of offenders. As with the court system, corrections facilities are operated at the federal and state levels. The system includes prisons and jails as well as a variety of programs such as probation, parole, and supervised community service.

## Historical Background

Punishments inflicted under the English common law were quite severe—the death penalty was prescribed for most felonies, and those convicted of misdemeanors were generally subjected to such corporal punishment as flogging in the public square. The new American colonies generally followed common-law practice; by the time of the American Revolution, the death penalty was in wide use for a variety of felonies, and corporal punishment, primarily flogging, was widely used for a variety of crimes.

**cruel and unusual punishments** Criminal penalties that shock the moral conscience of the community—for example, torture and other extreme forms of corporal punishment. Prohibited by the Eighth Amendment to the U.S. Constitution.

The Eighth Amendment to the U.S. Constitution prohibited the imposition of **"cruel and unusual punishments."** The framers sought to prevent the use of torture, which had been common in Europe as late as the eighteenth century; however, they did not intend to outlaw the death penalty or abolish all forms of corporal punishment.

**penitentiary** A synonym for prison. Literally, a place for doing penance.

During the nineteenth century, reformers introduced the concept of the **penitentiary**—literally, "a place to do penance." The idea was that criminals could be reformed through isolation, Bible study, and hard labor. This gave rise to the notion of *rehabilitation*—the idea that the criminal justice system could reform criminals and reintegrate them into society. Many of the educational, occupational training, and psychological programs found in modern prisons are based on this theory.

**death penalty** Capital punishment; a sentence of death for the commission of a crime.

## Contemporary Developments in Criminal Punishment

**monetary fines** Sums of money that offenders are required to pay as punishment for the commission of crimes.

By the twentieth century, incarceration largely replaced corporal punishment as the states, as well as the federal government, constructed prisons to house persons convicted of felonies. Even cities and counties constructed jails for the confinement of persons convicted of misdemeanors. The **death penalty**, an intensely controversial penalty, remains in effect today for certain federal offenses and in more than half the states for the most aggravated cases of murder. Today, the focus of criminal punishment is on the goal of incapacitation to prevent commission of further crimes.

**incarceration** Imprisonment.

**probation** Conditional release of a convicted criminal in lieu of incarceration.

**community service** A sentence or condition of probation requiring that the criminal perform some specific service to the community for some specified period of time.

There are procedural as well as substantive issues in the area of sentencing and punishment. Sharp disagreements exist regarding the roles that legislatures, judges, and corrections officials should play in determining punishments. Specifically, criminal punishment is limited by the Eighth Amendment prohibition of cruel and unusual punishments, the Due Process Clauses of the Fifth and Fourteenth Amendments, and by similar provisions in all fifty state constitutions. Today the criminal law provides for a variety of criminal punishments, including **monetary fines, incarceration**, **probation**, **community service**, and, of course, the death penalty.

As with courts, there is a federal corrections system and fifty separate state corrections systems. Each of these systems is responsible for supervising those persons sentenced to prison by courts of law. Originally, prisons were conceived as places for criminals to reflect on their misdeeds and repent; hence the term "penitentiary." In the twentieth century, the emphasis shifted to rehabilitation through psychological and sociopsychological methods. Unfortunately, these efforts were less than successful. Ironically, prisons appear to "criminalize" individuals more than they rehabilitate them. Inmates are exposed to an insular society with norms of conduct antithetical to those of civil society. As essentially totalitarian institutions, prisons do not encourage individuals to behave responsibly; furthermore, prisons provide an excellent venue for the spreading of criminal techniques. It is probably unrealistic to expect rehabilitation programs to succeed in such an environment. Today, prisons are generally regarded as little more than a way to punish and isolate those persons deemed unfit to live in civil society.

## America's Massive Prison Population

At midyear 2010, there were more than 2.2 million inmates in the United States. About 1.5 million prisoners were incarcerated in the federal or state prison systems; nearly 750,000 more were held in local jails or other correctional facilities. In 2010, more than seven million people were in jail or prison or on probation or parole, which is roughly more than three percent of all adult residents in the United States (or one in every 33 adults). (U.S. Department of Justice, Office of Justice Programs, Bureau of Justice Statistics, "Correctional Population in the United States, 2010," December 2011, NCJ 236319).

After decades of very rapid growth, the last several years have seen slower growth rates in state and federal prison populations. Nevertheless, most prisons are operating beyond design capacity and some state prisons are seriously overcrowded. Responding to lawsuits based on the Eighth Amendment's Cruel and Unusual Punishments Clause, federal courts have imposed limits on some prison populations. In 2005, about one in eight state prisons were under federal court orders to reduce prison populations (U.S. Department of Justice, Office of Justice Programs, Bureau of Justice Statistics Bulletin, "Census of State and Federal Correctional Facilities, 2005," October 2008, NCJ 222182).

## The Future Outlook

The public continues to demand harsh sentences for convicted felons, but legislators (and taxpayers) are often unwilling to pay the price of constructing more prisons. Moreover, local residents often object to prisons being built in their "backyards." Even those states that have been aggressive in prison construction have found that demand for cell space continues to exceed supply. In many instances, federal courts have ordered prison officials to reduce overcrowding to comply with the U.S. Constitution's prohibition against "cruel and unusual punishments."

In many state prisons, cells originally designed for one or two inmates now house three or four prisoners. Increasingly, state prison systems must rely on local jails to house inmates, a situation that presents its own set of problems relating both to security and to conditions of confinement. Aside from the threat of federal judicial intervention, overcrowded prisons are more likely to produce inmate violence and even riots.

In addition to prisons, corrections systems include agencies that supervise probation, parole, community service, and other forms of alternative sentences. With burgeoning prison populations, these alternatives to incarceration are assuming more importance and consuming more resources, especially at the state level.

## Conclusion

The American system of criminal justice is extremely complicated. The primary reason for this complexity is the principle of federalism, which refers to the division of political and legal authority in this country between one national government and fifty state governments. The U.S. Congress on behalf of the national government and each state legislature on behalf of its respective state enact their own criminal laws. The national government and all fifty state governments have their own law enforcement agencies, prosecutors, courts, and prison systems. No two systems are exactly alike. Indeed, there is tremendous variation from one jurisdiction to the next, both in the substantive criminal law and in the practices and procedures used by the various components of the criminal process. Yet, despite their substantive and procedural differences, all jurisdictions share two basic goals: to protect society from crime and, at the same time, to protect the rights of the individuals suspected of having committed offenses. Much of the conflict and inefficiency inherent in our criminal justice system stems from the need to balance these two competing objectives.

## Chapter Summary

- Learning Objective 1

  - Under our system of federalism, the national government and each of the fifty states operates its own system of criminal justice. Each has its own legislature, law enforcement and corrections agencies, and courts of law.
  - Because the federal government and the government of each state enacts its own criminal laws and has its own system of courts to interpret those laws, there are significant variations across the states and between the state and federal systems.

- Learning Objective 2

  - The U.S. Congress enacts laws defining federal crimes and setting punishments for those crimes. State legislatures define offenses and set punishments for their states and authorize local governing bodies to enact ordinances defining minor offenses and setting penalties.
  - Federal courts interpret and apply acts of Congress; state courts do likewise with regard to their respective states' laws.
  - Federal law enforcement agencies enforce federal laws; state and local agencies enforce state criminal prohibitions.

- Learning Objective 3

  - State legislatures have inherently broad powers to enact laws to further the public safety, order, health, and welfare.
  - Congress's legislative powers are restricted to constitutionally enumerated and implied powers, although in the modern era these powers have been exercised and interpreted quite broadly.

o Criminal laws are written in general terms and sometimes the meaning of criminal prohibitions is unclear. Courts must interpret statutes to determine their meaning as applied to particular cases.

o American courts basically adhere to the doctrine of following precedent (*stare decisis*). This provides predictability and stability in the law.

o Where legislative bodies use certain terms that are not defined, judges look to the common law for definitions and follow certain canons of construction for interpreting statutes that are unclear.

- Learning Objective 4

o Numerous federal and state agencies are responsible for enforcement of the criminal law. They investigate suspected criminal activity, arrest suspected criminals, and detain arrested persons until their cases come before the appropriate courts.

o Unlike their medieval forebears, modern law enforcement agencies are highly constrained by law and emphasize professionalism.

- Learning Objective 5

o The U.S. Attorney General heads the Department of Justice. U.S. Attorneys and their assistants prosecute federal offenses. At the state level a state or district attorney is the prosecutor.

o The prosecutor serves a vital function in the criminal justice system and is vested with broad discretion in determining whether to bring charges and, if so, the level of those charges.

o Defense counsel are guardians of the defendant's constitutional rights and the legality of the system. Defense attorneys serve as counselors to assist defendants in determining their best course of action and represent a defendant at trial when he or she elects to plead not guilty.

o In all but criminal prosecutions except for petty offenses, indigent defendants are entitled to government-furnished counsel, usually a public defender.

- Learning Objective 6

o At the federal level and in many states, grand juries review evidence of criminal activity and determine whether to hand down an indictment or presentment.

o Grand juries are not trial juries; they do not determine guilt or innocence, but only whether a criminal charge is warranted.

o An alternative mechanism for charging defendants is an "information" filed by a prosecutor followed by a preliminary hearing.

- Learning Objective 7

o The judicial branch operates through trial and appellate courts at both the national and state levels.

o At the national level U.S. District Courts are staffed by judges and U.S. Attorneys who prosecute federal offenses. The U.S. Courts of Appeal hear appeals from decisions of these courts.

o At the state level, where most criminal trials occur, trial courts conduct trials, sentence defendants found guilty and deal with posttrial functions. Appellate courts correct errors made at the trial level and, where it becomes necessary, fill in the gaps of the statutory law by exercising a lawmaking function.

o At the apex of the system is the U.S. Supreme Court, where nine justices who serve for life become the final arbiters of whether federal and state laws pass constitutional muster.

- The Supreme Court has jurisdiction to review, either on appeal or by writ of certiorari (discretionary review), all the decisions of the lower federal courts and many decisions of the highest state courts.

- Learning Objective 8

  - Military tribunals are empowered to try any offense by military personnel under the Uniform Code of Military Justice. A military commander convenes a court-martial composed of military officers and, in some instances, enlisted personnel. A trial counsel serves as prosecutor and defendants are furnished military lawyers unless they choose to employ civilian attorneys. Jurisdiction and the level of authorized punishment depends on whether the court-martial is summary, special, or general.
  - A military judge presides at special and general courts-martial. Military courts basically follow federal court procedures and rules of evidence. The military has an appellate system consisting of courts of review and the U.S. Court of Appeals for the Armed Forces.

- Learning Objective 9

  - Every state has its own system for administering justice to juveniles. The system has evolved from an informal system that focused on rehabilitation to an adversarial system that emphasizes due process.
  - Today the juvenile justice system includes specialized courts, law enforcement agencies, social services agencies, and corrections facilities that address juvenile delinquency and child neglect and abuse.
  - In addition to statutory offenses, juveniles are subject to punishment for certain status offenses. Juveniles are entitled to most constitutional rights afforded to adults but they are not entitled to jury trials.

- Learning Objective 10

  - Federal and state corrections facilities include prisons and jails as well as probation, parole, and supervised community service.
  - The correctional system administers the death penalty for certain federal offenses and for murder under the laws of many states.
  - Additional corrective procedures include incarceration, monetary fines, probation, and parole.
  - Today, the focus of criminal punishment is on the goal of incapacitation to prevent commission of further crimes rather than the rehabilitation of offenders.
  - Increasingly, the public demands that those who commit the most serious felonies be sentenced to lengthy prison terms. As a result, prisons are overflowing, and in many instances federal courts have ordered prison officials to reduce overcrowding to comply with the U.S. Constitution's prohibition against "cruel and unusual punishments."

## Key Terms

| | |
|---|---|
| appellate courts | corrections system |
| Attorney General | Court of Appeals for the Armed Forces |
| canons of construction | court-martial |
| community policing | courts of general jurisdiction |
| community service | courts of limited jurisdiction |

cruel and unusual punishments

death penalty

defense attorney

Department of Justice (DOJ)

*en banc* hearing

enumerated powers

Federal Bureau of Investigation (FBI)

federalism

grand jury

implied exception

implied powers

incarceration

independent counsel

indictment

indigent defendants

intermediate appellate courts

jurisdiction

jury

juvenile court

juvenile delinquency

legislative intent

legislature

monetary fines

no bill

*nolle prosequi*

order maintenance

*parens patriae*

penitentiary

petit (trial) jury

plain meaning rule

plea bargaining

police departments

probation

prosecutor

prosecutor's information

public defender

rules of procedure

rules of statutory interpretation

session laws

sheriff

special agents

speedy and public trial

state supreme court

state's attorneys

status offenses

statute

sworn officers

trial courts

true bill

U.S. Code

Uniform Code of Military Justice (UCMJ)

United States Attorneys

United States Code Annotated (U.S.C.A.)

United States Congress

United States Courts of Appeals

United States District Courts

United States Marshals Service

United States Supreme Court

void for vagueness

writ of certiorari

## Questions for Thought and Discussion

1. How does the concept of federalism complicate the administration of criminal justice in the United States?
2. Describe the functions of federal and state law enforcement agencies.
3. Compare and contrast the functions of trial and appellate courts. How are they similar? How are they different?
4. What function does a grand jury serve? Does replacement of the indictment function of grand juries at the state level with prosecutors authorized to charge crimes by filing a sworn information impair the rights of citizens charged with crimes?

5. Is there a justification for the broad discretion vested in a prosecutor?
6. To what extent does the United States Constitution protect the right to trial by jury in a criminal case?
7. What are the arguments for and against allowing trial judges broad discretion in criminal sentencing?
8. What factors do you think a prosecutor should take into consideration in determining whether to prosecute an individual the police have arrested for possession of illegal drugs?
9. What chief characteristics distinguish the military justice system under the Uniform Code of Military Justice from civilian criminal prosecutions?
10. What factors should a judge consider in determining whether to sentence a convicted felon to prison?

# The Substantive Criminal Law

# Constitutional Limitations on the Prohibition of Criminal Conduct

## CHAPTER OUTLINE

## JURISPRUDENCE

## LEARNING OBJECTIVES

After reading this chapter, you should be able to explain

1. what judicial review is and why it is important to the criminal law

2. how and why the U.S. Congress has created a body of federal criminal law

3. how the federal constitution limits prosecution for treason and prohibits the enactment of bills of attainder and *ex post facto* laws

4. how and why the Bill of Rights impacts the criminal law at both the federal and state levels

5. how the First Amendment freedoms of speech, religion, and assembly limit the enactment and enforcement of certain criminal prohibitions

6. the different interpretations of the Second Amendment right to keep and bear arms and the implications of these different interpretations for the criminal law

*Continued*

*Continued*

7. how and why the U.S. Constitution prohibits criminal laws that are overbroad and/or excessively vague

8. how the freedom from compulsory self-incrimination limits laws that require parties to report certain types of information to the government

9. how and why the Eighth Amendment's prohibition against cruel and unusual punishments makes it unconstitutional for government to criminalize "status"

10. how the constitutional right of privacy protects people from criminal prohibitions of consensual sexual conduct and how and why courts have recognized a "right to die"

11. why the provision of the Fourteenth Amendment regarding equal protection of the laws is important in limiting the enforcement of criminal prohibitions

12. the standards that courts employ when reviewing statutes challenged as being unconstitutional and why the state constitutions also provide significant constraints on the enactment and enforcement of statutes

# CHAPTER OPENING VIGNETTE

The Second Amendment to the U.S. Constitution provides, "A well regulated Militia, being necessary to the security of a free State, the right of the people to keep and bear Arms, shall not be infringed." Over the years this language has been the source of considerable scholarly commentary and political controversy. In recent decades governments at all levels have enacted laws regulating, and in some instances prohibiting, the possession and use of firearms. Many of these prohibitions are criminal in nature. Are such gun control laws consistent with the Second Amendment? Until recently the Supreme Court, stressing the "well regulated Militia" language of the Amendment, seemed to have little problem with gun control laws. However, in *District of Columbia v. Heller*, 554 U.S. 570, 128 S.Ct. 2783, 171 L.Ed.2d 637 (2008), the Court held that the Second Amendment protects an individual's right to possess a firearm in the home for personal protection. In so holding, the Court struck down a Washington, D.C. ordinance that effectively banned possession of handguns in the District, even in one's home.

The *Heller* decision left open the question of whether this personal right to bear arms limits state and local governments from enforcing similar prohibitions. After all, the Second Amendment, like the other amendments found in the Bill of Rights, was adopted as a limitation on the national government. Because Washington, D.C. is a federal enclave, there was never any question that the Second Amendment applied to it. Immediately after the *Heller* decision, gun

p3. 1

rights activists sought to challenge handgun bans in cities across America. In 2010 one of these challenges resulted in a decision by the Supreme Court.

In *McDonald v. Chicago*, 561 U.S. 3025, 130 S.Ct. 3020, 177 L.Ed.2d 894 (2010), the Supreme Court held that the Second Amendment applies to state and local governments via the Fourteenth Amendment, which prohibits states from depriving persons of liberty without due process of law. The Court basically held that the right to keep and bear arms is an essential aspect of liberty. Furthermore, the Court reaffirmed what it said in *Heller*—that the right to keep and bear arms is a personal right irrespective of any service in a militia.

Both *Heller* and *McDonald* were 5–4 decisions. Both produced strongly worded dissenting opinions from justices in the minority. Both show the ongoing relevance of the U.S. Constitution to the criminal law. Congress, the state legislatures, and city and county lawmaking bodies cannot enact just any criminal prohibition that they deem to be in keeping with the public interest. Criminal laws must be consistent with the federal and state constitutions. This chapter examines the most important constitutional limitations on the enactment and enforcement of criminal laws.

## Introduction

In most democratic countries, legislative bodies are supreme in enacting statutes defining crimes and providing penalties. The only overarching authority is the will of the people, as manifested through the ballot box. Being very familiar with the English monarchy and its parliamentary system, the framers of the U.S. Constitution understood that unbridled power to make and enforce criminal prohibitions constitutes a serious threat to liberty. Thus, they framed a constitution that limits the power of Congress and state legislatures to enact criminal statutes. Although federal and state legislative bodies have authority to enact statutes defining crimes and setting penalties, various provisions of the U.S. Constitution and state constitutions limit that power.

Our goal in this chapter is to provide an overview of the various constitutional provisions that limit legislative authority to define conduct as criminal and prescribe penalties for violations or offenses. We discuss the effect of judicial interpretations of criminal statutes and the power of courts to declare void laws that violate the constitutional principles.

## The Importance of Judicial Review

**judicial review** The power of courts to strike down legislation and other governmental actions determined to be unconstitutional.

Constitutional limits on the enactment and enforcement of criminal statutes do not depend for their vitality only on the voluntary compliance of legislators, prosecutors, and police officers. Under the doctrine of **judicial review**, courts are empowered to declare null and void laws that violate constitutional principles. In a landmark decision in 1803, the Supreme Court first asserted the power to invalidate legislation that is in conflict with the Constitution. *Marbury v. Madison*, 5 U.S. (1 Cranch) 137, 2 L.Ed. 60 (1803). Speaking for the Court in *Marbury*, Chief Justice John Marshall said, "It is emphatically the province and duty of the judicial department to say what the law is." 5 U.S. (1 Cranch) at 177, 2 L.Ed. at 175. Although the power of judicial review is generally associated with the Supreme Court, all courts of record, whether state or federal, can exercise the power to strike down unconstitutional legislation. It is doubtful whether constitutional limitations on governmental power would be meaningful in the absence of judicial review.

Throughout this textbook, we will be discussing constitutional limitations on the criminal justice system. Many of these principles are procedural in nature, imposing restrictions and obligations on law enforcement, prosecution, adjudication, and sentencing. In this chapter we are concerned only with those constitutional provisions that place limits on the substantive criminal law, both in the types of laws that legislatures are barred from enacting and the situations in which police and prosecutors are barred from enforcing existing statutes.

## Unconstitutional Per Se and Unconstitutional as Applied

**unconstitutional per se** Refers to a law that is unconstitutional on its face, meaning that it is invalid under any given circumstances.

**unconstitutional as applied** Refers to a declaration by a court of law that a statute is invalid insofar as it is enforced in some particular context.

In addressing constitutional assaults on criminal statutes, courts are sometimes asked to declare that a statute is unconstitutional under any circumstances, whereas in other instances a court might simply be asked to rule that the statute cannot constitutionally apply to certain conduct. A statute may be declared **unconstitutional per se** in that it inherently trenches on some constitutionally protected liberty or exceeds the constitutional powers of government. For example, a law that would restrict citizens' freedom to profess their religious beliefs would be inherently unconstitutional. Alternatively, a law that is facially valid, such as an ordinance prohibiting disorderly conduct, may be declared **unconstitutional as applied** if it is enforced in a way that impermissibly restricts or punishes the exercise of constitutional rights.

## The Power to Enact Criminal Laws

Because our nation is committed to the rule of law, "there is no crime, there is no punishment, without law." As we saw in Chapter 1, no one can be guilty of a crime in the absence of a law that prohibits a particular type of wrongful conduct. As Chapter 2 pointed out, it is the role of legislatures to enact statutes that define crimes and provide for punishments.

## Police Powers of State Legislatures

**police power** The power of government to enact legislation to protect the public health, safety, order, and welfare.

The **police power** of government is the authority to enact legislation to protect the public health, safety, order, and welfare. Under our system of federalism, the police power of government is vested primarily in the state legislatures. State legislatures have comprehensive power to adopt statutes regulating the activities of individuals and corporations as long as these statutes do not violate limitations contained in the state and federal constitutions. State legislatures, in turn, may delegate some of this power to local governments, which enact ordinances defining criminal offenses within their jurisdictions.

## The Federal Lawmaking Power

Unlike the state legislatures, the U.S. Congress does not possess plenary legislative authority (except over the District of Columbia and federal territories). As James Madison observed in 1788,

> The powers delegated by the proposed Constitution to the federal government are few and defined. Those which are to remain in the State governments are numerous and indefinite. *The Federalist* No. 45, pp. 292–293 (C. Rossiter, ed., 1961).

**enumerated powers** Governmental powers explicitly granted by that government's constitution.

Article I, Section 8 of the U.S. Constitution enumerates Congress's legislative powers. Several of these **enumerated powers** allow Congress to enact criminal laws in certain areas. These include the power to establish rules governing immigration and naturalization, to "define and punish piracies and felonies committed on the high seas," and to "provide for the punishment of counterfeiting the securities and current coin of the United States."

**implied powers** Governmental powers not explicitly stated in that government's constitution but fairly implied by it.

**doctrine of implied powers** Judicial doctrine interpreting the Necessary and Proper Clause of Article I, Section 8 of the U.S. Constitution to allow Congress to exercise powers that are plainly adapted to the goal of furthering one or more of Congress's enumerated powers.

Congress also possesses a reservoir of **implied powers**, which are justified by the Necessary and Proper Clause of Article I, Section 8. The **doctrine of implied powers** was established by the Supreme Court in *McCulloch v. Maryland,* 17 U.S. (4 Wheat.) 316, 4 L.Ed. 579 (1819). Writing for the Court, Chief Justice Marshall articulated the doctrine as follows: "Let the end be legitimate, let it be within the scope of the Constitution, and all means which are plainly adapted to that end, which are not prohibited, but consist with the letter and spirit of the Constitution, are constitutional." 17 U.S. (4 Wheat.) at 421, 4 L.Ed. at 605.

The doctrine of implied powers expands the legislative capabilities of Congress but does not give Congress the plenary legislative authority possessed by state legislatures. To qualify as a valid expression of implied powers, federal legislation must be plainly adapted to the goal of furthering one or more of Congress's enumerated powers. For example, Congress had the authority under its enumerated spending power to establish the Social Security system in 1935. *Steward Machine Co. v. Davis*, 301 U.S. 548, 57 S.Ct. 883, 81 L.Ed. 1279 (1937). Under the doctrine of implied powers, Congress also had the authority to make Social Security fraud a federal offense. See 42 U.S.C.A. § 408(a)(1)–(8). Criminalizing Social Security fraud is a "necessary and proper" means of protecting a system that Congress had the authority to create.

Of course, in some instances, the connection between enumerated and implied powers is not so clear. In *United States v. Comstock*, 560 U.S. —, 130 S.Ct. 1949, 176 L.Ed.2d. 878 (2010), the Supreme Court upheld a federal statute that permits federal courts to order the confinement of violent sexual predators who have completed their criminal sentences. The Court concluded that "the statute is a 'necessary and proper' means of exercising the federal authority that permits

Congress to create federal criminal laws, to punish their violation, to imprison violators, to provide appropriately for those imprisoned, and to maintain the security of those who are not imprisoned but who may be affected by the federal imprisonment of others." 560 U.S. at —, 130 S.Ct. at 1965, 176 L.Ed.2d. at 885. In dissent, Justice Clarence Thomas averred that the Court had come "perilously close to transforming the Necessary and Proper Clause into a basis for the federal police power that 'we *always* have rejected.'" 560 U.S. at —, 130 S.Ct. at 1983, 176 L.Ed.2d. at 919.

## The Commerce Clause

**interstate commerce** Economic activity between or among states or affecting more than one state.

In terms of the criminal law, by far the most significant of Congress's enumerated powers is the power to regulate **interstate commerce**. For example, Congress is not empowered to prohibit prostitution per se, but Congress may make it a crime to transport persons across state lines for "immoral purposes" by drawing on its broad power to regulate interstate commerce. *Hoke v. United States*, 227 U.S. 308, 33 S.Ct. 281, 57 L.Ed. 523 (1913).

Over the years Congress has relied on the Commerce Clause to enact a wide variety of criminal laws, including prohibitions against the following:

- interstate transportation of kidnapped persons (see 18 U.S.C.A. § 1201)
- interstate transportation of stolen automobiles (see 18 U.S.C.A. § 2312)
- manufacture, sale, distribution, and possession of controlled substances (see 21 U.S.C.A. § 801 *et seq.*)
- carjacking (see 18 U.S.C.A. § 2119)
- fraudulent schemes that use interstate television, radio, or wire communications (see 18 U.S.C.A. § 1343)
- conspiracies to restrain trade (see 15 U.S.C.A. § 1 *et seq.*)
- loan sharking (see 18 U.S.C.A. § 891 *et seq.*)
- computer crimes (see 18 U.S.C.A. § 1030)
- racketeering and organized crime (see 18 U.S.C.A. §§ 1961–1963)
- air pollution (see 42 U.S.C.A. §§ 7401–7642)
- water pollution (see 33 U.S.C.A. §§ 1251–1376)
- violations of regulations protecting endangered species (see 16 U.S.C.A. §§ 1531–1544)

In the modern era, Congress has stretched the concept of interstate commerce to justify broader authority to enact criminal statutes. For the most part, the courts have been willing to accommodate this expansion of federal legislative power. For example, in *Perez v. United States,* 402 U.S. 146, 91 S.Ct. 1357, 28 L.Ed.2d 686 (1971), the Supreme Court upheld the federal law against loansharking. However, in recent years the Supreme Court has circumscribed this authority somewhat. In *United States v. Lopez,* 514 U.S. 549, 115 S.Ct. 1624, 131 L.Ed.2d 626 (1995), the Court struck down the Gun-Free School Zones Act of 1990, which made it a federal crime for any person to knowingly possess a firearm while close to a school. Writing for the Court, Chief Justice William Rehnquist observed that "the challenged statute has nothing to do with 'commerce' or any sort of economic enterprise, however broadly one might define those terms." 514 U.S. at 560, 115 S.Ct. at 1631, 131 L.Ed.2d at 639. Similarly, in *United States v. Morrison,* 529 U.S. 598, 120 S.Ct. 1740, 146 L.Ed.2d 658 (2000), the Court struck down a provision of the Violence Against Women Act of 1994 that provided a federal civil remedy to victims of gender-motivated violence.

Together, *Lopez* and *Morrison* called into question a number of the criminal statutes enacted by Congress under the Commerce Clause. One of these was the federal Controlled Substances Act, 21 U.S.C.A. § 801 *et seq.,* which defines federal drug crimes (see Chapter 10). In *Gonzales v. Raich*, 545 U.S. 1, 125 S.Ct. 2195, 162 L.Ed.2d 1 (2005), the Supreme Court rejected a challenge to the federal prohibition of possession of marijuana. *Gonzales v. Raich* suggests that despite the decisions in *Lopez* and *Morrison,* Congress retains broad authority under the Commerce Clause to deal with social problems of national scope.

# Delimiting the Crime of Treason

**treason** The crime of making war against one's own government or giving aid and comfort to its enemies.

**Treason** involves betrayal of one's country, either by making war against it or by giving aid and comfort to its enemies. At common law, treason was the most heinous crime a person could commit. It was in a category by itself, considered far worse than any felony. English kings had used the crime of treason to punish and deter political opposition. For example, in 1683 one Algernon Sidney was executed for treason based primarily on published writings deemed to be subversive of the Crown. Being aware of these abuses of the criminal law, the framers of the U.S. Constitution sought to prohibit the federal government from using the offense of treason to punish political dissenters. Thus, they specifically defined treason against the United States in Article III, Section 3, paragraph 1, saying it "shall consist only in levying War against them, or in adhering to their Enemies, giving them Aid and Comfort." To make it more difficult for the government to prosecute people for treason, the same paragraph included the following injunction: "No Person shall be convicted of Treason unless on the Testimony of two Witnesses to the same overt Act, or on Confession in open Court." Thus, no one may be convicted of treason against the United States based solely on circumstantial evidence. In large part due to these constitutional limitations, treason is a rarely prosecuted offense in the modern era. (For further discussion, see Chapter 12.)

# Bills of Attainder and *Ex Post Facto* Laws

Two historic abuses of the English Parliament that the framers of the Constitution sought to correct were bills of attainder and *ex post facto* laws. Article I, Section 9 of the Constitution prohibits Congress from adopting bills of attainder and *ex post facto* laws. Article I, Section 10 extends these same prohibitions to the state legislatures.

## Bills of Attainder

**bill of attainder** A legislative act imposing punishment without trial upon persons deemed guilty of treason or felonies. Bills of attainder are prohibited by the U.S. Constitution.

A **bill of attainder** is a legislative act inflicting punishment on an individual or on a group of easily identifiable individuals. Laws of this character are antithetical to the basic principle that a person accused of wrongdoing is entitled to a fair trial in a court of law. Writing for the Supreme Court in *United States v. Lovett*, 328 U.S. 303, 66 S.Ct. 1073, 90 L.Ed. 1252 (1946), Justice Hugo Black reflected on the constitutional prohibition against bills of attainder:

> When our Constitution and Bill of Rights were written, our ancestors had ample reason to know that legislative trials and punishments were too dangerous to liberty

to exist in the nation of free men they envisioned. And so they proscribed bills of attainder. 328 U.S. at 318, 66 S.Ct. at 1080, 90 L.Ed. at 1261.

In *United States v. Brown*, 381 U.S. 437, 85 S.Ct. 1707, 14 L.Ed.2d 484 (1965), the Supreme Court struck down a law barring Communist Party members from holding positions as officers of labor unions. The Court found the prohibition to constitute a bill of attainder in that it punished easily identifiable members of a class by imposing upon them the sanction of a mandatory forfeiture of a position to which they would otherwise be entitled. Subsequently, in *Nixon v. Administrator of General Services*, 433 U.S. 425, 97 S.Ct. 2777, 53 L.Ed.2d 867 (1977), the Supreme Court said that in reviewing a law challenged as a bill of attainder, a court must consider (1) whether the statute falls within the historic meaning of legislative punishment; (2) whether the statute, viewed in terms of the type and severity of the burdens imposed, reasonably can be said to further nonpunitive legislative purposes; and (3) whether the legislative record evinces a legislative intent to punish. A statute that fails any of the prongs of the test may be declared unconstitutional.

## Ex Post Facto Laws

Sir William Blackstone, the great commentator on the English common law, wrote that an ***ex post facto* law** exists "when after an action (indifferent in itself) is committed, the legislator then for the first time declares it to have been a crime, and inflicts a punishment upon the person who has committed it." 1 W. Blackstone, *Commentaries* 46. Because the essence of the *ex post facto* law is retroactivity, it is flatly inconsistent with the **principle of legality**, which holds that individuals are entitled to know in advance if particular contemplated conduct is illegal. The framers of the U.S. Constitution viewed *ex post facto* laws as one of the "favorite and most formidable instruments of tyranny." *The Federalist* No. 84, p. 512 (C. Rossiter ed. 1961) (A. Hamilton). In his *Commentaries on the Constitution of the United States,* Justice Joseph Story expressed strong support for the prohibition of *ex post facto* laws:

> If the laws in being do not punish an offender, let him go unpunished; let the legislature, admonished of the defect of the laws, provide against the commission of future crimes of the same sort. The escape of one delinquent can never produce so much harm to the community, as may arise from the infraction of a rule, upon which the purity of public justice, and the existence of civil liberty, essentially depend. 3 J. Story, *Commentaries on the Constitution* § 1338, at 211, n. 2.

Although the phrase "*ex post facto* law" literally includes any law passed "after the fact," the Supreme Court has long recognized that the constitutional prohibition applies only to criminal statutes. Writing for the Supreme Court in *Calder v. Bull,* 3 U.S. (3 Dall.) 386, 1 L.Ed. 648 (1798), Justice Samuel Chase identified four types of laws that fall within the prohibition of the *ex post facto* laws:

> 1st. Every law that makes an action done before the passing of the law, and which was innocent when done, criminal, and punishes such action. 2d. Every law that aggravates a crime, or makes it greater than it was when committed. 3d. Every law that changes the punishment, and inflicts a greater punishment, than the law annexed to the crime when committed. 4th. Every law that alters the legal rules of evidence and receives less or different testimony than the law required at the time of the commission of the offense in order to convict the offender. 3 U.S. (3 Dall.) at 390, 1 L.Ed. at 651.

*ex post facto* law A retroactive law that criminalizes an action that was legal at the time it was performed or increases punishment for a criminal act after it was committed.

principle of legality The principle that there can be no crime or punishment in the absence of law.

## JURISPRUDENCE

*Carmell v. Texas*, 529 U.S. 513, 120 S.Ct. 1620, 146 L.Ed.2d 577 (2000)

In 1997 Scott Leslie Carmell was convicted in a Texas court of sexual assault, aggravated sexual assault, and indecency with a child. Evidence showed that between 1991 and 1995, Carmell committed various sex acts with his stepdaughter, starting when she was only twelve years old. Carmell was sentenced to life in prison on two convictions for aggravated sexual assault and twenty years in prison on thirteen other counts. The U.S. Supreme Court reversed four of Carmell's convictions by a vote of 5–4. These convictions were for sexual assaults that were alleged to have occurred in 1991 and 1992, when Texas law provided that a defendant could not be convicted merely on the testimony of the victim unless she was under fourteen. At the time of the alleged assaults in question, the victim was fourteen or fifteen. The law was later amended to extend the "child victim exception" to victims under eighteen years old. Carmell was convicted under the amended law, which the Supreme Court held to be an unconstitutional *ex post facto* law.

Although modern statutes are seldom invalidated as *ex post facto* laws, the courts continue to recognize Justice Chase's formulation. For example, in *Miller v. Florida*, 482 U.S. 423, 107 S.Ct. 2446, 96 L.Ed.2d 351 (1987), the Supreme Court held that Florida's sentencing guidelines, as revised by the state legislature in 1984, violated the *Ex Post Facto* Clause of the federal constitution insofar as their application caused an increase in punishment to persons whose crimes occurred before the effective date of the 1984 act.

More recently, in *Carmell v. Texas*, 529 U.S. 513, 120 S.Ct. 1620, 146 L.Ed.2d 577 (2000), the Supreme Court reversed a conviction for sexual assault of a minor because the state had applied retroactively a law altering the requirement that a victim's testimony be corroborated. The Court held that laws changing the rules of evidence to disadvantage defendants may not be applied retroactively.

Similarly, in *Stogner v. California*, 539 U.S. 607, 123 S.Ct. 2446, 156 L.Ed.2d 544 (2003), the Supreme Court broadened the prohibition against *ex post facto* laws. In 1994, California enacted a law lifting the statute of limitations in child molestation cases where the victim remembers the abuse after the statute of limitations runs out. In 2001, seventy-two-year-old Marion Stogner was charged with molesting his daughters nearly fifty years earlier. Before the enactment of the new law, the state's statute of limitations would have barred Stogner's prosecution, as it prohibited prosecution more than three years after the crime had occurred. In a 5–4 decision, the Supreme Court held that California's new law extending the statute of limitations could not be constitutionally applied to allow prosecution of cases in which prosecution would have been foreclosed by the statute of limitations prior to the enactment of the new law.

## The Bill of Rights

**First Amendment** Article I of the Bill of Rights, which recognizes the freedoms of religion, speech, press, and assembly, as well as the right to petition government for a redress of grievances.

Although the original Constitution contained few express limitations on legislative power, the Bill of Rights added several important constraints on Congress. Ratified in 1791, the Bill of Rights consists of the first ten amendments to the Constitution. From the standpoint of the substantive criminal law the most significant of these are the **First Amendment** freedoms of expression, religion, and assembly; the Second Amendment protection of "the right to keep and bear arms"; the Fifth Amendment Due Process Clause; the Eighth Amendment Cruel and Unusual

Punishments Clause; and the Ninth Amendment guarantee of "rights retained by the people."

The First Amendment begins with the injunction that *"Congress* shall make no law . . ." [emphasis added]. Unlike certain provisions in the original, unamended Constitution, the Bill of Rights makes no mention of limitations on the state and local governments. Throughout much of the nineteenth century, the Bill of Rights was viewed as imposing limitations only on Congress, having no effect on state legislatures or local governing bodies. The Supreme Court officially adopted this view in *Barron v. Baltimore*, 32 U.S. (7 Pet.) 243, 8 L.Ed. 672 (1833). Under this interpretation of the Bill of Rights, citizens had to look to their state constitutions and state courts for protection against state and local actions that infringed on their rights and liberties.

## Application of the Bill of Rights to State and Local Laws

**Fourteenth Amendment** Amendment to the U.S. Constitution ratified after the Civil War in 1868. Prohibits states from denying due process and equal protection of law to persons within their jurisdictions and provides Congress legislative power to enforce these prohibitions.

**Due Process Clause** The clause of the Fifth Amendment to the U.S. Constitution that prohibits the federal government from depriving persons within its jurisdiction of life, liberty, or property without due process of law. A similar provision in the Fourteenth Amendment imposes the same prohibition on state governments.

The ratification of the **Fourteenth Amendment** in 1868 provided a justification for extending the scope of the Bill of Rights to apply against the states. Section 1 of the Fourteenth Amendment enjoins the states from depriving "any person of life, liberty, or property, without due process of law." It also prohibits states from adopting laws that "abridge the privileges and immunities of citizens of the United States."

In a series of decisions, the Supreme Court has held that the **Due Process Clause** of the Fourteenth Amendment makes enforceable against the states those provisions of the Bill of Rights that are "implicit in the concept of ordered liberty." *Palko v. Connecticut*, 302 U.S. 319, 58 S.Ct. 149, 82 L.Ed. 288 (1937). This doctrine of incorporation has been employed by the Court to enforce the procedural guarantees of the Bill of Rights in state criminal prosecutions. For example, in *Wolf v. Colorado*, 338 U.S. 25, 69 S.Ct. 1359, 93 L.Ed. 1782 (1949), the Court said that the Fourth Amendment protection against unreasonable searches and seizures is applicable to state and local, as well as federal, law enforcement authorities. Similarly, in *Duncan v. Louisiana*, 391 U.S. 145, 88 S.Ct. 1444, 20 L.Ed.2d 491 (1968), the Court held that the Fourteenth Amendment requires states to observe the jury trial requirement of the Sixth Amendment.

In addition to incorporating the procedural protections of the Bill of Rights into the Fourteenth Amendment, the Court has extended the substantive limitations of the Bill of Rights to the states. In 1925 the Supreme Court recognized that the First Amendment protections of free speech and free press apply to state as well as federal laws. *Gitlow v. New York*, 268 U.S. 652, 45 S.Ct. 625, 69 L.Ed. 1138 (1925). Likewise, in *Cantwell v. Connecticut*, 310 U.S. 296, 60 S.Ct. 900, 84 L.Ed. 1213 (1940), the Court held that the Fourteenth Amendment embraces the First Amendment's protection of free exercise of religion.

As noted earlier, in 2010 the Supreme Court held that the Second Amendment's right to keep and bear arms applies to state and local governments via the Fourteenth Amendment. *McDonald v. Chicago*, 561 U.S. 3025, 130 S.Ct. 3020, 177 L.Ed.2d 894 (2010). McDonald was the latest, and quite possibly the last, in a series of decisions incorporating provisions of the Bill of Rights into the Fourteenth Amendment (see Table 3.1). With the exception of the Fifth Amendment's Grand Jury Clause and the Eighth Amendment's prohibitions of excessive bail and excessive fines, all the provisions of the Bill of Rights have been incorporated into the Fourteenth Amendment, making them applicable to state and local governments. Thus, the U.S. Constitution,

## JURISPRUDENCE

*Cantwell v. Connecticut*, 310 U.S. 296, 60 S.Ct. 900, 84 L.Ed. 1213 (1940)

In *Cantwell v. Connecticut* (1940), the Court struck down a state law that prohibited door-to-door solicitation for any religious or charitable cause without prior approval of a state agency. The law was challenged by Newton Cantwell, a member of the Jehovah's Witnesses, a sect committed to active proselytizing. Cantwell and his sons routinely went from door to door or stopped people on the street in order to communicate a message that was highly critical of the Roman Catholic Church and other organized religions. Eventually they were arrested and charged with failure to obtain approval for solicitation under the state law, as well as with common law breach of the peace. The Court reversed the breach-of-the-peace conviction and invalidated the state statute. In so doing the Court applied the First Amendment's Free Exercise of Religion Clause to the states via the Fourteenth Amendment.

| **TABLE 3.1** | Incorporation of the Bill of Rights | | |
|---|---|---|---|
| **Amendment** | **Clause** | **Case** | **Year** |
| 1 | Establishment of Religion | *Everson v Board of Education* | 1947 |
| 1 | Free Exercise of Religion | *Cantwell v. Connecticut* | 1940 |
| 1 | Freedom of Speech | *Gitlow v. New York* | 1925 |
| 1 | Freedom of the Press | *Near v. Minnesota* | 1931 |
| 1 | Freedom of Assembly | *DeJonge v. Oregon* | 1937 |
| 1 | Petition for Redress of Grievances | *Edwards v. South Carolina* | 1963 |
| 2 | Right to Keep and Bear Arms | *McDonald v. Chicago* | 2010 |
| 4 | Unreasonable Search and Seizure | *Wolf v. Colorado* | 1949 |
| 5 | Double Jeopardy | *Benton v. Maryland* | 1969 |
| 5 | Self-Incrimination | *Malloy v. Hogan* | 1964 |
| 5 | Just compensation | *Chicago, B&Q RR v. Chicago* | 1897 |
| 6 | Right to Speedy Trial | *Klopfer v. North Carolina* | 1967 |
| 6 | Right to Public Trial | *In re Oliver* | 1948 |
| 6 | Right to Trial by Impartial Jury | *Duncan v. Louisiana* | 1968 |
| 6 | Right to Confront Witnesses | *Pointer v. Texas* | 1965 |
| 6 | Right to Compulsory Process | *Washington v. Texas* | 1967 |
| 6 | Right to Counsel | *Gideon v. Wainwright* | 1963 |
| 8 | Cruel and Unusual Punishment | *Robinson v. California* | 1962 |

© Cengage Learning 2014

and in particular the Bill of Rights, now stands as a barrier to unreasonable or oppressive criminal laws, whether they are enacted by Congress, a state legislature, or a local governing body.

# The First Amendment Freedom of Expression

Perhaps the most treasured of our liberties, and the rights most essential to maintaining a democratic polity, are the First Amendment freedoms of speech and press. Often, freedom of speech and freedom of the press are referred to jointly as "freedom of expression." Although the concept of free expression is fundamental to our democratic society, the Supreme Court has said that the First Amendment has "never been thought to give absolute protection to every individual to speak whenever or wherever he pleases, or to use any form of address in any circumstances that he chooses." *Cohen v. California*, 403 U.S. 15, 19, 91 S.Ct. 1780, 1785, 29 L.Ed.2d 284, 290 (1971). The task of the courts, of course, is to strike a reasonable balance between the right of expression and the legitimate interests of society in maintaining security, order, peace, safety, and decency. In what has become a classic phrase, Justice Oliver Wendell Holmes Jr. observed that the "most stringent protection of free speech would not protect a man in falsely shouting fire in a theater, and causing a panic." *Schenck v. United States*, 249 U.S. 47, 51, 39 S.Ct. 247, 249, 63 L.Ed. 470, 473 (1919). Moreover, the Supreme Court has said that certain types of speech are so inherently lacking in value as not to merit any First Amendment protection:

> There are certain well-defined and narrowly limited classes of speech, the prevention and punishment of which have never been thought to raise any constitutional problem. These include the lewd and obscene, the profane, the libelous, and the insulting or "fighting" words—those which by their very utterance inflict injury or tend to incite an immediate breach of the peace. It has been well observed that such utterances are no essential part of any exposition of ideas, and are of such slight social value as a step to truth that any benefit that may be derived from them is clearly outweighed by the social interest in order and morality. *Chaplinsky v. New Hampshire*, 315 U.S. 568, 571, 62 S.Ct. 766, 769, 86 L.Ed. 1031, 1035 (1942).

## Advocacy of Unlawful Conduct

One of the most basic problems posed by the First Amendment is whether speech advocating unlawful conduct might itself be made unlawful. The Supreme Court first encountered this problem in *Schenck v. United States,* supra, where an official of the Socialist Party had been convicted under the Espionage Act of 1917, 40 Stat. at L. 217, 219, of conspiring to cause insubordination in the military services and obstruct military recruitment during World War I. Speaking for a unanimous Supreme Court, Justice Oliver Wendell Holmes, Jr. observed that

> the question in every case is whether the words used are used in such circumstances and are of such a nature as to create clear and present danger that they will bring about the substantive evils that Congress has a right to prevent. . . . When a nation is at war many things that might be said in time of peace are such a hindrance to its effort that their utterance will not be endured so long as men fight, and that no court could regard them as protected by any constitutional right. 249 U.S. at 52, 39 S.Ct. at 249, 63 L.Ed. at 473.

**clear and present danger doctrine** In constitutional law, the doctrine that the First Amendment does not protect those forms of expression that pose a "clear and present danger" of bringing about some substantive evil that government has a right to prevent.

**imminent lawless action** Unlawful conduct that is about to take place and that is inevitable unless there is intervention by the authorities.

The Supreme Court first invoked the **clear and present danger doctrine** to reverse a criminal conviction in a case involving a Georgia man who had been prosecuted under a state law prohibiting "any attempt, by persuasion or otherwise" to incite insurrection. *Herndon v. Lowry*, 301 U.S. 242, 57 S.Ct. 732, 81 L.Ed. 1066 (1937).

The modern Supreme Court has refined the clear and present danger doctrine so that public advocacy may be prohibited only in situations when it is directed to inciting **imminent lawless action** and is likely to produce such action. *Brandenburg v. Ohio*, 395 U.S. 444, 89 S.Ct. 1827, 23 L.Ed.2d 430 (1969). Today, it is highly unlikely the courts would uphold a conviction in circumstances similar to those in the

---

**JURISPRUDENCE**

*Schenck v. United States*, 249 U.S. 47, 51, 39 S.Ct. 247, 249, 63 L.Ed. 470, 473 (1919)

Charles T. Schenck, general secretary of the Socialist party, was tried, convicted, and sentenced to prison for "causing and attempting to cause insubordination in the military and naval forces of the United States," in violation of the Espionage Act of 1917. The conviction stemmed from Schenck's activities in mailing out 15,000 leaflets attacking American participation in the First World War and urging young men to oppose the military draft, which the leaflet equated with involuntary servitude. The Supreme Court upheld Schenck's conviction, saying that the First Amendment does not protect speech that creates a "clear and present danger" of bringing about something that the government has the right to prevent, namely the disruption of military recruitment during wartime.

---

**JURISPRUDENCE**

*Hess v. Indiana*, 414 U.S. 105, 94 S.Ct. 326, 38 L.Ed.2d 303 (1973)

Gregory Hess was arrested during an antiwar demonstration on a college campus after he yelled out to the crowd, "We'll take the fucking street later" or similar words to that effect. Hess was convicted under the Indiana disorderly conduct statute and the state supreme court upheld the conviction. The U.S. Supreme Court reversed, holding that Hess's words were not directed to any person or group and were not likely to produce imminent lawless action.

---

*Schenck* case. The courts probably would find that mailing a leaflet or standing on a street corner urging resistance to the draft—activities that were fairly common during the Vietnam War—are not fraught with imminent lawless action and therefore do not constitute a clear and present danger. In *Hess v. Indiana*, 414 U.S. 105, 94 S.Ct. 326, 38 L.Ed.2d 303 (1973), a case that came out of the anti-Vietnam War movement, the Supreme Court clarified its *Brandenburg* holding, saying that advocacy of lawlessness must be directed at a specific person or group *and* must be likely to produce imminent disorder. This is a difficult standard for the government to meet, which gives wide latitude to free expression in the public arena.

## Symbolic Speech and Expressive Conduct

**freedom of expression** The right of the individual to express thoughts and feelings through speech, writing, and other media of expression; protected by the First Amendment to the U.S. Constitution.

**symbolic speech** Expression by displaying symbols, making gestures, and so forth.

**Freedom of expression** is a broad concept embracing speech, publication, performances, and demonstrations. Even wearing symbols is considered to be constitutionally protected **symbolic speech**. *Tinker v. Des Moines Independent Community School District*, 393 U.S. 503, 89 S.Ct. 733, 21 L.Ed.2d 731 (1969). The Supreme Court has recognized a wide variety of conduct as possessing "sufficient communicative elements to bring the First Amendment to play." *Texas v. Johnson*, 491 U.S. 397, 404, 109 S.Ct. 2533, 2539, 105 L.Ed.2d 342, 353 (1989). The Court has accorded First Amendment protection to, among other things, "sit-ins" to protest racial segregation, *Brown v. Louisiana*, 383 U.S. 131, 86 S.Ct. 719, 15 L.Ed.2d 637 (1966); civilians wearing American military uniforms to protest the Vietnam War, *Schacht v. United States*, 398 U.S. 58, 90 S.Ct. 1555, 26 L.Ed.2d 44 (1970); and "picketing" over a variety of issues, *Amalgamated Food Employees Union v. Logan Valley Plaza, Inc.*, 391 U.S. 308, 88 S.Ct. 1601, 20 L.Ed.2d 603 (1968).

**Flag Burning**

Without question, the most controversial applications of the concept of expressive conduct have been the Supreme Court's decisions holding that the public burning of the American flag is protected by the First Amendment. In *Texas v. Johnson*, supra, the Court invalidated a Texas statute banning flag desecration. The Supreme Court's decision to reverse Mr. Johnson's conviction and strike down the Texas law resulted in a firestorm of public criticism of the Court as well as the enactment of a new federal statute. The Flag Protection Act of 1989, amending 18 U.S.C.A. § 700, imposed criminal penalties on anyone who knowingly "mutilates, defaces, physically defiles, burns, maintains upon the floor or ground, or tramples upon" the American flag. In *United States v. Eichman,* 496 U.S. 310, 110 S.Ct. 2404, 110 L.Ed.2d 287 (1990), the Supreme Court invalidated this federal statute as well, saying that "punishing desecration of the flag dilutes the very freedom that makes this emblem so revered, and worth revering." 496 U.S. at 319, 110 S.Ct. at 2410, 110 L.Ed.2d at 296. On several occasions, Congress has attempted to pass a constitutional amendment to overturn the Supreme Court's flag burning decisions, but in every instance the measure has failed to receive the necessary two-thirds vote in the Senate.

## Free Expression versus Maintenance of the Public Order

One type of expression that sometimes transgresses the criminal law is public speech that threatens the public peace and order. Numerous state and local laws prohibit incitement to riot and disturbing the peace. The Supreme Court has said, "[w]hen clear and present danger of riot, disorder, interference with traffic upon the public streets, or other immediate threat to public safety, peace, or order appears, the power of the State to prevent and punish is obvious." *Cantwell v. Connecticut*, 310 U.S. at 308, 60 S.Ct. at 905, 84 L.Ed. at 1220. Moreover, the Court has held that so-called **fighting words** are unprotected by the Constitution. *Chaplinsky v. New Hampshire*, supra. Fighting words are "those personally abusive epithets which, when addressed to the ordinary citizen, are, as a matter of common knowledge, inherently likely to provoke violent reaction." *Cohen v. California*, 403 U.S. at 20, 91 S.Ct. at 1785, 29 L.Ed.2d at 291.

Although government must have the authority to maintain order, it may not, under the guise of preserving public peace, unduly suppress free communication of views. Again, the challenge for courts is to strike a reasonable balance between

**fighting words** Utterances that are inherently likely to provoke a violent response from an individual or group to which they are directed.

## JURISPRUDENCE

*Texas v. Johnson*, 491 U.S. 397, 404, 109 S.Ct. 2533, 2539, 105 L.Ed.2d 342, 353 (1989)

Gregory Johnson was convicted of desecrating the American flag after he publicly burned the flag outside the Republican National Convention in Dallas in 1984. The Texas Court of Criminal Appeals reversed the conviction, holding that the Texas law under which Johnson was convicted was unconstitutional as applied to his particular conduct. The U.S. Supreme Court agreed, noting that Johnson was not prosecuted for burning the flag per se; rather it was the unpopular message the burning was intended to convey that led to his arrest and conviction.

legitimate competing interests in the context of the particular facts in the case at hand.

## Hate Speech

**hate speech** Offensive speech directed at members of racial, religious, sexual, or ethnic minorities.

In recent decades, legislatures and courts increasingly have become concerned with the problem of **hate speech.** Hate speech refers to any instance of hateful expression, whether verbal, written, or symbolic, that is based on racial, ethnic, or religious prejudice or some other similar animus. Because it constitutes expression, hate speech is generally protected by the Constitution unless it falls within one of the recognized exceptions to the First Amendment.

Would a public cross burning by the Ku Klux Klan in a black neighborhood qualify as fighting words, or would it be considered expressive conduct protected by the First Amendment? What about the display of swastikas by Nazis parading through the streets of a predominantly Jewish city? Would police be justified in these instances to make arrests for incitement to riot? These questions became more real than hypothetical during the 1980s, when the country witnessed a resurgence of racist organizations, and cities and states countered with laws proscribing hate speech. One such law, the St. Paul, Minnesota, Bias-Motivated Crime Ordinance, provided,

> Whoever places on public or private property a symbol, object, appellation, characterization or graffiti, including, but not limited to, a burning cross or Nazi swastika, which one knows or has reasonable grounds to know arouses anger, alarm or resentment in others on the basis of race, color, creed, religion or gender commits disorderly conduct and shall be guilty of a misdemeanor. St. Paul, Minn. Legis. Code 292.02 (1990).

In *R.A.V. v. City of St. Paul*, 505 U.S. 377, 112 S.Ct. 2538, 120 L.Ed.2d 305 (1992), the Supreme Court declared this ordinance unconstitutional in the context of a criminal prosecution of a white teenager who burned a cross on the front lawn of a black family's home. Lest the public be tempted to conclude that the Supreme Court condoned racially motivated cross burnings, the Court stated the following:

> Let there be no mistake about our belief that burning a cross in someone's front yard is reprehensible. But St. Paul has sufficient means at its disposal to prevent such behavior without adding the First Amendment to the fire. 505 U.S. at 396, 112 S.Ct. at 2550, 120 L.Ed.2d at 326.

Despite its earlier decision in *R.A.V. v. City of St. Paul*, the Supreme Court in 2003 upheld a Virginia law banning cross burning with "an intent to intimidate a person or group of persons." Va. Code Ann. § 18.2-423 (1996). Writing for a plurality of justices, Justice O'Connor concluded that the "First Amendment permits Virginia to outlaw cross burnings done with the intent to intimidate because burning a cross is a particularly virulent form of intimidation." *Virginia v. Black*, 535 U.S. 343, 363, 123 S.Ct. 1536, 1549, 155 L.Ed.2d 535, 554 (2003).

## Obscenity

Traditionally, state and local governments have proscribed speech, pictures, films, and performances regarded as obscene, generally classifying these as misdemeanors. Despite challenges to the constitutionality of such obscenity laws, the Supreme

**JURISPRUDENCE**

*Virginia v. Black*, 535 U.S. 343, 363, 123 S.Ct. 1536, 1549, 155 L.Ed.2d 535, 554 (2003)

Barry Black led a Ku Klux Klan rally on private property in Cana, Virginia, that concluded with the traditional Klan cross-burning. The county sheriff, who had observed the rally from the side of a nearby highway, arrested Black for burning a cross with the intent of intimidating a person or group of persons, in

violation of Virginia law. After a jury trial, Black was found guilty and fined $2,500. The Court of Appeals of Virginia reversed Black's conviction and declared the state law unconstitutional. The U.S. Supreme Court affirmed as to the reversal of Black's conviction, holding that the trial jury had been improperly instructed. However, the justices allowed that the State could prohibit cross-burning with the intent to intimidate.

**obscenity** Explicit sexual material that is patently offensive, appeals to a prurient or unnatural interest in sex, and lacks serious scientific, artistic, or literary content.

Court has held that **obscenity** is beyond the pale of the First Amendment and thus subject to criminal prosecution. *Roth v. United States*, 354 U.S. 476, 77 S.Ct. 1304, 1 L.Ed.2d 1498 (1957).

The problem for the legislatures, police, prosecutors, and courts is to determine what is obscene and therefore unprotected by the First Amendment. The Supreme Court has held that for expression to be obscene, it must (1) appeal to a prurient interest in sex; (2) depict sexual conduct in a patently offensive way; and (3) lack serious literary, artistic, political, or scientific value. *Miller v. California*, 413 U.S. 15, 93 S.Ct. 2607, 37 L.Ed.2d 419 (1973). Despite this test, the concept of obscenity remains somewhat vague. Nevertheless, the Supreme Court has made it clear that obscenity refers only to "hard-core" pornography. *Jenkins v. Georgia*, 418 U.S. 153, 94 S.Ct. 2750, 41 L.Ed.2d 642 (1974). Today, with the easy availability of pornography on the Internet, police and prosecutors have shifted their focus away from the enforcement of traditional obscenity laws and toward enforcement of more recent statutes criminalizing child pornography. (Obscenity and pornography are examined more fully in Chapter 10.)

## Profanity

Historically, states and local communities enacted laws prohibiting public profanity. In many instances these prohibitions were incorporated into broader prohibitions of offensive or disorderly conduct (see Chapter 12 ). Although in *Chaplinsky v. New Hampshire,* supra, the Supreme Court specifically enumerated profanity as being among those categories of speech so lacking in value as not to merit First Amendment protection, this view no longer prevails. In *Cohen v. California,* supra, the Supreme Court invalidated the "offensive conduct" conviction of a man who entered a courthouse wearing a jacket emblazoned with the slogan "Fuck the Draft." Writing for the Court, Justice John Marshall Harlan opined that

> while the particular four-letter-word being litigated here is perhaps more distasteful than others of its genre, it is nevertheless often true that one man's vulgarity is another's lyric. Indeed, we think it is largely because government officials cannot make principled distinctions in this area that the Constitution leaves matters of taste and style so largely to the individual. 403 U.S. at 25, 91 S.Ct. at 1788, 29 L.Ed.2d at 294.

Despite the Supreme Court's decision in *Cohen v. California,* most states and many cities retain laws proscribing public profanity. These laws are seldom enforced,

### The Case of the Cussing Canoeist

Profanity prosecutions are quite rare, but one notable exception is the case of the "cussing canoeist" that made national news in 1998. When Timothy Boomer, age twenty-five, fell out of his canoe and into the Rifle River in Michigan, he let loose a three-minute tirade of profanity. Two sheriff's deputies patrolling the river heard Boomer and ticketed him. Boomer was charged with violating an 1897 Michigan statute that provides, "Any person who shall use any indecent, immoral, obscene, vulgar or insulting language in the presence or hearing of any woman or child shall be guilty of a misdemeanor." M.C.L. § 750.337.

Standing before the Arenac County Circuit Court, Boomer said, "[I]f my words offended anyone, I'm sorry. I've said from the beginning that I did not know that there were children in the area and I would not

have said what I said if I had known there were children around." A jury found Boomer guilty, and the court sentenced him to four days' community service and imposed a $75 fine.

On appeal the Michigan Court of Appeals reversed Boomer's conviction, noting, "Allowing a prosecution where one utters 'insulting' language could possibly subject a vast percentage of the populace to a misdemeanor conviction, M.C.L. § 750.337 fails to provide fair notice of what conduct is prohibited, and it encourages arbitrary and discriminatory enforcement. . . . Here, it would be difficult to conceive of a statute that would be more vague than M.C.L. § 750.337. There is no restrictive language whatsoever contained in the statute that would limit or guide a prosecution for indecent, immoral, obscene, vulgar, or insulting language."

*People v. Boomer*, 655 N.W.2d 255 (Mich. App. 2002).

but when they are challenged, courts tend to strike them down. In some instances, courts have upheld the facial validity of such laws but ruled that they can be applied only where the defendant's language consists of "fighting words" or the defendant's conduct threatens a breach of the peace (see Chapter 12).

## Freedom of Assembly

The First Amendment specifically protects the "right of the people peaceably to assemble." Yet, as we have seen, one of the most important purposes of the criminal law is to maintain public peace and order. Sometimes these values conflict, as in the civil rights struggle of the 1960s, when public demonstrations became an important part of a powerful political movement. See, e.g., *Cox v. Louisiana*, 379 U.S. 559, 85 S.Ct. 476, 13 L.Ed.2d 487 (1965); *Adderley v. Florida*, 385 U.S. 39, 87 S.Ct. 242, 17 L.Ed.2d 149 (1966); *Walker v. City of Birmingham*, 388 U.S. 307, 87 S.Ct. 1824, 18 L.Ed.2d 1210 (1967).

In one of the most memorable cases from the civil rights era, the Supreme Court reversed the breach-of-the-peace convictions of 187 students who participated in a civil rights demonstration on the grounds of the South Carolina statehouse. *Edwards v. South Carolina*, 372 U.S. 229, 83 S.Ct. 680, 9 L.Ed.2d. 697 (1963). The Court characterized the students' conduct not as a breach of the peace but as "an exercise of . . . basic constitutional rights in their most pristine and classic form."

Governments may not ban assemblies in the **public forum** as long as they are peaceful and do not impede the operations of government or the activities of other citizens. Yet, to promote the interests of safety, order, and peace, governments may impose reasonable **time, place, and manner regulations** on public assemblies. The character of a given place and the pattern of its normal activities determine the type of time, place, and manner regulations that the courts consider reasonable.

**public forum** A public space generally acknowledged as appropriate for public assemblies or expressions of views.

**time, place, and manner regulations** Government limitations on the time, place, and manner of expressive activities in the public forum.

**JURISPRUDENCE**

*Edwards v. South Carolina*, 372 U.S. 229, 83 S.Ct. 680, 9 L.Ed.2d. 697 (1963)

In this case the Supreme Court reversed breach-of-the-peace convictions of 187 African American college students who had participated in a peaceful, if somewhat boisterous, civil rights demonstration on the grounds of the state capitol in Columbia, South Carolina. The Court held that in "arresting, convicting and punishing" these students, South Carolina had infringed their "constitutionally protected rights of free speech, free assembly, and freedom to petition for redress of their grievances." In his opinion for the majority, Justice Potter Stewart observed that "the Fourteenth Amendment does not permit a state to make criminal the peaceful expression of unpopular views." This decision is frequently cited by appellate courts in cases where demonstrators are charged with breach of the peace.

*© Cengage Learning 2014*

*Grayned v. City of Rockford*, 408 U.S. 104, 92 S.Ct. 2294, 33 L.Ed.2d 222 (1972). For example, a restriction against the use of sound amplifiers near a courthouse or library might well be judged reasonable, whereas a ban on "picketing" on the steps of the same buildings would not. In imposing time, place, and manner regulations, governments must be careful not to deprive demonstrations or protests of their essential content by imposing excessive or unnecessarily burdensome regulations. *United States v. Grace*, 461 U.S. 171, 103 S.Ct. 1702, 75 L.Ed.2d 736 (1983).

## Free Exercise of Religion

**freedom of religion** The First Amendment right to the free exercise of one's religion without undue interference by government.

The value of **freedom of religion** is so deeply rooted in American culture that rarely have legislatures sought to impinge directly on that right. Yet from time to time lawmakers have sought to prevent certain unpopular religious groups from proselytizing. The Supreme Court has been quick to invalidate such efforts. In one leading case, the Court struck down a state statute that made it a misdemeanor for any person to solicit door to door for religious or philanthropic reasons without prior approval from local officials, who were authorized to make determinations as to whether solicitors represented *bona fide* religions. The law was successfully challenged by a member of the Jehovah's Witnesses sect who had been prosecuted for engaging in door-to-door proselytizing without a permit. *Cantwell v. Connecticut*, supra.

### Unusual Religious Practices

Much more problematic are government attempts to enforce criminal statutes designed to protect the public health, safety, and welfare against religious practices deemed inimical to these interests. Does the right to exercise one's religion freely permit a person to violate an otherwise valid criminal statute? In 1878 the Supreme Court answered this question in the negative by upholding the prosecution of a polygamist. *Reynolds v. United States*, 98 U.S. (8 Otto) 145, 25 L.Ed. 244 (1878). More recently, however, the Supreme Court granted to members of the Old Order Amish sect an exemption to the Wisconsin compulsory education law. The Court found that the law significantly interfered with the Amish way of life and thus violated their right to freely exercise their religion. *Wisconsin v. Yoder*, 406 U.S. 205, 92 S.Ct. 1526, 32 L.Ed.2d 15 (1972).

Several state courts have decided cases arising from unusual forms of worship. The Tennessee Supreme Court upheld the validity of a statute making it a crime to handle poisonous snakes in religious ceremonies against the claim that the law

---

**JURISPRUDENCE**

*Wisconsin v. Yoder*, 406 U.S. 205, 92 S.Ct. 1526, 32 L.Ed.2d 15 (1972)

Jonas Yoder and several other members of the Old Order Amish religion were convicted and fined $5 for violating a state law requiring school attendance through age sixteen. On appeal, the Amish claimed that the compulsory school attendance law was unconstitutional as applied to them. Invoking the Free Exercise Clause of the First Amendment, they argued

that sending their children to school beyond the eighth grade would be psychologically and spiritually damaging to them and would ultimately have a destructive effect on their tight-knit community. The Wisconsin Supreme Court agreed and reversed their convictions. The state of Wisconsin obtained review by the U.S. Supreme Court, which ruled unanimously that the compulsory school attendance law as applied to the Amish was in violation of the Free Exercise Clause.

---

violated the right to free exercise of religion guaranteed by the state constitution. *Harden v. State*, 216 S.W.2d 708 (Tenn. 1949).

In a decision that cuts the other way, the California Supreme Court reversed the convictions of several members of the Native American Church for possession of peyote, which contains an illegal hallucinogen. *People v. Woody*, 394 P.2d 813 (Cal. 1964). In the court's view, the sacramental use of peyote was central to the worship by members of the Native American Church and thus protected by the First Amendment. In 1990, however, the U.S. Supreme Court held that the sacramental use of peyote by members of the Native American Church was not protected by the Free Exercise Clause of the First Amendment. *Employment Division v. Smith*, 494 U.S. 872, 110 S.Ct. 1595, 108 L.Ed.2d 876 (1990). In our federal system, however, state courts are free to provide greater levels of protection to individual rights under the terms of their state constitutions than those provided by the federal constitution.

The principle that underlies *Employment Division v. Smith* is that the Free Exercise Clause does not provide the basis for an exemption to a generally applicable criminal statute. A law aimed specifically at the practices of one religious group is another matter, as the Supreme Court made clear in striking down a Hialeah, Florida, ordinance prohibiting animal sacrifices. After receiving a number of complaints about the practice of animal sacrifice associated with the Santeria religion, the city of Hialeah adopted an ordinance making it an offense to "unnecessarily kill,

---

**JURISPRUDENCE**

*Employment Division v. Smith*, 494 U.S. 872, 110 S.Ct. 1595, 108 L.Ed.2d 876 (1990)

Two members of the Native American Church, Alfred Smith and Galen Black, worked as drug rehabilitation counselors for a private social service agency in Oregon. Along with other church members, Smith and Black ingested peyote, a hallucinogenic drug, at a sacramental ceremony practiced by Native Americans for hundreds of years. Citing their use of peyote as "job-related misconduct," the social service agency fired Smith and Black. On review, the Supreme Court

rejected the claim that the ritualistic use of peyote was protected as free exercise of religion. In the view of Justice Scalia, "if prohibiting the exercise of religion [is] merely the incidental effect of a generally applicable and otherwise valid [criminal] law, the First Amendment has not been offended." Dissenting, Justice Blackmun concluded that "Oregon's interest in enforcing its drug laws against religious use of peyote [was] not sufficiently compelling to outweigh respondents' right to the free exercise of their religion."

## JURISPRUDENCE

*Church of the Lukumi Babalu Aye, Inc. v. City of Hialeah*, 508 U.S. 520, 113 S.Ct. 2217, 124 L.Ed.2d 472 (1993)

The Church of the Lukumi Babalu Aye was established in Hialeah, Florida by Ernesto Pichardo and other practitioners of the Santeria religion. In 1987, after receiving a number of complaints about animal sacrifices being performed at the Church, the city of Hialeah adopted an ordinance making it an offense to "unnecessarily kill, torment, torture, or mutilate an animal in a public or private ritual or ceremony not for the primary purpose of food consumption." The Church then filed suit seeking to have the Hialeah ordinance declared unconstitutional. The federal district court in Miami upheld the ordinance, as did the U.S. Court of Appeals for the EleventhCircuit. In a unanimous decision, the U.S. Supreme Court reversed and declared the ordinance unconstitutional. The crux of the Court's opinion was that government cannot criminalize an activity only insofar as it takes place in a religious setting.

---

torment, torture, or mutilate an animal in a public or private ritual or ceremony not for the primary purpose of food consumption." Practitioners of Santeria sued to challenge the constitutionality of the ordinance. In a unanimous decision, the Supreme Court declared the ordinance unconstitutional. Writing for the Court, Justice Anthony Kennedy observed that "the laws in question were enacted by officials who did not understand, failed to perceive, or chose to ignore the fact that their official actions violated the Nation's essential commitment to religious freedom." *Church of the Lukumi Babalu Aye, Inc. v. City of Hialeah*, 508 U.S. 520, 524, 113 S.Ct. 2217, 2222, 124 L.Ed.2d 472, 477 (1993). The crux of the decision was that the City had violated the First Amendment by criminalizing an activity practiced by a religious group, as distinct from enacting a general criminal prohibition against the slaughter of animals.

## Refusal of Medical Treatment

One of the more troubling and tragic situations in which the Free Exercise Clause potentially conflicts with the criminal law involves the refusal of medical treatment. Certain religious groups, such as the Christian Scientists, believe that physical healing is to be achieved through spiritual power. Thus, when faced with an illness or injury, they are likely to refuse medical treatment. Other groups—for example, the Jehovah's Witnesses—believe that blood transfusions are specifically enjoined by scripture.

The courts have recognized the right of a competent adult to refuse medical treatment on religious grounds, even if the refusal results in death. See, e.g., *In re Estate of Brooks*, 205 N.E.2d 435 (Ill. 1965); *In re Milton*, 505 N.E.2d 255 (Ohio 1987). It is another matter entirely when parents refuse to allow medical treatment for their children. The Supreme Court has recognized that

> parents may be free to become martyrs themselves. But it does not follow that they are free in identical circumstances to make martyrs of their children before they have reached the age of full legal discretion when they can make that choice for themselves. *Prince v. Massachusetts*, 321 U.S. 158, 170, 64 S.Ct. 438, 444, 88 L.Ed. 645, 654 (1944).

Accordingly, courts seldom allow freedom of religion as a defense to a criminal charge stemming from a situation in which parents refused to seek or allow medical treatment for their children. In one recent case, a member of the Christian Scientist faith was prosecuted for involuntary manslaughter after failing to seek medical treatment of her daughter's meningitis, which turned out to be fatal. The California Supreme Court rejected the defendant's free-exercise-of-religion defense, saying that "parents have no right to free exercise of religion at the price of a child's life." *Walker v. Superior Court*, 763 P.2d 852 (Cal. 1988).

# The Right to Keep and Bear Arms

**right to keep and bear arms** Right to possess certain weapons; protected against governmental infringement by the Second Amendment to the U.S. Constitution.

There are numerous criminal prohibitions—at the federal, state, and local levels—against the sale, possession, and use of certain types of firearms. "Gun control" laws are seen by many as antithetical to the **right to keep and bear arms**. The Second Amendment to the U.S. Constitution provides, "A well regulated Militia, being necessary to the security of a free state, the right of the people to keep and bear arms, shall not be infringed."

In *United States v. Miller*, 307 U.S. 174, 59 S.Ct. 816, 83 L.Ed. 1206 (1939), the Supreme Court upheld a federal law criminalizing the interstate shipment of sawed-off shotguns, saying that "the right to keep and bear arms" had to be interpreted in relation to the "well regulated militia." The Court concluded that possession of sawed-off shotguns had no reasonable relationship to serving in the militia. In reaffirming *Miller*, the Court said that "the Second Amendment guarantees no right to keep and bear a firearm that does not have some reasonable relationship to the preservation or efficiency of a well regulated militia." *Lewis v. United States*, 445 U.S. 55, 65 n.8, 100 S.Ct. 915, 921 n.8, 63 L.Ed.2d 198, 209 n.8 (1980). However, in *District of Columbia v. Heller*, 554 U.S. 570, 128 S.Ct. 2783, 171 L.Ed.2d 637 (2008), the Court declared the right to keep and bear arms to be a personal right irrespective of actual or potential service in any militia. In *Heller*, the Court struck down a District of Columbia ordinance that effectively created a complete ban on handguns within the District. The Court did not define the scope of the right to keep and bear arms, nor did it indicate whether the right is secured against state action by the Fourteenth Amendment. It did indicate, though, that the right is subject to reasonable government regulations.

Like the federal constitution, many state constitutions contain language dealing with the right to keep and bear arms. Yet state courts tend to give wide latitude to state and local gun control laws. Conservatives and libertarians tend to criticize the courts for failing, in their view, to protect adequately the constitutional right to

---

## JURISPRUDENCE

*District of Columbia v. Heller*, 554 U.S. 570, 128 S.Ct. 2783, 171 L.Ed.2d 637 (2008)

Dick Heller, a D.C. special police officer authorized to carry a handgun while on duty at the Federal Judicial Center, applied for a registration certificate for a handgun that he wished to keep at home. Citing its strict gun control ordinances, which effectively banned the possession of handguns even in private homes, the District of Columbia refused to provide a registration certificate. Heller filed a lawsuit in the federal district court for the District of Columbia seeking, on Second Amendment grounds, to enjoin the city from enforcing its prohibition against possession of handguns in the home. On review, the U.S. Supreme Court held that D.C.'s ban on handgun possession in the home violated the Second Amendment.

© *Cengage Learning*

### The Right to Keep and Bear Arms

Article I, Section 2-a of the New Hampshire Constitution provides, "All persons have the right to keep and bear arms in defense of themselves, their families, their property and the state." At the same time, a New Hampshire statute proscribes possession of firearms by convicted felons. N.H. Rev. Stat. Ann. § 159: 3. Scott Smith, who was convicted in the Rockingham Superior Court of being a felon in possession of a firearm, challenged the constitutionality of the statute. The New Hampshire Supreme Court affirmed the conviction and sustained the validity of the statute, saying, "the State constitutional right to keep and bear arms is not absolute and may be subject to restriction and regulation. . . . The governmental interest served by the statute, protection of human life and property, is patently significant."

*State v. Smith*, 571 A.2d 279, 281 (N.H. 1990).

keep and bear arms. Members of the law enforcement community, however, are typically more supportive of legislative efforts to control the dissemination and use of firearms.

## The Doctrines of Vagueness and Overbreadth

The Fifth Amendment to the U.S. Constitution provides that "no person . . . shall be deprived of life, liberty or property without due process of law." The two fundamental aspects of due process are fair notice and fair hearing. The principle of fair notice implies that a person has a right to know whether particular contemplated conduct is illegal. Indeed, the Supreme Court has emphatically stated that "[n]o one may be required at peril of life, liberty or property to speculate as to the meaning of penal statutes." *Lanzetta v. New Jersey*, 306 U.S. 451, 453, 59 S.Ct. 618, 619, 83 L.Ed. 888, 890 (1939).

A criminal law that is excessively vague in its proscriptions offends this principle and is thus invalid under the Due Process Clause of the Fifth or Fourteenth Amendments (depending on whether it is a federal or state statute). However, we must realize that the **vagueness doctrine** is "designed more to limit the discretion of police and prosecutors than to ensure that statutes are intelligible to persons pondering criminal activity." *United States v. White*, 882 F.2d 250, 252 (7th Cir. 1989). Accordingly, the Supreme Court has held that the requisite specificity of criminal statutes may be achieved through judicial interpretation. *Rose v. Locke*, 423 U.S. 48, 96 S.Ct. 243, 46 L.Ed.2d 185 (1975). As interpreted by the Seventh Circuit Court of Appeals in *United States v. White*, "provided that conduct is of a sort widely known among the lay public to be criminal . . . , a person is not entitled to clear notice that the conduct violates a particular criminal statute." *United States v. White*, supra at 252.

In a landmark decision, the Supreme Court struck down a Jacksonville, Florida, ordinance that prohibited various forms of vagrancy, including loitering and "prowling by auto." *Papachristou v. City of Jacksonville*, 405 U.S. 156, 92 S.Ct. 839, 31 L.Ed.2d 110 (1972). Writing for the Court in *Papachristou*, Justice William O. Douglas objected to the "unfettered discretion" the ordinance placed in the hands of the police, allowing for "arbitrary and discriminatory enforcement of the law." (For further discussion of the vagueness doctrine as it relates to the crimes of vagrancy and loitering, as well as a discussion of the *Papachristou* case, see Chapter 12.)

**vagueness doctrine** Doctrine of constitutional law holding unconstitutional (as a violation of due process) legislation that fails to clearly inform the person of what is required or proscribed.

Closely related to the concept of vagueness, the **doctrine of overbreadth** was developed exclusively in the context of the First Amendment and concerns criminal laws that are written so broadly that they potentially infringe First Amendment freedoms. The evil of overbreadth of a law is that it may permit police to make arrests for constitutionally protected conduct, such as political speech, as well as for unprotected activity, such as inciting people to violence through the use of fighting words.

*Coates v. City of Cincinnati*, 402 U.S. 611, 91 S.Ct. 1686, 29 L.Ed.2d 214 (1971), illustrates both the vagueness doctrine and the doctrine of overbreadth. In *Coates* the Supreme Court struck down a Cincinnati ordinance that made it unlawful for "three or more persons to assemble . . . on any sidewalks and there conduct themselves in a manner annoying to persons passing by." The Court found the ordinance to be excessively vague in that "men of common intelligence must necessarily guess at its meaning." The Court also found that the ordinance was so broad that it criminalized speech and assembly protected by the First Amendment.

Ordinarily a person can contest only a law that has been directed against him or her. However, the doctrine of overbreadth enables a person to contest a law imposing restrictions on First Amendment freedoms even when that person has not been charged with violating the law. This doctrine was designed to bring to the courts' attention laws that have a "chilling effect" on the exercise of First Amendment rights.

In the 1980s, the Supreme Court appeared to be retreating somewhat from the overbreadth doctrine. In *New York v. Ferber*, 458 U.S. 747, 102 S.Ct. 3348, 73 L.Ed.2d 1113 (1982), for example, the Court rejected an overbreadth challenge to a child pornography statute that criminalized child pornography well beyond the legal test of obscenity delineated in *Miller v. California*, supra. Although expressing concern that the statute might possibly be applied to punish constitutionally protected artistic expression, the Court concluded that the law was not "substantially

---

## JURISPRUDENCE

*Coates v. City of Cincinnati*, 402 U.S. 611, 91 S.Ct. 1686, 29 L.Ed.2d 214 (1971)

Coates was involved in a demonstration stemming from a labor dispute and as a result was arrested, charged, and convicted of violating a Cincinnati ordinance making it a crime for "three or more persons to assemble . . . on any of the sidewalks . . . and there conduct themselves in a manner annoying to persons passing by. . . ." On appeal, Coates argued the ordinance was unconstitutional under the First and Fourteenth Amendments of the Constitution. In analyzing the language of the ordinance, the Supreme Court noted that "conduct that annoys some people does not annoy others." The Court held "the ordinance vague, not in the sense that it requires a person to conform his conduct to an imprecise but comprehensible normative standard, but rather in the sense that no standard of conduct is specified at all." Therefore, "men of common intelligence must necessarily guess at its meaning." In addition to invalidating the ordinance under the vagueness doctrine, the Court further held the ordinance overbroad. While the ordinance is "broad enough to encompass many types of conduct clearly within the city's constitutional power to prohibit," the City of Cincinnati is not permitted to enact and enforce ordinances "whose violation may entirely depend upon whether or not a policeman in annoyed." Municipalities are "free to prevent people from blocking sidewalks, obstructing traffic, littering streets, committing assaults, or engaging in countless other forms of antisocial conduct," but it must "do so through the enactment and enforcement of ordinances directed with reasonable specificity toward the conduct to be prohibited."

## JURISPRUDENCE

*Reno* v. *American Civil Liberties Union*, 521 U.S. 844, 117 S.Ct. 2329, 138 L.Ed.2d 874 (1997)

In 1996, Congress adopted the Communications Decency Act, which made it a crime to display "indecent" material on the Internet in a manner that might make it available to minors. The American Civil Liberties Union and other plaintiffs filed suit to challenge the constitutionality of the Act. A federal district struck down the statute and the government appealed. The Court declared the CDA unconstitutional on First Amendment grounds. Writing for the Supreme Court, Justice Stevens concluded that, with respect to cyberspace, "the interest in encouraging freedom of expression in a democratic society outweighs any theoretical but unproven benefit of censorship."

overbroad" and that impermissible applications of the statute should be addressed on a case-by-case basis. According to the *Ferber* Court, a statute should not be invalidated for overbreadth if its legitimate reach "dwarfs its arguably impermissible applications." 458 U.S. at 773, 102 S.Ct. at 3363, 73 L.Ed.2d at 1133.

The overbreadth doctrine was given new life by the Supreme Court in 1997, when the Court struck down provisions of the Communications Decency Act (CDA) of 1996, 47 U.S.C.A. §§ 223(a), 223(d) (Supp. 1997). Under the CDA, Congress had attempted to ban "indecent" as well as "obscene" speech from the Internet. Criminal penalties were provided for persons who transmitted such messages in a fashion that they could be received by children. The Court found that the law swept within its ambit constitutionally protected speech as well as obscenity. *Reno* v. *American Civil Liberties Union*, 521 U.S. 844, 117 S.Ct. 2329, 138 L.Ed.2d 874 (1997).

# Freedom from Compulsory Self-Incrimination

The Fifth Amendment to the U.S. Constitution provides that no person "shall be compelled in any criminal case to be a witness against himself." We normally think of the prohibition against compulsory self-incrimination in terms of a defendant's right not to testify in a criminal trial or a suspect's right to remain silent in the face of police interrogation. However, the courts have held that this clause also limits the degree to which legislatures can write statutes that require parties to report information to the government that can place them in jeopardy of criminal prosecution. Consider the following Supreme Court decisions from the late 1960s:

- In *Marchetti v. United States*, 390 U.S. 39, 88 S.Ct. 697, 19 L.Ed.2d 889 (1968), the defendant was convicted for conspiring to evade payment of an occupational tax relating to illegal wagers as required by 26 U.S.C.A. § 4411. The Supreme Court ruled that the requirements relative to registration and payment of the tax would have had the "direct and unmistakable consequence of incriminating" the defendant and were thus unconstitutional under the Self-Incrimination Clause.
- In *Haynes v. United States*, 390 U.S. 85, 88 S.Ct. 722, 19 L.Ed.2d 923 (1968), the Court held that the privilege against self-incrimination provided a defense to prosecution either for failure to register a firearm under 26 U.S.C.A. § 5841 or for possession of an unregistered firearm under 26 U.S.C.A. § 5851.
- In *Leary v. United States*, 395 U.S. 6, 89 S.Ct. 1532, 23 L.Ed.2d 57 (1969), the Court held that the privilege against self-incrimination is a complete defense to

## JURISPRUDENCE

*Leary v. United States*, 395 U.S. 6, 89 S.Ct. 1532, 23 L.Ed.2d 57 (1969)

Dr. Timothy Leary, along with his daughter, son and two others, drove across the International Bridge from Mexico into Texas, where a customs officer discovered some marijuana in the car and on Leary's daughter. Leary was subsequently indicted and convicted under the federal Marihuana Tax Act. Citing the Self-Incrimination Clause of the Fifth Amendment, the Supreme Court reversed his conviction. The Court held that the Act's requirements effectively required Leary to identify himself as a criminal, since possession of marijuana was unlawful in every state at that time.

CASE-IN-POINT

### A Constitutional Challenge to Reporting Requirements of the Federal Gun Control Act

Virgilio Patricio Flores was convicted under the Federal Gun Control Act, 18 U.S.C.A. § 922(e), for failing to provide written notice to a carrier before shipping firearms. On appeal, citing the Supreme Court decisions in *Marchetti, Haynes,* and *Leary,* Flores argued that the reporting requirement violated his Fifth Amendment privilege against self-incrimination. The Ninth Circuit Court of Appeals rejected his arguments. The court noted that the cited decisions are distinguishable because in each the Supreme Court invalidated a notice requirement in an area of activity permeated with criminal statutes or directed at a group of persons inherently suspect of criminal activities. The court found that in those cases, compliance with the reporting requirements produced an immediate or real and appreciable hazard of self-incrimination. In contrast, the court determined that the Gun Control Act is a general regulatory statute. It is not directed at catching illegal firearm exporters, but rather at helping the states regulate firearm distribution for the safety of their citizens by shutting off the flow of weapons across their borders. A divided court affirmed Flores's conviction; however, dissenting judges argued that the Gun Control Act has penal aspects that go beyond mere regulation and is a law designed to facilitate the discovery of criminal activity.

*United States v. Flores*, 753 F.2d. 1499 (9th Cir. 1985).

---

**cruel and unusual punishments** Criminal penalties that shock the moral conscience of the community—for example, torture and other extreme forms of corporal punishment. Prohibited by the Eighth Amendment to the U.S. Constitution.

a prosecution under 26 U.S.C.A. § 4744(a), the provision of the Marihuana Tax Act of 1937 that required payment of a tax when a person purchased marijuana (which was illegal under state laws at the time the statute was passed).

The Supreme Court's decisions in this area indicate that a statutory reporting requirement violates the freedom from compulsory self-incrimination if it (1) applies to an area of activity that is "permeated with criminal statutes," (2) is directed at a "highly selective" group of persons that is "inherently suspect of criminal activities," and (3) poses a "substantial hazard" or "direct likelihood" of self-incrimination.

## The Prohibition Against Cruel and Unusual Punishments

The Eighth Amendment prohibits the imposition of **cruel and unusual punishments**. This principle applies both to the procedures by which criminal sentences are imposed, *Furman v. Georgia,* 408 U.S. 238, 92 S.Ct. 2726, 33 L.Ed.2d 346 (1972), and to the substantive laws that define punishments. For example, in *Coker* *v. Georgia,* 433 U.S. 584, 97 S.Ct. 2861, 53 L.Ed.2d 982 (1977), the Supreme Court invalidated a provision of a state death penalty law that allowed capital punishment in cases of rape. Writing for the plurality, Justice Byron White concluded that "the death penalty, which is 'unique in its severity and its irrevocability,' is an excessive penalty for the rapist who, as such, does not take human life." 433 U.S. at 598, 97 S.Ct. at 2869, 53 L.Ed.2d at 993.

On occasion, the Eighth Amendment has even been employed to limit the definition of crimes. In *Robinson v. California,* 370 U.S. 660, 82 S.Ct. 1417, 8 L.Ed.2d 758 (1962), the Supreme Court, relying on the Cruel and Unusual Punishments Clause, struck down a state law that made it a crime for a person to be "addicted to the use of narcotics." The Court found it unacceptable that an individual could be punished merely for a "status" without regard to any specific criminal conduct. In effect, the Court "constitutionalized" the traditional requirement that a crime involve a specific *actus reus.* (For further discussion of the *Robinson* case, see Chapter 4.)

# The Constitutional Right of Privacy

**constitutional right of privacy** Implied constitutional right allowing individuals to be free of government interference in intimate activities, especially those involving sex and reproduction.

Although there is no mention of "privacy" in the text of the Constitution, the Supreme Court has held that a sphere of intimate personal conduct is immune from legislative interference. In its first explicit recognition of this **constitutional right of privacy**, *Griswold v. Connecticut,* 381 U.S. 479, 85 S.Ct. 1678, 14 L.Ed.2d 510 (1965), the Court relied in part on the Ninth Amendment, which provides that "[t]he enumeration in the Constitution, of certain rights, shall not be construed to deny or disparage others retained by the people."

In the *Griswold* case, the Supreme Court invalidated a state law proscribing the use of birth control devices as it applied to married couples. In *Eisenstadt v. Baird,* 405 U.S. 438, 92 S.Ct. 1029, 31 L.Ed.2d 349 (1972), the Court extended the principle to protect single individuals from a similar anticontraception statute. Writing for the Court in *Eisenstadt,* Justice William J. Brennan stated that the right of privacy is "the right of the individual, married or single, to be free from unwarranted governmental intrusion into matters so fundamentally affecting a person as the decision whether or not to beget a child." 405 U.S. at 453, 92 S.Ct. at 1038, 31 L.Ed.2d at 362. In reversing Baird's conviction and striking down the Massachusetts law, the Court established the constitutional right of privacy as an individual right, not a right enjoyed solely by married couples.

---

## JURISPRUDENCE

*Griswold v. Connecticut,* 381 U.S. 479, 85 S.Ct. 1678, 14 L.Ed.2d 510 (1965)

Estelle Griswold, the director of Planned Parenthood in Connecticut, was convicted and fined $100 for aiding and abetting persons in using contraceptive devices, an offense under Connecticut law. The Connecticut courts upheld her conviction, rejecting the contention that the state law was unconstitutional. The Supreme Court struck down the Connecticut birth control law by a vote of 7–2, holding that it violated a constitutional guarantee of marital privacy implicit in the Bill of Rights and applicable to the states under the Fourteenth Amendment. Writing for the Court, Justice William O. Douglas posed and answered a rhetorical question: "Would we allow the police to search the sacred precincts of marital bedrooms for telltale signs of the use of contraceptives? The very idea is repulsive to the notions of privacy surrounding the marriage relationship."

## JURISPRUDENCE

*Eisenstadt v. Baird*, 405 U.S. 438, 92 S.Ct. 1029, 31 L.Ed.2d 349 (1972)

William Baird, a former medical student, was arrested after he delivered a lecture on birth control at Boston University, during which he provided some contraceptive foam to a female student. Baird was convicted of violating a Massachusetts law that made it a felony "for anyone to give away a drug, medicine, instrument, or article for the prevention of conception except in the case of (1) a registered physician administering or prescribing it for a married person or (2) an active registered pharmacist furnishing it to a married person presenting a registered physician's prescription." Baird sought habeas corpus relief in federal district court, which denied his petition; however the Court of Appeals vacated the dismissal and held the statute to be "a prohibition on contraception per se," and that the statute conflicted "with fundamental human rights" under *Griswold v. Connecticut*. The Supreme Court, speaking through Justice Brennan, affirmed stating "by providing dissimilar treatment for married and unmarried persons who are similarly situated, the statute violates the Equal Protection Clause of the Fourteenth Amendment."

## Abortion

The Supreme Court's *Griswold* and *Eisenstadt* decisions paved the way for its landmark decision in *Roe v. Wade*, 410 U.S. 113, 93 S.Ct. 705, 35 L.Ed.2d 147 (1973). In *Roe*, the Court held that the right of privacy was broad enough to include a woman's decision to terminate her pregnancy. This 7–2 decision invalidated the Texas antiabortion statute and rendered unenforceable similar laws in most states.

The essential holding in *Roe v. Wade* has been reaffirmed by the Supreme Court on several occasions, most notably in 2000 when it struck down a Nebraska law banning a procedure commonly described as "partial-birth abortion." *Stenberg v. Carhart*, 530 U.S. 914, 120 S.Ct. 2597, 147 L.Ed.2d 743 (2000). In April 2007, the Court upheld a similar federal enactment, but in so doing restated *Roe's* essential holding that, before fetal viability, the government may not prohibit a woman from exercising her right to terminate a pregnancy. *Gonzales v. Carhart*, 550 U.S. 124, 127 S.Ct. 1610, 167 L.Ed.2d 480 (2007).

## JURISPRUDENCE

*Roe v. Wade*, 410 U.S. 113, 93 S.Ct. 705, 35 L.Ed.2d 147 (1973)

Norma McCorvey, a.k.a. Jane Roe, was a twenty-five-year-old unmarried Texas woman who was faced with an unwanted pregnancy. Because abortion was illegal in Texas, Roe brought suit in federal court to challenge the constitutionality of the antiabortion statute. The district court declared the Texas law unconstitutional, but refused to issue an injunction, invoking the doctrine of abstention. Roe appealed directly to the Supreme Court, which handed down a 7–2 decision striking down the Texas law. Justice Blackmun wrote the majority opinion, concluding that the right of privacy was broad enough to encompass a woman's decision to terminate her pregnancy. However, Blackmun noted, "the right [to abortion] is not unqualified and must be considered against important state interests." Although a fetus was not, in the Court's view, a "person" within the language of the Constitution, states would be permitted (except in cases where the mother's life was endangered by carrying the fetus to term) to ban abortion after "viability" (that point in gestation where the fetus is capable of surviving outside the mother's womb). Dissenting, Justice Rehnquist wrote that "the fact that a majority of the States . . . have had restrictions on abortion for at least a century is a strong indication . . . that the right to an abortion is not 'so rooted in the traditions and conscience of our people to be ranked as fundamental'."

The continuing "pro-life" and "pro-choice" demonstrations around the country attest to the extremely controversial nature of legal abortion. (The abortion issue is discussed more thoroughly in Chapter 6.) Few questions today have greater philosophical, religious, ethical, medical, and political saliency than the issue of abortion. Seemingly irreconcilable views on the subject of abortion exist, and the issue continues to spawn legislative and judicial attention. The continuing clashes with demonstrators, resulting in injuries and even death, have caused some states to respond by restricting the proximity of demonstrators to clinics. In *Madsen v. Women's Health Center,* 512 U.S. 753, 114 S.Ct. 2516, 129 L.Ed.2d 593 (1994), the U.S. Supreme Court attempted to balance the constitutional rights of those seeking access to abortion clinics against the First Amendment rights of the protesters. In a 6–3 decision, the Court upheld the basic provisions of a state court injunction intended to keep disruptive protesters from blocking access to the clinics.

On May 26, 1994, President Bill Clinton signed the Freedom of Access to Clinic Entrances (FACE) Act, 18 U.S.C.A. § 248. This federal law was prompted by the 1993 killing outside a Pensacola, Florida, clinic of a doctor who performed abortions, as well as by numerous episodes around the country in which persons working at or seeking access to abortion clinics had been harassed and threatened by antiabortion activists. The new act provides civil and criminal remedies against whomever

> by force or threat of force or by physical obstruction, intentionally injures, intimidates or interferes with or attempts to injure, intimidate or interfere with any person because that person is or has been, or in order to intimidate such person or any other person or any class of persons from, obtaining or providing reproductive health services. 18 U.S.C.A. § 248(a)(1).

The Fourth Circuit held that the FACE Act does not violate the First Amendment's Free Speech or Free Exercise of Religion Clauses and is neither overbroad nor vague. *American Life League, Inc. v. Reno,* 47 F.3d 642 (4th Cir. 1995).

## Privacy and Sexual Conduct

Prior to the 1960s, it was generally assumed that government had the authority to enforce traditional sexual mores through the criminal law. Even though laws against adultery, fornication, and sodomy were seldom enforced and had in fact been abolished in many states, few questioned the right of state and local governments to enact and enforce such prohibitions. Beginning in the 1960s, commentators began to question this assumption. The constitutional right of privacy recognized in *Griswold v. Connecticut* (1965), *Roe v. Wade* (1973), and similar decisions came to be viewed by many commentators as a shield against governmental interference with private, consensual sexual conduct between adults. Beginning in the 1970s, activists in the gay rights movement sought to use the right of privacy to attack laws criminalizing homosexual conduct.

In 1986 the Supreme Court declined to extend the right of privacy to protect homosexual conduct between consenting adults. In *Bowers v. Hardwick,* 478 U.S. 186, 106 S.Ct. 2841, 92 L.Ed.2d 140 (1986), the Court upheld a Georgia sodomy law as applied to homosexual conduct. After the decision in *Bowers v. Hardwick,* however, a number of state courts invalidated sodomy laws on state constitutional grounds. See, e.g., *Powell v. State,* 510 S.E.2d 18 (Ga. 1998); *Campbell v. Sundquist,* 926 S.W.2d 250 (Tenn. App. 1996).

In 2003, the Supreme Court revisited and overturned *Bowers v. Hardwick*. *Lawrence v. Texas*, 539 U.S. 558, 123 S.Ct. 2472, 156 L.Ed.2d 508 (2003). Writing for the Court, Justice Kennedy asserted that a Texas law criminalizing private, consensual homosexual conduct intruded upon personal liberty and autonomy without a sufficient justification. Dissenting, Justice Antonin Scalia argued that the Court had undercut the foundations of other long-standing criminal prohibitions such as those against incest, bestiality, and bigamy. Whether Justice Scalia was correct as a matter of legal reasoning, it was clear that by 2003 public attitudes about homosexuality had changed to the point that most Americans did not believe that the state should concern itself with such conduct. On the other hand, society continues to condemn bigamy, incest, and bestiality, and it is unlikely that courts will interpret constitutional principles so as to prevent government from expressing this condemnation through the criminal law.

## JURISPRUDENCE

*Lawrence v. Texas*, 539 U.S. 558, 123 S.Ct. 2472, 156 L.Ed.2d 508 (2003)

Two men were convicted of having sex with each other in violation of a Texas law that made it an offense "to engage in deviate sexual intercourse with another individual of the same sex." A Texas appellate court, in a divided opinion, rejected the defendants' federal constitutional arguments under both the Equal Protection and Due Process Clauses of the Fourteenth Amendment and affirmed the defendants' convictions. When the Supreme Court granted certiorari in *Lawrence v. Texas*, the stage was set for the continuing campaign to obtain a reversal of the 1986 decision in *Bowers v. Hardwick*. Justice Kennedy, writing for the Supreme Court in a 6–3 decision, opined that the Texas statute "furthers no legitimate state interest which can justify its intrusion into the personal and private life of the individual." The Court expressly overruled its decision in *Bowers v. Hardwick* on the ground that the Due Process Clause of the Fourteenth Amendment prohibits states from making private consensual sexual conduct of adults a crime.

**CASE-IN-POINT**

### The Virginia Supreme Court Strikes Down the State's Fornication Law

As recently as 2005, Virginia state law provided, "Any person, not being married, who voluntarily shall have sexual intercourse with any other person, shall be guilty of fornication, punishable as a Class 4 misdemeanor." Va. Code Ann. § 18.2-344. Although the law had not been enforced against consenting adults for more than a century, the constitutionality of the statute was raised in a civil suit brought by a woman who accused a man of infecting her with a sexually transmitted disease. The defendant in the suit argued that the plaintiff could not recover damages inasmuch as she voluntarily participated in an unlawful act, to wit, the consensual sexual intercourse with him that resulted in her infection. The plaintiff then challenged the constitutionality of the fornication law, but the trial court upheld the statute as a rational means of protecting the public health. On appeal, the Virginia Supreme Court invalidated the prohibition as applied to consenting adults. Invoking the U.S. Supreme Court's decision in *Lawrence v. Texas* (2003), the state high court observed, "Because Code § 18.2-344, like the Texas statute at issue in *Lawrence*, is an attempt by the state to control the liberty interest which is exercised in making these personal decisions, it violates the Due Process Clause of the Fourteenth Amendment." *Martin v. Ziherl*, 607 S.E.2d 367, 370 (Va. 2005).

**CASE-IN-POINT**

### The Landmark Karen Quinlan Case

Karen Quinlan was a healthy young woman who became permanently comatose after she ingested large quantities of drugs and alcohol. In this condition, she was unable to maintain normal breathing without a ventilator. After it became clear that Karen Quinlan would not regain consciousness, her parents asked her physicians to remove the respirator. The physicians refused, no doubt concerned about possible criminal prosecution or civil liability. The Quinlans went to court and obtained an order allowing removal of the life-support machine. According to the New Jersey Supreme Court, the right of privacy was "broad enough to encompass [Karen Quinlan's] decision to decline medical treatment under certain circumstances, in much the same way as it is broad enough to encompass a woman's decision to terminate pregnancy. . . ." Of course, Karen Quinlan, lying comatose in the hospital, was unable to communicate her intentions to exercise this aspect of the right of privacy. According to the Court's opinion, the "only practical way to prevent destruction of [Karen Quinlan's] right is to permit the guardian and family . . . to render their best judgment as to whether she would exercise [the right to decline treatment] in these circumstances." After Karen Quinlan was taken off the breathing machine, she lived for nine years in a coma, taking food and water through a nasogastric tube. Her parents never asked that this feeding be discontinued.

*In re Quinlan*, 355 A.2d 647 (N.J. 1976).

## The Right to Die

Since the mid-1970s, the right of privacy has been successfully asserted in state courts as a basis for refusing medical treatment. It is now settled law that a competent adult with a terminal illness has the **right to refuse medical treatment** that would unnaturally prolong his or her life. See, e.g., *Satz v. Perlmutter*, 379 So.2d 359 (Fla. 1980). Under certain circumstances courts have allowed the family of a comatose individual to direct removal of extraordinary means of life support. See, for example, *In re Quinlan*, 355 A.2d 647 (N.J. 1976), featured in the Case-in-Point that follows. This manifestation of rights of privacy and personal autonomy came to be known as the **right to die**.

The right to die, if extended beyond the right of a terminally ill person to refuse artificial means of life support, runs headlong into criminal prohibitions against suicide and, potentially, homicide (see Chapter 6). As yet, courts have been unwilling to extend the right of privacy this far. For example, in *Gilbert v. State*, 487 So.2d 1185 (Fla. App. 1986), a Florida appeals court rejected Roswell Gilbert's "euthanasia" defense to the charge that he committed premeditated murder against his wife, who suffered from osteoporosis and Alzheimer's disease. A decade later the U.S. Supreme Court upheld a state law criminalizing doctor-assisted suicide against a constitutional challenge based on the right of privacy. *Washington v. Glucksberg*, 521 U.S. 702, 117 S.Ct. 2258, 138 L.Ed.2d 772 (1997). (This decision and the issue of doctor-assisted suicide are discussed in Chapter 6.)

**right to refuse medical treatment** The right of a patient—or a patient's surrogate in some instances—to refuse to allow doctors to administer medical treatment.

**right to die** The asserted right to terminate one's own life under certain circumstances; also refers to termination of extraordinary means of life support.

**equal protection of the laws** Constitutional principle enshrined in the Fourteenth Amendment by which law is supposed to apply equally to all persons without regard to race and other irrelevant characteristics.

## Equal Protection of the Laws

The Fourteenth Amendment of the U.S. Constitution forbids states from denying persons **equal protection of the laws**. The Due Process Clause of the Fifth Amendment has been interpreted to impose a similar prohibition on the federal

## JURISPRUDENCE

*Loving v. Virginia,* 388 U.S. 1, 87 S.Ct. 1817, 18 L.Ed.2d 1010 (1967)

The Lovings, an interracial couple who were residents of Virginia, had been married in the District of Columbia but returned to Virginia to live. They were indicted by a grand jury, tried, convicted, and sentenced to one year in jail for violating the state law forbidding interracial marriage. The judge suspended the sentence on the condition that they leave the state and not return together for twenty-five years. Writing for a unanimous Supreme Court, Chief Justice Earl Warren concluded that "[t]here can be no doubt that restricting the freedom to marry solely because of racial classification violates the central meaning of the Equal Protection Clause."

government. *Boling v. Sharpe,* 347 U.S. 497, 74 S.Ct. 693, 98 L.Ed. 884 (1954). Most state constitutions contain similar requirements. On occasion, the concept of equal protection has been used to challenge the validity of criminal statutes. For example, in *Loving v. Virginia,* 388 U.S. 1, 87 S.Ct. 1817, 18 L.Ed.2d 1010 (1967), the Supreme Court relied on the Equal Protection Clause of the Fourteenth Amendment in striking down a state statute that criminalized interracial marriage. The effect of *Loving* was that any law that criminalized conduct solely on the basis of the race of the parties was rendered null and void.

In *Eisenstadt v. Baird,* supra, the Court invoked the Equal Protection Clause in striking down a Massachusetts law that criminalized the use of birth control devices by single persons but not by married couples. And in *Craig v. Boren,* 429 U.S. 190, 97 S.Ct. 451, 50 L.Ed.2d 397 (1976), the Court invalidated an Oklahoma law that forbade the sale of beer containing 3.2 percent alcohol to females under the age of eighteen and males under the age of twenty-one. The Court concluded that the state lacked a sufficient justification for discriminating between the sexes regarding the legal availability of the contested beverage.

In recent years, women have challenged the constitutionality of laws that permit men but not women to go topless in public. For the most part these challenges have failed. See, e.g., *State v. Vogt,* 775 A.2d 551 (N.J. App. 2001). However, as the public's moral sensibilities evolve, it is likely that such restrictions will continue to be challenged.

**CASE-IN-POINT**

### A Woman Challenges Her Conviction for Going Topless on a Public Beach

Arlene Vogt was arrested for going topless on a public beach and was convicted of violating the Lower Township, New Jersey ordinance that prohibited "indecent or unnecessary exposure" of the human body in public. On appeal to the New Jersey Superior Court, Vogt argued, among other things, that the application of the law to topless women but not men "creates an invidious discrimination on the basis of gender in violation of both the federal and state constitutional guarantees of equal protection." The Superior Court rejected the challenge and upheld Vogt's conviction, noting that the "restrictions on exposure of the female breast are supported by the important governmental interest in safeguarding the public's moral sensibilities, and [are] substantially related to that interest." *State v. Vogt,* 775 A.2d 551 (N.J. App. 2001).

# Standards of Judicial Review

**rational basis test** The judicial requirement that legislation must be rationally related to a legitimate government objective in order to survive constitutional challenge.

**fundamental rights** Those constitutional rights that have been declared to be fundamental by the courts. Include First Amendment freedoms, the right to vote, and the right to privacy.

**strict judicial scrutiny** Judicial review of government action or policy in which the ordinary presumption of constitutionality is reversed.

**compelling government interest** A government interest sufficiently strong that it overrides the fundamental rights of persons adversely affected by government action or policy.

At a minimum, a criminal law prohibition that touches on a constitutionally protected interest must be "rationally related to furthering a legitimate government interest." *Massachusetts Board of Retirement v. Murgia*, 427 U.S. 307, 96 S.Ct. 2562, 49 L.Ed.2d 520 (1976). For example, a state law that makes it a crime for a person to perform surgery without a license is obviously a rational means of advancing the state's legitimate interests in public health and safety. Thus, even though the law deprives laypersons of their right to make contracts freely and discriminates against those unable to obtain a license, there is little doubt it would withstand judicial review under the **rational basis test**.

Criminal laws that infringe **fundamental rights** such as the First Amendment freedoms of speech and press are judged by a more stringent standard of review. Such laws are subject to **strict judicial scrutiny**, which means, in effect, that they are presumed to be unconstitutional. To survive judicial review, government must show that the challenged law furthers a **compelling government interest** and is narrowly tailored to that purpose. *Shapiro v. Thompson*, 394 U.S. 618, 89 S.Ct. 1322, 22 L.Ed.2d 600 (1969). This is a heavy burden for the government to carry. Consequently, most laws subjected to strict judicial scrutiny are declared unconstitutional. However, the application of strict scrutiny is not necessarily equivalent to a declaration of unconstitutionality. For example, in *New York v. Ferber*, supra, the Supreme Court upheld a child pornography law that impinged on the First Amendment freedom of expression because, in the view of the Court, the law served a compelling interest in protecting children from the abuse typically associated with the pornography industry.

# The Importance of State Constitutions

Under our federal system of government, the highest court of each state possesses the authority to interpret with finality its state constitution and statutes. A decision by a state court is not subject to review by the U.S. Supreme Court, except insofar as the state law on which it is based is being challenged as a violation of the federal constitution or statutes. Because every state constitution contains language protecting individual rights and liberties, many state court decisions implicate both state and federal constitutional provisions. Under the relevant language of their constitutions and statutes, state courts are free to recognize greater (but not lesser) protections of individual rights than are provided by the U.S. Constitution as interpreted by the federal courts. As a result of the increased conservatism of the federal judiciary, and in particular the Supreme Court, over the last two decades, there has been a resurgence of interest in state constitutional law as it relates to civil rights and liberties.

In *Michigan v. Long*, 463 U.S. 1032, 1040, 103 S.Ct. 3469, 3476, 77 L.Ed.2d 1201, 1214 (1983), the U.S. Supreme Court said that "when a state court decision fairly appears to rest primarily on federal law, or to be interwoven with the federal law, and when the adequacy and independence of any possible state law ground is not clear from the face of the opinion, we will accept as the most reasonable explanation that the state court decided the case the way it did because it believed that federal law required it to do so." However, the Court also indicated that "if the state court decision indicates clearly and expressly that it is alternatively based on *bona fide* separate, adequate, and independent grounds, we, of course, will not undertake to review the decision." 463 U.S. at 1041, 103 S.Ct. at 3476, 77 L.Ed.2d at 1214 (1983).

*Michigan v. Long* effectively invited the state courts to consider the parallel provisions of their state constitutions independently. Some state courts have accepted the invitation. For example, in 1989 the Florida Supreme Court struck down as a violation of the right of privacy a statute that required parental consent in cases where minors sought abortions. *In re: T.W.*, 551 So. 2d 1186 (Fla. 1989). The Florida court made it clear that it was basing its decision on an amendment to the Florida Constitution that (unlike the federal constitution) explicitly protects the right of privacy. These decisions, and many others like them, mean that a person interested in constitutional limitations on the prohibition of criminal conduct must not ignore the provisions of state constitutions that parallel the U.S. Constitution.

## Conclusion

Enacting laws defining crimes and specifying punishments is a legislative function carried out by Congress and by state legislatures. The power to exercise that function is subject to the limitations in various provisions of the U.S. Constitution and state constitutions. Criminal laws must be rationally related to a legitimate public interest and must be specific to avoid being declared void for vagueness. Moreover, laws that restrict fundamental rights such as First Amendment freedoms are subject to strict judicial scrutiny. Courts address not only definitions of crimes but also the application of those definitions to specific conduct. These serious constraints on the definition of criminal conduct and the enforcement of the criminal law are sustained through the well-established power of judicial review. This protects the constitutional rights of the individual and ensures that the rule of law will prevail in the nation.

## Chapter Summary

- Learning Objective 1

    o In *Marbury v. Madison* (1803) the U.S. Supreme Court ruled that courts have the power of judicial review, which allows them to strike down criminal laws that violate the U.S. Constitution. Without this power of judicial review, legislative compliance with the Constitution would be ineffective. Both federal and state courts exercise this power.

    o Some statutes inherently trench on a constitutionally protected liberty or exceed the constitutional powers of government. Courts can declare them unconstitutional per se. Other laws may be facially valid, such as an ordinance prohibiting disorderly conduct, but may be declared unconstitutional as applied if enforced in a way that impermissibly restricts or punishes the exercise of constitutional rights.

- Learning Objective 2

    o Congress has used its enumerated powers, most notably the power to regulate interstate commerce, as well as its implied powers to create a substantial body of federal criminal law.

    o At times Supreme Court decisions have questioned the extent of Congress's legislative authority to criminalize certain conduct. In recent years, however, the Court has been inclined to view Congress as having broad authority to enact statutes to define crimes in order to deal with social problems of national scope.

- Learning Objective 3

  o The framers of the U.S. Constitution recognized serious abuses that occurred in England during the development of the common law. Thus, to prohibit the federal government from using the offense of treason to punish political dissenters, they narrowly defined treason to consist only of levying war against the nation or giving aid or comfort to its enemies. They then specified that "No Person shall be convicted of Treason unless on the Testimony of two Witnesses to the same overt Act, or on Confession in open Court."

  o The framers also sought to correct two other abuses by the English Parliament by constitutionally prohibiting federal and state governments from enacting bills of attainder and *ex post facto* laws. Bills of attainder are legislative acts imposing punishment without trial upon persons deemed guilty of crimes. *Ex post facto* laws are those that criminalize actions that were legal at the time they were performed or increase punishment for criminal acts after they have been committed.

- Learning Objective 4

  o The Bill of Rights to the U.S. Constitution was ratified in 1791 to afford citizens protection against the new federal government. Initially these provisions were held by the courts to apply only to the federal government.

  o Over the years the Supreme Court has incorporated virtually all the provisions of the Bill of Rights into the Fourteenth Amendment, thereby making these protections applicable to state and local governments.

- Learning Objective 5

  o The First Amendment, which protects freedom of speech, has been broadened in its application by the U.S. Supreme Court to protect publication, performances, demonstrations, and even expression such as wearing symbols.

  o The Court has stated that obscenity is not entitled to constitutional protection, yet the definition of "obscenity" remains somewhat vague. Today only hard core pornography is considered to meet the test of obscenity and prosecutions are infrequent.

  o Probably the greatest reaction to the Court's First Amendment jurisprudence has been to its decisions protecting the burning of the American flag as political expression.

  o In addition to the libelous and obscene, the First Amendment allows government to criminalize the utterance of "fighting" words—words that tend to incite an immediate breach of the peace—as well as those that create a "clear and present danger."

  o The Court has refined the clear and present danger doctrine so that public advocacy may be prohibited only when there is imminent lawless action.

  o Government may impose reasonable time, place, and manner regulations on public assemblies but may not otherwise ban peaceful assemblies that do not disrupt its government activities in the public forum.

  o The First Amendment "free exercise" clause also protects religious liberty. The Supreme Court has been liberal in its approach to the right to worship in unusual ways and has invalidated ordinances prohibiting door-to-door solicitation for religious or philanthropic reasons. But it has upheld laws proscribing dangerous practices such as snake handling in religious ceremonies.

o While competent adults may refuse medical treatments, courts seldom allow freedom of religion as a defense to criminal charges stemming from parental refusal to seek medical treatment for their children.

- Learning Objective 6

  o The Second Amendment protects the right "to keep and bear arms." A long controversy over whether this protection is limited to the militia or whether it confers a personal right culminated in 2008, when the Supreme Court declared the right to keep and bear arms to be a personal right irrespective of actual or potential service in any militia.

  o In 2010 the Court extended coverage of the Second Amendment to the states via the Fourteenth Amendment.

- Learning Objective 7

  o The Fifth Amendment provides that "no person . . . shall be deprived of life, liberty or property without due process of law." Similar language in the Fourteenth Amendment requires states to observe due process as well.

  o The two fundamental aspects of due process are fair notice and fair hearing.

  o Courts have developed a void-for-vagueness doctrine that requires that statutes define criminal offenses with sufficient definiteness so that people can understand what conduct is prohibited. An excessively vague criminal statute offends this principle and is thus invalid under the Due Process Clause of the Fifth or Fourteenth Amendments (depending on whether it is a federal or state statute).

  o A similar doctrine known as overbreadth is used to scrutinize broad criminal laws that have the potential to intrude on freedoms protected by the First Amendment.

- Learning Objective 8

  o The Fifth Amendment provides that no person "shall be compelled in any criminal case to be a witness against himself." This protects a defendant's right not to testify in a criminal trial and a suspect's right to remain silent in the face of police interrogation.

  o It also limits the degree to which legislatures can write statutes that require parties to report information to the government that can place them in jeopardy of criminal prosecution.

- Learning Objective 9

  o The Eighth Amendment prohibits cruel and unusual punishments and applies to sentencing procedures as well as to the substantive laws that define punishments.

  o The Supreme Court gave it even a broader application when, in 1962, it struck down a state law that made it a crime for a person to be "addicted to the use of narcotics."

- Learning Objective 10

  o Prior to the 1960s it was generally assumed that government had the authority to enforce traditional sexual mores through the criminal law. The Constitution does not mention "privacy," but in 1965 the Court explicitly recognized a constitutional "right of privacy" when it invalidated a Connecticut law proscribing the use of birth control devices.

    ○ This paved the way for the Court's landmark 1973 decision, which held that the right of privacy was broad enough to include a woman's decision to terminate her pregnancy.

    ○ Subsequently, the Court in 2005 invalidated a Texas statute criminalizing private, consensual homosexual conduct on the ground that it intruded upon personal liberty without a sufficient justification.

    ○ Courts have considered the right of privacy as sufficiently broad to encompass decisions to decline medical treatment under certain circumstances. But as yet the right to die, if extended beyond the right of a terminally ill person to refuse artificial means of life support, runs into criminal prohibitions against suicide and, potentially, homicide. Courts have been unwilling to extend the right of privacy that far.

- Learning Objective 11

    ○ The Fourteenth Amendment expressly forbids states from denying equal protection of the laws to persons in their jurisdictions. The Due Process Clause of the Fifth Amendment has been interpreted to apply the same injunction to the federal government.

    ○ In ruling on challenges based on equal protection of the law, courts closely scrutinize laws that make racial distinctions or treat men and women differently.

- Learning Objective 12

    ○ At a minimum, a criminal law prohibition that touches on a constitutionally protected interest must be "rationally related to furthering a legitimate government interest."

    ○ Criminal laws that infringe fundamental rights such as the First Amendment freedoms of speech and press are judged by a more stringent standard of review. Such laws are subject to strict judicial scrutiny, which means, in effect, that they are presumed to be unconstitutional. To survive judicial review, government must show that the challenged law furthers a compelling government interest and is narrowly tailored to that purpose.

    ○ State courts can declare state laws invalid under both the federal constitution and their own state constitutions.

    ○ The Supreme Court has said that if the state court decision indicates clearly and expressly that it is alternatively based on separate, adequate, and independent grounds, it will not undertake to review the decision. Thus it does not undertake to review decisions on state laws that are based on state constitutional authority that grants greater constitutional liberties than does the U.S. Constitution.

## Key Terms

| | |
|---|---|
| bill of attainder | enumerated powers |
| clear and present danger doctrine | equal protection of the laws |
| compelling government interest | *ex post facto* law |
| constitutional right of privacy | fighting words |
| cruel and unusual punishments | First Amendment |
| doctrine of implied powers | Fourteenth Amendment |
| doctrine of overbreadth | freedom of expression |
| Due Process Clause | freedom of religion |

| | |
|---|---|
| fundamental rights | right to die |
| hate speech | right to keep and bear arms |
| imminent lawless action | right to refuse medical treatment |
| implied powers. | strict judicial scrutiny |
| interstate commerce | symbolic speech |
| judicial review | time, place, and manner regulations |
| obscenity | treason |
| police power | unconstitutional as applied |
| principle of legality | unconstitutional per se |
| public forum | vagueness doctrine |
| rational basis test | |

## Questions for Thought and Discussion

1. Can you think of an example of an *ex post facto* law?
2. Is it possible for the criminal law to define the crime of obscenity precisely enough to avoid the "vice of vagueness" or the problem of overbreadth?
3. Can a municipality enforce an ordinance totally banning religious organizations from canvassing neighborhoods in search of new members? What about an ordinance that prohibits such canvassing between the hours of 8 P.M. and 8 A.M.?
4. Should the constitutional right of privacy invalidate criminal statutes that require a minor to obtain parental consent to obtain an abortion?
5. Would the constitutional right of privacy provide a defense to a charge of possession of obscene materials where videos were viewed only by the defendant in the privacy of his or her home?
6. Could a father who, without judicial approval, unplugs the respirator sustaining the breathing of his comatose, terminally ill child be prosecuted for murder?
7. Would a law making it an offense for a person to carry prescription medicine in other than the original, labeled container meet the test of being rationally related to a legitimate government interest?
8. How does the doctrine of judicial review affect the power of a state legislature to define criminal conduct? Would the constitutional limitations on legislative power be effective without the power of courts to declare laws unconstitutional?
9. Give an example of a law that would be constitutional per se, and point out how such a law might be unconstitutional in its application to a specific conduct.
10. Give an example of a law defining a crime that, although held to be constitutional by the U.S. Supreme Court, has been declared unconstitutional by some state courts. Why can such a result occur in our federal system?

## Problems for Discussion and Solution

1. A federal statute enacted in 1999 makes it a crime for anyone to publish depictions of animal cruelty for commercial gain. A company operates a website that streams live videos of cockfights. The company claims that the cockfights take place in Puerto Rico, where cockfighting is not prohibited. The company is challenging the constitutionality of the federal statute on basis of the First Amendment, although it has not yet been prosecuted or even threatened with

prosecution under the law. What are the company's chances of prevailing in its lawsuit?

2. Amelia Eyeland has been arrested for trespass, disorderly conduct, and resisting arrest. The charges stem from an incident in which Amelia and other members of the Green Warriors staged a raucous protest in a privately owned shopping mall during regular business hours. The protest was aimed at the decision of the mall's owners to expand the mall's parking lot into a wetlands area known to be a habitat for a number of animals. Amelia's attorney is considering a defense based on the First Amendment freedoms of speech and assembly. What chance does the attorney have at being successful with this defense?

3. John Masters, a licensed psychotherapist, has been charged with violating a new state statute making it a crime for "any licensed psychologist, psychiatrist, or psychotherapist to have sexual intercourse with a patient during the existence of the professional relationship." Masters is challenging the constitutionality of the statute on two principal grounds: (a) that it intrudes on his right of privacy and (b) that it violates the Equal Protection Clause of the Fourteenth Amendment in that it fails to apply the same prohibition to other health care professionals. Do you think Masters is likely to prevail in his challenge to the statute? If you were a judge faced with these constitutional questions, how would you be inclined to rule? What additional information would you need to render your decision?

## CHAPTER 4

# Elements of Crimes and Parties to Crimes

## JURISPRUDENCE

*Robinson v. California* (1962)

*Powell v. Texas* (1968)

*Morissette v. United States* (1952)

## LEARNING OBJECTIVES

After reading this chapter, you should be able to explain

1. why a prohibited act is the one indispensable element of a crime

2. how possession can be considered a criminal act and the difference between actual and constructive possession

3. why one's status cannot be the basis for criminal prosecution

4. why criminal intent historically has been an important element of common-law crimes

5. the difference between general-intent and specific-intent crimes

6. how the Model Penal Code recognizes "culpable mental states"

7. why many modern *mala prohibita* crimes are considered strict liability offenses and why strict liability offenses do not require proof of criminal intent

8. how "principals" differ from "accessories" and how "accessories before the fact" differ from "accessories after the fact"

9. how and why the modern criminal law has largely abolished the distinction between principals and accessories before the fact

## CHAPTER OPENING VIGNETTE

Police stopped Lawrence Robinson on a Los Angeles street and noticed scarring and discoloration on his arms. Upon questioning, Robinson admitted to occasional intravenous drug use. Robinson was arrested, tried, and convicted under a California statute that made it a misdemeanor for a person to "be addicted to the use of narcotics." The Appellate Department of the Los Angeles County Superior Court affirmed the conviction without opinion. After unsuccessful attempts to obtain further appellate review in the California courts, Robinson appealed to the U.S. Supreme Court. In *Robinson v. California*, 370 U.S. 660, 82 S.Ct. 1417, 8 L.Ed.2d 758 (1962), the high court overturned the conviction and declared unconstitutional the statute under which Robinson had been prosecuted. Speaking for the Court, Justice Potter Stewart noted that the law "makes the 'status' of narcotic addiction a criminal offense, for which the offender may be prosecuted 'at any time before he reforms.'" 370 U.S. at 663, 82 S.Ct. at 1418, 8 L.Ed.2d at 761. In what was at that time a novel interpretation of the Eighth Amendment, the Court held that "a state law which imprisons a person thus afflicted as a criminal, even though he has never touched any narcotic drug within the State or been guilty of any irregular behavior there, inflicts a cruel and unusual punishment. . . ." 370 U.S. at 667, 82 S.Ct. at 1421, 8 L.Ed.2d at 763.

The *Robinson* case has come to stand for the proposition that one's status cannot be the basis for criminal liability. Criminal liability can exist only where there is a wrongful act that is specifically prohibited by the law. Thus, although theft is a crime, the status of *being a thief* is not. Normally, but not always, this wrongful act must be accompanied by some culpable mental state. These are the basic elements of criminal liability that we have inherited from the English common law. These elements, along with the classification of parties to crimes, are the subjects of this chapter.

# Introduction

As we noted in the opening vignette, the traditional elements of a crime are a wrongful act, often referred to as the *actus reus*, and the culpable state of mind or criminal intent, frequently called the *mens rea*. To establish that a defendant is guilty of a crime, the prosecution must prove the defendant committed some legally proscribed act or failed to act when the law required certain action. In most instances the prosecution must also prove that such act or failure to act occurred with a concurrent criminal intent. It would be contrary to our common-law heritage to punish someone who accidentally or unwittingly committed a wrongful act without any intent to commit a crime, but there are some exceptions to this common-law principle. Likewise, a person cannot be punished for a mere intention, however wrongful that intention may be.

Certain offenses, primarily regulatory and public-welfare–type offenses, are classified as strict liability crimes and are exceptions to the common-law concept of requiring proof of a defendant's criminal intent. They came into prominence in America during the Industrial Revolution, and today they form a significant part of the substantive criminal law, particularly the so-called public welfare offenses such as food and drug laws and traffic offenses.

In addition to the basic requirement of establishing a physical act and intent, in some instances the prosecution must establish that certain circumstances existed at the time the act was committed. For example, in some sexual battery offenses the prosecution must establish that the defendant's acts occurred without the victim's consent. Moreover, in other situations the prosecution must establish that a defendant's acts caused specific results. For instance, in homicide cases the prosecution must prove a causal relationship between the defendant's act and the victim's death.

**principals** Parties whose conduct involves direct participation in a crime.

**accessories before the fact** Persons who aid or assist others in commission of an offense.

**accessories after the fact** Persons who, with knowledge that a crime has been committed, conceal or protect the offender.

The English common law classified crimes as *felonies* and *misdemeanors*. Felonies were very serious crimes; misdemeanors were lesser offenses. Early English common law imposed the death penalty on felons but developed categories of offenders to lessen the punishment meted out to those who assisted in the commission of felonies. At common law, parties to crimes were classified as **principals** in the first and second degree, **accessories before the fact**, and **accessories after the fact**. Crimes were classified as felonies and misdemeanors. An awareness of the history of these terms leads to a better understanding of their function in contemporary American criminal law and the procedure of federal and state court systems. In this chapter we first explain the elements of a crime; then we discuss parties to crimes.

# The *Actus Reus* (The Act Requirement)

The term *actus reus* means "the act of a criminal." But simply committing a wrongful act does not mean that one has committed a crime. To fulfill the requirements of the criminal law, the actor must willfully commit a proscribed physical act or intentionally fail to act where the law requires a person to act. The rationale for the *actus reus* requirement is to prevent a person from being guilty of an offense based on thoughts or intent alone. Common-law crimes required commission of an act or omission and not merely possession of an evil state of mind. Of course, in the United States, a law that made it a criminal offense simply to entertain an evil thought would be patently unconstitutional.

## What Is an Act?

Probably the most complete definition of an "act" as contemplated by the criminal law is found in the Model Penal Code (MPC), which we introduced in Chapter 1. In § 1.13(2) the MPC defines "act" as a "bodily movement whether voluntary or involuntary"; however, § 2.01(1) states that "a person is not guilty of an offense unless his liability is based on conduct that includes a voluntary act or the omission to perform an act of which he is capable." Indeed, courts have generally held that some outward manifestation of voluntary conduct must occur to constitute the physical act necessary in criminal law. The rationale for the requirement of a voluntary act is simple: Only those persons whose acts result from free choice should be criminally punished. Most acts are voluntary. For example, when you raise your hand, it is considered a voluntary act, but when your hand moves as a result of a muscle spasm, it is not a voluntary act. Likewise, movements committed by a person who is unconscious, or acts by someone having an epileptic seizure or sleepwalking, are not regarded as voluntary acts. On the other hand, a driver who takes sleeping pills before beginning to operate an automobile and then falls asleep at the wheel would generally be held criminally responsible for a traffic accident because the driver voluntarily committed the act of taking the pills. Consider the following examples:

- John enters Tom's house and strikes Tom. John has quite obviously committed an "act."
- John picks up a pistol and fires it in the direction of Tom. John, by pulling the trigger of the gun, has committed an "act."
- John hands Tom a glass of liquid to be given to Bob. Unknown to Tom, John added poison to the glass of liquid before handing it to Tom. Tom gives the liquid to Bob, who drinks it and dies. Here John has acted through Tom, an innocent agent; thus, John has committed the "act."
- While riding as a passenger on a bus, John suffers an unexpected attack of epilepsy. As a consequence, John violently kicks his leg, inflicting an injury on Tom, a fellow passenger. John would not be criminally responsible for the injury to Tom.

## When Does Failure to Act Constitute an Act?

**act of omission** The failure to perform an act required by law

The requirement for an act is usually fulfilled by an affirmative act. But even a person's failure to act—that is, an **act of omission**—can satisfy the requirements of a physical act in the criminal law. To be guilty of a crime for failure to act, there must have been a legal duty to act in the first place. Such a duty can arise in one of three ways: (1) by relationship of the actor to the victim, for example, parent–child or husband–wife; (2) by a statutory duty; or (3) by contract between the actor and the victim. Consider these examples:

- Mark, an expert swimmer, is lying on the beach and sees a young girl, unrelated to him, struggling to stay afloat and crying for help. Mark disregards her cries, and she drowns. Is Mark criminally liable? The answer is no, for although we might agree that Mark had a strong moral obligation to attempt to save the child, there was no legal obligation to do so. If, on the other hand, Mark were the child's parent or guardian, or a lifeguard on duty, then Mark's failure to act would most likely qualify as a criminal act.

### The *Actus Reus* Requirement

**CASE-IN-POINT**

Law officers found two whiskey stills and all the paraphernalia for making liquor on the defendant's land. Seeing no activity, they drove away. As they did, they met a car driven by the defendant heading toward the property. The car contained a quantity of sugar and other indicators of the illegal activity the officers suspected. The defendant committed no act of making liquor in the presence of the officers, but on the basis of what they observed, they arrested the defendant, and he was convicted of making liquor unlawfully.

On appeal, the South Carolina Supreme Court reversed the conviction, observing that "the evidence overwhelmingly tends to show an intention to manufacture liquor. . . . But intent alone, not coupled with some overt act . . . is not cognizable by the court. [T]he act must always amount to more than mere preparation, and move directly toward the commission of the crime." Citing respectable textbook authority, the court explained that the law does not concern itself with mere guilty intention unconnected with any overt act.

*State v. Quick*, 19 S.E.2d 101 (S.C. 1942).

---

- Jennifer receives an annual income of $50,000 from the operation of her business. She fails to file a federal income tax return as required by the laws of the United States. Is Jennifer's omission a criminal act? Clearly it is, for she has violated a statutory obligation, the breach of which is punishable by law.
- Dr. Gore, a surgeon, undertakes to perform an operation on a patient for a fee. Before completing the operation, Dr. Gore decides to cease his efforts. As a result of such inattention, the patient dies. Would Dr. Gore's failure to complete what he undertook professionally qualify as an act within the meaning of the criminal law? Yes, because Dr. Gore had a contractual relationship with his patient.

**administrative-type act** A ministerial act performed by executive officers in carrying out a duty assigned by law.

In some instances, failure to perform an **administrative-type act** required by law might not be a crime. In *Lambert v. California*, 355 U.S. 225, 78 S.Ct. 240, 2 L.Ed.2d 228 (1957), the U.S. Supreme Court reviewed a case where the defendant, a convicted felon, was charged with failing to register with authorities as required by a Los Angeles city ordinance. The Court held that as applied to one who has no actual knowledge of a duty to register and where no showing is made of the probability of such knowledge, the ordinance violates the Due Process Clause of the Fourteenth Amendment to the U.S. Constitution. In contrasting the ordinance requiring felon registration with various public welfare offenses it had upheld, the Court noted that public welfare offenses punish failure to act only in "circumstances that should alert the doer to the consequences of his deed." *Lambert v. California,* 355 U.S. at 228, 78 S.Ct. at 243, 2 L.Ed.2d at 231. However, *Lambert's* reach has been limited. In *Texaco, Inc. v. Short,* 454 U.S. 516, 537–538 n. 33, 102 S.Ct. 781, 70 L.Ed.2d 738 (1982), the Supreme Court noted that its application has been so circumscribed that it gives "some credence to Justice Frankfurter's colorful prediction in dissent [in *Lambert*] that the case would stand as 'an isolated deviation from the strong current of precedents—a derelict on the waters of the law'" (quoting *Lambert,* 355 U.S. at 232, 78 S.Ct. at 245 [Frankfurter, J., dissenting]).

## Possession as a Criminal Act

**possession** The actual or constructive control or occupancy of real or personal property.

In certain crimes, **possession** alone is considered to be the wrongful act. For example, in the offense of carrying a concealed weapon, the possession of the weapon concealed from ordinary observation is the wrongful act. Likewise, possession of contraband such as illegal drugs or untaxed liquors constitutes the wrongful act element of certain offenses. Possession is not usually defined in criminal statutes; however, courts generally define possession as the power to control something. The law recognizes two classes of possession: actual and constructive. **Actual possession** exists when a person has something under his or her direct physical control. An example of actual possession would be when an item is on your person, within your reach, or located in a place where you alone have access. **Constructive possession**, on the other hand, is a more difficult concept. A person who has the power and intention to control something either directly or through another person is said to be in constructive possession. The exact meaning of these terms is usually determined by the context of the situation. The difficulty is exacerbated when two or more persons are in joint possession of the premises or vehicle where an object is found. Consider the following examples:

> **actual possession** Possession of something with the possessor having immediate control.

> **constructive possession** Being in the position effectively to control something, even if it is not actually in one's possession.

- Sarah and Tiffany rent and share an apartment. A police search yields contraband: Drugs are found on the coffee table in the living room, which is used by both Sarah and Tiffany. Can both be charged with possession of the contraband? They probably can. Possession by both Sarah and Tiffany can be inferred because the drugs are in plain view and located in a place to which both have access.

- Under the same circumstances of a shared apartment, drugs are found in a privately owned, closed container in a dresser drawer where only Sarah keeps her clothes. Because Tiffany has no access to this area, the law does not infer that Tiffany has constructive possession of the contents of the drawer. Of course, there might be circumstances under which the prosecution could prove that Tiffany actually had rights to the drugs, knowledge of their whereabouts, and/or access to

**CASE-IN-POINT**

### Divergent Judicial Perspectives on Constructive Possession of Contraband

Valot was charged and convicted of "possession and control of marijuana," and under Michigan state law, possession and control are separate offenses. The trial judge's "recited findings . . . made it clear that the conviction was based on findings of control" rather than possession. The Michigan Court of Appeals affirmed Valot's conviction. Speaking for the Court Judge Churchill noted that "the trial judge conceded the possibility that someone, unbeknownst to [Valot], brought the marijuana into the room, but nevertheless did not have a reasonable or fair doubt as to the Valot's control." Judge Churchill held this "was a fact question," and in this case, there "was strong circumstantial evidence to support the [trial court's] finding" that Valot had "control of the marijuana in the room as a fact reasonably inferred from the evidence." However, Judge Levin's dissenting opinion stated, "it is not a crime to be in control of a room where marijuana is found." For Judge Levin, "the People failed to prove that the defendant . . . was in possession or control of marijuana." Judge Levin opined that "to infer from the fact that a person is in control of a room that he is in control of marijuana in the possession of other persons in the room is not a reasonable inference."

*People v. Valot*, 189 N.W.2d 873 (Mich. App. 1971).

them. Then the prosecution could establish that Tiffany was in constructive possession of the contraband.

## Status as a Criminal Act

**status** One's condition or situation.

**Status** refers to a person's state of being, and ordinarily the state cannot criminalize a person's status. For example, a person's race or gender represents a status. But is addiction to narcotics a status that cannot be criminalized? As we saw in the chapter opening vignette, in *Robinson v. California,* 370 U.S. 660, 82 S.Ct. 1417, 8 L.Ed.2d 758 (1962), the U.S. Supreme Court declared unconstitutional a California statute that made it an offense for a person "to be addicted to the use of narcotics." The Court observed that

> we deal with a statute which makes the "status" of narcotic addiction a criminal offense, for which the offender may be prosecuted "at any time before he reforms. . . ." We hold that a state law which imprisons a person thus afflicted as a criminal, even though he has never touched any narcotic drug within the State or been guilty of any irregular behavior there, inflicts a cruel and unusual punishment in violation of the Fourteenth Amendment. 370 U.S. at 666–667, 82 S.Ct. at 1420–1421, 8 L.Ed.2d at 762–763.

The issue of when a criminal statute proscribes status, as opposed to conduct, can be very close. This is illustrated by the Supreme Court's decision in *Powell v. Texas,* 392 U.S. 514, 88 S.Ct. 2145, 20 L.Ed.2d 1254 (1968). Powell was a chronic alcoholic who was convicted of public intoxication. Four justices held that Powell had been punished for being in a public place on a particular occasion while intoxicated rather than for his status as a chronic alcoholic. A fifth justice concurred in affirming Powell's conviction. But the four dissenting justices thought the case was indistinguishable from *Robinson v. California,* supra. In their view, both cases involved defendants who were prosecuted for being in a condition that they had no capacity to alter or avoid.

## JURISPRUDENCE

*Robinson v. California,* 370 U.S. 660, 82 S.Ct. 1417, 8 L.Ed.2d 758 (1962)

The California legislature enacted a statute that made it a misdemeanor "for any person to be addicted to the use of narcotics." Robinson was arrested and convicted under the statute. At trial, the evidence showed that Officer Brown of the Los Angeles Police Department "had [an] occasion to examine [Robinson's] arms" and saw "scar tissue and discoloration on the inside" of Robinson's right arm "and 'what appeared to be numerous needle marks.'" Testimony also revealed that Robinson admitted "occasional use of narcotics." Robinson's conviction was upheld on appeal in the California courts. The Supreme Court reversed, holding as construed and applied by the California courts, "the statute inflicts a cruel and unusual punishment in violation of the Eighth and Fourteenth Amendments." Justice Stewart, speaking for the majority, stated that a "state law which imprisons a person thus afflicted [with an illness] as a criminal, even though he has never touched any narcotic drug within the State or been guilty of any irregular behavior there, inflicts a cruel and unusual punishment . . . . Even one day in prison would be a cruel and unusual punishment for the 'crime' of having a common cold."

---

## JURISPRUDENCE

*Powell v. Texas*, 392 U.S. 514, 88 S.Ct. 2145, 20 L.Ed.2d 1254 (1968)

Leroy Powell was convicted of public intoxication in Austin, Texas. Powell challenged his conviction, saying that he was a "chronic alcoholic" who did not appear intoxicated in public by his own volition. Citing *Robinson v. California* (1962), Powell argued that it would be cruel and unusual punishment to punish him

for being an alcoholic. The Supreme Court rejected that argument and upheld his conviction. Writing for a plurality of justices, Thurgood Marshall concluded that Powell was convicted not for being a chronic alcoholic, but for being in public while drunk on a particular occasion. The case was thus distinguishable from *Robinson v. California*.

---

# The *Mens Rea* (The Criminal Intent Requirement)

The common law developed the doctrine that there should be no crime without a *mens rea*, or "guilty mind." This element is customarily referred to as the criminal intent. To constitute a crime, there must be a concurrence of the *actus reus* with a person's criminal intent. Strict liability offenses, discussed later, are an exception to this principle.

**motive** A person's conscious reason for acting; what someone seeks to accomplish by engaging in particular conduct.

Criminal intent must be distinguished from **motive**. To obtain a conviction, a prosecutor must establish the defendant's criminal intent but not necessarily the defendant's motive for committing a crime. A person's motive often equates with an impulse, an incentive, or a reason for certain behavior, and proof of one's motive can assist in establishing criminal intent. To illustrate, if the prosecution relies on circumstantial evidence to establish the defendant's guilt in a homicide case, the fact that the defendant had vowed "to get even" with the victim might be a relevant factor in the proof. Yet the failure to establish a defendant's motive is not fatal to proving guilt. On the other hand, good motives do not exonerate a person from a crime. Thus, one who steals food to feed a poor, hungry family might have a noble motive. Nevertheless, such a person would be guilty of a crime because of his or her act and intent.

The basic reason that the law requires proof of a criminal intent as well as an act or omission is to distinguish those acts or omissions that occur accidentally from those committed by a person with a "guilty mind." As the California Supreme Court observed in *In re Hayes*, 442 P.2d 366, 369 (Cal. 1968), "an essential element of every orthodox crime is a wrongful or blameworthy mental state of some kind."

## Concurrence of Act and Intent

To constitute a crime, there must be a concurrence of the *mens rea* and the *actus reus*. Many years ago, the Massachusetts Supreme Court articulated this traditional common-law standard when it observed, "An evil intention and an unlawful action must concur in order to constitute a crime." *Commonwealth v. Mixer*, 93 N.E. 249 (Mass. 1910). In 1872, California stipulated in § 20 of the California Penal Code that "the defendant's wrongful intent and his physical act must concur in the sense that the act must be motivated by the intent." See *People v. Green*, 609 P.2d 468, 500 (Cal. 1980). Concurrence of the act and intent usually, but not always, occurs simultaneously. For example, suppose an owner accidentally starts a fire in his or her building without any intention to defraud. The owner then takes no steps to extinguish the fire or notify the fire department. The owner's omission to act concurs with the owner's intent to defraud the insurer of the premises. See *Commonwealth v. Cali,* 141 N.E. 510 (Mass. 1923). On the other hand, suppose Andrew forms an intent to kill his enemy, Bryan, but after completely abandoning the idea, Andrew later inadvertently kills Bryan in a traffic accident. There would be no concurrence of the original intent with the subsequent act.

## General and Specific Intent

At common law, crimes were classified as requiring either general intent or specific intent. American courts followed that tradition. **General intent** is the intent to do an act but not necessarily to cause the results that occur from that act.

Where a crime requires only proof of a general intent, the fact finder (that is, the judge or jury) may infer the defendant's intent from the defendant's acts and the circumstances surrounding those acts. Thus, the prosecution does not have to prove that the defendant had any specific intent to cause a particular result when the act was committed: "General intent exists when from the circumstances the prohibited result may reasonably be expected to follow from the offender's voluntary act, irrespective of a subjective desire to have accomplished such result." *Myers v. State,* 422 N.E.2d 745, 750 (Ind. App. 1981).

Historically, many trial judges instructed juries that "the law presumes that a person intends the ordinary consequences of his voluntary acts." In 1979, in *Sandstrom v. Montana,* 442 U.S. 510, 99 S.Ct. 2450, 61 L.Ed.2d 39, the Supreme Court ruled that it is unconstitutional for a judge so to instruct the jury. The Court held that such a presumption conflicts with the presumption of innocence of the accused and violates the Due Process Clause of the Fourteenth Amendment, which requires that the state prove every element of a criminal offense beyond a reasonable doubt.

Most criminal statutes that prohibit particular voluntary acts are classified as **general-intent statutes**. "General intent means the intent to do that which the law prohibits; an individual need not have intended the precise harm or precise result which eventuated." *State v. Poss,* 298 N.W.2d 80, 83 (S.D. 1980). Statutory words such as "willfully" or "intentionally" generally indicate that the offender must have only intended to do the act and not to accomplish any particular result. Thus, a statute making it the crime of arson "willfully and unlawfully" to set fire to a building is generally viewed as defining a general-intent crime. *Linehan v. State,* 476 So.2d 1262 (Fla. 1985).

On the other hand, **specific intent** refers to an actor's mental purpose to accomplish a particular result beyond the act itself. Again, in the context of the crime of arson, suppose the statute stated that it was an offense for any person "to willfully and with the intent to injure or defraud an insurance company set fire to any building." In this instance the prosecution would be required to prove that the defendant had the specific intent to injure or defraud an insurance company when the proscribed act was perpetrated. Specific intent is the intent to accomplish the precise act that the law prohibits. *State v. Poss,* 298 N.W.2d 80, 83 (S.D. 1980). Again, a statute defining murder that includes the language "premeditated killing of a human being" requires the prosecution to prove the defendant's specific intent. Courts have consistently said that a **specific-intent statute** designates "a special mental element which is required above and beyond any mental state required with respect to the *actus reus* of the crime." *State v. Bridgeforth,* 750 P.2d 3, 5 (Ariz. 1988). Thus, in its decision in *Holloway v. United States,* 526 U.S. 1, 119 S.Ct. 966, 143 L.Ed.2d 1 (1999), the U.S. Supreme Court referred to the federal carjacking statute, 18 U.S.C.A. § 2119, which

---

**general intent** The state of mind to do something prohibited by law without necessarily intending to accomplish the harm that results from the illegal act.

**general-intent statutes** Statutes defining crimes that require only general intent, as distinct from specific intent, on the part of the violator.

**specific intent** The mental purpose to accomplish a particular thing prohibited by law, such as the death of another person.

**specific-intent statute** A statute defining criminal conduct in which the offender must harbor a specific intent to accomplish a prohibited result.

defines carjacking as "tak[ing] a motor vehicle . . . from . . . another by force and violence or by intimidation . . . with the intent to cause death or serious bodily harm," as a law including a specific-intent element.

Assume that State X charged a defendant with burglary of a dwelling under a specific-intent statute that defines the offense as "the unauthorized entry of a dwelling by a person with the intent to commit theft therein." Three basic elements must be established to convict the defendant. First, the state must prove the defendant made an unauthorized entry. Second, it must prove that the entry was made into a dwelling. Finally, it must establish that the defendant made such unauthorized entry with the intent to commit a theft. Intent, of course, is a state of mind, but it can be (and almost always is) inferred from the defendant's actions and surrounding circumstances. Therefore, if some of the dwelling owner's property had been moved and other items left in disarray, the inference would be that the defendant who made the unauthorized entry intended to commit theft from the dwelling. Moreover, this would be true whether the defendant did in fact commit a theft within the dwelling.

The Michigan Supreme Court summed up the difference between specific and general intent in 2000 when it observed that its decisions have held that "the distinction between specific intent and general intent crimes is that the former involve a particular criminal intent beyond the act done, while the latter involve merely the intent to do the physical act." *People v. Nowack,* 614 N.W.2d 78, 84 (Mich. 2000).

In a situation where the defendant might not have had a specific intent to cause a particular result but there was a substantial likelihood of the result occurring, and the act was done with conscious disregard or indifference for the consequences, some courts have developed the concept of **constructive intent** as a substitute for the defendant's specific intent.

**constructive intent** Criminal intent inferred by law as a result of circumstances surrounding a party's actions.

There are two reasons why it is essential to determine whether a particular offense is a general-intent or a specific-intent crime or, in some recent statutory revisions, whether it meets the MPC culpability requirements: First, the intent requirement in a criminal statute determines the extent of proof that must be offered by the prosecution. Second, as we will explain in later chapters, in certain crimes the intent required to be proven determines whether particular defenses are available to the defendant.

---

**CASE-IN-POINT**

### The *Mens Rea* Requirement

The defendant was convicted under a statute that made it an offense to fondle or caress the body of a child less than sixteen years old "with the intent to gratify the sexual desires or appetites of the offending person or . . . to frighten or excite such child." On appeal, the Indiana Supreme Court noted that the strongest evidence in favor of the prosecution was that both the defendant's daughters admitted that during playfulness the father touched and came in contact with the breasts of one of his daughters. However, there was no evidence that this was done with the intent to gratify the sexual desires of the defendant or to frighten the child.

In reversing the defendant's conviction, the court observed that "[a] crime has two components—an evil intent coupled with an overt act. The act alone does not constitute the crime unless it is done with a specific intent declared unlawful by the statute in this state. . . . There must also be proved beyond a reasonable doubt, the specific intent at the time of touching to gratify sexual desires or to frighten the child as stated in the statute."

*Markiton v. State,* 139 N.E.2d 440, 441 (Ind. 1957).

## The Model Penal Code Approach to Intent

Over the years, the common-law classifications of general and specific intent have become subject to many variations in court decisions in the various jurisdictions. In the chapters of this text that discuss substantive offenses, the reader will find a variety of terms that legislatures and courts have used to describe the *mens rea* requirements of various crimes. Such terms include "unlawfully," "feloniously," "willfully," "maliciously," "wrongfully," "deliberately," "recklessly," "negligently," "with premeditated intent," "with culpable negligence," "with gross negligence," and numerous others. In some instances courts have even disagreed on whether these *mens rea* requirements apply to every material element of an offense. The wide variety of terms used to describe the mental element of crimes and the dichotomy between general and specific intent have led to considerable difficulty in determining intent requirements in statutory crimes.

In 1962 the American Law Institute (ALI) published the Model Penal Code (MPC) and in 1980 published a somewhat revised version with commentaries. The MPC has had a profound impact on the criminal law, especially with regard to the formulation of *mens rea*. The MPC rejects the common-law terms for intent. Instead, it simplifies the terms describing culpability and proposes four states of mind: purposely, knowingly, recklessly, and negligently. M.P.C. § 2.02(2). Section 2.02(4) states that the prescribed culpability requirement applies to all material elements of an offense. (The term "purposely" seems to correspond roughly to the common-law specific-intent requirement, while other MPC categories seem to fall within the general-intent category.)

Several legislative revisions of state criminal codes have followed the MPC in setting standards of culpability. For example, in 1977 Alabama adopted § 13A-2-2 of its Criminal Code. The commentary following the new section notes that it attempts "to identify, define and reasonably delimit the main culpable mental states involved in the criminal law." It provides that the following definitions of culpability apply:

1. *Intentionally.* A person acts intentionally with respect to a result or to conduct described by a statute defining an offense, when his purpose is to cause that result or to engage in that conduct.
2. *Knowingly.* A person acts knowingly with respect to conduct or to a circumstance described by a statute defining an offense when he is aware that his conduct is of that nature or that the circumstance exists.
3. *Recklessly.* A person acts recklessly with respect to a result or to a circumstance described by a statute defining an offense when he is aware of and consciously disregards a substantial and unjustifiable risk that the result will occur or that the circumstance exists. The risk must be of such nature and degree that disregard thereof constitutes a gross deviation from the standard of conduct that a reasonable person would observe in the situation. A person who creates a risk but is unaware thereof solely by reason of voluntary intoxication, as defined in § 13A-3-2(e)(2), acts recklessly with respect thereto.
4. *Criminal negligence.* A person acts with criminal negligence with respect to a result or to a circumstance that is defined by statute as an offense when he fails to perceive a substantial and unjustifiable risk that the result will occur or that the circumstance exists. The risk must be of such nature and degree that the failure to perceive it constitutes a gross deviation from the standard of care that a reasonable person would observe in the situation. A court or jury may consider statutes or ordinances regulating the defendant's conduct as bearing upon the question of criminal negligence.

Commentary following § 13A-2-2 further notes that this section "is derived principally from Michigan Revised Criminal Code § 305, which followed New York Penal Law § 15.05, which in turn is based on the Model Penal Code § 2.02." Some other states have essentially adopted the MPC proposals, and, like Alabama, several have opted to use the term "intentionally" instead of the MPC term "purposely" in the first category of culpability. This difference appears to be only one of terminology.

Section 13A-6-3 of Alabama's Criminal Code now begins defining "manslaughter" by stating, in part, that "[a] person commits the crime of manslaughter if (1) He recklessly causes the death of another person ...," whereas a state that has not adopted the MPC classifications might define manslaughter in terms of "an unlawful killing of a person by culpable negligence" or "a killing of a human being without malice aforethought."

In addition to understanding traditional concepts of general and specific intent, a student should become acquainted with previously quoted sections of the MPC that define "act" and relate to levels of culpability. While these are among the most widely relied-on provisions of the MPC, in later chapters dealing with substantive crimes we refer to instances where the MPC has been influential in the revision of criminal statutes.

In 1978 Arizona adopted the four MPC culpable mental states of intention, knowledge, recklessness, and criminal negligence, as defined in Ariz. Rev. Stat. § 13-105; M.P.C. § 2.02(2). These replaced all previous mental states used in Arizona's criminal laws. See *State v. Robles*, 623 P.2d 1245, 1246 (Ariz. App. 1981).

Congress has not adopted the Model Penal Code, although in 1980 the Supreme Court alluded to the merits of the MPC classification of *mens rea*, *United States v. Bailey*, 444 U.S. 394, 100 S.Ct. 624, 62 L.Ed.2d 575 (1980), and often has made use of the MPC approach to *mens rea* in interpreting federal criminal statutes. See, e.g., *United States v. United States Gypsum Co.*, 438 U.S. 422, 98 S.Ct. 2864, 57 L.Ed.2d 854 (1978).

## The Doctrine of Transferred Intent

**doctrine of transferred intent** Doctrine originating in common law under which an actor's criminal intent associated with an act against an intended victim is transferred to an unintended victim who suffers the consequences of the defendant's act.

The **doctrine of transferred intent** transfers an actor's original intent against an intended victim to an unintended victim who suffers the consequences. An English court invoked the doctrine in 1575 in the classic case *Regina v. Sounders & Archer*, 75 Eng. Rep. 706, where Saunders gave his wife a poisoned apple. After tasting it but suffering no consequences, the wife gave the apple to her daughter, who died from the poison. The court found that Saunders caused his daughter's death despite the fact he intended no harm to her. American courts apply the doctrine primarily in assaultive and homicide cases, often referred to as the "missed aim" cases, but it can apply to other crimes such as, for example, arson. Because the doctrine supplies an intent to commit a crime against a person where no such intent existed, it is often referred to as a "legal fiction." It is designed to avoid an otherwise unjust result by obviating the need for the prosecution to establish that it was predictable that an accused's actions would have caused harm to an unintended victim. Instead of following the doctrine of transferred intent, the MPC deals with such a situation on the basis of causation. M.P.C. § 2.02(2)(a).

In *State v. Gardner*, 203 A.2d 77 (Del. 1964), the Delaware Supreme Court ruled that where a defendant whose express malice aforethought was directed toward an intended victim but not in fact toward the actual victim who was killed, a defendant can nevertheless be convicted of first-degree murder. The court noted that

### California Court Reaffirms the Doctrine of Transferred Intent

On May 28, 2000, Lori Gonzalez, age 20, was sitting in the driver's seat of a Chevrolet Caprice that was stopped in the drive-through lane at a Popeye's Chicken and Biscuits restaurant in Los Angeles. Defendant Samuel Shabazz, a gang member, walked up to the passenger side and fired several shots at Gonzalez's passenger, Ernest Gray, a member of a rival gang. Gray ducked when he saw the firearm and the shots hit and killed Gonzalez. A jury found the defendant guilty of first-degree murder carried out by the defendant while he was an active participant in a street gang.

On appeal the defendant contended that the gang-murder statute that requires special circumstances was inapplicable to him because it requires that the defendant intentionally kill the victim, and that he had intended to kill Ernest Gray, not Lori Gonzalez. In rejecting his contention that the doctrine of transferred intent was inapplicable, the California Supreme Court held that the gang-murder special circumstances statute is directed against murderers who kill as part of any gang-related activity and not simply against those who kill their intended targets. The court observed: "Under the classic formulation of California's common law doctrine of transferred intent, a defendant who shoots with the intent to kill a certain person and hits a bystander instead is subject to the same criminal liability that would have been imposed had the fatal blow reached the person for whom intended."

*People v. Shabazz*, 130 P.3d 519, 523 (Cal .2006).

courts in the great majority of other states consider the defendant guilty of the same crime as if the defendant had accomplished the original purpose. As more recently explained by the North Carolina Supreme Court,

> [U]nder the doctrine of transferred intent, it is immaterial whether the defendant intended injury to the person actually harmed; if he in fact acted with the required or elemental intent toward someone, that intent suffices as the intent element of the crime charged as a matter of substantive law. *State v. Locklear*, 415 S.E.2d 726, 730 (N.C. 1992).

Most transferred intent cases involve homicides. As the doctrine developed, some courts expressed disagreement as to whether a defendant's specific intent to kill an individual is transferred to an unintended victim. But even if the actor's *specific intent* is not transferred, the killing of an unintended victim can be prosecuted as a homicidal crime or other offense not requiring proof of the defendant's specific intent. Because the doctrine is designed to punish an offender who "misses aim" and kills or injures an unintended victim, jurisdictions have split on whether it also applies when the accused kills or injures both the intended and the unintended victims. Some courts reason that it is unnecessary to apply the doctrine in such cases. But in *Poe v. State*, 671 A.2d 501 (Md. 1996), Maryland's highest court held that the doctrine of transferred intent applied where the defendant, intending to kill a woman, fired a shot that wounded the woman who was targeted, passed through her, and killed a child standing nearby.

## Strict Liability Offenses

As we previously noted, common-law crimes consist of a criminal act or omission known as the *actus reus* and the mental element known as the *mens rea*. However, legislative bodies have the power to dispense with the necessity for the mental

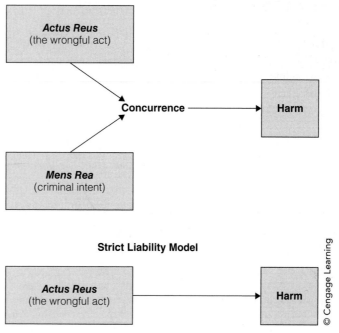

**FIGURE 4.1** Elements of a Crime: Traditional and Strict Liability Models.

element and authorize punishment of particular acts without regard to the actor's intent (see Figure 4.1). Such crimes are known as "strict liability offenses."

As we pointed out in Chapter 1, *mala in se* offenses are inherent wrongs, whereas *mala prohibita* offenses are considered wrongs because they are so defined by the law. In such common-law felonies as murder, rape, robbery, and larceny, the proscribed conduct is considered *mala in se* and the intent is deemed inherent in the offense. This holds true today even if the statute proscribing such conduct fails to specify intent as an element of the offense.

Many of the *mala prohibita* crimes are defined as strict liability offenses. For the most part, these include "regulatory" or "public welfare" types of offenses, which often are tailored to address public safety, environmental, and public health concerns. We see some of the earliest examples of strict liability in cases involving the sale of liquor and adulterated milk. Examples of strict liability laws today include mostly traffic regulations, food and drug laws, and laws prohibiting the sale of liquor and cigarettes to minors. Strict liability offenses now constitute a substantial part of the criminal law.

The fact that a statute is silent on the matter of criminal intent does not necessarily mean that it defines a strict liability offense. If the prohibited conduct falls within a traditional common-law crime category, courts will likely interpret such statutes to contain a *mens rea* requirement. For example, in *Morissette v. United States*, 342 U.S. 246, 72 S.Ct. 240, 96 L.Ed. 288 (1952), the defendant had been convicted of violating federal law by taking some old bomb casings from a government bombing range. At trial, the district court refused to instruct the jury on the issue of intent, in effect holding that the government was required to prove only the defendant's act, not his intent, because the statute required proof of only the prohibited act. The Supreme Court reversed Morissette's conviction, holding that the crime for which he was prosecuted

## JURISPRUDENCE

*Morissette v. United States*, 342 U.S. 246, 72 S.Ct. 240, 96 L.Ed. 288 (1952)

On a large piece of uninhabited and wooded land in Michigan, the federal government "established a practice bombing range over which the Air Force dropped simulated bombs at ground targets." Signs were posted at various places on the land reading "Danger—Keep Out—Bombing Range." However, the land was well known for being "good deer county and was extensively hunted." Spent bomb casings were "thrown into piles" on the land, which had accumulated over a period of four years or longer. Morissette, a scrap metal dealer, went hunting in the area in 1948 and collected three tons of the spent bomb casings worth about $84. Morissette was subsequently indicted and convicted of "unlawfully, willfully and knowingly steal[ing] and convert[ing]" property of the United States. At trial, Morissette argued "he believed the casings were cast-off and abandoned, that he did not intend to steal the property, and took it with no wrongful or criminal intent." However, the district court "refused to submit or to allow counsel to argue to the jury whether Morissette

acted with innocent intention." The Court of Appeals affirmed. The Supreme Court concluded that "criminal intent is an essential element of an offense . . . which provides that 'whoever . . . steals . . . or knowingly converts' property of the United States is punishable by fine and imprisonment." The Supreme Court went on to say that "the mere omission [from the statute] of any mention of intent is not to be construed as eliminating that element from the crimes defined." In an examination of the legislative history of the statute, the Supreme Court concluded that there was "no ground for inferring any affirmative instruction from Congress to eliminate intent from the offense of 'knowingly converting' or stealing government property." In summation, the Court held "where intent of the accused is an ingredient of the crime charged, its existence is a question of fact which must be submitted to the jury for determination in the light of all relevant evidence, and the trial court may not withdraw or prejudge the issue by instructing the jury that the law raises a presumption of intent from a single act." Therefore, Morissette's conviction was overturned.

was a variant of the common-law offense of larceny and that failure to include the intent requirement in the statute did not eliminate the element of intent.

In *United States v. United States Gypsum Co.*, 438 U.S. 422, 98 S.Ct. 2864, 57 L.Ed.2d 854 (1978), the Supreme Court was called on to decide whether a criminal violation of the Sherman Act required proof of criminal intent or whether intent may be presumed conclusively from the anticompetitive effect of the defendants' actions. Despite the fact that the Sherman Act does not use the words "willfully" or "knowingly," the Court held that intent is an essential element of a criminal antitrust offense and must be established not only by proof of anticompetitive effects but by proof that the defendants had knowledge that the proscribed effects were probable.

Critics of strict liability offenses argue that they run counter to the standards of criminal culpability. Others argue that it is desirable to classify these offenses as regulatory or administrative, thereby removing the "criminal" stigma. Still others counter that to remove the criminal aspect from these offenses would remove their deterrent factor. One thing seems certain: If the prohibited conduct falls within a traditional common-law crime category, courts will likely interpret such statutes to contain a *mens rea* requirement. In the chapters that follow, note that as penalties for statutory offenses become heavier, courts are more reluctant to dispense with proof of intent. This is true in environmental crimes (see Chapter 11) and in some serious motor vehicle violations. For example, many state courts have addressed the issue of whether proof of a criminal intent is necessary to convict someone of the statutory crime of driving with a revoked or suspended license. In *Jeffcoat v. State*, 639 P.2d 308 (Alaska App. 1982), the Alaska Court of Appeals held that even though the statute is silent, the element of *mens rea* must be read into it by implication. In *State*

### Court Implies a *Mens Rea* Requirement as an Element of a Federal Election Offense

Ricardo Knight, an alien resident of the United States, was convicted of improperly voting in the 2000 presidential election, in violation of 18 U.S.C.A. § 611(a). On appeal he contended that Congress's failure to have incorporated a *mens rea* requirement into the law rendered the statute unconstitutional, and that the court was precluded from reading an implied intent into the statute.

In rejecting Knight's contention the Court of Appeals observed, "The existence of a *mens rea* is the rule of, rather than the exception to, the principles of Anglo-American criminal jurisprudence." Further, the court pointed out that the U.S. Supreme Court has held that some congressional intent is required to dispense with *mens rea* as an element of a federal crime. Despite Congress's failure to incorporate a *mens rea* requirement into the statute prohibiting aliens from voting in federal elections, the statute includes an implied general intent and is not unconstitutional because the government must prove that a defendant knowingly engaged in the conduct prohibited by 18 U.S.C.A. § 611.

*United States v. Knight*, 490 F.3d 1268 (11th Cir. 2007).

---

*v. Keihn*, 530 N.E.2d 747 (Ind. 1989), the Indiana Supreme Court agreed that in a prosecution for driving with a suspended license, the State was required to prove the defendant's knowledge of the suspension. However, in 1998 the Connecticut Supreme Court disagreed with the Indiana Supreme Court's decision in *State v. Keihn* and held that actual knowledge of a license suspension is not an essential element of the crime of operating a motor vehicle with a suspended license as long as there was proof of a bulk certified mailing of the suspension notice. *State v. Swain*, 718 A.2d 1 (Conn. 1998).

## The Causation Requirement

**causation** The linkage between cause and effect. X can be said to cause Y if X precedes Y and Y could not have occurred in the absence of X.

**proximate cause** The cause that is nearest to a given effect in a causal relationship.

When an offense is defined in a manner that a specific result must occur, the concept of **causation** becomes important. This is most commonly associated with homicide offenses. For example, the various degrees of homicide require that to be guilty of murder or manslaughter, the accused's conduct must have resulted in the death of a human being. Sometimes lawyers refer to legal causation as **proximate cause**, defined as "a cause that in a natural, continuous sequence, unbroken by any intervening causes, produces the consequences that occur." Proximate cause is satisfied if the result that occurs was foreseeable. Sometimes the "but-for" test is employed here, meaning that "but for" the accused's actions, the harm would not have occurred. This can be illustrated by an instance where, but for the accused's firing a pistol, the victim would not have been killed. But suppose the victim was only slightly injured by the accused's having fired a pistol and was later taken to a hospital, where through the negligence of health care providers the victim died? If the victim's death occurred from such an intervening cause, it would likely result in the perpetrator's being charged with a lesser offense such as assault with a dangerous weapon.

Although causation is important in many crimes to link the elements of the accused's act and intent, in Chapter 5 we will study the incomplete offenses of attempt, solicitation, and conspiracy, which are classified as inchoate (incomplete) offenses. These offenses, among others that we will later study, do not require that specified results occur.

# Parties to a Crime

**accomplices** Persons who voluntarily unite with others in the commission of an offense.

Historically, the common law classified parties to crimes as either principals or accessories. Principals were persons whose conduct involved direct participation in a crime; accessories were **accomplices** or those who gave aid and comfort to principals. The common law classified crimes other than treason as felonies and misdemeanors. Felonies were very serious; in fact, at times, a person found guilty of a felony could be deprived of all worldly possessions and suffer either death or lengthy imprisonment. Because of the serious nature of felonious conduct and because all persons involved might not be equally guilty, the common law developed several technical distinctions among the various participants.

## Common-Law Distinctions among Participants in Crime

To comprehend present criminal law regarding participants in a crime, a basic knowledge of the common-law scheme is essential. At common law, a person directly involved in committing a felony was classified as a principal; a person whose conduct did not involve direct participation was classified as an accessory. Principals were further classified by the degree of their participation. A person who directly or through the acts of an innocent agent actually committed the crime was a principal in the first degree. A principal in the second degree was a person not directly involved, but actually or constructively present at the commission of the crime, who aided and abetted the perpetrator. To be constructively present, one had to be sufficiently close to render assistance to the perpetrator. For example, suppose a man led a woman's escort away from her so that another man could sexually attack the woman. The man who led the escort away would probably be constructively present and would be classified as a principal in the second degree because he was **aiding and abetting** a crime. Aiding and abetting another in the commission of a crime means assenting to an act or lending countenance or approval, either by active participation in it or by encouraging it in some other manner.

**aiding and abetting** Assisting in or otherwise facilitating the commission of a crime.

An accessory at common law was classified as either an accessory before or after the fact. An accessory before the fact was one who procured or counseled another to commit a felony but who was not actually or constructively present at the commission of the offense. An accessory after the fact was one who, with knowledge of the other's guilt, rendered assistance to a felon in an effort to hinder the felon's arrest or punishment.

Because misdemeanors were far less serious than felonies, the common law found it unnecessary to distinguish between participants in misdemeanor offenses. As with treason, all participants in misdemeanors were regarded as principals.

Accessories to felonies were not regarded as being as culpable as the principals, so they were punished less severely at common law. Moreover, under the common law there were some procedural distinctions applicable to principals and accessories; for example, a party had to be charged either as a principal or as an accessory. The principal had to be tried first, and if the principal were found not guilty, the accessory could not be tried for the offense.

## The Modern American Approach

The American approach has been to abolish both the substantive and procedural distinctions between principals and accessories before the fact. Federal law stipulates that "[w]hoever commits an offense against the United States or aids, abets, counsels, commands, induces, or procures its commission, is punishable as a principal. . . ." 18 U.S.C.A. § 2(a). The federal statute reflects the law of most of the states insofar as it abolishes the distinction between principals and accessories before the fact. As early as 1872, California enacted a statute defining principals as "all persons concerned in the commission of a crime, whether it be felony or misdemeanor, and whether they directly commit the act constituting the offense, or aid and abet in its commission, or, not being present, have advised and encouraged its commission." West's Ann. Cal. Penal Code § 31. As explained by the Supreme Court of Appeals of West Virginia in *State v. Fortner*, 387 S.E.2d 812, 822 (W.Va. 1989),

> Being an accessory before the fact or a principal in the second degree is not, of itself, a separate crime, but is a basis for finding liability for the underlying crime. . . . In essence, evidence of such complicity simply establishes an alternative theory of criminal liability, i.e., another way of committing the underlying crime.

The common-law distinction between principals and accessories before the fact has been largely abolished, but the concept of accessory after the fact as a separate offense has been retained by many jurisdictions. Modern statutes view an accessory after the fact as less culpable than someone who plans, assists, or commits a crime. Thus, statutes generally define being an accessory after the fact as a separate offense and provide for a less severe punishment. See, e.g., West's Ann. Cal. Penal Code § 33. In most states, a lawful conviction as an accessory after the fact requires proof that a person knew that the person he or she aided or assisted had committed a felony. The gist of being an accessory after the fact lies essentially in obstructing justice,

**CASE-IN-POINT**

### Defendant with Intent to Commit Felony Convicted as an Accomplice Irrespective of Active Participation in Killing a Victim

Defendant Vernell Dixon appealed his conviction of capital felony murder that occurred during the course of an aggravated robbery. He argued that his conviction should not stand because the evidence showed that he did not take an active part in the killing of the victim.

In rejecting Dixon's argument the Arkansas Supreme Court observed,

A defendant must only have the requisite intent for the underlying felony. Substantial evidence established defendant as an accomplice to the underlying aggravated robbery, and it was committed under circumstances manifesting extreme indifference to the value of human life.

Under the capital murder statute, Ark. Code Ann. § 5-10-101(a)(1) (Repl. 1993), it is not necessary that the State show that the defendant took an active part in the killing so long as he assisted in the commission of the underlying crime. . . . A defendant must only have the requisite intent for the underlying felony. . . . The proof showed that [the defendant] was an accomplice and had the requisite intent for the aggravated robbery, supplied the .25 caliber pistol used in the robbery, and was present when the victim was killed in the course of the robbery. Such proof is sufficient to sustain the conviction for capital felony murder.

*Dixon v. State*, 891 S.W.2d 59 (Ark. 1995).

and a person is guilty who knows that an offense has been committed and receives, relieves, comforts, or assists the offender to hinder his or her apprehension, trial, or punishment. *United States v. Brown*, 33 F.3d 1002 (8th Cir. 1994). However, federal law does not distinguish whether the person assisted has committed a felony or a misdemeanor. 18 U.S.C.A. § 3.

The common-law rule that a woman who gave comfort and aid to her husband was exempt from being an accessory after the fact no longer prevails, yet some state statutes exempt spouses and other classes of relatives from penalty for being accessories after the fact. For example, Florida law has long prevented the prosecution as an accessory after the fact of any person standing in the relation of husband or wife, parent or grandparent, child or grandchild, or brother or sister, either by blood or marriage. West's Fla. Stat. Ann. § 777.03(1)(a). In 1999 the legislature amended the statute to add that, regardless of relation to the offender, a person who maintains or assists a principal or accessory before the fact knowing the offender has committed child abuse or a related offense is subject to prosecution as an accessory after the fact unless the court finds that such person is a victim of domestic violence. West's Fla. Stat. Ann. § 777.03(1)(b).

## Conclusion

The concepts discussed in this chapter, though technical, are basic to an understanding of the criminal law in the United States. At this stage, concepts like *actus reus* and *mens rea* may seem abstract, but they will become more concrete in later chapters as we relate them to specific offenses.

Common-law crimes were considered *mala in se*, or wrongs in themselves, and required proof of a general or specific intent. The classification of intent as general or specific remains viable; however, in some criminal code revisions today, these traditional categories of intent are being replaced by categories of culpability recommended by the Model Penal Code. In contrast, many modern statutory offenses are classified as *mala prohibita*—that is, they are offenses simply because a legislative body has classified them as wrongs, and they are considered strict liability crimes. Yet even where a statute describes a strict liability crime, courts will imply an intent requirement if the crime is basically of common-law origin or imposes a heavy punishment.

The elements of crimes discussed in this chapter will be relevant throughout the text. In contrast, except for the offense of being an accessory after the fact, the common-law designation of parties to crimes is largely of historical importance. This is because modern criminal law at the federal and state levels treats parties who are complicit in crimes as principals, whether perpetrators or accomplices. Some jurisdictions make an exception for accessories after the fact where a close family relationship is involved. Society has found this approach necessary, and this principle has become firmly ingrained in modern criminal law.

## Chapter Summary

- Learning Objective 1

  - The traditional elements of a crime are a person's wrongful act (*actus reus*) and criminal intent or guilty state of mind (*mens rea*).

- o To be found guilty of a crime a person must commit a voluntary act, and in most instances, such act must be committed with a criminal intent.
- o A wrongful act is the indispensable element in all crimes. A person cannot be found guilty of an offense based solely on criminal intent.
- o The *actus reus* requirement can be fulfilled by a person's failure to act where there is a family relationship or statutory or contractual duty to act.

- Learning Objective 2

  - o In some instances possession can be a criminal act; examples include possession of concealed weapons and contraband.
  - o The law recognizes two classes of possession: actual possession, where a person has something under direct physical control; and constructive possession, where a person has the power and intention to control something either directly or through another person.

- Learning Objective 3

  - o The law recognizes that a person's status cannot be criminalized, but there has been disagreement on the Supreme Court as to what constitutes status in certain instances. The law cannot criminalize the status of being addicted to narcotics, but it can punish an alcoholic for the act of public intoxication.

- Learning Objective 4

  - o Criminal intent is the conscious mental purpose to do a prohibited act.
  - o In most instances a prosecutor must establish the defendant's criminal intent as well as the commission of a prohibited act. This is because, unlike the civil law, the criminal law generally does not punish people for unintentional wrongs.
  - o Laws allowing criminal liability irrespective of intent or in cases where there is culpable negligence are exceptions to this rule.

- Learning Objective 5

  - o At common law, crimes were classified as requiring either general intent or specific intent.
  - o General intent is the intent to do an act but not necessarily to cause the results that occur from that act, while specific intent refers to an actor's mental purpose to accomplish a particular result beyond the act itself.
  - o There are two reasons why it is essential to determine whether a particular offense is a general-intent or a specific-intent crime. First, the intent requirement in a criminal statute determines the extent of proof that must be offered by the prosecution; second, in certain crimes the intent that must be proven determines whether particular defenses are available to the defendant.
  - o When an offense is defined in a manner that requires that a specific result must occur, the concept of causation becomes important. This is most commonly associated with homicide offenses, where various degrees of homicide require that to be guilty of murder or manslaughter, the accused's conduct must have resulted in the death of a human being. Legal

causation or "proximate cause" is defined as "a cause that in a natural, continuous sequence, unbroken by any intervening causes, produces the consequences that occur." Proximate cause is satisfied if the result that occurs was foreseeable.

- Learning Objective 6

  o The Model Penal Code (MPC), which has influenced the criminal laws of some states, rejects the common-law terms for intent.
  o The MPC recognizes four states of mind—purposely, knowingly, recklessly, and negligently—and states that the prescribed culpability requirement applies to all material elements of an offense.
  o Congress has not adopted the Model Penal Code, although in 1980 the Supreme Court alluded to the merits of the MPC classification of *mens rea* and often has made use of the MPC approach to *mens rea* in interpreting federal criminal statutes.

- Learning Objective 7

  o Certain offenses are classified as strict liability crimes and are exceptions to the common-law concept of requiring proof of a defendant's criminal intent.
  o Many *mala prohibita* crimes, usually "regulatory" or "public welfare" types of offenses, are strict liability offenses and do not require proof of intent.
  o The fact that a statute is silent on the matter of criminal intent does not necessarily mean that it defines a strict liability offense. If the prohibited conduct falls within a traditional common-law crime category, courts will likely interpret such statutes to contain a *mens rea* requirement.

- Learning Objective 8

  o At common law, parties to felonies were denominated as principals in the first and second degree, and accessories before and after the fact.
  o A person directly involved in committing a felony was a principal; a person whose conduct did not involve direct participation was an accessory.
  o An accessory before the fact was one who procured or counseled another to commit a felony but who was not actually or constructively present at the commission of the offense.
  o An accessory after the fact was one who, with knowledge of the other's guilt, rendered assistance to a felon in an effort to hinder the felon's arrest or punishment.

- Learning Objective 9

  o The American approach has been to abolish both the substantive and procedural distinctions between principals and accessories before the fact.
  o Federal law stipulates that "[w]hoever commits an offense against the United States or aids, abets, counsels, commands, induces, or procures its commission, is punishable as a principal. . . ." This reflects the statutory law of most of the states insofar as it abolishes the common-law distinction between principal and accessories before the fact.
  o In many states, the concept of an accessory after the fact remains as a separate offense.

## Key Terms

| | |
|---|---|
| accessories after the fact | doctrine of transferred intent |
| accessories before the fact | general intent |
| accomplices | general-intent statutes |
| act of omission | motive |
| actual possession | possession |
| administrative-type act | principals |
| aiding and abetting | proximate cause |
| causation | specific intent |
| constructive intent | specific-intent statute |
| constructive possession | status |

## Questions for Thought and Discussion

1. Distinguish between the concepts of motive and intent in the criminal law. Can you cite an instance where, despite good motives, a person would be guilty of a crime?
2. What justifies the criminal law making mere possession of contraband articles illegal? Do you think this rationale extends to criminalizing the mere possession of such innocent items as a screwdriver, a pair of pliers, or an ice pick, which could be used to commit burglary?
3. Given the fact that the common-law requirement of intent is not an element of strict liability crimes, what rationale supports legislative enactment of such offenses? Name some examples of offenses that are classified as strict liability.
4. Should the criminal law punish a person whose mere carelessness, as opposed to willfulness, causes harm to another? Give reasons for your answer.
5. Is there a justification for the criminal law not punishing a person for failing to act when there is a clear moral duty to act?
6. Has the moral integrity of the criminal law been jeopardized by the increasing number of offenses for which a person can be convicted without proof of any criminal intent?
7. Why has the common-law doctrine distinguishing between principals and accessories before the fact diminished in importance in contemporary criminal law?
8. Contrast an offense that requires proof of causation with one that does not.
9. Is it fair to assess the same degree of fault and impose the same punishment on an accomplice as on a perpetrator? What rationale supports your conclusion?
10. Is there a valid reason to exempt close family relatives from punishment as accessories after the fact to felonious conduct?

## Problems for Discussion and Solution

1. Arthur and Bob were friends and co-workers in an auto assembly plant. Arthur became enraged at Bob because he believed that Bob had sex with Charlotte, his girlfriend. Arthur had made statements that he hated Bob and wanted to see him dead. A few months later, after neither Arthur nor Bob were dating Charlotte, they resumed their friendship. While Arthur and Bob were hunting together, Arthur accidentally shot and killed Bob. Knowing of Arthur's previously

expressed hate for Bob, Bob's family sought to have Arthur prosecuted for murder. What result would likely occur? Why?

2. Fred, experienced in rowing and canoeing, was hired by a boys' camp to supervise campers in their rowing and canoeing. During a teaching exercise, a boy who was not a good swimmer fell from a canoe. Fred took no action and the boy drowned. Does Fred have any criminal liability? What principle is applicable here?

3. A municipality enacts an ordinance making it an offense for a person who is addicted to narcotics to appear in public. Richard, who is addicted to heroin, is arrested for violating the ordinance when he is leaving the grocery store with his purchases. He argues that the ordinance is unconstitutional because he has not committed any crime. What result should occur?

4. Nancy was charged with exceeding the posted speed limit by driving 50 m.p.h. in a 30-m.p.h. zone. She explains to the traffic court judge that she was distracted by thoughts of the unfortunate death of her younger sister, which had occurred a few days before. She contends that she had no intent to violate the speed limit. Evaluate her contention.

5. A state statute reads, "Any person, who with intent to defraud, files a claim for disability benefits under an insurance policy shall, upon conviction, be fined $500." What category of *mens rea* does this statute illustrate?

6. Sol Toolmaker visited his long-time friend, I. N. Mate, a prisoner in a state institution. Mate had previously told Toolmaker how much he wanted to escape from the prison. So, on this occasion, Toolmaker brought Mate two small saws. Mate hid the saws in a place where he thought the prison guards would not find them, but the guards promptly discovered and confiscated the saws. The warden turned this evidence over to the prison's legal counsel with a request that charges be prepared against Mate for attempting to escape from prison. Assuming Mate intended to escape from prison, did his conduct constitute a criminal act?

7. Alice Alpha had a long-standing grievance against Benjamin Beta and had threatened to kill him. When Alpha saw Beta standing on a street corner amidst a crowd of people, Alpha pulled out a gun and fired a shot. The bullet grazed Beta's arm, injuring him slightly. But it struck and killed Gerry Gamma, who was unknown to Alpha. Considering the concepts discussed in this chapter, what crime or crimes has Alpha committed?

CHAPTER **5**

# Inchoate Offenses

## CHAPTER OUTLINE

Introduction

Attempt

Solicitation

Conspiracy

Conclusion

Chapter Summary

Key Terms

Questions for Thought and Discussion

Problems for Discussion and Solution

## JURISPRUDENCE

*Callanan v. United States* (1961)

*Pinkerton v. United States* (1946)

## LEARNING OBJECTIVES

After reading this chapter, you should be able to explain

1. why the law criminalizes inchoate offenses

2. why an attempt often requires a substantial step toward the commission of a crime

3. why an attempt usually merges into the target offense when the latter is committed

4. how solicitation differs from attempt

5. why courts differ on whether solicitation is more heinous than attempt

6. how conspiracy differs from solicitation

7. why the federal government and some states require proof of an overt act in furtherance of a conspiracy

8. how Wharton's Rule prevents prosecution for conspiracy with respect to certain target crimes

9. why, under the *Pinkerton* Rule, a member of a conspiracy is vicariously liable for offenses committed by others in furtherance of the conspiracy

10. the defenses available in cases of attempt, solicitation and conspiracy

# CHAPTER OPENING VIGNETTE

By the end of the 1990s, Enron Corporation was one of the most successful companies in the United States and a world leader in the field of energy. But after revelations of widespread accounting fraud, the company collapsed into bankruptcy in 2001. Some 20,000 employees lost their jobs and investors lost billions of dollars.

In one of the most dramatic white-collar crime cases ever prosecuted in the United States, Enron founder Kenneth Lay and former chief executive Jeffrey Skilling were convicted in federal court in May of 2006 of conspiracy to commit securities fraud and wire fraud. The government charged that Lay and Skilling entered into a conspiracy to defraud investors and employees by giving them false information about the giant energy company's financial health. In her closing argument to the jury, prosecutor Kathryn Ruemmler insisted that Lay and Skilling committed their crimes "through accounting tricks, fiction, hocus-pocus, trickery, misleading statements, half-truths, omissions and outright lies. . . ." Prosecution witnesses included eight former Enron employees who had pleaded guilty to other charges stemming from the scandal or entered into immunity agreements with the government. The jury deliberated for six days before returning guilty verdicts against Lay and Skilling. In July 2006, before sentences were imposed, Lay died of a heart attack. Because he died before he had an opportunity to challenge his conviction on appeal, the court dismissed the case against Lay.

In October 2006, Skilling, who was convicted of conspiracy, securities fraud, making false representations to auditors, and insider trading, was sentenced to twenty-four years and four months in prison, three years' supervised release, and $45 million in restitution. After the Fifth Circuit Court of Appeals affirmed his convictions, *United States v. Skilling*, 554 F.3d 529 (2009), Skilling petitioned the Supreme Court to review the case. On June 24, 2010, the Court ruled that one of the statutes Skilling was found guilty of conspiring to violate, 18 U.S.C.A. § 1346, had been improperly interpreted by the lower courts. *Skilling v. United States*, 561 U.S. —, 130 S.Ct. 2896, 177 L.Ed.2d 619 (2010). The Supreme Court remanded the case to the Fifth Circuit for reconsideration, giving Skilling hope that his conspiracy conviction ultimately would be overturned. That hope was dashed when the Fifth Circuit reaffirmed Skilling's conviction, *United*

*States v. Skilling*, 638 F.3d 480 (5th Cir. 2011), and the Supreme Court subsequently denied review. The Skilling case shows the complexity of the contemporary criminal law, especially in the area of white-collar crime. It also shows that the offense of conspiracy is a powerful tool for prosecutors.

# Introduction

**inchoate offense** An offense preparatory to committing a crime. Inchoate offenses include attempt, conspiracy, and solicitation.

The word "inchoate" means "underdeveloped" or "unripened." Thus, an **inchoate offense** is one involving activity or steps directed toward the completion of a crime. There are three such offenses: attempt, solicitation, and conspiracy. These are not crimes in themselves; rather there must be an attempt to commit a crime—for example, attempted murder—the solicitation of someone to commit a crime, or a conspiracy to commit an offense—for example, to sell contraband. Although preparatory to the commission of other offenses, they are separate and distinct crimes. During the 1800s, too late to become a part of the common law under the reception statutes adopted by most new American states, each was recognized as a misdemeanor at English common law. Most American jurisdictions now define these offenses by statute, frequently classifying them as felonies.

The development of the law in this area has been primarily through the courts. Courts have often found it difficult to determine when mere noncriminal activity has reached the stage of criminal conduct. Yet, by recognizing an actor's design toward commission of an offense, the law permits police to apprehend dangerous persons who have not yet accomplished their criminal objectives, thereby affording them an opportunity to terminate such conduct at an early stage.

# Attempt

**attempt** An intent to commit a crime coupled with an act taken toward committing the offense.

**Attempt** is the most frequently charged of the inchoate crimes. Attempt, of course, means an effort to accomplish a particular purpose. As the Tennessee Supreme Court has explained, "An attempt, by nature, is a failure to accomplish what one intended to do." *State v. Kimbrough*, 924 S.W.2d 888 (Tenn. 1996). State penal codes often specifically provide for attempts to commit the most serious crimes, such as murder. The remaining offenses are then covered by a general attempt statute. A typical statute that covers all attempts provides that "[w]hoever attempts to commit an offense prohibited by law and in such attempt does any act toward the commission of such an offense, but fails in the perpetration or is intercepted or prevented in the execution of the same, commits the offense of criminal attempt."

**overt act** A visible act by an individual.

West's Fla. Stat. Ann. § 777.04(1). The "act" requirement contemplates an **overt act** that constitutes a **substantial step** toward the commission of an offense. Although

**substantial step** A significant movement toward completion of an intended result.

the quoted statute makes no distinction between felony and misdemeanor offenses, statutes in some states limit the crime of attempt to attempts to commit felonies or certain specified crimes. No specific federal statute proscribes or defines attempts generally; rather, various statutes focus on attempts to commit specific offenses. For example, 18 U.S.C.A. § 1113 proscribes attempts to commit murder or manslaughter. In general, federal courts have recognized the requisite elements of attempt as (1) an intent to engage in criminal conduct and (2) the performance of an act that constitutes a substantial step toward the completion of the substantive offense. See *United States v. Manley*, 632 F.2d 978 (2d Cir. 1980). This follows the Model Penal Code § 5.01 view that the requisite elements of attempt are intent to engage in criminal conduct and the performance of acts, which constitute a "substantial step" toward the commission of the substantive offense. *United States v. Jackson*, 560 F.2d 112 (2d Cir. 1977).

## The Act Requirement

**preparatory conduct** Actions taken in preparation to commit a crime.

As we have noted, the "act" element in the crime of attempt requires an act that constitutes a substantial step toward the commission of an offense; that is, it must be conduct beyond mere preparation. The Model Penal Code distinguishes **preparatory conduct** from an attempt. It allows conviction for the crime of attempt, where the actor engages in "an act or omission constituting a substantial step in a course of conduct planned to culminate in the commission of the crime." M.P.C. § 501 (1)(c). Federal courts apply this test. In *United States v. Mandujano*, 499 F.2d 370, 376 (5th Cir. 1974), the court observed, "A substantial step must be conduct strongly corroborative of the firmness of the defendant's criminal intent." In a similar vein, the Supreme Judicial Court of Maine has recognized that the State must prove more than mere preparation; it must prove "a positive action . . . directed towards the execution of the crime." *State v. Charbonneau*, 374 A.2d 321, 322 (Me. 1977).

Where multiple intentions underlie an act, one act may establish several different criminal attempts. For example, in *State v. Walters*, 804 P.2d 1164 (Or. 1991), the court held that the defendant's conduct established an intention to engage in conduct that constituted a substantial step toward commission of kidnapping, rape, and sodomy.

Many state statutes also include the term "substantial step" in defining the act requirement. Where they do not, courts usually imply that the act must constitute a substantial step toward the commission of a substantive offense. In either instance, it becomes necessary to distinguish between mere preparatory acts of planning or arranging means to commit a crime and those acts that constitute a direct movement toward the commission of an offense. Appellate courts have taken various approaches as to how close that act must be to accomplishment of the intended crime. This issue frequently turns on the specific factual situation involved. An early, and demanding, test held that an actor must have engaged in the "last proximate act necessary to accomplish the intended crime," but most courts have now rejected that test and apply a more realistic test that the actor's conduct must be "within dangerous proximity to success." An Illinois decision is illustrative. Two men armed with guns were found hiding behind a service station. One had a black nylon stocking in his pocket. The Illinois Supreme Court affirmed their convictions for attempted armed robbery because it found their act of "lying in wait . . . reconnoitering the place contemplated for the commission of the crime [while in] possession of materials to be employed in the commission of the crime" to be conduct sufficient to constitute a substantial step toward the commission of armed robbery. *People v. Terrell*, 459 N.E.2d 1337 (Ill. 1984).

New York courts have summed it up in a practical manner, opining simply that an accused's conduct must be "very near" to the completion of the intended crime. *People v. Mahboubian*, 543 N.E.2d 34 (N.Y. 1989).

**CASE-IN-POINT**

### The Mississippi Supreme Court Reverses a Conviction for Attempt

Mayor Henry Bucklew of Laurel, Mississippi was convicted of attempted embezzlement for attempting to use city tax dollars to pay for personal vehicle repairs. Under the relevant state statute, an attempt crime "consists of three elements: (1) an intent to commit a particular crime; (2) a direct ineffectual act done toward its commission; and (3) the failure to consummate its commission." The question before the Mississippi Supreme Court was "whether the State established that Bucklew had committed an overt act in furtherance of the attempted embezzlement." In an examination of the relevant state case law to determine the definition of an overt act, the court determined that defendants must "reach a point in the proceedings to commit a crime beyond mere preparation, so that they actually begin to commit the alleged crime." Applying this rule to the case, the court held that "the acts done by [Bucklew] were mere acts in preparation to the submission of the bill to the clerk for payment. The testimony shows that it was necessary for the mayor to sign the bill before submitting it to the clerk for payment, and the proof shows that the mayor did not submit the bill to the clerk for payment." Additionally, no evidence suggested there was "any extraneous cause that prevented the mayor from attempting to collect the amount due to the automobile company." As a result, Bucklew's conviction was reversed; the evidence did "not show an overt act . . . to commit the crime charged, before . . . he abandoned his alleged purpose."

*Bucklew v. State*, 206 So.2d 200 (Miss. 1968).

## The Requisite Criminal Intent

**target crime** A crime that is the object of an attempt, solicitation, or conspiracy.

To find a defendant guilty of the crime of attempt, most courts require the prosecution to prove that the defendant had a specific intent to commit the intended offense, frequently referred to as the **target crime**. See, e.g., *Thacker v. Commonwealth*, 114 S.E. 504 (Va. 1922); *State v. Earp*, 571 A.2d 1227 (Md. 1990). The rationale for this view is that it is logically impossible to attempt an unintended result.

The specific intent requirement raises an issue on which courts disagree: Can a person intend to commit a crime by unintentionally causing a result? Because specific intent is not an element of certain offenses, for example, manslaughter, some courts hold that a defendant cannot be convicted of an attempt to commit such a crime. See, e.g., *State v. Zupetz*, 322 N.W.2d 730 (Minn. 1982). Other courts hold that if the prosecution is not required to show a defendant's specific intent in order to prosecute the completed crime successfully, it is not required to establish specific intent in order to prosecute an attempt to commit such a crime. In *Gentry v. State*, 437 So.2d 1097 (Fla. 1983), the Florida Supreme Court held, "If the state is not required to show specific intent to successfully prosecute the completed crime, it will not be required to show specific intent to successfully prosecute an attempt to commit that crime." In any event, courts require at least the level of intent that must be established in proof of the target crime.

## Attempts in Relation to Substantive Crimes

When a criminal attempt completes a substantive crime, the attempt usually merges into the target offense. The actor is then guilty of the substantive crime, rather than merely an attempt to commit it. Thus, a person who is successful in an attempt to commit murder is guilty of murder. However, there can be no attempt to commit certain crimes because some substantive offenses by definition embrace an attempt.

To illustrate, consider the statutory crime of uttering a forged instrument. Statutes usually define the crime as including an attempt to pass a forged instrument to someone to obtain something of value. Therefore, one who makes such an attempt would be guilty of uttering a forged instrument, not merely an attempt to do so. In effect, the attempt is subsumed in the very definition of the substantive crime. Needless to say, it would be redundant to charge someone with attempting to attempt to commit a given crime.

## Defenses to the Crime of Attempt

The Model Penal Code proposes that an accused who "purposely engages in conduct that would constitute the crime if the attendant circumstances were as he believed them to be" is guilty of an attempt. M.P.C. § 5.01(1)(a). Although many state statutes track this Model Penal Code language, it raises the issue of whether the law should pursue a conviction for an attempt to commit a crime that is impossible to commit.

> **legal impossibility** A defense allowed in some jurisdictions when, although the defendant intended to commit a crime, it was impossible to do so because the completed act is not a crime.

The rule developed in most jurisdictions is that **legal impossibility** is a defense to the crime of attempt but **factual impossibility** is not. The distinction can be very close. For example, attempted rape requires a human victim. Therefore, a man who assaults a mannequin dressed as a woman would not be guilty of attempted rape because it would be legally impossible to commit that offense. Yet this example must be distinguished from the classic illustration in *State v. Mitchell*, 71 S.W. 175 (Mo. 1902). There, a man was held responsible for attempted murder when he shot into the room in which his target usually slept. Fortuitously, that person was sleeping elsewhere in the house at the time of the shooting. Although the bullet struck the target's customary pillow, attainment of the criminal objective was factually impossible. Likewise, a person who picks another's pocket intending to steal money may be found guilty of attempted theft even if the victim's pocket is empty. In these instances courts have said that although it was factually impossible to commit the crime, it was legally possible to do so.

> **factual impossibility** That which is in fact impossible to achieve. Unlike legal impossibility, this is not a defense to a charge of attempt.

New York law now provides that it is no defense to a prosecution that the crime charged to have been attempted was either factually or legally impossible to commit if it could have been committed had the circumstances been what the defendant believed them to be. McKinney's N.Y. Penal Law § 110.10; *People v. Davis*, 526 N.E.2d 20 (N.Y. 1988). The trend is toward finding an attempt to commit a crime in instances where the actor's intent has been frustrated merely because of some factor unknown at the time. Thus, if the accused believed a victim was alive when the accused shot at the victim, it follows that such an attempt to kill a dead person would constitute an attempt under New York law. *People v. Dlugash*, 363 N.E.2d 1155 (N.Y. 1977).

Some jurisdictions have laws providing that it is a defense to the crime of attempt if the defendant abandons an attempt to commit an offense or otherwise prevents its consummation. See, e.g., Vernon's Tex. Ann. Penal Code § 15.04(a). Where recognized as a defense, abandonment must be wholly voluntary. It cannot be the result of any outside cause such as the appearance of the police on the scene. See, e.g., *People v. Walker*, 191 P.2d 10 (Cal. 1948).

## Solicitation

> **solicitation** The inchoate offense of requesting or encouraging someone to engage in illegal conduct.

By the 1800s, the English common law specified that a person who counseled, incited, or solicited another to commit either a felony or a misdemeanor involving breach of the peace committed the offense of **solicitation**. A person who solicited another to commit a crime was guilty of solicitation even if the crime counseled, incited, or solicited was not committed. The offense of solicitation is now defined by statute in most American jurisdictions. Numerous federal statutes define solicitation as a crime in various contexts. See, e.g., 18 U.S.C.A. § 373, which proscribes solicitation to commit a crime of violence.

Conviction under federal law requires the solicitation to be of a federal offense. *United States v. Korab*, 893 F.2d 212 (9th Cir. 1989). In explaining why its penal code makes solicitation an offense, a California appellate court offered two reasons: first, to protect individuals from being exposed to inducement to commit or join in the commission of crime, and second, to prevent solicitation from resulting in the commission of the crime solicited. *People v. Cook*, 199 Cal. Rptr. 269 (Cal. App. 1984).

## The Act Requirement

The request, command, or enticement constitutes the *actus reus* required for solicitation. The statutory definition of solicitation in Illinois is typical: "A person commits solicitation when, with intent that an offense be committed, other than first-degree murder, he commands, encourages, or requests another to commit the offense." 720 Ill. Comp. Stat. Ann. § 5/8-1.1. (A separate statute defines solicitation for first-degree murder.) The gist of the offense is the solicitation itself, so the offender may be found guilty irrespective of whether the solicited crime is ever committed.

Commission of the crime of solicitation does not require direct solicitation of another; it may be perpetrated through an intermediary. Thus, if Abel solicits Barnes

**CASE-IN-POINT**

### Solicitation Does Not Require Acquiescence by the Party Being Solicited

Patrick Alan Keen was convicted of soliciting Blaine Bacon and Ben Wade to murder his wife. At trial, the evidence revealed that Keen agreed to pay Bacon $5,000 from a life insurance policy for the murder of his wife. "Bacon immediately attempted to contact several law enforcement officers with whom he had become acquainted when he had worked as an informer or undercover agent." Bacon "finally reached a U.S. Treasury agent and informed him" of what Keen had proposed. The "agent advised him to keep in contact," and "Bacon's actions thereafter were generally directed by law enforcement officers." Keen visited Bacon again wanting an answer to his proposal and at this time, "Ben Wade, an agent of the State Bureau of Investigation, was concealed in Bacon's rear office so that he could overhear their conversation." At this meeting, Keen pressed Bacon for an answer and Bacon stated he knew a professional killer who "was an expert at making deaths appear accidental." Bacon, Wade and Keen met a few days later where Keen gave Wade "a photograph and physical description of" his wife, and told Wade "that his wife's death

must appear accidental and must occur prior to the cancellation of her life insurance policy on the first of October." Payment for the murder was also discussed, and when Keen left the meeting, police immediately arrested him. Keen testified on his own behalf claiming that "he did not originally intend to have his wife killed but Bacon implanted the idea in his mind." Keen also testified that Bacon suggested that Keen "knock her off" and collect on the insurance policy. On appeal, Keen argued "that there could have been no completion of the crime since all parties with whom he spoke were connected with law enforcement." The North Carolina Court of Appeals held "that the interposition of a resisting will, by a law enforcement officer or anyone else, between the solicitation and the proposed felony is of no consequence." The court supported the holding by stating "the solicitation was complete before the resisting will of another had refused its assent and cooperation." As a result, the court held "the crime of solicitation to commit a felony is complete with the solicitation even though there could never have been an acquiescence in the scheme by the one solicited."

*State v. Keen*, 214 S.E.2d 242 (N.C. App. 1975).

to solicit Cummings to commit a crime, Abel would be liable even though he did not directly contact Cummings, because Abel's solicitation of Barnes itself involves the commission of the offense.

Recall that in Chapter 3 we discussed the fact that the "void for vagueness doctrine" requires a penal statute to define an offense with sufficient definitiveness that ordinary people can understand what conduct is prohibited. In the next Case-in-Point, the court rejected a challenge that a child solicitation statute was unconstitutionally vague and explains that child solicitation is complete upon urging a child to perform a sexual act.

## Is an Uncommunicated Solicitation an Offense?

The Model Penal Code states, "It is immaterial . . . that the actor fails to communicate with the person he solicits to commit a crime if his conduct was designed to effect such communication." M.P.C. § 5.02(2). Nevertheless, courts have been reluctant to uphold a conviction of solicitation where there has been no communication of the solicitation to the intended solicitee. For example, in *State v. Cotton*, 790 P.2d 1050 (N.M. App. 1990), the New Mexico Court of Appeals explained that the language of its criminal code describes the offense of criminal solicitation in a manner that differs in several material respects from the Model Penal Code by specifically omitting that portion of the Model Penal Code subsection that declares that an uncommunicated solicitation to commit a crime may constitute the offense of criminal solicitation. Thus, the court concluded that the legislative intent was to require some form of actual communication from the defendant to either an intermediary or the intended solicitee. In *People v. Saephanh*, 94 Cal.Rptr.2d 910 (Cal. App. 2000), a corrections officer intercepted the defendant's letter of solicitation to commit murder. In a case of first impression, a California appellate court held that solicitation of murder requires receipt of solicitation by the intended recipient. The court, however, held that the defendant could be convicted of attempted solicitation of murder.

---

**CASE-IN-POINT**

### Child Solicitation Is Complete upon Urging the Performance of a Sexual Act

In July 2002, Detective Mike Widner of the Noblesville, Indiana Police Department logged on to an Internet chat room and impersonated a thirteen-year-old girl. Allegedly, after two sessions with Michael LaRose, which included sexually explicit remarks, LaRose agreed to meet at a Wal-Mart parking lot. Upon arrival he was arrested and charged with felony child solicitation under Indiana Code § 35-42-4-6, which makes it an offense for a person eighteen years of age or older to knowingly or intentionally solicit a child under fourteen years of age, or an individual the person believes to be a child under fourteen years of age, to engage in sex acts. LaRose moved to dismiss the charges, arguing there was no allegation that he solicited an individual to engage in an act "at some immediate time." Additionally, he contended the statute was unconstitutionally vague. The trial court denied LaRose's motion and the Court of Appeals accepted jurisdiction.

Noting that the crime of child solicitation is complete upon urging a child to perform a sexual act and rather than upon performance of the urged act, the Court of Appeals rejected LaRose's argument. Additionally, the court rejected LaRose's challenge that the statute was unconstitutionally vague, noting that it unequivocally informs individuals they may not use a computer to sexually solicit a child under the age of fourteen. The court affirmed the trial court's denial of LaRose's motion to dismiss.

*LaRose v. State*, 820 N.E.2d 727 (Ind. App. 2005).

## The Requisite Criminal Intent

The statutory language making solicitation a crime might not seem to require the prosecution to establish the defendant's specific intent. However, most courts hold that to commit solicitation, the solicitor must have specifically intended to induce or entice the person solicited to commit the target offense. See, e.g., *Kimbrough v. State*, 544 So.2d 177 (Ala. Crim. App. 1989). If the particular jurisdiction does not require proof of the defendant's specific intent, the prosecution must at least establish that the actor who solicits someone to commit a crime had the requisite intent for the crime solicited.

## Solicitation Distinguished from Other Inchoate Crimes

The offenses of solicitation and attempt are different crimes, analytically distinct in their elements. Although each is an inchoate offense, solicitation is complete when the request or enticement to complete the intended offense is made, and it is immaterial whether the solicitee agrees, the offense is carried out, or any steps are taken toward consummation of the offense. In contrast, mere solicitation is generally not sufficient to constitute an attempt, because attempt requires proof of an overt act to commit the intended criminal act. This principle was succinctly explained by the Idaho Supreme Court: "The solicitation of another, assuming neither the solicitor nor solicitee proximately acts toward the crime's commission, cannot be held for an attempt." *State v. Otto*, 629 P.2d 646, 650 (Idaho 1981).

Is solicitation more serious than attempt? The Tennessee Supreme Court has suggested that it is not, stating, "There is not the same degree of heinousness in solicitation as in attempts, nor is solicitation as likely to result in a completed crime, there not being the same dangerous proximity to success as found in attempts." *Gervin v. State*, 371 S.W.2d 449, 451 (Tenn. 1963). The Connecticut Supreme Court has taken the contrary point of view, observing, "The solicitation to another to [commit] a crime is as a rule far more dangerous to society than the attempt to commit the same crime. For the solicitation has behind it an evil purpose, coupled with the pressure of a stronger intellect upon the weak and criminally inclined." *State v. Schleifer*, 121 A. 805, 809 (Conn. 1923).

If the crime solicited is committed or attempted by the solicitee, then the offense of solicitation ordinarily merges into the target crime. For example, if Andrew solicits Bob to murder Carl and Bob then murders or attempts to murder Carl, then Andrew would become an accessory before the fact to murder or attempted murder. As discussed in Chapter 4, this complicity would make Andrew a principal to the crime of murder or attempted murder. If, however, Bob refuses Andrew's solicitation, Andrew would still be guilty of solicitation.

Solicitation is distinguished from conspiracy because although solicitation requires an enticement, conspiracy, as we explain later, requires an agreement. Sometimes a solicitation results in a conspiracy, and some courts have regarded the offense of solicitation as "an offer to enter into a conspiracy." See, e.g., *Commonwealth v. Carey*, 439 A.2d 151, 155 (Pa. Super. 1981).

## Defenses to the Crime of Solicitation

Generally, the fact that the solicitor countermands the solicitation is not a defense to the crime of solicitation. Nor is it a defense that it was impossible for the person solicited to commit the crime. The Model Penal Code provides that a complete and

**CASE-IN-POINT**

### When Is the Crime of Solicitation Committed?

Defendant Roger Gardner, an alleged contract killer, subcontracted the killing of Alvin Blum to a man named Tim McDonald for a fee of $10,000. Gardner met with McDonald and gave him some expense money, a gun, and ammunition. In talking with McDonald, Gardner said that he (Gardner) would first kill a man named Hollander, and if this did not create the desired result, then McDonald would be directed to kill Blum. Gardner's attempts were foiled when he was arrested and charged with solicitation to murder. It turned out that McDonald was a police informant whose assistance led to Gardner's arrest.

On appeal, Gardner argued that he did not commit the crime of solicitation because he did not actually direct McDonald to proceed with the murder of Blum or pay him all of the money he had promised. In affirming Gardner's conviction, the Maryland Court of Appeals said, "the crime of solicitation was committed when he asked McDonald to commit the murder." The Court explained that "[n]either a final direction to proceed nor fulfillment of conditions precedent (paying of the money) was required." In holding that the crime of solicitation was committed, the court observed that "[t]he gist of the offense is incitement."

*Gardner v. State*, 408 A.2d 1317, 1322 (Md. 1979).

voluntary renunciation of the accused's criminal purpose is a defense to a charge of solicitation. M.P.C. § 5.02(3). Some states have adopted this position. Kentucky law agrees; however, § 506.060 of the Kentucky Statutes stipulates,

> A renunciation is not "voluntary and complete" . . . when it is motivated in whole or in part by: (a) A belief that circumstances exist which pose a particular threat of apprehension or detection of the accused or another participant in the criminal enterprise or which render more difficult the accomplishment of the criminal purpose; or (b) A decision to postpone the criminal conduct until another time or to transfer the criminal effort to another victim or another but similar object.

## Conspiracy

**conspiracy** The inchoate offense of two or more persons agreeing or planning to commit a target crime.

Under English common law, **conspiracy** consisted of an agreement by two or more persons to accomplish a criminal act or to use unlawful means to accomplish a noncriminal objective. The gist of the offense was the unlawful agreement between the parties, and no overt act was required.

The common law regarded a husband and wife as one person for most purposes; therefore, a husband and wife could not be guilty of conspiring with each other. In recent years courts have recognized the separate identities of spouses, and there is no valid reason to continue the common-law approach. See, e.g., *People v. Pierce*, 395 P.2d 893 (Cal. 1964). Thus, a husband and wife who conspire only between themselves ordinarily cannot claim immunity from prosecution for conspiracy on the basis of their marital status.

Today the offense of conspiracy is defined by statute in all jurisdictions. Most state laws define the elements of the offense along the lines of the common law. Thus, the agreement becomes the *acts reus* of the offense. Typically, as the Florida law states, "A person who agrees, conspires, combines, or confederates with another person or persons to commit any offense commits the offense of criminal conspiracy." West's Fla. Stat. Ann. § 777.04(3). Thus, under Florida law, both an agreement and an intention to commit an offense are necessary elements to support a conviction for conspiracy. *Webster v. State*, 646 So.2d 752 (Fla. App. 1994).

Several states, however, require proof of an overt act to convict someone for conspiracy. Where an overt act is required, courts simply require that the act be one taken in furtherance of the conspiracy without the qualifications required of an act required in an attempt to commit a crime. For example, Texas law provides that "[a] person commits criminal conspiracy if, with intent that a felony be committed, (1) he agrees with one or more persons that they or one or more of them engage in conduct that would constitute the offense, and (2) he or one or more of them performs an overt act in pursuance of the agreement." Vernon's Tex. Penal Code Ann. § 15.02 (a). Note that the Texas statute also requires an intent that a felony be committed, whereas in many states it is necessary only to prove an intent to commit a criminal offense.

Federal law (with some exceptions) requires proof of an overt act by one or more persons to effect the object of a conspiracy to commit an offense or to defraud the United States. 18 U.S.C.A. § 371. In *United States v. Jobe,* 101 F.3d 1046, 1063 (5th Cir. 1996), the court stated, "In order to establish a conspiracy under 18 U.S.C.A. § 371, the government must prove beyond a reasonable doubt the existence of an agreement between two or more people to violate a law of the United States and that any one of the conspirators committed an overt act in furtherance of that agreement."

Because of the variations encountered in statutory language, in reviewing any statute defining conspiracy it is necessary to determine at the outset (1) the type of the offense or unlawful activity the statute proscribes and (2) whether it requires proof of an overt act in furtherance of the parties' agreement.

## Justification for Making Conspiracy a Crime

Why is conspiracy considered an offense distinct from the substantive offense the conspirators agree to commit? The late U.S. Supreme Court Justice Felix Frankfurter articulated one of the most cogent responses to this question. In *Callanan v. United States*, 364 U.S. 587, 593–594, 81 S.Ct. 321, 325, 5 L.Ed.2d 312, 317 (1961), Frankfurter observed,

> Concerted action both increases the likelihood that the criminal object will be successfully attained and decreases the probability that the individuals involved will depart from their path of criminality. Group association for criminal purposes often, if not normally, makes possible the attainment of ends more complex than those which one criminal could accomplish. . . . Combination in crime makes more likely the commission of crimes unrelated to the original purpose for which the group was formed. In sum, the danger that a conspiracy generates is not confined to the substantive offense that is the immediate aim of the enterprise.

---

### JURISPRUDENCE

*Callanan v. United States*, 364 U.S. 587, 593–594, 81 S.Ct. 321, 325, 5 L.Ed.2d 312, 317 (1961)

Lawrence Callanan was convicted under the Hobbs Act, 18 U.S.C. § 1951, of both extortion and conspiracy to commit extortion. He was sentenced to consecutive terms of twelve years for each offense. On appeal, Callanan argued that in passing the Hobbs Act, Congress did not intend for defendants to be convicted of both offenses. The Supreme Court disagreed, holding that under the Act, extortion and conspiracy to commit extortion are separate offenses, thus separate consecutive sentences may be imposed for each offense. Writing for the Court, Justice Felix Frankfurter observed that "the danger that a conspiracy generates is not confined to the substantive offense that is the immediate aim of the enterprise."

## The Range of Conspiracies in Society

The range of conspiracies cuts across socioeconomic classes in society. Traditionally, state prosecutions for conspiracy have been directed at criminal offenses such as homicide, arson, perjury, kidnapping, and various offenses against property. In recent years an increasing number of both state and federal conspiracy prosecutions have been related to illicit drug trafficking. In addition to the numerous narcotics violations, federal prosecutions include a variety of conspiracies not found under state laws. Among these are customs violations, counterfeiting of currency, copyright violations, mail fraud, lotteries, and violations of antitrust laws, laws governing interstate commerce, and other areas of federal regulation. On September 15, 2008 a federal appellate court affirmed a defendant's conviction for violation of 18 U.S.C.A. § 371 for conspiracy to commit wire fraud in connection with a scheme to defraud mortgage lenders in mobile home financing. *United States v. Price,* 532 F.3d 617 (8th Cir. 2008). Recently, several federal prosecutions have involved conspiracies to deprive persons of civil rights secured by the Constitution or laws of the United States. See 18 U.S.C.A. § 241. Lower federal courts have held that this section, which prohibits conspiracy against rights of citizens, does not require proof of an overt act. See, e.g., *United States v. Morado,* 454 F.2d 167 (5th Cir. 1972).

## The Act Element in Conspiracy

In general, the *actus reus* of the crime of conspiracy is the unlawful agreement. But the agreement need not be formal or written. A simple understanding is sufficient. Where an overt act is required, such act need not be a substantial movement toward the target offense. For example, in California, where the law requires an overt act, the courts have said that an overt act tending to effect a conspiracy may merely be a part of preliminary arrangements for the commission of the ultimate crime. *People v. Buono,* 12 Cal. Rptr. 604 (Cal. App. 1961). In *Bannon v. United States,* 156 U.S. 464, 15 S.Ct. 467, 39 L.Ed. 494 (1895), the U.S. Supreme Court held that an act committed by any one of the conspirators applies to all present members of the conspiracy. In fact, a single act, such as a telephone conversation arranging a meeting, has been held to be sufficient proof of an overt act. *United States v. Civella,* 648 F.2d 1167 (8th Cir. 1981).

In *State v. Dent,* 869 P.2d 392 (Wash. 1994), the Supreme Court of Washington articulated the difference between the *actus reus* requirements in the crimes of attempt and conspiracy. The court observed that the two crimes differ in the nature of the conduct sought to be prohibited and in the significance of the "substantial step" requirement (known as the "overt act" requirement in some jurisdictions) in each context. "A substantial step," the court noted, "is required in the context of attempt to prevent the imposition of punishment based on intent alone." But the court explained that the purpose of the substantial step or overt act requirement is different in the context of conspiracy: "The purpose of the 'substantial step' requirement is, therefore, to manifest that the conspiracy is at work, and is neither a project still resting solely in the minds of the conspirators nor a fully completed operation no longer in existence." 869 P.2d at 397.

Contrary to some popular views, the participants in a conspiracy need not even know or see one another as long as they otherwise participate in common deeds. The essence of the offense is the mutual agreement of the parties to the conspiracy, not the acts done to accomplish its objective. Moreover, the agreement need not be explicit. In fact, it seldom is. In most instances, the agreement is implied from the acts of the parties and the circumstances surrounding their activities. Furthermore, the conspirators do not all have to join the conspiracy at the same time.

## The Requisite Criminal Intent

Statutes frequently fail to encompass the intent requirement in the offense of conspiracy. This difficulty is compounded by failure of the courts to define clearly the intent required for a conviction. In general, the prosecution must prove that a defendant intended to further the unlawful object of the conspiracy, and such intent must exist in the minds of at least two of the parties to the alleged conspiracy. *People v. Cohn,* 193 N.E. 150 (Ill. 1934). Many courts refer to the crime as requiring a specific intent. See, e.g., *People v. Marsh,* 376 P.2d 300 (Cal. 1962). As previously noted relative to attempts, such intent may be inferable from the conduct of the parties and the surrounding circumstances. Although many federal court decisions have not required proof of a specific intent, the U.S. Supreme Court has said that in federal prosecutions there must be proof of at least the criminal intent necessary for the requirements of the substantive offense. *United States v. Feola,* 420 U.S. 671, 95 S.Ct. 1255, 43 L.Ed.2d 541 (1975).

## Conspiracy Distinguished from Aiding and Abetting and Attempt

As we noted in Chapter 4, aiding and abetting someone in the commission of a crime makes a person either a principal or an accessory before the fact. Conspiracy is a separate offense and must be distinguished from aiding and abetting. Conspiracy involves proof of an agreement between two or more persons, an element often present in, but not essential to, proving that a defendant aided and abetted a crime. On the other hand, aiding and abetting requires some actual participation. Conspiracy differs from the crime of attempt in that it focuses on intent, whereas attempt places more emphasis on the defendant's actions.

## The *Pinkerton* Rule

*Pinkerton* **Rule** Rule enunciated by the Supreme Court in *Pinkerton v. United States* (1946) holding that a member of a conspiracy is liable for all offenses committed in furtherance of the conspiracy.

*In Pinkerton v. United States,* 328 U.S. 640, 66 S.Ct. 1180, 90 L.Ed. 1489 (1946), the U.S. Supreme Court held that a member of a conspiracy is liable for all offenses committed in furtherance of the conspiracy. This has come to be known as the **Pinkerton Rule**. It is based on the theory that conspirators are agents of one another, and just as principals are bound by the acts of their agents within the scope of the agency relationship, so too conspirators are bound by the acts of their coconspirators. See *United States v. Troop,* 890 F.2d 1393 (7th Cir. 1989).

The *Pinkerton* doctrine has broad implications, and not all courts have accepted it. For example, in *People v. McGee,* 399 N.E.2d 1177 (N.Y. 1979), the court rejected the *Pinkerton* doctrine and observed,

> It is not offensive to permit a conviction of conspiracy to stand on the overt act committed by another, for the act merely provides corroboration of the existence of the agreement and indicates that the agreement has reached a point where it poses a sufficient threat to society to impose sanctions. . . . But it is repugnant to our system of

*Pinkerton v. United States,* 328 U.S. 640, 66 S.Ct. 1180, 90 L.Ed. 1489 (1946)

Brothers Walter and Daniel Pinkerton were both indicted on nine counts of tax evasion and one count of conspiracy to commit tax evasion. A jury found Walter Pinkerton guilty of all nine counts of tax evasion as well as the conspiracy. The evidence showed that Daniel Pinkerton did not participate in any of the substantive offenses although he was party to the conspiracy that led to Walter's offenses. Yet Daniel was convicted not only of conspiracy, but of six substantive offenses in furtherance thereof. The U.S. Supreme Court upheld Daniel's conviction, stating that a member of a conspiracy is liable for all offenses committed in furtherance of that conspiracy. The Court did indicate that a different result may occur if the offenses were not reasonably foreseeable as a natural consequence of the unlawful agreement of the conspirators. Justice Wiley Rutledge dissented, claiming that the Court had set a "dangerous precedent."

jurisprudence, where guilt is generally personal to the defendant . . . to impose punishment, not for the socially harmful agreement to which the defendant is a party, but for substantive offenses in which he did not participate. 399 N.E.2d at 1182.

## Some Unique Aspects of the Offense of Conspiracy

Because the courts view each conspirator as an agent of the others, it follows that each will be held responsible for the acts of the others within the context of their common design. *Commonwealth v. Thomas,* 189 A.2d 255 (Pa. 1963). This principle permits an exception to the rule of evidence that ordinarily excludes hearsay statements from being used in a trial over the defendant's objection. Thus, statements made "in furtherance of" the conspiracy may be admitted into evidence. These include statements to inform other conspirators of the activities or status of the conspiracy and those identifying other conspirators. Federal courts have upheld the use of statements to establish the source or purchaser of controlled substances. Before receiving this type of evidence, a court must receive independent evidence that a conspiracy exists. In some instances, courts receive the hearsay evidence subject to its being tied into the offense by independent evidence of the conspiracy. Court procedures in this area are very technical because the court must determine the scope of the conspiracy and the inception of the conspirator's participation.

In *Territory v. Goto,* 27 Hawaii 65 (1923), the Supreme Court of Hawaii properly characterized the judicial approach to conspiracy: "In the eyes of the law conspirators are one man, they breathe one breath, they speak one voice, they wield one arm, and the law says that the acts, words, and declarations of each, while in the pursuit of the common design, are the words and declarations of all."

Courts have held that once formed, a conspiracy continues to exist until consummated, abandoned, or otherwise terminated by some affirmative act. *Cline v. State,* 319 S.W.2d 227 (Tenn. 1958). Consequently, upon joining a conspiracy and not withdrawing, a conspirator is not insulated from the actions of his or her coconspirators.

These unique aspects are significant. They assist the prosecution in proof of cases that might be otherwise unprovable. Perhaps the law has established these exceptions in recognition of the difficulties of prosecuting persons involved in conspiracies, which are generally formed in secret.

Conspiracy is among the most commonly charged federal offenses. A law review article explains why this is the case:

> Conspiracy, the prosecutor's "darling," is one of the most commonly charged federal crimes. The offense of conspiracy is construed broadly by courts and is therefore applied by prosecutors to a variety of situations. . . . A conspiracy charge gives the prosecution certain unique advantages and . . . one who must defend against such a charge bears a particularly heavy burden. Raphael Prober and Jill Randall, *Federal Criminal Conspiracy,* 39 Am. Crim. L. Rev. 571 (Spring 2002).

## Conspiracy Does Not Merge into the Target Crime

Conspiracy is regarded as a separate and distinct crime; therefore, it does not merge into the target offense. See *People v. Carter,* 330 N.W.2d 314 (Mich. 1982). A pragmatic consideration is that by not merging conspiracy into the target offense, the law can more effectively deal with organized crime, criminal street gangs, and other dangerous collective efforts to commit crimes.

## The Wharton's Rule Exception

**Wharton's Rule** This rule holds that two people cannot conspire to commit a crime such as adultery, incest, or bigamy inasmuch as these offenses necessarily require two participants; they cannot be committed by one person acting alone.

**Wharton's Rule**, named after Francis Wharton, a well-known commentator on criminal law, provides an exception to the principle that conspiracy does not merge into the target crime. Wharton's Rule holds, "An agreement by two persons to commit a particular crime cannot be prosecuted as a conspiracy when the crime is of such a nature as to necessarily require the participation of two persons for its commission." 1 R. Anderson, Wharton's Criminal Law and Procedure 89, p. 191 (1957). Thus, Wharton's Rule holds that two people cannot conspire to commit a crime such as adultery, incest, or bigamy because these offenses require two participants—they cannot be committed by one person acting alone.

The rationale behind Wharton's Rule is that, unlike the usual conspiracy (often viewed as a wheel with many spokes or as a chain of circumstances), the offenses named do not endanger the public generally. Wharton's Rule has been applied in many state and federal courts, but it has its limitations. In holding Wharton's Rule inapplicable to various federal gambling offenses under the Organized Crime Control Act of 1970, the Supreme Court pointed out that the rule itself is simply an aid to the determination of legislative intent and must defer to a discernible legislative judgment. *Iannelli v. United States,* 420 U.S. 770, 786, 95 S.Ct. 1284, 1294, 43 L.Ed.2d 616, 628 (1975).

## Criticism of the Conspiracy Laws

There has been an increased tendency in recent years to prosecute defendants for conspiracies as well as target crimes. The offense of conspiracy is a potent weapon for prosecutors, particularly as they try to cope with the problem of organized crime. Because the intent requirement and the form of agreement required are somewhat imprecise, a conspiracy is easier to prove than specific substantive crimes. On this basis, some critics argue that prosecutors, judges, and juries are given too much latitude in finding a defendant guilty.

Critics also argue that prosecution for conspiracy can chill a person's exercise of freedom of speech under the First Amendment, especially in matters involving political dissent. Courts, however, have ruled that conduct is not protected by the First Amendment merely because it involves the use of language. This became an issue in

### Conspiracy to Deliver Controlled Substances

Cook, an undercover police officer, agreed to purchase fifty doses of LSD from Erickson at a park in Snohomish, Washington. Erickson asked Smith for a ride there, ostensibly to meet Hensler (who owed Smith $600). When Smith and Erickson arrived in Smith's vehicle, Cook approached the car and asked Erickson if he had the LSD. When Erickson produced a bag of LSD, Cook asked Smith if he had tried it. Smith replied that "he was going to college . . . and couldn't afford to get messed up, but that his wife had taken some of it, and . . . 'it really [messed] her up.'" At that point Cook agreed to purchase the LSD, handed the money to Erickson, and arrested both Smith and Erickson. Smith was found guilty of conspiracy to deliver LSD.

On appeal, Smith argued that there was no proof beyond a reasonable doubt (1) that he agreed to engage in delivery of LSD and (2) that he intended that it be delivered. The appellate court rejected both contentions and affirmed Smith's conviction. The court first pointed out that "a formal agreement is not necessary to the formation of a conspiracy." Then the court observed that although Smith's primary purpose in giving Erickson a ride to the park was to meet Hensler, his secondary purpose was to assist in delivering LSD. In finding the evidence sufficient to show that Smith intended to assist Erickson, the court opined that "there was evidence not only of knowledge of Erickson's unlawful purpose, but an agreement to assist with the plan by providing the necessary transportation. . . . Here there were two overt acts: first, that Smith drove Erickson to Snohomish knowing, according to Cook, Erickson's purpose for the trip; and second, that Smith provided encouragement for the sale by assuring the officer of the potency of the drug."

*State v. Smith*, 828 P.2d 654, 656, 657 (Wash. App. 1992).

the 1968 prosecution of the late Dr. Benjamin M. Spock, the renowned pediatrician and author. Dr. Spock and three alleged coconspirators were convicted of violating the Universal Military Training and Service Act, § 12(a) as amended, 50 U.S.C.A. App. § 462(a), for conspiring to urge men to evade the military draft. The U.S. Court of Appeals found that the evidence at Spock's trial was insufficient and set aside his conviction. *United States v. Spock,* 416 F.2d 165 (1st Cir. 1969). The court explained in dicta that the First Amendment did not, per se, require acquittal on the charge of conspiracy to counsel men to resist the draft.

## Defenses to the Charge of Conspiracy

In some states, statutes specifically provide for a defense of withdrawal from and renunciation of a conspiracy. As an illustration, Missouri law specifies that "[n]o one shall be convicted of conspiracy if, after conspiring to commit the offense, he prevented the accomplishment of the objectives of the conspiracy under circumstances manifesting a renunciation of his criminal purpose." Vernon's Mo. Ann. Stat. § 564.016(5)(1). In the absence of statutory authority, courts have been reluctant to approve a person's withdrawal as a defense. One difficulty in approving withdrawal as a defense is that even though a conspirator withdraws, the criminal objective of the conspiracy may proceed. Therefore, it seems reasonable to require that a person who would rely on such defense not only renounce any criminal purpose but also take the necessary steps to thwart the objective of the conspiracy. To accomplish this result, the conspirator would probably have to notify law enforcement authorities of the pertinent details of the conspiracy. In any event, if an accused is allowed to offer such a defense, the defendant has the burden of establishing his or her withdrawal from the conspiracy.

### Evidence Sufficient to Support a Conspiracy Conviction

Joyce Gomez and Roberta Taylor were jointly tried and convicted in a Colorado court of conspiracy to commit larceny. The evidence revealed that Edward Cook, a locomotive engineer, left work traveling home in his automobile when he encountered Gomez and Taylor after being stopped at a traffic light. Once stopped at the traffic light, Gomez and Taylor opened the right-hand door of Cook's vehicle and got in. Gomez sat in the front passenger seat and "ordered him to drive on stating: 'help us out; that girl's [Taylor's] husband is going to kill her,' and that one of the two women stated that Taylor's husband was armed with a gun." Cook drove on for a while, but then pulled over to the side of the road and ordered both women out of his vehicle. After physically removing the women from his vehicle, Cook realized his wallet was missing. Gomez and Taylor both "broke and ran, whereupon he gave hot pursuit, and after a four-to-five-block chase espied the two crouching down on the floor of the front seat of an abandoned automobile." As Cook attempted to pull the women from this vehicle, the police arrived and Gomez cried "rape." Cook's wallet was found inside this vehicle; however, some of the money contained within was missing. Gomez argued there was insufficient evidence to submit the case to the jury for deliberation, but the trial court disagreed. On appeal the Colorado Supreme Court held "the trial court did not commit error in submitting the case to the jury, and that there [was] ample evidence to support the jury's [guilty] verdict."

*Gomez v. People*, 381 P.2d 816 (Colo. 1963).

Entrapment, a defense to be examined in Chapter 14, may be a defense to conspiracy under some circumstances. For example, in *Stripling v. State,* 349 So.2d 187 (Fla. App. 1977), the court found reversible error in the trial judge's having instructed the jury that the defense of entrapment was not available to a defendant if the officer acted in good faith and merely furnished an opportunity for commission of a crime by one who already had the intent to commit the crime. As the appellate court said, "A defendant could deny being a party to a conspiracy and yet raise the issue that any overt acts done by him or her were done because of entrapment; that rationale being that inconsistencies in defenses in criminal cases are allowable so long as the proof of one does not necessarily disprove the other." *Id.* at 191.

## Conclusion

By criminalizing attempt, solicitation, and conspiracy, the law endeavors to prevent the occurrence of criminal acts that pose prospective harm to persons. These inchoate offenses often pose substantial problems for law enforcement agencies, courts, and legislative bodies.

Police and courts experience difficulty determining the stage at which an act tends toward commission of a crime such that it qualifies as criminal attempt. Moreover, there are difficulties in distinguishing between what is legally impossible and what is factually impossible.

Solicitation poses a major problem because the solicitor often exerts power by manipulating the solicitee to commit a crime. There remains controversy over whether legislatures should make it a criminal offense to solicit another person to commit a misdemeanor.

In conspiracy, group action can accomplish criminal purposes not otherwise likely from individual efforts. The offense of conspiracy affords prosecutors considerable leeway in proving offenses sometimes remote from a conspirator's intention.

Yet, as will become apparent in later chapters, the offense of conspiracy has become a vital tool in coping with racketeering, drug trafficking, and white-collar crime. It is also an essential weapon in the ongoing war on terrorism.

Despite the problems associated with inchoate offenses, there is strong public support for criminalizing conduct directed toward future injuries to society. Most American jurisdictions have statutes making it an offense to attempt to commit a crime; some are directed at attempts to commit specific crimes. Not all jurisdictions make solicitation a crime, and those that do sometimes limit solicitation to certain classes of felonies. Conspiracy has been made a crime by statute in all jurisdictions. Criminalizing such incomplete and preparatory conduct permits timely intervention of law enforcement agencies to restrain dangerous persons and prevent intended crimes.

## Chapter Summary

- Learning Objective 1

  - The law criminalizes inchoate conduct that involves steps taken toward completion of a crime—attempt, solicitation, and conspiracy—to allow police to apprehend dangerous persons before they accomplish their criminal objectives.
  - To be a criminal offense there must be an attempt to commit a crime, solicitation of someone to commit a crime, or a conspiracy of persons to commit a criminal offense. Most American jurisdictions define these offenses by statute, frequently classifying them as felonies, but their development has been primarily through the courts.

- Learning Objective 2

  - With respect to criminal attempt, to prevent a person from being punished simply based on intent, laws often require an overt act that constitutes a substantial step toward the commission of an offense.
  - Most courts require proof that the defendant has a specific intent to commit the target crime; if not, they require at least the level of intent required for proof of the target crime.

- Learning Objective 3

  - An attempt that completes a substantive crime merges into the target offense, making the actor guilty of the substantive crime. But there can be no attempt to commit a crime which, by definition, embraces an attempt. For example, an attempt to pass a forged instrument to someone to obtain something of value is itself a substantive crime.

- Learning Objective 4

  - Statutes generally provide that whoever commands, encourages, or requests another to commit an offense is guilty of solicitation. Solicitation of another is not an attempt, assuming neither the solicitor nor solicitee proximately acts toward the crime's commission. If the crime solicited is committed or attempted by the solicitee, then the offense of solicitation ordinarily merges into the target crime.

- Learning Objective 5

  ○ Numerous federal statutes define solicitation in various contexts. Some jurisdictions specifically define the crime of solicitation to murder. Irrespective of the statutory language courts often require the prosecution to establish the defendant's specific intent, but in any event the prosecution must establish that the solicitor had the requisite intent for the crime solicited.

- Learning Objective 6

  ○ Federal and state statutes define the offense of conspiracy as involving an agreement by one or more persons to commit any offense.
  ○ In general, the *actus reus* of conspiracy is the unlawful agreement, which need not be formal or written. A simple understanding is sufficient. Some statutes require proof of an overt act; some state statutes require proof of intent to commit a felony.
  ○ Conspiracy is a separate and distinct crime. The danger it generates is usually not confined to the immediate aim of the conspiracy, therefore, conspiracy does not merge into the target offense.
  ○ Federal conspiracy prosecutions often relate to illicit drug trafficking and conspiracies not found under state laws, for example, customs violations, counterfeiting of currency, copyright violations, mail fraud, wire fraud, lotteries, and antitrust violation; state prosecutions are commonly directed at criminal homicide, arson, perjury, kidnapping, and property offenses as well as illicit drug trafficking.

- Learning Objective 7

  ○ The purpose of some statutes requiring an overt act is to manifest that a conspiracy is at work. Because the intent requirement and form of agreement required are somewhat imprecise, a conspiracy is easier to prove than specific substantive crimes, leading critics to argue that conspiracy covers too broad a sphere and can chill exercise of First Amendment freedom of speech.

- Learning Objective 8

  ○ Wharton's Rule holds that two people cannot conspire to commit a crime such as adultery, incest, or bigamy because these offenses require only two participants.

- Learning Objective 9

  ○ The *Pinkerton* Rule holds that conspirators are agents of one another bound by the acts of their coconspirators, so each conspirator is responsible for the acts of the others within the context of their common design. Thus, statements made in furtherance of the conspiracy may be admitted into evidence—an exception to the rule that ordinarily excludes admission of hearsay statements at trial over the defendant's objection.

- Learning Objective 10

  ○ In many jurisdictions it is a defense to a charge of committing an attempt if it would be legally impossible to commit the crime. But if it is simply factually impossible to commit a crime, it is no defense.

- ○ Some jurisdictions allow a defense of abandonment of an attempt or a showing that the defendant prevented the consummation of the offense.
- ○ Neither the fact that the solicitor countermanded the solicitation nor a showing that it was impossible for the person solicited to commit the crime is recognized as a defense, but the Model Penal Code provides that the accused's complete and voluntary renunciation of his or her criminal purpose is a defense to a charge of solicitation, and some states have adopted this position.
- ○ In some states, statutes specifically provide for a defense of withdrawal from and renunciation of a conspiracy. To accomplish this result, the conspirator would probably have to notify law enforcement authorities of the pertinent details of the conspiracy.
- ○ Entrapment, which we examine in a later chapter, may be a possible defense to a conspiracy charge.

## Key Terms

| | |
|---|---|
| attempt | *Pinkerton* Rule |
| conspiracy | preparatory conduct |
| factual impossibility | solicitation |
| inchoate offense | substantial step |
| legal impossibility | target crime |
| overt act | Wharton's Rule |

## Questions for Thought and Discussion

1. What justifies criminalizing attempt, solicitation, and conspiracy?
2. How does the criminal law distinguish between mere preparatory conduct and the overt act required for a criminal attempt? Can you think of a situation in which preparatory conduct might have the appearance of prospective criminal conduct but would not constitute a criminal attempt?
3. Should it be a defense to a charge of attempt that the accused voluntarily abandoned the attempt?
4. What is the rationale for making solicitation a crime even where a solicitor's requests are completely unheeded?
5. Which do you think poses a more serious threat to society: an attempt or a solicitation to commit murder? Why?
6. Should statutes defining conspiracy require proof of an overt act in furtherance of the conspirators' agreement? Why or why not?
7. Given the First Amendment protections of freedom of expression and association, under what circumstances can members of a revolutionary political organization be prosecuted for conspiring to overthrow the government of the United States?
8. Name some instances where the offense of conspiracy provides a means to protect the public from dangers incident to group activities.
9. What distinguishes the offense of conspiracy from the crime of aiding and abetting, discussed in Chapter 4?
10. What are the arguments for and against making the statute proscribing conspiracy require an overt act in furtherance of the conspiracy?

# Problems for Discussion and Solution

1. To prove attempted rape, the prosecution must prove the defendant took a substantial step toward commission of the crime of rape. If a male physically forced a female into a bedroom and onto the bed, tried to force his hand under her clothing, and attempted to kiss her, do you think this would establish the substantial step required for attempted rape? What, if any, other crime might the male have committed?

2. Two adults, Alice and Joe, committed adultery in a public place in violation of an old state statute. Each was charged with conspiracy to violate the statute as well as with the violation itself. Would their actions constitute a conspiracy? Why or why not?

3. In an exchange of e-mails, Alex and Peter agreed to sell illicit drugs in a state where the law defining conspiracy requires an unlawful agreement and an overt act. Alex called a third party whom he believed could supply the drugs. Would Alex's actions be sufficient as an overt act or would the law require that there be a more substantial movement toward arranging to sell drugs?

4. Jill's friend, Bob, works at an electronics store at the mall. Jill urges Bob to steal a new laptop computer for her to use at college. Is Jill guilty of solicitation?

5. Leo Lothario was having an affair with Lucy Slarom, a woman separated from her husband, Joe. One night while Lothario and Lucy were playing tennis in her backyard, Joe appeared on the scene. Lothario demanded that Joe leave, but he declined and sat in one of the yard chairs. Lothario went to the garage, picked up a rifle, pointed it at Joe, and from a distance of approximately seventy-five feet, fired a shot in the direction of Joe. The bullet missed Joe by about eighteen inches. Lothario explained to the police that he was simply trying to scare Lucy's estranged husband so he would not bother her. On the strength of these facts, do you think there is a basis to charge Lothario with attempted murder?

6. John and Jane were running a student loan scam. They were convicted of soliciting several students to make false applications in exchange for a portion of the loan proceeds, and also for aiding and abetting those same students in making false applications for loans. On appeal, they argue that the solicitation charges merged into their convictions for aiding and abetting the making of the false applications. The state responds that John and Jane were guilty of both crimes because the solicitation offenses were completed before John and Jane assisted the students in making the false applications. How should the appellate court rule on this appeal? Why?

7. A state statute makes it a criminal offense for "three or more persons to conduct, direct, or own a gambling business." Several defendants were convicted of "conspiring to violate the statute." In addition, each was convicted of the substantive offense of gambling. On appeal, each defendant argues that the conspiracy offense merged into the substantive offense of gambling because the offense of gambling required participation of a number of persons. The state counters that the harm attendant upon commission of the offense of gambling is not limited to the parties to the conspiracy. Moreover, it points out that those prosecuted for the conspiracy would not necessarily be identical to those who are prosecuted for the substantive offense of gambling. How do you think an appellate court should rule in this instance? Why?

# CHAPTER 6
# Homicidal Offenses

## CHAPTER OUTLINE

## JURISPRUDENCE

*Washington v. Glucksberg* (1997)
*Stenberg v. Carhart* (2000)

## LEARNING OBJECTIVES

After reading this chapter, you should be able to explain

1. the common-law background of the modern criminal law of homicide

2. how modern statutes classify homicide by degrees of culpability, and the difference between first- and second-degree murder

3. the felony–murder doctrine

4. the difference between voluntary and involuntary manslaughter

5. why states now have laws specifically aimed at vehicular homicide

6. the difference between justifiable and excusable homicide

7. the unique prosecutorial burdens in proving homicide cases

8. how modern criminal law treats suicide and assisted suicide

9. how the law regards the removal of medical life-support systems

10. how the criminal law treats abortion and killing of the human fetus

# CHAPTER OPENING VIGNETTE

In 2001, Diane Whipple was attacked outside her San Francisco apartment by two dogs owned by her neighbors, Marjorie Knoller and her husband Robert Noel. Another neighbor, who witnessed part of the attack, called 911. Shortly after arriving at the hospital, Whipple died from massive loss of blood due to more than seventy-five lacerations from dog bites. The attack made national news and attracted considerable media attention. Appearing on *Good Morning America*, Knoller and Noel denied any responsibility for the attack. Nevertheless, Knoller was charged with second-degree murder; her husband, who was not home during the attack, was charged with involuntary manslaughter. After a jury trial, which was moved to Los Angeles, both defendants were convicted of their respective homicide charges. However, the trial judge granted Knoller's motion for a new trial on the charge of second-degree murder on the ground that her culpability did not rise to the level required for second-degree murder. Ultimately, in August 2010, a California appellate court ruled that the trial judge had erred in granting a new trial. In its unpublished opinion the appellate court held that Knoller had been properly convicted of second-degree murder based on "implied malice." The court observed that Knoller's "deliberate act of leaving her apartment with an unmuzzled Bane [one of the dogs] knowing that she could not control him, as well as the evidence that she knew he was dangerous to human life provided substantial support for the jury's finding that she acted with conscious disregard for human life." *People v. Knoller*, 2010 Cal. App. Unpub. (Aug. 20, 2010). The California Supreme Court subsequently denied review, thus bringing the case to a conclusion nine years after the incident occurred. See *People v. Knoller*, 2010 Cal. Lexis 12088 (Dec. 1, 2010). This case suggests the complexity of modern criminal law with respect to homicide. While the English common law divided criminal homicide into murder and manslaughter, modern American statutes provide for gradations of criminal homicide based on degrees of culpability. The modern law of homicide is sufficiently complex that we have decided to devote an entire chapter to it.

# Introduction

**homicide** The killing of a human being.

**murder** At common law, the unlawful killing of one person by another with malice aforethought (premeditation).

**manslaughter** The crime of unlawfully killing another person without malice.

**malice aforethought** The mental predetermination to commit an illegal act.

**heat of passion** A violent and uncontrollable rage resulting from a provocation that would cause such a response by a reasonable person.

**suicide** The intentional taking of a person's own life.

The word **homicide** means the taking of the life of one human being by another. The English common law recognized both criminal and noncriminal homicides. The killing of a human being was the common factor in all classes of homicide; however, the perpetrator's state of mind was significant in determining whether an offense had been committed and, if so, the category of that offense. At common law, criminal homicide embraced the crimes of **murder** and **manslaughter**; noncriminal homicide included those killings of humans deemed either justifiable or excusable. Homicide was justifiable if performed by the command or permission of the law; it could be excusable if it occurred accidentally or when committed in self-defense.

Under English common law, murder was the unlawful killing of one person by another with **malice aforethought**. The required malice could be either express or implied. There were no degrees of murder. Manslaughter was the unlawful killing of one human being by another when no malice was involved. There were two categories: voluntary and involuntary. Voluntary manslaughter consisted of an intentional, unlawful killing that occurred in the **heat of passion** as a result of some adequate provocation. Involuntary manslaughter was the unintentional killing of another by the accused's gross or wanton negligence. Simply stated, the difference between the two was that the former was intentional whereas the latter was unintentional.

English common law viewed **suicide** as a serious offense against the Crown, inasmuch as the decedent had deprived the monarch of one of his or her subjects. It was also regarded as a serious moral offense by ecclesiastical authorities and by the English people. Suicide was punished by forfeiture of the decedent's personal property to the Crown and denial of a proper burial. William Blackstone observed that "the law has . . . ranked [suicide] among the highest crimes" but admitted that the punishment for it "border[s] a little upon severity." 4 W. Blackstone, *Commentaries* at 189–90.

At common law, abortion was not considered murder or manslaughter, as the law required the victim of a criminal homicide to have been born alive. Abortion was recognized as a misdemeanor, but only after the "quickening" of the fetus.

With respect to homicide, modern American criminal law has evolved considerably from its common-law origins. Yet certain basic terms and concepts remain viable. The criminal law still addresses murder, manslaughter, suicide, and abortion, but the law today is considerably more complex and nuanced.

## The Modern Approach to Homicide

**premeditation** Deliberate decision or plan to commit a crime.

**voluntary manslaughter** The intentional killing of a human without malice or premeditation and usually occurring during a sudden quarrel or in the heat of passion.

**involuntary manslaughter** The unintentional killing of another person as the result of gross or wanton negligence.

Under modern statutes, criminal homicide is classified based on the degree of the offender's culpability (see, e.g., the overview of Tennessee's homicide offenses contained in Table 6.1). Most jurisdictions now classify murder as either first or second degree. First-degree murder is usually defined as requiring either malice aforethought or **premeditation**. Second-degree murder commonly requires proof that the accused was guilty of imminently dangerous or outrageous conduct, albeit not malicious conduct in the common-law sense of malice aforethought.

All states make manslaughter a crime, although some statutes have abolished the distinction between **voluntary manslaughter** and **involuntary manslaughter**. Additionally, modern statutes extend the offense of manslaughter to embrace a person's responsibility for a person's death resulting from an omission to act in instances where the law imposes a duty to act.

| TABLE 6.1 | Levels of Criminal Homicide in Tennessee |
|---|---|
| **Level of Criminal Homicide** | **Statutory Definition** |
| First-degree murder | "the premeditated and intentional killing of another" or the "killing of another committed in the perpetration of or attempt to perpetrate any first-degree murder, arson, rape, robbery, burglary, theft, kidnapping, aggravated child abuse, aggravated child neglect or aircraft piracy" or the "killing of another committed as the result of the unlawful throwing, placing or discharging of a destructive device or bomb" |
| Second-degree murder | "the knowing killing of another" or the "killing of another which results from the unlawful distribution of any Schedule I or Schedule II drug when such drug is the proximate cause of the death of the user" |
| Voluntary manslaughter | "the intentional or knowing killing of another in a state of passion produced by adequate provocation sufficient to lead a reasonable person to act in an irrational manner" |
| Vehicular homicide | "the reckless killing of another by the operation of an automobile, airplane, motorboat or other motor vehicle: (1) As the proximate result of conduct creating a substantial risk of death or serious bodily injury to a person; or (2) As the proximate result of the driver's intoxication. . . ." |
| Reckless homicide | "the reckless killing of another" |
| Criminally negligent homicide | "criminally negligent conduct which results in death" |

Source: Tennessee Code Annotated § 39-13-201 *et seq.*

**justifiable homicide** Killing another in self-defense or defense of others when there is serious danger of death or great bodily harm to self or others or when authorized by law.

**excusable homicide** A death caused by accident or misfortune.

**doctor-assisted suicide** The commission of suicide with the aid of a physician.

**right to die** Controversial "right" to terminate one's own life under certain circumstances.

Modern criminal codes generally provide that it is **justifiable homicide** for one to take another's life by authority of the law (e.g., an executioner performing a duty). It is usually considered **excusable homicide** if death results from the inadvertent taking of another's life when the actor is not guilty of criminal negligence (e.g., death occurring from an unavoidable traffic accident).

The overwhelming majority of homicide prosecutions are brought under state laws. However, federal statutes provide jurisdiction over the killing of certain officers and employees of the United States engaged in performance of their official duties, 18 U.S.C.A. § 1114, as well as certain foreign officials, 18 U.S.C.A. § 1116. Federal statutes classify criminal homicide as murder in the first degree, felony murder, and manslaughter (voluntary and involuntary). 18 U.S.C.A. § 1111–1112.F.

Suicide statutes are now designed primarily to punish those who assist others in committing suicide. Such laws, especially those prohibiting **doctor-assisted suicide,** have become problematic, as courts have recognized a **right to die** in certain instances.

# First-Degree Murder

The California Penal Code illustrates a modern statutory approach to homicide. It defines murder as the "unlawful killing of a human being, or a fetus, with malice aforethought," but stipulates that the death of a fetus is not murder when an abortion is performed by a physician when the mother's life is endangered or with the mother's consent. West's Ann. Cal. Penal Code § 187. The malice required by the code may be either express or implied. When a deliberate intention is manifested to take a person's life unlawfully, the malice is considered express. Intent may be

**provocation** Conduct that prompts another person to react through criminal conduct.

implied when no considerable **provocation** appears or under other circumstances indicating malice. West's Ann. Cal. Penal Code § 188. In defining degrees of murder, the California code states that

> all murder which is perpetrated by means of a destructive device or explosive, knowing use of ammunition designed primarily to penetrate metal or armor, poison, lying in wait, torture, or by any other kind of willful, deliberate, and premeditated killing, or which is committed in the perpetration of, or attempt to perpetrate, arson, rape, carjacking, robbery, burglary, mayhem, kidnapping . . . is murder of the first degree; and all other kinds of murder are of the second degree. West's Ann. Cal. Penal Code § 189.

The penalties in California and other jurisdictions for first-degree murder are the most severe, with decreasing penalties provided for second-degree murder and manslaughter.

**first-degree murder** The highest degree of unlawful homicide, usually defined as "an unlawful act committed with the premeditated intent to take the life of a human being."

**First-degree murder** is the highest classification of homicide. It contemplates a true "intent to kill" and, as noted, usually requires proof of either malice aforethought or premeditation. Thus, to obtain a conviction, the prosecution must establish the defendant's specific intent to take another's life.

The California Supreme Court has said that "when a defendant with a wanton disregard for human life, does an act that involves a high degree of probability that it will result in death, he acts with malice aforethought." Moreover, the court has opined that "willful, deliberate, and premeditated," as used in the statute, indicates the legislature's intent to require as an essential element of first-degree murder substantially more reflection "than the mere amount of thought

---

**CASE-IN-POINT**

### What Constitutes Premeditation in First-Degree Murder?

Corder was convicted of first-degree murder in a South Dakota court and sentenced to life in prison. During the trial, Corder moved for a judgment of acquittal on the ground that the state had provided insufficient proof of premeditation. The trial court denied the motion and Corder appealed on this basis. In addressing the issue, the Supreme Court of South Dakota held "the fact of premeditation may be inferred from the facts and circumstances surrounding the killing" and is a question for the jury to decide. The court stated, "[I]n determining the sufficiency of evidence to establish a premeditated design to effect death in murder cases, the courts generally consider the following factors of importance: the use of a lethal or deadly weapon; the manner of the killing; the accused's conduct before and after the killing; and a determination of the presence or absence of

provocation." The evidence at trial revealed that the victim "was beaten repeatedly about the head and chest areas" and the cause of death was determined to be "multiple head and abdominal trauma." As a result of the beating, the victim "suffered a laceration to his liver and had multiple rib fractures." After beating the victim with a log, Corder "threw it into the river." The court stated that "surely there was sufficient time for Corder to form the intent to kill and an opportunity for him to reconsider the matter and not strike [the victim] with the log." Also, "in an apparent attempt to conceal evidence, Corder removed [the victim's] shirt and jacket and tried to burn them in order to destroy any fingerprints." In affirming Corder's conviction, the court stated that "sufficient evidence was produced to support a reasonable inference of premeditation and that, therefore, the jury's finding of this fact should not be disturbed."

*State v. Corder*, 460 N.W.2d 733 (S.D. 1990).

necessary to form the intention to kill." *People v. Cruz*, 605 P.2d 830, 834 (Cal. 1980). The Pennsylvania Supreme Court has defined malice aforethought more elaborately, saying it is "not only a particular ill will, but a hardness of heart, cruelty, recklessness of consequences, and a mind regardless of social duty." *Commonwealth v. Buzard*, 76 A.2d 394, 396 (Pa. 1950). Such malice may be expressed or may be implied from the circumstances under which a homicidal act is performed. However, that court has noted that a single punch to a victim's face was insufficient to support a finding of malice. *Commonwealth v. Thomas*, 594 A.2d 300 (Pa. 1991).

Many jurisdictions define first-degree murder based on the "premeditated intent" of the offender. For example, Florida classifies a homicide as a first-degree murder if the unlawful killing of a human being is "perpetrated from a premeditated design to effect the death of the person killed or any human being." West's Fla. Stat. Ann. § 782.04. Initially, one might be inclined to think of a premeditated act as requiring a lengthy period of deliberation. Indeed, dictionaries commonly define "premeditation" as a conscious and deliberate preplanning over a period of time. However, judicial decisions defining premeditation emphasize that although it requires thought beforehand, no particular length of time is required. The length of time necessary to deliberate, or to form a specific intent to kill, need only be time enough to form the required intent before the killing. It matters not how short that time may be, as long as the process of premeditation occurs at any point before the killing. See, e.g., *State v. Corn*, 278 S.E.2d 221 (N.C. 1981). (On the issue of premeditation, courts consider defendants' acts and comments before and after killing, use of grossly excessive force or infliction of lethal blows after the deceased has been felled, and history of altercations or ill will between the parties.)

The prosecution usually attempts to establish either malice aforethought or premeditation by introducing a variety of evidentiary facts and circumstances bearing on the defendant's motive and state of mind. These include the defendant's previous relationship with the victim, encompassing threats, quarrels, and expressions of ill will as well as conversations of the defendant at the time of and before and after the act of killing. Prosecutors also point to the nature of the wound inflicted, prior attacks on the victim, the defendant's actions before and after the crime, and the circumstances of the killing itself, including the weapon used and the nature and location of wounds inflicted.

---

### First-Degree Murder: Evidence of Premeditation

**CASE-IN-POINT**

Defendant Phillip Lee Young suggested to his two companions that they rob and kill John Cooke in order to obtain money to buy liquor. After the three men used a ruse to gain entry to Cooke's house, Young stabbed Cooke twice in the chest, and one of the companions stabbed the victim several times in the back. Cooke died as a result of the injuries.

A jury found Young guilty of first-degree murder, and he appealed. After explaining that first-degree murder is the unlawful killing of a person with malice and with premeditation and deliberation, the North Carolina Supreme Court rejected Young's contention that the evidence was insufficient to support a conviction.

*State v. Young*, 325 S.E.2d 181 (N.C. 1985).

# Felony Murder

**felony murder** A homicide committed during the course of committing another felony other than murder (e.g., armed robbery). The felonious act substitutes for the malice aforethought ordinarily required in murder.

The common law developed a doctrine that where an accused was engaged in the commission of a felony and a homicide occurred, the felonious act was regarded as a substitute for the proof of malice aforethought required to find the defendant guilty of murder. Thus, it became **felony murder** when an accused unintentionally killed a human being while committing, or attempting to commit, such common-law felonies as burglary, arson, rape, or robbery. The theory was that if a killing resulted, even though unintentional or accidental, the required malice was carried over from the original felony. Consequently, the felon would be found guilty of murder.

The felony murder doctrine has been incorporated into most criminal codes in the United States. See *People v. Aaron*, 299 N.W.2d 304 (Mich. 1980). With the proliferation of crimes classified as felonies, legislatures have generally limited the applicability of felony murder to felonies involving violence or posing great threat to life or limb (e.g., rape, robbery, kidnapping, arson, and burglary). See, e.g., West's Ann. Cal. Penal Code § 189, quoted above. Some state legislatures have sought to equate certain felonious drug offenses with violent felonies. Some statutes provide for degrees of felony murder depending on the seriousness of the felony attempted or perpetrated by the accused, whether the killing occurred by a person other than the person perpetrating or attempting to perpetrate the felony, and whether the accused was present at the scene when the killing occurred. See, e.g., West's Fla. Stat. Ann. § 782.04. Felony murder statutes have produced much litigation in the criminal courts. Some of the pertinent questions raised include the following:

- Can a felon who perpetrates an offense be guilty of felony murder where the victim of the intended offense kills a co-felon?
- Should a felon committing a crime such as robbery be guilty of felony murder if a police officer mistakenly kills the felon's intended victim?
- Can a felon be guilty of felony murder when a co-felon accidentally kills a bystander or a police officer?

Most courts have held that the doctrine of felony murder does not extend to a killing stemming from the commission of the felony if it is directly attributable to the act of someone other than the defendant or those actively participating with the defendant in the unlawful enterprise. Nevertheless, courts have arrived at different solutions to these and other problems arising under felony murder laws.

Perhaps questions such as these led the Michigan Supreme Court in 1980 to abrogate the felony murder doctrine. After commenting on how its prior decisions had already significantly restricted the doctrine, the court concluded that the rule that substitutes the intent to commit the underlying felony for the malice element of murder had to be abolished. Its abrogation of the doctrine does not make irrelevant the fact that a death occurred in the course of a felony. Rather, the court noted that a jury could properly infer malice from evidence that a defendant intentionally set in motion a force likely to cause death or great bodily harm. However, Michigan juries are no longer instructed to find malice if they are satisfied from all the evidence that it does not exist. *People v. Aaron*, supra.

A cogent argument can be made that the felony murder rule violates the basic requirement of moral culpability in the criminal law. Moreover, critics point out that under the early common law, conviction of a felony was punishable by death. Consequently, they note, when a death occurred in the commission of a felony and the accused was guilty of felony murder, no additional consequences resulted. With the exception of certain federal offenses recently classified as capital crimes, no felony except murder committed under aggravating circumstances is punishable by death.

Nevertheless, the felony murder doctrine is well established in most jurisdictions. With legislatures perceiving the need to take a "hard line" on crime, it is doubtful that many states will be motivated to repeal felony murder statutes. Therefore, courts have become increasingly conscious of the need to interpret such statutes strictly. Observing that it is the commission of a specified felony that supplants the requirement of premeditation for first-degree murder, the Florida Supreme Court declared that for the felon to be guilty of felony murder there must be some causal connection between the homicide and the underlying felony. *Bryant v. State*, 412 So.2d 347 (Fla. 1982). The State must prove that there was no break in the chain of circumstances beginning with the felony and ending with the murder. *Santiago v. State*, 874 So.2d 617 (Fla. App. 2004).

## Second-Degree Murder

**second-degree murder** A killing perpetrated by any act imminently dangerous to another and evincing a depraved mind regardless of human life, although without any premeditated design to effect the death of any particular individual.

**depraved mind or heart** A serious moral deficiency; a high level of malice often linked to second-degree murder.

In many jurisdictions, **second-degree murder** is a residual classification applied to unlawful homicides not evidenced by malice aforethought or premeditation, not occurring in conjunction with other felonies, and not falling within the statutory definition of manslaughter. More commonly, second-degree murder is defined as an unlawful killing of a human being by a person having a **depraved mind or heart**. For example, in South Dakota second-degree murder is defined as follows:

> Homicide is murder in the second degree when perpetrated by any act imminently dangerous to others and evincing a depraved mind, regardless of human life, although without any premeditated design to effect the death of any particular individual, including an unborn child. S.D. St. § 22-16-7.

The South Dakota Supreme Court has held that the statutory language "although without any premeditated design" distinguishes premeditated murder from second-degree murder. *State v. Satter*, 543 N.W.2d 249 (S.D. 1996). Two years later that court held that a trial court properly defined the phrase "evincing a depraved mind" as conduct demonstrating an indifference to the life of others, that is, not only disregard for the safety of another but also a lack of regard for the life of another. *State v. Hart*, 584 N.W.2d 863 (S.D. 1998).

Shooting a firearm into a crowd or into an occupied house or automobile is a classic example of a depraved-heart-or-mind murder. But courts have also found such conduct as a parent spanking and shaking a young child so hard as to cause death, a driver running a police roadblock at a high rate of speed, a golfer swinging a golf club with great force against a victim, and a person tossing heavy stones from a building onto a busy street below to be conduct evincing a depraved heart or depraved mind.

We began the chapter by referring to a case where Diane Whipple was killed by dogs belonging to neighbors. In that case, a conviction for second-degree murder was sustained under a California statute that allows for conviction of second-degree murder based on "implied malice." The statute provides that malice "is implied, when no considerable provocation appears, or when the circumstances attending the killing show an abandoned and malignant heart." West's Ann. Cal. Penal Code § 188. In *People v. Phillips*, 414 P.2d 353, 587 (1966), the California Supreme Court held that malice can be implied when the death of another results from "an act, the natural consequences of which are dangerous to life, which act was deliberately performed by a person who knows that his conduct endangers the life of another and who acts with conscious disregard for life."

### Second-Degree Murder Conviction Reduced to Manslaughter

In a high-profile case, in October 1997 a Massachusetts jury found Louise Woodward, a young British *au pair* serving an American family, guilty of second-degree murder in the death of an eight-month-old child under her care. The child died a few days after receiving a severe head trauma while in Woodward's care. There was no evidence the defendant had ever abused or injured the child prior to the fatal injury. Fearing a compromise verdict, Woodward's counsel requested that the court not instruct the jury on the offense of manslaughter. After the jury returned a verdict of second-degree murder, the trial judge found that the defendant's actions "were characterized by confusion, inexperience, frustration, immaturity and some anger, but not malice" and reduced the defendant's conviction to manslaughter. The prosecution challenged the trial judge's action; however, the Massachusetts Supreme Judicial Court concluded that the trial judge did not abuse his discretion.

*Commonwealth v. Woodward*, 694 N.E.2d 1277 (Mass. 1998).

## Manslaughter

As we have noted, there were two classes of manslaughter at common law: voluntary and involuntary. California, like many states, preserves that distinction and defines manslaughter as the "unlawful killing of a human being without malice." California law enumerates three categories: voluntary, involuntary, and vehicular. Voluntary manslaughter refers to instances where death of the victim occurs in a sudden quarrel or in the heat of passion. Involuntary manslaughter occurs where a death results from the commission of a lawful act that might produce death in an unlawful manner, or without due caution and circumspection. The third category, vehicular homicide, involves death resulting from the perpetrator's driving a vehicle while in the commission of an unlawful act not amounting to a felony and not with gross negligence, or driving a vehicle in the commission of a lawful act that might produce death in an unlawful manner, and with gross negligence. West's Ann. Cal. Penal Code § 192.

Many other states define manslaughter without categorizing it as voluntary or involuntary. Still other state legislatures have defined manslaughter by degrees. For example, New York law provides that a person who recklessly causes the death of another person, commits an unlawful abortion on a female that causes her death, or intentionally causes or aids another to commit suicide commits manslaughter in the second degree. McKinney's N.Y. Penal Law § 125.15. However, a person who inflicts certain intentional serious injuries that cause the death of another under circumstances that do not constitute murder may be guilty of the more serious offense of manslaughter in the first degree if he or she (1) acts under the influence of extreme emotional disturbance or (2) commits an unlawful abortional act that causes the death of a female pregnant for more than twenty-four weeks, unless it is an abortional act deemed justifiable by statutory exceptions. McKinney's N.Y. Penal Law § 125.20. Irrespective of whether a statute classifies manslaughter as voluntary, involuntary, or by degree, certain situations generally fall within the definition of the offense. Common examples include death resulting from mutual combat and killing someone by use of excessive force while defending oneself or a family member or acting in defense of property.

The intent the prosecution must establish to obtain a conviction of manslaughter may depend on the nature of the charge and whether the particular statute defines voluntary or involuntary manslaughter. To establish voluntary man-slaughter, the prosecution may have to establish the defendant's specific intent. On the other hand, in a prosecution for involuntary manslaughter, the prosecution need only establish the defendant's general intent, and that may be inferred from the defendant's act and surrounding circumstances. Often a charge of involuntary manslaughter is based on allegations of criminal negligence. For example, in 2011, Dr. Conrad Murray was convicted of involuntary manslaughter in a California court for administering a fatal dose of the drug propofol to pop star Michael Jackson. At trial, Murray's lawyers contended that Jackson had self-administered the fatal dose of the drug, but prosecutors countered by arguing that Murray acted with gross negligence, irrespective of who administered the lethal dose of propofol.

Provocation is frequently a factor in manslaughter trials. Provocation that would cause a reasonable person to lose control may be sufficient to convert an otherwise intentional killing of another to manslaughter. Mere words, however gross or insulting, are not sufficient to constitute provocation. Rather, to reduce a homicide from murder to manslaughter, it must generally be shown that there was sufficient provocation to excite in the defendant's mind such anger, rage, or terror as would obscure an ordinary person's reasoning and render the person incapable of cool reflection. A classic example is discovering one's spouse in an act of adultery with significant sexual contact taking place. The Maryland Court of Special Appeals has observed that

> if one spouse discovers another in an unexpected act of adultery, a killing of a spouse or paramour in hot-blooded fury may lower the blameworthiness from the murder level to the manslaughter level. The blood, however, must indeed be hot and, generally speaking, only the hot-blooded killer can attest to that. By an objective standard, moreover, the time frame must be close enough so that an average and reasonable man would not have had an adequate "cooling period" for the first fury to abate. *Bartram v. State*, 364 A.2d 1119, 1153 (Md. App. 1976).

The Indiana Supreme Court has noted that

> all that is required to reduce a homicide from murder to voluntary manslaughter is sufficient provocation to excite in the mind of the defendant such emotions as either anger, rage, sudden resentment, or terror as may be sufficient to obscure the reason of an ordinary man, and to prevent deliberation and premeditation, to exclude malice, and to render the defendant incapable of cool reflection. *Hardin v. State*, 404 N.E.2d 1354, 1357 (Ind. 1980).

Modern statutes often provide that negligent performance of a legal duty or the doing of a lawful act in an unlawful manner constitutes manslaughter. In addition to the more common instances, courts have upheld manslaughter convictions under such statutes for death occurring because of criminal negligence of medical practitioners or because of parental failure to provide medical attention or adequate nourishment for their children. See, e.g., *People v. Ogg*, 182 N.W.2d 570 (Mich. App. 1970) (the mother of a young child who left the home while her child was locked in a bedroom and the child was killed in a fire of undetermined origin was guilty of manslaughter). The California Supreme Court held that the mother of a child who died of meningitis after receiving treatment by prayer in lieu of medical attention may be guilty of such criminal negligence that the parent can be found guilty of involuntary manslaughter or child endangerment. *Walker v. Superior Court*, 763 P.2d 852 (Cal. 1988). Other

### Manslaughter by Culpable Negligence

William Burge and Juanita Calloway became involved in an argument over an alleged sexual indiscretion. When Calloway displayed a knife, Burge pulled a gun that he carried to kill snakes that lurked in the walls of his house. Burge pointed the gun at Calloway and cocked it. Burge then pushed Calloway in an attempt to get her into his car. When he did, Calloway's hand hit the gun and it went off, severely wounding Calloway. While driving her to the hospital, Burge ran out of gas and called an ambulance. Calloway died en route to the hospital. Despite his plea of self-defense, a jury found Burge guilty of manslaughter by culpable negligence. In affirming the conviction, the Mississippi Supreme Court rejected the defendant's contentions of self-defense and excusable and justifiable homicide. The court observed that the jury could reasonably have determined that although the victim was holding a knife, the defendant was not in danger of great personal injury.

*Burge v. State*, 472 So.2d 392 (Miss. 1985).

courts have rejected the First Amendment right to free exercise of religion as a defense in such situations.

## Vehicular Homicide

**vehicular homicide** A homicide resulting from the unlawful and negligent operation of a motor vehicle.

The carnage on American highways has prompted many states to enact statutes making **vehicular homicide** a specific felony rather than opting to rely on prosecutors to charge a defendant with manslaughter for causing a traffic death. Such statutes were originally directed at operators of motor vehicles but now frequently apply to operators of boats and airplanes as well.

In Kansas the legislature has provided that vehicular homicide is a class A misdemeanor and defines the offense as follows:

> Vehicular homicide is the unintentional killing of a human being committed by the operation of an automobile, airplane, motor boat or other motor vehicle in a manner which creates an unreasonable risk of injury to the person or property of another and which constitutes a material deviation from the standard of care which a reasonable person would observe under the same circumstances. Kans. Stat. Ann. § 21-3405.

Many states have opted to classify vehicular homicide as a felony. See, e.g., West's Fla. Stat. Ann. § 782.071. ("Vehicular homicide" is the killing of a human being, or the killing of a viable fetus by any injury to the mother, caused by the operation of a motor vehicle by another in a reckless manner likely to cause the death of, or great bodily harm to, another.) The Florida Supreme Court has said that in enacting its vehicular homicide statute, the legislature created a separate offense with a lesser standard of proof than is required for conviction under the state's manslaughter statute. Thus, the statute enables the prosecution to secure a conviction where the state is unable to meet the level of proof otherwise required in establishing manslaughter. The court said the state could charge a defendant with manslaughter for operating a motor vehicle in a culpably negligent manner that causes the death of a human being or could proceed under vehicular homicide, a lesser included offense. *State v. Young*, 371 So.2d 1029 (Fla. 1979).

**CASE-IN-POINT**

### Vehicular Homicide: Criminal Liability for Second Accident

On the evening of February 14, 1987, Gary Dawson was a passenger in a car driven by Richard Peaslee, Jr., on a snow-packed, icy road in Maine. As a result of Peaslee's intentional "fish-tailing," the car went out of control and overturned, throwing Dawson onto the road. Dawson, unable to move, lay on the road, where he was run over by another vehicle several minutes later. Dawson died before help arrived on the scene. A jury found Peaslee guilty of vehicular manslaughter, and he appealed. In affirming Peaslee's conviction, the Maine Supreme Court rejected his contention that he was not criminally responsible for the second accident. "The separate accidents were not independent of each other," said the court, "because Dawson would not have been lying immobile on the road in the path of the other car were it not for Peaslee's conduct." Moreover, the court concluded that "[w]hether Dawson was killed by the first or second impact makes no difference."

*State v. Peaslee*, 571 A.2d 825 (Me. 1990).

# Justifiable and Excusable Homicide

As do most jurisdictions, California classifies nonculpable homicide as excusable or justifiable. It is excusable "when committed by accident or misfortune or in doing any other lawful act by lawful means, with usual and ordinary caution, and without any unlawful intent." It may also be excusable "when committed in the heat of passion, or on sudden and sufficient provocation, or on sudden combat where no undue advantage is taken nor any dangerous weapon is used and the killing is not done in a cruel or unusual manner." West's Ann. Cal. Penal Code § 195. Examples of excusable homicide include killing someone while resisting a murder attempt; when in defense of a person's home under certain circumstances; or in some instances of self-defense where there is a reasonable ground to apprehend imminent danger of great bodily harm to a person's self, spouse, parent, or child. See West's Ann. Cal. Penal Code § 196; *People v. Collins*, 11 Cal. Rptr. 504 (Cal. App. 1961).

Under California law, homicide is justifiable when committed by public officers and those acting by their command in their aid and assistance,

1. In obedience to any judgment of a competent Court; or,
2. When necessarily committed in overcoming actual resistance to the execution of some legal process, or in the discharge of any other legal duty; or,
3. When necessarily committed in retaking felons who have been rescued or have escaped, or when necessarily committed in arresting persons charged with felony, and who are fleeing from justice or resisting such arrest. West's Ann. Cal. Penal Code § 196; *People v. Young*, 29 Cal. Rptr. 595 (Cal. App. 1963).

## Removal of Life-Support Systems

Another area of contemporary concern has resulted from technological advances in medicine that have enabled physicians to use sophisticated life-support systems to prolong life for indefinite periods. In a landmark case involving Karen Quinlan, the New Jersey Supreme Court in 1976 reviewed the request of Karen's parents to remove the life-support systems sustaining the life of their daughter, who lay in a comatose state with no reasonable medical probability of regaining a sapient

### The Terri Schiavo Case

Problems can result in acrimonious litigation when a patient has no living will or other written instructions on the issue of removal of life support and close family members disagree. In 1990, Terri Schiavo, age twenty-six, suffered cardiac arrest and remained in a coma for several weeks. She was then diagnosed as being in a persistent vegetative state. In 1998, Michael, her husband and guardian, petitioned a Florida court to remove her feeding tube. She had no living will. Over the strong objections of her parents, the court found the evidence revealed that Schiavo did not wish to be kept alive and ordered her feeding tube removed. The court's decision engendered numerous unsuccessful appeals in state courts. The Florida legislature became involved in the controversy, and even the U.S. Congress passed a law granting federal court jurisdiction over this particular case, an action that raised critical constitutional issues. The U.S. Supreme Court denied review of court decisions, denying the parents relief. Subsequently even Florida governor Jeb Bush was unsuccessful in an attempt to prohibit removal of the feeding tube. Finally, Schiavo's feeding tube was removed for the third time. Throughout the controversy, the media kept the public advised of the progress of the legal proceedings, Schiavo died on March 31, 2005, at the age of forty-one.

The Schiavo case did not develop any new legal principles or procedures. But it did focus national attention on the need for individuals to execute legal directives clearly defining the extent of extraordinary medical procedures to be taken in the event they are in a persistent vegetative state.

© *Cengage Learning*

existence. The court ruled that withdrawal of such life-support systems, under the circumstances, would not constitute a criminal homicide. *In re Quinlan*, 355 A.2d 647 (N.J. 1976).

A significant body of decisional law has now developed on the issue of when life-sustaining measures should be initiated and when they may be removed. Generally, a competent adult who is terminally ill may decide to forgo such extraordinary measures or may order such measures discontinued. *McKay v. Bergstedt*, 801 P.2d 617 (Nev. 1990). Moreover, the Florida Supreme Court has held that terminally ill incompetent persons have the same right to refuse extraordinary measures as competent persons and that family members or guardians may exercise such rights on their behalf. *John F. Kennedy Memorial Hosp., Inc. v. Bludworth*, 452 So.2d 921 (Fla. 1984).

Judicial opinions vary as to when, under what circumstances, and by whom discontinuance of medical treatments may be ordered for minors and incompetents. Statutes in several states now address many of the problems in this area, yet there is no statutory or judicial consensus on the procedures to effect discontinuance. However, courts have been cautious not to allow criminal prosecutions where life-sustaining medical procedures have been discontinued in good faith based on competent medical advice and consent of a competent patient or the patient's family. See, e.g., *Barber v. Superior Court*, 195 Cal. Rptr. 484 (Cal. App. 1983).

## Prosecutorial Burdens in Homicide Cases

To obtain a conviction in a homicide case, the prosecution bears several burdens peculiar to homicide cases. The victim of the crime must have been alive; the defendant's actions must be the cause of the victim's death; and, in some jurisdictions, death of the victim must occur within a stated period of time. Although these might appear to be matters easily proven, sometimes they pose problems for prosecutors.

## The Requirement That the Victim was Alive Before the Homicidal Act

By definition, a criminal homicide consists of someone taking another person's life. It follows that before the accused can be found guilty of a homicidal crime, the prosecution must establish that the victim was alive before the accused's criminal act. In *People v. Dlugash*, 363 N.E.2d 1155 (N.Y. 1977), the New York Court of Appeals reviewed a case where a defendant (Dlugash) had been convicted of murder after he had fired shots into a body that had been shot by another person (Bush) several minutes earlier:

> While the defendant admitted firing five shots at the victim approximately two to five minutes after Bush had fired three times, all three medical expert witnesses testified that they could not, with any degree of medical certainty, state whether the victim had been alive at the time the latter shots were fired by the defendant. Thus, the People failed to prove beyond a reasonable doubt that the victim had been alive at the time he was shot by the defendant. Whatever else it may be, it is not murder to shoot a dead body. Man dies but once. 363 N.E.2d at 1158–1159.

## The *Corpus Delicti* Requirement

**corpus delicti** "The body of the crime." The material thing upon which a crime has been committed.

In addition to establishing that a human being was alive before a killing took place, the prosecution must always establish the **corpus delicti**, or body of the crime. The *corpus delicti* consists of the fact that a human being is dead and that the death was caused by the criminal act or agency of another person.

In most jurisdictions the *corpus delicti* rule requires independent evidence beyond a defendant's confession. Some argue that this requirement is simply a technicality that impedes the search for truth. They argue that modern constitutional protections of confessions render the rule unnecessary. Others contend that by requiring some independent evidence to link a defendant to the crime charged ensures that no one is convicted based on a mistake or a coerced or fabricated confession. This rule is firmly implanted in American law, although several states have modified the rule in the last few decades. To prove the *corpus delicti*, the prosecution must show by either direct or circumstantial evidence, independent of the accused's statements, that the victim died as a result of a criminal act. Usually, the victim's body is available for medical examination, and a physician can testify about the cause of death. If the deceased's body is not recovered and the victim's death cannot be determined to have resulted from a criminal act, a conviction cannot be lawfully obtained. Consider the case of *Ex parte Flodstrom*, 277 P.2d 101 (Cal. 1954). There, it could not be determined if a baby died from the mother's alleged homicidal act or if death occurred as a result of natural causes. Consequently, because there was no evidence available to establish the *corpus delicti*, the appellate court discharged the accused mother from custody on the ground that she was being held to answer charges of murder without probable cause.

**proximate cause** The cause that is nearest to a given effect in a causal relationship.

To hold a defendant responsible for the death of a victim, the prosecution must also establish that the defendant's act was the **proximate cause** of the victim's death. This means that the victim's death must have been the natural and probable consequence of the defendant's unlawful conduct. Where A shoots or physically beats B, A pushes B out of a window or overboard from a boat, or A administers poison to B, medical evidence can usually establish the cause of the victim's death.

However, killings can be accomplished in hundreds of ways. For example, death can be precipitated by fright, shock, or other means not involving physical contact with the victim. The accused's acts or omissions need not be the immediate cause of the victim's death as long as the death results naturally from the accused's conduct.

Some situations present perplexing issues for medical experts and courts. For example, a defendant fired a shot into the water about six feet from a boat occupied by two boys. When a second shot struck nearer to the boat than the first, one of the boys leaped out of the boat into the water. The boat capsized with the remaining boy in it. Both boys drowned. The defendant argued that he could not be guilty of causing the death of the boy who drowned when the boat overturned. The Tennessee Supreme Court rejected his contention and upheld the defendant's conviction for involuntary manslaughter, concluding that it was his shots, not the act of the boy who caused the boat to capsize, that caused the decedent's death. *Letner v. State*, 299 S.W. 1049 (Tenn. 1927).

In another instance, a wife who had been severely beaten by her husband in the past was impelled by fear of another beating at his hands to jump from a moving automobile. She died from injuries sustained. Her husband was charged with her murder and was found guilty of the lesser offense of manslaughter. On appeal, the Florida Supreme Court upheld the conviction. *Whaley v. State*, 26 So.2d 656 (Fla. 1946).

In a recent prosecution for several counts of attempted murder, the evidence revealed that the defendant was aware that he had tested positive for human immunodeficiency virus (HIV). The defendant's probation officer had even informed him that if he passed HIV to another person, "he would be killing someone." Nevertheless, he repeatedly and intentionally engaged in sexual activity with multiple partners and refused to take "safe sex" precautions. The defendant was convicted and appealed. He argued that he meant only to satisfy himself sexually and such was insufficient to prove intent to cause death. The Oregon Court of Appeals rejected his appeal and held that the defendant did not act impulsively merely to satisfy his sexual desire; rather, he acted deliberately to cause his victims serious bodily injury and death. *State v. Hinkhouse*, 912 P.2d 921 (Or. App. 1996).

Prosecutions of HIV-positive defendants under statutes proscribing attempted murder pose difficult problems for prosecutors. For example, proof of the element of intent is problematic, and proof of causation can pose great difficulty when the victim has had sexual relations with multiple partners. In *Smallwood v. State*, 680 A.2d 512 (Md. 1996), an HIV-positive defendant who pleaded guilty to attempted first-degree rape and robbery was then convicted of assault with intent to murder and attempted murder. On appeal, the Maryland Court of Appeals reversed the defendant's convictions for assault with intent to murder and attempted murder. The court held that evidence that the defendant knew he was HIV positive when he raped three women was insufficient to prove that he had an intent to kill.

Some states allow for the prosecution of persons who are HIV positive under reckless endangerment statutes, thus eliminating proof of intent and causation. A number of states have adopted statutes that proscribe a person who has been diagnosed with HIV from engaging in sexual activity with another person without first informing that person of the HIV diagnosis.

## When Death Occurs

Just as it is necessary to determine that a homicide victim was alive before the injury that caused death, it is also necessary to establish that death has occurred. In most instances, the classic definition will suffice: death occurs when the heart stops beating and respiration ends. However, technological advances have rendered this definition obsolete as the sole means of determining when death occurs. Many state legislatures have now adopted a definition of **brain death** that specifies that irreversible cessation of total brain functions constitutes death. For example, North Carolina law states,

**brain death** The complete cessation of activity of the central nervous system.

> Brain death, defined as irreversible cessation of total brain function, may be used as a sole basis for the determination that a person has died, particularly when brain death occurs in the presence of artificially maintained respiratory and circulatory functions. This specific recognition of brain death as a criterion of death of the person shall not preclude the use of other medically recognized criteria for determining whether and when a person has died. West's N.C.G.S.A. § 90-323.

All states and the District of Columbia, either by statute or judicial decision, now recognize brain death as a criterion for death.

## The "One-Year-and-a-Day" Rule

**one-year-and-a-day rule** A common-law rule that to convict a defendant of homicide, not more than a year and a day can intervene from the defendant's criminal act to the death of the victim.

Another obstacle to the prosecution of homicide cases can be the **one-year-and-a-day rule**. Although the rule originated during the early development of the English common law, in 1894 the U.S. Supreme Court acknowledged its applicability to criminal prosecutions in this country, stating,

> In cases of murder the rule at common law undoubtedly was that no person should be adjudged "by any act whatever to kill another who does not die by it within a year and a day thereafter. . . ." And such is the rule in this country in prosecutions for murder, except in jurisdictions where it may be otherwise prescribed by statute. *Louisville, Evansville, & St. Louis R.R. Co. v. Clarke*, 152 U.S. 230, 239, 14 S.Ct. 579, 581, 38 L.Ed. 422, 424 (1894).

This inflexible rule continued because of uncertainties of medical science in establishing the cause of a victim's death after a lengthy period had elapsed. But in an age of advancing medical technology, the "one-year-and-a-day" rule has little relevance.

Either by statute or judicial decision the vast majority of states have abolished the rule; a few have modified it. California amended its statute in 1969 to stipulate that "[i]f death occurs beyond the time of three years and a day, there shall be a rebuttable presumption that the killing was not criminal." West's Ann. Cal. Penal Code § 194. Tennessee was one of the latest states to abolish the rule by judicial decision. In *State v. Rogers*, 992 S.W.2d 393 (Tenn. 1999), the Tennessee Supreme Court concluded that the reasons that prompted common-law courts to recognize the rule no longer exist, observing, "Modern pathologists are able to determine the cause of death with much greater accuracy than was possible in earlier times." *Id.* at 400. The U.S. Supreme Court upheld the Tennessee Supreme Court's retroactive abolition of the one-year and-a-day rule. Justice Sandra Day O'Connor, writing for the majority of the Court, pointed out that the rule was an outdated relic of the common law and that modern medicine no longer necessitated the rule. Further, her opinion held that judicial abrogation of the year-and-a-day rule was not unexpected, and thus Rogers had fair warning that the rule may be abolished and there was no violation of the Ex Post Facto Clause of the Constitution. *Rogers v. Tennessee*, 532 U.S. 451, 121 S.Ct. 1693, 149 L.Ed.2d 697 (2001).

## Defenses to Homicide Charges

Defendants charged with murder or manslaughter frequently plead either self-defense or insanity. These defenses are discussed in detail in Chapter 14. Where an accused defends against a charge of murder, the heat-of-passion defense discussed earlier may be available in some instances, as would be the defense of reasonable care or accidental killing in others.

# Suicide and Assisted Suicide

The early English common law defined the offense of suicide as the intentional taking of a person's life by self-destruction. Suicide was not only regarded as being contrary to nature; it was regarded as an offense against the biblical commandment "Thou shalt not kill." Suicide was a species of felony punishable by forfeiture of the decedent's goods and chattels because it deprived the king or queen of one of his or her subjects.

**assisted suicide** The act of aiding or assisting a person to take his or her life. An offense in some jurisdictions.

In the United States, the thrust of the criminal law has been to make it an offense to cause or aid another person to commit suicide, with many states making **assisted suicide** a crime. New York law provides that a person who "intentionally causes or aids another person to commit suicide" is guilty of manslaughter in the second degree. McKinney's N.Y. Penal Law § 125.15. In Texas, a person who, with intent to promote or assist in the commission of suicide, aids or attempts to aid another to commit suicide is guilty of a misdemeanor. If the actor's conduct causes a suicide or an attempted suicide that results in serious bodily injury, the offense becomes a felony. Vernon's Tex. Penal Code § 22.08. Until recently, the validity of laws of this character went unchallenged. As we explain in the following sections, this is no longer the case.

## Oregon's Death with Dignity Act

On November 8, 1994, Oregon voters adopted the Death with Dignity Act that allows terminally ill adult patients to obtain a physician's prescription for a lethal dose of medication. Two doctors must determine that the patient has less than six months to live and is mentally competent. The patient must request a lethal dose of medicine both orally and in writing and must wait at least fifteen days to obtain it. Although a federal district court originally enjoined the enforcement of the act, the U.S. Court of Appeals vacated the injunction. *Lee v. State of Oregon*, 107 F.3d 1382 (9th Cir. 1997). The U.S. Supreme Court declined to review the case. 522 U.S. 927, 118 S.Ct. 328, 139 L.Ed.2d 254 (1997).

On November 6, 2001, U.S. Attorney General John Ashcroft advised the Drug Enforcement Administration that assisting suicide was not a "legitimate medical purpose" and that the use of controlled substances to do so would violate the Controlled Substances Act (CSA). He pointed out that prescribing controlled substances for assisting suicide would make a physician's license subject to suspension or revocation. The State of Oregon filed suit, arguing that the Attorney General's actions exceeded his authority under the CSA. A federal court issued a permanent injunction against enforcement of the Attorney General's directive on the ground that the directive exceeded authority delegated to the Attorney General by the CSA. *Oregon v. Ashcroft*, 192 F.Supp.2d 1077 (D. Or. 2002). The Ninth Circuit Court of Appeals agreed. The U.S. Supreme Court granted review and held that the CSA did not authorize the Attorney General to prohibit doctors from prescribing regulated drugs for use in physician-assisted suicide, as authorized by the Oregon Death with Dignity Act. *Gonzales v. Oregon*, 546 U.S 243, 126 S.Ct. 904, 163 L.Ed.2d 748 (2006).

## The Michigan Experience

Over the past several years, a series of judicial decisions have held that physicians may withhold or withdraw medical treatment at a patient's request. But the courts recognized a sharp distinction between such activity and administering drugs to assist a person to take his or her own life. Michigan, and several other states, had no laws against assisted suicide. This was dramatized on June 4, 1990, when a fifty-four-year-old woman suffering from Alzheimer's disease took her life by pressing a button that injected a lethal substance into her system through use of a suicide machine developed by Dr. Jack Kevorkian, a retired Michigan pathologist. Murder charges filed against the doctor were dismissed on the grounds that Michigan had no law against assisted suicide and that the prosecutors failed to show that the doctor tripped the device used to effect the death. After additional instances of assisted suicide of terminally ill patients, the Michigan legislature enacted a bill banning assisted suicide. It became effective on April 1, 1993.

In succeeding years, the media reported numerous instances of alleged participation by Kevorkian in assisting terminally ill persons to commit suicide. After several unsuccessful attempts to prosecute Kevorkian, in 1999 a Michigan jury found him guilty of second-degree murder in the death of a man suffering from Lou Gehrig's disease. The court sentenced him to serve ten to twenty-five years in prison. The Michigan Court of Appeals affirmed his conviction and sentence. *People v. Kevorkian*, 639 N.W.2d 291 (Mich. App. 2001). The Supreme Court of Michigan denied his request for a further appeal, *People v. Kevorkian*, 642 N.W.2d 681 (Mich. 2002), and the U.S. Supreme Court denied his petition for a writ of certiorari. *Kevorkian v. Michigan*, 537 U.S. 881, 123 S.Ct. 90, 154 L.Ed.2d 137 (2002). Kevorkian was paroled on June 1, 2007, after having served eight years of his sentence. One of the conditions of his parole was that he could not help anyone else die.

During the 1990s, state laws that prohibit assisted suicide were challenged on constitutional grounds in instances where terminally ill patients seek to end their lives with the aid of a physician. Soon the state of Washington became the venue for a direct challenge to a state statute prohibiting assisted suicide, a challenge that would eventually lead to a seminal decision by the U.S. Supreme Court.

## The Washington Experience

In 1994 the Washington legislature enacted a law providing that "[a] person is guilty of promoting a suicide attempt when he knowingly causes or aids another person to attempt suicide." Wash. Rev. Code § 9A.36.060(1) (1994). "Promoting a suicide attempt" is a felony, punishable by up to five years' imprisonment and up to a $10,000 fine. § 9A.36.060(2). However, Washington's Natural Death Act, enacted in 1979, as amended in 1992, states that the "withholding or withdrawal of life sustaining treatment" at a patient's direction "shall not, for any purpose, constitute a suicide or a homicide." Wash. Rev. Code § 70.122.070(1).

In 1996 in *Compassion in Dying v. Washington*, 79 F.3d 790, the U.S. Court of Appeals for the Ninth Circuit, in an en banc decision, found a substantive due process right to physician-assisted suicide and held unconstitutional the Washington statute. In *Vacco v. Quill*, 80 F.3d 716 (2d Cir. 1996), the U.S. Court of Appeals for the Second Circuit addressed a similar New York statute and found that the Equal Protection Clause rendered it unconstitutional.

*Washington v. Glucksberg*, 521 U.S. 702, 117 S.Ct. 2258, 138 L.Ed.2d 772 (1997)

Here the Supreme Court unanimously upheld a prohibition of physician-assisted suicide enacted by the State of Washington. The case was brought originally by doctors who treated terminally ill, suffering patients. They stated that they would assist such patients in ending their lives were it not for Washington's ban on assisted suicide. The Supreme Court held that the Constitution provides no general right to doctor-assisted suicide under the

constitutional guarantee of due process. Applying a "rational basis test," the Court concluded that the "assisted suicide ban implicates a number of state interests," most notably an "unqualified interest in the preservation of human life." Writing for the Court, Chief Justice Rehnquist observed: "Throughout the Nation, Americans are engaged in an earnest and profound debate about the morality, legality, and practicality of physician assisted suicide. Our holding permits this debate to continue, as it should in a democratic society."

The U.S. Supreme Court granted certiorari and heard the two cases in tandem. In *Washington v. Glucksberg*, 521 U.S. 702, 117 S.Ct. 2258, 138 L.Ed.2d 772 (1997), the U.S. Supreme Court reversed the Ninth Circuit's decision. Writing for a unanimous Court, Chief Justice William Rehnquist pointed out that in almost every state it is a crime to assist in a suicide and that the statutes banning assisted suicide are long-standing expressions of the states' commitment to the protection and preservation of all human life. Rehnquist analyzed the interests that come into play in determining whether a statute banning assisted suicide passes constitutional muster. In doing so, the Court rejected any parallel between a person's right to terminate medical treatment and the "right" to have assistance in committing suicide. In *Vacco v. Quill*, 521 U.S. 793, 117 S.Ct. 2293, 138 L.Ed.2d 834 (1997), the Court held that New York's assisted-suicide ban did not violate the Equal Protection Clause of the Fourteenth Amendment.

## Competing Values in Suicide Laws

Laws against assisted suicide bring into play significant policy issues and require legislatures to balance carefully competing claims of individual liberty, ethics, and the interest of society. Some proponents of allowing assisted suicide argue that it simply enables a person who has a rational capacity to make a choice. Those who reject this view argue that the state has an interest in the preservation of life and that some individuals may elect to die needlessly as a result of misdiagnosis. Moreover, opponents of legalizing assisted suicide argue that allowing it leads to an indifference to the value of life. As a result of the Supreme Court's 1997 decision in *Washington v. Glucksberg*, supra, the states may enforce statutory bans on assisted suicide with more assurance, yet as the terminally ill population continues to increase, the debate is destined to continue. The Supreme Court's decision places that debate in the state legislatures and the state judicial tribunals.

Public opinion would seem to support the legalization of doctor-assisted suicide, at least in some instances. In a series of national surveys conducted between 1996 and 2005, the Gallup Organization asked, "When a person has a disease that cannot be cured and is living in severe pain, do you think doctors should or should not be allowed by law to assist the patient to commit suicide if the patient requests it?" In 1996, 52 percent of respondents said yes; in 2005, 58 percent answered in the affirmative. The Gallup Organization, Inc., The Gallup Poll, December 29, 2005.

### CASE-IN-POINT

### Doctor-Assisted Suicide

In 1997 Charles E. Hall, a mentally competent but terminally ill patient, and his physician, Cecil McIver, M.D., sought to have a Florida court declare that § 782.08, Florida Statutes, which prohibits assisted suicide, violated the Privacy Clause of the Florida Constitution and the Due Process and Equal Protection Clauses of the Fourteenth Amendment to the U.S. Constitution. They sought an injunction to keep the state attorney from prosecuting the physician for giving deliberate assistance to Hall in committing suicide. Basing its conclusion on Florida's privacy provision and the federal Equal Protection Clause, the trial court held that the Florida law could not be constitutionally enforced against Hall and McIver. The

Florida Supreme Court granted an expedited review. By the time it rendered its decision on July 17, 1997, the U.S. Supreme Court had ruled that state laws prohibiting assisted suicide pass muster under the federal constitution. On the basis of that decision, the Florida Supreme Court summarily disposed of the contention that the Florida law violated the U.S. Constitution. The court then proceeded to find that the explicit privacy provision in the Florida constitution was not violated by the state's 129-year-old statute prohibiting assisted suicide. In concluding its opinion, the court opted to leave "social policy" to the state legislature when it observed, "We do not hold that a carefully crafted statute authorizing assisted suicide would be unconstitutional."

*Krischer v. McIver*, 697 So.2d 97 (Fla. 1997).

Less than one month after the Supreme Court's decision in *Washington v. Glucksberg*, the Florida Supreme Court ruled that the state statute prohibiting assisted suicide did not offend the state constitution. *Krischer v. McIver*, 697 So.2d 97 (Fla. 1997). (See the Case-in-Point on assisted suicide.) In 2001 the Alaska Supreme Court held that the state constitution's guarantees of privacy and liberty do not afford terminally ill patients the right to a physician's assistance in committing suicide. *Sampson v. State*, 31 P.3d 88 (Alaska 2001).

## The Abortion Controversy

**abortion** The intentional termination of a pregnancy.

Abortion has been legally defined as the willful bringing about of the miscarriage of a pregnant woman. Under English common law, **abortion** was a misdemeanor, but only after quickening (that point in the pregnancy where the mother can feel the movement of the fetus inside her). As the Supreme Court recognized in *Roe v. Wade*, 410 U.S. 113, 132, 93 S.Ct 705, 716, 35 L.Ed 2d 147, 165 (1973), "It is undisputed that at common law, abortion performed before 'quickening'—the first recognizable movement of the fetus *in utero*, appearing usually from the 16th to the 18th week of pregnancy—was not an indictable offense." This was based on the belief that the soul entered the fetus at the time of quickening, thus making it alive.

In the late nineteenth century most states adopted statutes increasing the penalties for abortion and abolishing the quickening distinction. However, there was a tendency to provide that abortion was justified if physicians found it essential to save the mother's life. More-liberal statutes allowed abortions to be performed when one or two physicians advised that it was necessary to preserve the life or health of the mother. By 1970, a few states had even repealed criminal penalties for abortions where they were performed under medical supervision in the very early stages of a woman's pregnancy.

The 1960s and 1970s, a period of liberalized views on sexual practices, witnessed a clamor for liberalization of abortion laws. But before significant reforms occurred in most states, the U.S. Supreme Court entertained a challenge to the constitutionality of a Texas law that made it a felony to procure or attempt an abortion except one "procured or attempted by medical advice for the purpose of saving the life of the mother." Texas Rev. Crim. Stat., Arts. 1071–1076 (1911). In *Roe v. Wade*, supra, the Court held that this statute impermissibly interfered with a woman's constitutional right of privacy, which the Court determined to be "broad enough to encompass a woman's decision whether or not to terminate her pregnancy." 410 U.S. at 153, 93 S.Ct at 727, 35 L.Ed 2d at 177. Moreover, the Court held that the fetus is not a person and therefore has no constitutional right to life. At the same time the Court recognized the state's interest in protecting the unborn, an interest that becomes compelling at the point of **fetal viability**. The Court summarized its holding as follows:

**fetal viability** That point in pregnancy at which the fetus is capable of prolonged life outside the mother's womb.

(a) For the stage prior to approximately the end of the first trimester, the abortion decision and its effectuation must be left to the medical judgment of the pregnant woman's attending physician.

(b) For the stage subsequent to approximately the end of the first trimester, the State, in promoting its interest in the health of the mother, may, if it chooses, regulate the abortion procedure in ways that are reasonably related to maternal health.

(c) For the stage subsequent to viability, the State in promoting its interest in the potentiality of human life may, if it chooses, regulate, and even proscribe, abortion except where it is necessary, in appropriate medical judgment, for the preservation of the life or health of the mother. 410 U.S. at 164–165, 93 S.Ct at 732, 35 L.Ed 2d at 183–184.

The Court's decision had the effect of invalidating most state laws proscribing or regulating abortions, giving rise to an intense national debate that rages on today. As part of the national debate, Congress in the early 1980s considered but rejected a constitutional amendment to restrict abortions. In the 1980s and early 1990s, a more conservative Supreme Court modified *Roe* to allow states greater leeway in regulating abortions in such areas as waiting periods and required counseling. In the wake of one of these decisions, *Planned Parenthood v. Casey*, 505 U.S. 833, 112 S.Ct. 2791, 120 L.Ed.2d 674 (1992), supporters of abortion rights clamored for Congress to adopt a statute that would codify the holding in *Roe v. Wade*. In January 2004, supporters of abortion rights introduced into Congress the Freedom of Choice Act (FOCA), the express intent of which is to "prohibit, consistent with *Roe v. Wade*, the interference by the government with a woman's right to choose to bear a child or terminate a pregnancy, and for other purposes." Despite support from the Obama Administration, the bill did not pass Congress in 2009–2010 and was not reintroduced in 2011.

**partial-birth abortion** A method of abortion in which the fetus is partially delivered before its life is terminated and it is removed from the mother's body.

## Partial-Birth Abortion

In 1995 and 1997, Congress passed bills banning the medical procedure known as intact dilation and extraction, commonly referred to as **partial-birth abortion**. In each instance President Bill Clinton vetoed these measures. Several states, however, enacted laws proscribing partial-birth abortion; they were usually declared unconstitutional by

**JURISPRUDENCE**

*Stenberg v. Carhart*, 530 U.S. 914, 120 S.Ct. 2597, 147 L.Ed.2d 743 (2000)

LeRoy Carhart, a Nebraska physician, brought suit to challenge the constitutionality of a Nebraska law banning partial-birth abortions. In a sharply divided decision, the Supreme Court invalidated the Nebraska law. Writing for the Court in *Stenberg v. Carhart* (2000), Justice Stephen Breyer found that the law went well beyond the prohibition of late-term abortions and could be invoked to prohibit certain early-term abortions as well. In Breyer's view, the law, if allowed to stand, could be interpreted to prohibit the "dilation and evacuation" procedure, "the most commonly used method for performing previability second trimester abortions." In dissent, Justice Anthony Kennedy objected that the Court had repudiated the Court's earlier decision in *Planned Parenthood v. Casey* "by invalidating a statute advancing critical state interests, even though the law denies no woman the right to choose an abortion and places no undue burden upon the right." Kennedy characterized partial birth abortion as "a procedure many decent and civilized people find so abhorrent as to be among the most serious of crimes against human life. . ."

federal courts. The Nebraska Legislature enacted a statute defining partial-birth abortion as "an abortion procedure in which the person performing the abortion partially delivers vaginally a living unborn child before killing the unborn child and completing the delivery." Neb. Rev. Stat. Ann. § 28-326(9). In *Stenberg v. Carhart*, 530 U.S. 914, 120 S.Ct. 2597, 147 L.Ed.2d 743 (2000), the U.S. Supreme Court, in a 5–4 decision, invalidated the Nebraska law because it lacked an exception for the preservation of the health of the mother and imposed an undue burden on a woman's right to choose to have an abortion.

In November 2003 Congress enacted a new statute proscribing partial-birth abortions. Lower federal courts found the law unconstitutional, primarily because it contained no exception for performing the procedure where necessary for preserving the health of the mother. But the Supreme Court, dividing 5–4, reversed and upheld the statute. *Gonzales v. Carhart*, 550 U.S. 124, 127 S.Ct. 1610, 167 L.Ed.2d 480 (2007). Justice Anthony Kennedy, writing for the majority, explained that the government has a legitimate and substantial interest in preserving and promoting fetal life and in banning abortions that involve partial delivery of a living fetus. Relying on Congress's findings that the partial-birth abortion procedure is not necessary to protect the health of a pregnant woman, he further found there had been no showing that the act imposes an undue burden on a woman's right to an abortion based on a lack of a "health-of-the mother" exception. Dissenting, Justice Ruth Bader Ginsburg (joined by Justices Stephen Breyer, John Paul Stevens, and David Souter) viewed the decision as alarming in that the law contains no provision safeguarding a woman's health.

Abortion rights advocates see *Gonzales v. Carhart* as being harmful to a woman's health and interfering with a woman's decision making. Moreover, many view it as "chipping away" at women's rights under the Court's landmark 1973 decision in *Roe v. Wade*. On the other hand, prolife supporters herald the new decision as a recognition of the rights of the unborn and one that may open the door for state legislatures to enact further restrictions on abortion procedures.

## Laws Criminalizing Other Acts Resulting in the Death of a Fetus

Under common law a child was not considered born until the umbilical cord had been severed and the child's circulation became independent of its mother's. In the highly publicized case of *Keeler v. Superior Court*, 470 P.2d 617 (Cal. 1970), the California Supreme Court held that in enacting its homicide statute, the legislature intended it to follow the common-law rule that in order for there to be a homicide, the victim must be "born alive." Consequently, the court overturned a murder conviction where the defendant stomped on a pregnant woman's abdomen, thereby causing the death of her fetus. As a result, California amended § 187(a) of its penal code, which defines murder, to include the present language, *"the unlawful killing of a human being, or a fetus, with malice aforethought"* [emphasis added].

Nearly all states have laws criminalizing intentional acts other than medical abortion that result in death to a fetus. Some statutes explicitly limit the offense to instances where the fetus is "viable." See, e.g., Tenn. Code Ann. § 39-13-214. Other states, such as Michigan, prohibit the killing of an "unborn quick child." See, e.g., Mich. Stat. Ann. § 28.554. The Michigan Supreme Court has said that this law applies only to those fetuses that are viable. *Larkin v. Cahalan*, 208 N.W.2d 176 (Mich. 1973). Other state courts have generally followed the same approach in defining the term "unborn quick child."

In Tennessee, the killing of a viable fetus can be first-degree murder, second-degree murder, voluntary manslaughter, vehicular homicide, reckless homicide, or criminally negligent homicide, depending on the mental state of the perpetrator. Tenn. Code Ann. § 39-13-201 *et seq.*

The California Supreme Court has held that "viability is not an element of fetal homicide," but the state must demonstrate "that the fetus has progressed beyond the embryonic stage of seven to eight weeks." *People v. Taylor*, 86 P.3d 881 (Cal. 2004). Thus, under California state law, when a defendant commits murder of a pregnant woman, the prosecution can also charge the defendant with murder of an unborn child only if fetal development has progressed beyond the embryonic stage.

In some of the more conservative states, the killing of a fetus (other than through abortion) is a crime throughout pregnancy. For example, in South Carolina,

> (A)(1) A person who commits a violent crime . . . that causes the death of, or bodily injury to, a child who is *in utero* at the time that the violent crime was committed, is guilty of a separate offense under this section.
>
> (2)(a) Except as otherwise provided in this subsection, the punishment for a separate offense . . . is the same as the punishment provided for that criminal offense had the death or bodily injury occurred to the unborn child's mother. S.C. Code Ann. § 16-3-1083.

The South Carolina statute is controversial inasmuch as it does not require the unborn child to be viable. Under the South Carolina statute, the killing of a woman who is in the earliest stage of pregnancy can result in two counts of first-degree murder. In Virginia, by contrast, one "who unlawfully, willfully, deliberately and maliciously kills the fetus of another" is guilty of a Class 2 felony, which is punishable by five to forty years in prison. Va. Code Ann. § 18.2–32.2.

## Conclusion

The English common law provides the starting point for study of the law of homicide. But unlike England, America insisted that homicidal offenses be precisely defined. Crimes involving homicide bring into play separate categories of public opinion, which are represented by legislative judgments. While the public may disagree to some extent on definitions and degrees of culpability, there is near-universal support for proscribing murder, manslaughter, and vehicular homicide. Although courts and legislatures have restricted, and in some instances abolished, the felony murder rule, application of the rule remains controversial. Finally, ethical and religious opinions and secular views evoke considerable controversy on issues of suicide and abortion. These reactions are apparent in legislative proscriptions and in litigation involving the constitutionality of statutes proscribing suicide and abortion.

## Chapter Summary

- Learning Objective 1

    ○ Modern American laws on homicide are based on the English common law, which classified murder and manslaughter as criminal homicide, and classified noncriminal homicide as justifiable or excusable.

- Learning Objective 2

    ○ Modern statutes generally classify taking another's life with either malice aforethought or premeditation as first-degree murder. To obtain a conviction the prosecution must establish the defendant's specific intent to take the life of the accused. Comments made by a defendant before and after killing, use of grossly excessive force or infliction of lethal blows, and a history of altercations or ill will between the parties all bear on establishing malice aforethought or premeditation.

    ○ Second-degree murder is now frequently defined as "an unlawful killing of a human being by a person having a depraved mind or heart." It often becomes a residual classification applied to unlawful homicides not evidenced by malice aforethought or premeditation, not occurring in conjunction with other felonies, and not falling within the statutory definitions of manslaughter. Convictions often reflect a "jury pardon" where a jury concludes that circumstances surrounding the killing do not justify the penalty for first-degree murder, which is often death.

- Learning Objective 3

    ○ The common law developed a doctrine under which, where an accused was engaged in the commission of a felony and a homicide occurred, the felonious act substituted for proof of malice aforethought. Thus it became felony murder when an accused unintentionally killed a human being while committing, or attempting to commit, such common-law felonies as burglary, arson, rape, or robbery.

    ○ Today federal law and statutes in many states define felony murder, often limiting its applicability to specified felonies. A few states have abolished felony murder; in other jurisdictions the doctrine poses numerous questions and is subject to considerable criticism.

- Learning Objective 4

    ○ Today statutes often define manslaughter as the "unlawful killing of a human being without malice." Some abolish the common-law distinction between voluntary and involuntary manslaughter, but federal law and the laws of many states preserve the common-law distinction.

    ○ Irrespective of whether a killing is classified as voluntary or involuntary, certain scenarios typify manslaughter. These include death resulting from mutual combat, use of excessive force in defense of a family member or property, criminal negligence, and parental failure to provide medical attention for their children. Taking the life of another in a hot-blooded fury may lower the blameworthiness of an accused from murder to the manslaughter level.

- Learning Objective 5

  o Vehicular homicide is a common statutory offense often defined as "killing of a human being, or the killing of a viable fetus by any injury to the mother, caused by operation of a motor vehicle (or boat or other vehicle) in a reckless manner likely to cause the death of, or great bodily harm to, another."

- Learning Objective 6

  o Homicide is *justifiable* when a person takes another's life in obedience to a court judgment or when necessarily committed in overcoming actual resistance to execution of legal process.
  o Homicide is *excusable* when a person kills someone while resisting the decedent's attempts to murder or to inflict great bodily injury upon another; in defense of a person's home under certain circumstances; or in some instances of self-defense where there is a reasonable ground to apprehend imminent danger of great bodily harm to another.

- Learning Objective 7

  o The prosecution bears several burdens unique to homicide cases: First, it must establish the *corpus delicti*, or body of the crime. This requires proof that a person's death was caused by the criminal act or agency of another person.
  o Ordinarily death occurs when the heart stops beating and respiration ends; however, all jurisdictions have now adopted laws specifying that irreversible cessation of total brain functions constitutes death.
  o Second, the victim must have been alive before a killing took place and that the defendant's act was the proximate cause of the victim's death.
  o Finally, some jurisdictions follow the common-law rule that death of the victim must occur "within a year and a day." But today this rule has little relevance and most jurisdictions have abolished the rule by statute or judicial decision.

- Learning Objective 8

  o Common law imposed harsh penalties on the body and the estate of a person who committed suicide and against a person who assisted another in committing suicide.
  o Modern criminal laws make it an offense to cause or aid another person to commit suicide.
  o In 1997, the Supreme Court reversed federal appellate courts and held that statutes banning assisted suicide are long-standing expressions of the states' commitment to the protection and preservation of all human life.
  o On the other hand, in 2006, the Court held that the federal Controlled Substances Act did not authorize the Attorney General to prohibit doctors from prescribing regulated drugs for use in physician-assisted suicide as authorized by Oregon's Death with Dignity Act, which allows terminally ill adult patients to obtain a physician's prescription for a lethal dose of medication.

- Learning Objective 9

  ○ Judicial opinions vary as to when, under what circumstances, and by whom discontinuance of medical treatments may be ordered for minors and incompetents. Statutes in several states now address many of the problems in this area. Yet there is no statutory or judicial consensus on the procedures to effect discontinuance, and courts are cautious not to allow criminal prosecutions where life-sustaining procedures are removed based on medical advice and patient and family consent.

- Learning Objective 10

  ○ Under English common law, abortion was a misdemeanor, but only after quickening (that point in the pregnancy where the mother can feel the movement of the fetus inside her).

  ○ In its landmark decision in *Roe v. Wade* in 1973, the Supreme Court held that a woman's constitutional right to privacy allows her to obtain an abortion, effectively invalidating most state laws proscribing or regulating abortions.

  ○ In the 1980s and early 1990s, the Supreme Court modified *Roe* to allow states greater leeway in regulating abortions in such areas as waiting periods and required counseling.

  ○ In the 1990s several states enacted laws proscribing a procedure commonly referred to as "partial-birth abortion" and these laws were declared unconstitutional by lower federal courts. In 2000 the US Supreme Court struck down a Nebraska partial birth abortion statute. But relying on Congress's findings that the partial-birth abortion procedure is not necessary to protect the health of a pregnant woman, in 2007 the Supreme Court, in a 5–4 decision, upheld a 2003 act of Congress that bans abortions involving partial delivery of a living fetus. Dissenting justices argued that the act is unconstitutional because it does not include an exception for the mother's health.

  ○ Nearly all states now have laws criminalizing intentional acts (other than medical abortions) that result in death to a fetus. Some limit the offense to instances where the fetus is "viable." In some of the more conservative states, the killing of a fetus (other than through medical abortion) is a crime throughout pregnancy.

## Key Terms

| | |
|---|---|
| abortion | malice aforethought |
| assisted suicide | manslaughter |
| brain death | murder |
| *corpus delicti* | one-year-and-a-day rule |
| depraved mind or heart | partial-birth abortion |
| doctor-assisted suicide | premeditation |
| excusable homicide | provocation |
| felony murder | proximate cause |
| fetal viability | right to die |
| first-degree murder | second-degree murder |
| heat of passion | suicide |
| homicide | vehicular homicide |
| involuntary manslaughter | voluntary manslaughter |
| justifiable homicide | |

# Questions for Thought and Discussion

1. What circumstances are usually presented by the prosecution to bear on the issue of whether a killing was premeditated or with malice aforethought?
2. Describe some scenarios that might typify a conviction for second-degree murder.
3. Is it legitimate for a jury to find a defendant guilty of manslaughter in a case where there is evidence of premeditation, simply because members of the jury feel that the defendant was somewhat justified in taking the life of the victim?
4. How can the prosecution establish the *corpus delicti* in a murder case when the body of the victim cannot be found?
5. Compare the U.S. Supreme Court's 1997 opinion holding that there is no constitutional right to have assistance in committing suicide with the constitutional right of privacy discussed in Chapter 3. Can these views be logically reconciled?
6. Why has the common-law doctrine of felony murder become controversial among courts and legal scholars in recent years?
7. Is a state law making it a felony to kill an unborn child at any stage of development constitutional, notwithstanding the Supreme Court's decision in *Roe v. Wade*?

# Problems for Discussion and Solution

1. During a domestic quarrel, a wife continually taunted her husband by degrading him and telling him he was a "lousy lover" and that she wanted to be rid of him. When the husband tried to persuade her to relent she continued to taunt him in a louder voice. Finally, he grabbed a kitchen knife and stabbed her. As a result she died. The husband was convicted of second-degree murder. On appeal he argues his actions were taken during a "fit of passion" and seeks to have his conviction reduced from second-degree murder to manslaughter. Is he likely to succeed? Why or why not?
2. Shortly before midnight, a man is driving through a residential area in an attempt to get his wife, who is in labor, to the hospital. The posted speed limit is 30 m.p.h., but the anxious husband is driving 50 m.p.h. In a dark area, the car strikes and kills a ten-year-old boy who is playing in the middle of the street. Can the driver be convicted of (a) manslaughter or (b) vehicular homicide?
3. A male who is aware that he has been diagnosed with acquired immunodeficiency syndrome (AIDS) engages in sexual intercourse with a female. He does not inform the female that he has AIDS. As a result, the female contracts AIDS and dies from the disease two years later. Under the laws of your state, could the male be convicted of a homicidal act?
4. An intoxicated driver recklessly drove his vehicle into a car being driven by a woman who was seven months pregnant. As a result of the accident, the woman's baby was born prematurely, suffered from extensive brain damage, and died two days later. The state law defines a "person" as an individual "who has been born and is alive." Nevertheless, the state prosecuted the intoxicated driver, and a jury found him guilty of manslaughter. Do you think an appellate court should uphold the defendant's conviction? Why or why not?

## CHAPTER 7

# Other Offenses against Persons

## CHAPTER OUTLINE

## JURISPRUDENCE

*Smith v. Doe* (2003)

*United States v. Lanier* (1997)

## LEARNING OBJECTIVES

After reading this chapter, you should be able to explain

1. how the common law defined assault and battery and how modern statutes treat those offenses

2. why mayhem is no longer a frequently charged offense

3. the distinctly modern offenses of hazing, stalking, and cyberstalking

4. how the crime of rape has evolved significantly from its common-law origins

5. why statutory rape is a strict liability offense

6. why in some states certain nonconsensual sexual acts may be prosecuted as sodomy rather than rape or sexual battery

7. the controversy over sex offender registration laws

8. how and why legislatures have criminalized child abuse, spousal abuse, and elder abuse

9. how false imprisonment and kidnapping have evolved from their common-law origins

10. why Congress created federal civil rights offenses and hate crimes

# CHAPTER OPENING VIGNETTE

For thirty years prior to his retirement in 1999, Jerry Sandusky was a respected assistant coach for the Penn State Nittany Lions football team. He was twice named Assistant Coach of the Year by the American Football Coaches Association. He authored several books on coaching and even founded a charity to help underprivileged youth. He was a family man with six adopted children. In short, Sandusky appeared to be a pillar of the community and the consummate role model. However, Sandusky's public image was radically altered in November 2011 when a grand jury indicted him on charges of sexually abusing boys over a fifteen-year period. A month later, after additional victims came forward, the indictment was amended to add more charges. Sandusky's trial took place in June 2012 in Bellefonte, Pennsylvania. During the trial, jurors heard from eight victims, the youngest of which testified to more than twenty instances of sexual abuse beginning when he was only eleven years old. Sandusky publicly denied all the charges but did not take the witness stand at trial, as was his constitutional right. Rather, his attorney concentrated on raising doubts about the credibility of the prosecution witnesses. After an eight-day trial, the jury convicted Sandusky of forty-five charges, including multiple counts of "involuntary deviate sexual intercourse," "indecent assault," "unlawful contact with minors," and "endangering the welfare of children." Under Pennsylvania law, the sixty-eight-year-old Sandusky faced more than four hundred years in prison, effectively a life sentence.

In recent years American society has come to recognize the seriousness and prevalence of child sexual abuse. Victimization extends far beyond the injury and suffering inflicted during the act, as victims often develop serious psychological problems later in life. The criminal law has sought to deal with the problem of child sexual abuse by creating offenses beyond those recognized at common law, relaxing statutes of limitations, and by establishing registries to keep track of sex offenders. Nevertheless, because victims often do not come forward until many years after the abuse has occurred, these cases are difficult to prosecute. Clearly, dealing with child sexual abuse is one of the major challenges facing our criminal justice system today.

# Introduction

As with homicide offenses, the English common law provided the basis for other crimes against persons. But by the 1800s America's quest for representative government and its penchant for definiteness and certainty, combined with the standards of written constitutions, resulted in legislative definitions of crimes. Defining offenses against persons became primarily a state rather than a federal legislative function, and the new states followed the common-law themes, making variations deemed necessary in the new social, economic, and political environment. As the United States became urbanized, more densely populated, and increasingly mobile, the areas of conduct initially defined as criminal offenses against persons required revision and, in many instances, enlargement.

Under modern statutes, assault and battery are classified according to their seriousness, the character of the victim, and the environment in which these crimes are committed, and legislatures have created new crimes against persons such as stalking and, more recently, "cyberstalking." Conduct that constituted the offense of mayhem at common law is now often prosecuted under various forms of assaultive crimes.

In recent years contemporary moral standards have caused the offense of rape to be expanded into a more comprehensive, gender-neutral offense of sexual battery, with new emphasis on the victim's age and vulnerability. And laws prohibiting consensual sodomy between adults, a felony at common law, have been found unconstitutional by the U.S. Supreme Court. *Lawrence v. Texas*, 539 U.S. 558, 123 S.Ct. 2472, 156 L.Ed.2d 508 (2003).

The offense of false imprisonment is essentially the same as at common law, but the crime of kidnapping, which today focuses on child abduction, serves a much different role in American society than it did under the English common law.

As noted in Chapter 4, common-law crimes required proof of a criminal intent. In contrast, many statutory crimes—for example, the sale of intoxicants to minors and consensual sexual relations between an adult and a minor—now fall in the category of strict liability offenses. In contemporary society there is a new emphasis on enforcement of civil rights laws that originated in the post–Civil War environment and have been supplemented by modern enactments. Finally, in an effort to curb intimidation, many states now proscribe certain conduct as "hate crimes."

# Assaultive Offenses

**assault** The attempt to inflict bodily injury upon another person.

**battery** The unlawful use of force against another person that entails some injury or offensive touching.

**Assault** and **battery**, though commonly referred to together, were separate misdemeanor offenses at common law. An assault was basically an attempted battery. It consisted of an attempt to do bodily harm to another using force and violence, while a battery was a completed or consummated assault. Although an actual touching was not required, words alone did not constitute an assault. The common law made no distinction between classes or degrees of assault and battery, but dealt more severely with aggravated cases.

## Modern Statutory Developments

Today all jurisdictions make assault a crime, and most make battery a crime as well. Assault is defined by statute, as is battery, and sometimes the term "assault and battery" is used to indicate one offense. Simple assaults and batteries generally remain misdemeanors, whereas those perpetrated against public officers

**aggravated assault** An assault committed with a dangerous weapon or with intent to commit a felony.

**aggravated battery** A battery committed by use of an instrument designed to inflict great bodily harm on the victim.

(e.g., fire and police personnel) are frequently classified as felonies. Legislatures commonly classify as felonies more egregious assaultive conduct such as **aggravated assault**, **aggravated battery**, and assault with intent to commit other serious crimes.

The California Penal Code defines an assault as "an unlawful attempt, coupled with a present ability, to commit a violent injury on the person of another." West's Ann. Cal. Penal Code § 240. It imposes increased penalties for an assault committed on a person engaged in performing the duties of a peace officer, firefighter, lifeguard, process server, paramedic, physician, or nurse. West's Ann. Cal. Penal Code § 241(c). Like most states, California makes it a felony to commit an assault with a deadly weapon or with force likely to produce great bodily injury. West's Ann. Cal. Penal Code § 245. Many states classify this latter offense as aggravated assault. For example, under Florida law, a person who commits an assault with a deadly weapon without intent to kill or an assault with intent to commit a felony is guilty of aggravated assault, a felony offense. West's Fla. Stat. Ann. § 784.021.

The California Penal Code defines as battery "any willful and unlawful use of force or violence upon the person of another." West's Ann. Cal. Penal Code § 242. The code also specifies increased punishment for batteries committed against specific classes of officers, West's Ann. Cal. Penal Code § 243.6, or those committed on school property, park property, or hospital grounds, West's Ann. Cal. Penal Code § 243.2. Consistent with its handling of aggravated assaults, Florida law classifies a battery resulting in great bodily harm, permanent disability, or permanent disfigurement, or one committed with a deadly weapon, as an aggravated battery, an even more serious felony than aggravated assault. West's Fla. Stat. Ann. § 784.045.

Although most assault and battery prosecutions occur under state laws, the federal government also has a role in this area. Federal statutes proscribe assault within the maritime and territorial jurisdiction of the United States. 18 U.S.C.A. § 113. Interestingly, federal courts have held that the statute covers the entire range of assaults, *United States v. Eades*, 615 F.2d 617 (4th Cir. 1976), and that the word "assault" includes acts that would constitute batteries under most state laws. *United States v. Chaussee*, 536 F.2d 637 (7th Cir. 1976). Additional federal statutes proscribe assaults on federal officers, including members of the uniformed services engaged in the performance of official duties, 18 U.S.C.A. § 111, and assaults on foreign diplomatic and other official personnel, 18 U.S.C.A. § 112.

**CASE-IN-POINT**

### Assault with a Deadly Weapon

Rasor, a police officer, stopped a vehicle and attempted to arrest the driver, Jackson, for driving while intoxicated. As he did, a fight broke out between the officer and Jackson. At that point, the defendant, Lloyd Gary, a passenger in Jackson's car, approached the two combatants, removed the officer's pistol, and pointed it at Rasor and Jackson. Gary was convicted of assault with a deadly weapon. On appeal, he argued that the trial judge erred in not directing the jury to return a verdict of not guilty because the evidence showed no attempt to commit a physical injury. The Arizona Supreme Court rejected Gary's argument, saying that "[t]he pointing of a gun may constitute 'an assault' . . . and it is not necessary to show in addition that there was an intent to do physical harm to the victim."

*State v. Gary*, 543 P.2d 782, 783 (Ariz. 1975).

## Common Illustrations of Simple and Aggravated Assault and Battery

Statutory definitions vary, but under most statutes a simple assault would include a threat to strike someone with the fist or a small stone, or simply a missed punch. Firing a shot in the direction of a person or threatening someone with a weapon would probably qualify as aggravated assault. A battery, on the other hand, involves some physical contact with the victim. Common illustrations of simple battery include hitting or pushing someone, a male hugging and kissing a female—or even an offensive touching—if against her will; using excessive force in breaking up a fight; intentionally tripping another individual; or using excessive force (by a parent or teacher) in disciplining a child. The acts referred to above as constituting aggravated assault, if completed, would most likely be prosecuted as aggravated batteries. When courts must determine whether an assault or battery is "aggravated," two questions commonly arise: first, what constitutes a "deadly weapon," and second, whether the defendant's conduct results in "great bodily harm." For example, the South Carolina Supreme Court observed,

> Circumstances of aggravation include the use of a deadly weapon, the intent to commit a felony, infliction of serious bodily injury, great disparity in the ages or physical conditions of the parties, a difference in gender, the purposeful infliction of shame and disgrace, taking indecent liberties or familiarities with a female, and resistance to lawful authority. *State v. White*, 605 S.E.2d 540 (S.C. 2004).

Courts have no difficulty in finding that a gun, a knife, a club, or an axe is a deadly weapon. Other objects such as a pocketknife, hammer, rock, or walking cane, while not dangerous instruments per se, may under certain circumstances cause death or serious bodily injury.

What constitutes great or serious bodily injury is a factual determination not subject to a precise definition; however, the Indiana Supreme Court has stated that the term "great bodily harm" means "great as distinguished from slight, trivial, minor or moderate harm, and as such does not include mere bruises as are likely to be inflicted in a simple assault and battery." *Froedge v. State*, 233 N.E.2d 631, 636 (Ind. 1968). In making factual determinations of whether an injury constitutes a "serious" or "great" bodily injury, courts consider the type of injury the victim has suffered, as well as the instrument by which the injury was inflicted, and any disability that the victim will suffer. In many instances courts make the determination of whether the use of one's body can be a "deadly weapon" by focusing on the manner in which such body parts are used in committing an assault or battery. For example, in *Jefferson v. State*, 974 S.W.2d 887 (Tex. App. 1998), the court upheld a defendant's conviction for aggravated assault where the defendant struck the victim in the face four times with his fist and the victim suffered a broken nose, lacerations, and bleeding. In *State v. Bolarinho*, 850 A.2d 907, 910 (R.I. 2004), the Rhode Island Supreme Court noted that it is the object's capability and manner of use that is determinative of whether an object qualifies as a dangerous weapon. The court held that a person's foot can qualify as a dangerous weapon, particularly when employed with karate-like precision. Many other courts have considered hands and fists to be deadly weapons for purposes of assault with a deadly weapon, given the manner in which they were used and the relative size and condition of the parties involved. See, e.g., West's N.C.G.S.A. § 14-33; *State v. Yarrell*, 616 S.E.2d 258 (N.C. App. 2005).

In *State v. Flemming*, 19 S.W.3d 195, 197 (Tenn. 2000), the Tennessee Supreme Court took a contrary view and held that feet and fists are not deadly weapons

## Aggravated Assault and Battery

**CASE-IN-POINT**

Towers was arrested and convicted of aggravated assault and battery. The evidence during the bench trial revealed that Towers "visited a friend's house to return a car bed." The victim, a thirteen-year-old girl, "was in the house 'babysitting' for a child two years of age and an infant of six months." The victim knew Towers and prior to the incident in question Towers "had always acted toward her as a gentleman." After a brief conversation, Towers grabbed her "and kissed her on the cheek and lips." The victim "immediately asked" Towers to leave her alone, "but Towers continued to hold her and proceeded to touch her breasts and place one of his hands between her legs in contact with her 'private part' from outside her clothing." Upon further demands by the victim to stop, Towers complied and left the premises. Towers argued on appeal that the finding of "aggravated" was unsupported by the evidence. In addressing the issue, the Supreme Court of Maine examined the relevant precedents and concluded "assault and battery may become 'high and aggravated in nature' by the presence of "circumstances of aggravation, such as . . . great disparity between the ages and physical conditions of the parties, a difference in the sexes, indecent liberties or familiarities with a female, and the purposeful infliction of shame and disgrace." Furthermore, the court stated, "What intention could the respondent have had other than an evil intention to indulge his own lustful desires? By his indecent acts he violated the person and dignity of the child in a manner abhorrent to society." As a result, the Supreme Court of Maine affirmed Towers's conviction.

*State v. Towers*, 304 A.2d 75 (Me. 1973).

---

under Tennessee Code Annotated § 39-11-106(a)(5). The court commented, "Were we to interpret the statute to be written broadly enough to include one's fists and feet within the statutory definition of 'deadly weapon,' it would lead to an absurd result—the merger of simple and aggravated offenses—which would contradict the expressed intent of the General Assembly."

## The Burden of the Prosecution

The proof required to establish assaultive offenses depends on the statutory language of the offense. To convict a defendant of simple assault or battery, the prosecution generally needs only to prove the act and the defendant's general, not specific, intent. In aggravated assault and aggravated battery prosecutions, courts have arrived at different interpretations of the intent requirement, but proof of the defendant's general intent is usually sufficient. In contrast, if a defendant is prosecuted for committing an assault or battery "with the intent to do great bodily harm" or "with the intent to commit a specific felony, for example, murder," courts generally require the prosecution to prove the defendant's specific intent to accomplish those results.

## Defenses to Charges of Assault and Battery

Many forms of conduct involving intentional use of physical force do not constitute batteries. In many instances, there is an express or implied consent of the person against whom the physical force is exerted. Reasonableness is the test applied in sports contests and friendly physical encounters. Everyday examples include such contact sports as football, in which the participants obviously consent to forceful bodily contact. The physician who performs surgery with consent of the patient provides another example of physical contact that, if properly applied, does not constitute a battery. Reasonableness is also the test applied to interpersonal relationships. Thus, although a person might imply consent to a friendly kiss or caress, seldom could a person imply consent to an act of violence, even when done under the guise of affection.

Statutory law regulates the degree of force that can be used by teachers, police officers, and correction officials, and an excessive use of force may constitute a battery. Likewise, parents, guardians, and those standing *in loco parentis* have a right to impose reasonable punishment when disciplining a child but must consider the child's age, health, size, and all other relevant circumstances. Parents who inflict injury on a child or who impose excessive punishment may be guilty of committing a simple or even an aggravated battery. They may also be subject to prosecution under modern statutes proscribing child abuse.

A person charged with battery can defend the action by showing that the touching or hitting was unintentional, that the physical force used was reasonable, or that the action was taken in self-defense. Self-defense is subject to qualifications, as we explain in Chapter 14. Defenses applicable to the offense of battery generally apply as well to a charge of assault. The theory is that a person who fails to make physical contact with another can defend on the same basis of reasonableness or self-defense as a person who successfully commits a battery.

## Mayhem

**mayhem** At common law, the crime of injuring someone so as to render that person less able to fight.

At common law, **mayhem** consisted of willfully and maliciously injuring another so as to render the victim less able to fight. Mayhem became a statutory crime in most states, with some statutes extending the common law definition to include injuries that disfigure a person. In most instances it is a general-intent offense; however, some statutes require proof of the actor's specific intent to maim or disfigure the victim. Mayhem statutes are less common today because many of the acts formerly prosecuted under these laws are now prosecuted under such statutory crimes as aggravated battery and attempted murder.

## Hazing

**hazing** Intentional or reckless physical or mental harassment, abuse, or humiliation, often as part of an initiation.

**Hazing** consists of intentional or reckless physical or mental harassment, abuse, or humiliation. It frequently occurs in the process of initiation into clubs, fraternities, sororities, athletic teams, and other groups. Hazing sometimes merely consists of foolish pranks, but too often it has resulted in serious injuries to the initiate. In recent years state legislatures in the great majority of states have enacted statutes making hazing in all schools and colleges either a misdemeanor or felony, depending on the degree of injury to the initiate. The objective of antihazing statutes is to prevent or severely curtail the practice of hazing. Currently many national fraternities and sororities have adopted prohibitions or restrictions on the hazing activities of local chapters. Likewise, many colleges and universities have explicit prohibitions on hazing. See, e.g., *Buttny v. Smiley*, 281 F. Supp. 280 (D. Colo. 1968) (upholding antihazing rule at University of Colorado). Hazing is also prohibited in the armed forces academies. See 10 U.S.C.A. §§ 4352, 6964, 6965, 9352. Moreover, antihazing statutes do not restrict prosecutions, and, in some instances, egregious conduct can be prosecuted under other statutes as a felony, for example, aggravated battery.

The Maryland legislature has enacted a rather typical antihazing statute:

(a) A person may not recklessly or intentionally do an act or create a situation that subjects a student to the risk of serious bodily injury for the purpose of an initiation into a student organization of a school, college, or university.

(b) A person who violates this section is guilty of a misdemeanor and on conviction is subject to imprisonment not exceeding 6 months or a fine not exceeding $500 or both.

(c) The implied or express consent of a student to hazing is not a defense under this section. Md. Code, Crim. Law § 3-607.

In rejecting an attack on the constitutionality of the statute, the Maryland Court of Special Appeals held that the state has a compelling interest in preventing violent or dangerous initiation activities on campuses and found that the law is not vague and does not violate freedoms of association and assembly guaranteed by the First Amendment. The court further observed that the statute "does not reach students' rights to participate in fraternities, sororities, or other organizations, does not reach such conduct as yelling at or insulting pledges, and does not reach such conduct as requiring pledges to don matching tee shirts, memorize silly songs, or run errands for and serve meals to regular members. . . ." *McKenzie v. State*, 748 A.2d 67, 72 (Md. App. 2000).

# Stalking

**stalking** Following or placing a person under surveillance and threatening that person with bodily harm, sexual assault, confinement, or restraint, or placing that person in reasonable fear of bodily harm, sexual assault, confinement, or restraint.

By the late 1980s, persons who were being continually followed, threatened, or harassed by others were beginning to file complaints with law enforcement officers. Most complainants were women targeted by former suitors or celebrities who were being constantly followed by obsessive fans. Police began to refer to this type of behavior as **stalking**, which consists of repeatedly following, watching or harassing another person, often to enforce a relationship. But they were hampered in taking action to protect victims until after harm occurred to them. Police and prosecutors who felt that the traditional protections of the criminal law were not always sufficient to protect victims from stalking urged legislators to adopt statutes to help them combat the problem.

In 1989 an obsessed fan shot and killed actress Rebecca Schaeffer in California after stalking her for two years. In 1990 this led the California legislature to enact the first law making stalking a crime. By 1994 all states and the District of Columbia had enacted laws defining stalking and making it either a misdemeanor or a felony. Some stalking statutes require proof of a stalker's specific intent, while in others proof of a general intent suffices. Some require that stalking must have frightened the victim; others require only that the stalking would cause a reasonable person to experience fear.

In 1996 Congress enacted a law to protect persons against stalking when the perpetrator has crossed state lines to commit the crime. The federal statute was amended as part of the Violence against Women Act (VAWA) of 2000. It makes it a crime to stalk someone across state or tribal lines where the stalker has the intent to kill, injure, harass, or intimidate a victim. 18 U.S.C.A. § 2261A(1). In a report entitled *Stalking Victimization in the United States* (January 2009), the Bureau of Justice Statistics noted that during 2006 an estimated 3.4 million persons age eighteen or older were victims of stalking.

In what is often considered to be one of the toughest laws on stalking, the Illinois Criminal Code makes stalking another person a felony and provides that a person guilty of aggravated stalking is guilty of an even more serious felony. As amended, Illinois law now provides:

(a) A person commits stalking when he or she, knowingly and without lawful justification, on at least two separate occasions follows another person or places the person under surveillance or any combination thereof and:

(1) at any time transmits a threat of immediate or future bodily harm, sexual assault, confinement or restraint and the threat is directed towards that person or a family member of that person; or

(2) places that person in reasonable apprehension of immediate or future bodily harm, sexual assault, confinement or restraint; or

(3) places that person in reasonable apprehension that a family member will receive immediate or future bodily harm, sexual assault, confinement, or restraint.

(a-5) A person commits stalking when he or she has previously been convicted of stalking another person and knowingly and without lawful justification on one occasion:

(1) follows that same person or places that same person under surveillance; and

(2) transmits a threat of immediate or future bodily harm, sexual assault, confinement or restraint; and

(3) the threat is directed towards that person or a family member of that person.

Subsection (d) of the statute states that a defendant "places a person under surveillance" by: (1) remaining present outside the person's school, place of employment, vehicle, other place occupied by the person, or residence other than the residence of the defendant; or (2) placing an electronic tracking device on the person or the person's property. Subsection (e) stipulates that the words "follows another person" mean "(i) to move in relative proximity to a person as that person moves from place to place or (ii) to remain in relative proximity to a person who is stationary or whose movements are confined to a small area." However, subsection (e) points out that following another person does not include following within the residence of the defendant. Subsection (g) defines "transmit[ting] a threat" as giving a "verbal or written threat or a threat implied by a pattern of conduct or a combination of verbal or written statements or conduct." Finally, subsection (h) broadly defines "family member." 720 Ill. Comp. Stat. Ann. § 5/12-7.3.

In Illinois a person commits aggravated stalking when he or she, in conjunction with committing the offense of stalking, also does any of the following:

(1) causes bodily harm to the victim;
(2) confines or restrains the victim; or
(3) violates a temporary restraining order, an order of protection, or an injunction prohibiting the behavior described in subsection (b)(1) of Section 214 of the Illinois Domestic Violence Act of 1986. 720 Ill. Comp. Stat. Ann. § 5/12-7.4(a).

During the 1990s a number of defendants attacked stalking laws on grounds that the laws violated the First Amendment to the U.S. Constitution. In *People v. Bailey*, 657 N.E.2d 953 (Ill. 1995), the Illinois Supreme Court upheld its stalking laws against challenges that the statutes were unconstitutionally vague and overbroad and that they intruded on the right to freedom of speech. As pointed out in *People v. Baer*, 973 P.2d 1225 (Colo. 1999), the majority of courts have upheld the constitutionality of stalking laws in various states. In 2007 a Colorado appellate court upheld a defendant's conviction for harassment and stalking where he repeatedly contacted a victim through letters and phone calls and threatened to overwhelm her with lawsuits to bring her to financial ruin if she would not communicate with him. *People v. Richardson*, 181 P.3d 340 (Colo. App. 2007).

Nevertheless, in some instances defendants have prevailed in such attacks. For example, in *Commonwealth v. Kwiatkowski*, 637 N.E.2d 854 (Mass. 1994), the Massachusetts Supreme Judicial Court held the state's stalking statute to be unconstitutional because the uncertain meaning of "repeated patterns of conduct" and "repeated series of acts" rendered the statute vague, thereby failing to give a person of ordinary intelligence fair notice of what conduct is forbidden. Where appellate courts have found infirmities in statutory language, state legislatures usually have made necessary changes in wording to avoid such further challenges. For example, litigation over what constitutes a "credible threat" caused some state legislatures to eliminate that term from their stalking statutes.

## Cyberstalking

**cyberstalking** Harassing and threatening a person through persistent online contact so that the person is placed in fear for his or her safety.

Following the increased use of computers, many people complained of being victims of relentless e-mail messages. **Cyberstalking**, sometimes referred to as "stalking by proxy," often involved some prankster or disappointed suitor placing a female's name online with suggestive data directed to third parties. But today cyberstalking is not limited to female victims; often males complain. The anonymity of the Internet makes it extremely difficult for law enforcement agencies to track down cyberstalkers. The problem is exacerbated by the availability of personal data on the Internet and, in addition to e-mail messages, cyberstalking often includes such electronic forms as blogs, bulletin boards, chat rooms, and Internet sites.

Title 18 U.S.C.A. § 2261A(2) makes it a federal crime to stalk someone across state, tribal, or international lines using regular mail, e-mail, or the Internet with the intent to kill or injure the victim, or to place the victim, a family member, or a spouse or intimate partner of the victim in fear of death or serious bodily injury.

**CASE-IN-POINT**

### Evidence Sufficient to Affirm Defendant's Conviction for Menacing by Stalking

Christopher G. Schwab appealed his conviction for "menacing by stalking" in violation of Ohio Rev. Code § 2903.211, which prohibits a person from engaging in a pattern of conduct causing mental distress to another person. In his appeal Schwab argued that the evidence did not show that he caused the victim mental distress and did not establish his guilt beyond a reasonable doubt.

The evidence at the defendant's trial disclosed that Schwab and his female victim had lived together in a romantic relationship for about two years. On March 5, 1996, she moved out of their apartment and moved in with her parents. When the defendant phoned her the next day at her parents' home she informed him they were "broken up" and that she did not love him or want to be with him or talk to him. She told Schwab not to call her because the calls were upsetting her and her family. Between the time she moved out and April 1, 1996, Schwab sent the victim a number of unwanted letters and flowers. He followed the victim on more than one occasion and tried to obtain information about her college class schedule from the university she attended. These actions, the victim testified, caused her to become frightened. The court found that the evidence was sufficient to establish that the defendant's actions caused the victim mental distress and to support the defendant's conviction for menacing by stalking.

*State v. Schwab*, 695 N.E.2d 801 (Ohio App. 1997).

Illinois has now specifically criminalized cyberstalking as a felony, providing:

(a) A person commits cyberstalking when he or she, knowingly and without lawful justification on at least 2 separate occasions, harasses another person through use of electronic communication and:

> (1) at any time transmits a threat of immediate or future bodily harm, sexual assault, confinement, or restraint and the threat is directed toward that person or a family member of that person, or

> (2) places that person or a family member of that person in reasonable apprehension of immediate or future bodily harm, sexual assault, confinement, or restraint. 720 Ill. Comp. Stat. Ann. § 5/12-7.5.

Several other states have amended their statutory definitions of stalking to include cyberstalking. For example, in 2004 the Florida legislature amended West's Fla. Stat. Ann. § 784.048 to define cyberstalking as "to engage in a course of conduct to communicate, or to cause to be communicated, words, images, or language by or through the use of electronic mail or electronic communication, directed at a specific person, causing substantial emotional distress to that person and serving no legitimate purpose."

# Rape and Sexual Battery

**carnal knowledge** An antiquated term for sexual intercourse.

**common-law rape** Rape as it was defined by the English common law, i.e., sexual intercourse by a male with a female, other than his wife, by force and against the will of the female.

**forcible rape** Sexual intercourse by force and against the will of the victim.

**statutory rape** The strict liability offense of having sexual intercourse with a minor, irrespective of the minor's consent.

**marital exception** The traditional common-law principle that a husband could not be guilty of raping his wife.

**Hale's Rule** English common law doctrine credited to Sir Matthew Hale, Lord Chief Justice in the seventeenth century, holding that a husband could not be charged with the rape of his wife.

There are early biblical accounts of the offense of rape; however, the law of rape, as it exists today, has its roots in the early English common law. It was a felony for a male to have unlawful **carnal knowledge** of (that is, sexual intercourse with) a female by force and against her will. This is usually referred to as **common-law rape** or **forcible rape**. In later stages of the English law, it became a statutory offense for a man to have carnal knowledge of a female child less than ten years of age with or without the child's consent. This latter offense came to be known as **statutory rape**.

The common-law offenses required penetration, however slight, of the female's sexual organ by the male sexual organ; no emission of seed was required. At common law, there was a conclusive presumption that a male under age fourteen could not commit the crime of rape.

Common-law rape contemplated unlawful intercourse; therefore, a husband could not be guilty of raping his wife. Although this **marital exception** is of somewhat dubious judicial origin, it is generally referred to as **Hale's Rule** and is credited to the writings of Sir Matthew Hale, who served as Lord Chief Justice in England from 1671 to 1676. Of course, in egregious cases the husband could be charged with assault or battery of his wife. Furthermore, a husband or even another woman could be charged as an aider or abettor if he or she assisted or procured another man to rape a wife.

More than two centuries after Hale's demise, in March 1991, England's Court of Appeal dismissed an appeal by a man who was convicted of an attempted rape of his estranged wife. In delivering the opinion of the five-judge court, the Lord Chief Justice observed that a rapist remains a rapist irrespective of his relationship with his victim. Further, the court observed that the centuries-old legal doctrine that a husband could not be guilty of raping his wife no longer represented the law, considering the position of a wife in contemporary society.

## The American Approach

The new American states followed the common-law scheme in statutorily defining rape; however, two principal changes soon occurred. First, many states explicitly rejected the common-law presumption that males under age fourteen could not commit the offense. Second, legislatures in most states made consensual intercourse with a young female an offense (statutory rape) if the female was younger than sixteen or eighteen, rather than ten. Some, however, added the qualification that the female must have been "of previous chaste character."

American courts disagreed on the intent required for a defendant to be guilty of rape, and most held that no intent other than that evidenced by the act of intercourse was needed. See, e.g., *Walden v. State*, 156 S.W.2d 385 (Tenn. 1941).

Courts in American jurisdictions struggled with the requirements of **force** and **consent** in the law of rape. Some judges instructed juries that "for the defendant to be found guilty of rape, you must find that the woman resisted to her utmost." Later cases recognized degree of resistance as a relative matter dependent on all the circumstances surrounding the incident. Yet courts continued to recognize that resistance generally had to be more than a mere negative verbal response by a female.

All courts recognized that to constitute common-law rape, intercourse had to be without the female's consent. However, consent by a woman who was asleep, unconscious, or mentally deficient and consent obtained by fraud or impersonation or through pretext were invalid. Thus, if a man impersonated a woman's husband and caused her to submit to sexual intercourse, he would be guilty of rape. Likewise, a physician who had intercourse with female patients who were not conscious of the nature of the doctor's acts because of the treatments being administered was properly found guilty of rape. *People v. Minkowski*, 23 Cal.Rptr. 92 (Cal. App. 1962).

**force** The element of compulsion in such crimes against persons as rape and robbery.

**consent** Voluntarily yielding to the will or desire of another person.

## Statutory Rape Laws

In America, state legislatures enacted laws to protect young women from sexual intercourse. These statutory rape laws usually stipulate that carnal knowledge (sexual intercourse) with a female under age sixteen, seventeen, or eighteen is a crime. In contrast with common-law rape, the elements of force and consent are irrelevant in statutory rape laws. In effect, underage females are deemed unable to validly consent to sexual relations. A few states have allowed a male to defend against a charge of statutory rape on the basis that he was mistaken about the female's age, but most hold a male defendant strictly liable even if he made a reasonable inquiry in good faith to determine the victim's age. (The concept of a strict liability offense is explained in Chapter 4.)

Statutory rape laws are now gender-neutral in most states, and some impose penalties only if there is at least a two- to five-year disparity between the ages of the perpetrator and the underage party. Obviously, it would be inconceivable to prosecute every minor who has a consensual sexual relationship. The original objective of statutory rape laws was to protect the chastity of young females; however, those who support these laws now emphasize both the psychological effects and the threat of disease that accompany sexual encounters involving minors. They also point out that it is adult males who impregnate most teenage mothers and that, when vigorously enforced, statutory rape laws that focus on sexual relationships involving age discrepancies of several years are one solution to the problem of teenage pregnancy. Some states have graded voluntary sexual battery offenses by considering the age of a perpetrator who engages in sex with a minor. For example, in 1996 the Florida legislature made it a second-degree felony for a person age twenty-four or older to engage in sex with a person age sixteen or seventeen. West's Fla. Stat. Ann. § 794.05.

There is universal agreement that very young children should be protected from sexual predators, but there is considerable opposition to statutory rape laws. Opponents argue that these laws are out of touch with present-day sexual mores. Some see statutory rape laws as depriving women in their late teens of exercising a personal choice; others point out that these laws are largely unobserved and lend themselves to selective enforcement along the lines of race and social class. Despite the conflict in views, it appears that for the foreseeable future statutory rape laws, now often termed "voluntary sexual assault or battery" laws, will remain on the American legal scene.

## Reform in the American Law of Rape

During the late 1970s and the 1980s, protests led to several statutory and judicial reforms in the law of rape. As societal awareness increased, legislatures and courts came to realize that marriage in contemporary society is regarded as a partnership and should not be deemed a license to enjoy sex on demand by a forcible encounter with one's spouse.

Legislative reforms focused on revising statutes by

**gender-neutral offense** A crime that may be committed by members of either sex against members of either sex.

- Defining rape as a **gender-neutral offense**, whereby the offender and victim may be of either sex
- Criminalizing forced sexual relations between spouses or cohabitants. For example, Connecticut law defines "sexual intercourse" very broadly and states, "No spouse or cohabiter shall compel the other spouse or cohabiter to engage in sexual intercourse by the use of force against such other spouse or cohabiter, or by the threat of the use of force against such other spouse or cohabiter which reasonably causes such other spouse or cohabiter to fear physical injury." Conn. Gen. Stat. Ann. § 53a-70b.
- Expanding common-law definitions to include anal, oral, or vaginal penetrations by a sex organ or another object, excepting acts performed for *bona fide* medical purposes.
- Dividing the offense of sexual battery into classifications and degrees, and providing punishment based on the type of sexual conduct or contact, the force used, and the age and vulnerability of the victim.
- Enacting **rape shield laws**, which preclude presentation of evidence of a victim's prior sexual activity with anyone other than the defendant.

**rape shield laws** Statutes that protect the identity of a rape victim and/or prevent disclosure of a victim's sexual history.

## Rape Shield Laws

Rape shield laws are designed "to protect the victims of sexual assault from humiliating and embarrassing public fishing expeditions into their sexual conduct; to overcome victims' reluctance to report incidents of sexual assault; and to protect victims from psychological or emotional abuse in court as the price of their cooperation in prosecuting sex offenders." *State v. Guthrie*, 518 S.E.2d 83, 96 (W.Va. 1999). Even where the defendant seeks to introduce evidence of prior relations with a victim, statutes commonly require such evidence to be first presented to the court *in camera* (in the judge's private chambers) for the court to determine whether the evidence of the defendant's prior relationship with the victim is relevant to the victim's consent. For example, New Jersey law provides:

> In prosecutions for the crime of rape, assault with intent to commit rape, and breaking and entering with intent to commit rape, evidence of the complaining witness's previous sexual conduct shall not be admitted nor reference made to it in the presence of the jury except as provided in this act. N.J. Stat. Ann. § 2A:84A-32.1.

The New Jersey statute goes on to state that before permitting evidence of a complaining witness's sexual history, the court must first conduct a hearing *in camera* to determine whether such evidence is relevant and whether its probative value is not outweighed by the prejudice or confusion it will create or by its unwarranted invasion of the complaining witness's privacy.

Rape shield laws are based on the theory that a victim's prior sexual activity is not probative of whether the victim has been violated in the instance for which the defendant stands accused. Thus, in *State v. Madsen*, 772 S.W.2d 656 (Mo. 1989), the Missouri Supreme Court held that neither evidence of a victim having a live-in boyfriend nor of having two illegitimate children was relevant in a prosecution for rape. But can a female victim offer testimony of a prior rape to explain her conduct in failing to resist an attacker? In *Raines v. State*, 382 S.E.2d 738 (Ga. App. 1989), the appellate court found this to be appropriate.

In interpreting the applicability of rape shield laws to some unusual factual situations, courts have faced some difficult judgments. In a Massachusetts decision, the court ruled that a defendant charged with rape should have been allowed to question the complainant as to whether she had sexual intercourse with anyone else on the night of the attack. The court concluded that such evidence would not constitute an attack on the complainant's credibility. Rather, the court held that such evidence tended to support the defendant's theory that someone else had attacked the complainant and that she had wrongly accused him. *Commonwealth v. Fitzgerald*, 590 N.E.2d 1151 (Mass. 1992).

A Virginia appellate court ruled that evidence a victim did not report her alleged rape until a month after the incident, when she learned that she had contracted gonorrhea, was admissible to show ill will of the complainant. The court found that such evidence did not relate to the sexual conduct of the victim and therefore was not barred by the Virginia rape shield statute. *Evans v. Commonwealth*, 415 S.E.2d 851 (Va. App. 1992).

### Judicial Reforms

Significant judicial reforms have also occurred in the law of rape, as courts

- No longer instruct juries that the uncorroborated testimony of a victim of sexual battery deserves more scrutiny than the testimony of other crime victims.
- No longer insist that a woman must "resist to the utmost" to establish that her sexual privacy has been violated. (This is consistent with the advice of law enforcement officers, who frequently caution women that violent resistance to a rapist's attack can result in the victim's serious injury or death.) Now, in considering whether a victim's resistance has been overcome, courts consider such factors as the extent of the offender's force, the physical capacity of the victim to resist, and the psychological and emotional stress of a victim whose sensibilities are outraged by fear of violation of her bodily integrity.
- Have generally disavowed the unity concept of marriage, abrogating Hale's Rule, discussed previously, which American courts generally followed until the 1970s. By the mid-1990s, about half the states had abolished the marital exception completely; the majority of the remaining states had abolished the exception where the spouses were living apart from each other. In 1981 the New Jersey Supreme Court held that the state's rape statute, which used the language "any person who has carnal knowledge of a woman forcibly against her will," did not except from its operation a husband who was living apart from his wife. *State v. Smith*, 426 A.2d 38 (N.J. 1981). In *People v. Liberta*, 474 N.E.2d 567 (N.Y. 1984), New

York's highest court termed the notion of a wife's implied consent to intercourse as "irrational and absurd" and emphasized that a married woman should have the same right to bodily autonomy as a single woman. Either statutes or judicial decisions in many states now provide that a husband may be charged with rape of his wife.

## A Contemporary Statutory Treatment of Sexual Offenses

Michigan has modern, comprehensive laws that classify criminal sexual conduct by various degrees, depending on whether it involves sexual penetration or sexual contact with another person as well as other factors. Sexual contact is defined as including the intentional touching of the victim's intimate parts or the intentional touching of the clothing covering the immediate area of the victim's intimate parts, if that intentional touching can reasonably be construed as being for the purpose of sexual arousal or gratification (Mich. Comp. Laws § 750.520a(q)). **Sexual penetration** is defined as sexual intercourse, cunnilingus, fellatio, anal intercourse, or any other intrusion, however slight, of any part of a person's body or of any object into the genital or anal openings of another person's body, but emission of seed is not required. Mich. Comp. Laws § 750.520a(r).

**sexual penetration** Sexual intercourse, cunnilingus, fellatio, anal intercourse, or any other intrusion, however slight, of any part of a person's body or any object into the genital or anal openings of another person's body.

Sec. 720.520b deals with first-degree criminal sexual conduct and provides:

1. A person is guilty of criminal sexual conduct in the first degree if he or she engages in sexual penetration with another person and if any of the following circumstances exists:

   (a) That other person is under 13 years of age.

   (b) That other person is at least 13 but less than 16 years of age and any of the following:

   (i) The actor is a member of the same household as the victim.

   (ii) The actor is related to the victim by blood or affinity to the fourth degree.

   (iii) The actor is in a position of authority over the victim and used this authority to coerce the victim to submit.

   (iv) The actor is a teacher, substitute teacher, or administrator of the public or nonpublic school in which that other person is enrolled.

**CASE-IN-POINT**

### Does Asking an Attacker to Wear a Condom Constitute Consent to Sex?

In May 1993, in Travis County, Texas, Joel Valdez, a twenty-eight-year-old defendant who was charged with rape, claimed that the female with whom he admittedly had sexual intercourse had asked him to wear a condom. Valdez testified that he complied with the woman's request and that accordingly they were simply "making love."

But the twenty-six-year-old complainant explained that she pleaded with her attacker to wear a condom only to protect herself from acquired immunodeficiency syndrome (AIDS). The jury in Austin, Texas, found Valdez guilty of rape, implicitly finding that asking the attacker to wear a condom does not constitute consent to sexual intercourse.

*© Cengage Learning*

(c) Sexual penetration occurs under circumstances involving the commission of any other felony.

(d) The actor is aided or abetted by 1 or more other persons and either of the following circumstances exists:

    (i) The actor knows or has reason to know that the victim is mentally incapable, mentally incapacitated, or physically helpless.

    (ii) The actor uses force or coercion to accomplish the sexual penetration. Force or coercion includes but is not limited to any of the circumstances listed in subdivision (f).

(e) The actor is armed with a weapon or any article used or fashioned in a manner to lead the victim to reasonably believe it to be a weapon.

(f) The actor causes personal injury to the victim and force or coercion is used to accomplish sexual penetration. Force or coercion includes but is not limited to any of the following circumstances:

    (i) When the actor overcomes the victim through the actual application of physical force or physical violence.

    (ii) When the actor coerces the victim to submit by threatening to use force or violence on the victim, and the victim believes that the actor has the present ability to execute these threats.

    (iii) When the actor coerces the victim to submit by threatening to retaliate in the future against the victim, or any other person, and the victim believes that the actor has the ability to execute this threat. As used in this subdivision, "to retaliate" includes threats of physical punishment, kidnapping, or extortion.

    (iv) When the actor engages in the medical treatment or examination of the victim in a manner or for purposes which are medically recognized as unethical or unacceptable.

    (v) When the actor, through concealment or by the element of surprise, is able to overcome the victim.

(g) The actor causes personal injury to the victim, and the actor knows or has reason to know that the victim is mentally incapable, mentally incapacitated, or physically helpless.

(h) The other person is mentally incapable, mentally disabled, mentally incapacitated, or physically helpless, and any of the following:

    (i) The actor is related to the victim by blood or affinity to the fourth degree.

    (ii) The actor is in a position of authority over the victim and uses this authority to coerce the victim to submit.

**sexual contact** The intentional touching of the victim's intimate parts or the intentional touching of the clothing covering the immediate area of the victim's intimate parts, if that intentional touching can reasonably be construed as being for the purpose of sexual arousal or gratification.

Second-degree criminal sexual conduct follows substantially along the lines of the preceding section, but instead of penetration it makes sexual contact with a victim unlawful. Third-degree criminal sexual conduct includes two of the same elements as a first-degree offense (that is, penetration and use of force or coercion) but does not include the element that the defendant was aided or abetted in the act by one or more persons. § 750.520d. Fourth-degree criminal sexual conduct involves **sexual contact** with another person involving force or coercion; an actor who knows or has reason to know that the victim is mentally incapable, mentally incapacitated, or physically helpless; or a victim who is under jurisdiction of the department of corrections and an actor who is associated with that department.

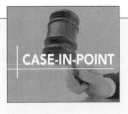

### CASE-IN-POINT

## Must a Rape Victim Scream or Attempt to Escape?

The defendant, Studham, and the victim were involved in long term, and sometimes volatile relationship, which ended with the imposition of an order of protection. Early one morning, the victim "was awakened at her apartment by a knocking and ringing of her doorbell." Studham, "who had been drinking, was at the door and [stated] he wanted to talk to her, but she refused to let him in[side]." Studham "kicked the door open and entered; and he remained in the apartment for about two hours, during which there was some kissing and amorous advances." The victim testified at Studham's rape trial that Studham "threatened her, pinned her to the floor during a struggle, put his hand over her mouth so that she had difficulty breathing, and forced intercourse upon her against her will." The victim also testified that "she did not scream or attempt to run from her apartment . . . due to its futility and the fact that her young son was asleep in the adjoining room." Studham argued insufficiency of the evidence to support his conviction because it was based "almost solely upon [the victim's] own self-interested testimony," which "is inherently improbable and inconsistent because, though she claims force and denies consent, she did not scream, or try to escape from the apartment even though during the time he was there she had opportunity to do so." The Supreme Court of Utah held "the question of guilt or innocence often depends upon the weighing of the credibility of the victim against that of the accused; accordingly, the rule is that if there is nothing so inherently incredible about the victim's story that reasonable minds would reject it, a conviction may rest upon her testimony alone." In addressing the victim's failure to scream, the court held "whether an outcry was made, or should have been made, depends upon how practical and effective it might have been." However, "mere failure to make such an outcry does not render a conviction unsupportable." In addressing the victim's failure to attempt escape, the court held "even though it is necessary that the rape be against the victim's will, manifest by a determined effort on her part to resist, it is not necessary that it be shown that she engaged in any heroics which subjected her to great brutality or that she suffered or risked serious wounds or injuries." As a result, Studham's rape conviction was affirmed.

*State v. Studham*, 572 P.2d 700 (Utah 1977).

Note that the Michigan law makes no distinction as to the sex of the actor or victim. In other words, it is gender neutral. It broadly defines sexual penetration and sexual contact and divides the offense of criminal sexual conduct into degrees considering the conduct of the actor and the vulnerability of the victim. Thus, it is a comprehensive sexual battery statute that embodies many of the reforms discussed earlier.

Violations of the Michigan law for first-, second-, and third-degree sexual conduct constitute felonies; fourth degree sexual conduct that involves contact is a serious misdemeanor.

## Prosecutorial Burdens in Rape and Sexual Battery Cases

As in all criminal cases, the prosecution must prove the *corpus delicti*—that is, the fact that the crime has been committed. Proof that an act of sexual intercourse (or other sexual imposition, depending on the statutory definition of the offense) has taken place with the victim is usually sufficient in a sexual battery case. In addition, in a statutory rape case, proof must be offered of the age of the victim (usually the female) and, in some instances, the age of the offender (usually the male). In sexual battery prosecutions, proof of the defendant's general intent is usually sufficient, absent a statute requiring proof of the defendant's specific intent.

One common problem in sexual battery prosecutions is the lack of independent eyewitness testimony. Consequently, it frequently becomes the victim's word against the defendant's word. Thus, police and prosecutors place paramount importance on a "fresh complaint" by a victim. Preservation of semen, photographs of bruises, torn clothing, and even pubic hairs become valuable evidence to corroborate a victim's testimony. Seldom is the credibility of a complaining witness as vital as in sexual battery prosecutions. To appear in court and testify concerning a sexual assault is a traumatic experience for a victim of sexual assault. This is particularly true for young children. To assist youngsters, many courts permit them to illustrate their testimony through the use of anatomically detailed dolls.

## Rape Trauma Syndrome

**rape trauma syndrome** A recurring pattern of physical and emotional symptoms experienced by rape victims.

In 1974, to describe a recurring pattern of physical and emotional symptoms experienced by rape victims, psychiatrists coined the term **rape trauma syndrome**, which refers to a set of psychological manifestations (e.g., fear, depression, and a sense of guilt) of victims usually following a sexual assault. Since then, prosecutors have sought to introduce expert testimony at rape trials to establish that a victim's symptoms are consistent with those of the syndrome. This type of evidence has particular relevance to prosecutions where the defendant claims consent of the victim as a defense. On review of convictions, appellate courts have disagreed on whether such evidence is admissible. The Kansas Supreme Court was the nation's first appellate court to address the question of the admissibility of expert testimony concerning rape trauma syndrome. The court allowed the introduction of psychiatric testimony that a rape victim suffered from rape trauma syndrome, noting that such expert evidence is relevant where the defendant claims consent. *State v. Marks*, 647 P.2d 1292 (Kan. 1982). Other state supreme courts have reached a similar conclusion. *State v. Liddell*, 685 P.2d 918 (Mont. 1984); *State v. Huey*, 699 P.2d 1290 (Ariz. 1985). An Ohio appellate court held that such expert psychiatric testimony is admissible but only where its value outweighs its prejudicial impact. The court noted that expert opinions of this type assist laypersons in interpreting reactions of a victim, especially in child rape cases. *State v. Whitman*, 475 N.E.2d 486 (Ohio App. 1984).

There is respectable judicial authority to the contrary. In 1982 the Minnesota Supreme Court ruled that the diagnosis of rape trauma syndrome is not a fact-finding tool but rather a therapeutic tool and that admission of expert testimony on the subject at a rape trial is erroneous. *State v. Saldana*, 324 N.W.2d 227 (Minn. 1982). Several other appellate courts have held that expert testimony concerning the syndrome is not admissible to prove that a rape in fact occurred. For example, in *People v. Pullins*, 378 N.W.2d 502 (Mich. App. 1985), the court held evidence of rape trauma syndrome inadmissible to establish that a rape occurred. This came the year after the Missouri Supreme Court, in *State v. Taylor*, 663 S.W.2d 235 (Mo. 1984), concluded that such testimony was beyond the proper basis of expert opinion.

In 1990 New York's highest court concluded that the scientific community has now generally accepted that rape is a highly traumatic event that triggers the onset of certain identifiable symptoms. The court agreed that expert testimony of the rape trauma syndrome may be admitted to aid the jury's understanding of the victim's behavior after the assault. Nevertheless, the court observed that identifiable symptoms in rape victims do not indicate whether an incident did or did not occur; thus, trial judges cannot allow such testimony to be introduced for this purpose. *People v. Taylor*, 552 N.E.2d 131 (N.Y. 1990). In *People v. Nelson*, 837 N.Y.S.2d 697

**CASE-IN-POINT**

## Sufficiency of Evidence to Support a Conviction for Sexual Assault

Rothenberg met the complainant in a bar. After dancing with her, Rothenberg asked the complainant to accompany him to a party at a friend's condominium. The complainant agreed and drove to the condominium in her own car. When she arrived at the condo, there appeared to be no one there except Rothenberg. The complainant and Rothenberg sat on a couch in the living room where they kissed and exchanged back massages. The complainant then told Rothenberg that she wanted to leave, but he refused to let her go. She ran to the front door and attempted to open it, but Rothenberg closed the door and prevented her from leaving. The complainant then locked herself in the bathroom where she remained for thirty minutes. Rothenberg promised to let the complainant leave if she would come out of the bathroom. When she came out, Rothenberg forced her onto the couch. At that point the complainant submitted to sexual intercourse. In sustaining Rothenberg's conviction for sexual assault, the Connecticut Supreme Court noted that "the complainant's unambiguous request to leave the condominium disabused the defendant of any misinterpretation of her wishes" and that "the defendant's conduct thereafter was knowingly coercive."

*State v. Rothenberg*, 487 A.2d 545 (Conn. 1985).

(2007), the court held that expert testimony regarding rape trauma syndrome was properly admitted, in a prosecution for sexual abuse, to aid the jury in understanding the victim's unusual behavior.

Appellate courts still disagree on the admissibility of evidence of the rape trauma syndrome. Much of the controversy focuses on the purpose of the evidence and the qualifications of experts. Yet the trend is to allow such evidence. As the New Mexico Court of Appeals recently pointed out, an expert's testimony on victimization and impact of trauma on victims is relevant in a trial for sex offenses. *State v. Maestas*, 112 P.3d 1134 (N.M. App. 2005).

Can a defendant charged with rape introduce expert testimony concerning the rape trauma syndrome to establish that a rape did not occur? In *Henson v. State*, 535 N.E.2d 1189 (Ind. 1989), the defense presented a witness who testified to seeing the victim dancing and drinking at a bar on the evening after the alleged rape. The defense then sought to introduce expert testimony on the subject, but the trial judge would not allow it. The state supreme court ruled that the testimony must be permitted because it would be unfair to allow the prosecution to present expert testimony on rape trauma syndrome but deny a defendant the same opportunity.

## Sex Offender Registration Laws

**Megan's Law** Name applied to statutes that require convicted sex offenders, upon release from prison, to register with local law enforcement agencies. (The statute was named in memory of Megan Kanka, who died in 1994 at the hands of a released offender.)

On June 20, 1997, a Trenton, New Jersey, court sentenced Jesse Timmendequas to death for the rape and murder of seven-year-old Megan Kanka in 1994. The case attracted national attention after it was revealed that Timmendequas had a record of committing sex offenses against children. Public outrage led the New Jersey legislature to enact a law requiring convicted sex offenders who are released from prison, move into the state, or simply change their address to register with local law enforcement agencies. Registration must include the individual's address, description, and other personal data along with a complete criminal history. These agencies in turn must make this information available to the public. The New Jersey statute became widely known as **Megan's Law** in memory of Megan Kanka. Failure to comply with the registration requirement is itself a criminal offense. After fifteen years with no violations, an offender may request a court to terminate sex offender status. See, generally, N.J. Stat. Ann. § 2C:7-1 *et seq.*

Similar laws have been enacted in most states, and most of these laws have survived constitutional attack. In 1996 Congress enacted a federal version of Megan's Law. 42 U.S.C.A. § 14071. The federal statute sets forth guidelines for state programs and encourages states to adopt such programs by threatening them with the loss of federal funds. All states and the District of Columbia have adopted variations of Megan's Law.

It remains to be seen how effective the various versions of Megan's Law will be in protecting children from sexual predators. There is also concern that these laws may be too inclusive, in that persons convicted in the past of minor sexual offenses are subjected to undeserved community scorn. Megan's Law and similar laws are also subject to the criticism that they impose penalties based on status rather than on wrongful acts. However, the public has demanded that the justice system do more to protect people from sexual predators, and such individuals often remain a serious threat to the community even after they have paid their debt to society.

State registration laws modeled after Megan's Law have survived constitutional attacks based on double jeopardy, vagueness, equal protection, the right to privacy, and cruel and unusual punishment. For example, in *Cutshall v. Sundquist*, 193

## JURISPRUDENCE

*Smith v. Doe,* 538 U.S. 84, 123 S.Ct. 1140, 155 L.Ed.2d 164 (2003)

The Alaska Sex Offender Registration Act provides: any sex offender or child kidnaper incarcerated in the State must register with the Department of Corrections within 30 days before his release, providing his name, address, and other specified information. If the individual is at liberty, he must register with local law enforcement authorities within a working day of his conviction or of entering the State. If he was convicted of a single, non-aggravated sex crime, the offender must provide annual verification of the submitted information for 15 years. If he was convicted of an aggravated sex offense or of two or more sex offenses, he must register for life and verify the information quarterly.

In this case, two defendants "were convicted of aggravated sex offenses," and "both were released from prison and completed rehabilitative programs for sex offenders." Although the defendants were "convicted before the Act's passage," they were covered by it. The defendants filed a civil action under 42 U.S.C. § 1983, seeking to "declare the Act void as applied to them under the *Ex Post Facto* Clause." The district court denied the defendant's relief; however, the Ninth Circuit disagreed, "holding that, because its effects were punitive, the Act violates the *Ex Post Facto Clause.*"

The Supreme Court held the Act to be "nonpunitive" and as a result held "its retroactive application does not violate the *Ex Post Facto* Clause." The Supreme Court concluded that the Alaska legislature's intention behind the Act "was to enact a regulatory scheme that is civil and nonpunitive." The "statutory text states the legislature's finding that sex offenders pose a high risk of reoffending, [and] identifies protecting the public from sex offenders as the law's primary interest, and declares that release of certain information about sex offenders to public agencies and the public will assist in protecting the public safety." The Court, speaking through Justice Kennedy, held "where a legislative restriction is an incident of the State's power to protect the public health and safety, it will be considered as evidencing an intent to exercise that regulatory power, and not a purpose to add to the punishment." In dissent, Justice Ruth Bader Ginsburg (joined by Justice Stephen Breyer) asserted that the legislative intent behind the act was ambiguous but that its effect was punitive. In her view, the act was an unconstitutional *ex post facto* law. Justice John Paul Stevens also dissented, noting the severe stigma that sex offender registration places on the convicted sex offender. In Stevens's view, it was "clear beyond peradventure that these unique consequences of conviction of a sex offense are punitive."

F.3d 466 (6th Cir. 1999), a federal appeals court rejected a challenge to Tennessee's sex offender registration law based on the Double Jeopardy Clause of the Fifth Amendment.

In March 2003 the U.S. Supreme Court upheld Alaska's version of Megan's Law against an attack based on the constitutional prohibition against *ex post facto* laws. *Smith v. Doe*, 538 U.S. 84, 123 S.Ct. 1140, 155 L.Ed.2d 164 (2003). The majority found that although the act was retroactive, it was nonpunitive in nature; therefore, the *Ex Post Facto* Clause did not apply.

## Defenses to Charges of Sexual Battery

Beyond a general denial of the charges, the most common defense asserted in a rape case is that the victim consented. For consent to be a defense, it must be voluntarily given before the sexual act. As we pointed out previously, the defense of consent is not available where the victim is unconscious, asleep, or mentally deficient.

The defense of consent would not be valid in a case of voluntary sexual battery (that is, statutory rape) because persons under a certain age are legally incapable of consent. Moreover, it is usually not a defense to a charge of voluntary sexual battery that the defendant believed the victim was older than the prohibited age. In the majority of states this is true despite the victim's appearance or misrepresentation of his or her age. The Model Penal Code allows a defense when the victim is over the age of ten, but it requires the actor "to prove by a preponderance of the evidence that he reasonably believed the child to be above the critical age." M.P.C. § 213.6. Legislatures in about one-third of the states have enacted statutes allowing a mistake-of-age defense, often with variations such as the age of the victim and in instances when a mistake is based on declarations of age by the victim.

**impotency** Lacking in power; in reference to a male, the inability to achieve an erection.

**Impotency** (that is, the inability to engage in sexual intercourse) can be asserted as a defense to a charge of rape. The majority of cases where the defense of impotency is asserted involve charges against young males and men of an advanced age. However, this defense is seldom successful. Modern laws have so broadened the definition of sexual battery as to render impotency irrelevant in many sexual impositions.

Finally, if the statute under which the defendant is prosecuted requires proof of a specific intent, the defendant may be able to show an inability to form such intent due to voluntary intoxication (see Chapter 14).

## Sodomy

**sodomy** Oral or anal sex between persons or sex between a person and an animal. The latter act is commonly referred to as "bestiality."

**Sodomy** refers to oral or anal sex between humans and sexual intercourse between humans and animals (the latter is often termed bestiality). In his landmark commentaries on the English common law, Sir William Blackstone defined sodomy as "the infamous crime against nature" and asserted that it was an offense of "deeper malignity" than rape. Sodomy can be consensual or nonconsensual. Nonconsensual sodomy is considered a crime against a person and is often charged along with rape in states with older, narrower statutory definitions of rape. (Of course, in jurisdictions with more modern rape statutes, any nonconsensual sexual penetration is considered rape.) Consensual sodomy, on the other hand, was viewed traditionally as an offense against public morality. Prior to 2003, many states had abolished the offense either through legislative or judicial action. In June 2003 the U.S. Supreme Court found a Texas law that proscribed private, consensual sodomy between same-sex partners to be unconstitutional. *Lawrence v. Texas*, 539 U.S. 558, 123 S.Ct. 2472, 156 L.Ed.2d

508 (2003). The Supreme Court's decision sounded the death knell for state laws prohibiting sodomy between consenting adults.

# Abusive Offenses

Laws proscribing abuse of one person by another are modern concepts. Many of these laws have been proposed by social agencies that bear the responsibility of coping with problems of members of society who require protection from abusive behavior. Increasingly, legislatures and, even more recently, Congress have responded by enacting laws designed to protect children, spouses and other intimate partners, and, in some instances, the elderly.

## Child Abuse

**child abuse** Actions that physically, mentally, or emotionally endanger the welfare of a child.

Since the 1980s, complaints of **child abuse** have increased dramatically. Many cases involve commission of assault, battery (or aggravated categories thereof), or some category of sexual assault or sexual battery and are prosecuted under one or more of such statutes. Nevertheless, with the rise of neglect and abuse of and violence against children, many states have enacted specific child abuse laws to cover a broader range of abusive behavior. These laws often refer to **endangering the welfare of a child**, and they hold a parent or guardian responsible for abuse of a child regardless of the source of the mistreatment. These concerns appear to be reflected in McKinney's N.Y. Penal Law § 260.10. That law makes endangering the welfare of a child a misdemeanor and provides that a person is guilty of endangering the welfare of a child when

**endangering the welfare of a child** Knowingly acting in a manner likely to be injurious to the physical, mental, or moral welfare of a child.

1. He knowingly acts in a manner likely to be injurious to the physical, mental or moral welfare of a child less than seventeen years old or directs or authorizes such child to engage in an occupation involving a substantial risk of danger to his life or health; or
2. Being a parent, guardian or other person legally charged with the care or custody of a child less than eighteen years old, he fails or refuses to exercise reasonable diligence in the control of such child to prevent him from becoming an "abused child," a "neglected child," a "juvenile delinquent," or a "person in need of supervision," as those terms are defined in articles ten, three and seven of the family court act.

Because of the age and vulnerability of minors, statutes proscribing child abuse are strict liability crimes in many states. Since 2000, several states have enacted statutes making it a misdemeanor to allow young children to remain unattended in a vehicle. For example, a defendant's actions in leaving a three-week-old child locked in a van on a hot summer day posed substantial risk of harm to the child and thus was a violation of an Ohio child endangerment statute that provided "[n]o person, who is the parent . . . or person *in loco parentis* of a child under eighteen years of age . . . shall create a substantial risk to the health or safety of the child, by violating a duty of care, protection, or support." *State v. Morton*, 741 N.E.2d 202 (Ohio App. 2000).

The prosecution of parents for leaving a child unattended in a vehicle has engendered some debate. Some argue that parents should not be punished criminally for their lack of judgment. But the more prevalent view is that punishing parents for such lapses of judgment forces parents to face the consequences of their actions. Moreover, such statutes raise public awareness as to the danger of leaving children alone in vehicles. In other instances, a parent has been charged with endangering a child's welfare by transporting a child in an auto while the parent was driving under the influence of intoxicating beverages.

Statutes now commonly require medical professionals and social workers to report instances of suspected child abuse to the enforcement authorities. When such cases of child abuse reach the courts, they often involve legal issues as to whether parents, social workers, and others who discuss these matters with an abused child are to be permitted to testify in court concerning communications with the child. Moreover, expert testimony of physicians, psychologists, and social workers is often relied on to explain a child's sometimes-curious behavior that might be a result of certain types of abuse.

The widespread drug problem has led to prosecutions of women for child abuse when, during pregnancy, they ingested cocaine or other controlled substances and demonstrable adverse medical effects were present in their children at birth. Courts have generally declined to hold that such action constitutes child abuse, often based on their interpretation of statutes proscribing child endangerment or delivery of controlled substances. For example, Kentucky Revised Statute § 508.110 criminalizes abuse of "another person of whom [the offender] has actual custody" which "places him in a situation that may cause . . . serious physical injury" to a person twelve years of age or less or who is physically or mentally helpless.

In a leading decision on the subject, the Kentucky Supreme Court held that the statute does not apply to a mother whose baby suffered injuries as the result of the mother's ingestion of drugs during her pregnancy. *Commonwealth v. Welch*, 864 S.W.2d 280 (Ky. 1993). In reaching its decision, the court cited *Johnson v. State*, 602 So.2d 1288 (Fla. 1992). There, the Florida Supreme Court held that cocaine passing through a baby's umbilical cord after birth but before the cord was cut did not violate a Florida law making it a crime for an adult to deliver a controlled substance to a minor.

In *Reinesto v. Superior Court*, 894 P.2d 733 (Ariz. App. 1995), the state prosecuted a mother for having knowingly caused injury to her unborn child under circumstances likely to produce death or serious physical injury in violation of Ariz. Rev. Stat. § 13-3623.B. The statute makes it a felony for "any person" who "[u]nder circumstances likely to produce death or serious physical injury . . . causes a child . . . to suffer physical injury. . . ." The statute defines a child as "an individual who is under eighteen years of age" and physical injury as "the impairment of physical condition . . . or any physical condition which imperils health or welfare." Ariz. Rev. Stat. § 13-3623.A. The defendant challenged the right of the state to bring charges against her. The appellate court granted her petition and held,

> The plain language of section 13-3623 indicates that the legislature intended to proscribe conduct by any person that causes physical harm to a child. Applying the ordinary meaning of these words leads us to conclude that the statute refers to conduct that directly endangers a child, not to activity that affects a fetus and thereby ultimately harms the resulting child. *Id*. at 735–736.

Because it concluded that Arizona's child abuse statute does not reach the defendant's conduct, the court declined to reach the constitutional issue of whether the statute violated her right of privacy.

Many court decisions hold that maternal conduct before the birth of the child does not give rise to criminal prosecution under state child abuse/endangerment or drug distribution statutes. However, in *Whitner v. State*, 492 S.E.2d 777 (S.C. 1997), the South Carolina Supreme Court held that a mother of a newborn infant could be criminally prosecuted on the statutory theory of child abuse or endangerment for injuries to her child resulting from prenatal substance abuse.

## Spousal Abuse

**spousal abuse** Physical, emotional, or sexual abuse of one's husband or wife.

In recent years, legislatures and courts have given increased attention to **spousal abuse**. Many of these abuses constitute criminal violations of one or more traditional statutes of the types previously discussed. Nevertheless, laws have been enacted in many states to provide for issuance of court injunctions to protect spouses from domestic violence and provide for the arrest of those who violate these orders. In many instances, courts issue protective orders of this character during litigation. In *Cole v. Cole*, 556 N.Y.S.2d 217 (Fam. Ct. 1990), a wife petitioned the court to have her husband held in contempt for violating such an order. A question arose about the effectiveness of such an order when the wife voluntarily seeks reconciliation with her husband. The court explained that a victim of domestic violence who has procured such an order is entitled to the court's protection from violence throughout the duration of the order, even if the victim is desirous of pursuing a goal of voluntary reconciliation with the offending spouse.

Prosecutions for spousal abuse are sometimes hindered by the difficulty of showing which instances of domestic violence have occurred in which legal jurisdiction. Recognizing this, Congress included in the Violent Crime Control and Law Enforcement Act of 1994 (commonly referred to as the "federal crime bill") an offense of "interstate domestic violence." Section 40221 of the act inserts a new chapter titled "Domestic Violence" so that now 18 U.S.C.A. § 2261 provides:

(a) Offenses.—

(1) Travel or conduct of offender.—A person who travels in interstate or foreign commerce or enters or leaves Indian country or within the special maritime and territorial jurisdiction of the United States with the intent to kill, injure, harass, or intimidate a spouse, intimate partner, or dating partner, and who, in the course of or as a result of such travel, commits or attempts to commit a crime of violence against that spouse or intimate partner, shall be punished as provided in subsection (b).

(2) Causing travel of victim.—A person who causes a spouse, intimate partner, or dating partner to travel in interstate or foreign commerce or to enter or leave Indian country by force, coercion, duress, or fraud, and who, in the course of, as a result of, or to facilitate such conduct or travel, commits or attempts to commit a crime of violence against that spouse or intimate partner, shall be punished as provided in subsection (b).

Shortly after the new act took effect, Christopher Bailey was charged with violating it for assaulting his spouse and driving her around West Virginia and Kentucky until he finally carried her into an emergency room. A jury found Bailey guilty of kidnapping and interstate domestic violence under the new federal act. The U.S. Court of Appeals for the Fourth Circuit affirmed his convictions for violating 18 U.S.C.A. § 1201(a)(1), kidnapping, and 18 U.S.C.A. § 2261(a)(2), the new act. The court rejected Bailey's constitutional argument that the new federal statute was beyond the power of Congress to enact. *United States v. Bailey*, 112 F.3d 758 (4th Cir. 1997). The court in *United States v. Lankford*, 196 F.3d 563 (5th Cir. 1999), held that the enactment of the Violence Against Women Act, 18 U.S.C.A. § 2261(a)(1), did not exceed the scope of Congress's authority under the Commerce Clause.

# Abuse of the Elderly

**abuse of the elderly** Infliction of physical or mental harm on elderly persons.

**Abuse of the elderly** is often handled through state and local regulatory agencies. Frequently, this has involved resorting to civil court processes, but in recent years some state legislatures have created criminal offenses to punish caregivers who abuse, neglect, or exploit elderly persons. Generally these statutes define caregivers broadly to include adults who are close relatives and persons appointed by agencies or otherwise employed to assist the elderly and disabled. New York and Illinois have been leaders in enacting legislation that provides criminal sanctions for endangering the welfare of a vulnerable elderly person.

McKinney's N.Y. Penal Law, Chapter 260, makes it a felony for a caregiver to endanger the welfare of a vulnerable elderly person. A "caregiver" is defined as one who assumes responsibility for the care of a vulnerable elderly person pursuant to a court order or who receives monetary or other valuable consideration for providing care for a vulnerable elderly person. A "vulnerable elderly person" is one sixty years of age or older who is suffering from a disease or infirmity associated with advanced age and manifested by demonstrable physical, mental, or emotional dysfunction to the extent that the person is incapable of adequately providing for his or her own health or personal care. It is endangering in the second degree (and a felony) for a caregiver for a vulnerable elderly person to recklessly cause physical injury to such person or subject the person to sexual contact without that person's consent (§ 260.32). It is endangering in the first degree (and a felony) for a caregiver to intentionally or recklessly cause injury to a vulnerable elderly person (§ 260.34).

Under Illinois law, the caregiver of an elderly or disabled person commits a felony if he or she knowingly

(1) performs acts which cause the elderly or disabled person's life to be endangered, health to be injured, or preexisting physical or mental condition to deteriorate; or

(2) fails to perform acts which he knows or reasonably should know are necessary to maintain or preserve the life or health of the elderly or disabled person and such failure causes the elderly or disabled person's life to be endangered, health to be injured or preexisting physical or mental condition to deteriorate; or

(3) abandons the elderly or disabled person. 720 Ill. Comp. Stat. Ann. § 5/12-21 (West 1994).

In *People v. Simester*, 678 N.E.2d 710 (Ill. App. 1997), Janice and Dale Simester, husband and wife, were convicted of two counts of criminal neglect of an elderly person and sentenced to thirty months probation and one thousand hours of community service. The victim, Stanley Pierzga, the wife's seventy-four-year-old uncle, had lived with the couple for several years. At trial the evidence revealed that when paramedics responded to a call to the home they found Mr. Pierzga lying on the floor in a coma in a fetal position. An emergency room physician found him covered with dried urine and crusted feces. Medical evidence further revealed the victim had had no nutritional intake for at least one week, that his rigid fetal position took at least two weeks to develop, and that his deep coma had to have existed for several days before his hospitalization.

On appeal the defendants argued that the statute (quoted above) presumptively imposes medical and psychiatric knowledge on a layperson for diagnosing and correctly treating the preexisting ailments of the elderly or disabled and that by making it an offense to fail to give adequate care to the victim on the basis that one "should reasonably know" the proper care, the statute "impermissibly adopts a civil negligence standard and enforces it as a criminal felony." The appellate court rejected their contentions and, in affirming their convictions, observed that both defendants should have reasonably known of the victim's condition long before the paramedics were summoned.

## Bullying

In recent years society has grown painfully aware of the problem of bullying in schools and the related problem of "cyberbullying." Most states have now enacted legislation requiring public school authorities to establish and enforce rules against bullying in schools, but few of these laws contain criminal provisions. Of course, extreme cases of bullying may constitute crimes such as assault, battery, or stalking and can be prosecuted as such. Cyberbullying is a more difficult legal problem, in that it typically takes place outside the school environment and involves expression rather than any physical contact. Nevertheless, the consequences of cyberbullying can be devastating to victims—a number of suicides have been linked to cyberbullying. In extreme cases, perpetrators can be prosecuted for cyberstalking or sued for intentional infliction of emotional distress.

# False Imprisonment and Kidnapping

**false imprisonment** Also known as false arrest, this is the tort or crime of unlawfully restraining a person.

**kidnapping** The forcible abduction and carrying away of a person against that person's will.

In recognition of the need to protect an individual's freedom of movement, the common law developed two misdemeanor offenses: **false imprisonment** and **kidnapping**. False imprisonment consisted of confining someone against the person's will, whereas kidnapping involved forcibly abducting and taking a person to another country.

## The Statutory Offense of False Imprisonment

Not all states have adopted statutes making false imprisonment an offense. Those that have generally classify it as a misdemeanor and define it much as did the common law, which defined the offense as the unlawful detention of a person.

One typical example, the Texas statute, states that "[a] person commits an offense if he intentionally and knowingly restrains another person." Vernon's Tex. Penal Code Ann. § 20.02(a). Texas law declares the offense to be a misdemeanor but provides that it becomes a felony if the offender recklessly exposes the victim to a substantial risk of serious bodily injury. Vernon's Tex. Penal Code Ann. § 20.02(c). Usually, a prosecution for false imprisonment requires only proof of a defendant's general intent, although this depends on the language of the particular statute.

Four hypothetical situations illustrate the crime of false imprisonment:

- A police officer takes a person into custody under an unlawful arrest.
- A prison warden fails to release a prisoner who has served his or her term.
- A storekeeper detains a customer when the storekeeper has a hunch the customer has shoplifted but has no reasonable basis for such suspicion.
- An overzealous male refuses to allow his female companion to leave his apartment without yielding to his sexual demands.

In recent years, false imprisonment has not been a commonly charged offense. Three reasons chiefly account for this: (1) Serious charges involving restraint of a person frequently reveal elements constituting the statutory offense of kidnapping;

### Does the Evidence Support Convictions for False Imprisonment and Assault?

The defendant, Snider, was drinking in a bar. The victim in the case was working as the bartender. The victim asked Snider to finish his drink so she could close the bar. They were the only two people there at the time. Snider went behind the bar, grabbed the victim by the arms, took her from behind the bar, pushed her about ten feet, and pinned her against a pool table for about fifteen minutes. Snider then left the bar. The victim's boyfriend arrived two minutes later to pick her up, discovered what had transpired, and called police. Snider was convicted of false imprisonment and assault.

Addressing the level of evidence to sustain his conviction, the Court of Appeal of Iowa noted that "the essential elements of false imprisonment are (1) detention or restraint against one's will, and (2) the unlawfulness of such detention or restraint." The court first looked "to whether the period of confinement or distance of removal exceeded that which would normally be incidental to an assault." In order to make this determination, the court assessed "whether the confinement or removal was significantly independent from the assault because it either (1) substantially increased the risk of harm to the victim, (2) lessened the risk of detection, or (3) significantly facilitated the defendant's escape following the assault."

The court stated "a pivotal question is whether holding the victim against the pool table substantially increased her risk of harm." The court held "the facts of this case do not show the victim's freedom was substantially restricted." As a result, Snider's conviction for false imprisonment was reversed. However, one judge dissented, saying "forcible confinement for almost fifteen minutes is not merely incidental to the initial assault," and "the facts show the confinement was separate from the assault."

*State v. Snider*, 479 N.W.2d 622 (Iowa App. 1991).

(2) persons claiming to have been falsely imprisoned often seek to recover damages in a civil suit rather than press criminal charges; and (3) on close investigation, many restraints undoubtedly are determined to have been imposed based on authority, or at least a reasonable belief that there was authority to have restrained the complaining party.

## Modern Statutory Treatment of Kidnapping

Unlike false imprisonment, the crime of kidnapping is a serious felony proscribed by all state and federal jurisdictions. It plays a far greater role in our society than it did at common law, where kidnapping required taking the victim to another country.

**asportation** The carrying away of something; in kidnapping, the carrying away of the victim; in larceny, the carrying away of the victim's property.

Under modern legislation the elements of the crime necessarily depend on the precise wording of the statute in a particular jurisdiction but, in general, for an act to constitute kidnapping, there must be an unlawful taking and forcible carrying away (sometimes called **asportation**) of a victim without that person's consent. Intimidation and coercion can substitute for the required force, and even where consent has been given, a person who has the capacity to consent must have voluntarily given it. Therefore, young children and incompetent persons cannot legally consent to an act of asportation.

**simple kidnapping** The abduction of another person without a demand for ransom.

Most states classify kidnapping as **simple kidnapping** and **kidnapping for ransom**. Others classify the offense by degrees. In New York, kidnapping in the second degree is a felony that merely involves the abduction of another person. McKinney's N.Y. Penal Law § 135.20. Kidnapping in the first degree is a more serious felony, and the statute proscribing it states,

**kidnapping for ransom** The offense of unlawfully taking and confining a person until a specified payment is made to the offender.

A person is guilty of kidnapping in the first degree when he abducts another person and when:

1. His intent is to compel a third person to pay or deliver money or property as ransom, or to engage in other particular conduct, or to refrain from engaging in particular conduct; or

2. He restrains the person abducted for a period of more than twelve hours with intent to:

    (a) Inflict physical injury upon him or violate or abuse him sexually; or

    (b) Accomplish or advance the commission of a felony; or

    (c) Terrorize him or a third person; or

    (d) Interfere with the performance of a governmental or political function; or

3. The person abducted dies during the abduction or before he is able to return or to be returned to safety. McKinney's N.Y. Penal Law § 135.25.

## The Requirement of Asportation in Kidnapping

The asportation or movement of the victim distinguishes the crime of kidnapping from the offense of false imprisonment. One of the more commonly litigated issues in kidnapping prosecutions concerns the extent of movement of the victim required to meet this element of the crime. In *People v. Martinez*, 973 P.2d 512 (Cal. 1999), the California Supreme Court noted that there are two requirements under the asportation standard. First, the movement of the victim must not be merely incidental to the commission of the underlying crime, and second, it must increase the risk of harm to the victim over and above that necessarily present in the underlying crime itself. See West's Ann. Cal. Penal Code § 209(b)(2).

In recent years, courts have tended to limit the scope of kidnapping statutes by deciding that the required movement of a victim must be something more than that inherent in or incidental to the commission of another felony. The proliferation of court decisions on this subject might be the result of prosecutors' tendencies to levy multiple charges against a criminal defendant for conduct arising from a single criminal episode.

When is the offender's movement of a victim in conjunction with an independent offense such as assault, rape, or robbery sufficient to constitute an independent offense of kidnapping? If the movement is merely incidental to a crime and does not involve an additional significant risk to the victim, courts generally will not sustain a conviction for kidnapping in addition to the other offense. Appellate court decisions are instructive. The New Hampshire Supreme Court has held that a defendant was properly convicted for kidnapping as an accomplice of a defendant who forced a woman into a car and drove her to an apartment where the principal defendant assaulted her. *State v. Goodwin*, 395 A.2d 1234 (N.H. 1978). In the same vein, two years later, the North Carolina Supreme Court sustained a kidnapping conviction where a handyman forced a woman off the street and into her home for purposes of sexually assaulting her. *State v. Adams*, 264 S.E.2d 46 (N.C. 1980).

Two 1983 appellate court decisions addressed the extent of movement required to meet the asportation element of kidnapping. The Florida Supreme Court held that the statutory requirement of "confining, abducting, or imprisoning another person . . . with intent to commit or facilitate commission of any felony" does not include movement or confinement that is inconsequential or inherent in the nature of the felony. *Faison v. State*, 426 So.2d 963 (Fla. 1983). In applying this rationale, a

California appellate court held that moving a robber's victim across a room or from one room to another was an insufficient movement to meet the requirement for kidnapping. *People v. John*, 197 Cal. Rptr. 340 (Cal. App. 1983).

## Federal Kidnapping Laws

Perhaps the most notorious kidnapping to have occurred in the United States was the abduction of the infant son of Charles A. Lindbergh, the "Lone Eagle" who, in 1927, made the first nonstop solo flight across the Atlantic Ocean. The Lindbergh baby was abducted from the family home in New Jersey in 1932. Bruno Richard Hauptmann was convicted of the crime after a spectacular trial and was executed in 1936. The Lindbergh kidnapping led to a demand for federal laws to enable the FBI to become involved in apprehending kidnappers. This, in turn, led to sweeping changes in state and federal laws on kidnapping. The Federal Kidnapping Act, commonly called the Lindbergh Law, provides, "Whoever unlawfully seizes, confines, inveigles, decoys, kidnaps, abducts, or carries away and holds for ransom or reward or otherwise any person, except in the case of a minor by a parent thereof . . . shall be punished by imprisonment." 18 U.S.C.A. § 1201(a). Subsection (b) of the statute raises a presumption that if the kidnapped victim is not returned within twenty-four hours after the taking, then the defendant did, in fact, take the victim across state lines. This presumption effectively allows the federal government to act promptly to bring federal agents into the investigation of an alleged kidnapping.

> **hostage taking** The act in which the perpetrator of a robbery or some other crime forcibly detains innocent bystanders.

A recent federal statute makes **hostage taking** an offense. 18 U.S.C.A. § 1203. Other federal statutes make it a crime to knowingly receive, possess, or dispose of any money or property that has been delivered as ransom for a victim of a kidnapping, 18 U.S.C.A. § 1202, or for a bank robber to avoid apprehension by forcing someone to accompany him, 18 U.S.C.A. § 2113(e).

## Defenses to Charges of False Imprisonment and Kidnapping

It is not false imprisonment for a person to detain another under authority of the law. Thus, an officer, or even a private citizen, who makes a lawful arrest or a jailer who detains a prisoner lawfully committed to custody is not guilty of an offense. Likewise, a parent who reasonably disciplines a child or a teacher who reasonably restrains a pupil would not be guilty of false imprisonment.

Consent can also be a defense to false imprisonment or kidnapping. Of course, the consent must not have been induced by threat, coercion, or misrepresentation and must have been given by a person competent to give consent. A person who relies on consent as a defense has the burden of establishing the validity of such consent.

Finally, as we have noted, a defendant may challenge whether there was sufficient movement of the victim to constitute the asportation element of kidnapping.

## Child Snatching

> **child snatching** Action taken by one parent to deliberately retain or conceal a child from the other parent.

In recent years, marital disputes have given rise to many serious problems concerning the custody of children of divorced or separated parents. It has been estimated that in excess of 300,000 children are abducted by family members each year. The term **child snatching** is now commonly applied to situations in which one parent deliberately retains or conceals a child from the other parent. The problem has resulted partly from the ability of one parent to seize a child from the custodial parent, travel to another state, and petition the court in the latter state for custody of the child.

In 1995 the Supreme Judicial Court of Maine affirmed the conviction of a father who took his children from their home, where their mother had equal legal custody rights. The evidence revealed that the defendant's purpose was to keep the children away from their mother and to hold them in a place where they were not likely to be found. The court found this evidence sufficient to support the conviction of the father for violating a statute defining criminal restraint to include taking a child "from the custody of his other parent." *State v. Butt*, 656 A.2d 1225 (Me. 1995).

Most states have made child snatching a felony, thereby subjecting violators to extradition for prosecution in the state where the offense occurred. In addition, child snatching is now being curbed by several approaches:

- In many states, trial judges include a provision in a divorce judgment requiring court approval to remove a child from the state where the divorce is granted. Violation may subject the offending party to being held in contempt of court or, in some states, to be prosecuted for a felony.
- The **Uniform Child Custody Jurisdiction and Enforcement Act (UCCJEA)**, proposed in 1968 and now in force in all fifty states, generally continues jurisdiction for custody in the home or resident state of the child. Cooperation between the courts in the different states is becoming increasingly effective in preventing "judge shopping."
- In 1980 Congress enacted the **Parental Kidnapping Prevention Act (PKPA)**. The federal act is designed to prevent jurisdictional conflicts over child custody, and it takes precedence over any state law, including the UCCJA. Its primary goal is to reduce any incentive for parental child snatching.
- Federal and state governments, as well as religious and civic organizations and the media, have initiated programs for identifying children and for collecting and disseminating information on missing children.

Prosecuting international parental kidnapping presents additional problems, most notably the difficulties encountered in dealing with a foreign legal system.

**Uniform Child Custody Jurisdiction and Enforcement Act (UCCJEA)** A law in force in all fifty states that generally continues jurisdiction for custody of children in the home or resident state of the child.

**Parental Kidnapping Prevention Act (PKPA)** A federal act adopted in 1980 designed to prevent jurisdictional conflicts over child custody matters. The primary goal of the statute is to reduce any incentive for parental child snatching.

---

**CASE-IN-POINT**

## Rape and Kidnapping: Required Resistance in the Face of Threats

Late one night after leaving work, a woman responded to a request by two men to assist them in getting their car off the road. When she began to leave, both men grabbed her, ordered her into the back seat of the car, and threatened to kill her unless she cooperated. The men told her that they had escaped from prison and were holding her as a hostage. They then drove their victim to a tent, disrobed her, and forced her to submit to sexual acts with each of them. When they drove her back to her car the next morning, they told her that they would kill her if she reported the incident to the police.

The defendants were convicted of rape, kidnapping, and several other offenses. On appeal, they argued that the victim had cooperated in their endeavors; hence, they were not guilty of either rape or kidnapping. The Indiana Supreme Court rejected their contentions and explained that the resistance necessary to protect against sexual attack is dependent on all circumstances. Further, the court noted that a victim need not physically resist after being confronted with threats and being in fear of injury. *Ballard v. State*, 385 N.E.2d 1126 (Ind. 1979).

# Civil Rights Offenses

**civil rights** In general, this term refers to all the rights protected by the federal and state constitutions and statutes. The term is often used to denote the right to be free from unlawful discrimination.

A category of offenses unknown to the common law involves injuries to the **civil rights** of individuals. After the Civil War, Congress adopted a series of laws designed to protect the civil rights of the newly freed former slaves. Today, these statutes as amended can be used to initiate federal prosecutions against individuals who conspire or use their official positions to deprive persons of rights guaranteed by the U.S. Constitution or the laws of the United States. The relevant provisions are as follows:

### 18 U.S.C.A. § 241. Conspiracy against rights

If two or more persons conspire to injure, oppress, threaten, or intimidate any inhabitant of any State, Territory, Commonwealth, Possession, or District in the free exercise or enjoyment of any right or privilege secured to him by the Constitution or laws of the United States, or because of his having so exercised the same; or

If two or more persons go in disguise on the highway, or on the premises of another, with intent to prevent or hinder his free exercise or enjoyment of any right or privilege so secured—

They shall be fined under this title or imprisoned not more than ten years, or both; and if death results from the acts committed in violation of this section or if such acts include kidnapping or an attempt to kidnap, aggravated sexual abuse or an attempt to commit aggravated sexual abuse, or an attempt to kill, they shall be fined under this title or imprisoned for any term of years or for life, or both, or may be sentenced to death.

### 18 U.S.C.A. § 242. Deprivation of rights under color of law

Whoever, under color of any law, statute, ordinance, regulation, or custom, willfully subjects any person in any State, Territory, or District to the deprivation of any rights, privileges, or immunities secured or protected by the Constitution or laws of the United States, or to different punishments, pains, or penalties, on account of such person being an alien, or by reason of his color, or race, than are prescribed for the punishment of citizens, shall be fined under this title or imprisoned not more than one year, or both; and if bodily injury results from the acts committed in violation of this section or if such acts include the use, attempted use, or threatened use of a dangerous weapon, explosives, or fire, shall be fined under this title or imprisoned not more than ten years, or both; and if death results from the acts committed in violation of this section or if such acts include kidnapping or an attempt to kidnap, aggravated sexual abuse, or an attempt to commit aggravated sexual abuse, or an attempt to kill, shall be fined under this title, or imprisoned for any term of years or for life, or both, or may be sentenced to death.

These statutes are used most frequently to prosecute in federal court individuals who engage in criminal acts that are racially motivated. Thus, although a conspiracy to commit arson may be prosecuted as such under state law, if it is racially motivated, it may also constitute a federal civil rights violation under 18 U.S.C.A. § 241. Instances of police brutality are sometimes prosecuted under 18 U.S.C.A. § 242. Increasingly, section 242 is being used to prosecute state officials who engage in other types of egregious conduct. See, e.g., *United States v. Lanier*, 520 U.S. 259, 117 S.Ct. 1219, 137 L.Ed.2d 432 (1997).

To be guilty of willfully depriving a person of constitutional rights under this section, the defendant must act under color of law; where use of force is involved, the force used must be unreasonable and unnecessary. *United States v. Stokes*, 506 F.2d 771 (5th Cir. 1975). As a result of judicial interpretation, federal civil rights laws now

*United States v. Lanier*, 520 U.S. 259, 117 S.Ct. 1219, 137 L.Ed.2d 432 (1997)

In 1982 David W. Lanier was elected judge of the Chancery Court in the small town of Dyersburg, Tennessee. Soon he developed a reputation for taking liberties with women who appeared before him as litigants or worked with him in the courthouse. Because Judge Lanier's family was prominent and because his brother was district attorney, the women whom Lanier victimized were reluctant to come forward. Eventually, federal authorities in Memphis heard of the allegations and launched an investigation. Five women agreed to appear before a federal grand jury. They testified that Judge Lanier had sexually assaulted them in his chambers and in his courtroom. One woman, a litigant in a child custody dispute, told the grand jury how Lanier threatened to deny her custody of her children in order to extort sexual favors from her.

Judge Lanier was indicted on eleven counts of violating 18 U.S.C.A. § 242, a civil rights law enacted after the Civil War. Had the case been prosecuted in state court, the charge would have been straightforward—sexual assault. But that option was not available to federal prosecutors. In a somewhat novel theory of the scope of 18 U.S.C.A. § 242, the indictment alleged that the judge, acting willfully and under color of state law, had deprived his victims of their federal constitutional right to be free from sexual assault. After trial, Lanier was convicted and sentenced to twenty-five years in prison and a $25,000 fine. The U.S. Supreme Court upheld the conviction and in so doing signaled the breadth of conduct that is susceptible to prosecution under the federal civil rights laws. After the Supreme Court's decision, Judge Lanier was apprehended in Mexico, where he had fled to avoid imprisonment. He is currently serving his sentence in federal prison.

protect individuals from a wide range of injurious conduct by public officials or other persons acting under the authority of the government.

Among the most common types of civil rights offenses is the excessive use of force by police. In a highly publicized case in March 1991, four Los Angeles police officers were charged with the beating of Rodney King, an African American motorist who was stopped by the police after a high-speed automobile chase. After the officers were acquitted in a state court trial, highly destructive riots erupted in South Central Los Angeles. Federal authorities then prosecuted the officers under 18 U.S.C.A. § 242 for violating King's civil rights, in particular, his Fourth Amendment right to be free from an unreasonable seizure. In April 1993, two of the officers, Stacey Koon and Laurence Powell, were convicted and sentenced to prison; the two other officers were found not guilty. Their convictions were upheld by the U.S. Court of Appeals, *United States v. Koon*, 34 F.3d 1416 (9th Cir. 1994). (Later review by the Supreme Court was limited to issues regarding sentencing. *Koon v. United States*, 518 U.S. 81, 116 S.Ct. 2035, 135 L.Ed.2d 392 [1996].)

## | Hate Crimes

**hate crimes** Crimes in which the victim is selected on the basis of race, ethnicity, religion, gender, or sexual orientation.

**Hate crimes** are offenses motivated by bias against a person's race, religion, nationality, gender, disability, or sexual orientation. Hate crimes can be offenses against property—for example, an instance of synagogue vandalism that is motivated by anti-Semitism. But most hate crimes are violent crimes against persons. In recent years there have been a number of highly publicized homicides where the only apparent motive was animus based on the victim's race, religion, gender, or sexual orientation. One of the most grisly such crimes was the racially motivated murder of James Byrd, Jr., in Jasper, Texas in 1998. Byrd, an African American, was chained by his ankles to the back of a pickup truck and dragged for three miles. He died when he was decapitated when his body struck a culvert. A Texas court sentenced two of the three white males convicted of Byrd's murder to death; the third was sentenced to life in prison.

Until recently, federal law limited federal prosecution of hate crimes to civil rights offenses under 18 U.S.C.A. § 245, which criminalizes interference with "federally protected activities" such as voting. But in 2009 Congress enacted the Matthew Shepard and James Byrd, Jr. Hate Crimes Prevention Act, 18 U.S.C.A. § 249, which eliminated the requirement that the victim be engaging in a federally protected activity. The new law also expanded federal hate crimes to include those motivated by a victim's actual or perceived gender, sexual orientation, gender identity, or disability.

Of course, hate crimes are also subject to state legislation. For example, New Jersey Statutes § 16-1 provides, "A person is guilty of the crime of bias intimidation if he commits, attempts to commit, conspires with another to commit, or threatens the immediate commission of an offense specified [in certain chapters of New Jersey Statutes] (1) with a purpose to intimidate an individual or group of individuals because of race, color, religion, gender, handicap, sexual orientation, or ethnicity. . . ." The law goes on to provide for a grading of the offense and specifies that "the court shall impose separate sentences upon a conviction for bias intimidation and a conviction of any underlying offense."

Most states now have laws permitting courts to enhance criminal penalties when defendants are convicted of hate crimes. The Supreme Court has upheld hate crime laws of the penalty enhancement variety—see *Wisconsin v. Mitchell*, 508 U.S. 476, 113 S.Ct. 2194, 124 L.Ed.2d 436 (1993)—but it has also said that the factual question of whether a crime was motivated by animus against a particular group is an element of the crime that must be proved beyond a reasonable doubt. In a jury trial, this question must be submitted to the jury. *Apprendi v. New Jersey*, 530 U.S. 466, 120 S.Ct. 2348, 147 L.Ed.2d 435 (2000).

## Conclusion

Over the centuries the assaultive, sexual, and detention crimes have been a stable base for prosecuting persons whose antisocial conduct offended the basic norms of civilized people. Yet laws must change to cope with the economic, social, and cultural needs of a dynamic society. In addition to the well-known offenses involving persons, in this chapter we have attempted to broaden the scope of the usual coverage of crimes against persons by explaining the impact of newer offenses such as stalking; abuse of children, spouses, and the elderly; and child snatching, as well as federal laws concerning violations of civil rights, which have become integral parts of the criminal justice system.

## Chapter Summary

- Learning Objective 1

  - The common law treated assault and battery as separate misdemeanors with an assault consisting of an offer to do bodily harm to another by using force and violence and a battery consisting of a completed assault.
  - Today all jurisdictions make assault an offense; most classify simple assaults and batteries as misdemeanors, while grading as felonies those perpetrated against public officers or involving more egregious conduct (aggravated assault, aggravated battery, and assault with intent to commit a serious crime). Most prosecutions occur under state laws, but federal statutes proscribe assaults within the maritime and territorial jurisdiction of the United States and assaults on federal officers, military personnel engaged in official duties, and foreign diplomatic personnel.

- Learning Objective 2

  - At common law, mayhem consisted of willfully and maliciously injuring another so as to render the victim less able in fighting.
  - Mayhem became a statutory crime in most states, but most of the acts formerly prosecuted under mayhem statutes now result in prosecutions for aggravated battery and attempted murder.

- Learning Objective 3

  - Hazing consists of intentional or reckless physical or mental harassment, abuse, or humiliation and frequently occurs in initiations into clubs, fraternities, sororities, athletic teams, and other groups. Although most hazing involves foolish pranks and seldom results in serious injuries, most states have laws that make hazing in all schools and colleges either a misdemeanor or felony, depending on the degree of injury to the initiate. Hazing laws usually stipulate that implied or express consent by the initiate is not a defense.
  - Statutes in all states now proscribe the offense of stalking. It is usually defined as consisting of repeatedly following, watching, or harassing another person. Federal law proscribes interstate stalking. Generally, stalking is a misdemeanor while aggravated stalking involving physical injury to a victim is a felony.
  - Most statutes either proscribe electronic forms of stalking or include it in their statutory definitions of stalking. Where courts have found constitutional infirmities in stalking statutes, legislatures have revised laws to make definitions more precise.

- Learning Objective 4

  - Under early English common law it was a felony for a male to have unlawful carnal knowledge of a female by force and against her will. Rape required *unlawful* intercourse; consequently, a husband could not be guilty of raping his wife. The law of rape required penetration, however slight, of the female's sexual organ by the male's sexual organ; no emission of seed was required.
  - During the late 1970s and the 1980s, protests led to reforms that focused on making rape a gender-neutral offense embracing all anal, oral, or vaginal penetrations by a sex organ or by another object, excepting acts performed for *bona fide* medical purposes, and dividing the offense of sexual battery into categories.
  - In many states, either by statutes or judicial decisions, a husband may be charged with rape of his wife. Marriage in contemporary society is regarded as a partnership and not as a license to enjoy sex on demand by a forcible encounter.
  - A significant reform was the enactment of rape shield laws that preclude presentation of evidence of a victim's prior sexual activity with anyone other than the defendant. Even where the defendant seeks to introduce evidence of prior relations with a victim, such evidence must usually be first presented to the court *in camera* to determine its relevancy to the victim's consent.
  - Appellate courts still disagree on the admissibility of evidence of expert evidence regarding the rape trauma syndrome. Courts no longer insist that a woman must "resist to the utmost" to establish that her sexual privacy has been violated. Neither do they instruct juries to scrutinize a victim's testimony.
  - Because a prosecution for rape frequently involves the victim's word against the defendant's word, police and prosecutors place paramount importance

on a "fresh complaint" by a victim. Preservation of semen, photographs of bruises, torn clothing, and even pubic hairs become valuable evidence to corroborate a victim's testimony.

○ Beyond a general denial of the charges, the most common defense asserted in a rape case is that the victim consented. Impotency is sometimes asserted but it is rarely accepted as a defense.

- Learning Objective 5

○ At common law a male under age fourteen was conclusively presumed not to be able to commit rape. It later became statutory rape for a male to have carnal knowledge of a female child under age ten with or without the child's consent.

○ American courts generally followed the English common law but early on states explicitly rejected the common law presumption that males under age fourteen could not commit rape and determined that consensual intercourse with a female younger than sixteen or eighteen, rather than ten, was statutory rape.

○ A few states have allowed a male to defend against a charge of statutory rape on the basis that he was mistaken about a female's age, but most hold a male defendant strictly liable. Most statutory rape laws are now gender neutral. Some impose penalties only if there is at least a two- to five-year disparity between the ages of the perpetrator and the underage victim.

○ There is universal agreement that very young children should be protected from sexual predators, but there is considerable opposition to statutory rape laws. Opponents argue that these laws are out of touch with present-day sexual mores, deprive women in their late teens of exercising a personal choice, and lend themselves to selective enforcement along the lines of race and social class.

- Learning Objective 6

○ Sodomy refers to oral or anal sex between humans and sexual intercourse between humans and animals. Consensual sodomy was formerly viewed as an offense against public morality, but in 2003 the U.S. Supreme Court found unconstitutional a Texas law that proscribed private, consensual sodomy between same-sex partners. This sounded the death knell for laws prohibiting consensual sodomy.

○ Nonconsensual sodomy is considered a crime against a person and is often charged under statutes proscribing sexual battery.

- Learning Objective 7

○ To protect children from sexual predators, states now require sexual offenders who are released from prison, move into a state, or simply change their address to register with local law enforcement agencies. These laws have survived a variety of constitutional attacks.

- Learning Objective 8

○ Recently, Congress and state legislatures have enacted laws designed to protect from abuse children, spouses, other intimate partners, and, in some instances, the elderly. Many offenses against children are subject to traditional crimes against persons, yet many states have enacted specific child abuse laws to cover a broader range of abusive behaviors and violence against children, which are prosecuted as strict liability offenses.

○ Prosecutions for maternal conduct before a birth—for example, ingestion of harmful drugs—are problematical under child abuse/endangerment or drug distribution statutes.

- o Many states have enacted laws to provide for issuance of court injunctions to protect spouses and intimate partners from domestic violence and provide for the arrest of violators. Federal courts have upheld the constitutionality of the federal law that criminalizes interstate abuses of spouses and intimate partners.
- o Abuse of the elderly is usually handled through regulatory agencies, but some state legislatures have made it a felony in order to punish caregivers who abuse, neglect, or exploit elderly persons.

- Learning Objective 9

  - o In recognition of the need to protect an individual's freedom of movement, the common law developed two misdemeanor offenses: false imprisonment and kidnapping. False imprisonment consisted of confining someone against his or her will, whereas kidnapping involved forcibly abducting and taking a person to another country.
  - o Today, most cases of false imprisonment involve civil litigation, but where states make it a misdemeanor they generally define it, as did the common law, as "the unlawful detention of a person."
  - o Kidnapping is a serious felony proscribed by all states and by federal law. Unlike the common law, where kidnapping required that the victim be taken to another country, federal and state statutes generally require that there be "an unlawful taking and forcible carrying away (asportation) of a victim without that person's consent." Intimidation and coercion can substitute for force. Consent must be voluntarily given. Young children and incompetents cannot legally consent to an act of asportation. Courts generally do not allow movement incidental to another crime that does not involve additional significant risk to the victim to fulfill the asportation requirement.
  - o The Federal Kidnapping Act criminalizes interstate kidnapping for ransom. A recent federal statute makes hostage taking an offense. Most defenses to false imprisonment or kidnapping contend that the acts were done as authorized by law. Defendants charged with kidnapping often challenge whether there has been proper asportation.
  - o A category of offenses unknown to the common law involves injuries to the civil rights of individuals. After the Civil War, Congress adopted a series of laws designed to protect the civil rights of the newly freed former slaves. As a result of judicial interpretation, federal civil rights laws now protect individuals from a wide range of injurious conduct by public officials or other persons acting under the authority of the government.
  - o Today, these statutes are also used to prosecute individuals who conspire to use their official positions to deprive persons of rights guaranteed by the U.S. Constitution or federal laws and to prosecute individuals who engage in criminal acts that are racially motivated and police who use excessive force.
  - o Hate crimes are motivated by bias against members of certain groups. Until recently, federal law limited federal prosecution of hate crimes to interference with "federally protected activities." In 2009 Congress enacted the Matthew Shepard and James Byrd, Jr. Hate Crimes Prevention Act, which eliminated this requirement and expanded federal hate crimes to include those motivated by a victim's actual or perceived gender, sexual orientation, gender identity, or disability.
  - o Hate crimes are also subject to state legislation, which often takes the form of enhancing criminal penalties for persons convicted of crimes motivated by bias.

## Key Terms

abuse of the elderly

aggravated assault

aggravated battery

asportation

assault

battery

carnal knowledge

child abuse

child snatching

civil rights

common-law rape

consent

cyberstalking

endangering the welfare of a child

false imprisonment

force

forcible rape

gender-neutral offense

Hale's Rule

hate crimes

hazing

hostage taking

impotency

kidnapping

kidnapping for ransom

marital exception

mayhem

Megan's Law

Parental Kidnapping Prevention Act (PKPA)

rape shield laws

rape trauma syndrome

sexual contact

sexual penetration

simple kidnapping

sodomy

spousal abuse

stalking

statutory rape

Uniform Child Custody Jurisdiction and Enforcement Act (UCCJEA)

## Questions for Thought and Discussion

1. What elements, in addition to those required for assault or battery, must the prosecution prove to convict a defendant of aggravated assault or battery?
2. What interests does the law seek to protect in proscribing (a) forcible rape and (b) statutory rape?
3. Which statutory and judicial reforms of the 1970s and 1980s in the law of rape were the most significant from a female victim's standpoint? Are there other biases against female victims of sexual assault that should be addressed?
4. Does Hale's Rule, which creates a marital exception in the law of rape, apply in your state?
5. What role do the Uniform Child Custody Jurisdiction and Enforcement Act (UCCJEA) and the Parental Kidnapping Prevention Act (PKPA) play in controlling child snatching?
6. Do the federal statutes that make it unlawful to deprive persons of their civil rights under color of law have a significant deterrent effect on misconduct of law enforcement personnel? Or do these statutes hamper effective police action?
7. Explain the necessity for the prosecution to prove asportation in order to establish the offense of kidnapping.

8. Why have most state courts rejected prosecution of a mother whose child suffers adverse medical effects from the mother's ingestion of cocaine during her pregnancy?

9. Assume you are a staff member of a state criminal justice agency. The director asks you to compose a draft of a statute to prohibit endangerment to children. What key points would you include in your draft?

## Problems for Discussion and Solution

1. Daniel grabbed a large stick and in a threatening manner advanced toward William. Before he came within striking distance of William, a third party stopped him. Based on this evidence is it likely that Daniel will be found guilty of assault?

2. A state law defines false imprisonment as "the intentional restraint of another person without lawful authority." Alan drove his girlfriend, Olivia, to the shopping mall. He insisted she wait in the car while he shopped. When she protested he locked the car and was gone for forty-five minutes. Olivia filed a complaint with the police. Is it likely that the state will prosecute Alan for false imprisonment?

3. A store manager observes Lucy Grabit stuffing a pair of nylon hose into her purse before going through the checkout counter in a supermarket. The manager detains her and promptly directs his employee to call the police. Is the store manager guilty of false imprisonment? Why or why not?

4. Several college freshmen enter the dean's private office and remain there for several hours. They refuse to let the dean leave until he yields to their demands to allow unrestricted visitation in all dormitories. Under contemporary criminal statutes, what offense, if any, have the students committed? Explain.

5. The defendant was convicted of battery under a statute that provides that "a person commits a battery who either intentionally or knowingly, and without legal justification, makes physical contact of an insulting or provoking nature with an individual." The evidence disclosed that one morning the male defendant picked up a female friend whom he had invited to have breakfast with him. En route to the restaurant he unbuttoned her blouse and placed his hand on her breast; after she removed his hand and asked him to stop, he again placed his hand on her breast. On appeal, the defendant argues that his conviction should be reversed because his acts were not insulting, there was no struggle, and the female did not testify that she was traumatized or disturbed by his acts. Moreover, he points out that the evidence disclosed that after the incident the female complainant accompanied him to a restaurant where they had breakfast together. Should the appellate court reverse this conviction on the ground that the evidence is insufficient? Why or why not?

6. The defendant and her husband have two sons, ages five and three. Without notifying her husband, the defendant left the family home with both children. At that time, no court proceedings were pending concerning either their marriage or custody of their children. Two weeks later, and without the wife's knowledge, the husband obtained a court order granting him custody of the two children. An arrest warrant was eventually issued for the wife. She was arrested in another state and brought back to her home state, where she now faces prosecution under a statute that provides, "Whoever, being a relative of a child . . . without lawful authority, holds or intends to hold such a child permanently or for a protracted period, or takes or entices a child from his lawful custodian . . . shall be guilty of a felony." The wife's attorney stipulates that the facts are correct as

stated but contends that the wife cannot be convicted of parental kidnapping under the quoted statute. What result do you think should occur? Why?

7. A nineteen-year-old woman returns home from an evening at the beach. She tells her mother that she has been raped and sodomized by an attacker she does not know. Some hours later, the woman identifies her attacker to her mother, and they notify the police. At trial, the prosecution seeks to admit expert testimony on rape trauma syndrome to explain the victim's reticence in promptly identifying her attacker. The defense objects. Should the court allow expert testimony on this subject to explain the reactions of the female victim in the hours following her attack and to explain why she may initially have been unwilling to report the defendant who attacked her? Why or why not?

# CHAPTER 8

# Property Crimes

## CHAPTER OUTLINE

## JURISPRUDENCE

*McLaughlin v. United States* (1986)

*Holloway v. United States* (1999)

## LEARNING OBJECTIVES

After reading this chapter, you should be able to explain

1. how the common-law theft offenses have evolved under modern statutory law to include sophisticated forms of theft

2. why robbery is considered more heinous than other property crimes

3. why Congress created the offense of carjacking

4. how extortion differs from robbery

5. how forgery differs from passing a worthless check

6. how and why burglary is defined more broadly today than it was under the common law

7. why arson is no longer merely an offense against habitation

8. how malicious mischief can be either a misdemeanor or a felony

9. the defenses against prosecution for property crimes

## CHAPTER OPENING VIGNETTE

In March 2010, Robert Halderman pleaded guilty in a New York courtroom to the crime of extortion. His was far from a run-of-the-mill property crime. Halderman, who worked as a producer at CBS, apparently uncovered information about the private life of late-night comic David Letterman. Halderman then demanded $2 million from Letterman in exchange for not revealing the information. Halderman presented the extortion threat under the guise of a "treatment," which is industry jargon for an idea for a television program. Appearing to give in to the threat, Letterman's attorney delivered a bogus $2 million check to Halderman. Reading from a prepared statement in court, Halderman acknowledged that the treatment he presented "was just a thinly veiled threat to ruin Mr. Letterman if he did not pay me a lot of money." He also admitted, "I knew throughout this time that I was not engaged in a legitimate business transaction with Mr. Letterman and that what I was doing was against New York law."

The statute under which Halderman was convicted, McKinney's N.Y. Penal Law § 155.05(2), provides, in relevant part, that a person commits extortion when "he compels or induces another person to deliver . . . property to himself or to a third person by means of instilling in him a fear that, if the property is not so delivered, the actor or another will . . . expose a secret or publicize an asserted fact, whether true or false, tending to subject some person to hatred, contempt or ridicule." Like most of the property crimes discussed in this chapter, extortion is rooted in the English common law, but it has become a broader offense under modern statutes.

As part of a plea bargain with prosecutors, Robert Halderman agreed to plead guilty to extortion and publicly admit responsibility for the crime. He was sentenced to six months in jail and one thousand hours of community service. Under New York law, he could have faced a prison term of up to fifteen years.

# Introduction

Private property is a basic value of American society and a fundamental tenet of American law. In early America, property interests beyond raw land were often meager, consisting primarily of possessions necessary for survival. Most people's dwellings were modest. At that time, enforcement of the law largely depended on "self-help."

As the nation developed, property interests became a vital part of the American economy, and professional law enforcement became the rule rather than the exception. The law recognized the need to deter people from infringing on the property interests of others and to punish transgressors. In today's affluent society and with the rapid technological advances of the past few decades, crimes against property have assumed even greater significance. In this chapter we examine the background of basic common-law property and habitation offenses and provide a sampling of the present-day statutory crimes in this area.

## The Common-Law Background

When the common law emerged, England was an agrarian country with relatively little commercial activity. Possession of private property was an important concept, but beyond the right to occupy a dwelling, the property interests of most people consisted largely of what the law refers to as **tangible property** (such things as animals, cooking implements, and tools). Today, in addition to tangible property (such as automobiles, household goods, and books), a majority of households own some intangible property, such as bank accounts, stocks, bonds, and notes. Thus, in contrast to the early common-law period, intangible assets are now of great economic importance.

**tangible property** Property that has physical form, substance, and value in itself.

The common-law offenses involving property reflect the environment in which they matured. It was a very serious offense for someone to permanently deprive another of the possession of personal property, whether through stealth or through force, violence, or intimidation. However, it was of far less consequence to cheat someone by the use of false tokens or false weights and measures. When it came to such breaches of ethics as misrepresentations and violations of trust, the common law generally left victims to their civil remedies. This view gave rise to such early maxims as *caveat emptor*, meaning, "let the buyer beware." Because commercial transactions were not a major concern, forgery remained a misdemeanor. Likewise, extortion and malicious mischief were misdemeanors, because the conduct involved in these offenses did not qualify for the severe punishment meted out for felonies. Finally, offenses concerning the rights of landholders were dealt with largely through the civil law.

## The Common-Law Theft Offenses

By 1776 the English common law recognized two offenses dealing with theft: larceny and false pretenses. Theft offenses of embezzlement and receiving stolen property were later created by statutes passed by the English Parliament.

### Larceny

The basic common-law offense against infringement of another's personal property was **larceny**, the crime from which all other theft offenses developed. Larceny was a felony that consisted of (1) the wrongful taking and carrying away of (2) the personal property of another (3) with the intent to permanently deprive the other person of the property. The taking was called the "caption," the carrying away was called the "asportation," and the personal property had to have a "corporeal" (that is, a physical) existence. The wrongful act of taking was described as a "trespass," and the intent to permanently deprive the victim of the property was known as the *animus furundi*. Although many of these terms are not in common use today, the reader will find that courts frequently use them in judicial opinions when interpreting modern-day theft statutes.

**larceny** A synonym for theft. At common law, larceny was defined as the unlawful taking of property with the intent of permanently depriving the owner of same.

To constitute common-law larceny, the taking had to be a deprivation of the owner's or possessor's interest in personal property. Real estate and the property attached to it were not subject to larceny; neither were trees nor crops wrongfully severed from the land. But if the owner of property had already severed crops and a thief carried them away, it was larceny because the thief was carrying away personal property rather than merely infringing on the owner's real property.

These distinctions are difficult to appreciate today, but they were significant in the development of the common law, where wrongs concerning a person's land gave rise to civil, as opposed to criminal, remedies. Also, at common law, anyone wrongfully deprived of possession of personal property was entitled to recover damages based on the tort (civil wrong) of conversion. Thus, there was overlap between the crime of larceny and the tort of conversion.

As the common law developed, personal property consisted largely of tools, household items, and domestic animals. Items such as promissory notes were not subject to larceny because they represented intangible legal rights; however, coins and bills were, because they had a physical existence.

A taking by a person who had a lawful right to possession was not larceny. As we will discuss later, this led Parliament to legislatively create the crime of embezzlement. Because the property had to be taken from another, a co-owner or partner did not commit larceny by taking jointly owned property. Nor did a spouse commit larceny by taking the other spouse's property, because at common law, both spouses were considered one entity.

To find an accused guilty of larceny, it was necessary to prove that the taker carried the property away. This element was usually satisfied by even a slight removal of the property. It was also essential to prove the taker's intent to permanently deprive the owner or possessor of the property. A person could not be convicted for borrowing property or for using property under a reasonable belief of a right of possession. Consequently, a person who temporarily took another's horse would not be guilty of larceny because there was no intent to permanently deprive the owner of the horse. Furthermore, had someone taken a horse that reasonably appeared to be the taker's own, the taker would likely have been acting under a *bona fide* mistake of fact and hence would not have been guilty of larceny. (See Chapter 14 for a discussion of the mistake-of-fact defense.) Yet a person who secured possession of goods through trickery could be found guilty of larceny if there was proof that the trickster intended to permanently deprive the owner of the goods.

## False Pretenses, Embezzlement, and Receiving Stolen Property

Many technical and often subtle distinctions developed in the common-law crime of larceny. Perhaps one reason for this was that courts were reluctant to find a thief guilty of larceny because the penalty at early common law was death. As commerce became more significant in England, the crime of larceny was not adequate either to deal with those who obtained financial advantage through false pretenses or to deter or punish servants who fraudulently appropriated property that rightfully came into their possession. Consequently, by the late 1700s, the English Parliament created two supplemental misdemeanor offenses: **false pretenses** and embezzlement. The offense of false pretenses came into being in 1757, before the

**false pretenses** The crime of obtaining money or property through misrepresentation.

**embezzlement** The crime of using a position of trust or authority to transfer or convert the money or property of another to oneself.

American Revolution. The offense thereby became a part of the common law of those states that adopted it with the statutory modifications made by Parliament before the American Revolution. **Embezzlement**, on the other hand, did not become a statutory crime until an enactment by Parliament in 1799. Although as early as 1691 a receiver of stolen goods could be prosecuted as an accessory after the fact to larceny, not until 1827 did Parliament enact a statute making receiving stolen property a misdemeanor. Thus, embezzlement and receiving stolen property became English laws too late to become part of the common law adopted by the new American states. By subsequent enactments, the English Parliament broadened the scope of embezzlement.

A charge of false pretenses (actually, "obtaining property by false pretenses") usually involves (1) the accused obtaining wares or merchandise of another (2) by false pretenses and (3) with the intent to cheat or defraud the other person. Parliament's enactment of the offense of false pretenses during the Industrial Revolution represented an important development in the English criminal law. Because false pretenses became an offense just before the American Revolution, few English court decisions interpreting this offense became a part of the common law adopted by the new American states. Even so, the English law in this area influenced both American legislation and judicial decisions.

In contrast with larceny, embezzlement occurred where a person who had lawful possession of another's property (e.g., a servant or employee) wrongfully appropriated that property. A series of enactments by the English Parliament brought not only servants but also brokers, bankers, lawyers, and trustees within the scope of embezzlement. Thus, an embezzlement occurred when someone occupying a position of trust converted another's property to his or her own use, whereas larceny required proof of a wrongful taking and carrying away of the personal property of another. Nevertheless, to convict a defendant of embezzlement, it was necessary to prove that the accused intended to defraud the victim. **Receiving stolen property** consisted of receiving possession and control of another's personal property knowing it was stolen and with the intent to permanently deprive the owner of possession of such property.

**receiving stolen property** Knowingly receiving possession and control of personal property belonging to another with the intent to permanently deprive the owner of possession of such property.

---

**CASE-IN-POINT**

## Receiving Stolen Property: Sufficient Evidence to Convict

Defendant Lynn Belt was convicted of receiving stolen property in violation of Utah Code Ann. § 76-6-408(1) (Supp. 1989), which makes it a crime for a person to receive property of another "knowing that it has been stolen or believing that it probably has been stolen . . . with a purpose to deprive the owner thereof." Belt appealed, contending that the evidence was legally insufficient to support his conviction. The evidence revealed that the defendant purchased videocassette recorders from Sgt. Illsley of the Metro Major Felony Unit during an undercover operation involving the purchase and sale

of stolen property. Defendant met Illsley at an empty parking lot, where Illsley offered the new recorders to the defendant at a very low price, explaining that the store name and serial numbers had been cut off. Defendant replied, "I don't want to hear about the serial number or store names—just do our business." Illsley testified that at one point the defendant said, "I wish you wouldn't cut the serial numbers off. That makes it look hot." The Court of Appeals of Utah held that the evidence was sufficient for the jury to have found that the defendant believed the goods he purchased were stolen and affirmed Belt's conviction.

*State v. Belt*, 780 P.2d 1271 (Utah App. 1989).

# The Modern Approach to Theft Offenses

A review of the various technical distinctions that developed in the common-law offenses of larceny, receiving stolen property, and false pretenses and the early statutory offenses of embezzlement and receiving stolen property makes it obvious that significant reforms were needed. A redefinition of these basic property offenses was required to cope with the various aspects of theft in American society. Modern theft includes not only forms of larceny known to the common law but also theft of vehicles, shoplifting, looting, carjacking, extortion, and other sophisticated forms of theft (see Figure 8.1). We deal with the more sophisticated forms of larceny in Chapter 9 under the heading of "white-collar crimes."

## Federal Approaches

Congress has enacted a series of statutes comprehensively proscribing theft and embezzlement. The first, 18 U.S.C.A. § 641, provides,

> Whoever embezzles, steals, purloins, or knowingly converts to his use or the use of another, or without authority, sells, conveys or disposes of any record, voucher, money, or thing of value of the United States or any department or agency thereof, or any property made or being made under contract for the United States or any department or agency thereof; or
>
> Whoever receives, conceals, or retains the same with intent to convert it to his use or gain, knowing it to have been embezzled, stolen, purloined or converted; . . .
>
> Shall be fined. . . .

The purpose of 18 U.S.C.A. § 641 is to place in one part of the criminal code crimes so kindred as to belong in one category. The Supreme Court has said that despite the failure of Congress to include expressly the common-law intent requirement for larceny, § 641 should not be construed to eliminate that intent requirement. The statute has been held to apply not only to larceny and embezzlement, but also to all instances in which a person may obtain wrongful advantage from another's property. *Morissette v. United States*, 342 U.S. 246, 72 S.Ct. 240, 96 L.Ed. 288 (1952).

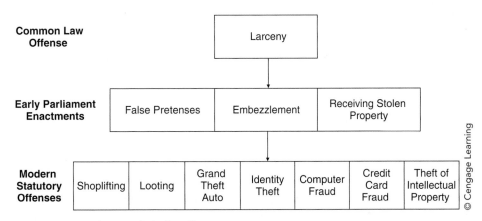

**FIGURE 8.1** Evolution of Theft Offenses.

Another federal statute, 18 U.S.C.A. § 659, provides penalties for embezzling or unlawfully taking the contents of any vehicle moving in interstate or foreign commerce or from any passenger therein. Federal appellate courts have characterized the intent requirement under this statute as the intent to appropriate or convert the property of the owner. Furthermore, the federal appellate courts have said that a simultaneous intent to return the property or make restitution does not make the offense any less embezzlement. See, e.g., *United States v. Waronek*, 582 F.2d 1158 (7th Cir. 1978).

A variety of other federal statutes define embezzlement and theft by public officers or employees of the United States, custodians of federal funds, bank examiners, and bank officers and employees. See 18 U.S.C.A. §§ 641–665. During the 1990s Congress added statutes creating new offenses involving theft. These included theft from programs involving federal funds, theft of livestock and artwork, and theft or embezzlement in connection with health care. 18 U.S.C.A. §§ 666–669.

## State Approaches

All states have enacted statutes expanding the common-law concept of larceny to include all types of tangible and intangible property. Historically, the states maintained numerous statutes that adopted the basic concepts of common-law larceny and false pretenses as well as the later English statutes proscribing embezzlement and receiving stolen property. As new problems developed, legislative bodies attempted to fill the gaps by creating new offenses. This resulted in the legislative creation of numerous statutory offenses proscribing various forms of stealing and dishonest dealings. These statutes often were confusing and in many instances were contradictory.

In recent years, many states have replaced their various theft statutes with a consolidated theft statute that proscribes stealing in very broad terms. These new statutes make it unlawful for a person to commit any of the common-law theft offenses mentioned, as well as other crimes, and impose penalties based on the amount and character of the property stolen.

Florida, for example, passed the Florida Anti-Fencing Act in 1977. Despite its narrow title, the act defines theft as including all the common-law theft offenses, several former statutory offenses, possession of property with altered or removed identifying features, and dealing in stolen property (that is, fencing). As do other modern theft statutes, the statute defines theft by degrees based on the seriousness of the offender's conduct. West's Fla. Stat. Ann. § 812.012–037. Section 812.014(1) provides:

> A person commits theft if he or she knowingly obtains or uses, or endeavors to obtain or to use, the property of another with intent to, either temporarily or permanently:
> (a) Deprive the other person of a right to the property or a benefit from the property.
> (b) Appropriate the property to his or her own use or to the use of any person not entitled to the use of the property.

Under the comprehensive Florida theft statute, the phrase "obtains or uses" replaces the old common-law requirement of "taking and carrying away." The law defines "obtains or uses" as

> any manner of (a) taking or exercising control over property; (b) making any unauthorized use, disposition, or transfer of property; (c) obtaining property by fraud, willful misrepresentation of a future act, or false promise; or (d) by conduct previously known as stealing, larceny, purloining, abstracting, embezzlement, misapplication, misappropriation, conversion, or obtaining money or property by false pretenses, fraud, or deception; or (e) other conduct similar in nature. § 812.012(1)(2).

"Property" is broadly defined to include "(a) Real property, including things growing on, affixed to, and found in land; (b) Tangible or intangible personal property, including rights, privileges, interests, and claims; and (c) Services." § 812.012(4).

"Property of another" means "property in which a person has an interest upon which another person is not privileged to infringe without consent, whether or not the other person has an interest in the property." § 812.012(5).

"Services" means "anything of value resulting from a person's physical or mental labor or skill, or from the use, possession, or presence of property, and includes: (a) Repairs or improvements to property. (b) Professional services. (c) Private, public, or government communication, transportation, power, water, or sanitation services. (d) Lodging accommodations. (e) Admissions to places of exhibition or entertainment." § 812.012(6).

**grand theft** Major form of larceny; theft of a sufficient value of property to make the crime a felony.

The value and type of property stolen categorize the seriousness of the offense. **Grand theft** in the first degree is the most serious felony. It includes stealing property valued at $100,000 or more or cargo valued at $50,000 or more, as well as committing any grand theft in the course of which the offender uses a motor vehicle as an instrumentality, other than merely as a getaway vehicle, to assist in committing the offense and thereby damages the real property of another or causes damage to the real or personal property of another in excess of $1,000. §§ 812.014(2)(a)–(b).

Grand theft in the second degree, a somewhat less serious felony, involves theft of property valued at $20,000 or more but less than $100,000, cargo valued at less than $50,000, or emergency medical equipment or law enforcement equipment

**CASE-IN-POINT**

## The Nebraska Supreme Court Reverses a Conviction for Shoplifting

The defendant, Richard, was convicted of larceny in a Nebraska court. The evidence revealed that Richard entered Alexander's Super Market where he "examined the bacon displayed for sale, picked up a 1-pound package, and walked by the meat counter." The meat manager followed defendant, and testified at trial that Richard thrust his hand into his coat, went toward the checkout lane, and didn't have the bacon [in his hand] anymore." The store manager testified that he "approached [Richard], talked to him about the bacon, and Richard took the pound of bacon from his coat." However, the manager could "not remember whether [Richard] told him that he was going to pay for the bacon, but did remember that defendant handed the bacon to him and walked out of the store after the confrontation." Richard testified that "he had examined different types of bacon, selected one pound, did not put it in his coat, was stopped by the store personnel, showed them his wallet with 'seventy-some' dollars in it, offered to pay, and when that offer was refused told the store personnel that he was not trying to steal the bacon; and said 'either you're going to take

my money or . . . I'm going to walk back, . . . I'm going to put it down, [and] I'm going to walk out of here.'" The Supreme Court of Nebraska concluded that "the bacon was not removed from the store by defendant." As a result, the question before the court was whether Richard's actions constituted the crime of "stealing" where there is a "taking and 'asportation' with intent to steal." The court held "to constitute larceny the object stolen must be removed from the premises of the owner, with intent to steal, before the larceny is complete." The court went on to hold "where merchandise in a store is involved, . . . the case [law] appear[s] to be in agreement that in a self-service store, where customers select and pick up articles to be paid for at the checkout counter, the mere picking up of an article in the display area does not constitute asportation." Simply because Richard "placed the goods in a shopping bag provided no valid reason for the trial court to infer a criminal intent or a possession clearly adverse to the interest of the store." Thus, Richard's conviction was reversed and the case remanded for a new trial.

*State v. Richard*, 216 Neb. 832, 346 N.W.2d 399 (Neb. 1984).

valued at $300 or more. § 812.014(2)(b). It is grand theft in the third degree, and a lesser felony, if the property stolen is valued at $300 or more but less than $20,000, or if the property stolen is a will, codicil, or other testamentary instrument; firearm; motor vehicle; livestock; fire extinguisher; 2,000 or more pieces of citrus fruit; a stop sign; property taken from an identified construction site; or anhydrous ammonia. § 812.014(2)(c). If the property stolen is valued at $100 or more but less than $300 and is taken from a dwelling or from the unenclosed curtilage of a dwelling, the offense is also classified as a third-degree felony. § 812.014(2)(d). Otherwise, except for the specified articles, theft of property having a value under $300 is petit theft, a misdemeanor. § 812.014(2)(e).

**petit theft** Minor form of larceny; theft of property of sufficiently small value that the offense is classified as a misdemeanor.

Finally, a person previously convicted of theft who commits **petit theft** is guilty of a more serious misdemeanor, § 812.014(3)(b). One who has been convicted of theft two or more times commits a felony of the third degree, § 812.014(3)(c). Special penalties include suspension of the driver's license of a person who drives away from a filling station without paying for gasoline, § 812.014(5). Penalties are also upgraded where the victim of theft is over age 65. § 812.0145.

**intent to deprive** The willful design to take goods or services from another without permission or authority of law.

Theft remains a specific-intent crime, but like many newer theft statutes, the Florida statute simply refers to the **intent to deprive**. The Florida Supreme Court has said this means the "intent to steal" and not necessarily the intent to permanently deprive the owner of the property. *State v. Dunmann*, 427 So.2d 166 (Fla. 1983). Because the statutory definition of theft includes an endeavor to commit theft, the crime is fully proved when an attempt, along with the requisite intent, is established. *State v. Sykes*, 434 So.2d 325 (Fla. 1983) (see Chapter 5).

## A Unique Prosecutorial Burden in Theft Offenses

Except where statutorily specified articles are stolen, theft offenses are usually classified as grand theft or petit theft. Statutes commonly grade the felony and misdemeanor offenses based on ranges of market value of goods stolen. Therefore, the prosecution must establish the market value of goods or services stolen. The determining factor is generally the market value at the time and in the locality of the theft. *State v. Kimbel*, 620 P.2d 515 (Utah 1980). This may be shown by proof of the original market cost, the manner in which the property stolen has been used, and its general condition and quality. *Negron v. State*, 306 So.2d 104 (Fla. 1974). Judges customarily instruct juries that if the value of the property cannot be ascertained, they

**CASE-IN-POINT**

### Larceny Committed through a Phony Night-Deposit Box

A Massachusetts jury convicted Brian Donovan and Robert Grant of larceny. Evidence introduced at trial showed that they had constructed a phony night-deposit box and attached it to the wall of a bank building. The box was constructed of heavy-gauge steel just like a real depository. Seven depositors lost an estimated $37,000 by making deposits to the phony box. Although the phony box was never recovered, a witness testified that he overheard the defendants in a bar talking about the phony deposit box as "a helluva'n idea." Another witness stated that Grant had admitted to her that he had robbed a bank using a phony deposit box. On appeal, the Massachusetts Supreme Court rejected the defendants' contentions that certain testimony had been improperly admitted into evidence and that the evidence produced at trial was legally insufficient to prove the crime of larceny.

*Commonwealth v. Donovan*, 478 N.E.2d 727 (Mass. 1985).

must find the value to be less than that required for grand theft. However, consider the theft of a credit card. Usually, these cards have set credit limits that are only available to the holder on proper signature. Therefore, a credit card has no market value to a third person in lawful channels. In *Miller v. People*, 566 P.2d 1059 (Colo. 1977), the Colorado Supreme Court held that the amount that could be purchased on the stolen card in the "illegitimate" market could be considered in determining whether a defendant was guilty of felony theft. In *Owolabi v. Commonwealth*, 428 S.E.2d 14 (Va. App. 1993), a Virginia appellate court disagreed. Where there was no evidence of the value of the credit cards stolen, but only of the lines of credit they represented, the evidence did not support a finding that the card had a value greater than $200. Thus, the court held that the defendant could be convicted only of petit larceny, not grand larceny.

Proof of value is very important in a theft case because it can often mean the difference between a misdemeanor conviction and a felony conviction, or even between felonies of various degrees. For this reason, courts often receive expert testimony on this issue.

# Robbery

**robbery** The crime of taking money or property from a person against that person's will by means of force or intimidation.

At common law, **robbery** was a felony that consisted of (1) a taking of another's personal property of value (2) from the other person's possession or presence (3) by force or placing the person in fear and (4) with the intent to permanently deprive the other person of that property. In reality, robbery was an aggravated form of larceny where the taking was accomplished by force or threats of force and had the same specific-intent requirement as common-law larceny. The intent to steal (*animus furundi*), for example, was the same as in larceny and the taking of property had to be from the victim's actual or constructive possession. To constitute robbery, the violence or intimidation had to overcome the victim's resistance and precede or accompany the actual taking of property. Property in the victim's dwelling or vicinity was regarded as being in the victim's possession. To illustrate a significant difference between larceny and robbery, a person who spirited a person's wallet from his pocket would be guilty of larceny, but if the victim resisted and the thief took the wallet by force or violence, the offense constituted robbery.

## Statutory Approaches to Robbery

In some respects, robbery is an offense against the person because it usually involves an assault or battery. See, e.g., *State v. Shoemake*, 618 P.2d 1201 (Kan. 1980). Yet it also involves a taking of property and is generally classified as an offense against property.

### Federal Laws

A federal statute makes it an offense to take, or attempt to take, by force and violence or intimidation from the person or presence of another any property or money belonging to or in the care of a bank, credit union, or savings and loan association. 18 U.S.C.A. § 2113(a). The statute also proscribes bank robbery "by the use of a dangerous weapon." 18 U.S.C.A. § 2113(d). The Supreme Court has ruled that using an unloaded gun during a bank robbery qualifies as using a "dangerous weapon." *McLaughlin v. United States*, 476 U.S. 16, 106 S.Ct. 1677, 90 L.Ed.2d 15 (1986).

In addition, 18 U.S.C.A. § 1951 (Hobbs Act) defines the obstruction of interstate commerce in the context of robbery. Federal jurisdiction is established where the

*McLaughlin v. United States*, 476 U.S. 16, 106 S.Ct. 1677, 90 L.Ed.2d 15 (1986)

On the morning of July 26, 1984, Lamont Julius McLaughlin and a companion, both wearing masks, entered a bank in Baltimore. McLaughlin brandished a handgun and told those in the bank to put up their hands and not to move. While McLaughlin held the gun, his companion leaped over the counter and stuffed several thousand dollars into a brown paper bag. Police officers were waiting outside and promptly arrested the pair. It was then determined that McLaughlin's gun was not loaded. McLaughlin was found guilty in federal court of bank robbery "by the use of a dangerous weapon" in violation of 18 U.S.C.A. § 2113(d). On appeal, McLaughlin argued that his unloaded gun did not qualify as a "dangerous weapon"

under the statute. The U.S. Supreme Court rejected the argument and upheld McLaughlin's conviction. Justice John Paul Stevens opined,

Three reasons, each independently sufficient, support the conclusion that an unloaded gun is a "dangerous weapon." First, a gun is an article that is typically and characteristically dangerous; the use for which it is manufactured and sold is a dangerous one, and the law reasonably may presume that such an article is always dangerous even though it may not be armed at a particular time or place. In addition, the display of a gun instills fear in the average citizen; as a consequence, it creates an immediate danger that a violent response will ensue. Finally, a gun can cause harm when used as a bludgeon.

bank is a federally chartered institution or where its deposits are federally insured. *United States v. Harris*, 530 F.2d 576 (4th Cir. 1976). The statutory offense varies from the common-law crime of robbery in that the government need only establish the defendant's general intent. *United States v. Klare*, 545 F.2d 93 (9th Cir. 1976).

**State Laws**

Robbery is an offense in every state. Many states have enacted statutes simply defining it as did the common law, a practice sometimes referred to as *codifying the common law*. Other states classify robbery according to degree, with the seriousness of the offense usually based on whether the assailant is armed, the degree of force used, and, in some instances, on the vulnerability of the victim. The value of the property taken does not usually affect the degree of the crime of robbery, as it does that of theft.

The Colorado Criminal Code provides a good illustration of classification of robbery offenses: "A person who knowingly takes anything of value from the person or presence of another by the use of force, threats, or intimidation commits robbery." West's Colo. Stat. Ann. § 18-4-301(1). Property is taken from the "presence of another" under Colorado law when it is so within the victim's reach, inspection, or observation that he or she would be able to retain control over the property but for the force, threats, or intimidation directed by the perpetrator. *People v. Bartowsheski*, 661 P.2d 235 (Colo. 1983). This is "simple robbery," in contrast with the statutory offense of **aggravated robbery**. The Colorado statute further provides:

**aggravated robbery** A robbery made worse by one or more aggravating factors, such as the perpetrator being armed with a dangerous weapon or actually inflicting harm on the victim.

(1) A person who commits robbery is guilty of aggravated robbery if during the act of robbery or immediate flight therefrom:

    (a) He is armed with a deadly weapon with intent, if resisted, to kill, maim, or wound the person robbed or any other person; or

    (b) He knowingly wounds or strikes the person robbed or any other person with a deadly weapon or by the use of force, threats, or intimidation with a deadly

### Robbery During an Escape

**CASE-IN-POINT**

Jerry Earl Jones, was being transported by automobile from one correctional facility to another. En route, Jones threatened the deputy who was transporting him by brandishing an object that appeared to be a gun. As a result, the deputy surrendered his vehicle to Jones, who escaped with both the automobile and the deputy's pistol. The gun Jones used to perpetrate the escape turned out to be a fake. In its opinion, the Virginia Court of Appeals court cited the elements of robbery, which include a "taking, with intent to steal, of the personal property of another, from his person or in his presence, against his will, by violence or intimidation." On the facts as summarized here, the Court had no difficulty sustaining the conviction.

*Jones v. Commonwealth* (1992), 414 S.E.2d 193 (Va. App. 1992).

weapon knowingly puts the person robbed or any other person in reasonable fear of death or bodily injury; or

(c) He has present a confederate, aiding or abetting the perpetration of the robbery, armed with a deadly weapon, with the intent, either on the part of the defendant or confederate, if resistance is offered, to kill, maim, or wound the person robbed or any other person, or by the use of force, threats, or intimidation puts the person robbed or any other person in reasonable fear of death or bodily injury; or

(d) He possesses any article used or fashioned in a manner to lead any person who is present reasonably to believe it to be a deadly weapon or represents verbally or otherwise that he is then and there so armed.

West's Colo. Stat. Ann. § 18-4-302.

The Colorado Supreme Court has said that the gist of the crime of robbery under the Colorado statutes is "the putting in fear and taking of property of another by force or intimidation." *People v. Small*, 493 P.2d 15 (Colo. 1972). Aggravated robbery is distinguished from simple robbery by the fact that an accomplice or confederate is armed with a dangerous weapon with intent, if resisted, to maim, wound, or kill. The Colorado Supreme Court has observed that simple and aggravated robbery are but two degrees of the same offense. *Atwood v. People*, 489 P.2d 1305 (Colo. 1971).

## The Temporal Relationship of Force to the Taking

Is it essential to the crime of robbery that the element of violence or intimidation occur before or at the same time as the taking of the victim's property? State appellate courts are divided on this issue, often based on the specific statutory language. Note that the Colorado statute in addressing aggravated robbery includes the language "if during the act of robbery or immediate flight therefrom." The Colorado Supreme Court has said that force used in robbery need not occur simultaneously with the taking. *People v. Bartowsheski*, supra. Other courts have agreed. In *Hermann v. State*, 123 So.2d 846 (Miss. 1960), a defendant, after stealthily obtaining gasoline, made a getaway from a filling station by pointing a deadly weapon at the attendant. The attendant stuck his hand through the window of the vehicle but was pushed away by the offender. The Mississippi Supreme Court held that this act of pushing the victim away constituted the force element of robbery. Again, in *People v. Kennedy*, 294 N.E.2d 788 (Ill. App. 1973), the court held that while the taking may be without force, the offense is robbery if the departure with the property is accomplished by the use of force. Likewise, a Utah appellate court noted that if force or fear is used at any time prior to or concurrent with the victim actually losing the ability to control his chattel (personal property), then a robbery has occurred. *State in Interest of D.B.*, 925 P.2d 178 (Utah App. 1996).

In 1986 the Florida Supreme Court held that defendants who used force while fleeing a retail store after committing theft in the store could not be convicted of robbery. The court followed the traditional common-law view that the use of force must occur before or at the same time as the taking of property. *Royal v. State*, 490 So.2d 44 (Fla. 1986). The state legislature promptly amended the statutory definition of robbery to add "an act shall be deemed 'in the course of committing the robbery' if it occurs in an attempt to commit robbery or in flight after the attempt or commission." West's Fla. Stat. Ann. § 812.13(3)(a). The statute also added that "an act shall be deemed 'in the course of taking' if it occurs either prior to, contemporaneous with, or subsequent to the taking of the property and if it and the act of taking constitute a continuous series of acts and events." § 812.13(3)(b). See *Perry v. State*, 801 So.2d 78 (Fla. 2001) (recognizing the change under the revised statute).

# Carjacking

**carjacking** Taking a motor vehicle from someone by force and violence or by intimidation.

Depending on the circumstances, a person who forcibly takes another's vehicle may be subject to prosecution for grand larceny and robbery. Recognizing the serious national threat that forcible auto theft poses to persons and their motor vehicles, and after a nationwide spree of **carjacking**, Congress enacted the Anti-Car Theft Act of 1992. 18 U.S.C.A. § 2119. As originally enacted, the statute made it a crime for anyone who "takes a motor vehicle that has been transported, shipped, or received in interstate or foreign commerce from the person or presence of another by force and violence or by intimidation, or attempts to do so." The Ninth Circuit interpreted the 1992 statute as creating a general-intent offense. *United States v. Martinez*, 49 F.3d 1398 (9th Cir. 1995).

In 1994 Congress amended § 2119 to provide:

Whoever, *with the intent to cause death or serious bodily harm* [emphasis added] takes a motor vehicle that has been transported, shipped, or received in interstate or foreign commerce from the person or presence of another by force and violence or by intimidation or attempts to so shall

(1) be fined under this title or imprisoned not more than 15 years, or both,

(2) if serious bodily injury (as defined in section 1365 of this title, including any conduct that, if the conduct occurred in the special maritime and territorial-jurisdiction of the United States, would violate section 2241 or 2242 of this title) results, be fined under this title or imprisoned not more than 25 years, or both, and

(3) if death results, be fined under this title or imprisoned for any number of years up to life, or both, or sentenced to death.

Thus, the amended statute describes three offenses with different statutory elements: (1) a carjacking (or attempted carjacking), § 2119(1); (2) a carjacking (or attempted carjacking) resulting in a serious bodily injury, § 2119(2); and (3) a carjacking (or attempted carjacking) resulting in a death, § 2119(3). In 1999, the Supreme Court held that § 2119 merely requires proof of a conditional intent to kill or seriously harm the driver if necessary to steal the car. *Holloway v. United States*, 526 U.S. 1, 119 S.Ct. 966, 143 L.Ed.2d 1 (1999).

*Holloway v. United States*, 526 U.S. 1, 119 S.Ct. 966, 143 L.Ed.2d 1 (1999)

Holloway was charged with three counts of carjacking in violation of 18 U.S.C.A. § 2119. In each case, he and an armed accomplice approached an occupied vehicle, brandished a handgun, and threatened to shoot the driver unless he turned over the car keys. At trial, the accomplice testified that the plan was to steal the cars without harming the victims, but that he would have used his gun if any of the drivers had given him "a hard time." The trial judge instructed the jury that the intent requisite under § 2119 may be "conditional," and that this element of the offense is met as long as the defendant intended to cause death or serious bodily harm if the victims refused to surrender their automobiles. The conviction was upheld by the Court of Appeals, which rejected petitioner's view that the trial judge misconceived the *mens rea* requirement under § 2119. The Supreme Court affirmed, holding that the federal carjacking law applies to defendants with the conditional intent of harming drivers who resist. Two justices dissented, objecting to the introduction of the concept of conditional intent into the federal criminal law.

Although the offense of carjacking originated with the enactment of the federal statute, today a number of states have enacted their own prohibitions against carjacking. These laws are modeled after the federal statute and there is little variation in how the offense is defined.

## Extortion

**extortion** Also known as blackmail; the crime of obtaining money or property by threats of force or the inducement of fear.

In describing common-law **extortion**, William Blackstone said it was "the taking by color of an office of money or other thing of value, that is not due, before it is due, or more than is due." Under most modern statutes, extortion has been extended beyond acts by public officers. As the California law provides, extortion is "the obtaining of property from another, with his consent, or the obtaining of an official act of a public officer, induced by a wrongful use of force or fear, or under color of official right." West's Ann. Cal. Penal Code § 518.

In the vignette at the beginning of the chapter, we recounted a high-profile extortion case prosecuted by the state of New York. Robert Halderman, who attempted to extort $2 million from David Letterman, was convicted of violating the following statute:

A person obtains property by extortion when he compels or induces another person to deliver such property to himself or to a third person by means of instilling in him a fear that, if the property is not so delivered, the actor or another will:

(i) Cause physical injury to some person in the future; or

(ii) Cause damage to property; or

(iii) Engage in other conduct constituting a crime; or

(iv) Accuse some person of a crime or cause criminal charges to be instituted against him; or

(v) Expose a secret or publicize an asserted fact, whether true or false, tending to subject some person to hatred, contempt or ridicule; or

(vi) Cause a strike, boycott or other collective labor group action injurious to some person's business; except that such a threat shall not be deemed extortion when the property is demanded or received for the benefit of the group in whose interest the actor purports to act; or

(vii) Testify or provide information or withhold testimony or information with respect to another's legal claim or defense; or

(viii) Use or abuse his position as a public servant by performing some act within or related to his official duties, or by failing or refusing to perform an official duty, in such manner as to affect some person adversely; or

(ix) Perform any other act which would not in itself materially benefit the actor but which is calculated to harm another person materially with respect to his health, safety, business, calling, career, financial condition, reputation or personal relationships.

McKinney's N.Y. Penal Law § 155.05(2).

## Extortion Distinguished from Robbery

There are both similarities and distinctions between the offenses of extortion and robbery. As explained by a California appellate court,

> The crime of extortion is related to and sometimes difficult to distinguish from the crime of robbery. . . . Both crimes have their roots in the common law crime of larceny. Both crimes share the element of an acquisition by means of force or fear. One distinction between the robbery and extortion frequently noted by courts and commentators is that in robbery property is taken from another by force or fear "against his will" while in extortion property is taken from another by force or fear "with his consent." The two crimes, however, have other distinctions. Robbery requires a "felonious taking" which means a specific intent to permanently deprive the victim of the property. . . . Robbery also requires the property be taken from the victim's "person or immediate presence." . . . Extortion does not require proof of either of these elements. . . . Extortion does, however, require the specific intent of inducing the victim to consent to part with his or her property. *People v. Torres*, 39 Cal.Rptr.2d 103, 110–111 (Cal. App. 1995).

## Extortion under Federal Law

**blackmail** The vernacular term for extortion.

In many instances, the statutory offense of extortion has become synonymous with the common understanding of **blackmail**. In fact, 18 U.S.C.A. § 873—a federal statute that provides that "[w]hoever, under a threat of informing, or as a consideration for not informing, against any violation of any law of the United States, demands, or receives any money or other valuable thing, shall be fined . . ."—is often referred to as the "blackmail statute." Another federal statute, 18 U.S.C.A. § 876, makes it a crime to mail using the U.S. Postal Service a demand for ransom or a threat to injure a person's property or reputation. The only specific intent required to support a conviction under § 876 is that the defendant knowingly deposited a threatening letter in the mail, not that he or she intended to carry out the threat. *United States v. Chatman*, 584 F.2d 1358 (4th Cir. 1978). Finally, 18 U.S.C.A. § 879 makes it a felony to "knowingly and willfully threaten to kill, kidnap, or inflict bodily harm upon . . . persons protected by the Secret Service."

# Forgery and Uttering a Forged Instrument

**forgery** The crime of making a false written instrument or materially altering a written instrument with the intent to defraud.

Blackstone defined common-law **forgery** as "the fraudulent making or alteration of a writing to the prejudice of another man's right." The early cases reveal that such writings as wills, receipts, and physicians' certificates were subject to forgery. To convict a defendant of forgery under common law, it was essential to establish the accused's intent to defraud. **Uttering a forged instrument** was also a common-law offense, but one separate and distinct from forgery. "Utter," a term of art synonymous with "publish," distinguishes the actual forgery from the act of passing a forged instrument to someone. As an indication of the lesser importance of commercial matters in early English society, the common law classified both forgery and uttering a forged instrument as misdemeanors.

**uttering a forged instrument** The crime of passing a false or worthless instrument, such as a check, with the intent to defraud or injure the recipient.

## Statutory Expansion of Forgery Offenses

Unlike the common law, federal and state statutes generally classify forgery as a felony. Reflecting the importance of written and printed documentation in our modern economy, statutes in all American jurisdictions have extended the crime of forgery to almost every type of public or private legal instrument.

### Federal Statutes

Under federal law, "[w]hoever, with intent to defraud, falsely makes, forges, counterfeits, or alters any obligation or other security of the United States" commits the crime of forgery. 18 U.S.C.A. § 471. Federal courts have stated that the manifest purpose of these laws is to protect all currency and obligations of the United States, *United States v. LeMon*, 622 F.2d 1022 (10th Cir. 1980), and that the prosecution must prove not only the passing but also the defendant's "intent to pass the bad money," *United States v. Lorenzo*, 570 F.2d 294, 299 (9th Cir. 1978).

Title 18, § 472 provides that "[w]hoever, with intent to defraud, passes, utters, publishes, or sells, or attempts to pass, utter, publish, or sell, or with like intent brings into the United States or keeps in possession or conceals any falsely made, forged, counterfeited, or altered obligation or other security of the United States, shall be fined under this title or imprisoned. . . ." In *United States v. Drumright*, 534 F.2d 1383 (10th Cir. 1976), a defendant seeking a reversal of his conviction under § 472 argued that the Federal Reserve bill he uttered was not of an appearance calculated to deceive an unsuspecting person of ordinary observation. The court disagreed, pointing out that the bill was "a falsely made and altered obligation of the United States because it was composed of parts of three genuine bills which had been fastened together with transparent tape. When folded with the right half of the obverse side showing, it has the appearance of a good $50 bill. . . . Although the workmanship on the bill was crude, it was of such character that under favorable circumstances it could be uttered and accepted as genuine." *Id.* at 1385. The court concluded that the circumstances presented in the case's peculiar facts were sufficient to establish a violation of the statute.

**counterfeiting** Making an imitation of something with the intent to deceive—for example, making imitations of U.S. coins and currency.

Several other federal statutes relate to forgery and the **counterfeiting** of federal securities, postage stamps, postage meters, money orders, federal and state securities, public records, judges' signatures, and court documents. See 18 U.S.C.A. §§ 472–520. Many prosecutions are brought under 18 U.S.C.A. § 495, which provides that

> Whoever falsely makes, alters, forges, or counterfeits any deed, power of attorney, order, certificate, receipt, contract, or other writing, for the purpose of obtaining or receiving, or of enabling any other person, either directly or indirectly, to obtain or receive from the United States or any officers or agents thereof, any sum of money; or

Whoever utters or publishes as true any such false, forged, altered, or counterfeited writing, with intent to defraud the United States, knowing the same to be false, altered, forged, or counterfeited; or

Whoever transmits to, or presents at any office or officer of the United States, any such writing in support of, or in relation to, any account or claim, with intent to defraud the United States, knowing the same to be false, altered, forged, or counterfeited—

Shall be fined under this title or imprisoned. . . .

To convict someone under this statute, the government must establish the defendant's specific fraudulent intent. *United States v. Sullivan*, 406 F.2d 180 (2d Cir. 1969).

### State Statutes

Most states have substantially adopted the common-law definition of forgery but have expanded the types of instruments that can be forged to include a lengthy list of public and private documents. For example, the Arizona Criminal Code makes forgery a felony and provides the following:

A. A person commits forgery if, with intent to defraud, the person:

1. Falsely makes, completes or alters a written instrument; or
2. Knowingly possesses a forged instrument; or
3. Offers or presents, whether accepted or not, a forged instrument or one which contains false information. (Ariz. Rev. Stat. § 13-2002.)

Under this section, the offenses of forgery and uttering have been coupled under the term "forgery," but their status as separate offenses must still be observed because the elements of the offenses are not the same and the proof required can differ. *State v. Reyes*, 458 P.2d 960 (Ariz. 1969). Thus, under Arizona law the crime of forgery has three elements: (1) signing the name of another person, (2) intending to defraud, and (3) knowing that there is no authority to sign. *State v. Nettz*, 560 P.2d 814 (Ariz. App. 1977). On the other hand, uttering is the passing or publishing of a false, altered, or counterfeited paper or document. *State v. Reyes*, supra. Proof of the intent to defraud is essential to obtain a conviction of forgery, *State v. Maxwell*, 445 P.2d 837 (Ariz. 1968), but such intent may be inferred from circumstances in which the false instrument is executed or issued, *State v. Gomez*, 553 P.2d 1233 (Ariz. App. 1976). Note that based on the wording of the Arizona statute proscribing forgery, a conviction for "attempt to pass" is a conviction of forgery, not of an attempt. *Ponds v. State*, 438 P.2d 423 (Ariz. App. 1968) (see Chapter 5).

## Common Examples of Forgery and Uttering a Forged Instrument

Among the more common examples of forgery today are the following:

- Signing another's name to an application for a driver's license
- Printing bogus tickets to a concert or sports event
- Signing another's name to a check on his or her bank account without authority
- Altering the amount of a check or note
- Signing another's name without authority to a certificate transferring shares of stock
- Signing a deed transferring someone's real estate without authorization

- Making an unauthorized change in the legal description of property being conveyed under a deed
- Altering the grades or credits on a college transcript

Uttering a forged instrument commonly occurs when a person knowingly delivers a forged check to someone in exchange for cash or merchandise, knowingly sells bogus tickets for an event, or submits a deed with forged signatures for official recording.

Falsification of computerized records such as college credits and financial records poses new challenges to laws proscribing forgery. The increasing use of computers gives rise to the need for new applications of statutes proscribing forgery and uttering a forged instrument.

## Forgery and Embezzlement

**CASE-IN-POINT**

Emma Cisneros purchased a Volkswagen bus, and a certificate of title was conveyed to her, which assigned title. Cisneros came in contact with Gomez "while dining at the Coronado Inn" where Gomez "expressed interest in purchasing [the vehicle], predicated upon a one-hour test drive." Cisneros agreed; however, Gomez "failed to return." Cisneros was unable to locate her vehicle or Gomez for three months; however, subsequently, Cisneros observed her vehicle at Diaz Garage. Diaz, a mechanic, testified that "the vehicle was delivered for repairs to his garage" by Gomez's uncle. Once Cisneros saw her vehicle, she "removed the ignition keys and told Diaz to send the person who claimed the van to her office at the Wager Insurance Agency." Gomez "appeared at the Wager Insurance Agency to pick up the keys to the vehicle," but Cisneros refused "to give up the keys." Gomez left but "later returned with the certificate of title," giving it to Cisneros. Cisneros's name and address "had been removed from the certificate and replaced" with Gomez's information. Gomez was subsequently convicted of forgery and embezzlement. Gomez appealed his forgery conviction, arguing that the State failed to produce evidence that Gomez in fact altered the vehicle's title. The Court of Appeals of Arizona held that "intent to defraud is an essential element of forgery. However, intent to defraud may be, and often must be, inferred from the circumstances in which the false instrument is executed or issued." The court went on to hold that "we do not require direct evidence" that Gomez "physically obscur[ed] or obliterat[ed]

Cisneros's name and address with liquid paper and insert[ed] his own" because "to do so would place a virtually impossible burden on the State." The court concluded "that the circumstances of the disappearance and recovery of the vehicle, along with [Gomez's] physical possession of the altered document, provided sufficient evidence to support the jury's determination that he altered the document with intent to defraud or aided and abetted the alteration with the same intent." As a result, Gomez's forgery conviction was upheld. Gomez also argued that the State failed to produce sufficient evidence that he embezzled the vehicle. The Court held "that the gist of the crime of embezzlement is a breach of trust," and "the elements necessary to establish embezzlement are a trust relation, possession or control of property by virtue of the trust relation, and a fraudulent appropriation of the property to a use or purpose not in the due and lawful execution of the trust." Applying the facts to the rule, the court held "there is ample evidence to support [Gomez's] conviction of embezzlement" because Gomez "requested possession and control of the vehicle for the purpose of a test drive and stated that he would return 'in about an hour or so.'" Based on this, Cisneros waited for approximately ninety minutes before leaving the restaurant. The court inferred the requisite intent from these facts along with the facts that "the vehicle was never returned and at no time did [Gomez] tender payment for it or notify Cisneros of its whereabouts." Therefore, the embezzlement conviction was affirmed as well.

*State v. Gomez*, 27 Ariz. App. 248, 553 P.2d 1233 (1976).

# Worthless Checks

As commercial banking developed, the passing of "bad checks" became a serious problem. A person who writes a worthless check on his or her bank account does not commit a forgery. In early cases, some courts referred to issuance of checks without funds in the bank as use of a "false token." These cases were prosecuted under statutes making it unlawful to use false pretenses to obtain property.

States have now enacted a variety of statutes making it unlawful to issue checks with insufficient funds to cover payment. Earlier statutes often provided that to be guilty of false pretenses for issuing a worthless check, a person had to fraudulently obtain goods. This proved to be an impracticable method to control issuance of checks by depositors who misgauged their checking account balances. The widespread use of commercial and personal banking led legislatures to enact **worthless-check statutes** to cope with the problem. These statutes usually classify such an offense as a misdemeanor, and legislatures have increasingly opted to allow offenders to make restitution of losses caused by worthless checks. State laws often allow a recipient of a bad check to assess a fee against one who issues or transfers a bad check. Many retail stores have signs posted notifying customers of such fees.

Ohio law makes it an offense to "issue or transfer or cause to be issued or transferred a check or other negotiable instrument, knowing that it will be dishonored." Ohio Rev. Code § 2913.11(B). The statute further provides that one who issues or transfers such a negotiable instrument is presumed to know that it will be dishonored if either (1) the drawer had no account with the drawee bank, or (2) the negotiable instrument was properly refused payment for insufficient funds upon presentment within thirty days and the liability of any person liable on the instrument was not discharged by payment or satisfaction within ten days after receiving notice of dishonor. See Ohio Rev. Code §§ 2913.11(C) (1)–(2). If a bad check is for less than $500, the offense is a misdemeanor; beyond that amount it becomes a felony, the degree of which is dependent on the amount of the check, with a check for $100,000 or more becoming a felony of the third degree. See Ohio Rev. Code § 2913.11(F). Ohio courts have held that where the payee of a check knows that the check is not collectible at the time it is tendered, there is no criminal violation of passing a bad check. *State v. Edwards*, 751 N.E.2d 510 (Ohio App. 2001).

**worthless-check statutes** Laws making it an offense to knowingly pass a worthless check.

# Burglary

English common law emphasized the sanctity of one's dwelling, as reflected in the well-known dictum, "A man's home is his castle." According to Blackstone, common-law **burglary** consisted of (1) breaking and entering of (2) a dwelling of another (3) during the nighttime (4) with intent to commit a felony therein. The "breaking" at common law could be either "actual" or "constructive." An actual breaking could be merely technical, such as pushing open a door or opening a window. An entry gained through fraud or deception was considered a "constructive" breaking. Even the slightest entry was deemed sufficient; for instance, a hand, a foot, or even a finger within the dwelling was regarded as a sufficient entry. Proof of the defendant's intent to commit a felony was essential: A breaking and entering did not constitute burglary at common law unless the perpetrator had a specific intent to commit a felony (e.g., murder, rape, or larceny); however, it was not necessary to prove that any felony was committed. "Dwelling" was defined as the house or place of habitation used by the occupier or member of the family "as a place to sleep in." Finally, to constitute burglary at common law, it was essential that the offense be committed at nighttime, generally defined as the period between sunset and sunrise.

**burglary** At common law, breaking and entering a dwelling of another during the nighttime with the intent to commit a felony therein. Modern statutes typically expand the offense beyond dwellings and eliminate the "nighttime" element.

## Statutory Revisions of Burglary

**breaking and entering** Forceful, unlawful entry into a building or conveyance.

Many states have enacted statutes proscribing **breaking and entering**, thereby placing a new label on the common-law crime of burglary. At a minimum, these statutes expand the offense of burglary beyond dwelling houses and eliminate the requirement that the offense take place in the nighttime. Most states retain the common-law requirement that the accused break and enter with intent to commit a felony, and others include the language "or theft." Even where the offense is still labeled burglary, legislatures have made significant changes in the common-law definition. In addition to eliminating the nighttime requirement, they have broadened the offense to include buildings and structures of all types. Today, most criminal codes include vehicles, aircraft, and vessels either in the definition of burglary or by a separate statute. Finally, modern statutes frequently provide that a person who enters a structure with consent but who remains therein with intent to commit a felony may be found guilty of burglary notwithstanding an original lawful entry. An example of this would be someone intentionally remaining in a department store with the intent to commit an offense therein after the store closes for the day.

Mich. Comp. Laws Ann. § 750.110 deals with breaking and entering and provides:

> A person who breaks and enters with intent to commit any felony, or any larceny therein, a tent, hotel, office, store, shop, warehouse, barn, granary, factory or other building, structure, boat or ship, shipping container, or railroad car shall be guilty of a felony.

**home invasion** A more heinous form of burglary, in which the perpetrator is armed with a dangerous weapon or persons are present in the home at the time of the break-in.

Increasingly, state statutes recognize **home invasion** as a more heinous form of burglary in that the perpetrator is armed with a dangerous weapon or persons are present in the home at the time of the break-in.

Michigan law defines home invasion as follows:

> (2) A person who breaks and enters a dwelling with intent to commit a felony, larceny, or assault in the dwelling, a person who enters a dwelling without permission with intent to commit a felony, larceny, or assault in the dwelling, or a person who breaks and enters a dwelling or enters a dwelling without permission and, at any time while he or she is entering, present in, or exiting the dwelling, commits a felony, larceny, or assault is guilty of home invasion in the first degree if at any time while the person is entering, present in, or exiting the dwelling either of the following circumstances exists:
>
> (a) The person is armed with a dangerous weapon.
>
> (b) Another person is lawfully present in the dwelling.
>
> (3) A person who breaks and enters a dwelling with intent to commit a felony, larceny, or assault in the dwelling, a person who enters a dwelling without permission with intent to commit a felony, larceny, or assault in the dwelling, or a person who breaks and enters a dwelling or enters a dwelling without permission and, at any time while he or she is entering, present in, or exiting the dwelling, commits a felony, larceny, or assault is guilty of home invasion in the second degree.
>
> (4) A person is guilty of home invasion in the third degree if the person does either of the following:
>
> (a) Breaks and enters a dwelling with intent to commit a misdemeanor in the dwelling, enters a dwelling without permission with intent to commit a misdemeanor in the dwelling, or breaks and enters a dwelling or enters a

### What Constitutes "Entry" Within the Meaning of a Burglary Statute?

On February 4, 1998, a man later identified as the defendant was seen removing a screen from a bathroom window of the Floreas's house and unsuccessfully attempting to open the window itself. Then, after unsuccessfully attempting to open the front door of the house, the defendant banged on the wall and drove away. Shortly thereafter he was arrested and charged with burglary under California law, which provides that the crime of burglary is committed when a person "enters any . . . building," including a "house," "with intent to commit . . . larceny or any felony." A jury found the defendant guilty of burglary in the first degree because the crime involved an inhabited dwelling house. The trial court sentenced him to four years in prison. In 2001, a California appellate court reversed his conviction on the ground that penetration into the area behind a window screen did not constitute an entry as required by the burglary statute.

The California Supreme Court granted review, and in reversing the court of appeals' decision, opined, "We recognize that penetration into the area behind a window screen without penetration of the window itself usually will effect only a minimal entry of a building in terms of distance. But it has long been settled that '[a]ny kind of entry, complete or partial . . . will' suffice." *Id.* at 927. A dissenting judge argued that the defendant committed attempted burglary because he tried, but failed, to enter the house.

*People v. Valencia*, 46 P.3d 920 (Cal. 2002).

dwelling without permission and, at any time while he or she is entering, present in, or exiting the dwelling, commits a misdemeanor.

(b) Breaks and enters a dwelling or enters a dwelling without permission and, at any time while the person is entering, present in, or exiting the dwelling, violates any of the following ordered to protect a named person or persons:

   (i) A probation term or condition.

   (ii) A parole term or condition.

   (iii) A personal protection order term or condition.

   (iv) A bond or bail condition or any condition of pretrial release.

Mich. Comp. Laws § 750.110(a)

Home invasion of the first, second, and third degrees is a felony, the imprisonment and fine varying in severity based on the degree of the offense.

Courts tend to construe liberally the terms "breaking" and "entering" commonly found in burglary statutes. In *State v. Jaynes*, 464 S.E.2d 448, 466 (N.C. 1995), the North Carolina Supreme Court said that for purposes of burglary, "any force, however slight, employed to effect entrance through any usual or unusual place of ingress, whether open, partly open, or closed . . . by any use of force, however slight, . . . will suffice as the 'breaking' required for burglary." A New York appellate court has said that a defendant "enters" a building within the meaning of that state's burglary statute when a defendant's person or any part of a defendant's body intrudes. *People v. Jackson*, 638 N.Y.S.2d 140 (1996).

**possession of burglar's tools** The knowing control of instruments, machines, or substances designed to enable one to forcefully break into buildings or vaults in order to carry out the intent to steal or destroy property.

## Possession of Burglar's Tools

Michigan, like most states, makes **possession of burglar's tools** a felony if the possessor has the intent to use the tools for burglarious purposes. Michigan law provides,

Any person who shall knowingly have in his possession any nitroglycerine, or other explosive, thermite, engine, machine, tool or implement, device, chemical or substance, adapted and designed for cutting or burning through, forcing or breaking open any building, room, vault, safe or other depository, in order to steal therefrom any money or other property, knowing the same to be adapted and designed for the purpose aforesaid, with intent to use or employ the same for the purpose aforesaid, shall be guilty of a felony. Mich. Comp. Laws Ann. § 750.116.

Many years ago, the Michigan Supreme Court emphasized that to obtain a conviction, the state must prove the accused knowingly had possession of burglar's tools, knew the tools could be used for a criminal purpose, and intended to use them for such purpose. *People v. Jefferson*, 126 N.W. 829 (Mich. 1910).

# Arson

**arson** The crime of intentionally burning someone else's house or building; now commonly extended to other property as well.

Like burglary, **arson** was a felony at common law designed to protect the security of the dwelling place. The crime consisted of (1) the willful and malicious burning (2) of a dwelling (3) of another. There was no requirement that the dwelling be destroyed or even that it be damaged to a significant degree. In fact, a mere charring was sufficient, but scorching or smoke damage did not constitute arson at common law. The common law gave the term "dwelling" the same meaning as in burglary. Consequently, the burning of buildings within the curtilage constituted arson. The common law regarded arson as a general-intent crime, with the required malice being presumed from an intentional burning of someone's dwelling. Setting fire to one's own home was not arson at common law. Yet some early English cases indicate that under circumstances where burning one's own house posed a danger to others, "houseburning" was a misdemeanor offense.

## Statutory Revision of Arson

Modern statutes have extended the offense of arson to include the intentional burning of buildings, structures, and vehicles of all types. Frequently, this even includes a person's own property. Several states have enacted statutes that provide that the use of explosives to damage a structure constitutes arson. As in burglary, the modern offense of arson is designed to protect many forms of property. Therefore, arson can no longer be considered strictly a habitation offense. By categorizing arson, legislatures can make appropriate distinctions and provide penalties accordingly.

Michigan law embraces four categories of arson. Mich. Comp. Laws § 750.72 provides,

> Any person who willfully or maliciously burns any dwelling house, either occupied or unoccupied, or the contents thereof, whether owned by himself or another, or any building within the curtilage of such dwelling house, or the contents thereof, shall be guilty of a felony.

In *People v. Williams*, 318 N.W.2d 671 (Mich. App. 1982), the court held that to establish the *corpus delicti* of arson of a dwelling house, the state must show not only a burning of the house but also that it resulted from an intentional criminal act. The court explained that where only a burning is shown, a presumption arises that it was accidentally caused.

Section 750.73 makes it a lesser felony for anyone to willfully or maliciously burn any building or other real property or contents thereof, other than a dwelling house, while § 750.74 makes it a misdemeanor or felony to willfully and maliciously

**CASE-IN-POINT**

### Proving the Crime of Arson

Early on the morning of September 23, 1981, a fire destroyed a log cabin belonging to Henry Xavier Kennedy. Investigators determined that the fire was incendiary in origin. A hot plate with its switch in the "on" position was found in the most heavily burned area of the cabin. Investigators also determined that kerosene poured around the area of the hot plate had accelerated the fire.

Five days before the fire, Kennedy had renewed a $40,000 insurance policy on the cabin. Evidence was also presented that Kennedy's building business was slow. Kennedy introduced evidence of an alibi from midnight until 4:00 a.m. Although the fire was reported at 3:42 a.m., investigators testified that the incendiary device could have been set before midnight.

Kennedy was convicted of arson, and his conviction was upheld on appeal.

*Kennedy v. State*, 323 S.E.2d 169 (Ga. App. 1984).

burn personal property, the level of offense being determined by the value of the property involved. A fire "willfully" set by the accused requires that the defendant commit such act stubbornly and for an unlawful purpose. Mere proof of carelessness or accident is not sufficient to establish guilt. *People v. McCarty*, 6 N.W.2d 919 (Mich. 1942).

In contrast with Michigan's law, many state statutes broaden the scope of the offense by referring to "damage caused by fire" rather than "burning." In further contrast with the common law, under many modern statutes proof of damage by smoke or scorching is sufficient to constitute arson. See, e.g., *State v. McVeigh*, 516 P.2d 918 (Kan. 1973).

## Burning Property with the Intent to Defraud an Insurance Company

Most jurisdictions have enacted statutes making it a crime to burn any property with the intent to defraud an insurance company, usually requiring the prosecution to prove the defendant's specific intent to defraud. In this respect, Mich. Comp. Laws § 750.75 stipulates the following: "Any person who shall willfully burn any building or personal property which shall be at the time insured against loss or damage by fire with intent to injure and defraud the insurer, whether such person be the owner of the property or not, shall be guilty of a felony."

## Malicious Mischief

**malicious mischief** Synonym for vandalism; the willful destruction of the property of another person.

**vandalism** Synonym for malicious mischief; the willful destruction of the property of another person.

A mere trespass to land or personal property was not a crime at common law unless it was committed forcibly or maliciously. However, it was a common-law misdemeanor called **malicious mischief** for a person to damage another's real or personal property. Modern statutes usually define the offense much as did the common law, often referring to the offense as **vandalism** and imposing penalties based on the extent of damage inflicted on the victim's property.

Section 806.13(1)(a), West's Florida Statutes Annotated, is a good illustration of present-day statutes. It provides that "[a] person commits the offense of criminal mischief if he or she willfully and maliciously injures or damages by any means any real or personal property belonging to another, including, but not limited to, the

### Malicious Mischief

**CASE-IN-POINT**

The defendant, Tonnisen, was convicted of malicious mischief, which the relevant New Jersey statute states, "any person who willfully or maliciously destroys, damages, injures or spoils any real or personal property of another, either of a public or private nature, for which no punishment is otherwise provided by statute, is guilty of a misdemeanor." The incident took place during a labor dispute at the Peter J. Schweitzer Plant where workers on strike who "were on a picket line across the entrance to the plant" blocked the entrance to a truck attempting to make a delivery. The local authorities cleared a path for the truck to enter the plant. One police officer observed Tonnisen "stick his hand in between the tractor and the trailer," and "when he withdrew his hand there was grease on it." As the truck driver attempted to drive forward, the "tractor pulled ahead and separated from the trailer which fell down on the road causing the bottom of the tank to crack and the contents . . . to leak out on the road." The "safety mechanism of the coupling between the tractor and trailer had been pulled." Tonnisen denied any involvement. On appeal, Tonnisen argued that the "State failed to prove criminal willfulness or malice." However, the Superior Court of New Jersey disagreed, holding the elements of malicious mischief "are rarely if ever susceptible of direct proof." Normally "they are inferred from the totality of the State's case," and the court found "ample credible evidence from which a jury could have found that beyond a reasonable doubt [Tonnisen] pulled the safety mechanism and did so willfully or maliciously within the intent of the statute." Therefore, Tonnisen's conviction was affirmed.

*State v. Tonnisen*, 224 A.2d 21 (N.J. App. 1966).

placement of graffiti thereon or other acts of vandalism thereto." The offense is a misdemeanor, and the value of property determines the punishment. But if the damage is $1,000 or greater, or if there is interruption or impairment of a business operation or public communication; transportation; supply of water, gas or power; or other public service which costs $1,000 or more in labor and supplies to restore, or the defendant has had one or more previous convictions, the offense is a felony of the third degree. Florida appellate courts have held that to be found guilty of the offense, the actor must possess the specific intent to damage the property of another. *In Interest of J.G.*, 655 So.2d 1284 (Fla. App. 1995).

## Defenses to Property Crimes

At common law, the offenses of larceny and robbery were specific-intent crimes. This intent requirement has been carried over in statutes proscribing theft, either comprehensively or in various descriptive crimes, but the intent requirement in modern robbery statutes varies. Therefore, in a prosecution for theft, a defendant may raise the defense of mistake of fact, but this does not necessarily follow when defending a charge of robbery (see Chapter 14). This means that a defendant who takes items of property from another person in the good-faith belief that they belong to the defendant may have a defense. A classic example: Sherry leaves a jacket on a coat rack, and later Mary does also. The jackets are similar, and Sherry mistakenly walks away with Mary's jacket. The problem becomes more acute if Mary has left a wallet in her jacket with hundreds of dollars of currency in it. These mistakes justify requiring the prosecution to prove a defendant's specific intent in theft offenses. Have you ever opened the door of a car like yours in a shopping center parking lot, thinking the car was your own?

In some theft prosecutions, mistake of law has been held to be a defense. This is limited to situations where there are exceedingly technical questions concerning ownership rights (see Chapter 14).

In a prosecution for forgery, an accused can defend by proving that he or she was authorized to sign another's name. Under certain circumstances, a person accused of forgery can also assert the defense of "mistake of fact" (see Chapter 14).

In some instances, a person charged with burglary can also assert mistake of fact as a defense. For example, an intoxicated person who enters a "row house" identical to his or her own may have a defense. And, of course, the requirement that the prosecution prove "an intent to commit a felony" would make it difficult to prove that a person who took refuge from a storm on the porch of an unoccupied dwelling did so with intent to commit a felony therein (see Chapter 14). Arson, on the other hand, is usually a general-intent crime. This imposes a limitation on defenses beyond consent, where a person intentionally commits the proscribed acts. Because statutes proscribing the commission of arson with the intent to defraud an insurer usually require proof of the defendant's specific intent to defraud, the lack of such intent can be shown in defense. As we point out in Chapter 14 the defenses of alibi, insanity, duress, and, in some instances, intoxication may be defenses to property crimes.

## Conclusion

Most statutory property crimes parallel the basic common-law scheme but have been broadened to meet the demands of our changing society. Although the common-law crimes against property and habitation provide a good starting point for legislating against offenses involving property, there is a need for continuing statutory revision to consolidate the laws proscribing certain property offenses that have proliferated over the years.

Consumers are no longer willing to acquiesce in outmoded doctrines such as *caveat emptor*. Thus, laws concerning representations made in commercial transactions assume an important role in today's society. Consumer fraud, intentional false advertising, credit card fraud, and a variety of other scams need to be specifically proscribed or included in omnibus definitions in theft and forgery statutes and in statutes specifically addressing computer fraud and access device fraud.

The laws proscribing burglary and arson must protect more than homes. These offenses pose serious threats to lives and property, regardless of whether they are committed in a residential or business property; whether the structure involved is private or public; and whether it is a vehicle, vessel, building, or other structure. These offenses have changed from crimes against habitation to crimes against property. Modern statutes tend to make these offenses crimes against persons as well. With the almost-universal dependence on insurance to protect against casualty losses, the need for a close look at statutes proscribing insurance fraud is also essential.

## Chapter Summary

- Learning Objective 1

  ○ At the time the United States was founded, the common law recognized two theft offenses: larceny and false pretenses.
  ○ Larceny was a felony that consisted of the wrongful taking and carrying away of the personal property of another with intent to permanently deprive the owner of the property.

- Obtaining property by false pretenses was a misdemeanor that involved obtaining wares or merchandise of another with the intent to cheat or defraud the other person.
- Later, the English Parliament created the misdemeanor offenses of embezzlement and receiving stolen property. Whereas larceny required proof of a wrongful taking and carrying away of another's personal property, embezzlement made it unlawful for servants and others with a fiduciary relationship to wrongfully convert assets.
- The common law that America inherited included larceny and false pretenses but left matters involving real property and commercial transactions to the civil law.
- As America matured, most households acquired intangible property, and commercial transactions assumed a role of greater importance. Congress enacted statutes comprehensively proscribing theft and embezzlement and expanding larceny to include all types of tangible and intangible property.
- A proliferation of statutes addressing various forms of theft led many states to adopt comprehensive theft statutes that proscribe all types of theft and make temporary as well as permanent deprivation of all classes of property subject to theft laws.
- Theft remains a specific-intent crime. Because penalties are graded according to the value of items stolen, prosecutors must produce evidence to prove the value of goods or services stolen.

- Learning Objective 2

  - At common law, robbery was a felony that consisted of taking another's personal property from the other person's possession or presence by force or by placing the person in fear, with the intent to permanently deprive the other person of that property. Force had to occur at the time of taking of property.
  - Many states simply define robbery as did the common law; others classify it according to degree, with the seriousness of the offense usually based on whether the assailant is armed, the degree of force used, and the vulnerability of the victim. Where courts have followed the common-law view that the use of force must occur before or at the same time as the taking of property, legislatures have amended their robbery statutes to provide that the force can occur at or after the criminal act.
  - Federal statutes make it an offense "to take, or attempt to take, by force and violence or intimidation from the person or presence of another any property or money belonging to or in the care of a bank, credit union, or savings and loan association."

- Learning Objective 3

  - The Federal Anti-Car Theft Act of 1992, as amended, makes carjacking a crime by stipulating that "[w]hoever, with the intent to cause death or serious bodily harm, takes a motor vehicle that has been transported, shipped, or received in interstate or foreign commerce from the person or presence of another by force and violence or by intimidation or attempts to so . . ." is guilty of a felony.
  - Although the offense of carjacking originated with the enactment of the federal statute, today a number of states have enacted their own prohibitions against carjacking. These laws are modeled after the federal statute and there is little variation in how the offense is defined.

- Learning Objective 4

  o Extortion is the obtaining of property from another, with his or her consent, induced by a wrongful use of force or fear, or under color of official right or the obtaining of an official act of a public officer, induced by a wrongful use of force or fear, or under color of official right.

  o Today extortion has often become synonymous with the common understanding of blackmail. It differs from robbery because of its consensual nature.

- Learning Objective 5

  o At common law, forgery was a felony defined as "the fraudulent making or alteration of a writing to the prejudice of another man's right."

  o Federal law provides that "[w]hoever, with intent to defraud, falsely makes, forges, counterfeits, or alters any obligation or other security of the United States" commits the crime of forgery and that "Whoever, with intent to defraud, passes, utters, publishes, or sells, or attempts to pass, utter, publish, or sell, or with like intent brings into the United States or keeps in possession or conceals any falsely made, forged, counterfeited, or altered obligation or other security of the United States" commits the offense of "uttering."

  o Most states have substantially adopted the common-law definition of forgery (in some instances coupling it with the offense of uttering) and make it a felony. But states have expanded the number of instruments that can be forged to include a lengthy list of public and private documents.

  o Uttering a forged instrument is commonly a felony and occurs when a person knowingly delivers a forged check to someone in exchange for cash or merchandise, knowingly sells bogus tickets for an event, or submits a deed with forged signatures for official recording.

  o The widespread use of commercial and personal banking led state legislatures to enact worthless-check statutes that usually classify issuing a worthless check as a misdemeanor. These statutes frequently allow offenders to make restitution of losses caused by worthless checks.

- Learning Objective 6

  o The common-law offenses of burglary and arson gave credence to the old English saying "A man's home is his castle." These offenses protected the dwelling house and buildings within the curtilage, an enclosed area around the dwelling.

  o At common law, burglary consisted of breaking and entering a dwelling of another during the nighttime with intent to commit a felony.

  o In America, state laws soon eliminated the nighttime requirement and extended the coverage to include buildings and structures of all types. Today these laws usually include vehicles, aircraft, and vessels either in the definition of burglary or by a separate statute.

  o Moreover, modern statutes frequently provide that a person who enters a structure with consent but who remains therein with intent to commit a felony may be found guilty of burglary notwithstanding an original lawful entry.

  o State statutes usually provide for greater penalties for those who break and enter a dwelling.

  o Most states also have statutes that make possession of burglar's tools a felony.

- Learning Objective 7

  o Arson at common law consisted of the willful and malicious burning of another's dwelling.
  o Early on, states broadened the scope of arson laws to include the intentional burning of buildings, structures, and vehicles of all types. Frequently, this includes burning a person's own property.
  o Several states have enacted statutes that provide that the use of explosives to damage a structure constitutes arson.
  o Most jurisdictions also have statutes making it a crime to burn any property with the intent to defraud an insurance company, usually requiring the prosecution to prove the defendant's specific intent to defraud.

- Learning Objective 8

  o A mere trespass to land or personal property was not a crime at common law unless it was committed forcibly or maliciously.
  o Malicious mischief was a common-law misdemeanor consisting of damaging another's real or personal property.
  o Modern statutes usually define the offense much as did the common law, often calling the offense "vandalism" and imposing penalties based on the extent of damage inflicted on the victim's property.

- Learning Objective 9

  o At common law, the offenses of larceny and robbery were specific-intent crimes. This intent requirement has been carried over to statutes proscribing theft; by contrast, the intent requirement in modern robbery statutes varies. Therefore, in a prosecution for theft and burglary (and under some robbery statutes), a defendant may raise the defense of mistake of fact.
  o In some instances consent may apply as a defense to forgery.

## Key Terms

| | |
|---|---|
| aggravated robbery | home invasion |
| arson | intent to deprive |
| blackmail | larceny |
| breaking and entering | malicious mischief |
| burglary | petit theft |
| carjacking | possession of burglar's tools |
| counterfeiting | receiving stolen property |
| embezzlement | robbery |
| extortion | tangible property |
| false pretenses | uttering a forged instrument |
| forgery | vandalism |
| grand theft | worthless check statutes |

## Questions for Thought and Discussion

1. What advantages do you see for a state that adopts a comprehensive theft statute?
2. How does the criminal law of your state distinguish between grand theft and petit theft?
3. How does the crime of burglary as it is typically defined under modern statutes differ from the definition of this offense under English common law?
4. Is it more important for theft offenses to be classified as specific-intent crimes or for robbery to be so classified? Why?
5. What provisions would you include in a model statute making arson a crime? Would you provide for separate degrees of the offense?
6. Should the offense of forgery be divided into degrees based on the importance of the forged documents? If so, what criteria would you propose for the various degrees of the crime?
7. Give some examples of actions that would probably fall within the conduct proscribed by (a) extortion statutes and (b) vandalism or malicious mischief statutes.
8. Identify some important similarities and distinctions between the offenses of robbery and extortion.
9. What is the rationale for courts to require that to obtain a conviction for possession of burglar's tools the state must prove that the accused knowingly had possession of burglar's tools, knew the tools could be used for a criminal purpose, and intended to use them for such purpose?
10. Assume you are working as a staff assistant to a legislator who desires to introduce a bill to assist merchants who are experiencing losses from bad checks. What types of provisions and penalties would you recommend?

## Problems for Discussion and Solution

1. Larry Lightfingers steals a package of filet mignon priced at $19.99 from the meat counter in a supermarket. As he leaves the store, he is approached by a security guard. Lightfingers kicks and injures the security guard in his attempt to leave with the meat he has stolen. In your state, would Mr. Lightfingers be charged with petit theft, grand theft, or robbery? Why?
2. Sally Spendthrift has an established bank account at a local bank. She gives a check to a merchant for the purchase of a new stereo. Her bank returns the check to the merchant because Spendthrift's account has insufficient funds to cover payment. Do you think Spendthrift should face criminal charges or simply be required to compensate the bank and anyone else who suffered a loss?
3. Phillip, a jilted boyfriend, demanded that Michelle, his ex-girlfriend, reimburse him for expenses incident to their dating experiences. When she refused, Phillip threatened to distribute to patrons of a local bar copies of explicit videos of Michelle engaged in sexual activity along with her phone number and a suggestion to contact her for sex. What offense does this scenario suggest?

## CHAPTER 9

# White-Collar and Organized Crime

## CHAPTER OUTLINE

## JURISPRUDENCE

## LEARNING OBJECTIVES

After reading this chapter, you should be able to explain

1. the nature of white-collar crime and organized crime

2. the basis of criminal laws dealing with white collar and organized crime

3. how and why a corporation may be guilty of a crime

4. how federal antitrust laws define criminal conduct

5. how the law deals with computer crimes

6. the offenses of access device fraud and identity theft

7. the various offenses involving intellectual property

*Continued*

*Continued*

8. money laundering and other currency-related offenses

9. the different species of fraud, including tax fraud, bankruptcy fraud, securities fraud, and mail and wire fraud

10. the importance of the federal RICO law in the prosecution of racketeering

## CHAPTER OPENING VIGNETTE

Bernie Madoff was a major player on Wall Street for decades. His investment firm, Bernard L. Madoff Investment Securities, had numerous high-profile clients, including banks, foundations, and universities. Madoff was widely sought after as an expert on stock markets and had close ties to the Securities and Exchange Commission (SEC). In March 2009, Madoff pleaded guilty to eleven federal crimes, including securities fraud, mail fraud, wire fraud, and money laundering, all of which are offenses discussed in this chapter. In pleading guilty, Madoff admitted to a massive Ponzi scheme that defrauded billions of dollars from thousands of investors. A Ponzi scheme is one in which money from new investors is used to provide bogus returns to earlier investors. Investors are attracted by the promise of exceptional returns on their investments. When someone of Madoff's résumé and reputation is running the scam, it proves to be irresistible to many. Madoff's Ponzi scheme started as far back as the 1980s. The SEC had investigated Madoff on several occasions, but those investigations never bore fruit. In December 2008, Madoff's sons came to the SEC with information that their father had confessed to them that he was perpetrating a fraud. Investigators subsequently found that more than $65 billion was missing from client accounts. A court-appointed trustee determined that actual losses to investors were in the vicinity of $18 billion. In June 2009, Madoff was sentenced to 150 years in prison, the maximum sentence for his offenses. Today Madoff resides in a medium-security facility at the Federal Correctional Complex in Butner, North Carolina. He is, without question, America's most notorious white-collar criminal.

# Introduction

In the previous chapter we delineated what might be called "traditional" property crimes. In this chapter we examine a set of distinctly modern economic offenses. Some of these offenses can be viewed as extensions of the ancient common-law offense of larceny. But most of them are decidedly modern creations—the products of statutes enacted by Congress or the state legislatures. These offenses are often referred to as **white-collar crimes** because perpetrators typically come from the middle and upper socioeconomic strata of society, whereas the offenses described in the previous chapter are often termed "street crimes." However, it is important to understand that anyone, regardless of his or her social status, can commit any of the crimes described in this chapter, just as anyone can commit larceny, robbery, burglary, or any of the other traditional property crimes. While crimes such as burglary, robbery, and carjacking are often associated with violence, white-collar crimes are almost always nonviolent. Instead, they are characterized by deception or abuse of trust and often involve the use of computers or other modern technologies.

**white-collar crimes** Economic offenses characterized by deception or abuse of trust and often involving the use of computers or other modern technologies.

The rapid growth of the Internet has opened up new vistas of opportunity for criminals. Identity theft, theft of intellectual property, and numerous types of fraudulent schemes have been propelled to unprecedented levels by means of the Internet. In 2000, the FBI received roughly 17,000 complaints of Internet-based crimes; by 2011 that number had risen to more than 314,000. Federal Bureau of Investigation, Internet Crime Complaint Center, *2011 Internet Crime Report*, http://www.ic3.gov/media/annualreport/2011_IC3Report.pdf, page 6.

**organized crime** Syndicates involved in racketeering and other criminal activities.

**Organized crime** involves offenses committed by persons or groups who conduct their business through illegal enterprises. Organized crime figures, or "racketeers," often attempt to gain political influence through graft and corruption, and they frequently resort to threats and acts of violence in the commission of white-collar offenses. Organized crime gained its greatest foothold during the Prohibition era, when the Eighteenth Amendment to the U.S. Constitution, prohibiting the sale and distribution of alcoholic beverages, was in effect. By the time Prohibition was repealed in 1933, organized crime had become involved in many phases of our economy, often pursuing its interests through such illegal activities as **loan-sharking**, gambling, prostitution, and drug trafficking. Protection rackets and other forms of **racketeering** have become the methodology of organized crime as it has infiltrated many legitimate business operations.

**loan-sharking** The practice of lending money at illegal rates of interest.

**racketeering** A system of organized crime traditionally involving the extortion of money from businesses by intimidation, violence, or other illegal methods.

White-collar crime is responsible for the loss of billions of dollars annually by government, businesses, and citizens nationwide. The FBI has special units that handle investigations of economic crimes, financial institution fraud, government fraud, and public corruption. In addition, the Internal Revenue Service, the Secret Service, the Environmental Protection Agency, and the Securities and Exchange Commission are active in the enforcement of federal white-collar crime legislation. In recent years the states have become more active in establishing agencies to enforce state laws in this area.

The U.S. Department of Justice also has an Organized Crime and Racketeering Section (OCRS), which coordinates the department's program to combat organized crime. OCRS coordinates with other investigative agencies such as the FBI and the Drug Enforcement Administration and works with the Attorney General's Organized Crime Council. OCRS also reviews all proposed federal prosecutions under the Racketeer Influenced and Corrupt Organizations (RICO) statute and provides advice to prosecutors.

# Legal Principles Governing White-Collar Crimes

The principles discussed in relation to the elements of crimes and parties generally also apply to white-collar offenses. Requirements under both state and federal laws for an *actus reus*, *mens rea*, their concurrence, and causation of harm, as well as the definition of principals and accessories, are explained in Chapter 4. In prosecuting white-collar crimes in federal court, the government is usually required to prove that the accused committed the prohibited act "knowingly and willfully." Frequently, federal prosecutors charge white-collar defendants with conspiracy, either under 18 U.S.C.A. § 371 or under one of the conspiracy provisions pertaining to substantive offenses. As pointed out in Chapter 5, the prosecution enjoys certain procedural advantages in using conspiracy as a basis for criminal charges.

Most white-collar crimes prosecuted as federal violations are based on statutes enacted by Congress under the authority of Article I, Section 8 of the U.S. Constitution, which grants Congress power over postal, bankruptcy, and taxing matters and authority to regulate interstate domestic and foreign commerce. Of course, state legislatures have broad authority to proscribe such offenses as contrary to the public welfare.

While the most notable prosecutions of white-collar crimes involve large-scale corporate frauds, white-collar offenses more frequently entail telephone, mail, and e-mail solicitations by those who commit frauds and swindles as they furnish their victims with "opportunities" to buy unregistered securities, obtain undeserved diplomas, participate in phony contests, and the like. Also common are scams involving fraudulent home-improvement schemes, bogus land sales, and spurious investments.

Many statutes defining offenses that have become known as white-collar crimes also provide civil remedies designed to compensate those who have suffered pecuniary losses as a result of a defendant's activities. These laws provide an example of the overlap between the civil and criminal law discussed in Chapter 1. In instances where a civil proceeding and a criminal proceeding are conducted at the same time, courts often stay the civil proceeding pending resolution of the criminal action.

## Prosecution of Corporate Defendants

Under common law, a corporation was not held criminally responsible for its acts. This was because a corporation is an artificial being that cannot form the mental element necessary for imposition of criminal liability and cannot be imprisoned. Nevertheless, its members could be held responsible. As strict liability offenses not requiring proof of a *mens rea* developed, corporations were held criminally responsible. Eventually, courts began to interpret the words "person" and "whoever" in criminal statutes to include corporations. Where statutes prescribed punishment other than death or incarceration, courts began to impose criminal liability based on acts of the corporation's agents and to punish corporations by imposing fines. In some jurisdictions, however, a corporation cannot be held criminally liable for crimes against persons unless the offense is one based on the corporation's negligence rather than a crime based on specific intent. The rationale for this is that the corporation cannot form the necessary *mens rea*.

## Acts by Corporate Agents

**corporate defendants** Corporations charged with criminal offenses.

**scope of an agent's authority** In white-collar crime cases, the scope of an agent's authority depends on whether the commission of the offense was authorized, requested, commanded, performed, or recklessly tolerated by the board of directors or by a high managerial agent acting in behalf of the corporation within the scope of his or her office or employment.

Today, prosecutions of white-collar crime are frequently directed against **corporate defendants**, and corporations are held criminally liable for the acts of their agents committed within the **scope of an agent's authority**. In 1909 the U.S. Supreme

Court first held that a corporation could be held criminally liable based on acts of its agents attributed to the corporation. *N.Y. Cent. & Hudson River R.R. Co. v. United States*, 212 U.S. 481, 29 S.Ct. 304, 53 L.Ed. 613 (1909). Today, corporations are held criminally liable for the unlawful acts of their agents, provided that such conduct is within the scope of the agent's actual or apparent authority. *United States v. Bi-Co Pavers, Inc.*, 741 F.2d 730 (5th Cir. 1984). An agent's knowledge is imputed to the corporation where the agent is acting within the scope of his or her authority and where the knowledge relates to matters within the scope of that authority. See *In re Hellenic, Inc.*, 252 F.3d 391, 395 (5th Cir. 2001). State and federal courts tend to define broadly what constitutes scope of authority, generally holding that the agent's acts must be intended to benefit the corporation in some way.

A few states have adopted § 2.07 of the Model Penal Code or some version of it. Section 2.07(1) provides that a corporation may be convicted of an offense under the following guidelines:

(a) the offense is a violation defined by a statute in which a legislative purpose to impose liability on corporations plainly appears and the conduct is performed by an agent of the corporation acting in behalf of the corporation within the scope of his office or employment, except that if the law defining the offense designates the agents for whose conduct the corporation is accountable or the circumstances under which it is accountable, such provisions shall apply; or

(b) the offense consists of an omission to discharge a specific duty of affirmative performance imposed on corporations by law; or

(c) the commission of the offense was authorized, requested, commanded, performed or recklessly tolerated by the board of directors or by a high managerial agent-acting in behalf of the corporation within the scope of his office or employment.

In other jurisdictions, courts simply seek to determine whether the corporate agent or employee was acting within the scope of his or her authority. If so, the courts impute that action to the corporation. Although a corporation may be prosecuted for crimes, that does not exonerate individuals who commit unlawful acts. In fact, in prosecutions for white-collar crimes committed by or on behalf of a corporation, it is not uncommon for corporate executives to be individually punished, generally by the imposition of large fines.

## Antitrust Violations

**Sherman Antitrust Act** A federal statute prohibiting any contract, combination, or conspiracy in restraint of trade. The act is designed to protect and preserve a system of free and open competition. Its scope is broad and reaches individuals and entities in for-profit and nonprofit activities as well as local governments and educational institutions.

The **Sherman Antitrust Act**, 15 U.S.C.A. § 1 *et seq.*, makes it a crime to enter into any contract or engage in any combination or conspiracy in restraint of trade or to monopolize or attempt to monopolize trade. The act is designed to protect and preserve a system of free and open competition. Its scope is broad and reaches individuals and entities in for-profit and nonprofit activities as well as local governments and educational institutions. The act includes civil remedies as well as criminal sanctions. The criminal provisions are enforced by the Antitrust Division of the U.S. Justice Department.

To prove a criminal violation of the act, the government must establish that (1) two or more entities formed a combination or conspiracy; (2) the combination or conspiracy produces, or potentially produces, an unreasonable restraint of trade or commerce; (3) the restrained trade or commerce is interstate in nature; and (4) the defendant's general intent is to violate the law.

**antitrust violations** Violations of laws designed to protect the public from price-fixing, price discrimination, and monopolistic practices in trade and commerce.

Principles outlined in Chapter 5 concerning conspiracies come into play in prosecutions for **antitrust violations**. The antitrust statutes are unclear regarding whether intent must be proven to convict a defendant. In *United States v. U.S. Gypsum Co.*, 438 U.S. 422, 98 S.Ct. 2864, 57 L.Ed.2d 854 (1978), a case involving alleged price-fixing, the Supreme Court rejected any idea that criminal violations of the act were intended to be strict liability crimes. Rather, the Court observed that intent is an indispensable element of a criminal antitrust case, just like any other criminal offense.

The essence of a Sherman Antitrust Act violation is a combination and conspiracy in restraint of trade. For example, in 1998 the Tenth Circuit Court of Appeals held that the NCAA's rules restricting earnings of a class of coaches to an annual salary of $16,000 was an unreasonable restraint of trade that had an anticompetitive effect. *Law v. National Collegiate Athletic Association*, 134 F.3d 1010 (10th Cir. 1998).

**price-fixing** Sellers unlawfully entering into agreements as to the price of products or services.

Among the more common violations are **price-fixing** and **bid rigging**. As previously suggested, price-fixing occurs when sellers unlawfully enter into agreements to control the prices of products or services. Bid rigging involves interference with competitive bidding for the award of a contract. Illustrative convictions are the following:

**bid rigging** Illegally manipulating the submission of bids to obtain a contract, usually from a public body.

- Parties made an agreement not to bid competitively at a bankruptcy auction and to hold a later auction and then split the profits. *United States v. Seville Industrial Machinery Corp.*, 696 F. Supp. 986 (D.N.J. 1988).
- An agent for a public contractor agreed to rig bids with another on a county construction project. *United States v. Bi-Co Pavers, Inc.*, 741 F.2d 730 (5th Cir. 1984).
- Parties entered into a conspiracy to submit collusive noncompetitive bids on a project. *United States v. Mobile Materials, Inc.*, 881 F.2d 866 (10th Cir. 1989).
- Defendant corporations conspired to fix prices for fiberglass materials. *United States v. Therm-All, Inc.*, 373 F.3d 625 (5th Cir. 2004).

The U.S. Justice Department alone is authorized to enforce the criminal sanctions of the Sherman Act. Criminal violations are felonies; the act provides that those convicted shall be punished by a fine not exceeding $100,000,000 if a corporation; or, if any other person, $1,000,000; or by imprisonment not exceeding ten years; or by both punishments, in the discretion of the court. 15 U.S.C.A. § 1.

Corporate defendants often seek to avoid liability for violations committed by their agents. But courts have generally held that as long as an agent acts within the scope of employment or apparent authority, the corporation may be held legally responsible.

Most state legislatures have enacted statutes under which intrastate violations of securities laws are prosecuted. The text of state statutes and their judicial interpretations often parallel the federal ones.

## Computer Crimes

**Computer Fraud and Abuse Act** Federal law criminalizing fraud and related activity in connection with computers.

Once computers became common in society, criminals began to employ them to commit a variety of offenses. Indeed, the pervasiveness of computers poses some unique challenges to federal and state law enforcement agencies and prosecutors. In 1984 Congress enacted the **Computer Fraud and Abuse Act**, 18 U.S.C.A. §. 1030. The statute has been amended several times, most recently in 2008. The act proscribes crimes involving "protected computers"—those used in interstate commerce or communications—including computers connected to the Internet. As amended

**CASE-IN-POINT**

### A Federal Computer Crime

The federal government charged John Larking Trotter with intentionally causing damage to a Salvation Army computer without authorization in violation of the Computer Fraud and Abuse Act, 18 U.S.C.A. § 1030(a)(5)(A)(i). Trotter admitted that the Salvation Army's computer that he accessed was a protected computer, but on appeal he argued that the statute was unconstitutional as applied to him because "the statute cannot possibly be so broad as to cover the computer network of a not-for-profit organization like the Salvation Army." The federal appellate court rejected his argument, explaining that the Salvation Army's computers are intertwined with interstate commerce and thus are within the realm of Congress's power to regulate interstate commerce. The court further observed, "The Salvation Army's status as a not-for-profit entity has no bearing on our analysis; it is the characteristics of the computer or computer network, not the entity using the network, that is the focus of the statutes."

*United States v. Trotter*, 478 F.3d 918 (8th Cir. 2007).

in 1996, 18 U.S.C.A. § 1030(a)(5)(A) makes it a crime to "knowingly cause the transmission of a program, information, code, or command" in interstate commerce with intent to cause damage to a computer exclusively used by a financial institution or the U.S. government. In addition, the act prohibits "knowingly and with intent to defraud, trafficking in passwords to permit unauthorized access to a government computer, or to affect interstate or foreign commerce." 18 U.S.C.A. § 1030(a)(6)(A)(B). Subsection 1030(a)(7) makes it illegal to transmit in interstate or foreign commerce any threat to cause damage to a protected computer with intent to extort something of value.

It is also a federal crime to "knowingly with intent to defraud" produce, use, or traffic in counterfeit **access devices**. 18 U.S.C.A. § 1029(a). Access devices include cards, plates, codes, electronic serial numbers, mobile identification numbers, personal identification numbers, telecommunications services, equipment, instrument identifiers, or other means that can be used to obtain goods or services. 18 U.S.C.A. § 1029(e). To obtain a conviction for unauthorized access devices, the government must prove that a defendant acted knowingly and with intent to defraud, but proof of such intent may be established with circumstantial evidence. *United States v. Ismoila*, 100 F.3d 380 (5th Cir. 1996).

> **access devices** Cards, plates, codes, electronic serial numbers, personal identification numbers, and telecommunications services, equipment, instrument identifiers, and other means that can be used to obtain goods or services.

## The USA PATRIOT Act

After the terrorist attacks of September 11, 2001, Congress hastily passed important legislation officially known as the Uniting and Strengthening America by Providing Appropriate Tools Required to Intercept and Obstruct Terrorism Act of 2001. Better known by its acronym, the **USA PATRIOT Act** was signed into law by President George W. Bush on October 25, 2001. This 342-page statute was designed to deter and punish terrorist acts in the United States and around the world and to enhance the federal government's law-enforcement investigatory tools. On March 9, 2006, President Bush signed legislation essentially renewing the USA PATRIOT Act. Section 814 of the act makes a number of changes in federal statutes designed to strengthen the Computer Fraud and Abuse Act, 18 U.S.C.A. § 1030.

Section 814 of the PATRIOT Act amends the definition of "protected computer" to include computers outside of the United States that affect "interstate or foreign

> **USA PATRIOT Act** Controversial act of Congress enacted in 2001 to strengthen the federal government's efforts to combat terrorism.

commerce or communication of the United States." 18 U.S.C.A. § 1030(e)(2)(B). Section 814 of the act raises the maximum penalty for violations for damaging a protected computer to ten years for first-time offenders and twenty years for repeat offenders. 18 U.S.C.A. § 1030(c)(4). Under previous law, first-time offenders who violate § 1030(a)(5) by damaging a protected computer could be punished by no more than five years' imprisonment, while repeat offenders could receive up to ten years.

Section 814 of the act added 18 U.S.C.A. §§ 1030(c)(2)(C) and (e)(8), which clarify that a hacker need only intend to damage a protected computer or the information on it, not to cause a specific dollar amount of loss or other special harm.

## State Laws Proscribing Computer Offenses

Since 1978 nearly every state has enacted laws specifically defining computer crimes. These laws define *access, computer program, software, database, hacking, financial instrument,* and other terms used in modern computer parlance and address such activities as computer manipulation, theft of intellectual property, telecommunications crimes, and software piracy. They also create such offenses as **theft of computer services**, **computer fraud**, and **computer trespass**.

The Virginia legislature has addressed each of these offenses by enacting the Virginia Computer Crimes Act, § 18.2-152.3 of which provides:

> Any person who uses a computer or computer network without authority and with the intent to:
>
> 1. Obtain property or services by false pretenses;
>
> 2. Embezzle or commit larceny; or
>
> 3. Convert the property of another is guilty of the crime of computer fraud.

Depending on the value of property or services actually obtained, the offense is either a felony or a serious misdemeanor.

Section 18.2-152.4 provides:

> A. It shall be unlawful for any person, with malicious intent, to:
>
> 1. Temporarily or permanently remove, halt, or otherwise disable any computer data, computer programs or computer software from a computer or computer network;
>
> 2. Cause a computer to malfunction, regardless of how long the malfunction persists;
>
> 3. Alter, disable, or erase any computer data, computer programs or computer software;
>
> 4. Effect the creation or alteration of a financial instrument or of an electronic transfer of funds;
>
> 5. Use a computer or computer network to cause physical injury to the property of another; or
>
> 6. Use a computer or computer network to make or cause to be made an unauthorized copy, in any form, including, but not limited to, any printed or electronic form of computer data, computer programs or computer software residing in, communicated by, or produced by a computer or computer network.

Depending on the damages caused, an offense under this statute is either a felony or a serious misdemeanor.

**theft of computer services** Stealing software, data, computer access codes, computer time, and so on.

**computer fraud** An offense consisting of obtaining property or services by false pretenses through use of a computer or computer network.

**computer trespass** An offense consisting of the unauthorized copying, alteration, or removal of computer data, programs, or software.

## Antispam Laws

As everyone who uses e-mail knows, "spam" refers to unsolicited e-mail messages sent to thousands, even millions, of e-mail accounts. Spam is a nuisance to e-mail users and causes real problems for Internet service providers. A number of states have enacted laws regulating commercial spam. Arizona law, for example, provides:

> A person shall not knowingly transmit commercial electronic mail if any of the following apply:
> 1. The person falsifies electronic mail transmission information or other routing information for unsolicited commercial electronic mail.
> 2. The mail contains false or misleading information in the subject line.
> 3. The person uses a third party's Internet address or domain name without the third party's consent for the purpose of transmitting electronic mail in a way that makes it appear that the third party was the sender of the mail.
>
> Ariz. Rev. Stat. § 44-1372.01(A).

In enacting regulations of unsolicited bulk e-mail, states must be aware of First Amendment considerations. Virginia's antispam law was declared unconstitutional by the Virginia Supreme Court because it prohibited transmission of any unsolicited e-mails, including those containing political, religious, or other protected speech. *Jaynes v. Commonwealth*, 666 S.E.2d 303 (Va. 2008).

## International Efforts to Combat Cybercrime

**cybercrimes** Crimes committed using computers and the Internet.

Because of its global reach, Internet crime poses an especially difficult challenge to domestic law enforcement agencies. In 2006, the United States joined more than forty other countries by ratifying the Convention on **Cybercrime**, a treaty designed to harmonize national laws and strengthen international cooperation in this area. In addition to its provisions dealing with sexual exploitation of children, terrorism, and "hate crimes," the treaty addresses several problems in the area of international white-collar crime, including computer-related fraud, "hacking," the dissemination of computer viruses, and electronic attacks on financial institutions.

---

**CASE-IN-POINT**

### The Virginia Supreme Court Strikes Down an Antispam Law

On three separate occasions Jeremy Jaynes sent more than 10,000 unsolicited e-mails to America Online (AOL) subscribers. Jaynes intentionally falsified the header information and sender domain names before transmitting the e-mails, but investigators used a sophisticated database to identify Jaynes as the sender. After a jury trial, Jaynes was convicted of violating the Virginia Computer Crimes Act and was sentenced to nine years in prison. The state appeals court affirmed the conviction, but the Virginia Supreme Court reversed and struck down the provision of the statute under which Jaynes was prosecuted. The court held that provision to be "unconstitutionally overbroad on its face because it prohibits the anonymous transmission of all unsolicited bulk e-mails including those containing political, religious or other speech protected by the First Amendment to the United States Constitution."

*Jaynes v. Commonwealth*, 666 S.E.2d 303 (Va. 2008).

### Unauthorized Access to a Voice Mailbox

Andrea M. Gerulis was convicted in a bench trial of two counts of unlawful use of a computer and two counts of violating a statute that criminalized intentionally obtaining various electronic services "available only for compensation" by deception, unauthorized connection, etc. Gerulis was ordered to make restitution. The evidence revealed that Gerulis had deposited and retrieved information from voice mailboxes (VMBs) of a hospital and a telephone message company without authority from either to do so. By altering passwords, she thereby prevented authorized users from using their VMBs. Gerulis appealed, contending the evidence was insufficient to sustain her convictions.

The appellate court found that VMBs are "computers" within the meaning of the statute, and Gerulis's disruption of normal use of the VMBs violated the statute. The court then addressed Gerulis's convictions for theft of services. The court observed that the prosecution had charged Gerulis under a statute that makes it an offense if a person "intentionally obtains services for himself or for another which he knows are available only for compensation." Because the evidence revealed that the VMBs that Gerulis accessed were provided by the hospital and message company without charge for their employees, the court found that Gerulis's mere intent to obtain free services did not violate that statute. Accordingly, the court affirmed Gerulis's convictions for unlawful use of a computer, reversed her convictions for theft of services, and remanded the case to the trial court to modify the restitution order imposed as Gerulis's sentence.

*Commonwealth v. Gerulis*, 616 A.2d 686 (Pa. Super. 1992).

## Access Device Fraud

Debit cards and credit cards, automated teller machine (ATM) cards, account numbers, personal identification numbers (PINs), and other means are now commonly available to named persons who assume the obligation of their use. Because of their widespread use, state legislatures have realized the necessity to enact comprehensive statutes proscribing the fraudulent use of devices to secure cash, goods, and services through means beyond the traditional credit card.

In 1998 Pennsylvania rewrote its statute titled "Credit Card Fraud" to proscribe a variety of means of gaining fraudulent access to money, goods, and services. As amended, the revised section of Purdon's Pennsylvania Consolidated Statutes Annotated now provides:

Section 4106. Access device fraud

(a) Offense defined.—A person commits an offense if he:

    (1) uses an access device to obtain or in an attempt to obtain property or services with knowledge that:

        (i)   the access device is counterfeit, altered or incomplete;

        (ii)  the access device was issued to another person who has not authorized its use;

        (iii) the access device has been revoked or canceled; or

        (iv) for any other reason his use of the access device is unauthorized by the issuer or the device holder; or

    (2) publishes, makes, sells, gives, or otherwise transfers to another, or offers or advertises, or aids and abets any other person to use an access device knowing that the access device is counterfeit, altered or incomplete, belongs to another person who has not authorized its use, has been revoked or canceled or for any reason is unauthorized by the issuer or the device holder; or

(3) possesses an access device knowing that it is counterfeit, altered, incomplete or belongs to another person who has not authorized its possession.

(a.1) Presumptions.—For the purpose of this section as well as in any prosecution for theft committed by the means specified in this section:

(1) An actor is presumed to know an access device is counterfeit, altered or incomplete if he has in his possession or under his control two or more counterfeit, altered or incomplete access devices.

(2) Knowledge of revocation or cancellation shall be presumed to have been received by an access device holder seven days after it has been mailed to him at the address set forth on the access device application or at a new address if a change of address has been provided to the issuer.

(b) Defenses.—It is a defense to a prosecution under subsection (a)(1)(iv) if the actor proves by a preponderance of the evidence that he had the intent and ability to meet all obligations to the issuer arising out of his use of the access device.

Subsection (c) of the Pennsylvania statute stipulates that if the value involved is $500 or more, the offense constitutes a felony; if less than $500, the offense constitutes a misdemeanor. The degree of felony or misdemeanor depends on the value involved.

Subsection (d) includes the following definitions:

- "Access device." Any card, including, but not limited to, a credit card, debit card and automated teller machine card, plate, code, account number, personal identification number or other means of account access that can be used alone or in conjunction with another access device to obtain money, goods, services or anything else of value or that can be used to transfer funds.
- "Altered access device." A validly issued access device which after issue is changed in any way.
- "Counterfeit access device." An access device not issued by an issuer in the ordinary course of business.
- "Device holder." The person or organization named on the access device to whom or for whose benefit the access device is issued by an issuer.

**access device fraud** The crime of knowingly producing, using, or trafficking in counterfeit credit cards, personal identification numbers, access codes, account numbers, etc. with the intent to fraudulently obtain money, goods, or services.

Because of the widespread use of access devices, many states have adopted statutes prohibiting **access device fraud**. Offenses proscribed by the above statute could likely be prosecuted under modern comprehensive theft or forgery statutes; however, given such statutes, an issue has arisen as to whether the existence of a statute proscribing credit card use (more recently included in statutes proscribing access device fraud) precludes prosecution under a theft or forgery proscribing more severe penalties. Several courts have held that such specific statutes did not preclude prosecution under a statute based on theft or forgery. See, e.g., *People v. James*, 497 P.2d 1256 (Colo. 1972); *Garcia v. State*, 669 S.W.2d 169 (Tex. App. 1984).

In *Commonwealth v. Sargent*, 823 A.2d 174 (Pa. Super. 2003), a Pennsylvania appellate court rejected a defendant's argument that, because he obtained property valued at $450 through fraudulent use of a credit card, he could not be convicted under a statute making forgery a felony. He argued that because of the existence of § 4106, his offense would be a misdemeanor because he obtained property valued at only $450. The court held that the defendant's action of signing the victim's name to credit card receipts was a felony of the third degree because the receipts constituted documents within the meaning of a statute providing that forgery is a felony of the third degree. The court concluded, "We find meritless Appellant's argument that the Legislature did not intend the fraudulent signing of credit card receipts to constitute a felony of the third degree under the facts in this case since the Legislature specifically provided for the unauthorized use of credit cards in 18 Pa. C.S.A. § 4106." *Id.* at 177.

### College Student Prosecuted for Hacking into Sarah Palin's E-mail Account

In September 2008, David Kernell, a University of Tennessee student, hacked into Sarah Palin's Yahoo account and posted several of her emails and photos to the Web. Kernell later admitted that he hoped to derail her campaign to be elected Vice President. In October, Kernell was arrested and was charged with four federal crimes—identity theft, wire fraud, obstruction of justice and intentionally accessing an account without authorization—carrying a maximum sentence of twenty years in prison and $250,000 fine. In 2010, Kernell was tried before a jury and convicted of obstruction of justice (a felony) and intentionally accessing an account without authorization (a misdemeanor). The obstruction charge was based on the fact that Kernell deleted files from his hard drive in an attempt to destroy evidence. The jury deadlocked on the identity theft charge and acquitted Kernell of wire fraud. In November 2010, Judge Thomas W. Phillips sentenced Kernell to one year in custody and three years probation. At sentencing, Kernell apologized to Sarah Palin, who testified at trial that the incident had caused emotional distress to her and her family. In January 2012, a federal appeals court affirmed Kernell's conviction and sentence for obstruction of justice.

*United States v. Kernell,* 667 F.3d 746 (6th Cir. 2012).

Many states have adopted statutes similar to the Pennsylvania law. Courts have generally held that the existence of a statute specifically addressing access devices does not preclude the state from prosecution of an access device offense as forgery, where the facts warrant it, under a forgery statute proscribing more severe penalties. See, e.g., *Garcia v. State,* 669 S.W.2d 169 (Tex. App. 1984); *People v. James,* 497 P.2d 1256 (Colo. 1972).

## Identity Theft

**identity theft** The crime of using someone else's personal information—such as their name, social security number, or credit card number—without their permission to commit fraud or other crimes.

The theft or misappropriation of personal identifying information and documents, commonly referred to as **identity theft**, has become a theft offense of major proportions in the United States. In 2010, an estimated 8.1 million adults in the United States were victimized by identity thieves (Javelin Strategy and Research, "2011 Identity Fraud Survey Report: Consumer Version," Pleasanton, CA: Javelin, February 2011).

A person's identity is closely tied to personal and numerical identification of bank accounts; credit cards; Social Security, Medicare, telephone, insurance, and utility accounts; and many other identifying documents. Thieves obtain information about a person through many means. These include such obvious means as theft of wallets and purses, mail, and computer data, and gathering information from home and car burglaries. They also obtain information from such less obvious means as "shoulder surfing" when someone is paying by check or credit card, and "dumpster diving" into trash to obtain discarded identifying documents such as unused preapproved credit card applications. Information obtained from e-mail and other computer transactions, including responses to requests for passwords and other information, is increasingly becoming a source of identifying information. Armed with such information, a thief can then assume the victim's identity, change the victim's address, open new accounts, buy a car, borrow money, and otherwise injure the victim's assets, credit standing, and reputation. Most victims of identity theft are unaware of how a thief obtained their personal information. Often the victim is unaware of the fraud until substantial damage has been inflicted. Victims often incur large expenses and expend considerable time in opening new accounts and repairing their credit ratings.

## Federal Legislation

To address the growing problem of identity theft, Congress enacted the Identity Theft and Assumption Deterrence Act of 1998 (ITADA), which amends 18 U.S.C.A. § 1028 by adding subsection (a)(7). This subsection makes it a felony to "knowingly transfer, possess or use, without lawful authority, a means of identification of another person with the intent to commit, or to aid or abet, any unlawful activity that constitutes a violation of Federal law, or that constitutes a felony under any applicable State or local law." Conduct involving identity theft or fraud may in some instances also be a violation of 18 U.S.C.A. § 1341 (credit card fraud); 18 U.S.C.A. § 1030 (computer fraud); 18 U.S.C.A. § 1341 (mail fraud); 18 U.S.C.A. § 1343 (wire, radio and television fraud); or 18 U.S.C.A. § 1344 (financial institution fraud).

The Federal Trade Commission maintains a website (www.ftc.gov/idtheft) that furnishes considerable information about identity theft. It explains how the crime occurs, what steps can be taken to prevent it, and what measures should be taken when people discover that they have been victimized by identity theft. The site also features a comprehensive survey of federal and state legislation criminalizing identity theft.

## State Legislation

By 2003 most states had enacted specific statutes criminalizing identify theft and fraud, but even without specific statutes such activity could be prosecuted under statutes proscribing theft and fraud. Section 943.201(2) of the Wisconsin Statutes, as recently amended, provides that

> (2) Whoever, for any of the following purposes, intentionally uses or attempts to use or possess with intent to use any personal identifying information or personal identification document of an individual, including a deceased individual, without the authorization or consent of the individual and by representing that he or she is the individual, that he or she is acting with the authorization or consent of the individual, or that the information or document belongs to him or her is guilty of a Class H felony:
>
> > (a) To obtain credit, money, goods, services, employment, or any other thing of value or benefit.
> >
> > (b) To avoid civil or criminal process or penalty.
> >
> > (c) To harm the reputation, property, person, or estate of the individual.

In *State v. Ramirez*, 633 N.W.2d 656 (Wis. App. 2001), the court upheld the conviction of a defendant found guilty under Wis. Stat. § 943.201(2) for misappropriating the personal identifying information of another. The defendant had used someone else's social security number without authorization to obtain employment.

In 2005, the Washington Court of Appeals rejected a defendant's contention that the state's choice to prosecute him for the felony of identity theft rather than the misdemeanor offense of use of a false name or a false identity denied him his constitutional right to equal protection of the laws. The court rejected his contention because the misdemeanor offense did not require assuming the identity of an actual person. *State v. Presba*, 26 P.3d 1280 (Wash. App. 2005).

In *People v. Montoya*, 868 N.E.2d 389 (Ill. App. 2007), defendant Montoya used another person's name and social security number to get a job with Terra Harvest Foods. Over more than three years she received over $50,000 in wages and approximately $31,000 in medical insurance benefits under the name and social security number of her victim. The Illinois appellate court found the evidence of identity theft sufficient to support her conviction.

### Georgia Supreme Court Affirms a Conviction for Identity Theft

Nohe Gomes Hernandez, an illegal immigrant, was convicted under a Georgia statute that makes it a crime to access the resources of a person unlawfully through the use of identifying information. The evidence at trial revealed that Hernandez misappropriated Jason Smith's social security number to obtain a social security card and a driver's license in Smith's name. Next, posing as Smith, Hernandez used these means of identification to obtain a job at a poultry processing plant. Hernandez's wages, under Smith's name, were reported to the Internal Revenue Service. In 2005, when Smith contacted the IRS to inquire about a tax refund he was expecting, an IRS agent informed him that he owed approximately $12,000 in back taxes. This led to the discovery that Hernandez had assumed Smith's identity.

On appeal, Hernandez argued that although he used Smith's identifying information to obtain a job there was no evidence that he used the information to access any of Smith's resources. In rejecting his contention the court pointed out that Ga. Code Ann. § 16-9-120(f)(F), which states that a person's resources includes "[a]ny account, . . . including a national bank . . . is sufficiently broad to include the U.S. Treasury, the nation's foremost banking institution." The appellate court affirmed Hernandez's conviction. *Hernandez v. State*, 639 S.E.2d 473 (Ga. 2007).

## Intellectual Property Offenses

**intellectual property**
Products of the human intellect, such as inventions, plays, stories, films, music, and trade secrets.

The term **intellectual property** refers to products of the human intellect such as patents, copyrights, trademarks, and trade secrets. In the Information Age, intellectual property is as important as real estate or tangible personal property. The U.S. Constitution, Article 1, Section 8, clause 8, grants Congress the power to secure for a limited time to authors and inventors the exclusive rights to their writings and discoveries. Congress has legislated pursuant to such authority and has granted federal courts exclusive jurisdiction over civil and criminal actions based on federal statutes. See 28 U.S.C.A. §§ 1338, 1355. While most disputes involving intellectual property are civil matters, there are several important criminal prohibitions in this area, most notably patent infringement, copyright infringement, trademark counterfeiting, and theft of trade secrets.

### Patent Infringement

**patent** A government grant of the right to exclude others from producing or using a discovery or invention for a certain period of time.

A **patent** is a federal government grant of the right to exclude others from producing or using a discovery or invention. Patents are issued by the U.S. Patent and Trademark Office for inventions and discoveries that are novel, useful, and not something of an obvious nature. See 35 U.S.C.A. §§ 101–103. Patents are issued for a period of twenty years. 35 U.S.C.A. § 154.

Patent infringements are generally remedied through civil litigation. Indeed, there are few instances of criminal penalties being imposed. The Patent Act, however, establishes criminal liability of $500 per infringement for falsely affixing or marking in connection with sales or advertising of any imitation the name of the patentee or the patent number, or using the words "patent," "patentee," "patent applied for," or "patent pending" to falsely convey the status of a patent. To prove any of the above violations, the prosecution must show the deceitful intent of the defendant. 35 U.S.C.A. § 292. Title 18 U.S.C.A. § 497 makes it an offense for "[w]hoever passes, utters, or publishes, or attempts to pass, utter, or publish as genuine, any such letters patent, knowing the same to be forged, counterfeited or falsely altered." The statute calls for a fine or imprisonment.

## Copyright Infringement

**copyright** A form of legal protection provided to the authors of original literary, musical, artistic, and architectural works as well as videos, computer software, and databases.

A **copyright** is a form of legal protection that is provided to the authors of original works. Congress has enacted statutes to expand the protection of literary work to include musical, artistic, and architectural works as well as videos, computer software, and databases. Copyrights are registered in the Copyright Office in the Library of Congress, and a copyright for a work created after January 1, 1978, is given statutory protection for the life of the author plus seventy years after the author's death. 17 U.S.C.A. § 302(a). Section 506 of the Copyright Act provides for the criminal prosecution of certain types of infringement.

Section 506(a) of the Copyright Act, 17 U.S.C.A. § 506(a), provides that anyone "who infringes a copyright willfully either (1) for purposes of commercial advantage or private financial gain, or (2) by the reproduction or distribution, including by electronic means of one or more copies or phonorecords . . . shall be punished as provided in 18 U.S.C.A. § 2319." (The term "willfully" distinguishes the crime from infringement in civil litigation.) Under this latter statute the determination of whether such violation is a felony or misdemeanor depends on the quantity and value of items distributed in a specified period of time. Penalties are also provided for fraudulent removal of copyright notices and for false representations in copyright applications. 17 U.S.C.A. §§ 506(d) & (e).

**bootlegging** The crime of knowingly trafficking in counterfeit labels affixed or designed to be affixed to copies of musical recordings, computer programs, motion pictures, etc.

Knowingly trafficking in counterfeit labels affixed or designed to be affixed to a phonorecord or copy of a computer program, motion pictures, or other audiovisual works is **bootlegging**, an offense punishable by fine or imprisonment under 18 U.S.C.A. § 2318.

Section 506(b) of the Copyright Act provides for the "forfeiture and destruction . . . of all infringing copies or phonorecords and all implements, devices, or equipment used in the manufacture of such infringing copies or phonorecords." 17 U.S.C.A. § 506(b).

It is a misdemeanor to fraudulently place a copyright notice on an article, to distribute such an article, to fraudulently remove the copyright notice from a validly copyrighted article, or to knowingly make false representations in an application for copyright. 17 U.S.C.A. §§ 506(c), (d), & (e). Some states have also enacted laws making bootlegging of copyrighted materials an offense.

In 1994 Congress adopted 18 U.S.C.A. § 2319A, which, as amended, provides:

Whoever, without the consent of the performer or performers, knowingly and for commercial advantage or private financial gain

(1) fixes the sounds or sounds and images of a live musical performance in a copy or phonorecord, or reproduces copies or phonorecords of such a performance from an unauthorized fixation;

(2) transmits or otherwise communicates to the public the sounds or sounds and images of a live musical performance; or

(3) distributes or offers to distribute, sells or offers to sell, rents or offers to rent, or traffics in any copy or phonorecord fixed as described in paragraph (1) shall be imprisoned for up to five years and for up to ten years for a second offense.

## Internet-Based Copyright Infringement

In 1997, Congress enacted the No Electronic Theft (NET) Act, 111 STAT. 2678, Public Law 105-147, specifically to address Internet-based copyright infringement. Prior to this legislation, copyright infringement could be prosecuted only where the

## Criminal Copyright Infringement

**CASE-IN-POINT**

In August of 1999, Jeffrey G. Levy, a twenty-two-year-old senior at the University of Oregon, pleaded guilty to criminal copyright infringement. According to a statement issued by the U.S. Attorney's Office in Oregon, Levy admitted that he illegally posted computer software, music files, and digitally recorded movies on the Internet, which allowed anyone accessing his site to download and copy these products. Officials at the University of Oregon brought the matter to the attention of the FBI after noting an unusually large volume of bandwidth traffic being generated from Levy's website, which was hosted

on the University's file server. The FBI's investigation confirmed that thousands of computer programs, movies, and musical recordings had been made available for downloading from Levy's site. Although Levy faced a possible $250,000 fine and three years in prison, his negotiated guilty plea led to a sentence of two years' probation. As a condition of probation, Levy was ordered not to access the Internet from his home computer.

*Source:* United States Attorney's Office, District of Oregon, "Defendant Sentenced for First Criminal Copyright Conviction Under the 'No Electronic Theft' (NET) Act for Unlawful Distribution of Software on the Internet," November 23, 1999.

defendant derived a financial benefit from the infringement. The proliferation of file sharing via the Internet prompted Congress to change the law. The NET Act amended 17 U.S.C.A. § 506 and 18 U.S.C.A. § 2319 to make it unlawful to reproduce or distribute copyrighted works even where a defendant lacks a commercial or financial motive. One who reproduces or distributes ten or more copyrighted works that have a total value of more than $2,500 can be charged with a felony punishable by up to three years in prison and a fine of up to $250,000. A defendant who reproduces or distributes one or more copies of copyrighted works with a value of more than $1,000 can be charged with a misdemeanor punishable by up to one year in prison and a fine of up to $100,000.

## Trademark Counterfeiting

**trademark** A distinctive word, phrase, or graphic symbol used to distinguish a commercial product.

A **trademark** is a distinctive word, phrase, or graphic symbol used to distinguish a product. To be protected by federal law, trademarks used in interstate or foreign commerce maybe registered with the U.S. Patent and Trademark Office. Once registered, a trademark has nationwide protection. See 15 U.S.C.A. §§ 1051–1072. Trademark disputes are generally resolved in civil courts, but federal law does provide criminal penalties for **trademark counterfeiting**. The Trademark Counterfeiting Act of 1984 provides:

**trademark counterfeiting** The offense of using a registered trademark to falsely market a product or service.

> Whoever intentionally traffics or attempts to traffic in goods or services and knowingly uses a counterfeit mark on or in connection with such goods or services shall, if an individual, be fined not more than $2,000,000 or imprisoned not more than ten years, or both, and, if a person other than an individual, be fined not more than $5,000,000. 18 U.S.C.A. § 2320.

The statute defines "counterfeit mark" to mean "a spurious mark . . . that is identical with, or substantially indistinguishable from, a mark registered in the United States Patent and Trademark Office . . . and the use of which is likely to cause confusion, to cause mistake, or to deceive. . . ." 18 U.S.C.A. § 2320(e). When a genuine trademark is affixed to a counterfeit product, it becomes a "spurious mark" within the meaning of the statutory prohibition against trafficking in counterfeit goods. To establish a violation of the statute, the government must prove that the mark is counterfeit and that the defendant knew the mark was counterfeit. Section 2320 requires the government to establish, beyond a reasonable doubt, four elements: (1) that the defendant trafficked or attempted to traffic in goods or services; (2) that such trafficking, or the attempt to traffic, was intentional; (3) that the defendant used a "counterfeit mark" on or in connection with such goods or services; and (4) that the defendant "knew" that the counterfeit mark was so used. *United States v. Sultan*, 115 F.3d 321, 325 (5th Cir. 1997).

## Theft of Trade Secrets

**trade secret** A formula, pattern, physical device, idea, process, compilation of information, or other information that provides a business with a competitive advantage.

A **trade secret** is generally a formula, pattern, physical device, idea, process, compilation of information, or other information that provides a business with a competitive advantage. Trade secrets include "all forms and types of financial, business, scientific, technical, economic, or engineering information . . . whether tangible or intangible, and whether or how stored, compiled, or memorialized physically, electronically, graphically, photographically, or in writing." 18 U.S.C.A. § 1839(3).

Controversies concerning the use and misuse of trade secrets are frequently handled in civil courts where state statutes and the common law provide remedies. However, Congress enacted the Economic Espionage Act of 1996 (EEA), creating the first national criminal penalty for theft of trade secrets. The EEA prohibits foreign governments from stealing trade secrets (18 U.S.C.A. § 1831) and criminalizes domestic trade secret theft (18 U.S.C.A. § 1832). Title 18 U.S.C.A. § 1832, provides that

(a) Whoever, with intent to convert a trade secret, that is related to or included in a product that is produced for or placed in interstate or foreign commerce, to the economic benefit of anyone other than the owner thereof, and intending or knowing that the offense will, injure any owner of that trade secret, knowingly—

(1) steals, or without authorization appropriates, takes, carries away, or conceals, or by fraud, artifice, or deception obtains such information;

(2) without authorization copies, duplicates, sketches, draws, photographs, downloads, uploads, alters, destroys, photocopies, replicates, transmits, delivers, sends, mails, communicates, or conveys such information;

(3) receives, buys, or possesses such information, knowing the same to have been stolen or appropriated, obtained, or converted without authorization;

(4) attempts to commit any offense described in paragraphs (1) through (3); or

(5) conspires with one or more other persons to commit any offense described in paragraphs (1) through (3), and one or more of such persons do any act to effect the object of the conspiracy, shall, except as provided in subsection (b), be fined under this title or imprisoned not more than 10 years, or both.

(b) Any organization that commits any offense described in subsection (a) shall be fined not more than $5,000,000. 18 U.S.C.A. § 1832.

Title 18 U.S.C.A. § 1834 provides for forfeiture to the United States of any profits and proceeds derived from violation of § 1832.

In July 2006 the media reported that three people had been arrested for allegedly violating the EEA. An employee of the Coca-Cola Company and two others were charged with stealing the confidential files and a sample of a new drink product and offering to sell these items to Coca-Cola's main rival, PepsiCo. Reportedly, the plot was foiled when Coca-Cola learned of the crime and reported it to the FBI. On February 2, 2007, a federal jury in Atlanta convicted Joya Williams, a former executive assistant at Coca-Cola, of conspiracy to steal trade secrets.

**CASE-IN-POINT**

### Violation of the Economic Espionage Act

Dr. Victor Lee was employed by Avery Dennison Inc. to conduct scientific research on adhesives. In 1989, while making a presentation in Taiwan, Lee was introduced to Pin-Yen Yang, the head of Four Pillars Enterprise Co., Ltd., a competing firm. According to the indictment, Yang and Lee agreed that Lee would receive $25,000 to serve as a secret consultant to Four Pillars. Some time later Lee provided Yang with confidential materials belonging to Avery Dennison, including information regarding a new adhesive product. After learning of Lee's activities, the FBI confronted him and persuaded him to participate in a "sting" operation in which the FBI videotaped a meeting between Lee and Yang at which Lee provided Yang with confidential Avery Dennison materials. After a jury trial, Yang was convicted of attempt and conspiracy to commit theft of a trade secret. The U.S. Court of Appeals for the Sixth Circuit upheld the conviction.

*United States v. Yang*, 281 F.3d 534 (6th Cir. 2002).

## False Statements, Bankruptcy Fraud, and False Claims

**False Statements Act** A federal statute making it a crime for a person to knowingly make a false and material statement to a U.S. government agency to obtain a government benefit or in connection with performing work for the government.

The federal **False Statements Act** (18 U.S.C.A. § 1001) prohibits knowingly and willfully making a false statement that is material to a matter within the jurisdiction of any department or agency of the United States. "Congress intentionally drafted § 1001 in an expansive fashion in order that it be accorded the broadest possible interpretation regarding the situations in which it would come into play." *Moser v. United States*, 18 F.3d 469, 473 (7th Cir. 1994).

When proceeding under the False Statements Act, the government must prove that the accused knowingly and willfully submitted to a government agency or department a statement that was false and material. The issue of materiality is one for the court to consider. *United States v. Rodgers*, 466 U.S. 475, 104 S.Ct. 1942, 80 L.Ed.2d 492 (1984). (A false statement in any matter within the jurisdiction of any department or agency of the United States encompasses criminal investigations conducted by the FBI and Secret Service.)

**bankruptcy fraud** Dishonest or deceitful acts committed by one who seeks relief under laws designed to protect honest debtors from their creditors.

Federal statutes criminalize **bankruptcy fraud**, which is defined as the knowing and fraudulent concealment of assets, avoiding distribution of nonexempt assets, taking false oaths, and related conduct in connection with bankruptcy proceedings. 18 U.S.C.A. § 152. To convict, the government must prove that the defendant acted willfully; however, one who acts with "willful blindness" can be found to have acted with the requisite criminal intent. Although the statute does not expressly state a materiality requirement, 18 U.S.C.A. § 152 has been construed "to require that [a] false oath be given in relation to some material matter." *United States v. O'Donnell*, 539 F.2d 1233, 1237 (9th Cir. 1976).

Medicare and Medicaid provide health care benefits to millions of Americans. Medicare is designed to provide medical care primarily to older citizens, whereas Medicaid is a program that furnishes health care services to the needy.

**False Claims Act** A federal statute that makes it unlawful for a person to knowingly present a false or fraudulent claim to the U.S. government.

Historically, criminal violations of the federal statutes providing these benefits, as well as other false claims to federal entitlements, have been prosecuted under the **False Claims Act**, 18 U.S.C.A. § 287, and the False Statements Act. To prove Medicare or Medicaid fraud under the False Claims Act, the government must prove that (1) the defendant presented a claim seeking reimbursement from the government for medical services or goods, (2) the claim was false or fraudulent, and (3) the accused knew of the claim's falsity. See *United States v. Upton*, 91 F.3d 677 (5th Cir. 1996), where the court, after reciting these elements of proof, affirmed the defendants' convictions under 18 U.S.C.A. § 287 for filing a false claim with the U.S. Air Force for reimbursement of unpaid bond premiums.

### Criminal Prosecution under the False Claims Act

Evidence at trial disclosed that the defendant had submitted false claims to Pennsylvania Blue Shield and the Travelers Insurance Co. but not to any federal agency or official. These insurance companies processed and paid the claims and were reimbursed by the federal government for their payments and costs of processing the claims. The defendant was convicted and appealed. A question arose whether the insurance carriers could be considered "agencies" of the United States for purposes of criminal prosecution. The court doubted that the insurance carriers were agencies of the United States; however, it cited another federal statute, 18 U.S.C.A. § 2(b), which provides that "[w]hoever willfully causes an act to be done which if directly performed by him or another would be an offense against the United States, is punishable as a principal." Finding the proof established that the defendant "caused" the private carriers to submit false claims to the government, the court affirmed the defendant's conviction.

*United States v. Catena*, 500 F.2d 1319 (3d Cir. 1974).

## The Health Insurance Portability and Accountability Act (HIPAA)

The **Health Insurance Portability and Accountability Act (HIPAA)** A federal statute designed to protect patient privacy, promote portability of health insurance coverage, and deter fraud in the provision of medical services.

In 1996 Congress enacted the **Health Insurance Portability and Accountability Act (HIPAA)** of 1996, Public Law 104–191. Section 244 of the act, codified at 18 U.S.C.A. § 1035, establishes a new false-statement offense that prohibits making material false or fraudulent statements or entries in connection with delivery of or payment for health care benefits. This new section covers statements and concealments made to private insurers that could not be prosecuted under the False Statements Act. The new act also includes several other criminal provisions. Section 242 makes it an offense for any person to knowingly and willfully execute or attempt to execute a scheme or artifice to defraud any health care benefit program or to fraudulently obtain money or property of such programs in connection with the delivery of or payment for health care benefits, items, or services. 18 U.S.C.A § 1347. Section 243 proscribes knowingly and willfully embezzling assets of a health care benefit program. 18 U.S.C.A. § 669. Section 245 creates a new crime that prohibits willfully obstructing, misleading, or delaying communication of information

### Criminal Prosecution under the Health Insurance Portability and Accountability Act

Three defendants participated in staged automobile accidents and fabricated personal injury claims to take advantage of the operation of the New York No-Fault Act. They contended that they were not subject to prosecution under 18 U.S.C.A. § 1347 because they were not health professionals. The court rejected their contention and held that

[W]hether that person is a medical professional, a patient, or otherwise—who purposefully endeavors to defraud a health care benefit program may be found guilty of health care fraud, if his or her conduct otherwise conforms to the elements of the offense. The broad language of § 1347 shows that Congress intended for this statute to include within its scope a wide range of conduct so that all forms of health care fraud would be proscribed, regardless of the kind of specific schemes unscrupulous persons may concoct.

*United States v. Lucien*, 347 F.3d 45, 51 (2d Cir. 2003).

or records to a criminal investigator relating to a violation of a federal health care offense. 18 U.S.C.A. § 1518.

# Mail and Wire Fraud

**mail fraud** A scheme devised or intended to defraud or to obtain money or property by fraudulent means, or using or causing the use of the mails in furtherance of the fraudulent scheme.

The Federal Mail Fraud Statute, 18 U.S.C.A. § 1341, makes it a crime to use the mail to defraud. **Mail fraud** consists of (1) a scheme devised or intended to defraud or to obtain money or property by fraudulent means and (2) the use of or causing to use the mails in furtherance of the fraudulent scheme. Courts have held that to obtain a conviction, the government must prove the existence of a scheme committed by the defendant with a specific intent to defraud through use of the U.S. Postal Service or some other interstate commercial carrier. The government is not required to prove that the scheme to defraud was successful. It is sufficient for the government to prove that a scheme existed in which use of the mails was reasonably foreseeable and that an actual mailing occurred in furtherance of the scheme. *United States v. Dick*, 744 F.2d 546, 550 (7th Cir. 1984).

**wire fraud** A fraudulent scheme that uses interstate television, radio, or wire communications.

A companion statute, the Federal Wire Fraud Statute, 18 U.S.C.A. § 1343, parallels the mail fraud statute and criminalizes fraudulent schemes that use interstate television, radio, or wire communications. Although the U.S. Constitution grants Congress jurisdiction over the postal service, Congress enacted the **wire fraud** statute under its authority to regulate interstate commerce. U.S. Const., Art. I, § 8. Therefore, a violation of this statute exists only if the communication crosses state lines.

Shortly after the tragedy of 9/11, Americans were again shocked by allegations of fraud affecting the rights of employees and shareholders of once–highly regarded corporations. One of the most highly publicized was that involving the Enron Corporation, an energy company that had become one of the largest corporations in America. In July 2004, a federal jury convicted a former Enron financial executive and four former investment brokers of conspiracy and fraud. On May 25, 2006, a federal jury convicted former Enron chief executive Jeffrey Skilling and founder Kenneth Lay of conspiracy to commit securities and wire fraud. Lay died before sentencing. Because his demise occurred before the sentencing and appeal

---

## JURISPRUDENCE

*Schmuck v. United States*, 489 U.S. 705, 109 S.Ct. 1443, 103 L.Ed.2d (1989)

Wayne T. Schmuck, a used-car distributor, purchased used cars, rolled back their odometers, and then sold the automobiles to Wisconsin retail dealers for prices artificially inflated because of the low mileage readings. The dealers, in turn, mailed the title applications to the state transportation department. Schmuck was indicted on twelve counts of mail fraud under 18 U.S.C.A. § 1341. Prior to trial, Schmuck moved to dismiss the indictment on the ground that the mailings were not in furtherance of the fraudulent scheme and, thus, did not satisfy the mailing element of mail fraud. The federal district court denied

the motion. Schmuck was tried before a jury and convicted on all twelve counts and the conviction was upheld by the U.S. Court of Appeals. Ultimately, the U.S. Supreme Court upheld Schmuck's conviction as well. Justice Harry Blackmun, writing for the Court, noted that "[t]here are two elements in mail fraud: (1) having devised or intending to devise a scheme to defraud (or to perform specified fraudulent acts), and (2) use of the mail for the purpose of executing, or attempting to execute, the scheme (or specified fraudulent acts)." Finding that the mailings by the dealers were essential to Schmuck's fraudulent acts, the Court concluded that Schmuck had been properly convicted of mail fraud.

process was completed, on October 17, 2006 the U.S. District Judge in Houston, Texas, vacated the proceedings against Lay. See *United States v. Moehlenkamp*, 557 F.2d 126, 127–128 (7th Cir. 1977) (Defendant's death pending appeal from final judgment of conviction deprives the defendant of the right to an appellate decision and requires vacating of a conviction). At a sentencing hearing on October 23, 2006, the court sentenced Skilling to serve twenty-four years and four months in confinement.

# Money Laundering and Currency Violations

**money laundering** The offense of disguising illegal income to make it appear legitimate.

**Money laundering** is the crime of disguising illegal income to make it appear legitimate and is prohibited by the Money Laundering Control Act of 1986, 18 U.S.C.A. §§ 1956, 1957. Section 1956(a)(1) provides as follows:

> Whoever, knowing that the property involved in a financial transaction represents the proceeds of some form of unlawful activity, conducts, or attempts to conduct such a financial transaction which in fact involves the proceeds of specified unlawful activity
>
> (A)(i) with the intent to promote the carrying on of specified unlawful activity; or (ii) with intent to engage in conduct constituting a violation of section 7201 or 7206 of the Internal Revenue Code of 1986; or
>
> (B) knowing that the transaction is designed in whole or in part (i) to conceal or disguise the nature, the location, the source, the ownership, or the control of the proceeds of specified unlawful activity; or (ii) to avoid a transaction reporting requirement under State or Federal law, shall be sentenced to a fine of not more than $500,000 or twice the value of the property involved in the transaction, whichever is greater, or imprisonment for not more than twenty years, or both.

Crimes under § 1956 fall into three categories: (1) acts committed with intent to promote unlawful activity; (2) those committed with knowledge that a transaction is to conceal ownership, control, or source of funds; and (3) those designed to avoid certain currency reporting laws. Section 1957 makes it a crime to engage in or attempt to engage in a transaction involving criminally derived property. To convict a defendant of money laundering, the government must show that (1) the defendant took part in a financial transaction and knew that the property in the transaction involved proceeds of illegal activity; (2) the property involved was in fact proceeds of illegal activity; and (3) the defendant knew that the transaction was designed in whole or part to conceal or disguise the nature, source, location, ownership, or control of illegal proceeds. The government bears a heavy burden to establish that a defendant is guilty of money laundering. It must show that the accused has "actual knowledge" or is guilty of "willful blindness" to the criminal acts; simply showing that a defendant "should have known" is insufficient to establish guilt.

Often, federal appellate courts have had to determine whether certain acts constitute a financial transaction within the meaning of the statute. In *United States v. Jackson*, 935 F.2d 832 (7th Cir. 1991), the defendant appealed his conviction on three counts of money laundering in violation of § 1956(a) and other violations. The evidence revealed that the defendant had deposited funds derived from both legitimate and illegal activities in a local savings and loan institution and had written checks on the account. After first pointing out that writing a check on an account in a financial institution is a "transaction" within the money laundering statute, the court of appeals rejected the defendant's argument that the prosecution failed to establish that the financial transactions involved the proceeds of unlawful activity within the meaning of the statute, because the checks involved were written on an account that contained both legitimate funds and drug profits. The court held that it was sufficient for the government to show that the transaction in question involved the proceeds of one of the types of criminal conduct specified. Federal courts have also held that the term "financial transaction" includes making a deposit into an account. See *United States v. Reynolds*, 64 F.3d 292 (7th Cir. 1995). But the Fifth Circuit has held that transportation of drug proceeds by car does not constitute a financial transaction within the meaning of § 1956. *United States v. Puig-Infante*, 19 F.3d 929 (5th Cir. 1994).

## Structuring Cash Transactions to Avoid Reporting Requirements

Federal statutes require financial institutions to file currency transaction reports with the Secretary of the Treasury for cash transactions in excess of $10,000. 31 U.S.C.A. § 5313. A related provision, 31 U.S.C.A. § 5324, prohibits a person from causing or attempting to cause a financial institution from making the required reports or from **structuring** or assisting in structuring a transaction with one or more institutions to evade the requirement, and provides penalties for persons who conduct a transaction to evade this structuring requirement.

**structuring** Engaging in multiple smaller transactions to avoid currency reporting requirements.

In *Ratzlaf v. United States*, 510 U.S. 135, 114 S.Ct. 655, 126 L.Ed.2d 615 (1994), the U.S. Supreme Court held that the structuring provisions required proof that the defendant knew that banks have a duty to report cash deposits in excess of $10,000, and that it was unlawful to structure deposits to avoid this reporting. Shortly after *Ratzlaf*, Congress amended 31 U.S.C.A. § 5324 to remove the requirement that the defendant acted "willfully." Apparently the only mental state now required is a purpose to evade the reporting requirement. See *United States v. Vazquez*, 53 F.3d 1216, 1218 n. 2 (11th Cir. 1995).

---

### JURISPRUDENCE

*Ratzlaf v. United States*, 510 U.S. 135, 114 S.Ct. 655, 126 L.Ed.2d 615 (1994)

On October 20, 1988, Waldemar Ratzlaf ran up a debt of over $100,000 playing blackjack at a casino in Reno, Nevada. The casino gave him one week to pay. On the due date, Ratzlaf returned to the casino with cash totaling $100,000 in hand. When Ratzlaf offered to pay $100,000 on his gambling debt, the casino informed him that payment by a check in that amount would trigger the currency reporting requirements under federal law. Ratzlaf then proceeded to obtain a series of $10,000 cashier's checks from various banks to pay his debt. The government charged him with "structuring transactions" in violation of 31 U.S.C.A. § 5322 and § 5324. Section 5324 provides that it is illegal to "structure" financial transactions "for the

purpose of evading" a financial institution's reporting requirements. Section 5322(a) established that "a person willfully violating" the antistructuring provision (§ 5324) is subject to criminal penalties. A jury found him guilty. On review, the U.S. Supreme Court, in a 5–4 decision, interpreted "willfully" in 31 U.S.C.A. § 5322 to require the government to prove that a defendant acted with knowledge that his conduct was unlawful, and reversed his conviction. The Court based its holding upon a strict reading of the statutory language of the two sections. Section 5324 provides that it is illegal to "structure" financial transactions "for the purpose of evading" a financial institution's reporting requirements. Section 5322(a) establishes that a person "willfully violating" the antistructuring provision (§ 5324) is subject to criminal penalties.

# Securities Fraud

**insider trading** Transactions in securities by a person who operates inside a corporation and, by using material nonpublic information, trades to his or her advantage without first disclosing that information to the public.

**Securities and Exchange Act** The 1934 act of Congress regulating the sale of securities in interstate commerce.

A variety of federal and state statutes criminalize conduct involving misrepresentations, omissions, **insider trading**, and other aspects of fraud in securities dealing. The most significant federal acts are the Securities Act of 1933, 15 U.S.C.A. § 77a *et seq.*, and the **Securities and Exchange Act** of 1934, 15 U.S.C.A. § 78a *et seq.* Again, these statutes provide for civil remedies as well as criminal sanctions. The Securities and Exchange Commission (SEC) refers most criminal prosecutions to the Department of Justice. Convictions can result in fines in the millions of dollars and imprisonment.

Not all misrepresentations or omissions involving securities give rise to criminal violations. Rather, the government must prove the accused's *willful* intent to commit a substantive fraud in connection with the purchase or sale of a security or in the offering or sale of a security involving interstate commerce or through use of the mails. Courts uniformly hold that to sustain a conviction, the omission or misrepresentation must be material and be made in reckless disregard for the truth or falsity of the information provided. See, e.g., *United States v. Farris*, 614 F.2d 634 (9th Cir. 1979). The specific intent that must be proven to sustain a criminal prosecution can be found in a defendant's deliberate and intentional acts or reckless disregard for the facts. *United States v. Boyer*, 694 F.2d 58 (3d Cir. 1982).

## Churning and Insider Trading

**churning** Making purchases and sales of securities in a client's account simply to generate commissions for the broker.

In recent years, many financial executives and securities brokers have been prosecuted under the Securities and Exchange Act for fraudulent conduct known as churning and insider trading. **Churning** is a term applied to transactions made in a customer's account without regard to the customer's investment objectives; rather, they are made simply to generate commissions for the broker. When determining whether a broker is guilty of churning, courts often focus on whether the trading by a broker was disproportionate to the size of the customer's account.

Insider trading usually occurs when a person who operates within a corporation has access to material, nonpublic information and uses that information to trade securities without first disclosing that information to the public.

## JURISPRUDENCE

*Chiarella v. United States*, 445 U.S. 222, 100 S.Ct. 1108, 63 L.Ed.2d 348 (1980)

From 1975 to 1976, Vincent Chiarella worked as a "markup man" for a company that printed announcements of corporate takeover bids. From the copy submitted for printing, he discerned information that enabled him to purchase stock in companies targeted for takeover before this information was disclosed to the general public. Chiarella made a profit in excess of $30,000 from the purchase, and later sale, of stock in the targeted companies. He was convicted in federal district court for violating section 10(b) of the Securities Exchange Act of 1934. 15 U.S.C.A. §§ 78b,

78j(b). In 1978 the U.S. Court of Appeals for the Second Circuit affirmed his conviction. On review, the Supreme Court recognized that a corporate insider must not trade in shares of a corporation without having first disclosed all material insider information. But the Court ruled that the obligation to disclose is based on having the "duty to disclose arising from a relationship of trust and confidence between parties to a transaction." Thus, the Court held that the trial court erred when, in effect, it instructed the jury that Chiarella owed a duty to everyone, including all sellers—indeed, to the market as a whole. Accordingly, the Court reversed his conviction.

### Domestic Diva Investigated for Insider Trading

In one of the most highly publicized insider trading cases in history, "domestic diva" Martha Stewart was investigated by the Securities and Exchange Commission in 2002 for selling 4,000 shares of stock in a company called ImClone after allegedly receiving insider information that the company's new cancer drug was going to be rejected by the Food and Drug Administration (FDA). The day after Stewart sold her stock, the FDA announced its rejection of the cancer drug and ImClone stock declined 16 percent. The SEC charged Stewart with insider trading via a civil complaint; additionally, she was charged criminally with conspiracy, obstructing an agency proceeding, making false statements to investigators, and securities fraud. Although Stewart was acquitted of securities fraud, a federal jury found her guilty of the other offenses. On July 16, 2004, a federal district judge sentenced Stewart to five months in prison followed by two years of supervised release (including five months of house arrest and electronic monitoring). On January 6, 2006, a federal appeals court upheld Stewart's conviction.

*United States v. Stewart*, 433 F.3d 273 (2d Cir. 2006).

Securities and Exchange Commission rule 10(b) proscribes (1) using any "deceptive device" (2) "in connection with the purchase or sale of any security," in contravention of rules promulgated by the SEC. Insider trading qualifies as a "deceptive device" because the insider occupies a position of trust and confidence with regard to the corporation's shareholders. This position of trust requires the insider to abstain from trading based on information he or she has acquired by virtue of the insider status. *Chiarella v. United States*, 445 U.S. 222, 100 S.Ct. 1108, 63 L.Ed.2d 348 (1980).

The late 1980s witnessed sensational cases involving insider trading by prominent Wall Street financiers. Since then, the SEC has secured indictments under rule 10(b) against numerous prominent individuals and corporations for securities violations.

**Ponzi Schemes**

A "Ponzi scheme," also known as a "pyramid scheme," is a form of securities fraud in which unknowing investors are paid abnormally high rates of return using money from new investors. The funds are never really invested, so the scheme must constantly bring in new money in order to pay the initial investors the promised high returns. The scheme is named for Charles Ponzi, who ran a notorious pyramid scheme in the early twentieth century. In 2008, Wall Street icon Bernard Madoff was charged by federal authorities with operating a Ponzi scheme that defrauded investors of more than $50 billion. The scheme collapsed when, during the financial panic of late 2008, Madoff's clients began to withdraw their funds. In March 2009, after waiving an indictment, Madoff pleaded guilty to all eleven counts he was charged with, including fraud, perjury, and theft from an employee benefit plan and two counts of international money laundering.

## Tax Fraud

**tax fraud** False or deceptive conduct performed with the intent of violating revenue laws, especially the Internal Revenue Code.

Prosecutions for white-collar crime often include charges of violating federal tax statutes. Although the government can employ a wide variety of federal criminal statutes to prosecute those who commit **tax fraud**, most prosecutions are based on the Internal Revenue Code, 26 U.S.C.A. § 7201 *et seq.* Some of the more common violations include deliberately underreporting or omitting income and overstating the amount of deductions. Whether violations are felonies or misdemeanors, to obtain a conviction the government must prove the defendant's willfulness to commit the proscribed act. *United States v. Bishop*, 412 U.S. 346, 93 S.Ct. 2008, 36 L.Ed.2d 941 (1973). To establish "willfulness," the government must prove the defendant's "intentional violation of a known legal duty." *United States v. Pomponio*, 429 U.S. 10, 97 S.Ct. 22, 50 L.Ed.2d 12 (1976). In reaffirming this standard of proof, the Supreme Court observed in *Cheek v. United States*, 498 U.S. 192, 111 S.Ct. 604, 112 L.Ed.2d 617 (1991), that the term "willfully" as used in federal criminal tax statutes serves to "carve out an exception to the traditional rule [that ignorance of the law or mistake of law is no defense to prosecution]." 498 U.S. at 200, 111 S.Ct. at 609, 112 L.Ed.2d at 628.

Many prosecutions for tax evasion occur under § 7201, which makes it a felony to willfully attempt to evade or to evade federal taxes. A successful prosecution requires that the government prove willfulness, the existence of a tax deficiency, and an affirmative act of evasion or attempted evasion of the tax. *Sansone v. United States*, 380 U.S. 343, 85 S.Ct. 1004, 13 L.Ed.2d 882 (1965).

Section 7202 also makes it a crime to willfully fail to collect, account truthfully for, or pay over taxes. Although most employers do not fail to collect taxes, a more common violation is the employer's failure to pay over those taxes to the Internal Revenue Service (IRS).

Section 7203 makes it a misdemeanor to willfully fail to pay an estimated tax, file a tax return, keep records, or supply information required by law. To successfully prosecute an accused, the government must establish that the accused had knowledge of a duty to file a return and willfully failed to file.

Section 7206 makes it a felony to commit fraud or make false statements in conjunction with tax obligations. To convict a person of "tax perjury," under § 7206 the government must prove the defendant (1) acted willfully, (2) filed a return containing a written declaration (3) made under penalty of perjury, (4) did not believe that the return was true and correct as to every material matter, and (5) exercised willfulness with the specific intent to violate the law. The defendant's willfulness may be inferred from the existence of unreported or misreported tax information. In *United States v. Tarwater*, 308 F.3d 494 (6th Cir. 2002), the court pointed out that § 7206 is an antiperjury statute that criminalizes lying on any document filed with the IRS and that "the government need only prove that a defendant willfully made and subscribed a return, that the return contained a written declaration that it was made under penalties of perjury, and that the defendant did not believe the return to be true and correct as to every material matter." *Id.* at 504.

Section 7206(2) makes it a felony to willfully aid and assist another in a material falsity. To convict, the government must prove (1) an act of aiding and assisting in the preparation of a return or other document, (2) material falsity, and (3) willfulness. Tax preparers are sometimes prosecuted under this provision of the statute.

Additional sections of 26 U.S.C.A. criminalize the furnishing of false and fraudulent statements to the IRS, interfering with the administration of the tax laws, and delivering a fraudulent tax return.

# Racketeering and Organized Crime

**crime syndicates** An association or group of people that carries out organized crime activities.

During the Prohibition era, organized gangs trafficked in liquor and became involved in prostitution and other vices. After the repeal of the Eighteenth Amendment in 1933, these **crime syndicates** expanded into loan-sharking, gambling, narcotics, and extortion. As they did, they infiltrated legitimate businesses and conducted widespread illegal operations through their own complex and secretive structures.

As we have pointed out in other chapters, the common-law development of crimes and the legislative acts defining crimes focused on particular acts of wrong-doing and on inchoate activities. This approach did not cover the ongoing criminal activity by organized groups. To that extent, the traditional definitions of crime left a void in the criminal justice system.

## The Hobbs Act

**Hobbs Act** A 1946 act of Congress authorizing criminal penalties for whoever in any way or degree obstructs, delays, or affects commerce or the movement of any article or commodity in commerce by robbery or extortion or attempts or conspires so to do, or commits or threatens physical violence to any person or property in furtherance of a plan or purpose to do anything in violation of the act.

Congress enacted the Anti-Racketeering Act of 1934 in an effort to control rack-eteering activities. However, the act did not specifically mention racketeering, and as a result of certain judicial interpretations, in 1946 Congress enacted the **Hobbs Act**. 18 U.S.C.A. § 1951. Subsection (a) provides:

> Whoever in any way or degree obstructs, delays, or affects commerce or the movement of any article or commodity in commerce, by robbery or extortion or attempts or conspires so to do, or commits or threatens physical violence to any person or property in furtherance of a plan or purpose to do anything in violation of this section shall be fined under this title or imprisoned not more than twenty years, or both.

Note that the act includes the inchoate offenses of attempt and conspiracy. Other subsections define "robbery," "extortion," and "commerce." The Hobbs Act was enacted under the power of Congress to regulate interstate commerce; however, the courts have held that it is sufficient if the government simply proves that an act

---

### JURISPRUDENCE

*Evans v. United States*, 504 U.S. 255, 112 S.Ct. 1881, 119 L.Ed.2d 57 (1992)

During the course of a federal investigation into allegations of public corruption in Georgia, an FBI agent posed as a real estate developer and "initiated a number of conversations with Evans, an elected member of the DeKalb County Board of Commissioners," in "effort[s] to [have Evans] rezone a tract of land." In exchange for the desired zoning, the FBI agent offered, and Evans accepted, $7,000 in cash. Additionally, Evans "failed to report [the funds] on his state campaign-financing disclosure form or his federal income tax return." Evans was ultimately convicted of extortion, under the Hobbs Act, which is defined as "the obtaining of property from another, . . . induced by wrongful use of actual or threatened force, violence, or fear, or under color of official right." The Court of Appeals upheld the conviction holding "that the trial court's jury instruction did not require a finding that Evans had demanded or requested the money, or that he had conditioned the performance of any official act upon its receipt." It also held that "passive acceptance of the benefit" was sufficient for a Hobbs Act violation if the public official knew that he was being offered the

payment in exchange for a specific requested exercise of his official power." The Supreme Court, speaking through Justice Stevens, held that "an affirmative act of inducement by a public official, such as a demand, is not an element of the offense of extortion 'under color of official right' prohibited by the Hobbs Act." The Court noted that while the Hobbs Act has been expanded over time, "the portion of the Act referring to official misconduct continues to mirror the common-law definition," and "there is nothing in the sparse legislative history or the statutory text that could fairly be described as a contrary direction . . . from Congress to narrow the offense's scope." The Court concluded that the "offense is completed when the public official receives payment in return for his agreement to perform specific official acts; fulfillment of the *quid pro quo* is not an element of the offense. Nor is an affirmative step on the official's part an element of the offense on which an instruction need be given." Supreme Court held that "the Government need only show that a public official has obtained a payment to which he was not entitled, knowing that the payment was made in return for official acts." Thus, Evans's conviction was upheld.

has an effect on interstate commerce. Courts allow this to be established by proof of an actual impact, however small, or, in the absence of actual impact, by proof of a probable or potential impact.

Originally, most prosecutions under the Hobbs Act were based on extortion by public officials using force, violence, or fear. Now prosecutors frequently rely on the act as a basis to prosecute state and local officials based on extortion "under color of official rights."

In 1961 Congress enacted three statutes to combat the growing problem of organized crime. These acts gave the FBI jurisdiction over: gambling violations and interstate and foreign travel or transportation in aid of racketeering, 18 U.S.C.A. § 1952; interstate transportation of wagering paraphernalia, 18 U.S.C.A. § 1953; prohibition of illegal gambling, 8 U.S.C.A. § 1955; and laundering of monetary instruments, 18 U.S.C.A. § 1956. In 1968 Congress passed the Omnibus Crime Control and Safe Streets Act. This act provided for the conduct of court-authorized electronic surveillance. 18 U.S.C.A. §§ 2510–2521.

## The Organized Crime Control Act of 1970

Notwithstanding the FBI's increased attention to organized crime, the problem continued to grow. Congress found that organized crime had weakened the stability of the nation's economy through infiltration of legitimate businesses and labor unions and threatened to subvert and corrupt democratic processes. Under its power to regulate foreign and interstate commerce, Congress enacted the **Organized Crime Control Act of 1970**. Title IX of the act, titled **Racketeer Influenced and Corrupt Organizations (RICO)**, prohibits the infiltration of legitimate organizations by racketeers where foreign or interstate commerce is affected. 18 U.S.C.A. §§ 1961–1963. In addition to increased criminal penalties, RICO provided for forfeiture of property used in criminal enterprises and permitted the government to bring civil actions against such enterprises.

RICO created new crimes and a new approach to criminal prosecution. First, it makes it a crime for any person "who has received any income derived, directly or indirectly, from a pattern of racketeering activity or through collection of an unlawful debt . . . to use or invest [in] any enterprise which is engaged in interstate or foreign commerce." 18 U.S.C.A. § 1962(a). Second, RICO makes it unlawful for any such person to participate, directly or indirectly, in the conduct of the enterprise's affairs through a "pattern of racketeering." 18 U.S.C.A. § 1962(b). Third, it is a crime for any person "employed by or associated with any enterprise engaged in, or the activities of which affect, interstate or foreign commerce, to conduct or participate, directly or indirectly, in the conduct of such enterprise's affairs through a pattern of racketeering activity or collection of unlawful debt." 18 U.S.C.A. § 1962(c). This last subsection has become the provision most frequently used by prosecutors. Finally, the act prohibits conspiracies to violate any of these proscriptions. 18 U.S.C.A. § 1962(d).

### The Expansive Scope of RICO

RICO broadly defines racketeering activity to include a variety of federal offenses as well as nine state crimes that are characteristically felonies. 18 U.S.C.A. § 1961(1). Establishing a **pattern of racketeering** activity requires proof of at least two of these acts of racketeering having occurred within a period of ten years, excluding any period of imprisonment. 18 U.S.C.A. § 1961(5). Courts frequently refer to these

**Organized Crime Control Act of 1970** Federal law dealing with organized crime. Title IX of the act is entitled "Racketeer Influenced and Corrupt Organizations" and is commonly referred to by the acronym RICO.

**Racketeer Influenced and Corrupt Organizations (RICO)** A federal law enacted in 1970 imposing civil and criminal liability where two or more acts of racketeering show a pattern of criminal activity carried on by an enterprise. (Many states now have adopted RICO laws.)

**pattern of racketeering** To obtain a conviction under the federal RICO statute, the government must establish the defendant's involvement in a "pattern of racketeering" that requires proof of the occurrence of at least two predicate acts of racketeering within a period of ten years, excluding any period of imprisonment.

**CASE-IN-POINT**

### Court Holds that Predicate Acts Satisfy Relatedness under RICO

Louis Daidone was found guilty of racketeering, racketeering conspiracy, witness tampering by murder, conspiracy to make extortionate loans, and conspiracy to collect extensions of credit by extortionate means. On appeal Daidone argued that the government failed to prove that the three predicate acts alleged in the racketeering counts formed a unitary "pattern of racketeering activity as required by 18 U.S.C.A. § 1962(c)" because these acts "were committed years apart, by different people and for entirely different reasons." He contended that instead of independently establishing the requirements for proving a pattern of racketeering activity—which requires proving both horizontal and vertical relatedness—the government improperly used what was essentially the same evidence to prove both avenues of relatedness.

In rejecting his contention, the court pointed out that racketeering Act One was the murder and the conspiracy to murder Thomas Gilmore; racketeering Act Two was the murder and conspiracy to murder Bruno Facciolo; and racketeering Act Three was the loansharking business. The court found that sufficient evidence established that as a member of an organized crime family Daidone orchestrated predicate acts of murdering two associates and participating in loansharking operations. The court concluded that each of the defendant's three predicate acts were related to the organized crime family's enterprise, as well as to each other, as required to satisfy the relatedness requirement in defendant's RICO prosecution, and affirmed his conviction.

*United States v. Daidone*, 471 F.3d 371 (2d Cir. 2006).

---

**predicate acts** Prior acts of racketeering used to demonstrate a pattern of racketeering in a RICO prosecution.

acts as **predicate acts**, and any combination of two or more can constitute a pattern of racketeering. To obtain a conviction under RICO, the government must establish the defendant's involvement in a "pattern of racketeering or collection of an unlawful debt." A pattern of racketeering is not established merely by proving two predicate acts. Rather, to form a pattern of racketeering activity, predicate acts must be related to each other and to the enterprise. Therefore, to establish a RICO violation requires proof of a specified relationship between racketeering acts and a RICO enterprise. *United States v. Indelicato*, 865 F.2d 1370 (2d Cir. 1989). There is no requirement that a state conviction be obtained before the state offense can be used as a predicate act of the racketeering activity charged. *United States v. Malatesta*, 583 F.2d 748 (5th Cir. 1978). RICO provides for a maximum of twenty years' imprisonment, a heavier penalty than many of the predicate offenses on which a RICO conviction can be based.

RICO does not criminalize a person for being a racketeer—it criminalizes that person's conduct of an enterprise through a pattern of racketeering. Therefore, a jury that finds a defendant has committed the required predicate acts must still find that these acts were committed in connection with a pattern of racketeering or collection of an unlawful debt.

### What Constitutes an Enterprise?

**enterprise** An individual, partnership, corporation, association, union or other legal entity.

In RICO, Congress defined **enterprise** broadly to include "any individual, partnership, corporation, association, or other legal entity, and any union or group of individuals associated in fact although not a legal entity." 18 U.S.C.A. § 1961(4). The Supreme Court has said that the term encompasses both legitimate and illegitimate entities and groups. *United States v. Turkette*, 452 U.S. 576, 101 S.Ct. 2524, 69 L.Ed.2d 246 (1981). Lower federal courts have held that the term includes both private and public entities such as corporations, banks, and decedents' estates, as well as state agencies, police departments, traffic courts, and prostitution rings.

## JURISPRUDENCE

*Salinas v. United States*, 522 U.S. 52, 118 S.Ct. 469, 139 L.Ed.2d 352 (1997)

The federal government charged Mario Salinas, a deputy sheriff of Hidalgo County, Texas, with one count of violating RICO, 18 U.S.C.A. § 1962(c); one count of conspiracy to violate RICO, § 1962(d); and other offenses. The government alleged that Deputy Salinas accepted two watches and a truck in exchange for permitting women to make "contact visits" to a federal prisoner housed in the county jail. A jury acquitted Salinas of the substantive RICO count but convicted him on the conspiracy charge. The U.S. Court of Appeals for the Fifth Circuit affirmed, and the Supreme Court granted review. Salinas contended that he could not be convicted

of conspiracy under the RICO statute because he was found not guilty of the substantive RICO offense. In rejecting his contention, Justice Anthony Kennedy, writing for the Court, noted that the RICO conspiracy statute provides, "It shall be unlawful for any person to conspire to violate any of the provisions of subsection (a), (b), or (c) of this section." Kennedy stated, "There is no requirement of some overt act or specific act in the statute before us, unlike the general conspiracy provision applicable to federal crimes, which requires that at least one of the conspirators have committed an 'act to effect the object of the conspiracy'." "The RICO conspiracy provision, then, is even more comprehensive than the general conspiracy offense in § 371."

### Extension of RICO beyond Its Original Scope

RICO was conceived as a weapon for prosecution of organized crime, but it has become the basis of prosecution against white-collar criminals as well. Prosecutors have long experienced difficulty in securing convictions of organized crime leaders for violating specific criminal statutes. In part, this occurs because the evidence of a specific statutory violation might be unconvincing to a judge or jury. The reaction of a judge or jury is likely to be different when the prosecution parades before the court evidence of a series of violations that reveal a pattern of criminal behavior.

RICO has been justified because the harm that organized crime inflicts on society is far greater than the harm inflicted by those who commit statutory crimes. It can be an effective tool to help prosecutors fight against crime syndicates. Yet membership in organized crime is not a necessary element for a conviction under RICO. Unlike conventional criminal statutes, which historically have been narrowly construed, Congress provided that RICO is to be liberally interpreted to effect its remedial purposes. The liberal construction of the enterprise requirement and the fact that the pattern requirement of racketeering activity is cast in numerical terms have engendered some criticism. Critics contend that RICO is a catchall statute that gives prosecutors too much discretion to expand the range of indictable offenses. Examples of RICO prosecutions include the following:

- Several members of the Outlaws Motorcycle Club were prosecuted for a RICO violation based on narcotics and prostitution offenses. *United States v. Watchmaker*, 761 F.2d 1459 (11th Cir. 1985).
- A U.S. Customs Service Officer accepted payment for information that was used to facilitate a drug smuggling operation. The bribe money was invested in foreign bank accounts, thus constituting a money laundering enterprise. *United States v. Vogt*, 910 F.2d 1184 (4th Cir. 1990).
- A gambler and a police officer were convicted for their involvement in a police protection racket. *United States v. Sanders*, 962 F.2d 660 (7th Cir. 1992).
- Gang members were convicted of racketeering offenses for extorting protection money from local Chinese businesses; committing robberies; and kidnapping and murdering rival gang members, potential witnesses, and business owners who refused to pay protection money. *United States v. Wong*, 40 F.3d 1347 (2d Cir. 1994).

### RICO, Predicate Offenses, and Double Jeopardy

**CASE-IN-POINT**

Sixty members of the Nicodemo Scarfo crime family allegedly controlled Mafia operations in parts of Pennsylvania and New Jersey. The government alleged that over the course of eleven years the family's activities included a number of felony offenses. All the defendants were found guilty of conspiring to participate and participating in an enterprise through a pattern of racketeering in violation of 18 U.S.C.A. § 1962.

On appeal, Scarfo contended that the use of his former convictions as predicate offenses on which to base the RICO prosecution violated his constitutional right not to be placed in jeopardy twice for the same offense. In rejecting Scarfo's claims, the

U.S. Court of Appeals pointed out the following: (1) As to state convictions used as predicate offenses, there could be no double jeopardy because different sovereigns were involved; and (2) as to federal convictions used as predicate offenses, the court in previous cases has ruled that a RICO offense "is not, in a literal sense, the 'same' offense as one of the predicate offenses" because a RICO violation requires proof of a "pattern of racketeering" and is intended to deter continuous criminal conduct, whereas the predicate offenses are intended to deter discrete criminal acts. Accordingly, the court rejected Scarfo's contentions.

*United States v. Pungitore*, 910 F.2d 1084 (3d Cir. 1990).

- An attorney was convicted of violating RICO based on participating in a scheme involving bribery of judges, where evidence revealed that the defendant had agreed to seek to use the court system corruptly by bribing judges to appoint attorneys as special assistant public defenders. *United States v. Massey*, 89 F.3d 1433 (11th Cir. 1996).

RICO has been extended beyond its original purpose to target non–organized criminals such as white-collar criminals and corrupt government officials. Thus, through RICO a prosecutor can circumvent statutes of limitation and seek to inflict multiple punishments for the same offenses.

Most states have adopted RICO-type statutes. Some closely parallel the federal act, whereas others have varying provisions concerning prohibited acts, sanctions, forfeitures of property, and the procedures involved.

Despite criticism, RICO is firmly established as a weapon in the arsenal of federal and, in many instances, state prosecutors. It has proved to be a useful tool in the war against racketeering and corruption, both private and public, whether organized or not.

### Constitutional Assaults on Rico

Since its enactment in 1970, RICO has withstood a number of constitutional assaults. In *United States v. Martino*, 648 F.2d 367 (5th Cir. 1981), the Fifth Circuit found that RICO does not violate the *ex post facto* prohibition of the U.S. Constitution, nor does it violate the Ninth and Tenth Amendments by intruding on state sovereignty. Prior to that the Ninth Circuit had rejected a contention that the RICO term "pattern of racketeering" is vague and ambiguous, concluding that any ambiguity was cured by the definitions of "pattern" and "racketeering activity" in § 1961. *United States v. Campanale*, 518 F.2d 352, 364 (9th Cir. 1975). Perhaps a more serious challenge to RICO has been the allegation that it violates the Double Jeopardy Clause of the Constitution. But because a RICO violation involves a separate criminal proceeding, courts have generally denied such contentions. For example, the Fifth Circuit has held that the Double Jeopardy Clause of the Fifth

Amendment does not prohibit the government from prosecuting a defendant for a RICO charge where the defendant has been previously prosecuted for a substantive offense used as one of the predicate crimes. *United States v. Smith*, 574 F.2d 308 (5th Cir. 1978).

# Defenses in White-Collar and Organized Crime Cases

Many of the defenses available to defendants charged with white-collar and organized crime offenses are similar to those available to defendants generally. The most common defense to prosecutions involving fraud is that the defendant had a good-faith belief that allegedly "fraudulent" representations were, in fact, true. In a prosecution under a statute that requires the government to prove that the defendant acted willfully, an effective defense is one that negates the defendant's willfulness. In tax prosecutions, a defendant who in good faith relied on the advice of a professional tax preparer can assert such reliance as a defense, provided the taxpayer disclosed all relevant information to the tax preparer.

In prosecutions under RICO, the defenses of entrapment, double jeopardy, and selective prosecution appear more frequently than in other situations (see Chapter 14). In organized crime prosecutions, the defense often attacks the validity of the underlying predicate offenses. Moreover, the complexities involved in many federal statutes aimed at organized crime raise more issues of statutory construction and legislative intent than do the more traditionally defined crimes.

## Conclusion

Unlike transactional criminal offenses, white-collar crime and organized crime are not easily defined, and the conduct involved is often elusive and not readily quantifiable. We know that white-collar crimes are usually characterized by deception or abuse of trust and often involve the use of computers or other modern technologies. But we lack the accurate data and statistical information that is available on the traditional defined offenses. Some conduct criminalized today as white-collar crimes might have been considered mere unethical business practices in our earlier history. Other behavior, although long recognized as offensive, did not fit into the molds developed at common law and has become statutorily forbidden only in recent years. In today's society, so dependent on electronic transactions, the computer criminal might become as significant a danger to our well-being as is the street criminal who robs, burglarizes, and steals.

Organized crime syndicates cater to people's desire for goods and services that cannot be legally supplied but that can be made available to them at minimal risks to the providers. Organized crime gained its greatest foothold during the Prohibition era, and by the time Prohibition was repealed in 1933, organized crime had permeated many phases of the American economy. On the positive side, today there is an increased awareness of organized crime operations and an increased emphasis, particularly at the federal level, on investigation and prosecution. RICO has introduced a new dimension to the criminal law and has provided the legal system with effective tools to prosecute criminal enterprise activity and those who engage in racketeering. If the public demands increased efforts in this area, we should see considerable progress in ferreting out and punishing those who threaten the safety and economic well-being of society.

# Chapter Summary

- Learning Objective 1

  - The substantive criminal offenses described in previous chapters are frequently associated with violence and are often termed "street crimes." In contrast, white-collar crimes typically come from the middle and upper socioeconomic strata of society and are usually nonviolent offenses characterized by deception or abuse of trust.

  - Today white-collar crimes often involve the use of computers or other modern technologies.

  - Organized crime involves offenses committed by persons or groups who often attempt to gain political influence through graft and corruption. Organized crime figures, sometimes called "racketeers," frequently conduct their business through illegal enterprises. They often resort to threats and acts of violence in the commission of white-collar offenses.

  - Organized crime gained its greatest foothold during the Prohibition era, when the Eighteenth Amendment to the U.S. Constitution, prohibiting the sale and distribution of alcoholic beverages, was in effect. By the time Prohibition was repealed in 1933, organized crime had become involved in many phases of the economy, often pursuing its interests through illegal activities.

- Learning Objective 2

  - White-collar crimes often are prosecuted based on federal statutes enacted by Congress under its constitutional power over postal, bankruptcy, and taxing matters and its authority to regulate interstate domestic and foreign commerce.

  - State legislatures have broad authority to proscribe other offenses as contrary to the public welfare.

  - Prosecutions involve not only large-scale corporate frauds but also unlawful telephone, mail, and e-mail solicitations; sales of unregistered securities and undeserved diplomas; phony contests; fraudulent home improvement schemes; and bogus land sales. In some instances statutes also provide civil remedies.

- Learning Objective 3

  - Under common law, a corporation (as opposed to its members) was not held criminally responsible for its acts. Eventually courts imposed criminal liability based on acts of the corporation's agents; however, a corporation cannot be held criminally liable for crimes against persons unless the offense is one based on the corporation's negligence as opposed to a crime based on specific intent.

  - Prosecutions of white-collar crime are frequently directed against corporate defendants, with corporations held criminally liable for the acts their agents commit within the scope of their actual or apparent authority. State and federal courts broadly define "scope of authority" to include an agent's acts intended to benefit the corporation.

  - The fact that a corporation is prosecuted for crimes does not exonerate the individuals who commit the unlawful acts. In fact, it is not uncommon for corporate executives to be punished, generally by imposition of fines.

- Learning Objective 4

  o The Sherman Antitrust Act is a federal statute that makes it a crime to enter any contract or engage in any combination or conspiracy in restraint of trade or to monopolize or attempt to monopolize trade.

  o The act reaches individuals and entities in for-profit and nonprofit activities as well as local governments and educational institutions.

  o Price-fixing and bid rigging are among the most common violations.

  o To prove a criminal violation of the act, the government must establish that two or more entities formed a combination or conspiracy that produces, or potentially produces, an unreasonable restraint of interstate in trade or commerce with intent to violate the law.

  o The act includes civil remedies as well as criminal sanctions. Criminal violations are felonies.

  o The U.S. Department of Justice alone is authorized to enforce the criminal sanctions of the act.

  o Corporations may be fined as much as $100,000,000; individuals may be fined as much as $1,000,000, sentenced to imprisonment, or both.

- Learning Objective 5

  o In 1984 Congress enacted the Computer Fraud and Abuse Act. As amended in 1996, it makes it a crime to "knowingly cause the transmission of a program, information, code, or command" in interstate commerce with intent to cause damage to a computer exclusively used by a financial institution or the U.S. government.

  o In addition, the act prohibits "knowingly and with intent to defraud, trafficking in passwords to permit unauthorized access to a government computer, or to affect interstate or foreign commerce" or to transmit in interstate or foreign commerce any threat to cause damage to a protected computer with intent to extort something of value.

  o As amended, the USA PATRIOT Act defines "protected computer" to include computers outside of the United States that affect "interstate or foreign commerce or communication of the United States" and increases the penalty for violations for damaging a protected computer.

  o In 2006, the United States ratified the Convention on Cybercrime, a treaty designed to harmonize national laws and strengthen international cooperation in this area. The treaty addresses several problems in the area of international white-collar crime, including computer-related fraud, "hacking," the dissemination of computer viruses, and electronic attacks on financial institutions.

  o Federal and state statutes now proscribe theft of computer programs, computer fraud, and computer trespass.

- Learning Objective 6

  o The widespread use of debit and credit cards, automated teller machine cards, account numbers, personal identification numbers, and other access devices caused states to enact comprehensive statutes proscribing the fraudulent use of devices to secure cash, goods, and services through means beyond the traditional credit card.

  o A person who without authority uses an access device or one who uses a revoked access device to obtain or attempt to obtain property or services commits the offense.

- ○ The offenses are usually classified as misdemeanors or felonies depending on the amount involved.
- ○ To address the growing problem of identity theft, Congress enacted the Identity Theft and Assumption Deterrence Act of 1998 making it a felony to "knowingly transfer, possess or use, without lawful authority, a means of identification of another person with the intent to commit, or to aid or abet, any unlawful activity that constitutes a violation of Federal law, or that constitutes a felony under any applicable State or local law."
- ○ By 2003 most states had also enacted specific statutes making identify theft and fraud a felony.

- Learning Objective 7

  - ○ Intellectual property comprises patents, copyrights, trademarks, and trade secrets.
  - ○ Patents are issued for a period of twenty years by the U.S. Patent and Trademark Office for inventions and discoveries that are novel, useful, and not something of an obvious nature.
  - ○ A copyright affords legal protection to authors of original works, which now include musical, artistic, and architectural works as well as videos, computer software, and databases. For a work created after January 1, 1978, statutory protection is given for the life of the author plus seventy years after the author's death.
  - ○ A trademark is a distinctive word, phrase, or graphic symbol used to distinguish a product. To be protected by federal law, trademarks used in interstate or foreign commerce may be registered with the U.S. Patent and Trademark Office.
  - ○ Disputes involving intellectual property are mostly civil matters, but there are criminal prohibitions for patent and copyright infringement, trademark counterfeiting, and theft of trade secrets.
  - ○ The Economic Espionage Act of 1996 prohibits foreign governments from stealing trade secrets and criminalizes domestic trade-secret theft.

- Learning Objective 8

  - ○ The federal Money Laundering Control Act of 1986 makes it a crime to disguise illegal income to make it appear legitimate.
  - ○ Federal statutes require financial institutions to file currency transaction reports with the Secretary of the Treasury for cash transactions in excess of $10,000 and to cause or attempt to cause a financial institution from making the required reports or from structuring or assisting in structuring a transaction to evade the reporting requirements.

- Learning Objective 9

  - ○ The federal False Statements Act prohibits knowingly and willfully making a false statement that is material to a matter within the jurisdiction of any department or agency of the United States.
  - ○ Federal bankruptcy statutes criminalize fraudulent concealment of assets, avoiding distribution of nonexempt assets, taking false oaths, and related conduct in bankruptcy proceedings.
  - ○ The Health Insurance Portability and Accountability Act of 1996 (HIPAA) prohibits making material false or fraudulent statements or entries in connection with delivery of or payment for health care benefits.

- The Federal Mail Fraud Statute makes it a crime to use the mail to obtain money or property by fraudulent means and to use the mails in furtherance of the fraudulent scheme.

- The Federal Wire Fraud Statute, which parallels the mail fraud statute, criminalizes fraudulent schemes that use interstate television, radio, or wire communications.

- A variety of federal and state statutes criminalize conduct involving misrepresentations, omissions, insider trading, and other aspects of fraud in securities dealing. The most significant federal acts are the Securities Act of 1933 and the Securities and Exchange Act of 1934. These statutes provide for civil remedies as well as criminal sanctions.

- Prosecutions for white-collar crime often include charges of tax fraud. Although most federal tax violations are resolved through civil proceedings, the Internal Revenue Code criminalizes a host of offenses including deliberately failing to file tax returns, underreporting or omitting income, and overstating the amount of deductions. Most violations are felonies. To establish "willfulness," the government must prove the defendant's "intentional violation of a known legal duty."

- Learning Objective 10

  - After the Eighteenth Amendment was repealed in 1933 crime syndicates expanded into loan-sharking, gambling, narcotics, and extortion and infiltrated legitimate businesses. Common-law and statutory crimes focus on specific acts of wrongdoing and were not too effective in controlling ongoing criminal activity by organized groups. To combat this, Congress enacted the Anti-Racketeering Act of 1934; to increase its effectiveness it enacted the Hobbs Act in 1946. Prosecutions under the Hobbs Act originally focused on extortion by public officials using force, violence, or fear; now prosecutors frequently rely on the act to prosecute state and local officials based on extortion "under color of official rights."

  - A gigantic legal step in fighting organized crime occurred in 1970 when Congress enacted the Organized Crime Control Act, which includes the Racketeer Influenced and Corrupt Organizations (RICO) Act. RICO makes it a crime for any person "who has received any income derived, directly or indirectly, from a pattern of racketeering activity or through collection of an unlawful debt . . . to use or invest [in] any enterprise which is engaged in interstate or foreign commerce."

  - RICO makes it unlawful for any such person to participate, directly or indirectly, in the conduct of the enterprise's affairs through a "pattern of racketeering." It broadly defines racketeering activity to include a variety of federal offenses as well as nine state crimes that are characteristically felonies, and it defines "enterprise" to include "any individual, partnership, corporation, association, or other legal entity, and any union or group of individuals associated in fact although not a legal entity."

  - Establishing a pattern of racketeering activity requires the government to prove that at least two acts of racketeering (called predicate acts) have occurred within a period of ten years, excluding any period of imprisonment. The predicate acts must be related to each other and to the enterprise.

  - RICO also provides for forfeiture of property used in criminal enterprises and permits the government to bring civil actions against such enterprises.

○ RICO was conceived as a weapon for prosecution of organized crime, but it has become the basis for prosecution of white-collar criminals as well.
○ Unlike other criminal statutes that historically have been narrowly construed, Congress provided that RICO is to be liberally interpreted. RICO has withstood a number of constitutional challenges.
○ The most serious challenge was that it violates the Double Jeopardy Clause of the Constitution. Because a RICO violation involves a separate criminal proceeding, courts have generally denied such contentions.

## Key Terms

access device fraud

access devices

antitrust violations

bankruptcy fraud

bid rigging

bootlegging

churning

computer fraud

Computer Fraud and Abuse Act

computer trespass

copyright

corporate defendants

crime syndicates

cybercrimes

enterprise

False Claims Act

False Statements Act

Health Insurance Portability and Accountability Act (HIPAA)

Hobbs Act

identity theft

insider trading

intellectual property

loan-sharking

mail fraud

money laundering

organized crime

Organized Crime Control Act of 1970

patent

pattern of racketeering

predicate acts

price-fixing

Racketeer Influenced and Corrupt Organizations (RICO)

racketeering

scope of an agent's authority

Securities and Exchange Act

Sherman Antitrust Act

structuring

tax fraud

theft of computer services

trade secret

trademark

trademark counterfeiting

USA PATRIOT Act

white-collar crimes

wire fraud

## Questions for Thought and Discussion

1. Why do federal criminal statutes figure so prominently in the context of white-collar offenses?
2. Under what circumstances can a corporation be held legally responsible for a white-collar offense committed by one of its agents or employees?
3. Is it a crime to share digital music files with friends if one receives no payment for the files?

4. What is the federal constitutional authority for enacting (a) antitrust and wire fraud laws? (b) postal offenses? (c) securities laws? (d) bankruptcy laws?
5. What is the extent of prohibitions under the Sherman Antitrust Act? Give some examples of violations of the act.
6. Why does the rationale for federal antitrust and securities laws require the availability of both civil and criminal sanctions?
7. Describe a factual scenario that could occur in the operation of a municipal or county government in your state and that could likely result in a person being prosecuted under the Hobbs Act.
8. What led Congress to the realization that the traditional common-law transactional approach to crime was inadequate to deal with organized crime?
9. What is required to establish a "pattern of racketeering activity" under RICO?
10. How does RICO define "enterprise," and what is its significance in prosecution of RICO offenses?

## Problems for Discussion and Solution

1. Ima Hacker is a skilled computer operator at a business office. Through stealthy operation of her computer, she successfully obtains a list of names and addresses of a competitor's customers without the knowledge or consent of the competitor. For what offense would Ms. Hacker most likely be prosecuted in your state?
2. Men's Fashions, a clothing store, was an incorporated business that was experiencing financial problems. Some of the principals of the business organized a new corporation and sold a substantial portion of the inventory of Men's Fashions to the new corporation for considerably less than the wholesale cost of the merchandise. A few weeks after the sale, Men's Fashions filed a bankruptcy petition, listing as assets a greatly diminished inventory without disclosing the recent sale of inventory to the new corporation. Does this scenario suggest bankruptcy fraud? Why or why not?
3. An elderly widow whose income was derived primarily from Social Security and a small pension owned $100,000 in government bonds that she inherited from her late husband. Other than her home and a modest checking account, her bonds constituted her estate. On advice of A. Brokero, a licensed securities broker, she converted the bonds into cash and deposited the proceeds with Brokero to manage. She explained her financial situation and investment objectives. She and Brokero agreed that her funds should be invested in conservative, income-producing investments. Instead, Brokero, who had trading authorization from the widow, bought and sold numerous issues of aggressive stocks for the account, and at the end of two years the account had dwindled to $28,500. During the two-year period, Brokero had earned thousands of dollars in commissions for buying and selling the investments. What, if any, criminal violation is suggested by this scenario?
4. At a state peace officers' convention, two police officers from Sedateville, a small rural community, developed a friendship with two officers from Trendville, a metropolitan city. Gambling, except for a state lottery, was prohibited in the state. As their friendship developed, they enjoyed "a friendly game of poker" with modest betting. They all agreed that "after all, gambling is really not all bad" and probably should not be prohibited. As the rural officers began to lament their modest salaries, the Trendville officers introduced them to some "prominent businessmen." They all agreed that "it would hurt no one" to allow these businessmen

to conduct some private gambling operations in Sedateville. But, of course, the operation would require some protection by the local police. With cooperation of the officers, the businessmen opened a bar where gambling was conducted in a back room. The new operation also accommodated male patrons seeking prostitutes by transporting the men to Trendville for a weekend "sports event." Through the cooperation of the officers, the new operation was "overlooked" by the Sedateville police. In turn, the officers from Trendville and Sedateville enjoyed some of the profits from the gambling and prostitution activities. The four officers' gains eventually exceeded their salaries as police officers, and as they later said, "No one was hurt in this operation—people were just allowed to have a good time." Under what circumstances would this scenario present a basis for a RICO prosecution?

## CHAPTER 10

# Vice Crimes

## CHAPTER OUTLINE

## JURISPRUDENCE

*Barnes v. Glen Theatre, Inc.* (1991)

*Jenkins v. Georgia* (1974)

*New York v. Ferber* (1982)

*Mackey v. Montrym* (1979)

*Gonzales v. Raich* (2005)

## LEARNING OBJECTIVES

After reading this chapter, you should be able to explain

1. how and why offenses involving consensual sexual conduct have largely disappeared from the criminal law

2. how the criminal law treats prostitution, public nudity, voyeurism, and erotic dancing in places of public accommodation

3. why courts and prosecutors have struggled with obscenity and why child pornography is viewed differently

4. how the laws regarding gambling have changed and why enforcement of gambling laws is so difficult

5. how the law protects domestic animals from abandonment, neglect, and abuse

6. the various crimes involving the use of alcohol, including offenses involving drivers of motor vehicles

7. the origin and development of the "war on drugs"

8. how and why the marijuana laws have evolved

9. the particular problems police and prosecutors face in proving drug charges

10. how and why specialized drug courts have been developed to deal with drug offenders

## CHAPTER OPENING VIGNETTE

Lindsey Lohan was already an established model when she made her acting debut at age eleven, starring in the 1998 Disney film *The Parent Trap.* From there her career took off and she appeared in numerous films, television programs, and magazines and even recorded several music CDs. Like so many celebrities, Lohan developed problems with substance abuse. A May 2007 traffic accident led to her arrest for driving under the influence of alcohol (DUI). Later that year she was arrested again for DUI and possession of cocaine. A plea agreement required her to spend one day in jail, perform ten days of community service, and undergo drug and alcohol treatment as conditions of the three-year term of probation. In October 2009 Lohan's probation was extended another year after the judge learned that she had not completed her alcohol treatment program. In the summer of 2010 Lohan was jailed for thirty days for violating the terms of her probation. In September 2010 the judge revoked Lohan's probation and issued a bench warrant for her arrest after learning that Lohan had failed a court-ordered drug test. Lohan served a day in jail and then checked into another treatment facility. The Lohan case, although tragic, is all too common. For centuries people have struggled with addictions to drugs and alcohol, as well as many other vices discussed in this chapter. The question is, "What is the appropriate role of the criminal law in dealing with such vices?"

## Introduction

**vice** Conduct widely considered immoral such as prostitution, gambling, and drug abuse.

The word "vice" comes from the Latin *vitium*, meaning "fault" or "defect." In the criminal justice system, the term **"vice"** is associated with a number of crimes traditionally classified as offenses against public decency or morality. Some of these offenses, such as indecent exposure, bigamy, and obscenity, have their roots in English common law. Others, like prostitution, gambling, and alcohol and drug offenses, were created legislatively at various times in our nation's history. All of these offenses have evolved substantially in recent decades, reflecting tremendous changes in our society.

It is not uncommon today for critics to question whether the furtherance of decency and morality is a legitimate goal of the criminal justice system. Many believe that morality, like religion, is a personal matter and that the state should be neutral in matters of morality, much as it is with respect to religion. Others, stressing the practical aspect of the problem, cite the aphorism "you can't legislate morality." However, critics must realize that the moral basis of the law extends far beyond the prohibition of vice. Many proscriptions of the criminal law, from animal cruelty to insider stock trading, are based on collective societal judgments about what is right and what is wrong. Writing for the U.S. Supreme Court in *Bowers v. Hardwick*, 478 U.S. 186, 106 S.Ct. 2841, 92 L.Ed.2d 140 (1986), Justice Byron White observed that "the law . . . is constantly based on notions of morality, and if all laws representing essentially moral choices are to be invalidated . . . , the courts will be very busy indeed." 478 U.S. at 196, 106 S.Ct. at 2846, 92 L.Ed.2d at 149. It should also be pointed out that many of the crimes discussed in this chapter can be viewed as threats to other societal interests beyond morality. For example, prostitution is often seen as a public health issue. Alcohol-and drug-related offenses are often real threats to the public safety and order.

# Criminal Prohibitions of Sexual Conduct

Reflecting its common-law origins, American criminal law traditionally proscribed a wide range of consensual sexual conduct, including fornication, adultery, seduction, sodomy, prostitution, and incest. Today the prevalent view is that such behavior is, or at least ought to be, private in character and thus beyond the reach of the law. However, many people still subscribe to the classical conservative view that such prohibitions are necessary to maintain a proper moral climate. In any event, changes in attitudes about such matters have led state legislatures to abolish many of these offenses. Others have been invalidated by courts of law on the basis of the constitutional **right of privacy**. Judicial decisions in this area have given rise to the constitutional principle that competent adults have the right to make their own decisions in matters of sex and reproduction (see Chapter 3).

**right of privacy** Constitutional right to engage in intimate personal conduct or make fundamental life decisions without interference by the government.

## Fornication, Adultery, and Seduction

**Fornication** is sexual intercourse between unmarried persons. **Adultery** is generally defined as sexual intercourse between a male and female, at least one of whom is married to someone else. Fornication and adultery were regarded as offenses against morality and were punishable in the ecclesiastical courts in England. Neither was considered a common-law crime unless committed openly. In such instances the act was prosecuted as a public nuisance. Historically, the rationale for criminalizing these acts was threefold: (1) to avoid disharmony in family relationships, (2) to prevent illegitimate births, and (3) to prevent the spread of sexually transmitted diseases.

**fornication** Sexual intercourse between unmarried persons; an offense at common law.

**adultery** Voluntary sexual intercourse between a married person and someone other than that person's spouse.

Because of changing societal attitudes, these offenses are rarely prosecuted today. Indeed, as suggested above, many states have eliminated these offenses altogether. Adultery and fornication might be widespread, but they generally occur under the most private of circumstances. Consequently, complaints about these sexual encounters are seldom reported to the authorities. In instances where sexual conduct is the subject of a complaint by a participant, it may fall under the classification of sexual battery (see Chapter 7). As we noted in Chapter 3, in 2005 the Virginia Supreme Court struck down that state's prohibition of fornication as a violation of the liberty guaranteed by the Fourteenth Amendment. *Martin v. Ziherl*, 607 S.E.2d 367 (Va. 2005).

**seduction** The crime of inducing a woman to have sexual intercourse outside of wedlock on the promise of marriage.

**Seduction** was not a crime at common law, but it was a tort. In the early nineteenth century a number of American states enacted statutes criminalizing seduction. By the mid-twentieth century most states had this offense on the books. The essence of the offense was that a male obtained sexual intercourse from a virtuous female on the unfulfilled promise of marriage. Historically, prosecution for seduction served the role of persuading a recalcitrant suitor to marry the woman he seduced. One could avoid criminal liability by agreeing to marry the complainant. Most states have repealed their seduction statutes, and where such laws remain on the books, prosecution is extremely rare.

## Sodomy: The Demise of a Historic Offense

**sodomy** Oral or anal sex between persons or sex between a person and an animal; the latter is commonly referred to as bestiality.

The word "sodomy" is derived from the biblical account of Sodom, the city that was destroyed because of its vices. **Sodomy** consists of committing acts that were once commonly referred to as "crimes against nature." Sodomy was originally an ecclesiastical offense but became a felony in sixteenth-century England, the later stages of the common law. In general, the offense includes oral or anal sex between humans and sexual intercourse between humans and animals. (The latter is often termed *bestiality*.) Until 1961 all states had statutes outlawing sodomy; however, during the 1970s and 1980s many of these statutes were either repealed or invalidated by courts. The few that remained on the books were not actively enforced.

In *Lawrence v. Texas*, 539 U.S. 558, 123 S.Ct. 2472, 156 L.Ed.2d 508 (2003), the Supreme Court struck down one of the few remaining sodomy laws, saying that it "furthers no legitimate state interest which can justify its intrusion into the personal and private life of the individual." 539 U.S. at 578, 123 S.Ct. at 2484, 156 L.Ed.2d at 526. The *Lawrence* decision signaled the demise of consensual sodomy as a criminal offense in the United States. However, as we pointed out in Chapter 7, forcible sodomy can be prosecuted as a species of rape or sexual battery.

## Incest

**incest** Sexual intercourse with a close blood relative or, in some cases, a person related by affinity.

**Incest** is sexual intercourse within or outside the bonds of marriage between persons related within certain prohibited degrees. *Haller v. State*, 232 S.W.2d 829 (Ark. 1950). Incest was not a crime at common law but was punishable by the ecclesiastical courts.

There are strong religious and moral taboos against incest. Furthermore, it has been almost universally believed that incest not only disrupts family relationships but also leads to genetically defective offspring. For these reasons, all states prohibit marriage or sexual relations between certain close relatives. Once the prosecution establishes the defendant's knowledge of the prohibited relationship, proof of the act of sexual intercourse is sufficient to show violation of the statute.

Statutes that prohibit intermarriage or sexual relations between persons within certain degrees of kinship usually refer to relationship by consanguinity (that is, blood relationships). But some went further and classified as incestuous close relationships between persons related by affinity (that is, marriage) as well as relationships by the bloodline.

There is little support for repealing laws forbidding incest. The practice of incest among those related by consanguinity is widely condemned in Western civilization, and laws forbidding it will undoubtedly remain intact. Those who do advocate the repeal of these laws advance the same arguments as those advanced for legalizing fornication, adultery, and sodomy. Others who see incest as a genuine concern urge that government should approach the problem through counseling and by furnishing psychiatric assistance to transgressors, rather than by making incest a penal offense.

## Bigamy and Polygamy

**bigamy** The crime of being married to more than one person at the same time.

Like most sexual offenses, **bigamy** was originally a canonical offense punishable by the ecclesiastical courts in England; later it became a common-law offense. All

### CASE-IN-POINT

### Criminal Prosecution of a Polygamist

In what was described in the press as the country's first major polygamy case in nearly five decades, Thomas Arthur Green was found guilty on four counts of bigamy and one count of child rape in May of 2001. Green, a fundamentalist Mormon polygamist, had five wives and thirty children by them.

Upon conviction, Green was sentenced to five years in prison. In reviewing the case in 2004, the Utah Supreme Court rejected Green's argument that the state bigamy statute violated the federal constitutional right to free exercise of religion. It also held that the bigamy statute was not unconstitutionally vague as applied.

*State v. Green*, 99 P.3d 820 (Utah 2004).

American jurisdictions prohibit bigamy (that is, marriage between two persons when one is already legally married to another). Usually these statutes require the prosecution to prove that the defendant had knowledge of the prior marital status of the person whom he or she married. Since everyone is presumed to know the consequences of his or her acts, no further intent need be shown.

**polygamy** The state or practice of having more than one spouse simultaneously.

During the 1800s arguments were advanced that **polygamy**—the practice of one person being married to several spouses at the same time—was a religious practice protected by the First Amendment. The U.S. Supreme Court soundly rejected these contentions when it held that a religious belief cannot be made a justification for commission of an overt act made criminal by the state. *Reynolds v. United States*, 98 U.S. (8 Otto) 145, 25 L.Ed. 244 (1878). The *Reynolds* case involved a Mormon polygamist who challenged the constitutionality of the federal statute prohibiting polygamy in federal territories. Subsequently the Church of Jesus Christ of Latter-day Saints disavowed the practice of polygamy, but the practice continues to this day in some fundamentalist Mormon communities in the western United States. Prosecutions for bigamy or polygamy are rare (but see Case-in-Point above).

## Prostitution

**prostitution** The practice of selling sexual favors.

A prostitute is a person who indulges in indiscriminate sexual activity for hire. Although **prostitution** was not a crime at common law, statutes proscribing prostitution have been part of the laws directed against public immorality since the early history of the United States. Lawmakers have officially deplored the existence of prostitution, and law enforcement authorities have long linked the activity with other forms of vice, including narcotics offenses, as well as the exploitation of women.

Today, prostitution is illegal in all states except Nevada, where it exists by local option in some counties, although it is strictly regulated by law. See Nev. Rev. Stat., Chapter 201, Crimes Against Public Decency and Good Morals. Despite the limited legalization in Nevada, arrests for prostitution are still quite numerous in that state. This is largely explained by the fact that prostitution is rampant in Las Vegas, where it remains illegal.

Historically, laws prohibiting prostitution were directed almost exclusively at the prostitute, usually at females who have sexual intercourse with males for compensation. However, newer statutes provide for conviction of customers as well as prostitutes. Indeed, if the statutes are not so construed, they might be vulnerable to constitutional attack as a denial of equal protection under the law. In recent years, as prostitution by males has increased, enforcement has come to be directed at males as well.

In addition to making prostitution an offense, most states make it an offense to solicit for a prostitute or to live off the earnings of a person engaged in prostitution. Statutes also commonly declare brothels and houses of prostitution as public nuisances.

Texas statutes provide that a person who offers or agrees to engage or engages in sexual conduct for a fee, or who solicits another in a public place to engage in such conduct, commits the misdemeanor offense of prostitution. Vernon's Tex. Penal Code Ann. § 43.02. Texas also makes promotion of prostitution a misdemeanor offense. § 43.03. One who owns or manages a prostitution enterprise that uses two or more prostitutes commits a felony. § 43.04. Finally, Texas law makes it a serious felony for a person to knowingly cause another by force, threat, or fraud or to cause by any means a person younger than seventeen years to commit prostitution. § 43.05.

Those who oppose the prostitution laws now extant in the United States point to the fact that the "oldest profession" has survived many centuries of condemnation yet exists as a cultural institution. Thus, they argue, it fulfills a socially desirable function because it furnishes an outlet for sexual impulses and tends to lessen the incidence of sexual attacks on women. In addition to the need to conserve scarce resources to fight serious crime and the futility of trying to eradicate an ingrained institution, reformers contend that legalization of prostitution would lead to needed regulation. This, they point out, could provide for medical inspections to diminish the spread of sexually transmitted diseases. Finally, many critics of the present laws concerning prostitution contend that legalization would allow the police to take this activity from the grips of organized crime and control more effectively many of the problems that now accompany unregulated prostitution.

Despite the cries for reform, any decriminalization of prostitution will most likely be in selected locations only and will confine activities to prescribed areas. The inherent privacy of the scene of offenses makes it very difficult to apprehend prostitutes and their customers. Therefore, enforcement is more effective when it is

**CASE-IN-POINT**

### Prostitution

Kimberli Austin was found guilty of prostitution in a Texas state court and she appealed on the grounds that there was insufficient evidence to sustain her conviction. The State of Texas alleged that Austin "did . . . knowingly agree to engage in sexual intercourse with [Officer] J. Hutto for a fee." Officer Hutto testified "he and other officers were in the process of investigating massage parlors and modeling studios." Hutto stated he entered the Satin Spa where a male told him "to select one of the females, and Hutto selected . . . Austin." Austin told "Hutto the 'Basic Rub' was a 'fingertip' massage, and the 'Swedish Deep Muscle Rub' was a 'more thorough and stimulating rub.'" Hutto testified that he "had experience with the terminology and understood that 'Swedish Deep Muscle Rub' was 'a catch phrase' for prostitution." Hutto gave payment for the "highest price 'Swedish' rub." Austin inquired as to how Hutto "would 'like to end the session,'" and Hutto "pretended not to understand." Hutto asked if he could get something more whereupon Austin stated "yes." Austin and Hutto ultimately agreed to sexual intercourse and that the cost would be included in the payment already rendered. In affirming Austin's conviction for prostitution, the Court of Criminal Appeals of Texas held that a "trial judge in a bench trial is the sole trier of the facts, the credibility of the witnesses and the weight to be given to their testimony, and may accept any part of or all the testimony given by the witnesses." While Austin argued that the State failed to establish that she agreed to sexual intercourse for "a fee," the court held that the trial judge, as the trier of fact, was free to determine the credibility of the officer's testimony and the weight to be given to such testimony. Austin's conviction was upheld.

*Austin v. State*, 794 S.W.2d 408 (Texas Crim. App. 1990).

focused on procurers of prostitutes and solicitors for their services, and not merely on those who render those services.

## Human Trafficking

**human trafficking** The illegal trade in human beings for the purpose of migration, labor, or commercial sexual exploitation.

Closely related to prostitution is the problem of **human trafficking**, which is the illegal trade in human beings for the purpose of migration, labor or, more commonly, commercial sexual exploitation. According to the Bureau of Justice Statistics, federally funded human trafficking task forces investigated 2,515 suspected incidents of human trafficking between January 2008 and June 2010. Approximately 80 percent of these incidents were classified as sex trafficking (U.S. Department of Justice, Bureau of Justice Statistics, "Characteristics of Suspected Human Trafficking Incidents, 2008–2010," April 2011, NCJ 233732). The legalization of brothels does not address the problem of human trafficking and in fact may increase it.

Federal law provides that "[w]hoever knowingly transports any individual in interstate or foreign commerce, or in any Territory or Possession of the United States, with intent that such individual engage in prostitution, or in any sexual activity for which any person can be charged with a criminal offense, or attempts to do so, shall be fined under this title or imprisoned not more than 10 years, or both." 18 U.S.C.A. § 2421. This statute, first enacted as the Mann Act in 1910, originally prohibited taking women across state lines for "immoral purposes." Long viewed as a relic of a more prudish age, the law is now being applied to cases of human trafficking for sexual exploitation.

The Trafficking Victims Protection Act (TVPA), first enacted in 2000 and reauthorized twice since, represented an ambitious effort by the federal government to identify and assist victims of human trafficking. The Act also contains provisions to enhance the prosecution and punishment of human traffickers under existing criminal statutes. See 22 U.S.C.A. §§ 7101–7112 (2010).

## Indecent Exposure and Voyeurism

At common law, it was a misdemeanor for persons to expose their "private parts" intentionally in a public place. Today, statutes and local ordinances in most jurisdictions make it a misdemeanor to expose one's private parts to the view of another under offensive circumstances. However, such laws have been generally interpreted not to prohibit public exposure of the buttocks. See, e.g., *Duvallon v. District of Columbia*, 515 A.2d 724 (D.C. App. 1986). Frequently state statutes and local ordinances specify that the prohibited exposure must be in public or visible to the public. Questions are often raised as to what constitutes being "in public" or "visible to the public."

Some statutes proscribing indecent exposure do not include the requirement that the exposure must be open to the public. For example, in *People v. Neal*, 702 N.W.2d 696 (Mich. App. 2005), the defendant exposed his erect penis to a minor victim while they were in his home and not in a public place. The court held that the Michigan statute providing that "[a]ny person who shall knowingly make any open or indecent exposure of his or her person or of the person of another is guilty of a misdemeanor . . ." does not require that the offending act take place in public.

**indecent exposure** The intentional exposure in public of private areas of a person's body.

**lewd and lascivious conduct** Indecent exposure of a person's private parts in public; indecent touching or fondling of a child.

Several state courts have upheld laws criminalizing **indecent exposure** against a variety of constitutional challenges. See, e.g., *Keller v. State*, 738 P.2d 186 (Okla. Crim. App. 1987); *State v. Ludwig*, 468 So.2d 1151 (La. 1985). Frequently, the offense of indecent exposure is termed **lewd and lascivious conduct**. Because a person can expose himself or herself either accidentally or of necessity, laws generally

### CASE-IN-POINT

### Indecent Exposure

A man exposing himself in a second-story apartment in New Orleans was seen from below by persons in the apartment parking lot. He was prosecuted for indecent exposure under a statute that had been interpreted as criminalizing indecent exposure if it was viewable from any location open to the public. In upholding his conviction, the Louisiana Supreme Court noted that the parking lot from which the victims observed the man exposing himself was not enclosed, nor was it posted as private property, and was open to any visitors to the apartment complex.

*State v. Clark*, 372 So.2d 1218 (La. 1979).

provide that indecent exposure must be done willfully and in an offensive manner. See, e.g., *People v. Randall*, 711 P.2d 689 (Colo. 1985).

Often, statutes require that offensive exposure must be in the *presence* of another person. Interpreting the term "presence" has become problematic. In 1992, the Florida Supreme Court ruled that presence "encompasses sensory awareness as well as physical proximity." Consequently, the court reversed the conviction of a man who admitted to masturbating in the presence of his thirteen-month-old child. In the court's view, the child did not have "sensory awareness" of the act in question. *State v. Werner*, 609 So.2d 585 (Fla. 1992). The Supreme Court of Kansas took a contrasting view. In *State v. Bryan*, 130 P.3d 85 (Kan. 2006), the court held that there is no awareness requirement associated with the offense of publicly exposing a sex organ in the presence of a person.

## Erotic Dancing in Places of Public Accommodation

Generally, laws against indecent exposure are applied in situations where individuals expose themselves in public or in private to unwilling viewers. But what if the exposure takes place by mutual consent, such as in a nightclub that features nude dancing? Often regulation of "exotic dancing" is accomplished through local ordinances aimed at places of public accommodation that serve alcohol. The Supreme Court has recognized that exotic dancing is entitled to First Amendment protection under certain circumstances, but has also expressed a willingness to uphold reasonable regulations, especially involving establishments that serve alcoholic beverages. *Doran v. Salem Inn*, 422 U.S. 922, 95 S.Ct. 2561, 45 L.Ed.2d 648 (1975). In *Barnes v. Glen Theatre, Inc.*, 501 U.S. 560, 111 S.Ct. 2456, 115 L.Ed.2d 504 (1991), the Court upheld an Indiana statute requiring that nightclub dancers wear "pasties" and "G-strings" when they dance. In an opinion expressing the view of three justices, Chief Justice William H. Rehnquist observed that "Indiana's requirement that the dancers wear at least pasties and a G-string is modest, and the bare minimum necessary to achieve the state's purpose." 501 U.S. at 571, 111 S.Ct. at 2463, 115 L.Ed.2d at 515.

After the Supreme Court's decision in *Barnes v. Glen Theatre*, the City of Erie, Pennsylvania, adopted an ordinance making it an offense for anyone to "knowingly or intentionally appear in public in a state of nudity." To comply with the ordinance, erotic dancers were required to wear pasties and G-strings. The owners of Kandyland, a club that featured all-nude erotic dancers, filed suit in a state court to challenge the constitutionality of the new ordinance. The Court of Common Pleas declared the ordinance unconstitutional under the First Amendment, and the Pennsylvania Supreme Court agreed, concluding that the unstated purpose of

## JURISPRUDENCE

*Barnes v. Glen Theatre, Inc.*, 501 U.S. 560, 111 S.Ct. 2456, 115 L.Ed.2d 504 (1991).

Two Indiana business establishments, including Glen Theatre, wanted to "provide totally nude dancing as entertainment;" however, under the Indiana public indecency law, exotic dancers were required to "wear pasties and a G-string." As a result, Glen Theatre and individual dancers employed there "brought suit in the District Court to enjoin enforcement of the state law . . . asserting that the law's prohibition against total nudity in public places violates the First Amendment." The district court "held that the nude dancing involved here was not expressive conduct," but the Court of Appeals reversed holding "that nonobscene nude dancing performed for entertainment is protected expression, and that the statute was an improper infringement of that activity because its purpose was to prevent the message of eroticism and sexuality conveyed by the dancers." The Supreme Court reversed. Chief Justice Rehnquist and Justices O'Connor and Kennedy "concluded that the enforcement of Indiana's public indecency law to prevent totally nude dancing does not violate the First Amendment's guarantee of freedom of expression." Furthermore, they asserted that "the law is clearly within the State's constitutional power," and "it furthers a substantial governmental interest in protecting societal order and morality." The Chief Justice noted in his opinion that "public indecency statutes reflect moral disapproval of people appearing in the nude among strangers in public places, and this particular law follows a line of state laws, dating back to 1831, banning public nudity." Justice Scalia, concurring in judgment, concluded that the statute, "as a general law regulating conduct and not specifically directed at expression, either in practice or on its face, is not subject to normal First Amendment scrutiny, and should be upheld on the ground that moral opposition to nudity supplies a rational basis for its prohibition." Justice Souter, also concurring in judgment, "agreed that the nude dancing at issue here is subject to a degree of First Amendment protection," but concluded "that the State's interest in preventing the secondary effects of adult entertainment establishments—prostitution, sexual assaults, and other criminal activity—is sufficient to justify the law enforcement against nude dancing."

the ordinance was the suppression of expression. On certiorari, the U.S. Supreme Court reversed and upheld the ordinance. Writing for a plurality of justices, Justice Sandra Day O'Connor concluded that the requirement that dancers wear pasties and G-strings was "a minimal restriction" that left dancers "ample capacity" to convey their erotic messages. *City of Erie et al. v. Pap's A. M.*, 529 U.S. 277, 120 S.Ct. 1382, 146 L.Ed.2d 265 (2000).

## Nudity and Seminudity on Public Beaches

Historically, public nudity has been taboo in Western societies. Yet only a few states have imposed outright bans. Many states maintain that public nudity on beaches and other recreational areas violates laws proscribing lewd and lascivious conduct or indecent exposure. For example, in Florida, where public beaches are popular attractions, signs are commonly posted notifying beachgoers that nude sunbathing is a violation of Florida Statutes § 877.03. Actually, that law prohibits "such acts as are of a nature to corrupt the public morals, or outrage the sense of public decency, or affect the peace and quiet of persons who may witness them." In 1976 the Florida Supreme Court held that the legislative intent of the statute prohibits adult females from openly exposing their breasts on public beaches. *Moffett v. State*, 340 So.2d 1155 (Fla. 1976). Arrests under this provision are not common. In fact, Miami Beach and other Florida cities that attract large numbers of tourists have set aside specified areas where topless or nude sunbathing is permitted. In 2001 a Florida appellate court held that a state statute and a county ordinance that prohibited exposure of

CASE-IN-POINT

## "Up-skirt" Video Voyeurism

Tony O. Morris was convicted of "interference with privacy" under Minnesota Statutes § 609.746 (2000). The evidence showed that Morris carried a bag containing a concealed video camera into a J.C. Penney department store and surreptitiously positioned the lens underneath a sales clerk's skirt so as to photograph her underwear. Morris was sentenced to ninety days in jail and fined $1,000. On appeal, the conviction was affirmed. The appellate court concluded that "[b]ecause appellant surreptitiously positioned a video camera lens underneath [the victim's] skirt, a place where [the victim] had a reasonable expectation of privacy, so as to photograph the clothing covering the immediate area of the intimate parts of her body, with the intent to intrude upon or interfere with her privacy, he was lawfully found guilty of interference with privacy. . . ."

*State v. Morris*, 644 N.W.2d 114 (Minn. App. 2002).

the female breast in circumstances where the exposure of the male breast would not be prohibited did not violate the equal protection guarantee of the state constitution because the classification served an important governmental objective. *Frandsen v. County of Brevard*, 800 So.2d 757 (Fla. App. 2001). The Florida Supreme Court denied review. 828 So.2d 386.

## Voyeurism

**voyeurism** The practice of seeking sexual gratification by observing the naked bodies or sexual acts of others, usually from a hidden vantage point.

**Voyeurism** refers to obtaining sexual gratification from seeing another person's sexual organs or sexual activities. Historically voyeurism has been addressed under "Peeping Tom" statutes and ordinances based on a trespass theory. Modern photography and the availability to publish photos on the Internet have caused some states to revisit such prohibitions in order to protect the privacy of persons, not only in their homes but also in public where a person would ordinarily expect a reasonable degree of privacy.

Although most state statutes defining voyeurism prohibit nonconsensual viewing only in "private" places, Florida statutes now take a modern approach to prohibiting voyeurism. Section 810.14 provides, "A person commits the offense of voyeurism when he or she, with lewd, lascivious, or indecent intent, secretly observes, photographs, films, videotapes, or records another person when such other person is located in a dwelling, structure, or conveyance and such location provides a reasonable expectation of privacy." Another recently enacted statute makes it unlawful for any merchant to directly observe or make use of video cameras or other visual surveillance devices to observe or record customers in the merchant's dressing room, fitting room, changing room, or restroom when such room provides a reasonable expectation of privacy. West's Fla. Stat. Ann. § 877.26.

## | Obscenity and Pornography

**obscenity** Explicit sexual material that is patently offensive, appeals to a prurient or unnatural interest in sex, and lacks serious scientific, artistic, or literary content.

At common law, vulgar and obscene language and indecent public exhibitions were considered public nuisances, punishable as misdemeanors. Historically, federal and state governments in the United States passed laws banning various forms of **obscenity**. By the late 1800s, Congress had made it an offense to mail any "obscene, lewd or lascivious paper or writing" and provided that the word "obscene" should be given fully as broad a significance as it had at common law. The states and many municipalities also passed laws making the sale or distribution of obscene materials a crime, but seldom did these laws attempt to define obscenity. As questions arose, the courts tended to define obscenity as sexual or erotic speech or conduct. The word "obscene" came to mean something offensive to the senses—that is, repulsive, disgusting, foul, or filthy.

## Changing Constitutional Standards

As mass communications developed, laws banning obscene speech, materials, and performances became subject to scrutiny under the First Amendment. The Supreme Court's first direct encounter with regulating obscenity came in *Roth v. United States*, 354 U.S. 476, 77 S.Ct. 1304, 1 L.Ed.2d 1498 (1957). Roth was found guilty of sending erotic materials through the mail, and his conviction was affirmed on appeal. The Supreme Court granted review and held that obscenity was not constitutionally protected; rather, the Court viewed it as "utterly without redeeming social importance." After observing that "sex and obscenity are not synonymous," the Court said the test for determining obscenity was whether "to the average person applying contemporary community standards, the dominant theme of the material taken as a whole, appeals to the prurient interest." 354 U.S. at 489, 77 S.Ct. at 1311, 1 L.Ed.2d at 1509 (1957).

By the late 1950s, there was a flood of erotic materials on the market. *Roth* effectively made the definition of obscenity a matter of federal constitutional law. It also evidenced the Court's concern for First Amendment freedoms and for protecting the free flow of expression from local interpretations of what constituted obscenity. But under the *Roth* standards, law enforcement officers experienced great difficulty in enforcing obscenity laws.

**hard-core pornography** Material that is extremely graphic in its depiction of sexual conduct.

From 1957 to 1973, the Supreme Court granted review of several lower court decisions determining that particular books, plays, and movies were obscene, often explicating due process guidelines to be followed by lower courts in determining what constitutes obscenity. In 1964, Justice Potter Stewart, in expressing the view that obscenity is limited to **hard-core pornography**, made his oft-quoted remark on obscenity: "I know it when I see it." *Jacobellis v. Ohio*, 378 U.S. 184, 197, 84 S.Ct. 1676, 1683, 12 L.Ed.2d 793, 804 (1964) (Stewart, J. concurring).

## The *Miller* Test

When the Supreme Court decided the seminal case of *Miller v. California*, 413 U.S. 15, 93 S.Ct. 2607, 37 L.Ed.2d 419 (1973), it referred to "the intractable obscenity problem." 413 U.S. at 16, 93 S.Ct. at 2610, 37 L.Ed.2d at 426. In *Miller*, the defendant had mailed unsolicited material containing explicit sexual drawings in violation of a California law. A jury found him guilty, and an appellate court upheld the judgment without opinion. At the outset, Chief Justice Warren Burger reiterated that obscene materials were unprotected by the Constitution. Then the Court suggested that local juries could base their judgments on local and not national standards. Most significantly, the Court redefined the standards for determining obscenity, saying that the

**prurient interest** An excessive or unnatural interest in sex.

**patently offensive** That which is obviously offensive or disgusting.

basic guidelines for the trier of fact must be: (1) whether "the average person, applying contemporary community standards" would find that the work, taken as a whole, appeals to the **prurient interest**; (b) whether the work depicts or describes, in a **patently offensive** way, sexual conduct specifically defined by the applicable state law; and (c) whether the work, taken as a whole, lacks serious literary, artistic, political, or scientific value. 413 U.S. at 24, 93 S.Ct. at 2614, 37 L.Ed.2d at 431.

Finally, the Court expressly rejected any requirement that the challenged materials be found to be "utterly without redeeming social importance." 413 U.S. at 24, 93 S.Ct. at 2614, 37 L.Ed.2d at 431. The Court gave examples of "patently offensive" by saying it meant "representations or descriptions of ultimate sexual acts, normal or perverted, actual or simulated . . . , representations or descriptions of masturbation, excretory functions, and lewd exhibition of genitals." 413 U.S. at 25, 93 S.Ct. at 2615, 37 L.Ed.2d at 431. The Court made it clear that no one would be subject to prosecution unless the materials alleged to be obscene described patently offensive, "hardcore" sexual conduct.

In a companion case, *Paris Adult Theatre I v. Slaton*, 413 U.S. 49, 93 S.Ct. 2628, 37 L.Ed.2d 446 (1973), the Court observed that the states have a right to "maintain a decent society" and may challenge obscene material even if it is shown only to consenting adults.

## Significant Post-*Miller* Developments

*Miller* may have clarified the tests for obscenity, but it did not satisfy those who sought to ban pornographic materials. For example, *Carnal Knowledge*, a very successful movie in the early 1970s, was held not to be obscene under the *Miller* test. There were scenes in which "ultimate sexual acts" were understood to be taking place; however, the camera did not focus on the bodies of the actors, nor was there any exhibition of genitals during such scenes. The Court said that the film was not a "portrayal of hard core sexual conduct for its own sake, and for the ensuing commercial gain" and did not depict sexual conduct in a patently offensive way. *Jenkins v. Georgia*, 418 U.S. 153, 161, 94 S.Ct. 2750, 2755, 41 L.Ed.2d 642, 650 (1974).

**JURISPRUDENCE**

*Jenkins v. Georgia*, 418 U.S. 153, 161, 94 S.Ct. 2750, 2755, 41 L.Ed.2d 642, 650 (1974).

Billy Jenkins was convicted, prior to the Supreme Court's decision in *Miller v. California*, of "violating Georgia's obscenity statute for showing the film 'Carnal Knowledge' in a motion picture theater." The jury had been instructed on obscenity under that statute, which defined obscene material in terms similar to the definition in *Memoirs v. Massachusetts*. The Georgia Supreme Court affirmed Jenkins's conviction. The Supreme Court held that Jenkins was "entitled to any benefit available" under the Court's prior decision in *Miller* since his conviction was on appeal at the time the *Miller* opinion was announced. Justice Rehnquist, writing for the majority, held "there is no constitutional requirement that juries be instructed in state obscenity cases to apply the standards of a hypothetical state-wide community . . . and jurors may properly be instructed to apply 'community standards,' without a specification of the 'community' by the trial court." However, Rehnquist went on to say that "juries do not have unbridled discretion in determining what is 'patently offensive,' since 'no one will be subject to prosecution for the sale or exposure of obscene materials that do not depict or describe patently offensive 'hard core sexual conduct'.'" The Supreme Court held that the film was not obscene under the First and Fourteenth Amendments. The Court noted in this particular film that "the camera does not focus on the bodies of actors during scenes of 'ultimate sexual acts', nor are the actor's genitals exhibited during those scenes. The film shows occasional nudity, but nudity alone does not render material obscene."

**CASE-IN-POINT**

### Obscenity

In the first federal appeals court decision applying the *Miller v. California* obscenity test to a musical composition, the Eleventh Circuit Court of Appeals ruled that the recording *As Nasty as They Wanna Be* by 2 Live Crew was not obscene. The Eleventh Circuit ruled that even assuming the work was "patently offensive" and appealed to a "prurient interest," the trial judge erred in concluding, simply on the basis of his own listening to a tape recording, that the work lacked "serious artistic value."

*Luke Records, Inc. v. Navarro*, 960 F.2d 134 (11th Cir. 1992).

In *Pope v. Illinois*, 481 U.S. 497, 107 S.Ct. 1918, 95 L.Ed.2d 439 (1987), the Supreme Court said that the application of "contemporary community standards" is appropriate in evaluating the first two prongs of the *Miller* test for obscenity— that is, the work's appeal to the prurient interest and its patent offensiveness. However, the Court concluded that the third prong must be determined on an objective basis, with the proper inquiry being not whether an ordinary member of any given community would find serious literary, artistic, political, or scientific value in allegedly obscene material, but whether a reasonable person would find such value in the material taken as a whole. 481 U.S. at 500, 107 S.Ct. at 1921, 95 L.Ed.2d at 445.

Noting that the First Amendment protection extends to rap music and is not weakened because the music takes on an unpopular or even dangerous viewpoint, in 2000 a federal district court in Louisiana found that "gangsta rap" did not lack serious artistic value so as to constitute obscene speech devoid of First Amendment protection. *Torries v. Hebert*, 111 F.Supp.2d 806 (W.D. La. 2000).

## State and Local Regulation of Obscenity

States, of course, may interpret their own constitutions to allow greater freedom of expression than is allowed under the current federal constitutional interpretations. In that vein, in 1987 the Oregon Supreme Court held that "any person can write, print, read, say, show or sell anything to a consenting adult even though that expression may be generally or universally condemned as 'obscene'." *State v. Henry*, 732 P.2d 9, 18 (Or. 1987).

Some states classify violations of their obscenity statutes by degree. For example, in New York a person is guilty of obscenity in the third degree when, knowing its content and character, he or she

1. Promotes, or possesses with intent to promote, any obscene material; or
2. Produces, presents or directs an obscene performance or participates in a portion thereof which is obscene or which contributes to its obscenity.

McKinney's N.Y. Penal Law § 235.05.

A person is guilty of obscenity in the second degree "when he commits the crime of obscenity in the third degree . . . and has been previously convicted of obscenity in the third degree." § 235.06. A person is guilty of obscenity in the first degree "when, knowing its content and character, he wholesale promotes or possesses with intent to wholesale promote, any obscene material." § 235.07. New York law makes third-degree obscenity a misdemeanor, whereas second-degree or first-degree obscenity is a felony.

States generally set higher penalties for exposing juveniles to pictures or shows where obscenity or even pornography is involved, and some state laws have been updated to proscribe disseminating indecent material to minors through computers. For example, McKinney's N.Y. Penal Law § 235.22 provides that disseminating indecent material to minors in the first degree is a class D felony. In *People v. Foley*, 731 N.E.2d 123 (N.Y. 2000), the New York Court of Appeals, the state's highest court, upheld the constitutionality of § 235.22 against challenges that it is vague and that, by its content-based restrictions, it violates the First Amendment. The court distinguished its decision from the U.S. Supreme Court's decision in *Reno v. American Civil Liberties Union*, 521 U.S. 844, 117 S.Ct. 2329, 138 L.Ed.2d 874 (1997). In *Reno*, the Court struck down the Communications Decency Act (47 U.S.C.A. § 223), which prohibited the knowing transmission of "obscene or indecent" comments to any person under the age of eighteen. (We discuss the *Reno* decision in a later topic in this chapter.)

## Defenses to Charges of Obscenity

New York law provides a defense for those charged with obscenity if they can establish that the allegedly obscene material was disseminated to or performed for an audience of persons having scientific, educational, governmental, or other similar justification for possessing or viewing the material. McKinney's N.Y. Penal Law § 235.15. Moreover, it is a defense for disseminating indecent material to minors if the defendant had reasonable cause to believe that the minor involved was seventeen years old or older and exhibited official documentation to the defendant to establish that fact. McKinney's N.Y. Penal Law § 235.23. This latter provision was undoubtedly inserted to protect theater personnel from conviction on a strict liability basis.

## Problems of Enforcement

Police and prosecutors often experience difficulty in determining what is to be considered obscene based on "contemporary community standards." Juries in most instances now determine the issue of obscenity simply by reviewing the material. As a result, it is not unusual for a given work to be determined obscene by a jury in one locality and not obscene by another jury in a different locality. For example, the rock musical stage production *Hair* was found not to be obscene by a federal court in Georgia. *Southeastern Promotions, Ltd. v. Atlanta*, 334 F. Supp. 634 (N.D. Ga. 1971). The following year, it was found to be obscene by another federal court in Tennessee, but this decision was reversed by the Supreme Court. *Southeastern Promotions, Inc. v. Conrad*, 341 F. Supp. 465 (E.D. Tenn. 1972), aff'd, 486 F.2d 894 (6th Cir. 1973), rev'd, 420 U.S. 546, 95 S.Ct. 1239, 43 L.Ed.2d 448 (1975).

Legal problems incident to searches and seizures of allegedly obscene materials can be very technical. Because books, movies, and even live performances are presumptively protected by the First Amendment, the Supreme Court has held that police must obtain a search warrant before conducting searches and seizures of such materials. *Roaden v. Kentucky*, 413 U.S. 496, 93 S.Ct. 2796, 37 L.Ed.2d 757 (1973). However, the Court has explained that the Fourth Amendment does not prohibit undercover police officers from purchasing allegedly obscene materials, because such a purchase would not constitute a "seizure." *Maryland v. Macon*, 472 U.S. 463, 105 S.Ct. 2778, 86 L.Ed.2d 370 (1985).

## Pornography on the Internet

Amid growing public concerns about the prevalence of sexually explicit material on the Internet, and especially the relatively easy access of children to such material, Congress enacted the Communications Decency Act of 1996 (CDA). One provision, codified at 47 U.S.C.A. § 223(a) (Supp. 2000), prohibited the knowing transmission of obscene or indecent messages to any recipient under eighteen years of age. In *Reno v. American Civil Liberties Union*, 521 U.S. 844, 117 S.Ct. 2329, 138 L.Ed.2d 874 (1997), the Supreme Court struck down this provision on First Amendment grounds. Focusing on the statute's proscription of "indecent" transmissions, the Court concluded that the CDA presented a real threat of censoring expression entitled to First Amendment protection. Thus, the Court held that the statute was unconstitutionally overbroad.

In an attempt to overcome some of the constitutional defects of the CDA, in 1998 Congress passed the Child Online Protection Act (COPA). 47 U.S.C.A. § 231. COPA states,

> Whoever knowingly and with knowledge of the character of the material, in interstate or foreign commerce by means of the World Wide Web, makes any communication for commercial purposes that is available to any minor and that includes any material that is harmful to minors shall be fined not more than $50,000, imprisoned not more than 6 months, or both.

Subsection (6) of COPA relies on "community standards" to determine whether materials are harmful to minors. Lower federal courts enjoined enforcement of COPA on the ground that it improperly relied on community standards to identify what material is harmful to minors and was unconstitutionally overbroad in violation of the First Amendment. The Supreme Court then held that COPA's reliance on community standards did not by itself render the statute substantially overbroad for First Amendment purposes; however, it remanded the case to the Third Circuit Court of Appeals to determine whether COPA suffers from substantial overbreadth for other reasons. *Ashcroft v. American Civil Liberties Union*, 535 U.S. 564, 122 S.Ct. 1700, 152 L.Ed.2d 771 (2002). On March 6, 2003, the Third Circuit found that the plaintiffs established a substantial likelihood of prevailing on their claim that COPA is unconstitutionally overbroad and continued a preliminary injunction against enforcement of the act. 322 F.3d 240 (3d Cir. 2003). The Supreme Court granted review and held that the district court did not abuse its discretion when it entered the preliminary injunction. However, the Court remanded the case to enable the district court to consider whether recent technological developments in the Internet and recent Congressional enactments might enable the government to meet its constitutional burden of showing that COPA is the least restrictive alternative available to accomplish Congress's goal. *Ashcroft v. American Civil Liberties Union*, 542 U.S. 656, 124 S.Ct. 2783, 159 L.Ed.2d 690 (2004).

On March 22, 2007, a federal district judge in Philadelphia again struck down COPA, finding it to be impermissibly vague and overbroad and not narrowly tailored to the compelling interest of the government in protecting children. In his final order, Judge Lowell A. Reed, Jr., concluded that COPA "is facially violative of the First and Fifth Amendments of the United States Constitution" and ordered that the government is "PERMANENTLY ENJOINED from enforcing or prosecuting matters premised upon 47 U.S.C. § 231 at any time for any conduct." *American Civil Liberties Union v. Gonzales*, 478 F.Supp.2d 775 (E.D. Pa. 2007). On July 22, 2008 the U.S. Court of Appeals for the Third Circuit upheld the district court, *American Civil*

*Liberties Union v. Mukasey*, 532 F.3d 181 (2008). When the Supreme Court denied review in *Mukasey v. ACLU*, 555 U.S. 1137, 129 S.Ct. 1032, 173 L.Ed.2d 293 (2009), the decade-long battle over COPA finally ended in defeat for the federal government.

## Child Pornography

**child pornography** Material depicting persons under the age of legal majority in sexual poses or acts.

In *New York v. Ferber*, 458 U.S. 747, 102 S.Ct. 3348, 73 L.Ed.2d 1113 (1982), the Supreme Court unanimously held that **child pornography**, like obscenity, is unprotected by the First Amendment to the Constitution. The Court upheld a New York law prohibiting persons from distributing materials that depict children engaging in lewd sex. The Court found such laws valid even if the material does not appeal to the prurient interest of the average person and is not portrayed in a patently offensive manner. The Court found a compelling state interest in protecting the well-being of children and perceived no value in permitting performances and photo reproductions of children engaged in lewd sexual conduct.

Most states have also criminalized the possession of child pornography. For example, Ohio law makes it a crime to "possess or view any material or performance that shows a minor who is not the person's child or ward in a state of nudity." Ohio Rev. Code Ann. 2907.323(A)(3) (Supp. 1989). In 1990, the Supreme Court upheld this prohibition against a constitutional challenge that the statute was overbroad. *Osborne v. Ohio*, 495 U.S. 103, 110 S.Ct. 1691, 109 L.Ed.2d 98 (1990). Together, the *Ferber* and *Osborne* decisions suggested that the Supreme Court would not be sympathetic to any First Amendment claim that would protect from criminal prosecution those who produce, distribute, or consume child pornography.

---

## JURISPRUDENCE

*New York v. Ferber*, 458 U.S. 747, 102 S.Ct. 3348, 73 L.Ed.2d 1113 (1982).

New York passed a statute that made it a crime to "knowingly promote sexual performances by children under the age of 16 by distributing material which depicts such performances." Paul Ferber, "the proprietor of a Manhattan bookstore specializing in sexually oriented products, sold two films to an undercover police officer" that "depicted young boys masturbating." Ferber was indicted on two counts under the statute and two additional counts under a second statute "controlling dissemination of child pornography." Ferber was acquitted of the two counts of promoting an obscene sexual performance, but was found guilty of the two counts related to the dissemination of child pornography, "which did not require proof that the films were obscene." The Appellate Division of the New York State Supreme Court affirmed Ferber's convictions,

but the New York Court of Appeals reversed, holding that the statute "violated the First Amendment." Ferber did not argue "that the State is unjustified in pursuing those who distribute child pornography." Instead, Ferber argued "that it is enough for the State to prohibit the distribution of materials that are legally obscene under the *Miller* test," which is "whether a work, taken as a whole, appeals to the prurient interest of the average person bears no connection to the issue of whether a child has been physically or psychologically harmed in the production of the work." The Court held the statute "not substantially overbroad" and felt "it unnecessary to consider its application to material that does not depict sexual conduct of a type that New York may restrict consistent with the First Amendment." The Court held "as applied to Ferber, the statute does not violate the First Amendment . . . [under] the Fourteenth Amendment."

Having determined that virtual child pornography is as destructive as pornography using real children, and in an effort to keep up with developing technology, Congress enacted the Child Pornography Prevention Act of 1996 (CPPA). 18 U.S.C.A. § 2252A. The Act prohibited any type of virtual or simulated child pornography, even if real children were not involved. In *Ashcroft v. Free Speech Coalition*, 535 U.S. 234, 122 S.Ct. 1389, 152 L.Ed.2d 403 (2002), the Supreme Court surprised some observers in striking down the prohibition of virtual child pornography. The Court noted that in upholding the ban on child pornography *Ferber* focused on how the depictions of child pornography were made, not on what was communicated, and held that *virtual* child pornography is distinguishable from *real* child pornography, which, under *New York v. Ferber*, supra, may be banned without regard to whether it depicts works of value. The Court found that the ban on virtual child pornography in the CPPA abridges the freedom to engage in a substantial amount of lawful speech, and thus is overbroad and therefore unconstitutional under the First Amendment. Three justices dissented from this ruling.

# Gambling

**gambling** Operating or playing a game for money in the expectation of gaining more than the amount played.

Traditionally, to gamble has meant to risk money on an event, chance, or contingency in the hope of realizing a gain. See *State v. Stripling*, 21 So. 409 (Ala. 1897). The common law did not regard gambling as an offense. However, many of the new American states, by either constitution or statute, made all or certain forms of **gambling** illegal. Today, federal laws and a variety of state statutes and local ordinances prohibit gambling. Laws regulating gambling come under the police power of the state. The U.S. Supreme Court has recognized that there is no constitutional right to gamble. *Lewis v. United States*, 348 U.S. 419, 75 S.Ct. 415, 99 L.Ed. 475 (1955).

**lottery** A drawing in which prizes are distributed to winners selected by lot from among those who have participated by paying consideration.

Bingo, craps, baccarat, poker, raffles, bookmaking, and slot machines are just a few common forms of gambling. Gambling also includes betting on sports events and card games. Many forms of gambling are legal; therefore, when considering gambling, we must separate the legal from the illegal. For example, those who pay something of value to take a chance to win a prize in a **lottery** are gambling. In many jurisdictions, this is a criminal offense. Yet in several states, lotteries are not only legal—they are an important source of public revenue. In effect, it is only unregulated gambling that is illegal. A common form of unregulated gambling is "numbers." To play, you place a bet on a number with the hope that it will correspond to a preselected number. The **numbers racket** is widespread and, along with prostitution, is a major source of income for organized crime.

**numbers racket** A common form of illegal gambling in which one places a bet on a number with the hope that it will correspond to a preselected number.

## What Constitutes Gambling?

**consideration, prize, and chance** The legal elements that constitute gambling under most statutes that make it an offense to gamble.

To constitute gambling, gaming activity must generally include three elements: **consideration, prize, and chance**. Retail stores conduct a variety of promotional schemes; local carnivals and fairs offer opportunities to play a variety of games for prizes. When are they gambling, and when are they games of skill? And if they are games of skill, are they exempt from laws prohibiting gambling? Some statutes regulating gambling provide the answer. In other instances, courts may be called on to determine whether a particular activity offends a statutory prohibition against gambling.

### What Constitutes an Illegal Gaming Machine?

The Michigan Liquor Control Commission imposed a $250 fine on the Sanford Eagles Club for having a "video poker" machine on its premises. The machine had five windows, and when a quarter was deposited, a playing card appeared in each window. Essentially, the contestant played a game of five-card draw against the machine. A "winner" could gain credits entitling the player to free replays based on a random "reshuffling" of the cards. After administrative and judicial hearings, the court of appeals held that the machine was not an illegal gaming device because there was no monetary payoff. The Michigan Supreme Court reversed. The court based its decision on a provision of the statute addressing gambling devices that exempted mechanical amusement devices that reward a player with replays as long as the device is not allowed to accumulate more than fourteen replays at one time. Because the video poker machine at issue in this case permitted the player to accumulate more than fourteen replays, it did not fall within the statutory exemption.

*Automatic Music and Vending Corp. v. Liquor Control Comm.*, 396 N.W.2d 204 (Mich. 1986).

Most statutes prohibiting gambling are interpreted to exclude athletics or other contests in which participants pit their physical or mental skills against one another for a prize. Courts tend to be practical in their interpretations. For example, an Ohio appellate court found that a pinball machine that allowed the outcome of its operation to be determined largely by the skill of the user was not "a game of chance," and the pinball operators were not in violation of the Ohio gambling statute. *Progress Vending, Inc. v. Department of Liquor Control*, 394 N.E.2d 324 (Ohio App. 1978).

## Statutory Regulation of Gambling

A federal statute called the Travel Act, 18 U.S.C.A. § 1952, prohibits interstate travel in aid of gambling. The act is not aimed at local criminal activity; rather, its purpose is to attack crime that has a definite interstate aspect. *United States v. O'Dell*, 671 F.2d 191 (6th Cir. 1982).

Many states broadly proscribe gambling much the same as Florida law, which provides:

> Whoever plays or engages in any game at cards, keno, roulette, faro or other game of chance, at any place, by any device whatever, for money or other thing of value, shall be guilty of a misdemeanor of the second degree. West's Fla. Stat. Ann. § 849.08.

Typically, Florida law creates certain exemptions. Nonprofit organizations are permitted to conduct bingo games under strict regulations, § 849.0931, and charitable and nonprofit organizations are allowed to conduct certain drawings by chance, § 849.0935. Subject to specific restrictions, certain retail merchandising promotions with prizes awarded to persons selected by lot are permitted. § 849.092. Another exception allows penny-ante card games with participants age eighteen or older provided that the games are conducted in a dwelling in which the winnings of any player in a single round or game do not exceed $10 in value. § 849.085.

Where gambling is prohibited, states customarily make it unlawful to possess gambling devices and provide for their confiscation. See, e.g., West's Fla. Stat. Ann. §§ 849.231, 849.232.

## Prosecutorial Problems and Defenses

Because of the consensual nature of gambling, apprehension of violators largely depends on the use of informants by police. Procedures for obtaining search and arrest warrants are technical and require close adherence to Fourth Amendment standards. In most instances, the prosecution must prove a consideration, a prize, and a chance; however, some statutes have eliminated the consideration requirement. If the statute prohibiting gambling makes intent an element of the offense, the prosecution must prove the defendant's intent; otherwise, it is sufficient merely to prove the act of gambling.

Texas law makes it an offense to bet on results of games, contests, political nominations, or elections or to play games with cards and dice. See Vernon's Tex. Penal Code Ann. § 47.02(a). The Texas legislature has taken a pragmatic approach by providing that it is a defense to prosecution under that section of the statute if

> (1) the actor engaged in gambling in a private place; (2) no person received any economic benefit other than personal winnings; and (3) except for the advantage of skill or luck, the risks of losing and the chances of winning were the same for all participants. Vernon's Tex. Penal Code Ann. § 47.02(b).

Section 47.02(c) provides that it is a defense to prosecution if the actor reasonably believed that the gambling conduct was permitted under bingo or a charitable raffle or occurred under a lottery approved by a parks and wilderness agency for determination of hunting privileges.

In some instances a defendant charged with gambling might succeed in establishing entrapment, a defense discussed in Chapter 14.

## The Paradox of Gambling Laws

The law on gambling seems paradoxical. Some laws authorize nonprofit organizations to conduct certain forms of gambling that are otherwise forbidden. In some states, people can legally bet at dog tracks and horse tracks, yet may still be prosecuted for betting in their own homes on the World Series or the Kentucky Derby. Many reformers contend that present laws are ineffective to suppress gambling. Instead, they claim these laws actually lend support to the activities of organized crime.

Certain forms of legalized gambling, particularly state lotteries and state-franchised dog and horse tracks, have become increasingly acceptable. Yet unregulated forms of gambling will most likely continue to be prohibited in most instances. In any event, if inroads are to be made in controlling unregulated gambling, enforcement efforts must be directed primarily toward gambling activity that is under the control of organized crime syndicates.

Today, gambling via the Internet is widespread and very easily accessible. Because gambling websites tend to be hosted on servers located in foreign countries, prosecution of those who operate the sites is not possible. And it is very difficult to obtain the identities of persons in this country who use the sites. Thus, prosecutions for Internet-based gambling are extremely rare.

# Animal Cruelty

Today there are a number of interest groups advocating the cause of "animal rights." Domestic animals do not have rights as such under American law. Nevertheless they can be, and in many instances are, protected by law. For example, the Tennessee Code provides:

> (a) A person commits an offense who intentionally or knowingly:
>
> (1) Tortures, maims or grossly overworks an animal;
>
> (2) Fails unreasonably to provide necessary food, water, care or shelter for an animal in the person's custody;
>
> (3) Abandons unreasonably an animal in the person's custody;
>
> (4) Transports or confines an animal in a cruel manner; or
>
> (5) Inflicts burns, cuts, lacerations, or other injuries or pain, by any method, including blistering compounds, to the legs or hooves of horses in order to make them sore for any purpose including, but not limited to, competition in horse shows and similar events.
>
> (b) It is a defense to prosecution under this section that the person was engaged in accepted veterinary practices, medical treatment by the owner or with the owner's consent, or bona fide experimentation for scientific research. Tenn. Code Ann. § 39-14-202.

Violation of these animal cruelty laws is a misdemeanor; however, a second or subsequent conviction for cruelty to animals is a felony.

Tennessee law also proscribes cockfighting, dog fighting, and other forms of animal fighting, Tenn. Code Ann. § 39-14-203, as well as the intentional killing of animals belonging to other persons, except where necessary to protect oneself, Tenn. Code Ann. § 39-14-205. There is also a statute governing offenses involving farm animals and animal research facilities. Tenn. Code Ann. § 39-14-803. Tennessee law classifies all of these offenses as crimes against property, but these behaviors are prohibited because people are repulsed by the wanton or unnecessary infliction of suffering on animals.

When Atlanta Falcons star quarterback Michael Vick was arrested and charged by federal authorities with conspiracy for his alleged role in a commercial dog-fighting operation during the summer of 2007, the nation became aware that Congress has also enacted legislation prohibiting animal fighting. The statute, codified at 7 U.S.C.A. § 2156, makes it a crime "for any person to knowingly sponsor or exhibit an animal in an animal fighting venture, if any animal in the venture was moved in interstate or foreign commerce." 7 U.S.C.A. § 2156(a)(1). Vick, who ultimately pleaded guilty to conspiracy and other related charges, was sentenced to twenty-three months in federal prison.

# Alcohol-Related Offenses

Alcohol is the oldest and most widely abused drug known to mankind. Nearly 2000 years B.C., the Code of Hammurabi regulated commercial establishments where alcoholic beverages were consumed. In Judeo-Christian culture, consumption of alcoholic beverages was tolerated, even encouraged, and wine took on a ceremonial importance in Judaism and a sacramental importance in Christianity. However, Judeo-Christian culture frowned upon drunkenness. Islam, which dates from the seventh century A.D., has from its inception prohibited the consumption of alcohol.

In England, the common law had little to say about alcohol, except that drunkenness was not regarded as a defense to a criminal prosecution (see Chapter 14).

However, in 1603 an English court took the view that not only was intoxication no defense, but it was a wrong in itself in the sense that it aggravated a crime committed. *Beverly's Case*, 4 Co. Rep. 125 (1603).

In colonial America, alcohol use was very widespread, the favorite libations being beer, ale, and rum. In 1697 New York adopted the first law requiring that drinking establishments be closed on Sundays. The sale of alcohol was prohibited altogether by the State of Georgia in 1735, but this early experiment in "prohibition" proved unsuccessful and was repealed after only seven years. The rise of evangelical Protestantism in the early nineteenth century led to the temperance movement, which condemned the use of alcohol, and by the mid-1800s, thirteen states had enacted laws prohibiting the sale of alcohol. The Civil War dealt a setback to the temperance movement, but the movement was revitalized in the early twentieth century as women became politically active and acquired the right to vote.

## "Prohibition"

In response to growing, but far from unanimous, public sentiment, Congress proposed the Eighteenth Amendment to the U.S. Constitution, which was ratified by the states in 1919. This amendment, widely referred to as "Prohibition," made unlawful the "manufacture, sale, or transportation of intoxicating liquors" within the United States. Prohibition actually began with the passage of the National Prohibition Act of 1920, 41 Stat. 305, better known as the Volstead Act, which implemented the Eighteenth Amendment to the Constitution.

Prohibition was widely violated and contributed greatly to the development of organized crime syndicates in this country. Rates of murder and other violent crimes rose dramatically during Prohibition—and then declined steadily after Prohibition was repealed. Many commentators believe that Prohibition also weakened public respect for the law, the courts, and law enforcement agencies. Jury nullification was common during Prohibition, as citizens were reluctant to convict people for doing something (albeit illegal) they themselves did on a regular basis. By the beginning of the 1930s, public opinion demanded that Prohibition be repealed.

Ultimately, Prohibition was repealed by the Twenty-First Amendment, ratified in 1933. Under the Twenty-First Amendment, however, state and local governments retain the authority to ban or regulate the manufacture, sale, and use of alcohol within their borders. As the U.S. Supreme Court recognized in *California Retail Liquor Dealers Association v. Midcal Aluminum, Inc.*, 445 U.S. 97, 110, 100 S.Ct. 937, 946, 63 L.Ed.2d 233, 246 (1980), the "Twenty-First Amendment grants the States virtually complete control over whether to permit importation or sale of liquor and how to structure the liquor distribution system." Indeed, there are still a number of so-called "dry counties" throughout the United States, mainly in the South and Midwest, where the sale of all or some alcoholic beverages is prohibited. Although no state has chosen to ban the sale of alcohol altogether, all states regulate the sale and use of alcoholic beverages and retain a number of alcohol-related offenses.

## Offenses Related to the Consumption of Alcohol by Minors

All states prohibit minors from purchasing, possessing, and consuming alcoholic beverages and also make it an offense for an adult to sell, serve, or otherwise provide alcohol to a minor. Such offenses are misdemeanors, but the recent trend is to punish these offenses severely. For example, Texas law makes furnishing alcohol to a minor a class A misdemeanor punishable by up to one year in jail and a fine of up to $4,000. Texas Alcoholic Beverages Code § 106.03(c). However, it is not a strict liability offense; an adult who furnishes alcohol to a minor is not guilty of a crime if the minor uses a plausible but false identification card to represent himself or herself as an adult. Texas Alcoholic Beverages Code § 106.03(b).

Although states are free to set their own drinking ages, Congress has used its considerable fiscal power to induce states to raise the drinking age to twenty-one. Under 23 U.S.C.A. § 158, the Secretary of Transportation is required to withhold a percentage of a state's otherwise allocable federal highway funds if the state does not establish a minimum age of twenty-one for "the purchase or public possession" of alcoholic beverages. The act has effectively established twenty-one as the minimum age for drinking. In *South Dakota v. Dole*, 483 U.S. 203, 107 S.Ct. 2793, 97 L.Ed.2d. 171 (1987), the Supreme Court upheld this measure as a valid exercise of congressional spending power.

## Public Intoxication

**public drunkenness** The offense of appearing in public while intoxicated.

Laws and ordinances making **public drunkenness** an offense have long been enforced by all jurisdictions, with most states and municipalities simply providing that whoever shall become intoxicated from the voluntary use of intoxicating liquors shall be punished. The offense merely involves a person being found in a public place in a state of intoxication. This offense is usually classified as a minor misdemeanor. A common police practice has been to take offenders into custody and release them once they have sobered up, a practice sometimes described as a "revolving door." In a great many cases, people who are repeatedly arrested for public intoxication suffer from alcoholism and are in need of treatment. For such individuals, the application of a criminal sanction is not likely to curb their unlawful behavior.

There is a growing awareness that alcoholism is a disease, and many have argued that the criminal law is an inappropriate mechanism to deal with it. In addition, some reformers have contended that criminalizing the public presence of an intoxicated person is contrary to the Eighth Amendment's prohibition of cruel and unusual punishments. However, the Supreme Court has declined to accept such a view. Instead, in *Powell v. Texas*, 392 U.S. 514, 88 S.Ct. 2145, 20 L.Ed.2d 1254 (1968), the Court upheld a public intoxication law. In effect, the Court ruled that the defendant, Powell, was not being punished for his status as an alcoholic but rather for his presence in a public place in an inebriated condition.

In recent years, some states have enacted statutes directing police officers to take persons found intoxicated in public places to treatment facilities rather than to incarcerate them. Consistent with this approach, many statutes now criminalize only disorderly intoxication. This newer offense involves the offender's being intoxicated in a public place or on a public conveyance and endangering the safety of others, not merely being in a state of intoxication in public. See, e.g., Vernon's Tex. Penal Code § 49.02. In 1992 a Texas appellate court ruled that a police officer had sufficient probable cause for a warrantless arrest for public intoxication. The officer believed that the defendant could have fled from the scene, posing a danger to himself and others. Witnesses testified that the defendant ran into a parked car while intoxicated. *Segura v. State*, 826 S.W.2d 178 (Tex. App. 1992).

## Public Intoxication

Joseph W. Findlay, Jr. was convicted of the offense of public intoxication and was fined $25.00. At trial in Tulsa Municipal Court, the arresting officer testified that he had been called to a Seven-Eleven store at approximately 3:00 A.M. There he observed Findlay "leaning against a food counter . . . eating Fritos with a can of dip opened beside him; he was staring with a dazed look on his face; his eyes were dilated and very bloodshot; his face was dirty; and, he had an odor of alcohol on his breath." The officer also testified that the defendant's speech was slurred and that he staggered when he attempted to walk. Testifying in his own defense, Findlay admitted to having consumed three double scotches between 11:00 P.M. and 2:30 A.M. and three beers earlier in the evening. He also testified that he took a prescription drug to control stomach pains and that the drug made him "kind of woozy." The defense also called to the stand a pharmacist who testified that the drug Findlay had taken was known to cause stupor, which might account for the staggering and slurred speech.

On appeal, Findlay claimed, among other things, that the ordinance under which he was convicted was unconstitutionally vague. That ordinance provided, "It shall be an offense for any person to be drunk or in a state of intoxication in any street, avenue, alley, park or other place open to the public." The Oklahoma Court of Criminal Appeals affirmed the conviction and upheld the ordinance. In rejecting the constitutional challenge the court opined, "The condition of being in a state of intoxication is a matter of general knowledge, the meaning of which is sufficiently 'settled and commonly understood' so that definite and sensible definition may be made of the words of the ordinance in question." The court observed, "This is true whether the term "intoxication" is used in reference to intoxication as a result of consumption of intoxicating liquor or any other intoxicating substance."

*Findlay v. City of Tulsa*, 561 P.2d 980 (Okla. Cr. App. 1977).

## Driving Under the Influence

The carnage on the American highways attests to the urgent need for states to take stern measures to keep drunk drivers off the road, and all states have enacted laws attempting to accomplish this goal. Perhaps these measures contributed to the decline from over 1.5 million arrests for driving while under the influence of intoxicants in 1985 to approximately 871,000 in 2000, a decrease of 41 percent (U.S. Department of Justice, Bureau of Justice Statistics, *Sourcebook of Criminal Justice Statistics* 2001, p. 358).

**driving while intoxicated (DWI)** The crime of driving while intoxicated by alcohol or drugs.

**driving under the influence (DUI)** The crime of driving under the influence of alcohol or drugs.

**driving with an unlawful blood-alcohol level (DUBAL)** The offense of operating a motor vehicle while one's blood-alcohol level is higher than allowed by law.

The "classic" offense in this area is **driving while intoxicated (DWI)** or, more accurately, operating a motor vehicle while intoxicated. In the 1950s the laws in many states stipulated that a level of 0.15 percent or more alcohol in the bloodstream evidenced intoxication. In the 1960s and 1970s, many jurisdictions expanded the offense to prohibit **driving under the influence (DUI)** of intoxicating liquors or drugs. DWI and DUI laws sometimes allowed a defendant to avoid conviction because of the ambiguity of his or her subjective behavior. In response to this problem, most states have modified their statutes to prohibit **driving with an unlawful blood-alcohol level (DUBAL)**. For many years most states defined "an unlawful blood-alcohol level" as 0.10 percent or more alcohol in the bloodstream. Today, as a result of federal fiscal incentives, all fifty states have lowered the prohibited blood-alcohol level to 0.08 percent. Moreover, most states now impose harsher penalties on DUBAL offenders whose blood-alcohol levels are especially high, typically defined as 0.15 to 0.20 percent.

Most states now require mandatory minimum jail terms (usually twenty-four or forty-eight hours) for first-time DWI, DUI, or DUBAL offenders. Jail terms increase with subsequent offenses. Other penalties include monetary fines, suspension, or revocation of driving privileges, and alcohol education or treatment programs. In several states, repeat offenders may have their vehicles confiscated. A number of states allow judges to require repeat offenders to install devices that measure the driver's blood-alcohol level before the vehicle can be started.

## Zero Tolerance for Juveniles

**zero tolerance law** A statute that the enacting authority claims will be enforced zealously and without exception.

In 1996 Kentucky enacted a "**zero tolerance law**," also known as the juvenile DUI law, which makes it an offense for a person under age twenty-one to drive with a blood-alcohol content of 0.02 percent or higher. In *Commonwealth v. Howard*, 969 S.W.2d 700 (Ky. 1998), the Kentucky Supreme Court upheld the law as being rationally related to the legitimate legislative purpose of reducing teenage traffic fatalities and protecting all members of the public. Therefore, the court held that it does not violate the equal protection rights of those who are prosecuted. By 2003, all fifty states had followed Kentucky's lead in establishing a lower permissible blood-alcohol level for juveniles (in most states, 0.02 percent).

## Prosecution of DWI, DUI, and DUBAL Charges

To obtain a conviction for DWI, DUI, or DUBAL, the prosecution must first establish that the defendant charged with driving while intoxicated or driving under the influence was operating the vehicle. This may be accomplished by either eyewitness testimony or circumstantial evidence. In *State v. Harrison*, 846 P.2d 1082 (N.M. App. 1992), the court reviewed a DUI conviction where the defendant's only contention was that the prosecution failed to prove he was driving a vehicle. Evidence at the defendant's trial revealed that he was found asleep behind the steering wheel of his car parked on the roadway with the key in the ignition, the motor running, and the transmission in drive. The court determined that this evidence established that the defendant was in actual physical control of the vehicle and therefore was sufficient to prove that the defendant was driving the automobile.

**contraband** Any property that is inherently illegal to produce or possess.

Next, the prosecution must establish the intoxication. Statutes, it should be noted, often refer to intoxication occurring as a result of alcohol or from ingestion of **contraband** substances. Intoxication is often a difficult state to articulate. Therefore, in addition to frequently offering evidence of a defendant's blood and urine alcohol content, law enforcement officers who observed the defendant are permitted to testify as to the defendant's appearance, speech, or conduct and whether the officer detected the odor of an alcoholic beverage on the defendant's person. These factors are relevant evidence of the defendant's mental and physical impairment.

**field sobriety test** A test administered by police to people suspected of driving while intoxicated. Usually consists of requiring the suspect to demonstrate the ability to perform such physical acts as touching one's finger to one's nose or walking backward.

In *Berkemer v. McCarty*, 468 U.S. 420, 104 S.Ct. 3138, 82 L.Ed.2d 317 (1984), the U.S. Supreme Court held that an officer's roadside questioning and administration of a **field sobriety test** to an individual stopped for irregular driving was not a "custodial interrogation" that required giving the suspect the *Miranda* warnings. However, the Court cautioned that the *Miranda* warnings apply once the suspect is under arrest.

Evidence indicates that field sobriety tests can be somewhat unreliable, and courts are beginning to scrutinize cases that rely solely on field sobriety tests without supporting chemical testing of the blood, urine, or breath of the suspect. Still, most courts permit persons to be convicted of DUI without chemical tests, especially when multiple sobriety tests have been performed by more than one officer.

breathalyzer A device that detects the amount of alcohol in a sample of a person's breath.

Increasingly, police videotape suspects' performance on field sobriety tests and make audiotape recordings of suspects' speech. Many police agencies today have mobile blood-alcohol testing units ("Batmobiles") equipped with **breathalyzer** testing machines, videotape equipment, and voice recorders. These vans, available at the call of the arresting officer, give the police the opportunity to collect evidence promptly at or near the scene of the arrest.

One of the most sophisticated methods of alcohol detection is measuring the grams of alcohol in a volume of breath by use of a spectrophotometer, which measures the absorption of infrared light by a sample of a gas. The sampled gas is human breath, and the absorption of infrared light by a sample of the gas is affected by the concentration of alcohol in the gas. A formula can be used to determine the concentration of alcohol. An instrument called the Intoxilyzer, which performs this calculation electronically and provides a printout of the results, is increasingly used by law enforcement.

Although generally regarded as superior to field sobriety tests from an evidentiary standpoint, chemical tests are not devoid of problems. We mention some of these problems in the following topic. Ideally, to obtain a conviction, a prosecutor would like to have evidence that the defendant was driving abnormally, smelled of alcohol, exhibited slurred speech, failed a battery of field sobriety tests administered by several officers, and registered an impermissibly high blood-alcohol level on one or more chemical tests performed by a trained technician. Of course, in the real world of law enforcement, such thorough evidence is seldom obtained.

## Defense of DWI, DUI, and DUBAL Charges

Historically, counsel who represent a defendant charged with DWI, DUI, or DUBAL have challenged the methodology of an officer's administration of field sobriety tests, particularly where the defendant suffers from any physical impairment or has been taking medication that might make it difficult to perform these tests. Today defense counsel must have a basic knowledge of scientific evidence and also be prepared to challenge the reliability and validity of chemical testing equipment and the operator's level of competence. Defense counsel may present expert testimony challenging the chemicals that breath analysis machines measure and offer evidence of a defendant's illnesses and the medications a defendant was taking at the time of the tests.

States have administrative rules that specify the procedure to be followed in administering a breath test. Defense counsel often seeks to suppress the results of Intoxilyzer tests on grounds that the prosecution has not established a proper predicate for their admissibility. For example, in *Davis v. State*, 712 So.2d 1115 (Ala. Crim. App. 1997), the defense objected to the introduction of the results of the Intoxilyzer tests on the ground that the instrument was not properly calibrated at the time the blood-alcohol test was performed. The trial court denied the motion. On appeal, the Alabama Criminal Appeals Court agreed with the defense. The court held there was no evidence the equipment used to perform the tests had been inspected as required by rules of the Alabama Department of Forensics.

State administrative rules usually require an observation period before administration of a breath test to ensure that no substance enters the defendant's mouth that might affect the validity of the test results. For example, an Illinois administrative rule governing alcohol breath tests stipulated that the test was valid only if the driver did not regurgitate within an observation period of twenty minutes before the test. In *People v. Bonutti*, 817 N.E.2d 489 (2004), defense counsel objected to the introduction of the tests, asserting what has become known as the "acid reflux defense." The Illinois Supreme Court reversed the lower court's ruling and suppressed the results of the breath alcohol test because the evidence revealed that the defendant suffered an acid reflux episode while waiting to take the breath test.

Defense counsel often challenge the results of breath tests made by the Intoxilyzer instruments. The manufacturer of these instruments has been unwilling to release their source codes, claiming that this information does not satisfy the "materiality" requirement and that they are protected as trade secrets. Several trial courts in Florida have found that nondisclosure of the source codes denies defendants material evidence in support of their defense and that the instruments are not an "approved test" as required by the Florida implied consent statute. Thus, in some cases nondisclosure of the source codes has resulted in exclusion of all Intoxilyzer evidence at trial or in denying the prosecution the presumptions and shortened predicate for admissibility of the breath test results allowed under Florida law.

**implied consent statutes** Laws providing that by accepting a license, a driver arrested for a traffic offense consents to urine, blood, and breath tests to determine blood-alcohol content.

## Implied Consent Statutes

To facilitate chemical testing in DWI, DUI, and DUBAL cases, California and most other jurisdictions have enacted **implied consent statutes**. Under these laws, a person who drives a motor vehicle is deemed to have given consent to a urine test for drugs and to blood, breath, or urine testing to determine blood-alcohol content. The

---

### JURISPRUDENCE

*Mackey v. Montrym*, 443 U.S. 1, 99 S.Ct. 2612, 61 L.Ed.2d 321 (1979).

The Massachusetts legislature enacted statute that mandates the "suspension of a driver's license for refusing to take a breath-analysis test upon arrest for operating a motor vehicle while under the influence of intoxicating liquor." Upon refusal to undergo a breath-analysis test, the Registrar of Motor Vehicles "must order a 90-day suspension upon receipt of the police report," whereupon the driver is entitled to an immediate hearing before the Registrar. Montrym's license was suspended under the statute, which prompted him to file a federal lawsuit claiming that the statute was unconstitutional in that it authorized the suspension of his driver's license without affording him a presuspension hearing. The federal district court held that Montrym "was entitled as a matter of due process to some sort of presuspension hearing," and held the "statute unconstitutional on its face as violative of the Due Process Clause of the Fourteenth Amendment." The Supreme Court, speaking through Chief Justice Burger, reversed. While the Court recognized that the "suspension of a driver's license for statutorily defined cause implicates a property interest protected by the Due Process Clause," Massachusetts has a "compelling interest in highway safety . . . in making a summary suspension effective pending the outcome of the available prompt post-suspension hearing." The Court went on to state that the compelling state interests are "substantially served by the summary suspension because (i) it acts as a deterrent to drunk driving; (ii) provides an inducement to take the breath-analysis test, permitting the Commonwealth to obtain a reliable form of evidence for use in subsequent criminal proceedings; and (iii) summarily removes from the road licensees arrested for drunk driving who refuse to take the test." Requiring states to provide for a presuspension hearing "would substantially undermine the . . . interest in public safety by giving drivers an incentive to refuse the breath-analysis test and demand such a hearing as a dilatory tactic, which, in turn, would cause a sharp increase in the number of hearings sought, and thus impose a substantial fiscal and administrative burden. . . ."

testing is made incident to a lawful arrest of a driver. See, e.g., West's Ann. Cal. Vehicle Code § 23612. In most instances, refusal to submit to the tests required by an implied consent law will result in an administrative suspension of licensing privileges. The Supreme Court has upheld the validity of the Massachusetts implied consent law, which provides for suspension of the driver's license of a person who refuses to take a breathalyzer test. *Mackey v. Montrym*, 443 U.S. 1, 99 S.Ct. 2612, 61 L.Ed.2d 321 (1979).

# Drug Offenses

Though not as widespread as alcohol, drugs like marijuana and opium have been used by people in various parts of the world for thousands of years. The indigenous peoples of South America knew of the stimulating properties of coca leaves, although cocaine was not invented until the nineteenth century. In that century, cocaine and opium derivatives were widely used by Americans with no legal prohibitions or regulations. Opium derivatives were routinely used to treat diarrhea, sleeplessness, and anxiety. In 1875, the City of San Francisco prohibited the smoking of opium, a common practice among Chinese immigrants. But the city did not criminalize other means of ingesting opium that were popular among white citizens, such as in the liquid preparation called laudanum. As the twentieth century dawned, Americans were becoming more aware of the addictive nature of narcotics, and people began to call for governmental restrictions on such products.

## The Harrison Act

The Harrison Act of 1914, 38 Stat. 785, was the first attempt by the federal government to regulate the sale and use of opium and cocaine. Ostensibly a revenue measure, the act levied criminal penalties on those who distributed cocaine or opium and failed to register and pay the requisite taxes. Although the act allowed doctors to prescribe cocaine and opiates for legitimate medical reasons, it criminalized their prescription merely to satisfy the cravings of addicts. The Supreme Court upheld the Harrison Act against the challenge that it was not a valid revenue measure and usurped the police powers of the states. *United States v. Doremus*, 249 U.S. 86, 39 S.Ct. 214, 63 L.Ed. 493 (1919). In the wake of the Harrison Act, state legislatures enacted statutes criminalizing the sale and possession of opiates and cocaine. By the 1930s, these prohibitions were nearly universal among the states. During this period, rates of cocaine and opium use declined, but the country also saw the emergence of an underground drug economy that persists to this day.

## Prohibition of Marijuana

Marijuana or hemp, which has been used in parts of the world for thousands of years, was widely cultivated in the United States in the nineteenth century. Used primarily as a source of fiber for making rope, marijuana was also used as medicine, both for people and animals. Smoking marijuana for "recreational" purposes was not widespread in the United States until the early twentieth century, when an influx of immigrants from Mexico brought the practice to this country. During Prohibition, many people turned to marijuana as a cheap and legal alternative to alcohol. After Prohibition was repealed in 1933, federal and state authorities turned their attention to marijuana.

By 1937, forty-six of the forty-eight states had banned the cultivation, sale, possession, and use of the cannabis plant. Marijuana use declined dramatically during the 1940s and 1950s, at least partly due to the new criminal prohibitions, but rose again in the 1960s.

The Marihuana Tax Act of 1937 was the federal government's first attempt to control marijuana. Not a direct prohibition, the act criminalized the failure to pay a tax on the transfer of cannabis. Of course, compliance with the law exposed a person to criminal prosecution under state laws, which is why the U.S. Supreme Court declared the statute unconstitutional in 1969. *Leary v. United States*, 395 U.S. 6, 16, 89 S.Ct. 1532, 1537, 23 L.Ed.2d 57, 70 (1969).

Go to the companion website for an edited version of *Leary v. United States*.

## Modern Federal Drug Laws

In the 1960s, the United States saw a resurgence of illicit drug use. Whereas illegal drug use had previously been concentrated in big cities, among ethnic minorities, and among the lower socioeconomic strata, in the 1960s drug use proliferated within the middle-class white population, especially young people. During the 1960s marijuana use increased dramatically and new hallucinogenic drugs like LSD came on the scene. The use of such drugs was encouraged by a "counterculture" movement that eschewed middle-class conventions and encouraged young people to experiment with alternative lifestyles.

**Controlled Substances Act** A federal law listing controlled substances according to their potential for abuse. States have similar statutes.

Responding to concern over the rise in drug use, Congress enacted the Comprehensive Drug Abuse Prevention and Control Act of 1970. 21 U.S.C.A. § 801 *et seq*. The act, commonly referred to as the **Controlled Substances Act**, establishes the criteria for classification of substances and lists controlled substances according to their potential for abuse. Offenses involving the manufacture, sale, distribution, and possession with intent to distribute are defined and the penalties are prescribed in 21 U.S.C.A. § 841. Penalties for simple possession of controlled substances are prescribed in 21 U.S.C.A. § 844. Provision is made in 21 U.S.C.A. § 823 for registered practitioners to dispense narcotics for approved purposes.

## Modern State Drug Laws

In 1972 the Uniform Controlled Substances Act was drafted by the Commission on Uniform Laws, whose purpose was to achieve uniformity among state and federal laws. There are three versions of the Uniform Controlled Substances Act: 1970, 1990, and 1994. Provisions within each version are similar. All fifty states and the Virgin Islands have adopted one of the three versions. Like the federal statute, the uniform act classifies controlled substances according to their potential for abuse. For example, opiates are included in Schedule I because they are unsafe for use even under medical treatment, whereas Schedule II includes drugs that have a high potential for abuse but may be medically acceptable under certain conditions. The remaining schedules include controlled substances that have lesser potential for abuse and dependency. The range of controlled substances includes such well-known drugs as cocaine, amphetamines, tranquilizers, and barbiturates (see Table 10.1).

**controlled substances** Drugs designated by law as contraband.

All states make the manufacture, sale, and possession of **controlled substances** illegal. Offenses involving drugs that have a high potential for abuse (e.g., heroin and cocaine) are usually very serious felonies. Although it is constitutionally permissible to enact such laws, the U.S. Supreme Court has ruled that states may not

| TABLE 10.1 | Schedule of Controlled Substances under Tennessee Law | |
|---|---|---|
| Schedule I | High potential for abuse; no accepted medical use in treatment or lacks accepted safety for use in treatment under medical supervision. | This includes certain opiates (e.g., heroin); hallucinogens (e.g., LSD); depressants (e.g., methaqualone); and stimulants (e.g., MDMA). |
| Schedule II | High potential for abuse; has currently accepted medical use in treatment, or currently accepted medical use with severe restrictions; abuse of the substance may lead to severe psychic or physical dependence. | Examples: Cocaine, morphine, amphetamines, amobarbital. |
| Schedule III | Potential for abuse less than the substances listed in Schedules I and II; has currently accepted medical use in treatment; and may lead to moderate or low physical dependence or high psychological dependence. | Examples: Anabolic steroids. |
| Schedule IV | Low potential for abuse relative to substances in Schedule III; has currently accepted medical use in treatment; and may lead to limited physical dependence or psychological dependence relative to the substances in Schedule III. | Example: Phenobarbital. |
| Schedule V | Low potential for abuse relative to the controlled substances listed in Schedule IV; has currently accepted medical use in treatment in the United States; and has limited physical dependence or psychological dependence liability relative to the controlled substances listed in Schedule IV. | Example: A medicine containing not more than two hundred (200) milligrams of codeine per one hundred (100) grams. |
| Schedule VI | Tetrahydrocannabinols. | Marijuana; hashish; synthetic equivalents. |
| Schedule VII | Butyl nitrite and any isomer thereof. | |

Source: Tennessee Drug Control Act of 1989, T.C.A § 39-17-401 *et seq.*

criminalize the mere status of being addicted to such drugs. *Robinson v. California*, 370 U.S. 660, 82 S.Ct. 1417, 8 L.Ed.2d 758 (1962).

Like most states, California statutes proscribe possession or purchase for sale of designated controlled substances and provide penalties according to the harmfulness of the substance. See West's Ann. Cal. Health & Safety Code §§ 11350–11352. In most states offenses involving the mere possession of less harmful substances are often classified as lesser-degree felonies or, where a very small quantity of marijuana is involved, are frequently classified as misdemeanors.

During the 1970s several states decriminalized their antimarijuana laws by removing the threat of a jail sentence for possession offenses. In Nebraska, where the legislature amended its laws in 2008, possession of less than one ounce of marijuana is considered an "infraction" for which a first-time offender may be fined no more than three hundred dollars and assigned to attend a drug education course. Neb. Rev. Stat. § 28–416(13)(a). Possession of more than one ounce but less than one pound of marijuana is a misdemeanor, see Neb. Rev. Stat. § 28-416(11); possession of more than one pound is a felony. Neb. Rev. Stat. § 28-416(12).

## The Marijuana Controversy

Marijuana violations lead to nearly half of all drug arrests in the United States. Despite aggressive law enforcement, marijuana remains widely available, a situation that exemplifies the difficulty of enforcing a law that has less-than-universal public support. Nevertheless, courts have generally declined to reassess legislative judgments in this area, and statutes making it a criminal offense to possess marijuana have withstood numerous constitutional challenges. For example, in *State v. Smith*, 610 P.2d 869 (Wash. 1980), the Supreme Court of Washington held that criminal penalties for possession of marijuana did not violate the constitutional prohibition against cruel and unusual punishments. More recently, in *State v. Harland*, 556 So.2d 256 (La. App. 1990), a Louisiana appellate court rejected the contention that such penalties violated a state constitutional provision protecting the right of privacy.

Perhaps the most notable court ruling dealing with marijuana use is an Alaska Supreme Court decision in 1975. In *Ravin v. State*, 537 P.2d 494 (Alaska 1975), the court held that the explicit right to privacy contained in the Alaska state constitution protects the possession and personal use of marijuana by an adult in the home. In interpreting the right to privacy under the Alaska Constitution, the court took note of the individualistic nature of Alaska's political culture. The court concluded that, given the relatively innocuous nature of marijuana, the state had an insufficient basis for criminalizing its use in the home. The court recognized that the distribution of marijuana could still be criminalized.

Responding to the *Ravin* decision, the Alaska legislature in 1982 decriminalized the possession by an adult of up to four ounces of marijuana for personal use. However, in 1990 Alaska voters approved a ballot initiative that stated,

> Under Alaska law it is currently legal for adults over 18 years old to possess less than four ounces of marijuana in a home or other private place. The penalty for adults over 18 years old for possessing less than one ounce in public is a fine of up to $100. This initiative would change Alaska's laws by making all such possession of marijuana criminal, with possible penalties of up to 90 days in jail and/or up to a $1000 fine.

In *Noy v. State*, 83 P.3d 545 (Alaska App. 2003), the Alaska Court of Appeals struck down the statute adopted by voter initiative in 1990. The court noted that the voters are bound, as is the legislature, to respect the provisions of the state constitution as interpreted by the state's highest court. The court determined that the legislature had acted properly in its 1982 enactment decriminalizing possession of up to four ounces of marijuana for personal use. Unless and until the Alaska Supreme Court says otherwise, or the people of Alaska amend their state constitution, Alaskans have a constitutional right to possess up to four ounces of cannabis in their homes for personal use. As noted in *State v. Crocker*, 97 P.3d 93, 95 (Alaska App. 2004), "Not all marijuana possession is a crime in Alaska. Under *Ravin* and *Noy*, an adult may possess any amount of marijuana less than four ounces in their home, if their possession is for personal use."

### Marijuana for Medicinal Use

As we noted earlier in the chapter, marijuana was sometimes used in the nineteenth century for medicinal purposes. Today, there is a growing demand that marijuana be made legal for medical use, especially for the relief of nausea experienced by persons undergoing chemotherapy for cancer or acquired immunodeficiency syndrome (AIDS). In 1991 a Florida appellate court permitted a husband and wife suffering from AIDS to assert a medical necessity defense (see Chapter 14) in a marijuana possession case. *Jenks v. State*, 582 So.2d 676 (Fla. App. 1991). That decision and similar decisions in other states helped to give rise to a national movement to legalize marijuana for medicinal use.

Between 1996 and 2012, seventeen states (Alaska, Arizona, California, Colorado, Connecticut, Delaware, Hawaii, Maine, Michigan, Montana, Nevada, New Jersey, New Mexico, Oregon, Rhode Island, Vermont, and Washington) and the District of Columbia passed laws legalizing the possession of small quantities of marijuana for medical uses. Most of these laws resulted from referenda. In fifteen of these states, only state residents can qualify for the medical exemption from the law prohibiting marijuana possession.

Opponents of medical marijuana initiatives claim that they are a cleverly disguised first step toward drug legalization rather than a genuine effort to alleviate suffering due to cancer or AIDS. Indeed, in California today it is easy for people suffering from stress to obtain a prescription so that they can legally purchase and use cannabis. Some might say California has already legalized marijuana on a *de facto* basis.

The federal authorities have thus far taken the position that marijuana has no legitimate medical use. In *United States v. Oakland Cannabis Buyers' Cooperative*, 532 U.S. 483, 121 S.Ct. 1711, 149 L.Ed.2d 722 (2001), the Court refused to recognize a "medical necessity exception" to the Controlled Substances Act. As yet, Congress has not amended the act to create a medical necessity exception.

The legalization of marijuana for medical use creates a conflict between state and federal law. As we noted in Chapter 3, in *Gonzales v. Raich*, 545 U.S. 1, 125 S.Ct. 2195, 162 L.Ed.2d 1 (2005), the Supreme Court held that Congress does have the power under the Commerce Clause to prohibit the mere possession of small quantities of marijuana, even if it is solely for personal medicinal use authorized by state law. Thus, a person using marijuana with a doctor's prescription pursuant to a state "compassionate use" statute is still subject to arrest and prosecution by federal authorities, although it is safe to say that the enforcement of the marijuana prohibition against such individuals is not a high priority for federal prosecutors or law enforcement agencies.

## JURISPRUDENCE

*Gonzales v. Raich*, 545 U.S. 1, 125 S.Ct. 2195, 162 L.Ed.2d 1 (2005).

The case involved two women who used marijuana for medical reasons based on the recommendation of their doctor as authorized by California's Compassionate Use Act of 1996. Under the federal Controlled Substances Act (CSA), the possession or use of marijuana is a crime and there is no exception for medicinal use. When agents of the federal Drug Enforcement Administration learned that one of the women was cultivating marijuana in her home, they obtained a search warrant and seized and destroyed the plants. Subsequently, the women brought suit in federal court, claiming that Congress had no authority under the Commerce Clause to prohibit the possession and use of marijuana that is not intended for interstate distribution. Although the district court rejected the claim, the U.S. Court of Appeals for the Ninth Circuit reversed. The Supreme Court reversed the Ninth Circuit, however, holding that Congress may criminalize the possession and medicinal use of marijuana. Writing for the Court, Justice John Paul Stevens stressed the commercial aspects of the marijuana prohibition. In a dissenting opinion joined by Chief Justice Rehnquist and Associate Justice Thomas, Justice O'Connor suggested that the Court had backtracked from the commitment to principles of federalism expressed in earlier decisions. *Gonzales v. Raich* suggests that Congress retains broad authority under the Commerce Clause to deal with social problems of national scope.

## The Crystal Meth Crisis

In the 1980s, cocaine (especially "crack") emerged as the leading drug problem in this country. Today, law enforcement agencies are confronting a new epidemic—that of homemade methamphetamines. Also known as "crystal meth" or "crank," this powerful stimulant can be easily made by amateur chemists with products readily available in the marketplace. However, the making of the drug is itself extremely dangerous, as it involves highly volatile, explosive, and noxious chemicals. The process also produces highly toxic by-products that, when disposed of, present a serious threat to the natural environment. Meth labs tend to be located in rural areas where they can operate without detection. Often the authorities become aware of them only after a fire, explosion, or serious environmental contamination has occurred. Prosecutors have begun to take a new and dramatic approach to the meth lab problem. They have begun to charge operators of labs with environmental crimes (see Chapter 11).

### The Combat Methamphetamine Epidemic Act

In 2005, Congress passed an important measure to address the crystal meth crisis. In addition to increasing penalties for smuggling and selling methamphetamine, the Combat Methamphetamine Epidemic Act of 2005, now codified in various sections of Title 21 of the U.S. Code, is designed to make it more difficult to acquire the precursor chemicals used to make meth. The new law limits purchases of ephedrine, pseudoephedrine, and phenylpropanolamine, which are commonly found in over-the-counter cold and sinus products as well as appetite suppressants. The law requires stores to keep products containing these ingredients behind the counter or in locked display cases. Vendors are prohibited from selling more than 3.6 grams per day or 9 grams per month of these chemicals to any customer, regardless of the number of transactions. Of course, those who are intent on acquiring large quantities of these products can go from store to store. That is why vendors are required to keep a logbook in which they record the names and addresses of purchasers, who must show valid identification in order to purchase the regulated products. These logbooks must be made available on demand to state and federal authorities investigating meth production.

## Prohibition of Drug Paraphernalia

**drug paraphernalia** Items closely associated with the use of illegal drugs.

Under federal law, it is a crime to import, export, sell, offer for sale, or use the mails to transport any **drug paraphernalia**. 21 U.S.C.A. § 863(a). Violation of this prohibition is punishable by a fine and imprisonment up to three years. 21 U.S.C.A. § 863(b). Federal law defines drug paraphernalia to include "any equipment, product, or material of any kind which is primarily intended or designed for use in manufacturing, compounding, converting, concealing, producing, processing, preparing, injecting, ingesting, inhaling, or otherwise introducing into the human body a controlled substance, possession of which is unlawful under this subchapter." 21 U.S.C.A. § 863(d). Under federal law, drug paraphernalia is subject to confiscation. 21 U.S.C.A. § 863(c). In *United States v. Janus Industries*, 48 F.3d 1548 (10th Cir. 1995), a federal appeals court upheld the federal prohibitions and penalties associated with drug paraphernalia. Possession of drug paraphernalia is also commonly a criminal offense under state laws and many local ordinances.

## Problems of Drug Enforcement and Prosecution

Federal and state laws on controlled substances mirror one another in many respects. Federal enforcement is usually directed against major interstate or international drug traffickers; states usually concentrate on those who possess or distribute controlled substances. Many drug-trafficking violations of federal law involve prosecution for conspiracy. Unlike many state laws, the federal law proscribing conspiracy to violate the Controlled Substances Act does not require proof of an overt act. 21 U.S.C.A. § 846; *United States v. Pulido*, 69 F.3d 192 (7th Cir. 1995); *United States v. Wilson*, 657 F.2d 755 (5th Cir. 1981).

Because those involved in narcotics transactions are usually willing participants, enforcement often depends on the use of confidential informants by police. Obtaining search warrants and making arrests based on probable cause often present difficult Fourth Amendment problems.

The level of intent that the prosecution must establish in contraband cases can vary according to the particular statutory offense (see Chapter 4). However, courts have generally held that statutes making possession, distribution, or trafficking of contraband unlawful require the prosecution to prove only the defendant's general intent. See, e.g., *State v. Williams*, 352 So.2d 1295 (La. 1977) (intent established by mere proof of voluntary distribution); *State v. Bender*, 579 P.2d 796 (N.M. 1978).

### Actual and Constructive Possession

In drug possession cases, a critical problem is proving that the defendant was in possession of a controlled substance. The prosecution may prove either actual or constructive possession of contraband to satisfy the possession requirement. Proof of actual possession is established by evidence that the contraband was found on the accused's person or that the accused was in exclusive possession of the premises or vehicle where the contraband was discovered. Where the accused is not in actual possession, however, or where the accused and another person jointly occupy a dwelling or automobile where contraband is discovered, the prosecution must attempt to prove what the law calls *constructive possession*.

A person has constructive possession of contraband if he or she has ownership, dominion, or control over the contraband itself or over the premises in which it is concealed. *United States v. Schubel*, 912 F.2d 952 (8th Cir. 1990). The prosecution usually attempts to establish constructive possession by evidence of incriminating statements and circumstances from which the defendant's ability to control the contraband may be inferred. This can pose a formidable difficulty.

In *State v. Somerville*, 572 A.2d 944 (Conn. 1990), the defendant appealed his conviction for possession of cocaine with intent to sell sixty-nine vials of crack cocaine. He argued that no evidence was presented at his trial to establish that he possessed the drugs in question. He pointed to the fact that no drugs and no large sums of money were found on his person. The evidence revealed that the police found the sixty-nine vials of cocaine underneath a garbage can at the defendant's neighbor's house. Witnesses had seen the defendant selling crack cocaine in small vials before his arrest. They testified that he had been stooping near the garbage can under which the police found the vials of cocaine. The Connecticut Supreme Court rejected the defendant's contention and found the evidence sufficient to establish that the defendant had dominion and control over the cocaine and had knowledge of the character of the contraband and its presence.

### Proof of Intent to Sell or Distribute Drugs

Intent to distribute controlled substances may be proved by either direct or circumstantial evidence. It may be inferred from the presence of equipment to weigh and

## Constructive Possession of Drugs

After Minneapolis police obtained a tip that crack cocaine was being sold out of cars parked in front of a certain duplex, an officer observed a blue Cadillac parked in front of the building. A female later identified as the defendant, Nina Knox, made several trips between the car and the duplex. At one point she drove the car from the scene, but she returned shortly and sat in the car for a period of time while a number of men approached the car and walked away after brief encounters. The officer, who was experienced in dealing with drug offenses, believed the activities he witnessed to be drug transactions, although he was unable to observe money and drugs being exchanged. Knox was arrested, and a search of the car produced 14.3 grams of crack cocaine and $2,200 in cash. A search of Knox's purse produced a large amount of money and food stamps. Knox was convicted in federal court of possession with intent to distribute a controlled substance.

On appeal, Knox argued that the evidence failed to establish that she was in physical control of the cocaine and was intending to sell it. The U.S. Court of Appeals rejected Knox's contention, concluding that the evidence supported a finding that Knox had exercised "dominion over the premises in which the contraband [was] concealed" since she was observed driving the car, sitting in the car, and entering it on several occasions. The court further concluded that intent to distribute could be inferred from the fact that sizable amounts of cash and cocaine were found at the scene. Knox's conviction was affirmed.

*United States v. Knox*, 888 F.2d 585 (8th Cir. 1989).

measure narcotics and paraphernalia used to aid in their distribution. Large sums of cash and narcotics are common indicia of circumstantial evidence of intent to distribute illegal drugs. See, e.g., *United States v. Brett*, 872 F.2d 1365 (Mo. 8th Cir. 1989).

## Defenses in Drug Cases

Defendants on trial for drug offenses sometimes assert that they were entrapped by the police, a defense discussed in Chapter 14. More frequently, defense counsel attempt to suppress the contraband seized by police on the ground that it was obtained in violation of the Fourth Amendment prohibition against unreasonable searches and seizures. In some instances, a defendant presents an expert witness to contest the type of contraband introduced in evidence, and frequently defendants challenge the chain of custody of the contraband from the time it was seized until the time it was introduced into evidence. Because the gravity of the offense is often based on the amount of contraband seized, defendants sometimes challenge the weight of the contraband being introduced into evidence. Possession with intent to deliver drugs within a certain proximity of a school is a more serious offense that can carry severe penalties. Defendants charged with this offense often challenge the measurement of the distance between the school and the place where the offense allegedly occurred.

In a number of cases, courts have rejected such defenses as economic coercion and duress, but, as we noted above, in some instances courts have accepted the defense of "medical necessity" in possession of marijuana cases.

## The "War on Drugs"

President Richard Nixon first "declared war" on illegal drugs in 1973. President Ronald Reagan "redeclared" the war in 1982, as did President George H. W. Bush in 1988. Since 1973 the war on drugs has been waged on numerous fronts, from elementary schools to Colombian coca farms, and law enforcement agencies have employed a number of controversial weapons and tactics. Federal and state drug laws have been made more stringent; budgets for drug enforcement activities have been increased dramatically, teachers, police officers and other public employees have been subjected to random drug testing; and constitutional restrictions on searches and seizures have been relaxed. Millions of dollars have been spent on public information campaigns on the dangers of drug abuse. To supporters of the drug war, it is a war for national survival, nearly as important as the current war on terrorism. Its detractors see it as a war on people or, alternatively, a war on the Constitution.

### The Drug Enforcement Administration

In 1973, President Nixon issued an executive order creating the Drug Enforcement Administration (DEA) within the Department of Justice to concentrate federal drug enforcement responsibilities within one agency of government. Since then, the DEA has been involved in all facets of the drug war, including joint operations with state and local law enforcement agencies as well as agencies in other countries. The DEA has even worked in tandem with the Coast Guard in an effort to interdict smuggling operations into the United States. The DEA has employed a number of controversial tactics, including **drug courier profiling**, in which a set of behavioral characteristics believed to typify drug smugglers is employed to identify, monitor and sometimes detain suspected drug couriers. Such tactics have generated considerable litigation—with disparate results. See, e.g., *Reid v. Georgia*, 448 U.S. 438, 100 S.Ct. 2752, 65 L.Ed.2d 890 (1980); *United States v. Sokolow*, 490 U.S. 1, 109 S.Ct. 1581, 104 L.Ed.2d 1 (1989).

**drug courier profiling** The practice of employing a set of characteristics thought to typify people engaged in drug smuggling in order to identify such persons.

The DEA employs more than 9,000 people, including more than 4,500 special agents. Its annual budget exceeds $1.8 billion. Yet according to a Performance and Management Assessment released by the White House in February 2003, the DEA "is unable to demonstrate its progress in reducing the availability of illegal drugs in the U.S." The report cited a lack of cooperation with other law enforcement agencies, misplaced priorities, and a lack of internal evaluation and accountability mechanisms, all of which may be valid criticisms. The reality may well be the problem that DEA is tasked with solving is beyond the capabilities of any government agency.

### Mandatory Minimum Sentences

In 1969, amidst public outcry over drugs and street crime, the New York legislature enacted the first of the so-called Rockefeller Drug Laws, which required mandatory prison terms for persons convicted of serious drug crimes. In 1973, the legislature strengthened these laws by establishing more severe penalties and by restricting plea bargaining in drug cases. By and large, these laws remain in effect today. As an example of the harshness of the laws, a person convicted of selling two ounces or possessing four ounces of cocaine or heroin is required to serve at least fifteen years in prison before being eligible for parole. While their effect on deterring illegal drug use is debatable, the Rockefeller Drug Laws have certainly had the effect of dramatically increasing the size of the prison population in New York. In 1998 the prison population in New York State stood at roughly 70,000 inmates, nearly three times as many prisoners as in 1979. By 1998, nonviolent drug offenders accounted for 30 percent of the state prison population. (See Spiros A. Tsimbinos, *Is It Time to Change the Rockefeller Drug Laws?*, 13 St. John's J. Legal Comment 613–34, Spring 1999.)

In the late 1970s and 1980s, other states and the federal government followed New York's example. Beginning in 1986, Congress required mandatory minimum prison terms for drug felonies. For example, a person charged with possession with the intent to distribute more than five kilograms of cocaine is subject to a mandatory minimum sentence of ten years in prison. See 21 U.S.C.A. § 841(b)(1)(A). Consequently, the federal prison population has swelled with drug offenders who theretofore received probation. In 1991, 58 percent of federal prisoners were convicted of drug offenses; by 1997 the proportion had risen to 63 percent. (U.S. Department of Justice, Bureau of Justice Statistics, *Sourcebook of Criminal Justice Statistics*, 2001, p. 499). As of November 2004 there were 143,864 federal offenders sentenced to prison. Of these, 77,867 or 54.1 percent were sentenced for drug offenses. (*Sourcebook of Criminal Justice Statistics*, 2003, p. 519). As a result of mandatory sentencing under federal law, a significantly higher percentage of federal drug defendants are sentenced to prison than are state drug defendants.

### Drug Testing of Public Employees and Public School Students

As a means of reducing drug use among public employees, numerous local, state, and federal government agencies in the 1980s adopted **drug-testing requirements** for their employees. In 1989 the U.S. Supreme Court sustained a Customs Service policy requiring drug tests for persons seeking positions as customs inspectors. *Treasury Employees Union v. Von Raab*, 489 U.S. 656, 109 S.Ct. 1384, 103 L.Ed.2d 685 (1989). As yet, the Supreme Court has not addressed the issue of general, random drug testing of public employees. However, it has invalidated a policy under which all political candidates were required to submit to drug testing as a condition of qualifying for the ballot. *Chandler v. Miller*, 520 U.S. 305, 117 S.Ct. 1295, 137 L.Ed.2d 513 (1997). Several state courts have addressed the question of random drug testing of public employees, and at least one state appellate court has found such a policy to be unconstitutional. *City of Palm Bay v. Bauman*, 475 So.2d 1322 (Fla. App. 1985).

In many school districts around the country, teachers and students are subjected to drug testing. Teachers are required to submit to drug testing as a condition of employment, and this requirement has generally been upheld by the courts. See, e.g., *Knox County Education Association v. Knox County Board of Education*, 158 F.3d 361 (6th Cir. 1998). With respect to students, most policies require drug testing as a condition of participation in sports or other extracurricular activities. One such policy established by the City of Tecumseh, Oklahoma, was upheld by the U.S. Supreme Court in 2002. See *Board of Education v. Earls*, 536 U.S. 822, 122 S.Ct. 2559, 153 L.Ed.2d 735 (2002). Writing for the Court, Justice Clarence Thomas concluded, "Given the nationwide epidemic of drug use, and the evidence of increased drug use in Tecumseh schools, it was entirely reasonable for the School District to enact this particular drug testing policy." 536 U.S. at 836, 122 S.Ct. at 2568, 153 L.Ed.2d at 748.

### Asset Forfeiture

In passing the Comprehensive Drug Abuse Prevention and Control Act of 1970, Pub.L. No. 91-513, 84 Stat. 1276, Congress for the first time provided for forfeiture of property used in connection with federal drug crimes. Today federal law authorizes forfeiture of illegal drugs themselves, drug paraphernalia, money and other assets furnished or intended to be furnished in drug exchanges, proceeds from illegal drug transactions, real estate used or intended to be used in illegal drug transactions, as well as aircraft, vessels, and vehicles used to transport or otherwise facilitate illegal drug transactions. Most states have enacted similar laws. See, e.g., Oklahoma's Uniform Controlled Dangerous Substances Act, 63 Okla. St. Ann. § 2-503.

Federal asset forfeitures can be criminal or civil. In a **criminal forfeiture**, a person convicted of a federal drug offense is ordered to forfeit property involved in that offense. However, in order for that to occur, the property sought by the government

---

**drug-testing requirements** Laws, regulations, or policies that require students or employees to undergo chemical testing of their urine to determine whether they are free of illicit drugs.

**criminal forfeiture** Government confiscation of private property obtained through or otherwise involved in criminal activity pursuant to a criminal conviction of the owner of said property.

must be specifically identified in the indictment so that the owner has the opportunity to contest the forfeiture. Furthermore, the standard of proof with respect to the forfeiture is lower than that required to convict the defendant. As in any criminal prosecution, the government must prove the defendant's guilt beyond a reasonable doubt. But the standard of proof with respect to the associated forfeiture of property is merely "by a preponderance of the evidence." The two principal statutes governing criminal forfeiture in federal drug cases are 18 U.S.C.A. § 982 and 21 U.S.C.A. § 853.

**civil forfeiture** Taking of property used in or obtained through unlawful activity pursuant to a civil proceeding in which the property itself is named as the defendant.

In contrast to a criminal forfeiture, a **civil forfeiture** (see 18 U.S.C.A. § 983) does not require a criminal conviction, or even prosecution of the owner, because the legal action is brought against the property itself in what is known as an *in rem* action. Thus, a civil forfeiture case is likely to be styled something like *United States v. 2003 Porsche 911 Carrera Cabriolet*. Property may be seized as long as agents have probable cause to believe it is subject to forfeiture. A subsequent civil proceeding determines whether the property is to be forfeited or returned to the owner. Civil forfeiture thus rests on the legal fiction that the property itself is in violation of the law and can be the target of legal action. Of course, the real target of the action is the property owner, who may or may not be simultaneously defending against a criminal prosecution.

### Criticism and Reform

In the 1980s, the federal government became much more aggressive in the use of civil forfeitures as part of the war on drugs. The Comprehensive Crime Control Act of 1984, Pub. L. 98-473, 98 Stat. 1976, directed that proceeds of forfeitures be disbursed to law enforcement agencies that made seizures, thus creating a powerful incentive for the seizure of assets in connection with drug arrests. As a result, civil forfeitures increased dramatically. Critics charged that the practice was being abused and called on Congress and the courts to limit the government's power in this area.

The Supreme Court limited civil forfeitures in several important decisions handed down in 1993. In *United States v. A Parcel of Land*, 507 U.S. 111, 113 S.Ct. 1126, 122 L.Ed.2d 469 (1993), the Court ruled that although proceeds traceable to an unlawful drug transaction are subject to forfeiture, an owner's lack of knowledge that her home had been purchased with proceeds of illegal drug transactions constitutes a defense to a forfeiture proceeding under federal law. In *United States v. Good Real Property*, 510 U.S. 43, 114 S.Ct. 492, 126 L.Ed.2d 490 (1993), the Court held that due process requires government to provide property owners adequate notice and a meaningful opportunity to be heard before seizing real estate that is subject to civil forfeiture. And in *Austin v. United States*, 509 U.S. 602, 113 S.Ct. 2801, 125 L.Ed.2d 488 (1993), the Court ruled that civil *in rem* forfeitures, although not technically criminal proceedings, are subject to the Excessive Fines Clause of the Eighth Amendment. However, the Court declined to establish any test for determining when a forfeiture is constitutionally excessive.

Responding to continuing criticism of civil forfeitures, Congress enacted the Civil Asset Forfeiture Reform Act (CAFRA) of 2000, Pub. L. No. 106-185, 114 Stat. 202. Previously, the property owner carried the burden of proving by a preponderance of the evidence that the property seized by the government is not subject to forfeiture. CAFRA reversed the burden of proof so that it now rests on government. 18 U.S.C.A. § 983(c). It also established a uniform "innocent owner defense" applicable to all federal forfeiture statutes. To prevail in this defense, owners must prove either that they did not know of the unlawful activity associated with their property or that they did all they could reasonably be expected to do to prevent or halt it. 18 U.S.C.A. § 983(d). The new law also provides counsel to indigent property owners who have standing to challenge forfeitures. 18 U.S.C.A. § 983(b)(2). While CAFRA represents a serious attempt to reform civil forfeitures, it does not severely retard the government's ability to use this powerful weapon in the war on drugs.

### The Office of National Drug Control Policy

In 1988, Congress enacted the Anti-Drug Abuse Act, which established the Office of National Drug Control Policy (ONDCP) within the Executive Office of the President to coordinate federal and state drug control policies. The ONDCP spends considerable time, effort, and money on public relations and advertising in an attempt to persuade people not to use illicit drugs and to defeat efforts by various interest groups to ease existing drug laws. The director of the ONDCP is known colloquially as the "drug czar." To emphasize the importance of the war on drugs, President Reagan made the drug czar a member of his cabinet, and subsequent presidents have followed suit. As the official responsible for coordinating federal drug policy, the drug czar deals with every federal agency involved in the war on drugs, including the FBI, the Customs Service, the DEA, the Department of Transportation, the Department of Health and Human Services, the State Department, and even the Department of Defense. But the role is more than one of coordinator. The drug czar helps set the tone for national policy on illicit drug use, including the use of criminal prohibitions. By rhetoric and directive, the drug czar is in a position to greatly influence whether the war on drugs continues along its present course.

### Assessing the War on Drugs

Some commentators, believing that the national "war on drugs" has failed, have argued for the legalization of such drugs as marijuana, cocaine, and heroin. These commentators would prefer to see the use of these drugs legalized, although highly regulated, with increased efforts directed toward educational and treatment programs. Advocates of legalization contend that criminal prohibition of drug use has led to a vast underground economy and that the war on drugs has debased the rule of law by ineffective attempts to alter personal conduct. They argue that imprisonment of nonviolent drug offenders is excessive, unjust, and ruinous to lives that might otherwise be productive. They also object to what they perceive to be the curtailment of individual rights that has accompanied the drug war. Although the number of Americans who are sympathetic to such arguments appears to be increasing, there remains substantial public support for maintaining criminal prohibitions in this area.

Despite widespread criticism, the war on drugs continues. There were more than 1.7 million drug arrests in the United States in 2008. (See 2008 Crime in the United States, FBI Uniform Crime Reports, Washington, DC: U.S. Dept. of Justice, September 2009.)

Libertarians argue that drug use should be strictly a moral question, where each person is free to decide his or her own limits. Yet drug abuse affects more than just the individual user. Drug abuse creates many dramatic economic, social, and health problems in our society. Illegal trafficking in drugs has led to many violent crimes as well as to instances of official corruption. Moreover, many violent crimes are committed by people under the influence of illicit drugs. The correlation between drug abuse and crime is demonstrated by the fact that in twenty-three of the largest cities in the United States, between 50 and 77 percent of male arrestees test positive for drugs. In 2009, anywhere from 56 percent (Charlotte) to 82 percent (Chicago) of arrestees . . . tested positive for the presence of some substance at the time of arrest. Office of National Drug Control Policy, ADAM II 2009 Annual Report, p. 23. Most Americans want their government to continue to fight the war on drugs, although citizens and officials are often frustrated with the rate of progress.

## Drug Courts: A New Approach to an Old Problem

By the late 1980s, judges began to recognize that traditional court processes were neither deterring substance abusers nor addressing the medical, social, and economic problems associated with drug abuse. In an effort to use the court's authority to divert certain offenders to closely monitored programs, courts began to develop the concept of a drug court. Rather than sending nonviolent defendants to jail, a **drug court**—in collaboration with prosecutors, defense counsel, and other professionals—would monitor their progress through status hearings and prescribe sanctions and rewards and thus reduce substance abuse, rehabilitate participants, and thereby reduce recidivism.

**drug court** A specialized court or division of a court designed to deal specifically with defendants charged with violating laws proscribing the possession and use of controlled substances. Drug courts emphasize rehabilitation of offenders.

The first drug court was implemented in 1989 in Miami, Florida. Since then there has been a continual expansion in the number of drug courts. The Bureau of Justice Assistance Drug Court Clearinghouse Project, February 11, 2009, listed 2,018 drug courts operating in all fifty states, the District of Columbia, Northern Mariana Islands, Puerto Rico, and Guam, with another 257 drug court programs in the planning stages. Drug court procedures vary from standard postarrest processes. After an individual who has not committed a violent crime is arrested for possession of a controlled substance, a background check is made. If the arrestee meets the drug court eligibility requirements and the prosecuting attorney agrees, the defendant may opt to be diverted to a drug court program. Prosecution is deferred as long as the participant progresses. Once in the program, the participant must obtain a sponsor, attend certain meetings and counseling sessions, give frequent urine samples, and attend required court status hearings. The participant signs a "contract" to complete the program within a specified period, usually twelve months. The treatment phases consist of detoxification, counseling sessions, and often assistance in job training or obtaining employment. In some programs a participant who agrees is given acupuncture treatments to aid in detoxification and to make the participant more receptive to counseling sessions.

The status hearings before the drug court are central to the program. They are held in open court with all participants present. The judge may begin with a short orientation emphasizing the need for sobriety and gainful employment. The judge then reviews each participant's progress file and commends those whose urine samples are "clean" and who are in complete compliance with their contract. Participants applaud those with outstanding records of performance. The judge encourages those who have minor deviations in their performance and admonishes those who have relapsed. Often the court prescribes additional counseling, treatment, community service, or a short stay in jail for those who have seriously relapsed in their efforts.

Most programs countenance some relapse; however, positive urine tests, additional arrests, or failure to attend status hearings or treatment sessions may cause a participant to be terminated and prosecution resumed. Successful completion of a drug court program usually results in the charges against the participant being dropped or the plea of guilty being stricken from the record.

There are many variations on the drug court model. Some focus on women or juveniles; others handle both male and female adults. Some provide support services such as health and housing assistance and job placement; others do not. Some operate with a professional staff; in other instances, the assigned judge might have minimal professional assistance. These factors, along with the relative newness of the programs and the problem of comparing a given group of drug court participants with a control group of those whose offenses are handled in the traditional manner, make it difficult to evaluate the success of the drug court program. Nevertheless, the relapse rate of the participants and the frequency of new arrests are criteria that can be used to assess the program's effectiveness. And, though still new and innovative institutions, drug courts appear to hold considerable promise to deter repetitive criminal behavior of drug abusers. They also hold a promise to relieve courts and other functionaries in the criminal justice system of the burden of repetitive arrests and overloaded trial and sentencing dockets of criminal cases where drugs play an important role.

## Conclusion

The criminal law proscribes certain forms of conduct that offend the norms of societal morality. Chief among these prohibitions are laws prohibiting certain forms of sexual activity, public indecency, obscenity, profanity, and gambling. As societal consensus changes—as it surely has with respect to sexual activities, pornography, and gambling—the prohibitions of the criminal law must, and do, change as well. But offenses involving the use of alcohol and drugs, although sometimes categorized as offenses against public morality, can also be viewed as threats to public order, safety, and peace.

The American public is committed to strict enforcement of laws proscribing drunk driving, where positive results are being achieved through education and through law enforcement officers' use of sophisticated technological methods. In other areas the control of the use of illegal drugs has been less promising. The widespread abuse of drugs is a serious social problem with many undesirable consequences. Society has responded to this problem largely through the criminal justice system, and the American public has generally supported this approach. However, there are those who believe that criminalizing drug possession is undesirable public policy. Because efforts to control the supply of illegal drugs has proved extremely difficult, the public now appears to place primary emphasis on criminal enforcement against drug dealers while being receptive to increasing education designed to control demand by educating the public of the consequences of drug abuse, minimizing penalties for the possession of small amounts of marijuana, and rehabilitating minor nonviolent offenders through treatments administered by drug courts.

## Chapter Summary

- Learning Objective 1

  - Vice crimes were viewed traditionally as offenses against public decency and it was widely assumed that the protection of the public morals was an important function of the criminal law.
  - Today, critics question whether the furtherance of decency and morality is a legitimate goal of the criminal justice system. However, the moral basis of the law extends far beyond the prohibition of vice. Many proscriptions of the criminal law are based on collective societal judgments about what is right and what is wrong.
  - Vice crimes have implications for the public health, safety and welfare and therefore should not be viewed solely as offenses against public morality.
  - Fornication, adultery, seduction, and consensual sodomy, which were prohibited at common law, are today generally regarded as private matters, and statutes prohibiting such conduct either have been repealed or are seldom enforced.

- o There remains strong support for prohibiting bigamy and incest (inter-marriage or sexual relations between persons within certain degrees of consanguinity).

- Learning Objective 2

  - o Although **prostitution** was not a crime at common law, statutes proscribing prostitution have been part of the laws directed against public immorality since the early history of the United States. Today, prostitution is illegal in all states except Nevada, where it exists by local option in some counties, although it is strictly regulated by law.
  - o Closely related to prostitution is the problem of human trafficking, which is the illegal trade in human beings for the purpose of migration, labor or, more commonly, commercial sexual exploitation. Federal law prohibits human trafficking for the purpose of prostitution.
  - o Reformers contend that legalization of prostitution would remove this activity from the grips of organized crime and allow authorities to control more effectively many of the problems that now accompany unregulated prostitution.
  - o It was a common-law misdemeanor for persons intentionally to expose their "private parts" in public. Today, state statutes and local ordinances make it a misdemeanor, often called "lewd and lascivious conduct," intentionally to expose one's private parts under offensive circumstances. Courts vary as to whether such exposure must be in the presence of another.
  - o Voyeurism, which refers to obtaining sexual gratification from viewing another person's sexual organs or sexual activities, has been addressed under "Peeping Tom" statutes and ordinances that make it a misdemeanor.
  - o The Supreme Court has recognized that erotic dancing in places of public accommodation is entitled to First Amendment protection under certain circumstances, but has also expressed a willingness to uphold reasonable regulations, especially involving establishments that serve alcoholic beverages.

- Learning Objective 3

  - o At common law, vulgar and obscene language and indecent public exhibitions were public nuisances and punishable as misdemeanors. In America federal and state governments enacted laws banning various forms of obscenity, but questions arose as to the definition of obscenity.
  - o In a series of landmark decisions the Supreme Court ruled that obscenity is not entitled to First Amendment protection, but made it clear that no one would be subject to prosecution unless the materials alleged to be obscene described "hard-core" sexual conduct.
  - o Public concern about the prevalence of sexually explicit material on the Internet, and especially the easy access of children to such material, caused Congress, in 1997, to enact the Communications Decency Act of 1996 (CDA). The Supreme Court found the statute to be unconstitutionally overbroad.
  - o Congress passed the Child Online Protection Act of 1998 (COPA), which made it an offense to post material to the Internet that could be harmful to minors. Lower federal courts found COPA unconstitutional and enjoined the government from enforcing the law. The Supreme Court denied review and the battle over COPA ended in defeat for the federal government.
  - o In 1982 the Supreme Court unanimously held that child pornography, like obscenity, is unprotected by the First Amendment and upheld state laws prohibiting persons from distributing materials that depict children engaging in lewd sex.

- ○ Congress enacted the Child Pornography Prevention Act of 1996 (CPPA) prohibiting any type of virtual or simulated child pornography, even if real children were not involved. The Supreme Court struck down the prohibition of virtual child pornography, finding that it abridged freedom of speech under the First Amendment.

- Learning Objective 4

  - ○ The common law did not regard gambling as an offense. However, many of the new American states, by either constitution or statute, made all or certain forms of gambling illegal.
  - ○ Today, the Federal Travel Act prohibits interstate travel in aid of gambling. The Supreme Court has recognized that there is no constitutional right to gamble and has upheld a variety of state statutes and local ordinances that prohibit gambling. Gambling must generally include three elements: consideration, prize, and chance. Gambling laws present a paradox.
  - ○ In many jurisdictions it is a criminal offense to buy a chance in a lottery; yet many states sponsor lotteries as a source of public revenue.
  - ○ Most laws prohibiting gambling either include exceptions for, or are interpreted to exclude, contests in which participants pit their physical or mental skills against one another for a prize, retail promotions that award prizes by lot, and penny-ante card games played in dwellings.
  - ○ Where gambling is prohibited, states customarily make it unlawful to possess gambling devices, and provide for their confiscation.
  - ○ Today, gambling via the Internet is widespread, but because these websites tend to be hosted on servers in foreign countries, prosecution is rare and usually not possible.

- Learning Objective 5

  - ○ Every state today has laws protecting animals from unnecessary harm.
  - ○ State laws also proscribe cockfighting, dog fighting, and other forms of animal fighting, as well as the intentional killing of animals belonging to other persons, except where necessary to protect oneself.
  - ○ There also are laws governing offenses involving farm animals and animal research facilities.

- Learning Objective 6

  - ○ Until 1603, when an English court viewed drunkenness as aggravating a crime, the common law had little to say about alcohol. In America, when alcohol use became widespread, public sentiment caused the states in 1919 to ratify the Eighteenth Amendment to the U.S. Constitution, making unlawful the "manufacture, sale, or transportation of intoxicating liquors" within the United States. Prohibition was widely disregarded, and contributed to increased criminal activity and a lack of respect for the law. Ultimately, it was repealed by the Twenty-First Amendment, ratified by the states in 1933.
  - ○ State and local governments retain the authority to ban or regulate the manufacture, sale, and use of alcohol, and while no state has completely banned the sale of alcohol, states regulate the sale and use of alcoholic beverages.
  - ○ Laws usually make it a misdemeanor to sell alcoholic beverages to minors or for minors to purchase or consume alcoholic beverages. Federal incentives to states have effectively established twenty-one as the minimum age for drinking.

o Historically, states and cities prohibited public drunkenness. After the Supreme Court ruled in 1968 that a person convicted of public drunkenness could be punished for being in public in an inebriated condition, many states began to criminalize only disorderly intoxication.

o Most early driving while intoxicated (DWI) laws stipulated that a level of 0.15 percent or more alcohol in the bloodstream of a driver evidenced intoxication. But in the 1970s, many states expanded the offense to prohibit driving under the influence (DUI) of intoxicating liquors or drugs. Most states modified their statutes to prohibit driving with an unlawful blood-alcohol level (DUBAL), and as a result of federal fiscal incentives, all fifty states have lowered the prohibited blood-alcohol level to 0.08 percent. By 2003, all fifty states had followed Kentucky's lead in establishing a lower permissible blood-alcohol level for juveniles (in most states, 0.02 percent).

o Most states now require mandatory minimum jail terms (usually twenty-four or forty-eight hours) for first-time DWI, DUI, or DUBAL offenders. Other penalties include fines, suspension or revocation of driving privileges, and alcohol education or treatment programs. Some states allow judges to require repeat offenders to install devices that measure the driver's blood-alcohol level before the vehicle can be started; in others repeat offenders may have their vehicles confiscated.

o To facilitate chemical testing in DWI, DUI, and DUBAL cases most jurisdictions have enacted implied consent statutes stipulating that a person who drives a motor vehicle is deemed to consent to a urine test for drugs and to blood, breath, or urine testing to determine blood-alcohol content incident to the arrest of a driver.

• Learning Objective 7

o In 1970 Congress enacted the Comprehensive Drug Abuse Prevention and Control Act (the Controlled Substances Act), which defines offenses involving the manufacture, sale, distribution, and possession with intent to distribute, sets penalties, and establishes criteria for classification of controlled substances according to their potential for abuse.

o Federal and state laws on controlled substances mirror one another in many respects. Federal enforcement is usually directed against major interstate or international drug traffickers; states usually concentrate on those who possess or distribute controlled substances.

o In 1973, President Nixon issued an executive order creating the Drug Enforcement Administration (DEA) within the Department of Justice to concentrate federal drug enforcement responsibilities within one agency of government. Since then, the DEA has been involved in all facets of the drug war. Yet the DEA has been unable to demonstrate much progress in reducing the availability of illegal drugs in the United States.

o Beginning in 1986, Congress required mandatory minimum prison terms for drug felonies, and many states did the same. In 1988, Congress enacted the Anti-Drug Abuse Act, which established the Office of National Drug Control Policy (ONDCP) within the Executive Office of the President to coordinate federal and state drug control policies. The ONDCP spends considerable time, effort, and money on public relations and advertising in an attempt to persuade people not to use illicit drugs.

o Congress also has provided for forfeiture of property used in connection with federal drug crimes. Federal asset forfeitures can be criminal or civil. In a criminal forfeiture, a person convicted of a federal drug offense is ordered to forfeit property involved in that offense; however, the owner has the opportunity to contest the forfeiture.

o Under federal law, it is a crime to import, export, sell, offer for sale, or use the mails to transport any drug paraphernalia. Possession of drug paraphernalia is also commonly a criminal offense under state laws.

o Some employees, and teachers and students in many school districts, are subjected to drug testing, and these programs generally have been upheld by the courts.

o Advocates of legalization contend that criminal prohibition of drug use has led to a vast underground economy and that the war on drugs has debased the rule of law by ineffective attempts to alter personal conduct.

- Learning Objective 8

  o Marijuana violations lead to nearly half of all drug arrests in the United States. Despite aggressive law enforcement, marijuana remains widely available, a situation that exemplifies the difficulty of enforcing a law that has less-than-universal public support. Nevertheless, courts have generally declined to reassess legislative judgments in this area, and statutes making it a criminal offense to possess marijuana have withstood numerous constitutional challenges.

  o During the 1970s several states decriminalized their antimarijuana laws by removing the threat of a jail sentence for possession offenses. Between 1996 and 2012, seventeen states and the District of Columbia passed laws legalizing marijuana for medical use.

  o Legalization of marijuana creates a conflict between state and federal law because in 2005 the Supreme Court held that Congress has the power under the Commerce Clause to prohibit the mere possession of small quantities of marijuana, even if it is solely for personal medicinal use authorized by state law.

- Learning Objective 9

  o Because those involved in narcotics transactions are usually willing participants, enforcement often depends on the use of confidential informants by police. Obtaining search warrants and making arrests based on probable cause often present difficult Fourth Amendment problems.

  o In drug possession cases, a critical problem is proving that the defendant was in actual or constructive possession of a controlled substance. Defendants on trial for drug offenses sometimes assert that they were entrapped by the police.

  o More frequently, defense counsel attempt to suppress the contraband seized by police on the ground that it was obtained in violation of the Fourth Amendment prohibition against unreasonable searches and seizures.

- Learning Objective 10

  o The establishment of drug courts has been an important development in the criminal justice system. Rather than sending nonviolent defendants to jail, a drug court—in collaboration with prosecutors, defense counsel, and other professionals—monitors their progress through status hearings and prescribes sanctions and rewards. There is evidence that this approach can reduce substance abuse, rehabilitate participants, and thereby reduce recidivism.

## Key Terms

adultery

bigamy

breathalyzer

child pornography

civil forfeiture

consideration, prize, and chance

contraband

controlled substances

Controlled Substances Act

criminal forfeiture

driving under the influence (DUI)

driving while intoxicated (DWI)

driving with an unlawful blood-alcohol
    level (DUBAL)

drug courier profiling

drug court

drug paraphernalia

drug-testing requirements

field sobriety test

fornication

gambling

hard-core pornography

human trafficking

implied consent statutes

incest

indecent exposure

lewd and lascivious conduct

lottery

numbers racket

obscenity

patently offensive

polygamy

prostitution

prurient interest

public drunkenness

right of privacy

seduction

sodomy

vice

voyeurism

zero tolerance law

## Questions for Thought and Discussion

1. Assume you are a legislative assistant for a member of the state house of representatives. Your representative intends to introduce a bill to prohibit up-skirt videography in public shopping areas. She asks you to prepare a memo suggesting language for the bill. What do you think should be included in the text of the bill?

2. Would prostitution be more injurious or less injurious to the public health, welfare, and morality if it were legalized and regulated?

3. Is "mooning," a common adolescent prank, a form of indecent exposure in your state?

4. How are laws proscribing obscenity susceptible to the overbreadth and vagueness challenges discussed in Chapter 3?

5. Given the fact that there are millions of Internet users throughout the United States, is it appropriate for courts to apply the "contemporary community standards" test in making determinations concerning obscenity on the Internet?

6. Do you think Congress can devise a law that will pass constitutional muster to protect children from Internet pornography? What suggestions do you have in this area?

7. What, if any, constitutional objections could be raised against a city ordinance making it a criminal offense "to use profane language in a public place"?

8. What forms of gambling are legal and illegal in your state? Are there any particular games that fall into a gray area between permitted and prohibited activity? Is church bingo legal in your state?

9. Should chronic alcoholism be a defense to intoxication offenses such as public drunkenness or driving under the influence?

10. Is requiring a person suspected of driving while intoxicated to submit to a blood-alcohol test a violation of the Fifth Amendment prohibition against compulsory self-incrimination?

11. Is it sensible to maintain the criminal prohibitions against illicit drugs, or should these substances be legalized and carefully regulated, and their abuse dealt with through other means?

12. What are the typical difficulties facing prosecutors in drug possession cases?

13. Why, according to *Robinson v. California*, may a person not be held criminally liable for being addicted to illicit narcotics? Is this decision distinguishable from *Powell v. Texas*?

14. Is the drug court method of dealing with nonviolent drug offenders superior to the traditional methods of imposing a fine or jail term or placing the defendant on probation? Should drug courts limit eligibility to participate to first-time offenders?

15. How does the prosecution establish that a defendant is in constructive possession of illicit drugs?

16. To what extent have the federal courts approved drug testing of students in public institutions?

17. To what extent has the U.S. Supreme Court placed restrictions on forfeiture of real estate involved in drug trafficking operations?

18. Has your state legalized possession of marijuana for medical use? If so, what are the requirements and restrictions?

## Problems for Discussion and Solution

1. Gerald N. runs a video game arcade. One of his most popular games is called Video Blackjack. Essentially, the game is a computerized form of blackjack in which the contestant plays against the computer. The cost of playing the game is fifty cents. The contestant who wins the game is issued a token that can be used to play any other game in the arcade. Suppose your state gambling statute prohibits all "games involving valuable consideration, chance, and a possible prize." If you were the prosecutor, would you be concerned about the legality of this game?

2. A popular social networking website targets teenage users and is supported solely by advertising revenue. Users create accounts, share music clips, post announcements about their interests and activities, and communicate with their peers through the site. In recent months, several pedophiles have been caught using the site to solicit young victims across the country. In response to public outcry, the Sylvania state legislature passed a law making it illegal for children under the age of eighteen to visit the site. Violators are to be fined $100 and compelled to attend a six-hour diversionary program on Internet safety. Two challenges to the new law are pending in the courts. Sylvania resident Rachel Rebel (age sixteen) was caught maintaining an account on the site to promote her new band and to solicit gigs. Ms. Rebel was adjudged delinquent by her county's juvenile court system. She is now appealing that decision. Does she have a case? What would be her contentions on appeal?

3. Suppose you were elected to the state assembly. In your first week on duty, a colleague asks you to cosponsor a bill she plans to introduce that would decriminalize all drug possession offenses in your state, as long as the quantity of drugs

possessed is relatively small. The bill would require offenders to complete a drug education and treatment program in lieu of payment of a substantial civil fine, but it would not permit the state to incarcerate anyone for drug possession. Would you be willing to cosponsor the bill? Why or why not? If not, are there amendments you might propose that would engender your support for the legislation?

4. Late one night, a deputy sheriff found Ronald Rico in his car parked on the side of a road in a rural area of the county. Rico was at the wheel, the headlights were on, and the radio was playing at a loud volume. The motor was not running. No one else was in the vehicle. A field sobriety test and a later chemical test indicated that Rico had a 0.14 blood alcohol concentration level. Under these circumstances, should Rico be prosecuted for driving under the influence of alcohol? What defenses would a lawyer representing Rico likely raise?

5. Police were called to quell a disturbance at a motel where the management had reported some disorderly conduct and apparent drug use. Outside the motel, the police observed Henry Egad standing by a tree. About eighteen inches from Egad's feet, the police discovered a matchbox on the ground. Their examination revealed that the matchbox contained a substance that later proved to be PCP, an illegal drug. Police placed Egad under arrest and charged him with possession of a controlled substance. Based on these facts alone, do you think the prosecutor can establish that Egad was in possession of the PCP?

CHAPTER **11**

# Offenses against Public Health and the Environment

## CHAPTER OUTLINE

Introduction

Public Health Legislation

Planning and Zoning Laws

The Scope of Federal and State Environmental Statutes

Noise Pollution

Antismoking Legislation

Wildlife Protection Laws

Conclusion

Chapter Summary

Key Terms

Questions for Thought and Discussion

Problems for Discussion and Solution

## JURISPRUDENCE

*United States v. Wiesenfeld Warehouse Co.* (1964)

*United States v. Dotterweich* (1943)

*United States v. Pennsylvania Industrial Chemical Corp.* (1973)

## LEARNING OBJECTIVES

After reading this chapter, you should be able to explain

1. why government has criminalized offenses against the public health and the natural environment and why most offenses in this area do not have antecedents in the English common law

2. why many offenses in this area are strict liability crimes and why laws carrying more severe penalties are apt to include a *mens rea* requirement

3. the importance of the federal Food, Drug, and Cosmetic Act in criminalizing offenses to the public health

4. why violations of zoning ordinances seldom result in criminal prosecutions

5. the range of federal environmental laws and the agencies involved in the enforcement of those laws

6. how and why corporations and responsible corporate officers can be held criminally liable for offenses against the public health and the natural environment

7. how Congress and local governing bodies have addressed the problem of noise pollution

8. why states and cities are prohibiting smoking in certain places

9. how federal and state laws protect wildlife and, in particular, endangered species

## CHAPTER OPENING VIGNETTE

When BP's Deepwater Horizon offshore drilling rig exploded and burned on April 20, 2010, it touched off the largest oil spill in the history of the United States. Oil gushed from the severed wellhead 5,000 feet below the surface of the Gulf of Mexico at a rate of more than a million gallons per day. It was not until mid-July that BP was able to stop the flow of oil, and not until mid-September that the well was permanently sealed. By then, more than 200 million gallons of oil had leaked into the Gulf. Despite efforts by BP, the government, and others to mitigate the effects of the spill and begin the cleanup of the Gulf, wetlands, and beaches, much of the ecology and economy of the Gulf Coast had been devastated. Without a doubt, the oil spill of 2010 was the worst environmental disaster in American history. Most economists agreed that the economic cost of the spill was far greater than the $20 billion that BP agreed to place in a fund to compensate victims of the disaster.

On June 1, 2010, Attorney General Eric Holder announced that the Department of Justice had opened a criminal investigation of the BP oil spill. Holder mentioned that several laws may have been broken: the Clean Water Act, the principal federal statute dealing with water pollution; the Migratory Bird Act, a federal law making it a crime to kill migratory birds; and the Refuse Act, which prohibits illegal dumping in the nation's waterways. In this chapter we discuss all three of these important environmental statutes. In contemplating criminal prosecution under these and other environmental laws, one must consider carefully the culpable mental state (*mens rea*) required for criminal violations. Obviously, BP and the company that operated the Deepwater Horizon did not intentionally spill millions of barrels of oil into the Gulf of Mexico. What, then, would be the basis for holding BP criminally liable? Think about this question as you read this chapter.

## Introduction

In the wake of the Industrial Revolution, people recognized the need for government to protect the public health. In the latter decades of the twentieth century, society became aware of the need for governmental action to protect the natural environment as well. Obviously, these two societal interests are closely related, as public health is greatly dependent on a healthy natural environment. Increasingly, governments at all levels (i.e., federal, state, and local) are making use of criminal sanctions as means of protecting the public health and the environment.

In addition to offenses involving the adulteration or misbranding of foods, medicines, and cosmetics and the unlawful exposure of others to germs or toxins, this chapter examines **environmental crime**, which includes, among other things, the unlawful pollution of the air and water; unlawful transportation, handling, or storage of hazardous materials; and unlawful destruction of protected animal and plant species or their habitats.

Beyond protecting natural resources and public health, the criminal law seeks to promote aesthetic values. Laws forbidding **littering** or dumping of refuse along the roadside are based on aesthetic considerations as well as environmental and public health concerns. **Antismoking laws**, which we discuss later in this chapter, are motivated by aesthetic as well as public health concerns. **Noise ordinances** also seek to protect the aesthetic quality of the living environment that people share.

## Sources of Law Defining Crimes against the Public Health and the Environment

As we have seen throughout the foregoing chapters, common-law crimes were originally recognized by courts and later revised and expanded by legislatures. But crimes against public health and the environment do not have their origin in the English common law. Rather, these offenses originated directly from Congress and state legislatures in response to the needs of a changing society. Offenses relating to public health originated in the late nineteenth and early twentieth centuries as a result of the widespread distribution of food, drugs, and cosmetics and the need to control communicable diseases. By the early 1900s, municipalities perceived the need for zoning to control nuisances and to regulate land use. Since the middle of the twentieth century, pollution of the ground, water, and air has been recognized as a major threat to the health and welfare of the people and, indeed, to the ecological balance of the Earth.

Enforcing regulations in these fields is accomplished largely through regulatory agencies and measures imposing civil liability. Nevertheless, legislatures have found it necessary to impose criminal sanctions to enforce standards effectively and to deter violators. Although not faced with the severe environmental problems of our age, the common law did regard wildlife, game, and fish as resources to be preserved by government. In the United States, the state and federal governments have for many years imposed criminal sanctions against **poaching** to protect these resources for the benefit of the public.

In contrast with the typical common-law crimes, many offenses against the public health and environment consist of an offender's neglect to comply with required standards or failure to take action required by law. These offenses are *mala prohibita*, and statutes criminalizing conduct in these areas generally contemplate a lower level of intent, frequently imposing a standard of **strict liability** (a concept we introduced in Chapter 4). For example, in *State v. Budd Co.*, 425 N.E.2d 935 (Ohio App. 1980), the defendant was convicted under a state law that made it a criminal offense to dispose of garbage or other pollutants in any ditch, pond, stream, or other watercourse. On appeal, the court rejected the appellant's argument that it was necessary for the state to prove his criminal intent. The court observed that the law did not require proof of intent and that "the destruction of wildlife through pollution will occur whenever the waterways are intentionally or accidentally polluted." 425 N.E.2d at 938.

---

**environmental crime** A violation of a criminal provision of an environmental statute such as the Clean Air Act, the Clean Water Act, the Refuse Act, and so forth.

**littering** The crime of disposing of garbage or other waste material along a public street or road, or in public parks, beaches, or waterways.

**antismoking laws** State statutes or local ordinances prohibiting or restricting smoking in all or specified public places.

**noise ordinances** Local laws restricting the making of excessive noise.

**poaching** Taking of game illegally, either by hunting protected species, hunting out of season, hunting in areas in which hunting is prohibited, or violating restrictions as to the number or size of animals that may be taken.

**strict liability** Criminal responsibility based solely on the commission of a prohibited act.

# Public Health Legislation

The authority of government to enact laws to protect the public health is a basic-component of the police power of the state. Statutes delegating to public health agencies the power to declare quarantines, and later to require inoculations to control communicable diseases, were among the earliest applications of this police power. At the turn of the century, the U.S. Supreme Court reviewed a defendant's sentence to pay a fine for refusing to be vaccinated for smallpox as required by a Cambridge, Massachusetts, ordinance. The defendant argued that a compulsory vaccination law invaded his liberty under the Constitution. Rejecting this contention, the Court observed that "persons and property are subjected to all kinds of restraints and burdens in order to secure the general comfort, health, and prosperity of the state." *Jacobson v. Massachusetts*, 197 U.S. 11, 26, 25 S.Ct. 358, 361, 49 L.Ed. 643, 650 (1905). Today all states require vaccinations of public school students; however, they often provide exemptions where parents show that vaccinations are contrary to their religious beliefs.

Today, numerous federal, state, and local laws address health concerns, providing criminal penalties for serious violations. Modern statutes address a variety of contemporary problems. California, like other states, has a comprehensive collection of laws concerning prevention and control of communicable disease and sexually transmitted disease. Section 120600 of the California Health and Safety Code stipulates the following:

> Any person who refuses to give any information to make any report, to comply with any proper control measure or examination, or to perform any other duty or act required by this chapter, or who violates any provision of this chapter or any rule or regulation of the state board issued pursuant to this chapter, or who exposes any person to or infects any person with any venereal disease; or any person infected with a venereal disease in an infectious state who knows of the condition and who marries or has sexual intercourse, is guilty of a misdemeanor.

In *Reynolds v. McNichols*, 488 F.2d 1378 (10th Cir. 1973), a federal appeals court upheld a Denver, Colorado, "hold and treat" ordinance authorizing detention and treatment, if necessary, of a woman arrested for prostitution who was reasonably suspected of having a venereal disease. Indeed, many states now have statutes imposing criminal penalties on health care professionals who fail to report communicable diseases. See, e.g., West's Colo. Stat. Ann. § 25-4-402. A California appellate court has held that under the "special needs" doctrine, the state, without individualized suspicion, may require that a person convicted of prostitution be tested for AIDS. *Love v. Superior Court*, 276 Cal. Rptr. 660 (Cal. App. 1990). In *Fosman v. State*, 664 So.2d 1163 (Fla. App. 1995), the court held that a court order requiring a defendant charged with sexual battery to submit to an HIV test did not constitute an unreasonable search and seizure. Florida has also enacted laws criminalizing intentional sexual transmission of HIV without a partner's consent and making it a felony for a person who knows that he or she is HIV-positive to donate blood or organs. West's Fla. Stat. Ann. §§ 381.0041(11), 384.24(1). In Nevada, a licensed prostitute who practices with knowledge of a positive HIV test result is guilty of a felony. Nev. Rev. Stat. § 201.358. Most public health laws that impose criminal penalties create strict liability offenses in that they do not include any intent requirement. In those instances the government need only prove that the defendant violated the statute.

# The Federal Food, Drug, and Cosmetic Act

In 1848 Congress first enacted legislation to prevent the importation of adulterated drugs and medicines. Today, numerous federal acts relate to foods and drugs, but the basic **Food, Drug, and Cosmetic Act (FDCA)** dates back to 1906. It was comprehensively amended in 1938 and subsequently amended many times. 21 U.S.C.A. §§ 301–392. The present law prohibits traffic in food, drugs, and cosmetics being prepared or handled under unsanitary circumstances or under conditions that render them injurious to health. Included in its broad sweep are prohibitions against misbranding and adulteration of food, drugs, and cosmetics, as well as requirements for truthful labeling.

> **Food, Drug, and Cosmetic Act (FDCA)** Federal law that prohibits traffic in food, drugs, and cosmetics prepared or handled under unsanitary circumstances or under conditions that render them injurious to health.

The U.S. Supreme Court has declared that the purpose of the FDCA is "to safeguard the consumer by applying the act to articles from the moment of their introduction into interstate commerce all the way to the moment of their delivery to the ultimate consumer." *United States v. Sullivan*, 332 U.S. 689, 696, 68 S.Ct. 331, 336, 92 L.Ed. 297, 303 (1948). Violations of the FDCA are punishable by criminal penalties, civil fines, and injunctive relief, and, in some instances, by seizure of the articles found to be adulterated or misbranded. Specifically, the FDCA prohibits

(a) The introduction or delivery for introduction into interstate commerce of any food, drug, device, or cosmetic that is adulterated or misbranded.

(b) The adulteration or misbranding of any food, drug, device, or cosmetic in interstate commerce.

(c) The receipt in interstate commerce of any food, drug, device, or cosmetic that is adulterated or misbranded, and the delivery or proffered delivery thereof for pay or otherwise. 21 U.S.C.A. § 331.

The FDCA defines adulterated food, 21 U.S.C.A. § 342; sets out standards for considering whether drugs and devices are adulterated, 21 U.S.C.A. § 351; and sets out criteria for adulterated cosmetics, 21 U.S.C.A. § 361. In general an item is considered adulterated if its ingredients are poisonous, filthy, putrid, or otherwise unsanitary or if it has come into contact with unsanitary substances.

Misbranding includes false or misleading labels, packaging, and containers. Specifically, 21 U.S.C.A. § 343 defines misbranded foods; 21 U.S.C.A. § 352 classifies misbranded drugs and devices; and 21 U.S.C.A. § 362 defines misbranded cosmetics.

In 1952, the Eighth Circuit declared, "It is not necessary that [food] actually become contaminated. . . . [T]he statute is designed to prevent adulterations 'in their incipiency' by condemning unsanitary conditions which may result in contamination." *Berger v. United States*, 200 F.2d 818, 821 (8th Cir. 1952). Numerous federal court decisions have interpreted what constitutes adulteration and misbranding under the FDCA. Illustrative decisions include:

- *United States v. Kohlback*, 38 F.3d 832 (6th Cir. 1994), where the court found that orange juice had been adulterated by adding beet sugar, other additives, and preservatives in order to extend the product's shelf life.
- *United States v. Bhutani*, 175 F.3d 572 (7th Cir. 1999), where the court noted the jury had found that a manufacturer adulterated a liver drug by "spiking" it with sodium hydroxide and repacking it with falsified expiration dates.
- *United States v. Haas*, 171 F.3d 259 (5th Cir. 1999), where the court upheld a conviction for aiding and abetting the illegal delivery of misbranded drugs into interstate commerce by sale of non-FDA-approved drugs.

*United States v. Wiesenfeld Warehouse Co.*, 376 U.S. 86, 84 S.Ct. 559, 11 L.Ed.2d 536 (1964)

Section 301(k) of the Federal Food, Drug, and Cosmetic Act prohibits the "alteration, mutilation, destruction, obliteration, or removal of the whole or any part of the labeling of, or the doing of any other act with respect to, a food, drug, device, or cosmetic, if such act is done while such article is held for sale after shipment in interstate commerce and results in such article being adulterated. . . ." The Court addressed whether a public storage warehouseman's holding of food after interstate shipment but before sale in a building accessible to rodents, birds

and insects violated § 301(k). The U.S. District Court for the Middle District of Florida concluded that § 301(k) did not apply to "the mere act of 'holding' goods" on the ground that the Act was too vague and indefinite. The Supreme Court reversed, relying in part on legislative history. The Court concluded that the Congressional intent showed a desire to prohibit the holding of food in unsanitary conditions causing contamination. The Court noted that in the area of food and drug regulation, criminal intent, or an awareness of wrongdoing, was not always a requirement to justify criminal responsibility.

In addition to provisions prohibiting adulteration and misbranding, the FDCA proscribes

> The alteration, mutilation, destruction, obliteration, or removal of the whole or any part of the labeling of, or the doing of any other act with respect to, a food, drug, device, or cosmetic, if such act is done while such article is held for sale (whether or not the first sale) after shipment in interstate commerce and results in such article being adulterated or misbranded. 21 U.S.C.A. § 331(k).

The Supreme Court has held that § 331(k) defines two distinct offenses with respect to products held for sale after interstate shipment: (1) acts relating to misbranding and (2) acts relating to adulteration of the product. *United States v. Wiesenfeld Warehouse Co.*, 376 U.S. 86, 84 S.Ct. 559, 11 L.Ed.2d 536 (1964).

## Strict Liability Offenses

**regulatory offenses** Criminal offenses of statutory origin dealing with public health and the environment. The term is also used to denote noncriminal violations of regulations promulgated by government agencies in the executive branch.

As do most public health laws, violations of federal food and drug laws fall in the category of **regulatory offenses**. Therefore, unless the statute criminalizing conduct or failure to act requires an intent element, criminal liability can attach without proof of the defendant's intent. *United States v. Wiesenfeld Warehouse Co.*, supra; *United States v. Park*, 421 U.S. 658, 670, 95 S.Ct. 1903, 1910, 44 L.Ed.2d 489, 500 (1975).

In *United States v. Dotterweich*, 320 U.S. 277, 64 S.Ct. 134, 88 L.Ed. 48 (1943), the U.S. Supreme Court established a standard of strict liability for violations of the FDCA by holding that proof of the defendant's intent to commit a violation was not required to obtain a misdemeanor conviction. In felony prosecutions, however, the government must prove the defendant's intent. Moreover, in prosecutions under certain sections of the FDCA, lower federal courts have held that to obtain a felony conviction, the government must establish the defendant's specific intent. See, for example, *United States v. Mitcheltree*, 940 F.2d 1329 (10th Cir. 1991), where the defendant was prosecuted for violating 21 U.S.C.A. §§ 331(a) and 333(a)(2) for introducing a misbranded drug into interstate commerce with the intent to mislead or defraud.

Many legal scholars criticize the imposition of strict liability in regulatory offenses, such as violations of food, drug, and health laws. They contend that it brands

**negligence standard** The basic standard for liability in civil cases; the failure to exercise ordinary care or caution.

as criminals people who are without moral fault. Arguing against making the violation of such laws punishable by incarceration, critics suggest decriminalization, with liability predicated on a **negligence standard** rather than on strict liability, or punishment by only a monetary fine. These criticisms notwithstanding, Congress has determined that the interest of society requires a high standard of care and has been unwilling to eliminate either the strict liability standard or incarceration. The courts follow *United States v. Park*, supra, and hold that a corporate agent who bears a responsible relationship to the operation of the enterprise, and has power to take measures necessary to ensure compliance, can be found guilty of violating such regulatory statutes.

## Criminal Liability of Responsible Corporate Officers

**responsible corporate officer** A person who holds a supervisory position in an organization, and may be subject to criminal liability for regulatory offenses committed by subordinates.

Food, drugs, and cosmetics are usually produced and distributed by corporate enterprises. To enforce regulatory laws imposing criminal sanctions in these areas effectively, government agencies must be able to affix responsibility on individuals in supervisory positions as well as on corporate entities. The Supreme Court first recognized the concept of a **responsible corporate officer** in *United States v. Dotterweich*, supra. There, a pharmacy company and Dotterweich, its president and general manager, were charged with shipping misbranded and adulterated drugs in violation of the FDCA. The U.S. Supreme Court upheld Dotterweich's conviction, and held that a "responsible corporate officer" could be held accountable for corporate violations of the FDCA.

Until 1975 there were conflicting federal court decisions about whether a corporate officer who failed to take measures to prevent violations of the food and drug laws from occurring could be held criminally liable. Recognizing this conflict, the Supreme Court again addressed the standard of liability of corporate officers under the FDCA in *United States v. Park*, 421 U.S. 658, 95 S.Ct. 1903, 44 L.Ed.2d 489 (1975). There, a national retail food chain and its president and chief executive officer were charged with causing food shipped in interstate commerce to be held in a building accessible to rodents and exposed to contamination. The food chain pled guilty, but its president contested the charges against him. He argued that although he retained authority over corporate affairs, he delegated "normal operating duties," including sanitation, to lower-level personnel. In rejecting his contention as a basis of

### JURISPRUDENCE

*United States v. Dotterweich*, 320 U.S. 277, 64 S.Ct. 134, 88 L.Ed. 48 (1943)

Buffalo Pharmacal Co., Inc., and its president and general manager, Joseph H. Dotterweich, were indicted for violating the Federal Food, Drug, and Cosmetic Act on the ground that the company purchased drugs from various pharmaceutical manufacturers, shipped the medications, and repackaged the medications with its own label. The Act prohibited "the introduction or delivery from introduction into interstate commerce of any drug that is . . . misbranded." The jury declined to find

the company guilty but did find Dotterweich guilty of three violations of the Act in his capacity as a corporate officer. A federal appellate court reversed his conviction, but the Supreme Court reversed again and upheld Dotterweich's conviction. The court addressed whether a corporate officer could be criminally responsible for the acts of the corporation and held that under the Act, a corporation and those individuals who aid and abet a corporation's criminal acts are "equally guilty." The Court reasoned that Dotterweich was in a responsible position to prevent any public danger.

nonliability, the Court explained that the prosecution established a *prima facie* case of the guilt of the accused when it established that the defendant had, by reason of his position in the corporation, responsibility and authority either to prevent in the first instance or promptly to correct the violation complained of and that he failed to do so. The Court left open a means for a defendant to establish that he or she was powerless to prevent or correct a violation but noted, "If such a claim is made, the defendant has the burden of coming forward with evidence, but this does not alter the Government's ultimate burden of proving . . . the defendant's guilt, including his power, in light of the duty imposed by the Act, to prevent or correct the prohibited condition." *United States v. Park*, 421 U.S. at 673, 95 S.Ct. at 1912, 44 L.Ed.2d at 502. The Court agreed with the government that Park was subject to strict criminal liability because he failed to use his authority in operating the company to prevent the storage of food in an area where it could be contaminated by rodents.

## Defenses under the FDCA

Defendants charged with violations of the FDCA have challenged warrantless inspections, but in most cases this has not proved to be successful because the courts have ruled that the Fourth Amendment allows considerable latitude in inspection of commercial establishments. A corporate officer charged with a violation of the act may assert the defense of objective impossibility. In *United States v. Gel Spice Co., Inc.*, 773 F.2d 427 (2d Cir. 1985), the court noted that to establish the impossibility defense, the corporate officer must introduce evidence that he or she exercised extraordinary care but was nevertheless powerless to prevent or correct violations of the act. The defense is very difficult to establish and fails in most situations. In cases where the government prosecutes for misbranding of articles, the defense will sometimes rely on experts to establish the validity of the defendant's branding.

## Product Tampering

In 1982 seven people in the Chicago area died after taking Tylenol that had been adulterated after it was shipped to retail stores. No one was ever arrested, but the bizarre episode and the many "copycat" incidents that followed led drug manufacturers to improve greatly the security of their packaging. It also led to the enactment of

**CASE-IN-POINT**

### Responsibility Follows Authority

Dean Starr, secretary-treasurer of Cheney Brothers Food Corp., was convicted of violating the Federal Food, Drug, and Cosmetic Act, 21 U.S.C.A. §§ 301–391, for allowing contamination of food stored in a company warehouse over which he had operational responsibility. After an inspector from the Food and Drug Administration (FDA) pointed out the problem, the janitor for the warehouse was instructed to make corrections, but no action was taken. A month later, a second inspection

by the FDA disclosed that the problem had not been corrected. On appeal, Starr contended that he was not responsible because the janitor in charge had failed to comply with instructions to clean up the warehouse. The court rejected his argument, noting that Starr was aware of the problem after the first inspection and had ample time to remedy the situation. In affirming his conviction, the court also observed that supervisory officers have a duty to anticipate the shortcomings of their delegates.

*United States v. Starr*, 535 F.2d 512 (9th Cir. 1976).

the Federal Anti-Tampering Act of 1983, codified at 18 U.S.C.A. § 136. This statute prohibits product tampering and assigns investigative responsibility to the FDA and the U.S. Department of Agriculture (USDA) as well as the FBI. States have similar laws, of which the following Indiana statute is a good example:

… A person who:

(1) recklessly, knowingly, or intentionally introduces a poison, a harmful substance, or a harmful foreign object into a consumer product; or

(2) with intent to mislead a consumer of a consumer product, tampers with the labeling of a consumer product;

that has been introduced into commerce commits consumer product tampering, a Class D felony. However, the offense is a Class C felony if it results in harm to a person, and it is a Class B felony if it results in serious bodily injury to another person. Indiana Code § 35-45-8-2.

# Planning and Zoning Laws

Although sometimes used interchangeably, the terms "zoning" and "planning" are not synonymous. Zoning is primarily concerned with the use and regulation of buildings and structures, whereas planning is a broader term embracing the systematic and orderly development of a community. *State ex rel. Kearns v. Ohio Power Co.*, 127 N.E.2d 394, 399 (Ohio 1955).

In *Village of Euclid, Ohio v. Ambler Realty Co.*, 272 U.S. 365, 47 S.Ct. 114, 71 L.Ed. 303 (1926), the Supreme Court first upheld the concept of **zoning**, which allows local governments to divide areas of the community and to designate the permitted and prohibited land uses in the respective districts. Today land-use zoning has become widespread and sophisticated. For example, newer concepts such as the "planned unit development" (PUD) may permit a mixture of land uses on the same tract of land. See, e.g., *Rouse-Fairwood Development Ltd. Partnership v. Supervisor of Assessments for Prince George's County*, 773 A.2d 535 (Md. App. 2001). Comprehensive planning has evolved into complex land-use management that guides the development of a community. Such planning is implemented to a large degree by local zoning ordinances (their enactment usually preceded by studies and recommendations of professional consultants). Building codes are generally encompassed within the overall local zoning requirements. Local citizens are enlisted to sit on planning and zoning boards that make recommendations to the governing body. Any comprehensive zoning ordinance must provide for a board of adjustment to act in a quasijudicial capacity. The board must have the power to grant variances where strict enforcement of an ordinance would cause an undue hardship to property owners. It may also be empowered to approve special exceptions based on criteria specified in a zoning ordinance.

As with other regulatory measures, enforcement of local zoning codes is accomplished administratively in most instances. Failing this, local governments often resort to civil court actions, commonly seeking injunctive relief against violators. Most zoning ordinances classify violations as misdemeanors and provide for a fine and a jail term on conviction. Zoning ordinances, like most health regulations, generally do not include an intent requirement. Prosecution of violators is usually undertaken only as a last resort. But once a state or local government commences prosecution of a defendant for violating a zoning ordinance, it must meet all burdens placed on the prosecution in criminal proceedings. *People v. St. Agatha Home for Children*, 389 N.E.2d 1098 (N.Y. 1979).

**zoning** Local laws regulating the use of land.

**Environmental Protection Agency (EPA)** Independent agency within the executive branch of the national government with principal responsibility for the enforcement of federal environmental laws, promulgation of environmental regulations, and administration of environmental programs.

Numerous federal statutes and agencies play a part in regulating and enforcing the laws affecting our environment. Among the older agencies are the Army Corps of Engineers, the Coast Guard, and the Departments of the Interior, Commerce, Transportation, and Justice. A newer agency, the **Environmental Protection Agency (EPA)**, acts under the authority of major congressional enactments and has significant responsibilities in numerous areas, including hazardous wastes, toxic substances, and air and water pollution. State environmental agencies became active in the 1970s, and planning and coordinating councils now function at state, regional, and local levels. They play an important part in environmental regulation by establishing pollution controls, water management programs, and wastewater and solid-waste disposal programs.

# The Scope of Federal and State Environmental Statutes

The Commerce Clause found in Article I, Section 8 of the U.S. Constitution provides the authority for Congress to enact laws protecting the environment. Environmental regulation at the federal and state levels has become a vast undertaking. Laws enacted by federal and state governments are enforced by regulatory agencies, by civil suits, and by criminal prosecutions. At the federal level, the EPA, which came into being in 1970, coordinates national efforts to reduce environmental risks and enforces federal laws protecting health and the environment. During the 1970s government agencies relied almost exclusively on civil penalties as an enforcement tool. The concept changed in the 1980s and 1990s, when criminal enforcement of environmental laws became prominent, particularly in instances of egregious waste disposal, water pollution, and air pollution.

Most states now have environmental agencies that coordinate with the EPA in the enforcement of national environmental laws as well as in supervising the enforcement of state environmental laws. The California Environmental Protection Agency is a good example. In 1991 the governor, by executive order, established the agency as a cabinet-level position in order to restore, protect, and enhance the environment and to ensure public health, environmental quality, and economic vitality.

Some environmental crimes (usually punishable as misdemeanors) require only proof that the defendant committed a proscribed act or failed to comply with a required standard. In prosecutions of these strict liability offenses, the government may establish the defendant's guilt in a manner similar to that used in prosecuting many crimes against the public health. Other statutes (usually those that impose felony punishment) require the government to establish the defendant's negligent conduct or a willful or knowing violation, and many court decisions in environmental prosecutions turn on whether the evidence is sufficient to meet the required statutory standard.

**Rivers and Harbors Act** The first major environmental statute enacted by Congress. The Act authorizes the Army Corps of Engineers to regulate the use of the navigable waters of the United States.

**Refuse Act** A section of the Rivers and Harbors Act that makes it unlawful to discharge refuse matter of any kind into any navigable water of the United States.

## Major Federal Environmental Legislation Providing Criminal Sanctions

Congress enacted its first major environmental law, the **Rivers and Harbors Act**, 33 U.S.C.A. §§ 401–467, in 1899. Most of the Act deals with improvements to and regulation of the navigable waters of the country. But a section of the statute, 33 U.S.C.A. § 407, known commonly as the **Refuse Act**, makes it a misdemeanor to "throw, discharge, or deposit, or cause, suffer, or procure to be thrown, discharged, or deposited either from or out of . . . the shore (or) . . . manufacturing establishment . . . any

## JURISPRUDENCE

*United States v. Pennsylvania Industrial Chemical Corp.*, 411 U.S. 655, 93 S.Ct. 1804, 36 L.Ed.2d 567 (1973)

The Pennsylvania Industrial Chemical Corp. was convicted of violating the Rivers and Harbors Act of 1899 by discharging matter from iron and concrete pipes into navigable waters without a permit. The Act prohibited the "discharge or deposit into navigable waters of 'any refuse matter of any kind or description whatever other than that flowing from streets. . . .'" The Act also provided that "'the Secretary of the Army . . . may permit the deposit' of refuse matter deemed by the Army Corps of Engineers not to be injurious to navigation" as long as application was made to the Secretary of the Army before discharging any material. The Court held that the government could prosecute those who discharge refuse even without the promulgation of formal regulatory-permit program. Because Pennsylvania Industrial was not permitted to present evidence that it was misled by the Army Corps' regulations, the Court reversed and remanded for a new trial.

refuse matter of any kind or description . . . into any navigable water of the United States." Courts have held that the Refuse Act does not require the government to prove any culpable mental state. See, e.g., *United States v. White Fuel Corp.*, 498 F.2d 619 (1st Cir. 1978). A violation of the Act is thus a strict liability offense. Courts have interpreted "refuse" broadly to include oil. See, e.g., *United States v. White Fuel Corp.*, supra, where a company was prosecuted and fined after oil from its onshore tanks leaked into Boston Harbor. Thus, the Refuse Act provided a statutory basis for the federal government's criminal investigation into the calamitous BP oil spill of 2010.

In the 1970s and 1980s, Congress enacted a series of landmark statutes in the environmental field. In addition to providing regulatory authority for the Environmental Protection Agency and other federal agencies and providing for civil suits to address environmental torts, these laws contain important criminal provisions:

- Clean Air Act of 1970, 42 U.S.C.A. §§ 7401–7642.
- Federal Water Pollution Control Act of 1972 (Clean Water Act), 33 U.S.C.A. §§ 1251–1376.
- Resource Conservation and Recovery Act of 1976 (RCRA), 42 U.S.C.A. §§ 6901–6992.
- Toxic Substances Control Act of 1976 (TSCA), 15 U.S.C.A. §§ 2601–2692.
- Comprehensive Environmental Response, Compensation and Liability Act of 1980 (CERCLA), 42 U.S.C.A. §§ 9601–9675.

## The Clean Air Act

**Clean Air Act** A federal statute designed to enhance the quality of the air by regulating, deterring, and penalizing polluters.

The **Clean Air Act** sets federal standards designed to enhance the quality of the air by deterring air polluters. In 1977 Congress passed a series of amendments establishing stricter standards for air quality. As amended, the act provides criminal sanctions for the violation of any provisions for which civil penalties apply and for any person who knowingly makes any false representation in a document filed under the act.

The Clean Air Act recognizes that the prevention and control of air pollution at its source is the primary responsibility of states and local governments. It provides that enforcement may be delegated to the states pursuant to the State Implementation Plan (SIP), 42 U.S.C.A. § 7410, but the states are not required to enact minimum criminal provisions to receive EPA approval of their implementation plans.

Nevertheless, states are increasingly toughening criminal penalties in this area. State penalties for violations of air pollution laws vary. For example, violation of Oklahoma's Clean Air Act entails a fine of $25,000 or up to one year in jail per day for misdemeanor violations and a fine of $250,000 or up to ten years' imprisonment for violations classified as felonies. 27A Okla. Stats. Ann. § 2–5–116. Rhode Island law provides for substantial fines and imprisonment for violations of air pollution laws and regulations, yet it stipulates:

> No person shall be convicted or found liable in any criminal prosecution . . . brought by or on behalf of the state, the director or the public to enjoin, suppress, prohibit, or punish air pollution unless he or she knowingly violated a rule or regulation or order of the director, issued under the authority conferred upon him or her by [Ch. 23]. R.I. Gen. Laws.

There have been fewer criminal prosecutions for violation of air pollution laws than for violations of hazardous waste and water pollution laws. Two reasons have been advanced: first, the cost of criminal enforcement in this area is apparently great; second, the problems of enforcement are made exceedingly difficult for states because air pollution is a less stationary category of pollution.

## The Clean Water Act

**Clean Water Act (CWA)** A federal statute designed to enhance the quality of bodies of public water by regulating, deterring, and penalizing polluters.

**point source** Any discernible, confined, and discrete conveyance from which pollutants are or may be discharged.

The Federal Water Pollution Control Act of 1972, better known as the **Clean Water Act (CWA)**, 33 U.S.C.A. §§ 1251–1376, is designed to control water pollution and regulate industrial and other discharges into navigable waters. What constitutes "navigable waters" under the CWA is important because it defines the extent of EPA jurisdiction. The term has been subject to debate. In *Rapanos v. United States*, 547 U.S. 715, 126 S.Ct. 2208, 165 L.Ed.2d 159 (2006), a plurality opinion of the Supreme Court said that navigable waters under the CWA includes only relatively permanent standing or flowing bodies of water and does not cover transitory puddles or ephemeral flows of water. The CWA prohibits the discharge of pollutants from any **point source** into the navigable waters of the United States unless such discharge complies with a permit issued by the EPA pursuant to the National Pollutant Discharge Elimination System (NPDES) or by an EPA-authorized state agency. See 33 U.S.C.A. §§ 1311(a) and 1342. Although the CWA is enforced primarily through civil means, criminal sanctions have been imposed for willful or negligent violations of certain provisions concerning permits and the making of false statements. Amendments in 1987 substituted the term "knowingly" for the earlier intent requirement of "willfully" and imposed more stringent penalties for negligent violations and even more severe penalties for knowing violations of the act's criminal provisions. 33 U.S.C.A. § 1319(c)(2).

Courts have construed the term "knowingly" to find that a defendant's acts violate the CWA if those acts are proscribed, even if the defendant was not aware of the proscription. Thus, courts have held that the government need only prove that the defendant performed acts intentionally; it is not required to prove that the defendant knew those acts violated the CWA. *United States v. Hopkins*, 53 F.3d 533 (2d Cir. 1995).

Courts tend to construe the penal provisions of the CWA broadly and generally hold supervisory personnel vested with authority to a high standard of compliance. The trend in the federal courts is to hold responsible corporate officers criminally liable in environmental offenses despite their lack of "consciousness of wrongdoing."

### The *Exxon Valdez* Prosecution and Subsequent Civil Suit

In March 1989, the supertanker *Exxon Valdez* ran aground and ruptured, spilling more than 240,000 barrels of oil into Alaska's Prince William Sound and wreaking havoc on the natural environment. Subsequently, the federal government brought criminal charges against the Exxon Shipping Co. and its parent, Exxon Corporation, under the Clean Water Act, the Migratory Bird Act, the Ports and Waterway Safety Act, and the Dangerous Cargo Act. In October 1991, one week before the case was scheduled to go to trial, Exxon accepted a plea bargain under which it agreed to plead guilty and pay $25 million in federal fines and another $100 million in restitution, split between the federal and state governments. The $125 million fine was the largest environmental criminal fine in U.S. history.

In 1994, a federal district court in Anchorage, Alaska, ordered Exxon to pay roughly $287 million in compensatory damages to commercial salmon and herring fishermen, plus $5 billion in punitive damages. However, the Ninth Circuit Court of Appeals remanded the case to the district court to reconsider the punitive damages. *In re Exxon Valdez*, 270 F.3d 1215 (9th Cir. 2001). On remand, the district court concluded that the $5 billion in punitive damages was still fair, but in compliance with the Ninth Circuit mandate, it reduced the award to $4 billion. *In re Exxon Valdez*, 236 F. Supp.2d 1043 (2002). After further litigation, on December 22, 2006, the Ninth Circuit Court of Appeals ordered the district court to reduce the punitive damage award against Exxon to $2.5 billion.

*In re Exxon Valdez*, 472 F.3d 600 (9th Cir. 2006).

In *United States v. Hanousek*, 176 F.3d 1116 (9th Cir. 1999), Edward Hanousek Jr., a roadmaster for a railroad company, was convicted under a *respondeat superior* (supervisory responsibility) theory for the negligent discharge of oil into navigable waters, a violation of 33 U.S.C.A. § 1319(c)(1). The accident occurred due to a backhoe's puncture of a high-pressure oil line and resulted in the release of up to 5,000 gallons of oil directly into the Skagway River. Although Hanousek held a supervisory position of responsibility for construction and maintenance of the railroad track, he was home at the time of the accident. On appeal, he argued that the trial judge had violated his right to due process of law by failing to instruct the jury that the government had to prove that he acted with *criminal* and not ordinary negligence. The U.S. Court of Appeals for the Ninth Circuit rejected his argument, observing, "The criminal provisions of the CWA constitute public welfare legislation. . . . Public welfare legislation is designed to protect the public from potentially harmful or injurious items . . . and may render criminal 'a type of conduct that a reasonable person should know is subject to stringent public regulation and may seriously threaten the community's health or safety.'" The court then noted that "a public welfare statute may subject a person to criminal liability for ordinary negligence without offending due process." *Id.* at 1121–1122. The Ninth Circuit's decision sends a message to those who occupy supervisory roles that a supervisor can be held criminally liable for ordinary negligence in failing to take precautions to prevent another person from committing a violation of the CWA. Thus, in *United States v. Ortiz*, 427 F.3d 1278 (10th Cir. 2005), the Tenth Circuit Court of Appeals upheld the conviction of an operator of a chemical distillation facility for negligently discharging propylene glycol wastewater by pouring it into a toilet where the storm drain led to a navigable river.

A majority of the states have programs approved by the EPA. Although states vary somewhat in their approaches, many provide penalties similar to those in the federal act for either willful or negligent violations of water pollution provisions.

## The Government's Requirement of Proof of Violation of the Clean Water Act

In *United States v. Wilson*, 133 F.3d 251, 264 (4th Cir. 1997), the court stated:

> To establish a felony violation of the Clean Water Act, we hold [the government] must prove:

1. that the defendant knew that he was discharging a substance, eliminating a prosecution for accidental discharges;
2. that the defendant correctly identified the substance he was discharging, not mistaking it for a different, unprohibited substance;
3. that the defendant knew the method or instrumentality used to discharge the pollutants;
4. that the defendant knew the physical characteristics of the property into which the pollutant was discharged that identify it as a wetland, such as the presence of water and water-loving vegetation;
5. that the defendant was aware of the facts establishing the required link between the wetland and waters of the United States; and
6. that the defendant knew he did not have a permit.

## The Point Source Problem

As noted, the CWA prohibits the discharge of pollutants from any point source into the navigable waters of the United States unless such discharge complies with a permit issued by the EPA. The CWA states:

> The term "point source" means any discernible, confined and discrete conveyance, including but not limited to any pipe, ditch, channel, tunnel, conduit, well, discrete fissure, container, rolling stock, concentrated animal feeding operation, or vessel or other floating craft, from which pollutants are or may be discharged. This term does not include agricultural storm water discharges and return flows from irrigated agriculture. 33 U.S.C.A. 1362 (14)

Courts generally have interpreted "point source" broadly. For example, in *Froebel v. Meyer*, 217 F.3d 928, 938 (7th Cir. 2000), the court noted that several circuit courts have even considered that dams can act as point sources if an artificial mechanism introduces pollutants. In *Avoyelles Sportsmen's League, Inc. v. Marsh*, 715 F.2d 897 (5th Cir. 1983), the U.S. Court of Appeals for the Fifth Circuit held that bulldozers and backhoes are point sources within the meaning of the CWA.

The issue of whether a human being can be a point source came into sharp focus in 1988 after schoolchildren on a field trip discovered glass vials of blood in the Hudson River. The vials were traced to Plaza Health Laboratories, Inc. (Plaza Health), a blood-testing laboratory in Brooklyn, New York. In 1989 a federal grand jury handed down a four-count indictment against Plaza Health and its co-owner and vice president, Geronimo Villegas, for violating the CWA. At Villegas's trial the evidence revealed that Villegas had thrown the vials into water with his hands. The court instructed the jury that under the CWA, the act of physically throwing the pollutants into the water constituted a discharge from a point source. The jury found Villegas guilty on all four counts. On appeal by Villegas, the U.S. Court of Appeals for the Second Circuit found that the language and legislative history of the CWA and the case law interpreting the term "point source" supported a conclusion that "the statute was never designed to address the random, individual polluter like Villegas." Rather, the court noted that the term "point source" in the CWA was defined to include a "pipe, ditch, channel, tunnel, conduit, well, [and] discrete fissure" and to "evoke images of physical structures and instrumentalities that systematically act as a means of conveying pollutants from an industrial source to navigable waterways." Thus, applying the rule of lenity (a rule often applied in criminal prosecutions), the court found that the CWA did not clearly proscribe Villegas's conduct and therefore did not give him fair warning that he was violating the law. *United States v. Plaza Health Laboratories, Inc.,* 3 F.3d 643, 646 (2d Cir. 1993). A dissenting judge pointed out "the discharge was directly into the water, and came from an identifiable point," *Id.* at 653, and concluded that Villegas had fair warning that his actions were illegal and proscribed by the CWA. At the time this book was written, Congress had not acted to indicate that under the intent of the CWA a discharge of pollutants into the water by an individual is illegal, although many observers had expected that it would do so.

## The Resource Conservation and Recovery Act

**Resource Conservation and Recovery Act (RCRA)** The major federal law dealing with the transportation, storage, and disposal of hazardous waste.

Enactment of the **Resource Conservation and Recovery Act (RCRA)** in 1976 was a significant step in environmental control. It establishes detailed provisions for the regulation of hazardous wastes. Its objective is to encourage the states—through grants, technical assistance, and advice—to establish standards and provide for civil and criminal enforcement of state regulations. The EPA sets minimum standards requiring the states to enact criminal penalties against any person who knowingly stores or transports any hazardous waste to an unpermitted facility, who treats such waste without a permit, or who makes false representations to secure a permit. All states have enacted criminal statutes pursuant to the criteria specified in the RCRA.

The RCRA proscribes a comprehensive list of illegal actions and imposes criminal penalties on any person who

1. knowingly transports or causes to be transported any hazardous waste to an unpermitted facility, 42 U.S.C.A. § 6928(d)(1);
2. knowingly treats, stores, or disposes of any hazardous waste without a permit, in knowing violation of any material condition or requirement of the interim status, 42 U.S.C.A. § 6928(d)(2)(A)—(C); or one who
3. knowingly omits material information or makes any false statement or representation in any record or document required to be maintained under the regulations or submitted to the [EPA] or any state which is authorized to run RCRA programs. 42 U.S.C.A. § 6928(d)(3).

RCRA contains criminal penalties of up to five years' imprisonment and $50,000 per day in fines, or both. In addition, § 6928(e), often referred to as the "knowing endangerment" provision, makes it a criminal offense knowingly to place another person in imminent danger of death or serious bodily injury in conjunction with the transportation, storage, or disposal of hazardous wastes. This provision carries fines of up to $250,000 and up to fifteen years' imprisonment, or both. A defendant that is an organization is subject to a fine of not more than $1,000,000.

RCRA has become an important tool for enforcement, and prosecutors frequently rely on it when prosecuting persons who illegally dispose of hazardous wastes. In *United States v. Johnson & Towers, Inc.,* 741 F.2d 662, 664 (3d Cir. 1984), the court held that the term "person" in RCRA § 6928(d) includes employees as well as owners and operators, but that employees can be subject to criminal

## Criminal Prosecution under the Clean Water Act

David W. Boldt was the chemical engineering manager for Astro Circuit Corp., a Massachusetts company that manufactured circuit boards using an electroplating process. Boldt's duties included supervising the company's pretreatment process, a part of the pollution control system. He was charged with six counts of violating the Clean Water Act. He was convicted on two counts: one for knowingly aiding and abetting the discharge of pollutants into a municipal sewer in 1987, when the copper level in Astro's effluent greatly exceeded the federal standards, and another for ordering a subordinate in 1988 to dump 3,100 gallons of partially treated industrial wastewater containing excessive metals into the municipal sewer. At trial, Boldt asserted the defense of impossibility to the first incident, arguing he was only a mid-level manager who was not responsible for the discharge. Boldt

acknowledged responsibility for the second discharge but pleaded the defense of necessity, arguing it was necessary to authorize the discharge to avoid a worse harm.

In upholding both convictions, the appellate court observed that the evidence showed that pollution control was part of Boldt's area of responsibility and that, regarding the 1987 violation, he was aware of the practice of bypassing the pollution control system and had condoned it on the occasion at issue. Regarding the 1988 incident, the court found that the undisputed evidence showed Boldt directly ordered his subordinate to dump the copper wastewater, a conclusion bolstered by his subordinate's testimony that Boldt attempted to cover up the incident. Finally, the appellate court observed that the record of the trial disclosed that the president of Astro testified that Boldt was authorized to shut down the plant.

*United States v. Boldt*, 929 F.2d 35 (1st Cir. 1991).

prosecution only if they knew or should have known that there had been no compliance with the permit requirement of § 6925. Proof of the knowledge element required may be inferred for those individuals holding responsible corporate positions.

In *United States v. Hayes International Corp.*, 786 F.2d 1499 (11th Cir. 1986), the court affirmed a conviction under § 6928(d)(1) for unlawfully transporting hazardous waste materials to an unpermitted facility and ruled that neither a lack of knowledge that paint waste was a hazardous material nor ignorance of the permit requirement was a defense.

Conviction for the treatment, storage, or disposal of hazardous waste without an RCRA permit has been more problematic. In *United States v. Hoflin*, 880 F.2d 1033 (9th Cir. 1989), the court held that the government is not required to prove the defendant's knowledge of the lack of a permit to secure a conviction in either transport or storage cases; nevertheless, a person who does not know that the waste material he or she is disposing of is hazardous cannot be guilty of violating § 6928(d)(2)(a).

One of the most serious cases brought under the RCRA involved § 6928(e) (the knowing endangerment provision), which makes it a criminal violation to knowingly place employees "in imminent danger of death or serious bodily injury." *United States v. Protex Industries, Inc.*, 874 F.2d 740 (10th Cir. 1989), involved a company that operated a drum-recycling facility and, in connection with its business, purchased drums that previously contained toxic chemicals. The evidence revealed that the company's safety provisions were inadequate to protect its employees and, as a result, certain company employees suffered from solvent poisoning and exhibited serious maladies. The court upheld a conviction of Protex for placing employees in an industrial environment without sufficient protection against exposure to toxic chemicals.

### Prosecution of a "Responsible Corporate Officer" under the Clean Water Act

During 1996, Avion Environmental employees discharged untreated wastewater directly into the Richmond, Virginia, sewer system in violation of Avion's discharge permit. Based on these activities, the government charged James Hong, as a responsible corporate officer of Avion, with thirteen counts of negligently violating pretreatment requirements under the CWA, 33 U.S.C.A. § 1319(c)(1)(A) (West Supp. 2000). Hong, the sole shareholder of Avion Environmental, was convicted. Although he played a substantial role in the corporation's operations, Hong was not identified as an officer or as having direct oversight responsibility for operations from which the releases occurred. On appeal, Hong contended that the government failed to prove that he was a formally designated officer of Avion Environmental. Alternatively, he argued that there was no proof that he had sufficient control over the operations of Avion to be liable for violations of the CWA. The U.S. Fourth Circuit Court of Appeals rejected his arguments. The court held that the government was not required to prove that Hong was formally designated an officer of Avion. Rather, the court stated, "[T]he pertinent question is whether the defendant bore such a relationship to the corporation that it is appropriate to hold him criminally liable for failing to prevent the charged violations of the CWA." Holding that he did not prevent the violations, the court affirmed his convictions.

*United States v. Hong*, 242 F.3d 528, 531 (4th Cir. 2001).

## The Government's Requirement of Proof of RCRA Offenses

Actions that violate the RCRA are often quite evident, yet proof of an offending person's intent is often the key to successful prosecution under the RCRA. To successfully prosecute a defendant charged with illegally transporting hazardous materials to a facility that lacks a permit, the government must prove that the substance being transported fit within the parameters of the definition of "hazardous waste," not that the defendant had knowledge that the material was hazardous and waste. *United States v. Kelly,* 167 F.3d 1176 (7th Cir. 1999). A corporate officer who does not "directly" cause the violations may still be culpable. *United States v. Hansen,* 262 F.3d 1217, 1243 (11th Cir. 2001).

It is not necessary that the government prove that the defendant knew a chemical waste had been defined as a "hazardous waste" by the EPA. *United States v. Goldsmith,* 978 F.2d 643, 646 (11th Cir. 1992). The government need only prove that a defendant had knowledge of "the general hazardous character" of the chemical. *United States v. Dee,* 912 F.2d 741, 745 (4th Cir. 1990).

## The Toxic Substances Control Act

**Toxic Substances Control Act (TSCA)** Federal statute authorizing the Environmental Protection Agency to prohibit the manufacture, distribution, or use of chemicals that present unreasonable risks to the environment and to regulate the disposal of such chemicals.

The **Toxic Substances Control Act (TSCA)** of 1976 authorizes the EPA to require testing of, and to prohibit the manufacture, distribution, or use of, certain chemical substances that present an unreasonable risk of injury to health or the environment and to regulate their disposal. Section 14 of TSCA prohibits the commercial use of substances that the user knew or had reason to know were manufactured, processed, or distributed in violation of any provision of TSCA. 15 U.S.C.A. § 2614(2). Although the act depends primarily on civil penalties, a person who knowingly or willfully fails to maintain records or to submit reports as required violates the criminal provisions of the act. 15 U.S.C.A. §§ 2614, 2615(b).

## Criminal Prosecution under the RCRA: No Requirement that Defendant Knew Waste Would Be Harmful if Improperly Disposed

James Ralph Sellers was convicted of knowingly and willfully disposing of methylethylketone (M.E.K.), a hazardous waste, without obtaining a permit, a violation of 42 U.S.C.A. § 6928(d)(2)(A) (RCRA). At his jury trial the evidence revealed that residents discovered sixteen 55-gallon drums of hazardous paint waste on the embankment of a creek that flows into the Leaf River. These drums contained paint waste and M.E.K., a paint solvent. The evidence further revealed that Sellers did not have a permit for disposing of hazardous waste, nor did he take the waste to a licensed disposal area.

The trial court instructed the jury that the government must prove (1) that the defendant knowingly disposed of, or commanded and caused others to dispose of, wastes as charged in the indictment; (2) the

defendant knew what the wastes were; (3) the wastes were listed or identified or characterized by the EPA as a hazardous waste pursuant to the RCRA; and (4) the defendant had not obtained a permit from either the EPA or the state of Mississippi authorizing the disposal under the RCRA.

On appeal, Sellers argued that the jury charge should have required the government to prove that Sellers knew that the paint waste could be hazardous or harmful to persons or the environment. The U.S. Court of Appeals rejected Sellers's contention and held that in a prosecution for knowingly and willfully disposing of M.E.K., a hazardous waste, without obtaining a permit, there was no requirement that the defendant knew that waste would be harmful if improperly disposed of.

*United States v. Sellers*, 926 F.2d 410 (5th Cir. 1991).

There have been relatively few criminal prosecutions under TSCA; however, in 1982 a court upheld the conviction of Robert Earl Ward Jr., the chairman of the board of Ward Transformer Co., on eight counts of the unlawful disposal of toxic substances (PCB-containing oils from used transformers) and the willful aiding and abetting of the unlawful disposal of toxic substances. The evidence at trial revealed that although the defendant himself did not dispose of the toxic substances, the company's employees performed the task while he was kept advised of the progress. *United States v. Ward*, 676 F.2d 94 (4th Cir. 1982). In 1995 the U.S. Court of Appeals for the First Circuit found sufficient evidence to uphold a conviction of a defendant who allowed others to take PCB-laden transformers, knowing they would dump them unlawfully. *United States v. Catucci*, 55 F.3d 15 (1st Cir. 1995).

**Comprehensive Environmental Response, Compensation, and Liability Act (CERCLA)** Federal statute commonly known as the Superfund Law. Its purpose is to finance cleanup and provide for civil suits by citizens. The act also imposes reporting requirements for the collection and disposal of solid wastes. CERCLA imposes criminal penalties on those who act in a supervisory capacity and who are in a position to detect, prevent, and abate a release of hazardous substances.

## The Comprehensive Environmental Response, Compensation, and Liability Act

In 1980 Congress enacted the **Comprehensive Environmental Response, Compensation, and Liability Act (CERCLA)**, commonly known as the Superfund Law. Its purpose is to finance cleanup and provide for civil suits by citizens. As revised in 1986, the act requires notice to federal and state agencies of any "release" of a "reportable quantity" of a listed hazardous substance. "Release" is broadly defined, and "reportable quantity" is related to each of the several hundred "hazardous substances." CERCLA also allows the EPA to promulgate regulations for the collection and disposal of solid wastes. The act imposes criminal sanctions against those who fail to report as required or who destroy or falsify records. 42 U.S.C.A. § 9603(d)(2).

## Standard of Liability of Corporate Officers

Many violations in the public health area are caused by corporate entities; therefore, courts often focus on whether an accused, by reason of his or her position in the corporate enterprise, had sufficient responsibility and authority to either prevent or correct the violation charged. Courts hold responsible corporate officers liable in environmental crimes just as in prosecutions under the FDCA. In fact, Congress has adopted the "responsible corporate officer" doctrine in the Clean Air Act, 42 U.S.C.A. § 7413(c)(6), and the Clean Water Act, 33 U.S.C.A. § 1319(c)(3)(6). The doctrine has been upheld by federal appeals courts in CERCLA cases. For example, in *United States v. Carr*, 880 F.2d 1550 (2d Cir. 1989), the court rejected a maintenance supervisor's argument that he could not be guilty because he was a relatively low-level employee. The court explained that CERCLA imposes criminal responsibility on a person "even of relatively low rank" who acts in a supervisory capacity and is "in a position to detect, prevent, and abate a release of hazardous substances." 880 F.2d at 1554. Thus, a responsible corporate officer not only cannot avoid criminal liability by delegating tasks to others but also must remedy any violations that occur. At the state level, corporate executives have been charged with criminally negligent homicide and manslaughter where employees' deaths have resulted from the improper use of hazardous substances. See, e.g., *State ex rel. Cornellier v. Black*, 425 N.W.2d 21 (Wis. App. 1988).

## Lack of Uniformity in Environmental Laws

Disparate environmental standards, enforcement policies, and sanctions in the areas of water and air pollution and disposal of hazardous wastes can lead industrial companies to "shop" for locations that will enable them to be more competitive by not having to comply with stringent environmental standards. Significant differences exist among the fifty states in the standards of proof required and in the sanctions imposed for criminal violations of hazardous waste, water pollution, and air pollution laws.

Compare the differences between the statutory language in the Kentucky and Vermont offenses set out in Tables 11.1 and 11.2. What level of proof should be required for establishing a defendant's guilt under the "knowingly" standard of the Kentucky laws? Would a different standard of proof be required under Vermont's laws concerning hazardous wastes and air pollution?

Unfortunately, fines imposed on violators of environmental laws are too often regarded as "costs of doing business" because in reality these costs can be passed on to the ultimate consumer. The threat of imprisonment, on the other hand, is one cost that cannot be passed on to consumers; therefore, it is a powerful deterrent to those who would pollute the environment. As states more aggressively prosecute environmental crimes, more uniformity of criminal sanctions will undoubtedly develop, much as it has for the more common criminal offenses.

## Defenses to Environmental Crimes

Defendants' attacks on most environmental statutes, alleging them to be vague and ambiguous, have largely failed. Defenses asserting that a criminal prosecution constitutes double jeopardy (see Chapter 14 ) because the government has previously exacted a civil fine against the defendant have also been unsuccessful. Nevertheless, courts must provide an opportunity for assertion of defenses. In *United States*

| TABLE 11.1 | Kentucky Environmental Laws Imposing Criminal Penalties Concerning Hazardous Wastes, Water Pollution, and Air Pollution | |
|---|---|---|
| | **Unlawful Acts** | **Penalties** |
| Hazardous Wastes | Knowingly engaging in the generation, treatment, storage, transportation, or disposal of hazardous wastes in violation of this chapter, or contrary to a permit, order, or administrative regulation issued or promulgated under the chapter; or knowingly making a false statement, representation, or certification in an application for, or form pertaining to, a permit, or in a notice or report required by the terms and conditions of an issued permit. § 224.99-010(6). | Imprisonment between one and five years or a fine up to $25,000 per day of violation, or both. § 224.99-010(6). |
| Water Pollution | Knowingly violating any of the following: § 224.70-110 (water pollution) § 224.73-120 (monitoring and reporting) § 224.40-100 (waste disposal) § 224.40-305 (unpermitted waste disposal facilities) Or violating any determination, permit, administrative regulation, or order of the Cabinet promulgated pursuant to those sections which have become final; or knowingly providing false information in any document filed or required to be maintained under this chapter; or knowingly rendering inaccurate any monitoring device or method required to be maintained. § 224.99-010(4). | Imprisonment between one and five years or a fine up to $25,000 per day of violation, or both. § 224.99-010(4). |
| Air Pollution | Knowingly violating § 224.20-110 (air pollution), or any determination, permit, administrative regulation, or order of the Cabinet promulgated pursuant to those sections which have become final; or knowingly providing false information in any document filed or required to be maintained under this chapter; or knowingly rendering inaccurate any monitoring device or method required to be maintained. § 224.99-010(4). | Imprisonment between one and five years or a fine up to $25,000 per day of violation, or both. § 224.99-010(4). |

Source: Kentucky Revised Statutes Annotated.

*v. Pennsylvania Industrial Chemical Corp.*, 411 U.S. 655, 93 S.Ct. 1804, 36 L.Ed.2d 567 (1973), a manufacturing corporation was convicted under the Rivers and Harbors Act of discharging refuse into navigable waters without a permit. The Court reversed the defendant's conviction after the trial court failed to allow the defendant to present evidence at trial that he had been misled deliberately by the government about required permits, and thus deprived of presenting a defense.

Environmental cases can be very technical. Frequently they involve challenging the government's test results that form the basis of the charges. Some prosecutions under the CWA where defendants have eventually prevailed provide illustrations of defenses under environmental statutes. For example, in *United States v. Borowski*, 977 F.2d 27 (1st Cir. 1992), the First Circuit reversed a conviction where company officers directed employees to pour toxic chemicals into a drain that led to a public treatment plant. While observing that the defendants' conduct was reprehensible, the court held that they did not violate the CWA because prosecution for knowing endangerment under the CWA cannot be premised upon danger that occurs before a pollutant reaches publicly owned sewer or treatment works. As noted in *United States v. Plaza Health Labs* earlier in this chapter, in a prosecution under the CWA, defense counsel succeeded in establishing a restrictive application of what constitutes a discharge from a point source.

In *Village of Oconomowoc Lake v. Dayton Hudson Corp.*, 24 F.3d 962 (7th Cir. 1994), the Seventh Circuit held that a six-acre artificial retention pond that discharged only to groundwater did not constitute "waters of the United States," a predicate

| TABLE 11.2 | Vermont Environmental Laws Imposing Criminal Penalties Concerning Hazardous Wastes, Water Pollution, and Air Pollution | |
|---|---|---|
| | **Unlawful Acts** | **Penalties** |
| Hazardous Wastes | Violating any provision of the waste management chapter (transportation, storage, disposal, or treatment of hazardous waste; permit and manifest requirements), rules promulgated therein, or terms or conditions of any order of certification. Title 10, § 6612(a). | Imprisonment up to six months or a fine up to $25,000 per day of violation, or both. Title 10, § 6612(a). |
| | Violating any provision of the waste management chapter by the knowing or reckless (1) transport, treatment, storage or disposal of any hazardous waste; (2) transport, treatment, storage or disposal of more than one cubic yard of solid waste or more than 275 pounds of solid waste; or release of any hazardous material. Title 10, § 6612(d). | Imprisonment up to five years; or a fine not to exceed $250,000 or both. Title 10, § 6612(d). |
| Water Pollution | Violating any provision of the water pollution control subchapter, or failing, neglecting, or refusing to obey or comply with any order or the terms of any permit issued under this subchapter. Title 10, § 1275(a). | Imprisonment up to six months or a fine up to $25,000 per day of violation, or both. Title 10, § 1275(a). |
| | Knowingly making any false statement, representation, or certification in any document filed or required to be maintained under the water pollution control subchapter, or by any permit, rule, regulation, or order issued thereunder; or falsifying, tampering with, or knowingly rendering inaccurate any monitoring device or method required to be maintained under this subchapter, or by any permit, rule, regulation, or order issued thereunder. Title 10, § 1275(b). | Imprisonment up to six months or a fine up to $10,000 or both. Title 10, § 1275(b). |
| Air Pollution | Violating a provision of the air pollution control chapter (discharge of air contaminants without a permit or in violation of pollution standards) except § 563 and § 567 (relating to motor vehicles and confidential records), or any rule issued thereunder. Title 10, § 568(a). | Imprisonment up to five years, a fine up to $100,000 per violation, or both. Title 10, § 568(a). |
| | Knowingly making any false statement, representation or certification in any application, record, report, plan or falsifying, tampering with, or knowingly rendering inaccurate any monitoring devices required to be maintained under chapter or by permit, rule, regulation, or order issued under chapter. Title 10, § 568(b). | Imprisonment up to one year, a fine up to $50,000 per violation, or both. Title 10, § 568(b). |

Source: Vermont Statutes Annotated.

for conviction under the CWA's proscription on discharges of pollutants into navigable waters. In *Solid Waste Agency of Northern Cook County v. United States Army Corps of Engineers*, 531 U.S. 159, 121 S.Ct. 675, 148 L.Ed.2d 576 (2001), the U.S. Supreme Court held that isolated ponds, some used only seasonally as a habitat by migratory birds, did not fall within the CWA's definition of "navigable waters" merely because these waters served as a habitat for migratory birds. The Court's decision has caused speculation as to the viability of the so-called Migratory Bird Rule.

# Noise Pollution

**Quiet Communities Act** Federal law enacted in 1978 to protect the environment against noise pollution.

Congress enacted the **Quiet Communities Act** of 1978, 42 U.S.C.A. §§ 4901–4918, to protect the environment against noise pollution, which has become perceived as a growing danger to the health and welfare of the population. Section 4909 details prohibited acts, and § 4910 provides criminal penalties for those who knowingly or willfully import, manufacture, or distribute products that fail to comply with noise standards specified in the statute. However, the act recognizes that the primary responsibility for protecting communities against noise pollution lies with state and local governments.

Historically, local governments have adopted ordinances that prohibit excessive noise. In the twentieth century, ordinances have reflected concern about amplified sound equipment. Noise control ordinances often prohibit the use of loud audio equipment in an apartment building where residents live in close quarters. These ordinances are directed at loud late-night parties that disturb neighbors or against persons whose car stereos are played so loudly as to be an annoyance or even a safety hazard.

Most persons charged with violations of noise ordinances do not choose to contest the charges. Instead, they pay a small fine or agree to abate the violation. Those who do choose to contest the charge often attack the constitutionality of the ordinance. As we pointed out in Chapter 3, the vagueness doctrine requires that a statute that defines a criminal offense must be definite so that ordinary persons can understand what conduct is prohibited. Local ordinances that vaguely prohibit unnecessary noise are subject to constitutional challenge. In 1991 the Supreme Court of Mississippi held that Gulfport's noise control ordinance, by prohibiting "unnecessary or unusual noises . . . which either annoys, injures or endangers the comfort, repose, health or safety of others . . . fails to provide clear notice and sufficiently definite warning of the conduct that is prohibited." As a result, the court said that persons of "common intelligence must necessarily guess at its meaning and differ as to its application." *Nichols v. City of Gulfport*, 589 So.2d 1280, 1282 (Miss. 1991). Likewise the Supreme Court of Georgia invalidated a county ordinance that prohibited "any . . . unnecessary or unusual sound or noise which . . . annoys . . . others." The court held that the ordinance failed to provide the requisite clear notice and sufficiently definite warning of the conduct that is prohibited. *Thelen v. State*, 526 S.E.2d 60, 62 (Ga. 2000).

The city of Sarasota, Florida adopted an ordinance that amended its zoning code by prohibiting all amplified sound in nonenclosed structures in an area zoned "Commercial Business–Newtown" during specified times of day. Daley, who owned a restaurant that provided both live and recorded musical entertainment for its customers, challenged the ordinance's validity. A Florida appellate court invalidated the ordinance. *Daley v. City of Sarasota*, 752 So.2d 124 (Fla. App. 2000). The court recognized that music, as a form of expression and communication, is protected under the First Amendment and observed,

> The goal of regulating unreasonable sound is unquestionably a matter within the city's province. However, that goal, no matter how laudable, cannot be achieved by the overbroad regulation of activities protected by the First Amendment. As currently written, the city's ordinance can be used to suppress First Amendment rights far more severely than can be justified by the city's interest in regulating unreasonable sound. 752 So.2d at 126.

Narrowly drafted noise control ordinances fare better before judicial tribunals. In *City of Janesville v. Garthwaite*, 266 N.W.2d 418 (Wis. 1978), the city charged the defendant with violation of an ordinance that states, "No person shall make unnecessary and annoying noise with a motor vehicle by squealing tires, excessive acceleration of engine or by emitting unnecessary and loud muffler noises." The Supreme Court of Wisconsin held that the ordinance was a valid exercise of the city's police power to manage and control its streets.

In 2001 the Ohio Court of Appeals upheld the village of Kelleys Island's antinoise ordinance, which provides:

> No person shall generate or permit to be generated noise or loud sound which is likely to cause inconvenience or annoyance to persons of ordinary sensibilities by means of a live performance, radio, phonograph, television, tape player, compact disc player, loudspeaker or any other sound amplifying device which is plainly audible at a distance of 150 feet or more from the source of the noise or loud sound.

The owner of a bar that featured karaoke or live bands on an outdoor patio was cited for violation of the ordinance. The owner contended that the ordinance was vague and therefore unconstitutional under the First Amendment to the U.S. Constitution. The court, however, found that the ordinance was sufficiently definite to allow a person to determine what conduct violated the ordinance and prevent arbitrary enforcement. Addressing concerns as to the ordinance's constitutionality, the court explained that the "noise or loud sound" is made definite by adding that it must be "plainly audible" or "clearly heard" by a person using his or her "normal hearing faculties." Also, the noise or sound must be inconvenient or annoying to persons of "ordinary sensibilities." "Time and distance limitations also aid in providing fair warning of the nature of the unlawful conduct." The distance requirement puts "an objective quantifiable number into the ordinance, thus narrowing the scope of its operations." Thus, it held that the ordinance was a valid exercise of police power and not unconstitutionally vague. *Kelleys Island v. Joyce,* 765 N.E.2d 387, 393 (Ohio App. 2001).

# Antismoking Legislation

As society has become more aware of the ill effects of smoking and, in particular, the hazards of "secondhand smoke," governments have restricted smoking in public buildings and places of public accommodation and transportation. Perhaps the best-known example is the Federal Aviation Administration regulation prohibiting all smoking on domestic passenger airline flights. The last few years have witnessed enactment of no-smoking laws by states; by 2003 most states had laws restricting smoking in public places, and several have laws restricting smoking in private workplaces. In some instances state laws have preempted the subject, and local communities have been prevented from enacting conflicting ordinances. In other instances local communities have acted where the states have not. Often antismoking laws carry minor civil penalties, and local ordinances frequently impose penalties analogous to parking fines.

## The Florida Initiative

In November 2002 Florida voters, by a margin in excess of 70 percent, adopted a state constitutional amendment that required the state legislature to enact a comprehensive ban on smoking in restaurants and other public places. The state legislature promptly enacted laws that require proprietors to implement policies regarding smoking prohibitions in indoor workplaces and generally prohibit smoking in restaurants, with exceptions that allow smoking in "stand-alone" bars that serve incidental snacks, on outdoor patios at restaurants, at membership associations, in designated smoking rooms at public lodging establishments, and at designated smoking areas at airports. The new laws make violations noncriminal and impose civil fines for violators. West's Fla. Stat. Ann., Ch. 386.

## New York's Comprehensive Smoking Ban

In 2003 the New York legislature enacted a comprehensive antismoking law. McKinney's Public Health Law § 1399-o provides that smoking shall not be permitted and no person shall smoke in places of employment, indoor areas of bars and restaurants, subways, and numerous other enclosed areas. Smoking is permitted in private automobiles and homes, unless the home is used to provide day care. This far-ranging and controversial statute is enforced through administrative fines, not criminal penalties. The statute is praised by public health authorities and antismoking groups and severely criticized by "smokers' rights" organizations.

## The Future of Smoking Bans

As noted, the clear trend is to prohibit or restrict smoking in public places. Thus, the great majority of the other states have enacted laws prohibiting or restricting smoking in a variety of areas—for example, public transportation vehicles, hospitals, medical offices, public offices and meeting rooms, schools, child care centers, libraries, motion picture theaters, stage performance theaters, restaurants, waiting and meeting rooms owned or operated by the executive and judicial branches of the state and local governments, and specified areas of sports arenas. Many smokers resent laws that they see as infringements on their freedom and often assert that their decision to smoke is no one else's business. But because smoking negatively affects others who are in close proximity, there is little question that government has a legitimate basis upon which to restrict smoking in public places. How far government chooses to go in this area is a political issue, not a constitutional one, as most constitutional attacks on nonsmoking regulations based on equal protection and due process grounds and the right of privacy have failed.

# Wildlife Protection Laws

Since the early common law, fish and game have been viewed as *ferae naturae* (wild animals), meaning that the state as sovereign owns them in trust for the people. *Bayside Fish Flour Co. v. Gentry*, 297 U.S. 422, 56 S.Ct. 513, 80 L.Ed. 772 (1936). As trustee, the state has the duty to preserve and protect wildlife by regulating fishing in public and private streams and by controlling the taking of game. *Shively v. Bowlby*, 152 U.S. 1, 14 S.Ct. 548, 38 L.Ed. 331 (1894). Federal courts have said that under the public trust doctrine, the U.S. and state governments have the right and the duty to protect and preserve the public's interest in natural wildlife resources. See, e.g., *Toomer v. Witsell*, 334 U.S. 385, 68 S.Ct. 1156, 92 L.Ed. 1460 (1948). Owners of private property retain a qualified interest, so those seeking to take fish or game from the confines of private property must secure the owner's permission.

## The Migratory Bird Act

**Migratory Bird Act** Federal law protecting certain species of migratory birds from hunting within the United States and its territories.

Although it is generally within the jurisdiction of the states to regulate wildlife, fish, and game, the federal government has jurisdiction to enact statutes to carry out treaties for migratory birds. The jealous regard that the states have over wildlife within their borders led Missouri to challenge the constitutionality of the **Migratory Bird Act**, 16 U.S.C.A. §§ 703–712, a statute Congress enacted to enforce the provisions of the Migratory Bird Treaty entered into by the United States in 1916. Missouri claimed the federal statute infringed rights reserved to the states by the Tenth Amendment to the U.S. Constitution. The Supreme Court rejected that challenge, thereby settling the issue of federal control. The Court held that Article II, Section 2 of the Constitution grants the president the power to make treaties, and Article I, Section 8 gives Congress the power to enact legislation to enforce those treaties. *Missouri v. Holland*, 252 U.S. 416, 40 S.Ct. 382, 64 L.Ed. 641 (1920). Of course, the federal government retains jurisdiction to protect all wildlife, game, and fish within national game preserves. *Hunt v. United States*, 278 U.S. 96, 49 S.Ct. 38, 73 L.Ed. 200 (1928).

Enforcement of the Migratory Bird Act (MBA) remains a viable part of the federal environmental enforcement program. In *Humane Society v. Glickman*, 217 F.3d 882 (D.C. Cir. 2000), the U.S. Court of Appeals for the D.C. Circuit held that federal agencies are subject to the provisions of the MBA. Its broad proscription makes it

> unlawful . . . to pursue, hunt, take, capture, kill, attempt to take, capture, or kill, possess, offer for sale, sell, offer to barter, barter, offer to purchase, purchase, deliver for shipment, ship, export, import, cause to be shipped, exported, or imported, deliver for transportation, transport or cause to be transported, carry or cause to be carried, or receive for shipment, transportation, carriage, or export birds protected under the treaty. 16 U.S.C.A. §§ 703–712.

A violation of a regulation issued under the MBA is a misdemeanor, but a person guilty of knowingly taking a migratory bird with intent to sell or offer for sale or barter is guilty of a felony and subject to up to two years' imprisonment and a substantial fine. 16 U.S.C.A. § 707.

In 1986 Congress inserted the word "knowingly" into the section of the act providing criminal sanctions, thus requiring the prosecution to prove the defendant's *mens rea* as well as *actus reus* to establish a violation (see Chapter 4 ). Although § 707 requires the government to prove a knowing act, it does not require it to establish that a defendant's act is willful. Thus, in *United States v. Pitrone*, 115 F.3d 1 (1st Cir. 1997), in upholding the defendant's conviction for unlawfully selling a Harlequin duck, the appellate court rejected the defendant's contention that the government was required to prove his specific intent in order to establish that he knowingly violated the law. In effect, the government must show that the defendant's actions were intentional but need not show that the defendant knew they were illegal.

In an appeal from a conviction for possessing more migratory game birds than the daily bag limit imposed under 16 U.S.C.A. § 703, another defendant argued that his hunting dog had simply picked up birds from other hunters. Thus, he contended, he had no intent to violate the law. But the U.S. Court of Appeals for the Fifth Circuit rejected his argument, holding that a misdemeanor violation of the MBA for possessing more migratory game birds than the daily limit allowed is a strict liability offense. *United States v. Morgan*, 283 F.3d 322 (5th Cir. 2002).

## The Endangered Species Act

**Endangered Species Act (ESA)** Federal statute designed to conserve ecosystems by preserving wildlife, fish, and plants. The act imposes criminal penalties against any person who knowingly violates regulations issued under the act.

Modern efforts of the federal government to preserve the environment through protection of wildlife is illustrated by the Federal **Endangered Species Act** of 1973 (ESA), 16 U.S.C.A. §§ 1531–1544. This act is designed to conserve ecosystems by preserving wildlife, fish, and plants. And although enforcement is largely through civil penalties, criminal liability is imposed against any person who knowingly violates regulations issued under the act. 16 U.S.C.A. § 1540(b). The ESA prohibits several specific acts regarding endangered species, and the Secretary of the Interior is further authorized to prohibit any of those acts with regard to threatened species.

The powerful role the ESA plays in the preservation of endangered species was dramatized in 1978 when the U.S. Supreme Court upheld a permanent injunction against construction of the Tellico Dam and Reservoir, a nearly complete $100 million water project in Tennessee. According to the plaintiffs in the case, the project would have eradicated or destroyed the remaining habitat of the only known population of an endangered species of fish, the snail darter. In upholding an injunction against the continuance of the project, the Court held that "the plain intent of Congress in enacting this statute was to halt and reverse the trend toward species extinction, whatever the cost." *Tennessee Valley Authority v. Hill*, 437 U.S. 153, 184, 98 S.Ct. 2279, 2297, 57 L.Ed.2d 117, 140 (1978). Subsequently, Congress enacted legislation restarting the project and the Tellico Dam was completed in 1979.

Under the ESA, criminal liability is imposed for the knowing violation of one of the specific prohibitions listed in the act, a regulation issued to implement those prohibitions, or a permit or certificate issued pursuant to the act. Violators may be fined up to $50,000 or imprisoned for up to a year, or both. ESA also authorizes fines of up to $25,000 or imprisonment for up to six months, or both, for violations of any other regulation promulgated under the act.

In *United States v. Billie,* 667 F. Supp. 1485 (S.D. Fla. 1987), the defendant was charged with killing a Florida panther, an endangered species. He argued that the prosecution had to prove his specific intent—that is, that he knew the animal he shot was a Florida panther, as opposed to a species of panther not on the list of "endangered species." The district court rejected his argument and held that the government "need prove only that the defendant acted with general intent when he

**CASE-IN-POINT**

### A Federal Appellate Court Grants Protection to Nesting Sea Turtles

In 1978 the U.S. Fish and Wildlife Service listed the loggerhead sea turtle as a threatened species and the green sea turtle as an endangered species. In the spring, the female sea turtles come ashore on the beaches in Volusia County, Florida, deposit their eggs in the sand, and return to the ocean. Nesting females avoid bright lights. Months later, the hatchlings break out of their shells at night and instinctively crawl toward the brightest light on the horizon, which on an undeveloped beach is the moon's reflection off the surf. But on a developed beach, the brightest light can be artificial and can lead to disorientation of the turtles. Citizens acting on behalf of the endangered turtles sought an injunction against the county's refusal to ban beach driving and beachfront artificial light sources that adversely impact sea turtles during sea turtle nesting season, arguing that the county had violated the "take" prohibition of 16 U.S.C.A. § 1538(a)(1)(B). The county responded that it had implied permission to "take" federally protected sea turtles through artificial beachfront lighting because it had a federal permit conditioned on its implementation of detailed lighting-related mitigatory measures. The district court enjoined the county from permitting beach driving during the nesting season but denied relief as to the beachfront lighting. The turtles appealed. In a case of first impression, the U.S. Court of Appeals for the Eleventh Circuit held that the ESA's incidental-take permit exception to its "take prohibition" did not apply to an activity performed as a purely mitigatory measure upon which the permit is conditioned, and thus did not authorize the county to take protected sea turtles through measures associated with artificial beachfront lighting.

*Turtles v. Volusia County,* 148 F.3d 1231 (11th Cir. 1998).

shot the animal in question." 667 F. Supp. at 1493. The court discussed the fact that the defendant was charged with violating a regulatory statute enacted to conserve and protect endangered species and that its purposes would be eviscerated if the government had to prove that a hunter who killed an animal recognized the particular subspecies as being protected under the act. 667 F. Supp. at 1492–1493. The following year a defendant was convicted for illegally taking a grizzly bear. The court held that the government had to establish that the defendant knowingly took the bear without a permit, but the government was not required to prove that the defendant knew he was shooting at a grizzly bear. *United States v. St. Onge*, 676 F. Supp. 1044 (D. Mont. 1988).

Despite the existence of criminal penalties for the violation of environmental laws, often the most effective means of enforcement is to secure an injunction against actual or threatened violations. This is illustrated by an action against Volusia County, Florida, filed under the citizen-suit provision of the ESA, 16 U.S.C.A. § 1540(g)(1)(A), discussed in the 1998 decision from the Fifth Circuit Court of Appeals in *Turtles v. Volusia County*, illustrated in the Case-in-Point.

## State Regulation of Wildlife

State legislatures may make it a strict liability offense to take or possess fish and game in violation of regulations. *Cummings v. Commonwealth*, 255 S.W.2d 997 (Ky. 1953). Most states have done so, usually imposing strict liability for taking quantities of game or fish in excess of permitted allowances and for hunting and fishing during closed seasons. But it can be quite difficult to determine whether a given law that imposes a criminal penalty for violating a fishing or game regulation is a strict liability statute. If a wildlife penal statute includes language incorporating a *mens rea* requirement, it is clear that the prosecution must prove the defendant's intent. Although it is difficult to generalize, if a wildlife penal law does not explicitly require intent by including such words as "willfully" or "knowingly," only proof of the *actus reus* of the offense is required. The courts have tended to make an exception to imposing strict liability where the offense is of a more serious criminal character (e.g., smuggling and chemical trafficking) or where the offense is designated as a felony or otherwise carries a severe punishment.

In *State v. Rice*, 626 P.2d 104 (Alaska 1981), the court considered a game regulation that lacked any requirement for criminal intent. As we have noted, this type of regulation is generally treated as a strict liability offense, much like a traffic law. The Alaska Supreme Court took a different approach, saying, "strict liability is an exception to the rule that requires criminal intent" and that criminal statutes will be "strictly construed to require some degree of *mens rea* absent a clear legislative intent to the contrary." *Id.* at 108.

Statutes also commonly make it a strict liability offense to use improper types of fishing nets, to hunt with artificial lights, and to shoot over baited fields. In addition, statutes provide for forfeiture of illegal equipment used to hunt or fish in violation of laws. See, for example, *State v. Billiot*, 229 So.2d 72 (La. 1969), where the Louisiana Supreme Court upheld the forfeiture of seines and other devices used in trawling for shrimp during a closed season.

Irrespective of whether a penal statute imposes strict liability or requires proof of intent, the prosecution is not required to establish that a person accused of fishing in a closed season actually caught fish, *State v. Parker*, 167 A. 854, 855 (Me. 1933), nor is it a defense that a hunter has failed to kill any game, *Key v. State*, 384 S.W.2d 22 (Tenn. 1964).

## What Constitutes Possession?

Recall that in Chapter 10 we discussed the difference between actual and constructive possession and the elements of joint possession, concepts that often come into play in regard to possession of illegal drugs and drug paraphernalia. These same concepts become important in wildlife laws where proof of violation of game and fish laws can be based on constructive possession, and even constructive joint possession, as well as actual possession of game and fish.

The concept of constructive possession of wildlife is illustrated by the Vermont Supreme Court's decision in *State v. Letourneau,* 503 A.2d 553 (Vt. 1985). There, the defendants appealed their convictions for illegal possession of moose where a game warden had searched their premises and found packages of moose meat in the defendants' freezers. The trial judge had instructed the jury that if a person deposited unlawful property in a place of concealment on his own premises or otherwise, he nevertheless had possession of the property even though he might have been absent from the place he was using for its concealment. The court rejected the defendants' contention that the instruction was improper and held that the instruction was consistent with statutory and case law.

In *Ford v. State,* 344 S.E.2d 514 (Ga. App. 1986), a Georgia appellate court reviewed a conviction for possession of a wild turkey with the knowledge that it had been taken in violation of Ga. Code Ann. § 27-1-31. The court reversed the defendant's conviction because there was no evidence that the defendant knew or reasonably should have known that the turkey was taken in violation of the law. Nevertheless, the court took the occasion to explain the law of constructive possession of the turkey. The court observed that the jury could have inferred the defendant's joint constructive possession of a turkey where the defendant waited for a companion who shot a wild turkey. The court found that the defendant knew her companion was to hunt for turkey on the morning in question; she waited for him during the hunt and cooked and ate the game he killed.

## Defenses Rejected

Defendants have attacked certain wildlife regulations as being vague and ambiguous, but in most cases such challenges have failed. In other cases defendants have challenged warrantless searches as violations of the Fourth Amendment to the U.S. Constitution. Historically, a "subsistence" defense—that is, a contention that game or fish was taken as a means of subsistence—may have been allowed, but this defense generally fails today. See *State v. Eluska,* 742 P.2d 514 (Alaska 1986). In *State v. Gibbs,* 797 P.2d 928 (Mont. 1990), a defendant charged with illegal possession of a bobcat pelt claimed he had killed the bobcat in defense of his son, whom the animal had attacked. (We discuss defense of another person in Chapter 14.) He based his defense on Mont. Code Ann. § 87-3-112, which provided that there was no criminal liability for the taking of wildlife that was molesting or threatening to kill a person. The trial court refused to submit the issue of defense of another person to the jury, noting the statute that the defendant relied upon required notification to the Department of Fish, Wildlife, and Parks within seventy-two hours and that the defendant failed to comply with the statutory reporting requirement. The Montana Supreme Court upheld the trial court's action in refusing to submit the defense to the jury and affirmed the defendant's conviction.

In *State v. Billie,* 497 So.2d 889 (Fla. App. 1986), a Florida appellate court held that the state of Florida had jurisdiction to charge a member of the Seminole tribe with unlawfully killing a panther pursuant to Florida Statutes § 372.671. The court rejected claims that the ESA preempted state law, finding that the state law in this area was more protective than the federal ESA.

## Conclusion

The authority of state governments to enact laws to protect the public health is a basic component of their police powers. The federal government has acquired a virtual police power through an expansive interpretation of the Commerce Clause of Article I, Section 8 of the U.S. Constitution and has exercised this power to legislate extensively with respect to the public health and environmental protection. The Food, Drug, and Cosmetic Act, the Clean Air Act, the Clean Water Act, and the Endangered Species Act are some of the more prominent manifestations of this power.

Many of the offenses in this area are strict liability crimes. Formerly, governmental agencies relied almost exclusively on civil penalties to punish violators of environmental laws, but the regulatory climate has changed. The coming years will continue to witness an increased reliance by federal and state authorities on criminal sanctions, often with greatly increased penalties. As this trend continues, legislatures (or, in their absence, courts of law) will most likely include a *mens rea* requirement in regulatory statutes that subject violators of environmental laws to severe punishment.

Strict liability is also applied to transgressors of wildlife regulations, although—whenever a violation rises to the level of a felony or involves a substantial penalty—courts are inclined to require proof of the defendant's intent before upholding a conviction that visits serious consequences on the offender.

Noise pollution and smoking in public places are increasingly viewed by society as detrimental. Increased concern about the deleterious effects of secondhand smoke has caused the public to demand restrictions on smoking in public buildings, restaurants, bars, and workplaces.

## Chapter Summary

- Learning Objective 1

  - Crimes against public health and the environment originate from Congress and state legislatures, which have responded to public concerns. States exercise this authority through their police powers; the Commerce Clause in the U.S. Constitution has been interpreted to grant similar authority to the federal government.
  - Although enforcement is accomplished largely through regulatory agencies, Congress and state legislatures impose criminal sanctions to enforce standards and deter violators.

- Learning Objective 2

  - Many of the offenses in this area are *mala prohibita,* usually strict liability misdemeanor offenses that consist of neglect to comply with required standards.
  - In felony prosecutions, however, the government must generally prove the defendant's intent.

- Learning Objective 3

  - First passed in 1905, the Food, Drug, and Cosmetic Act (FDCA) was comprehensively amended in 1938 and has since been amended many times.

- o The FDCA defines adulterated food, sets standards for determining whether drugs and devices are adulterated, and defines misbranding by false or misleading labels and packaging.
- o Violations are punishable by criminal penalties, civil fines, injunctive relief, and, in some instances, by seizure of adulterated or misbranded articles.
- o Misdemeanor offenses are generally strict liability, but in felony prosecutions the government must usually prove the defendant's intent.
- o Because food, drugs, and cosmetics are usually produced and distributed by corporate enterprises, government agencies affix responsibility on supervisory personnel as well as corporate entities for violations and for failure to prevent violations from occurring.

- Learning Objective 4

  - o In 1926 the Supreme Court upheld the concept of land use zoning, which allows local governments to designate permitted and prohibited land uses.
  - o Today land-use zoning is widespread. Enforcement is usually accomplished administratively or by civil law proceedings.
  - o Most zoning ordinances classify violations as misdemeanors and provide for a fine and a jail term on conviction. Zoning ordinances, like most health regulations, generally do not include an intent requirement. Prosecution of violators is usually undertaken only as a last resort.

- Learning Objective 5

  - o Governments still rely on civil penalties for enforcement of environmental regulations, but Congress has enacted a number of landmark statutes defining environmental crimes. By and large states have adopted counterparts to these federal laws. States vary in the standards of proof required and the sanctions imposed for criminal violations of hazardous waste, water pollution, and air pollution laws.
  - o The Clean Air Act sets federal standards to enhance the quality of the air and provides criminal sanctions for violations. As amended, the act provides criminal sanctions for the violation of any provisions for which civil penalties apply and for any person who knowingly makes any false representation in a document filed under the act.
  - o The Clean Water Act prohibits the discharge of pollutants from any *point source* (pipe, ditch, etc.) into navigable waters unless such discharge complies with a permit issued by the EPA or by an EPA-authorized state agency. Although enforced primarily through civil means, criminal sanctions are imposed for *knowingly* discharging pollutants, for violations concerning permits, and for making false statements.
  - o The Resource Conservation and Recovery Act (RCRA) imposes criminal penalties on those who knowingly transport or cause any hazardous waste to be transported to an unpermitted facility, or who treat, store, or dispose of hazardous waste without a permit. It also makes it a crime to omit material information or make false statements in any record or document required under the regulations or submitted to the EPA or to any state authorized to run RCRA programs.
  - o The Toxic Substances Control Act (TSCA) authorizes the EPA to require testing of and to prohibit the manufacture, distribution, or use of certain chemical substances that present an unreasonable risk of injury to health or the environment, and to regulate their disposal. The TSCA also prohibits commercial use of substances that the user knew or had reason to know were

manufactured, processed, or distributed in violation of any provision of the TSCA. Most enforcement is by civil means but one who knowingly or willfully fails to maintain records or submit reports as required violates the criminal provisions of the act.

o The Comprehensive Environmental Response, Compensation, and Liability Act (CERCLA), the "Superfund Law," finances environmental cleanup and provides for civil suits by citizens. The act now requires notice to federal and state agencies of any "release" of a "reportable quantity" of a listed hazardous substance. CERCLA imposes criminal penalties on supervisors who are in a position to detect, prevent, and abate a release of hazardous substances.

- Learning Objective 6

  o Many violations in the public health area are caused by corporate entities; therefore, courts often focus on whether an accused, by reason of his or her position in the corporate enterprise, had sufficient responsibility and authority to either prevent or correct the violation charged.

  o Courts hold responsible corporate officers liable for environmental crimes as well. Congress has adopted the "responsible corporate officer" doctrine in the Clean Air Act and the Clean Water Act; the doctrine has been upheld in CERCLA cases by federal appeals courts.

- Learning Objective 7

  o The Quiet Communities Act of 1978 protects against noise pollution and provides criminal penalties for knowingly or willfully importing, manufacturing, or distributing products that do not comply with specified noise standards. But it recognizes that states and local communities have primary responsibility in these areas.

  o Local governments often enact ordinances prohibiting the use of loud audio equipment and loud and annoying car stereos. Ordinances attacked on First Amendment grounds have met with mixed success.

- Learning Objective 8

  o States have adopted laws restricting smoking in public transportation vehicles, hospitals, medical offices, public offices and meeting rooms, schools, child care centers, libraries, theaters, restaurants, and specified areas of sports arenas.

  o Antismoking laws and ordinances often carry minor civil penalties.

- Learning Objective 9

  o To protect and preserve the public's interest in natural wildlife resources, states regulate the taking of wildlife and fish, but the federal government has jurisdiction to enforce the Migratory Bird Act (MBA) and migratory bird treaties. In 1986 Congress inserted the word "knowingly" into the act, providing criminal sanctions.

  o Most wildlife and fish statutes proscribe strict liability offenses, but if a law includes terms such as "willfully" or "knowingly," the prosecution must prove the defendant's intent.

  o The Endangered Species Act of 1973 (ESA) is designed to conserve ecosystems by preserving wildlife, fish, and plants. The law prohibits specific acts regarding endangered species. Enforcement is largely through civil penalties, but criminal liability is imposed against anyone who knowingly violates regulations issued under the act.

## Key Terms

environmental crime

littering

antismoking laws

noise ordinances

poaching

strict liability

Food, Drug, and Cosmetic Act (FDCA)

regulatory offenses

negligence standard

responsible corporate officer

zoning

Environmental Protection Agency (EPA)

Rivers and Harbors Act

Refuse Act

Clean Air Act

Clean Water Act

Resource Conservation and Recovery Act (RCRA)

Toxic Substances Control Act (TSCA)

Comprehensive Environmental Response, Compensation, and Liability Act (CERCLA)

point source

Quiet Communities Act

Migratory Bird Act

Endangered Species Act (ESA)

## Questions for Thought and Discussion

1. Are criminal sanctions essential to the effective enforcement of food, drug, and cosmetic laws?
2. Should the term "responsible corporate officer" be explicitly defined by statute, or should courts make this determination on a case-by-case basis?
3. Does your community impose criminal penalties for violations of zoning regulations? If so, are violations treated as strict liability offenses? Why is it often more effective for a local governmental body to seek injunctive relief against zoning violators?
4. Should efforts be made to formulate a model state code of environmental regulations?
5. Should environmental crimes that carry major penalties be strict liability offenses, or should prosecutors be required to prove that a defendant knowingly or willfully committed an offense?
6. Do you think hunting and fishing violations should be decriminalized and treated as civil infractions in the way that many states treat less serious traffic offenses? Give reasons for your view.
7. Can you describe some instances where it is advisable to seek injunctive relief rather than impose criminal penalties for violations of environmental laws?
8. Where smoking is prohibited by law in workplaces, restaurants, and bars, should violations be treated as civil or criminal infractions? What, if any, exceptions should be provided in such laws?

## Problems for Discussion and Solution

1. Two boys died of asphyxiation after playing in a dumpster in which a toxic solvent was disposed of improperly. The solvent was placed in the dumpster by workers at a nearby industrial plant. Under which, if any, federal statute can the plant manager be prosecuted?
2. After purchasing an old automobile repair shop, Jerry Huxley hires a crew to clean up the shop. The crew finds numerous rusty unmarked cans containing

unknown liquids. These cans, along with various other junk and garbage, are loaded onto the bed of Huxley's pickup truck and hauled to the county landfill. At the landfill, Huxley signs a form certifying that none of the cans contains any hazardous waste. Subsequently, Huxley is indicted under 42 U.S.C.A. § 6928(d)(1) for "knowingly transporting hazardous wastes, including various industrial solvents and petrochemicals, to an unpermitted facility." What will be Huxley's defense? Is that defense likely to be successful?

3. Mal Hocus decides to go bass fishing. Before putting his boat in the lake, he stops at a nearby fish camp to renew his fishing license. The proprietor informs him that she is out of license forms, but that a camp across the lake has them. Mal puts his boat in the water and heads across the lake. En route, he notices a group of boats anchored at a spot where he has had good luck in the past. Mal stops his boat but does not anchor. At the very moment he casts his lure for the first time, a state wildlife officer approaches in another boat. Upon discovering that Mal has no current license, the officer cites him for fishing without a license, a misdemeanor punishable by a $50 fine. When Mal protests that he was just about to obtain his license at the camp across the lake, the officer responds, "Tell it to the judge." Does Mal have a defense, or would he be better advised to simply mail in the fine?

4. Hoss Tile is arrested after police are called to the scene of a private social club where Tile is a member. The police are called because Tile refuses to extinguish his cigarette in the dining room and is becoming belligerent. He is charged with a misdemeanor under a new ordinance that prohibits smoking in "restaurants and other places of public accommodation other than those in which alcoholic beverages are sold for consumption on the premises." The club in which he was arrested does not sell or serve alcohol. How might Tile defend himself in this case?

5. The Acme Oil Refining Corporation operates several oil refineries along the Gulf Coast. For the last decade, Acme officials have known that a pipeline bringing crude oil into one of its refineries has been leaking and that as a result thousands of gallons of crude oil have leached into the ground and have contaminated the groundwater. During this time Acme took no action to rectify the problem, nor did it report the problem to the Environmental Protection Agency or any other regulatory agency. Now that the EPA has learned of the problem from a corporate "whistleblower," Acme is taking steps to repair the pipeline. In addition to announcing fines against Acme for violating its regulations, EPA is considering referring the matter to the Department of Justice for prosecution. Under what statute(s) could Acme Corporation or its corporate officers be prosecuted?

## CHAPTER 12

# Offenses against Public Order, Safety, and National Security

## CHAPTER OUTLINE

Introduction

Breaches of the Peace

Vagrancy, Loitering, Curfews, and Panhandling

Motor Vehicle Violations

Weapons Offenses

Offenses against National Security

Terrorism and Weapons of Mass Destruction

Immigration Offenses

Conclusion

Chapter Summary

Key Terms

Questions for Thought and Discussion

Problems for Discussion and Solution

## JURISPRUDENCE

*United States v. Grace* (1983)

*Edwards v. South Carolina* (1963)

*Papachristou v. City of Jacksonville* (1972)

*City of Chicago v. Morales* (1999)

## LEARNING OBJECTIVES

After reading this chapter, you should be able to explain

1. how the common law defined breaches of the peace

2. how local, state, and federal laws define breaches of the peace today

3. why the common law criminalized vagrancy and why vagrancy laws have been declared unconstitutional

4. why laws governing loitering and panhandling and laws imposing curfews are controversial

5. how cities and states deal with traffic violations and other automobile safety issues

6. why gun control laws often are challenged under the Second Amendment to the U.S. Constitution

7. the various offenses against national security and why treason and sedition pose constitutional problems

8. how the modern criminal law has attempted to combat various forms of terrorism, piracy and weapons of mass destruction

9. why immigration offenses are the primary responsibility of the federal government

# CHAPTER OPENING VIGNETTE

On the night of May 1, 2010, New York City police received a call from a street vendor about a vehicle parked in Times Square and emitting smoke. Upon arriving on the scene, police discovered a Nissan Pathfinder containing a crude bomb consisting of fireworks, cans of gasoline, and propane tanks. Times Square was evacuated while the bomb squad defused the device. Had the bomb exploded, as many as fifty people might have been killed and many more injured. After attempting to detonate the device, the perpetrator had escaped on foot, leaving behind his getaway car with the keys still in the ignition. It did not take long for the FBI to catch up to the would-be bomber. They arrested him two days later at JFK Airport as he was boarding a plane to the Middle East.

In June 2010, a thirty-year-old Pakistani American named Faisal Shahzad pleaded guilty in federal court to an indictment that charged, among other things, attempted use of a weapon of mass destruction, transportation of an explosive device, and conspiracy to commit an act of terrorism. Shahzad, the son of a Pakistani air force officer, had come to the United States when he was eighteen. After graduating from college, he worked as a financial analyst and lived what seemed to be a normal middle-class life in suburban Connecticut. But he became disillusioned with the West and angry at the United States for its actions in the Islamic world. He travelled to Pakistan for a year and affiliated with the Taliban. While in Pakistan he received weapons training and made a video in which he proclaimed, "You will see the Muslim war has just started, until Islam spreads war over the whole world." Upon returning to America, he began his efforts to commit a bombing in Times Square. On October 5, 2010, Shahzad was sentenced to life in prison.

The Shahzad case is one of a string of terrorism cases in the United States in the decade since September 11, 2001. Terrorism-related offenses are crimes against public order, safety, and national security and thus are examined in this chapter along with many other much more prosaic offenses. Since 9/11 there have been a number of developments in the substantive criminal law relative to terrorism, including the controversial USA PATRIOT

Act. Obviously, terrorism presents a formidable challenge to law enforcement, and combating terrorism strains our national commitment to civil rights and liberties. It is a problem that is likely to remain with us for decades to come.

# Introduction

Government has a fundamental obligation to protect the public order and safety. The criminal law is one means by which government performs this function—by criminalizing acts that threaten society's interests in order and safety. Government is also obligated to protect the security of the nation itself. It does this primarily through its military capabilities and intelligence agencies, but the criminal law also plays a role in the protection of national security. Since the attacks of 9/11, protection of the homeland against acts of terrorism has become a high priority for the criminal law.

As with most basic criminal offenses, the crimes against public order and safety are rooted in the English common law. The common law recognized the right of the people to assemble peaceably for lawful purposes. Nevertheless, maintaining public order was given a high priority. To maintain order, the common law developed three misdemeanors: **unlawful assembly, rout,** and **riot**. If three or more persons met together with the intention of cooperating to disturb the public peace by doing an unlawful act, their gathering was considered an unlawful assembly. If they took steps to achieve their purpose, it was a rout, and if they actually executed their plans, they committed a riot.

Modern statutes have modified these common-law crimes somewhat. Today, the category of offenses known as **breaches of the peace** includes unlawful assembly, riot, **inciting a riot**, and **disorderly conduct**, as well as violations of noise ordinances. While these offenses are very important in carrying out the day-to-day peacekeeping function of the police, they do raise constitutional problems in certain instances. The First Amendment guarantees the rights of free expression and assembly. Of course, the exercise of these freedoms sometimes poses a threat to public order and safety. The line between what the Constitution protects and what the criminal law legitimately forbids can sometimes be difficult to perceive (see Chapter 3).

To discourage idleness, the common law also developed the offense of **vagrancy**, which was the crime of "going about without visible means of support." Historically, this offense allowed the police tremendous discretion in dealing with suspicious persons. Accordingly, it has been the subject of considerable controversy. Today, the offense of vagrancy has been largely supplanted by the modern offense of **loitering**, although it too is subject to criticism. Numerous vagrancy and loitering laws have been attacked as being excessively vague and therefore in violation of the constitutional requirement that criminal laws provide fair notice as to what specific conduct is prohibited.

**unlawful assembly** A group of individuals, usually five or more, assembled to commit an unlawful act or to commit a lawful act in an unlawful manner.

**rout** At common law, a disturbance of the peace that was similar to a riot but failed to carry out the intended purpose.

**riot** A public disturbance involving acts of violence, usually by three or more persons.

**breaches of the peace** Crimes that disturb the public tranquility and order; a generic term encompassing disorderly conduct, riot, etc.

**inciting a riot** The crime of instigating or provoking a riot.

**disorderly conduct** Illegal behavior that disturbs the public peace or order.

**vagrancy** The common-law offense of going about without any visible means of support.

**loitering** Standing around idly; "hanging out."

**motor vehicle violations** Minor crimes or infractions involving the operation of motor vehicles.

**weapons offenses** Violations of laws restricting or prohibiting the manufacture, sale, transfer, possession, or use of certain firearms.

**gun control laws** Laws regulating the manufacture, importation, sale, distribution, possession, or use of firearms.

**USA PATRIOT Act** Controversial act of Congress enacted in 2001 to strengthen the federal government's efforts to combat terrorism.

Offenses against public order and safety also include **motor vehicle violations** and **weapons offenses**, which, while unknown to the common law, exist by virtue of modern legislation aimed at protecting the public safety. While there is little constitutional debate over traffic safety laws, weapons offenses are sometimes challenged under the Second Amendment to the Constitution, which protects the right to keep and bear arms. Today, there is a strident political debate taking place in this country on both the desirability and constitutionality of **gun control laws**.

In the wake of the horrific terrorist attacks of September 11, 2001, offenses against national security have taken on renewed importance. Many offenses that were far less prominent before 9/11, such as sabotage, espionage, and sedition, are receiving renewed attention. So too are immigration offenses, not only due to the threat of terrorists entering the country illegally but also because in the last two decades the country has experienced an enormous wave of unlawful immigrants, primarily coming across the Mexican border.

The **USA PATRIOT Act**, enacted shortly after 9/11 and essentially reauthorized in 2006, has updated many federal criminal laws by relating new technologies to new terrorist threats. In interpreting these laws, the courts will bear the responsibility of balancing the need to effectively combat terrorism against the need to preserve the freedoms and due process of law guaranteed by the U.S. Constitution.

# Breaches of the Peace

In the United States, the responsibility for maintaining public order and peace rests primarily with state and local governments, although the federal government has a significant role as well. A variety of state statutes and local ordinances prohibit unlawful assemblies, riots, and disorderly conduct. Control of unlawful assemblies and riots is aimed at group behavior, whereas laws proscribing disorderly conduct are aimed at both group and individual behavior. By enforcing laws prohibiting disorderly conduct, state and local governments attempt to prevent such undesirable conduct as violent and tumultuous behavior, excessive noise, offensive language and gestures, actions impeding movement of persons on public sidewalks and roads, and disturbances of lawfully conducted meetings.

On the other hand, the First Amendment to the U.S. Constitution guarantees citizens the rights of free speech and free assembly in the public forum. Courts must carefully weigh the community's interests in maintaining order and peace against these fundamental freedoms. The exercise of freedom of speech and assembly in the public forum may be restricted only where necessary to achieve a compelling public interest. *United States v. Grace*, 461 U.S. 171, 103 S.Ct. 1702, 75 L.Ed.2d 736 (1983).

## Unlawful Assembly and Riot

Most states have enacted statutes proscribing unlawful assemblies and riots. For example, the Indiana Code defines unlawful assembly as "an assembly of five or more persons whose common object is to commit an unlawful act, or to commit a lawful act by unlawful means," and further defines tumultuous conduct as "conduct that results in, or is likely to result in, serious bodily injury to a person or substantial damage to property." Ind. Code § 35-45-1-1. A person who is a "member of an unlawful assembly who recklessly, knowingly, or intentionally engages in tumultuous conduct commits rioting." Under Indiana law, the offense is punishable as a misdemeanor

*United States v. Grace*, 461 U.S. 171, 103 S.Ct. 1702, 75 L.Ed.2d 736 (1983).

Mary Grace stood on the sidewalk in front of the Supreme Court building in Washington, D.C., and held up a sign displaying the text of the First Amendment. A police officer approached Grace and informed her that she would be arrested if she did not move across the street. Grace complied with the officer's request but later filed suit to challenge the constitutionality of 40 U.S.C.A. § 13k, which made it unlawful to "parade, stand, or move in processions or assemblages in the Supreme Court Building or grounds," or "display therein any flag, banner, or device designed or adapted to bring into public notice any party." The federal district court dismissed the suit, but Grace appealed and the case eventually reached the Supreme Court. The Court declared the statute unconstitutional insofar as it restricted expression on the sidewalk in front of the Supreme Court building. In his opinion for the Court, Justice Byron White observed that "[t]here is nothing to indicate to the public that these sidewalks are part of the Supreme Court grounds or are in any way different from other public sidewalks in the city." White concluded that there was "insufficient justification for [the] prohibition of carrying signs, banners, or devices on the public sidewalks surrounding the building."

unless committed while armed with a deadly weapon, in which case it becomes a felony. Ind. Code § 35-45-1-2.

## The Federal Anti-Riot Act

Historically, federal statutes have made it a crime to riot. However, the controversy over the Vietnam War, racial unrest, poverty, and a host of other social ills during the 1960s became catalysts for riotous behavior beyond proportions previously experienced. To cope better with riots, Congress enacted the **Federal Anti-Riot Act** of 1968. The act applies to persons who travel in or use any facility of interstate and foreign commerce. It proscribes interstate travel and use of the mail, telegraph, telephone, radio, or television with intent to incite, encourage, participate in, or carry on a riot; or to aid or abet any person in inciting or participating in a riot or committing any act of violence in furtherance of a riot. 18 U.S.C.A. § 2101(a).

**Federal Anti-Riot Act** A federal law enacted in 1968 that made it a crime to travel or use interstate or foreign commerce facilities in connection with inciting, participating in, or aiding acts of violence.

The act comprehensively defines riot by stating that

the term "riot" means a public disturbance involving (1) an act or acts of violence by one or more persons part of an assemblage of three or more persons, which act or acts shall constitute a clear and present danger of, or shall result in, damage or injury to the property of any other person or to the person of any other individual or (2) a threat or threats of the commission of an act or acts of violence by one or more persons part of an assemblage of three or more persons having, individually or collectively, the ability of immediate execution of such threat or threats, where the performance of the threatened act or acts of violence would constitute a clear and present danger of, or would result in, damage or injury to the property of any other person or to the person of any other individual. 18 U.S.C.A. § 2102(a).

The federal law defines "to incite a riot" by explaining that

the term "to incite a riot," or "to organize, promote, encourage, participate in, or carry on a riot," includes, but is not limited to, urging or instigating other persons to riot, but shall not be deemed to mean the mere oral or written (1) advocacy of ideas or (2) expression of belief, not involving advocacy of any act or acts of violence or assertion of the rightness of, or the right to commit, any such act or acts. 18 U.S.C.A. § 2102(b).

**CASE-IN-POINT**

### Evidence Sustaining a Conviction for Inciting a Riot

A jury convicted Powell of inciting a riot. He appealed, challenging the sufficiency of the evidence. The jury heard evidence that after fourteen-year-old Anderson rejected Powell's request to have sex with him, Powell threatened to have his eighteen-year-old girlfriend, Johnson, beat her. Powell then informed Johnson that Anderson had been talking about her and suggested that Johnson go up the street to meet Anderson. As Anderson and her friends Lattimore and Faust walked down the street, Johnson cursed them, and at Powell's direction, Johnson jumped on Lattimore's back and began pulling her hair and punching her. When Lattimore's sister attempted to break up the fight, Powell insisted on keeping the fight going and shoved away everyone who tried to stop it. Before Faust returned with Lattimore's mother and uncle, who ended the fight, between twenty-five and sixty onlookers had gathered.

In affirming Powell's conviction, the Georgia Court of Appeals noted that the essential elements of inciting a riot are (1) engaging in conduct which urges, counsels, or advises others to riot; (2) with intent to riot; and (3) at a time and place and under circumstances which produce a clear and present danger of a riot. Ga. Code Ann. § 16-11-31(a). The court observed that Powell encouraged Johnson to confront Anderson and that after Johnson attacked Lattimore, Powell directed Johnson's moves and yelled, "You ought to be beating this bitch" and "Don't stop the fight, the bitch got too much mouth." Further, Powell shoved and bullied several people in the gathering crowd in order to prevent any interference with the fight.

*Powell v. State*, 462 S.E.2d 447 (Ga. App. 1995).

In 1972 the U.S. Court of Appeals for the Seventh Circuit held that the Anti-Riot Act is not unconstitutionally vague or overbroad in relation to the First Amendment. *United States v. Dellinger*, 472 F.2d 340 (7th Cir. 1972).

## Disorderly Conduct

In *Commonwealth v. Young*, which is reproduced on the companion website, a Pennsylvania court upholds a defendant's conviction for disorderly conduct.

Closely related to statutes prohibiting unlawful assembly and riot are laws making disorderly conduct an offense. The Indiana Code concisely, yet comprehensively, proscribes disorderly conduct by providing that

> [a] person who recklessly, knowingly or intentionally: (1) engages in fighting or in tumultuous conduct; (2) makes unreasonable noise and continues to do so after being asked to stop; (3) disrupts a lawful assembly of persons; commits disorderly conduct. . . . Ind. Code § 35-45-1-3.

Statutes and ordinances similar to those in Indiana are found in virtually every state. There is no constitutional problem when such laws are applied to conduct that is violent or threatens to produce imminent lawless action. *Brandenburg v. Ohio*, 395 U.S. 444, 89 S.Ct. 1827, 23 L.Ed.2d 430 (1969). Nor is there any constitutional barrier against applying such statutes to the utterance of fighting words. *Chaplinsky v. New Hampshire*, 315 U.S. 568, 571, 62 S.Ct. 766, 769, 86 L.Ed. 1031, 1035 (1942). However, the Constitution "does not permit a State to make criminal the peaceful expression of unpopular views." *Edwards v. South Carolina*, 372 U.S. 229, 237, 83 S.Ct. 680, 684, 9 L.Ed.2d 697, 703 (1963). (For more discussion of these First Amendment concepts, see Chapter 3.)

It is instructive to compare *Edwards v. South Carolina* with *Adderley v. Florida*, 385 U.S. 39, 87 S.Ct. 242, 17 L.Ed.2d 149 (1966). Here the Supreme Court affirmed the convictions of African American student protesters who blocked a driveway to the local jail. Emphasizing the use of the driveway for vehicles providing service to

*Edwards v. South Carolina*, 372 U.S. 229, 237, 83 S.Ct. 680, 684, 9 L.Ed.2d 697, 703 (1963).

On the morning of March 2, 1961, a large group of African American students congregated on the lawn of the statehouse in Columbia, South Carolina, to protest the state's segregation laws. Speeches were made; songs were sung. The students responded by clapping and stomping their feet. A large crowd of onlookers gathered nearby. Nobody among the crowd caused or threatened any trouble, and there was no obstruction of pedestrian or vehicular traffic. A contingent of thirty or more police officers was present to meet any foreseeable possibility of disorder. After refusing to obey a police order to disperse, many of the students were arrested and found guilty of breach of the peace. In reversing their convictions, the U.S. Supreme Court noted that the students "were convicted upon evidence which showed no more than that the opinions which they were peaceably expressing were sufficiently opposed to the views of the majority of the community to attract a crowd and necessitate police protection." In an oft-quoted line, the Court concluded that "[t]he Fourteenth Amendment does not permit a State to make criminal the peaceful expression of unpopular views."

the jail, the Supreme Court observed, "The State, no less than a private owner of property, has power to preserve the property under its control for the use to which it is lawfully dedicated." 385 U.S. at 47, 87 S.Ct. at 247, 17 L.Ed.2d at 156.

In *People v. Barron*, 808 N.E.2d 1051 (Ill. App. 2004) the defendant was convicted of disorderly conduct for violating an Illinois statute proscribing specific categories of conduct, 720 Ill. Comp. Stat. Ann. § 5/26-1(a)(3, which provided:

> A person commits disorderly conduct when he knowingly . . . [t]ransmits or causes to be transmitted in any manner to another a false alarm to the effect that a bomb or other explosive of any nature . . . is concealed in such place that its explosion or release would endanger human life, knowing at the time of such transmission that there is no reasonable ground for believing that such bomb . . . is concealed in such place.

The evidence at the defendant's trial disclosed that although the defendant was not actually in possession of a concealed explosive device, he informed two airline ticket agents that he had a bomb in his shoe. He claimed the ticket agents knew he was joking; however, one of the agents called the police, who used bomb-searching dogs and arrested the defendant. On appeal, the defendant argued that § 5/26-1(a)(3) requires that, once transmitted, the alarm must cause actual fear in the mind of the listener. In a case of first impression, the court rejected his arguments and held that the crime of disorderly conduct is complete upon the transmission of a false alarm to another person, regardless of the effect the false alarm has upon the individual who receives it. The court affirmed the defendant's conviction.

In *Colten v. Kentucky*, 407 U.S. 104, 92 S.Ct. 1953, 32 L.Ed.2d 584 (1972), the Supreme Court upheld a conviction for disorderly conduct arising from a confrontation between a police officer and a student protester. After conducting a political demonstration, several students got into their cars and formed an entourage. A police officer stopped one of the vehicles after noting that its license plate had expired. The other cars in the group were also pulled over. One of the students approached the officer to find out what was wrong. After explaining the situation, the officer asked the student to leave. The student refused to do so and was arrested for violating § 437.016(1)(f) of the Kentucky Revised Statutes, which provided that a person was guilty of disorderly conduct "if, with intent to cause public inconvenience, annoyance or alarm, or recklessly creating a risk thereof," he "congregates with other persons in a public place and refuses to comply with a lawful order of the police to disperse." A conviction for disorderly conduct was upheld by the Kentucky Court of Appeals. *Colten v. Commonwealth*, 467 S.W.2d 374 (Ky. 1971). In upholding the conviction, the U.S. Supreme Court said this:

> As the Kentucky statute was construed by the state court, . . . a crime is committed only where there is no *bona fide* intention to exercise a constitutional right—in which event, by definition, the statute infringes no protected speech or conduct—or where the interest so clearly outweighs the collective interest sought to be asserted that the latter must be deemed to be insubstantial. . . . Individuals may not be convicted under the Kentucky statute merely for expressing unpopular or annoying ideas. The statute comes into operation only when the individual's interest in expression, judged in the light of all relevant factors, is "minuscule" compared to a particular public interest in preventing that expression or conduct at that time and place. 407 U.S. at 111, 92 S.Ct. at 1958, 32 L.Ed.2d at 590.

In a similar case, *Hess v. Indiana*, 414 U.S. 105, 94 S.Ct. 326, 38 L.Ed.2d 303 (1973), the Supreme Court reversed a conviction of a student protester who had been arrested after the sheriff heard him shout, "We'll take the fucking street later." The Supreme Court found that the defendant's language did not amount to fighting words or represent imminent lawless action.

In *Cavazos v. State*, 455 N.E.2d 618 (Ind. App. 1983), an Indiana appellate court found that a defendant calling a police officer an "asshole" and continuing to debate with him about the arrest of her brother was insufficient to support her conviction for disorderly conduct. The court reasoned that the defendant's words to the police officer did not constitute fighting words or fall within any of the other unprotected classes of speech.

In 1999 a Georgia appellate court reversed a defendant's conviction for disorderly conduct. The court held that although the defendant's statement to a female medic that she had "nice tits" was crude and socially unacceptable, such words were not such as to incite a breach of the peace. *Lundgren v. State*, 518 S.E.2d 908 (Ga. App. 1999). But vulgar language, when combined with physical action, may constitute disorderly conduct. In 1999 the Supreme Judicial Court of Maine affirmed a defendant's conviction for disorderly conduct where, in addition to the use of foul

---

## Allegations of Disorderly Conduct and Inciting a Riot

**CASE-IN-POINT**

Reggie Upshaw was charged with disorderly conduct and inciting a riot. He moved to dismiss the charges, contending that the complaint failed to allege facts from which it could be inferred that he intended to cause a riot or disturbance or to present a clear and present danger of creating unrest. The court found that the complaint was supported by sworn allegations that shortly after the 9/11 terrorist attacks on the World Trade Center, the defendant and several accomplices confronted a gathering street crowd in the vicinity of Times Square in New York City. They allegedly boasted that they supported the attacks and were disappointed the carnage had not been greater, yelling in the faces of the crowd, "We've got something for your asses." The complaint further alleged that the defendant and his accomplices refused to disperse after police officers asked them to do so. In ruling against the motion to dismiss, the court concluded that the defendant's remarks went beyond speech protected by the First Amendment and constituted a real threat of violence.

*People v. Upshaw*, 741 N.Y.S.2d 664 (N.Y. City Crim. Ct. 2002).

and vulgar language, the defendant, an emergency room patient, "head butted" a physician. *State v. McKenzie*, 605 A.2d 72 (Me. 1999).

## Excessive Noise

**excessive noise** Unnecessarily loud sounds that interfere with the public peace and endanger the public health and welfare; sounds emitted that exceed the levels permitted by law or ordinance.

Local governments often use disorderly conduct ordinances to control **excessive noise**. To sustain a conviction based on unreasonable noise, the prosecution must show that the speech at issue infringed on the peace and tranquility enjoyed by others. *Hooks v. State*, 660 N.E.2d 1076 (Ind. App. 1996). For example, the noise produced by a late-night party with a live band might be actionable under a breach of the peace ordinance, but only if the party is in fact disturbing the peace of the neighborhood. Courts are inclined to uphold the application of ordinances that proscribe making excessive noise in areas such as hospitals and nursing homes. Police officers responding to complaints about excessive noise usually first request that the offending party "turn it down." If this fails, the offender may be charged with a breach of the peace.

# Vagrancy, Loitering, Curfews, and Panhandling

Elites in feudal England placed great emphasis on able-bodied serfs performing labor and not straying from their assigned tasks. This was motivated by both the need for laborers and the desire to prevent idle persons from becoming public charges. With the breakup of feudal estates, England found it necessary to prevent workers from moving from one area to another in search of improved working conditions. Thus, to regulate the economics of the populace, the common law developed the misdemeanor offense of vagrancy. The offense comprised three elements: (1) being without visible means of support, (2) being without employment, and (3) being able to work but refusing to do so. *Fenster v. Leary*, 229 N.E.2d 426 (N.Y. 1967). In sixteenth-century England, persons who loitered idly for three days were subject to punishment under the Enslavement Acts.

Eventually the emphasis shifted from merely punishing idleness toward the prevention of crime, as England enacted statutes defining vagrancy. The objective then became to protect the people and their property from persons considered potential criminals or simply regarded as undesirables. Thus, by the time the American colonists settled in their new environment, the concept of punishing vagrants had become firmly implanted, and the colonists found it to be a desirable way to prevent idleness and to outlaw conduct offensive to their social mores.

## The American Approach to Vagrancy

During the 1800s, virtually all American states and most cities enacted statutes and ordinances punishing a wide variety of conduct as vagrancy. Statutory language was intentionally rather vague, presumably to allow police broad discretion to arrest persons they deemed undesirable to the community. Vagrancy laws not only proscribed such acts as disorderly conduct, begging, and loitering; they also criminalized the conditions of being poor, idle, or of bad reputation, or simply "wandering around without any lawful purpose." By 1865, Alabama's vagrancy statute included "runaways" and "stubborn servants." By making a person's status an offense, these laws ran counter to the historical concept that a crime consisted of the commission of an unlawful act or the failure to perform a required act. Frequently, vagrancy laws were directed against persons without the means to contest their validity or to challenge the application of such laws to them. Moreover, the U.S. Supreme Court had sanctioned these laws in 1837 by saying that

> [w]e think it [is] as competent and as necessary for a state to provide precautionary measures against the moral pestilence of paupers, vagabonds, and possibly convicts; as it is to guard against . . . physical pestilence. . . . *City of New York v. Miln*, 36 U.S. (11 Pet.) 102, 142, 9 L.Ed. 648, 664 (1837).

In the first half of the 1900s, arrests and convictions for vagrancy were common, as were appellate court decisions upholding convictions in a variety of circumstances. For example, in Minnesota a defendant's conviction for wandering about the streets with no place of abode and without giving a good account of himself was affirmed. *State v. Woods*, 163 N.W. 518 (Minn. 1917). In Virginia, an appellate court held that a defendant's conduct in consorting with gamblers and idlers constituted the offense of vagrancy. *Morgan v. Commonwealth*, 191 S.E. 791 (Va. 1937). Even a defendant's conduct as part of "a group of 4 or 5 suspicious men" at a saloon was, under the particular circumstances, held to be vagrancy. *State v. Carroll*, 30 A.2d 54 (N.J. 1943).

The wide range of vaguely proscribed conduct in vagrancy laws made them susceptible to arbitrary enforcement by law enforcement agencies. In their efforts to prevent crime and control "undesirables," these laws became somewhat of a catch-all of the criminal justice system. Police commonly used them as a basis to arrest a suspect, who was then held pending investigation, or as a method of getting the suspect to confess. Vagrancy laws also furnished a convenient basis for police to justify a search incident to arrest as an exception to the warrant requirement of the Fourth Amendment.

By the 1950s, the vagrancy laws were enforced primarily against alcoholics and derelicts when they left the environs of "skid row" and ventured into the more respectable neighborhoods, where residents found their presence offensive. The constitutionality of the vagrancy laws was frequently challenged on grounds that they were vague, violated due process of law requirements, and exceeded the police power of the states. Such challenges were rejected by state and federal courts, which generally upheld the right of the legislature to define what constitutes being a vagrant. During the 1960s, however, a number of statutes defining a vagrant as a person "without visible means of support," who "wanders around the streets at late hours," or who "fails to give account of himself" were declared unconstitutional.

## The Death Knell of Vagrancy Laws

In 1972 the U.S. Supreme Court issued an opinion that had a profound effect on the enforcement of vagrancy laws in the United States. *Papachristou v. City of Jacksonville*, 405 U.S. 156, 92 S.Ct. 839, 31 L.Ed.2d 110 (1972). In Jacksonville, Florida, eight defendants were convicted under a municipal ordinance that broadly defined vagrancy and levied criminal penalties on violators of as many as ninety days in jail, a $500 fine, or both. The ordinance included language common to many of the statutes and ordinances extant at the time:

> Rogues and vagabonds, or dissolute persons who go about begging, common gamblers, persons who use juggling or unlawful games or plays, common drunkards, common night walkers, thieves, pilferers or pickpockets, traders in stolen property, lewd, wanton and lascivious persons, keepers of gambling places, common railers and brawlers, persons wandering or strolling around from place to place without any

**JURISPRUDENCE**

*Papachristou v. City of Jacksonville*, 405 U.S. 156, 92 S.Ct. 839, 31 L.Ed.2d 110 (1972).

Eight defendants were convicted of violating a Jacksonville vagrancy ordinance, and appealed to the Supreme Court. Justice Douglas, writing for the majority,

held the statute unconstitutional and "void for vagueness, both in the sense that it 'fails to give a person of ordinary intelligence fair notice that his contemplated conduct is forbidden by the statute,' . . . and because it encourages arbitrary and erratic arrests and convictions. . . ."

lawful purpose or object, habitual loafers, disorderly persons, persons neglecting all lawful business and habitually spending their time by frequenting houses of ill fame, gaming houses, or places where alcoholic beverages are sold or served, persons able to work but habitually living upon the earnings of their wives or minor children shall be deemed vagrants. . . . Quoted in *Papachristou*, 405 U.S. at 158–159, n. 1, 92 S.Ct. at 841, 31 L.Ed.2d at 112.

Speaking for a unanimous Supreme Court, Justice William O. Douglas said that the Jacksonville ordinance was void for vagueness, both in the sense that it "fails to give a person of ordinary intelligence fair notice that his contemplated conduct is forbidden by the statute and because it encourages arbitrary and erratic arrests and convictions." 405 U.S. at 162, 92 S.Ct. at 843, 31 L.Ed.2d at 115.

Despite the Supreme Court's ruling in *Papachristou*, the effects of the vagrancy ordinances lingered on. In 1968 a Nevada police officer arrested Lloyd Powell under a Henderson, Nevada, vagrancy ordinance. In a search incident to the arrest, the officer discovered a .38-caliber revolver with six spent cartridges in the cylinder. Laboratory analysis determined that the weapon had been used in a recent murder. Powell was convicted of second-degree murder, and although a federal court later declared the vagrancy ordinance unconstitutional, the use of the evidence against Powell, and his conviction for murder, were ultimately sustained. *Stone v. Powell*, 428 U.S. 465, 96 S.Ct. 3037, 49 L.Ed.2d 1067 (1976).

State legislatures and local governments continued to enact ordinances in an attempt to control conduct they deemed objectionable; however, courts have invalidated such laws when they criminalize a person's status (e.g., homelessness or intoxication) as opposed to proscribing a person's actions, frequently on the ground that such laws are vague and lead to arbitrary enforcement. One state supreme court took the view that a vagrancy statute that made it an offense to be a habitual drunkard violated the constitutional prohibition against cruel and unusual punishment for punishing a person's status. *State v. Pugh*, 369 So.2d 1308 (La. 1979).

## Loitering

After the Supreme Court's decision in *Papachristou*, a new generation of laws making loitering a crime came on the scene. These new laws are narrower and often focus on preventing such crimes as prostitution and drug dealing. Courts scrutinize these ordinances carefully because they often prohibit or restrict constitutionally protected activities. Some have met the same fate as the traditional vagrancy ordinances.

One such ordinance enacted by Akron, Ohio, made it an offense to loiter "for the purpose of engaging in drug-related activity." The ordinance then listed eleven factors that may be considered in determining whether such purpose is manifested. The Ohio Supreme Court found the ordinance to be unconstitutionally vague under both the federal and state constitutions because it did not give persons of ordinary intelligence a reasonable opportunity to know what conduct was prohibited. Moreover, the court held that the enumerated factors to be considered—for example, looking like a drug user, being in an area known for unlawful drug use, and so on—could well be innocent and constitutionally protected conduct. Finally, the court pointed out that the ordinance was flawed because it delegated matters to enforcement authorities without providing necessary objective standards. *Akron v. Rowland*, 618 N.E.2d 138 (Ohio 1993).

In 1992 the Nevada Supreme Court held that the Nevada statute and Las Vegas Municipal Code provision criminalizing "loitering" on private property when the person has "no lawful business with owners or occupant thereof" lacked guidelines to avoid arbitrary and discriminatory enforcement and were unconstitutionally vague under the Due Process Clauses of the federal and state constitutions. *State v. Richard*, 836 P.2d 622 (Nev. 1992).

Any ordinance that proscribes loitering without clearly defining the activities prohibited and without providing objective guidelines for enforcement is vulnerable to constitutional objections; however, courts have upheld loitering ordinances with a more narrow scope. For example, in 1989 the Oregon Supreme Court rejected a defendant's argument that the phrase "loiter in a manner and under circumstances manifesting the purpose of soliciting prostitution" did not meet the required constitutional standard of certainty. *City of Portland v. Levi*, 779 P.2d 192 (1989).

Police often use loitering ordinances and statutes to remove suspected drug dealers from the streets. At least one appellate court has approved this approach. See *Griffin v. State*, 479 S.E.2d 21 (Ga. App. 1996), where the court held that the sale of drugs on the streets violated a state loitering statute.

### Chicago's Gang Loitering Ordinance

In 1992 the Chicago City Council enacted the "Gang Congregation Ordinance," which made it a criminal offense for gang members to loiter with one another in any public place "with no apparent purpose." The ordinance required police to order a group of people who were standing around "with no apparent purpose" to move along if an officer believed that at least one of them belonged to a street gang. Those who disregarded an order to disperse were subject to arrest. Some 45,000 people were arrested in the three years the ordinance was enforced before the Illinois Supreme Court struck down the ordinance as violating due process of law by giving the police too much discretion and impermissibly restricting personal liberty. *City of Chicago v. Morales*, 687 N.E.2d 53 (Ill. 1997). On review, the Supreme Court agreed with the Illinois Supreme Court. Writing for a divided Court, Justice John Paul Stevens criticized the ordinance for requiring police to tell people to disperse without inquiring about their purpose for standing around. He wrote that the ordinance "affords too much discretion to the police and too little notice to citizens who wish to use the public streets." *City of Chicago v. Morales*, 527 U.S. 41, 119 S.Ct. 1849, 144 L.Ed.2d 67 (1999).

To withstand constitutional attack, it appears that any ordinance proscribing loitering must, at a minimum, focus on a person's conduct and not a person's status or association, give fair notice as to what is proscribed, and afford a person an opportunity to explain his or her presence before being ordered to disperse.

### Homeless Persons Sleeping On Public Property—The Florida Experience

In recent years Florida municipalities have attempted to control the problem of homeless persons sleeping on public property in attempts to remove such persons

## JURISPRUDENCE

*City of Chicago v. Morales*, 527 U.S. 41, 119 S.Ct. 1849, 144 L.Ed.2d 67 (1999).

The City of Chicago enacted its Gang Congregation Ordinance, which "prohibit[ed] 'criminal street gang members from loitering in public places'." Under the ordinance, when a "police officer observes a person whom he reasonably believes to be a gang member loitering in a public place with one or more persons, he shall order them to disperse." Accordingly, anyone who does "not promptly obey such an order" violates the ordinance. In order to limit police discretion in the application of the ordinance, the police department's General Order 92-4 "confine[d] arrest authority to designated officers, establishing detailed criteria for defining street gangs and membership therein, and provid[ed] for designated, but publicly

undisclosed, enforcement areas." On two occasions, trial judges "upheld the ordinance's constitutionality, but [eleven] others ruled it invalid." The Illinois Appellate Court held the ordinance unconstitutional, and the Illinois Supreme Court affirmed, "holding that the ordinance violates due process in that it is impermissibly vague on its face and an arbitrary restriction on personal liberties." Justice Stevens delivered the opinion of the U.S. Supreme Court, holding the ordinance unconstitutional on the grounds "that the ordinance's broad sweep violates the requirement that a legislature establish minimal guidelines to govern law enforcement." Additionally, the Court held "because the ordinance fails to give the ordinary citizen adequate notice of what is forbidden and what is permitted, it is impermissibly vague."

from the streets and parks. These attempts were preceded by a history of courts invalidating ordinances. In *State v. Penley*, 276 So.2d 180 (Fla. App. 1973), the court invalidated a city ordinance that provided, "No person shall sleep upon or in any street, park, wharf or other public place." The appellate court determined that the ordinance was unconstitutional in that it might result in arbitrary and erratic arrests and convictions.

A decade later, in *City of Pompano Beach v. Capalbo*, 455 So.2d 468 (Fla. App. 1984), another Florida appellate court reviewed a municipal ordinance that provided, "It shall be unlawful for any person to lodge or sleep in, on, or about any automobile, truck, camping or recreational vehicle or similar vehicle in any public street, public way, right of way, parking lot or other public property, within the limits of the city." The court found the ordinance void for vagueness "because it leaves in the unbridled discretion of the police officer whether or not to arrest one asleep in a motor vehicle on a public street or way or in a parking lot. A wide range of persons may violate [the ordinance] from the tired child asleep in his car-seat while a parent drives or while the car is parked, to the alternate long-distance driver asleep in the bunk of a moving or parked tractor-trailer, to the tired or inebriated driver who has . . . chosen to go to sleep in his parked car rather than take his life or others' lives in his hands." 455 So.2d at 470.

Against this background, § 43.52 of the city of Orlando's Code prohibited "camping" on public property, which was defined to include, among other things, "sleeping out-of-doors." After James Joel, a homeless person, was arrested for violating the ordinance, he filed suit against the city, contending that the ordinance violated his rights under the Fifth, Eighth, and Fourteenth Amendments to the U.S. Constitution. He contended that the ordinance (1) encouraged discriminatory, oppressive, and arbitrary enforcement, (2) was unconstitutionally vague, (3) bore no rational relationship to a legitimate governmental purpose, (4) violated his right to travel, and (5) violated his right to be free from cruel and unusual punishment. He sought a declaratory judgment, injunctive relief, and monetary damages under 42 U.S.C.A. § 1983. The federal district court ruled in favor of the city, and Joel appealed. On appeal, the U.S. Court of Appeals affirmed, noting the ordinance was rationally related to the city's interest in promoting aesthetics, sanitation, public health, and safety and did not violate equal protection rights of the homeless, notwithstanding that it may have had disproportionate impact on homeless persons. *Joel v. City of Orlando*, 232 F.3d 1353 (11th Cir. 2000).

## Curfews

**curfew ordinances** Local laws requiring people, typically minors, to be off the streets by a certain time of night.

In an attempt to combat juvenile crime and protect children by keeping them off the streets at night, most large cities and many counties have enacted **curfew ordinances**. While restrictions vary considerably, most curfew laws define juveniles as unmarried persons under age eighteen and prohibit them from being on public streets or in other public places from midnight to 6:00 A.M. unless accompanied by a parent or guardian or another adult approved by the juvenile's parent or guardian. Many curfew ordinances provide that parents and guardians violate the ordinance if they knowingly allow their child to commit a violation. Curfew laws often provide exceptions concerning work, school and civic events, travel, and emergencies.

Considerable litigation has ensued concerning the validity of curfews. Those who seek to sustain them argue that a juvenile curfew is a valid exercise of the government's police power. They liken the curfew regulations to requirements that minors are required to attend school, are prohibited from purchasing alcoholic beverages, and are subject to restrictions on operation of motor vehicles. Challengers contend that curfew regulations are vague and violate First Amendment rights of association, abridge Fourth Amendment rights to be free from unreasonable detention, deny juveniles the equal protection of the law, and interfere with parental rights.

In *City of Wadsworth v. Owens*, 536 N.E.2d 67 (Ohio 1987), a city ordinance prohibited anyone under age eighteen from being on the streets, sidewalks, or other public places during certain nighttime hours unless accompanied by a parent or some other responsible adult having the parent's permission. The court found the ordinance unconstitutionally overbroad, pointing out that it contained no exceptions, thereby restricting a minor's church, school, and work activities. Courts in New Jersey, Ohio, Hawaii, and the state of Washington have also found curfew ordinances unconstitutional. On the other hand, in *Panora v. Simmons*, 445 N.W.2d 363 (Iowa 1989), the Iowa Supreme Court upheld an ordinance making it unlawful for any minor to be or remain upon any street or in any public place between 10:00 P.M. and 5:00 A.M. The ordinance provided exceptions for a minor accompanied by a parent or other adult custodian and for a minor traveling between home and places of employment, and to church, civic, or school functions.

More recent curfew ordinances that have been upheld have included an expanded number of exceptions. For example, in May 1997, Pinellas Park, Florida, adopted a curfew ordinance along the lines described above. In addition to permitting a juvenile to be accompanied by a parent or an adult authorized by a custodial parent, the ordinance includes numerous exceptions such as when a juvenile is exercising First Amendment rights to attend religious, political, and governmental meetings or events sponsored by civic and governmental groups, during or going to and from lawful employment and school-sponsored or theme-park events, when on the sidewalk at home or at a neighbor's home with the neighbor's permission, or when involved in interstate travel. The trial court, applying a strict scrutiny test (see Chapter 3), invalidated the ordinance on the basis that it violates a juvenile's parents' fundamental right to raise their children without governmental intrusion. On appeal, the court applied a "heightened scrutiny" test and reversed the trial court's ruling, noting that the ordinance includes adequate exceptions to limit the scope of the curfew. *State v. T.M.*, 761 So.2d 1140 (Fla. App. 2000). On review, the Florida Supreme Court ruled that the appellate court had erred in applying "heightened scrutiny" test and remanded the case to the appellate court to apply a "strict standard" in reviewing the ordinance. *T.M. v. State*, 784 So.2d 442 (Fla. 2001). On remand, the district court of appeals held that the city's juvenile curfew ordinance was unconstitutional under the "strict scrutiny test." 832 So.2d 118 (Fla. App. 2002).

Courts in Texas, Virginia, and Washington, D.C., have also upheld curfew ordinances. Those people who oppose curfews recognize the authority of parents to impose restrictions, but they claim the government should not intrude into the parental sphere. They also point to studies showing no correlation between arrests for curfew violations (which are quite common) and the incidence of juvenile crime. The American Civil Liberties Union (ACLU) has been very active in attacking curfew laws in the courts. In excerpts from a March 2009 letter to the Wisconsin Equal Opportunity Commission, explaining its position on juvenile curfews, the ACLU observed,

> Juvenile curfew laws inherently discriminate against young people and give police unlimited discretion to give citations or even arrest youth engaged in otherwise noncriminal or constitutionally protected freedoms. Limits on young people's freedom of movement should come from parents, not police.

Despite the controversial nature of juvenile curfews, law enforcement officials and local governing bodies overwhelmingly support these measures. They are likely to remain on the scene as long as juvenile crime continues to plague our nation's cities, although to be upheld the ordinances must recognize reasonable exceptions.

### Emergency Curfews

Although most curfews involve restrictions on juveniles, the law recognizes that governments can also impose curfews to cope with emergencies. Curfews restrict a person's right of movement, but the Supreme Court has stated that the constitutional right to travel may be legitimately curtailed when a community has been ravaged by flood, fire, or disease and its safety and welfare are threatened. *Zemel v. Rusk*, 381 U.S. 1, 85 S.Ct. 1271, 14 L.Ed.2d 179 (1965).

State laws usually grant local governments the authority to impose limited curfews during emergencies where floods, fires, riots, looting, and other situations threaten the safety and welfare of a community. West's Ann. Cal. Gov. Code § 8634 is illustrative. It provides:

> During a local emergency the governing body of a political subdivision, or officials designated thereby, may promulgate orders and regulations necessary to provide for the protection of life and property, including orders or regulations imposing a curfew within designated boundaries where necessary to preserve the public order and safety. Such orders and regulations and amendments and rescissions thereof shall be in writing and shall be given widespread publicity and notice.

Courts generally uphold the exercise of emergency powers by local governing bodies or their authorized representatives to declare a curfew where life and property are threatened, as long as the curfew regulations are reasonable. To be reasonable, curfew regulations must not be directed at any one class of persons, must not unduly restrict the right of expression, and must allow necessary exemptions.

In April 1992, widespread rioting, looting, and arson occurred in Los Angeles County following the jury verdict acquitting police officers in the Rodney King beating. Long Beach, California, imposed curfew regulations that prohibited anyone from being on the public streets and in public places between 7:00 P.M. and 6:00 A.M. so long as the emergency existed. The regulations were not directed at any particular class or group, regulated conduct and not the content of speech, exempted law enforcement officers and firefighters, and permitted arrest of only those who refused, after notice, to obey the curfew. A California appellate court upheld the curfew regulations. *In re Juan C*, 33 Cal.Rptr.2d 919 (Cal. App. 1994).

## Panhandling

Before the Supreme Court's 1972 seminal decision in *Papachristou v. City of Jacksonville*, supra, vagrancy ordinances commonly included a prohibition on begging on public streets and sidewalks. Once catchall vagrancy ordinances were invalidated, cities began to look for new ways to prohibit begging, often called **panhandling**. Some local ordinances proscribe all begging on public ways; others prohibit "aggressive begging." Prohibitions against begging subordinate a beggar's right of expression on the public ways to a pedestrian's right to be left alone. The issue becomes whether the activity of begging is conduct that can be proscribed under local "police power" or whether such activity constitutes expression protected by the First Amendment. In some instances courts have analyzed the problem based on the "time, place, and manner" doctrine that guides the regulation of expressive conduct in the public forum (see the discussion in Chapter 3).

**panhandling** Begging for money in public.

The U.S. Supreme Court has held that government can regulate, but not prohibit, solicitation of funds for charities on public ways. *Village of Schaumburg v. Citizens for a Better Environment*, 444 U.S. 620, 100 S.Ct. 826, 63 L.Ed.2d 73 (1980). But the Court has not yet spoken directly on the issue of begging on public streets and sidewalks. Decisions from lower federal and state courts make it difficult to generalize as to whether such ordinances pass constitutional muster. Federal courts have held that any ordinance that restricts begging must be narrowly drawn to avoid conflict with the First Amendment.

In 1990 the U.S. Court of Appeals for the Second Circuit upheld a prohibition against begging and panhandling in the New York City subway system. The court observed that begging and panhandling in the city subway system was not expression protected by the First Amendment and that the regulations furthered the government's interest in preventing disruption and startling of passengers. *Young v. New York City Transit Authority*, 903 F.2d 146 (2d Cir.), cert. denied, 498 U.S. 984, 111 S.Ct. 516, 112 L.Ed.2d 528 (1990). Seven years later, in *Loper v. New York City Police Dept.*, 999 F.2d 699, 705 (2d Cir. 1993), the same federal appellate court declared unconstitutional a New York statute that provided, "A person is guilty of loitering when he loiters, remains or wanders about in a public place for the purpose of begging. . . ." The court distinguished its 1990 decision in *Young v. New York City Transit Authority*, supra, saying, "[W]e observed that the prohibition on panhandling in the subway did not foreclose begging throughout all of New York City." *Young*, 903 F.2d at 160. The court found that the regulation was neither content-neutral nor justifiable as a proper time, place, or manner restriction on protected speech. Finally, the court found no compelling state interest was served by excluding those who beg in a peaceful manner from communicating their messages of indigency to their fellow citizens.

State courts have commonly struck down local ordinances that prohibit begging on the public streets. For example, in *Ledford v. State*, 652 So.2d 1254 (Fla. App. 1995), a Florida appellate court struck down a St. Petersburg Beach ordinance that provided:

It shall be unlawful for any person to beg for money in the City while about or upon any public way, and it shall be unlawful for any persons to be in or upon any public way in the City for the purpose of begging money for themselves or any other person.

In holding the ordinance unconstitutional, the court stated,

> [B]egging is communication entitled to some degree of First Amendment protection. . . . [S]ince the ordinance restricts speech on the 'public ways,' a traditional public forum, the regulation is subject to intense scrutiny. Such regulations survive only if: (1) they are narrowly drawn to achieve a compelling governmental interest; (2) the regulations are reasonable; and (3) the viewpoint is neutral. *Id.* at 1256.

In subjecting the ordinance to strict scrutiny, the court pointed out that it was vague and neither defined the terms "beg" or "begging" nor distinguished between "aggressive" and "passive" begging.

In recent years federal appellate courts have approved ordinances that restrict "aggressive panhandling." An Indianapolis ordinance restricting panhandling is illustrative. The ordinance prohibited solicitation of cash on any day after sunset or before sunrise. It also prohibited solicitation at a bus stop, near a public transportation vehicle or facility, at a parked or stopped vehicle, at a sidewalk cafe, or in an area within twenty feet in any direction of an automatic teller machine or entrance to a bank. It also made it unlawful to engage in an act of panhandling in an aggressive manner, which entails blocking the path of a person being solicited or the entrance to any building or vehicle; following behind, ahead, or alongside a person who walks away from the panhandler after being solicited; or using profane or abusive language, either during the solicitation or following a refusal to make a donation. In 2000 the U.S. Court of Appeals for the Seventh Circuit held that the ordinance was narrowly tailored to promote the city's legitimate interest in safety and convenience of its citizens on public streets and that it allowed feasible alternatives to reach both daytime and nighttime downtown crowds. In upholding the ordinance the court pointed out, "Under the ordinance, panhandlers may ply their craft vocally or in any manner they deem fit (except for those involving conduct defined as aggressive) during all the daylight hours on all of the city's public streets." *Gresham v. Peterson*, 225 F.3d 899, 907 (7th Cir. 2000).

## Motor Vehicle Violations

States, and many municipalities, have adopted laws defining a wide range of motor vehicle violations. These are generally strict liability offenses; therefore, there is generally no requirement to prove criminal intent to find a defendant guilty of a traffic violation (see Chapter 4). Among other offenses, these laws proscribe speeding; failing to yield the right-of-way; failing to observe traffic officers, signs, and signals; and driving without required equipment.

By the 1980s, many states adopted a number of "model" laws, providing legal uniformity to the **rules of the road**. Such uniformity is highly desirable given the mobility of today's populace and the volume of traffic on the nation's highways. People driving along the nation's highways, often passing through several states on a single trip, would be ill served by variance in state traffic laws.

**rules of the road** Rules for the operation of motor vehicles on the public streets.

When a driver is stopped for a traffic violation, police may observe conduct or evidence that gives rise to probable cause to conduct a search or make an arrest. Frequently drugs, alcohol, and weapons are discovered by police officers stopping automobiles for routine traffic violations.

## Decriminalization of Traffic Offenses

Historically, traffic offenders were treated like persons committing other misdemeanors: they were arrested and required to post bond to avoid confinement pending the adjudication of their cases. Since the 1960s, most states and municipalities have decriminalized minor traffic offenses, which means that these offenses are now considered **civil infractions** rather than misdemeanors. For example, consider the following excerpt from the Maine Revised Statutes, Title 29-A:

**civil infractions** Noncriminal violations of a law; often refer to minor traffic violations.

§ **103. Traffic infraction**

1. Traffic infraction. A traffic infraction is not a crime. The penalty for a traffic infraction may not be deemed for any purpose a penal or criminal punishment.

2. Jury trial. There is no right to trial by jury for a traffic infraction.

3. Exclusive penalty. The exclusive penalty for a traffic infraction is a fine of not less than $25 nor more than $500, unless specifically authorized, or suspension of a license, or both.

In Maine and most other states, traffic violators are now commonly issued citations or "tickets" instead of being subject to arrest. Offenders may avoid a court appearance by simply paying a fine according to a predetermined schedule of fines. Of course, offenders may elect to contest the charge by appearing in the appropriate court, often a municipal court or **traffic court**. In addition to fines, most states assess "points" against a driver for traffic violations, and an accumulation of points can lead to suspension or revocation of a driver's license.

**traffic court** Court of limited jurisdiction whose main function is the adjudication of traffic offenses and other minor misdemeanors.

The **decriminalization of routine traffic offenses** has proved to be an expeditious and efficient means of maintaining discipline and order on the public thoroughfares. Under most traffic codes, however, the more serious motor vehicle offenses—such as driving while intoxicated, eluding a police officer, and reckless driving—are still defined as misdemeanors, and offenders are subject to arrest.

**decriminalization of routine traffic offenses** The recent trend toward treating minor motor vehicle offenses—for example, speeding—as civil infractions rather than crimes.

## Seat Belts, Cell Phones, and Text Messaging

During the 1980s and the 1990s many state legislatures enacted **mandatory seat belt laws** and **mandatory child restraint laws**. Such laws usually require a violator to pay a small fine and have generally been accepted by the driving public and upheld by the courts. But it came as a surprise to many observers when the Supreme Court in 2001 upheld a custodial arrest for the violation of a seat-belt law. A police officer in Lago Vista, Texas, arrested Gail Atwater for driving without wearing a seat belt as required by Texas law. The law provided for punishment by payment of a fine, and police officers had discretion to issue citations to violators. Instead of simply issuing a citation, the officer arrested and detained Atwater in jail. The Court held that the warrantless custodial arrest did not violate Atwater's Fourth Amendment rights. *Atwater v. City of Lago Vista*, 532 U.S. 318, 121 S.Ct. 1536, 149 L.Ed.2d 549 (2001). Dissenting, Justice Sandra Day O'Connor contended that the majority "cloaks the pointless indignity that Gail Atwater suffered with the mantle of reasonableness." 532 U.S. at 373, 3121 S.Ct. at 1567, 149 L.Ed.2d at 589 (2001).

**mandatory seat belt laws** Laws requiring automobile drivers and passengers to wear seat belts.

**mandatory child restraint laws** Laws requiring that children below a specified age be restrained by approved safety devices when riding in automobiles.

By 2000 state legislatures had begun to express concern that using a cell phone had become a mental and visual distraction from driving. In 2001 New York enacted the first prohibitory law. McKinney's N.Y Vehicle and Traffic Law § 1225-c provides:

2. (a) Except as otherwise provided in this section, no person shall operate a motor vehicle upon a public highway while using a mobile telephone to engage in a call while such vehicle is in motion.

(b) An operator of a motor vehicle who holds a mobile telephone to, or in the immediate proximity of his or her ear while such vehicle is in motion is presumed to be engaging in a call within the meaning of this section. The presumption established by this subdivision is rebuttable by evidence tending to show that the operator was not engaged in a call. The law makes exceptions for use of mobile phones in emergency communications; by fire, police, and other persons in the performance of official duties; and for use of a hands-free mobile phone. A violation of the statute is treated as a traffic infraction and is punishable by a fine not to exceed $100.

In an initial assault on the statute, a New York Justice Court upheld its constitutionality. *People v. Neville*, 737 N.Y.S.2d 251 (N.Y. Just. Ct. 2002). But the law has been held not to apply to a parking lot in a public shopping center because such property does not qualify as a "public highway" under the above-quoted statute. *People v. Moore*, 765 N.Y.S.2d 218 (N.Y. Just. Ct. 2003).

In 2004 New Jersey became the second state to ban the use of handheld cell phones while driving, and by 2008 four states had enacted laws making the use of a cell phone while driving a primary offense—an offense where an officer may issue a traffic ticket irrespective of any other traffic violation taking place. Legislators in other states are considering similar proposals. In January 2009, the National Safety Council called on motorists to stop using cell phones and messaging devices while driving, and urged legislators in all fifty states and the District of Columbia to pass laws banning that behavior.

Another recent advance in communications technology is text messaging, which has become extremely popular among young people. But it has also brought problems when drivers of motor vehicles engage in text messaging. Some regulation was inevitable. Washington became the first state to make text messaging by drivers a traffic infraction. Effective January 2, 2008, a person operating a moving motor vehicle in that state who, by means of an electronic wireless communications device, other than a voice-activated global positioning or navigation system, sends, reads, or writes a text message, is guilty of a traffic infraction. Wash. Rev. Code Ann. § 46.61.668. California's Wireless Communications Device Law, effective January 1, 2009, makes it a traffic infraction to write, send, or read a text-based communication on an electronic wireless communications device, such as a cell phone, while driving a motor vehicle. West's Ann. Cal. Vehicle Code § 23123.5. These laws include exceptions for emergencies.

Today, thirty-nine states and the District of Columbia ban **texting while driving**. In most of these states, texting while driving is considered a **primary offense**, which means that police officers can stop drivers and issue citations for this activity alone. In a few jurisdictions, texting while driving is a **secondary offense**, which means officers cannot stop and cite drivers solely for this offense. In Ohio, a state law enacted in 2012 makes texting while driving a secondary offense (except for minors). However, the city of Beachwood, Ohio passed an ordinance making texting while driving within the city a primary offense for all drivers.

**texting while driving** The offense of using a cell phone or other handheld device to send text messages or emails while operating a motor vehicle.

**primary offense** An offense that in and of itself justifies police stopping and citing or arresting a motorist.

**secondary offense** An offense that does not in and of itself justify police stopping and citing a motorist. Police can issue a citation for a secondary offense only if they have stopped a driver for a primary offense.

## Weapons Offenses

Firearms are commonly used in the perpetration of serious crimes. Although the incidence of firearm-related crime has declined significantly in the last two decades, more than 300,000 violent crimes were perpetrated with firearms in 2008 alone. The FBI estimated that nearly seven of ten murders in 2007 were committed with guns (U.S. Department of Justice, Bureau of Justice Statistics, "Firearms and Crime Statistics," http://bjs.ojp.usdoj.gov/content/guns.cfm, accessed July 24, 2012). And, of course, many cities have experienced very high rates of gun violence associated with criminal street gangs. In the first six months of 2012, homicides rose nearly 38 percent from the same period in 2011, mainly due to gang-related gun violence (David Heinzmann, "Homicide numbers reveal stark contrast," *Chicago Tribune*, July 12, 2012). And in July 2012, the nation was shocked when a man opened fire in an Aurora, Colorado movie theater, killing twelve people and wounding fifty-eight others.

In an attempt to lessen gun-related crime, governing bodies have enacted laws restricting access to and limiting use of firearms. However, gun rights activists insist that many of these measures violate the Second Amendment to the U.S. Constitution, which provides that "a well regulated Militia, being necessary to the security of a free state, the right of the people to keep and bear Arms, shall not be infringed." Nevertheless, there are numerous state and federal statutory prohibitions against the manufacture, sale, possession, and use of firearms and other weapons.

## The Meaning of the Second Amendment

**well-regulated militia** This phrase, from the Second Amendment to the U.S. Constitution, refers to a citizen army subject to government regulations. In the early history of the United States, the militia was the set of able-bodied men who could be pressed into military service by the governor of the state. The National Guard is its modern counterpart.

In 1939 and again in 1980 the Supreme Court said that the Second Amendment protects the keeping and bearing of arms only in the context of a **well-regulated militia**. See *United States v. Miller*, 307 U.S. 174, 59 S.Ct. 816, 83 L.Ed. 1206 (1939); *Lewis v. United States*, 445 U.S. 55, 100 S.Ct. 915, 63 L.Ed.2d 198 (1980). But in *District of Columbia v. Heller*, 554 U.S. 570, 128 S.Ct. 2783, 171 L.Ed.2d 637 (2008), the Court reversed course and declared that the Second Amendment does protect a personal right to possess a firearm for "traditionally lawful purposes" irrespective of one's service in any militia. In *Heller* the Court struck down a District of Columbia ordinance effectively prohibiting the possession of handguns, even in the home. Writing for a sharply divided Court, Justice Antonin Scalia observed,

> Undoubtedly some think that the Second Amendment is outmoded in a society where our standing army is the pride of our Nation, where well-trained police forces provide personal security, and where gun violence is a serious problem. That is perhaps debatable, but what is not debatable is that it is not the role of this Court to pronounce the Second Amendment extinct. 554 U.S. at 636, 128 S.Ct. at 2822, 171 L.Ed.2d at 684.

The Supreme Court's decision in *District of Columbia v. Heller* is excerpted on the companion website.

However, Justice Scalia noted that "nothing in our opinion should be taken to cast doubt on longstanding prohibitions on the possession of firearms by felons and the mentally ill, or laws forbidding the carrying of firearms in sensitive places such as schools and government buildings, or laws imposing conditions and qualifications on the commercial sale of arms." 554 U.S. at 626, 128 S.Ct. at 2816, 171 L.Ed.2d at 678.

As we mentioned in Chapter 3, the Supreme Court in 2010 reaffirmed its *Heller* decision and also held that the Second Amendment applies to the state and local governments via the Due Process Clause of the Fourteenth Amendment. *McDonald v. Chicago*, 561 U.S. 3025, 130 S.Ct. 3020, 177 L.Ed.2d 894 (2010). This means that state and local gun control laws are now subject to challenge as infringements of the federal constitutional right to keep and bear arms. However, in *McDonald*, as in *Heller*, the Court made clear that the Second Amendment allows for the reasonable regulations of firearms. Clearly, the Court's decisions in *Heller* and *McDonald* have set the stage for widespread legal challenges to federal, state, and local gun control measures.

## State Gun Laws

Under Iowa law, any unauthorized person who knowingly possesses an "offensive weapon" commits a class D felony, Iowa Code Ann. § 724.3. "Offensive weapons" include machine guns, short-barreled rifles and shotguns, bombs, grenades, mines, poison gases, ballistic knives, bullets, and projectiles containing any explosive mixtures or chemical compounds. § 724.1. The statute makes exceptions for peace officers and certain other instances. In *State v. Winders*, 366 N.W.2d 193 (Iowa App. 1985), the court held that the term "knowingly" in § 724.3 merely requires that the defendant had knowledge that he or she possessed a weapon within the general meaning of such term, rather than knowledge that he or she possessed an "offensive weapon" as statutorily defined. "To hold otherwise," the court said, "would only serve to undermine the very purpose of the provision in regulating possession of weapons in the interest of public safety." 366 N.W.2d at 196.

**concealed weapon** A weapon carried on or about a person in such a manner as to hide it from the ordinary sight of another person.

States commonly enact statutes making it unlawful to carry a **concealed weapon**. Iowa law stipulates that "A person who goes armed with a dangerous weapon concealed on or about the person, or who, within the limits of any city, goes armed with a pistol or revolver, or any loaded firearm of any kind, whether concealed or not, or who knowingly carries or transports in a vehicle a pistol or revolver, commits an aggravated misdemeanor." Iowa Code Ann. § 724.4. "A 'dangerous weapon' is any instrument or device designed primarily for use in inflicting death or injury upon a human being or animal, and which is capable of inflicting death upon a human being when used in the manner for which it was designed." *State v. Mitchell*, 371 N.W.2d 432 (Iowa App. 1985). Exceptions include peace officers whose duties require carrying weapons and members of the armed forces whose members are required to carry weapons.

Most laws define a concealed weapon as one that is carried on or about a person in such a manner as to conceal it from the ordinary sight of another person. It follows that a defendant was properly convicted of carrying a concealed weapon in her purse when it was disclosed by a metal detector at a courthouse. *Schaaf v. Commonwealth*, 258 S.E.2d 574 (Va. 1979). But more often, litigation involves less than absolute concealment. For example, a Georgia appellate court ruled that even though the handle of a pistol tucked in a defendant's pants was visible to some extent through a slit in his shirt, the weapon was concealed. *Marshall v. State*, 200 S.E.2d 902 (Ga. App. 1973). Similarly, in *People v. Charron*, 220 N.W.2d 216 (Mich. App. 1974), a Michigan appellate court held that a knife slightly protruding from a defendant's rear pocket was a concealed weapon.

**CASE-IN-POINT**

### Unlawful Possession of a Firearm

South Carolina law provides that it is unlawful for any person to carry a pistol about his or her person, regardless of whether the pistol is concealed. S.C. Code Ann. § 16-23-20. The statute provides twelve exceptions to the prohibition. Barry Clarke was convicted of violating the statute after he was stopped for a traffic violation and the police officer noticed a gun in a holster next to the driver's seat. On appeal, Clarke argued that the burden of proof should have been on the prosecution to show that he did not qualify to carry the weapon under any of the twelve exceptions to the prohibition. The South Carolina Supreme Court disagreed, saying that "[t]he general rule, when dealing with statutory crimes to which there are exceptions, is that the defendant 'has the burden of excusing or justifying his act; and hence the burden may be on him to bring himself within an exception in the statute or to prove the issuance of a license or permit'."

*State v. Clarke*, 396 S.E.2d 827 (S.C. 1990).

Many concealed-weapons statutes also make it an offense to carry a concealed weapon in a vehicle, and in numerous cases courts have been asked to rule on the application of these laws. For example, a defendant reached into his automobile and withdrew a revolver from a shelf behind the driver's seat. In affirming the defendant's conviction, the Wisconsin Supreme Court said that "[i]f the weapon is hidden from ordinary observation, it is concealed." The court noted that "absolute invisibility to other persons" was not "indispensable to concealment." The question was this: "Was [the weapon] carried so as not to be discernible by ordinary observation?" *Mularkey v. State*, 230 N.W. 76, 77 (Wis. 1930). More recently, an Illinois appellate court observed that "[i]t is well settled . . . that a weapon is 'concealed' . . . even though there is some notice of its presence to an alert police officer who can see part of the gun when he approaches the vehicle." *People v. Williams*, 350 N.E.2d 81, 83 (Ill. App. 1976).

## Federal Gun Control Laws

The **Federal Gun Control Act** of 1968, 18 U.S.C.A. § 921 *et seq.*, established a fairly comprehensive regime governing the distribution of firearms. The statute prohibits firearms dealers from transferring handguns to persons who are under twenty-one, nonresidents of the dealer's state, or are otherwise prohibited by state or local laws from purchasing or possessing firearms. 18 U.S.C.A. § 922(b). The law also forbids possession of a firearm by, and transfer of a firearm to, persons in several categories, including convicted felons, users of controlled substances, persons adjudicated as incompetent or committed to mental institutions, persons dishonorably discharged from the military, persons who are illegally in the United States, persons who have renounced their citizenship, and fugitives from justice. 18 U.S.C.A. §§ 922(d) and (g).

In the early 1990s, Congress enacted three important gun control statutes. The **Gun-Free School Zones Act** of 1990, 18 U.S.C.A. § 922, makes it unlawful for any individual knowingly to possess a firearm in a school zone, regardless of whether the school is in session. The 1993 **Brady Bill**, also codified at 18 U.S.C.A. § 922, requires a five-working-day waiting period for the purchase of a handgun. And the 1994 Crime Bill banned the manufacture, transfer, or possession of firearms classified as "assault weapons." 18 U.S.C.A. § 922(v)(1).

In 1995 the U.S. Supreme Court struck down the Gun-Free School Zones Act of 1990 and reversed a student's conviction for carrying a handgun to school. The Court found that the law, in its full reach, was beyond the power of Congress to regulate interstate commerce. *United States v. Lopez*, 514 U.S. 549, 115 S.Ct. 1624, 131 L.Ed.2d 626 (1995).

In 1997 the Court dealt another blow to federal gun control efforts when it invalidated a section of the Brady Bill requiring local law enforcement officers to conduct background checks of prospective gun purchasers. The Court held that, absent exigent circumstances, Congress could not commandeer state law enforcement authorities to implement a federal program. *Printz v. United States*, 521 U.S. 898, 117 S.Ct. 2365, 138 L.Ed.2d 914 (1997).

## Recent State Developments

After several catastrophic incidents involving firearms, state legislatures began to focus on gun safety legislation. Many states have enacted laws that require background checks of gun buyers at gun shows. Most states require registration or permits to purchase firearms and prohibit sales to persons convicted of serious felonies.

**Federal Gun Control Act** This 1968 statute prohibits firearms dealers from transferring handguns to people who are younger than twenty-one, nonresidents of the dealer's state, and those who are otherwise prohibited by state or local laws from purchasing or possessing firearms. It also forbids possession of a firearm by, and transfer of a firearm to, people in a number of categories, including convicted felons, users of controlled substances, those adjudicated as incompetent or committed to mental institutions, illegal aliens, those dishonorably discharged from the military, those who have renounced their citizenship, and fugitives from justice.

**Gun-Free School Zones Act** Federal statute making it a crime "for any individual knowingly to possess a firearm at a place that the individual knows, or has reasonable cause to believe, is a school zone." This law was declared unconstitutional by the U.S. Supreme Court in *United States v. Lopez* (1995).

**Brady Bill** Legislation passed by Congress in 1993 requiring a five-day waiting period before the purchase of a handgun, during which time a background check of the buyer is conducted.

The Supreme Court's decisions in *United States v. Lopez* and *Printz v. United States* are excerpted on the companion website.

New Jersey has been very active in enacting gun safety laws. Licensing of retail dealers and their employees is strictly regulated. No handgun can be delivered to any person unless such person possesses and exhibits a valid permit to purchase a firearm and at least seven days have elapsed since the date of application for the permit. Applications must be submitted to designated officials. The purchaser of a firearm must be personally known to the seller or present evidence of his or her identity. N.J. Stat. Ann. § 2C:58-2. Trigger locks are required on handguns. N.J. Stat. Ann. § 2C:58-2. Sawed-off shotguns and silencers are prohibited. N.J. Stat. Ann. § 2C:39-3. Further, New Jersey laws strictly regulate the possession and use of handguns. Any person who knowingly has in his or her possession any handgun, including any antique handgun, without having obtained a permit to carry the same as provided in N.J. Stat. Ann. § 2C:58-4, is guilty of a crime of the third degree. N.J. Stat. Ann. § 2C:39-5.

# Offenses against National Security

The preamble to the U.S. Constitution appropriately refers to the role of the federal government "to promote the common defense." The federal government performs this function by relying on the immense military capabilities of the United States and also upon various agencies devoted to the gathering of foreign intelligence. But it also relies on the criminal justice system to deter and punish violations of national security. While there are a number of specific offenses in this category, the principal crimes against national security are **treason**, **espionage**, **sabotage**, and **sedition**.

**treason** The crime of making war against one's own government or giving aid and comfort to its enemies.

**espionage** The crime of turning over state secrets to a foreign government.

**sabotage** The crime of infiltrating and destroying a nation's war-making capabilities.

**sedition** The crime of advocating or working toward the violent overthrow of one's own government.

## Treason

As we discussed in Chapter 3, Article III, Section 3 of the U.S. Constitution provides that treason against the United States "shall consist only in levying War against them, or in adhering to their Enemies, giving them Aid and Comfort." Following this constitutional language, the current federal statute on treason provides:

> Whoever owing allegiance to the United States, levies war against them or adheres to their enemies, giving them aid and comfort within the United States or elsewhere, is guilty of treason and shall suffer death, or shall be imprisoned not less than five years and fined under this title but not less than $10,000; and shall be incapable of holding any office under the United States. . . . 18 U.S.C.A. § 2381.

No one has been convicted of treason since the Second World War. Many people incorrectly believe that Julius and Ethel Rosenberg, who provided the Soviet Union with top-secret information about the construction of the atomic bomb, were convicted of treason. Prosecutors considered charging the Rosenbergs with treason but concluded that they could not obtain a conviction due to the constitutional two-witness requirement. Instead, they elected to charge the Rosenbergs with espionage. The defendants were convicted in 1951 and sentenced to death.

Some people believed that John Walker Lindh, the so-called American Taliban, was guilty of treason based on his involvement with the Taliban regime in Afghanistan and Osama bin Laden's al-Qaeda terrorist organization. Lindh, an American citizen, was captured by American forces after a battle in Afghanistan in December 2001. As in the Rosenberg case, federal prosecutors elected not to charge Lindh with treason. Rather, he agreed to plead guilty to two lesser offenses and was sentenced to twenty years in prison.

# Espionage

Known in the popular parlance as "spying," **espionage** consists of turning over state secrets to a foreign government. First criminalized by the Espionage Act of 1917, 40 Stat. 217, espionage is now covered by a number of federal statutes. 18 U.S.C.A. § 793 criminalizes gathering or transmitting defense information "with intent or reason to believe that the information is to be used to the injury of the United States, or to the advantage of any foreign nation." 18 U.S.C.A. § 794(b) prohibits collection or transmission of information about American military activities during time of war "with intent that the same shall be communicated to the enemy."

In recent years there have been a number of high-profile espionage cases in the United States. In 1986, Jonathan Pollard, a former U.S. Navy intelligence analyst, was sentenced to life imprisonment after he was convicted of selling classified information to Israel. Pollard admitted that he provided Israel with American intelligence about weapons programs in Syria, Iraq, Pakistan, and Libya. In 1994, former CIA analyst Aldrich Ames was sentenced to life in prison after he was convicted of selling classified information to the Soviet Union. The investigation revealed that Ames had received $2.7 million from Moscow for exposing covert American operations and betraying fellow CIA agents. In 2001, former FBI agent Robert Hanssen pleaded guilty to fifteen counts of espionage and conspiracy to commit espionage and was sentenced to life in prison. The government's investigation revealed that Hanssen received nearly $1.5 million from Russia in exchange for classified information.

The Intelligence Identities Protection Act of 1982, 50 U.S.C.A. § 421 *et seq.*, prohibits disclosure of the identities of undercover intelligence officers, agents, informants, and their "sources." The public became acutely aware of this law in the fall of 2003 when the FBI began an investigation of the Bush administration after it was alleged that senior administration officials had intentionally exposed an undercover CIA operative as an act of political retaliation. The operative was married to a former ambassador who had accused the Bush administration of selectively using intelligence to exaggerate the threat from Iraq in order to justify making war against Saddam Hussein's regime. A *Washington Post/BBC* News survey reported on October 2, 2003, found that more than eight in ten Americans viewed the allegation as "serious" and more than seven in ten thought it likely that a White House official was behind the leak. Ultimately, after a two-year investigation, it was determined that the leak came from an official in the State Department and not the White House.

# Sabotage

Sabotage is the intentional destruction of a country's military infrastructure by an enemy agent or a civilian with the objective of hindering that country's war efforts or reducing its military capabilities. Several federal statutes criminalize particular forms of sabotage, but the broadest of these statutes is found at 18 U.S.C.A. § 2155. It provides:

> (a) Whoever, with intent to injure, interfere with, or obstruct the national defense of the United States, willfully injures, destroys, contaminates or infects, or attempts to so injure, destroy, contaminate or infect any national-defense material, national-defense premises, or national-defense utilities, shall be fined under this title or imprisoned not more than twenty years, or both, and, if death results to any person, shall be imprisoned for any term of years or for life.

18 U.S.C.A. § 2153 prohibits sabotage during time of war or national emergency and carries a thirty-year maximum prison term. Most states have similar laws, many of them enacted during World War II.

## Sedition

Sedition is the incitement of insurrection or revolution. At common law there was no offense of sedition per se, but English law did proscribe seditious libel, seditious meetings, and seditious conspiracies. In 1798, the U.S. Congress enacted the infamous Sedition Act, which prohibited "false, scandalous and malicious" utterances and publications against the federal government or any of its officials. Thomas Jefferson and his followers assailed the act as a violation of the First Amendment to the U.S. Constitution. After Jefferson was elected president in 1801 and his party won both houses of Congress, the Sedition Act was promptly repealed.

In 1918, during the First World War, Congress enacted a new Sedition Act aimed primarily at communists, socialists, anarchists, and other radicals. More than 2,000 persons were prosecuted under this prohibition. In *Abrams v. United States*, 250 U.S. 616, 40 S.Ct. 17, 63 L.Ed. 1173 (1919), the Supreme Court upheld the conviction of five Russian immigrants who published leaflets criticizing America's role in World War I and attacking the capitalist system. In dissent, Justice Oliver Wendell Holmes questioned the need for governmental suppression of dissent, saying "the best test of truth is the power of the thought to get itself accepted in the competition of the market. . . ." 250 U.S. at 630, 40 S.Ct. at 22, 63 L.Ed. at 1180.

In 1940, Congress adopted the Smith Act, 54 Stat. 670, 671. The act has been amended several times. In its present form, codified at 18 U.S.C.A. § 2385, the act makes it a crime if a person

> knowingly or willfully advocates, abets, advises, or teaches the duty, necessity, desirability, or propriety of overthrowing or destroying the government of the United States or the government of any State, Territory, District or Possession thereof, or the government of any political subdivision therein, by force or violence, or by the assassination of any officer of any such government.

In *Dennis v. United States*, 341 U.S. 494, 71 S.Ct. 857, 95 L.Ed. 1137 (1951), the Supreme Court upheld the convictions under the Smith Act of eleven officials of the Communist Party, rejecting their First Amendment challenge to the statute. But in *Yates v. United States*, 354 U.S. 298, 77 S.Ct. 1064, 1 L.Ed.2d 1356 (1957), the Court set aside the convictions of another set of Communist Party officials. In so doing, the Court distinguished between "advocacy of abstract doctrine and advocacy directed at promoting unlawful action" and held that the Smith Act prohibited only the latter. In 1969, in *Brandenburg v. Ohio*, 395 U.S. 444, 89 S.Ct. 1827, 23 L.Ed.2d 430, the Court went so far as to hold that mere advocacy could never be criminalized in the absence of "imminent lawless action." Although the *Brandenburg* case did not arise under the Smith Act, but rather under a state law prohibiting "criminal syndicalism," most commentators have concluded that the "imminent lawless action" doctrine applies equally to federal prosecutions under the Smith Act. Today, however, such prosecutions are rare.

# Terrorism and Weapons of Mass Destruction

**terrorism** The crime of inflicting terror on a population through the indiscriminate killing of people and destruction of property, often with explosive devices.

Before the 1980s some sporadic acts of **terrorism** were committed in the United States by radical political protesters and by persons involved in protests during the fight for racial equality. The 1980s and 1990s witnessed a series of attacks by Theodore Kaczynski, the so-called Unabomber, who sent packages with bombs in his protest against modern technology. Antiabortion extremists committed sporadic acts of terrorism at abortion clinics. During the 1980s and 1990s terrorists attacked several American military bases overseas. Militant Islamists were convicted of damaging the

World Trade Center in 1993. Timothy McVeigh and Terry Nichols, who bore extreme hatred for the government, were convicted of the massive bombing of a federal government building in Oklahoma City in 1995. And everyone is familiar with the tragic loss of thousands of lives when hijackers crashed aircraft into the World Trade Center and the Pentagon on 9/11.

## Antiterrorism Legislation

**Antiterrorism and Effective Death Penalty Act** A federal statute designed to effectuate reforms in administration of the death penalty by curtailing successive petitions for habeas corpus by prisoners sentenced to death.

The Omnibus Diplomatic Security and Antiterrorism Act of 1986, Pub. L. 99-399, now codified as 18 U.S.C.A. § 2332, makes it a federal offense for a terrorist overseas to kill, attempt to kill, conspire to kill, or engage in physical violence with the intent to cause serious bodily injury to an American citizen. The **Antiterrorism and Effective Death Penalty Act** of 1996, Pub. L. 104-132, 110 Stat. 1214, enacted after the Oklahoma City bombing of 1995, expanded federal jurisdiction with respect to investigation and prosecution of international terrorism. It also made it a crime for persons in the United States or subject to U.S. jurisdiction to provide material support to groups designated as terrorist organizations by the U.S. Department of State. 18 U.S.C.A. § 2339B.

Since terrorists attacked the United States on September 11, 2001, the federal government has responded in new ways in attempts to maintain the security of the country. These include the creation of the Department of Homeland Security; stricter safety measures in mass transportation systems; increased protective measures to safeguard borders, ports, utility systems, and government buildings; and training police, fire, and medical personnel to cope with the potential use of weapons of mass destruction. From a legislative standpoint, the USA PATRIOT Act has become an important part of the criminal justice system.

**The USA PATRIOT Act**

As we explained in Chapter 10, Congress enacted the **USA PATRIOT Act** shortly after the terrorist attacks of 9/11. Title VIII of the USA PATRIOT Act strengthens numerous federal criminal laws against terrorism. Section 801 creates a detailed new offense for willfully attacking mass transportation facilities. Section 802 defines domestic terrorism as "activities that occur primarily within U.S. jurisdiction, that involve criminal acts dangerous to human life that appear to be intended to intimidate or coerce a civilian population, to influence government policy by intimidation or coercion, or to affect government conduct by mass destruction, assassination, or kidnapping." Section 803 prohibits knowingly harboring persons who have committed or who are about to commit an act of terrorism.

The act establishes federal jurisdiction over crimes committed at U.S. facilities abroad (§ 804) and, by amending 18 U.S.C.A. § 2339A, applies prohibitions against providing material support for terrorism offenses outside of the United States (§ 805). It also subjects to civil forfeiture all assets, foreign or domestic, of individuals and terrorist organizations that plan or perpetrate domestic or international terrorism against the United States (§ 806).

Section 809 extends the statute of limitations for certain offenses and provides that there shall be no statute of limitations for certain terrorism offenses if the commission of such an offense resulted in, or created a foreseeable risk of, death or serious bodily injury to another person. Section 810 provides for alternative maximum penalties for specified terrorism crimes, while § 811 provides the same penalties for attempts and conspiracies as for terrorist acts and provides for postrelease supervision for terrorists whose offenses resulted in foreseeable risk of death or serious bodily injury. Certain acts of terrorism are deemed to be racketeering activity (§ 813), and penalties regarding fraud and related activity in connection with specified cyberterrorism offenses are included (§ 814). Finally, § 817 creates a new offense of possession of biological weapons when not justified for research or other specified purposes.

On March 9, 2006, President George W. Bush signed legislation making permanent all but two provisions of the USA PATRIOT Act. In signing the USA PATRIOT Improvement and Reauthorization Act of 2005, President Bush stated,

> The law allows our intelligence and law enforcement officials to continue to share information. It allows them to continue to use tools against terrorists that they use against drug dealers and other criminals. It will improve our nation's security while we safeguard the civil liberties of our people. The legislation strengthens the Justice Department so it can better detect and disrupt terrorist threats. And the bill gives law enforcement new tools to combat threats to our citizens from international terrorists to local drug dealers.

Although recognizing the need to protect the security of the United States, critics argue that certain sections of the act unduly restrict personal liberties, thereby offending basic constitutional protections. For example, they cite language in § 802, which defines terrorism to include "activities . . . that appear . . . to influence government policy by intimidation or coercion," as having the potential to chill political dissent. Among the sharpest critics of the PATRIOT Act is the American Civil Liberties Union, which has challenged several of the act's provisions in court.

## Aircraft Piracy and Related Offenses

**aircraft piracy** Wrongfully seizing control of an aircraft by force, violence, the threat of force or violence, or any other form of intimidation.

Among the numerous offenses committed by the 9/11 terrorists was the hijacking of four commercial airliners. Of course, **aircraft piracy** has long been a concern in the United States and around the world. Chapter 46 of Title 49 of the U.S. Code is entitled "Special Aircraft Jurisdiction of the United States." As provided in 49 U.S.C. § 46501, the term "special aircraft jurisdiction of the United States" includes any of the following aircraft in flight:

(A) a civil aircraft of the United States.

(B) an aircraft of the armed forces of the United States.

(C) another aircraft in the United States.

(D) another aircraft outside the United States—

    (i)   that has its next scheduled destination or last place of departure in the United States, if the aircraft next lands in the United States;

    (ii)   on which an individual commits an offense . . . if the aircraft lands in the United States with the individual still on the aircraft; or

    (iii)   against which an individual commits an offense . . . if the aircraft lands in the United States with the individual still on the aircraft.

(E) any other aircraft leased without crew to a lessee whose principal place of business is in the United States or, if the lessee does not have a principal place of business, whose permanent residence is in the United States.

Title 49, Chapter 46 of the U.S. Code contains several criminal prohibitions pertaining to aircraft under the special aircraft jurisdiction of the United States:

§ 46502. Aircraft piracy

§ 46503. Interference with security screening personnel

§ 46504. Interference with flight crew members and attendants

§ 46505. Carrying a weapon or explosive on an aircraft

§ 46506. Application of certain criminal laws to acts on aircraft

§ 46507. False information and threats

**naval piracy** Under the law of nations, a robbery at sea.

## Naval Piracy

Article I, Section 8, paragraph 10 of the U.S. Constitution authorizes Congress to make laws to "define and punish Piracies . . . committed on the high Seas. . . ." Thus, 18 U.S.C. § 1651 provides, "Whoever, on the high seas, commits the crime of piracy as defined by the law of nations, and is afterwards brought into or found in the United States, shall be imprisoned for life." Historically, the law of nations defined **naval piracy** essentially as a robbery at sea. *United States v. Smith*, 18 U.S. 153, 5 L.Ed. 57 (1820).

In April 2009, the U.S. Navy killed two Somali pirates who had attacked an American vessel, the *Maersk Alabama*, and were holding the ship's captain at gunpoint. Another pirate was captured and brought to the U.S. for prosecution. In May 2009, a federal grand jury indicted Abduwali Abdukhadir Muse for piracy, conspiracy to commit hostage-taking, and other offenses. As the quoted statute indicates, the defendant was facing a life sentence for the piracy offense alone. In February 2011, Muse was sentenced to thirty-three years in federal prison.

## Weapons of Mass Destruction

**weapons of mass destruction (WMDs)** Weapons designed to kill large numbers of people and/or damage extensive areas. Includes nuclear, radiological, biological, and chemical weapons.

While terrorism using conventional explosives can produce massive destruction and widespread panic, as we saw in New York City on 9/11, the prospect of terrorists using chemical, biological, or nuclear weapons is almost too horrible to contemplate. In recent years Congress has enacted a number of statutes that provide criminal jurisdiction over the use of **weapons of mass destruction** (WMDs). For example, 18 U.S.C. A. § 175(a) provides:

Whoever knowingly develops, produces, stockpiles, transfers, acquires, retains, or possesses any biological agent, toxin, or delivery system for use as a weapon, or knowingly assists a foreign state or any organization to do so, or attempts, threatens, or conspires to do the same, shall be fined under this title or imprisoned for life or any term of years, or both. There is extraterritorial Federal jurisdiction over an offense under this section committed by or against a national of the United States.

Additional provisions found in Title 18 of the U.S. Code impose similar prohibitions with respect to toxic chemicals, § 229, and nuclear materials, § 831.

Title 18 § 2332a criminalizes the use of weapons of mass destruction within the United States or against an American national anywhere in the world. It provides:

§ 2332a. Use of weapons of mass destruction

(a) Offense Against a National of the United States or Within the United States.—A person who, without lawful authority, uses, threatens, or attempts or conspires to use, a weapon of mass destruction—

(1) against a national of the United States while such national is outside of the United States;

(2) against any person or property within the United States, and

(A) the mail or any facility of interstate or foreign commerce is used in furtherance of the offense;

(B) such property is used in interstate or foreign commerce or in an activity that affects interstate or foreign commerce;

(C) any perpetrator travels in or causes another to travel in interstate or foreign commerce in furtherance of the offense; or

**CASE-IN-POINT**

### Court Affirms Defendants' Convictions for Threats to Use Weapons of Mass Destruction

Johnie Wise and Jack Abbott Grebe were convicted of threatening to use a biological agent and a weapon involving a disease organism in violation of 18 U.S.C.A. § 2332a(a)(2). That statute makes it a crime even to threaten to use a weapon of mass destruction if using such a weapon would affect interstate commerce. On appeal the defendants challenged the sufficiency of the evidence, which disclosed that they sent e-mails to government agencies outside their state of Texas, threatening to use weapons with biological or chemical agents. The defendants argued that this was insufficient to support their convictions because the government failed to present any testimony or documentary evidence that the use of the weapon specified in the threat would have affected interstate commerce. In rejecting their contention, the court pointed out that the statute on its face makes clear that, in the case of a threat, it applies where the results would have affected interstate or foreign commerce and that the trial jury was so instructed. In its opinion the court said, "In any event, the e-mails, which had been sent from Texas, were received by government agencies outside of Texas. For example, the FBI received the e-mails in California; the United States Customs received the e-mails at its website in Virginia; the ATF, the Secret Service, and the Office of Correspondence for the President all received the e-mails in Washington, D.C. The threat itself crossed state boundaries; therefore, it cannot be argued that an effect on interstate commerce is lacking in this case." The U.S. Court of Appeals for the Fifth Circuit affirmed the defendants' convictions.

*United States v. Wise*, 221 F.3d 140 (5th Cir. 2000).

(D) the offense, or the results of the offense, affect interstate or foreign commerce, or, in the case of a threat, attempt, or conspiracy, would have affected interstate or foreign commerce;

(3) against any property that is owned, leased or used by the United States or by any department or agency of the United States, whether the property is within or outside of the United States; or

(4) against any property within the United States that is owned, leased, or used by a foreign government, shall be imprisoned for any term of years or for life, and if death results, shall be punished by death or imprisoned for any term of years or for life.

## Immigration Offenses

**immigration offenses** Violations of criminal provisions of the Immigration and Nationality Act, a federal law that relates to immigration.

Article I, Section 8 of the U.S. Constitution vests in Congress the power "[t]o establish an uniform Rule of Naturalization. . . ." The courts have interpreted this language as giving Congress plenary power over immigration. In exercising this power, Congress has created several **immigration offenses**. Section 1325 of Title 8 U.S.C.A. prohibits improper entry by aliens, while 8 U.S.C.A. § 1326 makes it an offense for an alien who has been removed from the United States to reenter the country. Specific immigration offenses include entering or attempting "to enter the United States at any time or place other than as designated by immigration officers," 8 U.S.C.A. § 1325(a)(1); eluding "examination or inspection by immigration officers," 8 U.S.C.A. § 1325(a)(2); attempting to enter or obtaining entry to the United States "by a willfully false or misleading representation or the willful concealment of a material fact," 8 U.S.C.A. § 1325(a)(3); knowingly entering into a marriage "for the purpose of evading any provision of the immigration laws," 8 U.S.C.A. § 1325(c); and knowingly establishing "a commercial enterprise for the purpose of evading any provision of the immigration laws," 8 U.S.C.A. § 1325(d).

Lax enforcement of immigration laws in the face of massive illegal immigration across the nation's southern border has led to a divisive political battle over "immigration reform." On one hand, there is broad public support for tightening security at the borders and more vigorously enforcing existing laws. The need for greater border control is particularly acute in an age of international terrorism and when Mexican drug cartels carry out violent forays into the United States. On the other hand, it is unrealistic to deport or prosecute the millions of immigrants who have come to this country illegally, most simply looking to improve their lives through hard work at low wages, performing jobs that many Americans are unwilling to do.

In 2006 the president and Congress began to seriously address the problem of illegal immigration. The president sent National Guard troops to augment the U.S. Border Patrol's operations on the southern border, and additional funds were provided to increase measures to protect the border. The U.S. Senate and the U.S. House of Representatives crafted very different approaches to the problems of border protection and the resolution of the status of illegal immigrants. But by 2007 major political differences continued to thwart congressional action to achieve a unified approach to resolve the numerous issues surrounding immigration and border control.

## Conclusion

Offenses against public order, safety, and security present a picture of the dynamic development of the law in a constitutional democracy. The needs to maintain order and protect the public safety are high-priority items for any organized society. Yet the U.S. Constitution mandates that government maintain a delicate balance between these interests and the rights of citizens. Of particular relevance to offenses against public order are the protections of the First Amendment. Today, our society faces a new threat, that of terrorism, which adds more pressure to limit individual rights and freedoms and grant more power to law enforcement agencies. Americans today are engaged in a great debate about where the balance should be struck between freedom on one hand and order, safety, and security on the other.

## Chapter Summary

- Learning Objective 1
  - The English common law recognized the right of the people to assemble peaceably for lawful purposes, but made unlawful assemblies, routs, and riots misdemeanor offenses.
  - If three or more persons met together with the intention of cooperating to disturb the public peace by doing an unlawful act, their gathering was considered an unlawful assembly. If they took steps to achieve their purpose, it was a rout, and if they actually executed their plans, they committed a riot.

- Learning Objective 2
  - A variety of state statutes and local ordinances prohibit unlawful assemblies, riots, and disorderly conduct.
  - An unlawful assembly is a group of persons who seek to commit unlawful acts or to use unlawful means to commit lawful acts.

- A riot is a public disturbance of three or more persons who threaten or commit acts of violence to persons or property. Inciting a riot involves instigating others to riot.
- Disorderly conduct laws target individual as well as group behavior and usually make it an offense to engage in fighting or making unreasonable noise.
- States have primary responsibility for controlling breaches of the peace.
- Laws applied to violent or threatened conduct, imminent lawless action, or utterance of fighting words seldom invoke constitutional challenges; however, laws proscribing loitering and begging and curfew ordinance require courts to weigh the need to maintain order and peace against First Amendment guarantees of freedom of speech and assembly.
- The Federal Anti-Riot Act of 1968 proscribes interstate travel and use of the mail or other media to encourage or carry on a riot; or to aid or abet any person in inciting or participating in a riot. In 1972 a federal appellate court held that the act is not unconstitutionally vague or overbroad in relation to the First Amendment.

- Learning Objective 3

  - The common law developed the offense of vagrancy to criminalize idleness. American colonists, and later, states and local governments, found it desirable to punish idleness and offensive conduct and to control alcoholics and derelicts. The wide range of conduct prohibited by vagrancy laws made them susceptible to arbitrary enforcement by police to justify arrests and searches of suspects.
  - In 1972 the U.S. Supreme Court declared unconstitutional a typical vagrancy law because it "fails to give a person of ordinary intelligence fair notice that his contemplated conduct is forbidden by the statute and because it encourages arbitrary and erratic arrests and convictions."

- Learning Objective 4

  - States and cities have enacted loitering ordinances designed to focus on conduct and not status, to give fair notice as to what is proscribed, and to afford persons an opportunity to explain their presence before being ordered to disperse.
  - Like vagrancy ordinances, those that target homeless persons, such as by making it an offense to sleep in public places, have often been invalidated as being vague and subject to arbitrary enforcement. Others have been upheld as promoting aesthetics, sanitation, public health, or safety.
  - In 1999 the U.S. Supreme Court invalidated Chicago's "gang violence ordinance," which police had used to prevent gang members from loitering in any public place "with no apparent purpose."
  - Most courts have held unconstitutional curfew laws that prohibit young people unaccompanied by a parent or guardian from being on the streets during nighttime hours. Some courts have upheld such ordinances when they include numerous exceptions. On the other hand, the Supreme Court has stated that the constitutional right to travel may be legitimately curtailed by curfews on an emergency basis when the safety and welfare of a community has been ravaged by flood, fire, or disease.
  - Once vagrancy ordinances were declared unconstitutional local governments began to enact ordinances that prohibit begging (panhandling). That raised the issue of whether begging activity constitutes expression protected by the First

Amendment. Courts have frequently declared unconstitutional ordinances that proscribe all begging on public ways, but federal appellate courts have recently approved narrowly drawn ordinances that restrict only "aggressive panhandling."

- Learning Objective 5

  o During the 1960s, most states and municipalities decriminalized minor traffic offenses, with violations considered as civil infractions rather than misdemeanors. Drivers are issued citations (tickets) instead of being arrested.

  o In order to provide legal uniformity to the "rules of the road," states, and many municipalities, have adopted "model" laws defining a wide range of more serious motor vehicle (generally strict liability) offenses.

  o Since the 1980s many states have enacted mandatory seat belt and child restraint laws. Most states have enacted prohibitions on using a cell phone or text messaging while driving.

- Learning Objective 6

  o The common belief that the Second Amendment protects keeping and bearing of arms only in the context of a well-regulated militia was dispelled in 2008 when the Supreme Court struck down a District of Columbia ordinance that effectively prohibited possession of handguns. The Court held that the Second Amendment protects a personal right to possess a firearm for "traditionally lawful purposes" irrespective of one's service in any militia.

  o The Federal Gun Control Act of 1968 prohibits firearms dealers from transferring handguns to persons who are under twenty-one, nonresidents of the dealer's state, or those who are otherwise prohibited by state or local laws from purchasing or possessing firearms.

  o A variety of state laws prohibit possession of offensive weapons by other than law enforcement personnel. States also commonly proscribe carrying a weapon concealed from ordinary sight on or about a person or in a vehicle.

  o Many states have laws that require background checks of gun buyers at gun shows, require registration of firearms or permits to purchase them, and prohibit sales to persons convicted of serious felonies. A 2010 decision of the U.S. Supreme Court makes state and local laws subject to constitutional challenge under the Second Amendment.

- Learning Objective 7

  o The principal crimes against national security are treason, espionage, sabotage, and sedition. The U.S. Constitution provides that treason against the United States "shall consist only in levying War against them, or in adhering to their Enemies, giving them Aid and Comfort."

  o Espionage (spying) consists of turning over state secrets to a foreign government and is covered by a number of federal statutes which criminalize gathering or transmitting defense information "with intent . . . that the information . . . be used to the injury of the United States, or to the advantage of any foreign nation." The Intelligence Identities Protection Act of 1982 prohibits disclosure of the identities of undercover intelligence officers, agents, informants, and their "sources."

  o Sabotage is the intentional destruction of the country's military infrastructure by an enemy agent or civilian and is proscribed by federal and state laws.

  o Sedition is the incitement of insurrection or revolution. In 1940, Congress adopted the Smith Act, which in its present form makes it a crime for a person to knowingly or willfully advocate the overthrow of federal, state, or local government by force or violence, or by assassination of any governmental officer. In 1957, the Supreme Court set aside the convictions of Communist Party officials, distinguishing between "advocacy of abstract doctrine and advocacy directed at promoting unlawful action" and held that the Smith Act prohibited only the latter. In a landmark decision, the Court held that mere advocacy could never be criminalized in the absence of "imminent lawless action."

- Learning Objective 8

  ○ The Omnibus Diplomatic Security and Antiterrorism Act of 1986 makes it a federal offense for a terrorist overseas to kill, attempt to kill, conspire to kill, or engage in physical violence with the intent to cause serious bodily injury to, an American citizen.

  ○ The Antiterrorism and Effective Death Penalty Act of 1996 expanded federal jurisdiction with respect to investigation and prosecution of international terrorism.

  ○ After the attacks on 9/11, the federal government created the Department of Homeland Security. Since then the federal government has taken stricter safety measures to safeguard mass transportation, borders, ports, utility systems, and government buildings. It has also undertaken to train police, fire, and medical personnel to cope with the potential use of weapons of mass destruction.

  ○ The USA PATRIOT Act, enacted after the attacks of 9/11, amends various federal statutes; creates new offenses for attacks on mass transportation facilities and for possession of biological weapons, when not justified for research; deems certain acts of terrorism to be racketeering activity; and extends statutes of limitations. The act increases the ability of law enforcement agencies to search telephone, e-mail communications, medical, and financial records and subjects assets of individuals involved in terrorism to civil forfeiture. Critics argue that by restricting personal liberties certain sections of the act offend basic constitutional protections.

  ○ In March 2006, Congress made permanent all but two provisions of the USA PATRIOT Act.

  ○ Federal law also prohibits naval and aircraft piracy; interference with security screening personnel, flight crew members, and flight attendants; and carrying weapons or explosives onto an aircraft.

  ○ Other federal criminal laws forbid the use of weapons of mass destruction within the United States or against an American national anywhere in the world.

- Learning Objective 9

  ○ The U.S. Constitution vests in Congress the power "[t]o establish an uniform Rule of Naturalization. . . ." Federal statutes prohibit improper entry by aliens; make it an offense for an alien who has been removed from the United States to reenter the country; and include a variety of offenses that make it unlawful to enter the country by false and misleading actions, by knowingly entering into a marriage, or by establishing a commercial enterprise to evade the immigration laws.

  ○ Lax enforcement of immigration laws in the face of massive illegal immigration across the nation's southern border has led to a divisive political battle over "immigration reform." In 2006 the president and Congress began to seriously address the problem, but by 2009 major political differences continued to thwart Congressional action to achieve a unified approach to the numerous issues surrounding immigration and border control.

## Key Terms

aircraft piracy

Antiterrorism and Effective Death
    Penalty Act

Brady Bill

breaches of the peace

civil infractions

concealed weapon

curfew ordinances

decriminalization of routine traffic
    offenses

disorderly conduct

espionage

excessive noise

Federal Anti-Riot Act

Federal Gun Control Act

gun control laws

Gun-Free School Zones Act

immigration offenses

inciting a riot

loitering

mandatory child restraint laws

mandatory seat belt laws

motor vehicle violations

naval piracy

panhandling

primary offense

riot

rout

rules of the road

sabotage

secondary offense

sedition

terrorism

texting while driving

traffic court

treason

unlawful assembly

USA PATRIOT Act

vagrancy

weapons of mass destruction (WMDs)

weapons offenses

well-regulated militia

## Questions for Thought and Discussion

1. Why has it been necessary for American courts to interpret laws proscribing breach of peace and vagrancy more strictly than did the English common-law courts?

2. How does the Federal Anti-Riot Act seek to prevent the definition of "to incite a riot" from being applied in such a way that it violates First Amendment guarantees of freedom of expression?

3. Is an ordinance that defines "disturbing the peace" simply as "tumultuous or offensive conduct" sufficiently precise to meet the constitutional standard of giving a person of ordinary intelligence fair notice of what conduct is forbidden?

4. How did the Jacksonville, Florida, vagrancy ordinance invalidated by the Supreme Court in the *Papachristou* case offend the Constitution of the United States? Have the reforms in vagrancy laws at the state and local levels sufficiently removed the threat of criminalizing a person's status? Are they now written with the precision necessary to protect citizens from arbitrary enforcement of the law?

5. Based on the ruling of the Supreme Court in *City of Chicago v. Morales*, what protections of the individual do you think must be included in an ordinance proscribing loitering?

6. Assume you are working as a staff assistant to a state legislator who intends to introduce a law making it an offense to solicit funds by "panhandling" on streets

and in parks. You are asked to prepare a memorandum of provisions to be considered in order to avoid the proposed act's being declared unconstitutional. What basic provisions would you recommend?

7. Have traffic offenses been decriminalized in your state? Should drivers who use cell phones for conversing or for text messaging be charged with civil infractions? To what extent? What procedures are available to contest a traffic ticket?

8. Why have the courts refused to interpret the Second Amendment's protection of the "right to keep and bear arms" to prohibit gun control legislation? On what bases other than the Second Amendment can one make constitutional attacks on federal gun control laws?

9. To what extent does the First Amendment protect the right of citizens to advocate on behalf of groups that have been labeled as terrorist organizations by the federal government?

10. Under what circumstances does the law permit the government to prosecute a person who publicly advocates the violent overthrow of the U.S. government? What constitutional considerations come into play?

11. Evaluate the criticism leveled against the USA PATRIOT Act that the sections quoted in the text unconstitutionally deprive individuals of their civil liberties by such vague terms as "acts intended to influence government policy by intimidation or coercion."

12. Are acts of terrorism perpetrated against the United States by foreign nationals more appropriately viewed as crimes or acts of war? Is the criminal justice system the appropriate means of dealing with foreign terrorists?

13. What should be done about the millions of foreign nationals who have entered the United States illegally? Should they be prosecuted for immigration offenses, deported to their countries of origin, or granted some sort of amnesty whereby they can remain in this country and work legally?

## Problems for Discussion and Solution

1. Consider the following hypothetical case: Members of the American Nazi Party announced a demonstration to be held in Pleasant Ridge, a predominantly Jewish suburb of Metropolis. The Pleasant Ridge City Council quickly adopted an ordinance requiring groups planning demonstrations to obtain a permit from the police department. Under the ordinance, to hold a demonstration without a permit was a misdemeanor, punishable by a $1,000 fine and sixty days in jail. The Nazis applied for a permit, which was denied on the ground that their presence in Pleasant Ridge constituted a "clear and present danger to the public order." The Nazis held their demonstration anyway. Approximately one hundred demonstrators congregated on the city square. Many were dressed in Nazi uniforms, others carried banners emblazoned with swastikas, and others held signs on which were printed anti-Semitic slogans. Pleasant Ridge police arrived at the scene and asked the demonstrators to disperse. When they refused, police arrested some demonstrators; others ran to avoid arrest. The leader of the Nazi group, Adrian Maples, was convicted of a number of offenses, including violation of the new ordinance. On appeal, Maples is challenging the constitutionality of the ordinance. What do you think the court's ruling should be? Explain your reasoning.

2. The City of Dystopia experienced difficulties with groups of rowdy individuals congregating on downtown sidewalks and harassing passersby. When the local

police were unable to control the situation by enforcing the disorderly conduct statute, the city council enacted the following ordinance:

Sec. 1. It shall be unlawful for three or more persons to assemble on any public sidewalk or walkway within the city while conducting themselves in a manner that is annoying or bothersome to surrounding persons.

Sec. 2. Anyone found guilty of violating this ordinance shall be punished as provided in the city charter.

After the ordinance went into effect, three college students congregated on a public sidewalk and made loud, obnoxious remarks to passersby. The police arrested the students and charged them under the ordinance. The students admit that they were rowdy but argue that the ordinance unduly restricts their First Amendment rights. What constitutional arguments could they, or their counsel, present to a court in an effort to reverse their convictions? Do you think they would prevail? In your opinion, should they prevail?

## CHAPTER 13

# Offenses against Justice and Public Administration

## JURISPRUDENCE

*United States v. Gaudin* (1995)

*United States v. Bailey* (1980)

*Sacher v. United States* (1952)

*Watkins v. United States* (1957)

## LEARNING OBJECTIVES

After reading this chapter, you should be able to

1. explain how the common law defined offenses against the administration of justice

2. understand why the offense of bribery has been extended beyond bribing of judges and other public officials

3. explain the offenses of perjury, subornation of perjury, and making false statements

4. explain the defenses available in perjury cases

5. understand how obstruction of justice includes a number of related offenses

6. explain how compounding a crime differs from misprision of felony

7. know the circumstances under which one may lawfully escape from confinement

8. explain how criminal contempt differs from civil contempt and how a direct contempt differs from an indirect contempt

# CHAPTER OPENING VIGNETTE

On December 9, 2008, federal agents arrested Illinois governor Rod Blagojevich on charges of solicitation of bribery and conspiracy to commit mail and wire fraud. The arrests came after an investigation by the FBI into whether Blagojevich attempted to profit from the appointment to fill Barack Obama's vacant U.S. Senate seat. The scandal led the Illinois legislature to impeach the governor and remove him from office in January 2009. In April a federal grand jury indicted Blagojevich on a variety of federal charges. In February 2010, a superseding indictment charged the former governor with additional federal crimes.

On June 3, 2010, Blagojevich went to trial on twenty-four counts, including racketeering, solicitation of bribery, conspiracy to commit bribery, attempted extortion, and conspiracy to commit extortion. On August 17, the jury returned a conviction on only one count—making false statements to the FBI. The jury was deadlocked on the remaining counts, forcing the judge to declare a mistrial on twenty-three counts. Subsequent television interviews with jurors in the case revealed that one juror had held out for acquittal, thus deadlocking the jury on all but the one count. Blagojevich celebrated the mistrial and portrayed himself as the victim of a runaway prosecution launched by an overzealous prosecutor. The prosecution vowed to retry the former governor.

The one crime of which Blagojevich was convicted, making false statements to the FBI, is a serious offense against the administration of justice and carries a maximum prison term of five years. The applicable federal statute, 18 U.S.C.A. § 1001, is a controversial one. Critics say it allows prosecutors to pile on criminal charges by making it a crime to simply deny an accusation made by law enforcement agents. Certainly it goes well beyond the common-law offense of perjury.

Making good on their promise to retry the governor, prosecutors dropped three charges and proceeded to trial on twenty of the charges that had resulted in mistrial. On June 27, 2011, after a second jury trial, Blagojevich was convicted of seventeen of these charges. The jury found him not guilty of one charge and failed to return a verdict on two others. On December 7, the former governor was sentenced to fourteen years in federal prison.http:// en.wikipedia.org/wiki/Rod_Blagojevich-cite_note-88. In announcing the sentence, Judge James B. Zagel observed that the harm caused by Blagojevich's crimes was "not measured in the value of property or money," but rather "the erosion of public trust in government."

# Introduction

The English common-law judges found it necessary to create a number of offenses to maintain the integrity of the law and the administration of justice. Principally, these offenses were bribery, perjury and subornation of perjury, resisting arrest, obstruction of justice, compounding a crime, and escape. At common law, these offenses were misdemeanors. In addition, the common law developed the concept of criminal contempt to enable judges to maintain the dignity and authority of the courts and the respect due judicial officers. All of these common-law crimes remain an important part of contemporary criminal law in the United States, although they have been expanded and augmented by a variety of modern statutes. The offenses against public administration and the administration of justice in particular serve as a means to punish those who breach the public trust and whose actions corrupt the orderly processes of government and the justice system.

# Bribery

**bribery** The crime of offering, giving, requesting, soliciting, or receiving something of value to influence a decision of a public official.

The concept of **bribery** dates back to biblical times, when it was regarded as sinful to attempt to influence a judge with a gift because the judge represented the divine. Thus, when the common law developed the crime of bribery, it sought to penalize only persons whose actions were designed to improperly influence those identified with the administration of justice. Later, it was considered bribery for anyone to give or receive anything of value or any valuable service or promise with the intent to influence any public officer in the discharge of a legal duty. Bribery is generally a felony under modern law. The seriousness with which the founders of this country regarded bribery is demonstrated by Article II, Section 4 of the U.S. Constitution, which specifically authorizes impeachment of public officials who commit "Treason, *Bribery*, or other high Crimes and Misdemeanors" (emphasis added).

## The Modern Statutory Offense of Bribery

Today, a variety of federal statutes proscribe bribery of specific public officers and witnesses as well as of jurors and government employees and functionaries. The most prominent among these is 18 U.S.C.A. § 201, which makes it a crime if anyone "directly or indirectly gives, offers, or promises anything of value to any public official, former public official, or person selected to be a public official, for or because of any official act performed or to be performed by such public official, former public official, or person selected to be a public official. . . ." 18 U.S.C.A. § 201(c)(1)(A). The law also makes it a crime if "a public official, former public official, or person selected to be a public official, otherwise than as provided by law for the proper discharge of official duty, directly or indirectly demands, seeks, receives, accepts, or agrees to receive or accept anything of value personally for or because of any official act performed or to be performed. . . ." 18 U.S.C.A. § 201(c)(1)(B). Other subsections of the statute make it a crime to offer a bribe to a witness or for a witness to solicit or accept a bribe. 18 U.S.C.A. §§ 201(c)(2)–(3).

State statutes generally define bribery in broad terms and frequently address specific situations as well. The trend has been to enlarge the common-law approach by extending the offense to new categories of persons and conduct and by making the punishment more severe. The broad statutory definition of bribery is illustrated by a Florida law that makes bribery a felony and provides:

> "Bribery" means corruptly to give, offer, or promise to any public servant, or, if a public servant, corruptly to request, solicit, accept, or agree to accept for himself or herself or another, any pecuniary or other benefit with an intent or purpose to influence the performance of any act or omission which the person believes to be, or the public servant represents as being, within the official discretion of a public servant, in violation of a public duty, or in performance of a public duty. West's Fla. Stat. Ann. § 838.015(1).

Section 838.015(2) makes explicit that the person sought to be bribed need not have authority to accomplish the act sought or represented. Courts generally construe such terms as "public servant" and "benefit" broadly to accomplish the intended legislative purpose of statutes defining bribery.

Arizona law adds the term "party officer" to its statute proscribing bribery. It defines that term as "a person who holds any position or office in a political party, whether by election, appointment or otherwise." Ariz. Rev. Stat. § 13-2601. Section 13-2602 of the Revised Arizona Statutes provides:

A. A person commits bribery of a public servant or party officer if with corrupt intent:

    1. Such person offers, confers or agrees to confer any benefit upon a public servant or party officer with the intent to influence the public servant's or party officer's vote, opinion, judgment, exercise of discretion or other action in his official capacity as a public servant or party officer; or

    2. While a public servant or party officer, such person solicits, accepts or agrees to accept any benefit upon an agreement or understanding that his vote, opinion, judgment, exercise of discretion or other action as a public servant or party officer may thereby be influenced.

B. It is no defense to a prosecution under this section that a person sought to be influenced was not qualified to act in the desired way because such person had not yet assumed office, lacked jurisdiction or for any other reason.

C. Bribery of a public servant or party officer is a class 4 felony.

Although the Florida statute is explicit on the subject, irrespective of statutes, courts generally hold that where the act intended to be influenced is connected with a person's public duty, it is immaterial whether the person bribed has, or has not, the authority to do a specific act. See, e.g., *State v. Hendricks*, 186 P.2d 943 (Ariz. 1947).

## The Range of Bribery Offenses

Bribery covers a wide range of conduct and is frequently associated with white-collar and organized crime situations (see Chapter 9). Common examples of bribery include obtaining the release or acquittal of an arrestee, securing an award of a government contract, and even obtaining a favorable vote by a legislator on a pending bill. The Arizona statute just quoted expands the traditional concept of "public servant" by recognizing the potential for bribery within the ranks of political parties. Although we commonly think of money being offered or requested as a bribe, a variety of other things are offered, sought, or exchanged. These not only include cash or its equivalent but also such tangible and intangible benefits as price advantages, use of vehicles, vacation homes, and even sexual favors. Bribes often occur in subtle or disguised ways. For example, a sale of property for less than its true value would likely be considered bribery if the seller's real purpose was to benefit the purchaser to influence his or her official governmental action.

## The Burden of the Prosecution

The gist of the crime of bribery is the unlawful offer or agreement to do something under color of office. Ordinarily, the prosecution must prove not only the offer or agreement or the request or acceptance of a benefit but also that the defendant had a false or corrupt intent. One difficulty encountered in prosecuting a bribery charge is establishing the corrupt intent element. For example, it can be extremely difficult to prove that a person received employment or was granted a contract as a result of a bribe. The difficulty is compounded because, not infrequently, bribes are disguised as gifts or even as political or charitable contributions.

**commercial bribery** Offering, soliciting, or accepting a benefit or consideration in respect to a business or professional matter in violation of a person's duty of fidelity.

**sports bribery** Offering anything of value to a participant or official in an amateur or professional athletic contest to vary his or her performance.

## Offenses Extending the Concept of Bribery

Many states have enacted statutes to extend the offense of bribery to encompass conduct of persons other than public officials and employees. The two principal areas of extension have been commerce and sports. Although **commercial bribery** and **sports bribery** are not offenses against the administration of justice or government, we include them here as they are extensions of the basic offense of bribery beyond its traditional context. For example, the commercial bribery statute quoted in the following section includes bribery in instances of arbitration, an extrajudicial method of settling disputes.

**CASE-IN-POINT**

### Bribery: What Constitutes a Thing of Value?

McDonald, a male trial court judge in Alabama, was prosecuted for solicitation of sexual favors in exchange for affording a female favorable treatment in pending court cases. He was convicted of bribery under a state statute that provided that it was bribery for any public official to accept "any gift, gratuity, or other thing of value." On appeal, McDonald argued that "sexual intercourse, or the promise of sexual intercourse, or the promise of other sexual favors or relationship" did not meet the test of being a "thing of value" under the bribery statute. The Alabama Court of Criminal Appeals rejected the defendant's contention, saying, "The word 'thing' does not necessarily mean a substance. . . . [I]t includes an act, or action."

*McDonald v. State*, 329 So.2d 583 (Ala. Crim. App. 1975).

# Commercial Bribery

Section 224.8 of the Model Penal Code outlines an offense known as commercial bribery. Some states have classified certain corrupt business practices, for example, fraudulent acts of purchasing agents, as commercial bribery. The New Jersey law making commercial bribery a crime includes many of the provisions outlined in the Model Penal Code. As amended in 1986, the statute provides:

a. A person commits a crime if he solicits, accepts or agrees to accept any benefit as consideration for knowingly violating or agreeing to violate a duty of fidelity to which he is subject as:

(1) An agent, partner or employee of another;

(2) A trustee, guardian, or other fiduciary;

(3) A lawyer, physician, accountant, appraiser, or other professional adviser or informant;

(4) An officer, director, manager or other participant in the direction of the affairs of an incorporated or unincorporated association;

(5) A labor official, including any duly appointed representative of a labor organization or any duly appointed trustee or representative of an employee welfare trust fund; or

(6) An arbitrator or other purportedly disinterested adjudicator or referee.

b. A person who holds himself out to the public as being engaged in the business of making disinterested selection, appraisal, or criticism of commodities, real properties or services commits a crime if he solicits, accepts or agrees to accept any benefit to influence his selection, appraisal or criticism.

c. A person commits a crime if he confers, or offers or agrees to confer, any benefit the acceptance of which would be criminal under this section. N.J. Stat. Ann. § 2C:21–10.

---

**CASE-IN-POINT**

## A State Supreme Court Upholds a Conviction for Sports Bribery

Following a bench trial, Angelo Trosclair III was convicted of two counts of bribery of sports participants on February 14, 1981, in violation of La. Rev .Stat. Ann. § 14:118.1. That statute defines bribery of a jockey as "the giving or offering to give, directly or indirectly, anything of apparent present or prospective value to any jockey with the intent to influence him to lose or cause to be lost, or corruptly to affect or influence the result of a horse race or to limit his mount or beast's margin of victory in any race." On appeal Trosclair contended that the evidence was legally insufficient to support a finding that he was guilty beyond a reasonable doubt.

In rejecting his contention, the Louisiana Supreme Court noted, "The state presented two witnesses who testified that they had been offered, and had actually received, significant sums of money in exchange for their promises not to finish first, second or third in the fourth race at the Fairgrounds on February 14, 1981. The testimony of the two jockeys, Hale and Durousseau, undoubtedly provided an adequate basis for a finding of guilt beyond a reasonable doubt by a rational trier of fact." Despite the defendant's claim that the credibility of these two witnesses was destroyed, the court further noted, "[I]t is not our function to assess credibility or reweigh the evidence. Our review for minimal constitutional sufficiency of evidence is a limited one which ends upon our finding that the rational trier–reasonable doubt standard has been satisfied." The court affirmed the defendant's convictions.

*State v. Trosclair*, 443 So.2d 1098 (La. 1983).

Under the New Jersey statute, the benefit offered, conferred, agreed to be conferred, solicited, accepted, or agreed to determines the degree of the crime and the penalty.

## Sports Bribery

Because of the increased role of both professional and amateur sports in society, most states now have made sports bribery a crime. Sports bribery statutes generally make it an offense for a person to offer anything of value to a participant or official in an amateur or professional athletic contest to vary his or her performance. Likewise, it is a crime for a participant or official in a sports event to accept a bribe under such circumstances. See, e.g., Iowa Code Ann. § 722.3; *State v. Di Paglia*, 71 N.W.2d 601 (Iowa 1955).

## Defenses to the Crime of Bribery

Of course, the fact that an offer to bribe is not legally enforceable is no defense. The only recognized defense to a charge of bribery, other than denial, is entrapment. See *State v. Harrington*, 332 So.2d 764 (La. 1976). We discuss the defense of entrapment in Chapter 14.

# Perjury

**perjury** The crime of making a material false statement under oath.

Like bribery, the crime of **perjury** has its roots in biblical times. The Mosaic Code included an admonition against the bearing of false witness. At common law, perjury came to consist of willfully giving under oath in a judicial proceeding false testimony material to the issue. Because of the narrow scope of the offense, it was eventually supplemented by the common-law offense of false swearing, a crime committed when an oath was taken in other than a judicial proceeding.

## Elements of the Offense of Perjury

The basic elements of the common-law offenses of perjury and false swearing have been codified by a federal statute, 18 U.S.C.A. § 1621, which provides

> Whoever (1) having taken an oath before a competent tribunal, officer, or person, in any case in which a law of the United States authorizes an oath to be administered, that he will testify, declare, depose, or certify truly, or that any written testimony, declaration, deposition, or certificate by him subscribed, is true, willfully and contrary to such oath states or subscribes any material matter which he does not believe to be true; or (2) in any declaration, certificate, verification, or statement under penalty of perjury as permitted under section 1746 of title 28, United States Code, willfully subscribes as true any material matter which he does not believe to be true; is guilty of perjury. . . .

The reference to 28 U.S.C.A. § 1746 covers certifications subscribed under a rule, regulation, or order pursuant to any law where the subscriber signs a document in substantially the following form: "I declare (or certify, verify, or state) under penalty of perjury under the laws of the United States of America that the foregoing is true and correct." Probably the most common example of this is the declaration a taxpayer signs when filing a federal income tax return. 26 U.S.C.A. § 6065.

All states have laws making perjury a criminal offense. For example, the California perjury statute provides that a person who has taken an oath to tell the truth and who "willfully and contrary to the oath, states as true any material matter which he or she knows to be false" is guilty of perjury. West's Ann. Cal. Penal Code § 118. Although § 118 relates to oaths in administrative and judicial proceedings, § 118a makes it perjury for a person to give a false affidavit to be used in those proceedings. Section 118 is applicable whether the statement, testimony, declaration, deposition, or certification is made or subscribed within or without the State of California. As in other jurisdictions, additional California statutes make it unlawful for anyone to give a false statement under oath in various applications, certificates, and reports. Courts have ruled that a grant of immunity (discussed in Chapter 14) will not protect a witness from prosecution for perjury if the witness testifies falsely. The courts reason that although a witness may be compelled to testify, nevertheless the witness is not compelled to testify falsely. See, e.g., *DeMan v. State*, 677 P.2d 903 (Alaska App. 1984).

## The Burden of the Prosecution

To convict a defendant of perjury, the prosecution must establish that the defendant took an oath to tell the truth and knowingly made a false statement of fact. Statutes usually permit anyone with scruples against taking an oath to affirm that a statement is true. In either event, a person cannot be lawfully convicted of perjury unless there is proof that he or she was administered the oath by, or made an affirmation before, someone with legal authority. *Whitaker v. Commonwealth*, 367 S.W.2d 831 (Ky. 1963). Furthermore, the defendant's statement must have been material. This means that the testimony given by the defendant must have been capable of influencing the tribunal on the issues before it. *United States v. Jackson*, 640 F.2d 614 (8th Cir. 1981).

Historically, courts in many jurisdictions held that the question of whether a witness's statement was material was a matter to be decided by the judge. In the 1990s some courts reasoned that because materiality is an element of the crime of perjury, a jury must determine that such element has been proved beyond a reasonable

---

### JURISPRUDENCE

*United States v. Gaudin*, 515 U.S. 506, 115 S.Ct. 2310, 132 L.Ed.2d 444 (1995)

Michael E. Gaudin was convicted of making false statements on Department of Housing and Urban Development (HUD) loan documents. At trial, the judge instructed the jury that the Government had to prove that the alleged false statements were material to HUD's decision with respect to the loan, but added that the issue of materiality was a matter for the court rather than the jury to decide. Holding that the question of materiality should be put to the jury, the U.S. Court of Appeals for the Ninth Circuit reversed Gaudin's conviction. The Supreme Court granted the government's petition for certiorari. In his opinion for the Court affirming the Ninth Circuit's ruling, Justice Antonin Scalia stated, "The Constitution gives a criminal defendant the right to have a jury determine, beyond a reasonable doubt, his guilt of every element of the crime with which he is charged. The trial judge's refusal to allow the jury to pass on the 'materiality' of Gaudin's false statements infringed that right."

doubt. See, e.g., *State v. Anderson*, 603 A.2d 928 (N.J. 1992). Their view prevailed in 1995, for as the Supreme Court pointed out in *United States v. Gaudin*, 515 U.S. 506, 115 S.Ct. 2310, 132 L.Ed.2d 444 (1995), the Constitution requires that in a perjury prosecution the materiality of the defendant's statements, like all other elements of a crime, is a jury question.

Some statutes that define perjury require the prosecution to prove that the defendant's statement was made with the "intent to deceive." See, e.g., Vernon's Tex. Penal Code § 37.02(a). Irrespective of statutory requirements, most jurisdictions require the prosecution to prove that the defendant's false statement was made "willfully and corruptly" because at common law, perjury was a specific-intent crime. Requiring the prosecution to prove the defendant's specific intent generally eliminates the likelihood of a defendant's being convicted for simply having made a careless or offhanded statement.

Perjury is one of the most difficult crimes to prove. The inherent difficulty of convicting a defendant of this offense is exacerbated by the **two-witness rule** that prevails in most jurisdictions. Under this rule the prosecution must prove the falsity of a defendant's statements by two witnesses. For example, McKinney's N.Y. Penal Code § 210.50 provides:

In any prosecution for perjury, except a prosecution based upon inconsistent statements pursuant to § 210.20, or in any prosecution for making an apparently sworn false statement, or making a punishable false written statement, falsity of a statement may not be established by the uncorroborated testimony of a single witness.

Most courts have held that the two-witness rule does not require the live testimony of two witnesses. As the Second Circuit Court of Appeals observed in *United States v. Maultasch*, 596 F.2d 19, 25, n. 9 (2d Cir. 1979), "Technically, the 'two witness' rule is a misnomer because the rule requires either the testimony of a second witness or other evidence of independent probative value."

> **two-witness rule** A requirement that to prove a defendant guilty of perjury, the prosecution must prove the falsity of the defendant's statements either by two witnesses or by one witness and corroborating documents or circumstances.

## Perjury by Contradictory Statements

Early American cases followed the common-law principle that a defendant could not be convicted of **perjury by contradictory statements** unless the prosecution established which one of the statements was false. Modern statutes make it unnecessary for the prosecution to establish which of two contradictory statements is false. See, e.g., McKinney's N.Y. Penal Law § 210.20 (inability of the prosecution to establish specifically which of the two statements is the false one does not preclude a prosecution for perjury).

> **perjury by contradictory statements** Commission of the offense of perjury by a witness who makes conflicting statements under oath.

## Subornation of Perjury

At common law, **subornation of perjury** consisted of instigating or procuring another person to commit perjury. Statutes now generally define subornation of perjury much as did the common law. To convict a defendant of the offense, the prosecution must first establish that the defendant induced another to testify falsely and that an actual perjury has been committed. *State v. Devers*, 272 A.2d 794 (Md. 1971). Thus, the Tennessee Supreme Court upheld a subornation of perjury conviction of an attorney for counseling four men charged with illegally selling whiskey to commit perjury. The attorney was prosecuted, however, only after his four clients were convicted. *Grant v. State*, 374 S.W.2d 391 (Tenn. 1964).

> **subornation of perjury** The crime of procuring someone to lie under oath.

## The Perjury Trial of the Twentieth Century

**CASE-IN-POINT**

On August 3, 1948, Whitaker Chambers, a magazine editor, acknowledged before a Congressional committee investigating subversive activities of governmental employees that he operated as a spy for the Soviet Union during 1934–1938. Chambers charged that during this time Alger Hiss, a highly respected official of the U.S. Department of State, had turned over U.S. government documents to him in his former role as a spy. Hiss appeared before the committee and categorically denied that he was, or ever had been, a communist or a communist sympathizer. He asserted that he did not know anyone by the name of Whittaker Chambers.

On December 15, 1948, Hiss testified under oath as a witness before a federal grand jury investigating charges of espionage activities by communists in the U.S. government. Hiss stated that he had never, nor had his wife in his presence, turned over any documents of the State Department to Chambers or to any other unauthorized person. He also testified before the same grand jury on the same day that he thought he could definitely say that he did not see Chambers after January 1, 1937. This grand jury indicted Hiss for having committed perjury when he testified that he did not turn over government documents to Chambers and when he denied knowing Chambers. (The statute of limitations had tolled, so the government could not charge Hiss with espionage.)

Hiss was tried by jury twice, the jury at the first trial having failed to agree upon a verdict. At the second trial, in 1950, the government presented Chambers

and a witness to corroborate Chambers's testimony. Hiss denied knowing Chambers, denied any involvement with the communists, and branded Chambers a liar. He presented excellent character witnesses and a well-known expert who categorized Chambers as a psychopathic personality given to repetitive lying. But the government also presented evidence of documents evidently prepared for espionage purposes that were typed on a typewriter owned by Hiss.

Hiss was convicted on both counts of perjury and sentenced to five years in prison. On appeal to the U.S. Court of Appeals for the Second Circuit, Hiss contended that the evidence was legally insufficient under the law of perjury. The court acknowledged that there must be either two witnesses who testify that the accused violated his oath or one witness to that and corroboration by other evidence the jury believes. The court affirmed, however, because in addition to Chambers's direct testimony, there was sufficient independent evidence of the documents of which Chambers produced copies and which were all available to the defendant at the Department of State. Further, the court found that the evidence established that the documents were copied on a typewriter when in the defendant's possession. As to count 2, the court noted that both Chambers and his wife testified that the defendant met and saw Chambers after January 1, 1937. Notwithstanding the decisions of the courts, Hiss stoutly maintained his innocence until his death in 1996.

*United States v. Hiss*, 185 F.2d 822 (2d Cir. 1951). Review denied, 340 U.S. 948, 71 S.Ct. 532, 95 L.Ed. 683 (1951).

# Defenses to the Crime of Perjury

Truth, of course, is a complete defense to a charge of perjury; therefore, a defendant who, while under oath, gives an answer that is "literally accurate, technically responsive or legally truthful" cannot lawfully be convicted of perjury. *United States v. Wall*, 371 F.2d 398, 400 (6th Cir. 1967).

After making a false statement under oath, a witness sometimes recants and tells the truth. Federal law provides for a **recantation** defense to a prosecution for perjury where in the same continuous court or grand jury proceeding in which a declaration is made, the person making the declaration admits such declaration to be false "if the declaration has not substantially affected the proceeding, or it has not become manifest that such falsity has been or will be exposed." 18 U.S.C.A. § 1623(d).

**recantation** The withdrawal or repudiation of previous statements. In some instances, a person who has lied under oath is permitted to recant to avoid being charged with perjury.

**CASE-IN-POINT**

### Perjury: The Truth Must Be Unequivocal

A police officer was convicted of committing perjury on the basis of his denial of having received money from certain persons while in performance of his police duties. On appeal, he argued that his answer, "No sir. Not for my duties," to the prosecutor's question whether he received any money from any persons while on official duty as a Chicago policeman was literally true and therefore formed no basis for his conviction. The U.S. Court of Appeals for the Seventh Circuit rejected his contention. The court explained that his initial response, "No sir," was directly responsive and false, so that his nonresponsive attempted hedge that followed was not effective.

*United States v. Nickels*, 502 F.2d 1173 (7th Cir. 1974).

In reviewing a state statute similar to the federal statute, in *Nelson v. State*, 500 So.2d 1308 (Ala. Crim. App. 1986), the court held that retraction of a false statement is a defense if the retraction occurs in the same proceeding and the statement is retracted before it becomes manifest that the fabrication is or will be exposed.

New York courts have held that recantation is a defense provided it occurs promptly, before the body conducting the inquiry (e.g., a grand jury) has been deceived or any prejudice has occurred and before the defendant's perjury has most likely become known to the authorities. *People v. Ezaugi*, 141 N.E.2d 580 (N.Y. 1957). The rationale for the recantation defense is that the object of judicial investigations and trials is to ascertain the truth. It follows, therefore, that the law should encourage a witness to correct a false statement without fear of perjury charges as long as the false statement has prejudiced no one.

## Federal Statute on Making False Statements to Government Agencies

We have seen that the federal perjury statute, 18 U.S.C.A. § 1621, criminalizes knowingly making false statements under oath. However, another federal statute, 18 U.S.C.A. § 1001, prohibits making false statements to government agencies irrespective of having taken an oath:

(a) Except as otherwise provided in this section, whoever, in any matter within the jurisdiction of the executive, legislative, or judicial branch of the Government of the United States, knowingly and willfully—

(1) falsifies, conceals, or covers up by any trick, scheme, or device a material fact;

(2) makes any materially false, fictitious, or fraudulent statement or representation; or

(3) makes or uses any false writing or document knowing the same to contain any materially false, fictitious, or fraudulent statement or entry;

shall be fined under this title, imprisoned not more than 5 years or, if the offense involves international or domestic terrorism . . . , imprisoned not more than 8 years, or both. . . . 18 U.S.C.A. § 1001(a).

This is the statute under which former Illinois governor Rod Blagojevich was convicted in 2010. Some have criticized this statute as giving prosecutors a means of "piling on" an additional felony charge when a suspect simply denies charges when confronted by investigators. Many people will instinctively deny criminal wrongdoing when first confronted by the authorities. Critics believe it is unfair for the government to be able to prosecute someone merely for such a denial. Commenting on this criticism, the Supreme Court in *Brogan v. United States*, 522 U.S. 398, 405, 118 S.Ct. 805, 810, 139 L.Ed.2d 830, 838 (1998), said,

> The supposed danger is that overzealous prosecutors will use this provision as a means of "piling on" offenses—sometimes punishing the denial of wrongdoing more severely than the wrongdoing itself. The objectors' principal grievance on this score, however, lies not with the hypothetical prosecutors but with Congress itself, which has decreed the obstruction of a legitimate investigation to be a separate offense, and a serious one.

Given the position taken by the Supreme Court in *Brogan*, it would seem advisable for anyone who faces the slightest possibility of criminal exposure to refrain from talking to federal agents in the absence of counsel.

# Obstruction of Justice

**obstruction of justice** The crime of impeding or preventing law enforcement or the administration of justice.

At common law it was a crime to commit an act obstructing or tending to obstruct public justice. Any act that prevented, obstructed, impeded, or hindered the administration of justice was considered a common-law misdemeanor. This included a host of acts such as obstructing an officer, tampering with jurors or witnesses, preparing false evidence, and secreting or destroying evidence. As statutory law came into being, some offenses that had been prosecuted as **obstruction of justice**, for example, escape, rescue and later resisting arrest, were dealt with as distinct crimes.

## Modern Statutory Developments

Federal statutes proscribe a lengthy list of actions that constitute obstruction of justice. Among the actions made unlawful are assault on a process server; theft or alteration of process; endeavoring to influence or impede grand or petit jurors; obstructing proceedings before departments, agencies, and committees; tampering with or retaliating against a witness, victim, or informant; and obstructing court orders. 18 U.S.C.A. §§ 1501–1518. Postal laws make it an offense to willfully and knowingly obstruct or retard the passage of the mail. 18 U.S.C.A. § 1701. Thus, in *United States v. Upshaw*, 895 F.2d 109 (3d Cir. 1990), a federal appeals court upheld a defendant's conviction for obstructing mail where a postal truck driver took home a package after he signed out from work.

All jurisdictions have statutes proscribing interference with police officers, prosecutors, jurors, and judges in the performance of their duties. Some laws define obstruction to embrace many forms of conduct. Common examples include statutes making it unlawful to

- Give false information to an officer with the intent to interfere with the officer's lawful performance of duties.
- Knowingly give a false fire or emergency alarm.
- Impersonate an officer.
- Intimidate a victim, witness, or juror.
- Destroy or tamper with public records or physical evidence to be offered in official proceedings.
- Fail to appear in court when required to do so by a summons or subpoena.
- Use jamming devices to interfere with radar equipment used by police to detect speeding.

## Is Swallowing Contraband Obstruction of Justice?

**CASE-IN-POINT**

Jason T. Brake was driving his father's car when he was stopped by police for driving with only one working headlight and having a cracked windshield. During the automobile stop, the officer noticed something in Brake's mouth, but before he could retrieve it, Brake swallowed it. Brake was transported to the hospital, where his stomach was pumped and a small bag of heroin was retrieved. In addition to being charged with possession of a controlled substance, Brace was charged with obstruction of justice for concealing evidence. A jury found Brake guilty of both offenses. In upholding the conviction for obstruction of justice, the appellate court commented, "Although defendant was currently engaged in a possessory crime, his action was designed to 'destroy, alter, conceal or disguise physical evidence' of that offense."

*People v. Brake,* 783 N.E.2d 1084 (Ill. App. 2003).

Federal statutes make it an offense for a person to falsely assume or pretend to be an officer or employee acting under the authority of the United States or any department, agency or officer thereof. 18 U.S.C.A. § 912. Likewise, states commonly proscribe impersonation of officers. For example in Tennessee, a person "who pretends to be a law enforcement officer for the purpose of: (1) Engaging in an activity that is ordinarily and customarily an activity established by law as a law enforcement activity; and (2) Causing another to believe that the person is a law enforcement officer" is guilty of criminal impersonation. Tenn. Code Ann. §39-16-301(a).

Obstruction of justice involves interference with the administration of the justice system. For example, under Illinois law it is obstruction of justice, a felony, to knowingly destroy, alter, conceal, or disguise physical evidence, plant false evidence, or furnish false information with the intent to prevent the apprehension or to obstruct the prosecution or defense of any person, 720 Ill. Comp. Stat. Ann. § 5/31-4(a). In 2003, an Illinois appellate court held that a defendant who swallowed a plastic bag containing drugs, of which an arresting officer was aware, was guilty of violating the statute by concealing or destroying evidence of the defendant's possessory offense. *People v. Brake,* 783 N.E.2d 1084 (Ill. App. 2003).

## The Citizen's Duty to Assist Law Enforcement Officers

The common law imposed a duty on citizens to assist the sheriff and, on request, to keep the peace and apprehend wrongdoers. Modern statutes impose on citizens the duty to come to the assistance of law enforcement officers on request. Rather typical is the Ohio law that makes it a misdemeanor to fail to aid a law enforcement officer. Ohio Rev. Code Ann. § 2921.23(a) states,

> No person shall negligently fail or refuse to aid a law enforcement officer, when called upon for assistance in preventing or halting the commission of an offense, or in apprehending or detaining an offender, when such aid can be given without a substantial risk of physical harm to the person giving it.

Many states also have comprehensive statutes making it an offense to prevent, hinder, or delay the discovery or apprehension of persons sought by law enforcement.

# Resisting Arrest

**resisting arrest** The crime of obstructing or opposing a police officer making an arrest.

All jurisdictions make **resisting arrest** a crime. The common law did not permit a person to resist a lawful arrest by an authorized officer of the law. It did, however, permit a person to use force to resist an unlawful arrest. *United States v. Heliczer*, 373 F.2d 241 (2d Cir. 1967). Until recently this rule of law was applied in most American jurisdictions, but the functioning of the rule in modern society brought about the need to change it. The legality of an arrest may frequently be a close call, and because officers will normally overcome resistance with necessary force, there is a great danger of escalating violence between the officer and the arrestee. Thus, in recent years many courts have reexamined this common-law doctrine and have held that there is no longer authority to use physical force to resist an arrest by a police officer, or by one the arrestee knows or has good reason to believe is an authorized peace officer performing his or her duties, whether such arrest is legal or illegal. See *Miller v. State*, 462 P.2d 421 (Alaska 1969).

Legislatures, too, have reexamined the issue of using physical force in resisting arrest. In 1980, the New York legislature amended its penal law to provide:

> A person may not use physical force to resist an arrest, whether authorized or unauthorized, which is being effected or attempted by a police officer or peace officer when it would reasonably appear that the latter is a police officer or peace officer. McKinney's N.Y. Penal Law § 35.27.

Oregon law now provides, "A person commits the crime of resisting arrest if the person intentionally resists a person known by the person to be a peace officer in making an arrest." Or. Rev. Stat. § 162.315(1). In *State v. Wright*, 799 P.2d 642 (Or. 1990), the Oregon Supreme Court held that a person may not lawfully resist arrest,

---

**CASE-IN-POINT**

### Court Dismisses Assault Charge but Upholds Conviction for Resisting Arrest

Officer Dennis Cole arrested Joshua Deer after witnessing an apparent assault by him in a restaurant parking lot on January 5, 2006. The officer charged Deer with assault and several other misdemeanors. The trial court dismissed the assault charge but found Deer guilty of other misdemeanors, including resisting arrest, and sentenced him to 217 days in the corrections center. Deer appealed. The appellate court pointed out that to prove the offense of resisting arrest the prosecution must first show that the arrest was lawful. To do so, the court observed, "[T]he state must prove not only that there was a reasonable basis to believe an offense was committed, but also that the offense was one for which the defendant could be lawfully arrested." The court further pointed out that the state must also show that the defendant knew he was under arrest before resisting. In this case

the evidence showed that Officer Cole had a reasonable basis to believe the defendant was assaulting the victim. Officer Cole located the defendant in a car, where he was pushing and holding the victim down and screaming at the victim, who was crying. He ordered Deer to release her, and when he refused the officer used his Taser. Deer then raised his hands in a fighting stance and challenged the officer by saying, "Is that all you have?" Officer Cole attempted to use the Taser again, but it was ineffective. The officer, who was in uniform, then told Deer that he was under arrest. Another officer arrived, and the two officers handcuffed Deer as he struggled, pushed, and cursed the officers. The court found that the state presented sufficient evidence to find that the defendant resisted arrest beyond a reasonable doubt and affirmed his conviction.

*State v. Deer*, 2007-Ohio-1866 (Ohio App. 2007).

even if the arresting officer lacks the legal authority to make the arrest, provided that the officer was acting under color of official authority. In addition, the court observed that if a police officer uses excessive force in making an arrest, the arrestee may use only such physical force as is reasonably necessary to defend against such excessive force.

The modern statutory and judicial revisions to the common-law approach make sense. It is not too great a burden today for a person who believes that he or she has been unlawfully arrested to submit to the officer and seek legal remedies in court. The circumstances surrounding an arrest are completely different from those that prevailed at common law. An arrestee today must be promptly taken before a magistrate, and legal counsel is readily available. Moreover, today's detention facilities do not resemble the crude dungeons where arrestees were incarcerated for lengthy periods before trial under the early English common law. The abandonment of the common-law rule is another example of a rule of law ceasing to exist when the rationale for it has ceased to exist.

# Compounding a Crime

**misprision of felony** The crime of concealing a felony committed by another.

At common law a person who accepted money or something else of value in exchange for agreeing not to prosecute a felony was guilty of compounding a felony. In the later history of the common law, it became a misdemeanor to compound a misdemeanor if the conduct constituted an offense against public justice and was dangerous to society. To conceal a felony was also a common-law offense known as **misprision of felony**, which was based on the common-law duty to inform authorities about any felony of which one had knowledge. A person who saw someone commit a felony and used no means to prevent the felony or apprehend the felon committed the offense of misprision of felony.

## The Modern Statutory Approach

**compounding a crime** The acceptance of money or something else of value in exchange for an agreement not to prosecute a person for committing a crime.

The legal theory underlying the offense of **compounding a crime** is that justice is debased when an offender bargains to escape the consequences of his or her crime. Most states have enacted statutes making it a crime to compound a felony, but some have expanded the common-law rule by making it a crime to compound any offense. To illustrate, New Hampshire law provides that a person is guilty of a misdemeanor who

1. Solicits, accepts, or agrees to accept any benefit as consideration for his refraining from initiating or aiding in a criminal prosecution; or

2. Confers, offers, or agrees to confer any benefit upon another as consideration for such person refraining from initiating or aiding in a criminal prosecution.

It is an affirmative defense that the value of the benefit did not exceed an amount which the actor believed to be due as restitution or indemnification for the loss caused, or to be caused by the offense. N.H. Rev. Stat. Ann. § 642:5.

Most states have not made misprision of felony a statutory crime, probably relying on enforcement of statutes making it an offense to become an accessory after the fact to an offense (see Chapter 4). The federal criminal code, however, specifically makes misprision of felony a crime, the gist of the offense being concealment and not merely the failure to report a felony. 18 U.S.C.A. § 4. The U.S. Court of Appeals for the Second Circuit has held that the elements of misprision of felony are that the defendant had full knowledge that the principal committed and completed an alleged felony and that the defendant failed to notify authorities and took steps to conceal the crime. *United States v. Cefalu*, 85 F.3d 964 (2d Cir. 1996).

## A Common Scenario of Compounding a Crime

The offense of compounding a crime often appears where a crime victim whose goods have been stolen agrees with the thief to take back the goods in exchange for not prosecuting. Such an action would ordinarily constitute an offense by the victim. But the New Hampshire statute makes it an affirmative defense that the value of the benefit did not exceed that which the victim believed was due as restitution for a loss. In some instances courts will approve dismissal of a prosecution based on an agreement for restitution to the victim, but persons should not reach such an agreement without prior court approval.

# Escape

**escape** Unlawfully fleeing to avoid arrest or confinement.

At common law a person who departed from lawful custody committed the crime of **escape**. Where the prisoner used force, the offense came to be known as *prison break*. A person who forcibly freed another from lawful custody was guilty of the offense of *rescue*.

## Modern Statutory Approaches to Escape

Statutes proscribing escape are generally broad enough to embrace all three common-law offenses relating to escape. Often the punishment is more severe when force has been used. Federal statutes prohibit a person who has been lawfully arrested or confined from escaping or attempting to escape from custody, 18 U.S.C.A. § 751, or from rescuing or attempting to rescue a federal prisoner, 18 U.S.C.A. § 752.

Most state statutes define escape in rather simple terms. For example, Texas law provides that a person commits the offense of escape "if he escapes from custody when he is: (1) under arrest for, charged with, or convicted of an offense; or (2) in custody pursuant to a lawful order of court." Vernon's Tex. Penal Code Ann. § 38.06.

## The Elements of the Offense of Escape

The gist of the offense of escape is the prisoner's unauthorized departure from lawful custody. Lawful custody is generally presumed once the prosecutor establishes that the escapee was confined to an institution specified by law. In other instances it may be essential for the prosecutor to establish proof of lawful custody; however, those who escape from a jail, juvenile detention home, penal institution, or reformatory are usually presumed to have been in lawful custody. Likewise, a person who fails to return to detention following a temporary release or furlough generally falls within the ambit of escape statutes.

Absent an explicit statutory requirement, courts differ on whether the prosecution must prove the defendant's specific intent to avoid lawful confinement. Of course, if a statute requires specific intent, the prosecution must establish this before a conviction can be lawfully obtained. The Supreme Court has held that under the

### Was the Defendant Released on Bail "In Custody" Within the Meaning of the Statute?

After Douglas Owen Davis pled guilty to several drug offenses, the trial court released him on bond pending a presentencing investigation. He was ordered to report to jail on August 1, 2003, prior to his sentencing date. When Davis failed to report as ordered, the trial court, in a bench trial, found him guilty of escape under Virginia statute, which provides, "[I]f any person lawfully confined in jail or lawfully in the custody of any court or officer thereof or of any law-enforcement officer on a charge or conviction of a felony escapes, otherwise than by force or violence or by setting fire to the jail, he shall be guilty of a Class 6 felony." Va. Code Ann. § 18.2-479(B).

In reviewing the conviction, the state appellate court framed the issue as whether Davis was in "the custody of [the] court" within the meaning of § 18.2-479(B) when he failed to report to jail after the trial court released him on bond. Noting the case presented an issue of first impression, the court observed, "Appellant in the instant case had been released from the trial court pending sentence and allowed to remain free on bond. At that point he was no longer in the physical custody or even presence of the court. Thus, the sufficient restraint to have physical control over him 'did not presently exist.'" Accordingly, the court ordered the trial court to dismiss the charges against Davis, commenting in a footnote, "We do not preclude by this holding the trial court's other remedies for failure to abide by its orders."

*Davis v. Commonwealth*, 608 S.E.2d 482 (Va. App. 2005).

federal statute, the government need only prove that the escapee knew that his or her actions would result in leaving confinement without permission. *United States v. Bailey*, 444 U.S. 394, 100 S.Ct. 624, 62 L.Ed.2d 575 (1980).

State appellate courts differ on whether the prosecution must prove that the escapee intended to leave or be absent from lawful custody. Recognizing that a slim majority of jurisdictions hold that intent is not an element of the crime, a Florida appellate court in 1975 held that the state must prove that a defendant intended to leave or be absent from lawful custody. Despite the lack of such a statutory requirement in Florida law, the court justified its position by raising some interesting "horribles" under which a defendant charged with escape could be improperly convicted if the state were not required to establish the escapee's specific intent to avoid lawful confinement. In one scenario the court hypothesized that a road gang member had fallen asleep under a tree and was left behind by a negligent guard. The prisoner awakened to find that the guards and work detail had returned to the prison. Because of such possibilities, the court opted for requiring the prosecution to establish the defendant's specific intent to escape. *Helton v. State*, 311 So.2d 381 (Fla. App. 1975).

## Defenses to the Charge of Escape

Occasionally an innocent person is unlawfully confined. Even if custody was lawful, the fact that a person was innocent is not generally recognized as a defense to a charge of escape. See *Woods v. Commonwealth*, 152 S.W.2d 997 (Ky. 1941). Of course, a person who escapes can always assert the defense of unlawful confinement or custody. *State v. Dickson*, 288 N.W.2d 48 (Neb. 1980).

During the 1970s there was considerable attention to the conditions of prisons, particularly at the state level. This is illustrated by a landmark 1974 California decision. Defendant Marsha Lovercamp was attacked by other inmates demanding sex. Prison authorities failed to provide Lovercamp with adequate protection, and she escaped. She was found guilty of escape, but an appellate court awarded her a new trial because the trial judge had denied her the opportunity to submit evidence of her plight as a justification for her escape. In reversing Lovercamp's conviction, the appellate court enumerated guidelines for asserting the defense of duress or necessity in these situations. *People v. Lovercamp*, 118 Cal. Rptr. 110 (Cal. App. 1974). The court opined that a limited defense is available if the following conditions exist:

(1) The prisoner is faced with a specific threat of death, forcible sexual attack or substantial bodily injury in the immediate future;

(2) There is no time for a complaint to the authorities or there exists a history of futile complaints which make any result from such complaints illusory;

(3) There is no time or opportunity to resort to the courts;

(4) There is no evidence of force or violence used toward prison personnel or other "innocent" persons in the escape; and

(5) The prisoner immediately reports to the proper authorities when he has attained a position of safety from the immediate threat.

In 1991, the Kansas Court of Appeals observed that the great majority of courts now follow the principles outlined in *Lovercamp*. *State v. Pichon*, 811 P.2d 517 (Kan. App. 1991). See, e.g., *People v. Unger*, 338 N.E.2d 442 (Ill. App. 1975), aff'd, 362 N.E.2d 319 (Ill. 1977); *State v. Alcantaro*, 407 So.2d 922 (Fla. App. 1981).

In 1980, the U.S. Supreme Court recognized the defense of necessity as being valid in the context of the crime of escape. To sustain the defense, the Court said a prisoner must demonstrate (1) that because of an imminent threat of harm, escape was the prisoner's only reasonable alternative; and (2) that the prisoner made a *bona fide* effort to surrender or return to custody as soon as the duress or necessity lost its coercive force. *United States v. Bailey*, supra.

Legislatures respond to public opinion, and improvement of prison conditions is not a high priority for most voters. Because courts tend to focus on issues where the legislative process affords no relief, they will undoubtedly continue to give attention

---

### JURISPRUDENCE

*United States v. Bailey*, 444 U.S. 394, 100 S.Ct. 624, 62 L.Ed.2d 575 (1980)

Clifford Bailey and three other prisoners escaped from the District of Columbia jail by crawling through a window from which a bar had been removed and sliding down a knotted bed sheet. Over the next several months, federal authorities recaptured all four escapees. At their trials for violating the federal escape statute, the defendants asserted that intolerable conditions at the DC jail made it necessary for them to escape. The trial judge refused to instruct the jury as to the defenses of necessity and duress because the

defendants failed to produce any evidence that they attempted to surrender to authorities once they had freed themselves from the conditions of the jail. The jury found the defendants guilty of escape, but the U.S. Court of Appeals for the D.C. Circuit reversed their convictions. The U.S. Supreme Court reversed the circuit court, holding that "where a criminal defendant is charged with escape and claims that he is entitled to an instruction on the theory of duress or necessity, he must proffer evidence of a bona fide effort to surrender or return to custody as soon as the claimed duress or necessity had lost its coercive force."

to complaints concerning prison conditions. As they do, prisoners will most likely seek to extend the defense of necessity to justify an escape based on the inadequacy of prison conditions. Some have already argued that the denial of needed medical care should be recognized as a defense to escape. See, e.g., *People v. Martin*, 298 N.W.2d 900 (Mich. App. 1980) (allowing defendant to present to jury whether lack of medical attention could rise to the defense of necessity). Courts, however, have generally refused to accept either lack of medical care or inhumane living conditions as a defense to escape.

# Contempt

**contemnor** A person found to be in contempt of court.

Early in the history of the common law, judges began to exercise the power to punish persons whose conduct interfered with the orderly functioning of the courts in the administration of justice. Federal and state courts exercise the power to hold an offender—sometimes called a **contemnor**—in either civil or criminal contempt.

In *Bessette v. W.B. Conkey Co.*, 194 U.S. 324, 327, 24 S.Ct. 665, 666, 48 L.Ed. 997, 1001 (1904), the U.S. Supreme Court observed,

> The power to punish for contempt is inherent in all courts; its existence is essential to the preservation of order in judicial proceedings, and to the enforcement of the judgments, orders, and writs of the courts, and, consequently to the due administration of justice. The moment the courts of the United States were called into existence and invested with jurisdiction over any subject, they became possessed of this power.
>
> State courts have universally recognized that the power to punish for contempt is an inherent one that springs from the nature and constitution of a judicial tribunal.

## Civil Contempt

**civil contempt** Being held in contempt of court pending the performance of some court-ordered act.

Because it is not considered a crime, we will deal very briefly with the concept of **civil contempt**. Usually it is a sanction imposed to coerce a recalcitrant person to obey a court order. For example, a court may hold someone in civil contempt for failing to pay court-ordered support for dependents. Perhaps the best known example of a civil contempt citation occurred in 1999 when Chief Judge Susan Webber Wright of the U.S. District Court in the Eastern District of Arkansas found former president William Jefferson Clinton in civil contempt in a sexual harassment suit filed by Paula Jones because "the President responded to plaintiff's questions by giving false, misleading and evasive answers that were designed to obstruct the judicial process." *Jones v. Clinton*, 36 F.Supp.2d 1118, 1127 (E.D. Ark. 1999). As a result, the court ordered Clinton to pay approximately $90,000 to attorneys and others for expenses they incurred as a result of his actions. *Jones v. Clinton*, 57 F.Supp.2d 719 (E.D. Ark. 1999).

## Criminal Contempt

**criminal contempt** Punishment imposed by a judge against a person who violates a court order or otherwise intentionally interferes with the administration of the court.

A court imposes **criminal contempt** to punish an offender whose deliberate conduct is calculated to obstruct or embarrass the court or to degrade a judicial officer in the role of administering justice. Intent is always an element in criminal contempt proceedings. Legislative bodies can regulate the power to punish for contempt, and, in recent years, the Supreme Court has referred to 18 U.S.C.A. § 401, where Congress has provided that

A court of the United States shall have power to punish by fine or imprisonment, or both, at its discretion, such contempt of its authority, and none other, as—

(1) Misbehavior of any person in its presence or so near thereto as to obstruct the administration of justice;

(2) Misbehavior of any of its officers in their official transactions;

(3) Disobedience or resistance to its lawful writ, process, order, rule, decree, or command.

## Direct and Indirect Criminal Contempt

**direct contempt** An obstructive or insulting act committed by a person in the immediate presence of the court.

**indirect contempt** An act committed outside the presence of the court that insults the court or obstructs a judicial proceeding.

Criminal contempt is classified as either direct or indirect. **Direct contempt** is contemptuous behavior committed in the presence of the court or so close to the court as to interrupt or hinder the judicial proceedings. Disruptions of the examination of a witness or an assault on a judge or juror are examples of direct contempt. **Indirect contempt**, sometimes called constructive contempt, refers to acts that occur outside the court's presence that tend to degrade the court or hinder the proceedings of the court. One illustration of indirect contempt is an attorney charged with responsibility for a case who is willfully absent from the courtroom; another is a juror who discusses the facts of a case with a news reporter before the trial of that case has been completed.

---

### JURISPRUDENCE

*Sacher v. United States*, 343 U.S. 1, 72 S.Ct. 451, 96 L.Ed. 717 (1952)

In 1949, after a turbulent trial lasting nine months, eleven officials of the Communist Party were found guilty of violating the Smith Act (now codified at 18 U.S.C.A. § 2385), which prohibits activities aimed at the violent overthrow of the U.S. government. When the trial was concluded, Judge Harold Medina held the five attorneys for the defense in contempt for "their persistent obstructive colloquies, objections, arguments, and many groundless charges against the court." Medina sentenced the lawyers to jail for terms ranging from thirty days to six months. On reviewing the case, the Supreme Court upheld the convictions for contempt. Speaking for the Court, Justice Robert Jackson rejected the argument that the lawyers were merely performing their duty by providing a vigorous defense of their clients:

But that there may be no misunderstanding, we make clear that this Court, if its aid be needed, will unhesitatingly protect counsel in fearless, vigorous and effective performance of every duty pertaining to the office of the advocate on behalf of any person whatsoever. But it will not equate contempt with courage or insults with independence. It will also protect the processes of orderly trial, which is the supreme object of the lawyer's calling.

In dissent, Justice Felix Frankfurter suggested that it would have been prudent for Judge Medina to refer the contempt charge to another judge:

The particular circumstances of this case compel me to conclude that the trial judge should not have combined in himself the functions of accuser and judge. For his accusations were not impersonal. They concerned matters in which he personally was deeply engaged. Whatever occasion may have existed during the trial for sitting in judgment upon claims of personal victimization, it ceased after the trial had terminated. It falls to this Court as head of the Federal judicial system to correct such abuse of judicial power.

One reason for classifying contempt as direct or indirect is to determine the processes that must be followed. Direct criminal contempt proceedings are usually handled summarily. The judge must inform the contemnor of the accusation and ask if he or she can show any cause to preclude the court from entering a judgment of contempt. The court then proceeds to enter its judgment accordingly. Courts justify the summary character of these proceedings because the contemptuous act has occurred in the presence of the judge.

The process is more formal in indirect contempt proceedings. The judge is required to issue a written order to the contemnor to show cause as to why he or she should not be held in contempt of court. The order must set forth the essential facts of the charge and allow the contemnor a reasonable time to prepare a defense. The judge tries all issues of law and fact, but the contemnor has the right to counsel, to compulsory process to secure witnesses, and to refuse to testify.

U.S. Supreme Court decisions have established basic due process rights that must be accorded contemnors in these proceedings. Of course, if there are statutes or court rules in a particular jurisdiction that prescribe the method of processing criminal contempt, the judge must not deviate from those rules to the prejudice of the contemnor's rights. In any contempt proceeding, if the contemnor is to be sentenced to a term of imprisonment for more than six months, he or she is entitled to a jury trial. *Baldwin v. New York*, 399 U.S. 66, 90 S.Ct. 1886, 26 L.Ed.2d 437 (1970).

## Direct Criminal Contempt

**CASE-IN-POINT**

Attorney Terrence M. Spears represented Gary Kaeding in an indirect criminal contempt proceeding. During the Kaeding proceeding, the judge stated that he would give Spears five days to file a motion for substitution of judge. Thereafter, the following exchange took place between the court and counsel for the parties:

THE COURT: Also I am going to *sua sponte* enter an order ordering Mr. Kaeding to be examined by a psychiatrist of the choice of the Court, because I do not know whether he is competent to stand trial.

MR. SPEARS: You cannot rule since there has been a Motion for Leave—

THE COURT: (Interrupting) I can; anybody can request a psychiatric examination. I am going to do that.

MR. SPEARS: I will be asking for one for you, Judge; have that on the record.

MR. SCHARF: [Prosecutor] Judge, I would ask he be found in contempt for that.

THE COURT: I am going to hold you in contempt, $500 fine.

MR. SPEARS: Praise God, praise the Lord Almighty God. May you—

MR. SCHARF: (Interrupting) I ask for jail.

MR. SPEARS: May you reap what you sow, Judge, by the good book.

THE COURT: You have 24 hours to pay the fine, or you are going to jail.

In affirming the trial court's finding that attorney Spears was in contempt, the appellate court found that Spears' comments "were calculated to embarrass the court and to derogate from the court's authority and dignity." Accordingly, the appellate court concluded that "the trial court's finding of direct criminal contempt was proper."

*People v. Kaeding*, 607 N.E.2d 580 (Ill. App. 1993).

## Is Criminal Contempt Really a Crime?

Until the 1960s there was considerable division of thinking on this subject. In 1968, the U.S. Supreme Court, in *Bloom v. Illinois*, 391 U.S. 194, 88 S.Ct. 1477, 20 L.Ed.2d 522 (1968), held that criminal contempt is a crime in the ordinary sense and may be punished by fine, imprisonment, or both. Writing for the Court in Bloom, Justice Byron White observed:

Criminally contemptuous conduct may violate other provisions of the criminal law; but even when this is not the case, convictions for criminal contempt are indistinguishable from ordinary criminal convictions, for their impact on the individual defendant is the same. Indeed, the role of criminal contempt and that of many ordinary criminal laws seem identical -- protection of the institutions of our government and enforcement of their mandates. 391 U.S. at 201, 88 S.Ct. at 1481–82, 20 L.Ed.2d at 528.

A person charged with criminal contempt is presumed innocent and must be afforded the rudiments of due process of law. Consequently, a contemnor must be proven guilty beyond a reasonable doubt before being held in criminal contempt. In some states, criminal contempt has been made a statutory crime. See, e.g., McKinney's N.Y. Penal Law § 215.50–51, which provides that contempt in the second degree includes such misbehavior before the court, a misdemeanor (§ 215.50), while contempt in the first degree is a felony and concerns refusal to be sworn before the grand jury or refusal to answer proper questions after having been sworn in. (§ 215.51).

## Legislative Contempt

Legislative bodies also have the power hold in contempt persons whose deliberate acts impede legislative activities. A dramatic example of this occurred in June 2012 when the U.S. House of Representatives voted to hold Attorney General Eric Holder in contempt for withholding documents sought by a House committee investigating an ill-fated "gun walking" operation run by the Bureau of Alcohol, Tobacco, Firearms and Explosives. This was the first time in history that a sitting Attorney General had been held in contempt of Congress.

A witness called to testify before Congress who "willfully makes default, or who, having appeared, refuses to answer any question pertinent to the question under inquiry" is guilty of a misdemeanor and subject to a maximum $1,000 fine and 12 month imprisonment. 2 U.S.C.A. § 192. In order for Attorney General Holder to be punished under this statute, however, he would have to be convicted in federal court, which requires a U.S. Attorney to initiate prosecution.

In *Quinn v. United States*, 349 U.S. 155, 75 S.Ct. 668, 99 L.Ed. 964 (1955), the Supreme Court overturned a conviction for contempt of Congress where there was not adequate proof that the witness deliberately and intentionally refused to answer a question. The court observed that this essential element of the offense must be proved beyond a reasonable doubt. And in *Watkins v. United States*, 354 U.S. 178, 77 S.Ct. 1173, 1 L.Ed.2d 1273 (1957), the Supreme Court invalidated a conviction for contempt of Congress because a witness was not adequately advised as to the pertinence of a subcommittee's questions.

Some states have enacted statutes to cover specific instances of criminal contempt in respect to legislative functions. New York, for example, makes criminal

**JURISPRUDENCE**

*Watkins v. United States*, 354 U.S. 178, 77 S.Ct. 1173, 1 L.Ed.2d 1273 (1957)

The Supreme Court reversed a conviction for contempt of Congress in a case where a witness had refused to answer questions put to him by a subcommittee of the House Un-American Activities Committee. The witness, John Watkins, answered questions about his own beliefs and activities, but refused to discuss the activities of other suspected Communists, saying: "I am not going to plead the Fifth Amendment, but I refuse to answer certain questions that I believe are outside the scope of your committee's activities. . . . I do not believe . . . that this committee has the right to undertake public exposure of persons because of their past activities." The Supreme Court reversed Watkins' conviction, holding that he had been denied due process of law. Writing for the Court, Chief Justice Earl Warren observed: "The statement of the Committee Chairman in this case, in response to the petitioner's protest, was woefully inadequate to convey sufficient information as to the pertinency of the questions to the subject under inquiry." The Court also expressed concern that First Amendment values were being threatened by HUAC's public hearings. In dissent, Justice Clark accused the majority of "mischievous curbing of the informing function of the Congress."

contempt of the legislature a misdemeanor. McKinney's N.Y. Penal Law § 215.60 provides:

A person is guilty of criminal contempt of the legislature when, having been duly subpoenaed to attend as a witness before either house of the legislature or before any committee thereof, he:

1. Fails or refuses to attend without lawful excuse; or
2. Refuses to be sworn; or
3. Refuses to answer any material and proper questions; or
4. Refuses, after reasonable notice, to produce books, papers, or documents in his possession or under his control which constitute material and proper evidence.

Some states follow the federal practice in referring those held in contempt of the legislature to the state attorney general's office for prosecution in the courts. In other states the law permits the legislature to conduct its own trial, at least for direct contempts. Courts are apt to closely scrutinize such trials to insure that due process is observed. In *Groppi v. Leslie*, 404 U.S. 496, 92 S.Ct. 582, 30 L.Ed.2d 632 (1972), the U.S. Supreme Court overturned a contempt citation issued by the Wisconsin legislature. Father James Groppi, a Roman Catholic priest and civil rights activist, was summarily held in contempt and sentenced to six months in jail for leading a sit-down demonstration in the state capital. The Court found the summary trial for contempt defective in that the legislature failed to provide notice to the alleged contemnor and failed to give him an opportunity to respond.

## Conclusion

The fair and impartial administration of justice and the orderly processes of democratic government depend on the honesty and integrity of those who occupy positions of authority. Hence, the basic common-law offenses described in this chapter have endured over the centuries. The offense of bribery seeks to avoid corruption of those in positions of trust, whereas the crime of perjury seeks to maintain the integrity of the judicial system and agencies of government.

To safeguard the security and effectiveness of law enforcement personnel, all jurisdictions make it a crime to resist arrest, even if the arrest is later declared to be unlawful. Society must ensure confinement of those it has chosen to incarcerate, so it is essential to maintain the offense of escape. With increased awareness of inhumane prison conditions and the rights of prisoners, however, courts have recognized that under some circumstances necessity can be a defense to a charge of escape. The abandonment of the common-law principle that allowed a person to forcibly resist an unlawful arrest and the recognition of the necessity defense in the law of escape both demonstrate the dynamic nature of the criminal law in response to societal change.

Finally, to maintain the effectiveness and the dignity of the judicial and legislative processes, courts and legislatures must have the authority to hold persons in contempt, although that power must be exercised with due regard for the rights of contemnors.

## Chapter Summary

- Learning Objective 1
  - English common-law created several misdemeanor offenses to aid the administration of justice.
  - Bribery involved improper actions identified with the administration of justice.
  - Perjury consisted of willfully giving false and material testimony under oath.
  - Obstruction of justice involved acts that hindered administration of justice.
  - The common law also made it an offense to conceal a felony (misprision) or accept something of value in exchange for not reporting a felony (compounding a felony).
  - It was an offense at common law to resist an arrest.
  - Escape at common law consisted of departing from lawful custody.
  - To maintain dignity and authority of the courts, the common-law judges developed the offense of contempt.

- Learning Objective 2
  - The gist of bribery is that it is unlawful to offer or to agree to do something under color of public office, irrespective of whether the person bribed has the authority to do a specific act.
  - Today, federal statutes proscribe bribery of specific public officers and of witnesses, jurors, and government functionaries.
  - State statutes generally define bribery in broad terms and require the prosecution to prove a defendant's false or corrupt intent. This can be difficult, as bribes are often disguised as political or charitable contributions.
  - Many state statutes now criminalize sports and commercial bribery.
  - Other than a denial, the only recognized defense is entrapment.

- Learning Objective 3
  - Federal statutes make it a crime to take false oaths in judicial proceedings or to falsely swear to a variety of certifications—for example, income tax returns.

○ All states make it a crime to take an oath to tell the truth and then to willfully state as true material matter which the oath taker knows to be false.

○ Historically, many courts held that the question of whether a witness's statement was material was to be decided by the judge. But in 1995, the U.S. Supreme Court ruled that the Constitution requires that the materiality of a defendant's statements is an issue for a jury to decide.

○ Perjury was a specific-intent crime at common law, which led most jurisdictions to require the prosecution to prove that the defendant's false statement was made "willfully and corruptly."

○ The "two-witness rule" that prevails in most jurisdictions requires the prosecution to prove the falsity of a defendant's statements by two witnesses; however, testimony of a second witness may be satisfied by evidence of independent probative value.

○ In "perjury by contradictory statements" scenarios, modern statutes make it unnecessary for the prosecution to establish which of two contradictory statements is false.

○ To prove subornation of perjury the prosecution must establish that the defendant induced another person to testify falsely and that an actual perjury has been committed.

- Learning Objective 4

  ○ Truth is a defense to a charge of perjury.

  ○ Federal law provides for a recantation defense where in the same continuous court or grand jury proceeding in which a declaration is made, a witness admits such declaration to be false "if the declaration has not substantially affected the proceeding, or it has not become manifest that such falsity has been or will be exposed."

  ○ Some state courts hold that retraction of a false statement is a defense if the retraction occurs in the same proceeding and the statement is retracted before it becomes manifest that the fabrication is or will be exposed.

- Learning Objective 5

  ○ Federal statutes proscribe impersonation of federal officers. They also proscribe a lengthy list of acts that influence or impede grand or petit jurors; obstruct proceedings before agencies and committees; tamper with witnesses, victims, or informants; or obstruct court orders.

  ○ All jurisdictions make resisting arrest a crime. Although the common law allowed a person to use force to resist an unlawful arrest, today many courts hold that a person may not lawfully resist arrest, even if the arresting officer lacks legal authority.

- Learning Objective 6

  ○ Most states have enacted statutes making it a crime to compound a felony. Some states have expanded the common-law rule by making it a crime to compound any offense.

○ Most states have not made misprision of felony a statutory crime, probably relying on enforcement of statutes that make it an offense to become an accessory after the fact. The federal criminal code, however, specifically makes misprision of felony a crime, with the gist of the offense being concealment and not merely the failure to report a felony.

- Learning Objective 7

  ○ Federal statutes prohibit a person who has been lawfully arrested or confined from escaping or attempting to escape from custody, or from rescuing or attempting to rescue a federal prisoner.

  ○ Most state statutes proscribe the offense of "escape" in similar terms. A person who escapes can always assert the defense of unlawful confinement or custody.

  ○ In 1980, the U.S. Supreme Court recognized the "defense of necessity" if a prisoner can demonstrate that because of an imminent threat of harm, escape was the only reasonable alternative and the prisoner made a *bona fide* effort to surrender or return to custody as soon as the duress or necessity lost its coercive force.

- Learning Objective 8

  ○ Federal and state courts exercise the power to hold an offender (contemnor) in contempt. Courts impose criminal contempt to punish an offender whose deliberate conduct is calculated to obstruct or embarrass the court or to degrade a judicial officer in the administration of justice.

  ○ Direct criminal contempt involves behavior committed in the presence of the court or so close to the court as to interrupt or hinder the judicial proceedings. Indirect criminal contempt consists of contemptuous acts that occur outside the court's presence.

  ○ Contempt procedures must follow strict processes to insure fairness, and a contemnor who is to be punished by more than six months' imprisonment is entitled to a jury trial.

  ○ Legislative bodies also have the power to punish by contempt those persons whose deliberate acts impede legislative activities. They frequently refer proceedings to a court.

## Key Terms

| | |
|---|---|
| bribery | misprision of felony |
| civil contempt | obstruction of justice |
| commercial bribery | perjury |
| compounding a crime | perjury by contradictory statements |
| contemnor | recantation |
| criminal contempt | resisting arrest |
| direct contempt | sports bribery |
| escape | subornation of perjury |
| indirect contempt | two-witness rule |

## Questions for Thought and Discussion

1. To what extent have contemporary legislative bodies expanded the scope of bribery to cover classes of persons beyond public officials?
2. How does the requirement that the prosecution prove a defendant's specific intent to deceive protect citizens from unwarranted prosecutions for perjury?
3. Should a simple denial of criminal wrongdoing when first confronted by federal agents constitute the offense of making false statements? Should Congress amend the statute to exclude such denials from criminal prosecution?
4. Contrast the common-law rule allowing a person to resist an unlawful arrest with the modern trend of requiring citizens to submit to unlawful arrests by police officers. Which approach makes more sense in today's society?
5. Is a state statute that makes it a criminal offense "to hinder or delay a law enforcement officer in the performance of his or her duties" likely to be held void for vagueness under the tests outlined in Chapter 3?
6. Would a person who accepts the return of stolen goods from a thief without agreeing to refrain from filing a criminal complaint be guilty of compounding a crime?
7. Name some acts that would likely be considered obstruction of justice under federal and state statutes.
8. Despite the wording of most statutes proscribing the offense of escape, courts increasingly require the prosecution to prove the defendant's specific intent to avoid lawful confinement. Are courts justified in imposing such a requirement on the statutory law?
9. Have courts aided society by allowing escapees from prison to defend their actions on the basis of intolerable prison conditions? Are such conditions likely to be remedied by the legislative process?
10. Should courts allow an escapee from prison to assert as a defense the prison's failure to provide essential medical treatment to the prisoner? If this is to be recognized as a basis for a defense of necessity, what stipulations would you recommend to protect the public?
11. Describe some specific acts that a trial judge could justifiably consider to be in direct contempt of court.
12. Why does the law require more formal proceedings in cases of indirect contempt than in cases of direct criminal contempt?

## Problems for Discussion and Solution

1. A pharmaceutical company's agent secretly gives a free three-day ski resort vacation to a hospital purchasing agent, urging the purchasing agent to "to keep in mind the pharmaceutical company's products" when ordering pharmaceuticals for the hospital. What, if any, offense has been committed? By whom?
2. George Fox is a prisoner at a men's reformatory. He is assigned to a work farm enclosed by a fence and instructed to remain inside the fence. On the second day of Fox's imprisonment, a guard discovers that Fox has not returned to his quarters by curfew. Early the next morning, Fox is found walking down a road outside the fence that bounds the work farm. In his trial for escape, Fox contends that this evidence is insufficient to establish his intent to escape. He claims that had he intended to escape he would not have allowed himself to be located so easily. He claims that he got lost on the prison farm and was trying to make his way back to his barracks. What result is likely? Why?

3. Harry Hamilton is arrested for grand theft. He signs a form stating that he has no prior convictions under oath before a deputy court administrator. Based on this representation, he is granted pretrial release on his own recognizance. There is no statute or court rule that authorizes the court administrator to authorize deputies to give oaths. He is prosecuted for perjury and at trial his statement is proven to be false. Based on this evidence, does Hamilton have a good defense to the charge of perjury?

4. The state charges Larcen Yee with escape from prison. The court appoints a public defender to represent him. You are assigned to investigate the case and report your findings to the public defender. Your investigation reveals that Yee was convicted of burglary of a dwelling and was serving the second year of a five-year sentence in the state prison. He complained to the warden that another inmate had sexually molested him and requested transfer to another prison, or at least another cell block. After confirming that an inmate in Yee's cell block had molested him on one occasion, the warden told Yee that he would place him in another cell block. During the next three days the warden took no action. On the fourth day, while Yee and other prisoners were on a work detail picking up trash from the roadside outside the prison, Yee left without permission and caught a ride to a nearby city where he obtained a construction job. He had no contact with the prison until two weeks later, when the local police apprehended him and returned him to prison. Based on your investigation, do you think the public defender can successfully establish the defense of necessity on behalf of Mr. Yee?

5. Early one evening Alden Dancio was sitting at a table in a tavern with his girlfriend and two other couples. They had been drinking beer and were talking and laughing. A local uniformed police officer, who was patrolling the area, stopped in to have a sandwich. Annoyed by the loud talking and laughing, the officer walked over to the table. There he saw Angela Mellow, a female he occasionally dated, sitting with her arm around Dancio. No one at the table was intoxicated. The officer demanded that Dancio produce some identification and, when he refused, the officer told him he was under arrest for disorderly conduct and ordered him to get in the patrol car. Dancio refused and, after an altercation between the two, the officer handcuffed Dancio and placed him in the patrol car. After reviewing the police file, the prosecutor acknowledged that Dancio should not have been arrested for disorderly conduct. He dismissed that charge. Nevertheless, the prosecutor decided to file charges against Dancio for resisting arrest. Is there a basis for charging Dancio with resisting arrest in the state where you live?

# CHAPTER 14

# Criminal Responsibility and Defenses

## CHAPTER OUTLINE

## JURISPRUDENCE

*Clark v. Arizona (2006)*

*Lambert v. California (1957)*

*Jacobson v. United States (1992)*

*Wayte v. United States (1985)*

## LEARNING OBJECTIVES

After reading this chapter, you should be able to explain

1. the difference between a negative defense and an affirmative defense

2. the defenses asserting incapacity to commit a crime

3. the origin and development of the insanity defense

4. the circumstances under which criminal acts are excusable

5. the degree to which one may use force to defend oneself, one's property and other people

6. the different forms of immunity

7. the constitutionally based defense of double jeopardy

8. why statutes of limitations are important in the criminal law

9. how and when governmental misconduct can be a defense

10. some of the more novel and innovative defenses that have been proposed in recent years

# CHAPTER OPENING VIGNETTE

John W. Hinckley, Jr., watched the 1976 movie *Taxi Driver* over and over and developed an obsession with actress Jodie Foster, who portrayed a teenage prostitute in the film. Hinckley moved to New Haven, Connecticut to be close to Foster, who was an undergraduate student at Yale. He never met Foster, but left letters and poems in her mailbox and spoke to her twice by telephone. Hinckley decided that to impress Foster he would assassinate the president of the United States. He followed President Jimmy Carter around the country but never took action against him. On March 30, 1981, Hinckley approached President Reagan's entourage outside the Washington Hilton and fired six shots from a .22 caliber handgun. The President's press secretary, a Secret Service agent, and a Washington, D.C. police officer were struck and wounded. One of the bullets ricocheted off the presidential limousine and struck President Reagan in the chest. Reagan was rushed to George Washington University Hospital, where surgeons removed the bullet and saved the president's life. Federal authorities charged Hinckley with attempted assassination of the president, attempted murder, use of a firearm in the commission of a federal crime, and multiple assault charges, as well as a weapons violation under the D.C. Code. Hinckley was found competent to stand trial but pleaded not guilty by reason of insanity. Although the defense had little difficulty producing evidence of Hinckley's mental illness, the nation was stunned and outraged when the jury returned a not-guilty verdict. Subsequently, Hinckley was committed to a mental institution, where he remains today. As you will see in this chapter, the Hinckley case would have a dramatic impact on the law as it relates to the insanity defense. Still, the insanity defense, which is seldom invoked and rarely successful, continues to evoke popular bewilderment and scorn.

# Introduction

**criminal responsibility** Refers to the set of doctrines under which individuals are held accountable for criminal conduct.

As the English common law developed, the concept of **criminal responsibility** became a significant consideration. As it did, various defenses to criminal conduct emerged. Incapacity to commit a crime because of infancy, insanity, or, under some circumstances, intoxication came to be recognized as defenses. Self-defense, defense of others, and defense of habitation and other property were also recognized as defenses because of justification for a defendant's use of force in those instances. Moreover, the common law allowed a defendant to assert certain matters as an excuse or justification for having committed a criminal act. Mistake of fact that occurred honestly, necessity, duress, and—under limited circumstances—consent were recognized as defenses.

Essentially these defenses have been recognized in various jurisdictions in the United States, although they have been modified over the years. The Fifth Amendment to the U.S. Constitution and corresponding provisions of the state constitutions furnish defendants two additional defenses: immunity and double jeopardy. Legislatures initiated the concept of a statute of limitations on the prosecution of most crimes. Through judicial development, entrapment has become a recognized defense where improper governmental conduct has induced an otherwise innocent person to commit a crime. In rare instances, defendants have successfully asserted the defense of selective prosecution—that is, being singled out for prosecution.

In previous chapters, we have mentioned some defenses applicable to specific substantive crimes. We revisit some of those defenses in this chapter, further examining the scope of common-law, constitutional, and statutory defenses to criminal charges.

# Negative and Affirmative Defenses

**negative defense** A defense in which the defendant denies committing the crime or claims that the prosecution lacks sufficient evidence of the defendant's guilt.

**affirmative defense** A defense to a criminal charge in which the defendant admits to the criminal act but denies criminal responsibility.

**beyond a reasonable doubt** The standard of proof that is constitutionally required to be met before a defendant can be found guilty of a crime or before a juvenile can be adjudicated as a delinquent.

**preponderance of the evidence** Evidence that has greater weight than countervailing evidence.

The most basic distinction in criminal defense is that between the **negative defense** and the **affirmative defense**. A negative defense is one in which the defendant denies committing the crime or claims that the prosecution lacks sufficient evidence of the defendant's guilt. An affirmative defense admits to the alleged act but denies criminal responsibility by claiming an excuse or justification for the defendant's otherwise illegal conduct or asserting that the defendant lacked the capacity to form criminal intent. While the prosecution always carries the burden of proving the defendant's guilt **beyond a reasonable doubt**, courts generally require a defendant to prove an affirmative defense by a **preponderance of the evidence**. The Supreme Court has said that the law may constitutionally place the burden on a defendant to establish an affirmative defense as long as that defense is not one that simply negates an element of the crime the prosecution must prove to convict the defendant. *Patterson v. New York*, 432 U.S. 197, 97 S.Ct. 2319, 53 L.Ed.2d 281 (1977). Affirmative defenses may be divided into five broad categories:

1. Those asserting lack of capacity (infancy, intoxication, insanity, automatism)
2. Those asserting excuse or justification (duress, necessity, consent, mistake)
3. Those justifying the use of force (self-defense, defense of others, defense of property and habitation, and using force to resist an arrest)
4. Those relying on constitutional or statutory rights (immunity, double jeopardy, statutes of limitation)
5. Those assailing governmental conduct (entrapment, selective prosecution)

## Is Alibi a Negative or Affirmative Defense?

**alibi** Defense to a criminal charge that places the defendant at some place other than the scene of the crime at the time the crime occurred.

*Alibi* means "elsewhere," and the defense of **alibi** may be interposed by a defendant who claims to have been at a place other than where the crime allegedly occurred. A criminal defendant who relies on an alibi as a defense does not deny that a crime was committed. Rather, he or she denies the ability to have perpetrated such crime because of having been elsewhere at the time.

The Colorado Supreme Court has pointed out that most jurisdictions that have addressed the issue have concluded that an alibi is not an affirmative defense. *People v. Huckleberry*, 768 P.2d 1235 (Colo. 1989). A defendant who asserts an affirmative defense essentially admits the conduct charged and seeks to excuse or justify or otherwise deny responsibility for it. One who claims an alibi does not admit this. Therefore, it seems logical not to classify alibi as an affirmative defense. As explained by the Missouri Supreme Court,

> The theory of alibi is that the fact of defendant's presence elsewhere is essentially inconsistent with his presence at the place where the alleged offense was committed and, therefore, defendant could not have personally participated. Although the defense is not an affirmative one, the fact of defendant's presence elsewhere is an affirmative fact logically operating to negative his presence at the time and place. *State v. Armstead*, 283 S.W.2d 577, 581 (Mo. 1955).

Yet the defense of alibi is similar to an affirmative defense in that it must be specifically pled. Statutes or court rules commonly require that to assert alibi as a defense, a defendant must notify the prosecution in advance of trial and furnish the names of witnesses the defendant intends to use to support the alibi. The Supreme Court has said that this requirement does not violate the defendant's right to due process of law. *Williams v. Florida*, 399 U.S. 78, 90 S.Ct. 1893, 26 L.Ed.2d 446 (1970). In 1973, however, the Court held that when the state requires such information, the prosecution must make similar disclosures to the defendant concerning refutation of the evidence that the defendant furnishes. *Wardius v. Oregon*, 412 U.S. 470, 93 S.Ct. 2208, 37 L.Ed.2d 82 (1973). Alibi-notice statutes and court rules now commonly require disclosure by both defense and the prosecution.

# Defenses Asserting Lack of Capacity to Commit a Crime

In proffering a defense asserting the lack of capacity to commit a crime, the defendant admits the *actus reus* alleged by the prosecution but denies criminal responsibility for that act on the ground that he or she lacked the mental capacity to form the requisite criminal intent. There are four principal defenses asserting the lack of capacity to commit a crime: infancy, intoxication, insanity, and automatism.

## Infancy

**infancy** The condition of being below the age of legal majority.

The common law regarded a child under age seven as incapable of forming criminal intent. Thus, **infancy** gave rise to a conclusive presumption of incapacity for a child younger than seven. This presumption of incapacity was rebuttable regarding a child between seven and fourteen years old, with the prosecution having the burden to demonstrate that a child younger than fourteen was capable of comprehending the wrongdoing involved in commission of an offense. Children over age fourteen were treated as adults. *Commonwealth v. Cavalier*, 131 A. 229 (Pa. 1925).

The rationale for these common-law presumptions was that young children require protection from the harshness of the adversarial processes of the law. Some jurisdictions have abolished these presumptions because legislatures have provided that children under certain ages, usually sixteen to eighteen, are subject to the jurisdiction of the juvenile courts, where the procedures are tailored toward less mature offenders. In establishing juvenile courts, the legislatures frequently intend to eliminate the common-law presumption of incapacity of infants. See *People v. Miller*, 334 N.E.2d 421 (Ill. App. 1975), for the court's perception of legislative intent under Illinois law. Under federal law, a juvenile is a person who has not attained age eighteen at the time of the commission of an offense. 18 U.S.C.A. § 5031.

Starting with Illinois in 1899, all states developed juvenile court systems. These courts traditionally handled juvenile offenders separately from adults in nonadversarial proceedings. The theory was that the state acted as *parens patriae*, taking a clinical and rehabilitative, rather than an adversarial or punitive, approach to youthful offenders. Nevertheless, the system suffered from many deficiencies, such as inadequate staffing and substandard facilities, and the results were disappointing. Many youthful offenders were not rehabilitated, nor were they afforded even the most basic constitutional rights afforded to adults in the criminal justice system. In the words of the U.S. Supreme Court, "[T]he child receives the worst of both worlds: that he gets neither the protections accorded to adults nor the solicitous care and regenerative treatment postulated for children." *Kent v. United States*, 383 U.S. 541, 556, 86 S.Ct. 1045, 1054, 16 L.Ed.2d 84, 94 (1966). Although juvenile courts remain a part of the judicial scene, statutes commonly provide that for certain offenses a juvenile may be tried as an adult.

## Intoxication

**intoxication** Condition in which a person has impaired physical or mental capacities due to the ingestion of drugs or alcohol.

**voluntary intoxication** The state of becoming drunk or intoxicated of one's own free will.

**involuntary intoxication** Intoxication that is not the result of a person's intentional ingestion of an intoxicating substance. A person may become involuntarily intoxicated through the trickery or fraud of another person or through the inadvertent ingestion of medicine.

**Intoxication** can result from ingestion of alcohol or drugs. The common law did not excuse from responsibility for criminal conduct a person who voluntarily became intoxicated. In an early English case, the court approved a death sentence for a homicide committed by an extremely intoxicated defendant. *Regina v. Fogossa*, 75 Eng. Rep. 1 (1550).

In evaluating whether intoxication is a defense, **voluntary intoxication** must first be distinguished from **involuntary intoxication**. In most jurisdictions, voluntary intoxication may be considered in determining whether a defendant can formulate the specific intent the prosecution must establish in such crimes as larceny, burglary, and premeditated murder. Most courts reject the defense of voluntary intoxication for general-intent crimes. See, e.g., *United States v. Hanson*, 618 F.2d 1261 (8th Cir. 1980) (assault on a federal officer); *Commonwealth v. Bridge*, 435 A.2d 151 (Pa. 1981) (voluntary manslaughter); *State v. Keaten*, 390 A.2d 1043 (Me. 1978) (gross sexual misconduct). These decisions are grounded in the public policy of not excusing conduct by those who voluntarily impair their own judgment. Three decades ago the South Carolina Supreme Court judicially adopted a rule that voluntary intoxication, where it has not produced permanent insanity, is never an excuse for or a defense to a general- or specific-intent crime. *State v. Vaughn*, 232 S.E.2d 328, 330 (S.C. 1977). Recent years have witnessed considerable activity by several state legislatures addressing the issue of voluntary intoxication as a defense.

In 1996 the U.S. Supreme Court, in a 5–4 decision, upheld a Montana law that does not allow a jury to consider a defendant's voluntary intoxication in determining

### Can Voluntary Intoxication Negate Specific Intent?

This case stems from a shooting in a bar in Troy, Alabama. Latimore, a juvenile, was transferred to the Circuit Court of Pike County, Alabama where he was prosecuted, convicted and sentenced to 50 years' imprisonment for murder. Latimore testified at trial that "he had smoked some marijuana and consumed some alcohol" prior to the shooting. On appeal Latimore argued, among other things, that "he was intoxicated to such an extent as to create a reasonable doubt of his ability to form a specific intent." The Court of Criminal Appeals of Alabama held that while "voluntary intoxication can never justify or excuse the commission of a crime," . . . "excessive intoxication may render an individual incapable of forming a specific intent." In this case, the court found that "although [Latimore] testified that he had smoked part of two marijuana cigarettes and had drunk over a pint of whiskey and several beers, there was no evidence to show as a matter of law that [he] was intoxicated to such an extent as to render him incapable of forming the requisite intent." The court said that "intoxication must be of such character and extent as to render the accused incapable of consciousness that he is committing a crime, incapable of discriminating between right and wrong—stupefaction of the reasoning faculty." This determination is also a jury question, which is free to weigh the witness's credibility in making its determination. The appellate court upheld Latimore's conviction for murder.

*Latimore v. State,* 534 So.2d 665 (Alabama Crim. App. 1988)

whether the defendant possessed the mental state necessary for the commission of a crime. *Montana v. Egelhoff,* 518 U.S. 37, 116 S.Ct. 2013, 135 L.Ed.2d 361 (1996). In 1999 the Florida Legislature enacted a statute that eliminates voluntary intoxication as a defense. The new law specifies that evidence of voluntary intoxication is not admissible to show a lack of specific intent or to show insanity at the time of the offense. However, the statute makes an exception for controlled substances taken pursuant to a doctor's prescription. West's Fla. Stat. Ann. § 775.051.

Florida courts have held that the statute excluding the right to assert the defense does not violate a defendant's constitutional right to due process. *Barrett v. State,* 862 So.2d 44 (Fla. App. 2003); *Cuc v. State,* 834 So.2d 378 (Fla. App. 2003). The trend is for states to disallow the defense of voluntary intoxication, on the theory that a defendant who voluntarily deprives himself or herself of the ability to distinguish between right and wrong is criminally responsible for acts committed. As of 2008, Alabama, Delaware, Florida, Georgia, Hawaii, Idaho, Indiana, Missouri, Montana, Ohio, Oklahoma, Pennsylvania, and Texas had statutes providing that voluntary intoxication is not a defense to crime.

Involuntary intoxication rarely occurs, but when it does, it removes the criminality of an act committed under its influence if, as a result of intoxication, the defendant no longer knows right from wrong. *State v. Mriglot,* 564 P.2d 784 (Wash. 1977). A person can become involuntarily intoxicated through the trickery or fraud of another person—see, e.g., *Johnson v. Commonwealth,* 115 S.E. 673 (Va. 1923)—or through inadvertent ingestion of medicine. See *People v. Carlo,* 361 N.Y.S.2d 168 (N.Y. App. Div. 1974). The New Hampshire Supreme Court summarized the law in this area:

> Generally the defense of involuntary intoxication will only be considered when it is shown that the intoxication was the product of external pressures such as fraud, force, or coercion, or when intoxication resulted from a medical prescription. *State v. Plummer,* 374 A.2d 431, 435 (N.H. 1977).

Involuntary intoxication as a defense to criminal liability has been codified in some jurisdictions. Section 939.42 of the Wisconsin Statutes is rather typical:

An intoxicated or a drugged condition of the actor is a defense only if such condition:
(1) Is involuntarily produced and renders the actor incapable of distinguishing between right and wrong in regard to the alleged criminal act at the time the act is committed; or
(2) Negatives the existence of a state of mind essential to the crime *except as provided in § 939.24(3)*. Wis. Stat. Ann. § 939.42.

The Wisconsin legislature inserted the italicized exception in 1987 to stipulate that a voluntarily produced intoxicated or drugged condition is not a defense to liability for criminal recklessness.

Wisconsin courts have said that to establish the defense of involuntary intoxication, the accused must show the inability to tell right from wrong at the time of the offense.

## Insanity

All persons are presumed sane unless previously adjudicated insane. Even a person who has been adjudicated legally insane may still be found guilty of a criminal act if it was committed during a lucid interval. Insanity is a legal concept and is defined differently in various jurisdictions in the United States. A person who meets the requirements of the definition at the time of commission of an offense may plead **insanity** as a defense to criminal conduct.

Few cases have caused as great a concern about how the criminal justice system functions as did the verdict of **not guilty by reason of insanity** in John Hinckley's federal court trial for the 1981 shooting of President Ronald Reagan, his press secretary, and two law enforcement officers. The defense of insanity has never been popular with the public. It has sometimes been called "a rich person's defense" because defendants who invoke it frequently expend considerable financial resources to present psychiatric testimony. The Hinckley verdict motivated Congress and several state legislatures to review the status of insanity defenses.

**insanity** A degree of mental illness that negates the legal capacity or responsibility of the affected person.

**not guilty by reason of insanity** A plea that admits criminal conduct but raises the insanity defense.

### Historical Roots of the Insanity Plea
The concept of mental responsibility has deep roots in Anglo-American law—the common-law crimes included a *mens rea* (mental element). Nevertheless, the common law was slow to develop any standard for a mental condition that would excuse a person from criminal responsibility. By the eighteenth century, some English courts applied what has sometimes been called a "wild beast" test. For example, one English judge opined that "a man . . . totally deprived of his understanding and memory, . . . and doth not know what he is doing, no more than an infant, than a brute, or a wild beast . . . is never the object of punishment." *Rex v. Arnold*, 16 Howell's State Trials 695 (Eng. 1724).

### The *M'Naghten* Rule
Little progress occurred in the development of the defense of insanity until 1843, when an event in England caused even greater consternation than the Hinckley verdict caused in the United States. Suffering from delusions that he was being persecuted by government officials, Daniel M'Naghten decided to kill Sir Robert Peel, the British Home Secretary. (Peel was the founder of the British police system; hence,

**M'Naghten rule** Under this rule, for a defendant to be found not guilty by reason of insanity, it must be clearly proved that, at the time of committing the act, the defendant was suffering such a defect of reason, from disease of the mind, as not to know the nature and quality of the act he was doing; or, if he did know it, that he did not know what he was doing was wrong.

**irresistible impulse** A test for insanity that allowed a person who knew an act was wrong but acted under an uncontrollable desire or duress of mental disease to be excused from a criminal act.

the term "bobbies" is still applied to British law officers.) From outside Peel's home, M'Naghten saw Peel's secretary, Edward Drummond, leave the house. Believing Drummond to be Peel, M'Naghten shot and killed him. At trial, M'Naghten's barristers argued that he was insane at the time of the shooting and therefore should be found not guilty. The jury agreed. Enraged by the verdict, Queen Victoria insisted that the law provide a yardstick for the defense of insanity. The House of Lords responded, and the test they developed is still referred to as the *M'Naghten rule*. It provides that insanity cannot be a defense to a crime unless "at the time of committing the act, the party accused was labouring under such a defect of reason, from disease of the mind, as not to know the nature and quality of the act he was doing; or, if he did know it, that he did not know what he was doing was wrong." *M'Naghten's Case*, 8 Eng. Rep. 718 (1843).

The *M'Naghten* **rule** became the test for insanity used in both federal and state courts in the United States. As psychology and psychiatry developed new theories of mental capacity, critics attacked the rule as being based solely on cognition (that is, a process of the intellect) and ignoring a person's emotions. In response, some courts accepted the **irresistible impulse** test, which stressed volition (that is, self-control), as a supplement to the *M'Naghten* rule. See *Parsons v. State*, 2 So. 854 (Ala. 1887). This allowed a person who knew an act was wrong but who acted under an uncontrollable desire or the duress of mental disease to be excused from a criminal act.

### The *Durham* Test

Another test for insanity evolved from *Durham v. United States*, where the U.S. Court of Appeals for the District of Columbia held that an accused is not

**CASE-IN-POINT**

## A Federal Court Reviews the Insanity Defense Reform Act

Dwayne Freeman was arrested and convicted of bank robbery in federal district court. Freeman appealed his conviction for reasons related to the "trial court's determination that he was sane at the time of the offense." Freeman argued that the Insanity Defense Reform Act of 1984 was unconstitutional and also asserted "that as a matter of law, he established his insanity by clear and convincing evidence." The Eighth Circuit Court of Appeals rejected these arguments and upheld Freeman's conviction. The Insanity Defense Reform Act shifted the burden of proof from the government to the defendant to prove insanity by clear and convincing evidence. The Eighth Circuit examined the relevant Supreme Court precedents, including *Leland v. Oregon* (1952), where the Court held that a state could constitutionally require a defendant to prove insanity beyond a reasonable doubt. The Eighth Circuit noted "the Supreme Court . . . has repeatedly reaffirmed the *Leland* holding [and]

*Leland* compels a holding that the aspect of the Insanity Reform Act of 1984 requiring a defendant to prove insanity by clear and convincing evidence is constitutional." As to Freeman's second argument, the district court held that he "failed to prove by clear and convincing evidence that he was unable to appreciate the nature and quality of his acts at the time of the offense." The Eighth Circuit found that "ample evidence exists indicating that Freeman knew his conduct was wrongful." The record revealed that "Freeman changed his clothes after robbing the bank to avoid identification," used a "mask, handgun and satchel to execute the robbery and avoid apprehension," and "informed bank personnel that if the police were called, he would come back and kill everyone." Furthermore, when Freeman was "spotted by the police, Freeman ran to avoid apprehension." Given the evidence, the Eighth Circuit held "the district court's decision was not clearly erroneous."

*United States v. Freeman*, 804 F.2d 1574 (11th Cir. 1986)

criminally responsible if that person's unlawful act was "the product of mental disease or defect." 214 F.2d 862, 876 (D.C. Cir. 1954). Many psychiatrists applauded the **Durham** test, but it gained little judicial support outside of the District of Columbia. It was eventually discarded even there. *United States v. Brawner*, 471 F.2d 969 (D.C. Cir. 1972).

### The ALI Standard

In 1962 the American Law Institute (ALI), an association of distinguished lawyers and judges, proposed a new standard combining both cognitive and volitional capacities as a test for insanity. It is sometimes referred to as the **ALI Standard** or **substantial capacity test** and reads as follows:

> A person is not responsible for criminal conduct if at the time of such conduct, as a result of mental disease or defect, a person lacks substantial capacity either to appreciate the wrongfulness of his conduct or to conform his conduct to the requirements of the law.

The ALI Standard was adopted by most federal courts and has sometimes been referred to as the *Freeman* rule, stemming from an endorsement of the test by the U.S. Court of Appeals for the Second Circuit in *United States v. Freeman*, 357 F.2d 606 (2d Cir. 1966). State courts, however, remained divided in their approaches to the defense of insanity. Many opted to follow the new substantial capacity test; the remainder adhered to the *M'Naghten* rule.

The substantial capacity concept was applied as the test for insanity in the infamous John Hinckley case. Under the ALI criteria, a showing of substantial impairment of a person's mental faculties is enough to meet the test of insanity. In contrast, establishing insanity under a strict *M'Naghten* approach requires a showing of total incapacity, and evidence that does not tend to prove or disprove the defendant's ability to distinguish right from wrong is irrelevant.

### The Current Federal Standard

Dissatisfied with the ALI test, Congress decided to eliminate the volitional prong in the federal test for insanity and to revert substantially to the *M'Naghten* rule when it enacted the **Insanity Defense Reform Act of 1984**. This act provides that in federal courts:

> It is an affirmative defense to a prosecution under any federal statute that, at the time of the commission of the acts constituting the offense, the defendant, as a result of a severe mental disease or defect, was unable to appreciate the nature and quality or the wrongfulness of his acts. Mental disease or defect does not otherwise constitute a defense. 18 U.S.C.A. § 17(a).

In addition, the act stipulates that "[t]he defendant has the burden of proving the defense of insanity by clear and convincing evidence." 18 U.S.C.A. § 17(b). The **clear and convincing evidence standard** is higher than the usual civil evidentiary standard of preponderance of the evidence but somewhat lower than the standard of beyond a reasonable doubt, the evidentiary standard required for criminal convictions. Although there has been some controversy concerning the legitimacy of placing the burden of proof of insanity on the defendant, the U.S. Supreme Court has held that this type of "burden shifting" does not violate the defendant's right of due process of law under the U.S. Constitution. *Patterson v. New York*, supra. Moreover, federal appellate court decisions in 1986 affirmed the

---

**Durham test** A test for determining insanity developed by the U.S. Court of Appeals for the District of Columbia Circuit in the case of *Durham v. United States* (1954). Under this test, a person is not criminally responsible for an unlawful act if it was the product of a mental disease or defect.

**ALI Standard** A test proposed by the American Law Institute to determine if a defendant is legally insane.

**substantial capacity test** The doctrine that a person is not responsible for criminal conduct if at the time of such conduct, as a result of mental disease or defect, the person lacked substantial capacity either to appreciate the wrongfulness of his or her conduct or to conform his or her conduct to the requirements of the law.

**Insanity Defense Reform Act of 1984** An act of Congress that specifies that insanity is an affirmative defense to a prosecution under a federal statute and details the requirements for establishing such a defense.

**clear and convincing evidence standard** An evidentiary standard that is higher than the standard of "preponderance of the evidence" but lower than the standard of "beyond a reasonable doubt."

constitutionality of this burden shifting under the 1984 federal act. *United States v. Freeman*, 804 F.2d 1574 (11th Cir. 1986); *United States v. Amos*, 803 F.2d 419 (8th Cir. 1986).

On April 4, 1995, a federal jury found Francisco Martin Duran guilty of attempting to assassinate President Bill Clinton. Duran pleaded insanity. His counsel argued that Duran was a paranoid schizophrenic who was shooting at the White House as a symbol of a government he hated. Unlike in the John Hinckley trial, the new federal standard for insanity applied in Duran's trial. The jury rejected Duran's plea of insanity and found him guilty of attempting to assassinate the president, as well as several other charges.

### The Insanity Defense Reform Act: The Effect on the Use of Psychiatric Evidence

Under the Insanity Defense Reform Act, psychiatric evidence of impaired volitional control is inadmissible to support an insanity defense. After passage of the new law, a question arose as to whether Congress also intended to prohibit the use of psychiatric evidence to negate a defendant's specific intent to commit an offense. In 1990 the U.S. Court of Appeals for the Eleventh Circuit addressed the issue: "Both Congress and the courts have recognized the crucial distinction between evidence of psychological impairment that supports an 'affirmative defense,' and psychological evidence that negates an element of the offense charged." The court ruled that the language of the new federal act does not bar the use of psychiatric evidence to negate specific intent where that level of intent is an element of the offense charged by the government. *United States v. Cameron*, 907 F.2d 1051, 1063 (11th Cir. 1990).

### Contemporary State Developments

Although Congress has placed the burden on defendants who plead insanity in federal courts to prove their defense, state courts are divided on the issue. In some states, where insanity is classified as an affirmative defense, the defendant bears the burden of proof of insanity, usually by a preponderance of the evidence. See, e.g., *State v. Baker*, 424 A.2d 171 (N.H. 1980).

Tennessee is now among the states that place the burden on the defendant to establish the affirmative defense of insanity by clear and convincing evidence. Tenn. Code Ann. § 39-11-501; *State v. Flake*, 114 S.W.3d 487 (Tenn. 2003). In many other states, because of the presumption of sanity, when a defendant pleads insanity and introduces some evidence of insanity, the presumption disappears and the prosecution must then establish the defendant's sanity, usually by proof beyond a reasonable doubt, the standard required for establishing a defendant's guilt. See, e.g., *State v. Milam*, 260 S.E.2d 295 (W.Va. 1979). Courts usually permit laypersons as well as expert witnesses to testify about a defendant's sanity.

Unlike a defendant who is simply found not guilty, a defendant who is found not guilty by reason of insanity is committed to indefinite institutionalization and may, in some circumstances, be committed to a mental institution. *Jones v. United States*, 463 U.S. 354, 103 S.Ct. 3043, 77 L.Ed.2d 694 (1983). This is generally accomplished subsequent to the verdict by the trial judge, who determines whether the protection of the public requires that the defendant be confined.

On the premise that a person should not be found not guilty on the basis of insanity, some states have recently resorted to verdicts of **guilty but mentally ill** in cases where the defendant's insanity has been established. For example, in *People v.*

**guilty but mentally ill** A form of verdict that may be rendered in some states where the jury finds that the defendant's mental illness does not deprive the defendant of substantial capacity sufficient to satisfy the insanity test but warrants the defendant's treatment in addition to incarceration.

### Insanity Defense

Joy Ann Robey was charged with involuntary manslaughter and child abuse in connection with the death of her ten-month-old daughter, Christina. At trial, Robey admitted to beating the child severely and repeatedly over a two-month period but pleaded not guilty by reason of insanity. The trial court found that the defendant was temporarily insane each time she beat the child but that she returned to sanity thereafter.

Accordingly, the defendant could not be held criminally liable for the beatings, but was responsible for her failure to seek medical care for her child. Robey was convicted of involuntary manslaughter and child abuse and sentenced to three concurrent ten-year terms in prison. Her conviction was upheld on appeal over her contention that the trial court erred in holding her criminally responsible after acknowledging that she was insane at the time of the beatings.

*Robey v. State*, 456 A.2d 953 (Md. App. 1983).

*Sorna*, the court explained that this category of verdict deals with situations "where a defendant's mental illness does not deprive him of substantial capacity sufficient to satisfy the insanity test but does warrant treatment in addition to incarceration." 276 N.W.2d 892, 896 (Mich. App. 1979).

Kansas became the fourth state to abolish the separate defense of insanity when it enacted Kans. Stat. Ann. § 22-3220, effective January 1, 1996. Montana, Idaho, and Utah had previously abolished insanity as a defense. In *State v. Cowan*, 861 P.2d 884 (Mont. 1993), the Montana Supreme Court held that its state law abolishing insanity as a defense did not violate the federal constitution. The defendant, asserting a constitutional right to plead the defense, asked the U.S. Supreme Court to review his case. In March 1994, the Court refused to review the *Cowan* decision. *Cowan v. Montana*, 511 U.S. 1005, 114 S.Ct. 1371, 128 L.Ed.2d 48 (1994). Although the Court declined to definitively settle the issue, its action suggests that the federal constitution does not require that states allow a defendant to plead insanity.

In 1995 the Nevada Legislature enacted a law effectively abolishing insanity as a complete defense to a criminal offense. In *Finger v. State*, 27 P.3d 66 (Nev. 2001), the Nevada Supreme Court held the new statutory scheme to be unconstitutional under both the Nevada and U.S. Constitutions and ordered that the insanity defense as it previously existed be reinstated. The court noted that "legal insanity is a well-established and fundamental principle of the law of the United States," and "it is therefore protected by the Due Process Clauses of both the United States and Nevada Constitutions." 27 P.3d at 84. The State of Nevada sought review of the court's decision by the U.S. Supreme Court, but the Court denied its request without opinion. *Nevada v. Finger*, 534 U.S. 1127, 122 S.Ct. 1063, 151 L.Ed.2d 967 (2002).

It is sometimes difficult to classify the results that occur from a plea of insanity when a jury acquits the defendant. For example, in 1994 Lorena Bobbitt was charged with severing her husband's penis, a fact that was not in controversy. She relied on insanity as a defense but in a novel way. She testified about her husband's alleged cruel and abusive behavior toward her and characterized herself as a victim. A jury in Manassas, Virginia, acquitted her. Some observers have characterized her acquittal as a jury nullification rather than a finding of not guilty by reason of insanity.

*Clark v. Arizona*, 548 U.S. 735, 126 S.Ct. 2709, 165 L.Ed.2d 842 (2006)

In 1993, the Arizona legislature deleted a reference to the defendant's knowledge of the "nature and quality" of his act, a traditional component of the *M'Naghten* Rule, thereby deleting the cognitive capacity aspect from its statutory test for insanity. Eric Clark, a young man, was charged with first-degree murder for the June 21, 2000, killing of a Flagstaff, Arizona, police officer, Jeff Moritz. Clark, who was suffering from paranoid schizophrenia at the time he shot the officer, pleaded "guilty, but insane" and waived the right to a jury trial. At a bench trial, the judge found that Clark did not establish that his schizophrenia distorted his perception of reality so severely that he did not know his actions were wrong. After the Arizona Court of Appeals affirmed his conviction, the U.S. Supreme Court granted review. Clark argued that the Arizona definition of insanity violates due process of law because it does not allow a defendant to be judged insane if he did not understand the "nature and quality of his act," as has historically been an essential part of the *M'Naghten* Rule. Thus, Clark contended that, by not allowing evidence of

mental disease or defect, the Arizona law violated his right to due process under the Fourteenth Amendment to the U.S. Constitution. Moreover, Clark's counsel pointed out that at least thirty-eight states, the District of Columbia, and the federal government employ insanity standards under which persons satisfying either part of the *M'Naghten* Rule qualify as legally insane.

In reviewing the case, the U.S. Supreme Court considered two questions: (1) whether due process prohibits Arizona's use of an insanity test stated solely in terms of the capacity to tell whether an act charged as a crime was right or wrong, and (2) whether the Arizona insanity statute violates due process in restricting the consideration of defense evidence of mental illness and incapacity to its bearing on a claim of insanity, thus eliminating its significance directly on the issue of the mental element of the crime charged. The Court concluded that there was no violation of due process in either instance. Thus, the Court upheld Arizona's elimination of the cognitive capacity aspect, not only from its statutory test for insanity, but also in refusing to allow psychiatric testimony short of insanity to negate the *mens rea* element of the crime charged.

## Automatism

**automatism** The condition under which a person performs a set of actions during a state of unconsciousness.

Older cases treated defendants who claimed that their unlawful acts were committed because of an involuntary condition such as somnambulism (that is, sleepwalking) within the context of the insanity defense. Newer cases tend to classify such involuntary actions as **automatism** and view automatism similarly to unconsciousness as a basis for an affirmative defense independent from insanity. In *State v. Morganherring*, 517 S.E.2d 622, 641 (N.C. 1999), the North Carolina Supreme Court stated that "where a person commits an act without being conscious thereof, the act is not a criminal act even though it would be a crime if it had been committed by a person who was conscious." The defense is usually limited to a situation where criminal conduct is beyond a person's knowledge and control. *Sellers v. State*, 809 P.2d 676 (Okla. Cr. App. 1991). In *Fulcher v. State*, 633 P.2d 142 (Wyo. 1981), the court explained that one reason for regarding automatism as a separate defense is that there are generally no follow-up consequences such as institutionalization, which usually occurs in an acquittal by reason of insanity. The defense of sleepwalking is infrequently pled. In November 1994, a defendant in Butler, Pennsylvania, contended that his sleep apnea disorder depleted his oxygen and caused him to shoot his wife. The prosecution countered by arguing that the man shot his wife because she had planned to leave him. The jury rejected the defendant's claim and found him guilty of murder.

# Defenses Asserting Excuse or Justification

A defendant who asserts an excuse admits the act charged by the prosecution but claims that under the circumstances his or her conduct should not result in punishment. A defendant who asserts a justification for conduct says, in effect, that it was justified under the circumstances. Five principal defenses are based on a defendant's asserting an excuse or justification: duress, necessity, consent, mistake of law, and mistake of fact.

## Duress

**duress** The use of illegal confinement or threats of harm to coerce someone to do something he or she would not do otherwise.

The common law recognized that **duress** can be a defense to criminal charges if the coercion exerted involved the use of threats of harm that were "present, imminent, and pending" and "of such nature as to include well-grounded apprehensions of death or serious bodily harm if the act was not done." Nevertheless, no form of duress, even the threat of imminent death, was sufficient to excuse the intentional killing of an innocent human being. American courts have generally followed this approach, with both federal and state courts having made it clear that threats of future harm are not sufficient to constitute duress. See, e.g., *United States v. Agard*, 605 F.2d 665 (2d Cir. 1979); *State v. Clay*, 264 N.W. 77 (Iowa 1935).

Today jurisdictions recognize the defense of duress, sometimes referred to as coercion or compulsion, by either statute or decisional law. Duress has been asserted most frequently by defendants who have committed robberies and thefts and by prisoners who have escaped from custody. Some courts look to duress as negating an element of the offense charged and classify it as a negative defense. See *People v. Graham*, 129 Cal. Rptr. 31 (Cal. App. 1976) (a defendant who raised a reasonable doubt as to whether he had acted in the exercise of free will did not have the burden of showing duress by a preponderance of evidence). However, most courts classify duress as an affirmative defense and require the defendant to prove the defense by the preponderance of the evidence.

The common-law presumption was that if a wife committed a felony other than murder or treason in her husband's presence, she did so under coercion of her husband. That presumption has little significance in modern America and has been abolished in some jurisdictions either by statute—see, e.g., Wis. Stat. Ann. § 939.46(2)—or by judicial decision—see *People v. Statley*, 206 P.2d 76 (Cal. App. 1949). However, in 1992 a California appellate court allowed a defense in which a female defendant claimed that she committed robbery because she was afraid the man she lived with would kill her if she did not do as he demanded. *People v. Romero*, 13 Cal. Rptr. 2d 332 (Cal. App. 1992).

Prisoners who escape custody frequently plead duress. As pointed out in Chapter 13, the requirement for establishing duress as a defense to escape requires the defendant to show that a *bona fide* effort was made to surrender or return to custody as soon as the claimed duress had ended or lost its coercive force. See *United States v. Bailey*, 444 U.S. 394, 100 S.Ct. 624, 62 L.Ed.2d 575 (1980).

There is a conflict among jurisdictions about whether a threat against persons other than the defendant is a sufficient basis for a defendant to invoke the defense of duress. Kans. Stat. Ann. § 21-3209 provides:

(1) A person is not guilty of a crime other than murder or voluntary manslaughter by reason of conduct which he performs under the compulsion or threat of the imminent infliction of death or great bodily harm, if he reasonably believes that death

**CASE-IN-POINT**

### Court Distinguishes Burden of Establishing Affirmative Defense of Duress from the Prosecution's Burden where a Defendant Raises an Issue of Self-Defense

John New, a prison inmate, was convicted after a jury trial of taking a hostage and carrying a weapon while an inmate. The evidence revealed that New and another inmate, Wesley Floyd, burst into a prison office, where the defendant put a knife to a female prison employee's throat and threatened to harm her unless the building was cleared immediately. At trial, the defendant testified that he had no choice but to do so as he was directed by inmate Floyd, a convicted murderer, who had threatened his life several times. Over the defendant's objection, the trial court instructed the jury that it was the defendant's burden to prove his defense of duress by a preponderance of the evidence. On appeal the defendant argued that the State should have the burden of disproving duress, just as it does when a defendant raises an issue of self-defense. In rejecting New's contention, the South Carolina Supreme Court pointed out that duress excuses the crime but does not negate any element of the offense, whereas self-defense goes to an element of the crime. Generally, affirmative defenses must be established by a preponderance of the evidence. Thus, it was defendant's burden to prove his affirmative defense of duress by a preponderance of the evidence. In a footnote, the court noted that in *Dixon v. United States*, 548 U.S. 1, 126 S.Ct. 2437, 165 L.Ed.2d 299 (2006), the U.S. Supreme Court upheld a jury instruction that placed the burden on a defendant to establish the defense of duress by preponderance of the evidence. The court affirmed the defendant's conviction.

*State v. New,* 640 S.E.2d 871 (S.C. 2007)

or great bodily harm will be inflicted upon him or upon his spouse, parent, child, brother or sister if he does not perform such conduct.

(2) The defense provided by this section is not available to one who willfully or wantonly places himself in a situation in which it is probable that he will be subjected to compulsion or threat.

## Necessity

**necessity** A condition that compels or requires a certain course of action.

Whereas in duress the situation has its source in the actions of others, in the defense of **necessity** forces beyond the actor's control are said to have required a person's choice of the lesser of two evils. Early common-law cases recognized that "a man may break the words of the law . . . through necessity." *Regina v. Fogossa*, supra. Contemporary American judicial authorities hold that if there is a reasonable legal alternative to violating the law, the defense of necessity fails.

Suppose several people are shipwrecked on a cold night. One person swims to shore, breaks into an unoccupied beach cottage, and takes food and blankets to assist the injured until help can be secured. Prosecution in such an event would be unlikely, but if prosecuted, the defendant would properly plead the defense of necessity.

Is the defense of necessity applicable to a person with a suspended license driving a motor vehicle? In South Carolina, a defendant admitted to the offense but justified his actions on the ground that he needed to get help for his pregnant wife, who was suffering. He had no telephone, and his neighbor who did was not at home. The defendant drove to the nearest phone booth to request a relative to take his wife to the hospital. As he left, the police stopped him for having a broken taillight. He was then arrested for driving with a suspended license. At his trial, the judge refused his request to instruct the jury on the defense of necessity. The jury found him guilty, and he appealed. In a 3–2 decision, the Supreme Court of South Carolina ruled that

### Rejecting Economic Duress as a Defense

The defendant was arrested on board a boat in the Gulf of Mexico just off the coast of Florida and was charged with trafficking in cannabis in excess of ten thousand pounds. He pled not guilty and asserted the defense of duress. At trial, the defendant and his wife testified that economic reasons forced him to participate in trafficking in cannabis by piloting the boat. The trial judge declined to instruct the jury on duress, and the defendant was convicted. On appeal, the court affirmed the conviction and said that such a claim of economic coercion was insufficient to call for a jury instruction on duress.

*Corujo v. State*, 424 So.2d 43 (Fla. App. 1982), rev. denied, 434 So.2d 886 (Fla. 1983).

under the circumstances the defendant was entitled to plead the defense of necessity. *State v. Cole*, 403 S.E.2d 117 (S.C. 1991).

In 1991 a Florida court of appeals allowed a husband and wife who contracted AIDS to assert the defense of necessity to charges of possession and cultivation of marijuana. *Jenks v. State*, 582 So.2d 676 (Fla. App. 1991). Courts in a few other states have allowed the medical necessity defense. Although Maryland has not legalized the use of medical marijuana, it has enacted legislation that allows a person prosecuted for use or possession of marijuana to have the court consider as a mitigating factor any evidence of medical necessity. If a conviction results, the maximum penalty is a fine not exceeding $100. Md. Code, Crim. Law § 5-601(c)(3).

In November 1996, California voters approved Proposition 215 (Compassionate Use Act of 1996) to make marijuana legally available as a medicine to patients or their caregivers on recommendation of a physician. The Oakland Cannabis Buyers' Cooperative began to distribute marijuana to qualified patients for medical purposes. In 1998, the United States sued to enjoin the cooperative's operation, arguing that its activities violated the Controlled Substances Act's prohibitions on distributing, manufacturing, and possessing with the intent to distribute or manufacture a controlled substance. The litigation culminated in 2001 with an 8–0 decision from the U.S. Supreme Court holding that there is no implied medical necessity exception to the Controlled Substances Act's prohibitions. Justice Clarence Thomas, writing for the Court, observed, "For purposes of the Controlled Substances Act, marijuana has 'no currently accepted medical use' at all." *United States v. Oakland Cannabis Buyers' Co-op.*, 532 U.S. 483, 491, 121 S.Ct. 1711, 1718, 149 L.Ed.2d 722, 732 (2001). Many commentators predict that Congress will eventually make provision for medical uses of marijuana. In the meantime the Court's decision has tended to thwart the use of medical necessity as a defense by those charged with marijuana offenses.

A number of defendants have attempted to justify actions involving "civil disobedience" on the ground of necessity in instances where they have forcefully asserted their personal or political beliefs. One of the most dramatic of these incidents occurred in 1980 when a group of antinuclear activists entered a factory in Pennsylvania, damaged components of nuclear bombs, and poured human blood on the premises. An appellate court approved of the defendants' pleading a defense of necessity; however, the Pennsylvania Supreme Court reversed the decision. *Commonwealth v. Berrigan*, 501 A.2d 226 (Pa. 1985). Other attempts to plead the necessity defense by antinuclear activists have also failed.

In most, but not all cases, the necessity defense has been unavailing to defendants espousing other social and political causes. In another instance, several defendants were charged with criminal trespass when they refused to leave an abortion clinic in Anchorage, Alaska. They claimed their actions were necessary to avert the imminent peril to human life that would result from abortions being performed. They were convicted, and on appeal they argued that the trial court erred in refusing to instruct the jury on their claim of necessity as a defense. In rejecting their contention, the Alaska Supreme Court outlined three requirements that must be met by a person who pleads the defense of necessity: (1) the act charged must have been done to prevent a significant evil, (2) there must have been no adequate alternative, and (3) the harm caused must not have been disproportionate to the harm avoided. *Cleveland v. Municipality of Anchorage*, 631 P.2d 1073, 1078 (Alaska 1981).

A Wisconsin statute codifies the defense of necessity by providing that

[p]ressure of natural physical forces which causes the actor reasonably to believe that his or her act is the only means of preventing imminent public disaster, or imminent death or great bodily harm to the actor or another and which causes him or her so to act, is a defense to a prosecution for any crime based on that act, except that if the prosecution is for first-degree intentional homicide, the degree of the crime is reduced to second-degree intentional homicide. Wis. Stat. Ann. § 939.47.

## Consent

Because in most instances a victim may not excuse a criminal act, American courts have said that consent is not a defense to a criminal prosecution. See, for example, *State v. West*, 57 S.W. 1071 (Mo. 1900). Yet there are exceptions to this general statement. For example, where lack of consent is an element of the offense, as in larceny, consent is a defense. This can also be true today in a prosecution for rape, but only where competent adults freely consent before having sexual relations. Thus, consent would not be a defense to a charge of statutory rape (the strict liability offense of having sexual intercourse with a minor).

Consent is commonly given to physicians who perform surgery. In contact sports, such as football and boxing, consent is implied and may be a defense to reasonable instances of physical contact that would otherwise be regarded as batteries. Some state legislatures have enacted statutes defining when consent is a defense. For example, § 565.080 of the Missouri Statutes specifies that for consent to be a defense, the physical injury consented to or threatened must result from conduct that is not intended to cause serious physical injury or that the conduct and harm are reasonably foreseeable occupational or athletic event hazards. Nevertheless § 565.080 does not apply to hazing or homicide cases, where consent is no defense.

Of course, a valid consent presupposes that it is voluntarily given by a person legally competent to do so and is not induced by force, duress, or deception. Moreover, a victim cannot ratify a criminal act by giving consent after the offense has been committed. *State v. Martinez*, 613 P.2d 974 (Mont. 1980).

## Mistake of Law

One of the oft-quoted maxims of the law is that "ignorance of the law is no excuse." The safety and welfare of society demand that persons not be excused from commission of criminal acts on the basis of their claims that they did not know they committed crimes. Although this is the generally accepted view, in some instances a defendant's honest but mistaken view of the law may be accepted as a defense.

*Lambert v. California*, 355 U.S. 225, 78 S.Ct 240, 2 L.Ed.2d228 (1957).

A Los Angeles, California, ordinance made it unlawful for any "convicted persons" to remain in the city for more than five days without registering with the police, or if they lived outside of the city, to enter the city on five or more occasions during a thirty-day period without registering. Virginia Lambert, a convicted felon, was found guilty of failing to register, fined $250,

and placed on probation for three years. On appeal to the U.S. Supreme Court, Lambert's conviction was reversed. Writing for the Court was Justice William O. Douglas: "Engrained in our concept of due process is the requirement of notice. Notice is sometimes essential so that the citizen has the chance to defend charges. Notice is required in a myriad of situations where a penalty or forfeiture might be suffered from mere failure to act."

**mistake of law** An erroneous opinion of legal principles applied to a set of facts.

One example is where such a mistake negates the specific-intent element of a crime. Thus, a **mistake of law** may be asserted as a defense in a larceny case where there is a technical question of who has legal title to an asset. *State v. Abbey*, 474 P.2d 62 (Ariz. App. 1970). Likewise, a defendant's good-faith but mistaken trust in the validity of a divorce has been held to be a defense to a charge of bigamy. *Long v. State*, 65 A.2d 489 (Del. 1949).

The Illinois Criminal Code lists four exceptions to the general rule that a person's ignorance of the law does not excuse unlawful conduct:

A person's reasonable belief that certain conduct does not constitute a criminal offense is a defense if:

(1) The offense is defined by an administrative regulation which is not known to him and has not been published or otherwise made reasonably available to him, and he could not have acquired such knowledge by the exercise of due diligence pursuant to facts known to him; or

(2) He acts in reliance upon a statute which later is determined to be invalid; or

(3) He acts in reliance upon an order or opinion of an Illinois Appellate or Supreme Court, or a United States appellate court later overruled or reversed; or

(4) He acts in reliance upon an official interpretation of the statute, regulation or order defining the offense, made by a public officer or agency legally authorized to interpret such statute. 720 Ill. Comp. Stat. Ann. § 5/4-8(b).

Citing the preceding statutory exceptions, the Illinois Supreme Court held that a taxpayer who contended that she reasonably believed that she would be subject only to civil penalties, not to criminal sanctions, for failure to file an occupational tax return did not present a mistake-of-law defense. *People v. Sevilla*, 547 N.E.2d 117 (Ill. 1989).

In *United States v. Moore*, 627 F.2d 830 (7th Cir. 1980), the court said that "the mistake of law defense is extremely limited and the mistake must be objectively reasonable." 627 F.2d at 833. Furthermore, a court will never recognize a dishonest pretense of ignorance of the law as a defense. *State v. Carroll*, 60 S.W. 1087 (Mo. 1901).

A defendant can always raise the unconstitutionality of a statute as a defense to a prosecution for its violation. But a person who violates a statute thinking it is unconstitutional does so at his or her peril; courts have said that a person's belief that a statute is unconstitutional, even if based on advice of counsel, does not constitute a valid defense for violating the law. *State v. Thorstad*, 261 N.W.2d 899 (N.D. 1978).

## Mistake of Fact

**mistake of fact** A defense asserting that a criminal defendant acted from an innocent misunderstanding of fact rather than from a criminal purpose.

In contrast with the ancient common-law maxim that "ignorance of the law is no excuse," at common law, ignorance or **mistake of fact**, guarded by an honest purpose, afforded a defendant a sufficient excuse for a supposed criminal act. American courts have agreed but have generally said that a mistake of fact will not be recognized as a defense to a general-intent crime unless the mistake is a reasonable one for a person to make under the circumstances. However, even an unreasonable mistake may be asserted as a defense to a crime that requires a specific intent. The decisions in recent years have indicated that a mistake of fact may be a defense as long as it negates the existence of the mental state essential to the crime charged. See, for example, *State v. Fuentes*, 577 P.2d 452 (N.M. App. 1978). Some jurisdictions have codified the mistake-of-fact defense. In Indiana, for example, mistake of fact is an affirmative defense by statute:

> It is a defense that the person who engaged in the prohibited conduct was reasonably mistaken about a matter of fact if the mistake negates the culpability required for commission of the offense. West's Ind. Code Ann. § 35-41-3-7.

In strict liability offenses, the defense of mistake of fact is unavailing because these offenses are not based on intent (see Chapter 4). In pointing out that this view represents the weight of authority, the Montana Supreme Court held that neither ignorance nor even a *bona fide* belief that a minor was of legal age constituted a defense to prosecution for selling intoxicating liquor to a minor, unless expressly made so by the statute. *State v. Parr*, 283 P.2d 1086 (Mont. 1955). Likewise, because having consensual sexual relations with a minor is generally considered a strict liability offense, a mistake of fact as to a minor's age is generally not a defense to a charge of statutory rape. Even if a court finds that a statutory rape statute requires proof of a general criminal intent to convict, a defendant's reasonable mistake of fact concerning a female's age is generally not available as a defense. *State v. Stiffler*, 788 P.2d 220 (Idaho 1990). In 1964, however, the California Supreme Court departed from this almost universally accepted rule and held that an accused's good-faith, reasonable belief that a female had reached the age of consent would be a defense to statutory rape. *People v. Hernandez*, 393 P.2d 673 (Cal. 1964).

Other state courts have noted, but not followed, the view of the Supreme Court of California. In 1993 the Court of Appeals in Maryland held that a rape statute prohibiting sexual intercourse with underage persons defines a strict liability offense. The court explained that the statute does not require the prosecution to prove *mens rea* and makes no allowance for a mistake-of-fact defense. *Garnett v. State*, 632 A.2d 797 (Md. App. 1993). A dissenting judge acknowledged the rationale for protecting very young females but challenged such statutes that protect young women: "But when age limits are raised to sixteen, eighteen, and twenty-one, when the young girl becomes a young woman, when adolescent boys as well as young men are attracted to her, the sexual act begins to lose its quality of abnormality and physical danger to the victim. Bona fide mistakes in the age of girls can be made by men and boys who are no more dangerous than others of their social, economic and educational level." *Id.* at 815.

In the past few years, in cases of statutory rape, some trial courts have heard arguments based on a minor's right to privacy. The contention is that because a minor female can consent to an abortion, she should be able to consent to sexual intercourse. Although this argument has generally fallen on deaf ears, some trial judges have questioned the need to continue to employ a strict liability standard in consensual sexual relationships where the female is a minor but appears to be an adult and represents herself as such.

**CASE-IN-POINT**

### Mistake of Fact

Robert Eric Freeman agreed to sell cocaine to Keith Hatcher who, unbeknownst to Freeman, was working with the police. Freeman gave Hatcher approximately two grams of what was supposed to be cocaine in exchange for $200. Freeman was convicted of "delivering a simulated controlled substance with respect to a substance represented to be cocaine." Freeman appealed, claiming that he could not be "convicted of delivering a simulated controlled substance when, in fact, he believed he was delivering deliver cocaine." The relevant Iowa statute defined "simulated controlled substance" as "a substance which is not a controlled substance but which is expressly represented to be a controlled substance, or a substance

which is not a controlled substance but which is impliedly represented to be a controlled substance and which because of its nature, packaging, or appearance would lead a reasonable person to believe it to be a controlled substance." Based on the literal reading of the statute and an examination of the relevant case law, the Iowa Supreme Court held "that a person who delivers a substance that is not a controlled substance, but who knowingly represents the substance to be a controlled substance, commits the offense of delivery of a simulated controlled substance regardless of whether the person believed that the substance was controlled or not controlled." Therefore, mistake of fact is no defense in this particular case; conviction affirmed.

*State v. Freeman*, 450 N.W.2d 826 (Iowa 1990)

Writing in the *University of Mississippi Law Journal,* Alexandra Hutton Oglesby has recommended that legislatures should at least provide "the availability of an affirmative defense of reasonable mistake of age when evidence suggests that the defendant honestly and reasonably believed he or she was conducting himself or herself within the boundaries of a constitutional 'safety zone' surrounding private consensual sexual activities engaged in with another legal adult." 76 Miss. L.J. 1067, 1099 (Spring 2007).

## Defenses Justifying the Use of Force

**justifiable use of force** The necessary and reasonable use of force by a person in self-defense, defense of another, or defense of property.

**deadly force** The degree of force that may result in the death of the person against whom the force is applied.

**nondeadly force** Force that does not result in death.

**self-defense** The protection of one's person against an attack.

When offering a defense justifying the use of force, a defendant admits to an offense but claims that his or her conduct was justified under the circumstances. The use of force may be a defense to a criminal charge that the defendant caused injury or death to another. Therefore, the defense of **justifiable use of force** applies to the assaultive and homicidal offenses.

As a starting point, the use of **deadly force** (that is, force likely to cause death or serious bodily injury) must be distinguished from the use of **nondeadly force**. In general, the use of deadly force in self-defense requires that the person using such force (1) be in a place where he or she has a right to be, (2) act without fault, and (3) act in reasonable fear or apprehension of death or great bodily harm. *Lilly v. State*, 506 N.E.2d 23 (Ind. 1987). In evaluating whether the use of deadly force is reasonable, courts consider numerous factors. Among these are the sizes, ages, and physical abilities of the parties; whether the attacker was armed; and the attacker's reputation for violence. Ordinarily, a person may use whatever nondeadly force appears reasonably necessary under the circumstances. *State v. Clay*, 256 S.E.2d 176 (N.C. 1979).

### Self-Defense

Defendants frequently admit the commission of acts that constitute an assaultive or homicidal offense but claim to have acted in **self-defense**. Unlike most other affirmative defenses, when a defendant raises the issue of self-defense, the prosecution generally must prove beyond a reasonable doubt that the accused did not act in self-defense. *Wash v. State*, 456 N.E.2d 1009 (Ind. 1983). Variations exist in the law on the permitted degree of force that can be used in self-defense, but the test of reasonableness appears common to all views. In determining the lawfulness of force used in self-defense, courts first look to see if the force used by the aggressor was unlawful. If so, the defender must show that there was a necessity to use force for self-protection and that the degree of force used by the defender was reasonable considering the parties and circumstances. The following Wisconsin statute nicely summarizes the general law on use of force in self-defense:

> A person is privileged to threaten or intentionally use force against another for the purpose of preventing or terminating what the actor reasonably believes to be an unlawful interference with his or her person by such other person. The actor may intentionally use only such force or threat thereof as he reasonably believes is necessary to prevent or terminate the interference. The actor may not intentionally use force which is intended or likely to cause death or great bodily harm unless the actor reasonably believes that such force is necessary to prevent imminent death or great bodily harm to himself or herself. Wis. Stat. Ann. § 939.48(1).

At common law, a person attacked had a duty "to retreat to the wall" before using deadly force in self-defense. *State v. Sipes*, 209 N.W. 458 (Iowa 1926). In *Scott v. State*, 34 So.2d 718 (Miss. 1948), the court explained that to justify the slaying of another in self-defense at common law, there must have been actual danger of loss of life or suffering of great bodily harm. But the court said that the American approach has been that the danger need not be actual but must be "reasonably apparent and imminent."

Most courts reject the common-law doctrine of requiring a person to retreat to the greatest extent possible before meeting force with force. Rather, they say that a person attacked or threatened may stand his or her ground and use any force reasonably necessary to prevent harm. Courts that take this view often state it in positive terms, as did the Oklahoma Court of Criminal Appeals when citing one of its 1912 precedents: "The law in Oklahoma is clear: There is no duty to retreat if one is threatened with bodily harm." *Neal v. State*, 597 P.2d 334, 337 (Okl. Crim. App. 1979).

A substantial minority of courts, however, have adopted the principle that a person who can safely retreat must do so before using deadly force. But courts that follow the **retreat rule** have generally adopted the principle that a person does not have to retreat in his or her own dwelling. *State v. Bennett*, 105 N.W. 324 (Iowa 1905).

**retreat rule** The common-law requirement that a person being attacked "retreat to the wall" before using deadly force in self-defense.

### "Stand Your Ground" Laws

In 2005, Florida enacted a new law expanding the right of self-defense for individuals. The law, which amended Florida Statutes § 776.013 effective October 1, 2005, provides:

> (1) A person is presumed to have held a reasonable fear of imminent peril of death or great bodily harm to himself or herself or another when using defensive force that is intended or likely to cause death or great bodily harm to another if
>
>> (a) The person against whom the defensive force was used was in the process of unlawfully and forcefully entering, or had unlawfully and forcibly entered, a dwelling, residence, or occupied vehicle, or if that person had removed or was attempting to remove another against that person's will from the dwelling, residence, or occupied vehicle; and

(b) The person who uses defensive force knew or had reason to believe that an unlawful and forcible entry or unlawful and forcible act was occurring or had occurred.

(2) [Includes provisions to protect anyone who has a right to be in a residence, those under lawful guardianship, and law enforcement officers]

(3) A person who is not engaged in an unlawful activity and who is attacked in any other place where he or she has a right to be has no duty to retreat and has the right to stand his or her ground and meet force with force, including deadly force if he or she reasonably believes it is necessary to do so to prevent death or great bodily harm to himself or herself or another or to prevent the commission of a forcible felony.

(4) A person who unlawfully and by force enters or attempts to enter a person's dwelling, residence, or occupied vehicle is presumed to be doing so with the intent to commit an unlawful act involving force or violence.

Florida law now allows individuals to use deadly force in public places without the duty to retreat. It also forbids the arrest, detention, or prosecution of those covered by the law and prohibits civil suits against them. In *State v. Smiley*, 927 So.2d 1000 (Fla. App. 2006), the defendant was prosecuted for first-degree murder occurring on November 6, 2004; he sought to have the jury instructed based on the expanded right of self-defense under Florida Statutes, § 776.013. When the trial court allowed the instruction the state sought review. Because the defendant was charged with an offense committed prior to the effective date of the new statute, the appellate court held that the new Florida law could not be applied retroactively.

Critics of the new law dubbed it a "shoot first" law and predicted that it would lead to preemptive shootings. But despite such criticism, the trend to expand the right of self-defense continued, and by 2009 twenty-five states had adopted **"stand your ground" laws**, rejecting the duty to retreat before using deadly force.

The use of deadly force presents the greatest issue in self-defense. As we noted earlier, deadly force may be used only where it reasonably appears necessary to use such force to prevent death or serious injury. In considering whether a defendant is justified in using deadly force, the law has traditionally applied an **objective test for the use of deadly force**. See, for example, *State v. Bess*, 247 A.2d 669 (N.J. 1968). Today, however, there is a conflict in the decisional law. Some courts apply a **subjective standard of reasonableness** to determine whether circumstances are sufficient to induce in the defendant an honest and reasonable belief that force must be used. See, for example, *State v. Wanrow*, 559 P.2d 548 (Wash. 1977). Although the objective test requires the jury to place itself in the shoes of a hypothetical "reasonable and prudent person," the subjective test permits a jury "to place itself in the defendant's own shoes."

Much of the impetus for courts' applying the subjective test to determine whether the use of deadly force is reasonable has resulted from cases where women charged with committing assaultive or homicidal offenses against men have defended their use of force. In *State v. Wanrow*, supra, a woman on crutches was convicted of second-degree murder and first-degree assault in her fatal shooting of a large, intoxicated man who refused to leave her home. In reversing her convictions, the Washington Supreme Court held that the trial judge erred by giving instructions to the jury that did not make it clear that Wanrow's actions were to be judged against her own subjective impressions and not those that the jury might determine to be objectively reasonable.

---

**"stand your ground" laws** Statutes providing that a person faced with a threat of bodily harm may use force to repel the threat and is not required to retreat.

**objective test for the use of deadly force** Under this test, the judge or jury places themselves in the shoes of a hypothetical reasonable and prudent person to determine whether a defendant's use of deadly force was permissible.

**subjective standard of reasonableness** A test used by courts to determine whether it was appropriate for a defendant to use deadly force in self-defense. Under this approach, the jury is asked to place itself in the shoes of the defendant.

**CASE-IN-POINT**

### The Trayvon Martin Shooting: Murder or Self-Defense?

On the night of February 26, 2012, George Zimmerman shot and killed Trayvon Martin inside a gated community in Sanford, Florida. Zimmerman, a twenty-eight-year-old Hispanic male, was the neighborhood watch coordinator for the community. Martin, seventeen-year-old African American male, was temporarily staying at a home in that community. While driving in his car, Zimmerman observed Martin walking around in the community and called police to report a suspicious person. Zimmerman, who was armed with a pistol, then left his vehicle and confronted Martin. There were no witnesses to what happened next, but when police arrived they found Martin dead from a single shot to the chest at close range. Zimmerman,

who was bleeding from the nose and had two lacerations on his head, told police that Martin had attacked him and that he fired his weapon in self-defense. After detaining and questioning him for five hours, police released Zimmerman without charging him with an offense. The incident was widely covered in the media and produced widespread outrage at what many perceived to be racism on the part of Zimmerman and the police. A special prosecutor appointed by the governor charged Zimmerman with second-degree murder. Zimmerman pleaded not guilty to the charge and was released on a $1 million bond pending trial. The case increased racial tensions throughout the country but also ignited a debate about Florida's "stand your ground" law.

*© Cengage Learning 2014*

### The Battered Woman Syndrome

Beyond the subjective standard of self-defense, in recent years the concept of self-defense by women has been expanded to include circumstances where a woman claims to have been continually battered by a man. The "battered spouse syndrome" soon became the **battered woman syndrome (BWS)**. It describes a pattern of psychological and behavioral symptoms of a woman living with a male in a battering relationship. Some jurisdictions now permit a woman who is charged with assaulting or killing a man to show that even though she did not face immediate harm, her plea of self-defense should be recognized because her actions were her response to constant battering by the man with whom she lived.

Decisional law is in the developing stage on the admissibility of expert testimony concerning the battered woman syndrome, with the trend being to hold that when a woman kills her batterer and pleads self-defense, expert testimony about BWS is admissible to explain how her particular experiences as a battered woman affected her perceptions of danger and her honest belief in its imminence. *State v. Hill*, 339 S.E.2d 121 (S.C. 1986); *People v. Aris*, 264 Cal. Rptr. 167 (Cal. App. 1989). In *Commonwealth v. Rodriquez*, 418 633 N.E.2d 1039 (Mass. 1994), the Supreme Judicial Court of Massachusetts found that the trial court erred in refusing to admit evidence of the battered woman syndrome where a defendant who stabbed her boyfriend during an argument claimed she did so in self-defense.

In some instances, legislatures have enacted statutes to provide for admission of such evidence. See, for example, § 563.033 of the Missouri Statutes Annotated, which provides, "Evidence that the actor was suffering from the battered spouse syndrome shall be admissible upon the issue of whether the actor lawfully acted in self-defense or defense of another."

Increasingly, courts are recognizing the role of the battered woman syndrome, not as an independent defense but as furnishing support for a woman's defense where a woman shows that she has been acting under coercion of a male. In *United*

**battered woman syndrome (BWS)** A group of symptoms typically manifested by a woman who has suffered continued physical or mental abuse, usually from a male with whom she lives.

*States v. Brown*, 891 F. Supp. 1501, 1505 (D. Kan. 1995), the court explained that although a woman cannot rely on the syndrome as a complete defense,

> it is some evidence to be considered to support a defense, such as self-defense, duress, compulsion, and coercion. Because women who suffer from the battered woman syndrome do not act in a typical manner as compared with women who do not suffer from it, evidence of the syndrome is used to explain their behavior. Evidence of the syndrome is presented through expert testimony to assist the jury's evaluation of the defendant's state of mind.

In *State v. Haines*, 860 N.E.2d 91 (Ohio 2006), the Ohio Supreme Court agreed that expert testimony regarding the battered woman syndrome can be admitted to help the jury determine whether the defendant had reasonable grounds for an honest belief that she was in imminent danger when considering the issue of self-defense. "Expert testimony on the battered woman syndrome," the court said, "would help dispel the ordinary lay person's perception that a woman in a battering relationship is free to leave at any time." 860 N.E.2d at 98.

### The Battered Child Syndrome

Where there is evidence that a child has been abused continually over an extended period, there is a movement now to assert the **battered child syndrome** (BCS) in defense of a child accused of assaulting or killing a parent. Many prosecutors claim that the use of BCS is undermining the law of self-defense, yet there are experts who claim that a child's perceptions of the need to use force are shaped by his or her experience of constant abuse by a parent. These experts argue that when juries hear such evidence, they may be persuaded that a child acted in self-defense and not out of retribution.

In the state of Washington, a boy who killed his stepfather was convicted of second-degree murder and two counts of second-degree assault. At his trial, the court held that evidence of the battered child syndrome could not, as a matter of law, support a finding of self-defense because there was no "imminent threat" to the defendant. In a much-discussed opinion, the appellate court held that this ruling was in error: "Neither law nor logic suggest any reason to limit to women recognition of the impact a battering relationship may have on the victim's actions or perceptions. . . . [T]he rationale underlying the admissibility of testimony regarding the battered women syndrome is at least as compelling, if not more so, when applied to children." *State v. Janes*, 822 P.2d 1238, 1243 (Wash. App. 1992).

In 1993 California charged Erik and Lyle Menendez, ages eighteen and twenty-one, respectively, with the murder of their parents. Although the defendants admitted killing their parents, they claimed to have been victims of parental abuse. Their first two trials ended in mistrials because the jurors could not agree on a verdict. In March 1996, the Menendez brothers were convicted and sentenced to life in prison without the possibility of parole.

## Defense of Others

At common law, a defender had the right to use reasonable force to prevent commission of a felony or to protect members of the household who were endangered, a principle that was codified in many jurisdictions. See, for example, *State v. Fair*, 211 A.2d 359 (N.J. 1965). The trend in American jurisdictions is to allow a person "to stand in the shoes of the victim" and to use such **reasonable force** as is necessary to defend

**battered child syndrome (BCS)** A group of symptoms typically manifested by a child who has suffered continued physical or mental abuse, often from a parent or person having custody of the child.

**reasonable force** The maximum degree of force that is necessary to accomplish a lawful purpose.

anyone, irrespective of relationship, from harm. As the court noted in *State v. Grier*, "What one may do for himself, he may do for another." 609 S.W.2d 201, 203 (Mo. App. 1980). Today a number of states have statutes that permit a person to assert force on behalf of another. To illustrate, the Wisconsin statute provides as follows:

> A person is privileged to defend a third person from real or apparent unlawful interference by another under the same conditions and by the same means as those under and by which the person is privileged to defend himself or herself from real or apparent unlawful interference, provided that the person reasonably believes that the facts are such that the third person would be privileged to act in self-defense and that the person's intervention is necessary for the protection of the third person. Wis. Stat. Ann. § 939.48(4).

Like the quoted Wisconsin statute, statutes in many other states limit a person's right to defend another individual from harm to those persons who "reasonably believe" that force is necessary to protect another. Some courts take a more restrictive view and hold that an intervenor is justified in using force to defend another only if the party being defended would have been justified in using the same force in self-defense. Under either standard, however, the right to go to the **defense of others** does not authorize a person to resort to retaliatory force.

> **defense of others** The defense asserted by one who claims the right to use reasonable force to prevent the commission of a felony against another person.

In *People v. Kurr*, 654 N.W.2d 651 (Mich. App. 2002), a Michigan appellate court held that the defense-of-others concept extends to the protection of a nonviable fetus from an assault against the mother. The court concluded that in enacting Mich. Comp. Laws Ann. § 750.90a *et seq.* (Fetal Protection Act), which provides penalties for harming a fetus or embryo during an intentional assault against a pregnant woman, the legislature determined that fetuses are worthy of protection as living entities.

## Defense of Habitation

The common law placed great emphasis on the security of a person's dwelling and permitted the use of deadly force against an intruder. *Russell v. State*, 122 So. 683 (Ala. 1929). This historical view was chronicled by the Illinois Supreme Court in *People v. Eatman*:

> As a matter of history the defense of habitation has been the most favored branch of self-defense from the earliest times. Lord Coke, in his Commentaries, says: "A man's home is his castle—for where shall a man be safe if it be not in his house?" 91 N.E.2d 387, 390 (Ill. 1950).

> **defense of habitation** The right of a defendant charged with an offense to assert that he or she used reasonable force to protect his or her home or property.

> **castle doctrine** An exception to the retreat rule allowing the use of deadly force by a person who is protecting his or her home and its inhabitants from attack, especially from a trespasser who intends to commit a felony or inflict serious bodily harm.

Referring to a person's **defense of habitation**, the *Eatman* court opined that "he may use all of the force apparently necessary to repel any invasion of his home." 91 N.E.2d at 390. This is sometimes referred to as the **castle doctrine**. Even though a householder may, under some circumstances, be justified in using deadly force, the householder would not be justified in taking a life to repel a mere trespass.

In *State v. McCombs*, 253 S.E.2d 906 (N.C. 1979), the North Carolina Supreme Court addressed the issue of using deadly force to protect one's home. The court said that the use of deadly force is generally justified to prevent a forcible entry into the habitation in circumstances such where the occupant is threatened, or reasonably apprehends death or great bodily harm to self or other occupants, or reasonably believes the assailant intends to commit a felony. Although this decision states the law generally applied by the courts, some statutory and decisional variations exist.

**CASE-IN-POINT**

## Defense of Habitation

Defendant Raines was charged with murder in connection with the death of Stinson. Stinson was the passenger in a car driven by Neese. The evidence showed that Neese had threatened to kill Raines and that Neese had driven past Raines's trailer and fired some shots out the window of his car. Raines was not home at the time, but when he returned, his live-in companion, Quates, told him what had happened. A few minutes later they heard a car approaching and went outside. Quates identified the car as the same one from which the shots had been fired. As the car drove away, Raines fired five shots from a semiautomatic rifle. Quates testified that Raines said that "he'd just shoot the tire out and stop it and we'd go get the law and find out who

it was." However, one of the bullets struck Stinson in the head, killing him. Despite his plea that he acted in self-defense and defense of his habitation, Raines was convicted of manslaughter.

The conviction was upheld on appeal, with the appellate court saying that "although Raines may well have been in fear of danger when the . . . car approached, such fear alone did not justify his firing at the car as it drove down the public road past his trailer." As the court further observed, "One assaulted in his house need not flee therefrom. But his house is his castle only for the purposes of defense. It cannot be turned into an arsenal for the purpose of offensive effort against the lives of others."

*Raines v. State*, 455 So.2d 967 (Ala. Crim. App. 1984).

## Defense of Property

The right to defend your property is more limited than the right to defend your home or yourself. The common law allowed a person in lawful possession of property to use reasonable, but not deadly, force to protect it. *Russell v. State*, supra. Today, the use of force to protect a person's property is often defined by statute. Typically, Iowa law provides that "[a] person is justified in the use of reasonable force to prevent or terminate criminal interference with his or her possession or other right to property." Iowa Code Ann. § 704.4. The quoted statutory language generally represents contemporary decisional law even in the absence of a statute. The prevailing view of the courts is that, in the absence of the felonious use of force by an aggressor, a person must not inflict deadly harm simply for the protection or recapture of property. *State v. McCombs*, supra. This is because the law places higher value on preserving the life of the wrongdoer than on protecting someone's property.

One method of defending property has been through the use of a mechanical device commonly known as a "spring gun" that is set to go off when someone trips a wire or opens a door. In the earlier history of the country, these devices were used on farms, in unoccupied structures, and sometimes in residences at night to wound or kill intruders. Some early court decisions said that use of a spring gun that resulted in the death of an intruder into a person's home was justified in instances where a homeowner, if present, would have been authorized to use deadly force.

Today, if someone is killed or injured as a result of a spring gun or similar mechanical device, the party who set it (and anyone who caused it to be set) generally will be held criminally responsible for any resulting death or injury. This is true even if the intruder's conduct would ordinarily cause a party to believe that the intrusion threatened death or serious bodily injury, conditions that might justify the use of deadly force.

The Model Penal Code § 3.06(5) takes the position that a device for the protection of property may be used only if

> (a) the device is not designed to cause or known to create a substantial risk of causing death or serious bodily harm; and

(b) the use of the particular device to protect the property from entry or trespass is reasonable under the circumstances, as the actor believes them to be; and

(c) the device is one customarily used for such a purpose or reasonable care is taken to make known to probable intruders the fact that it is used.

Even courts in jurisdictions that have not adopted the MPC view take a harsh view of the use of such mechanical devices, reasoning that to allow persons to use them can imperil the lives of innocent persons such as firefighters, police officers, and even children at play. Finally, some courts point to another reason: although a deadly mechanical device acts without mercy or discretion, there is always the possibility that a human being protecting property would avoid taking a human life or injuring someone. See *People v. Ceballos*, 526 P.2d 241 (Cal. 1974).

## Defense to Being Arrested

At common law, a person had the right to use such force as reasonably necessary, short of killing, to resist an unlawful arrest. The common-law rule developed at a time when bail was largely unavailable, arraignments were delayed for months until a royal judge arrived, and conditions in English jails were deplorable. Most American courts followed the English view. See, for example, *State v. Small*, 169 N.W. 116 (Iowa 1918). In some states a person may still forcibly resist an unlawful arrest.

As pointed out in Chapter 13, however, the rationale for the rule has substantially eroded. Increasingly, legislatures and courts recognize that resisting an arrest exposes both the officer and the arrestee to escalating violence. Moreover, defendants are now promptly arraigned, and counsel is generally available to debate the legality of an arrest in court. See *United States v. Ferrone*, 438 F.2d 381 (3d Cir. 1971). Today the majority of states, either by statute or judicial decision, provide that a person may not resist an arrest, even if it is illegal.

# Defenses Based on Constitutional and Statutory Authority

In earlier chapters we mentioned that, subject to certain exceptions, the First Amendment to the Constitution provides a defense for legitimate speech, press, assembly, and religious activities. We also discussed how the Due Process Clauses of the Fifth and Fourteenth Amendments permit one to defend against criminal charges based on statutes that are void for vagueness.

In this section we discuss two significant constitutional defenses asserted by defendants in criminal cases: immunity and double jeopardy. In addition, we mention here the defense provided by statutes of limitations, which are legislative enactments establishing time limits for prosecution of most offenses.

## Constitutional Immunity

Everyone is familiar with the scenario of the witness who invokes the constitutional privilege against self-incrimination based on the Fifth Amendment to the Constitution, which provides that "no person . . . shall be compelled in any criminal case to be a witness against himself." The privilege against self-incrimination is applicable to the states through the Fourteenth Amendment, *Malloy v. Hogan*, 378 U.S. 1, 84

S.Ct. 1489, 12 L.Ed.2d 653 (1964), although states have similar protections in their constitutions.

The privilege against self-incrimination guaranteed by the federal constitution is a personal one that applies only to natural persons and not corporations. *United States v. White*, 322 U.S. 694, 64 S.Ct. 1248, 88 L.Ed. 1542 (1944). A strict reading of the clause would limit the privilege to testimony given in a criminal trial. However, the Supreme Court has held that an individual may refuse "to answer official questions put to him in any . . . proceeding, civil or criminal, formal or informal, where the answers might incriminate him in future criminal proceedings." *Lefkowitz v. Turley*, 414 U.S. 70, 77, 94 S.Ct. 316, 322, 38 L.Ed.2d 274, 281 (1973). A classic example is the privilege of suspects in police custody to invoke their *Miranda* rights.

Frequently, when a witness invokes the Fifth Amendment and refuses to testify, the court is requested to compel the witness's testimony. This may be accomplished by conferring **immunity** on the witness, which is a grant of amnesty to protect the witness from prosecution through the use of compelled testimony. A witness compelled to give incriminating testimony thus receives **use immunity** (that is, the testimony given cannot be used against the witness). This form of immunity (sometimes referred to as "derivative immunity") is coextensive with the scope of the privilege against self-incrimination and meets the demands of the Constitution. *Kastigar v. United States*, 406 U.S. 441, 92 S.Ct. 1653, 32 L.Ed.2d 212 (1972).

In some states a witness who testifies under a grant of immunity is given **transactional immunity**, a broader protection than is required under the federal constitution. Transactional immunity protects a witness from prosecution for any activity mentioned in the witness's testimony. An example of requiring broader protection occurred in 1993 when the Alaska Supreme Court ruled that its state constitution requires that witnesses who are compelled to testify be given the more protective transactional immunity from prosecution, rather than the use immunity or derivative immunity required by the federal constitution. *State v. Gonzalez*, 853 P.2d 526 (Alaska 1993). A defendant may assert the defense of immunity by a pretrial motion. Despite a grant of immunity, a witness may be prosecuted for making material false statements under oath. *United States v. Apfelbaum*, 445 U.S. 115, 100 S.Ct. 948, 63 L.Ed.2d 250 (1980) (see Chapter 13).

## Other Forms of Immunity

Sometimes a prosecutor, with approval of the court, grants a witness **contractual immunity**. The purpose is to induce a suspect to testify against someone and thereby enable the prosecution to obtain a conviction not otherwise obtainable because of the constitutional protection against self-incrimination. This type of immunity is rarely granted if other available evidence will lead to a conviction. The authority to grant immunity in federal courts is vested in the U.S. Attorney with approval of the Attorney General or certain authorized assistants. 18 U.S.C.A. § 6003(b). At the state level, such authority is generally vested in the chief prosecuting officer (that is, the district or state attorney).

Under international law, persons who have diplomatic status and serve as part of a diplomatic mission, as well as members of their staff and households, are immune from arrest and prosecution, thus enjoying **diplomatic immunity**. The expectation, of course, is that American diplomats and their dependents and staff members will enjoy like immunity in foreign nations. Diplomatic immunity attaches to the sovereign state, not to the individual diplomat. In instances of egregious misconduct, a foreign state may be asked to waive the diplomat's immunity. In 1997, Republic of

**immunity** Exemption from civil suit or prosecution. See also **use immunity** and **transactional immunity**.

**use immunity** A grant of immunity that forbids prosecutors from using immunized testimony as evidence in criminal prosecutions.

**transactional immunity** A grant of immunity applying to all offenses that a witness's testimony relates to.

**contractual immunity** A grant by a prosecutor with approval of a court that makes a witness immune from prosecution in exchange for the witness's testimony.

**diplomatic immunity** A privilege to be free from arrest and prosecution that is granted under international law to diplomats, their staff, and their household members.

legislative immunity
Either of two special
immunities given to
members of Congress:
(1) the exemption from
arrest while attending a
session of the body to
which the member be-
longs, excluding an arrest
for treason, breach of the
peace or a felony; or (2)
the exemption from ar-
rest or questioning for any
speech or debate entered
into during a legislative
session.

Georgia envoy Gueorgui Makharadze was involved in a traffic accident in Washington, D.C., while driving while intoxicated. The accident resulted in the death of one person and injuries to four others. At the request of the U.S. government, Georgia withdrew Makharadze's diplomatic immunity. He pled guilty to involuntary manslaughter and aggravated assault and was sentenced to prison.

Another form of immunity is referred to as **legislative immunity** and is constitutionally based. Article I, Section 6 of the U.S. Constitution provides that members of Congress, in all cases except treason, felony, and breach of the peace, are privileged from arrest during attendance at and in going to and returning from legislative sessions. State constitutions generally include similar provisions for state lawmakers.

## Double Jeopardy

The concept of forbidding retrial of a defendant who has been found not guilty developed from the common law. *Ex parte Lange*, 85 U.S. (18 Wall.) 163, 21 L.Ed. 872 (1873). The Fifth Amendment to the U.S. Constitution embodies this principle: "[N]or shall any person be subject for the same offence to be twice put in jeopardy of life or limb." The Double Jeopardy Clause was made applicable to the states through the Fourteenth Amendment in *Benton v. Maryland*, 395 U.S. 784, 89 S.Ct. 2056, 23 L.Ed.2d 707 (1969). Even before that, all states provided essentially the same protection through their constitutions or statutes, or through judicial decisions recognizing common-law principles.

In a 1957 Supreme Court decision, Justice Hugo L. Black expressed the rationale underlying the Double Jeopardy Clause:

> The underlying idea, one that is deeply ingrained in at least the Anglo-American system of jurisprudence, is that the State with all its resources and power should not be allowed to make repeated attempts to convict an individual for an alleged offense, thereby subjecting him to embarrassment, expense and ordeal and compelling him to live in a continuing state of anxiety and insecurity, as well as enhancing the possibility that even though innocent he may be found guilty. *Green v. United States*, 355 U.S. 184, 187–188, 78 S.Ct. 221, 223, 2 L.Ed.2d 199, 204 (1957).

double jeopardy The
condition of being tried
twice for the same criminal
offense.

The subject of **double jeopardy** is very complex, but certain principles seem clear. Jeopardy attaches once the jury is sworn in, *Crist v. Bretz*, 437 U.S. 28, 98 S.Ct. 2156, 57 L.Ed.2d 24 (1978), or when the first witness is sworn in to testify in a nonjury trial, *Serfass v. United States*, 420 U.S. 377, 95 S.Ct. 1055, 43 L.Ed.2d 265 (1975). The defense of double jeopardy may be asserted by pretrial motion.

insufficient evidence Evidence that falls short of establishing what is required
by law, usually referring
to evidence that does not
legally establish an offense
or a defense.

weight of the evidence
The balance or prepon-
derance of the evidence.
Weight of the evidence is
to be distinguished from
"legal sufficiency of the
evidence," which is the
concern of an appellate
court.

The Double Jeopardy Clause forbids a second prosecution for the same offense after a defendant has been acquitted. *Ball v. United States*, 163 U.S. 662, 16 S.Ct. 1192, 41 L.Ed. 300 (1896). In recent years, this principle has been applied even after a conviction. *United States v. Wilson*, 420 U.S. 332, 95 S.Ct. 1013, 43 L.Ed.2d 232 (1975). But if a defendant appeals a conviction and prevails, it is not double jeopardy for the prosecution to retry the defendant, unless the appellate court rules that there was insufficient evidence to sustain the defendant's conviction. *Burks v. United States*, 437 U.S. 1, 98 S.Ct. 2141, 57 L.Ed.2d 1 (1978). Note the distinction between a conviction reversed by a higher court on the basis of **insufficient evidence** and a conviction that is vacated, with a new trial ordered, based on the **weight of the evidence**. In the latter case, a retrial of the defendant would not constitute double jeopardy. *Tibbs v. Florida*, 457 U.S. 31, 102 S.Ct. 2211, 72 L.Ed.2d 652 (1982). Nor is it double jeopardy to retry a defendant if the trial court, at the defendant's request, has declared a mistrial. *Oregon v. Kennedy*, 456 U.S. 667, 102 S.Ct. 2083, 72

### Double Jeopardy

In a high-profile case in 1992, four Los Angeles police officers were tried by jury in a California state court on charges arising out of the beating of Rodney King, an African American motorist stopped by the police for traffic infractions. The event was videotaped by an onlooker and televised nationally. The jury's verdict of not guilty was followed by considerable outrage and large-scale rioting in Los Angeles. Despite the acquittal on state charges, the federal government brought new charges against the officers for violating King's civil rights. Their pleas that the new federal charges were barred by the Double Jeopardy Clause of the Fifth Amendment were rejected by the U.S. District Court, and in April 1993 two of the four officers were convicted after a jury trial. 833 F. Supp. 769. On appeal, the Ninth Circuit said that "there is no evidence that the federal prosecution was a 'sham' or a 'cover' for the state prosecution."

*United States v. Koon*, 34 F.3d 1416 (9th Cir. 1994).

**manifest necessity** That which is clearly or obviously necessary or essential.

L.Ed.2d 416 (1982). If, however, the government moves for a mistrial, the defendant objects, and the court grants the mistrial, the prosecution must establish a **manifest necessity** for the mistrial in order for a retrial to be permitted. An example of a manifest necessity might be a highly improper opening statement by the defendant's counsel. *Arizona v. Washington*, 434 U.S. 497, 98 S.Ct. 824, 54 L.Ed.2d 717 (1978).

Some offenses are crimes against both the federal and state governments. The policy, and in some instances state law, forbids a second prosecution once an offender has been prosecuted in a different jurisdiction. Because separate sovereigns are involved, under our federal system the Double Jeopardy Clause does not preclude prosecution by both the federal and state governments. *Bartkus v. Illinois*, 359 U.S. 121, 79 S.Ct. 676, 3 L.Ed.2d 684 (1959). Nevertheless, this principle does not allow two courts within a state to try an accused for the same offense. Therefore, a person who has been prosecuted in a city or county court cannot be tried again in any court in the state for the same offense. *Waller v. Florida*, 397 U.S. 387, 90 S.Ct. 1184, 25 L.Ed.2d 435 (1970).

In addition to protecting against a second prosecution for the same offense after conviction or acquittal, the Double Jeopardy Clause protects against multiple punishments for the same offense. *North Carolina v. Pearce*, 395 U.S. 711, 89 S.Ct. 2072, 23 L.Ed.2d 656 (1969). However, the Constitution does not define "same offense." In 1932 the Supreme Court said the following:

> The applicable rule is that, where the same act or transaction constitutes a violation of two distinct statutory provisions, the test to be applied to determine whether there are two offenses or only one is whether each provision requires proof of an additional fact which the other does not. *Blockburger v. United States*, 284 U.S. 299, 304, 52 S.Ct. 180, 182, 76 L.Ed. 306, 309 (1932).

**Blockburger test** A test applied by courts to determine if the charges against a defendant would constitute a violation of the constitutional prohibition against double jeopardy—that is, being tried twice for the same offense. The *Blockburger* test holds that it is not double jeopardy for a defendant to be tried for two offenses if each offense includes an element that the other offense does not.

The ***Blockburger* test** compares the elements of the crimes in question. It is a tool of interpretation and creates a presumption of legislative intent, but it is not designed to contravene such intent. Rather, the Supreme Court has said that the "legislative intent," if clear, determines the scope of what constitutes "same offenses." *Missouri v. Hunter*, 459 U.S. 359, 103 S.Ct. 673, 74 L.Ed.2d 535 (1983); *Albernaz v. United States*, 450 U.S. 333, 101 S.Ct. 1137, 67 LEd.2d 275 (1981). In 1980 the Supreme Court reviewed a case where the defendant was first convicted of failing to slow down to avoid an accident with his car. Later he was charged with manslaughter arising from the same incident. After reciting the "elements" test in *Blockburger*, the Court stated that if in the pending manslaughter prosecution Illinois relies on and proves a failure to slow to avoid an accident as the reckless act necessary to prove manslaughter, Vitale [the defendant] would have a substantial claim of double jeopardy under the Fifth and Fourteenth Amendments of the U.S. Constitution. *Illinois v. Vitale*, 447 U.S. 410, 420, 100 S.Ct. 2260, 2267, 65 L.Ed.2d 228, 238 (1980).

The *Blockburger* test examines the elements, not the facts. Since the Supreme Court's decision in *Illinois v. Vitale*, supra, not all courts have regarded *Blockburger* as the exclusive method of determining whether successive prosecutions violate the principle of double jeopardy. Indeed, some courts look also to the evidence to be presented to prove those crimes. For example, the Connecticut Supreme Court, citing *Vitale*, held that the prosecution of a defendant for operating a vehicle under the influence of intoxicants after being acquitted for manslaughter with a motor vehicle while intoxicated was barred by the principle of double jeopardy. Even though the offenses were not the same under the *Blockburger* test, the evidence offered to prove that a violation of the offense charged in the first prosecution was to be the sole evidence offered to prove an element of the offense charged in the second prosecution. Thus, the court held that the second prosecution was barred by the principle of double jeopardy. *State v. Lonergan*, 566 A.2d 677 (Conn. 1989). Other courts continue to determine the issue of double jeopardy by applying the *Blockburger* test. See, for example, *Butler v. State*, 816 S.W.2d 124 (Tex. App. 1991).

In *Grady v. Corbin*, 495 U.S. 508, 110 S.Ct 2084, 109 L.Ed.2d 548 (1990), the Supreme Court, by a 5–4 vote, continued to follow the approach in *Vitale*. The Court said that "if to establish an essential element of an offense charged in that prosecution, the government will prove conduct that constitutes an offense for which the defendant has already been prosecuted," a second prosecution may not be undertaken. 495 U.S. at 510, 110 S.Ct. at 2087, 109 L.Ed.2d at 557. This became known as the

**same evidence test** A test applicable to the Double Jeopardy Clause of the Fifth Amendment. If, to establish an essential element of an offense charged, the government will prove conduct that constitutes an offense for which the defendant has already been prosecuted, a second prosecution is barred.

**same elements test** Test that bars separate punishment for offenses that have the same elements or for one offense that includes or is included in another offense.

**same evidence test** and barred a second prosecution based on the same conduct by the defendant that was at issue in the first prosecution. In June 1993, however, in *United States v. Dixon*, 509 U.S. 688, 113 S.Ct. 2849, 125 L.Ed.2d 556 (1993), by a 5–4 margin, the Court overruled *Grady v. Corbin*, replacing the same evidence test for double jeopardy analysis by a return to the **same elements test** from *Blockburger*, which bars punishment for offenses that have the same elements, or when one offense includes or is included in another offense. In *Dixon*, the Court also ruled that a criminal contempt conviction represents a "jeopardy" that triggers the bar against a second prosecution for the same offense. After the Supreme Court's decision in *United States v. Dixon*, the Connecticut Supreme Court revisited its decision in *State v. Lonergan*, 566 A.2d 677 (Conn. 1989) and adopted the *Blockburger* "same elements" approach. *State v. Alvarez*, 778 A.2d 938 (Conn. 2001).

In 1994 the U.S. Supreme Court invalidated a Montana tax on the possession of illegal drugs that was imposed on a party already convicted of possession of illegal drugs. The Court ruled that the added tax was punishment in violation of the Double Jeopardy Clause. *Dept. of Revenue of Montana v. Kurth Ranch*, 511 U.S. 767, 114 S.Ct. 1937, 128 L.Ed.2d 767 (1994). After a defendant won dismissal of DUI-related charges in Colorado on the basis that his driver's license had already been revoked because of the offense, defense attorneys began to assert a double jeopardy defense to DUI prosecutions. They argued that, on the basis of *Montana v. Kurth Ranch*, an administrative revocation of the accused's driver's license constituted "punishment" that barred a subsequent prosecution for DUI. In July 1996, the Colorado Supreme Court unanimously held that "imposition of criminal sanctions subsequent to an administrative driver's license revocation proceeding does not constitute the imposition of multiple punishments and does not violate the Double Jeopardy Clause." *Deutschendorf v. People*, 920 P.2d 53, 61 (Colo. 1996). The court's opinion appears to be consistent with what other courts have said on this issue. In *United States v. Reyes*, 87 F.3d 676 (5th Cir. 1996), the government imposed a three-day unpaid suspension of a civilian Air Force employee for operating a motor vehicle while intoxicated on an Air Force base. In that instance, the court held, the government was acting as an employer, not as a sovereign, and the suspension was not "punishment" under the Double Jeopardy Clause.

As we noted earlier, the dual sovereignty of the federal government and the states allow separate trials of a defendant for the same offense. In the past, this has not been a major problem because it has been governmental policy not to cause duplicate prosecutions. Some deviations from this policy have occurred in recent years, however.

## Statutes of Limitation

**statute of limitations** A law proscribing prosecutions for specific crimes after specified periods of time.

A **statute of limitations** is a legislative enactment that places a time limit on the prosecution of a crime. Common law placed no time limits on prosecution. There is no federal constitutional basis to limit the time in which a prosecution can be initiated. Nonetheless, the federal government and almost all states have enacted laws that prescribe certain time limits for prosecution of most offenses, excluding murder. There are two primary public policy reasons for enacting statutes of limitations on the prosecution of crimes. First, it is generally accepted that a person should not be under threat of prosecution for too long a period. Second, after a prolonged period, proof is either unavailable or, if available, may not be credible.

Statutes of limitations seldom place time limits on prosecutions for murder and other very serious offenses. This was dramatized in 1994, when Byron de la Beckwith was convicted for the June 1963 murder of Medgar Evers. Evers was an official of the National Association for the Advancement of Colored People, and his death galvanized support for the enactment of civil rights laws in the 1960s. Two trials in 1964 ended in deadlocked juries. But after extended litigation and a lapse of more than thirty years since the victim's death, a Mississippi jury found Beckwith guilty of killing Evers. On December 22, 1997, the Mississippi Supreme Court affirmed Beckwith's conviction. *Beckwith v. State*, 707 So.2d 547 (Miss. 1997).

Under most statutes of limitations, the period for prosecution begins when a crime is committed rather than when it is discovered. The period ends when an arrest warrant is issued, an indictment is returned, or an information is filed. The period of limitations is interrupted while a perpetrator is a fugitive or conceals himself or herself from authorities. This cessation of the statute of limitations is often referred to as the **tolling** of the statutory period.

**tolling** Causing to cease. For example, one who conceals himself or herself from the authorities generally causes a tolling of the statutes of limitation on the prosecution of a crime.

Federal statutes of limitations provide a five-year limitation on the prosecution of noncapital crimes. 18 U.S.C.A. § 3282 *et seq.* Although limitation periods vary among the states, the Ohio law appears representative:

Except as otherwise provided in this section, a prosecution shall be barred unless it is commenced within the following periods after an offense is committed:

(1) For a felony other than aggravated murder or murder, six years;
(2) For a misdemeanor other than a minor misdemeanor, two years;
(3) For a minor misdemeanor, six months. Ohio Rev. Code Ann. § 2901.13 (A).

There is a conflict among the various jurisdictions as to whether a statute of limitations in a criminal action is an affirmative defense. An affirmative defense that is not pled is ordinarily deemed waived, but some courts have said that such a waiver must be knowing and voluntary. In *State v. Pearson*, 858 S.W.2d (Tenn. 1993), the Tennessee Supreme Court treated the statute of limitations as waivable by a defendant when it is about to run out, indicating that a defendant may wish to waive the protection of the statute. The court cited an instance where a defendant needs to gain time for plea bargaining and another instance where a defendant who is charged with a more serious offense that is not time barred might want to waive the statute of limitations on a lesser included offense. But, as the court pointed out, any waiver of the statute of limitations must be knowingly and voluntarily entered. Other courts follow the rule that the statute of limitations is jurisdictional and that if the state's information or indictment discloses that the prosecution is initiated beyond the period allowed by the applicable statute of limitations, the prosecution is barred. See, for example, *People v. Ware*, 39 P.3d 1277 (Colo. App. 2001).

But what if the defendant is prosecuted for an offense not barred by the statute of limitations but found guilty of a lesser offense that is time barred? In *State v. Leonard*, 543 S.E.2d 655 (W.Va. 2000), the West Virginia Supreme Court of Appeals barred such a prosecution. It noted that numerous courts have held that a defendant cannot be convicted of a lesser offense upon prosecution for a greater crime that includes the lesser offense when the prosecution is commenced after the statute of limitations has run out on the lesser offense.

# Defenses Based on Improper Government Conduct

There are two defenses that are based on improper government conduct. The defense of entrapment aims to prevent the government from manufacturing crime. This defense is widely asserted in prosecution for narcotics violations, for these cases are frequently based on undercover police operations. The defense of selective prosecution is infrequently imposed and has achieved very limited success. Nevertheless, it is designed to prevent the government from singling out an individual for prosecution based on impermissible grounds.

## Entrapment

**entrapment** The act of government agents inducing someone to commit a crime that the person would not otherwise be disposed to commit.

Law enforcement officers may provide an opportunity for a predisposed person to commit a crime, but they are not permitted to "manufacture" crime by implanting criminal ideas into innocent minds. Therefore, a person who has been induced to commit an offense under these latter circumstances may plead the defense of **entrapment**. A defendant who claims to have committed an offense as a result of inducement by an undercover police officer or a confidential police informant often asserts the defense of entrapment. It is not available to a defendant who has been entrapped by a person not associated with the government or police. See *Henderson v. United States*, 237 F.2d 169 (5th Cir. 1956).

Entrapment was not a defense under the common law, and, strictly speaking, it is not based on the Constitution. Nevertheless, it has long been recognized in federal and state courts in the United States. In 1980 the Tennessee Supreme Court acknowledged that Tennessee was the only state in the Union that did not allow entrapment as a defense, and proceeded to remedy the situation by declaring, "From this day forward entrapment is a defense to a Tennessee criminal prosecution." *State v.*

*Jones*, 598 S.W.2d 209, 212 (Tenn. 1980). In 1989 the Tennessee legislature codified the law on entrapment and required a defendant who pleads entrapment to so advise the prosecution. Tenn. Code Ann. § 39-11-505.

In a landmark case arising during Prohibition days, the U.S. Supreme Court held that a federal officer had entrapped a defendant by using improper inducements to cause him to buy illegal liquor for the officer. The Court observed that the evidence revealed that the defendant, Sorrells, had not been predisposed to commit a crime but had been induced by the government agent to do so. The Court opined that entrapment occurs when criminal conduct involved is "the product of the creative activity of [law enforcement officers]." *Sorrells v. United States*, 287 U.S. 435, 451, 53 S.Ct. 210, 216, 77 L.Ed. 413, 422 (1932).

In *Sorrells*, the majority of the justices viewed entrapment as an issue of whether the defendant's criminal intent originated in the mind of the officer, or whether the defendant was predisposed to commit the offense. This focus on the predisposition of the defendant has come to be known as the **subjective test of entrapment**. A minority of justices in *Sorrells* would have applied what is now known as the **objective test of entrapment**. Under this view, the court would simply determine whether the police methods were so improper that they likely induced or ensnared a person into committing a crime.

In the past, the majority of federal and state courts followed the subjective view. Thus, a person who pled entrapment was held to have admitted commission of the offense. See, for example, *United States v. Sedigh*, 658 F.2d 1010 (5th Cir. 1981); *State v. Amodei*, 563 P.2d 440 (Kan. 1977). A jury would then proceed to determine whether the defendant committed the crime because of a predisposition, or instead was improperly induced to do so by the police.

The subjective approach to entrapment has the disadvantage of not providing the police with any bright lines for enforcement. Moreover, in proving predisposition, the prosecutor often brings in evidence of a defendant's past conduct that may be otherwise inadmissible. This can prejudice the jury with respect to arriving at a verdict on the principal offense charged.

In *United States v. Dion*, 762 F.2d 674 (8th Cir. 1985), modified, 476 U.S. 734 (1986), the U.S. Court of Appeals for the Eighth Circuit provided the following detailed list of factors appropriate for distinguishing predisposed defendants from non-predisposed defendants:

(1) whether the defendant readily responded to the inducement offered;
(2) the circumstances surrounding the illegal conduct;
(3) "the state of mind of a defendant before government agents make any suggestion that he shall commit a crime";
(4) whether the defendant was engaged in an existing course of conduct similar to the crime for which he is charged;
(5) whether the defendant had already formed the "design" to commit the crime for which he is charged;
(6) the defendant's reputation;
(7) the conduct of the defendant during the negotiations with the undercover agent;
(8) whether the defendant has refused to commit similar acts on other occasions;
(9) the nature of the crime charged; and
(10) "[t]he degree of coercion present in the instigation law officers have contributed to the transaction" relative to the "defendant's criminal background."

Although the traditional view of courts has been that a defendant who asserts entrapment as a defense admits the offense charged, there have been conflicting

**subjective test of entrapment** Whether the defendant's criminal intent originated in the mind of the police officer or the defendant was predisposed to commit the offense.

**objective test of entrapment** Under this approach to determining whether police engaged in entrapment, a court inquires whether the police methods were so improper that they were likely to induce or ensnare a reasonable person into committing a crime.

decisions in the federal courts between this view and the more modern view, which holds that a defendant may assert entrapment without being required to concede commission of the crime or any element thereof. The U.S. Supreme Court resolved the issue in *Mathews v. United States*, 485 U.S. 58, 108 S.Ct. 883, 99 L.Ed.2d 54 (1988). The Court ruled that a defendant who pleads entrapment does not necessarily admit to the crime charged or any element thereof. The Court's decision affects only the federal courts; state courts vary in their approach as to whether a defendant who pleads entrapment admits the crime charged, with their views sometimes being based on state laws providing for the defense of entrapment.

Where courts follow the objective view, the judge, not the jury, determines whether the police methods were so improper as to constitute entrapment. See, for example, *People v. D'Angelo*, 257 N.W.2d 655 (Mich. 1977). Some federal courts have simply said that where police conduct is outrageous, it becomes a question of law for the judge to determine whether governmental misconduct is so shocking as to be a violation of due process of law. See, for example, *United States v. Wylie*, 625 F.2d 1371 (9th Cir. 1980). In courts that strictly follow the objective view, the defendant's predisposition to commit an offense is irrelevant. The objective approach has the advantage of enabling the courts to scrutinize governmental action to ensure that outrageous methods are not employed in seeking to ferret out crime.

In 1993 the Wyoming Supreme Court declined to adopt the objective theory of entrapment. Nevertheless, it indicated that a defendant can rely on "outrageous government conduct" as a defense if the circumstances reveal police conduct that violates fundamental fairness and is shocking to the universal sense of justice mandated

---

**CASE-IN-POINT**

### Did Tampa Police Engage in Entrapment?

Tampa, Florida police "undertook a decoy operation in a high-crime area" where "an officer posed as an inebriated indigent, smelling of alcohol and pretending to drink wine from a bottle." The officer "plainly displayed from a rear pant pocket $150." Cruz and his female companion walked passed the officer without incident; however, they returned where Cruz "took the money" from the officer's pocket "without harming him in any way." Cruz was arrested for grand theft, and argued that his arrest constituted entrapment as a matter of law. The trial court granted the motion to dismiss; however the intermediate appellate court reversed. The Florida Supreme Court articulated the following threshold test stating that entrapment "has not occurred as a matter of law where police activity (1) has as its end the interruption of a specific ongoing criminal activity; and (2) utilizes means reasonably tailored to apprehend those involved in the ongoing criminal activity." In addressing the first prong, the court maintained that it "addresses the problem of police 'virtue testing,' that is, police activity seeking to prosecute crime where no

such crime exists but for the police activity engendering the crime." As to the second prong, the focus is the "problem of inappropriate techniques." The court directed lower courts to consider "whether a government agent 'induces or encourages another person to engage in conduct constituting such offense by either: (a) making knowingly false representations designed to induce the belief that such conduct is not prohibited or (b) employing methods of persuasion or inducement which create a substantial risk that such an offense will be committed by persons other than those who are ready to commit it.'" In applying this standard to Cruz, the court held that the police's "drunken bum decoy" constituted entrapment because under the first prong, it was undisputed that "none of the unsolved crimes occurring near this location involved the same *modus operandi* as the simulated situation created by the officers." As a result, the court stated the "police were apparently attempting to interrupt some kind of ongoing criminal activity," however no "specific activity was targeted." The trial court's decision to dismiss was reinstated.

*Cruz v. State*, 465 So.2d 516 (Fla. 1985)

by the Due Process Clauses of the Fifth and Fourteenth Amendments. *Rivera v. State*, 846 P.2d 1 (Wyo. 1993).

Recent decisions indicate that the subjective and objective tests can coexist. Some state courts now first determine whether a defendant who pleads entrapment has been ensnared by outrageous police methods. If so, the judge dismisses the charges against the ensnared defendant. If not, the court then allows the defendant to attempt to establish the defense of entrapment by proving improper inducement. The prosecution usually counters with evidence showing the defendant's prior criminal activity and ready acquiescence in committing the crime charged. The court then instructs the jury to determine whether the defendant committed the crime because of his or her predisposition or through inducement by the police. At least two states have adopted this general approach. See *Cruz v. State*, 465 So.2d 516 (Fla. 1985); *State v. Talbot*, 364 A.2d 9 (N.J. 1976).

Dissatisfied with the Florida Supreme Court's decision in *Cruz v. State*, supra, which provided for the trial court to first determine whether a defendant who pleads entrapment has been ensnared by outrageous police methods, the Florida legislature enacted a new subjective-model entrapment statute. West's Fla. Stat. 777.201. After passage of the statute, the Supreme Court of Florida held that, in enacting § 777.201, the legislature effectively eliminated the objective test in *Cruz*. Nevertheless, the court observed that the legislature cannot prohibit the judiciary from objectively reviewing the issue of entrapment to the extent that such a review involves the Due Process Clause of Article I, Section 9 of the Florida Constitution. *Munoz v. State*, 629 So.2d 90 (Fla. 1993).

Two principal reasons account for the increased assertion of the defense of entrapment in recent years. First, numerous violations of narcotics laws have been prosecuted on the basis of undercover police activity and evidence given by confidential police informants. Second, there has been increased attention to prosecuting corruption involving government officials.

One of the most highly publicized cases resulted from the 1980 Abscam operation, in which FBI agents posed as wealthy Arab businessmen and attempted to buy influence from members of Congress. Despite their claims of entrapment, several members of Congress were found guilty of offenses involving misuse of office. See, for example, *United States v. Jenrette*, 744 F.2d 817 (D.C. Cir. 1984).

## A Promise of Sex—Entrapment as a Matter of Law

**CASE-IN-POINT**

Law enforcement officers told a female that she might not be prosecuted for possession of cocaine if she would become a confidential informant. She agreed and met with the defendant, James Banks, a suspected drug dealer, on two nights. The meetings included "kissing and hugging," after which she told Banks that if he "could get her something [they] would get together for the weekend, fool around and party." The defendant obtained some cocaine for her, and as a result, he was arrested. The trial judge dismissed the charges because the uncontested facts established that the

officers used a method with a substantial risk of persuading or inducing the defendant to commit a criminal offense.

The state appealed the dismissal. The appellate court affirmed: "When law enforcement agencies utilize confidential informants who use sex, or the express or implied promise thereof, to obtain contraband the defendant did not already possess, there is no way for the courts or anyone else to determine whether such inducement served only to uncover an existing propensity or created a new one. This violates the threshold objective test."

*State v. Banks*, 499 So.2d 894 (Fla. App. 1986).

## JURISPRUDENCE

*Jacobson v. United States*, 503 U.S. 540, 112 S.Ct. 1535, 118 L.Ed.2d 174 (1992)

In 1987 Keith Jacobson was indicted for violating the Child Protection Act of 1984, 18 U.S.C.A. § 2252(a)(2)(A), which criminalizes the knowing receipt through the mails of a "visual depiction [that] involves the use of a minor engaging in sexually explicit conduct." At trial, Jacobson contended that the government entrapped him into committing the crime. A jury found him guilty, and his conviction was affirmed by the court of appeals. In evaluating the evidence at Jacobson's trial, the U.S. Supreme Court found that when it was still legal to do so, Jacobson ordered some magazines containing photos of nude boys. After Congress enacted the Child Protection Act, making this illegal, two government agencies learned that Jacobson had ordered the magazines. The agencies sent mail to Jacobson through fictitious organizations to explore his willingness to break the law. He was literally bombarded with solicitations, which included communications decrying censorship and questioning the legitimacy and constitutionality of the government's efforts to restrict availability of sexually explicit materials. He finally responded to an undercover solicitation to order child pornography and was arrested after a controlled delivery of the explicit sexual materials.

After pointing out that for twenty-six months government agents had made Jacobson the target of repeated mailings, the Court held that the prosecution failed to produce evidence that Jacobson was predisposed to break the law before the government directed its efforts toward him. Adding that government agents may not implant a criminal design in an innocent person's mind and then induce commission of a crime, the Court reversed his conviction, observing that Congress had not intended for government officials to instigate crime by luring persons otherwise innocent to commit offenses.

---

In 1994 the U.S. Court of Appeals for the Seventh Circuit rendered an *en banc* decision holding that when a defendant pleads entrapment, the government must prove that the defendant was not only "willing" to commit the offense charged but also that he or she was "ready" to commit the offense in the absence of official encouragement. *United States v. Hollingsworth*, 27 F.3d 1196 (7th Cir. 1994).

Because the Supreme Court's decision in *Jacobson v. United States* is not grounded on constitutional principles, it affects only federal law enforcement activities. Nonetheless, it signals that state enforcement authorities should not play on the weaknesses of innocent parties to beguile them into committing crimes.

## Selective Prosecution

**selective prosecution**
Singling out defendants for prosecution on the basis of race, religion, or other impermissible classifications.

Selective enforcement of the criminal law is not itself a constitutional violation; therefore, without more, it does not constitute a defense. *Oyler v. Boles*, 368 U.S. 448, 82 S.Ct. 501, 7 L.Ed.2d 446 (1962). There are many cases rejecting the defense of **selective prosecution**. To prevail, a defendant must ordinarily demonstrate that other similarly situated persons have not been prosecuted for similar conduct and that the defendant's selection for prosecution was based on some impermissible ground such as race, religion, or the exercise of the First Amendment right of free speech. *United States v. Jennings*, 991 F.2d 725 (11th Cir. 1993); *United States v. Arias*, 575 F.2d 253 (9th Cir. 1978).

In 1996 the Supreme Court reviewed a case where defendants indicted for federal narcotics violations filed a pretrial motion for the discovery of information that they contended would show that they were being selectively prosecuted because of their race. The Court held that the defendants failed to establish an entitlement to discovery based on their claim because they failed to produce any credible evidence that similarly situated defendants of other races could have been prosecuted but

**JURISPRUDENCE**

*Wayte v. United States*, 470 U.S. 598, 105 S.Ct. 1524, 84 L.Ed.2d 547 (1985)

In 1982 David Alan Wayte was indicted for willfully failing to register under the Military Selective Service Act. Wayte sought dismissal of the indictment on the ground of selective prosecution. He contended that he and the others being prosecuted had been singled out of an estimated 674,000 nonregistrants because they had voiced opposition to the Selective Service requirements. The district court dismissed the indictment on the ground that the government had failed to rebut Wayte's *prima facie* showing of selective prosecution. The case was eventually heard by the U.S. Supreme Court. The Court held that the government's passive enforcement policy, under which it prosecuted only those nonregistrants who reported themselves or were reported by others, did not violate the First or Fifth Amendments to the Constitution. Writing for the Court, Justice Lewis Powell noted that, at the time, "[p]assive enforcement was the only effective interim solution available to carry out the Government's compelling interest."

were not. *United States v. Armstrong*, 517 U.S. 456, 116 S.Ct. 1480, 134 L.Ed.2d 687 (1996).

In *United States v. Eagleboy*, 200 F.3d 1137 (8th Cir. 1999), the defendant, who was not a member of a federally recognized Indian tribe, was charged with possessing hawk parts in violation of the Migratory Bird Treaty Act (MBTA). Had the defendant been a member of a federally recognized Indian tribe, he would not have been charged with a violation of the MBTA. Pointing to this policy, the defendant moved to dismiss on the ground of selective prosecution. The U.S. Court of Appeals for the Eighth Circuit held that Eagleboy was not selectively prosecuted. The court said that the government's policy of not enforcing the act against recognized Indian tribes distinguished between persons on the basis of membership in a federally recognized Indian tribe, not on the basis of race.

# Nontraditional Defenses

Although they are seldom successful, defendants sometimes employ novel and innovative defenses. We previously discussed the status of the battered-woman– and battered-child–syndrome defenses, which, though not traditional, can no longer be considered novel. In this section, we discuss some of the more interesting novel defenses. These include unusual religious practices, the victim's negligence, premenstrual syndrome (PMS), compulsive gambling, posttraumatic stress syndrome (PTSS), the junk food defense, television intoxication, and pornographic intoxication. In instances where a novel defense leads to an acquittal, appellate courts do not have an opportunity to evaluate the legal basis of the defense. This is because the prosecution is not permitted to appeal an acquittal.

## Unusual Religious Beliefs and Practices

The courts have long rejected contentions by defendants that they have been commanded by God or the scriptures to commit illegal acts. See *Hotema v. United States*, 186 U.S. 413, 22 S.Ct. 895, 46 L.Ed. 1225 (1902). Moreover, laws prohibiting religious rites that endanger the lives, health, or safety of the participants or others are customarily upheld by the courts. This is illustrated by the decision of the Kentucky Court of Appeals in *Lawson v. Commonwealth*, 164 S.W.2d 972 (Ky. 1942). There, despite the defendants' contentions that their constitutional guarantees of freedom of religion were violated, the court upheld the constitutionality of a statute making it a misdemeanor for anyone to handle snakes or reptiles in connection with any religious service.

Courts have traditionally upheld the right of parents to raise their children by their own religious beliefs, ruling that the state's interest must yield to parental religious beliefs that preclude medical treatment, so long as the child's life is not immediately imperiled. See, for example, *In re Green*, 292 A.2d 387 (Pa. 1972). Nevertheless, the courts have held that where a child's life is imperiled, the parents have an affirmative duty to provide medical care that will protect the child's life. Thus, an appellate court upheld a conviction of parents for manslaughter when it found that a child's death was directly caused by the parents' failure to secure needed medical care. *Commonwealth v. Barnhart*, 497 A.2d 616 (Pa. Super. 1985). In about half of the states, child abuse and criminal neglect statutes permit parents to choose spiritual means or prayer as a response to illness without regard to a child's medical condition. In *State v. McKown*, 461 N.W.2d 720 (Minn. App. 1990), aff'd, 475 N.W.2d 63 (1991), the court upheld the dismissal of manslaughter charges against a parent and stepparent who relied on spiritual means and failed to secure medical treatment for an eleven-year-old boy. The child died allegedly as a result of medical problems resulting from diabetes.

The need to furnish medical care to children poses a problem of balancing the parents' interests in bringing up their offspring in accordance with their religious beliefs against the interest of the state in the preservation of life. In January 1988, the press reported that the American Academy of Pediatrics urged the repeal of laws allowing parents to reject medical treatment for their children on religious grounds. The academy pointed out that about three-fourths of the states have laws that permit some rejection of medical care on religious or philosophical grounds. However, the academy noted, courts have frequently intervened to order certain treatments for minors.

## Victim's Negligence

Federal and state courts hold that a victim's negligence, credulity, or wrongdoing is not a defense to a prosecution. *United States v. Kreimer*, 609 F.2d 126 (5th Cir. 1980); *State v. Lunz*, 273 N.W.2d 767 (Wis. 1979). Likewise, because a crime is an offense against society as well as against the victim, it follows that a victim's forgiveness or condoning does not relieve an actor of criminal responsibility.

## Premenstrual Syndrome

Premenstrual syndrome (PMS) refers to certain physiological changes that occur in some women, usually in the days close to the onset of menstruation. This results from hormonal imbalance and can cause serious depression and irritability. In certain cases, medical treatment is required. Some argue that a woman so affected should be allowed to assert PMS as a defense to criminal conduct because some physicians say that PMS directly affects behavior. Nevertheless, PMS has not been accepted as a defense in the United States. In England, it has been recognized as a basis for mitigating punishment.

## Compulsive Gambling

Evidence of compulsive gambling is generally not considered as a defense unless it rises to the level of insanity. For example, a defendant was convicted of entering a bank with intent to commit larceny and robbery. On appeal, he argued that the trial court erred in instructing the jury that "as a matter of law pathological gambling disorder is not a disease or defect within the meaning of the American Law Institute test for insanity." The U.S. Court of Appeals, which was still applying the former ALI standard, rejected his contention. *United States v. Gould*, 741 F.2d 45 (4th Cir. 1984).

## Posttraumatic Stress Syndrome

Posttraumatic stress syndrome (PTSS) commonly refers to the unique stresses suffered during combat, often manifesting in such symptoms as flashbacks, outbursts of anger, and blocked-out memories. After World War I, these conditions were usually referred to as "shell shock." Following World War II, the term "combat fatigue" was often used to describe such anxiety disorders. Present generations have heard these conditions described as "posttraumatic stress syndrome." Because of the bizarre type of warfare that service personnel endured in Vietnam, the unpopularity of the war, the availability of drugs, and the difficulties encountered in adjusting to civilian life, many veterans suffered severe psychological reactions. To a lesser extent, the stress of combat in Operation Desert Storm also caused delayed traumatic stress syndrome. Undoubtedly, the stress of combat operations in the present military operations in Afghanistan and Iraq can be expected to cause similar results.

Although not a legal defense in itself, in some instances PTSS may affect a defendant's understanding to the point of allowing a plea of insanity. More frequently, PTSS will be introduced as evidence bearing on a defendant's intent or offered at a sentencing hearing in an effort to mitigate punishment.

## The "Junk Food" Defense

Dan White, a former city supervisor, shot and killed the mayor of San Francisco in 1978. Following this, he killed another supervisor, who was a leader of the local gay community. In defense to charges of first-degree murder, White's counsel sought to establish that his client was depressed by having gorged himself on junk food. White was convicted of manslaughter instead of murder, giving some credence to reports that the jury may have accepted White's defense. This was jury action, so it set no precedent to establish any such defense.

## Television Intoxication

An adolescent boy was tried in Miami for the first-degree murder of an elderly woman. He attempted to establish insanity on the basis of psychiatric testimony concerning the effects of "involuntary subliminal television intoxication." The trial court rejected his claim. An appellate court, stating that the trial judge correctly limited the evidence to the requirements of the *M'Naghten* rule, found no difficulty in upholding the trial court's decision. *Zamora v. State*, 361 So.2d 776 (Fla. App. 1978).

## Pornographic Intoxication

There is a lively academic debate over the effect of pornography on the psyche. Does it stimulate sexual violence? Some defendants have attempted to employ a "pornography intoxication defense," but with little success. For example, in *Schiro v. Clark*, 963 F.2d 962 (7th Cir. 1992), a federal appellate court held that acting under the influence of pornography could not be used to mitigate the defendant's death sentence for rape and murder.

## Postpartum Depression

Postpartum depression refers to a group of symptoms a new mother may experience after giving birth. It involves severe depression, and in cases where it doesn't give rise to qualify for a defense of insanity, in cases involving infanticide it has been offered in an effort to mitigate punishment.

## XYY Chromosome Abnormality

Growing evidence indicates that a person's genes influence behavior, and there has been speculation in media reports that people accused of violent crimes might find a medical basis to assert a "my genes made me do it" defense. While this is not recognized as a specific defense, there is some medical evidence indicating that the presence of an extra Y chromosome may lead to physical and mental problems that cause an affected person to act aggressively. Some defendants have used evidence of this abnormality as a basis for the insanity defense.

## Multiple Personality Defense

One who asserts a multiple personality defense argues that he or she did not commit the offense alleged; rather, another personality of which the defendant has no memory and no control committed the crime. In October 2000, the press reported that a woman in Kansas City, Missouri, who pled not guilty by reason of insanity to several offenses, contended that her multiple personalities were responsible for the deaths of her two young sons in 1999. Her lawyers and expert witnesses said she had severe psychosis and an alternate personality named Sharon, who controlled her actions. Notwithstanding her claim, the defendant was found guilty of murder and a series of child abuse charges.

## Black Rage and Urban Survival Defenses

Based on claims that have developed over the years in response to perceptions of social needs are the "black rage defense" and the "urban survival defense." These are usually offered with the hope that a defendant's punishment will be mitigated by the social conditions they expose.

In the black rage defense, some African American defendants charged with violent crime against a white person have sought to absolve or mitigate their conduct on the basis of years of oppression and racist hostility endured at the hands of white Americans. Proponents contend that as a result of racism, substandard education, inadequate employment opportunities, and substandard housing and medical care, African American defendants can justify retaliatory action against white citizens. Critics point out that if courts were to accept black rage as a legal defense, it could lead to the impossible task of assessing claims of discrimination by criminal defendants of a variety of ethnic, and even religious, backgrounds.

Similar to the black rage defense is the advocacy of an "urban survival syndrome" defense based upon a defendant's having lived under substandard environmental conditions in a deteriorated urban neighborhood plagued with drug dealers and acts of violence that often include threats of deadly force.

## Conclusion

Despite the fact that the prosecution has met its burden of proving the elements of a crime, a defendant has the opportunity to not only dispute such proof but also to affirmatively assert defenses to the conduct charged. The traditional common-law defenses that allow a defendant to raise issues of lack of capacity, excuse, justification, and justifiable use of force have been augmented by constitutional and statutory defenses and defenses challenging improper government conduct. Concepts of criminal responsibility and criminal defenses will continue to evolve in response to our increased knowledge of human behavior and society's balance of the rights of the individual against society's legitimate demand for protection. Some nontraditional defenses could even become viable, given new social science and medical research.

## Chapter Summary

- Learning Objective 1
  - o Defenses may be divided into negative and affirmative defenses. A negative defense is one in which the defendant denies committing the crime or claims that the prosecution lacks sufficient evidence of the defendant's guilt. An affirmative is one in which the defendant admits to the criminal act but denies criminal responsibility by claiming an excuse or justification for the defendant's otherwise illegal conduct or asserting that the defendant lacked the capacity to form criminal intent.
  - o While the prosecution always carries the burden of proving the defendant's guilt beyond a reasonable doubt, courts generally require a defendant to prove an affirmative defense by a preponderance of the evidence.
  - o Alibi is an example of a negative defense, in that the defendant denies the ability to have perpetrated the alleged crime because of having been elsewhere at the time. Statutes or court rules commonly require that to assert alibi as a defense, a defendant must notify the prosecution in advance of trial and furnish the names of witnesses the defendant intends to use to support the alibi.

- Learning Objective 2
  - o Defenses asserting lack of capacity to commit a crime include infancy, intoxication, insanity, and automatism. What these defenses have in common is the assertion that the defendant was incapable of forming criminal intent and is therefore not responsible for a criminal act.
  - o English common law conclusively presumed that a child younger than seven could not commit a crime. This presumption was rebuttable for a child between seven and fourteen years old; children over fourteen were treated as adults. The defense of infancy still exists under modern American law, but instances of it are very rare. Today, most youthful offenders are dealt with in the juvenile justice system rather than in the adult criminal courts.
  - o The common law did not excuse those who became voluntarily intoxicated from criminal responsibility. Most American courts allow voluntary intoxication as a defense to specific-intent crimes but reject it for general-intent

crimes. But the trend is to prohibit voluntary intoxication as a defense to any crime. Involuntary intoxication relieves criminality if a defendant no longer knows right from wrong.

- ○ Older cases treated defendants who claimed that their unlawful acts were committed because of an involuntary condition such as somnambulism (that is, sleepwalking) within the context of the insanity defense. Newer cases tend to classify such involuntary actions as automatism and view automatism similarly to unconsciousness as a basis for an affirmative defense independent from insanity. The defense is usually limited to a situation where criminal conduct is beyond a person's knowledge and control.

- Learning Objective 3
  - ○ The insanity defense originated in England in 1843 in the form of the *M'Naghten* rule, which provided that insanity cannot be a defense unless "at the time of committing the act, the party accused was labouring under such a defect of reason, from disease of the mind, as not to know the nature and quality of the act he was doing; or, if he did know it, that he did not know what he was doing was wrong." The *M'Naghten* rule became the test for insanity in federal and state courts in the United States.
  - ○ As psychology and psychiatry developed new theories of mental capacity, some courts followed the ALI standard, which provides that persons are not responsible for criminal conduct if they lack substantial capacity either to appreciate the wrongfulness of their conduct or to conform their conduct to the requirements of the law.
  - ○ Most federal courts adopted the ALI standard, but after an assailant who shot President Reagan in 1981 was acquitted under the ALI standard, Congress enacted the Insanity Defense Reform Act of 1984. The new act essentially reestablished the *M'Naghten* rule in federal courts and made insanity an affirmative defense.
  - ○ Many state courts follow the *M'Naghten* standard; others follow more liberal tests. Some require the prosecution to refute claims of insanity; others classify insanity as an affirmative defense and require the defendant to prove insanity, usually by a preponderance of the evidence. Some states provide for verdicts of guilty but mentally ill. Others have abolished the defense of insanity altogether.

- Learning Objective 4
  - ○ Federal and state courts generally follow the common law and hold that duress can be a defense only when it involves present threats that cause well-grounded apprehensions of death or serious injury; duress cannot excuse an intentional killing of an innocent person.
  - ○ Early common law recognized that "a man may break the words of the law . . . through necessity." American courts hold that if there is a reasonable legal alternative to violating the law, the defense of necessity fails. In most cases, necessity has been unavailing to defendants espousing social and political causes.
  - ○ In some sexual offenses consent might be a defense, but this cannot apply in a prosecution for having sexual relations with a minor. Otherwise consent to criminal conduct is not a defense.
  - ○ The maxim "ignorance of the law is no excuse" remains the generally accepted view. Nevertheless, where a mistaken view of the law (such as title to property) negates the specific-intent element of a crime, mistake of law can be a defense.

- o Historically, American courts have held that a mistake of fact is not recognized as a defense to a general-intent crime unless the mistake is a reasonable one for a person to make under the circumstances. But even an unreasonable mistake may be asserted as a defense to a specific-intent crime. Recent court decisions indicate that a mistake of fact may be a defense if it negates the existence of the mental state essential to the crime charged. Mistake of fact is unavailing as a defense in strict liability crimes.

- Learning Objective 5
  - o The defense of justifiable use of force applies to claims of self-defense in assaultive and homicidal offenses. At common law, a person attacked had a duty "to retreat to the wall" before using deadly force in self-defense. Most courts reject that doctrine and hold that a person attacked or threatened may use any force reasonably necessary to prevent harm as long as the person using such force is where he or she has a right to be and acts without fault and in reasonable fear or apprehension of death or great bodily harm. A minority of courts hold that a person who can safely retreat must do so before using deadly force.
  - o The law has traditionally applied an objective test for the use of deadly force, but today many courts apply a subjective standard of reasonableness to determine whether circumstances are sufficient to induce an honest and reasonable belief that force must be used. Generally, when a defendant raises an issue of self-defense, the prosecution must prove that the accused did not act in self-defense.
  - o There is a developing trend that when a woman kills her batterer and pleads self-defense, expert testimony about battered woman syndrome (BWS) is admissible to explain how her experiences affected her perceptions of danger and honest belief in its imminence. There is a movement to allow a child who has been abused over an extended period to assert the battered child syndrome (BCS) in defense of charges for killing or injuring a parent.
  - o Common law allowed the use of reasonable force to prevent the commission of a felony or to protect household members who were endangered. This principle was codified in many jurisdictions. The trend in American jurisdictions is to allow a person "to stand in the shoes of the victim" and to use such reasonable force as is necessary to defend anyone, irrespective of relationship, from harm.
  - o The common law "castle doctrine" permits the use of deadly force against an intruder into a dwelling, but does not justify using deadly force in taking a life to repel a mere trespass. The right to defend other property is more limited and, if someone is killed or injured as a result of a spring gun or similar mechanical device, the party who set it or caused it to be set will generally be held criminally responsible for any resulting death or injury.
  - o The trend is to expand the right of self-defense, and half of the states have enacted "stand your ground" laws providing that a person does not have a duty to retreat before using deadly force.
  - o Today the majority of states, either by statute or judicial decision, provide that a person may not resist an arrest with force, even if the arrest is illegal.

- Learning Objective 6
  - o A witness compelled to give self-incriminating testimony receives use immunity. This means that the testimony given cannot be used against the witness.
  - o Some states grant transactional immunity to a witness who testifies under a grant of immunity. This protects a witness from prosecution for any activity mentioned in the witness's testimony.

- o A witness who testifies under a grant of immunity may be prosecuted for making material false statements under oath.
- o Contractual immunity is sometimes granted to a witness to enable the prosecutor to obtain a conviction not otherwise obtainable because of the constitutional protection against self-incrimination.
- o Authority to grant immunity in federal courts is vested in the U.S. Attorney with approval of the Attorney General or certain authorized assistants. At the state level, such authority is generally vested in the chief prosecuting officer.
- o Transactional immunity is a broader protection that protects a witness from prosecution for any activity mentioned in the witness's testimony.
- o A person with diplomatic status, who serves as part of a diplomatic mission, and members of the diplomat's staff and household enjoy diplomatic immunity from arrest and prosecution.
- o The U.S. Constitution provides that members of Congress, in all cases except treason, felony, and breach of the peace, are privileged from arrest during attendance at and in going to or from legislative sessions. State constitutions generally include similar provisions for state lawmakers.

- Learning Objective 7
  - o The Fifth Amendment to the U.S. Constitution provides: "[N]or shall any person be subject for the same offence to be twice put in jeopardy of life or limb." It is applicable to the states through the Fourteenth Amendment.
  - o The Double Jeopardy Clause forbids a second prosecution for the same offense after a defendant has been acquitted. But if a defendant prevails in an appeal, it is not double jeopardy to retry the defendant unless the appellate court rules that there was insufficient evidence to sustain the defendant's conviction.
  - o The Double Jeopardy Clause does not preclude a prosecution by both the federal and state governments, but the policy, and in some instances state law, forbids a second prosecution once an offender has been prosecuted in a different jurisdiction.
  - o Courts usually apply the *Blockburger* test, which bars punishment for offenses that have the same elements, or when one offense is included in another offense.

- Learning Objective 8
  - o Common law placed no time limits on prosecution. There is no federal constitutional basis for limiting the time in which a prosecution can be initiated.
  - o A statute of limitations is a legislative enactment that places a time limit on the prosecution of a crime, and the federal government and almost all states have enacted laws that prescribe certain time limits for prosecution of offenses, excluding murder.
  - o The twin rationales are that a person should not be under threat of prosecution for too long a period, and that after a prolonged period, proof is either unavailable or may not be credible.
  - o Statutes of limitations seldom place time limits on prosecutions for murder and other very serious offenses.

- Learning Objective 9
  - o Unknown at common law, entrapment consists of law enforcement inducing a person who is predisposed to commit a crime to commit that crime. It is a defense in all federal and state courts.
  - o This defense is designed to prevent the government from manufacturing crime and is widely asserted in drug cases based on testimony of confidential informants.

○ Most courts follow the subjective test, which focuses on whether a defendant's predisposition caused the defendant to commit the crime charged. A minority of courts apply an objective test whereby the court simply determines whether outrageous police methods induced a person to commit a crime. If the court so finds, the judge dismisses the charges against the ensnared defendant.

○ The selective prosecution defense is designed to prevent the government from singling out an individual for prosecution based on impermissible grounds. To prevail, a defendant who pleads selective prosecution must demonstrate that the defendant's prosecution is based on race, religion, or the exercise of the First Amendment rights of free speech, and that other similarly situated persons have not been prosecuted for similar conduct.

- Learning Objective 10
  ○ Some defendants employ novel and innovative defenses. These include unusual religious practices, victim's negligence, premenstrual syndrome (PMS), compulsive gambling, posttraumatic stress syndrome (PTSS), the junk food defense, television and pornographic intoxication, and other novel situations.
  ○ In isolated cases, reliance on one or more of these nontraditional offenses might result in a jury acquitting a defendant or a conviction for a lesser offense. In other instances reliance on one or more of these innovative theories might result in a lesser punishment.

## Key Terms

| | |
|---|---|
| affirmative defense | infancy |
| ALI Standard | insanity |
| alibi | insanity Defense Reform Act of 1984 |
| automatism | insufficient evidence |
| battered child syndrome (BCS) | intoxication |
| battered woman syndrome (BWS) | involuntary intoxication |
| beyond a reasonable doubt | irresistible impulse |
| *Blockburger* test | justifiable use of force |
| castle doctrine | legislative immunity |
| clear and convincing evidence standard | *M'Naghten* rule |
| contractual immunity | manifest necessity |
| criminal responsibility | mistake of fact |
| deadly force | mistake of law |
| defense of habitation | necessity |
| defense of others | negative defense |
| diplomatic immunity | nondeadly force |
| double jeopardy | not guilty by reason of insanity |
| duress | objective test for the use of deadly force |
| *Durham* test | objective test of entrapment |
| entrapment | preponderance of the evidence |
| guilty but mentally ill | reasonable force |
| immunity | retreat rule |

| | |
|---|---|
| same elements test | subjective test of entrapment |
| same evidence test | substantial capacity test |
| selective prosecution | tolling |
| self-defense | transactional immunity |
| "stand your ground" laws | use immunity |
| statute of limitations | voluntary intoxication |
| subjective standard of reasonableness | weight of the evidence |

## Questions for Thought and Discussion

1. In general, courts permit intoxication evidence only to the extent that it negates the *mens rea* of a specific-intent crime. Should evidence of voluntary intoxication be allowed for both general-intent and specific-intent crimes? Several states have recently enacted statutes making voluntary intoxication inadmissible as a defense to any crime. What position have the courts of your state taken on this issue?

2. What is the test for insanity in your state? Who bears the burden of proof once the defendant introduces some evidence of insanity? Do you think the test in your state adequately protects (a) the public and (b) the defendant's rights?

3. Should the courts recognize battered woman syndrome as a defense to assaultive and homicidal crimes by a woman living with a man who continually batters her? What position does your state take on this issue?

4. Explain the difference between the objective and subjective approaches to the defense of entrapment. Which approach is more just? Why?

5. Should the law require a person to retreat when attacked in his or her own home? Should the law make a distinction between co-occupant? Explain the justification for your view.

6. A few states have recently enacted statutes removing any duty to retreat if a person is attacked in a vehicle or other place where he or she has a right to be. Some allow a person attacked to presume that the attacker intends to do bodily harm and allow the vehicle occupant to use any force necessary in defense, with no duty to retreat. Supporters often characterize them as "stand your ground" laws. Some opponents call them "shoot first" laws. Do you think such laws are justifiable?

7. Increasingly, states have enacted "antihazing" laws aimed particularly at the initiation procedures of certain fraternal organizations. Most make it a misdemeanor; a few make it a felony where serious injury results from hazing. Should these laws permit defendants accused of hazing to assert the victim's consent as a defense?

8. The Fifth Amendment to the U.S. Constitution requires the court to grant use immunity to a witness who is required to testify over a legitimately invoked right of self-incrimination. In some states, a witness who testifies under a grant of immunity is given transactional immunity, a broader protection than the federal constitution requires. Explain the difference between the two categories of immunity.

9. To what extent, if at all, do you think the courts should interfere with the right of a parent to opt for spiritual, as opposed to medical, healing for a child who suffers from a curable disease?

10. Can one make a credible argument that any one of the nontraditional defenses outlined in the chapter should be accepted as a defense to criminal conduct?

11. The majority of courts hold that ignorance or even a *bona fide* belief that a minor is of legal age does not constitute a defense to prosecution of such strict liability

offenses as (a) voluntary sexual relations with a minor and (b) sale of intoxicating liquor to a minor. Do you think a state should adopt a statute that would excuse either or both of such offenses where the defendant made an inquiry as to a person's age and the person appeared to be of legal age?

12. The maxim "ignorance of the law is no excuse" is derived from an age when laws were much simpler than today's sophisticated legal codes. Assume you are working on the staff of a state legislator who tells you she intends to introduce a bill to "clearly define when a person's 'mistake of the law' should be excused." She asks you to do some research and prepare a memorandum of points that such a bill should include to enable her to discuss her proposal with a legislative committee. What are some of the key points that you would recommend?

## Problems for Discussion and Solution

1. Immediately following a catastrophic hurricane, Benjamin Saint entered several local stores that had suffered heavy damage and took food, water, and ice. He called himself a "proud looter" as he handed the items out to stranded persons who had taken refuge at a local school building. If prosecuted for looting, would Saint likely be able to establish the defense of necessity?

2. The state commenced prosecution of the defendant for grand theft within the statutory four-year period of limitations. The jury found the defendant not guilty of grand theft, but guilty of petit theft, a lesser included offense. The one-year statute of limitations for petit theft had run out before the prosecution commenced. Does the defendant have a viable issue to rise on appeal?

3. While taking his nightly walk, Charley Goodneighbor saw Joe Macho commit a battery on Charlene Lovely, a fourteen-year-old girl. Goodneighbor came to Lovely's defense and struck Macho so hard it fractured his skull. The police arrested both Macho and Goodneighbor. Goodneighbor explained to the police that he came to Lovely's aid to prevent her from being injured by Macho. What factors will the prosecutor probably consider in determining whether to file charges against Goodneighbor?

4. Nathan Ninja, who holds a black belt in karate, arrives at his home to find an intruder fleeing from the garage. Ninja pursues the intruder across the front yard and catches him in the street. An exchange of blows renders the intruder unconscious. A medical examination reveals substantial brain damage to the intruder as a result of the blows inflicted by Ninja. In a prosecution for aggravated battery, can Ninja successfully assert as a defense that his use of force was necessary to protect his habitation?

5. Sally Shopper drives a 1995 gray Honda Accord. She parks it in a shopping center lot while she shops. Two hours later, Shopper enters a car parked nearby that is almost identical to hers. As she drives away, the owner spots her and demands that a nearby police officer stop her. Just as the officer approaches her, Shopper realizes that she is in someone else's vehicle. Had she looked at the vehicle more carefully, she would have observed that it had a license tag from a different state and some unique bumper stickers. On complaint of the owner, the officer arrests Shopper and charges her with theft. What is Shopper likely to assert in her defense?

6. A destitute homeless man steals food from a convenience market. When prosecuted for theft, he pleads the defense of necessity. The prosecutor urges the trial judge to strike the defense on the ground that the defendant could have qualified for assistance from local welfare organizations. Should the defendant be allowed to present his defense to the jury? Do you think he has a credible defense? Why or why not?

7. A defendant was found guilty of having forcible sexual intercourse with a fifteen-year-old female of previous chaste character. He is charged, convicted, and sentenced for violating two statutes: (a) common-law rape involving force and lack of consent and (b) statutory rape involving intercourse with a minor of previous chaste character. On appeal, the defendant contends that his sentence violates the Double Jeopardy Clause of the Fifth Amendment. What arguments will his counsel likely present to the appellate court? What should be the appellate court's decision?

8. The police suspect Mary Jane Hemphill of having sold marijuana at the Sibannac Bar. An undercover agent approaches her and asks her to go out with him. After a movie, the agent says that he would like to buy some marijuana for his close friend. At first, Hemphill makes no response. They make another date, and after a very pleasant evening together, the undercover agent pleads with Hemphill to help him find marijuana for his friend. She agrees, and the next day she delivers a quantity of the contraband to the agent, who gives her $200. As he concludes his purchase, the undercover agent arrests Hemphill and charges her with the sale of contraband. Hemphill's attorney pleads entrapment at her trial. Do you think her defense will be successful? Why or why not?

9. Boris Bottlemore has just finished celebrating his new job promotion by consuming ten double shots of bourbon in a bar near his home. He staggers from the bar to his home, which is one of twenty identical row houses on his block. In his inebriated state, Bottlemore mistakes his neighbor's home for his own. Finding the door unlocked, he enters and promptly raids the refrigerator. He then collapses on a couch in the living room and passes out. The next morning, Patty Purebred is shocked to find a stranger sleeping in her living room and her refrigerator standing open, with food strewn across the kitchen floor. She telephones the police, who arrive and take Bottlemore into custody, charging him with burglary. What defense or defenses are available to Bottlemore? What would you assess his chances before a jury to be?

# PART THREE

# Law Enforcement and Criminal Procedure

# CHAPTER 15

# Search and Seizure

## CHAPTER OUTLINE

## JURISPRUDENCE

*Katz v. United States* (1967)

*California v. Greenwood* (1988)

*United States v. Ross* (1982)

*Terry v. Ohio* (1968)

*United States v. Jones* (2012)

*Mapp v. Ohio* (1961)

*United States v. Leon* (1984)

*Herring v. United States* (2009)

## LEARNING OBJECTIVES

After reading this chapter, you should be able to explain

1. when, where and to whom the Fourth Amendment applies

2. the scope of privacy protected by the Fourth Amendment

3. why searches based on consent are problematic

4. the meaning and importance of probable cause

5. the rules governing the issuance and execution of search warrants

6. the recognized exceptions to the warrant requirement

7. the circumstances under which police or other officials are permitted to conduct searches based on reasonable suspicion

8. how interpretation of the Fourth Amendment has evolved in response to electronic surveillance

9. how federal statutes, including the USA PATRIOT Act, affect electronic surveillance

10. the exclusionary rule and the good faith exception to the rule

# CHAPTER OPENING VIGNETTE

Federal agents suspected that Danny Kyllo was growing marijuana inside his home in Florence, Oregon. But mere suspicion is not enough to justify the issuance of a search warrant. So the agents, sitting in a parked car across the street, used a thermal imaging device to scan the home.

The scan revealed that the roof over the garage and a side wall of Kyllo's home were significantly hotter than the rest of the house and much warmer than neighboring homes. Based on these results, as well as utility bills showing inordinate use of electricity, the agents concluded that Kyllo was using high-intensity lamps to grow marijuana inside his home. A federal magistrate determined that there was probable cause and issued a search warrant. After executing the warrant, agents found what they had suspected: an indoor growing operation with more than a hundred cannabis plants. Kyllo was arrested and later indicted by a federal grand jury for manufacturing marijuana. Kyllo's attorney moved to have the evidence suppressed, claiming that the use of the thermal imager constituted an unconstitutional search of his home. When the motion was denied, Kyllo agreed to a guilty plea but reserved the right to appeal the ruling on the pretrial motion. In 2001, nine years after Kyllo was arrested, the case was decided by the U.S. Supreme Court.

The Fourth Amendment prohibits unreasonable searches and seizures, and the courts have long held that warrantless searches of the home are unreasonable in the absence of extraordinary circumstances. But was the thermal scan of Kyllo's home a "search"? At the time this case was being litigated, thermal imagers were being widely used by law enforcement agencies around the country as part of the national war on drugs. Police and prosecutors typically took the view that the thermal scan was not a search within the meaning of the Fourth Amendment, since it merely collected data on heat that was being released into the public space. In a 5–4 decision, the Supreme Court disagreed with this point of view. *Kyllo v. United States*, 533 U.S. 27, 121 S.Ct. 2038, 150 L.Ed.2d 94 (2001). Writing for the Court, Justice Antonin Scalia observed that "[w]here, as here, the Government uses a device that is not in general public use, to explore details of the home that would previously have been unknowable without physical intrusion, the surveillance is a search and is presumptively unreasonable without a warrant." 533 U.S. at 40, 121 S.Ct. at 2046, 150 L.Ed.2d at 106. As a result of the Supreme Court's decision, the evidence the government had obtained against Kyllo was thrown out. The case collapsed and the government dropped the charges. The *Kyllo* case is interesting because it shows how changing technology creates new and difficult Fourth Amendment problems. As technology advances, courts will continue to confront such issues.

# Introduction

**search** Inspection; attempt to locate a particular person or object.

**seizure** Action of police in taking possession or control of property or persons.

Search and seizure have always been essential tools of law enforcement. A **search** occurs when government agents look for evidence in a manner that intrudes into a person's legally protected zone of privacy. A **seizure** takes place when agents take possession or control of property or persons.

Today, as the United States simultaneously prosecutes a "war on drugs" and a "war on terrorism," search and seizure are crucial issues for law enforcement agencies, courts, and citizens. Without the powers to conduct searches and seize evidence, law enforcement agencies would be unable to perform their historic missions, let alone combat drug trafficking, organized crime, and international terrorism. On the other hand, unrestricted powers of search and seizure are antithetical to the American traditions of individual liberty, personal privacy, and limited government.

Because search and seizure often entails serious invasions of privacy, the power of law enforcement agencies to conduct searches and seizures is limited by the federal and state constitutions and by a number of federal and state statutes. Most important among these legal limitations is the Fourth Amendment to the U.S. Constitution, which provides:

> The right of the people to be secure in their persons, houses, papers and effects, against unreasonable searches and seizures, shall not be violated, and no Warrants shall issue but upon probable cause, supported by Oath or affirmation, and particularly describing the place to be searched and the persons or things to be seized.

**warrant** A judicial writ or order directed to a law enforcement officer authorizing the doing of a specified act, such as an arrest or a search.

**probable cause** A reasonable ground for belief in certain alleged facts.

**reasonable suspicion** A police officer's belief based on all relevant circumstances that criminal activity is afoot.

As a general rule, the Fourth Amendment requires law enforcement officers to obtain a **warrant** before conducting searches and seizures. Although some warrantless searches and seizures are permissible, they all must conform to a standard of reasonableness. Law enforcement officers are not permitted to conduct searches and seizures arbitrarily or even based on their hunches about criminal activity. For a search to be reasonable under the Fourth Amendment, police generally must have **probable cause** to believe that a search will produce evidence of crime. In certain instances, police may conduct limited searches based on the lesser standard of **reasonable suspicion**. Subject to certain exceptions, evidence obtained through unreasonable searches and seizures is not admissible in criminal prosecutions.

# Historical Background

**general warrant** A search or arrest warrant that is not particular as to the person to be arrested, place to be searched, or property to be seized.

Before the late seventeenth century, there was very little protection at common law against invasions of privacy by unreasonable searches and seizures. Although a system of warrants had long been in place to provide legal authority for arrests, searches, and seizures, executive as well as judicial authorities could issue warrants. Moreover, there was no requirement that a search warrant specify the location to be searched or the items to be seized. For hundreds of years, English subjects (and, later, American colonists) were subjected to the abuse of the **general warrant**—that is, a warrant authorizing searches of unspecified persons and places.

The Glorious Revolution of 1688 was the real beginning of democracy in England. It was then that Parliament achieved supremacy over the monarchy. In the wake of the Glorious Revolution, English courts began to place more stringent and effective limitations on the Crown's power. The power of search and seizure was one area in which courts moved to limit royal authority.

By far, the most significant English case in the area of search and seizure before the American Revolution was *Entick v. Carrington*, 95 Eng. Rep. 807 (1765). John Entick, who edited a newspaper highly critical of the government, was arrested on a charge of seditious libel. A warrant was issued calling for the seizure of all his books, letters, and papers. Entick successfully sued for trespass. On appeal, the judgment was upheld and the practice of general warrants declared illegal. The opinion in *Entick v. Carrington* proved to be very influential. The next year, Parliament declared the notorious general warrant invalid. Addressing the House of Commons, William Pitt (the elder) declared that

> [t]he poorest man may, in his cottage, bid defiance to all the forces of the Crown. It may be frail; its roof may shake; the wind may blow through it; the storm may enter; but the King of England may not enter; all his force dares not cross the threshold of the ruined tenement.

## Adoption of the Fourth Amendment

Although the common law provided some protection against general warrants, the framers of the American Bill of Rights adopted a more explicit, and more thorough, proscription of unreasonable searches and seizures. To a great extent they were motivated by a distaste for the Writs of Assistance, which gave customs officials in the American colonies unlimited power to search for smuggled goods. In a famous debate in 1761, James Otis called the Writs of Assistance "the worst instrument of arbitrary power, the most destructive of English liberty and the fundamental principles of law, that ever was found in an English lawbook." Quoted in *Boyd v. United States*, 116 U.S. 616, 625, 6 S.Ct. 524, 529, 29 L.Ed. 746, 749 (1886). The Fourth Amendment was adopted to ensure that officials of the U.S. government would never be able to exercise such unlimited powers of search and seizure.

Their distaste for general warrants led the framers of the Bill of Rights to write a particularity requirement into the Warrant Clause of the Fourth Amendment. The Supreme Court has recognized that "limiting the authorization to search to the specific areas and things for which there is probable cause to search . . . ensures that the search will be carefully tailored to its justifications, and will not take on the character of the wide-ranging exploratory searches the Framers intended to prohibit." *Maryland v. Garrison*, 480 U.S. 79, 84, 107 S.Ct. 1013, 1016, 94 L.Ed.2d 72, 80 (1987).

## Extension of the Fourth Amendment to Apply to Searches by State and Local Authorities

The Fourth Amendment, like all the protections of the Bill of Rights, was originally conceived as a limitation on the powers of the newly created national government. Under the original conception of the Bill of Rights, citizens seeking legal protection against actions of state and local governments had to look to their state constitutions and state courts for relief. *Barron v. Baltimore*, 32 U.S. (7 Pet.) 243, 8 L.Ed. 672 (1833). However, the protection of the Fourth Amendment, along with most of the protections contained in the Bill of Rights, has been extended to defendants in state criminal prosecutions on the basis of the Fourteenth Amendment's limitations on state action. In 1949 the Supreme Court held that the freedom from unreasonable searches and seizures is "implicit in 'the concept of ordered liberty' and as such enforceable against the States through the Due Process Clause [of the Fourteenth Amendment]." *Wolf v. Colorado*, 338 U.S. 25, 27–28, 69 S.Ct. 1359, 1361, 93 L.Ed. 1782, 1785 (1949).

The judicial extension of the Fourth Amendment and other protections of the Bill of Rights to limit the actions of the state and local governments are referred to as the **doctrine of incorporation**. Under this doctrine, provisions of the Bill of Rights deemed to be essential to a scheme of ordered liberty are incorporated into the Fourteenth Amendment's broad limitations on state and local authority. *Palko v. Connecticut*, 302 U.S. 319, 58 S.Ct. 149, 82 L.Ed. 288 (1937).

**doctrine of incorporation**
The doctrine under which provisions of the Bill of Rights are held to be incorporated within the Due Process Clause of the Fourteenth Amendment and are thereby made applicable to actions of the state and local governments.

## Judicial Federalism and the Fourth Amendment

As a result of *Wolf v. Colorado*, supra, the Fourth Amendment limits search and seizure activities by law enforcement agencies at all levels of government, whether federal, state, or local. The application of the Fourth Amendment to state prosecutions ensures a minimal national standard governing search and seizure. Under our system of federalism, state courts are free to provide higher levels of protection for individuals under applicable provisions of their state constitutions than are provided by the Fourth Amendment. But they cannot provide less protection to the individual without running afoul of the Fourteenth Amendment. Indeed, this is true of all constitutional protections. As long as state courts make clear that decisions that favor the rights of suspects, defendants, and prisoners rest on independent state constitutional grounds, those decisions are not subject to review by the federal courts. *Michigan v. Long*, 463 U.S. 1032, 103 S.Ct. 3469, 77 L.Ed.2d 1201 (1983).

State constitutional law in the search and seizure area has become extremely complex, as there are numerous issues on which certain state courts have refused to follow federal decisions restricting Fourth Amendment protections. We will mention a few examples on the pages that follow. In an attempt to reduce confusion and unnecessary complexity owing to different federal and state standards of search and seizure, Florida amended its constitution in 1982 to render its prohibition of unreasonable searches and seizures coextensive with that of the Fourth Amendment. West's Fla. Const. Art. 1, § 12 (as amended in 1982). Interpreting this novel amendment, the Florida Supreme Court has held that, in effect, the Florida Constitution incorporates all decisions of the U.S. Supreme Court interpreting the Fourth Amendment, regardless of when they were rendered. *Bernie v. State*, 524 So.2d 988 (Fla. 1988).

# When, Where, and to Whom the Fourth Amendment Applies

Because the Constitution limits government action, the Fourth Amendment protects a person's rights against the police and other government agents but not against searches and seizures conducted by private individuals. The Supreme Court has said that the Fourth Amendment "is wholly inapplicable to a search or seizure, even an unreasonable one, effected by a private individual not acting as an agent of the Government or with the participation or knowledge of any government official." *United States v. Jacobsen*, 466 U.S. 109, 113, 104 S.Ct. 1652, 1656, 80 L.Ed.2d 85, 94 (1984). In determining whether a private citizen has acted as an agent of the government, the court must consider (1) whether the government knew of and acquiesced in the activity and (2) whether the citizen was motivated on the basis of assisting the government. *United States v. Feffer*, 831 F.2d 734, 739 (7th Cir. 1987). Thus, a search by a privately employed security guard is ordinarily considered a search by a private citizen. Likewise, a search of a package by an employee of a common carrier is not considered a violation of the Fourth Amendment unless the search was instigated by government action. *United States v. Monroe*, 943 F.2d 884 (8th Cir. 1991).

On the other hand, states can interpret their own constitutional limitations more broadly to apply to searches by certain nongovernmental actors. Alternatively, they can enact statutes to that effect. For example, the Texas Code of Criminal Procedure provides, "No evidence obtained by an officer *or other person* [emphasis added] in violation of any provisions of the Constitution or laws of the State of Texas, or of the Constitution or laws of the United States of America, shall be admitted in evidence against the accused on the trial of any criminal case." Tex. Code Crim. Proc. Art. 38.23(a).

## Border Searches and Searches Outside the United States

**border searches** Searches of persons entering the borders of the United States.

Travelers crossing the borders of the United States are routinely subjected to searches even when they are not the targets of suspicion. Suspicionless **border searches** are justified by the view that persons crossing the national border are not entitled to the protections of the Fourth Amendment. *United States v. Ramsey*, 431 U.S. 606, 97 S.Ct. 1972, 52 L.Ed.2d 617 (1977). This is not to say that agents conducting border searches are beyond the law. Regardless of the applicability of the Fourth Amendment, methods of search and seizure may not be so severe or extreme as to "shock the conscience." *Rochin v. California*, 342 U.S. 165, 72 S.Ct. 205, 96 L.Ed. 183 (1952).

The border search exception to the Fourth Amendment extends to searches conducted at established stations near the border or other functional equivalents of a border search. An example would be the search of a ship when it first docks after entering the territorial waters of the United States. *United States v. Prince*, 491 F.2d 655 (5th Cir. 1974). On the other hand, in *Almeida-Sanchez v. United States*, 413 U.S. 266, 93 S.Ct. 2535, 37 L.Ed.2d 596 (1973), the Supreme Court invalidated a search by a roving patrol some twenty-five miles within the border because agents lacked probable cause.

The Fourth Amendment does not apply to searches and seizures conducted by U.S. agents outside the territory of the United States. The purpose of the amendment is to restrict only those searches and seizures conducted domestically. *United States v. Verdugo-Urquidez*, 494 U.S. 259, 110 S.Ct. 1056, 108 L.Ed.2d 222 (1990).

## The Home, Its Curtilage, and the Open Fields Doctrine

The English common law held that "a man's home is his castle," and it sought to protect persons in their homes by, among other things, creating the crime of burglary. The Fourth Amendment specifically mentions the right of the people to be secure in their houses. Of course, it also mentions their persons, papers, and effects. But it is fair to say that when a person is in his or her home, the protection afforded by the Fourth Amendment is at its maximum.

**curtilage** The enclosed space of ground surrounding a dwelling.

At common law, the concept of **curtilage** was developed to afford the area immediately surrounding a house the same protection under the law of burglary as the house itself. The term refers to the enclosed space of ground surrounding a dwelling. The Supreme Court has held that the Fourth Amendment provides the same protection to the curtilage as to the house itself. On the other hand, the open fields surrounding the house and curtilage are not entitled to Fourth Amendment protection. *Hester v. United States*, 265 U.S. 57, 44 S.Ct. 445, 68 L.Ed. 898 (1924). Writing for the Supreme Court in *Hester*, Justice Oliver Wendell Holmes noted that

> the special protection accorded by the Fourth Amendment to the people in their "persons, houses, papers and effects," is not extended to the open fields. The distinction between the latter and the house is as old as the common law. 265 U.S. at 59, 44 S.Ct. at 446, 68 L.Ed. at 900.

**open fields doctrine** The doctrine that the Fourth Amendment does not apply to the open fields around a home, even if these open fields are private property.

The **open fields doctrine** was reaffirmed by the Supreme Court in *Oliver v. United States*, 466 U.S. 170, 104 S.Ct. 1735, 80 L.Ed.2d 214 (1984). In *Oliver*, narcotics officers entered the defendant's land by going around a locked gate and ignoring "No Trespassing" signs. When they observed a field of marijuana, they arrested the owner of the property for manufacturing contraband. The Court upheld the search because it concluded that the Fourth Amendment did not apply to the open fields around the owner's home, despite his attempt to protect it by posting signs. State courts are divided on whether to provide greater protection under their state constitutions. But in *United States v. Cuevas-Sanchez*, 821 F.2d 248 (5th Cir. 1987), the Fifth Circuit Court of Appeals held that the use of a video camera mounted on a utility pole to conduct surveillance of a defendant's fenced-in backyard was a search entitled to Fourth Amendment protection.

In *People v. Scott*, 593 N.E.2d 1328 (N.Y. 1992), New York's highest court ruled that where property owners fence or post "No Trespassing" signs on their private property or, by some other means, indicate that entry is not permitted, they have a reasonable expectation of privacy that must be respected. The New York decision illustrates that a state is free to provide greater protection under its state constitution than the U.S. Supreme Court determines is required under the federal constitution. A New Jersey appellate court was unwilling to grant greater protection than afforded by the federal constitution when it excused a warrantless entry onto private lands by conservation officers investigating a suspected violation of fish and game law. *State v. Gates*, 703 A.2d 696 (N.J. Super. 1997).

## Searches of Abandoned Property

**abandoned property** Property over which the former owner has relinquished any claim of ownership.

Police may search abandoned premises and seize **abandoned property** without the necessity of legally justifying their actions. *Abel v. United States*, 362 U.S. 217, 80 S.Ct. 683, 4 L.Ed.2d 668 (1960). The key question in such cases is whether the property was abandoned at the time of the search. In a 1960 decision, the Supreme Court observed that a "passenger who lets a package drop to the floor of the taxicab in which he is riding can hardly be said to have 'abandoned' it. An occupied taxicab is not to be compared to an open field . . . or a vacated hotel room." *Rios v. United States*, 364 U.S. 253, 262, n. 6, 80 S.Ct. 1431, 1437, 4 L.Ed.2d 1688, 1694 (1960). Similarly, in 1990 the Supreme Court held that "a citizen who attempts to protect his private property from inspection, after throwing it on a car to respond to a police officer's inquiry, clearly has not abandoned that property." *Smith v. Ohio*, 494 U.S. 541, 543–544, 110 S.Ct. 1288, 1290, 108 L.Ed.2d 464, 468 (1990).

## Automobile Inventory Searches

**inventory search** An exception to the warrant requirement that allows police who legally impound a vehicle to conduct a routine inventory of the contents of the vehicle.

Most law enforcement agencies that impound automobiles for parking violations or abandonment, or pursuant to the arrest of a motorist, routinely conduct an inventory of the contents and remove any valuables for safekeeping. When conducted according to standard police procedures, an **inventory search** is generally regarded as an administrative search not subject to ordinary Fourth Amendment requirements. Inventory searches are justified by the need for protection of the owner's property while the vehicle remains in police custody, protection of the police from claims of lost property, and protection of the police from potential dangers that might be lurking inside closed automobiles. Of course, if a routine inventory search yields evidence of crime, it may be seized and admitted into evidence without violating the Fourth Amendment. *South Dakota v. Opperman*, 428 U.S. 364, 96 S.Ct. 3092, 49 L.Ed.2d 1000 (1976).

It should be recognized that police are not permitted to use an inventory search as a pretext for a criminal investigation. *Colorado v. Bertine*, 479 U.S. 367, 107 S.Ct. 738, 93 L.Ed.2d 739 (1987). Nevertheless, once the police have legitimately taken a vehicle into custody, they are not required to overlook contraband articles discovered during a valid inventory search, and such items may be used as evidence. Lower federal and state courts have emphasized that an inventory search must be in accordance with established inventory procedures. See, e.g., *United States v. Velarde*, 903 F.2d 1163 (7th Cir. 1990). In 1998, the Arkansas Supreme Court held that the fact that the defendant lacked a valid driver's license constituted good cause to justify a police officer's impounding his vehicle and completing a warrantless inventory of its contents pursuant to the police department's standards. *Thompson v. State*, 966 S.W.2d 901 (Ark. 1998).

## Searches Based on Consent

**consent to a search** The act of a person voluntarily permitting police to conduct a search of person or property.

Constitutional rights may be waived, and Fourth Amendment rights are no exception. Voluntary cooperation with police officers often results in fruitful searches and seizures. The Supreme Court has refused to require law officers to inform suspects of their right to refuse to **consent to a search**. *Schneckloth v. Bustamonte*, 412 U.S. 218, 93 S.Ct. 2041, 36 L.Ed.2d 854 (1973). More recently, the Court held that police are not required to inform motorists who are stopped for other reasons that they are "free to go" before asking them to consent to a search of their automobile. *Ohio v. Robinette*, 519 U.S. 33, 117 S.Ct. 417, 136 L.Ed.2d 347 (1996).

To be valid, consent must be truly voluntary. If a person actually assists the police in conducting a search, or consents after having been advised that consent is not required, courts have little difficulty in finding that consent was voluntary. Yet consent has to involve more than mere acquiescence to the authority of the police. Thus, in *Bumper v. North Carolina*, 391 U.S. 543, 88 S.Ct. 1788, 20 L.Ed.2d 797 (1968), the Court held that a claim of police authority based on a nonexistent warrant was so coercive as to invalidate the defendant's consent. Similarly, a Georgia appellate court invalidated an automobile search where the defendant and a companion were surprised by six heavily armed law officers, were searched at gunpoint, and were then asked to consent to a search of their automobile. *Love v. State*, 242 S.E.2d 278 (Ga. App. 1978).

When a person summons the police to the home to investigate a crime that has allegedly taken place there, there is an **implied consent** to a search of the premises related to the routine investigation of the offense. Of course, once police are lawfully on the premises, any evidence of crime that is in their plain view may be seized, even if the person who initially summoned the police may be ultimately prosecuted as a result of such evidence.

**implied consent** An agreement or acquiescence manifested by a person's actions or inaction.

A perennial problem in the area of consent searches is that of **third-party consent**. The problem is especially acute in situations where several persons share a single dwelling, as is common among college students. For example, may an apartment dweller consent to the search of his or her roommate's bedroom? The Supreme Court has said that the consent of a third party is valid only when there is mutual use of the property by persons generally having joint access or control. Thus, any of the co-occupants has the right to permit the inspection. The others have assumed the risk that one of their roommates might permit the common area to be searched. *United States v. Matlock*, 415 U.S. 164, 94 S.Ct. 988, 39 L.Ed.2d 242 (1974). *Matlock* stands for the principle that the validity of third-party consent is tested by the degree of dominion and control exercised by the third party over the searched premises and that a joint occupant may provide valid consent only if the other party is not present.

**third-party consent** Consent, usually to a search, given by a person on behalf of another—for example, a college roommate who allows the police to search his or her roommate's effects.

In *Illinois v. Rodriguez*, 497 U.S. 177, 110 S.Ct. 2793, 111 L.Ed.2d 148 (1990), the Supreme Court shifted the focus from the dominion and control of the third party to the police officer's subjective belief that the third party has the authority to grant consent to a search of the premises. Writing for the Court, Justice Antonin Scalia opined that a warrantless entry is valid when based on the consent of a third party that the police reasonably believe to possess common authority over the premises, even if the third party does not in fact have such authority.

There are a number of well-established situations in which third-party consent is not valid. Tenancy arrangements are a good example. A landlord does not have the implied authority to consent to the search of a tenant's premises. *Chapman v. United States*, 365 U.S. 610, 81 S.Ct. 776, 5 L.Ed.2d 828 (1961). Likewise, a hotel manager or clerk does not have the right to consent to the search of a guest's room during the time the guest has a legal right to occupy the room. *Stoner v. California*, 376 U.S. 483, 84 S.Ct. 889, 11 L.Ed.2d 856 (1964).

**exigent circumstances** Unforeseen situations that demand unusual or immediate action.

Courts have taken different approaches to searches of college dormitory rooms, often depending on the regulations the student agrees to when occupying the dormitory room. A search routinely performed by college officials for reasons of health or safety that reveals incriminating evidence in plain view would probably not be in violation of the Fourth Amendment. On the other hand, a search of a dormitory room by police would ordinarily require a search warrant issued on the basis of probable cause. In *Commonwealth v. McCloskey*, 272 A.2d 271 (Pa. Super. 1970), the court held that absent **exigent circumstances**, police entry into a college dormitory room by means of a pass key possessed by the head resident was improper. Even though the university had reserved the right to check the room for damage and use of unauthorized appliances, the court found that in the absence of exigent circumstances the university did not have authority to consent to a governmental search of the student's room.

Some current problems in the area of third-party consent involve parental consent to searches of premises occupied by their adult children and spousal consent to searches of the other spouse's property, such as an automobile. But again, the Supreme Court has shifted the focus to the police officer's subjective belief regarding the authority of third parties. In general, state courts have followed the *Matlock* approach. The Louisiana Supreme Court did that in 1999 by holding that a warrantless search may be valid even if consent was given by one without authority if the facts available to officers at the time of entry justified the officers' reasonable, albeit erroneous, belief that the one consenting to the search had authority over the premises. *State v. Edwards*, 750 So.2d 893 (La. 1999). But not all state courts have been willing to follow *Matlock*; some provide more protection to their citizens. For example, Oregon courts have ruled that the state constitution requires that consent by a third party must be based on actual authority. See *State v. Will*, 885 P.2d 715 (Or. App. 1994).

# The Scope of Privacy Protected by the Fourth Amendment

The term "seizure" refers to the taking into custody of physical evidence, property, or even a person. What constitutes a "search"? The answer is not so clear. Originally, the protection of the Fourth Amendment was limited to physical intrusions on one's person or property. *Olmstead v. United States*, 277 U.S. 438, 48 S.Ct. 564, 72 L.Ed. 944 (1928). Historically, courts looked at whether a trespass had taken place in deciding whether the Fourth Amendment was implicated. Thus, surveillance without physical contact with the suspect or the suspect's property was deemed to fall outside the protections of the Fourth Amendment. Accordingly, the Fourth Amendment was not deemed applicable to **wiretapping** or **electronic eavesdropping**.

In *Katz v. United States*, 389 U.S. 347, 88 S.Ct. 507, 19 L.Ed.2d 576 (1967), the Supreme Court overruled *Olmstead* and abandoned the trespass doctrine, saying "the Fourth Amendment protects people, not places." 389 U.S. at 361, 88 S.Ct. at 516, 19 L.Ed.2d at 582. The contemporary approach to determining the scope of protected privacy under the Fourth Amendment is nicely stated in Justice John M. Harlan's concurring opinion in *Katz*:

> My understanding of the rule as it has emerged from prior decisions is that there is a twofold requirement, first, that a person has exhibited an actual (subjective) expectation of privacy and, second, that the expectation be one that society is prepared to recognize as "reasonable." 389 U.S. at 361, 88 S.Ct. at 516, 19 L.Ed.2d at 587.

**wiretapping** The use of highly sensitive electronic devices designed to intercept electronic communications.

**electronic eavesdropping** Covert listening to or recording of a person's conversations by electronic means.

## Reasonable Expectations of Privacy

**reasonable expectation of privacy** Doctrine holding that the Fourth Amendment protects persons from official intrusions as long as they have a subjective expectation of privacy that society is prepared to accept.

Potentially, the term "search" applies to any official invasion of a person's reasonable expectation of privacy as to one's person, house, papers, or effects. In *Katz*, the Court held that a suspected bookie who was using a public telephone, allegedly to conduct a gambling business, enjoyed a **reasonable expectation of privacy** and that a police wiretap of the phone booth was a search within the meaning of the Fourth Amendment. This decision brought wiretapping and other forms of electronic eavesdropping within the limitations of the Fourth Amendment. Currently, any means of invading a person's reasonable expectation of privacy is considered a search for

---

**JURISPRUDENCE**

*Katz v. United States*, 389 U.S. 347, 88 S.Ct. 507, 19 L.Ed.2d 576 (1967)

Government agents, acting without a warrant, attached a "bug," or listening device, to the outside of a public telephone booth from which Charles Katz, a suspected bookie, often placed calls. Agents recorded Katz's conversations and obtained evidence that led to an eight-count indictment charging him with transmitting wagering information by telephone. Katz was convicted despite his claim that the government's key evidence had been obtained in violation of the Fourth Amendment. In affirming his conviction, the Court of Appeals, relying on *Olmstead v. United States* (1928), found no constitutional violation because "[t]here was no physical entrance into the area occupied by [Katz]." In a landmark ruling, the Supreme

Court reversed and overturned the conviction. The Court observed that "the underpinnings of [*Olmstead v. United States*] have been so eroded by our subsequent decisions that the 'trespass' doctrine there enunciated can no longer be regarded as controlling." Justice Potter Stewart's opinion for the Court concluded that "electronically listening to and recording the petitioner's words violated the privacy upon which he justifiably relied while using the telephone booth and thus constituted a "search and seizure" within the meaning of the Fourth Amendment." According to Justice Harlan's concurrence, which has come to be regarded as the most important opinion in *Katz*, the Fourth Amendment extends to any place or thing in which an individual has a "reasonable expectation of privacy."

---

Fourth Amendment purposes. The critical question that courts must address in reviewing cases where police conduct surveillance or eavesdropping without probable cause or prior judicial authorization is whether such surveillance intruded on a person's reasonable expectation of privacy.

The question of what constitutes a reasonable expectation of privacy has been litigated in hundreds of cases in federal and state courts. Police techniques such as canine sniffs are considered among the least intrusive means of government investigation. Thus, police were allowed to conduct a "sniff test" of a passenger's luggage at an airport without reasonable suspicion because it did not violate a person's reasonable expectation of privacy. *United States v. Place*, 462 U.S. 696, 106 S.Ct. 2637, 77 L.Ed.2d 110 (1983). In *City of Indianapolis v. Edmond*, 531 U.S. 32, 121 S.Ct. 447, 148 L.Ed.2d 333 (2000), the Supreme Court reviewed canine sniffs in context of vehicular traffic and observed that "walking a narcotics-detection dog around the exterior of each car . . . does not transform the seizure into a search." However, the uniqueness of individual situations has resulted in disparate views, with police frequently complaining that judicial decisions fail to furnish any "bright-line" rules. In a number of well-defined situations, however, courts have upheld minimally intrusive, suspicionless searches on the assumption that people's privacy expectations are reduced in such situations.

## Airport Security Procedures

With increased concern over airplane hijacking and terrorism has come increased security at the nation's airports. Passengers attempting to board aircraft routinely pass through metal detectors; their carry-on baggage and checked luggage are routinely subjected to X-ray scans. Should these procedures suggest the presence of suspicious objects, physical searches are conducted to determine what the objects are. There is little question that such searches are reasonable given their minimal intrusiveness, the gravity of the safety interests involved, and the reduced privacy expectations associated with airline travel. Indeed, travelers are often notified through airport public address systems and signs that "all bags are subject to search." Such announcements place passengers on notice that ordinary Fourth Amendment protections do not apply.

In 2010 a controversy erupted over enhanced screening procedures adopted by the Transportation Security Administration in response to recent attempts by terrorists to carry nonmetallic explosives onto aircraft. These procedures involved the use of full-body scans that revealed considerable anatomical detail and, for passengers who opted out of the scans, fairly extensive pat-down searches. Clearly the enhanced procedures were more intrusive and subjected passengers to considerable inconvenience and, in some cases, embarrassment. But most legal commentators agreed that, given the magnitude of the safety interests involved, the enhanced procedures were reasonable.

## Sobriety Checkpoints

**sobriety checkpoints**
Roadblocks set up for the purpose of administering field sobriety tests to motorists who appear to be intoxicated.

In the last twenty-five years society has become incensed about drunk driving and the resulting carnage on the nation's highways. One method increasingly used by law enforcement to combat this problem is the use of **sobriety checkpoints**, in which all drivers passing a certain point are stopped briefly and observed for signs of intoxication. To the extent that police officers at these checkpoints visually inspect the passenger compartments of stopped automobiles, these brief encounters involve searches, although in most instances these procedures entail only minor intrusion and inconvenience. Critics of sobriety checkpoints object to the fact that police temporarily detain and visually search cars without any particular suspicion. Yet the courts have generally approved such measures. See, e.g., *Michigan Dept. of State Police v. Sitz*, 496 U.S. 444, 110 S.Ct. 2481, 110 L.Ed.2d 412 (1990). It is noteworthy, however, that in 2000, the U.S. Supreme Court disallowed a checkpoint that was established primarily for the purpose of detecting illegal drugs. *City of Indianapolis v. Edmond*, 531 U.S. 32, 121 S.Ct 447, 148 L.Ed.2d 333 (2000). (This topic is explored further in the next chapter.)

## Jail and Prison Searches and Strip Searches

Obviously, anyone lawfully incarcerated in a prison or jail has no reasonable expectation of privacy. Jail and prison cells are routinely "swept" for weapons and other contraband, and inmates are routinely subjected to searches of their persons. The Supreme Court in *Bell v. Wolfish*, 441 U.S. 520, 99 S.Ct. 1861, 60 L.Ed.2d 447 (1979), upheld **strip searches** of prison inmates because of the demands for institutional security. But the Court did not give prison officials carte blanche. Rather, the Court held that the Fourth Amendment requires balancing the need for the particular search against the invasion of personal rights. Thus, courts must consider the justification and scope of the intrusion and the manner and place in which it is conducted.

**strip searches** Searches of suspects' or prisoners' private parts.

Absent cause for suspicion, visitors to a prison may be subjected to reasonable searches—for example, a pat-down search or a metal detector sweep. However, before conducting a strip search of a visitor, prison authorities must have at least a reasonable suspicion that the visitor is bearing contraband. *Spear v. Sowders*, 71 F.3d 626 (6th Cir. 1995).

Courts have generally disapproved of blanket policies that allow strip searches of all persons who have been arrested, particularly where traffic violators are concerned. Some courts hold that strip searches are violative of Fourth Amendment rights unless

**JURISPRUDENCE**

*California v. Greenwood*, 486 U.S. 35, 108 S.Ct. 1625, 100 L.Ed.2d 30 (1988)

A police officer asked a trash collector to turn over bags of garbage collected from the Greenwoods' home in Laguna Beach, California. The officer searched the garbage bags and found evidence indicating illicit drug use. She used this evidence as a basis for obtaining a warrant to search the Greenwood home. During the search, the police discovered cocaine and hashish. As a result, the police charged the defendants with possession of illicit drugs. The trial court dismissed the charges on the ground that the warrantless trash search violated the Fourth Amendment, and the California appellate court affirmed. The U.S. Supreme Court granted review and reversed on the ground that the defendants, by placing their garbage outside the curtilage, had exposed their garbage to the public, and regardless of whether they may have had an expectation of privacy in their garbage, it was not an expectation that society is prepared to accept as being objectively reasonable.

there is probable cause to believe that the arrestee is concealing weapons or contraband. See, e.g., *Mary Beth G. v. Chicago*, 723 F.2d 1263 (7th Cir. 1983). Other courts have permitted such searches where there is a reasonable suspicion that the arrestee is concealing weapons or contraband. See, e.g., *Weber v. Dell*, 804 F.2d 796 (2d Cir. 1986).

Strip searches can also have civil consequences. For example, in *Jones v. Edwards*, 770 F.2d 739 (8th Cir. 1985), Marlin E. Jones was arrested and taken into custody for failing to sign a summons and complaint on an animal leash law violation. He was subjected to a visual strip search of his anal and genital area. The court ruled that such a search, under these circumstances, subjected the police and jail personnel to liability for the violation of the arrestee's civil rights. The court emphasized that the police had no reason to suspect that Jones was harboring weapons or contraband on his person.

## The Warrant Requirement

As pointed out, when searches are challenged as being unreasonable, courts must first determine if the Fourth Amendment is applicable. The Fourth Amendment does not apply to border searches or searches conducted outside the United States, nor does it apply to open fields or abandoned property. Indeed, the Fourth Amendment does not apply to any situation where a person lacks a reasonable expectation of privacy. Where it does apply, the Fourth Amendment expresses a decided preference for searches and seizures to be conducted pursuant to a warrant. The warrant requirement is designed to ensure that the impartial judgment of a judge or a magistrate is interposed between the citizen and the state. The right of privacy is "too precious to entrust to the discretion of those whose job is the detection of crime and the arrest of criminals." *McDonald v. United States*, 335 U.S. 451, 455–456, 69 S.Ct. 191, 195–96, 93 L.Ed. 153, 158 (1948).

### Probable Cause

With the exception of warrants permitting administrative searches, search warrants must be based on probable cause. Like many legal terms, "probable cause" is not susceptible to precise definition. Probable cause exists when prudent and cautious police officers have trustworthy information leading them to believe that evidence of crime might be obtained through a particular search. See *Brinegar v. United States*,

338 U.S. 160, 69 S.Ct. 1302, 93 L.Ed. 1879 (1949); *Carroll v. United States*, 267 U.S. 132, 45 S.Ct. 280, 69 L.Ed. 543 (1925).

The Supreme Court has said that courts should view the determination of probable cause as a "commonsense, practical question" that must be decided in light of the **totality of circumstances** in a given case. *Illinois v. Gates*, 462 U.S. 213, 230, 103 S.Ct. 2317, 2328, 76 L.Ed.2d 527, 543 (1983). This approach has been amplified by lower federal courts, which have observed that even though an innocent explanation might be consistent with the facts alleged in an affidavit seeking a search warrant, this does not negate probable cause. See, e.g., *United States v. Fama*, 758 F.2d 834 (2d Cir. 1985).

Although state courts are free to impose a higher standard, most have followed this approach. For example, the Ohio Supreme Court ruled that an affidavit by a police agent saying that he observed a tall marijuana plant growing in an enclosed backyard furnished probable cause for a magistrate to conclude there was marijuana or related paraphernalia in the residence. *State v. George*, 544 N.E.2d 640 (Ohio 1989). Some state courts have declined to follow the *Gates* approach and have opted to provide their citizens more protection than allowed by the federal view. In some instances, these state views result from linguistic variations in state constitutional counterparts to the Fourth Amendment. For example, in *Commonwealth v. Upton*, 476 N.E.2d 548 (Mass. 1985), the court noted that the Massachusetts constitution provides more substantive protection to criminal defendants than does the Fourth Amendment to the U.S. Constitution in the determination of probable cause. Thus, the court held that an affidavit based on a telephone tip from an anonymous informer whose veracity was not shown did not establish probable cause for issuance of a warrant to search a mobile home.

## Issuance of the Search Warrant

Under normal circumstances, a police officer with probable cause to believe that evidence of a crime is located in a specific place must submit under oath an application for a search warrant to the appropriate judge or magistrate. Rule 41 of the Federal Rules of Criminal Procedure allows a federal agent to obtain a search warrant from a federal magistrate or a judge of a state court of record within the district wherein the property or person sought is located. Either by statute or judicial rules, states usually provide similar authorization.

In *Coolidge v. New Hampshire*, 403 U.S. 443, 91 S.Ct. 2022, 29 L.Ed.2d 564 (1971), the Supreme Court invalidated a warrant issued by the state attorney general. The Court said that a warrant must be issued by a neutral and detached magistrate and certainly not by an official responsible for criminal prosecutions. Similarly, in *United States v. United States District Court*, 407 U.S. 297, 92 S.Ct. 2125, 32 L.Ed.2d 752 (1972), the Court invalidated a statute that permitted electronic eavesdropping to be authorized solely by the U.S. Attorney General in cases involving national security. Writing for the Court, Justice Lewis Powell observed that "unreviewed executive discretion may yield too readily to pressures to obtain incriminating evidence and overlook potential invasions of privacy . . . " 407 U.S. at 317, 92 S.Ct. at 2136, 32 L.Ed.2d at 766.

## The Supporting Affidavit

An **affidavit** is a signed document attesting under oath to certain facts of which the **affiant** (the person submitting the affidavit) has knowledge (see Figure 15.1). Generally, an affidavit by a law enforcement officer requesting issuance of a search

**totality of circumstances** Circumstances considered in the aggregate as opposed to individually.

**affidavit** A written document attesting to specific facts of which the affiant has knowledge, and sworn to or affirmed by the affiant.

**affiant** A person who makes an affidavit.

ACODC NO. 29

# Commonwealth of Massachusetts

Middlesex _____, ss.

Concord District Court
Court

## AFFIDAVIT IN SUPPORT OF APPLICATION FOR SEARCH WARRANT*
G.L. c. 276, ss. 1 to 7; St. 1964, c. 557 As Amended

I, __Sam Buckley_____, being duly sworn, depose and say:

21   June   , 19 80

Name of applicant

1. I am ___Police Chief of Concord, Massachusetts____
(Describe position, assignment, office, etc.)

2. I have information based upon (describe sources, facts indicating reliability of source and nature of information; if based on personal knowledge and belief, so state) (If space is insufficient, attach affidavit or affidavits hereto)

Based on information from a Federal Drug Enforcement Officer, the above has reason to belive at 123 Smith Street, one-story red brick house, with garage, 2 bedrooms, kitchen, living room, and bathroom, there is a small brown suitcase containing a controlled substance believed to be heroin.

*3. Based upon the foregoing reliable information - and upon my personal knowledge and belief - and ~~searched affidavits~~ - there is probable cause to believe that the property hereinafter described - has been stolen - or is being concealed, etc.
and may be found in the possession of __Miss Francine Taggart_____
Name or person or persons

at premises _____123 Smith Street, Concord_____
(Identify number, street, place, etc.)

4. The property for which I seek the issuance of a search warrant is the following (here describe the property as particularly as possible).

One small brown suitcase taken from a station locker by Francine Taggart on June 19, 1980, containing heroin.

WHEREFORE, I respectfully request that the court issue a warrant and order of seizure, authorizing the search of (identify premises and the person or persons to be searched)

and directing that if such property or evidence or any part thereof be found that it be seized and brought before the court; together with such other and further relief that the court may deem proper.

Police Chief Sam Buckley
Signature of applicant

Then personally appeared the above named _Chief Buckley_____
and made oath that the foregoing affidavit by him subscribed is true.

Before me this __21__ day of __June__ , 19 80

J. P. Jones - Special Justice

Justice or Special Justice
Clerk or Assistant Clerk of the

Municipal
District Court.

* Strike inapplicable clauses

REVISED JULY 1965

APPROVED BY THE CHIEF JUSTICE OF THE DISTRICT COURTS

© Cengage Learning

**FIGURE 15.1** Application for a Search Warrant.

warrant is presented to a judge or magistrate. The manner in which the affidavit is recorded and transmitted may vary. For example, the Idaho Supreme Court, finding that electronically recorded testimony is no less reliable than a sworn, written statement, held that the word "affidavit" under the Idaho constitution was sufficiently broad to include a tape recording of oral testimony. *State v. Yoder*, 534 P.2d 771 (Idaho 1975).

Rule 41(d)(3)(A) of the Federal Rules of Criminal Procedure provides that a federal magistrate judge may issue a warrant based upon sworn oral testimony communicated by phone or other appropriate means, including facsimile transmission. Some states follow this approach—for example, California law permits police officers to complete affidavits using the telephone to expedite the issuance of a warrant. West's Ann. Cal. Pen. Code. § 1526(b).

The officer's affidavit in support of a search warrant must always contain a rather precise description of the place(s) or person(s) to be searched and the things to be seized. Moreover, the affidavit must attest to specific facts (merely on the affiant's suspicion) that establish probable cause to justify a search. The information on which an affidavit is based must be sufficiently fresh to ensure that the items to be seized are probably located on the premises to be searched. The issue of when a search warrant becomes invalid because the information the affidavit is based on is stale has been litigated in many cases, with varying results. No set rule can be formulated. For example, a Delaware appellate court invalidated a search warrant where there was a delay of twenty-three days between the last alleged fact and the issuance of the warrant. In *State v. Pulgini*, 374 A.2d 822 (Del. 1977), the Delaware Supreme Court reversed the decision, noting the affidavit for the warrant recited facts indicating activity of a protracted and continuous nature during the period of delay. The court said that under such circumstances the passage of time becomes less significant. In *United States v. Rosenbarger*, 536 F.2d 715 (6th Cir. 1976), a twenty-one-day time lapse between observation of the receipt of stolen property and issuance of the warrant did not invalidate the warrant because the magistrate could determine there was a reasonable probability that the stolen goods were still in the defendant's home.

In *State v. Carlson*, 4 P.3d 1122 (Idaho App. 2000), an Idaho appellate court held that a warrant to search a defendant's residence was not based upon stale information even though there was a lapse of twenty-four days between the informant's initial observations and the issuance of the search warrant. The court considered the fact that the information was supplemented by a second report regarding observation of a marijuana plant three days prior to the issuance of the warrant and the implication that a marijuana operation continued in the interim period.

In *Hemler v. Superior Court*, 118 Cal. Rptr. 564 (Cal. App. 1975), the court acknowledged that the question of "stale" information depends upon the facts of each case. The court stated that an affidavit clearly furnished probable cause for the issuance of a search warrant either immediately or within a short time after observation of the sale of narcotics in an apartment. Nevertheless, the court held that the affidavit did not furnish probable cause for the issuance of a search warrant thirty-four days later.

Most appellate courts have not set specific time limits as to when information supporting the issuance of a search warrant becomes stale. While a magistrate must consider time as an element of probable cause when issuing a warrant, in *Copeland v. State*, 616 S.E.2d 189, 192 (Ga. App. 2005), the court pointed out that "[t]he mere passage of time does not equate with staleness."

## Tips from Police Informants

A magistrate's finding of probable cause may be based on hearsay evidence. See, e.g., Fed. R. Crim. P. 41(c)(1), which permits police to obtain search warrants based on tips from anonymous or **confidential informants**. Confidential informants, or CIs, are often persons who have been involved with the police and are seeking favorable consideration in respect to their own offenses. Because their motivation may be suspect, their reliability is checked carefully. For many years the Supreme Court required magistrates to apply a rigorous two-pronged test to determine probable

**confidential informants** An informant known to the police but whose identity is held in confidence.

cause. See *Aguilar v. Texas*, 378 U.S. 108, 84 S.Ct. 1509, 12 L.Ed.2d 723 (1964); *Spinelli v. United States*, 393 U.S. 410, 89 S.Ct. 584, 21 L.Ed.2d 637 (1969). The *Aguilar–Spinelli* test required that the officer's affidavit satisfy two criteria: (1) it had to demonstrate that the informant was both credible and reliable, and (2) it had to reveal the informant's basis of knowledge.

The *Aguilar–Spinelli* test made it very difficult for police to use anonymous tips. In 1983 the Supreme Court relaxed the test and permitted magistrates to consider the totality of circumstances when evaluating applications based on hearsay evidence. *Illinois v. Gates*, supra. The following year, the Court held that the standard for determining probable cause announced in the *Gates* decision was to be given a broad interpretation by lower courts. *Massachusetts v. Upton*, 466 U.S. 727, 104 S.Ct. 2085, 80 L.Ed.2d 721 (1984).

Despite the Supreme Court's relaxed standard for determining probable cause based on tips from informants, several states have chosen to follow the stricter standards formerly imposed by the *Aguilar* and *Spinelli* decisions. This, of course, is the prerogative of the states. In a comprehensive opinion in *State v. Cordova*, 784 P.2d 30 (N.M. 1989), the New Mexico Supreme Court reviewed an affidavit for a search warrant that recited that Cordova had brought heroin into town and was selling it at the house in question. However, the affidavit was devoid of explanation about how the informant gathered this information. Further, although the affidavit stated that the informant had personal knowledge that "heroin users" had been at the residence in question, there was nothing to indicate the source of the informant's knowledge and no explanation of how the informant knew that the persons in question were heroin users. Because the affidavit did not establish that the informant was both credible and reliable, the court found it did not provide a substantial basis for believing the informant and for concluding that the informant gathered the information in a reliable manner. Further, the affidavit did not adequately state the informant's basis of knowledge that the defendant was selling heroin. In rejecting the state's appeal, the New Mexico Supreme Court declined to follow the *Gates* totality-of-circumstances rule and found the affidavit did not meet the requirements of the New Mexico Constitution and its rules of criminal procedure.

In 1985 the Connecticut Supreme Court criticized the totality-of-circumstances test as being "too amorphous" and an inadequate safeguard against unjustified police intrusions. Nevertheless, that court has recently held that if the information supplied by a CI fails the *Aguilar–Spinelli* test, probable cause may still be found if the affidavit sets forth other circumstances that bolster any deficiencies. *State v. Barton*, 594 A.2d 917 (Conn. 1991). Four years later, the Tennessee Supreme Court held that the two-pronged standard for probable cause inquiries incident to the issuance of a search warrant announced in the *Aguilar* and *Spinelli* cases, if not measured hypertechnically, is the standard to measure whether there is probable cause to issue a warrant. *State v. Jacumin*, 778 S.W.2d 430 (Tenn. 1989).

When a defendant demands to know the identity of the informant who provided the police with information on which they based their affidavit for a search warrant, courts face a delicate problem. There is a limited privilege to withhold the identity of the confidential informant. In determining whether to require disclosure, the court balances the interest of the public in preserving the anonymity of the informant against the defendant's need to have this information to prepare a defense, and where the questioned identity "is relevant and helpful to the defense of an accused, or is essential to a fair determination of a cause, the privilege must give way." *Roviaro v. United States*, 353 U.S. 53, 77 S.Ct. 623, 1 L.Ed.2d 639 (1957).

In *State v. Litzau*, 650 N.W.2d 177 (Minn. 2002), the Minnesota Supreme Court, citing *Roviaro*, pointed out that where an informant is merely a transmitter of information rather than an active participant in or a material witness to the crime, that disclosure is generally not required. But the court said, "Where an informant is an eyewitness to the crime, an *in camera* hearing is appropriate to determine whether there is a reasonable probability that the informer's testimony is necessary to a fair determination of guilt or innocence." *Id.* at 184. In considering a request for disclosure of the identity of an informant, the Minnesota court stated that the trial court considers (1) whether the informant is a material witness, (2) whether the informant's testimony will be material to the issue of guilt, (3) whether the state's evidence is suspect, and (4) whether the informant's testimony might disclose entrapment. *Id.* at 184.

## Required Specificity of a Search Warrant

The Fourth Amendment mandates that "no warrants shall issue" except those "particularly describing the place to be searched and the persons or things to be seized." Thus, the scope of a search and seizure is bound by the terms of the warrant (see Figure 15.2). Consequently, a warrant that described property to be seized as "various long play phonographic albums, and miscellaneous vases and glassware" was held insufficient. Nevertheless, in 1999 the Maine Supreme Judicial Court upheld a search warrant that authorized the seizure of all computer-related equipment in the defendant's house. The police knew only that images of minors who were allegedly sexually exploited were taken by digital camera and downloaded on a computer. *State v. Lehman*, 736 A.2d 256 (Me. 1999).

Courts tend to be less strict when it comes to the description of contraband (such as heroin), because it is illegal per se, but stricter in cases involving First Amendment rights. For example, a federal appeals court invalidated a warrant authorizing the seizure of "a quantity of obscene materials, including books, pamphlets, magazines, newspapers, films and prints." *United States v. Guarino*, 729 F.2d 864, 865 (1st Cir. 1984). In *United States v. Hall*, 142 F.3d 988 (7th Cir. 1998), the court held that search warrants were written with sufficient particularity "because the items listed on the warrants were qualified by . . . such phrases as 'child pornography,' 'minors engaged in sexually explicit conduct,' and 'sexual conduct between adults . . . and minors.'" *Id.* at 996–997.

**CASE-IN-POINT**

### Required Specificity of a Search Warrant

A police officer was executing a search warrant that specified a particular copyrighted software program, gave its serial number, and added "all other computer related software." The officer was unable to find a floppy disk containing the program but did locate the program on the hard drive of the defendant's computer. After making a diskette copy of the program, the officer seized the manuals for the program, the computer keyboard and terminal, and numerous related documents. In affirming the defendant's conviction for an offense involving intellectual property, the court held that these materials were properly seized even though not specifically listed in the warrant.

*State v. Tanner*, 534 So.2d 535 (La. App. 1988).

**FIGURE 15.2** A Typical Search Warrant.

**anticipatory search warrant** A search warrant issued based on an affidavit that at a future time evidence of a crime will be at a specific place.

## Anticipatory Search Warrants

The dramatic increase in drug trafficking over the last few decades has given rise to a countermeasure known as the **anticipatory search warrant**. Traditionally, police wait until a suspect receives contraband and then prepare an affidavit to obtain a search warrant. If the magistrate finds that probable cause exists at that time, a search warrant is issued. In the case of an anticipatory warrant, probable cause does not have to exist until the warrant is executed and the search conducted.

During the 1980s, several state appellate courts approved anticipatory search warrants. See, e.g., *State v. Coker*, 746 S.W.2d 167 (Tenn. 1987). In one of these cases, *Bernie v. State*, supra, a freight delivery service notified police that a package that broke in transit revealed a suspicious substance that later proved to be cocaine. An anticipatory warrant was issued to search the residence to which the package was addressed. Police were on the scene when the freight company delivered the package. The warrant was served, the cocaine seized, and the defendant taken into custody. On appeal, the search was upheld by the state supreme court, which observed that neither the federal nor the state constitutions prohibited issuance of a search warrant to be served at a future date in anticipation of the delivery of contraband.

The Alaska Supreme Court has cautioned that a magistrate issuing an anticipatory warrant should make its execution contingent on the occurrence of an event that evidences probable cause that the items to be seized are in the place to be searched rather than directing that the warrant be executed forthwith. *Johnson v. State*, 617 P.2d 1117 (Alaska 1980).

In January 2000, a Michigan appellate court first addressed the issue; following the trend of appellate courts, it concluded that an anticipatory search warrant does not violate the federal and state constitutional prohibitions against unreasonable searches and seizures. *People v. Kaslowski*, 608 N.W.2d 539 (Mich. App. 2000).

While there has been a split of authority, the majority of federal appellate courts have upheld the basic concept that contraband does not have to be currently located at the place described in a search warrant if there is probable cause to believe it will be there when the warrant is executed.

In 1986 the Ninth Circuit Court of Appeals held that an anticipatory search warrant is permissible "where the contraband to be seized is on a sure course to its destination." *United States v. Hale*, 784 F.2d 1465, 1468 (9th Cir. 1986). Two years later, the U.S. Court of Appeals for the Fourth Circuit upheld an anticipatory search warrant permitting an inspector to search an apartment for child pornography where the issuing magistrate conditioned the validity of the warrant on the contraband being placed in the mail. Thus, when the mailing was accomplished, the contraband was on a certain course to its destination. *United States v. Dornhofer*, 859 F.2d 1195 (4th Cir. 1988).

In *United States v. Grubbs*, 547 U.S. 90, 126 S.Ct. 1494, 164 L.Ed.2d 195 (2006), the Supreme Court held that anticipatory search warrants do not contravene the Fourth Amendment. In an opinion by Justice Scalia, the Court said,

> Anticipatory warrants are . . . no different in principle from ordinary warrants. They require the magistrate to determine (1) that it is now probable that (2) contraband, evidence of a crime, or a fugitive will be on the described premises (3) when the warrant is executed. It should be noted, however, that where the anticipatory warrant places a condition (other than the mere passage of time) upon its execution, the first of these determinations goes not merely to what will probably be found if the condition is met. . . . Rather, the probability determination for a conditioned anticipatory warrant looks also to the likelihood that the condition will occur, and thus that a proper object of seizure will be on the described premises. In other words, for a conditioned anticipatory warrant to comply with the Fourth Amendment's requirement of probable cause, two prerequisites of probability must be satisfied. It must be true not only that if the triggering condition occurs "there is a fair probability that

contraband or evidence of a crime will be found in a particular place," . . . but also that there is probable cause to believe the triggering condition will occur. The supporting affidavit must provide the magistrate with sufficient information to evaluate both aspects of the probable-cause determination. 547 U.S. at 96, 126 S.Ct. at 1500, 164 L.Ed.2d at 203.

By 2009 a majority of state courts approved issuance of anticipatory search warrants, but courts in at least eight states have held that statutory or constitutional provisions render such warrants invalid.

## Execution of a Search Warrant

Applicable federal and state laws and rules of criminal procedure govern the manner and time in which warrants are executed. Rule 41(e) of the Federal Rules of Criminal Procedure provides that the warrant

> shall command the officer to search, within a specified period of time not to exceed 10 days, the person or place named or the property or person specified. The warrant shall be served in the daytime, unless the issuing authority . . . authorizes its execution at times other than daytime.

Rule 41(a)(2)(B) defines "daytime" as the period between 6:00 A.M. and 10:00 P.M. according to local time. States have varying provisions governing the period of time within which a search warrant may be executed. Texas allows three days, excluding the date of issuance and the date of execution, Vernon's Ann. Texas C.C.P. Art. 18.07, whereas California allows ten, West's Ann. Cal. Penal Code § 1534. Likewise, state laws vary on the hours during which a search warrant may be executed. California law provides that upon a showing of good cause, the magistrate may, in his or her discretion, insert a direction in a search warrant that it may be served at any time of the day or night. In the absence of such a direction, the warrant shall be served only between the hours of 7 A.M. and 10 P.M. West's Ann. Cal. Penal Code § 1533. Some states, including Texas, do not impose restrictions on the hours when a warrant may be executed; others allow nighttime searches under special circumstances.

## The Knock-and-Announce Rule

**knock and announce** The provision under federal and most state laws that requires a law enforcement officer to first knock and announce his or her presence and purpose before entering a person's home to serve a search or arrest warrant.

At the time the Constitution was adopted, there was a principle of the English common law that law enforcement officers should ordinarily announce their presence and authority before entering a residence to conduct a search or make an arrest pursuant to a warrant. Under federal law an officer is required to **knock and announce** on arrival at the place to be searched. 18 U.S.C.A. § 3109. That section stipulates:

> The officer may break open any outer or inner door or window of a house, or any part of a house, or anything therein, to execute a search warrant, if, after notice of his authority and purpose, he is refused admittance or when necessary to liberate himself or a person aiding him in the execution of the warrant.

Most states have similar "knock-and-announce" requirements, but courts have created some exceptions to protect officers and to prevent the destruction of evidence. In *Wilson v. Arkansas*, 514 U.S. 927, 115 S.Ct. 1914, 131 L.Ed.2d 976 (1995), the U.S. Supreme Court elevated the knock-and-announce rule to constitutional status under the Fourth Amendment. However, the Court did recognize that exigent circumstances may render the knock-and-announce requirement unnecessary.

The purpose of the knock-and-announce requirement is to reduce the potential for violence and to protect the right of privacy of the occupants. Courts have generally ruled that there are no rigid limits as to the time that must elapse between the announcement and the officers' entry. A few seconds may even suffice. Moreover, courts frequently excuse compliance when to require it would endanger the lives of the officers or simply provide an occasion for occupants to dispose of evidence. The most common example of disposing of evidence after police have announced their presence is the flushing of contraband down a toilet. For example, in *State v. Stalbert*, 783 P.2d 1005 (Or. App. 1989), the court found no violation of the knock-and-announce rule where police officers arrived at the defendant's residence to execute a search warrant, yelled "Police officers, search warrant," and paused no more than two seconds between knocking and breaking through the door.

In *Wilson v. Arkansas*, supra, the Supreme Court noted that officers facing exigent circumstances such as the need to preserve evanescent evidence could dispense with the knock-and-announce requirement. But in *Richards v. Wisconsin*, 520 U.S. 385, 117 S.Ct. 1416, 137 L.Ed.2d 615 (1997), the Court ruled that states may not create a blanket "drug exception" to the requirement that police officers knock and announce prior to executing a search warrant. Writing for a unanimous bench, Justice John Paul Stevens observed that

> the fact that felony drug investigations may frequently present circumstances warranting a no knock entry cannot remove from the neutral scrutiny of a reviewing court the reasonableness of the police decision not to knock and announce in a particular case. Instead, in each case, it is the duty of a court confronted with the question to determine whether the facts and circumstances of the particular entry justified dispensing with the knock and announce requirement. 520 U.S. at 394, 117 S.Ct. at 1421, 137 L.Ed.2d at 624.

In *Hudson v. Michigan*, 547 U.S. 586, 126 S.Ct. 2159, 165 L.Ed.2d 56 (2006), the Supreme Court retreated from the position taken in *Wilson v. Arkansas*, holding that violations of the knock-and-announce requirement do not require the suppression of all evidence seized as the result of such violations. Speaking for a sharply divided Court, Justice Antonin Scalia concluded that when it comes to knock-and-announce violations, "[r]esort to the massive remedy of suppressing evidence of guilt is unjustified." 547 U.S. at 599, 126 S.Ct. at 2168, 165 L.Ed.2d at 69. Scalia also noted, "In addition to the grave adverse consequence that excluding relevant incriminating evidence always entails (viz. the risk of releasing dangerous criminals), imposing such a massive remedy would generate a constant flood of alleged failures to observe the rule. . . . " 547 U.S. at 595, 126 S.Ct. at 2165, 165 L.Ed.2d at 66. Writing for four dissenters, Justice Stephen Breyer observed that the decision "destroys the strongest legal incentive to comply with the Constitution's knock-and-announce requirement." 547 U.S. at 605, 126 S.Ct. at 2171, 165 L.Ed.2d at 73.

## Testing the Sufficiency of the Basis for Issuing a Search Warrant

In *Franks v. Delaware*, 438 U.S. 154, 98 S.Ct. 2674, 57 L.Ed.2d 667 (1978), the Supreme Court was faced with the issue of whether a defendant can challenge the affidavit for a search warrant in a pretrial proceeding. The Delaware Supreme Court had ruled that a defendant could not challenge the veracity of the statements made by the police to obtain their search warrant. The U.S. Supreme Court reversed and

*Franks* **hearing** A pretrial proceeding that allows a defendant to challenge the veracity of an affiant's statements in the affidavit that supports the issuance of a search warrant.

held that the Fourth Amendment requires an evidentiary hearing (called a *Franks* **hearing**) into the truthfulness of allegations in an affidavit in support of an application for a search warrant "where the defendant makes a substantial preliminary showing that a false statement knowingly and intentionally, or with reckless disregard for the truth, was included by the affiant in the warrant affidavit, and if the allegedly false statement is necessary to the finding of probable cause." 439 U.S. 154, 155–156, 98 S.Ct. 2674, 2676, 57 L.Ed.2d 667 (1978).

## Return of Seized Property

Illegally seized property must be returned to the owner; however, the government may retain property lawfully seized as long as the government has a legitimate interest in its retention. Whether seized legally or illegally, contraband or property subject to forfeiture is not subject to being returned. See *United States v. Carter*, 859 F. Supp. 202 (E.D. Va. 1994). The return of other seized property is generally handled expeditiously based on a motion of the party seeking return. See, e.g., Fed. R. Crim. P. 41(g).

# Exceptions to the Warrant Requirement

**warrantless searches** Searches made by police who do not possess search warrants.

Courts have recognized that an absolute warrant requirement would be impractical. Consequently, they have upheld the reasonableness of **warrantless searches** under so-called exigent circumstances. Yet, despite a number of exceptions, the warrant requirement remains a central feature of Fourth Amendment law. Whenever possible, police officers should obtain warrants, because their failure to do so can jeopardize the fruits of a successful search. The following are well-defined exceptions to the warrant requirement. However, it is important to understand that all these exceptions assume that police officers have probable cause to believe that a given search is likely to produce evidence of crime.

## Evidence in Plain View

The Supreme Court has said that evidence in plain view of a police officer is not subject to the warrant requirement. *Harris v. United States*, 390 U.S. 234, 88 S.Ct. 992, 19 L.Ed.2d 1067 (1968). Police officers are not required to close their eyes or wear blinders in the face of evidence of a crime. Police officers have long been permitted to seize evidence that comes to their attention inadvertently, provided that (1) the officer has a legal justification to be in a constitutionally protected area when the seizure occurs, (2) the evidence seized is in the plain view of the officer who comes across it, and (3) it is apparent that the object constitutes evidence of a crime. *Coolidge v. New Hampshire*, supra. An officer may not seize anything and everything in plain view—the officer must have probable cause.

The "inadvertent discovery" requirement announced in *Coolidge v. New Hampshire* remained in effect for more than a decade. However, in *Horton v. California*, 496 U.S. 128, 110 S.Ct. 2301, 110 L.Ed.2d 112 (1990), the Supreme Court noted that the inadvertence requirement was not an essential part of the plurality opinion in *Coolidge v. New Hampshire*. As the Court observed in 1983, "There is no reason [the police officer] should be precluded from observing as an officer what would be entirely visible to him as a private citizen." *Texas v. Brown*, 460 U.S. 730, 740, 103 S.Ct. 1535, 1542, 75 L.Ed.2d 502 (1983). Notwithstanding, some state courts have continued to insist that the inadvertence requirement is a limitation on the plain view exception to the warrant requirement. See, e.g., *State v. Davis*, 828 A.2d 293 (N.H. 2003) (inadvertence requirement is satisfied if, immediately prior to the discovery, the police lacked sufficient information to establish probable cause to obtain a warrant to search for the object).

**plain-view doctrine** The Fourth Amendment doctrine under which a police officer may seize evidence of a crime that is readily visible to the officer's naked eye as long as the officer is legally in the place where the evidence becomes visible.

The **plain-view doctrine** may apply both where the item seized is in plain view before the commencement of a search and where it comes into the plain view of an officer conducting an otherwise valid search or entry. For example, in *United States v. Pacelli*, 470 F.2d 67 (2d Cir. 1972), the court invoked the plain view doctrine to uphold the seizure of illegal chemicals found during a search based on a warrant to search for heroin. The search warrant gave police officers the right to enter and search the premises; other items of contraband found in plain view during the search were deemed properly seized.

In contrast with *Pacelli*, consider the case of *Arizona v. Hicks*, 480 U.S. 321, 107 S.Ct. 1149, 94 L.Ed.2d 347 (1987). There, police who had lawfully entered an apartment to search for weapons noticed stereo equipment that seemed out of place, given the squalid condition of the apartment. His suspicion aroused, an officer moved the stereo equipment to locate the serial numbers. A check of the numbers indicated that the equipment was stolen. The Supreme Court disallowed the "search" of the serial numbers because they were not in plain view when the police entered the apartment.

## Emergency Searches

Police frequently must respond to emergencies involving reports of crime or injuries. In other instances, they accompany firefighters to the scene of a fire. Increasingly, law enforcement authorities are called to investigate bomb threats where explosive devices are possibly sequestered inside buildings. Although these are among the most dramatic emergencies, in many other situations police are called to conduct **emergency searches**. The law recognizes that police do not have the time to obtain search warrants in such instances. Of course, police must possess probable cause to make warrantless emergency searches of dwellings. While they are on premises in response to an emergency, police may seize evidence in plain view during the course of their legitimate emergency activities. *Michigan v. Tyler*, 436 U.S. 499, 98 S.Ct. 1942, 56 L.Ed.2d 486 (1978).

**emergency searches** Searches by law enforcement officers in response to an emergency. In such an instance, police can seize evidence in plain view despite not having a search warrant.

Even when investigating a crime scene, police are not permitted to search anything and everything found. In *Flippo v. West Virginia*, 528 U.S. 11, 120 S.Ct. 7, 145 L.Ed.2d 16 (1999), the police responded to a 911 call reporting that a man and his wife had been attacked in a cabin at a state park. When they arrived, the police found the woman fatally wounded. While investigating the crime scene, they discovered a briefcase. They opened it and an envelope within it and found photographs that tended to incriminate the husband. The prosecutor attempted to justify the seizure based on a "crime scene" exception to the warrant requirement. While recognizing that police may make warrantless searches for perpetrators and victims at a crime scene, the Supreme Court rejected the contention that there is a "crime scene exception" to the Warrant Clause of the Fourth Amendment. In remanding the case to the lower court, the Court allowed that the police might have secured the evidence by consent, under the plain view doctrine, or under the inventory exception to the warrant requirement, but not on the basis of a claimed crime scene exception.

Police do not violate the Fourth Amendment if they stop a vehicle when they have adequate grounds to believe the driver is ill or falling asleep. *State v. Pinkham*, 565 A.2d 318 (Me. 1989). Likewise, police who make warrantless entries and searches when they reasonably believe that a person within is in need of immediate aid do not violate the protections against unreasonable search and seizure. Once inside, the police may justifiably seize evidence in plain view. See *Mincey v. Arizona*, 437 U.S. 385, 392, 98 S.Ct. 2408, 2413, 57 L.Ed.2d 290, 300 (1978). An officer's belief that an emergency exists must be reasonable, however. Judge Warren Burger (the future Chief Justice), in *Wayne v. United States*, 318 F.2d 205, 212 (D.C. Cir. 1963), opined that "the need to protect or preserve life or avoid serious injury is justification for what would be otherwise illegal absent an exigency or emergency." In *United States v. Al-Azzawy*, 784 F.2d 890 (9th Cir. 1985), the court upheld a warrantless search where a suspect was believed to be in possession of explosives and in such an agitated state as to create a risk of endangering the lives of others.

## Preservation of Evidence

**evanescent evidence**
Evidence that tends to disappear or be destroyed. Often, police seek to justify a warrantless search on the ground that destruction of the evidence is imminent.

A frequently invoked justification for a warrantless search and seizure is the preservation of **evanescent evidence**—evidence that might be lost or destroyed. Where there is a reasonable belief that loss or destruction of evidence is imminent, a warrantless entry of premises may be justified, *United States v. Gonzalez*, 967 F.2d 1032 (4th Cir. 1992), but a mere possibility of such is insufficient, *United States v. Hayes*, 518 F.2d 675, 678 (6th Cir. 1975). The leading case in this area is *Schmerber v. California*, 384 U.S. 757, 86 S.Ct. 1826, 16 L.Ed.2d 908 (1966), where the Supreme Court upheld a warrantless blood-alcohol test of a person who appeared to be intoxicated. The Court characterized the forcible blood test as a "minor intrusion" and noted that the test was performed by qualified medical personnel. However, the most significant fact of the case was that the suspect's blood-alcohol level was rapidly diminishing, and the time required for police to obtain a search warrant could well have changed the results of the test.

In 1984 the Supreme Court narrowed the doctrine, saying that destruction of evidence does not constitute exigent circumstances if the underlying offense is relatively minor. *Welsh v. Wisconsin*, 466 U.S. 740, 104 S.Ct. 2091, 80 L.Ed.2d 732 (1984). In particular, drug offenses, many of which may be either felonies or misdemeanors depending on the quantity of contraband involved, have proven vexing to police and courts trying to apply the "relatively minor" standard. In 1993 the Idaho Supreme Court said that a minor offense is one that is nonviolent; thus, drug possession offenses, even if felonies, are "minor offenses." The court announced its decision in a case where police, acting with probable cause but without a warrant, entered a home and seized marijuana they believed was about to be destroyed. *State v. Curl*, 869 P.2d 224 (Idaho 1993). Following the Idaho Supreme Court's decision, other courts have applied the "relatively minor" standard to such offenses as disorderly conduct, indecent exposure, and underage drinking.

## Search Incident to a Lawful Arrest

**search incident to a lawful arrest** Search of a person placed under arrest and the area within the arrestee's grasp and control.

A **search incident to a lawful arrest** is an exception to the warrant requirement in order that the police may disarm an arrestee and preserve evidence. It has long been recognized that such a search is permissible. *Weeks v. United States*, 232 U.S. 383, 34 S.Ct. 341, 58 L.Ed. 652 (1914). For many years, this rule was interpreted quite broadly.

For example, in *United States v. Rabinowitz*, 339 U.S. 56, 70 S.Ct. 430, 94 L.Ed. 653 (1950), the Supreme Court upheld a warrantless search of an entire home incident to a lawful arrest that occurred there. In 1969 the Supreme Court narrowed the permissible scope of searches incident to lawful arrests. *Chimel v. California*, 395 U.S. 752, 89 S.Ct. 2034, 23 L.Ed.2d 685 (1969). Under *Chimel*, police may search the body of an arrestee and the area within that person's immediate control. The area of immediate control is often defined as the area within the "grasp" or "lunge" of the arrestee. To conduct a more extensive search, police must generally obtain a search warrant.

Even if a formal arrest is not made until after a search, the search will be upheld as one incident to arrest if there was probable cause for the arrest before the search was begun. *Bailey v. United States*, 389 F.2d 305 (D.C. Cir. 1967). On the other hand, courts will not uphold a search where it is shown that the arrest was a mere pretext to conduct a warrantless search. See, e.g., *United States v. Jones*, 452 F.2d 884 (8th Cir. 1971).

There are definite limitations on police conducting a search incident to arrest. Despite the existence of probable cause, absent extraordinary circumstances, the police have no right to search a dwelling when an arrest occurs outside it. As the Supreme Court observed in *Payton v. New York*, 445 U.S. 573, 591, 100 S.Ct. 1371, 1382, 63 L.Ed.2d 639, 653 (1980), "The Fourth Amendment has drawn a firm line at the entrance to the house. Absent exigent circumstances, that threshold may not reasonably be crossed without a warrant." Exigent circumstances would most likely include a situation where, after an arrest, the officers have a reasonable basis to suspect that there may be others on the premises who pose a danger to the police or who may destroy evidence. See *Vale v. Louisiana*, 399 U.S. 30, 90 S.Ct. 1969, 26 L.Ed.2d 409 (1970). Thus, police who made an arrest outside a residence and had knowledge regarding cocaine trafficking taking place inside were not barred from entering the house to conduct a "protective sweep" for other persons who might pose a threat to their safety. *United States v. Hoyos*, 892 F.2d 1387 (9th Cir. 1989). Nevertheless, once a person is arrested and in custody, searching that person's car at another location is not a search incident to arrest. *Preston v. United States*, 376 U.S. 364, 84 S.Ct. 881, 11 L.Ed.2d 777 (1964).

## Hot Pursuit

**hot pursuit** (1) The right of police to cross jurisdictional lines to apprehend a suspect or criminal; (2) The Fourth Amendment doctrine allowing warrantless searches and arrests where police pursue a fleeing suspect into a protected area.

Officers in **hot pursuit** of a fleeing suspect already have probable cause to make an arrest. The Supreme Court has long recognized that police may pursue the suspect into a protected place, such as a home, without having to abandon their pursuit until a warrant can be obtained. *Warden v. Hayden*, 387 U.S. 294, 87 S.Ct. 1642, 18 L.Ed.2d 782 (1967). As the police enter a building and look for a suspect therein, they are by definition engaged in a search. If they find the suspect and make an arrest, they have in effect made a seizure. Once the suspect is in custody, police may engage in a warrantless search of the immediate area, which might produce evidence such as discarded weapons or contraband.

## Automobile Stops and Roadside Searches of Motor Vehicles

Police may stop an automobile without a warrant and temporarily detain the driver as long as they have probable cause to believe that criminal activity is taking place or that traffic laws or automobile regulations are being violated. *Whren v. United States*, 517 U.S. 806, 116 S.Ct. 1769, 135 L.Ed.2d 89 (1996). Sometimes, police use a minor traffic or equipment violation as a pretext for stopping an automobile that they wish to investigate. When police make such stops, evidence of drug or alcohol use or some other criminal violation may become readily apparent, which allows police to make a warrantless arrest and a warrantless search incident to that arrest.

Quite often, automobile stops involve fairly extensive roadside searches and seizures. The Supreme Court has long recognized the validity of the so-called **automobile exception** to the warrant requirement, as long as police have probable cause to believe the vehicle contains contraband or evidence of crime, on the premise that the mobile character of a motor vehicle creates a practical necessity for an immediate search. *Carroll v. United States*, supra. The Court has held that once begun under exigent circumstances, a warrantless search of an automobile may continue after the vehicle has been taken to the police station. *Chambers v. Maroney*, 399 U.S. 42, 90 S.Ct. 1975, 26 L.Ed.2d 419 (1970).

Several state supreme courts have refused to go along with *Chambers v. Maroney*. For example, in August 1993, the Connecticut Supreme Court refused to adopt *Chambers v. Maroney* as a matter of state constitutional law. In *State v. Miller*, 630 A.2d 1315 (Conn. 1993), the court noted that any exigent circumstances that might justify a roadside automobile search disappear once the vehicle has been impounded. Writing for the court was Chief Justice Ellen A. Peters:

> We tolerate the warrantless on-the-scene automobile search only because obtaining a warrant would be impracticable in light of the inherent mobility of automobiles and the latent exigency that that mobility creates. The balance between law enforcement interests and individuals' privacy interests thus tips in favor of law enforcement in the context of an on-the-scene automobile search. If the impracticability of obtaining a warrant no longer exists, however, our state constitutional preference for warrants regains its dominant place in that balance, and a warrant is required. 630 A.2d at 1325.

## The Scope of Warrantless Roadside Automobile Searches

One perennial problem associated with warrantless automobile searches is how closed containers, such as suitcases, found inside automobiles should be treated. In 1982 the U.S. Supreme Court held that a police officer who has probable cause to believe that evidence of a crime is concealed within an automobile may conduct a search as broad as one that could be authorized by a magistrate issuing a warrant. *United States v. Ross*, 456 U.S. 798, 102 S.Ct. 2157, 72 L.Ed.2d 572 (1982). This ruling effectively allowed police officers to search closed containers found during the course of an automobile search without first having to obtain a warrant.

In *United States v. Johns*, 469 U.S. 478, 105 S.Ct. 881, 83 L.Ed.2d 890 (1985), the Court upheld the warrantless search of plastic containers seized during an automobile search even though the police had waited several days before opening the containers. The Court reasoned that since police legitimately seized the containers during the original search of the automobile, no reasonable expectation of privacy could be maintained once the containers came under police control. The search of the containers, which produced a substantial quantity of marijuana, was therefore not unreasonable simply because it was delayed.

In 1998 a highway patrol officer in Wyoming stopped a speeding car. While speaking to the driver, the officer noticed a syringe in the driver's pocket. The driver admitted using the syringe to inject drugs. Having probable cause to search the car, the officer then opened a passenger's purse on the back seat and found contraband.

**automobile exception**
Exception to the Fourth Amendment warrant requirement. The exception allows the warrantless search of a vehicle by police who have probable cause to search but because of exigent circumstances are unable to secure a warrant.

---

## JURISPRUDENCE

*United States v. Ross*, 456 U.S. 798, 102 S.Ct. 2157, 72 L.Ed.2d 572 (1982)

District of Columbia Police received a tip from a reliable confidential informant that Albert Ross was selling narcotics from his car. The informant provided the location of the vehicle and the police immediately drove to where Ross's vehicle was allegedly located. When Ross entered the vehicle and began to drive away, the police stopped the vehicle and ordered Ross out of the car. Spotting a bullet on the front seat, one of the officers opened the glove compartment and found a pistol. Ross was then handcuffed and placed under arrest. Police then opened the "trunk, found a closed brown paper bag, and after opening the bag, discovered glassine bags containing white powder," which later tested positive for heroin. The vehicle was driven to police headquarters where a second warrantless search was performed, which

"revealed a zippered leather pouch containing cash." As a result of the two searches, Ross was tried and convicted of possession of heroin with intent to distribute, his objection to the admission of the seized evidence notwithstanding. The Supreme Court held where police officers have "legitimately stopped an automobile and have probable cause to believe that contraband is concealed somewhere within it may conduct a warrantless search of the vehicle that is as thorough as a magistrate could authorize by warrant." The Court applied the "automobile exception" articulated in *Carroll v. United States* (1925) to searches "of vehicles that are supported by probable cause to believe that the vehicle contains contraband." As a result, the search was not unreasonable as it was based on "objective facts that would justify the issuance of a warrant," even though a warrant was not actually obtained.

---

The Wyoming Supreme Court ruled that the search that yielded the contraband was not within the permissible scope of search of the vehicle and thus violated the Fourth Amendment. *Houghton v. State*, 956 P.2d 363 (1998). On review, the U.S. Supreme Court held that police officers who have probable cause to search a vehicle may search the belongings of passengers who are capable of concealing objects of the search. *Wyoming v. Houghton*, 526 U.S. 295, 119 S.Ct. 1297, 140 L.Ed.2d 408 (1999).

## Warrantless Automobile Searches Incident to the Arrest of an Occupant

In *New York v. Belton*, 453 U.S. 454, 101 S.Ct. 2860, 69 L.Ed.2d 768 (1981), the Supreme Court held that the police may search the passenger compartment of a vehicle and any containers therein, even absent probable cause, as a contemporaneous incident of an occupant's lawful arrest. *Belton*, provided police with a "bright-line" rule; however, it did not answer the question of whether officers may conduct such a search once the scene has been secured. *Belton* was criticized as moving beyond the rationale of *Chimel*. Most state courts have followed the *Belton* approach, but several have not. In *State v. Brown*, 588 N.E.2d 113 (Ohio 1992), the Ohio Supreme Court rejected *Belton*, which it characterized as allowing police "to search every nook and cranny of an automobile just because the driver is arrested for a traffic violation." 588 N.E.2d at 115.

Until 1998, Iowa law allowed an officer to conduct a full-blown search of an automobile and its driver when the officer stopped a motorist for speeding and issued a traffic citation. Pursuant to that rule, the officer searched the vehicle without consent or probable cause, and the search revealed a bag of marijuana and a "pot pipe." The search was upheld by the Iowa Supreme Court. *State v. Knowles*, 569 N.W.2d 601

(Iowa 1997). But the U.S. Supreme Court granted review and the following year held that a search under these circumstances (where a traffic citation was issued and no custodial arrest was involved) violates the Fourth Amendment. *Knowles v. Iowa*, 525 U.S. 113, 119 S.Ct. 484, 142 L.Ed.2d 492 (1998).

Some twenty-eight years after its decision in *Belton*, the Supreme Court in *Arizona v. Gant*, 556 U.S. 332, 129 S.Ct. 1710, 173 L.Ed.2d 485 (2009), substantially distinguished the rule that it had arrived at in the factual context of *Belton*. In doing so the Court placed limits on a search incident to arrest of an occupant of a vehicle. Writing for a 5–4 majority, Justice John Paul Stevens announced the new standard by saying,

> Police may search a vehicle incident to a recent occupant's arrest only if the arrestee is within reaching distance of the passenger compartment at the time of the search or it is reasonable to believe the vehicle contains evidence of the offense of arrest. When these justifications are absent, a search of an arrestee's vehicle will be unreasonable unless police obtain a warrant or show that another exception to the warrant requirement applies. 556 U.S. at 351, 129 S.Ct. at 1723–24, 173 L.Ed.2d at 501.

Dissenting, Justice Samuel Alito pointed out that the doctrine of *stare decisis* commands the "bright-line" rule adopted in *Belton* should not be discarded.

# Exceptions to the Probable Cause Requirement

Warrantless searches are now well established in the law, and although reasonable people might disagree about specific cases, there is consensus that warrantless searches are often necessary and proper. The same cannot be said for the next category of searches—those based on something less than probable cause. In these special situations, courts permit limited searches based on the lesser standard of reasonable suspicion. Reasonable suspicion is the belief, based on articulable circumstances, that criminal activity might be afoot. The classic application of the reasonable suspicion standard is to the so-called "stop-and-frisk."

## Stop-and-Frisk

**stop-and-frisk** An encounter between a police officer and a suspect during which the latter is temporarily detained and subjected to a pat-down search for weapons.

The **stop-and-frisk** is a routine law enforcement technique whereby police officers stop, question, and sometimes search suspicious persons. In *Terry v. Ohio*, 392 U.S. 1, 88 S.Ct. 1868, 20 L.Ed.2d 889 (1968), the Supreme Court upheld the authority of police officers to detain and conduct a limited "pat-down" search of several men who were acting suspiciously. Given the limited intrusiveness of the pat-down and the compelling need to protect officers in the field, the Court allowed the warrantless search for weapons on a reasonable suspicion standard instead of imposing the traditional probable cause requirement. Subsequently, the Court stressed the narrow scope of the stop-and-frisk exception by saying that "nothing in *Terry* can be understood to allow . . . any search whatever for anything but weapons." *Ybarra v. Illinois*, 444 U.S. 85, 93–94, 100 S.Ct. 338, 343, 62 L.Ed.2d 238, 247 (1979).

In *Michigan v. Long*, 463 U.S. 1032, 103 S.Ct. 3469, 77 L.Ed.2d 1201 (1983), the Supreme Court held that seizure of contraband other than weapons during a lawfully conducted *Terry* search was justified under the plain view doctrine. Going a step further in *Minnesota v. Dickerson*, 508 U.S. 366, 113 S.Ct. 2130, 124 L.Ed.2d 334 (1993), the Court said that police may seize nonthreatening

*Terry v. Ohio*, 392 U.S. 1, 88 S.Ct. 1868, 20 L.Ed.2d 889 (1968)

An experienced police officer on routine patrol in downtown Cleveland observed two men repeatedly walking up and down a street while stopping to stare into a store window. Each time one of the men walked up the street and stopped to look into the store window and returned, a conference was held between the two men and a third individual. The officer believed the men were "casing a job, a stick up." The officer approached the men, "identified himself as a policeman, and asked their names," but the men were less than forthcoming and mumbled something under their breaths. The officer "spun [Terry] around, patted down his outside clothing, and found in his overcoat pocket . . . a pistol." The officer then removed the overcoat from Terry, removed the pistol, and ordered the men "to face the wall with their hands raised." The officer repeated the same procedure with the other two men, finding a pistol during the pat-down on one, but nothing on the other. Terry and the second man with a pistol were charged with carrying a concealed weapon. The trial court denied defense's motion to suppress the evidence "on the ground that the officer had cause to believe the men were acting suspiciously, their interrogation was warranted, and the officer, for his own protection, had the right to pat down their outer clothing having reasonable cause to believe that they might be armed." The Supreme Court determined that the officer's actions to detain did constitute a search and seizure under the Fourth Amendment, but the search and seizure were not unreasonable. The Court expressly held that "where a reasonably prudent officer is warranted in the circumstances of a given case in believing that his safety or that of others is endangered, he may make a reasonable search for weapons of the person believed by him to be armed and dangerous."

contraband detected through their sense of touch during a protective pat-down search as long as that search stays within the bounds of a *Terry* search. This extension of *Terry* is sometimes referred to as a "plain feel" exception to the warrant requirement of the Fourth Amendment. Nevertheless, in *Dickerson* the Court found the search and seizure of contraband invalid because the officer conducting the search determined that the item he seized was contraband only after searching beyond the scope authorized in *Terry*. (More attention is given to the so-called *Terry* stop in Chapter 16.)

## Is a Stop-and-Frisk Permissible Based Solely on an Anonymous Tip?

In *Alabama v. White*, 496 U.S. 325, 110 S.Ct. 2412, 110 L.Ed.2d 301 (1990), police received an anonymous tip that a certain female was carrying cocaine and that she would leave a certain apartment at a specified time, get into a car matching a particular description, and drive to a particular motel. The police conducted surveillance of the woman, which verified elements of the tip. Only then did they move in to stop her car, detain her, and seize the cocaine.

Characterizing the case as a "close" one, the Supreme Court upheld the police procedure but said that the tip alone would not have justified the stop-and-frisk. It was on that basis that the Court invalidated a seizure of a firearm in *Florida v. J.L.*, 529 U.S. 266, 120 S.Ct. 1375, 146 L.Ed.2d 254 (2000). In the latter case, the Court observed that "an anonymous tip lacking indicia of reliability . . . does not justify a stop and frisk whenever and however it alleges the illegal possession of a firearm." 529 U.S. at 274, 120 S.Ct. at 1380, 146 L.Ed.2d at 262.

## Drug Courier Profiles

drug courier profiles Sets of characteristics that are believed to typify drug couriers.

In attempting to identify and to apprehend drug smugglers, law enforcement agencies have developed **drug courier profiles**. These profiles are sets of characteristics that typify drug couriers, such as paying for airline tickets in cash, appearing nervous, carrying certain types of luggage, and so forth. In *Reid v. Georgia*, 448 U.S. 438, 100 S.Ct. 2752, 65 L.Ed.2d 890 (1980), the Supreme Court suggested that fitting a drug courier profile was not in itself sufficient to give rise to the reasonable suspicion necessary to allow police to detain an airline passenger. Therefore, the stopping of an airline passenger on that basis violated the Fourth Amendment. However, in *United States v. Sokolow*, 490 U.S. 1, 109 S.Ct. 1581, 104 L.Ed.2d 1 (1989), the Court upheld a similar investigatory detention in which a drug courier profile was employed. It is instructive to examine these decisions side by side to determine how and why the Court distinguished the two situations.

## School Searches

In the First Amendment context, the Supreme Court has said that students in public schools do not "shed their constitutional rights . . . at the schoolhouse gate." *Tinker v. Des Moines Independent Community School District*, 393 U.S. 503, 506, 89 S.Ct. 733, 736, 21 L.Ed.2d 731, 737 (1969). Following this premise, the Court has held that the Fourth Amendment protects children in the public schools from unreasonable searches and seizures. However, the Court has said that such searches are to be judged by a reasonableness standard and are not subject to the requirement of probable cause. Moreover, the Court has said that the warrant requirement is particularly unsuited to the unique circumstances of the school environment. *New Jersey v. T.L.O.*, 469 U.S. 325, 105 S.Ct. 733, 83 L.Ed.2d 720 (1985). The pervasive problem of illicit drug use in the schools, as well as the notorious incidents of school violence in recent years, have added pressure to relax Fourth Amendment standards in the public school context.

Although there are certainly exceptions, most search and seizure policies implemented by public schools have been upheld by the courts. These include "sweeps" for drugs and guns using such devices as drug sniffing dogs and metal detectors, as well as routine searches of backpacks, lockers, and even automobiles coming onto school grounds. Courts have generally upheld searches of students in the public schools where the search is reasonably related to its objectives and not excessively intrusive in light of the age and sex of the student and the nature of the infraction. See *Brannum v. Overton County School Bd.*, 516 F.3d 489 (6th Cir. 2005). But the law has been unclear when it involves school officials going to the extent of strip searches. In 2003 Safford, Arizona school officials searching for ibuprofen ordered a search of a thirteen-year-old female student's backpack and pockets. Finding none, they conducted a strip search. In 2008 the Ninth Circuit Court of Appeals in a 6–5 decision held that the search was a violation of the student's Fourth Amendment right to privacy. *Redding v. Safford Unified School Dist. No. 1*, 531 F.3d 1071 (9th Cir. 2008). The Supreme Court has granted review and its decision could have major implications in balancing students' rights of privacy against the requirement of maintaining order on school campuses.

In *Commonwealth v. Cass*, 709 A.2d 350 (Pa. 1998), a leading case decided by the Pennsylvania Supreme Court, a public high school principal brought in police and drug sniffing dogs to detect drugs sequestered in student lockers. When a dog "alerted" to a particular locker, school officials would open it and search the contents. Eighteen lockers were searched, and one of them was found to contain a small amount of marijuana and some related paraphernalia. The student to whom that locker was assigned was suspended from school for ten days, required to attend drug counseling, and charged criminally with possession of marijuana and possession of drug paraphernalia. In rejecting a challenge to the constitutionality of the search that led to the discovery of the contraband, the Pennsylvania Supreme court observed:

> Common sense dictates that when a student is given permission to store his or her belongings in a locker designated for his or her personal and exclusive use, that student can reasonably expect a measure of privacy within that locker. Common sense further dictates that when the student's use of the locker is expressly conditioned upon the acknowledgment that the locker belongs to the school, that measure of privacy is necessarily limited. *Id*. at 359.

## Drug Testing

Because of the paramount interest in ensuring the public safety, courts have upheld the constitutionality of regulations permitting supervisory personnel to order urinalysis testing of public safety officers based on reasonable suspicion of drug abuse. See, e.g., *Turner v. Fraternal Order of Police*, 500 A.2d 1005 (D.C. App. 1985). In 1989 the U.S. Supreme Court upheld federal regulations requiring drug and alcohol testing of railroad employees involved in train accidents. *Skinner v. Railway Labor Executives' Association*, 489 U.S. 602, 109 S.Ct. 1402, 1411, 103 L.Ed.2d 639 (1989). The Court has also sustained a U.S. Customs Service policy requiring drug tests for persons seeking positions as customs inspectors. *Treasury Employees Union v. Von Raab*, 489 U.S. 656, 109 S.Ct. 1384, 103 L.Ed.2d 685 (1989). As yet, the Supreme Court has not addressed the issue of general, random **drug testing** of public employees. However, it has invalidated a policy under which all political candidates were required to submit to drug testing as a condition of qualifying for the ballot. *Chandler v. Miller*, 520 U.S. 305, 117 S.Ct. 1295, 137 L.Ed.2d 513 (1997).

**drug testing** Procedures, usually involving urinalysis, designed to test for the presence of illegal drugs in the body.

In 1995 the U.S. Supreme Court stated that a public school district's student athlete drug policy, which authorized random urinalysis drug testing of students who participated in athletic programs, did not violate a student's right to be free from unreasonable searches. While mandatory drug testing is a search, Justice Antonin Scalia, writing for a 6–3 majority of the Court, pointed out that given the decreased expectation of privacy of a public school student, the relative unobtrusiveness of the search, and the severity of the need, such a search was not unreasonable. *Vernonia School District v. Acton*, 515 U.S. 646, 115 S.Ct. 2386, 132 L.Ed.2d 564 (1995).

State courts have addressed random drug testing of municipal employees under both state and federal constitutional standards. In 2001 the Alaska Supreme Court held that where there was no documented history of substance abuse problems by firefighters and police employees, the random testing program violated the Alaska Constitution. *Anchorage Police Department Employees Ass'n v. Municipality of Anchorage*, 24 P.3d 547 (Alaska 2001). Three years later the Arizona Supreme Court found that the city of Mesa's random drug testing of firefighters was not justified by a generalized and unsubstantiated interest in deterring and detecting alcohol and drug use. Thus, it concluded that such random testing violated the Fourth Amendment privacy interests of the firefighters. *Petersen v. City of Mesa*, 83 P.3d 35 (Ariz. 2004). The U.S. Supreme Court denied review.

When administrative personnel turn over results of drug tests to law enforcement agencies for criminal prosecution, courts tend to exercise a higher level of scrutiny. The leading case in this regard is *Ferguson v. City of Charleston*, 532 U.S. 67, 121 S.Ct. 1281, 149 L.Ed.2d 205 (2001). There, the U.S. Supreme Court invalidated a policy under which a public hospital turned over to police urine samples of pregnant women who had tested positive for cocaine. The Court noted,

> The fact that positive test results were turned over to the police does not merely provide a basis for distinguishing our prior cases applying the "special needs" balancing approach to the determination of drug use. It also provides an affirmative reason for enforcing the strictures of the Fourth Amendment. 532 U.S. at 84, 121 S.Ct. at 1292, 149 L.Ed.2d at 220.

# Electronic Surveillance

The drafters of the Fourth Amendment obviously did not contemplate present-day technology. Yet, in framing the Bill of Rights, they used simple, straightforward language that has endured through the centuries—language capable of being adapted to the needs of the people. Today's technology makes possible silent and invisible intrusions on the privacy of the individual, and the courts are responding to these new, innovative means of surveillance, always cognizant that the touchstone of the Fourth Amendment is its prohibition of "unreasonable" searches and seizures. Of course, the interpretation of what is "reasonable" is apt to be affected by pressing public needs. The attacks on American cities on September 11, 2001, and the subsequent "war on terrorism" have had an enormous impact in the area of electronic surveillance, both in terms of what law enforcement agencies are now doing and what legislation and judicial opinions authorize.

## Expectations of Privacy with Respect to Electronic Surveillance

Generally speaking, the use of wiretaps, microphones, video recorders, and other devices that permit agencies to intercept the content of what would otherwise be private communications implicates the Fourth Amendment. *Katz v. United States*, supra. However, merely using technology to augment the senses does not necessarily trigger Fourth Amendment protections. For example, the Supreme Court has approved the use of searchlights, field glasses, aerial photography, and various other means of enhancing the police's powers of observation, even in the absence of a warrant or probable cause. *United States v. Lee*, 274 U.S. 559, 47 S.Ct. 746, 71 L.Ed. 1202 (1927); *Texas v. Brown*, 460 U.S. 730, 103 S.Ct. 1535, 75 L.Ed.2d 502 (1983). Lower federal courts have even approved miniaturized television camera surveillance. *United States v. Torres*, 751 F.2d 875 (7th Cir. 1984). The question is whether the police use methods that infringe on a person's reasonable expectations of privacy. If so, they need a warrant or some other form of judicial authorization before deploying these technologies.

## Cordless and Cellular Telephones

Changes in technology often create new legal questions. An excellent example is the proliferation of cordless telephones in the 1980s. When one uses a cordless phone, one is essentially broadcasting a low-power radio signal to a nearby receiver (the base unit) that is connected to a phone line. But any nearby receiver tuned to the correct frequency can intercept a conversation being conducted on a cordless phone. Analog cellular telephones operate in much the same way, although their signals are more powerful so they can communicate with towers located within "cells." The new digital cell phones are more difficult to eavesdrop upon because their signals are encrypted. Realizing the potential for monitoring conversations on cordless telephones and analog cellular phones, police sometimes employ receivers or scanners mounted in vehicles to eavesdrop on conversations. In doing this without a warrant or even probable cause, are police in violation of the Fourth Amendment?

In *Tyler v. Berodt*, 877 F.2d 705 (8th Cir. 1989), and *United States v. Smith*, 978 F.2d 171, 177 (5th Cir. 1992), two federal courts ruled that users of cordless phones had no reasonable expectation of privacy; therefore, the interception of their calls was not a "search" within the meaning of the Fourth Amendment. However, in *State v. Mozo*, 655 So.2d 1115 (Fla. 1995), the Florida Supreme Court held that nonconsensual interception of cordless phone calls without prior judicial approval violates a state statute protecting the privacy of communications. That court declined to reach the constitutional issues in the case, preferring to base its decision on statutory grounds. In 1986 Congress enacted a statute to provide nationwide protection against eavesdropping on cellular phone conversations, and in 1994 the statute was amended to provide protection for cordless phones as well. Thus, Congress provided through legislation protection to individual privacy that federal courts were unable or unwilling to provide via the Fourth Amendment.

## The Supreme Court's Major Decisions in the Area of Electronic Surveillance

The U.S. Supreme Court has rendered only a few decisions affecting the legality of electronic surveillance by police, but these decisions have had a major impact on law enforcement practices. In *Smith v. Maryland*, 442 U.S. 735, 99 S.Ct. 2577, 61 L.Ed.2d 220 (1979), the Court determined that the employment of a **pen register** is not a search within the meaning of the Fourth Amendment. A pen register is a device that records the phone numbers that are dialed from a particular phone number. Writing for the Court, Justice Harry Blackmun observed that merely by using the phone, the defendant "voluntarily conveyed numerical information to the telephone company and 'exposed' that information to its equipment in the ordinary course of business." 442 U.S. at 744, 99 S.Ct. at 2582, 61 L.Ed.2d at 229. Blackmun concluded that in so doing, the defendant "assumed the risk that the company would reveal to police the numbers he dialed." *Ibid*. In a vigorous dissenting opinion, Justice Potter Stewart asserted, "It is simply not enough to say, after *Katz*, that there is no legitimate expectation of privacy in the numbers dialed because the caller assumes the risk that the telephone company will disclose them to the police." 442 U.S. at 747, 99 S.Ct. at 2583, 61 L.Ed.2d at 231. In another dissenting opinion, Justice Thurgood Marshall observed that "[p]rivacy in placing calls is of value not only to those engaged in criminal activity" and predicted that "[t]he prospect of unregulated governmental monitoring will undoubtedly prove disturbing even to those with nothing illicit to hide." 442 U.S. at 751, 99 S.Ct. at 2586, 61 L.Ed.2d at 234.

In *Dow Chemical Co. v. United States*, 476 U.S. 227, 106 S.Ct. 1819, 90 L.Ed.2d 226 (1986), the Supreme Court held that high-altitude photography of a chemical plant was not a search within the meaning of the Fourth Amendment. The Court concluded that the means of surveillance was incapable of revealing intimate activities

**pen register** Device that enables law enforcement to obtain the numbers that have been dialed by use of a specific telephone instrument.

that would give rise to constitutional concerns. That same year, in *California v. Ciraolo*, 476 U.S. 207, 106 S.Ct. 1809, 90 L.Ed.2d 210 (1986), the Court upheld a conviction where police, acting on a tip, conducted a low-altitude flight and photographed marijuana plants growing in the defendant's backyard. The police then used the photos to obtain a warrant and seize the contraband. In upholding the search, the Court said, "[W]e readily conclude that [the defendant's] expectation that his garden was protected from [aerial] observation is unreasonable and is not an expectation that society is prepared to honor." 476 U.S. at 214, 106 S.Ct. at 1813, 90 L.Ed.2d at 217. Dissenting, Justice Lewis Powell suggested that the Court's decision was inconsistent with the broad interpretation of the Fourth Amendment suggested by the Court's seminal decision in *Katz v. United States*:

> Rapidly advancing technology now permits police to conduct surveillance in the home itself, an area where privacy interests are most cherished in our society, without any physical trespass. While the rule in *Katz* was designed to prevent silent and unseen invasions of Fourth Amendment privacy rights in a variety of settings, we have consistently afforded heightened protection to a person's right to be left alone in the privacy of his house. The Court fails to enforce that right or to give any weight to the longstanding presumption that warrantless intrusions into the home are unreasonable. 476 U.S. at 226, 106 S.Ct. at 1819, 90 L.Ed.2d at 225.

In the 1980s, police looking for marijuana being grown indoors under artificial light began to use infrared thermal imagers, which detect heat waves. These devices can provide a strong indication of whether marijuana is being grown inside a closed structure. Prior to 2001, most courts that considered this issue ruled that using thermal imaging devices was not a search within the meaning of the Fourth Amendment. See, e.g., *United States v. Pinson*, 24 F.3d 1056 (8th Cir. 1994); *United States v. Ford*, 34 F.3d 992 (11th Cir. 1994); and *United States v. Penny-Feeney*, 773 F. Supp. 220 (D.C. Hawaii 1991). A notable exception was *State v. Young*, 867 P.2d 593 (Wash. 1994), where the Washington Supreme Court held that the use of a thermal imaging device was a search within the meaning of the Washington state constitution. In *Kyllo v. United States*, 533 U.S. 27, 121 S.Ct. 2038, 150 L.Ed.2d 94 (2001), the U.S. Supreme Court adopted the view taken by the Washington Supreme Court. Writing for the Court, Justice Antonin Scalia concluded that when "the Government uses a device that is not in general public use, to explore details of the home that would previously have been unknowable without physical intrusion, the surveillance is a 'search' and is presumptively unreasonable without a warrant." 533 U.S. at 40, 121 S.Ct. at 2046, 150 L.Ed.2d at 106.

In *United States v. Jones*, 565 U.S. ___, 132 S.Ct. 945, 181 L.Ed.2d 911 (2012), the Supreme Court invalidated the use of GPS tracking devices without prior judicial authorization. Although the decision was a unanimous one, the justices split on the underlying rationale for the ruling, with five justices focusing on the physical intrusion of placing the GPS locator on the car and four justices focusing on the overall violation of a "reasonable expectation of privacy" entailed by lengthy electronic surveillance.

## Federal Legislation Governing Interception of Electronic Communications

As noted above, Congress has enacted legislation governing the interception of electronic communications. The cornerstone of this statutory edifice is Title III of the Omnibus Crime Control and Safe Streets Act of 1968, codified at 18 U.S.C.A.

---

**JURISPRUDENCE**

*United States v. Jones*, 565 U.S. \_\_\_, 132 S.Ct. 945, 181 L.Ed.2d 911 (2012)

Antoine Jones, a nightclub owner in the District of Columbia, was suspected by federal agents of trafficking in cocaine. Agents obtained a warrant authorizing them to install a GPS tracking device on Jones' car in D.C. within ten days. A day after the warrant expired, agents placed the tracking device on Jones vehicle while it was parked in Maryland. They then used the device to follow Jones for twenty-eight days. The investigation led to a multiple-count indictment charging Jones with conspiracy to distribute cocaine and other offenses. A jury found Jones not guilty on all charges

except for conspiracy, where they were not able to reach a verdict. Prosecutors then re-filed a single charge of conspiracy against Jones, who was convicted and sentenced to life in prison. The U.S. Court of Appeals for the D.C. Circuit reversed, holding that the warrantless use of the GPS device violated the Fourth Amendment. The U.S. Supreme Court affirmed the circuit court decision, holding that the government's physical intrusion into Jones' property for the purpose of obtaining information constituted a "search." In an opinion concurring only in the judgment, four justices focused on what they believed to be a violation of Jones's reasonable expectations of privacy.

---

§§ 2510–20. The act prohibits interception of electronic communications without a court order unless one party to the conversation consents. Interception is defined as "aural or other acquisition of the contents of any wire, electronic or oral communication through the use of any electronic, mechanical, or other device." 18 U.S.C.A. § 2510(4). In 1986 Congress expanded the meaning of "wire communications" to include conversations through "switching stations." 18 U.S.C.A. § 2510(1). Therefore, the statute now covers cellular telephones.

**wiretap orders** Court orders permitting electronic surveillance for a limited period.

Title III permits issuance of **wiretap orders** by federal and state courts on sworn applications authorized by the U.S. Attorney General, a specially designated assistant, or a state official at a similar level. The act expressly preempts state law. Therefore, to permit the use of electronic surveillance, a state must adopt legislation along the lines of the federal act, and many states have done so. See, e.g., the New Jersey Wiretapping and Electronic Surveillance Control Act of 1968, N.J. Stat. Ann. § 2A: 156A-(1), *et seq.*

An application for a wiretap order must contain considerable detailed information along with an explanation of why less intrusive means of investigation will not suffice. 18 U.S.C.A. § 2518(1)(c). The statute requires that normal investigative procedures be employed first. But it does not require an officer to exhaust all possible investigative methods before applying for a wiretap order. Before a court may issue a wiretap order, it must find probable cause that the subject of the wiretap has committed or is committing one of a series of enumerated crimes for which wiretapping is authorized and that conventional modes of investigation will not suffice. 18 U.S.C.A. § 2518(3). Originally these offenses included narcotics, organized crime, and national security violations. In 1986 the act was amended to include numerous other serious crimes, including interstate transportation of stolen vehicles; bribery in sports contests; weapons of mass destruction threats; sex trafficking of children by force, fraud, or coercion; mail fraud; and money laundering. 18 U.S.C.A. § 2516(1)(c).

Court orders permit surveillance for no longer than a thirty-day period. 18 U.S.C.A. § 2518(5). At the period's expiration, the recordings made of intercepted communications must be delivered to the judge who issued the order. They are then sealed under the judge's direction. 18 U.S.C.A. § 2518(8)(a).

The Electronic Communications Privacy Act of 1986 (ECPA), 18 U.S.C.A. § 2701 *et seq.*, established federal standards for access to e-mail and other electronic communications and to "transactional records," including subscriber identifying

**trap-and-trace devices**
Devices that capture incoming electronic impulses that identify the originating number of a device from which an electronic communication was transmitted.

information, call logs, phone bills, and so forth. The law established a high standard for access to the contents of electronic communications but allowed agencies to easily gain access to transactional records. One part of the act, 18 U.S.C.A. § 3121 *et seq.*, governs the use of pen registers and **trap-and-trace devices**. It requires judges to issue orders to allow the use of such devices when properly requested by prosecutors. There is no standard of proof that prosecutors have to meet in order to get such orders. The courts have generally taken the position that users of telephones have no reasonable expectations of privacy with regard to numbers associated with incoming or outgoing phone calls. Congress has chosen not to provide significant statutory protection in this area, much to the chagrin of civil libertarians.

In 2007 the Ninth Circuit Court of Appeals reviewed a case of first impression involving the use of computer surveillance. During its investigation of Defendants Forrester and Alba's Ecstasy manufacturing operation, the government used computer surveillance techniques to monitor Alba's e-mail and Internet activity. Alba argued that these techniques violated the Fourth Amendment. The court disagreed and pointed out that the messages are sent and the Internet protocol (IP) addresses are accessed through the equipment of their Internet service provider and other third parties. Therefore, e-mail and Internet users have no reasonable expectation of privacy in the to/from addresses of their messages or the IP addresses of the websites they visit. The court reasoned that because these computer surveillance techniques are constitutionally indistinguishable from the use of a pen register they do not violate the Fourth Amendment. *United States v. Forrester*, 495 F.3d 1041 (9th Cir. 2007).

## The USA PATRIOT Act

**USA PATRIOT Act** Controversial act of Congress enacted in 2001 to strengthen the federal government's efforts to combat terrorism.

Many of the measures enacted into law by the **USA PATRIOT Act** are outside the scope of this chapter; however, Title II, "Enhanced Surveillance Procedures," includes provisions of particular relevance to our discussion of search and seizure. Title II enables law enforcement agencies to access Internet communications and expands their authority to use pen registers and trap-and-trace surveillance. Listed below are several significant changes, most of which focus on expanding the government's power to conduct electronic surveillance:

- § 202. Computer fraud and abuse are added to the predicate crimes listed in 18 U.S.C.A. § 2516(1)(c) for seeking authorization for interception of wire, oral, or electronic communications.
- § 203. Rule 6(e)(3)(C), Federal Rules of Criminal Procedure and 18 U.S.C.A. § 2517 are amended to allow intelligence obtained in grand jury proceedings and from wiretaps to be shared with federal law enforcement and national security personnel for use in connection with their official duties.
- § 204. The act amends 18 U.S.C.A. § 2511(2)(f) in regard to interception and disclosure of electronic communications by inserting "wire, oral and electronic" in place of "wire and oral," thereby broadening the right of government to intercept electronic communications in foreign intelligence matters.
- § 206. The act also amends 18 U.S.C.A. § 1805(c)(2)(B) to authorize federal courts to issue "roving" surveillance orders in connection with foreign intelligence matters, enabling investigators to intercept e-mail and cell phone communications in circumstances where suspects frequently change their account numbers.
- § 209. The act amends 18 U.S.C.A. § 2510 to authorize law enforcement officers to seize voicemail messages pursuant to a search warrant instead of a wiretap order.

- § 210. The act amends 18 U.S.C.A. § 2703(c) to allow law enforcement officers to obtain by subpoena subscriber records of local and long-distance telephone connection records, "records of session times and durations," and means of payment including credit card numbers from Internet service providers (ISPs).

- § 212. ISPs are allowed to reveal data concerning their customers without first notifying them if the ISP reasonably believes that "death or serious physical injury to any person" requires such disclosure without delay.

- § 214. The government only has to certify that the information that it obtains would be relevant to an "ongoing investigation" to secure a pen register or trap-and-trace order. Formerly, under 50 U.S.C.A. § 1842(c)(3), the government had to certify that it had reason to believe that surveillance was being conducted on a line or device that is or was used in "communications with" someone involved in international terrorism or intelligence activities that may violate U.S. criminal law, or a foreign power or its agent whose communication is believed to concern terrorism or intelligence activities that violate U.S. law.

- § 215. Among the very controversial provisions of the act is an amendment to the Foreign Intelligence Security Act (FISA), 50 U.S.C.A. § 1861 *et seq.*, which removes the limitations on the FBI's ability to obtain business records pursuant to an *ex parte* court order and grants the FBI the power in terrorism investigations to obtain records and other "tangible things" from entities that include libraries and Internet providers. The act forbids those served such orders from disclosing such fact to other than official sources. Section 215 became the focus of the first direct constitutional assault on the act, in a suit filed by the American Civil Liberties Union and other organizations in July of 2003. (See amendments to the act in the topic that follows on the 2006 Reauthorization Act.)

- § 216. Sections of the Electronic Communications Privacy Act (ECPA), 18 U.S.C.A. §§ 3121, 3123 (previously discussed), are amended to add the terms "routing" and "addressing" to the phrase "dialing and signaling information," thus expanding the federal government's authority to monitor Internet activities, as well as telephone conversations, by using systems similar to pen registers and trap-and-trace devices. This enables a U.S. Attorney, acting at the behest of the FBI, to obtain a court order allowing use of technology that records e-mail addresses and URLs of websites being accessed from a particular computer.

- § 216. The act also amends 18 U.S.C.A. § 3123(a) to provide that the court shall enter an *ex parte* order authorizing the installation and use of a pen register or trap-and-trace device anywhere within the United States if the court finds that the attorney for the government has certified to the court that the information likely to be obtained by such installation and use is relevant to an ongoing criminal investigation. (Recall our previous discussion that a pen register or trap-and-trace device ordinarily reveals only such telephone transactions as numbers called from particular telephones.)

- § 219. The act also permits federal magistrate judges in any district in which terrorism-related activities may have occurred to issue search warrants for searches within or outside the district. This greatly facilitates the issuance of nationwide warrants for investigations involving terrorism.

As Americans come to rely more extensively on computers, e-mail, and the Internet, many see these new measures of exposing their electronic communications as a necessary evil in pursuit of a greater good, namely, prevention of terrorism. Others worry that their constitutional rights are being substantially diminished. While acknowledging that effective legislation is essential to protect the national security of the United States, they believe that greatly expanding the government's right to eavesdrop on e-mail and other Internet communications increases the potential for official mischief and diminishes individual liberty and privacy. Many Americans also see the right of law enforcement to share information revealed to a grand jury with intelligence-gathering agencies as unfairly infringing on the privacy of persons under investigation, many of whom are never indicted.

Although recognizing the imperatives of national security, many Americans would ask courts, legislatures, and their fellow citizens to heed the words of Justice Louis Brandeis written in a dissenting opinion more than seventy-five years ago:

> The makers of our Constitution undertook to secure conditions favorable to the pursuit of happiness. They recognized the significance of man's spiritual nature, of his feelings and of his intellect. They knew that only a part of the pain, pleasure and satisfactions of life are to be found in material things. They sought to protect Americans in their beliefs, their thoughts, their emotions and their sensations. They conferred, as against the government, the right to be let alone—the most comprehensive of rights and the right most valued by civilized men. To protect that right, every unjustifiable intrusion by the government upon the privacy of the individual, whatever the means employed, must be deemed a violation of the 4th Amendment . . . *Olmstead v. United States*, 277 U.S. 438, 478, 48 S.Ct. 564, 572, 72 L.Ed. 944, 956 (1928).

Soon after the hasty adoption of the USA PATRIOT Act in October 2001, controversy erupted about the necessity and constitutionality of several provisions of the act. Congress engaged in serious arguments concerning the act in general, and especially in respect to particular provisions. Some of the most significant complaints were lodged by libraries that could be directed to turn over records to the FBI and that, if served with § 215 orders, would be prohibited from disclosing that fact to anyone. Finally, Congress enacted—and on March 9, 2006, President George W. Bush signed—the Reauthorizing Amendments Act of 2006.

The new legislation contains a number of technical revisions of the original USA PATRIOT Act. Many are designed to clarify that individuals who receive Foreign Intelligence Service Act (FISA) orders can challenge nondisclosure requirements. Specifically, recipients of a § 215 order (often libraries) are granted the right to petition a judge of the special FISA court to modify or quash the nondisclosure requirement of such an order. The new act removes the requirement that recipients of § 215 orders or National Security Letters (NSLs) provide the FBI with the name of the attorney they consulted. Finally, it clarifies that libraries, whose services include offering patrons access to the Internet, are not subject to NSLs unless they are functioning as electronic communication service providers.

On September 6, 2007, the U.S. District Court for the Southern District of New York struck down the National Security Letter provisions of the USA PATRIOT Act on grounds that subsection 18 U.S.C.A. § 2709(c) (which incorporates the nondisclosure requirements referred to above) violates the First Amendment freedom of speech and the principle of separation of powers. *Doe v. Gonzales*, 500 F.Supp. 379 (S.D.N.Y. 2007). On appeal, the Second Circuit agreed that National Security Letter provisions violate the First Amendment. But the court said,

> We will adjudicate the constitutionality of the nondisclosure requirement in subsection 2709(c) by construing this requirement to apply only when senior FBI officials certify that disclosure may result in an enumerated harm that is related to "an authorized investigation to protect against international terrorism or clandestine intelligence activities." *Doe, Inc. v. Mukasey*, 549 F.3d 861, 875 (2d Cir. 2008).

# The Exclusionary Rule

**exclusionary rule** Judicial doctrine forbidding the use of evidence in a criminal trial where the evidence was obtained in violation of the defendant's constitutional rights.

The **exclusionary rule** is a judicially created rule that prohibits the use of illegally obtained evidence in a criminal prosecution of the person whose rights were violated by the police in obtaining that evidence. In 1914 the U.S. Supreme Court first held that evidence obtained through an unlawful search and seizure could not be used to convict a person of a federal crime. *Weeks v. United States*, supra. The rationale for the rule is to deter illegal searches and seizures by police and thereby enforce the constitutional requirements. In 1949, in *Wolf v. Colorado*, supra, the Supreme Court refused to require the states to follow the exclusionary rule, saying that it was not an essential element of Fourth Amendment protection. But in *Mapp v. Ohio*, 367 U.S. 643, 81 S.Ct. 1684, 6 L.Ed.2d 1081 (1961), the Court held that there was no other effective means of enforcing the protections of the Fourth Amendment. The Court reasoned that if the Fourth Amendment was applicable to the states under the Fourteenth Amendment, then the exclusionary rule was also because it was the only effective means of enforcing the Fourth Amendment against overzealous police officers. The *Mapp* decision had an immediate impact. In New York City, for example, in the year preceding *Mapp*, police officers had not bothered to obtain a single search warrant. In the year following *Mapp*, they obtained more than 800.

## The Fruit of the Poisonous Tree Doctrine

**fruit of the poisonous tree doctrine** A doctrine based on the judicial interpretation of the Fourth Amendment that holds that evidence derived from other, illegally seized evidence cannot be used by the prosecution.

The **fruit of the poisonous tree doctrine** holds that evidence derived from other evidence that is obtained through an illegal search or seizure is itself inadmissible. *Wong Sun v. United States*, 371 U.S. 471, 83 S.Ct. 407, 9 L.Ed.2d 441 (1963). The general rule is that where there has been an illegal seizure of property, such property cannot be introduced into evidence and no testimony may be given relative to any facts surrounding the seizure. However, the Fourth Amendment does not require evidence to be excluded, even if it was initially

---

## | JURISPRUDENCE

*Mapp v. Ohio*, 367 U.S. 643, 81 S.Ct. 1684, 6 L.Ed.2d 1081 (1961)

Cleveland, Ohio police arrived at Dollree Mapp's home pursuant to information that a bombing suspect was hiding there. They demanded access, but failing to produce a search warrant, were denied. Police returned some four hours later and forced their way into the home. Mapp, who protested the entry, was forcibly detained while officers searched the home. Although police failed to locate the bombing suspect, they did find in a trunk in the basement some sexually explicit materials. Mapp was arrested, tried, and convicted under the Ohio statute proscribing possession of obscene materials. The Ohio appellate courts upheld the conviction. Dividing 7–2, the U.S. Supreme Court reversed, holding that the evidence

had been improperly admitted against her since it had been obtained in violation of the Fourth Amendment warrant requirement. In this landmark decision, the Court overturned precedent and applied the exclusionary rule to the state courts via the Fourteenth Amendment. Dissenting, Justice Harlan asserted that the Court had "forgotten the sense of judicial restraint which, with due regard for *stare decisis*, is one element that should enter into deciding whether a past decision of this Court should be overruled." The majority, however, concluded that its decision "gives to the individual no more than that which the Constitution guarantees him, to the police officer no less than that to which honest law enforcement is entitled, and, to the courts, that judicial integrity so necessary in the true administration of justice."

discovered during an illegal search of private property, if that evidence is later discovered during a valid search that is wholly independent of the initial illegal activity. *Murray v. United States*, 487 U.S. 533, 108 S.Ct. 2529, 101 L.Ed.2d 472 (1988). The Supreme Court has also held that evidence obtained through a search guided by information obtained from an inadmissible confession is likewise inadmissible unless the search would inevitably have recovered the evidence in the absence of the tainted information. *Nix v. Williams*, 467 U.S. 431, 444, 104 S.Ct. 2501, 2509, 81 L.Ed.2d 377 (1984).

## Erosion of the Exclusionary Rule

The exclusionary rule is justified by the need to deter police misconduct, but it exacts a high price to society in that "the criminal is to go free because the constable has blundered." As crime rates rose dramatically during the 1960s and 1970s, the exclusionary rule came under attack from critics who argued that the social cost of allowing guilty persons to avoid prosecution outweighed the benefit of deterring police from violating the Fourth Amendment. During the 1970s, the Supreme Court used this sort of cost-benefit analysis in curtailing the scope of the exclusionary rule in a series of controversial decisions. In *United States v. Calandra*, 414 U.S. 338, 94 S.Ct. 613, 38 L.Ed.2d 561 (1974), the Court held that illegally obtained evidence could be used to obtain grand jury indictments. In *Michigan v. DeFillippo*, 443 U.S. 31, 99 S.Ct. 2627, 61 L.Ed.2d 343 (1979), the Court allowed the use of evidence obtained through a search incident to arrest pursuant to a law that was later ruled unconstitutional. But the most significant erosions of the rule came in the 1980s.

## The Good-Faith Exception

In the most significant exclusionary rule cases decided in the 1980s, the Supreme Court held that evidence obtained on the basis of a search warrant that is later

---

### JURISPRUDENCE

*United States v. Leon*, 468 U.S. 897, 104 S.Ct. 3405, 82 L.Ed.2d 677 (1984)

Police officers obtained a search warrant based on a tip from a confidential informant of unproven reliability. A subsequent search of a residence turned up a substantial amount of illegal drugs. At an evidentiary hearing prior to trial, a judge ruled that the warrant had been wrongly issued; that there was insufficient information to constitute probable cause. The Supreme Court ultimately held that the evidence could nevertheless be admitted against the defendants, because to exclude such evidence would have no deterrent effect on police misconduct. The error was made by the magistrate who issued the warrant, not by the police who

were deemed to be acting in good faith. Writing for the Court, Justice Byron White concluded that "that the marginal or nonexistent benefits produced by suppressing evidence obtained in objectively reasonable reliance on a subsequently invalidated search warrant cannot justify the substantial costs of exclusion." Dissenting, Justice William Brennan asserted that "it is clear that we have not been treated to an honest assessment of the merits of the exclusionary rule but have instead been drawn into a curious world where the 'costs' of excluding illegally obtained evidence loom to exaggerated heights and where the 'benefits' of such exclusion are made to disappear with a mere wave of the hand."

held to be invalid may be admitted as evidence at trial if the police officer who conducted the search relied on the warrant in "good faith." *United States v. Leon*, 468 U.S. 897, 104 S.Ct. 3405, 82 L.Ed.2d 677 (1984); *Massachusetts v. Sheppard*, 468 U.S. 981, 104 S.Ct. 3424, 82 L.Ed.2d 737 (1984). In *Illinois v. Krull*, 480 U.S. 340, 107 S.Ct. 1160, 94 L.Ed.2d 364 (1987), the Court held that the **good-faith exception** to the exclusionary rule permits the introduction of evidence obtained by an officer in reliance upon a statute authorizing warrantless administrative searches where the statute is later determined to be unconstitutional. It must be noted that the good-faith exception to the exclusionary rule, as it has been developed thus far by the Supreme Court, applies only to cases where police officers rely on warrants that are later held to be invalid; it does not apply to warrantless searches.

**good-faith exception** An exception to the exclusionary rule (which bars the use of evidence obtained by a search warrant found to be invalid). The exception allows use of the evidence if the police relied in good faith on the search warrant, even though the warrant is subsequently held to be invalid.

*In United States v. Leon*, supra, the Supreme Court identified four situations involving police reliance on a warrant where the good-faith exception to the exclusionary rule does not apply:

1. if the magistrate was misled by an affidavit that the affiant knew was false or would have known was false except for reckless disregard for the truth.
2. if the magistrate wholly abandons his or her judicial role
3. if the affidavit is so lacking in indicia of probable cause as to render belief in its existence unreasonable
4. if the warrant is so facially deficient that the executing officer cannot reasonably presume its validity

---

## JURISPRUDENCE

*Herring v. United States*, 555 U.S. 135, 129 S.Ct. 695, 172 L.Ed.2d 496 (2009)

On July 7, 2004, Investigator Mark Anderson of the Coffee County, Alabama, Sheriff's Department, learned that Bennie Dean Herring had driven in to retrieve something from his impounded truck. Anderson requested the county's warrant clerk, Sandy Pope, to check for any outstanding warrants for Herring's arrest. She found none. He then requested her to check with Sharon Morgan, her counterpart in the neighboring county. Morgan replied that there was an active arrest warrant for Herring's failure to appear on a felony charge. Pope then relayed the information to Anderson and he and a deputy followed Herring and arrested him. A search incident to arrest yielded methamphetamine in Herring's pocket and a pistol in his vehicle. There had, however, been a mistake about the warrant. When Morgan sought to retrieve the actual warrant to fax it to Pope, she learned it had been recalled five months earlier. Morgan immediately called Pope to alert her to the mix-up, and

Pope in turn contacted Anderson by radio, but by this time, Anderson had already arrested Herring and seized a gun and drugs incident to arrest. Herring was convicted in federal district court and the Eleventh Circuit Court of Appeal affirmed. The Supreme Court granted review.

Chief Justice John Roberts delivered the Court's 5–4 decision. Assuming the arrest was unlawful, the Court held that because the mistake was merely negligence, the evidence need not be suppressed. Pointing out that the exclusionary rule serves "to deter deliberate, reckless, or grossly negligent conduct," Roberts observed: "When a probable-cause determination was based on reasonable but mistaken assumptions, the person subjected to a search or seizure has not necessarily been the victim of a constitutional violation." In dissent, Justice Ruth Bader Ginsburg argued that negligent recordkeeping errors by law enforcement are susceptible to deterrence by the exclusionary rule and cannot effectively be remedied through other means.

## The Good-Faith Exception under State Constitutional Law

As previously noted, the Fourth Amendment sets a minimum national standard. Most states have adopted the good-faith exception. State courts are free to provide greater levels of protection under the search and seizure sections of state constitutions. This latter approach was followed by the New Jersey Supreme Court in *State v. Novembrino*, 519 A.2d 820 (N.J. 1987), where it refused to follow the good-faith exception to the exclusionary rule as a matter of state law. The court observed that the exclusionary rule was firmly embedded in its own jurisprudence and that a good-faith exception would "ultimately reduce respect for and compliance with the probable cause standard." 519 A.2d 854.

## Standing to Invoke the Exclusionary Rule

**standing** The right to initiate a legal action or challenge based on the fact that one has suffered or is likely to suffer a real and substantial injury.

A person who seeks the benefits of the exclusionary rule must have **standing** to invoke the rule. The concept of standing limits the class of defendants who may challenge an allegedly illegal search and seizure. In *Jones v. United States*, 362 U.S. 257, 80 S.Ct. 725, 4 L.Ed.2d 697 (1960), the Supreme Court granted automatic standing to anyone who was legitimately on the premises searched. In *Rakas v. Illinois*, 439 U.S. 128, 99 S.Ct. 421, 58 L.Ed.2d 387 (1978), however, the Court restricted the *Jones* doctrine by refusing to allow passengers of an automobile to challenge the search of the vehicle in which they were riding.

When police stop an automobile, the driver of the car is "seized" within the meaning of the Fourth Amendment. Therefore the driver has standing to challenge the constitutionality of the stop and everything that transpires during the stop. In *Brendlin v. California*, 551 U.S. 249, 127 S.Ct. 2400, 168 L.Ed.2d 132 (2007), the Supreme Court held that a passenger is seized as well and so has standing to challenge the constitutionality of the stop. However, under *Rakas v. Illinois*, supra, passengers have standing to challenge only searches and seizures of things in which they have a property interest. Therefore, while the passenger can challenge the validity of the automobile stop, under *Rakas v. Illinois* the passenger may not challenge the constitutionality of the stop of the automobile.

---

**CASE-IN-POINT**

### The Good-Faith Exception under State Constitutional Law

Acting on the basis of an informant's tip, police obtained a warrant to search a building owned by the defendant. Inside the building they discovered seventeen growing marijuana plants, as well as cultivating equipment. After a suppression hearing, the trial judge determined that the warrant upon which the search was based was defective in that it had not been adequately supported by probable cause. Nevertheless, the judge refused to suppress the evidence, citing the good-faith exception to the exclusionary rule created by the U.S. Supreme Court's decision in *United States v. Leon*. On appeal, the Pennsylvania Supreme Court interpreted its state constitution as affording more protection to a defendant against unreasonable searches and seizures than the federal constitution, as interpreted in *Leon*. Thus, the court concluded that the Pennsylvania constitution does not permit a *Leon*-style good-faith exception to the exclusionary rule.

*Commonwealth v. Edmunds*, 586 A.2d 887 (Pa. 1991).

In *United States v. Salvucci*, 448 U.S. 83, 100 S.Ct. 2547, 65 L.Ed.2d 619 (1980), the Court took the final step in overruling the automatic-standing rule of *Jones v. United States*. Salvucci was charged with possession of stolen mail. The evidence was recovered by police in a search of an apartment that belonged to the mother of Salvucci's accomplice. The federal district court granted Salvucci's motion to suppress the evidence, relying on the automatic-standing doctrine. The Supreme Court reversed, holding that Salvucci was not automatically entitled to challenge the search of another person's apartment. Justice William H. Rehnquist explained the Court's more conservative stance on the issue of standing:

> We are convinced that the automatic standing rule . . . has outlived its usefulness in this Court's Fourth Amendment jurisprudence. The doctrine now serves only to afford a windfall to defendants whose Fourth Amendment rights have not been violated. 448 U.S. at 95, 100 S.Ct. at 2554, 65 L.Ed.2d at 630.

Thus, a casual visitor to an apartment has no legitimate expectation of privacy in an apartment hallway that would grant the visitor standing to contest a search of those premises. *United States v. Burnett*, 890 F.2d 1233 (D.C. Cir. 1989). To successfully invoke the exclusionary rule now, a defendant must show that a legitimate expectation of privacy was violated.

In *United States v. Edwards*, 242 F.3d 928 (10th Cir. 2001), the court held that the defendant lacked standing to challenge the search of a rented car because it was rented in another person's name and the defendant was not an authorized driver of the vehicle, whereas in *United States v. Walker*, 237 F.3d 845 (7th Cir. 2001), the defendant had standing to challenge the search of a rental car because he was listed on the rental agreement as an authorized driver.

In 1983 the Pennsylvania Supreme Court determined that under its state constitution a defendant accused of a possessory crime who seeks to challenge a search and seizure must be accorded automatic standing notwithstanding the more restrictive view announced by the U.S. Supreme Court. *Commonwealth v. Sell*, 470 A.2d 457 (Pa. 1983). Of course, states may still grant automatic standing to challenge seized evidence. For example, "under Louisiana jurisprudence, any defendant against whom evidence is acquired as a result of an allegedly unreasonable search and seizure, whether or not it was obtained in violation of his rights, has standing to challenge the constitutionality of the search or seizure." *State v. Dakin*, 495 So.2d 344, 346 (La. 1986). Likewise, in *Commonwealth v. Amendola*, 550 N.E.2d 121, 126 (Mass. 1990), the court refused to abandon the automatic-standing rule: "When a defendant is charged with a crime in which possession of the seized evidence at the time of the contested search is an essential element of guilt, the defendant shall be deemed to have standing to contest the legality of the search and the seizure of that evidence." Courts in Michigan, New Hampshire, New Jersey, and Vermont have reached similar conclusions.

## Conclusion

The constitutional protection against unreasonable searches and seizures is a fundamental right, yet determining the precise scope and meaning of the right is not easy. The constitutional law governing search and seizure is extremely complex. Moreover, it is highly dynamic, as courts decide countless cases in this area each year. Figure 15.3 provides an overview of search and seizure law—actually, a decision tree that highlights the important questions that courts must answer in determining whether a particular search or seizure was lawful.

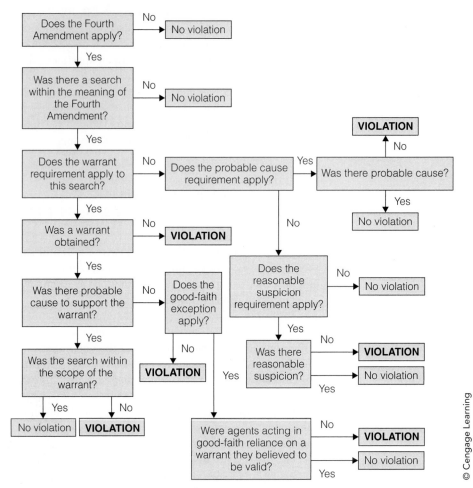

**FIGURE 15.3** Fourth Amendment Decision Tree. The decision tree depicted here is based on general principles of federal law and may not correctly portray applicable laws in all states.

© Cengage Learning

## Chapter Summary

- Learning Objective 1

  - The Fourth Amendment was conceived as a limitation on the powers of the national government but in 1949 the Supreme Court held that freedom from unreasonable searches and seizures is "implicit in the concept of ordered liberty" and ruled that the Fourth Amendment is enforceable against the States through the Due Process Clause of the Fourteenth Amendment.

  - State courts are free to provide higher levels of protection under their state constitutions but cannot provide less without running afoul of the Fourteenth Amendment.

  - The Fourth Amendment protects a person's rights against the police and other government agents from unreasonable searches and seizures but does not protect against searches and seizures by private individuals.

  - Persons crossing the national border or other functional equivalents, and searches and seizures conducted by U.S. agents outside the territory of the

United States, are not protected by the Fourth Amendment. Nor does it apply to open fields or to abandoned property.

o Fourth Amendment protection is at its maximum for persons in their home and its curtilage (the area immediately surrounding the house). Protections extend to stores, offices, and places of business, but not to those areas of commercial properties that carry an implied invitation for the public to enter.

• Learning Objective 2

o The term "seizure" refers to the taking into custody of physical evidence, property, or even a person. But what constitutes a "search" can be more difficult.

o Historically, courts looked at whether a trespass had taken place in deciding whether the Fourth Amendment was implicated. But in 1967 the Supreme Court abandoned the trespass doctrine, saying "the Fourth Amendment protects people, not places."

o Today courts employ a twofold requirement: first whether a person has exhibited an actual (subjective) expectation of privacy and, second, whether the expectation is one that society recognizes as "reasonable."

o Obviously, anyone lawfully incarcerated in a prison or jail has no reasonable expectation of privacy. Inmates are routinely subjected to searches of their persons, although some courts hold that strip searches violate Fourth Amendment rights unless there is probable cause to believe the arrestee is concealing weapons or contraband. Other courts permit such searches where there is a reasonable suspicion that the arrestee is concealing weapons or contraband.

o When conducted according to standard police procedures, an inventory search of a vehicle is regarded as an administrative search not subject to ordinary Fourth Amendment requirements. Inventory searches are justified by the need to protect the owner's property and to protect the police from claims of lost property and potential dangers lurking inside closed automobiles.

o Courts have approved properly established and conducted sobriety checkpoints where all drivers passing a certain point are stopped briefly for license checks and signs of intoxication.

• Learning Objective 3

o Consent to a search must be truly voluntary and involve more than mere acquiescence to the authority of the police.

o Courts have said that police may not search a home when one resident invites them in but another refuses to grant access.

o In 1990 the Supreme Court shifted the focus from the dominion and control of the third party to the police officer's subjective belief that the third party has the authority to grant consent to a search of the premises.

o The problem of consent is especially acute in situations where several persons share a single dwelling, as is common among college students.

• Learning Objective 4

o The Fourth Amendment expresses a preference for searches and seizures to be conducted pursuant to a warrant, which in turn must be supported by probable cause. Probable cause exists when prudent and cautious police officers have trustworthy information leading them to believe that evidence of crime might be obtained through a particular search.

- ○ Courts say officers are to determine probable cause as a "commonsense, practical question" in light of the totality of circumstances in a given case.

- Learning Objective 5

  - ○ To obtain a search warrant, agents submit an affidavit to a judge or magistrate who must then determine whether the stated facts support a finding of probable cause. The officer's affidavit must always contain a rather precise description of the place(s) or person(s) to be searched and the things to be seized. The information on which an affidavit is based must be sufficiently fresh to ensure that the items to be seized are probably located on the premises to be searched.

  - ○ A magistrate's finding of probable cause may be based on hearsay evidence, but because hearsay evidence is often provided by confidential informants (CIs), whose motivations may be suspect, their reliability and basis of knowledge must be carefully checked. The Supreme Court formerly required the officer's affidavit show that a CI was both credible and reliable, and give the basis of the CI's knowledge. In 1983 the Court relaxed the standards and permitted magistrates to consider the totality of circumstances when evaluating applications for search warrants based on hearsay evidence. Most states follow the relaxed standard but many have opted to adhere to the more strict requirements.

  - ○ The scope of a search and seizure is bound by the terms of the warrant. Courts tend to be less strict when it comes to the description of contraband because it is illegal per se, but stricter in cases involving First Amendment rights. Traditionally, police wait until a suspect receives contraband before obtaining a search warrant.

  - ○ Dramatic increases in drug trafficking over the last few decades gave rise to a number of state courts approving anticipatory search warrants where probable cause does not have to exist until the warrant is executed. In 2006 the Supreme Court approved anticipatory search warrants, noting that the magistrate must determine that it is probable that contraband will be on the described premises when the warrant is executed.

  - ○ The Federal Rules of Criminal Procedure provide that a warrant "shall command the officer to search, within a specified period of time not to exceed 10 days, the person or place named or the property or person specified. The warrant shall be served in the daytime, unless the issuing authority . . . authorizes its execution at times other than daytime."

  - ○ States have varying requirements that govern the period of time and hours for execution of a search warrant. An officer may break open door or window of a house to execute a search warrant, if, after notice of his or her authority and purpose, the officer is refused admittance. Giving notice is known as the "knock-and-announce requirement." Officers facing exigent circumstances such as the need to preserve evanescent evidence can dispense with the knock and announce requirement. But in 1997 the Court ruled that states may not create a blanket "drug exception" to the knock-and-announce requirement. In 2006 a divided Supreme Court held that violations of the knock-and-announce requirement do not require the suppression of all evidence seized as the result of such violations.

- Learning Objective 6

  - ○ Because an absolute warrant requirement would be impractical, courts uphold warrantless searches under "exigent circumstances." All exceptions assume that police officers have probable cause to believe that a given search is likely to produce evidence of crime.

- ○ Police may seize evidence that comes to their attention when they are lawfully in an area and the evidence is in plain view and apparently constitutes evidence of a crime.
- ○ Police in "hot pursuit" may continue to pursue a suspect into a protected place, such as a home, without having to wait until a warrant can be obtained. When police reasonably believe that a person is in need of immediate aid, they may make a warrantless entry of a dwelling. Once inside, they may justifiably seize evidence in plain view.
- ○ Where police have a reasonable belief that loss or destruction of evidence is imminent, a warrantless entry of premises may be justified. In 1984 the Supreme Court narrowed the doctrine, saying that destruction of evidence does not constitute exigent circumstances if the underlying offense is relatively minor.
- ○ In 1969 the Supreme Court limited the historic doctrine of search incident to arrest to allow police only to search the body of an arrestee and the arrestee's immediate "grasp" or "lunge" area. Police may not search a dwelling when an arrest occurs outside it.
- ○ Police may stop an automobile without a warrant and temporarily detain the driver as long as they have probable cause to believe that criminal activity is taking place or that traffic laws or automobile regulations are being violated.
- ○ In 1996 the Supreme Court held that police may use a minor traffic or equipment violation as a pretext for stopping an automobile that they wish to investigate. When evidence of drug or alcohol use or other criminal violation becomes apparent, police may make a warrantless arrest and search incident to that arrest.
- ○ Once begun under exigent circumstances, a warrantless search of an automobile may continue after the vehicle has been taken to the police station.
- ○ In 2009 the Supreme Court substantially revised the rule on a search incident to arrest of an occupant of a vehicle to provide that police may search a vehicle incident to a recent occupant's arrest only if the arrestee is within reaching distance of the passenger compartment at the time of the search or it is reasonable to believe the vehicle contains evidence of the offense of arrest.

- Learning Objective 7

  - ○ The courts have also recognized that certain types of searches may be reasonable in the absence of probable cause.
  - ○ To protect law enforcement personnel, in 1968 the Supreme Court upheld the authority of police officers to stop and frisk an individual and conduct a limited "pat-down" search for weapons based on reasonable suspicion.
  - ○ Stop-and-frisk laws generally also allow police to stop a motor vehicle on reasonable suspicion that crime is afoot and make a limited search for weapons. In attempting to identify and to apprehend drug smugglers, law enforcement agencies developed sets of characteristics that typify drug couriers.
  - ○ In 1980 the Supreme Court suggested that fitting a drug courier profile was not in itself sufficient to constitute the reasonable suspicion necessary to allow police to detain an airline passenger.
  - ○ The Supreme Court has also said searches of public school students can be based on a reasonableness standard rather than on probable cause.
  - ○ To insure public safety, courts have upheld the constitutionality of regulations permitting supervisory personnel to order urinalysis testing of public safety officers based on reasonable suspicion of drug abuse.

- Learning Objective 8

  - The use of technology searchlights, field glasses, aerial photography, and other means of enhancing observation does not necessarily trigger Fourth Amendment protections.
  - In 1979 the Supreme Court determined that use of a pen register to record phone numbers dialed from a particular phone number is not a search within the meaning of the Fourth Amendment.
  - In 1986 the Court held that neither the high-altitude photography of a chemical plant nor use in evidence of photos, taken in a low-altitude flight, of marijuana plants growing in a defendant's backyard constituted searches under the Fourth Amendment.
  - In 2001 the Court said, "when the Government uses a device that is not in general public use, to explore details of the home that would previously have been unknowable without physical intrusion, the surveillance is a 'search' and is presumptively unreasonable without a warrant."

- Learning Objective 9

  - The Omnibus Crime Control and Safe Streets Act of 1968 prohibits interception of electronic communications without a court order unless one party to the conversation consents. Interception is defined as "aural or other acquisition of the contents of any wire, electronic or oral communication through the use of any electronic, mechanical, or other device."
  - In 1986 Congress expanded the meaning of "wire communications" to include conversations through "switching stations," which covers cellular telephones. An application for a wiretap order must contain detailed information along with an explanation of why less intrusive means of investigation will not suffice.
  - The Electronic Communications Privacy Act of 1986 established federal standards for access to e-mail and other electronic communications and to "transactional records," including subscriber identifying information, call logs, phone bills, and so forth. The act requires judges to issue orders to allow using pen registers and trap-and-trace devices on request of prosecutors. Courts generally hold that users of telephones have no reasonable expectations of privacy with regard to numbers associated with incoming or outgoing phone calls.
  - In 2007 a federal appeals court reasoned that because computer surveillance techniques are constitutionally indistinguishable from the use of a pen register they do not violate the Fourth Amendment.
  - The USA PATRIOT Act enables law enforcement to access Internet communications, expands the authority for use of pen registers and trap-and-trace surveillance, and allows federal courts to issue "roving" surveillance orders in connection with foreign intelligence matters. Law enforcement officers are authorized to seize voicemail messages pursuant to a search warrant and to subpoena subscriber records of local and long-distance telephone connections and means of payment. The act also permits federal magistrate judges in any district in which terrorism-related activities may have occurred to issue search warrants for searches within or outside the district.
  - A section of the USA PATRIOT Act that prohibited libraries directed to turn over records to the FBI from disclosing that fact to anyone became controversial. Amendments in 2006 made a number of technical revisions to the

original USA PATRIOT Act and libraries now have the right to petition to modify or quash the nondisclosure requirement of such an order. In 2008 the Second Circuit said it would construe the nondisclosure requirement to apply only when senior FBI officials certify that disclosure may result in an enumerated harm related to "an authorized investigation to protect against international terrorism or clandestine intelligence activities."

- Learning Objective 10

  o The exclusionary rule was judicially created to prohibit the use of illegally obtained evidence in a criminal prosecution of a person whose rights were violated by the police in obtaining that evidence.

  o The "fruit of the poisonous tree doctrine" holds that evidence derived from other evidence that is obtained through an illegal search or seizure is itself inadmissible. Also, evidence obtained through a search guided by information obtained from an inadmissible confession is inadmissible unless the search would inevitably have recovered the evidence in the absence of the taint.

  o Evidence does not have to be excluded, even if it was initially discovered during an illegal search of private property, if that evidence is later discovered during a valid search wholly independent of the initial illegal activity.

  o In 1984 the Supreme Court instituted a "good-faith exception" to the exclusionary rule where the police officer who conducted the search relied in "good faith" on the validity of a search warrant. But the good-faith exception to the exclusionary rule does not apply if (1) the magistrate was misled by an affidavit that the affiant knew was false, or would have known was false except for reckless disregard for the truth; (2) the magistrate wholly abandons his or her judicial role; (3) the affidavit is so lacking in indicia of probable cause as to render belief in its existence unreasonable; or (4) the warrant is so facially deficient that the executing officer cannot reasonably presume its validity.

## Key Terms

| | |
|---|---|
| abandoned property | exigent circumstances |
| affiant | *Franks* hearing |
| affidavit | fruit of the poisonous tree doctrine |
| anticipatory search warrant | general warrant |
| automobile exception | good-faith exception |
| border searches | hot pursuit |
| confidential informants | implied consent |
| consent to a search | inventory search |
| curtilage | knock and announce |
| doctrine of incorporation | open fields doctrine |
| drug courier profiles | pen register |
| drug testing | plain-view doctrine |
| electronic eavesdropping | probable cause |
| emergency searches | reasonable expectation of privacy |
| evanescent evidence | reasonable suspicion |
| exclusionary rule | search |

| | |
|---|---|
| search incident to a lawful arrest | totality of circumstances |
| seizure | trap-and-trace devices |
| sobriety checkpoints | USA PATRIOT Act |
| standing | warrant |
| stop-and-frisk | warrantless searches |
| strip searches | wiretap orders |
| third-party consent | wiretapping |

## Questions for Thought and Discussion

1. Today many security personnel are "private police," yet Fourth Amendment protection has been extended only to those searches conducted by government officials. What arguments can be made for and against expanding the prohibitions of the Fourth Amendment to include security personnel?

2. What rationale supports the "search incident to arrest" exception to the warrant requirement? What limitations do the courts impose on such searches?

3. Should one have a reasonable expectation of privacy from infrared detectors and other high-tech devices that enable law enforcement officers to "see" heat emanating from a person's home? Why or why not?

4. Does a person using a public restroom in a government office building have a reasonable expectation of privacy from television security surveillance?

5. In *New Jersey v. T.L.O.* (1985), the Supreme Court adopted a reasonableness standard for public school searches. Should this standard be applied to searches of students in public colleges and universities? What about private colleges? Does it make a difference if the search is conducted in a public setting or in the student's dormitory room?

6. What is the rationale for excluding from trial evidence obtained in violation of the Fourth Amendment? Is this a compelling justification for the exclusion of criminal evidence from the trial of a defendant accused of a serious felony such as aggravated battery?

7. What alternatives to the exclusionary rule might be adopted to enforce the protections of the Fourth Amendment? How effective are such alternatives likely to be?

8. The Supreme Court has created a "good-faith" exception to the exclusionary rule where police rely on a search warrant that is later held to be invalid because the magistrate erred in finding probable cause for a search. Should the good-faith exception be extended to cases where police acting in good faith conduct *warrantless* searches that are later held to be unlawful?

9. What is meant by the "fruit of the poisonous tree doctrine" in relation to searches and seizures?

10. What is the "standing" requirement in the law of search and seizure? What is its purpose?

11. In 2006 in *Hudson v. Michigan*, Justice Antonin Scalia, writing for a sharply divided Supreme Court, concluded that when it comes to knock-and-announce violations, "[r]esort to the massive remedy of suppressing evidence of guilt is unjustified." Writing for the four dissenters, Justice Stephen Breyer contended that the decision "destroys the strongest legal incentive to comply with the Constitution's knock-and-announce requirement." Evaluate these opposing views.

12. In *United States v. Salvucci* (1980), the U.S. Supreme Court concluded that "the automatic standing rule . . . has outlived its usefulness in this Court's Fourth Amendment jurisprudence." Yet, several state courts have held that under their state constitutions a defendant accused of a possessory crime who challenges a search and seizure must be accorded automatic standing. What are the merits of states, based on their own constitutions, affording defendants more protection in this area than required by the Supreme Court?

## Problems for Discussion and Solution

1. Police observed an automobile traveling at a high rate of speed and swerving on the road. They gave pursuit and stopped the vehicle after a five-minute chase. The driver, later identified as Jerome Johnson, emerged from the car and began to verbally abuse and threaten the officers. Johnson appeared intoxicated but refused to take any of the standard field sobriety tests. Under state law, refusal to perform a sobriety test results in the loss of a driver's license for a period of one year. The law does not authorize police to force suspects to perform any sobriety tests against their will. Johnson was arrested and transported to a local hospital, where he was forcibly restrained and asked to submit to a blood-alcohol test. Johnson refused, saying "I'd rather lose my license than let you stick me with that needle." The test was administered over Johnson's objection, and the results indicated that Johnson's blood-alcohol level was substantially above the legal limit. Johnson was charged with driving under the influence of alcohol. Before trial, Johnson's attorney moved to suppress the results of the blood-alcohol test, arguing that it was taken without Johnson's consent, without probable cause, and in violation of the state's implied consent law. If you were the judge in this case, how would you be inclined to rule on the admissibility of this evidence? What additional information would you need to render your decision?

2. Acting without a search warrant, police arrive at a home after receiving an anonymous tip that a man has been making illegal explosives in his workshop. The officers find that the man is not at home. Can the man's wife consent to a warrantless search of her husband's workshop, or must police wait until the husband returns to obtain his consent? What would be the result if the man and his wife were both at home and the wife consented to the search but the man did not?

3. The sheriffs department in a rural north Georgia county receives an anonymous letter stating that there is a "meth lab" being operated in a trailer home belonging to Danny Dawgmire, and that children living in the trailer are being exposed to methamphetamine and other toxic chemicals. Without obtaining a warrant, deputies drive to the trailer home, where they detect strong chemical odors associated with the production of methamphetamines. The deputies knock and announce their presence, but no one answers. They then forcibly enter the trailer, where they discover large quantities of methamphetamines and associated equipment, paraphernalia, and supplies. No children are found in the trailer. The deputies call a hazardous materials disposal unit to the scene. Two hours later, as the meth lab is being cleaned up and evidence secured, Dawgmire arrives at the scene in his pickup truck and is promptly arrested and charged with manufacture of and possession with intent to distribute a controlled substance. In a pretrial motion, Dawgmire's attorney moves to suppress the evidence on the ground that no warrant had been obtained to authorize the search. The attorney claims that Dawgmire, who is unmarried, lives in the

trailer alone and that at no time have any children been inside the trailer. How would the state likely counter the motion? How would the judge likely rule on the motion to suppress?

4. Police receive a call from Johann Besch, who lives at 123 Pauline Place. Besch tells the police that he is convinced that his next door neighbor is running a drug dealing operation. Police go to Besch's residence. There they meet with Besch, who tells them of the many different cars that come and go at all hours of the day. Besch also says that he doesn't think his neighbor has a "real job" because he never sees him leaving the house. Based on Besch's statements, police drive by the neighbor's house several times over the next three days. Each time they drive by they observe different cars parked in the driveway. They check departmental records and discover that a search warrant had been executed at that home two years before and that the search had resulted in seizure of illegal drugs. At this point they go to a magistrate to obtain a search warrant. If you were the magistrate, would you issue the warrant based on the information police have obtained thus far? Why or why not?

# CHAPTER 16

# Arrest, Interrogation, and Identification Procedures

## CHAPTER OUTLINE

## JURISPRUDENCE

## LEARNING OBJECTIVES

After reading this chapter, you should be able to explain

1. why an arrest triggers the Fourth Amendment warrant requirement and when a warrantless arrest is permissible

2. the extent to which officers may use force to make an arrest

3. how an investigatory detention differs from an arrest and the applicable constitutional standards

4. the controversy over racial profiling as a basis for investigatory detentions

5. the legal issues surrounding the use of roadblocks and sobriety checkpoints

6. the circumstances under which police may require a person to produce identification

7. why police interrogation implicates constitutional rights and why the courts have required police to warn suspects in custody of their constitutional rights before questioning them

8. whether police can use deception to induce suspects to confess

9. why inadmissible confessions can result in the suppression of physical evidence as well

10. the various methods police employ to identify suspects, and the constitutional standards that apply to identification procedures

## CHAPTER OPENING VIGNETTE

The name "Miranda" is well known to the public. Countless movies and television programs have shown police officers advising suspects who have just been arrested of their right to remain silent and their right to have counsel present during questioning, as dictated by the Supreme Court's landmark decision in *Miranda v. Arizona*, 384 U.S. 436, 86 S.Ct. 1602, 16 L.Ed.2d 694 (1966). Indeed, a new verb, "Mirandize," has been coined to refer to the process of advising suspects of their rights. Ernesto Miranda, a suspect in a rape case, was interrogated for two hours without being advised of the aforementioned rights. The Supreme Court invalidated his confession, saying that unless police advise suspects of their rights, incriminating statements made by suspects in custody cannot be used as evidence against them. Probably more than any other decision, *Miranda* has come to represent the importance of the rule of law in criminal justice—the idea that everyone taken into custody by the police has constitutional rights that must be respected. In this chapter we examine those constitutional rights in depth.

## Introduction

**arrest** To take someone into custody or otherwise deprive that person of freedom of movement.

In its most general sense, the term **arrest** refers to the deprivation of a person's liberty by someone with legal authority. In the contemporary criminal justice system, an arrest usually occurs when police take an individual into custody and charge that person with the commission of a crime. Generally, an arrest is made by a police officer, although there are some circumstances in which an arrest can be effected by a private individual.

As a form of "seizure," an arrest is governed by requirements of the Fourth Amendment. However, the formal arrest is not the only type of encounter between police and citizens that implicates the Fourth Amendment. A seizure, for Fourth Amendment purposes, occurs when a police officer, "by means of physical force or show of authority, has in some way restrained the liberty of a citizen." *Terry v. Ohio*, 392 U.S. 1, 19 n. 16, 88 S.Ct. 1868, 1879 n. 16, 20 L.Ed.2d 889, 905 n. 16 (1968). The traditional full-blown arrest clearly constitutes a seizure. So, too, does a police officer's fatal shooting of a fleeing suspect. *Tennessee v. Garner*, 471 U.S. 1, 105 S.Ct. 1694, 85 L.Ed.2d 1 (1985). Other instances may not be so clear, however. In 1988 the Supreme Court declined to formulate a "bright-line" rule delineating what constitutes a seizure; rather, the Court asserted that the test requires an assessment of whether, in view of all the circumstances surrounding an incident, "a reasonable person would have believed that he was not free to leave." *Michigan v. Chesternut*, 486 U.S. 567, 108 S.Ct. 1975, 100 L.Ed.2d 565 (1988). The following year, the Court ruled that stopping a motorist at a police roadblock is a seizure for Fourth Amendment purposes. *Brower v. County of Inyo*, 489 U.S. 593,109 S.Ct. 1378, 103 L.Ed.2d 628 (1989).

Encounters between citizens and police range from formal arrests to situations in which police approach an individual and ask questions. Police–citizen encounters can be placed in four categories:

1. Arrest
2. Investigatory detention (also referred to as stop-and-frisk, as introduced in Chapter 15)
3. The use of roadblocks and sobriety checkpoints
4. The request for information or identification

Each type of encounter is unique from the standpoint of the Fourth Amendment. Accordingly, we examine each of these separately in this chapter.

**interrogation** Questioning of a suspect by police or questioning of a witness by counsel.

**Interrogation** refers to the questioning of a suspect by law enforcement officers to elicit a confession, an admission, or information that otherwise assists them in solving a crime. Typically, interrogation takes place behind closed doors in a law enforcement facility, although today a suspect being questioned is often accompanied by an attorney. Because interrogation of a suspect carries with it a risk of coercion, confessions obtained by police are subject to constitutional attack under the Self-Incrimination Clause of the Fifth Amendment.

**identification procedures** Scientific and nonscientific procedures employed by police to assist in the identification of suspects.

**Identification procedures** are techniques employed by law enforcement agencies to identify suspects. These fall into two basic categories: scientific means to match physical evidence taken from a suspect with that found at a crime scene, and procedures to determine whether victims or witnesses can identify perpetrators. Both types of identification procedure are extremely important in building cases against defendants, and both present unique legal problems.

## Arrest

Because arrest is the most serious type of police–citizen encounter, it is subject to the most stringent constitutional requirements. Specifically, arrest is subject to the probable cause and warrant requirements of the Fourth Amendment, although there are exceptions to the latter. The Supreme Court has said that the legality of arrests by state and local officers is to be judged by the same constitutional standards applicable to federal agents. *Ker v. California*, 374 U.S. 23, 83 S.Ct. 1623, 10 L.Ed.2d 726 (1963).

### The Probable Cause Requirement

For any arrest or significant deprivation of liberty to occur, police officers must have probable cause. Although not easy to define, probable cause in the context of arrest means the same thing as in the context of search and seizure (see Chapter 15). The Supreme Court has said that probable cause exists where "the facts and circumstances within [the officers'] knowledge and of which they had reasonably trustworthy information [are] sufficient in themselves to warrant a man of reasonable caution in the belief" that a particular crime had been or was being committed. *Carroll v. United States*, 267 U.S. 132, 162, 45 S.Ct. 280, 288, 69 L.Ed. 543, 555 (1925).

WARRANT OF ARREST

County of _____. State of _____.

To any peace officer of said state:

Complaint on oath having this day been laid before me that the crime of _____ (designating it generally) has been committed and accusing _____ (naming defendant) thereof, you are therefore commanded forthwith to arrest the above named defendant and bring him/her before me at _____ (naming the place), or in case of my absence or inability to act, before the nearest or most accessible magistrate in this county. Dated at _____ (place) this _____ day of _____, 20 ___.

_____
*(signature and full official title of magistrate)*

© Cengage Learning

**FIGURE 16.1** Typical Form of an Arrest Warrant.

Police can establish probable cause without personally observing the commission of a crime as long as they have sufficient information to conclude that the suspect probably committed it. Officers often obtain their information from crime victims, eyewitnesses, official reports, and confidential or even anonymous informants.

## The Warrant Requirement

**arrest warrant** A document issued by a magistrate or judge directing that a named person be taken into custody for allegedly having committed an offense.

**capias** "That you take." A general term for various court orders requiring that some named person be taken into custody.

An **arrest warrant** (see Figure 16.1) is routine in cases where an arrest is to be made based on an indictment by a grand jury. When a prosecutor files an accusatorial document known as an information, the court issues a *capias*, a document directing the arrest of the defendant. In such cases, suspects are often not aware that they are under investigation, and police officers have ample time to obtain an arrest warrant without fear that suspects will flee. However, most arrests are not made pursuant to secret investigations but instead are made by police officers who observe a criminal act, respond to a complaint filed by a crime victim, or have probable cause to arrest after completing an investigation. In such cases, it is often unnecessary for police to obtain an arrest warrant, but it is always essential that they have probable cause to make the arrest.

## Warrantless Arrests

**warrantless arrest** An arrest made by police who do not possess an arrest warrant.

At common law, police had the right to make a **warrantless arrest** if they observed someone in the commission of a felony or had probable cause to believe that a person had committed or was committing a felony. To make a warrantless arrest for a misdemeanor, an officer had to observe someone in the commission of the act.

*Dunaway v. New York*, 442 U.S. 200, 99 S.Ct. 2248, 60 L.Ed.2d 824 (1979)

On March 26, 1971, the owner of a pizza parlor in Rochester, New York, was killed during an attempted armed robbery. Acting without a warrant, police took Irving Dunaway into custody and interrogated him in connection with the attempted robbery and murder. Dunaway was not told that he was under arrest, but he was interrogated, he confessed, and he was ultimately convicted. On appeal, Dunaway contended that the police officers violated his rights under the Fourth and Fourteenth Amendments when, without probable cause, they seized him and transported him to the police station for interrogation. The state argued that although the police did not have probable cause to make an arrest, the "station-house detention" and interrogation of the suspect could be allowed on the lesser standard of reasonable suspicion. The Supreme Court reversed the conviction, saying that probable cause is necessary to justify a station-house detention and interrogation, irrespective of whether it is termed an "arrest."

**plain view** Readily visible to the naked eye.

Otherwise, to make an arrest, a warrant was required. Many states adopted common-law rules of arrest in statutes allowing police officers broad discretion to make warrantless arrests. As with warrantless searches and seizures, the Supreme Court has approved warrantless arrests (1) where crimes are committed in **plain view** of police officers or (2) where officers possess probable cause to make an arrest but exigent circumstances prohibit them from obtaining a warrant. Absent plain view or compelling exigencies, the need to obtain an arrest warrant is unclear. As a matter of policy, it makes sense for police officers to obtain arrest warrants when possible. However, given the time that it takes to obtain an arrest warrant and the fact that magistrates are not always available around the clock, it is not always feasible for police to obtain warrants before making arrests.

The Supreme Court has upheld the authority of police officers to make warrantless arrests in public, assuming they have probable cause to do so. *United States v. Watson*, 423 U.S. 411, 96 S.Ct. 820, 46 L.Ed.2d 598 (1976). More problematic are warrantless arrests involving the forcible entry of a dwelling. Here, we encounter the classic Fourth Amendment concern for the sanctity of the home. For example, in *Payton v. New York*, 445 U.S. 573, 100 S.Ct. 1371, 63 L.Ed.2d 639 (1980), the Supreme Court held that, absent exigent circumstances, a warrantless, nonconsensual entry into a suspect's home to make a routine felony arrest violates the Fourth Amendment. In a footnote, the Court pointed out that at that time, twenty-three states had laws permitting a warrantless entry into the home for the purpose of making an arrest, even in the absence of exigent circumstances. 445 U.S. at 598, n. 46, 100 S.Ct. at 1386, n. 46, 63 L.Ed.2d at 658, n. 46. Courts are generally inclined to uphold warrantless entries into homes for the purpose of making an arrest when the following conditions are met:

1. There is probable cause to arrest the suspect.
2. The police have good reason to believe the suspect is on the premises.
3. There is good reason to believe the suspect is armed and dangerous.
4. There is a strong probability that the suspect will escape or evidence will be destroyed if the suspect is not soon apprehended.
5. The entry can be effected peaceably.
6. The offense under investigation is a serious felony.

# The Right of an Arrestee to a Prompt Appearance before a Magistrate

Although the Supreme Court has recognized the practical necessity of permitting police to make warrantless arrests, it has stressed the need for immediate *ex post facto* judicial review of the detention of a suspect. Writing for the Supreme Court in *Gerstein v. Pugh*, 420 U.S. 103, 95 S.Ct. 854, 43 L.Ed.2d 54 (1975), Justice Potter Stewart observed that "once the suspect is in custody . . . the reasons that justify dispensing with the magistrate's neutral judgment evaporate." 420 U.S. at 114, 95 S.Ct. at 863, 43 L.Ed.2d at 65. When a suspect is in custody pursuant to a warrantless arrest, "the detached judgment of a neutral magistrate is essential if the Fourth Amendment is to furnish meaningful protection from unfounded interference with liberty." 420 U.S. at 114, 95 S.Ct. at 863, 43 L.Ed.2d at 65. In *County of Riverside v. McLaughlin*, 500 U.S. 44, 111 S.Ct. 1661, 114 L.Ed.2d 49 (1991), the Supreme Court ruled that if an arrested person is brought before a magistrate within forty-eight hours, the requirements of the Fourth Amendment are satisfied.

Actually, any person who is arrested, regardless of whether the arrest was based on a warrant, must be brought promptly before a court of law. Although this is not a federal constitutional right in instances where arrests are made pursuant to warrants, all states now have rules that require the police to promptly bring an arrestee before a magistrate. Similarly, as Fed. R. Crim. P. 5(a) states, "A person making an arrest within the United States must take the defendant without unnecessary delay before a magistrate judge, or before a state or local judicial officer as Rule 5(c) provides, unless a statute provides otherwise."

# Use of Force by Police Making Arrests

Because suspects frequently resist attempts to take them into custody, police officers often must use force in making arrests. An officer is entitled to use whatever reasonable force is necessary to effect an arrest. Sometimes, the use of force by police is challenged in civil suits seeking damages. Typically, in such cases, the courts have said that in making a lawful arrest, police officers may use such force as necessary to effect the arrest and prevent the escape of the suspect. See, e.g., *Martyn v. Donlin*, 198 A.2d 700 (Conn. 1964). Generally, a police officer has less discretion to use force in apprehending suspected misdemeanants than suspected felons. See, e.g., *City of Mason v. Banks*, 581 S.W.2d 621 (Tenn. 1979). Most states have statutes providing that police officers have the right to require bystanders to assist them in making arrests. See, e.g., West's Ann. Cal. Penal Code § 839. Nearly every state has a law governing the use of force by police attempting to make arrests. The Illinois statute is typical:

> (a) A peace officer, or any person he has summoned or directed to assist him, need not retreat or desist from efforts to make a lawful arrest because of resistance or threatened resistance to the arrest. He is justified in the use of any force which he reasonably believes to be necessary to effect the arrest and of any force which he reasonably believes to be necessary to defend himself or another from bodily harm while making the arrest. However, he is justified in using force likely to cause death or great bodily harm only when he reasonably believes that such force is necessary to prevent death or great bodily harm to himself or other such person, or when he reasonably believes both that:
>
> > 1. Such force is necessary to prevent the arrest from being defeated by resistance or escape; and

### JURISPRUDENCE

*Tennessee v. Garner*, 471 U.S. 1, 105 S.Ct. 1694, 85 L.Ed.2d 1 (1985)

At the time this case reached the Supreme Court, a Tennessee Statute provided that "if, after a police officer has given notice of an intent to arrest a criminal suspect, and the suspect flees or forcibly resists, 'the officer may use all the necessary means to effect the arrest'." A Memphis police officer, acting under this statute, shot and killed Garner's teenage son. The teenager was told to halt by the officer, but instead he "fled over a fence at night in the backyard of a house he was suspected of burglarizing." The officer "used deadly force despite being 'reasonably sure' the suspect was unarmed, 17 or 18 years old, and

of slight build". As a result, the father filed a lawsuit under 42 U.S.C. § 1983 for violating his son's constitutional rights. The district court held that the statute and the officer's actions were constitutional; however, the Court of Appeals reversed. The Supreme Court, speaking through Justice Byron White, held the Tennessee statute unconstitutional "insofar as it authorizes the use of deadly force against … an apparently unarmed, nondangerous fleeing suspect." Under these circumstances, "force may not be used unless necessary to prevent the escape and the officer has probable cause to believe that the suspect poses a significant threat of death or serious physical injury to the officer or others."

2. The person to be arrested has committed or attempted a forcible felony which involves the infliction or threatened infliction of great bodily harm or is attempting to escape by use of a deadly weapon, or otherwise indicates that he will endanger human life or inflict great bodily harm unless arrested without delay.

(b) A peace officer making an arrest pursuant to an invalid warrant is justified in the use of any force which he would be justified in using if the warrant were valid, unless he knows that the warrant is invalid. 720 Ill. Comp. Stat. Ann. § 5/7-5(a).

In *Tennessee v. Garner*, supra, the Supreme Court struck down a state statute that permitted police to use deadly force against fleeing suspects even when there was no threat to the safety of the officer or the public. This ruling effectively narrowed the discretion of police officers to use force to make arrests and broadened the possibility for civil actions against police for using excessive force.

### The Rodney King Episode

Concern over police brutality took center stage in 1991, when the nation viewed on television a videotape of what appeared to be the unnecessarily brutal beating of motorist Rodney King by Los Angeles police officers. In response to public outrage, four police officers involved in the incident were prosecuted by state authorities for assault and battery and related crimes. On the motion of the defense, the trial was moved from Los Angeles to a suburban community. A riot ensued in Los Angeles in April 1992 after the jury returned its verdict of not guilty. In response to the widespread perception that a miscarriage of justice had occurred, the U.S. Justice Department launched its own investigation of the case. In the summer of 1992, a federal grand jury indicted the four officers for violating Rodney King's Fourth Amendment rights. In April 1993, a trial jury returned verdicts of guilty against two of the officers; the other two were acquitted. See *Koon v. United States*, 518 U.S. 81, 116 S.Ct. 2035, 135 L.Ed.2d 392 (1996). In 1997, Rodney King was awarded $3.8 million in a civil suit he brought against the City of Los Angeles.

**The Amadou Diallo Case**

In February 1999, four New York City police officers looking for a serial rapist shot and killed Amadou Diallo, a recent immigrant from the African nation of Guinea. The officers cornered Diallo in the vestibule of his apartment building in the Bronx. It remains unclear as to whether the officers considered Diallo to be a suspect in the rapes. The officers later claimed that they had ordered Diallo to put his hands in the air and that he had not complied but instead turned around and reached into his pocket. The officers claimed that they believed that Diallo was armed and was going for a gun. Reacting immediately, the officers fired forty-one bullets, nine of which struck Diallo. It turned out that Diallo was unarmed. Some speculated that he might have been reaching into his pocket for his identification card. The shooting spawned a wave of protest and demands that the officers be held criminally responsible for Diallo's death. The state of New York charged the four police officers with second-degree murder and reckless endangerment. On the motion of the defense, the trial was moved upstate from the Bronx to Albany. In February 2000, after deliberating for roughly twenty hours, a jury composed of seven white males, one white female, and four African American females acquitted the police officers on all counts. The verdict prompted protests around the country and rekindled a debate over police treatment of minorities. Although the Diallo case was national news, there have been many such cases around the country. In many of these cases, what initially appears to be reckless or wanton use of force by the police appears more understandable when all of the evidence comes to light in court.

**Use of Police Dogs to Apprehend Suspects**

In addition to using trained dogs to sniff for drugs and other contraband, police often use dogs to assist them in apprehending uncooperative or fleeing suspects. Sometimes the use of a dog to take down a suspect results in serious injury to that person. Police dogs are trained to bite and hold a suspect on the arm. The bite of a German shepherd has a force in the range of 1,200 to 1,600 pounds per square inch. If the bite lasts more than a few seconds, it can result in a severe wound, a fracture, or possibly even the severing of the arm. Of course, police are trained that once the dog has subdued the suspect, the dog is to be called off. The dogs tend to be very well trained and almost always obey immediately when given the command to release the suspect. In an interesting case decided by the U.S. Court of Appeals for the Ninth Circuit in August of 2003, a deputy sheriff sent a police dog into a wooded area to apprehend a suspect who had fled on foot into the woods. Before the deputy dispatched the dog, he yelled into the woods, "This is the Sheriff's Office. You have five seconds to make yourself known, or a police dog will be sent to find you." When the suspect did not respond after five seconds, the deputy sent the dog into the woods. About a minute later loud screaming could be heard from the woods. The deputy moved toward the sound and within about forty-five seconds located the police dog with a firm bite on the suspect's arm. The deputy called off the dog and arrested the suspect, whose badly injured arm required immediate surgery. The suspect eventually brought suit under 42 U.S.C.A. § 1983 against the deputy and the county, claiming that the use of the police dog constituted excessive force in violation of the Fourth Amendment. The federal district judge who tried the case entered judgment in favor of the defendants, holding that the use of the dog was not unreasonable under the circumstances. In a unanimous opinion, the Ninth Circuit agreed. The court noted that the suspect was being sought for a felony, that the deputy had reason to believe the suspect was armed with a knife and therefore posed a danger, and that because it was nighttime the deputy would have had great difficulty in locating the suspect promptly without the assistance of the dog. Given the totality of the circumstances, the court determined that the deputy's use of the police dog was reasonable. *Miller v. Clark County*, 340 F.3d 959 (9th Cir. 2003).

**Use of Tasers to Subdue Persons Who Resist Arrest**
Taser is the trade name of a stun gun that shoots metal barbs attached to wires. The barbs stick into a person's skin or clothing, whereupon 50,000 volts of electricity are transmitted from the gun via the wires. Tasers are now in wide use among police departments and are certainly effective in incapacitating most suspects who resist arrest. Typically, persons subjected to Taser shocks experience tremendous pain for about five seconds, but in most cases there is no permanent injury. However, a number of persons subjected to Taser shocks have been hospitalized and, according to a February 2003 report by Amnesty International, at least three persons died in the United States in 2002 as the result of being struck by Tasers. Generally, the courts have upheld the use of Tasers as an alternative to more injurious force. For example, in *Ewolski v. City of Brunswick*, 287 F.3d 492 (6th Cir. 2003), a federal appeals court held that use of a Taser to subdue a potentially homicidal individual did not constitute excessive force. Of course, courts will not permit police to use Tasers against resisting suspects when equally effective but less risky measures are readily available.

## Arrest of Persons with Disabilities

There are special concerns stemming from police encounters with persons with disabilities. Persons who are deaf or mentally retarded may appear to be uncooperative. Persons experiencing epileptic seizures are likely to be perceived as "drunk and disorderly." Similarly, someone experiencing the effects of hypoglycemia may appear to be intoxicated. A disabled motorist who reaches behind the seat when stopped by the police may be trying to retrieve a walking assistance device, but this act might be perceived by police as an attempt to retrieve a weapon. Arresting and booking someone confined to a wheelchair poses obvious problems. According to the U.S. Department of Justice, the Americans with Disabilities Act requires public agencies "to make reasonable modifications in their policies, practices, and procedures that are necessary to ensure accessibility for individuals with disabilities, unless making such modifications would fundamentally alter the program or service involved." U.S. Department of Justice, Civil Rights Division, Disability Rights Section, "Commonly Asked Questions about the Americans with Disabilities Act and Law Enforcement," last revised April 4, 2006. The document recommends modifying the "regular practice of handcuffing arrestees behind their backs, and instead handcuff[ing] deaf individuals in front in order for the person to sign or write notes." The document also suggests that "[s]afe transport of other individuals who use manual or power wheelchairs might require departments to make minor modifications to existing cars or vans, or to use lift-equipped vans or buses."

## Citizen's Arrest

**citizen's arrest** An arrest made by a person who is not a law enforcement officer.

At common law, a private individual could make a **citizen's arrest** without a warrant for a felony or breach of the peace committed in the presence of that individual. The common-law rule prevails in some states; in others, it has been revised by statute.

A California law enacted in 1872 broadened the common law in that it permits a private person to make a warrantless arrest in any of three situations:

A private person may arrest another:

1. For a public offense committed or attempted in his presence.
2. When the person arrested has committed a felony, although not in his presence.
3. When a felony has been in fact committed, and he has reasonable cause for believing the person arrested to have committed it. West's Ann. Cal. Penal Code § 837.

## Arrests for Minor Traffic Offenses

In most states, a police officer is vested with discretion to make an arrest of or issue a citation to a person who commits a minor traffic violation. Generally, police exercise their discretion by giving the motorist a "ticket," yet there is little judicial guidance for the proper action to be taken in such situations. That this area of broad police discretion is subject to abuse was recognized in *State v. Hehman*, 578 P.2d 527 (Wash. 1978), where the Washington Supreme Court ruled that arrests for minor traffic offenses are unjustified if the defendant signs a promise to appear in court as provided by statute. By contrast, an Illinois appellate court upheld the arrest and jailing of a motorist for lacking a front license plate and being unable to produce a driver's license. *People v. Pendleton*, 433 N.E.2d 1076 (Ill. App. 1982).

In *Atwater v. City of Lago Vista*, 532 U.S. 318, 121 S.Ct. 1536, 149 L.Ed.2d 549 (2001), the U.S. Supreme Court ruled that the Fourth Amendment does not forbid a warrantless arrest for a minor traffic offense, specifically a seat belt violation. Writing for the Court, Justice David Souter concluded that

> Atwater's arrest was surely "humiliating," . . . but it was no more "harmful to . . . privacy or . . . physical interests" than the normal custodial arrest. She was handcuffed, placed in a squad car, and taken to the local police station, where officers asked her to remove her shoes, jewelry, and glasses, and to empty her pockets. They then took her photograph and placed her in a cell, alone, for about an hour, after which she was taken before a magistrate, and released on $310 bond. The arrest and booking were inconvenient and embarrassing to Atwater, but not so extraordinary as to violate the Fourth Amendment. 532 U.S. at 354, 121 S.Ct. at 1558, 149 L.Ed.2d at 577.

Four justices dissented, characterizing Atwater's arrest for not wearing a seat belt as a "pointless indignity." Writing for the dissenters, Justice Sandra Day O'Connor opined:

> The majority takes comfort in the lack of evidence of "an epidemic of unnecessary minor-offense arrests." . . . But the relatively small number of published cases dealing with such arrests proves little and should provide little solace. Indeed, as the recent debate over racial profiling demonstrates all too clearly, a relatively minor traffic infraction may often serve as an excuse for stopping and harassing an individual. After today, the arsenal available to any officer extends to a full arrest and the searches permissible concomitant to that arrest. An officer's subjective motivations for making a traffic stop are not relevant considerations in determining the reasonableness of the stop. . . . But it is precisely because these motivations are beyond our purview that we must vigilantly ensure that officers' poststop actions—which are properly within our reach—comport with the Fourth Amendment's guarantee of reasonableness. 532 U.S. at 372, 121 S.Ct. at 1567, 149 L.Ed.2d at 587.

State courts can interpret their state constitutions to provide more protection than does the federal constitution as interpreted in the *Atwater* decision. Perhaps a more feasible solution is for state legislatures to provide that misdemeanor offenses are subject to "ticketing" under a "cite and release" statute. For example, Tennessee law provides that "[a] peace officer who has arrested a person for the commission of a misdemeanor committed in such peace officer's presence . . . shall issue a citation to such arrested person to appear in court in lieu of the continued custody and taking of the arrested person before a magistrate." Tenn. Code Ann. § 40-7-118 (1997). In 1999 the legislature added, "No citation shall be issued under the provisions of this section if . . . [t]he person arrested cannot or will not offer satisfactory evidence of identification, including the providing of a field-administered fingerprint or thumbprint which a peace officer may require to be affixed to any citation. . . ." Tenn. Code Ann. § 40-7-118(c)(3) (Supp. 1999). The state's "cite and release" statute creates a presumptive right to be cited and released for the commission of a misdemeanor. *State v. Walker*, 12 S.W.3d 460 (Tenn. 2000).

## Search Incident to Arrest

When making an arrest, police usually conduct a limited search. As we noted in Chapter 15, the Supreme Court has said that such a search incident to arrest must be limited to the body of an arrestee and the area within that person's immediate control. *Chimel v. California*, 395 U.S. 752, 89 S.Ct. 2034, 23 L.Ed.2d 685 (1969).

Normally, a search incident to arrest takes place after the arrest has been effected. In *Rawlings v. Kentucky*, 448 U.S. 98, 100 S.Ct. 2556, 65 L.Ed.2d 633 (1980), however, the Supreme Court upheld a search incident to arrest even though the search briefly preceded the arrest. The key point is that probable cause to make the arrest must precede the search; police may not use the search as a means to justify the arrest.

The Supreme Court has limited the ability of police to conduct an automobile search incident to arrest when issuing a traffic citation. See *Knowles v. Iowa*, 525 U.S. 113, 119 S.Ct. 484, 142 L.Ed.2d 492 (1998). In some instances, police may opt to make an arrest rather than issue a citation so that they can conduct a search of the automobile. See *Gustafson v. Florida*, 414 U.S. 260, 94 S.Ct. 488, 38 L.Ed.2d 456 (1973). If a driver is arrested and there is no one else who is authorized to take possession of the vehicle, police will impound the vehicle and thoroughly search its contents. This will often lead to the discovery of incriminating evidence that has been sequestered in the vehicle. There is no Fourth Amendment barrier to using such evidence in a criminal prosecution. *South Dakota v. Opperman*, 428 U.S. 364, 96 S.Ct. 3092, 49 L.Ed.2d 1000 (1976). (For more information on inventory searches of impounded automobiles, see Chapter 15.)

# Investigatory Detention

**investigatory detention** Brief detention of a suspect by a police officer who has reasonable suspicion that criminal activity is afoot.

**pat-down search** A manual search by a police officer of the exterior of a suspect's outer garments.

The second major category of police-citizen encounters involves the so-called stop-and-frisk, discussed in Chapter 15. A more descriptive term for this type of encounter is **investigatory detention**. Police are permitted to detain persons temporarily for questioning as long as they have reasonable suspicion that criminal activity is afoot. If they have reasonable suspicion that the detained person is armed, police may perform a **pat-down search** of the suspect's outer clothing to locate weapons. *Terry v. Ohio*, supra. In conducting the "frisk," police may seize items that plainly feel like contraband. *Minnesota v. Dickerson*, 508 U.S. 366, 113 S.Ct. 2130, 124 L.Ed.2d 334 (1993).

*Minnesota v. Dickerson*, 508 U.S. 366, 113 S.Ct. 2130, 124 L.Ed.2d 334 (1993)

Police officers observed Timothy Dickerson leaving a building known for selling and trafficking cocaine. When the officers approached Dickerson, he seemed to make "evasive actions." Therefore, the police decided to investigate further and told Dickerson to submit to a "pat-down" *Terry* search. The search resulting in finding no weapons, but the officer "felt a small lump" in Dickerson's pocket, "believed it to be a lump of crack cocaine upon examining it with his fingers." The officer "then reached into the pocket and retrieved a small bag of cocaine." Dickerson moved to suppress the evidence at his trial for possession of a controlled substance, but the trial court denied the motion. The Supreme Court reversed the trial court stating that the "police may seize nonthreatening contraband detected through the sense of touch during a protective pat-down search of the sort permitted by *Terry*, so long as the search stays within the bounds marked by *Terry*." The Court refused to accept a "plain feel exception" to *Terry*. According to the Supreme Court, *Terry* "permits a brief stop of a person whose suspicious conduct leads an officer to conclude in light of his experience that criminal activity may be afoot, and a pat-down search of the person for weapons when the officer is justified in believing that the person may be armed and presently dangerous." This is a "protective search" that is "not meant to discover evidence of crime, [and] must be strictly limited to that which is necessary for the discovery of weapons which might be used to harm the officer or others." The Supreme Court explicitly held that if "the protective search goes beyond what is necessary to determine if the suspect is armed, it is no longer valid under *Terry* and its fruits will be suppressed."

## What Constitutes Reasonable Suspicion?

After the U.S. Supreme Court's 1968 decision in *Terry v. Ohio*, supra, the concept of what constitutes "reasonable suspicion" became extremely important both in law enforcement and in criminal procedure in the courts. The concept does not lend itself to a precise definition; however, in *United States v. Cortez*, 449 U.S. 411, 101 S.Ct. 690, 66 L.Ed.2d 621 (1981), after defining it in a rather technical way, Chief Justice Warren E. Burger offered a practical explanation. He said that a trained officer develops a reasonable suspicion that a person is, or is about to be, engaged in criminal activity from the officer's objective observations and from inference and deductions.

Thousands of federal and state judicial decisions have applied the standard of reasonable suspicion, often with degrees of variation. However, courts generally agree that the totality of the circumstances of any given scenario must be examined to determine whether a law officer had a reasonable suspicion as a basis for making an investigatory stop. In *United States v. Arvizu*, 534 U.S. 266, 122 S.Ct. 744, 151 L.Ed.2d 740 (2002), the Supreme Court said that courts are not to view in isolation the factors upon which police officers develop reasonable suspicion. Instead, courts should consider all of an officer's observations, giving appropriate weight to any inferences drawn by an officer based on his or her training or experience.

## The Length of an Investigatory Detention

The Supreme Court has said that investigatory detentions must be brief (unless, that is, they confirm police suspicions of criminal conduct). *Dunaway v. New York*, 442 U.S. 200, 99 S.Ct. 2248, 60 L.Ed.2d 824 (1979). Nevertheless, the Supreme Court has been disinclined to place an arbitrary time limit on detention. Instead, the Court

*Illinois v. Wardlow*, 528 U.S. 119, 120 S.Ct. 673, 145 L.Ed.2d 570 (2000)

Around noon on September 9, 1995, William Wardlow was standing in front of a building in a high crime area in Chicago known for narcotics trafficking. When he saw a caravan of four police cars pass by, he ran through an alley. Officers in one of the patrol cars pursued and eventually stopped him, patted him down in a protective search for weapons, and searched an opaque bag he was holding. They found him in possession of a handgun and arrested him. Wardlow sought to suppress the weapon on the ground that the officers had no reasonable suspicion to stop and frisk him. Therefore, he argued that the seizure of the handgun was in violation of the Fourth Amendment. His motion was denied, and he was convicted. The Illinois Supreme Court reversed, holding the stop illegal. On review, the U.S. Supreme Court, in a 5–4 decision, reversed the Illinois Supreme Court. The justices agreed that the "totality of the circumstances" governs in determining if there is reasonable suspicion for the stop, but they disagreed on the application of that test to the factual situation here. Writing for the majority, Chief Justice William Rehnquist found that the officers had a reasonable suspicion based on Wardlow's presence in a high crime area coupled with his headlong, unprovoked flight from the police. Four justices, in an opinion written by Justice John Paul Stevens, disagreed with the majority's conclusion that the Chicago police were justified in stopping Wardlow.

has considered the purpose of the stop and the reasonableness of the time required for the police to obtain any additional required information. This approach looks at the totality of the circumstances to determine whether there has been an infringement of the suspect's Fourth Amendment rights. In *Florida v. Royer*, 460 U.S. 491, 103 S.Ct. 1319, 75 L.Ed.2d 229 (1983), the Court held that a fifteen-minute detention of a suspect in a police room was unreasonable when the police detained the suspect while they brought his luggage to him. Yet a twenty-minute detention of a truck driver stopped on suspicion of transporting marijuana was found to be reasonable because the time was used by police in pursuing a second, related vehicle necessary to the investigation, and the suspect's actions contributed to the delay. *United States v. Sharpe*, 470 U.S. 675, 105 S.Ct. 1568, 84 L.Ed.2d 605 (1985). Consequently, although detention must be brief in stop-and-frisk situations, the time span must be evaluated in light of the totality of circumstances. In *State v. Merklein*, 388 So.2d 218 (Fla. App. 1980), a Florida appellate court said it was reasonable for officers to detain suspects for twenty to forty minutes pending arrival of another officer, witnesses, and the victim of a robbery. The key is whether the police are diligently investigating to confirm or dispel the suspicions that led to the stop. *State v. Werner*, 848 P.2d 11 (N.M. App. 1992).

In *United States v. Mayo*, 394 F.3d 1271 (9th Cir. 2005), the court held that although the duration of detention bears on whether a *Terry* stop is justified, there is no strict time requirement. In *Mayo* the court found that a detention of forty minutes was not unreasonable where after the initial investigation new grounds for suspicion of criminal activity continued to unfold.

## When May Police Conduct a Frisk?

*Terry* stop  An encounter between a police officer and a suspect during which the latter is temporarily detained and subjected to a pat-down search for weapons.

A valid ***Terry* stop** (a synonym for investigatory detention) does not necessarily permit an officer to conduct a frisk. Rather, the need for protecting the police justifies a frisk. Therefore, an officer who undertakes to frisk a suspect must be able to point to specific facts and reasonable inferences to believe that the individual is armed.

Initially, a frisk is limited to a pat-down search of an individual's outer garments. If during the pat-down search the officer feels an object that may be a weapon, the officer may seize it. If it turns out that the object is something other than a weapon, it may still be seized if it is contraband. As we have noted, a stop-and-frisk may be based on reasonable suspicion, but absent probable cause, an officer is not justified in simply searching a suspect for contraband when a pat-down does not reveal any weapon-like objects. *Terry v. Ohio*, supra.

In *Ybarra v. Illinois*, 444 U.S. 85, 100 S.Ct. 338, 62 L.Ed.2d 238 (1979), the Supreme Court ruled that because police could not point to any specific facts to support their belief that the suspect was armed and dangerous, they had no grounds for frisking him. The Court has made it amply clear that a frisk must be based on an officer's reasonable suspicion that the suspect is armed rather than on a desire to locate incriminating evidence. *Sibron v. New York*, 392 U.S. 40, 88 S.Ct. 1889, 20 L.Ed.2d 917 (1968). Under the doctrine of plain view (discussed in Chapter 15), however, contraband that is discovered during a legitimate pat-down for weapons may be admissible in evidence. For example, if during the course of a lawful frisk a police officer feels what the officer suspects is a knife concealed in the suspect's pocket, the officer may retrieve the object. If the object turns out to be a metal smoking pipe wrapped inside a plastic bag containing crack cocaine, the crack would most likely be admissible as evidence of crime under the plain-view doctrine.

## Investigatory Automobile Stops

Lower federal and state courts have routinely applied the stop-and-frisk doctrine to stops of vehicles as well as individuals. In many instances, this was stipulated in state statutes codifying the *Terry* standard; otherwise, it was based on the *Terry* rationale. A traffic stop involves a seizure of the driver under the Fourth Amendment "even though the purpose of the stop is limited and the resulting detention quite brief." Therefore, the police must have reasonable suspicion that criminal activity is afoot before stopping a motor vehicle. *Delaware v. Prouse*, 440 U.S. 648, 653, 99 S.Ct. 1391, 59 L.Ed.2d 660 (1979).

Normal police practice is for the officer who makes an automobile stop to examine the suspect's driver's license, vehicle registration, and license plate. A rapid computer check can reveal whether there are any outstanding warrants on the driver, whether the license has been suspended or revoked, and whether the automobile has been reported stolen. During the stop, the officer also visually scans the driver, any passengers, and any objects in plain view. Such visual scans sometimes provide probable cause to make an arrest or conduct a warrantless automobile search.

In *Michigan v. Long*, 463 U.S. 1032, 103 S.Ct. 3469, 77 L.Ed.2d 1201 (1983), the Supreme Court held "the search of the passenger compartment of an automobile, limited to those areas in which a weapon may be placed or hidden, is permissible if the police officer possesses a reasonable belief based on 'specific and articulable facts which, taken together with the rational inferences from those facts, reasonably warrant' the officers in believing that the suspect is dangerous and the suspect may gain immediate control of weapons." Among these are the knowledge, expertise, and experience of the officer; the physical appearance of a person or vehicle as fitting the description of a person or vehicle wanted for a crime; the item and place where the suspect or vehicle is seen; and their nearness to the scene of a crime. In addition, the suspect's demeanor and any furtive gestures or attempts to flee are relevant considerations. In *Arizona v. Gant*, 556 U.S. 332, 129 S.Ct. 1710, 173 L.Ed.2d 485 (2009), the Supreme Court held that

> Police may search a vehicle incident to a recent occupant's arrest only if the arrestee is within reaching distance of the passenger compartment at the time of the search or it is reasonable to believe the vehicle contains evidence of the offense of arrest. When these justifications are absent, a search of an arrestee's vehicle will be unreasonable unless police obtain a warrant or show that another exception to the warrant requirement applies.

## Automobile Stops Based on Anonymous Tips

**anonymous tip** Information given to the police by an unknown individual.

An issue that often comes before appellate courts is whether reasonable suspicion can be developed on the basis of an **anonymous tip**. In *Alabama v. White*, 496 U.S. 325, 110 S.Ct. 2412, 110 L.Ed.2d 621 (1990), the U.S. Supreme Court reviewed a case where the police stopped a vehicle based on an anonymous phone tip. The Court held that an anonymous tip corroborated by independent police work was sufficient to establish a reasonable suspicion to make an investigatory stop of the vehicle described by the one who gave police the tip.

Since the Supreme Court's decision in *Alabama v. White*, state courts have been addressing cases where police have made an investigatory stop based on an anonymous tip. State courts have been disinclined to approve an investigatory stop where the anonymous tip lacks indicia of credibility and is not sufficiently verified by independent evidence. See, e.g., *State v. Hjelmstad*, 535 N.W.2d 663 (Minn. App. 1995). Nevertheless, many state courts now agree that information supplied by an anonymous source can warrant an investigatory stop if verified by sufficient independent evidence of criminal activity. See, e.g., *People v. George*, 914 P.2d 367 (Colo. 1996). In 2000 the Supreme Court of Pennsylvania held that an uncorroborated anonymous tip alleging a defendant was selling marijuana did not create a reasonable suspicion that would justify an investigatory stop of the defendant's car. *Commonwealth v. Goodwin*, 750 A.2d 795 (Pa. 2000).

**CASE-IN-POINT**

### An Anonymous Tip as the Basis of Reasonable Suspicion

Police in Memphis, Tennessee received an anonymous telephone tip through a "drug hotline" that a number of African American men were dealing drugs at a particular street corner known to police as a "hot spot" for drug sales. When an officer and his partner approached the area, they saw a group of around eight African American males standing by the curb. When the officers approached the group, the men began to walk away. One of the men made a throwing motion toward the bushes. At this point the officers instructed the men to stop, take their hands out of their pockets, and place them on a nearby vehicle. A pat-down search of one of the men revealed a .40 caliber revolver tucked into his waistband. The man, who had been previously convicted of a felony, was subsequently convicted in federal court of violating 18 U.S.C. § 922(g), which prohibits the possession of a firearm by a convicted felon. In reversing the defendant's conviction, the U.S. Court of Appeals for the Sixth Circuit held that the anonymous tip the police received failed to provide sufficient specific information in support of reasonable suspicion and that, in the absence of the tip, the defendant's behavior was insufficient to support reasonable suspicion. One judge dissented, arguing that the court's approach departed from that required by the Supreme Court's 2002 decision in *United States v. Arvizu*, supra, which instructs lower courts not to consider in isolation the factors that support determinations of reasonable suspicion.

*United States v. Patterson*, 340 F.3d 368 (6th Cir. 2003).

## Pretextual Automobile Stops

Police have been known to use a minor or technical motor vehicle infraction as a pretext for stopping a vehicle and conducting an investigatory detention. In the past, most federal courts ruled that the police may not use minor traffic violations to justify **pretextual stops**. For example, in *United States v. Smith*, 799 F.2d 704 (11th Cir. 1986), the court said the appropriate analysis was whether a reasonable officer would have stopped the car absent an additional invalid purpose. Many state courts followed this approach.

**pretextual stops** An incident in which police stop a suspicious vehicle on the pretext of a motor vehicle infraction.

In *Whren v. United States*, 517 U.S. 806, 116 S.Ct. 1769, 135 L.Ed.2d 89 (1996), the U.S. Supreme Court ruled that the motives of an officer in stopping a vehicle are irrelevant as long as there is an objective basis for the stop. Thus, the Court held that there is no violation of the Fourth Amendment as long as there is probable cause to believe that even a minor violation has taken place. It remains to be seen whether the states, which may apply a stricter standard under their constitutions, will follow the federal standard.

## Can Police Require Drivers and Passengers to Exit Their Vehicles?

During automobile stops, police routinely request that drivers exit their cars. Sometimes they also request that passengers exit. These practices are justified by the need to protect police officers from weapons that might be concealed inside the passenger compartment of a stopped vehicle. In upholding these practices, the U.S. Supreme Court noted that in 1994 eleven police officers were killed and more than five thousand officers assaulted during traffic stops. *Maryland v. Wilson*, 519 U.S. 408, 117 S.Ct. 882, 137 L.Ed.2d 41 (1997). Of course, when drivers and passengers are required to exit their automobiles, police often discover contraband or observe behavior indicative of intoxication. Such was the case in *Maryland v. Wilson*,

### JURISPRUDENCE

*Whren v. United States*, 517 U.S. 806, 116 S.Ct. 1769, 135 L.Ed.2d 89 (1996)

Police were traveling in an unmarked police vehicle through a "high drug area" when they observed a truck waiting at a stop sign for an unusually long time. After some time, "the truck turned without signaling and sped off at an 'unreasonable' speed." The officers stopped the truck with the intention of giving the driver a warning; however, when they approached the truck, they saw "plastic bags of crack cocaine in Whren's hands and arrested him." Whren moved to suppress the drugs on the grounds that the officers did not have "reasonable suspicion or probable cause to believe" Whren was "engaged in illegal drug-dealing activity, and that the officers' traffic-violation ground

for stopping the truck was pretextual." The trial court denied the motion to suppress. The Supreme Court held that the "temporary detention of a motorist upon probable cause to believe that he has violated the traffic laws does not violate the Fourth Amendment's prohibition against unreasonable seizures, even if a reasonable officer would not have stopped the motorist absent some additional law enforcement objective." As long as the officer has probable cause to believe a traffic law has been violated, the detention of the motorist is reasonable. Furthermore, the Court held that "ulterior motives" will not invalidate police conduct on their own because "subjective intentions play no role in ordinary, probable-cause Fourth Amendment analysis."

where a passenger who had been ordered to exit a vehicle dropped a quantity of crack cocaine onto the ground. This evidence was used to secure a conviction for possession with intent to distribute; ultimately, the conviction was sustained by the Supreme Court. For the duration of a traffic stop, a police officer effectively seizes everyone in the vehicle. *Brendlin v. California*, 551 U.S. 249, 127 S.Ct. 2400, 168 L.Ed.2d 132 (2007). It followed therefore that in *Arizona v. Johnson*, 555 U.S. 323, 129 S.Ct. 781, 172 L.Ed.2d 694 (2009), the Supreme Court confirmed that during a traffic stop both the driver and passengers are lawfully detained. Accordingly, an officer may, without violating the Fourth Amendment, ask the driver and all passengers to exit the vehicle and submit to a frisk on reasonable grounds that they may be armed and dangerous.

## Drug Courier Profiles

**drug courier profiles** Sets of characteristics that are believed to typify drug couriers.

In recent years, police have developed **drug courier profiles** based on typical characteristics and behaviors of drug smugglers. The profiles include such factors as paying cash for airline tickets, taking short trips to drug-source cities, not checking luggage, and appearing nervous. Police often use these profiles to identify and detain suspected drug couriers, a controversial practice that has resulted in disparate court decisions. As we pointed out in Chapter 15, the Supreme Court has held that fitting a drug courier profile is not by itself sufficient to constitute the reasonable suspicion necessary to allow police to detain an airline passenger. *Reid v. Georgia*, 448 U.S. 438, 100 S.Ct. 2752, 65 L.Ed.2d 890 (1980). The critical question is whether the behavior of the suspect is inherently suspicious. In 1989 the Supreme Court upheld an investigative stop of an air passenger for which a number of circumstances, including the use of the profile, furnished the police a reasonable suspicion of criminal activity. Although the Court found that any one of the several factors relied on by the police may have been consistent with innocent travel, it observed that the evaluation of the stop requires a consideration of the "totality of the circumstances." *United States v. Sokolow*, 490 U.S. 1, 109 S.Ct. 1581, 104 L.Ed.2d 1 (1989).

---

### JURISPRUDENCE

*United States v. Sokolow*, 490 U.S. 1, 109 S.Ct. 1581, 104 L.Ed.2d 1 (1989)

When Drug Enforcement Agents stopped Andrew Sokolow at the Honolulu International Airport, agents found 1,063 grams of cocaine in his carry-on luggage. Prior to apprehending Sokolow, agents discovered during the course of an investigation that he paid cash for two round-trip plane tickets, traveled under a name that did not match the name under which his telephone number was listed, travelled to Miami, a city known for illicit drugs, stayed in Miami for only forty-eight hours when a trip from Hawaii takes twenty hours, appeared nervous during the flight, and failed to check any luggage. Sokolow was subsequently indicted for possession with intent to distribute cocaine. Sokolow moved to suppress the evidence; however, the trial court denied the motion on the grounds that the stop was justified by a reasonable suspicion that he was engaged in criminal activity, as required by the Fourth Amendment. The Supreme Court agreed that there was sufficient reasonable suspicion to believe Sokolow was transporting illegal drugs when they detained him; thus, the stop was justified under the premise of *Terry v. Ohio*. The Court said that the reasonableness of the stop does not turn on whether the police used the least restrictive means, but rather whether the stop was reasonable under the circumstances.

Although the Supreme Court has upheld the use of profiles in locating suspicious persons, courts must remain on guard against abuse of the practice. In 1990 a Minnesota appellate court reversed a conviction in which the defendant, who was in an automobile, had been stopped not on the basis of a particular suspicion but because the driver's behavior loosely fit the police profile of a person looking for prostitutes. In rejecting the use of the profile, the court distinguished the case from *Sokolow*, supra, saying that "the observable facts taken together do not approach the composite bundle available to the DEA in *Sokolow*." *City of St. Paul v. Uber*, 450 N.W.2d 623, 626 (Minn. App. 1990). The court concluded that "we cannot sustain what was, in effect, a random stop." 450 N.W.2d at 629.

## Racial Profiling

**racial profiling** Practice of singling out members of minority groups by law enforcement officers.

Recent years have seen a continuing controversy over **racial profiling**, a term loosely applied to a variety of police practices that are alleged to be racially biased. The Department of Justice defines racial profiling as "any police-initiated action that relies on the race, ethnicity or national origin rather than the behavior of an individual or information that leads the police to a particular individual who has been identified as being, or having been, engaged in criminal activity." Deborah Ramirez, Jack McDevitt, and Amy Farrell, *A Resource Guide on Racial Profiling Data Collection Systems: Promising Practices and Lessons Learned*, Washington, D.C.: U.S. Department of Justice, 2000, p. 3.

Most of the debate over racial profiling has focused on motor vehicle stops. The sarcastic phrase "driving while black" has been used to denote what critics allege to be a widespread police practice of stopping African American motorists solely or primarily based on their race. The movement to halt racial profiling has taken both legislative and judicial directions. Several state legislatures have passed laws to require data collection for police stops, while defendants who contend that they were stopped on the basis of race have sought to dismiss charges arising out of police stops, arguing they were denied due process and equal protection of the laws. Others have sought and won relief through civil litigation under 42 U.S.C.A. § 1983. See, e.g., *National Congress of Puerto Rican Rights v. City of New York*, 191 F.R.D. 52 (S.D.N.Y. 1999).

In the spring of 2010 controversy erupted over a proposed Arizona law (S.B. 1070) that provided, among other things, "For any lawful contact made by a law enforcement official or a law enforcement agency . . . where reasonable suspicion exists that the person is an alien who is unlawfully present in the United States, a reasonable attempt shall be made, when practicable, to determine the immigration status of the person. . ." Critics claimed that the new law would encourage racial profiling in that police would target persons who appeared to be Hispanic. On May 19, 2010, President Obama attacked the bill, saying, "In the United States of America, no law-abiding person—be they an American citizen, a legal immigrant, or a visitor or tourist from Mexico—should be subject to suspicion simply because of what they look like." Despite the President's protestations, the Arizona legislature enacted the law anyway. On July 6 the U.S. Department of Justice filed suit in federal court against the state of Arizona and Arizona's governor, claiming that S.B 1070 was a usurpation of the federal government's authority to regulate immigration. In 2012 the Supreme Court upheld the controversial provision pending a full hearing in the federal district court regarding its compatibility with federal law. *Arizona v. United States*, 567 U.S. ___, 132 S.Ct. 2492, 183 L.Ed.2d 351 (2012). As this book was being completed, the fate of S.B 1070 was still very much in doubt.

# Roadblocks, Sobriety Checkpoints, and Drug Checkpoints

**roadblocks** Barriers set up by police to stop motorists.

The third major category of police–citizen encounters includes **roadblocks** and sobriety checkpoints. Police often set up roadblocks for apprehending fleeing suspects, conducting field sobriety tests, or even for merely performing safety checks on automobiles. In addition to locating drunk drivers, roadblocks often lead to the discovery of illegal weapons, drugs, and other contraband. Because roadblocks do constitute a restraint on the liberty of the motorist, courts have held that they are susceptible to challenge under the Fourth Amendment. Therefore, police agencies must take care that roadblocks are established and operated according to guidelines that minimize the inconvenience to motorists and constrain the exercise of discretion by police officers.

In *Michigan Dept. of State Police v. Sitz*, 496 U.S. 444, 110 S.Ct. 2481, 110 L.Ed.2d 412 (1990), the Supreme Court recognized that a Fourth Amendment "seizure" occurs when a vehicle is stopped at a checkpoint but upheld the use of roadblocks for conducting field sobriety tests. In *Sitz*, the Michigan State Police operated a pilot roadblock program under guidelines drafted by an advisory committee. The guidelines set forth procedures governing checkpoint operations, site selection, and publicity. The sobriety checkpoints operated essentially as follows: Police set up roadblocks at predetermined points along state highways. All vehicles passing through the checkpoints were stopped, and drivers were briefly observed for signs of intoxication. The average length of the stop was less than thirty seconds, except where drivers appeared to be intoxicated. These drivers were instructed to pull their vehicles over to the side of the road for a license and registration check and, if indicated, a field sobriety test. Those who failed the test were placed under arrest. At one checkpoint, which was in operation for seventy-five minutes, 126 vehicles were stopped. Two drivers were given field sobriety tests, and one was arrested for driving under the influence of alcohol. One vehicle failed to stop at the roadblock but was apprehended and its driver arrested for driving under the influence.

## Drug Checkpoints

After the Supreme Court's 1990 decision upholding sobriety checkpoints, some police departments began running drug checkpoints that operated in much the same way but often involved the use of drug-sniffing dogs. In 2000, the U.S. Supreme Court invalidated an Indianapolis police practice of establishing checkpoints primarily for the purpose of detecting illegal drugs. Writing for the Court, Justice Sandra Day O'Connor distinguished between sobriety checkpoints, which are geared toward elimination of an imminent public safety threat, and drug checkpoints designed primarily to snare traffickers in contraband. *City of Indianapolis v. Edmond*, 531 U.S. 32, 121 S.Ct 447, 148 L.Ed.2d 333 (2000).

An interesting (and often productive) variation of the drug checkpoint procedure is for the police to place a sign on an interstate highway indicating, "Notice: Drug Checkpoint Ahead." The sign is placed just before an exit, tempting drivers who wish to avoid the checkpoint to take the exit. Of course, there really is no drug checkpoint on the interstate highway. Rather, police are waiting at the bottom of the exit ramp to see who takes the exit. Typically, the exit chosen is one where there is little or no commercial activity and no connection to a major road. When a van with out-of-state plates takes the exit, is this inherently suspicious? Can police

## JURISPRUDENCE

*City of Indianapolis v. Edmond*, 531 U.S. 32, 121 S.Ct 447, 148 L.Ed.2d 333 (2000)

In August 1998, the City of Indianapolis began to operate vehicle checkpoints in an effort to interdict unlawful drugs. The overall "hit rate" of the program was approximately 9 percent. The checkpoint locations were predetermined weeks in advance based on area crime statistics and traffic flow. The checkpoints were conducted during daylight hours and were identified with lighted signs reading, "NARCOTICS CHECK-POINT ___ MILE AHEAD, NARCOTICS K-9 IN USE, BE PREPARED TO STOP." Respondent James

Edmonds was stopped at a checkpoint and later filed a motion for injunctive relief claiming that the roadblocks violated the Fourth Amendment of the Constitution. The federal district court denied the motion for injunctive relief; however, the Court of Appeals for the Seventh Circuit reversed, holding that the checkpoints contravened the Fourth Amendment. The Supreme Court affirmed holding the checkpoints in violation of the Fourth Amendment because their primary purpose was indistinguishable from general interest crime control. The Court refused to validate suspicionless stops.

assume that the only reason the driver took the exit was to avoid the spurious drug checkpoint? Can police stop this vehicle, order the driver and passengers to exit the vehicle, and bring out a drug-sniffing canine? Federal courts have reached different conclusions on this issue. For example, in *United States v. Huguenin*, 154 F.3d 547 (6th Cir. 1998), the Sixth Circuit held that it was a pretextual seizure for police to selectively detain motorists without a traffic violation or reasonable suspicion of drug trafficking. But in *United States v. Brugal*, 209 F.3d 353 (4th Cir. 2000), the Fourth Circuit held that the totality of factors used by police in screening motorists eliminated a substantial portion of innocent travelers and that the conduct of the particular motorist involved gave officers reasonable suspicion that justified instructing him to pull his vehicle over.

After the Supreme Court's decision in the Indianapolis case, some law enforcement agencies expressed their intention to continue running drug checkpoints featuring the deceptive tactic described above. In their view, a drug checkpoint of this type is distinguishable from that which was invalidated in the Indianapolis case. It will be interesting to see if the Supreme Court examines this practice and whether it recognizes a distinction that can salvage the constitutionality of the deceptive drug checkpoint.

In *Illinois v. Lidster*, 540 U.S. 419, 124 S.Ct. 885, 157 L.Ed.2d 843 (2004), the Supreme Court reversed a state supreme court decision striking down a police checkpoint based on *Indianapolis v. Edmond*, supra. Police in Lombard, Illinois, set up a checkpoint along a highway, stopping motorists to ask them if they knew anything about a recent hit-and-run accident. Approaching the checkpoint in his minivan, Lidster swerved and nearly hit a police officer. Detecting the odor of alcohol, police performed a field sobriety test, determined that Lidster was impaired, and placed him under arrest. Lidster challenged his DUI conviction on the ground that the government obtained evidence through use of a checkpoint stop that violated the Fourth Amendment. The Illinois appellate courts agreed that, based on *Indianapolis v. Edmond*, the automobile stop was unconstitutional. The U.S. Supreme Court reversed, making clear in an opinion by Justice Stephen Breyer that *Indianapolis v. Edmond* was not intended to prevent the police from using checkpoints to obtain the motoring public's assistance in locating the perpetrator of a crime involving a traffic accident.

**CASE-IN-POINT**

### The Use of Roadblocks

On August 8, 1992, Deputy Sheriff Robert Starnes stopped Sarah Hutton Downey at a highway roadblock on Hixson Pike in Hamilton County, Tennessee. The roadblock had been set up without advance publicity by Lt. Ronnie Hill of the Tennessee Highway Patrol, who was assisted by members of the Chattanooga Police Department DUI task force, the Hamilton County DUI task force, and auxiliary sheriff's officers. Hill did not obtain the approval of a superior officer regarding the establishment, time, or location of the roadblock. When Deputy Starnes checked Downey's driver's license, he smelled an odor of alcohol. After field sobriety testing, he arrested her for driving under the influence.

At trial, evidence revealed the defendant did nothing to arouse the deputy's suspicion as she approached the roadblock; rather, she was stopped for the same purpose and in the same manner as other motorists. The defendant moved to suppress the evidence on grounds there was no suspicion that a crime had been committed before the stop, and therefore her detention violated the section of the state constitution that parallels the Fourth Amendment to the U.S. Constitution. The trial court denied her motion. The Court of Criminal Appeals ruled that use of the roadblock was not a per se violation of the state constitution, but in this case no General Order was in effect granting authority to set up highway roadblocks. Thus, the court ruled that the defendant's arrest constituted an unreasonable seizure. The Tennessee Supreme Court granted review to determine the constitutionality of highway roadblocks.

Referring to the U.S. Supreme Court's 1990 decision in *Michigan Dept. of State Police v. Sitz*, the court agreed that highway roadblocks established and operated in accordance with predetermined guidelines do not violate the Tennessee Constitution. But here, the court observed, "[T]he decision to set up a roadblock was made by an officer in the field . . . the site selected for the roadblock and the procedure to be used in operating the roadblock were matters left to the discretion of an officer in the field. No supervisory authority was sought or obtained, and no administrative decisions were made with regard to these critical factors." Because the roadblock was not conducted in accordance with proper, predetermined operational guidelines and supervisory authority, the court found it constituted an unreasonable seizure under the Tennessee Constitution and affirmed the Court of Criminal Appeals.

*State v. Downey*, 945 S.W.2d 102 (Tenn. 1997).

## Requests for Information or Identification

The lowest level of police–citizen encounter takes place when a police officer approaches an individual in public and asks questions or requests identification. Is there a legal duty to cooperate with the police in such instances? In a concurring opinion in *Terry v. Ohio*, supra, Justice Byron White observed,

> There is nothing in the Constitution which prevents a policeman from addressing questions to anyone on the streets. Absent special circumstances, the person approached may not be detained or frisked but may refuse to cooperate and go on his way. However, given the proper circumstances . . . the person may be briefly detained against his will while pertinent questions are directed to him. Of course, the person stopped is not obliged to answer, answers may not be compelled, and refusal to answer furnishes no basis for an arrest, although it may alert the officer to the need for continued observation. 392 U.S. at 34, 88 S.Ct. at 1886, 20 L.Ed.2d at 913.

Historically, many states had laws making it a misdemeanor for persons to refuse to identify themselves when asked to do so by police. In *Brown v. Texas*, 443 U.S. 47, 99 S.Ct. 2637, 61 L.Ed.2d 357 (1979), the Supreme Court reviewed the constitutionality of this Texas statute: "A person commits an offense if he intentionally refuses

**CASE-IN-POINT**

### Validity of an Ordinance Requiring Self-Identification

Section 17-13 of the Arlington, Virginia, County Code provides that "[i]t shall be unlawful for any person at a public place . . . to refuse to identify himself by name and address at the request of a uniformed police officer . . . if the surrounding circumstances are such as to indicate to a reasonable man that the public safety requires such identification." The defendant was convicted of failing to identify himself at the request of a police officer and appealed. The Virginia Supreme Court held that the police validly stopped the defendant under a *Terry v. Ohio* standard and that the "stop and identify" provision in the county code did not violate the Fourth Amendment. The court distinguished the case from the statute the U.S. Supreme Court struck down in *Kolender v. Lawson*, saying that the California statute at issue there required an individual to provide a credible and reliable identification and required a person to account for his or her presence.

*Jones v. Commonwealth of Virginia*, 334 S.E.2d 536 (Va. 1985).

to report or gives a false report of his name and residence address to a peace officer who has lawfully stopped him and requested the information." The Court held that the statute could not be constitutionally applied in the absence of reasonable suspicion that the individual who was asked for identification was engaged in or had engaged in criminal conduct.

In *Kolender v. Lawson*, 461 U.S. 352, 103 S.Ct. 1855, 75 L.Ed.2d 903 (1983), the Supreme Court reviewed a California statute that required persons who were loitering or wandering on the streets to provide a "credible and reliable" identification and

### JURISPRUDENCE

*Hiibel v. Sixth Judicial Dist. Court of Nevada*, 542 U.S. 177, 124 S.Ct. 2451, 159 L.Ed.2d 292 (2004)

Larry D. Hiibel was arrested after telling a deputy sheriff that he did not have to reveal his name or show any identification during his encounter with law enforcement officers. Hiibel was convicted under Nevada Revised Statute § 171.123(3), which authorizes *Terry* stops and provides, "Any person so detained shall identify himself, but may not be compelled to answer any other inquiry of any peace officer." After the Nevada Supreme Court upheld his conviction in 2002, the U.S. Supreme Court granted review. In a 5–4 decision the Court upheld the statute and affirmed Hiibel's conviction. Justice Anthony Kennedy, writing for the Court, pointed out that there was no issue here as to the validity of the *Terry* stop. Justice Kennedy then explained that unlike the Court's 1983 decision in *Kolender v. Lawson*, supra, where the law required a suspect to give an officer "credible and reliable" identification when asked to identify himself, the Nevada statute only required that a suspect disclose his or her name. Here, the officer's request for identification was reasonably related to circumstances justifying the *Terry* stop. Thus, the officer's request was a commonsense inquiry and Hiibel's arrest for failure to comply with the "stop and identify" law did not violate Fourth Amendment prohibition against unreasonable searches and seizures. Further, the Court held that the Nevada law did not violate Hiibel's Fifth Amendment rights against self-incrimination as there was no showing that disclosure of his name presented any reasonable danger of incrimination. Justice John Paul Stevens dissented on the grounds that the statute violates the Fifth Amendment privilege against self-incrimination. Also dissenting, Justices Stephen Breyer, David Souter, and Ruth Bader Ginsburg argued that while an officer is permitted to stop a suspect and ask a moderate number of questions in a *Terry* stop without having "probable cause", the Court's Fourth Amendment precedents invalidate laws that compel responses to police questioning.

to account for their presence when requested to do so by a police officer. The Court found that the statute was "unconstitutionally vague on its face because it encourages arbitrary enforcement by failing to describe with sufficient particularity what a suspect must do in order to satisfy the statute." 461 U.S. at 361, 103 S.Ct. at 1860, 75 L.Ed.2d at 911.

Over the last two decades, a number of states have enacted "stop and identify" statutes. These laws make it a misdemeanor for suspect to refuse to identify himself or herself during a valid police stop or detention. One such law, Nevada Revised Statute § 171.123(3), was upheld by the U.S. Supreme Court in *Hiibel v. Sixth Judicial District Court of Nevada*, 542 U.S. 177, 124 S.Ct. 2451, 159 L.Ed.2d 292 (2004). The decision was a close one, however, with four justices voting to strike down the law. For the majority, the determining factor appeared to be that the law only required suspects to identify themselves during a valid *Terry*-stop.

# Interrogation and Confessions

Although the courts have long recognized the need for police interrogation of suspects, they have also recognized the potential for abuse inherent in the practice of incommunicado interrogation. At early common law, any confession was admissible even if extracted from the accused by torture. As the common law progressed, judges came to insist on proof that a confession was made voluntarily before it could be admitted in evidence.

**coerced confession** A confession or other incriminating statements obtained from a suspect by police through force, violence, threats, intimidation, or undue psychological pressure.

In 1897 the Supreme Court held that to force a suspect to confess violates the Self-Incrimination Clause of the Fifth Amendment. *Bram v. United States*, 168 U.S. 532, 18 S.Ct. 183, 42 L.Ed. 568. In 1936 the Court held that a **coerced confession** deprived a defendant in a state criminal case of due process of law as guaranteed by the Fourteenth Amendment. *Brown v. Mississippi*, 297 U.S. 278, 56 S.Ct. 461, 80 L.Ed. 682 (1936). In 1964 the Self-Incrimination Clause was made applicable to state criminal prosecutions. *Malloy v. Hogan*, 378 U.S. 1, 84 S.Ct. 1489, 12 L.Ed.2d 653 (1964). As a result, federal and state police are held to the same standards in evaluating the voluntariness of confessions of guilt. In *Malloy*, the Court said that the Fifth Amendment prohibits the extraction of a confession by "exertion of any improper influence." 378 U.S. at 7, 84 S.Ct. at 1493, 12 L.Ed.2d at 659. A confession is voluntary when it is made with knowledge of its nature and consequences and without duress or inducement. *United States v. Carignan*, 342 U.S. 36, 72 S.Ct. 97, 96 L.Ed. 48 (1951).

In *Escobedo v. Illinois*, 378 U.S. 478, 84 S.Ct. 1758, 12 L.Ed.2d 977 (1964), the Supreme Court recognized the right of suspects to have counsel present during interrogation. Anticipating the criticism that the Court's decision would hamper

**CASE-IN-POINT**

### Coerced Confessions

As an example of psychological coercion, a confession was ruled involuntary where a defendant was incarcerated and subjected to questioning over a four-day period. The defendant's relatives were denied permission to see him, and he was unable to communicate with anyone outside the jail. At one point during the interrogation, the defendant was forced to hold for twenty-five minutes a gory picture of the deceased lying in a pool of blood.

*Davis v. State*, 308 S.W.2d 880, 882 (Tex. Crim. App. 1957).

law enforcement, Justice Arthur Goldberg observed the following: "If the exercise of constitutional rights will thwart the effectiveness of a system of law enforcement, then there is something very wrong with that system." However, the Court's work in this area was not finished. Two years later, in its landmark decision in *Miranda v. Arizona*, 384 U.S. 436, 86 S.Ct. 1602, 16 L.Ed.2d 694 (1966), the Supreme Court held that before interrogating suspects who are in custody, police must warn them of their right to remain silent and their right to have counsel present during questioning. The typical form of the **Miranda warnings** used by law enforcement is as follows:

> You are under arrest. You have the right to remain silent. Anything you say can and will be used against you in a court of law. You are entitled to have an attorney present during questioning. If you cannot afford an attorney, one will be appointed to represent you.

Unless these warnings have been given, no statement made by the suspect may be used in evidence, subject to certain narrow exceptions.

The *Miranda* decision was severely criticized by law enforcement interests when it was handed down in 1966. But now it is accepted, even supported, by most law enforcement agencies and has been integrated into routine police procedure. It is also firmly established in the Supreme Court's jurisprudence, as evidenced by the Court's recent decision in *United States v. Dickerson* (2000).

*Miranda* **warnings** Based on the Supreme Court's decision in *Miranda v. Arizona* (1966), these warnings are given by police to individuals who are taken into custody before they are interrogated. The warnings inform persons in custody that they have the right to remain silent and to have a lawyer present during questioning and that anything they say can and will be used against them in a court of law.

## The Fruit of the Poisonous Tree Doctrine

The *Miranda* decision essentially established an exclusionary rule applicable to statements made by suspects during custodial interrogation. But the loss of a confession or statement may have consequences for other evidence gathered by the police. Under the fruit of the poisonous tree doctrine, evidence that is derived from

---

**JURISPRUDENCE**

*Miranda v. Arizona*, 384 U.S. 436, 86 S.Ct. 1602, 16 L.Ed.2d 694 (1966)

Police arrested Ernesto Miranda, a twenty-three-year-old indigent with a ninth grade education, and charged him with raping an eighteen-year-old girl. At the police station, the victim picked Miranda out of a lineup. Two officers then took Miranda to a room where they interrogated him. After first denying his guilt, Miranda eventually confessed to the crime. Following his conviction, Miranda appealed on the ground that his confession had been coerced. The Supreme Court granted review, consolidating Miranda's appeal with three other cases involving the admissibility of confessions. The Court reversed Miranda's conviction, holding that his confession had been improperly admitted into evidence. As per Chief

Justice Earl Warren, the Court held that, henceforth, police must advise suspects of their right to remain silent and their right to have counsel present during interrogation. Failure to provide these warnings will result in the suppression of a confession, even if it is deemed reliable. These new requirements were based on the Court's conclusion that "without proper safeguards the process of in-custody interrogation . . . contains inherently compelling pressures which work to undermine the individual's will to resist and to compel him to speak where he would not otherwise do so freely." In a bitter dissent, Justice White complained that "[i]n some unknown number of cases the Court's rule will return a killer, a rapist or other criminal to the streets . . . to repeat his crime whenever it pleases him."

**derivative evidence** Evidence that is derived from or obtained only as a result of other evidence.

**independent source doctrine** The doctrine that permits evidence to be admitted at trial as long as it was obtained independently from illegally obtained evidence.

**inevitable discovery doctrine** The doctrine that holds that evidence derived from inadmissible evidence is admissible if it inevitably would have been discovered independently by lawful means.

inadmissible evidence is likewise inadmissible. *Wong Sun v. United States*, 371 U.S. 471, 83 S.Ct. 407, 9 L.Ed.2d 441 (1963). For example, if police learn of the location of a weapon used in the commission of a crime by interrogating a suspect who is in custody, that weapon is considered **derivative evidence**. If the police failed to provide the *Miranda* warnings, not only the suspect's responses to their questions but also the weapon discovered as the fruit of the interrogation are tainted. On the other hand, if the physical evidence was located on the basis of independently and lawfully obtained information, it may be admissible under the **independent source doctrine**. *Segurra v. United States*, 468 U.S. 796, 104 S.Ct. 3380, 82 L.Ed.2d 599 (1984). Thus, in our hypothetical case, if police learned of the location of the weapon from an informant, the weapon might well be admissible in court, even though the suspect's admissions are still inadmissible.

A variation on the independent source doctrine is what is termed the **inevitable discovery doctrine**. A grisly case that illustrates this doctrine is *Nix v. Williams*, 467 U.S. 431, 104 S.Ct. 2501, 81 L.Ed.2d 377 (1984). In a defendant's retrial for murder, the jury was not permitted to learn of the defendant's incriminating statements because the police had violated *Miranda*. He was convicted nevertheless, largely on evidence derived from the girl's corpse. The body was discovered when Williams, before meeting with his attorney, led police to the place where he had dumped it. On appeal, Williams argued that evidence of the body was improperly admitted at trial because its discovery was based on inadmissible statements and thus constituted the fruit of the poisonous tree. In reviewing the case, the U.S. Supreme Court held that the evidence of the body was properly admissible at trial because a search party operating in the area where the body was discovered would eventually have located the body, even without assistance from the defendant.

---

### JURISPRUDENCE

*Nix v. Williams*, 467 U.S. 431, 104 S.Ct. 2501, 81 L.Ed.2d 377 (1984)

Robert Anthony Williams was arrested in Davenport, Iowa for the kidnapping of a ten-year-old girl in Des Moines. He was given the *Miranda* warnings and indicated his desire to have counsel present during questioning. Des Moines police informed counsel that they would pick up Williams in Davenport and return him to Des Moines without questioning the suspect. During the car ride back to Des Moines, one of the police officers made a speech emphasizing the need for a "Christian burial" for the victim. In the ensuing conversation, Williams made incriminating statements and ultimately led police to where he had disposed of the victim's body. Prior to the beginning of this "conversation" a systematic search of the area was being conducted with the aid of two hundred volunteers. The search was terminated when Williams guided police to the body. At trial, Williams' counsel moved unsuccessfully for his client's incriminating statements to be suppressed along with evidence of the condition of the victim's body as it was found, articles and photographs of her clothing, and the results of tests on the body. Williams was convicted of first-degree murder. Then began an appellate odyssey lasting fifteen years and involving two decisions by the U.S. Supreme Court. In the latter of these decisions, the Court upheld the admissibility of the victim's body and related evidence. Speaking through Chief Justice Warren E. Burger, the Court reasoned that the body was not the fruit of the poisonous tree because the search that had been underway in the area would eventually have located the body anyway. Hence, the Court created the inevitable discovery exception to the fruit of the poisonous tree doctrine.

*New York v. Quarles*, 467 U.S. 649, 104 S.Ct. 2626, 81 L.Ed.2d 550 (1984)

Two New York City police officers were approached by a woman who claimed she had just been raped and that her assailant had gone into a nearby grocery store. The police were informed that the assailant was carrying a gun. The officers proceeded to the store and immediately spotted Benjamin Quarles, who matched the description given by the victim. Upon seeing the police, Quarles turned and ran. One of the police officers drew his service revolver and ordered Quarles to "freeze." Quarles complied with the officer's request. The officer frisked Quarles and discovered an empty shoulder holster. Before reading Quarles the *Miranda*

warnings, the officer asked where the gun was. Quarles nodded in the direction of some empty boxes and said, "The gun is over there." He was then placed under arrest and "Mirandized." Later Quarles moved to have his statement suppressed from evidence since it was made prior to the *Miranda* warnings. He also moved for suppression of the gun under the fruit of the poisonous tree doctrine. The Supreme Court allowed both pieces of evidence to be used against Quarles, notwithstanding the delay in the *Miranda* warnings. Obviously, the Court felt that the officers were justified in locating a discarded weapon prior to Mirandizing Quarles. In so holding, the Court created the public safety exception to *Miranda*.

## The Public Safety Exception to *Miranda*

**public safety exception** Exception to the requirement that police officers promptly inform suspects taken into custody of their rights to remain silent and have an attorney present during questioning. Under the public safety exception, police may ask suspects questions motivated by a desire to protect public safety without jeopardizing the admissibility of suspects' answers to those questions or subsequent statements.

Police generally provide the *Miranda* warnings immediately on arrest or as soon as is practicable to preserve as evidence any statements that the suspect might make, as well as any other evidence that might be derived from these statements. In some situations, however, the *Miranda* warnings are delayed because police are preoccupied with apprehending other individuals or taking actions to protect themselves or others on the scene. In *New York v. Quarles*, 467 U.S. 649, 104 S.Ct. 2626, 81 L.Ed.2d 550 (1984), the Supreme Court recognized a **public safety exception** to the *Miranda* exclusionary rule. Under *Quarles*, before providing the *Miranda* warnings police may ask suspects questions designed to locate weapons that might be used to harm the police or other persons. If this interaction produces incriminating statements or physical evidence, the evidence need not be suppressed.

## What Constitutes an Interrogation?

Although interrogation normally occurs at the station house after arrest, it may occur anywhere. For the purpose of determining when the *Miranda* warnings must be given, the Supreme Court has defined interrogation as "express questioning or its functional equivalent," including "any words or actions on the part of the police that the police should know are reasonably likely to elicit an incriminating response from the suspect." *Rhode Island v. Innis*, 446 U.S. 291, 301, 100 S.Ct. 1682, 1693, 64 L.Ed.2d 297, 308 (1980). Before police may engage in such interaction, they

**incriminating statements** Statements, typically made to police, that increase the likelihood that one will be found guilty of a crime.

must provide the *Miranda* warnings or risk the likelihood that useful **incriminating statements** will be suppressed as illegally obtained evidence.

## Waiver of *Miranda* Rights

It is axiomatic that all constitutional rights may be waived. A suspect may elect to waive the right to remain silent or the right to have counsel present during

**waiver of *Miranda* rights** A known relinquishment of the right to remain silent and/or have counsel present during police interrogation.

questioning as long as he or she does so knowingly and voluntarily. Courts are apt to strictly scrutinize a **waiver of *Miranda* rights** to make sure it is not the product of some coercion or deception by police. In *United States v. Carra*, 604 F.2d 1271 (10th Cir. 1979), the court observed that "[v]oluntary waiver of the right to remain silent is not mechanically to be determined but is to be determined from the totality of circumstances as a matter of fact." For example, in *United States v. Blocker*, 354 F. Supp. 1195 (D.D.C. 1973), a federal district court, citing decisions from the U.S. Court of Appeals for the Fifth Circuit, observed that a written waiver signed by the accused is not in itself conclusive evidence: "The court must still decide whether, in view of all the circumstances, defendant's subsequent decision to speak was a product of his free will." 354 F. Supp. at 1198 n. 11.

Although they must honor a suspect's refusal to cooperate, police are under no duty to inform a suspect who is considering whether to cooperate that arrangements have been made to provide counsel. In *Moran v. Burbine*, 475 U.S. 412, 106 S.Ct. 1135, 89 L.Ed.2d 410 (1986), police arrested a man on a burglary charge and subsequently linked him to an unsolved murder. The suspect's sister, not aware that a murder charge was about to be filed against her brother, arranged for a lawyer to represent her brother on the burglary charge. The attorney contacted the police to arrange a meeting with her client. The police did not mention the possible murder charge and told the attorney that her client was not going to be questioned until the next day. The police then began to interrogate Burbine, failing to tell him that a lawyer had been arranged for him and had attempted to contact him. Burbine waived his rights and eventually confessed to the murder. The Supreme Court upheld the use of the confession in evidence.

## *Miranda* Turned Upside Down?

Police "Mirandized" and then interrogated the suspect in a fatal shooting that occurred on January 10, 2000. At no point did the suspect, Van Chester Thompkins, indicate that he wished to remain silent or have a lawyer present during the interrogation. Three hours into the questioning, Thompkins answered, "Yes," when asked if he prayed to God to forgive him for his role in the shooting. After being charged with first-degree murder, Thompkins filed a pretrial motion to suppress that statement, claiming that it was obtained in violation of *Miranda*. The trial court denied the motion; in June 2010 the Supreme Court agreed. *Berghuis v. Thompkins*, 560 U.S. ___, 130 S.Ct. 2250, 176 L.Ed.2d 1098 (2010). Speaking through Justice Anthony Kennedy, a sharply divided Court held that a suspect's *Miranda* right to counsel must be invoked "unambiguously," which Thompkins failed to do. Moreover, Thompkins' answer to the question about prayer, albeit three hours into the interrogation, constituted a waiver of the right to remain silent. The fact that the waiver came three hours after interrogation began did not invalidate the interrogation. In dissent, Justice Sonia Sotomayor claimed that the Court's decision had turned *Miranda* "upside down."

> Criminal suspects must now unambiguously invoke their right to remain silent—which, counterintuitively, requires them to speak. At the same time, suspects will be legally presumed to have waived their rights even if they have given no clear expression of their intent to do so. Those results, in my view, find no basis in *Miranda* or our subsequent cases and are inconsistent with the fair-trial principles on which those precedents are grounded. 560 U.S. at ___, 130 S.Ct. at 2278, 176 L.Ed.2d at 1130.

## Coerced Confessions

Even where police officers provide the *Miranda* warnings and the suspect agrees to talk to police without having counsel present, a confession elicited from the suspect is inadmissible if it is obtained through coercion, whether in the form of physical intimidation or psychological pressure. *United States v. Tingle*, 658 F.2d 1332 (9th Cir. 1981). A classic example of psychological coercion is the so-called Mutt and Jeff strategy. Under this tactic, one police officer, the "bad guy," is harsh, rude, and aggressive, while another police officer, the "good guy," is friendly and sympathetic to the suspect. Obviously the objective of the strategy is to get the accused to confess to the "good guy," and many believe that it is an effective technique. There is controversy about whether the Mutt and Jeff tactic is a constitutional means of eliciting a confession from a suspect who has waived his or her *Miranda* rights and agreed to talk to police without the presence of counsel. In *Miranda*, the Supreme Court alluded to the Mutt and Jeff routine as a possible example of impermissible psychological coercion. 384 U.S. at 452, 86 S.Ct. at 1614, 16 L.Ed.2d at 711. Yet, absent other indications of coercion, courts have generally acquiesced in the practice.

## Police Deception

**voluntariness of a confession** The quality of a confession having been freely given.

The use of tricks or factual misstatements by police in an effort to induce a defendant to confess does not automatically invalidate a confession. A misstatement by police may affect the **voluntariness of a confession**, but the effect of any misstatements must be considered in light of the totality of surrounding circumstances. In *Frazier v. Cupp*, 394 U.S. 731, 89 S.Ct. 1420, 22 L.Ed.2d 684 (1969), the Supreme Court reversed a conviction where the police had falsely informed a suspect that his codefendant had confessed. Although the Supreme Court found the misstatement relevant to the issue of whether the confession had been given voluntarily, it did not find that the misstatement per se made the confession inadmissible. The Nebraska Supreme Court has held that even deceptive statements referring to nonexistent autopsies of victims will not automatically render a confession involuntary. *State v. Norfolk*, 381 N.W.2d 120 (Neb. 1986).

How far may police go in their use of deception? In 1989 a Florida appellate court affirmed a trial judge's order holding a confession involuntary where police had presented fabricated laboratory reports to the defendant to secure a confession. The "reports," which were on the stationery of a law enforcement agency and a DNA testing firm, indicated that traces of the defendant's semen had been found on the victim's underwear. Among the factors cited by the appellate court in support of the exclusion of the confession were the indefinite life span of manufactured documents, their self-authenticating character, and their ease of duplication. The court expressed concern that false documents could find their way into police files or the courtroom and be accepted as genuine. *State v. Cayward*, 552 So.2d 971 (Fla. App. 1989).

In *State v. Patton*, 826 A.2d 783 (N.J. Sup. 2003), a police officer, posing as an eyewitness, was "interviewed" on an audiotape and fabricated an account of the victim's murder. The tape was later played to the defendant. Despite his earlier denials of involvement, upon hearing the audiotape, the defendant confessed to the murder. The fabricated audiotape, identified as such, was later introduced into evidence at trial, and the defendant was found guilty. Relying heavily on the Florida court's opinion in *State v. Cayward*, supra, the New Jersey appellate court held that this fabrication of evidence violated due process. The court found the defendant's resulting confession to be inadmissible and reversed the defendant's conviction.

**police deception** Intentional deception by police in order to elicit incriminating statements from a suspect.

**Police deception** must be distinguished from cases where the police use or threaten force or promise leniency to elicit a confession. In instances where force is used or leniency is promised, courts will suppress confessions obtained. See *Spano v. New York*, 360 U.S. 315, 79 S.Ct. 1202, 3 L.Ed.2d 1265 (1959). Moreover, when the police furnish a suspect with an incorrect or incomplete advisory statement of the penalties provided by law for a particular crime, courts will generally suppress the suspect's confession. See, e.g., *People v. Lytle*, 704 P.2d 331 (Colo. App. 1985).

## Factors Considered by Judges in Evaluating Confessions

Judges consider several variables in determining whether a challenged confession was voluntary. These include the duration and methods of the interrogation, the length of the delay between arrest and appearance before a magistrate, the conditions of detention, the attitudes of the police toward the defendant, the defendant's physical and psychological state, and anything else that might bear on the defendant's resistance. *Commonwealth v. Kichline*, 361 A.2d 282, 290 (Pa. 1976). Courts are particularly cautious when receiving confessions by juveniles. See, e.g., *Haley v. Ohio*, 332 U.S. 596, 68 S.Ct. 302, 92 L.Ed. 224 (1948).

In a landmark ruling, *Arizona v. Fulminante*, 499 U.S. 279, 111 S.Ct. 1246, 113 L.Ed.2d 302 (1991), the Supreme Court said that the use of a confession that should have been suppressed does not automatically require reversal of a defendant's conviction. Rather, the appellate court must determine whether the defendant would have been convicted in the absence of the confession. If so, the admission of the confession is deemed to be a harmless error that does not require reversal. See, e.g., *State v. Tart*, 672 So.2d 116 (La. 1996).

---

### JURISPRUDENCE

*Arizona v. Fulminante,* 499 U.S. 279, 111 S.Ct. 1246, 113 L.Ed.2d 302 (1991)

Oreste Fulminante's eleven-year-old daughter was murdered in Arizona. After the murder, Fulminante left Arizona for New York, where he was convicted of an unrelated crime and sentenced to prison. While in prison, Fulminate became friends with a fellow inmate named Anthony Sarivola, who was a paid informant for the Federal Bureau of Investigation. In the course of conversation, Sarivola told Fulminante that the reason for his harsh treatment by other inmates was a rumor circulating that he had murdered a child. Sarivola told him that he would provide protection in exchange for the truth. Fulminante disclosed that he had killed his daughter in Arizona and gave details about the crime. After being released from prison in New York, Fulminante was indicted for first-degree murder in Arizona. The confession to Sarivola was the key piece of evidence, and Fulminate sought to have it suppressed. The trial court rejected the notion that the confession was coerced and barred by the Fifth and Fourteenth Amendments. The Arizona Supreme Court reversed holding that "the confession was coerced" and ordered a new trial without the use of the confession. The Supreme Court agreed that the confession was coerced because Fulminante's primary motivation to confess was to prevent physical violence. Thus, the confession could not be used against him under the Fifth and Fourteenth Amendments. However, the Court also ruled that the use in evidence of a confession that should have been suppressed does not automatically require reversal of a defendant's conviction. But the Court concluded that admitting Fulminante's confession was not harmless beyond a reasonable doubt, thus affirming the Arizona Supreme Court's conclusion that Fulminante was entitled to a new trial in which the confession was not to be used in evidence.

# Identification Procedures

Police identification procedures include those in which victims and witnesses are asked to identify perpetrators, such as **lineups**, **showups**, and **photo packs**. They also encompass scientific techniques comparing **forensic evidence** taken from a suspect with that found at a crime scene. All of these procedures are extremely important in police work, but each poses unique legal problems.

**lineups** Police identification procedure where suspects are included in a group with other persons and the group is exhibited to victims.

**showups** Events in which victims are taken to see suspects to make an identification.

**photo packs** Collections of "mug shots" exhibited to a victim or witness in an attempt to identify the perpetrator of a crime.

**forensic evidence** Evidence obtained through scientific techniques of analyzing physical evidence.

**handwriting exemplar** A sample of a suspect's handwriting.

**voice exemplar** A sample of a person's voice, usually taken by police for the purpose of identifying a suspect.

## Forensic Methods

Forensic methods involve the application of scientific principles to legal issues. In the context of police work, forensic methods commonly include fingerprint identification, comparison of blood samples, matching of clothing fibers, head and body hair comparisons, identification of semen, and, more recently, DNA tests. When these methods are conducted by qualified persons, the results are usually admissible evidence. Indeed, the courts have ruled that obtaining such physical evidence from suspects does not violate the constitutional prohibition of compulsory self-incrimination. *Schmerber v. California*, 384 U.S. 757, 86 S.Ct. 1826, 16 L.Ed.2d 908 (1966).

In *Gilbert v. California*, 388 U.S. 263, 87 S.Ct. 1951, 18 L.Ed.2d 1178 (1967), the U.S. Supreme Court held that a suspect could be compelled to provide a **handwriting exemplar**, explaining that it is not testimony but an identifying physical characteristic. Similarly, in *United States v. Dionisio*, 410 U.S. 1, 93 S.Ct. 764, 35 L. Ed.2d 67 (1973), the Court held that a suspect could be compelled to provide a **voice exemplar** on the ground that the recording is being used only to measure the physical properties of the suspect's voice, as distinct from the content of what the suspect has said.

Of course, police may not use methods that "shock the conscience" in obtaining physical evidence from suspects. *Rochin v. California*, 342 U.S. 165, 72 S.Ct. 205, 96 L.Ed. 183 (1952). Courts will scrutinize closely procedures that subject the suspect to major bodily intrusions. For example, in *Winston v. Lee*, 470 U.S. 753, 105 S.Ct. 1611, 84 L.Ed.2d 662 (1985), the prosecution sought a court order requiring a suspect to have surgery to remove a bullet lodged in his chest. The prosecution believed that ballistics tests on the bullet would show that the suspect had been wounded during the course of a robbery. The Supreme Court, weighing the risks to the suspect against the government's need for evidence and noting that the prosecution had other evidence against the suspect, disallowed the procedure. The Court declined to formulate a broad rule to govern such cases. Therefore, courts must consider such matters on a case-by-case basis, carefully weighing the interests on both sides.

As the 1995 O.J. Simpson murder trial demonstrated, defense lawyers can attack the methodology of forensic procedures as well as the qualifications of those administering them. If the evidence is inherently unreliable, it is inadmissible regardless of whether there were violations of the suspect's constitutional rights. In 1996 the FBI crime laboratory was criticized for allegedly sloppy procedures in the conduct of DNA and other forensic tests. This encouraged defense lawyers to challenge the reliability of the evidence in several cases where prosecutors were using evidence analyzed by the FBI crime lab.

With the rapid progress of science and technology, forensic procedures are constantly evolving and new procedures becoming available to the police. Evidence obtained through scientific and technological innovations can be both relevant and probative in a criminal case. Yet care must be taken to ensure that a new method is clearly supported by research.

Until recently, federal and state courts followed the test articulated in *Frye v. United States*, 293 F. 1013 (D.C. Cir. 1923), and admitted scientific evidence only if it was based on principles or theories generally accepted in the scientific community. In *Daubert v. Merrell Dow Pharmaceuticals, Inc.*, 509 U.S. 579, 113 S.Ct. 2786, 125 L.Ed.2d 469 (1993), the Supreme Court held that the Federal Rules of Evidence supersede *Frye* and govern the admissibility of scientific evidence in the federal courts. This approach causes admissibility of scientific evidence to hinge on such factors as whether the evidence can be tested and whether it has been subjected to peer review. State courts are now divided on whether to accept the newer *Daubert* standard or remain with the classic standard announced in 1923 in *Frye*. (This topic is discussed further in Chapter 18.)

## Lineups

Eyewitness identification may be more persuasive to juries than forensic evidence, but it can also present problems. One of the most common nonscientific methods of identification is the lineup. In a lineup, a group of individuals, one of whom is the suspect in custody, appears before a victim or witness, who is usually shielded from the suspect's view. Often, the individuals in the lineup are asked to walk, turn sideways, wear certain items of clothing, or speak to assist the victim or eyewitness in making a positive identification. The Supreme Court has held that there is no Fifth Amendment immunity against being placed in a lineup as an identification procedure. *United States v. Wade*, 388 U.S. 218, 87 S.Ct. 1926, 18 L.Ed.2d 1149 (1967).

---

### JURISPRUDENCE

*United States v. Wade*, 388 U.S. 218, 87 S.Ct. 1926, 18 L.Ed.2d 1149 (1967)

Billy Joe Wade was indicted for conspiracy and bank robbery. Several weeks afterwards, police placed Wade in a "lineup in which each person wore strips of tape on his face, as the robber allegedly had done, and, on direction, repeated words like those the robber allegedly had used." This was done without notice to Wade's appointed counsel. During the lineup, two bank employees identified Wade as the robber. At Wade's trial, the employees identified Wade as the robber when asked whether the guilty person was in the courtroom. However, Wade's attorney argued that the lineup "violated [Wade's] Fifth Amendment privilege against self-incrimination and his Sixth Amendment right to counsel, and filed a motion for judgment of acquittal or, alternatively, to strike the courtroom identifications." The trial court denied the motions and Wade was convicted. In reviewing the case, the Supreme Court held "neither the lineup itself nor anything required therein violated [Wade's] Fifth Amendment privilege against self-incrimination, since merely exhibiting his person for observation by witnesses and using his voice as an identifying physical characteristic involved no compulsion of the accused to give evidence of a testimonial nature against himself which is prohibited by that Amendment." However, the Court held that the postindictment lineup without the presence of his attorney violated Wade's Sixth Amendment right to counsel because such a right "guarantees an accused the right to counsel not only at his trial but at any critical confrontation by the prosecution at pretrial proceedings where the results might determine his fate and where the absence of counsel might derogate from his right to a fair trial." The postindictment lineup was held to be a "critical prosecutive stage," and therefore Wade was entitled to have counsel present. Yet the Court held that this violation did not necessitate reversal of Wade's conviction and said that his conviction could be upheld if the prosecution could show that the witnesses' in-court identification of Wade as the perpetrator was based on their observations of him during the crime.

However, courts must guard against the possibility that identification procedures, especially lineups, are unfair when a victim or witness is prompted to identify a particular suspect as the perpetrator. See, e.g., *Foster v. California*, 394 U.S. 440, 89 S.Ct. 1127, 22 L.Ed.2d 402 (1969). Obviously, if the perpetrator is known to be black, it is impermissibly suggestive for police to place one African American suspect in a lineup with five white individuals. In practice, however, the more subtle suggestiveness of lineups causes problems for the courts. To avoid such problems, police should place several persons with similar physical characteristics in a lineup.

To further protect the rights of the accused, the Supreme Court has said that after formal charges have been made against a defendant, the defendant has the right to have counsel present at a lineup. *Kirby v. Illinois*, 406 U.S. 682, 92 S.Ct. 1877, 32 L.Ed.2d 411 (1972). To ensure that police and prosecutors honor that right, the Supreme Court has said that a pretrial identification obtained in violation of the right to counsel is per se inadmissible at trial. *Gilbert v. California*, supra. A per se exclusionary rule was deemed necessary to ensure that the police and the prosecution would respect the defendant's right to have counsel present at a lineup. On the other hand, a pretrial identification obtained through impermissibly suggestive identification procedures is not per se inadmissible. Instead, such an identification may be introduced into evidence if the trial judge first finds that the witness's in-court identification is reliable and based on independent recall. In making this determination, the trial judge must consider (1) the opportunity of the witness to view the accused at the time of the crime, (2) the witness's degree of attention, (3) the accuracy of the witness's prior description of the accused, (4) the level of certainty demonstrated at the confrontation, and (5) the time that elapsed between the crime and the confrontation. *Neil v. Biggers*, 409 U.S. 188, 93 S.Ct. 375, 34 L.Ed.2d 401 (1972); see also *Wethington v. State*, 560 N.E.2d 496 (Ind. 1990).

## Showups

The showup is a frequently used method of identification of a suspect. In a showup, the police usually take the victim to the suspect to determine whether the victim can make an identification, and at least one state supreme court has held that the police may transport a person stopped for an investigatory stop a short distance for purposes of a showup. *People v. Lippert*, 432 N.E.2d 605 (Ill. 1982).

In 1967 the U.S. Court of Appeals for the District of Columbia Circuit approved the use of showups, commenting, "[W]e do not consider a prompt identification of a suspect close to the time and place of an offense to diverge from the rudiments of fair play that govern the due balance of pertinent interests that suspects be treated fairly while the state pursues its responsibility of apprehending criminals." *Wise v. United States*, 383 F.2d 206, 210 (D.C. Cir. 1967).

In *Stovall v. Denno*, 308 U.S. 293, 87 S.Ct. 198, 18 L.Ed.2d 1199 (1967), the Supreme Court recognized a defendant's due process right to exclude identification testimony that results from unnecessarily suggestive procedures that may lead to an irreparably mistaken identification. This form of "on-the-scene" confrontation between an eyewitness and a suspect is inherently suggestive because it is apparent that when law enforcement takes a victim for a showup of a suspect, they usually believe they have caught the offender. Therefore, courts review identification testimony carefully to make sure a witness's identification testimony is not based on impermissibly suggestive identification procedures. In making such a determination, courts often look to the length of time between the crime and the confrontation and the level of certainty demonstrated by the witness at the confrontation.

Although critics complain of the use of showups, such a confrontation may be justified by the necessity to preserve a witness's memory of a suspect before the suspect has had an opportunity to alter his or her clothing and appearance. Appellate courts consistently admonish caution in the use of showups; however, they generally approve of their use when the identification occurs shortly after the crime has been committed and the showup is conducted near the scene of the crime under circumstances that are not unduly suggestive. In approving showups, some courts have pointed out that a victim's or eyewitness's on-the-scene identification is likely to be more reliable than a later identification because the memory is fresher. See, e.g., *Jones v. State*, 600 P.2d 247, 250 (Nev. 1979). Courts base their judgments of the reliability of showups on many factors and circumstances. For example, in *United States v. Bautista*, 23 F.3d 726 (2d Cir. 1994), in its review of a challenge to an on-the-scene identification immediately following a nighttime narcotics raid, the court observed, "The fact that the suspects were handcuffed, in the custody of law enforcement officers, and illuminated by flashlights . . . did not render the pretrial identification procedure unnecessarily suggestive." *Id*. at 731. The court went on to explain that because the on-the-scene identification was necessary to allow the officers to release the innocent, the incidents of that identification were also necessary.

## Photo Packs

A photo pack is simply a set of "mug shots" that are shown individually to the victim or eyewitness in the hope that he or she will be able to identify the perpetrator. To produce a reliable, hence admissible, identification, the presentation of the photo pack should not emphasize one photo over the others. For example, in *Commonwealth v. Thornley*, 546 N.E.2d 350 (Mass. 1989), the Supreme Judicial Court of Massachusetts found that the photographic array was impermissibly suggestive because the witnesses admitted they made their selection of the defendant's photograph because the man in the photo was wearing glasses. The defendant was the only one of thirteen men in the photo array who was wearing glasses.

The words and actions of the officers making the presentation must manifest an attitude of disinterest. *State v. Thamer*, 777 P.2d 432 (Utah 1989). In analyzing a defendant's claim of being the victim of an impermissibly suggestive photo pack identification, courts generally apply a two-part test. First, did the photo array present the defendant in an impermissibly suggestive posture? Second, if so, under the totality of circumstances, did the procedure give rise to a substantial likelihood of misidentification? *State v. Bedwell*, 417 N.W.2d 66 (Iowa 1987).

## Conclusion

Police are permitted broad discretion in their interactions with the public. There are no legal prerequisites to the many consensual encounters through which police routinely perform their investigative and preventive duties. But the whole array of nonconsensual encounters with the public, including arrest, investigatory detention, interrogation, roadblocks, and identification procedures, are subject to strict constitutional requirements.

# Chapter Summary

- Learning Objective 1

  ○ Because an arrest is a form of "seizure," it must conform to the requirements of the Fourth Amendment. Thus, an arrest must be based on probable cause and, with certain exceptions, is subject to the warrant requirement of the Fourth Amendment.

  ○ At common law, and under contemporary American law, police who have probable cause to believe that a person has committed or is committing a felony or who observes someone committing a misdemeanor can make a warrantless arrest. Otherwise, an arrest requires a warrant.

  ○ An arrest warrant issues based on a grand jury indictment; a *capias* directs the defendant's arrest following a prosecutor's information.

  ○ The Supreme Court has approved warrantless arrests where crimes are committed in plain view of police officers or where officers possess probable cause but exigent circumstances prohibit obtaining a warrant.

  ○ The Fourth Amendment is very protective of homes. Nevertheless, courts generally uphold a peaceful warrantless entry into a home where there is probable cause to arrest an armed suspect for a serious felony and the suspect will likely escape or evidence will be destroyed.

  ○ By statute or court rules, federal and state officers are required to promptly take persons arrested before a magistrate, regardless of whether the arrest was based on a warrant.

  ○ At common law, a private individual could make a citizen's arrest without a warrant for a felony or breach of the peace committed in that person's presence. The rule prevails in some states; in others, it has been revised by statute.

  ○ In most states, a police officer has discretion to either make an arrest or issue a citation to a person who commits a minor traffic violation. In 2001, the Supreme Court ruled that the Fourth Amendment does not forbid a warrantless arrest, even for a minor traffic offense. Some states have "cite and release" statutes that create a presumptive right to be cited and released for the commission of a misdemeanor.

- Learning Objective 2

  ○ Laws typically allow police officers to use force reasonably necessary to make an arrest. This includes use of stun guns (Tasers) to incapacitate suspects who resist arrest and trained dogs to apprehend fleeing suspects.

  ○ In 2003, a federal appeals court held that use of a Taser to subdue a potentially homicidal individual did not constitute excessive force.

  ○ In 1985 the Supreme Court struck down a state statute that permitted police to use deadly force against fleeing suspects when there was no threat to the safety of the officer or the public.

- Learning Objective 3

  ○ Police who have "reasonable suspicion" that criminal activity is afoot may temporarily detain a person for questioning and, based on a reasonable suspicion that the detainee is armed, may perform a pat-down search of the suspect's outer clothing to locate weapons. An officer who feels an object that may be a weapon may seize it, and if it turns out to be something other than a weapon, it may be seized if it is contraband. Stops as long as forty minutes have been held to be reasonable.

o Courts have applied this rationale to stops of vehicles. An anonymous tip corroborated by independent police work is generally held to be sufficient to establish a reasonable suspicion to make an investigatory stop of a vehicle.

o In 1983 the Supreme Court held that when police stop an automobile based on reasonable suspicion, they may search the passenger compartment for weapons, assuming they have reason to believe that a suspect is dangerous. The search must be limited to areas in which a weapon may be placed or hidden. Passengers and the driver may be frisked if there is a reasonable suspicion they may be armed and dangerous. This often results in discovery of contraband or evidence of intoxication which police can use in a criminal prosecution.

o In 1996 the Court ruled that the motives of an officer in stopping a vehicle for a traffic violation are irrelevant if there is an objective basis for the stop.

o In 1989 the Supreme Court upheld an investigative stop of an air passenger for which a number of circumstances, including the use of a drug courier profile, gave the police reasonable suspicion of criminal activity.

- Learning Objective 4

  o Racial profiling involves "police-initiated action that relies on the race, ethnicity or national origin rather than the behavior of an individual or information that leads the police to a particular individual who has been identified as being, or having been, engaged in criminal activity."

  o Some defendants who claim to have been stopped on the basis of race have sought to dismiss charges, arguing they were denied due process and equal protection of the laws. The racial profiling debate was recharged in 2010 when Arizona enacted a law allowing officers to determine the immigration status of those persons reasonably suspected to be in this country illegally.

- Learning Objective 5

  o Police are permitted to stop motorists at roadblocks to perform safety checks on automobiles or apprehend fleeing suspects. They also may establish sobriety checkpoints designed to locate drunk drivers, as long as procedures are in place to ensure reasonableness. Roadblocks often reveal illegal weapons, drugs, and other contraband.

  o In 1990 the Supreme Court recognized that a "seizure" occurs when a vehicle is stopped at a checkpoint but upheld the use of roadblocks for conducting field sobriety tests, provided they are established and operated according to guidelines that minimize the inconvenience to motorists and constrain the exercise of discretion by police officers.

  o In 2000 the Court invalidated an ordinance establishing checkpoints primarily for snaring drug traffickers, but in 2004 the Court noted that its decision was not intended to prevent the police from using checkpoints to obtain assistance in locating perpetrators of a crime involving a traffic accident.

- Learning Objective 6

  - In 1979 the Supreme Court said that a law making it an offense to refuse to report or to give a false name and residence address to a peace officer could not be constitutionally applied in absence of reasonable suspicion that the individual asked for identification was engaged in or had engaged in criminal activity.
  - In 1983 the Court found unconstitutional a statute that required persons loitering or wandering on the streets to provide a "credible and reliable" identification and to account for their presence when requested to do so by a police officer.
  - In 2004, in a 5–4 decision, the Court affirmed a conviction of a defendant who violated an ordinance that provided, "Any person so detained shall identify himself, but may not be compelled to answer any other inquiry of any peace officer."

- Learning Objective 7

  - In 1897 the Supreme Court held that to force a suspect to confess violates the Self-Incrimination Clause of the Fifth Amendment; in 1936 it held that a coerced confession deprived a defendant in a state criminal case of due process of law.
  - Through a series of decisions in the 1960s the Supreme Court reformed the law on confessions. In 1964 it made the Self-Incrimination Clause applicable to state criminal prosecutions and recognized the right of suspects to have counsel present during interrogation.
  - In its seminal *Miranda* decision in 1966, the Court required police to advise suspects in custody of their rights to remain silent and to have counsel present during questioning. Before police engage in questioning, they must provide the *Miranda* warnings or risk the likelihood that incriminating statements will be suppressed as illegally obtained evidence.
  - A public safety exception allows police to ask suspects questions about the location of weapons before providing *Miranda* warnings.
  - A waiver of *Miranda* rights by a suspect must be knowing and voluntary. Courts scrutinize waivers closely, especially waivers by juveniles.
  - In 1986 the Court held that police are under no duty to inform a suspect considering whether to cooperate that arrangements have been made to provide counsel.
  - In 1991 the Court said that the use of a confession that should have been suppressed does not automatically require reversal of a defendant's conviction if an appellate court determines that the defendant would have been convicted in the absence of the confession.

- Learning Objective 8

  - The use of tricks or factual misstatements by police in an effort to induce a defendant to confess does not automatically invalidate a confession. This is distinguishable from instances where police furnish a suspect with an incorrect or incomplete advisory statement of the penalties the law provides for a particular crime or where they use threats to use force or promises of leniency to elicit a confession. In such instances courts will suppress confessions.

- Learning Objective 9

  o The Supreme Court held in 1963 that under the "fruit of the poisonous tree" doctrine, evidence derived from inadmissible evidence is likewise inadmissible to prove guilt.

  o Evidence obtained in violation of the *Miranda* rules is inadmissible in criminal prosecutions to prove guilt unless it was located on the basis of independently and lawfully obtained information (the independent source doctrine) or would have been discovered inevitably by an independent search (the inevitable discovery rule).

- Learning Objective 10

  o Law enforcement agencies use forensic means (such as fingerprints, blood samples, matching of clothing fibers, hair comparisons, identification of semen, and DNA tests) as well as witness identification of suspects.

  o The Supreme Court has held that neither obtaining such physical evidence nor compelling suspects to provide handwriting and voice exemplars violates the constitutional prohibition of compulsory self-incrimination.

  o Police use lineups wherein a group of individuals, one of whom is the suspect in custody, appears before a victim or witness, who is usually shielded from the suspect's view.

  o The Supreme Court held that there is no Fifth Amendment immunity against being placed in a lineup as a means of identification, but has recognized a defendant's due process right to exclude identification testimony that results from unnecessarily suggestive procedures that may lead to an irreparably mistaken identification.

  o After formal charges have been made against a defendant, the defendant has the right to have counsel present at a lineup and a pretrial identification obtained in violation of the right to counsel is per se inadmissible at trial.

  o In a showup police take the victim to the suspect to make an identification. This form of "on-the-scene" confrontation between an eyewitness and a suspect is inherently suggestive because when the police take a victim for a showup, they usually believe they have caught the offender.

  o A photo pack is simply a set of "mug shots" that are shown individually to the victim or eyewitness in the hope that he or she will be able to identify the perpetrator. In analyzing a defendant's claim of being the victim of an impermissibly suggestive photo pack identification, courts generally apply a two-part test. First, did the photo array present the defendant in an impermissibly suggestive posture? Second, if so, under the totality of circumstances, did the procedure give rise to a substantial likelihood of misidentification?

## Key Terms

| | |
|---|---|
| anonymous tips | lineups |
| arrest | *Miranda* warnings |
| arrest warrant | pat-down search |
| *capias* | photo packs |
| citizen's arrest | plain view |
| coerced confession | police deception |
| derivative evidence | pretextual stops |
| drug courier profiles | public safety exception |
| forensic evidence | racial profiling |
| handwriting exemplar | roadblocks |
| identification procedures | showups |
| incriminating statements | *Terry* stop |
| independent source doctrine | voice exemplar |
| inevitable discovery doctrine | voluntariness of a confession |
| interrogation | waiver of *Miranda* rights |
| investigatory detention | warrantless arrest |

## Questions for Thought and Discussion

1. Practically speaking, what is the difference between "probable cause" and "reasonable suspicion"? How long can police detain a suspect based on reasonable suspicion?

2. What are the practical arguments for and against allowing private citizens to make arrests when they observe criminal activity taking place? What is the law in your state governing "citizen's arrests"?

3. Does your state make any distinction between minor and serious traffic offenses in permitting arrests? Is the use of arrest procedures for relatively minor traffic offenses unnecessary? Is it better to give the individual police officer discretion in these matters or to adopt laws decriminalizing such infractions?

4. In the *Miranda* case, the Supreme Court released a convicted rapist when it imposed a requirement that police advise suspects of their constitutional rights before conducting interrogations. Was the Court's decision a wise one? What has been the impact of the *Miranda* decision on law enforcement?

5. What factors do courts consider in determining whether an individual is "in custody" when a police interrogation takes place?

6. What limitations do courts impose on police in the use of deception in interrogations of suspects?

7. How might police coerce a suspect into waiving the rights to counsel and to remain silent during interrogation? How can courts ensure that cooperation with police was voluntary?

8. What factors do courts consider in evaluating whether a confession has been coerced?

9. Are the courts correct in limiting the scope of the Fifth Amendment Self-Incrimination Clause to verbal statements so that there is no constitutional protection against compulsory police identification procedures? What would be the

implications for law enforcement if the courts included physical evidence like fingerprints or handwriting samples within the scope of the Fifth Amendment privilege?

10. Describe the methods of nonscientific identification used by law enforcement in their attempts to identify suspects. Which do you think is the most reliable?

11. Would it be permissible for police to construct a lineup including four visibly overweight persons along with a slim one where the victim told police that her assailant was "very thin"?

12. Discuss racial profiling, which results in a disproportionate number of minorities being stopped for disobeying traffic laws. Should this problem be addressed by (a) courts' dismissing charges or suppressing evidence seized as a result of racial profiling based on denial of due process and equal protection of the law, (b) civil litigation seeking financial redress, (c) disciplinary action against law enforcement officers responsible for racial profiling, or (d) some other proposed remedy?

## Problems for Discussion and Solution

1. Police obtained a warrant to search a single-family residence for "illegal amphetamines and equipment used in the manufacture of same." The warrant also authorized the search of the person of Harry Hampton, described in the warrant as a white male, thirty-two years of age, six feet two inches tall, and weighing 225 lbs. When police arrived at the scene, one officer began to search Hampton. When that search yielded contraband, another officer detained a second man sitting on the porch. (He was later identified as Jimmy Jaffers.) The officer subjected Jaffers to a pat-down search. No weapons were discovered on Jaffers's person, but the officer, having felt a "suspicious lump" in Jaffers's front pants pocket, retrieved a plastic bag of capsules that later proved to be illegal amphetamines. In a pretrial motion, Jaffers's counsel moves to suppress the contraband, arguing that his client was the victim of an unreasonable search. Is Jaffers likely to prevail in this contention? Why or why not?

2. A police officer on night patrol saw a car parked off a dirt road in an area known to be a "lovers' lane." As his cruiser approached the car, he observed a male and a female sitting inside. He noticed the male occupant make a movement that the officer interpreted as an attempt to hide something under the seat. The officer approached the vehicle and directed the occupants to get out. As they did, he observed a marijuana "roach" in the open ashtray. The officer then reached under the front seat and retrieved a small quantity of marijuana. The officer placed both individuals under arrest. In court, the officer admitted that he was not concerned for his safety but simply had a "hunch" that the couple could be "doing drugs." Did the officer make a legal arrest? Why or why not?

3. Deputy Dennis D. Mennis was conducting a routine patrol in his police cruiser at 4 A.M. in an area known to have high levels of gang, drug, and gun activity. He witnessed two young men standing near a parked car. He stopped to investigate. As he approached the two men, one of the men got into the car and attempted to drive away. Deputy Mennis ordered the man to stop and exit the vehicle, which he did. Deputy Mennis did not observe any criminal activity, but nevertheless ordered both men to place their hands on the hood of the car while he conducted a pat-down search of both of them. The pat-down search of one

of the men resulted in the seizure of a small caliber handgun, which was concealed in the man's jacket pocket. The man from whom the gun was seized was immediately arrested for possession of a concealed weapon. The other man, who turned out to be the owner of the vehicle, was permitted to leave the scene. Did Deputy Mennis act properly in conducting the pat-down searches, seizing the concealed firearm, and making the warrantless arrest? What standards would a judge employ in reviewing the deputy's actions?

4. Police were called to a residence by a homeowner who claimed she had just been the victim of a burglary and armed robbery. She gave the police a precise description of the perpetrator and informed police that the suspect had pointed a handgun at her during the crime. Thirty minutes later the same officers confronted a suspect who matched the homeowner's description walking down the road about a mile from the crime scene. When the police approached the suspect, he turned and ran toward nearby woods. The police gave chase while calling for the suspect to stop. Fearing that the suspect would avoid arrest, an officer drew his revolver and shot the suspect in the back, killing him. Was the officer's use of deadly force permissible in this instance? Why or why not?

5. Police got a phone call from someone who claimed he had just planted a bomb in a nearby high school and that it would go off in forty-five minutes. Police officers, including the bomb squad, rushed to the scene as the school was being evacuated. While surveying the area outside the school, an officer came upon a young man perched in a tree. The man appeared to be observing the scene with a pair of binoculars. The officer demanded that the man come down from the tree. As he was climbing down, a cell phone fell from his pocket. The officer picked up the phone and pushed the button to display the call history. The officer noticed that the last number called was the police station. The officer immediately placed the man in handcuffs and asked him, "Where's the bomb?" The man replied that there was no bomb and that the whole thing had been a prank. The man was arrested on a charge of making a false bomb threat. In a pretrial motion, his attorney moved to suppress the statements made by the suspect in response to the officer's questions. How would a judge likely rule on this motion? Why?

6. Police arrested Sam Shady for an alleged rape. Police required Shady, who was unusually tall and lean, to stand in a lineup with four other men, all of whom were of average height and weight. The victim did not hesitate to identify Shady as the perpetrator. Is this identification likely to withstand a challenge by the defense?

## CHAPTER 17

# The Pretrial Process

## CHAPTER OUTLINE

## JURISPRUDENCE

*Gideon v. Wainwright* (1963)

*Scott v. Illinois* (1979)

*Stack v. Boyle* (1951)

*United States v. Salerno* (1987)

*United States v. Armstrong* (1996)

*United States v. Calandra* (1974)

*Bruton v. United States* (1968)

*Bordenkircher v. Hayes* (1978)

## LEARNING OBJECTIVES

After reading this chapter, you should be able to explain

1. why constitutional rights, especially the right to counsel, are critically important during the pretrial process

2. why petty offenses are disposed of through summary trials and more serious charges entail more complex procedures

3. what factors determine whether a defendant will be granted pretrial release or remanded to custody

4. the different mechanisms by which formal charges are brought

5. the role and function of the grand jury in the pretrial process

6. how extradition works and why it is necessary

Continued

## CHAPTER OPENING VIGNETTE

On March 25, 1931, a sheriff's posse stopped a freight train in Paint Rock, Alabama and arrested nine young African-American men. The sheriff had been alerted by several white teenagers who had jumped off the train earlier and claimed that they had been assaulted by the African-Americans. Later that day, two young white women who also were on the train claimed that they had been raped by the African-Americans now in custody. The next day an angry mob surrounded the jail in Scottsboro, Alabama, where the suspects were being held. Thus began one of the most infamous cases in American legal history. The nine "Scottsboro boys," as they were dubbed by the press, were indicted for rape on March 30, 1931. Less than a week later they were tried before an all-white jury. During the rushed investigation and trial, conducted in an atmosphere of extreme racial animosity, the defendants were not represented by counsel in any meaningful sense. Eight of the nine defendants were convicted of rape and sentenced to death—the jury could not agree on whether one defendant should receive the death penalty or life imprisonment. In *Powell v. Alabama*, 287 U.S. 45, 53 S.Ct. 55, 77 L.Ed. 158 (1932), the U.S. Supreme Court reversed the convictions, holding that the defendants had been denied due process of law in violation of the Fourteenth Amendment. Saying that the Due Process Clause of the Fourteenth Amendment incorporates the "fundamental principles of liberty and justice which lie at the base of all our civil and political institutions," the Court foreshadowed modern judicial decisions protecting the rights of the accused. Unfortunately for the Scottsboro Boys, the High Court's decision did not end their legal troubles. The story of what happened in the years that followed is too long and complex to be recounted here. Suffice it to say that evidence later revealed that all of the defendants had been falsely accused. Ultimately, all were paroled or pardoned and the state of Alabama apologized for a horrific miscarriage of justice.

# Introduction

**petty offenses** Minor crimes for which fines or short jail terms are the only prescribed modes of punishment.

**criminal procedure** The rules of law governing the procedures by which crimes are investigated, prosecuted, adjudicated, and punished.

**initial appearance** After arrest, the first appearance of the accused before a judge or magistrate, at which the charges are read and the defendant is advised of his or her constitutional rights. Sometimes referred to as the "first appearance."

**preliminary hearing** A hearing held to determine whether there is sufficient evidence to hold an accused for trial.

**grand jury** A group of citizens convened either to conduct an investigation or to determine whether there is sufficient evidence to warrant the prosecution of an accused.

**arraignment** An appearance before a court of law for the purpose of pleading to a criminal charge.

The U.S. Constitution and the constitutions of all fifty states guarantee due process of law to all persons accused of criminal wrongdoing. Due process requires that persons accused of crimes be given fair notice of criminal charges and an adequate opportunity to contest them. As the Supreme Court has said,

> No principle of procedural due process is more clearly established than that of notice of the specific charge, and a chance to be heard in a trial of the issues raised by that charge, if desired, are among the constitutional rights of every accused in a criminal proceeding, in all courts, state or federal. *Cole v. Arkansas*, 333 U.S. 196, 201, 68 S.Ct. 514, 517, 92 L.Ed. 644, 647 (1948).

For **petty offenses** (minor misdemeanors), due process may require no more than the opportunity for the accused to contest the charge before a magistrate in a single, summary proceeding. For more serious offenses (treason, felonies, and major misdemeanors), the federal and state constitutions impose more elaborate procedural requirements.

As a practical matter, judicial decisions interpreting the generalities of the federal and state constitutions have greatly expanded the procedural rights that must be observed in criminal prosecutions. One result of this judicial activity is that the area of law known as criminal procedure has developed substantially over the past several decades.

Although many people equate the term **criminal procedure** with the criminal trial, the former term is actually much broader. Criminal procedure includes search and seizure, arrest, and interrogation (see Chapters 15 and 16), as well as a variety of other procedures that must occur before a trial can take place. The main components of the pretrial process are the **initial appearance** before a magistrate, the **preliminary hearing**, the **grand jury** proceeding, and the **arraignment** (see Figure 17.1). In addition, judges consider various motions made by the defense and prosecution at pretrial hearings. These pretrial procedures are designed to eliminate from the system those cases for which there is insufficient evidence of criminal wrongdoing and to set the stage for a fair and orderly resolution of cases for which the evidence is sufficiently strong to proceed to trial.

What happens during the pretrial process often determines the outcome of a criminal case. Indeed, the overwhelming majority of criminal cases never make it to trial. Some cases are dropped or dismissed for lack of sufficient evidence; many others result in convictions pursuant to guilty pleas. A substantial number of these guilty pleas result from negotiations between prosecutors and defense counsel. In such cases, trials are unnecessary. Where a defendant pleads guilty or no contest to an offense, there is a factual basis for the plea, and the court is satisfied that the plea

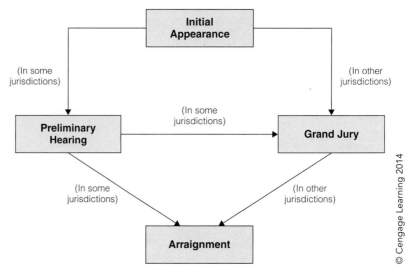

**FIGURE 17.1** Major Components of Pretrial Process.

has been entered voluntarily, guilt is pronounced and the process moves along to the sentencing stage. Given the relative infrequency of trials, pretrial procedures have great importance in the day-to-day operation of the criminal justice system.

# The Right to Counsel

**right to counsel** (1) The right to retain an attorney to represent oneself in court. (2) The right of an indigent person to have an attorney provided at public expense.

Before undertaking a detailed examination of pretrial procedures, we must consider the contours of the **right to counsel**, which is essential to preserving the fundamental fairness of all criminal procedures. The defense attorney not only represents the accused in pretrial court proceedings, but also advises on strategy, and often serves as the negotiator between the defendant and the prosecutor. Thus, the attorney for the defense plays an essential role in the criminal process. Indeed, in our adversarial legal system, the right to counsel may be the single most important right possessed by persons accused of serious crimes. As the Supreme Court has observed, "[T]he right of one charged with crime to counsel may not be deemed fundamental and essential in some countries, but it is in ours." *Gideon v. Wainwright*, 372 U.S. 335, 344, 83 S.Ct. 792, 796, 9 L.Ed.2d 799, 805 (1963).

## Common-Law Background of the Right to Counsel

Under the early English common law, there was no right to counsel for persons accused of treason or felonies. Somewhat ironically, by modern standards, the common law did recognize a right to counsel in misdemeanor cases. In 1698 Parliament enacted a law recognizing a right to counsel in cases of treason. By the late eighteenth century, the common law recognized a limited right to counsel in felony cases, and in 1836 Parliament passed legislation recognizing the right to counsel for all criminal defendants. Under the common law and the aforementioned acts of Parliament, the right to counsel meant the right to hire a barrister (a lawyer admitted to trial practice) at a person's own expense. It was not until 1903 that Parliament passed the Poor Prisoner's Defense Act, requiring that indigent defendants be provided counsel at public expense.

## The Modern American Approach

In the United States, the right to counsel has likewise evolved through both judicial decisions and legislation. As the Sixth Amendment to the U.S. Constitution provides, "In all criminal prosecutions, the accused shall enjoy the right . . . to have the Assistance of Counsel for his defense."

The Sixth Amendment has been consistently interpreted to allow defendants to employ counsel in all federal prosecutions, including treason, felony, and misdemeanor cases. Similar provisions in the fifty state constitutions have been interpreted to allow defendants to retain counsel in state criminal prosecutions. Irrespective of state constitutional protection, the accused is protected by the federal constitution. In 1963 the Supreme Court held that the Sixth Amendment right to counsel applies to prosecutions in the state courts by way of the Due Process Clause of the Fourteenth Amendment. *Gideon v. Wainwright*, supra. Today, criminal defendants have the right to retain attorneys to represent them in all types of criminal prosecutions, whether in state court, in federal court, or before military tribunals.

## Indigency and the Right to Counsel

Although criminal defendants have the right to employ attorneys to represent them, many defendants are too poor to afford private counsel. To what extent does the law mandate that they be provided counsel at public expense?

**indigency** Poverty. In context, the inability to afford an attorney.

In 1790 Congress first addressed the issue of **indigency** in the context of federal criminal prosecutions for capital crimes. The Federal Crimes Act of 1790, 1 Stat. 112, required federal judges to assign counsel to indigent defendants in capital cases, at least where defendants requested representation. Some states emulated the act of Congress by providing for appointed counsel in capital cases, but most did not.

### The Scottsboro Case

In a highly publicized case in the early 1930s, the Supreme Court held that the Fourteenth Amendment required states to observe the requirement long since imposed on federal courts by Congress. *Powell v. Alabama*, 287 U.S. 45, 53 S.Ct. 55, 77 L.Ed. 158 (1932). In the "Scottsboro case," as it has become known, several black youths were charged with raping two white women. Within a week of being arrested, the defendants were tried, convicted, and sentenced to death, all without meaningful assistance of counsel. The Supreme Court reversed their convictions:

> In light of the . . . ignorance and illiteracy of the defendants, their youth, the circumstances of public hostility, the imprisonment and the close surveillance of the defendants by the military forces, the fact that their friends and families were all in other states and communication with them necessarily difficult, and above all that they stood in deadly peril of their lives . . . we think that . . . the failure of the trial court to make an effective appointment of counsel was . . . a denial of due process within the meaning of the Fourteenth Amendment. 287 U.S. at 71, 53 S.Ct. at 65, 77 L.Ed. at 171 (1932).

Relying heavily on its reasoning in *Powell v. Alabama*, the Supreme Court held four years later that the Sixth Amendment requires federal courts to appoint counsel for indigent defendants in all felony cases. *Johnson v. Zerbst*, 304 U.S. 458, 58 S.Ct. 1019, 82 L.Ed. 1461 (1938). Subsequently, Congress passed the Criminal Justice Act of 1964, 18 U.S.C.A. § 3006A, which provided that all indigent defendants in federal criminal cases are entitled to appointed counsel.

In the wake of *Powell v. Alabama*, many states adopted laws creating a right to counsel at state expense, at least in capital cases. Some states went further by providing counsel for all indigent defendants in felony prosecutions. In states where appointed counsel was not a legal requirement, it was not uncommon for trial judges to appoint new members of the bar to represent indigent felony defendants *pro bono* (free of charge).

In *Betts v. Brady*, 316 U.S. 455, 62 S.Ct. 1252, 86 L.Ed. 1595 (1942), the Supreme Court held that state courts were under no federal constitutional obligation to provide counsel to indigent defendants. Writing for the Court, Justice Owen Roberts concluded that "while want of counsel in a particular case may result in a conviction lacking in such fundamental fairness, we cannot say that the Amendment embodies an inexorable command that no trial for any offense, or in any court, can be fairly conducted and justice afforded to a defendant who is not represented by counsel." 316 U.S. at 473, 62 S.Ct. at 1262, 86 L.Ed. at 1607.

**The *Gideon* Decision**

In 1963 the Supreme Court under Chief Justice Earl Warren overturned *Betts v. Brady* and held that the Fourteenth Amendment requires states to provide counsel to indigent defendants in all felony cases. In his opinion for a unanimous bench in *Gideon v. Wainwright*, supra, Justice Hugo Black observed,

> From the very beginning, our state and national constitutions and laws have laid great emphasis on procedural and substantive safeguards designed to assure fair trials before impartial tribunals in which every defendant stands equal before the law. This noble ideal cannot be realized if the poor man charged with crime has to face his accusers without a lawyer to assist him. 372 U.S. at 344, 83 S.Ct. at 796–797, 9 L.Ed.2d at 805.

> Because the *Gideon* decision was made retroactive, it allowed numerous persons serving time in state prisons to win their freedom by seeking writ of *habeas corpus* in the state and federal courts. In Florida, where the *Gideon* case originated, the state was forced to release or retry hundreds of convicted criminals. Other states experienced similar challenges. Today, *Gideon v. Wainwright* has come to be widely accepted by state officials who recognize that representation by counsel is essential to the fair and effective functioning of the adversary system of justice.

## JURISPRUDENCE

*Gideon v. Wainwright*, 372 U.S. 335, 83 S.Ct. 792, 9 L.Ed.2d 799 (1963)

Clarence Earl Gideon, a 51 year-old indigent "drifter" who had been in and out of jails all his adult life, was charged with felonious breaking and entering. At trial, he requested that the court appoint an attorney to represent him. The court refused, citing the Florida law that required appointment of counsel for indigent defendants only in capital cases. While serving his sentence in the Florida State Prison, Gideon unsuccessfully challenged his conviction in the Florida Supreme Court on a writ of *habeas corpus*. He then obtained review by the U.S. Supreme Court on a writ of certiorari. In a unanimous decision, the Court reversed Gideon's conviction. Writing for the Court, Hugo Black opined that "[t]he right of one charged with a crime to counsel may not be deemed fundamental and essential to fair trials in some countries, but it is in ours." Black observed that "any person haled into court, who is too poor to hire a lawyer, cannot be assured a fair trial unless counsel is provided for him."

## JURISPRUDENCE

*Scott v. Illinois*, 440 U.S. 367, 99 S.Ct. 1158, 59 L.Ed.2d 383 (1979)

Aubrey Scott was convicted of shoplifting and fined $50; however, Scott was unable to afford counsel to represent him. The statute under which Scott was prosecuted set the maximum penalty for shoplifting at a $500 fine and/or one year in jail. At his summary trial, Scott requested the appointment of counsel; however, the trial court denied his request. In a 5–4 decision, the Supreme Court held that the Sixth and Fourteenth Amendments require "that no indigent criminal defendant be sentenced to a term of imprisonment unless the State has afforded him the right to assistance of appointed counsel in his defense." However, the Court also held that the Sixth and Fourteenth Amendments "do not require a state trial court to appoint counsel for a criminal defendant, such as Scott, who is charged with a statutory offense for which imprisonment upon conviction is authorized but not imposed." Therefore, the Court explained that *Argersinger v. Hamlin* "limits the constitutional right to appointed counsel in state criminal proceedings to a case that actually leads to imprisonment." Dissenting, Justice William Brennan opined: "The Court, in an opinion that at best ignores the basic principles of prior decisions, affirms Scott's conviction without counsel because he was sentenced only to pay a fine. In my view, the plain wording of the Sixth Amendment and the Court's precedents compel the conclusion that Scott's uncounseled conviction violated the Sixth and Fourteenth Amendments and should be reversed."

### Indigent Misdemeanor Defendants

In 1972 the Supreme Court extended the *Gideon* decision to encompass defendants who were sentenced to jail terms for misdemeanors. *Argersinger v. Hamlin*, 407 U.S. 25, 92 S.Ct. 2006, 32 L.Ed.2d 530 (1972). But the Court's decision left unresolved the question of whether counsel had to be provided to misdemeanor defendants who faced possible jail terms, as distinct from those who are actually sentenced to jail. In 1979 the Court opted for the **actual imprisonment standard.** *Scott v. Illinois*, 440 U.S. 367, 99 S.Ct. 1158, 59 L.Ed.2d 383 (1979). The actual imprisonment standard poses a problem for judges, for if an indigent defendant to a misdemeanor charge is denied counsel and is subsequently found guilty, the judge is barred from imposing a jail term. To do so would be a constitutional violation likely to result in a reversal of the defendant's conviction. This places the judge in the anomalous position of having to consider the sentence before determining the guilt or innocence of the accused. As a result, several states have gone beyond the federal constitutional requirement announced in *Scott v. Illinois* by providing counsel to indigent defendants in all misdemeanor cases where defendants face possible jail terms.

**actual imprisonment standard** The standard governing the applicability of the federal constitutional right of an indigent person to have counsel appointed in a misdemeanor case. For the right to be violated, the indigent defendant must actually be sentenced to jail or prison after having been tried without appointed counsel.

### Representation of Indigent Persons at Pretrial Proceedings

Most people think of the right to counsel in terms of a defendant being represented at trial. Although this might be the most important stage of the criminal process for a defendant who pleads not guilty, most criminal cases do not go to trial. For the defendant who elects to plead guilty, the pretrial procedures are critically important. The right of indigent persons to be provided counsel extends to many pretrial procedures. The U.S. Supreme Court has specifically identified a number of critical stages where counsel must be provided to indigent persons. Such **critical pretrial stages** include preliminary hearings, *White v. Maryland*, 373 U.S. 59, 83 S.Ct. 1050, 10 L.Ed.2d 193 (1963); lineups after charges have been filed against the accused, *United States v. Wade*, 388 U.S. 218, 87 S.Ct. 1926, 18 L.Ed.2d 1149 (1967); postindictment interrogations, *Massiah v. United States*, 377 U.S. 201, 84 S.Ct. 1199, 12 L.Ed.2d 246 (1964); and arraignments, *Hamilton v. Alabama*, 368 U.S. 52, 82 S.Ct. 157, 7 L.Ed.2d 114 (1961).

**critical pretrial stages** Significant procedural steps that occur before a criminal trial. A defendant has the right to counsel at these critical stages.

**Alternative Means of Providing Counsel to Indigent Persons**

The representation provided to indigent defendants may take the form of a public defender or an attorney appointed ad hoc by the court. Many states have established successful public defender systems. In most states that use this system, the public defender is an elected official provided with funds to hire a staff of lawyers, much like the public prosecutor. In other states, indigent defendants still depend largely on ad hoc appointment of counsel. Very often the attorneys appointed to represent indigent defendants in noncapital cases are new members of the bar with limited trial experience. Remuneration for appointed counsel tends to be modest.

There remains considerable controversy over which method of providing counsel is more cost effective and which method more effectively meets a state's constitutional responsibilities. Proponents of the public defender system note that public defenders are full-time specialists in criminal law, whereas appointed counsel may be relatively inexperienced in the field. Critics of the public defender system express concern about the constant contact between public defenders and prosecutors. They argue that this undermines the adversary system, resulting in a routinization of the criminal process in which the interests of the accused become subordinated to a bureaucratic effort to maximize efficiency in the processing of cases.

Sometimes the public defender's office has a conflict in which codefendants want to pursue inconsistent defenses. In such instances, an outside attorney should be appointed. If trial counsel representing multiple defendants brings a conflict of interest to the judge's attention, separate counsel must be appointed unless the judge determines that the risk of conflict is remote. *Holloway v. Arkansas*, 435 U.S. 475, 98 S.Ct. 1173, 55 L.Ed.2d 426 (1978). Most states have statutes providing for the appointment of private counsel in instances where public defenders have conflicts, but even in the absence of such statutes, courts generally take the position that they have the inherent authority to make such appointments.

**Determining Who Is Indigent**

Federal law leaves the determination of indigency to the discretion of the courts. This is also the case in most states. See, e.g., Ala. Rule Crim. Proc. 6.3. Courts tend to be liberal in this regard, refusing to equate indigency with destitution, and are generally inclined to appoint counsel if the cost of hiring a lawyer would prevent the defendant from making bail.

After arrest, the accused is asked to complete a form to elicit information about employment, income, assets, and liabilities. Before the defendant's first appearance in court, judicial staff members will attempt to verify the accuracy of the defendant's statement. This information is then passed along to assist the magistrate in determining whether the defendant is entitled to appointed counsel. In most jurisdictions, more than 75 percent of felony defendants are classified as indigent. Some state statutes provide for an assessment of an attorney's fee against a defendant who is represented by the public defender's office. See, e.g., West's Ann. Cal. Penal Code § 987.8. An indigent defendant may be assessed the costs of appointed counsel, and these costs may be collected at some later time if the defendant becomes solvent. See *Fuller v. Oregon*, 417 U.S. 40, 94 S.Ct. 2116, 40 L.Ed.2d 642 (1974).

## Self-Representation

The Supreme Court has held that there is a constitutional right to represent oneself in a criminal prosecution. *Faretta v. California*, 422 U.S. 806, 95 S.Ct. 2525, 45 L.Ed.2d 562 (1975). In *Faretta*, the Court said that the defendant's legal knowledge or skill

**self-representation** Also
known as a pro se defense,
representing oneself in a
criminal case.

has no bearing on the right to **self-representation**. However, the Court stressed that the defendant who waives the right to counsel and proceeds *pro se* (Latin meaning "for oneself") must do so "knowingly and intelligently." Critics of the *Faretta* decision believe that criminal law and procedure have become too complex and technical to permit the nonlawyer defendant to engage in effective self-representation. They argue that due process requires that defendants be represented by trained counsel, lest fundamental fairness be denied. As the Supreme Court recognized in *Powell v. Alabama*,

> Even the intelligent and educated layman has small and sometimes no skill in the science of the law. If charged with a crime, he is incapable, generally, of determining for himself whether the indictment is good or bad. He is unfamiliar with the rules of evidence. Left without the aid of counsel he may be put on trial without a proper charge, and convicted upon incompetent evidence, or evidence irrelevant to the issue or otherwise inadmissible. He lacks both the skill and knowledge adequately to prepare his defense, even though he may have a perfect one. He requires the guiding hand of counsel at every step in the proceedings against him. Without it, though he be not guilty, he faces a danger of conviction because he does not know how to establish his innocence. 287 U.S. 45, 69, 53 S.Ct. 55, 64, 77 L.Ed. 158, 170 (1932).

Despite the potential dangers of the *pro se* defense, the Supreme Court held in *Faretta* that the Constitution places the defendant's "free choice" above the need for effective representation in a criminal trial. The constitutional issue aside, many lawyers have said that "the defendant who chooses to represent himself has a fool for a client."

In 1984 the Supreme Court ruled that "a defendant does not have a constitutional right to receive personal instruction from the trial judge on courtroom procedure. Nor does the Constitution require judges to take over chores for a *pro se* defendant that would normally be attended to by trained counsel as a matter of course." *McKaskle v. Wiggins*, 465 U.S. 168, 183–184, 104 S.Ct. 944, 954, 79 L.Ed.2d 122, 136–137 (1984). Numerous appellate decisions from state courts have emphasized that before approving self-representation by a criminal defendant, the trial court must conduct a thorough *Faretta* hearing to determine whether the defendant has competently and intelligently exercised the right to choose self-representation. Basic to the conduct of such a hearing is that the trial judge must make the defendant aware of the dangers and disadvantages of self-representation. The objective is to ensure that the defendant seeking to represent himself or herself makes such choice only after being fully informed of the disadvantages of self-representation. Failure to conduct a thorough *Faretta* hearing can result in reversal of a conviction. See, for example, *State v. Chavis*, 644 P.2d 1202 (Wash. App. 1982), in which the court held that the trial judge's questions to the defendant must reveal the defendant's understanding and not merely consist of questions that call for a simple "yes" or "no" response.

But once a defendant has made the choice "knowingly and intelligently," the trial court is not required to give the defendant instructions on the law. This is illustrated by a 1993 decision of the California Supreme Court, reversing lower state courts. In *People v. Barnum*, 64 P.3d 788 (Cal. 2003), the state supreme court ruled that a trial court is not required to advise self-represented defendants of the privilege against compelled self-incrimination. Moreover, the constitutional right to self-representation does not imply a right to obstruct the workings of the criminal process. A trial judge may terminate self-representation by a defendant who engages in obstructionist conduct. *Illinois v. Allen*, 397 U.S. 337, 90 S.Ct. 1057, 25 L.Ed.2d 353 (1970).

Judges sometimes appoint standby counsel to assist defendants who choose self-representation. There are two principal advantages: (1) standby counsel can be available to answer questions by a *pro se* defendant; and (2) if it is necessary to terminate the *pro se* defense because of misconduct, standby counsel is available to complete the case.

Although a defendant has the right to self-representation, he or she may not be represented by another person who is not a member of the bar. Nor may a defendant force an unwilling attorney to represent him or her. *Wheat v. United States*, 486 U.S. 153, 108 S.Ct. 1692, 100 L.Ed.2d 140 (1988). By the same token, a trial judge does have the discretion to deny an attorney's motion to withdraw from representation—after, of course, examining counsel's reasons for wanting to withdraw.

## Disposition of Petty Offenses

**citation** A summons to appear in court, often used in traffic violations and other minor offenses.

Petty (or petit) offenses are minor misdemeanors for which fines or short jail terms are the only prescribed modes of punishment. Usually, police issue citations rather than arrest people for such offenses. Common traffic violations fall under the category of petty offenses, as do most violations of local ordinances. Many states have decriminalized routine traffic violations altogether. This means that an officer who stops a motorist for committing such an infraction has no authority to make an arrest (unless, of course, there is probable cause to believe the motorist has committed another offense for which he or she may be arrested). Rather, the officer simply issues the motorist a **citation**. In other jurisdictions in which minor traffic violations are still considered criminal offenses, legislatures have passed **cite and release statutes** that instruct officers to issue citations rather than arrest motorists who are stopped only for minor traffic offenses.

**cite and release statutes** Laws permitting or requiring police officers to issue citations instead of making arrests for traffic violations or other minor misdemeanors or infractions.

One who is cited for an infraction or minor misdemeanor may simply elect to waive the right to appear in court to contest the charge, in which case he or she is required to pay a predetermined fine. If the individual appears in court to contest the charges, the entire matter is typically resolved in one proceeding. Under most statutes decriminalizing minor traffic violations, the court must find that there is a preponderance of evidence to support the citation. If the court so finds, the cited party is ordered to pay a fine (along with court costs), but there is no criminal record because the infraction is a civil one. In the case of the minor misdemeanor, the accused may plead guilty or no contest, in which case guilt is pronounced and the sentence is imposed immediately. If the plea is not guilty, the court conducts a **summary trial** and determines guilt or innocence according to the reasonable doubt standard.

**summary trial** A trial conducted by a trial court to determine guilt or innocence in minor misdemeanor cases where defendants plead not guilty.

Although defendants clearly have a right to hire attorneys to represent them in minor misdemeanor cases, few exercise this right. Most people would rather go it alone before the magistrate. If they lose, which is highly probable, they typically pay a fine, which tends to be substantially less expensive than hiring an attorney. As noted earlier, the Supreme Court has said that there is no constitutional right for indigent persons to have counsel appointed in such minor cases except where defendants are actually sentenced to jail terms. *Scott v. Illinois*, supra.

## The Initial Court Appearance

In major misdemeanor and felony cases, the procedure is much more complex and protracted. Typically, individuals charged with felonies are placed under arrest before any appearance in court. However, all persons placed under arrest must promptly be taken before a court of law. The purpose of the initial appearance is to begin the formal charging process. Essentially, the magistrate must perform three important functions at the initial appearance: (1) the charges must be read so that the accused knows exactly what he or she is being charged with; (2) the accused must be informed of relevant constitutional rights, including the right to remain silent and the right to counsel; and (3) a determination must be made of whether the accused should be released pending trial or remanded to custody to await the disposition of the case. As we shall discuss, the court may order the defendant to post bond in order to ensure future court appearances. If so, the amount of bail is determined at this time.

All jurisdictions require the prompt appearance of an arrestee before a court of law, but what constitutes "prompt"? Many jurisdictions require a suspect to be brought before a magistrate for an initial appearance within twenty-four hours after arrest. See, e.g., Fla. R. Crim. P. Rule 3.130(a). However, the U.S. Supreme Court has ruled that suspects may be detained for as long as forty-eight hours before being taken before a magistrate. *County of Riverside v. McLaughlin*, 500 U.S. 44, 111 S.Ct. 1661, 114 L.Ed.2d 49 (1991).

Rule 5(a) of the Federal Rules of Criminal Procedure provides that a person arrested for a federal offense shall be taken before a magistrate "without unnecessary delay" for a first appearance. Under the so-called *McNabb–Mallory* rule (see *McNabb v. United States*, 318 U.S. 332, 63 S.Ct. 608, 87 L.Ed. 819 [1943], and *Mallory v. United States*, 354 U.S. 449, 77 S.Ct. 1356, 1 L.Ed.2d 1479 [1957]), confessions made during periods of detention that violate the prompt presentment requirement of Rule 5(a) are inadmissible at trial. Under 18 U.S.C.A. § 3501(c), however, Congress provided that a confession made within six hours after arrest is not rendered inadmissible solely because of a delay in bringing the accused before the magistrate.

In *Alvarez-Sanchez v. United States*, 975 F.2d 1396 (9th Cir. 1992), the U.S. Court of Appeals for the Ninth Circuit reversed a federal counterfeiting conviction because of a delay in the pretrial process. The defendant was originally arrested on a Friday by state authorities on state charges. A search of his home turned up evidence of counterfeit U.S. currency. On Monday, federal agents took the defendant into custody and obtained a confession. Because of congestion in court, the defendant was not taken before a federal magistrate until Tuesday. The Ninth Circuit held that the confession could not be used as evidence because of the delay in the first appearance. In reversing the Court of Appeals, the Supreme Court held that the promptness requirement is inapplicable where an accused person is first arrested on state charges and is later turned over to federal authorities on related charges. As Justice Clarence Thomas explained, "Until a person is arrested or detained for a federal crime, there is no duty, obligation, or reason to bring him before a judicial officer 'empowered to commit persons charged with offenses against the laws of the United States,' and therefore, no 'delay' under § 3501(c) can occur." *United States v. Alvarez-Sanchez*, 511 U.S. 350, 358, 114 S.Ct. 1599, 1604, 128 L.Ed.2d 319, 328 (1994).

# Pretrial Release and Pretrial Detention

The immediate goal for anyone who has been arrested and confined to jail is to secure release as soon as possible. Beyond the obvious desirability of freedom, an accused who remains at liberty can be of considerable assistance to defense counsel in locating witnesses and being able to confer with counsel outside the jail setting. In addition, a person who remains at liberty can usually pursue gainful employment and discharge family responsibilities pending the disposition of the criminal charges.

**pretrial release** Release of a defendant on bail or personal recognizance pending adjudication of criminal charges.

Granting an accused **pretrial release** is commonly referred to as granting bail. Judicial authority to grant a defendant bail originated in English common law. Statutes or court rules commonly grant judges this authority today. In determining whether a defendant is entitled to pretrial release, the court usually considers the accused's prior convictions (if any), character, employment history, and ties to family and the community, as well as the nature and scope of the current charges. In making these determinations, judges rely on reports prepared by court personnel. In the federal system, these reports are prepared by an agency called Pretrial Services. Increasingly, courts are requiring that arrested persons be drug tested. Although not used as evidence, the results of the drug test help the judge decide whether to grant pretrial release and whether to impose conditions upon that release. As with probation and parole, pretrial release may be contingent on a defendant's willingness to abide by certain conditions, such as avoiding certain places or activities or remaining at home after dark.

## Modes of Pretrial Release

**release on personal recognizance** Pretrial release of a defendant based solely on the defendant's promise to appear for future court dates.

**surety bond** A sum of money or property that is posted or guaranteed by a party, usually an insurer, to ensure the future court appearance of another person.

Pretrial release can take several forms. The four most common are **release on personal recognizance**, release to the custody of another, posting an individual bond, and posting a **surety bond**.

- *Personal recognizance.* A recognizance is a person's promise to appear in court as required. The defendant signs a guarantee to appear at all required proceedings and, in some cases, acknowledges certain restrictions on his or her activities.
- *Release to the custody of another.* The magistrate may release the defendant to the custody of some responsible person, often the defendant's attorney, who agrees to exercise custodial supervision and to assume responsibility for the defendant's required court appearances.
- *Posting an individual bond.* The defendant posts a bond agreeing to appear in court as required. The defendant may or may not be required to post an amount of cash or other security to guarantee the undertaking.

**bail bond** Sum of money posted to ensure a defendant's subsequent appearance in court.

- *Posting a surety bond.* Also known as a **bail bond**, this is the common method of securing pretrial release by paying a premium to a third party that agrees to post the bond for the accused. The magistrate sets the amount of a bond for the particular offense. Often, this is based on a schedule of bonds set by the judge of the court having jurisdiction over the offense. The defendant signs the bond, agreeing to appear as required. The bond is guaranteed by the defendant's surety, which means that should the defendant default, the surety, or bonding company, is bound to pay the court the amount of the bond (called the "penal sum"). A defendant usually pays a premium of about 10 percent of the amount of the bond and in most instances provides the surety with collateral to induce the surety to sign the bond. Sureties bonding a defendant are responsible for ensuring the defendant's appearance; therefore, they are commonly given the statutory authority to arrest an absconding defendant. To this end, sureties often employ **skip tracers**, who are, in effect, modern bounty hunters who seek out and return absconding defendants. When a surety promptly produces a defendant, it can usually recover any money forfeited to the court because of the defendant's failure to appear.

**skip tracers** People who track down alleged offenders who have fled to avoid prosecution. Also known as bounty hunters.

## The Issue of Excessive Bail

Recognizing the common-law practice of allowing pretrial release on bail, the Eighth Amendment to the federal constitution states that "excessive bail shall not be required." The Supreme Court has made it clear that the purpose of bail is to ensure the appearance of the accused in court, not to inflict punishment: "Bail set at a figure higher than an amount reasonably calculated to fulfill this purpose is 'excessive' under the Eighth Amendment." *Stack v. Boyle*, 342 U.S. 1, 5, 72 S.Ct. 1, 3, 96 L.Ed. 3, 6 (1951). However, the Supreme Court has never held that the Excessive Bail Clause of the Eighth Amendment is enforceable against the states via the Fourteenth Amendment, leaving the matter of **excessive bail** in state criminal cases to the state constitutions, legislatures, and courts.

The Illinois Code of Criminal Procedure provides that "the amount of bail shall be: (1) Sufficient to assure compliance with the conditions set forth in the bail bond; (2) Not oppressive; (3) Considerate of the financial ability of the accused." 725 Ill. Comp. Stat. Ann. § 5/110-5(b). Similarly, the Texas Code of Criminal Procedure states that "the power to require bail is not to be so used as to make it an instrument of oppression." Vernon's Tex. Code Crim. P. § 17.15(2).

## Pretrial Detention

The Eighth Amendment prohibition of "excessive bail" is vague regarding the existence of a constitutional right to pretrial release. However, the Supreme Court has ruled that there is no right to bail under the Eighth Amendment. *United States v. Salerno*, 481 U.S. 739, 107 S.Ct. 2095, 95 L.Ed.2d 697 (1987). The **Federal Bail Reform Act of 1984**, 18 U.S.C.A. § 3141 *et seq.*, allows federal courts to detain arrestees without bail on the ground of the arrestee's danger to the community, as

**excessive bail** Where a court requires a defendant to post an unreasonably large amount or imposes unreasonable conditions as a prerequisite for a defendant to be released before trial. The Eighth Amendment to the U.S. Constitution prohibits courts from requiring "excessive bail."

**Federal Bail Reform Act of 1984** An act that provides that a defendant charged with a federal crime may be denied bail if the prosecution can show that the defendant poses a threat to public safety.

---

### JURISPRUDENCE

*Stack v. Boyle*, 342 U.S. 1, 72 S.Ct. 1, 96 L.Ed. 3 (1951)

Loretta Starvus Stack and eleven other members of the Communist Party were arrested and charged with "subversive activities" in violation of the Alien Registration Act of 1940, better known as the Smith Act. Their bail was initially set at different amounts ranging from $2,500 to $100,000, but later was fixed "pending trial in the uniform amount of $50,000." Each defendant moved for a reduction in bail under the theory that the $50,000 was "excessive under the Eighth Amendment." The Government's only argument against lowering the bail was that four other individuals previously convicted under the Smith Act "had forfeited bail." While the Government presented no evidence relating specifically to Stack and the other

defendants, the U.S. District Court denied the motion to reduce bond. The defendants, who could not make the $50,000 bail, sought unsuccessfully to challenge their pretrial detention via habeas corpus. In reviewing the denial of relief by the U.S. Court of Appeals, the Supreme Court held that the bail was not "fixed by proper methods." The Court stated that bail "set before trial at a figure higher than an amount reasonably calculated to fulfill the purpose of assuring the presence of the defendant is 'excessive' under the Eighth Amendment." The Court went on to establish the standards for setting bail by stating that the amount of bail "must be based upon standards relevant to the purpose of assuring the presence of that defendant." The Court sent the case back to the District Court for new bail hearings.

well as the need to ensure future court appearances. First, the court must determine whether the government has established "by a preponderance of the evidence that the defendant either has been charged with one of the crimes enumerated in Section 3142(f)(1) or that the defendant presents a risk of flight or obstruction of justice." *United States v. Friedman*, 837 F.2d 48, 49 (2d Cir. 1988). If the government satisfies that burden, the court must determine whether there are "conditions or a combination of conditions which reasonably will assure the presence of the defendant at trial." *United States v. Shakur*, 817 F.2d 189, 195 (2d Cir. 1987).

**pretrial detention** Holding a defendant in jail pending trial.

Congress has set forth various factors that a court must consider in weighing the appropriateness of **pretrial detention.** Among these are the nature of the offense, the weight of the evidence against the suspect, the history and character of the person charged, and the nature and seriousness of the risk to the community. 18 U.S.C.A. § 3142(g). The statute provides for an adversary hearing on the issue of detention. The government must show by clear and convincing evidence that pretrial release will not reasonably ensure the appearance of the accused or the safety of other persons and the community. *United States v. Orta*, 760 F.2d 887 (8th Cir. 1985).

The judge or magistrate who denies pretrial release must prepare a written statement justifying the decision to detain the accused and direct that the detainee be afforded a reasonable opportunity for private consultation with counsel. 18 U.S.C.A. § 3142(i). Finally, the law provides for a prompt appellate review of the detention decision. 18 U.S.C.A. § 3145(c). In upholding the Bail Reform Act of 1984 against an Eighth Amendment challenge, the Supreme Court in *United States v. Salerno* said that "when Congress has mandated detention on the basis of a compelling interest other than prevention of flight, as it has here, the Eighth Amendment does not require release on bail." 481 U.S. at 754–755, 107 S.Ct. at 2105, 95 L.Ed.2d at 713–714.

The *Salerno* decision, although technically limited to the constitutionality of federal pretrial detention, suggests the validity of state laws or court decisions that deny bail to persons accused of violent crimes, especially where arrestees have a record of violent crime.

## JURISPRUDENCE

*United States v. Salerno*, 481 U.S. 739, 107 S.Ct. 2095, 95 L.Ed.2d 697 (1987)

Anthony Salerno and Vincent Cafaro, members of the Genovese crime family, were arrested after being charged with violating the Racketeer Influenced and Corrupt Organizations (RICO) Act as well as mail fraud, wire fraud, extortion, and various gambling offenses. On the government's motion, they were denied bail under the Bail Reform Act of 1984, which allows pretrial detention when the prosecution establishes by clear and convincing evidence that no conditions of release will ensure the safety of the community or any person. Concluding that the statute allows defendants to be punished for crimes they might commit in the future, the U.S. Court of Appeals found the Bail Reform Act to be facially unconstitutional. The

Supreme Court reversed, "given the Act's legitimate and compelling regulatory purpose and the procedural protections it offers" to the accused. The Court's examination of the legislative history revealed that the Act was not intended as pretrial punishment, but rather "as a potential solution to the pressing societal problem of crimes committed by persons on release" and to prevent "danger to the community." In effect, the Court held that there is no constitutional right to bail under the Eighth Amendment. In a forceful dissenting opinion, Justice Thurgood Marshall noted that the case "brings before the Court for the first time a statute in which Congress declares that a person innocent of any crime may be jailed indefinitely, pending the trial of allegations which are legally presumed to be untrue. . . ."

In many states, a defendant is ineligible for pretrial release if charged with a crime that is punishable by death or life imprisonment and if the "proof is evident or the presumption [of guilt] is great." See, e.g., *State v. Arthur*, 390 So.2d 717, 718 (Fla. 1980). In the majority of these states, before denying pretrial release, courts must determine whether the facts, viewed in the light most favorable to the state, are legally sufficient to sustain a verdict of guilty. See *Fontaine v. Mullen*, 366 A.2d 1138 (R.I. 1976).

# The Formal Charging Process

**subpoenas** Judicial orders to appear at a certain place and time to give testimony.

Prosecutors occupy a uniquely important role in the criminal justice system. The prosecutor decides whether to proceed with a criminal case and whether to negotiate charges with the defense, and must, at various stages of the process, demonstrate the veracity of the government's case to the satisfaction of the court. The prosecutor causes the court to issue **subpoenas** to compel the attendance of witnesses to testify, to bring in documents, and to provide nontestimonial physical evidence such as handwriting specimens, *United States v. Mara*, 410 U.S. 19, 93 S.Ct. 774, 35 L.Ed.2d 99 (1973), and voice exemplars, *United States v. Dionisio*, 410 U.S. 1, 93 S.Ct. 764, 35 L.Ed.2d 67 (1973).

State and federal prosecutors have broad discretion in deciding whether to proceed with criminal charges initiated by a complainant or the police. The prosecutor may decide to drop a case for a variety of reasons, ranging from insufficient evidence to a judgment that the criminal sanction is inappropriate in a given situation. Alternatively, the prosecutor may decide to proceed on a lesser charge.

The American Bar Association's *Standards Relating to the Prosecution and Defense Function* offers prosecutors guidelines for the exercise of their discretion in making the decision to charge. The standards admonish prosecutors not to be influenced by personal or political motivations and not to bring more charges, in number or degree, than can reasonably be supported at trial.

**prosecutorial discretion** The leeway afforded to prosecutors in deciding whether or not to bring charges and to engage in plea bargaining.

**Prosecutorial discretion** facilitates the widespread yet controversial practice of plea bargaining, which we discuss later in the chapter. Although very broad, prosecutorial discretion is not unlimited. The Equal Protection Clause of the Fourteenth Amendment is offended by selective prosecution. Prosecutors may not single out defendants for prosecution on the basis of race, religion, or other impermissible classifications. *Oyler v. Boles*, 368 U.S. 448, 82 S.Ct. 501, 7 L.Ed.2d 446 (1962).

One of the long-standing controversies in the criminal justice field is whether police and prosecutors unfairly target people on the basis of race in the enforcement of certain types of criminal prohibitions. In 1996 the U.S. Supreme Court made it more difficult for criminal defendants to make prosecutors respond to claims that they are engaging in racially motivated selective prosecution. *United States v. Armstrong, 517 U.S. 456, 116 S.Ct. 1480, 134 L.Ed.2d 687 (1996)*. A party making such a claim must show that similarly situated individuals of a different race were not prosecuted. Obviously, this is a difficult showing to make.

**prosecutorial immunity** A prosecutor's legal shield against civil suits stemming from his or her official actions.

Courts have not only cloaked prosecutors with broad discretion in determining whether to prosecute, but they have also long held prosecutors immune from civil actions for malicious prosecution, as long as they are acting within the scope of their offices. *Griffith v. Slinkard*, 44 N.E. 1001 (Ind. 1896). More recently, the U.S. Supreme Court has ruled that the same considerations that underlie **prosecutorial immunity** in tort actions require that prosecutors be immune from damages for deprivation of defendants' constitutional rights under 42 U.S.C.A. § 1983. See *Imbler v. Pachtman*, 424 U.S. 409, 96 S.Ct. 984, 47 L.Ed.2d 128 (1976).

*United States v. Armstrong,* 517 U.S. 456, 116 S.Ct. 1480, 134 L.Ed.2d 687 (1996)

Five African Americans charged with selling crack cocaine persuaded lower courts to dismiss the charges against them because prosecutors refused to explain how they chose which crack cocaine cases to pursue. Dividing 8–1, the Court held that defendants who make selective prosecution claims must show that people of other races were not prosecuted for the same crimes. "To establish a discriminatory effect in a race case, the claimant must show that similarly situated individuals of a different race were not prosecuted," Chief Justice William H. Rehnquist wrote for the court. Because the defendants did not make such a showing, the prosecutors were not required to respond to their allegation of discrimination. In his solo dissent, Justice Stevens stressed "the need for judicial vigilance over certain types of drug prosecutions," referring to the fact that the overwhelming majority of individuals charged with offenses involving crack cocaine are black.

## Determining the Sufficiency of the Government's Case

**information** A document filed by a prosecutor under oath charging one or more persons with commission of a crime.

Assuming that the prosecutor decides to proceed with criminal charges, an examination of the sufficiency of the evidence generally follows. The purpose of this procedure is to ensure that there is probable cause for trial. This determination is made by a magistrate, a grand jury, or both. In some jurisdictions, the prosecutor files a document called an **information** in the appropriate court of law. An information is a formal accusatorial document detailing the specific charges against a defendant. After the filing of the information, a preliminary hearing may be requested to determine the sufficiency of the evidence in support of the information. In Florida, a defendant who is not charged in an information or indictment within twenty-one days from the date of arrest or service of the capias shall have a right to an adversary preliminary hearing on any felony charge. Fla. R. Crim. P. 3.133(b)(1). In other jurisdictions, the prosecutor must obtain an indictment from a grand jury. Some jurisdictions employ a combination of both mechanisms. In Tennessee, for example, a person accused of a felony must be indicted by a grand jury; a preliminary examination before the grand jury proceeding is available at the option of the accused. Tenn. R. Crim. P., Rule 5.

## The Preliminary Hearing

In a preliminary hearing (not to be confused with the initial appearance), a judge or magistrate examines the state's case to determine whether there is probable cause to bind the accused over to the grand jury or (in the absence of a grand jury

### Limitations on Prosecutorial Conduct

**CASE-IN-POINT**

E. J. Reagan was charged with torturing a child and assault with intent to do great bodily harm. The prosecutor agreed to drop the charges if Reagan could pass a lie detector test. The defendant agreed and passed the test. Pursuant to the agreement, the prosecutor filed a *nolle prose-qui* (Latin for "not wish to prosecute") and the charges were dismissed. Subsequently, the prosecutor became convinced that the polygraph examination was flawed. He then filed a new complaint on the same charges. The defendant was tried and convicted. The Michigan Supreme Court reversed the conviction and discharged the defendant. The court said that "a pledge of public faith in this instance gave force to an unwise agreement." *People v. Reagan,* 235 N.W.2d 581 (Mich. 1975).

requirement) hold the accused for trial. The Supreme Court has said that when an arrest is made without a warrant, a preliminary hearing is constitutionally required in the absence of grand jury review to determine the sufficiency of an information. *Gerstein v. Pugh*, 420 U.S. 103, 95 S.Ct. 854, 43 L.Ed.2d 54 (1975). *Gerstein* does not require preliminary hearings to be full-blown adversarial proceedings. Nevertheless, most states do provide for open hearings with both parties represented. Typically, in a preliminary hearing the defense has the privilege of cross-examining witnesses for the prosecution and can learn the details and strengths of the state's case. The state can preserve testimony of witnesses who may balk at testifying at the trial. Thus, the preliminary hearing serves the interests of both the prosecution and the defense by providing an inquiry into probable cause for arrest and detention, a screening device for prosecutors, and an opportunity for the defense to discover the prosecutor's case.

# The Grand Jury

In many jurisdictions, prosecutors must obtain an indictment or "true bill" from the grand jury in addition to, or instead of, the preliminary hearing. The Fifth Amendment to the U.S. Constitution states that "[n]o person shall be held to answer for a capital, or otherwise infamous crime, unless on a presentment or indictment of a grand jury."

The Supreme Court has held that states are not bound by the Fourteenth Amendment to abide by the grand jury requirement imposed on the federal courts by the Fifth Amendment. *Hurtado v. California*, 110 U.S. 516, 4 S.Ct. 111, 28 L.Ed. 232 (1884). Nevertheless, about half the states have constitutional provisions or statutes requiring the use of grand juries in certain types of criminal cases. Other states use grand juries primarily in an investigatory or supervisory capacity.

The grand jury is an institution deeply rooted in English common law. For a detailed discussion, see *Costello v. United States*, 350 U.S. 359, 362, 76 S.Ct. 406, 408, 100 L.Ed. 397, 401 (1956). At common law, the grand jury comprised twenty-three persons, at least twelve of whom had to agree to hand down an indictment. Today, federal grand juries comprise sixteen to twenty-three persons, Fed. R. Crim. P. 6(a), but the "twelve votes for indictment" rule applies in every case, Fed. R. Crim. P. 6(f). States vary in the size of grand juries, but in every state at least a majority of grand jurors must agree that there is probable cause in order to hand down an indictment against the accused. In Texas, for example, the grand jury consists of twelve jurors. Texas Const., Art. V, § 13. At least nine grand jurors must agree to hand down an indictment. Vernon's Tex. Code Crim. P. § 20.19.

## Exclusion of Minorities from Grand Juries

As with trial jurors, the selection of grand jurors must not systematically exclude certain groups in the community. A defendant may be able to obtain a reversal of a conviction on this basis. For example, in *Castaneda v. Partida*, 430 U.S. 482, 97 S.Ct. 1272, 51 L.Ed.2d 498 (1977), the Supreme Court reversed a conviction after finding that Mexican Americans had been grossly underrepresented on a grand jury that indicted a Mexican American defendant. In his opinion for the Court, Justice Harry Blackmun outlined the necessary steps to make a case that such a violation has occurred:

> [I]n order to show that an equal protection violation has occurred in the context of grand jury selection, the defendant must show that the procedure employed resulted

in substantial underrepresentation of his race or of the identifiable group to which he belongs. The first step is to establish that the group is one that is a recognizable, distinct class, singled out for different treatment under the laws, as written or as applied. . . . Next, the degree of underrepresentation must be proved, by comparing the proportion of the group in the total population to the proportion called to serve as grand jurors, over a significant period of time. . . . This method of proof, sometimes called the "rule of exclusion," has been held to be available as a method of proving discrimination in jury selection against a delineated class. . . . Finally, a selection procedure that is susceptible of abuse or is not racially neutral supports the presumption of discrimination raised by the statistical showing. . . . Once the defendant has shown substantial underrepresentation of his group, he has made out a *prima facie* case of discriminatory purpose, and the burden then shifts to the State to rebut that case. 430 U.S. at 494, 97 S.Ct. at 1280, 51 L.Ed.2d at 510–511 (1977).

## Functions and Powers of the Grand Jury

Historically, the grand jury acted as a shield to prevent unfounded charges and arbitrary and overzealous prosecution. Today, grand juries seldom refuse to hand down indictments sought by prosecutors, causing some critics to question the institution's use as a safeguard for the rights of the accused. Perhaps this perception has led several states to adopt the information/preliminary hearing mechanism in lieu of the grand jury. In most midwestern and western states, the grand jury is seldom used to charge persons with crimes.

The grand jury, like the magistrate presiding over the preliminary hearing, examines testimony and other evidence the prosecution has collected against the accused. Unlike the preliminary hearing, the grand jury proceeding is normally closed: the defendant is generally not represented by counsel or even present at the proceeding. Although controversial, grand jury secrecy encourages uninhibited testimony by witnesses and prevents the circulation of derogatory statements about persons who are ultimately not indicted. *Pittsburgh Plate Glass Co. v. United States*, 360 U.S. 395, 79 S.Ct. 1237, 3 L.Ed.2d 1323 (1959). Grand jury secrecy also protects grand jurors from intimidation and possible reprisals. In a federal grand jury, except while it is deliberating or voting, all proceedings must be recorded by a court reporter or by a suitable recording device. Traditionally, proceedings before a grand jury remain secret; however, a trial judge has discretion to allow disclosure subject to conditions. Fed. R. Crim. P. 6(e). In the states, testimony before the grand jury is not always transcribed, and if it is, access to transcripts is either limited or nonexistent.

After the prosecutor has presented testimony and physical evidence, the members of the grand jury vote on whether to hand down an indictment. Rules that determine grand jury indictments vary among jurisdictions, but in no case can a grand jury return a true bill unless a majority of grand jurors vote to indict.

Grand juries possess the authority to compel the appearance of witnesses, to subpoena documents, to hold individuals in contempt, and to grant immunity from prosecution in exchange for testimony. Immunity is of two kinds. Transactional immunity bars any further prosecution of the witness for the specific transaction as to which the witness testified. Use immunity is more limited, barring only the use of the witness's testimony against the witness in a subsequent prosecution. Federal grand juries are authorized to grant use immunity. 18 U.S.C.A. § 6002. The basic purpose of granting immunity is to permit compulsion of testimony that otherwise would be privileged by the Fifth Amendment. *United States v. Weiss*, 599 F.2d 730 (5th

Cir. 1979). Many states follow the federal statute; some states go further and permit grand juries to grant transactional immunity. The federal statutory bar against the use of immunized testimony applies equally to federal and state proceedings. *In re Grand Jury Proceedings*, 860 F.2d 11 (2d Cir. 1988).

## Rights of Witnesses and Suspects

The Supreme Court has held that grand jury witnesses retain their Fifth Amendment privileges against compulsory self-incrimination. *Lefkowitz v. Turley*, 414 U.S. 70, 94 S.Ct. 316, 38 L.Ed.2d 274 (1973). Nevertheless, through a limited grant of immunity, a grand jury can override a witness's refusal to answer questions on Fifth Amendment grounds. The Supreme Court has also held that a grand jury's grant of immunity must be coextensive with the privilege against self-incrimination. Use immunity satisfies this requirement; transactional immunity is not required by the Constitution. *Kastigar v. United States*, 406 U.S. 441, 92 S.Ct. 1653, 32 L.Ed.2d 212 (1972). Witnesses testifying before grand juries have no right to be represented by counsel, *In re Groban's Petition*, 352 U.S. 330, 77 S.Ct. 510, 1 L.Ed.2d 376 (1957), although some jurisdictions allow witnesses to consult with counsel outside the grand jury room. An attorney's appearance before a grand jury on behalf of a witness is generally thought to cause unnecessary delays and violate the secrecy of the proceeding.

In only a few states does the defendant have a right to appear before the grand jury to confront his or her accusers. Like witnesses, a suspect has no federal constitutional right to be represented by counsel inside the grand jury room. *United States v. Mandujano*, 425 U.S. 564, 96 S.Ct. 1768, 48 L.Ed.2d 212 (1976).

## Evidence before the Grand Jury

Many rules of evidence that apply to the criminal trial do not apply to the grand jury. *Costello v. United States*, 350 U.S. 359, 76 S.Ct. 406, 100 L.Ed. 397 (1956). For example, hearsay evidence is generally admissible, whereas at trial it is not admitted over the defendant's objection. Moreover, evidence excluded from trial on Fourth or Fifth Amendment grounds is admissible before the grand jury. *United States v. Calandra*, 414 U.S. 338, 94 S.Ct. 613, 38 L.Ed.2d 561 (1974). The theory is that the grand jury is an investigative body and that any infringement of the rights of the accused can be corrected in subsequent adversary court proceedings. Notwithstanding that a grand jury may consider evidence that is inadmissible at trial, it may not violate a valid evidentiary privilege (see Chapter 6) established under the Constitution, statutes, or the common law. *Branzburg v. Hayes*, 408 U.S. 665, 92 S.Ct. 2646, 33 L.Ed.2d 626 (1972).

## Right to a Prompt Indictment

Under federal law an indictment must be filed within thirty days of arrest, 18 U.S.C.A. § 3161. Where delay in filing an indictment prejudices the presentation of a defense and is engaged in for an improper purpose, it violates the Due Process Clause. *United States v. Lovasco*, 431 U.S. 783, 795, 97 S.Ct. 2044, 52 L.Ed.2d 752 (1977). Prejudice in this context means the sort of deprivation that impairs a defendant's right to a fair trial. See *United States v. Elsbery*, 602 F.2d 1054 (2d Cir. 1979). In *United States v. Mmahat*, 106 F.3d 89 (5th Cir. 1997), the court said the defendant must show actual prejudice and deliberate design by the government to gain tactical

---

## JURISPRUDENCE

*United States v. Calandra*, 414 U.S. 338, 94 S.Ct. 613, 38 L.Ed.2d 561 (1974)

Federal agents searched John Calandra's place of business pursuant to a warrant authorizing seizure of bookmaking records and wagering paraphernalia. During the course of the search, an agent discovered and seized a document implicating Calandra in loansharking. As a result, a grand jury was convened to investigate loansharking, which subpoenaed Calandra to appear before it for the purposes of questioning him on the seized evidence. Calandra refused to testify on Fifth Amendment grounds against self-incrimination. Calandra then moved to suppress the loansharking evidence seized during the search of his office on the grounds that the affidavit supporting the warrant was insufficient and that the search exceeded the scope of the warrant. The trial court granted the motion and further ordered that Calandra did not have to answer any questions posed by the grand jury related to the loansharking evidence. However,

the Supreme Court held that "a witness summoned to appear and testify before a grand jury *may not* refuse to answer questions on the ground that they are based on evidence obtained from an unlawful search and seizure." The Court, speaking through Justice Powell, reinforced the notion that the exclusionary rule is a "judicially created remedy designed to safeguard Fourth Amendment rights generally through its deterrent effect on future unlawful police conduct, rather than a personal constitutional right of the party aggrieved." As a result of this purpose, the Court held that "allowing a grand jury witness to invoke the exclusionary rule would unduly interfere with the effective and expeditious discharge of the grand jury's duties, and extending the rule to grand jury proceedings would achieve only a speculative and minimal advance in deterring police misconduct at the expense of substantially impeding the grand jury's role." As a result, the exclusionary rule does not apply in grand jury proceedings.

---

advantage to establish a claim of preindictment delay. Usually a defendant attempts to meet this standard by demonstrating that the prosecution's delay resulted in the loss of documentary evidence or the unavailability of a key witness.

State courts generally take a similar approach. Illustrative is *State v. Smith*, 699 P.2d 711 (Utah 1985), where the court observed,

> A hard and fast rule that a prosecutor must file charges as soon as he has probable cause could result in the charging of innocent persons. Such a rule could also result in the acquittal of guilty persons by hampering the investigation of crimes. Therefore, a prosecutor is not required to file charges as soon as probable cause exists but before the prosecutor is reasonably satisfied that he will be able to establish the suspect's guilt beyond a reasonable doubt. For preaccusation delay to constitute reversible error, the delay must cause actual prejudice to the defendant's case and result in a tactical advantage for the prosecutor. *Id*. at 713.

# | Extradition

**extradition** The surrender of a person by one jurisdiction to another for the purpose of criminal prosecution.

**Extradition** is the surrender, on demand, of an individual accused or convicted of an offense committed within the territorial jurisdiction of the demanding government and outside the territory of the ceding government. See *Terlinden v. Ames*, 184 U.S. 270, 22 S.Ct. 484, 46 L.Ed. 534 (1902). The objective is to prevent the escape of persons who stand accused or convicted of crimes and to secure their return to the jurisdiction from which they fled.

In a mobile society such as ours, it is not uncommon for persons accused of crimes to flee across state lines to avoid prosecution. Anticipating this problem,

Article IV, Section 2 of the Constitution provides, "A Person charged in any State with Treason, Felony or any other crime, who shall flee from Justice, and be found in another state, shall on demand of the executive Authority of the State from which he fled, be delivered up, to be removed to the State having Jurisdiction of the crime."

To effectuate the constitutional provision, Congress has enacted statutes governing interstate extradition. 18 U.S.C.A. § 3182. Interstate extradition is a summary executive proceeding designed to enable each state to bring offenders to trial swiftly in the state where the alleged crime was committed. *Michigan v. Doran*, 439 U.S. 282, 99 S.Ct. 530, 58 L.Ed.2d 521 (1978). Every offense punishable by law in the jurisdiction where it was committed can subject the offender to extradition, but extradition is usually sought only in serious offenses. Frequently it is used to regain custody of parole violators, prison escapees, or persons who have "jumped bail."

Most states have adopted the Uniform Criminal Extradition Law, which sets out procedural rules for handling interstate extradition. The governor of the "demanding" state issues a requisition warrant seeking return of the fugitive. This is presented to the governor of the "asylum" state (that is, the state in which the fugitive is located). After investigation, the governor of the asylum state issues a warrant for the fugitive's arrest. An opportunity exists for the person sought as a fugitive to contest the extradition in a court of law in the asylum state. Often this challenge takes the form of a petition for a writ of habeas corpus challenging whether the petitioner is in fact the person charged or attacking the regularity of the proceedings. See, e.g., N.J. Stat. Ann. § 2A:160-18. Extradition proceedings seek the release of the prisoner who is to be extradited but do not focus on the issue of the prisoner's guilt or innocence.

Extradition of suspects or convicted criminals between nations is regulated by treaties, which usually provide that the crime involved must be a serious one in both nations and that the penalty for the person extradited will not be disproportionate to the crime. The United States does not have extradition treaties with all nations. Even where treaties are in force, some countries, including many European nations, will not extradite unless they are assured that the death penalty will not be imposed on a suspect. In addition, many nations will not extradite persons charged with offenses regarded as political offenses, such as treason, sedition, and espionage.

# Jurisdiction and Venue

**jurisdiction** The authority of a court to hear and decide certain categories of legal disputes. Jurisdiction relates to the authority of a court over the person, subject matter, and geographical area.

Before it may hear and adjudicate a case, a court must possess **jurisdiction** over the subject matter and the parties to the case. State courts have jurisdiction only over persons who commit crimes in their particular states. Of course, it is necessary for a court to acquire jurisdiction over a person before that individual can be tried for an offense. When a person is arrested, a court with jurisdiction over the offense acquires jurisdiction over that person. In other instances, the court acquires jurisdiction when an arrest warrant is issued following an indictment or after a capias is issued once a prosecutor files an information.

**venue** The location of a trial or hearing.

The term **venue** is sometimes confused with the concept of jurisdiction, but it is a distinct concept. Venue refers to the place of the trial, and its importance is underscored by the fact that it is twice mentioned in the U.S. Constitution. Article III, Section 2 provides, in part, "Trial shall be held in the State where the said crimes shall have been committed; but when not committed within the State, the Trial shall be at such Place or Places as the Congress may by law have directed." And the Sixth Amendment provides, "In all criminal prosecutions, the accused shall enjoy the right to a . . . public trial, by an impartial jury of the State and district wherein the crime shall have been committed."

The Sixth Amendment applies to state criminal trials via the Fourteenth Amendment. *Duncan v. Louisiana*, 391 U.S. 145, 88 S.Ct. 1444, 20 L.Ed.2d 491 (1968). State constitutions, statutes, or court rules usually mirror the provisions of the Sixth Amendment.

Federal courts sit in all fifty states, as well as in federal territories. In some states, federal court jurisdiction is divided into two or more districts. A federal offense is normally tried in the particular federal district where the crime was committed. State courts are usually organized by districts of one or more counties. Likewise, a state criminal case is tried in the particular jurisdiction (district, county, circuit, and so forth) where the offense was committed.

Although venue lies in the district where the offense was committed, there are unique situations in which the nature of the crime makes it difficult to determine in which of two districts the crime occurred. For example, consider the situation where a person fires a rifle across a county or state line, killing a victim in the adjoining county or state. A more probable scenario is a kidnapping in which the perpetrator takes the victim across county or state lines. Courts must resolve these jurisdictional quandaries according to the relevant statutes and precedents.

**change of venue** The removal of a legal proceeding, usually a trial, to a new location.

Defendants commonly seek a **change of venue** if they believe it is impossible to obtain a fair trial in the venue in which the crime occurred. Rule 21(a) of the Federal Rules of Criminal Procedure stipulates,

> Upon the defendant's motion, the court must transfer the proceeding as to that defendant to another district . . if the court is satisfied that there exists in the district where the prosecution is pending so great a prejudice against the defendant that the defendant cannot obtain a fair and impartial trial at any place fixed for holding court in that district.

State statutes and court rules generally contain similar provisions. Indeed, some states permit prosecutors, as well as defendants, to seek a change of venue. See, e.g., Fla. R. Crim. P. 3.240. In determining whether to grant a change of venue, courts consider a variety of factors, including (1) the nature of the pretrial publicity and the degree to which it has circulated in the community, (2) the connection of government officials with the release of the publicity, (3) the length of time elapsing between the dissemination of the publicity and the trial, (4) the severity and notoriety of the offense, (5) the area from which the jury is to be drawn, (6) other events occurring in the community that either affect or reflect the attitude of the community or individual jurors toward the defendants, and (7) any factor likely to affect the candor and veracity of the prospective jurors. See, e.g., *State v. Bell*, 315 So.2d 307 (La. 1975).

A defendant seeking a change of venue bears the burden of showing the necessity for the change. Changing venue can offend the community sense of justice in not having a trial take place within the community. In addition, it can create hardships and inefficiencies because of the need to transport witnesses and court personnel to sometimes-distant locations. Because a decision to change venue depends on many factors that can best be determined by the local judge, trial courts are accorded considerable discretion in determining whether to grant a motion to change venue in a criminal case.

# Joinder and Severance

**joinder of offenses** The uniting of different charges or counts alleged in an information or indictment into one case for trial.

Very often, a defendant stands accused of several distinct offenses arising from one set of related facts. Conceivably, each offense could be prosecuted separately, but it would be more efficient, in most instances, to prosecute such offenses jointly. Most state rules of criminal procedure follow the federal rule on **joinder of offenses**:

> (a) Joinder of Offenses. The indictment or information may charge a defendant in separate counts with 2 or more offenses if the offenses charged—whether felonies or misdemeanors or both—are of the same or similar character, or are based on the same act or transaction, or are connected with or constitute parts of a common scheme or plan.

> Fed. R. Crim. P. 8(a).

In determining whether to proceed on multiple criminal charges jointly or separately, a prosecutor must consider the Double Jeopardy Clause of the Fifth Amendment. This clause bars successive prosecutions for the "same offense." A particular set of actions by the defendant may constitute distinct violations of criminal law and yet be considered part of the same offense under the Double Jeopardy Clause. For example, in *Harris v. Oklahoma*, 433 U.S. 682, 97 S.Ct. 2912, 53 L.Ed.2d 1054 (1977), the Supreme Court held that a defendant could not be prosecuted for armed robbery after being convicted of felony murder for a homicide committed during the armed robbery "because proof of the underlying felony, i.e., armed robbery, was required to prove the intent necessary for the felony-murder conviction."

The basic test laid down by the Supreme Court for determining whether there are two separate offenses is "whether each provision [of the criminal law] requires proof of an additional fact that the other does not." *Blockburger v. United States*, 284 U.S. 299, 304, 52 S.Ct. 180, 182, 76 L.Ed. 306, 309 (1932). Separate statutory crimes need not be identical—either in constituent elements or in actual proof—to be the "same offense" within the meaning of the Double Jeopardy Clause of the Fifth Amendment. Thus, a defendant cannot be convicted of an offense and a lesser included offense. *Brown v. Ohio*, 432 U.S. 161, 97 S.Ct. 2221, 53 L.Ed.2d 187 (1977). State courts have held that a person cannot be convicted of two separate homicide charges where there is only one victim. See, e.g., *Wilcox v. Leapley*, 488 N.W.2d 654 (S.D. 1992).

## Severance of Charges

**severance of the charges** Conducting multiple trials for multiple charges, as distinct from joinder, which refers to trying all charged offenses at once. Where two or more related offenses are charged in a single indictment or information, the trial judge often grants a severance of the charges on the motion of either the defense or the prosecution.

Where two or more related offenses are charged in a single indictment or information, the trial judge ordinarily grants a **severance of the charges** on the motion of either the defense or prosecution if it is necessary to achieve a fair determination of the defendant's guilt or innocence on each offense. A defendant seeking severance bears the burden of showing that a joint trial would be so unfairly prejudicial that it would result in a miscarriage of justice. *United States v. Williams*, 10 F.3d 1070 (4th Cir. 1993).

Trial judges have considerable discretion in this area, but there are certain situations in which severance seems mandatory. For example, a defendant charged with two offenses might want to testify in one case but decline to testify in the other. Or a defendant might be charged in one case with possession of a firearm by a convicted felon and in another case with robbery. To sustain the charge in the firearm case, the prosecution would have to show the defendant's prior conviction of a felony. Such a showing would obviously be prejudicial to defense of the robbery charge being heard by the same jury.

# Joinder and Severance of Parties

As with multiple offenses, prosecutors generally have broad discretion in deciding whether to prosecute multiple defendants separately or jointly. However, here too there are constitutional considerations. For example, it has been held that separate trials are required where the prosecution plans to use against one defendant evidence that has no relevance to the other defendants. *Kotteakos v. United States*, 328 U.S. 750, 66 S.Ct. 1239, 90 L.Ed. 1557 (1946).

Rule 8(b) of the Federal Rules of Criminal Procedure authorizes joinder of two or more defendants in the same indictment "if they are alleged to have participated in the same act or transaction or the same series of acts or transactions constituting an offense or offenses." However, rule 14(a) states that the court "may grant" a severance "if it appears that a defendant or the government is prejudiced by a joinder of offenses or of defendants." Thus, federal judges try to determine whether the failure to sever prevents the moving party from getting a fair trial. Denial of a motion for severance is generally held to be an abuse of discretion if the defendants present conflicting and irreconcilable defenses and if there is a danger that the jury will infer that such conflict demonstrates that both are guilty. *United States v. Tarantino*, 846 F.2d 1384 (D.C. Cir. 1988).

**joinder and severance of parties** The uniting or severing of two or more parties charged with a crime or crimes.

Rules governing **joinder and severance of parties** are usually spelled out in the rules of criminal procedure in each jurisdiction. The purpose of such rules is to ensure that when two or more persons are charged jointly, each will receive a fair determination of guilt or innocence. The Tennessee Rules of Criminal Procedure are fairly typical in this respect:

> The Court, on motion of the State or on motion of the defendant . . . shall grant a severance of defendants if:
>
> I. before trial, it is deemed necessary to protect a defendant's right to a speedy trial or it is deemed appropriate to promote a fair determination of the guilt or innocence of one or more defendants; or
>
> II. during trial, with the consent of the defendant to be severed, it is deemed necessary to promote a fair determination of the guilt or innocence of one or more defendants.
>
> Tenn. R. Crim. P., Rule 14(c)(2).

Severance of defendants is almost always granted when jointly charged defendants pursue inconsistent defenses, when their interests are otherwise antagonistic, or when one defendant chooses to testify and the other does not. Severance is required when a codefendant's confession implicates another, nontestifying codefendant. *Bruton v. United States*, 391 U.S. 123, 88 S.Ct. 1620, 20 L.Ed.2d 476 (1968).

The Florida courts developed the following procedural rule to cope with the *Bruton* problem. The rule gives the state three options when the trial court determines that a defendant's statement is not admissible against a codefendant.

> If a defendant moves for a severance of defendants on the ground that an oral or written statement of a co-defendant makes reference to him but is not admissible against him, the court shall determine whether the State will offer evidence of the statement at the trial. If the State intends to offer the statement in evidence, the court shall order the State to submit its evidence of such statement for consideration by the court and counsel for defendants and if the court determines that such

## JURISPRUDENCE

*Bruton v. United* States, 391 U.S. 123, 88 S.Ct. 1620, 20 L.Ed.2d 476 (1968)

Bruton and his codefendant, Evans, were tried jointly and convicted for armed postal robbery. While Evans did not testify, a postal inspector testified that Evans confessed that he and Bruton committed the robbery. As a result of the testimony, "the trial judge instructed the jury that, although Evans's confession was evidence against him it was inadmissible hearsay against [Burton] and had to be disregarded in determining [Bruton's] guilt or innocence." The Court of Appeals affirmed Bruton's conviction in view of the trial judge's jury instructions. The Supreme Court held that due to "the substantial risk that the jury, despite instructions to the contrary, looked to the incriminating statements in determining [Bruton's] guilt, the admission of Evans's confession in the joint trial violated his right of cross-examination secured by the Confrontation Clause of the Sixth Amendment." The Court reversed Bruton's conviction and remanded the case for a new trial.

statement is not admissible against the moving defendant, it shall require the State to elect one of the following courses: (i) a joint trial at which evidence of the statement will not be admitted; (ii) a joint trial at which evidence of the statement will be admitted after all references to the moving defendant have been deleted, provided the court determines that admission of such evidence with deletions will not prejudice the moving defendant; or (iii) severance of the moving defendant. Fla. R. Crim. P. 3.152.

## Redaction of Incriminating Statements Introduced in a Joint Trial

**redaction** Editing out portions of a transcript in order to maintain secrecy of someone's identity or other information.

One of the options allowed by the rule is **redaction** (editing) of a confession or incriminating statement made by one defendant so that it may be used at a joint trial without implicating any other defendant. In *Gray v. Maryland*, 523 U.S. 185, 118 S.Ct. 1151, 140 L.Ed.2d. 294 (1998), the Supreme Court addressed the redaction problem in a case that resulted in Kevin Gray's conviction for involuntary manslaughter. Gray's codefendant, Bell, had given a confession to the police in which he said that Bell, Gray, and Vanlandingham had participated in a beating that resulted in the victim's death. Vanlandingham later died, and Bell and Gray were tried jointly for murder. The trial judge, after denying Gray's motion for a separate trial, permitted a police detective to read Bell's redacted confession into evidence. The detective said the word "deleted" or "deletion" whenever Gray's name or Vanlandingham's name appeared. The state then introduced into evidence a written copy of Bell's confession with Gray's and Vanlandingham's names omitted, leaving in their place blank white spaces separated by commas. The Maryland Court of Appeals upheld Gray's conviction. A sharply divided Supreme Court vacated the decision and stated that "redactions that replace a proper name with an obvious blank, the word 'delete,' a symbol, or similarly notify the jury that a name has been deleted are similar enough to *Bruton's* unredacted confession as to warrant the same legal results." 523 U.S. at 195, 118 S.Ct. at 1156, 140 L.Ed.2d. at 302. Writing for the Court's four dissenters, Justice Antonin Scalia contended that allowing the confession to be admitted with limiting instructions "represents a reasonable practical accommodation of the interests of the state and the defendant in the criminal justice process." 523 U.S. at 200, 118 S.Ct. at 1159, 140 L.Ed.2d. at 306.

## Severance in Cases Where Defendants Pursue Mutually Contradictory Defenses

Lower federal courts have generally taken the position that defendants are entitled to separate trials if their defenses are mutually contradictory. See, e.g., *United States v. Tarantino*, supra. In 1993 the U.S. Supreme Court addressed the issue. Writing for the Court, Justice Sandra Day O'Connor made it clear that severance of defendants is not required, as a matter of law, when defendants present mutually antagonistic defenses. Rather, severance is required only if the trial court finds a serious risk that a joint trial would compromise a specific trial right of a properly joined defendant or prevent the jury from making a reliable judgment about guilt or innocence. Circumstances that may require a severance include a case in which joinder results in the admission of evidence that the jury could consider against one defendant but not another, or a case in which evidence exculpating one defendant would have to be excluded at a joint trial. But in federal courts, simply relying on antagonistic defenses without articulating any specific prejudice is not sufficient to require that a trial court sever the trial of a codefendant. *Zafiro v. United States*, 506 U.S. 534, 113 S.Ct. 933, 122 L.Ed.2d 317 (1993).

# Pretrial Motions

**pretrial motions** Requests for rulings or orders before the commencement of a trial.

**Pretrial motions** are written requests to the court on behalf of the government or the defendant. They are the means by which defense counsel and prosecutors seek to attain certain objectives before trial. Typically, many motions are available to both the defense and the prosecution during the pretrial phase of a criminal case. One common set of motions deals with joinder and severance of offenses and defendants, as previously discussed. Other common pretrial motions include the following:

**motion to dismiss** A formal request to a trial court to dismiss the criminal charges against the defendant.

1. *Motion to dismiss.* Frequently the defense files a **motion to dismiss** the indictment or information, alleging (a) that the government's allegations, assuming the truth thereof, do not allege a crime, or that the accusatorial document is not correct in form; or (b) that the undisputed facts do not establish a case of *prima facie* guilt against the defendant. Often the court's determination on a motion to dismiss is not final, as the government may be given an opportunity to amend its documentation. In addition, a defendant may file a motion to dismiss on grounds of double jeopardy or having been granted immunity.

2. *Motion to determine the competency of the accused to stand trial.* In cases where the defendant is mentally disturbed, the defendant may be declared incompetent to stand trial on the motion of the defense. In federal cases the trial judge must determine whether the defendant has (1) a rational and factual understanding of the pending proceedings and (2) the ability to consult with his or her lawyer with a reasonable degree of rational understanding. *Dusky v. United States*, 362 U.S. 402, 80 S.Ct. 788, 4 L.Ed.2d 824 (1960). State courts use varying standards to determine whether an accused person is competent to stand trial. The differences are largely semantic. Some state courts apply the federal standard, with the additional requirement that the accused must understand the range of penalties that would attend conviction and be able to perceive the adversarial nature of the trial process. A person restored to competency may then be tried for the criminal offense originally charged. States generally require a defendant to prove incompetency by a preponderance of the evidence. In *Cooper v. Oklahoma*, 517

U.S. 348, 116 S.Ct. 1373, 134 L.Ed.2d 498 (1996), the Supreme Court held that a law that required defendants to prove incompetence to stand trial by clear and convincing evidence violated the Due Process Clause.

3. *Motion to suppress evidence obtained through unlawful search or seizure.* Evidence obtained in violation of a defendant's Fourth Amendment rights cannot be used against the defendant in a criminal trial. *Weeks v. United States*, 232 U.S. 383, 34 S.Ct. 341, 58 L.Ed. 652 (1914); *Mapp v. Ohio*, 367 U.S. 643, 81 S.Ct. 1684, 6 L.Ed.2d 1081 (1961). When the defense moves to suppress evidence on Fourth Amendment grounds, the court generally holds an evidentiary hearing. If the defense is successful in causing the **suppression of evidence**, it may undermine the government's case, leading to a favorable ruling on a subsequent defense motion to dismiss. When the state's case depends solely on the evidence sought to be suppressed, the defense's attempt is often referred to as a **dispositive motion**.

4. *Motion to suppress confessions, admissions, or other statements made to the police.* A defendant is constitutionally entitled to a determination by the court of whether a confession is voluntary before the confession is made known to the jury. *Jackson v. Denno*, 378 U.S. 368, 84 S.Ct. 1774, 12 L.Ed.2d 908 (1964). The motion to suppress the confession is the means of bringing this issue before the court. The motion can initiate a number of related inquiries, such as whether the confession was obtained in violation of the *Miranda* rules. Generally, before ruling on a motion to suppress a confession, the court holds an evidentiary hearing. Again, the disposition of such a motion can have a significant impact on the prosecution of a criminal case. If the confession is crucial to the prosecution's case, a favorable ruling on the motion to suppress may lead to a dismissal of the charges.

5. *Motion to suppress a pretrial identification of the accused.* This motion by the defendant is designed to determine whether the pretrial identification procedures employed by the police in having an eyewitness identify the accused violated the due process standards outlined in *Neil v. Biggers*, 409 U.S. 188, 93 S.Ct. 375, 34 L.Ed.2d 401 (1972). The court's inquiry here focuses on whether the identification procedures were impermissibly suggestive to the witness (see Chapter 4).

6. *Motion to require the prosecution to disclose the identity of a confidential informant.* The prosecution is not ordinarily required to disclose the identity of a confidential informant who merely furnishes the probable cause on which an arrest or search is predicated. Nevertheless, if the informant was an "active participant" in the offense, the prosecution may be required to disclose the informant's identity. The test calls for balancing the public interest in protecting the free flow of information to the police against the individual's right to prepare a defense. See *Roviaro v. United States*, 353 U.S. 53, 77 S.Ct. 623, 1 L.Ed.2d 639 (1957). Trial judges have considerable discretion in ruling on this motion.

7. *Motion for change of venue.* The defendant, and in some instances the government, may move for a change of venue (that is, place of trial) on the ground that a fair and impartial trial cannot be had where the case is pending. In recent years, heightened media coverage of crime and criminal prosecutions has generated tremendous concern over the ability of defendants to receive a fair trial. The concern usually focuses on the difficulty of selecting an impartial jury when potential jurors have been exposed to intensive newspaper, radio, and television coverage of a crime. The Supreme Court, in *Sheppard v. Maxwell*, 384 U.S. 333, 86 S.Ct. 1507, 16 L.Ed.2d 600 (1966), established some guidelines for dealing with the effects of pretrial publicity (see Chapter 6). Since then, an increasing number of defendants have filed motions seeking a change of venue.

**suppression of evidence** Judicial rule forbidding the use of evidence in a criminal trial where the evidence was obtained in violation of the defendant's constitutional rights. See **exclusionary rule**.

**dispositive motion** A motion made to a court where the ruling on the motion will determine the outcome of the case.

**continuance** Delay of a judicial proceeding on the motion of one of the parties.

8. *Motion for a continuance.* Either the government or the defendant may seek a **continuance**, or postponement, of the trial. A variety of grounds may be asserted, including illness or emergency that makes it difficult or impossible for the defendant, prosecutor, defense counsel, or an important witness to be present as scheduled; the unavailability of a significant witness or piece of documentary evidence; or the lack of adequate time to prepare for trial. Appellate courts consistently hold that there is no abuse of discretion unless a party can show that specific prejudice has resulted to the defendant as a result of the denial of the requested continuance.

**deposition** The recorded sworn testimony of a witness; not given in open court.

9. *Other pretrial motions.* Other common pretrial motions include motions to take a **deposition** to preserve the testimony of an infirm witness or one who might not be available for trial; to appoint an interpreter; to inspect the minutes of the grand jury proceeding; to compel the prosecutor to disclose evidence that might be favorable to the accused; and to disqualify the trial judge on grounds of bias, close relationship to parties, or that the judge will be a material witness.

# Arraignment

**plea of not guilty** A formal answer to a criminal charge in which the accused denies guilt and thus exercises the right to a trial.

**plea of guilty** A formal answer to a criminal charge in which the accused acknowledges guilt and waives the right to a trial.

**Alford plea** A plea of guilty with a protestation of innocence.

**no-contest plea** Also called *nolo contendere,* a defendant's plea to a criminal charge that, although it is not an admission of guilt, generally has the same effect as a plea of guilty. A no-contest plea is usually not admissible in evidence in a subsequent civil suit.

**factual basis** When a defendant pleads guilty to an offense, the court requires a recitation of facts (usually by counsel) to establish that proof is available to show the defendant's guilt of the elements of the offense.

The arraignment is the accused's first appearance before a court of law with the authority to conduct a criminal trial. At this stage of the process, the accused must enter a plea to the charges contained in the indictment or information. There are several options. The accused may choose to enter a **plea of not guilty**, in which case the plea is noted and a trial date is set. The accused may enter a **plea of guilty**, in which case no trial is necessary. Instead, guilt is simply pronounced and sentencing follows, either immediately or at some future court appearance, after a presentence investigation has been completed (see Chapter 7). A plea of guilty containing a protestation of innocence, sometimes called an ***Alford* plea**, can be made when a defendant intelligently concludes that his or her interests require the entry of a guilty plea. *North Carolina v. Alford*, 400 U.S. 25, 91 S.Ct. 160, 27 L.Ed.2d 162 (1970). In some jurisdictions, the accused has the option of pleading *nolo contendere* (no contest). The **no-contest plea**, although functionally equivalent to a guilty plea has the advantage that it generally cannot be construed as an admission of guilt in a related civil suit. Although a judgment is entered on a no-contest plea, the defendant neither admits nor denies anything.

Because a plea of guilty or *nolo contendere* represents a waiver of constitutional rights, it is essential that the plea be made knowingly and voluntarily. The Federal Rules of Criminal Procedure preclude trial judges from accepting such a plea unless the court determines that the plea is "voluntary and not the result of force or threats or of promises apart from a plea agreement." Fed. R. Crim. P. 11(b)(2). In addition to determining voluntariness, a judge must decide whether a **factual basis** exists for a plea of guilty or *nolo contendere.* A factual basis is necessary to ensure that the accused does not admit to an offense when his or her conduct does not fall within the bounds of the government's accusations. See, e.g., *United States v. Montoya-Camacho*, 644 F.2d 480 (5th Cir. 1981).

Most states have adopted similar rules of procedure to ensure that pleas are voluntary and comply with constitutional requirements. For example, rule 3.170(k) of the Florida Rules of Criminal Procedure specifies that "[n]o plea of guilty or *nolo contendere* shall be accepted by a court without first determining . . . that the circumstances surrounding the plea reflect . . . its voluntariness and that there is a factual basis for the plea."

Rules concerning voluntariness and factual basis generally do not specify any precise method to be followed by the court. Judges employ various methods to determine voluntariness. Often these methods include interrogation of the defendant by the judge, and sometimes by the prosecutor and/or defense counsel. The extent of questioning often depends on the defendant's educational level and maturity. Frequently, judges ask indigent defendants about their satisfaction with court-appointed counsel. The objective is to establish that no improper inducements have been made to secure a plea, that the defendant understands the basic constitutional rights incident to a trial, that these rights are being waived, and that he or she comprehends the consequences of the plea. *Boykin v. Alabama*, 395 U.S. 238, 89 S.Ct. 1709, 23 L.Ed.2d 274 (1969).

In determining that a factual basis exists for the defendant's plea, judges often have the prosecutor briefly outline available proof to establish a *prima facie* case of the defendant's guilt. A more extensive inquiry is usually necessary for specific-intent crimes. The thoroughness of the court's determination of voluntariness and factual basis becomes important if a defendant later moves to withdraw a plea and enter a plea of not guilty.

Federal Rule of Criminal Procedure 11(d) provides that after a court accepts a plea, but before it imposes sentence, a defendant may withdraw a plea of guilty or *nolo contendere* if the defendant can show a just reason for requesting the withdrawal. "The fact that a defendant has a change of heart prompted by his reevaluation of either the Government's case against him or the penalty that might be imposed is not a sufficient reason to permit withdrawal of a plea." *United States v. Gonzalez*, 970 F.2d 1095, 1100 (2d Cir. 1992). Subsection (e) stipulates that after sentencing a defendant may not withdraw a plea, and that the plea may be set aside only on direct appeal or collateral attack. The rules of procedure in state courts generally allow the court, in its discretion, to permit a defendant to withdraw a plea for good cause before sentencing. But once a sentence has been imposed, a defendant must demonstrate that a manifest injustice requires correction in order to be permitted to withdraw a plea. See, e.g., *State v. Barney*, 570 N.W.2d 731 (1997).

## Plea Bargaining

In most jurisdictions, more than 90 percent of felony suspects arraigned plead guilty or no contest. Very often the guilty plea is the result of a bargain struck between the defense and the prosecution. In a plea bargain, the accused agrees to plead guilty in exchange for a reduction in the number or severity of charges or a promise by the prosecutor not to seek the maximum penalty allowed by law. Often bargains are quite specific in terms of punishment to be imposed, conditions of probation, restitution to the victim, and so forth.

Plea negotiations are subject to the approval of the trial court. In most instances, the bargain is arranged by experienced and knowledgeable counsel on both sides and is readily approved by the court. If the court is unwilling to approve the plea bargain, the defendant must choose between withdrawing the guilty plea (and thus going to trial) and accepting the plea bargain with such modifications as the judge may approve. Once the court has accepted a guilty plea pursuant to a plea bargain, the court cannot unilaterally alter it without permitting the defendant the opportunity to withdraw the plea.

In some jurisdictions, judges participate directly in plea bargaining discussions. The justification for this practice is that a judge can guide the parties to an equitable and expeditious resolution of the case. On the other hand, some courts disfavor the participation of a trial judge in plea bargaining discussions on the basis that the power and position of the judge may improperly influence the defendant to enter a guilty plea. See, e.g., *Perkins v. Court of Appeals*, 738 S.W.2d 276, 282 (Tex. Crim. App. 1987).

Plea bargaining has been sharply criticized by observers with different perspectives on the criminal process. Some critics fault plea bargaining for reducing the severity of criminal penalties. Others view plea bargaining as an unconstitutional effort to deprive defendants of their right to a fair trial. Plea bargaining has never been popular, but few who oppose the practice stop to consider the tremendous costs and delays that would result if the numerous cases currently resolved through plea bargaining were to go to trial.

Despite frequent criticism, the practice of plea bargaining is widespread among American jurisdictions today. In addition to permitting a substantial conservation of prosecutorial and judicial resources, plea bargaining provides a means by which, through mutual concession, the parties can obtain a prompt resolution of criminal proceedings with the benefits that flow from final disposition of a case. The plea bargain, or negotiated sentence, enables the parties to avoid the delay and uncertainties of trial and appeal, and it permits swift and certain punishment of law violators with a sentence tailored to the circumstances of the case at hand.

Despite constitutional attacks, the Supreme Court has upheld the practice of plea bargaining. In *Brady v. United States*, 397 U.S. 742, 753, 90 S.Ct. 1463, 1471, 25 L.Ed.2d 747, 759 (1970), the Court said that "we cannot hold that it is unconstitutional for the State to extend a benefit to a defendant who in turn extends a substantial benefit to the State." In a subsequent case, the Court was even more sanguine about plea bargaining:

> The disposition of criminal charges by agreement between the prosecutor and the accused, sometimes loosely called "plea bargaining," is an essential component of the administration of justice. Properly administered, it is to be encouraged. If every criminal charge were subjected to a full-scale trial, the States and the Federal Government would need to multiply by many times the number of judges and court facilities. *Santobello v. New York*, 404 U.S. 257, 260, 92 S.Ct. 495, 498, 30 L.Ed.2d 427, 432 (1971).

The plea bargain necessarily entails a waiver of the constitutional right to trial, so it must be examined by the trial court to determine whether the accused

---

**CASE-IN-POINT**

### The Realities of Plea Bargaining

Paul LaVallee was charged in a New Hampshire court with the crime of aggravated assault. He elected to plead not guilty, was convicted at trial, and was sentenced to ten to thirty years in prison. LaVallee brought a habeas corpus action challenging his sentence, arguing that it was disproportionate to the sentences given to defendants who agreed to plead guilty. He claimed that it was impermissible for the courts to give harsher sentences to defendants who insist on their constitutional right to a trial. The state supreme court rejected LaVallee's challenge. The court said that the defendant's argument ignored "the realities of the plea bargaining process." Further, it noted that "[i]n this state, we have rejected the notion that it is impermissible to compensate one who pleads guilty by extending him a proper degree of leniency."

*LaVallee v. Perrin*, 466 A.2d 932 (N.H. 1983).

*Bordenkircher v. Hayes*, 434 U.S. 357, 98 S.Ct. 663, 54 L.Ed.2d 604 (1978)

Here the Supreme Court held that the Due Process Clause of the Fourteenth Amendment "is not violated when a state prosecutor carries out a threat made during plea negotiations to have the accused reindicted on more serious charges on which he is plainly subject to prosecution if he does not plead guilty to the offense with which he was originally charged." Paul Lewis Hayes was charged with uttering a forged instrument, which carried a prison term of two to ten years. The prosecutor offered to recommend a sentence of five

years if Hayes would plead guilty. Hayes decided not to plead guilty and the prosecutor went back to the grand jury and obtained an indictment under Kentucky's habitual offender law. Hayes, who had two prior felony convictions, was found guilty and sentenced to life in prison as a habitual offender. Justice Potter Stewart, writing for the Supreme Court, stated that "though to punish a person because he has done what the law allows violates due process, there is no such element of punishment in the 'give-and-take' of plea bargaining as long as the accused is free to accept or reject the prosecutor's offer."

has knowingly waived his or her rights and agreed to plead guilty without coercion by the state. *Boykin v. Alabama*, supra. Despite such procedural protections, cases still arise challenging the fundamental fairness of certain plea bargaining tactics. See, e.g., *Bordenkircher v. Hayes*, 434 U.S. 357, 98 S.Ct. 663, 54 L.Ed.2d 604 (1978), where the Court found no due process violation when the prosecutor threatened during plea negotiations to reindict the defendant on a more serious charge if the defendant refused to plead guilty to the lesser crime originally charged.

## Availability of Compulsory Process

**compulsory process** The power to subpoena witnesses to appear in court.

The Sixth Amendment to the Constitution guarantees a defendant in a criminal case the right to "have the **compulsory process** of the law to obtain witnesses in his favor." The Compulsory Process clause was applied to the states in *Washington v. Texas*, 388 U.S. 14, 87 S.Ct. 1920, 18 L.Ed.2d 1019 (1967), although the right previously existed in state constitutions and laws. The method of securing this right is through use of a subpoena, which is a formal written demand available in all federal and state jurisdictions. Subpoenas are available to both the prosecution and defense.

Rule 17 of the Federal Rules of Criminal Procedure implements this right at the federal level by allowing a defendant to have the court issue a subpoena for witnesses, documents, and objects and providing for service of such subpoenas. Court clerks, and sometimes judges, issue subpoenas. They are usually served by a marshal in the federal system and by a sheriff or process server in the state system. There are costs associated with subpoenas, but the federal rule provides for issuance without cost when a defendant is financially unable to pay the costs, as long as the witness is "necessary to an adequate defense." States generally have statutes or court rules closely paralleling the federal rule.

In the pretrial stages, challenges may be made to the right to subpoena a witness, document, or object. Challenges are usually based on the contention that such witnesses or items are not material to issues in the case. Judges have considerable discretion in ruling on these challenges.

# Pretrial Discovery

The courts have long recognized a prosecutorial duty to disclose to the defense exculpatory information (that is, information that tends to vindicate the accused). This duty is based on the fundamental concept of our system of justice—that individuals accused of crimes must be treated fairly. The Supreme Court has stated that "the suppression by the prosecution of evidence favorable to the accused upon request violates due process where the evidence is material either to guilt or punishment, irrespective of the good faith or bad faith of the prosecution." *Brady v. Maryland*, 373 U.S. 83, 87, 83 S.Ct. 1194, 1996, 10 L.Ed.2d 215, 218 (1963).

The Supreme Court has held that, in addition to substantive exculpatory evidence, evidence tending to impeach (i.e., challenge the credibility of) prosecution witnesses falls within *Brady's* definition of evidence favorable to an accused. Therefore, under *Brady* a defendant is entitled to disclosure of information that might be used to impeach government witnesses. See *United States v. Bagley*, 473 U.S. 667, 105 S.Ct. 3375, 87 L.Ed.2d 481 (1985).

**exculpatory evidence**
That which exonerates or tends to exonerate a person from fault or guilt.

Generally, the defense must request the disclosure of the **exculpatory evidence**. If the defense is unaware of the existence of the evidence, however, such a request is impossible. The Supreme Court has held that failure to request disclosure is not necessarily fatal to a later challenge based on *Brady*, but it may significantly affect the standard for determining materiality. *United States v. Agurs*, 427 U.S. 97, 96 S.Ct. 2392, 49 L.Ed.2d 342 (1976).

In a similar vein, it has been held to be a denial of due process if a prosecutor knowingly allows perjured testimony to be used against the accused. *Mooney v. Holohan*, 294 U.S. 103, 55 S.Ct. 340, 79 L.Ed. 791 (1935); *Alcorta v. Texas*, 355 U.S. 28, 78 S.Ct. 103, 2 L.Ed.2d 9 (1957).

Evidence that impeaches the credibility of a prosecution witness is considered to be exculpatory. The Supreme Court of Virginia in 1993 held that before the prosecution is obliged to produce evidence, it must be established that the undisclosed evidence is exculpatory and material to the defendant's guilt or punishment. Accordingly, where the record did not establish that there was any exculpatory evidence in the defendant's accomplices' polygraph tests, the state supreme court said that the trial court did not err in denying the defendant's motion seeking to discover the results of the tests. *Ramdass v. Commonwealth*, 437 S.E.2d 566 (Va. 1993).

**pretrial discovery** The process by which the defense and prosecution interrogate witnesses for the opposing party and gain access to the evidence possessed by the opposing party prior to trial.

Most states have now adopted liberal rules pertaining to **pretrial discovery**, rules designed to avoid unfairness to the defense resulting from abdications of prosecutorial duty. Using appropriate pretrial motions, the defense and prosecution can gain access to the evidence possessed by the opposing party. Thus, pretrial discovery not only enhances the fairness of the criminal process but also militates against surprises at trial.

## Discovery in the Federal Courts

*Jencks* **Act** The common name for a federal statute that permits a defendant to review a witness's prior written or recorded statement, but only after the witness has testified on direct examination for the government.

Discovery in a criminal case is somewhat more limited in federal courts than in state courts. Under the provisions of 18 U.S.C.A. § 3500, a federal criminal defendant is not entitled to inspect a statement or report prepared by a government witness "until said witness has testified on direct examination in the trial of the case." After a witness testifies, the government, on proper request of the defense, must produce that portion of any statement or report that relates to the subject matter on which the witness has testified. The federal statute is commonly referred to as the *Jencks* **Act** because its effect was first recognized in *Jencks v. United States*, 353 U.S. 657, 77

### CASE-IN-POINT

## The Government's Failure to Preserve Evidence

Police obtained a warrant to search Barton's home based on an officer's affidavit that he had smelled marijuana during a prior consensual entry of the home. At a pretrial suppression hearing, Barton claimed that the officer could not have smelled the marijuana plants that were seized because they had no odor. But by the time of the suppression hearing, the plants had rotted because the police had not ventilated the bag in which they stashed the plants. The court recognized that the destruction by the government of evidence that tends to impeach allegations in an affidavit demonstrating

probable cause for a search warrant may violate due process principles. Nevertheless, the defendant did not prevail. Rather, the U.S. Court of Appeals for the Ninth Circuit court relied upon the principle declared by the U.S. Supreme Court in *Arizona v. Youngblood*, 488 U.S. 51, 109 S.Ct. 333, 102 L.Ed.2d 281 (1988). There, the Court held that the failure of law enforcement officers through mere negligence and not in bad faith to preserve evidence that might have been helpful to the defendant does not violate a defendant's right to due process of law.

*United States v. Barton*, 995 F.2d 931 (9th Cir. 1993).

---

S.Ct. 1007, 1 L.Ed.2d 1103 (1957). In *Jencks*, a defendant was allowed to obtain for impeachment purposes previous statements made to government agents by prosecution witnesses. Courts have indicated that the principal purpose of the *Jencks* Act is to aid a defendant's right to cross-examination. In some instances the trial judge must make an **in camera** **inspection** of documents where the government asserts that the documents contain statements not relevant to the subject matter to which the witness has testified. The government is not required under the *Jencks* Act to turn over victims' statements to defendants during a pretrial suppression hearing. *United States v. Williams*, 10 F.3d 1070 (4th Cir. 1993).

*in camera* inspection A trial judge's private consideration of evidence.

## The Right to a Speedy Trial

right to a speedy trial Constitutional right to have an open public trial conducted without unreasonable delay.

The Sixth Amendment to the Constitution guarantees the defendant the **right to a speedy trial**. In *Barker v. Wingo*, 407 U.S. 514, 92 S.Ct. 2182, 33 L.Ed.2d 101 (1972), the Supreme Court refused to mandate a specific time limit between the filing of charges and the commencement of trial but did adopt a balancing test to determine whether a defendant was denied the right to a speedy trial. Under this test, courts must consider (1) the length of the delay, (2) the reasons for the delay, (3) the defendant's assertion of the right, and (4) prejudice to the defendant.

Speedy Trial Act of 1974 This federal statute provides specific time limits for pretrial and trial procedures in the federal courts. For example, an indictment must be filed within thirty days of arrest, and trial must commence within seventy days after the indictment.

In response to the Court's decision in *Barker v. Wingo*, Congress enacted the **Speedy Trial Act of 1974**, 18 U.S.C.A. § 3161. The act provides specific time limits for pretrial and trial procedures in the federal courts. For example, an indictment must be filed within thirty days of arrest, and trial must commence within seventy days after the indictment. If the defendant's trial does not begin within the time limitations and the defendant enters a motion—before the trial's start or entry of a guilty plea—to dismiss the charges, the district court must dismiss the charges. There are a number of exceptions to the time limits, especially where delays are caused by defendants' motions. Questions have arisen in the lower federal courts as to whether a defendant can simply waive the application of the Speedy Trial Act. In *Zedner v. United States*, 547 U.S. 489, 126 S.Ct. 1976, 164 L.Ed.2d 749 (2006), the Supreme Court ruled that a defendant's prospective waiver of the application of the Speedy Trial Act was ineffective.

The Speedy Trial Clause of the Sixth Amendment applies to the states through the Fourteenth Amendment. *Klopfer v. North Carolina*, 386 U.S. 213, 87 S.Ct. 988, 18 L.Ed.2d 1 (1967). Most states have adopted legislation or court rules similar to the federal speedy trial law. See, e.g., 725 Ill. Comp. Stat. Ann. § 5/103-5. State laws frequently provide that the right to a speedy trial is activated either on the date of the filing of an indictment, information, or other formal accusatorial document or on the date that the accused is taken into custody. In *People v. Hillsman*, 769 N.E.2d 1100 (Ill. App. 2002), the court cites a number of Illinois appellate court decisions holding that an accused is entitled to discharge if his trial begins more than 120 days after he was placed in custody, and that a defendant in such a position is entitled to discharge on the day of his scheduled trial.

## Conclusion

The rights afforded by the Fourth, Fifth, Sixth, and Eighth Amendments to the U.S. Constitution (and similar provisions in the state constitutions) vitally affect the procedures used in criminal cases. Many of these rights were redefined or enlarged by the courts during the 1960s and 1970s, and they become significant considerations long before a criminal prosecution reaches the trial stage.

## Chapter Summary

- Learning Objective 1
  - Federal and state constitutions require that persons accused of crimes be given fair notice of criminal charges and an adequate opportunity to contest these charges at various stages. The right to counsel is fundamental and includes the right to representation at all critical pretrial stages.
  - Historically the Sixth Amendment to the U.S. Constitution, and similar provisions in state constitutions, were interpreted to allow defendants to retain counsel in criminal prosecutions. Through judicial developments, and eventually by Congressional legislation, counsel was appointed for indigent defendants in federal criminal cases. In 1963 the Supreme Court mandated that states provide counsel to indigent defendants in felony cases; in 1972 it extended the right to defendants sentenced to jail terms for misdemeanors.
  - Today most defendants charged with felonies or serious misdemeanors qualify for representation by a public defender or court-appointed counsel. In addition to representation at trial and sentencing, counsel represent the accused at such preliminary hearings, lineups after charges have been filed, postindictment interrogations, arraignments, and other critical pretrial stages.
  - In 1975 the Supreme Court said a defendant has the constitutional right to elect self-representation if that choice is made "knowingly and intelligently" and that the defendant's legal knowledge or skill has no bearing on the election. Judges sometimes appoint standby counsel to assist *pro se* defendants. In 2008, the Court held that the Constitution does not require a trial judge to allow a minimally competent defendant to elect self-representation at trial.

- Learning Objective 2
  - In routine traffic violations and minor misdemeanors, police usually issue citations rather than make arrests. Some states have "cite and release statutes." Many persons who are charged with minor offenses waive their right to appear in court and pay a predetermined fine. Those who contest charges

receive a summary trial where guilt or innocence is determined according to the reasonable doubt standard.

o In major misdemeanor and felony cases, pretrial procedure is complex and protracted. Typically, an individual arrested for a felony must promptly be taken before a court for an initial appearance where the charges are read to the accused, who is informed of relevant constitutional rights, including the right to remain silent and the right to counsel, and a determination is made as to whether to grant pretrial release or remand the accused to custody to await the disposition of the case.

o Federal Rules of Criminal Procedure provide that a person arrested for a federal offense must be taken before a magistrate "without unnecessary delay" for a first appearance. States have similar rules.

o Confessions made during periods of detention that violate the prompt presentment requirement are inadmissible at trial. Congress, however, has provided that a confession made within six hours after arrest is not inadmissible solely because of a delay in bringing the accused before the magistrate.

- Learning Objective 3
  o Pretrial release can take the form of release on personal recognizance or to the custody of another, or posting a cash or surety bond.
  o The Eighth Amendment states that "excessive bail shall not be required" and the Supreme Court has said that bail is to ensure the accused's appearance in court, not to inflict punishment: However, the Court has not held the Excessive Bail Clause of the Eighth Amendment to be enforceable against the states, leaving the matter of excessive bail in state criminal cases to the state constitutions, legislatures, and courts.
  o The Federal Bail Reform Act of 1984 allows federal courts to detain arrestees without bail on the ground of the arrestee's danger to the community, as well as to ensure future court appearances. Congress has set various factors a court must consider in weighing the appropriateness of pretrial detention, and the government must show that pretrial release will not reasonably ensure the appearance of the accused or the safety of the community. The Act only applies to federal cases, but it suggests the validity of state laws and court decisions that deny bail to persons accused of violent crimes.
  o In many states, a defendant charged with a crime punishable by death or life imprisonment is ineligible for pretrial release if the proof of guilt is evident.

- Learning Objective 4
  o Prosecutors occupy a unique role in deciding whether to proceed with a criminal case or negotiate charges. Prosecutorial discretion is very broad, but a prosecutor may not single out a defendant for prosecution on the basis of race, religion, or other impermissible classifications. The Supreme Court has ruled that prosecutors are immune from tort actions for violating a defendant's constitutional rights.
  o When an arrest is made without a warrant, a preliminary hearing is constitutionally required to determine if there is probable cause to bind the accused over to the grand jury or (in the absence of a grand jury requirement) to hold the accused for trial. In many jurisdictions, prosecutors must obtain an indictment or "true bill" from the grand jury in addition to, or instead of, the preliminary hearing.

- Learning Objective 5
  - The Fifth Amendment to the Constitution states that "[n]o person shall be held to answer for a capital, or otherwise infamous crime, unless on a presentment or indictment of a grand jury." The Supreme Court has held that states are not bound to abide by this requirement. Nevertheless, in about half of the states constitutions or statutes require the use of grand juries in certain types of criminal cases. Other states use grand juries primarily in an investigatory or supervisory capacity and prosecutors initiate prosecution by filing an information.
  - Selection of grand jurors must not systematically exclude certain groups in the community. A majority of jurors must agree to an indictment. Rules of evidence that apply in trials do not bind a grand jury, and although a witness retains Fifth Amendment rights against self-incrimination, a grand jury can override a witness's refusal to answer questions by granting the witness immunity coextensive with the privilege against self-incrimination.
  - Under federal law an indictment must be filed within thirty days of arrest, but to claim preindictment delay, a defendant must show actual prejudice and deliberate design by the government. State courts generally take a similar approach.

- Learning Objective 6
  - The U.S. Constitution provides, "A Person charged in any State with Treason, Felony or any other crime, who shall flee from Justice, and be found in another state, shall on demand of the executive Authority of the State from which he fled, be delivered up, to be removed to the State having Jurisdiction of the crime." Every offense punishable by law of a jurisdiction where it was committed can be subject to extradition, but extradition is usually sought only in serious offenses.
  - Extradition of suspects or convicted criminals between nations is regulated by treaties, which usually provide that the crime involved must be a serious one in both nations and that the penalty for the person extradited will not be disproportionate to the crime.

- Learning Objective 7
  - Defense counsel and prosecutors file motions seeking to attain certain objectives before trial. Common motions include those seeking severance of defendants and charges and motions to dismiss, to seek continuances, to suppress evidence, to change venue, to require disclosure of a confidential informant, and to determine competency of the accused.
  - Rules governing joinder and severance of parties and of charges against a defendant are usually spelled out in the rules of criminal procedure in each jurisdiction. Courts grant a severance of charges on the motion of either the defense or prosecution if necessary to achieve a fair determination of the defendant's guilt or innocence on each offense. Courts usually grant a severance of defendants when jointly charged defendants pursue inconsistent defenses, when their interests are otherwise antagonistic, or when one defendant chooses to testify and the other does not.
  - Venue refers to the place of the trial, and a federal offense is normally tried in the district where the crime was committed. State criminal cases are tried in the district, county, circuit, and so forth where the offense was committed. Courts exercise considerable discretion and consider many factors in deciding whether to grant a motion for change of venue.

- Learning Objective 8
  - ○ The arraignment is the accused's first appearance before a court with the authority to conduct a criminal trial. At this stage, the accused must enter a plea to the charges contained in the indictment or information. The accused may plead not guilty, in which case a trial date is set. Alternatively, the accused may enter a plea of guilty, in which case no trial is necessary. (An *Alford* plea is when a defendant intelligently concludes that his or her interests require the entry of a guilty plea.) Some jurisdictions allow an accused to plead *nolo contendere* (no contest). Although functionally equivalent to a guilty plea, a no-contest plea generally cannot be construed as an admission of guilt in a related civil suit. Before accepting a plea of guilty or no contest, a trial court must determine that a defendant's plea is voluntary and has a factual basis.
  - ○ In a plea bargain, the accused agrees to plead guilty in exchange for a reduction in the number or severity of charges or a promise by the prosecutor not to seek the maximum penalty allowed by law. Usually a plea bargain is arranged by experienced counsel on both sides and is readily approved by the court. Plea negotiations are subject to approval of the trial court, and if the court is unwilling to approve the plea bargain, or modifies it, the defendant may either withdraw the guilty plea and stand trial or accept the plea bargain as modified by the judge.
  - ○ Plea bargaining is controversial, but it is one of the realities of the criminal justice system. Despite constitutional attacks, the Supreme Court has upheld the practice.

- Learning Objective 9
  - ○ The Sixth Amendment to the Constitution guarantees a defendant in a criminal case the right to "have the compulsory process of the law to obtain witnesses in his favor." In 1967 the Supreme Court applied the Compulsory Process clause to the states. This allows a defendant to obtain witnesses and evidence in his or her favor. Most states have adopted liberal rules allowing pretrial discovery in criminal cases. Using appropriate pretrial motions, the defense and prosecution can gain access to the evidence possessed by the opposing party. (The Illinois rule on discovery quoted in the chapter presents a good summary of the type of rules that states allow on pretrial discovery.) Discovery in federal courts is more limited. Federal statutes and the *Jencks* Act provide that a federal criminal defendant is not entitled to inspect a statement or report prepared by a government witness "until said witness has testified on direct examination in the trial of the case."
  - ○ In 1963 the Supreme Court stated that "the suppression by the prosecution of evidence favorable to the accused upon request violates due process where the evidence is material either to guilt or punishment, irrespective of the good faith or bad faith of the prosecution." Under this rule defendants are entitled to obtain any exculpatory evidence from the police or prosecutor.

- Learning Objective 10
  - ○ The Sixth Amendment guarantees a defendant the right to a speedy trial. In 1967 the Supreme Court held that the speedy trial requirements apply to the states. In 1972, the Court refused to mandate a specific time limit between the filing of charges and the commencement of trial and adopted a balancing test to consider relevant factors to determine whether a defendant was denied the right to a speedy trial.

    o Congress enacted the Speedy Trial Act of 1974, which provides specific time limits for pretrial and trial procedures in the federal courts. If the defendant's trial does not begin within the time limitations and the defendant enters a motion—before the trial's start or the defendant's entry of a guilty plea—to dismiss the charges, the district court must dismiss the charges. But there are a number of exceptions to the time limits, especially when a defendant's actions are responsible for the delay. States have speedy trial rules roughly patterned after the federal rules.

## Key Terms

actual imprisonment standard

*Alford* plea

arraignment

bail bond

change of venue

citation

cite and release statutes

compulsory process

continuance

criminal procedure

critical pretrial stages

deposition

dispositive motion

excessive bail

exculpatory evidence

extradition

factual basis

Federal Bail Reform Act of 1984

grand jury

*in camera* inspection

indigency

information

initial appearance

*Jencks* Act

joinder and severance of parties

joinder of offenses

jurisdiction

motion to dismiss

no-contest plea

petty offenses

plea of guilty

plea of not guilty

preliminary hearing

pretrial detention

pretrial discovery

pretrial motions

pretrial release

prosecutorial discretion

prosecutorial immunity

redaction

release on personal recognizance

right to a speedy trial

right to counsel

self-representation

severance of the charges

skip tracers

Speedy Trial Act of 1974

subpoenas

summary trial

suppression of evidence

surety bond

venue

## Questions for Thought and Discussion

1. Have the courts gone too far or not far enough in requiring that indigent defendants be represented by counsel at public expense?

2. What are the arguments for and against allowing defendants without any legal training to represent themselves in felony prosecutions? How far should a trial judge go in advising a defendant of the pitfalls of proceeding without legal counsel?

3. In your opinion, does the Eighth Amendment guarantee the right to pretrial release on bail in a felony case? What about a misdemeanor case? Did the Supreme Court decide the *Salerno* case correctly? Why or why not?

4. How does a magistrate determine how much bail is appropriate and how much is "excessive"? What alternatives, if any, do you see to the traditional bail-bond system to ensure the appearance of the defendant in court?

5. Can you imagine a situation in which a prosecutor would run afoul of the Constitution by engaging in selective prosecution? In your state, can a prosecutor be sued for malicious prosecution? How is this proved?

6. Why does the law insist on a determination of voluntariness and a factual basis when a defendant pleads guilty or *nolo contendere*?

7. Do the courts in your state permit the *nolo contendere* plea? If so, what tactical advantage does the defendant gain by pleading *nolo contendere* rather than guilty?

8. How might a prosecutor persuade a defendant to plead guilty to a criminal charge without running afoul of due process? What prosecutorial tactics are likely to be viewed as fundamentally unfair?

9. Compare the advantages and disadvantages to the defendant of insisting on the right to a speedy trial.

10. Why do you think the U.S. Supreme Court has never held that the Fifth Amendment requirement of indictment by a grand jury applies to the states as well as to the federal government?

11. Does the grand jury still play a viable role in the criminal justice system? Are the criticisms of the grand jury valid? Why or why not?

12. Should plea bargaining be abolished? If not, what modifications might be necessary to protect (a) the defendant and (b) the public?

## Problems for Discussion and Solution

1. Lonnie London was cited by police officers for speeding and driving with an expired driver's license, minor offenses punishable only by fines. Appearing in court, Lonnie requests that the judge appoint counsel to represent him on the ground that he is indigent. When the judge refuses, Lonnie exclaims, "I've got a constitutional right to be represented here!" Does Lonnie have a valid constitutional claim?

2. Samuel Penurio was president of a community bank in a small town. He was well thought of in the community, but he was known to drink to excess occasionally. One June evening his bank hosted a cocktail party. About 10:00 P.M., after the party was over, Penurio offered to drive his secretary home. Each had drunk several cocktails. En route to her home, Penurio drove through an intersection controlled by a signal light. His car crashed into a car containing four students who had just left their high school football game. One student, the popular head female cheerleader, died as a result of the injuries she received from the accident.

Penurio's blood-alcohol level was 0.10. He was charged with vehicular homicide, which carries a maximum punishment of life imprisonment. Penurio and his secretary claim that he drove through the intersection just as the light was changing and that the car occupied by the students drove through the intersection at an excessive rate of speed. The driver of the students' car had not been drinking, and the surviving students all say Penurio drove through the red light. The local newspaper ran a front-page story with pictures of the students holding a school-wide memorial service for the deceased cheerleader, describing the students' version of the accident, and pointing out that Penurio had been convicted of DWI just a year earlier. Over the next several days, the newspaper and the local radio station carried adverse comments from their readers and listeners about Penurio's conduct. Penurio's counsel has filed a motion for a change of venue. Do you think it likely the court will grant the motion? What, if any, additional information should be sought to support the motion?

3. Willy Doolittle, age thirty-eight, is an unemployed construction worker. He is married with two children in middle school. He has been unable to support his family for the past few weeks because of lack of work. His wife takes care of their rented home but, in addition to being a high school dropout, she receives Medicaid assistance for a series of physical problems. One night after having a few beers, Doolittle, using a key he had kept from when he had worked in a grocery warehouse, entered the warehouse without permission and stole approximately $1,000 worth of snack foods. The state charged Doolittle with burglary. His bail was set under a standard schedule that calls for $10,000 cash or bond. Doolittle has no means to post cash or a bond. The public defender (PD) was appointed to represent him. Doolittle has no prior criminal record and has lived in the community for three years. He wants to be released, and the PD thinks he may be able to represent him more effectively if Doolittle is released and obtains employment. A social worker reports that the family is in need of support and has offered to assist Doolittle in obtaining employment at a new construction site. The PD asks you to prepare a memorandum to support an application for pre-trial release without posting cash or bond. What additional information should you seek? In seeking to obtain Doolittle's release without posting cash or bond, what conditions of release should the PD propose to the court?

4. Lauren L. is an eighteen-year-old woman who has just been arrested and charged with grand theft, possession of cocaine, and resisting arrest. She is being represented by the public defender's office. After being released on bail, Lauren is scheduled to meet with her attorney but fails to show up for the appointment. Minutes before her arraignment, Lauren meets with her lawyer, who informs her that he has made a "good deal" for her. Lauren agrees to take the deal and pleads guilty to misdemeanor theft. The judge asks Lauren if she understands the terms of the plea agreement and she responds in the affirmative. Under the deal, the court withholds adjudication of the drug possession charge on the condition that Lauren successfully completes a residential drug treatment program. Two weeks later, Lauren walks away from the treatment facility without having completed the program. She is arrested several days later and brought back to court, where the judge informs her that she must enter a plea to the cocaine possession charge. In response, Lauren says, "But your honor, nobody ever told me about that part of the deal." How should the judge proceed at this point?

5. Myron Minton, who suffers from schizophrenia, has been institutionalized on several occasions. After being released from a mental health facility, Myron refuses to take his medication and begins wandering the streets aimlessly. He

is soon arrested by police on a charge of aggravated battery. According to the police report, Minton has been identified by a homeless man who claims that Minton beat him severely with a pipe. At his first appearance in court, Minton refuses to be represented by the public defender's office. He tells the judge that he intends to represent himself and that he plans to plead not guilty by reason of insanity. How do you think a judge would be likely to handle this situation?

6. Wesley Watson was indicted by a Jefferson County grand jury for solicitation of murder. An undercover police officer posing as a "hit man" testified before the grand jury that Watson had offered him $50,000 to kill Benjamin Bratton, the district attorney. Because Bratton recused himself in the case, a local circuit judge convened the grand jury to investigate the case. After the indictment was handed down, Watson's attorney moved to quash the indictment on the ground that the convening of the grand jury by a member of the judiciary was unlawful and denied his client due process of law. Do you think a criminal court judge would be receptive to this argument? Why or why not?

# CHAPTER **18**

# The Criminal Trial

## CHAPTER OUTLINE

Introduction

Constitutional Rights Pertaining to the Criminal Trial

Selection and Composition of the Jury

Free Press versus Fair Trial

"Order in the Court"

The Rules of Evidence

The Trial Process

Conclusion

Chapter Summary

Key Terms

Questions for Thought and Discussion

Problems for Discussion and Solution

## JURISPRUDENCE

*Williams v. Florida* (1970)

*Batson v. Kentucky* (1986)

*Rivera v. Illinois* (2009)

*Sheppard v. Maxwell* (1966)

*Nebraska Press Association v. Stuart* (1976)

*Crawford v. Washington* (2004)

## LEARNING OBJECTIVES

After reading this chapter, you should be able to explain

1. the constitutional rights that apply to criminal trials
2. how juries are selected and composed
3. what the "death qualification" of a jury in a capital case is
4. the steps judges can take to insulate juries from prejudicial media coverage
5. what powers judges have to maintain order in the courtroom
6. the rules of evidence that apply to criminal trials
7. the role of expert witnesses and the test for admissibility of scientific evidence
8. the mechanics of a criminal trial
9. how and why juries are instructed by judges
10. the rules governing jury deliberations and verdicts

# CHAPTER OPENING VIGNETTE

On the evening of December 7, 1993, Jamaican-born Colin Ferguson boarded a commuter train in Long Island, New York, and began shooting passengers at random. Six people were killed and nineteen more were injured in the rampage. When Ferguson paused to reload his handgun, he was subdued by several passengers. Initially, Ferguson was represented by two prominent civil rights lawyers, William Kuntsler and Ron Kuby, who undertook the case *pro bono*. But Ferguson disapproved of the defense they intended to put on, namely, that Ferguson was legally insane at the time of the shooting due to an uncontrollable "black rage." Ferguson dismissed Kuntsler and Kuby and insisted on representing himself at trial.

The evidence produced at trial as to Ferguson's mental state, as well as his bizarre behavior in the courtroom, suggested that an insanity defense might have been effective, but Ferguson's defense amounted to little more than a denial and an insistence that he was a victim of mistaken identity. After hearing from a number of eyewitnesses to the shooting, the jury had little difficulty in convicting Ferguson of six counts of second-degree murder, nineteen counts of attempted second-degree murder, reckless endangerment, and criminal possession of a firearm. Ferguson was sentenced to consecutive prison terms that exceeded two hundred years. Today, he remains confined in New York's Attica prison.

Critics of the trial questioned how the trial judge could find Ferguson competent to stand trial, let alone to represent himself. However, in reviewing the case the Appellate Division of the New York Supreme Court determined that the trial court had properly determined that Ferguson was competent to stand trial. The appellate court held further that the trial court properly allowed Ferguson to represent himself, because a defendant who is deemed competent to stand trial is also competent to waive his right to counsel. *People v. Ferguson*, 248 A.D.2d 725, 670 N.Y.S.2d 327 (N.Y. App. 1998).

# Introduction

More than 90 percent of felony charges and an even higher percentage of misdemeanor cases are disposed of before trial. Nevertheless, the criminal trial is the centerpiece of the criminal justice system for several reasons. First, trials are generally held before juries drawn from the community. Second, trials are the most visible aspect of the justice system and often attract widespread media coverage. Finally, cases disposed of by trial often have an important impact on the administration of justice.

Before the arrival of William the Conqueror in England in 1066, criminal trials took the forms of compurgation or ordeal. In a trial by compurgation, a defendant who had denied guilt under oath attempted to recruit a body of men to attest to his or her honor. If a group would swear to the defendant's innocence, the law considered the defendant to be innocent. In a trial by ordeal, the defendant was tortured by fire or water. If the defendant survived the ordeal, people thought that God had intervened to prove the defendant's innocence before the law.

Jury trials as we know them today originated with the Magna Carta, which the English nobles forced King John to sign at Runnymede in 1215. The Magna Carta granted freemen the right of trial by their peers. Early juries comprised persons who had knowledge of the facts of a case—it was centuries before trial juries functioned in the role they now perform. The jury became characteristic of the English common law and was a feature that distinguished English law from the law of the European continent, which was based on Roman law.

# Constitutional Rights Pertaining to the Criminal Trial

Despite the protections of the common law, English subjects accused of crime were not always afforded fair trials. The notorious Star Chamber was established in the fifteenth century to punish offenses outside the common law. Its real purpose was to punish opponents of the monarch. It met in secret, dispensed with jury trials, and offered no legal protections to the accused. Accusation before the Star Chamber was tantamount to conviction. Its punishments were unduly harsh, often involving torture and disfigurement. Although the Star Chamber was abolished by Parliament in 1641, the framers of the American Bill of Rights wanted to make sure that no such institution would ever be established in this country. Thus, as the Sixth Amendment provides,

> In all criminal prosecutions, the accused shall enjoy the right to a speedy and public trial, by an impartial jury of the State and district wherein the crime shall have been committed, which district shall have been previously ascertained by law, and to be informed of the nature and cause of the accusation; to be confronted with the witnesses against him; to have compulsory process for obtaining witnesses in his favor, and to have the Assistance of Counsel for his defence.

Because they are deemed to be fundamentally important in securing liberty and ensuring fairness, the various rights protected by the Sixth Amendment are made applicable to state criminal trials by the Fourteenth Amendment. See, e.g., *Gideon v. Wainwright*, 372 U.S. 335, 344, 83 S.Ct. 792, 796, 9 L.Ed.2d 799, 805 (1963); *Pointer v. Texas*, 380 U.S. 400, 85 S.Ct. 1065, 13 L.Ed.2d 923 (1965); *Duncan v. Louisiana*, 391 U.S. 145, 88 S.Ct. 1444, 20 L.Ed.2d 491 (1968).

## The Right to Compulsory Process

The Sixth Amendment guarantees a defendant the right "to have compulsory process for obtaining witnesses in his favor." This affords the defendant the right to obtain court process (a subpoena) to compel witnesses to appear in court. There are some restrictions (e.g., a defendant cannot cause numerous witnesses to be subpoenaed simply to give cumulative testimony), but courts allow defendants a fair degree of liberality in causing witnesses to be subpoenaed. Of course, the prosecution can also compel the attendance of witnesses.

## The Right to an Open Public Trial

**open public trials** Trials that are held in public courtrooms that are open to spectators.

The Sixth Amendment guarantees "the right to a speedy and public trial" and the Supreme Court has recognized that **open public trials** are essential to our system of justice. *Richmond Newspapers v. Virginia*, 448 U.S. 555, 100 S.Ct. 2814, 65 L.Ed.2d 973 (1980). But the right to a public trial, even if waived by the defendant, does not allow a defendant to invoke the converse of that right—that is, there is no right to a private trial. *Singer v. United States*, 380 U.S. 24, 34–35, 85 S.Ct. 1783, 790, 13 L.Ed.2d 630, 638 (1965).

The right to an open public trial is not absolute. After pointing out that a public trial is for the benefit of the accused and to ensure that the judge and prosecutor carry out their duties responsibly, the Supreme Court in *Waller v. Georgia*, 467 U.S. 39, 45, 104 S.Ct. 2210, 2215, 81 L.Ed.2d 31, 38 (1984), explained that

> the right to an open trial may give way in certain cases to other rights or interests, such as the defendant's right to a fair trial or the government's interest in inhibiting disclosure of sensitive information. Such circumstances will be rare, however, and the balance of interest must be struck with special care.

The Supreme Court has ruled that the requirement of openness extends to all phases of the trial. Consequently, in 1982 it declared invalid a state statute requiring mandatory closing of the courtroom during the testimony of victims of sexual offenses. The Court said the issue of closing should be left to the discretion of the trial judge, who would determine on a case-by-case basis whether the state's legitimate interests in a victim's well-being necessitate closing the courtroom. *Globe Newspaper Company v. Superior Court*, 457 U.S. 596, 102 S.Ct. 2613, 73 L.Ed.2d 248 (1982).

Two years later, the Court held that *voir dire* proceedings (discussed later in this chapter) in criminal trials can be closed only by overcoming the presumption of openness. *Press-Enterprise Company v. Superior Court of California*, 464 U.S. 501, 104 S.Ct. 819, 78 L.Ed.2d 629 (1984). Accordingly, before a trial court orders the closing of court proceedings, it must make specific findings that closure is essential and explain why available alternatives are inadequate. Among the reasons frequently cited by courts for limiting public access to criminal proceedings are the need to protect rape victims or children who have been molested and the need to protect witnesses and jurors from embarrassment, trauma, or intimidation. Based on the *Press-Enterprise* decision, courts now apply a four-prong test for determining the propriety of closing judicial proceedings to spectators. First, the party seeking to close the hearing must advance an overriding interest that is likely to be prejudiced; second, the closure must be no broader than necessary to protect that interest; third, the trial court must consider reasonable alternatives to closing the proceeding; and fourth, it must make findings adequate to support the closure.

**CASE-IN-POINT**

### Court Upholds Closure of Defendant's Trial during Testimony of Juvenile Witnesses

Robert Morgan was charged with rape, deviate sexual assault, and two counts of aggravated incest committed against his minor stepdaughter. The state moved to close the trial to the public so as to protect the best interests of the minor victim and her brother and stepsister during their testimony against the defendant. Over the defendant's objection, the trial court granted the state's motion, limiting the exclusion order to the three juvenile witnesses. The trial court found that the intimate and embarrassing nature of the testimony warranted the limited closure and did not hamper the public nature of the trial. Morgan was found guilty and appealed, arguing that exclusion of the public during two days of his trial violated his Sixth Amendment right to a public trial. Applying the test developed by the U.S. Supreme Court in *Press-Enterprise v. Superior Court* (1984), the appellate court found that the trial court properly closed the courtroom to spectators during the testimony of the juvenile witnesses, held that the defendant was not denied his constitutional right to a public trial, and affirmed the defendant's conviction.

*People v. Morgan*, 504 N.E.2d 172 (Ill. App. 1987).

## The Right to Counsel

We examined the right to counsel fairly extensively in the previous chapter. However, there are a few specific issues that pertain to the conduct of a trial. In 1976 the Supreme Court ruled that it is a violation of a defendant's Sixth Amendment right to counsel for a trial judge to bar the defendant from conferring with defense counsel during an overnight recess of a trial. *Geders v. United States*, 425 U.S. 80, 96 S.Ct. 1330, 47 L.Ed.2d 592 (1976). More than a decade later, the Court held that it was not a denial of the right to counsel for a trial judge to bar a defendant from conferring with counsel during a brief trial recess that occurred after the defendant testified on direct examination but before cross-examination by the prosecutor. *Perry v. Leeke*, 488 U.S. 272, 109 S.Ct. 594, 102 L.Ed.2d 624 (1989). The Court's holdings in these cases acknowledge the importance of a close relationship between attorney and client during a trial but also recognize that the pursuit of truth is the purpose of the in-court examination of witnesses. Thus, there are valid reasons not to allow any witness to confer with counsel between the direct examination and the cross-examination.

### Self-Representation

We began the chapter with a vignette based on the infamous Colin Ferguson case, *People v. Ferguson*, 248 A.D.2d 725, 670 N.Y.S.2d 327 (N.Y. App. 1998). That case highlights the danger to a defendant, especially a defendant of questionable mental competency, of choosing to represent himself at trial. As we pointed out in the previous chapter, the Supreme Court has held that a defendant has the constitutional right to elect self-representation if that choice is made "knowingly and intelligently" and that the defendant's legal knowledge or skill has no bearing on the election. Any such waiver of counsel must be carefully documented in the court records, and the court, at its option, may appoint **standby counsel** to assist the defendant. *Faretta v. California*, 422 U.S. 806, 95 S.Ct. 2525, 45 L.Ed.2d 562 (1975).

In *State v. Bakalov*, 862 P.2d 1354 (Utah 1993), the Supreme Court of Utah cautioned trial judges to advise a defendant who elects to proceed *pro se* of the risks of presenting a *pro se* defense. A Pennsylvania appellate court has ruled that before the right to counsel may be waived, the trial court is required "to make searching and formal on-the-record inquiry to ascertain (1) whether the defendant is aware of

**standby counsel** An attorney appointed to assist an indigent defendant who elects to represent himself or herself at trial.

his right to counsel and (2) whether the defendant is aware of the consequences of waiving that right or not." *Commonwealth v. Owens*, 750 A.2d 872, 875 (Pa. Super. 2000). The Supreme Court has now held that the Constitution does not require a trial judge to allow a minimally competent defendant to elect self-representation at trial. *Indiana v. Edwards*, 554 U.S. 164, 128 S.Ct. 2379, 171 L.Ed.2d 345 (2008). At trial, a defense counsel who represents multiple defendants might discover a possible conflict in his or her representation of the defendants. In such an instance, it is the trial court's duty "either to appoint separate counsel or to take adequate steps to ascertain whether the risk was too remote to warrant separate counsel." *Holloway v. Arkansas*, 435 U.S. 475, 484, 98 S.Ct. 1173, 1178, 55 L.Ed.2d 426, 434 (1978).

## The Right to Trial by Jury

The Sixth Amendment also ensures the right to trial by jury. However, the amendment leaves unanswered questions concerning the qualifications of jurors, the method of their selection, and the requirements for a jury to convict a person accused of a crime.

**jury trial** A judicial proceeding to determine a defendant's guilt or innocence, conducted before a body of people sworn to render a verdict based on the law and the evidence presented.

**bench trial** A trial held before a judge without a jury present.

An accused may waive the right to a **jury trial**. Indeed, many persons who plead not guilty to misdemeanor charges elect a **bench trial**. On the other hand, most defendants who plead not guilty to felony charges choose to be tried by jury. The U.S. Supreme Court has ruled that the constitutional right to a jury trial extends to the class of cases for which an accused was entitled to a jury trial when the Constitution was adopted. This did not include juvenile cases; hence, there is no right to a jury trial for juveniles under the federal constitution. *McKeiver v. Pennsylvania*, 403 U.S. 528, 91 S.Ct. 1976, 29 L.Ed.2d 647 (1971). Furthermore, the right to trial by jury is not applicable to military tribunals. *Ex parte Quirin*, 317 U.S. 1, 63S.Ct. 1, 87 L.Ed. 3 (1942).

The constitutional requirement of a jury trial applies to the states, thereby guaranteeing a defendant a right to a jury trial in a state criminal prosecution if such a right would exist in a federal prosecution. *Duncan v. Louisiana*, supra. Interestingly, the Sixth Amendment right to a jury trial does not afford a defendant the corresponding right to be tried before a judge without a jury. *Singer v. United States*, 380 U.S. 24, 85 S.Ct. 783, 13 L.Ed.2d 630 (1965).

As now interpreted, the Sixth Amendment guarantees an accused the right to a jury trial in criminal cases where a penalty of more than six months' imprisonment can be imposed. *Codispoti v. Pennsylvania*, 418 U.S. 506, 94 S.Ct. 2687, 41 L.Ed.2d 912 (1974). Offenses that carry a possible penalty of no more than six months' imprisonment are generally termed "petty offenses," and a jury trial is not required under the Constitution. *Baldwin v. New York*, 399 U.S. 66, 90 S.Ct. 1886, 26 L.Ed.2d 437 (1970).

In *Blanton v. City of North Las Vegas*, 489 U.S. 538, 109 S.Ct. 1289, 103 L.Ed. 2d 550 (1989), the Supreme Court observed that a defendant might be entitled to a jury trial even if the penalty was no more than six months' imprisonment. The Court said this could occur where additional statutory penalties, in conjunction with the maximum authorized period of incarceration, are so severe as to clearly reflect a legislative determination that the offense is a "serious" one. But the Court held that the prospect of a $1,000 fine, attendance at an alcohol abuse clinic, and the loss of a driver's license for ninety days were not sufficient to make the offense of driving while intoxicated so "serious" as to require a jury trial.

In 1996, in a 5–4 decision, the Supreme Court ruled that a defendant charged with multiple petty offenses is not entitled to a jury trial under the federal constitution even though the possible sentence may add up to more than six months in prison. *Lewis v. United States*, 518 U.S. 322, 116 S.Ct. 2163, 135 L.Ed.2d 590 (1996).

Notwithstanding the federal constitutional requirements, under some states' constitutions or statutory laws, an accused has the right to a jury trial for certain offenses even though they may be classified as "petty offenses" from a federal constitutional standpoint. In Florida, for example, a defendant is entitled to a jury trial under the state constitution for any offense that was *malum in se* and indictable at common law even though the maximum punishment is less than six months' imprisonment. *Reed v. State*, 470 So.2d 1382 (Fla. 1985).

## Selection and Composition of the Jury

At common law, a jury consisted of twelve men. Rule 23(b), Federal Rules of Criminal Procedure, requires a twelve-member jury in criminal cases in federal courts unless the defendant stipulates to fewer in writing. If the court finds it necessary to excuse a juror after the jury has retired to consider its verdict, at the discretion of the court, a valid verdict may be returned by the remaining eleven jurors. All states require twelve-member juries in capital cases. Most require the same number for all felony prosecutions. However, many now use fewer than twelve jurors in misdemeanor cases. Florida uses six-person juries for all but capital felonies. Fla. R. Crim. P. 3.270. In *Williams v. Florida*, 399 U.S. 78, 90 S.Ct. 1893, 26 L.Ed.2d 446 (1970), the Supreme Court upheld the use of six-person juries in the trial of felony offenses in Florida. Subsequently, in *Ballew v. Georgia*, 435 U.S. 223, 98 S.Ct. 1029, 55 L.Ed.2d 234 (1978), the Court held that a jury of only five persons was not acceptable under the Sixth Amendment.

State and federal laws prescribe certain basic qualifications for jurors. Statutes commonly require that jurors be at least eighteen years of age and registered voters in the state or district from which they are to be selected. In contrast with past practices, laws prescribing qualifications cannot discriminate to prevent women as a class from serving as jurors. *Taylor v. Louisiana*, 419 U.S. 522, 95 S.Ct. 692, 42 L.Ed.2d 690 (1975). Convicted felons whose civil rights have not been restored are

### JURISPRUDENCE

*Williams v. Florida*, 399 U.S. 78, 90 S.Ct. 1893, 26 L.Ed.2d 446 (1970)

Williams was convicted of armed robbery and sentenced to life imprisonment. On appeal, one of Williams' arguments was that he had been tried by a jury composed of only six members. The Florida appellate courts rejected all of Williams' claims and sustained his conviction and sentence. In reviewing the case, the U.S. Supreme Court framed the issue as "whether the constitutional guarantee of a trial by 'jury' necessarily requires a trial by exactly 12 persons." The

Court held that a jury of twelve is not a requirement under the Sixth Amendment as it applies to the states via the Fourteenth Amendment. Writing for the Court, Justice Byron White concluded that "neither currently available evidence nor theory suggests that the 12-man jury is necessarily more advantageous to the defendant than a jury composed of fewer members." Justice John M. Harlan, one of three dissenters in the case, observed that "before today, it would have been unthinkable to suggest that the Sixth Amendment's right to a trial by jury is satisfied by a jury of six, or less . . ."

usually excluded from serving on juries. Beyond this, statutes frequently carve out exemptions for expectant mothers and mothers with young children; for persons over seventy years of age; and for physicians, dentists, attorneys, judges, teachers, elected officials, police, firefighters, and emergency personnel. The trend has been for states to restrict exemptions from jury duty so that the pool of prospective jurors reflects a representative cross-section of the community.

The Jury Selection and Service Act of 1968, 28 U.S.C.A. § 1861ff, was enacted to ensure that jury panels in federal courts are selected at random from a fair cross-section of the community. States also have statutes prescribing the process of selection. Local officials compile a list of persons qualified to serve as jurors, generally from the rolls of registered voters, driver's license lists, or some combination thereof. From this list, prospective jurors are randomly selected and summoned to court. Compensation paid to trial jurors ranges from meager to modest amounts for travel and per diem expenses. Most states prohibit an employer from discharging an employee who has been summoned for jury duty.

## Anonymous Juries

Ordinarily, the identities of members of a jury are a matter of public information. But in some cases courts find it necessary to impanel an anonymous jury, where information about the jurors such as their names, residences, employment information, and so forth is not disclosed to the public. Anonymous juries were unknown at common law; the first one was impaneled in the United States in 1979. Courts now employ anonymous juries where necessary to protect potential jurors and their families from threats, harassment, or intimidation, which can occur from organized crime, gang activity, or other sources. In *United States v. Paccione*, 949 F.2d 1183 (2d Cir. 1991), the court said a trial court "should not order the empanelling of an anonymous jury without (a) concluding that there is strong reason to believe the jury needs protection, and (b) taking reasonable precautions to minimize any prejudicial effects on the defendant and to ensure that his fundamental rights are protected." 949 F.2d at 1192.

In *United States v. Krout*, 66 F.3d 1420 (5th Cir. 1995), defendants were convicted in a federal district court of participating in a continuing criminal enterprise of murder, drug distribution, and firearms offenses. One ground asserted in their appeal was that they were denied a fair trial because the identities of the jurors who found them guilty were not publicly revealed. The U.S. Court of Appeals for the Fifth Circuit rejected their challenge and held that the trial court did not abuse its discretion in impaneling an anonymous jury. The appellate court mentioned that one of the objectives of the defendants' criminal organization was to interfere with potential witnesses. *United States v. Krout*, 66 F.3d 1420 (5th Cir. 1995).

In *State v. Ivy*, 188 S.W.3d 132 (Tenn. 2006), the Tennessee Supreme Court reviewed a defendant's murder conviction. Among other issues on appeal, the defendant argued that the trial court erred in impaneling an anonymous jury. The issue of impaneling anonymous juries was one of first impression with the court. The court upheld the trial court's finding that strong reasons existed to protect the jury, as one of the defendant's apparent motives in committing the charged offense included the defendant's desire to prevent the victim from going to the police. Following the rationale of federal appellate court decisions, the court approved the use of an anonymous jury where there is a strong reason to believe the jury needs protection and where reasonable precautions are taken to ensure that the defendant's fundamental rights are protected.

## The *Voir Dire*

**venire** The group of citizens from whom a jury is chosen in a given case.

The body of persons summoned to be jurors is referred to as the **venire**. After outlining the case to be tried and reciting the names of those expected to participate, the judge may excuse those whose physical disabilities or obvious conflicts of interest based on family relationships or business connections disqualify them from serving. After excusing those who do not qualify, the judge swears in the remaining members of the venire to answer questions put to them by the court and counsel. Then six or twelve of these prospective jurors are called at random to take their seats in the jury box, where either the judge or counsel for each side may ask further questions. This process is called the *voir dire*.

**voir dire** "To speak the truth." The process by which prospective jurors are questioned by counsel and/or the court before being selected to serve on a jury.

Lawyers for the prosecution and the defense are permitted to challenge prospective jurors either for cause or peremptorily. A challenge is a request that a juror be excused from serving. Challenges are customarily asserted at the *voir dire* (from the French, meaning "to tell the truth"). The function of the *voir dire* is to enable the court and counsel to obtain the information necessary to ensure the selection of a fair and impartial jury. To assist in obtaining background information and thereby expedite the *voir dire* process, it is not uncommon for courts to submit a series of written questions to be answered by prospective jurors in advance of their appearance in court. In some courts, the *voir dire* examination is conducted by the trial judge, who may invite the lawyers to suggest questions to ask the prospective jurors. In others, lawyers for each side conduct the *voir dire*. In either event, the presiding judge exercises broad discretion to keep the questioning within proper bounds. A *voir dire* examination is generally conducted before the six or twelve prospective jurors initially selected; however, under certain circumstances some courts have allowed the examination of individual jurors apart from the collective group.

The objective of the *voir dire* examination is to select jurors who can render a verdict fairly and impartially. However, it would be naive to expect that the prosecutor and defense counsel are both striving to seat a wholly objective panel of jurors. Obviously, each trial lawyer wants jurors who will be sympathetic to the cause he or she advocates. To accomplish this, trial lawyers must be well versed in the facts of the case and the relevant law. They must also display ingenuity in questioning the prospective jurors to determine whether to exercise their right to challenge jurors' qualifications to serve. Lawyers must be conversant with local court practices because judges have broad discretion in conducting the *voir dire*. Trial lawyers have their own theories on how to conduct a *voir dire* examination, but most would agree that a practical knowledge of psychology is helpful. In recent years, some have even retained social scientists for advice and assistance in the jury selection process. The process of excusing prospective jurors is accomplished by counsel exercising challenges, either "for cause" or "peremptorily"—that is, without assigning a reason.

## Challenges for Cause

**challenges for cause** Objections to a prospective juror on some specified ground (e.g., a close relationship to a party in the case).

**Challenges for cause** may be directed to the venire on the basis of the panel having been improperly selected. An example is when the defense counsel contends that the selection procedures exclude minority members. More commonly, challenges for cause are directed to a prospective juror individually concerning some fact or characteristic that would disqualify that person from serving on the particular case. Among the more common reasons for disqualification are having a close relationship with counsel, being significantly involved in the case as a witness or in some other capacity, or having formed a definite opinion about the case. However, it is not expected that the jurors be totally ignorant of the facts and issues involved in the case. Justice Tom C. Clark, writing for the Supreme Court, observed,

> In these days of swift, widespread and diverse methods of communication, an important case can be expected to arouse the interest of the public in the vicinity, and scarcely any of those best qualified to serve as jurors will not have formed some impression or opinion as to the merits of the case. *Irvin v. Dowd*, 366 U.S. 717, 722, 81 S.Ct. 1639, 1642, 6 L.Ed.2d 751, 756 (1961).

With our widespread access to television and the Internet, Justice Clark's observation is even more compelling today than in 1961. Nevertheless, prospective jurors who acknowledge that they have formed an opinion on the merits of the case and cannot disregard this opinion are generally excused for cause. Absent unusual circumstances concerning the parties involved in a case, a person will not be excused for cause because of religious or political affiliations.

## Peremptory Challenges of Prospective Jurors

It is not always possible to articulate a basis for dismissing a juror who appears to be biased. Therefore, each side in a criminal trial is also allowed a limited number of **peremptory challenges** that may be exercised on *voir dire* to excuse prospective jurors without stating any reason. The number of peremptory challenges is usually provided by statute or court rules.

In federal courts, each party in a criminal case where the offense is punishable by death is allowed twenty peremptory challenges. If the offense is punishable by more than one year in prison, the government is allowed six and the defendant is allowed ten. Each side is allowed three peremptory challenges where the offense carries a punishment of less than one year in prison. Fed. R. Crim. P. 24(b).

States vary in the number of peremptory challenges allowed in criminal trials. Rather typical is Article 35.15 of Vernon's Annotated Texas Code of Criminal Procedure, which allows the state and the defendant fifteen peremptory challenges each in capital cases where the state seeks the death penalty. Where two or more defendants are tried together, the state is entitled to eight peremptory challenges for each defendant, and each defendant is entitled to eight as well. In noncapital felony

**peremptory challenges** Objections to the selection of prospective jurors in which the attorney making the challenges is not required to state the reasons for the objections.

---

**CASE-IN-POINT**

### When Should a Juror Be Excused for Cause?

The defendant was tried by jury for rape, sodomy, and some weapons offenses. Prospective jurors were not asked during the *voir dire* if they had ever been raped or had a family member or friend who had been raped. After the jury had been selected, a female juror suggested to the court that she should be excused because her daughter had been raped five years earlier. After being closely questioned by the judge and defense lawyer, she expressed convincingly that she and her daughter had effectively recovered from the trauma of the rape and that she could be a fair and impartial juror. The court refused to excuse her from the jury panel. The defendant was convicted and appealed. The Georgia Court of Appeals affirmed the defendant's conviction. In rejecting the defendant's argument that the trial court erred in not excusing the juror for cause, the court said that the trial court had an ample basis upon which to believe the juror would perform her duty justly.

*Jamison v. State*, 295 S.E.2d 203 (Ga. App. 1982).

cases and in capital cases where the state does not seek the death penalty, the state and defendant are each entitled to ten peremptory challenges. Where two or more defendants are tried together, each defendant is entitled to six peremptory challenges, and the state is likewise entitled to six for each defendant. In misdemeanor cases, each side is allowed either three or five peremptory challenges, depending on the level of court where the defendant is tried.

To determine whether to exercise a peremptory challenge, an attorney conducting a *voir dire* examination attempts to determine the attitudes, backgrounds, and personalities of prospective jurors. Trial courts limit the questions that may be asked of prospective jurors, depending on the nature of the case. Some areas of questioning are considered very delicate and usually will not be permitted. For example, in *Alderman v. State*, 327 S.E.2d 168 (Ga. 1985), the Supreme Court of Georgia upheld a trial judge's refusal to allow a defendant to ask prospective jurors questions concerning the kinds of books and magazines they read, whether they were members of any political organizations, and what kinds of bumper stickers they had on their vehicles.

### Racially Based Peremptory Challenges

**racially based peremptory challenges** Peremptory challenges to prospective jurors that are based solely on racial animus or racial stereotypes.

To reduce the potential for racial discrimination in the exercise of **racially based peremptory challenges**, courts have recently reassessed the historic freedom afforded to counsel in exercising peremptory challenges. In 1965, in *Swain v. Alabama*, 380 U.S. 202, 85 S.Ct. 824, 13 L.Ed.2d 759, the Supreme Court said that it was a violation of the Equal Protection Clause of the Fifth Amendment to systematically exclude someone from serving on a jury because of the person's race. To make a *prima facie* case of purposeful discrimination, the defendant faced the formidable task of proving that the peremptory challenge system as a whole was being perverted. There was considerable criticism of the Court's ruling in *Swain v. Alabama*, and the Court again addressed the problem in *Batson v. Kentucky*, 476 U.S. 79, 106 S.Ct. 1712, 90 L.Ed.2d 69 (1986).

In *Batson*, the Supreme Court held that a prosecutor's peremptory challenges to exclude African Americans from a jury trying African-American defendants was ground for a defendant to claim discrimination under the Equal Protection Clause of the Fourteenth Amendment to the Constitution. *Batson* became the basis for trial courts to deny the prosecution's use of a peremptory challenge for exclusion of an African-American juror from a trial of a person of that race if the court was persuaded

---

### JURISPRUDENCE

*Batson v. Kentucky*, 476 U.S. 79, 106 S.Ct. 1712, 90 L.Ed.2d 69 (1986)

Batson, an African-American man, was on trial for burglary and receiving stolen goods. The prosecutor used his peremptory challenges to strike all four blacks from the venire, which led to an all-white jury being impaneled. The judge denied the defendant's motion to discharge the jury. Batson was convicted on both counts and the state supreme court affirmed. In a 7-2 decision, the U.S. Supreme Court reversed, holding that Batson had been denied a fair trial due

to the purposeful exclusion of blacks from the jury. The Court said that, henceforth, a trial judge must deny a prosecutor's peremptory challenge to an African-American juror where the defendant is also black if the judge is persuaded that the challenge is racially motivated. Justice Lewis Powell concluded his opinion for the Court by predicting that "public respect for our criminal justice system and the rule of law will be strengthened if we ensure that no citizen is disqualified from jury service because of his race."

the challenge was racially motivated. In 1991 the Supreme Court broadened the rule so that the racial motivation of the prosecutor became subject to challenge irrespective of the defendant and prospective juror being of the same race. *Powers v. Ohio*, 499 U.S. 400, 111 S.Ct. 1364, 113 L.Ed.2d 411 (1991).

In 1992 the Court revisited this area of the law and extended the *Batson* rule by holding that a defendant's exercise of peremptory challenges was state action and that the Equal Protection Clause also prohibits defendants from engaging in purposeful discrimination on the ground of race. *Georgia v. McCollum*, 505 U.S. 42, 112 S.Ct. 2348, 120 L.Ed.2d 33 (1992). And in 2000, the Court suggested that the *Batson* rule applies to ethnicity as well as race. *United States v. Martinez-Salazar*, 528 U.S. 304, 120 S.Ct. 774, 145 L.Ed.2d 792 (2000). In *Rico v. Leftridge-Byrd*, 340 F.3d 178 (3d Cir. 2003), the U.S. Court of Appeals for the Third Circuit relied on that dictum in holding that peremptory challenges to Italian American prospective jurors are within the scope of the *Batson* rule.

### Gender-Based Peremptory Challenges

**gender-based peremptory challenges** Challenges to a prospective juror's competency to serve that are based solely on the prospective juror's gender.

In the late 1980s and early 1990s, courts moved to restrict **gender-based peremptory challenges**. By 1993, federal appellate courts had issued disparate rulings on the issue. Finally, in *J.E.B. v. Alabama ex rel. T.B.*, 511 U.S. 127, 114 S.Ct. 1419, 128 L.Ed.2d 89 (1994), the U.S. Supreme Court resolved that conflict and held that the Equal Protection Clause of the Fourteenth Amendment also prohibits gender-based peremptory challenges. Writing for the majority, Justice Harry Blackmun emphasized the relationship between racially based and gender-based peremptory challenges: "Failing to provide jurors the same protection against gender discrimination as race discrimination could frustrate the purpose of *Batson* itself." 511 U.S. at 148, 114 S.Ct. at 1430, 128 L.Ed.2d at 107. Now that peremptory challenges based on race, ethnicity, and gender have been invalidated as violations of equal protection, some observers wonder whether the peremptory challenge itself is on the way out.

## Death-Qualified" Juries

In 1970 the Supreme Court expressed concern about some courts automatically excluding from juries trying capital cases persons who oppose or who have conscientious scruples against capital punishment. The Court held that opponents of

### JURISPRUDENCE

*Rivera v. Illinois*, 556 U.S. 148, 129 S.Ct. 1446, 173 L.Ed.2d 320 (2009)

Michael Rivera was tried on two counts of first-degree murder. During *voir dire*, his lawyer sought to use a peremptory challenge against a prospective juror. The judge disallowed the challenge without explaining why. The prospective juror was seated and Rivera was convicted and sentenced to eighty-five years in prison. On appeal, the Illinois Supreme Court remanded the case to the trial court, demanding that the trial judge explain why he overruled the peremptory challenge. The trial judge indicated that gender discrimination was the reason. The Illinois Supreme Court rejected this submission and held that the peremptory challenge had been wrongly denied. Nevertheless, the Illinois high court held that this mistake was a harmless error and upheld Rivera's conviction. In 2009, the U.S. Supreme Court unanimously agreed, holding that a trial judge's erroneous denial of a defendant's peremptory challenge to a prospective juror does not automatically require reversal of the defendant's conviction on appeal, as long the judge's ruling was made in good faith and all members of the jury were qualified and unbiased.

capital punishment could not be excluded from juries impaneled to hear cases where the death penalty could be imposed unless the prospective jurors indicated that they could not make an impartial decision on the issue of guilt or could never vote to impose the death penalty. *Witherspoon v. Illinois*, 391 U.S. 510, 88 S.Ct. 1770, 20 L.Ed.2d 776 (1968).

In *Wainwright v. Witt*, 469 U.S. 412, 424, 105 S.Ct. 844, 852, 83 L.Ed.2d 841, 851–852 (1985), the Court articulated the proper standard for determining when a prospective juror may be excluded for cause because of views on capital punishment. The test, the Court said, is whether the juror's views would "prevent or substantially impair the performance of his duties as a juror in accordance with his instructions and oath." Justice William J. Brennan, with whom Justice Thurgood Marshall joined in dissent, observed that "basic justice demands that juries with the power to decide whether a capital defendant lives or dies not be poisoned against the defendant." 469 U.S. at 439, 105 S.Ct. at 860, 83 L.Ed.2d at 861. In capital cases, the jury first hears the evidence bearing on the defendant's guilt or innocence; then, only if a guilty verdict is rendered, the jury receives evidence on whether the death penalty should be imposed. This practice is referred to as a bifurcated trial (see Chapter 19).

**death qualification of a jury** Questioning of prospective jurors in a death penalty case to insure that the jury is composed of people who do not entertain scruples against imposing capital punishment.

The Supreme Court has said that the **death qualification of a jury** (that is, the exclusion of prospective jurors who will not under any circumstances vote for imposition of the death penalty) is designed to obtain a jury that can properly and impartially apply the law to the facts at both the guilt and sentencing phases of a capital trial. On this rationale, the Court held that removal before the guilt phase in a capital trial of prospective jurors whose opposition to the death penalty would impair or prevent performance of their duties at the sentencing phase is not unconstitutional. *Lockhart v. McCree*, 476 U.S. 162, 106 S.Ct. 1758, 90 L.Ed.2d 137 (1986).

## Impaneling of the Jury

If the court anticipates that a trial might be protracted, it may have one or more alternate jurors selected to serve should any juror become ill or have to respond to an emergency. An alternate juror sits with the jury, but unless substituted for a regular juror, the alternate is excused just before the jury retires to deliberate. After selection of the jury is complete, it is sworn as a body by the judge or the clerk of the court to carry out its duties and is admonished not to discuss the case until instructed by the court to deliberate.

## Proposals for Jury Reform

In the nationally televised O. J. Simpson case in 1995, the public witnessed considerable bickering between counsel and long delays in impaneling a jury. A protracted jury trial with many delays ensued. Thus, the Simpson trial became a catalyst for reform in the jury processes. Polls taken after that trial revealed a great decline in interest in serving on juries. Many who have been called to serve complain of "just sitting around the courthouse and wasting time" with no explanation for the delay. They are demanding that court officials show them more concern and respect. Although some progress has been made in allowing jurors to remain on call until needed, there remains room for improvement in many jurisdictions.

Many who have served on juries feel that the jury selection process has become too competitive, with little focus on the goal of obtaining a fair and impartial jury. Others emphasize the need not only to expedite the process of impaneling a jury but also for jurors to be given a greater role during the trial. Suggestions for reform have

### What Happens When a Juror Becomes Emotionally Disabled?

**CASE-IN-POINT** Fred Mills was convicted of aggravated robbery in Dallas County, Texas. On the morning of his trial, one of the jurors impaneled to hear the case requested permission to attend a memorial service for his grandfather, who had died the previous evening. The trial judge found the juror was "emotionally disabled" and would not be able to concentrate if not allowed to attend the memorial service. Attempts to postpone the trial disclosed conflicts for other jurors and schedules for other docketed cases, so over Mills's objection, the judge proceeded with the trial with the remaining eleven jurors. On federal habeas corpus review, the U.S. Court of Appeals for the Fifth Circuit noted that Article 36.29 of the Texas Code of Criminal Procedure specifies a norm of twelve jurors in felony cases, yet it provides that if one juror becomes "disabled," the remaining eleven can render a verdict. The court declined to review the Texas court's finding that the juror was emotionally disabled due to death of a relative. Citing *Williams v. Florida*, 399 U.S. 78, 90 S.Ct. 1893, 26 L.Ed.2d 446 (1970), the court denied Mills's petition. The court observed that "since Texas provided Mills with a jury possessing the fundamental attributes of the jury guaranteed by the Sixth and Fourteenth Amendments, Mills has no claim for relief."

*Mills v. Collins*, 924 F.2d 89 (5th Cir. 1991).

included limiting the number of peremptory challenges by counsel, allowing jurors to take written notes as a trial proceeds, and permitting questioning of witnesses by jurors. Over the last decade, courts have been increasingly willing to allow jurors to play a more active role in the trial.

## Free Press versus Fair Trial

First Amendment guarantees of freedom of the press often collide with a defendant's right to a fair trial before an impartial jury. This is particularly true when heightened public interest results in mass media coverage of a trial, with potential prejudicial effects on witnesses and jurors. When this occurs, the trial court must protect the defendant's right to a fair trial by taking steps to prevent these influences from affecting the rights of the defendant. Failure to do so can result in a verdict of guilty being overturned by an appellate tribunal. The classic example of this is the Dr. Sam Sheppard Case, where the U.S. Supreme Court held that a defendant had been denied a fair trial in a sensational murder case because the trial judge failed to guard against pervasive and prejudicial media coverage. *Sheppard v. Maxwell*, 384 U.S. 333, 86 S.Ct. 1507, 16 L.Ed.2d 600 (1966).

Although the media cannot "take over" the courtroom, it is equally clear that because of First Amendment rights, the public and the press cannot ordinarily be excluded from criminal trials. In 1980 Chief Justice Warren Burger, writing for the Supreme Court, traced the history of criminal trials in Anglo-American jurisprudence and concluded that public access is an indispensable element of criminal trials. Therefore, the Court concluded that trials may not be closed without findings sufficient to overcome the presumption of openness. *Richmond Newspapers, Inc. v. Virginia*, 448 U.S. 555,100 S.Ct. 2814, 65 L.Ed.2d 973 (1980).

### Cameras in the Courtroom

In 1965, in a 5–4 decision, the Supreme Court held that the defendant, Billy Sol Estes, was denied due process of law because the proceedings of his criminal trial were televised over his objection. *Estes v. Texas*, 381 U.S. 532, 85 S.Ct. 1628, 14 L.Ed.2d

## JURISPRUDENCE

*Sheppard v. Maxwell*, 384 U.S. 333, 86 S.Ct. 1507, 16 L.Ed.2d 600 (1966)

In a high-profile homicide case, a jury found Dr. Sam Sheppard guilty of the 1954 murder of his wife, Marilyn. His conviction was affirmed on appeal. But in 1966 the Supreme Court reversed a federal appeals court's denial of Sheppard's petition for habeas corpus. Observing that jurors at Sheppard's trial were constantly exposed to intense media coverage until their deliberations and that the "newsmen took over practically the entire courtroom," the Court found that the highly prejudicial publicity contributed to the denial of due process of law to the defendant. Acknowledging that nothing proscribes the press from reporting events in the courtroom, the Court suggested that trial courts can combat the problem through such measures as (1) proscribing out-of-court statements by lawyers, parties, witnesses, or court officials concerning matters that could be prejudicial to the accused and (2) insulating the witnesses and sequestering the jury to prevent exposure to reports by the media. The prosecution was given a reasonable time to retry Sheppard. On retrial in 1966, he was acquitted. Sheppard died in 1970, but his son, Sam Reese Sheppard, brought a civil suit against the state of Ohio claiming that his father was wrongfully imprisoned for the crime for which he was later acquitted. In an attempt to clear Sheppard's reputation, counsel attempted to establish that the DNA of a third person—not Sheppard or his wife—was present at the crime scene. On April 10, 2000, a jury in Cuyahoga County, Ohio, unanimously rejected the claim.

543 (1965). This was consistent with the longtime ban that courts had imposed on allowing cameras in the courtroom. During the 1970s, many state courts began to allow radio, television, and still-camera coverage of court proceedings subject to limitations necessary to preserve the essential dignity of a trial (e.g., equipment must be noiseless, and strong lights are not permitted). Also, judges may limit coverage by requiring pooling of media equipment. Nevertheless, Rule 53 of the Federal Rules of Criminal Procedure still prohibits the taking of photographs in the courtroom during the progress of judicial proceedings in federal courts.

Florida is among the states that began permitting televised trials in the late 1970s. *In re Post-Newsweek Stations, Florida, Inc.*, 370 So.2d 764 (Fla. 1979). Thereafter, Noel Chandler and another defendant, who were charged with several offenses, requested the trial court to exclude live television coverage from their jury trial. The court denied their request, and they were found guilty. A state appellate court affirmed their convictions. *Chandler v. State*, 366 So.2d 64 (Fla. App. 1978). The U.S. Supreme Court granted review. At the outset, the Court acknowledged that it had no supervisory jurisdiction over state courts. Therefore, it confined its review to evaluating the constitutionality of Florida's program permitting radio, television, and photographic coverage of criminal proceedings over an accused's objection. The Court declined to prohibit television cameras from state courts but said that defendants have a right to show that such use prejudiced them in obtaining a fair trial. Finding that Chandler and his codefendant had not shown they were prejudiced in any way by the televising of their trials, the Court denied them any relief. *Chandler v. Florida*, 449 U.S. 560, 101 S.Ct. 802, 66 L.Ed.2d 740 (1981).

Today, cameras are allowed in the courtrooms of almost all state courts. And although there has been some backlash following the O. J. Simpson case, most still feel that cameras in the courtroom have enhanced the public's awareness of the judicial process. However, it is probably a fair generalization to conclude that, depending on the particular case, judges should be more assertive in exercising control over the televising of criminal proceedings.

The federal ban on cameras in the courtroom came to the forefront in March and April 1993, when four police officers, previously acquitted of criminal charges in a state court trial, were tried in a federal district court in Los Angeles on charges of violating the Fourth Amendment rights of Rodney King. Because this trial attracted widespread interest, the media voiced displeasure at their inability to bring live camera coverage to the public. Nevertheless, in 1994 the Judicial Conference of the United States voted to maintain the ban on television cameras in federal courts. There is less resistance to allowing television and still photography coverage of appellate proceedings. In March 1996, the U.S. Judicial Conference voted 14–12 to allow federal appeals courts to permit television, radio, and still photography in civil, but not criminal, appeals.

Almost all state courts now permit television and photographic coverage of court proceedings. In most states, the consent of the presiding judge is required, and judges generally have considerable discretion to control the coverage. Coverage of jurors is either prohibited or restricted, and most states prohibit coverage of cases involving juveniles and victims of sex crimes. Some states have such restrictive policies that television coverage of trials almost never takes place. However, in many states, television cameras that are permanent fixtures of the courtroom record court proceedings. Television stations and networks can simply pick up the signals, which they can edit or present live to their viewers.

The O. J. Simpson case, tried in California in 1995, shows how a sensational criminal trial can draw the mass media's attention. In that case, CNN and Court TV featured live coverage of many of the courtroom activities; other television networks carried daily "O. J. Updates" in their evening news programs.

## Gag Orders

**gag order** A court order prohibiting attorneys, witnesses, jurors and other persons associated with a trial from talking to the press about the case.

In order to keep the prosecutor and the defense counsel from "trying a case in the media," a judge can issue a **gag order** prohibiting the attorneys from talking to the press about the case. However, the U.S. Supreme Court has made it very difficult, if not impossible, for judges to extend gag orders to media members. *Nebraska Press*

---

**JURISPRUDENCE**

*Nebraska Press Association v. Stuart*, 427 U.S. 539, 96 S.Ct. 2791, 49 L.Ed.2d 683 (1976)

This case stems from the brutal murder of six members of the Henry Kelly family in Sutherland, Nebraska, on the night of October 18, 1975. Erwin Simants, an unemployed handyman, was accused of the crime. Evidence indicated that the victims died as a result of wounds inflicted with a .22-caliber rifle and that some of the victims had been sexually assaulted after the wounds had been inflicted. The grisly crime generated widespread publicity, much of which was prejudicial to the accused. Three days after Simants was arrested, attorneys for the state and the defense asked the local court to issue an order restricting media coverage of the case. The court complied and issued an order prohibiting

reportage of certain aspects of the case until a trial jury could be empaneled. The Nebraska Press Association then filed a civil suit challenging the constitutionality of the gag order. After the Nebraska Supreme Court upheld the lower court's order, the Nebraska Press Association took the case to the U.S. Supreme Court on a writ of certiorari. Before the Supreme Court handed down its decision, Erwin Simants was convicted and sentenced to death. Ultimately, however, his conviction was reversed by the Nebraska Supreme Court after it was found that the local sheriff had visited the trial jurors at the motel where they were sequestered during the course of the trial. After a second trial, Simants was found not guilty by reason of insanity and was committed to a mental institution.

*Association v. Stuart*, 427 U.S. 539, 96 S.Ct. 2791, 49 L.Ed.2d 683 (1976). Once the media finds out information about a trial, courts cannot restrict reportage of that information.

# "Order in the Court"

Occasionally a trial judge is confronted with a defendant or others in attendance at a trial whose disruptive behavior impedes the court from conducting a trial in a proper judicial atmosphere. As Justice Hugo Black observed, "The flagrant disregard in the courtroom of elementary standards of proper conduct should not and cannot be tolerated." *Illinois v. Allen*, 397 U.S. 337, 343, 90 S.Ct. 1057, 1061, 25 L.Ed.2d 353, 359 (1970).

This problem is more likely encountered in a so-called political trial, where there may be support for the cause the defendant claims to represent. One such highly publicized instance of courtroom disruption occurred in the 1969–1970 "Chicago Seven" conspiracy trial in federal court in Chicago. The seven defendants, including antiwar activist David T. Dellinger, were prosecuted under the Federal Anti-Riot Statute (18 U.S.C.A. §§ 2101–2102) for their actions at the August 1968 Democratic National Convention in Chicago. An eighth defendant, Black Panther party leader Bobby G. Seale, was tried separately on similar charges. Considerable antagonism developed among the trial judge, the defendants, and their counsel. As a result of their actions during their trials, all defendants and two of their attorneys were found guilty of contempt of court. Despite the number of unruly and disrespectful actions that took place, the contempt convictions were reversed because of procedural irregularities. *United States v. Seale*, 461 F.2d 345 (7th Cir. 1972); *In re Dellinger*, 461 F.2d 389 (7th Cir. 1972). Subsequently, the defendants' convictions were also reversed by the same federal court of appeals on the basis of judicial error. In this latter opinion the appellate court criticized the trial judge for his own antagonistic behavior during the trial. *United States v. Dellinger*, 472 F.2d 340 (7th Cir. 1972).

## Unruly Defendants

It is not too difficult for judges to exercise control over members of the public who attend court trials. The problem that confronts judges is a defendant who becomes unruly. In most instances, judges control disruption and defiance by defendants and others through exercise of the **power of contempt**. Yet in recent years, some courts have had to go further. In *Illinois v. Allen*, supra, the Supreme Court recognized that there is no one formula for maintaining the appropriate courtroom atmosphere, but indicated that

> there are at least three constitutionally permissible ways for a trial judge to handle an obstreperous defendant . . . : (1) bind and gag him, thereby keeping him present; (2) cite him for contempt; (3) take him out of the courtroom until he promises to conduct himself properly. 397 U.S. at 343–344, 90 S.Ct. at 1061, 25 L.Ed.2d at 359.

The Sixth Amendment protects the defendant's right to be present at every critical stage of criminal proceedings. *Snyder v. Massachusetts*, 291 U.S. 97, 54 S.Ct. 330, 78 L.Ed. 674 (1934). The right to be present at trial is fundamental; however, it may be forfeited if the defendant is disruptive or fails to comply with reasonable standards of the court. For example, in New York a defendant repeatedly insisted on appearing in court while wearing only his underwear covered by a sheet. After

**power of contempt** The authority of a court of law to punish someone who insults the court or flouts its authority.

warning him of the consequences of not wearing proper attire to court, the trial court allowed the trial to proceed in the defendant's absence. On appeal, the trial court's action was affirmed. *People v. Hinton*, 550 N.Y.S.2d 438 (N.Y. App. Div. 1990).

The Supreme Court in *Illinois v. Allen*, 397 U.S. 337, 90 S.Ct. 1057, 25 L.Ed.2d 353 (1970), explained that a trial judge is justified in employing necessary security measures to control a disruptive defendant. Accordingly, all courts insist that a defendant not disrupt courtroom proceedings. Thus, if there is a real threat of serious disruption by a defendant, or where threats of escape or danger to those in and around the courtroom exist, a defendant may be shackled. Federal and state courts are reluctant to shackle a defendant unless it becomes imperative because, in addition to concerns over the appearance of the defendant, shackling may have a prejudicial effect on a defendant's decision to testify at trial. See *People v. Duran*, 545 P.2d 1322 (Cal. 1976). Moreover, in some cases such restraints "may . . . impair [the defendant's] ability to confer with counsel, and significantly affect the trial strategy he chooses to follow." *Zygadlo v. Wainwright*, 720 F.2d 1221, 1223 (11th Cir. 1983).

Most state courts probably take the view of the Missouri Supreme Court. In 1996 that court observed that the use of restraints for courtroom security purposes is a matter within the discretion of the trial court. *State v. Kinder*, 942 S.W.2d 313 (Mo. 1996). In 1999 the Illinois Supreme Court, citing one of its earlier decisions, enumerated the following factors a trial judge should consider in determining whether to shackle a defendant:

> . . . the seriousness of the present charge against the defendant; defendant's temperament and character; his age and physical attributes; his past record; past escapes or attempted escapes, and evidence of a present plan to escape; threats to harm others or cause a disturbance; self-destructive tendencies; the risk of mob violence or of attempted revenge by others; the possibility of rescue by other offenders still at large; the size and mood of the audience; the nature and physical security of the courtroom; and the adequacy and availability of alternative remedies. *People v. Buss*, 718 N.E.2d 1, 40 (Ill. 1999).

## Behavior of Counsel

Dramatic, fictional presentations of courtroom proceedings now occupy a considerable part of television entertainment. A viewer is quite likely to gain an erroneous impression of courtroom proceedings, particularly in respect to the standards of conduct enforced against lawyers in criminal trials. Lawyers are seen asking inflammatory questions of a witness and expressing personal opinions concerning facts at issue. Others persist in interrogating a witness after the court has sustained an objection to such a line of questioning. It is not uncommon to see a lawyer continuing to press a point of law after the trial judge has made a ruling. Some actually appear to practice deceptive tactics on behalf of a client, justifying the means by the ultimate goal of helping a client. A prospective criminal justice professional could misapprehend the true role of a prosecutor or defense lawyer. Moreover, a prospective client who sees lawyers on television dramatically pursue such flagrant tactics may gain a false expectation of what a lawyer's role is in the courtroom, and as a result may someday expect his or her own lawyer to pursue such tactics.

In federal and state courts lawyers are subject to rather strict legal and ethical rules in presenting evidence, following trial procedures, and courtroom decorum. When making an opening statement, a lawyer must not express personal knowledge or opinion concerning facts in issue. Lawyers must avoid misstating a fact or point of law; must address their arguments to the court, not to opposing counsel; and must avoid disparaging remarks toward opposing counsel. They are expected to refer to adult witnesses by their surnames and refrain from any gestures of approval or disapproval during a witness's testimony. A lawyer is not permitted to express a personal opinion as to the guilt or innocence of a defendant, but may argue whether the evidence shows guilt or innocence. Furthermore, a lawyer should abstain from flattery or other comments designed to curry favor with a juror. And it goes without saying that a trial judge must maintain a position of dignity and neutrality during the course of a trial.

It is understandable that emotions can run high during a trial, but trial judges generally insist on proper decorum in the courtroom. The court may discipline a lawyer who fails to abide by these rules. An offending lawyer may be found in contempt of court and fined or even jailed in instances of egregious misconduct. However, because of the possible adverse effect on a case, trial judges are hesitant to reprimand a lawyer, particularly defense counsel, in the presence of a jury. Other forms of disciplinary action may be initiated by a bar association and can range from public reprimands to suspension or even disbarment where a lawyer intentionally deceives the court, knowingly makes a false statement or submits a false document, or improperly withholds material information that causes serious injury to a party or a significant adverse effect on a legal proceeding.

# The Rules of Evidence

In our adversary system, the purpose of a trial is to search for the truth. Guilt or innocence is determined based on the evidence produced at a trial. Evidence consists of verbal statements, writings, documents, photographs, and tangible items that tend to prove or disprove some fact in issue. Certain rules govern the introduction of evidence in a court of law. Sometimes a judge will tend to relax these rules in a nonjury trial because the judge is trained to "sort out" the probative evidence from the nonprobative. However, in a jury trial in a criminal case, the rules of evidence are strictly enforced.

The subject of evidence is complex. The rules of evidence prescribed by Congress for use in federal courts are known as the Federal Rules of Evidence and are found in Title 28 of the U.S. Code Annotated. Some states have legislatively or judicially adopted codes of evidence; in other states, the rules of evidence must be gleaned from a study of the decisional law of the state. Volumes have been written on the subject, and thousands of court decisions address its various aspects and refinements of general rules. From a basic text on criminal procedure, the reader can expect to gain only a very basic grasp of the principles involved.

## Judicial Notice

**judicial notice** The act of a court recognizing, without proof, the existence of certain facts that are commonly known.

Facts commonly known are accepted by courts without formal proof, a process known as the court taking **judicial notice** of certain established facts. Usually there is a request by counsel, but in some instances courts take judicial notice without request. The rationale for the doctrine of judicial notice is that courts should not exclude consideration of matters of general knowledge that are well known to informed members of the public. To illustrate, courts take judicial notice of who is president of the United States, that a particular date in a given month was on a certain day of the week, or that whiskey is an intoxicating liquor. In some instances it may be necessary to bring such commonly accepted facts to the court's attention by presentation of a calendar or an almanac. Courts in a particular area may be asked to take judicial notice of certain facts within the geographic area of the court's jurisdiction. However, judicial notice of a fact must never be used as a substitute for proof of an essential element of a crime. *State v. Welch*, 363 A.2d 1356 (R.I. 1976). Taking judicial notice is not conclusive, because a party can always offer proof to the contrary.

Courts also take judicial notice of the law. All courts take judicial notice of the U.S. Constitution and general acts of Congress, and federal courts take judicial notice of the federal laws and the laws of each state, including statutes or judicial opinions. *Lamar v. Micou*, 114 U.S. 218, 5 S.Ct. 857, 29 L.Ed. 94 (1885). State courts take judicial notice of their own state constitutions and state laws. Municipal ordinances and the laws of other states generally must be established by formal proof, but attorneys frequently stipulate as to the text of these laws. Of course, courts can require counsel to submit memoranda relative to the status of laws and judicial opinions to be judicially noticed.

## Proof beyond a Reasonable Doubt

**proof beyond a reasonable doubt** The standard of proof in a criminal trial or a juvenile delinquency hearing.

Historically, the requirement for **proof beyond a reasonable doubt** in a criminal trial has required proof whereby the fact finder would have "an abiding conviction, to a moral certainty, of the truth of the charge." *Commonwealth v. Webster*, 59 Mass. (5 Cush.) 295, 320 (1850). The historical requirement was elevated to a constitutional mandate in *In re Winship*, 397 U.S. 358, 90 S.Ct. 1068, 25 L.Ed.2d 368 (1970). There, the Supreme Court held that the Due Process Clause of the Fourteenth Amendment requires the prosecution to establish the elements of a charged crime beyond a reasonable doubt. Judges have defined "beyond a reasonable doubt" in a variety of ways. In *Victor v. Nebraska*, 511 U.S. 1, 114 S.Ct. 1239, 127 L.Ed.2d 583 (1994), the Supreme Court held that the Constitution does not require that any one particular form of words be employed. Rather, judges have wide discretion in instructing juries on the meaning of the reasonable doubt standard. In evaluating jury instructions on this issue, the question is whether the court's instruction, taken as a whole, conveys a correct sense of the concept of reasonable doubt. In *Victor*, the Court avoided defining reasonable doubt directly but said that trial courts must avoid definitions of reasonable doubt that permit juries to convict a person on a standard that is less than what is required by due process of law.

## Evidentiary Presumptions

**evidentiary presumptions** Establishment of one fact allows inference of another fact or circumstance.

This standard of requiring proof beyond a reasonable doubt is central to judicial consideration of the validity of **evidentiary presumptions**. At common law, a child younger than seven years old was conclusively presumed to be incapable of committing a crime. A legal presumption of this type is called an irrebuttable presumption. In other words, no evidence can be introduced in court to overcome it. In criminal law, an irrebuttable presumption that provides, based on proof of one fact, that the fact finder (judge or jury) must conclusively find that the existence of another fact is troublesome because it encroaches on a defendant's due process right to have the prosecution prove the defendant guilty beyond a reasonable doubt.

Today, most presumptions in criminal law are permissive. These are evidentiary devices designed to aid a party who has the burden of proof. For example, under this type of presumption, once evidence establishes a fact, the jury may infer that something else is true, provided there is a rational connection between the basic fact and the presumed fact.

In *County Court of Ulster County, New York v. Allen*, 442 U.S. 140, 99 S.Ct. 2213, 60 L.Ed.2d 777 (1979), the Supreme Court upheld the application of a New York statutory presumption that occupants of a car in which firearms were present are in illegal possession of them, as applied to a case in which three adults and a juvenile were tried for illegal possession of handguns. When the police stopped the vehicle in which the suspects were riding, they saw the handguns located crosswise in an open handbag. The juvenile admitted ownership of the bag. At the conclusion of the trial, the judge instructed the jury, in part, that "you may infer and draw a conclusion that such prohibited weapon was possessed by each of the defendants who occupied the automobile at the time when such instruments were found. The presumption, or presumptions, is effective only so long as there is no substantial evidence contradicting the conclusion flowing from the presumption, and the presumption is said to disappear when such contradictory evidence is adduced." The Supreme Court pointed out that "the presumption was merely a part of the prosecution's case, that it gave rise to a permissive inference available only in certain circumstances, rather than a mandatory conclusion of possession, and that it could be ignored by the jury even if there was no affirmative proof offered by defendants in rebuttal." 442 U.S. at 160–161, 99 S.Ct. at 2213, 60 L.Ed.2d at 794.

Shortly thereafter, in *Sandstrom v. Montana*, 442 U.S. 510, 99 S.Ct. 2450, 61 L.Ed.2d 39 (1979), the Court reviewed a case in which the State of Montana charged the defendant, David Sandstrom, with a homicidal crime where intent was a necessary element of the offense. The trial court instructed the jury that "the law presumes that a person intends the ordinary consequences of his voluntary act." Historically, many trial courts commonly instructed juries substantially as quoted. But in *Sandstrom*, the Supreme Court noted that because the jury was not told that the presumption could be rebutted, it may have interpreted the presumption as being conclusive or as shifting to the defendant the burden of persuasion on the element of intent. Thus, the Court viewed the issue to be whether such an instruction relieved the state of its

---

**CASE-IN-POINT**

### Constitutionality of a Statute that Creates a Permissive Inference

The state of Florida charged John Henry Rygwelski with violating Florida Statutes, § 812.155(4)(b), which provides that the failure to redeliver property within five days after receipt of, or within five days after return receipt from, the certified mailing of the demand for return "is prima facie evidence of fraudulent intent." The trial court found that the statute creates a mandatory presumption that relieves the state of its burden to prove an essential element of the offense, in violation of the Due Process Clauses of the federal and Florida constitutions. The appellate court granted the state's petition for review and held that under Florida Supreme Court precedents the statute creates a permissive inference, not a mandatory presumption. Therefore, a party challenging the law is required to demonstrate its invalidity *as applied to him or her*. The court said, "Rygwelski must make an as-applied challenge [of the statute] to its application under the facts of his case for the trial court to determine whether the presumed fact (fraudulent intent) is rationally connected to the proven fact (failure to return property within five days of receipt of demand for return). Given the procedural posture of this case—the only action taken was the ruling on the motion to dismiss; the parties have not submitted evidence as to the alleged violation—any consideration of an as-applied challenge is premature pending further factual development." The appellate court quashed the order under review and remanded this case for further proceedings consistent with its opinion.

*State v. Rygwelski*, 899 So.2d 498 (Fla. App. 2005).

burden to prove the defendant guilty beyond any reasonable doubt. The Court found that the instruction mandated a conclusive presumption that removed the need to prove the essential element of intent and ruled that such a presumption violated the defendant's due process rights under the Fourteenth Amendment.

A decade later, the Court reiterated the principle announced in *Sandstrom*. A defendant had been prosecuted for violating a statute that provided as follows: "Whenever any person who has . . . rented a vehicle willfully and intentionally fails to return the vehicle to its owner within 5 days after the . . . rental agreement has expired . . . shall be presumed to have embezzled the vehicle." The Court held that the jury instruction that included the mandatory presumption of the statute violated the defendant's due process rights. *Carella v. California*, 491 U.S. 263, 109 S.Ct. 2419, 105 L.Ed.2d 218 (1989).

## Requirements of Admissibility

As we pointed out in the previous chapters, a defendant has certain constitutional protections concerning the prosecution's use of forced admissions and confessions and of other evidence that has been illegally obtained. In addition, before evidence, whether real or testimonial and whether direct or circumstantial, may be admitted in court, it must meet specific legal requirements. All evidence must be relevant (that is, it must tend to prove or disprove a material fact in issue). For example, assume that a defendant is charged with armed robbery. It would be relevant to show where the defendant and victim were located when the offense occurred, the money or other articles stolen, the force applied by the defendant, details of any weapon used, the victim's resistance, and the defendant's fingerprints. Flight by the defendant when the police sought to make an arrest and, of course, any admissions or confessions of the defendant material to the crime would also be relevant. But offenses committed by the defendant completely unrelated to the crime of robbery would be irrelevant, as would be the defendant's individual likes, dislikes, and lifestyle.

## Similar Fact Evidence

**similar fact evidence**
Refers to evidence of facts similar to the facts alleged in the crime charged.

So-called **similar fact evidence** consists of facts similar to the facts in the crime charged. Such evidence might reveal the commission of a collateral crime. The test of admissibility is whether such evidence is relevant and has a probative value in establishing a material issue. Thus, under some limited circumstances, evidence of other crimes or conduct similar to that charged against the defendant may be admitted in evidence in a criminal prosecution. Although such evidence cannot be admitted to prove the defendant's bad character or propensity to commit a crime, in some instances it may be admitted to show motive, identity, or absence of mistake or accident. See, e.g., *Williams v. State*, 110 So.2d 654 (Fla. 1959). This is a very technical area of the law of evidence and is subject to varying interpretations by federal and state courts.

The trend is to admit similar fact evidence in cases involving prosecutions for sexual abuse of children. In these cases, it often becomes important to establish opportunity, motive, intent, identity, or the absence of a mistake or accident or even to establish a child's credibility as a witness if such credibility is attacked by the defendant. This last point is illustrated by *Gezzi v. State*, 780 P.2d 972 (Wyo. 1989). There, the Wyoming Supreme Court reviewed a defendant's conviction on two counts of committing indecent acts with the younger of his two daughters. During the defendant's trial, the older sister testified to a course of sexual misconduct occurring between her and the defendant similar to the molestation occurring between the defendant and the younger sister. Admission of this testimony was upheld because the younger sister's credibility was attacked and the evidence admitted at trial was inconclusive as to the cause of the younger sister's physical symptoms. In affirming the defendant's conviction, the court included an exhaustive footnote showing that about half of state courts now liberally recognize the admissibility of prior bad acts (similar acts) as evidence for various purposes in sexual offense cases.

## Classifications of Evidence

**real evidence** Refers to maps, blood samples, X-rays, photographs, stolen goods, fingerprints, knives, guns, and other tangible items introduced into evidence.

**testimonial evidence** Evidence received by a court from witnesses who have testified under oath.

**direct evidence** Evidence that applies directly to proof of a fact or proposition. For example, a witness who testifies to having seen an act done or heard a statement made is giving direct evidence.

**eyewitness testimony** Testimony given by a person based on personal observation of an event.

**indirect evidence** Inferences and presumptions that are probative of various facts in issue.

**circumstantial evidence** Indirect evidence from which the existence of certain facts may be inferred.

There are several classifications of evidence. First, evidence may be real or testimonial. **Real evidence** consists of maps, blood samples, X-rays, photographs, stolen goods, fingerprints, knives, guns, and other tangible items. **Testimonial evidence** consists of sworn statements of witnesses. Watching a television drama might give the impression that a criminal trial consists largely of real evidence, but the great majority of evidence presented in criminal trials comes from the mouths of the witnesses, both lay and expert.

Next, evidence may be direct or indirect. **Direct evidence** includes **eyewitness testimony**, whereas **indirect evidence** usually consists of circumstantial evidence—that is, attendant facts from which inferences can be drawn to establish other facts in issue at the trial. To illustrate, a person who testifies to having seen the defendant enter the victim's house is giving direct evidence. Testimony that reveals that the defendant's fingerprints were found on a windowpane of that house shortly after it was broken into is **circumstantial evidence** from which, depending on the circumstances, it may be inferred that the defendant entered the house through that window. The admissibility of circumstantial evidence in criminal trials is well established in American law. *Tot v. United States*, 319 U.S. 463, 63 S.Ct. 1241, 87 L.Ed. 1519 (1943).

The same evidence can be direct regarding one fact and circumstantial regarding another. The witness who testifies that the defendant had possession of a pistol is giving direct evidence of that fact. Depending on other circumstances, it might be inferable from proof of that fact that the defendant attacked the victim.

Actually, there is no real difference in the weight given to circumstantial as opposed to real evidence. Circumstantial evidence may once have been suspect, yet lawyers and judges can point to many instances where circumstantial evidence has proven to be more reliable than testimonial evidence. As the Supreme Court has observed:

> [C]ircumstantial evidence may in some cases point to a wholly incorrect result. Yet this is equally true of testimonial evidence. In both instances, a jury is asked to weigh the chances that the evidence correctly points to guilt against the possibility of inaccuracy or ambiguous inference. In both the jury must use its experience with people and events in weighing the probabilities. *Holland v. United States*, 348 U.S. 121, 140, 75 S.Ct. 127, 137–138, 99 L.Ed. 150, 166–167 (1954).

## The Requirement of Competency

**competent to testify** Having the legal capacity to offer evidence under oath in court.

To be admissible in court, evidence must also be competent. In determining whether a witness is **competent to testify**, the trial judge must consider the ability of the witness to receive and recollect impressions, to understand questions, and

**CASE-IN-POINT**

### Conviction Based Solely on Circumstantial Evidence Must Exclude Every Reasonable Hypothesis of a Defendant's Innocence

A Florida jury found John William Jackson guilty of first-degree murder and armed burglary based entirely on circumstantial evidence. On appeal, Jackson argued that the trial court erred in denying his motion for a judgment of acquittal.

The evidence revealed that on December 19, 1983, around 4:30 A.M., the victim was raped and stabbed in her house trailer. She sought help from a neighbor and described her assailant as "an orange picker, Michigan tag." Shortly thereafter she died from multiple stab wounds to her neck. The police arrived at the scene later that day and collected blood, semen, and saliva stains; fingerprints; and hair samples. Jackson later gave the police his fingerprints, impressions of his teeth, and samples of his pubic and head hair and his blood. An autopsy revealed that a bruise on the victim's right wrist was a bite mark. Jackson, a thirty-one-year-old Caucasian male, had lived in the vicinity of the victim's trailer from approximately July 1983 until a few days before the crime, when he moved a few miles away.

Dr. Richard Souviron, a forensic odontologist, testified that the bite mark on the victim's wrist was consistent with Jackson's teeth impressions. On January 31, 1984, Jackson had a conversation with Charles and Patricia Fuller, on whose property he had lived during the latter part of 1983. Jackson mentioned to them that when the police interrogated him, he learned that the victim had been raped, stabbed, and bitten. This occurred before the police had released the information that the victim had been bitten. Mrs. Fuller acknowledged that Jackson had told her that he had been picking oranges. Mr. Fuller testified that during the time he knew him, the defendant had worked as a heavy equipment operator. FBI Agent Michael Malone, an expert in hair and fiber analysis, identified two head hairs found on the victim's pajama top as being indistinguishable from Jackson's hair sample. Agent Malone also said that "Negroid hairs" were found in a window screen and in the combed pubic hair of the victim.

The appellate court found that the prosecution presented three items of crucial evidence: first, the consistent bite mark; second, Jackson's statement to the Fullers that the victim had been bitten; and third, the strands of hair matching Jackson's hair found on the victim. The court noted that although Dr. Souviron concluded that the bite marks on the victim's wrist were consistent with Jackson's teeth impression, he added, "this was not a positive bite. . . . I certainly hope [the detective] didn't arrest John Jackson on this bite." The court found that the fact that Jackson knew the victim had been bitten was not probative of his guilt. The court pointed out that prior to Jackson's conversation with the Fullers, the police had taken impressions of his teeth, an event that would be a strong indication to anyone that a bite mark was involved. The only other significant evidence against Jackson, the court noted, was Agent Malone's testimony that two strands of hair found on the victim's pajamas matched the defendant's hair samples. But Agent Malone also agreed that hair comparisons did not constitute a basis for positive personal identification and added, "It's not a fingerprint, no. I cannot say that that hair came from John Jackson and nobody else."

"Jackson's conviction," the court concluded, "hinges on two hairs found on the victim's clothing which match his hair sample. Hair comparison testimony, while admissible, does not result in identifications of absolute certainty. There was no evidence placing the defendant at the scene of the crime, no indication of a relationship of any kind between the defendant and the victim, or that they even knew each other. The victim's dying words pointed to an 'orange picker, Michigan tag.' Jackson's car, however, had a Florida tag. None of the fingerprints found at the scene of the crime matched Jackson's. This, plus the presence of Negroid pubic hair in the victim's pubic hair combings, adds support to a reasonable hypothesis that someone else committed the crime." Finally, the court explained that "[w]here the only proof of guilt is circumstantial, no matter how strongly the evidence may suggest guilt a conviction cannot be sustained unless the evidence is inconsistent with any reasonable hypothesis of innocence." Because the state failed to present evidence sufficient to enable the jury to exclude every reasonable hypothesis of the defendant's innocence, the court vacated the defendant's convictions.

*Jackson v. State*, 511 So.2d 1047 (Fla. App. 1987).

to appreciate the moral duty to tell the truth. A very young child may or may not be competent to testify. This depends on the court's finding regarding the child's ability to understand the meaning of telling the truth. No precise rule can be set forth about when a young child may be competent to testify. Rather, it is a matter for determination in the sound discretion of the trial judge. Considerations include the child's age, intelligence, and capacity to appreciate the requirement to tell the truth. See *Wheeler v. United States*, 159 U.S. 523, 16 S.Ct. 93, 40 L.Ed. 244 (1895). A determination that a child is competent to testify will generally not be overturned by an appellate court unless the trial court's judgment is clearly erroneous. *Trujillo v. State*, 880 P.2d 575 (Wyo. 1994). Persons of unsound mind may not be competent to testify, but again, a judge must determine this. The presiding judge and members of the jury would not be competent to testify at a trial where they serve.

## Expert Witnesses

**forensic experts** Persons qualified in the application of scientific knowledge to legal principles; usually applied to those who participate in discourse or who testify in court.

Today, **forensic experts** in nearly every field make a specialty of testifying in court. To qualify as an expert, a witness must present proper credentials and be received by the trial court as an expert. A court may call experts on its own motion, but usually the prosecution or defense produces experts. After one side offers a witness as an expert, opposing counsel may cross-examine the prospective witness about his or her qualifications. For example, a physician who is to give evidence as to the cause of the death of someone is first asked to relate his or her educational background and experience in the specialized area of medical practice in question. In many cases, attorneys for the prosecution and defense will stipulate that a particular witness is an expert in the field. The trial judge has considerable discretion in determining whether a witness is to be received as an expert.

**hypothetical questions** Questions based on an assumed set of facts. Hypothetical questions may be asked of expert witnesses in criminal trials.

Unlike lay witnesses, an expert witness may respond to **hypothetical questions** and may express opinions within the realm of his or her expertise. Fingerprint identification, ballistics tests, handwriting exemplars, and medical tests have been prominent among areas where expert evidence is commonly received in criminal cases. More recently, evidence from speed-detection devices as well as Breathalyzers and other devices to test blood-alcohol content has become commonplace. Judges and jurors are not necessarily scientists. Indeed, it is unlikely that many of them have more than a basic knowledge of scientific principles. Yet courts must make rational judgments about new scientific advances to determine their admissibility in court. To accomplish this, courts must depend on experts in the field.

An expert who has knowledge from personal observation may testify on that basis. For example, a psychiatrist who has examined the accused may offer an opinion as to the accused's sanity. If the expert is not acquainted with the subject from personal observation, the expert's opinion can be based on hypothetical questions that assume the existence of facts the evidence tends to establish. Medical experts and handwriting experts frequently are asked hypothetical questions in court, and experts on the subject of accident reconstruction frequently offer testimony about speed, braking, and other factors relevant to determining fault in cases involving auto accidents.

## Scientific Evidence in the Courtroom

Evidence obtained through scientific and technological innovations can be both relevant and probative in a criminal case. Yet care must be taken to ensure that a new principle or technique is well supported by research and is generally accepted by the

**scientific evidence**
Evidence obtained through scientific and technological innovations.

**general acceptance test** Also known as the *Frye* test, this test requires that the scientific principle from which the expert's deduction is made has gained general acceptance in its field.

scientific community. The basic issue the courts face is whether the expert **scientific evidence** is reliable. In *Frye v. United States*, 293 F. 1013 (D.C. Cir. 1923), the court said that "in admitting expert testimony deduced from a well-recognized scientific principle or discovery, the thing from which the deduction is made must be sufficiently established to have gained general acceptance in the particular field in which it belongs." 293 F. at 1014.

For seventy years the *Frye* test, or **general acceptance test**, was commonly applied in federal courts and in most state courts faced with the issue of whether new scientific tests should be admitted into evidence in criminal trials. In 1993, however, in *Daubert v. Merrell Dow Pharmaceuticals, Inc.*, 509 U.S. 579, 113 S.Ct. 2786, 125 L.Ed.2d 469, the U.S. Supreme Court rejected the general acceptance test. Rather, the Court ruled that the Federal Rules of Evidence supersede *Frye*. The Court held that admissibility of scientific evidence must be based on several factors, including whether the evidence can be tested and whether it can be subjected to peer review. Under *Daubert*, the trial judge must make a preliminary assessment of whether the reasoning or methodology underlying the expert's testimony is scientifically valid and whether that reasoning or methodology can be applied to the facts in issue. Once the court determines admissibility, the jury determines the weight to give to such evidence. Because the Court's ruling in *Daubert* is not one of constitutional dimension, state courts are not required to follow it.

In *Kumho Tire Co. v. Carmichael*, 526 U.S. 137, 119 S.Ct. 1167, 143 L.Ed.2d 238 (1999), the Court extended its *Daubert* reliability requirement beyond scientific testimony to include technical and other specialized expert testimony. State courts are now divided on whether to accept the newer *Daubert* standard or remain with the classic standard announced in 1923 in *Frye v. United States*.

## Hypnotically Enhanced Testimony

**hypnotically enhanced testimony** Testimony offered by a witness whose memory has been refreshed through hypnosis.

One controversial area of expert testimony concerns whether **hypnotically enhanced testimony** is admissible in a criminal trial. After examining extensive scientific literature, research, and testimony on the reliability of hypnotically refreshed memory and determining that the scientific community was divided on the subject, the California Supreme Court determined that hypnotically refreshed memory should not be admitted in judicial proceedings. *People v. Shirley*, 723 P.2d 1354 (Cal. 1982). In earlier years, some courts tended to admit such evidence—see, e.g., *Harding v. State*, 246 A.2d 302 (Md. App. 1968). However, the trend seems to have moved in the direction of not allowing such evidence. The majority of courts in the last decade have held that hypnotically enhanced testimony is not sufficiently reliable to be admissible. In *State v. Tuttle*, 780 P.2d 1203 (Utah 1989), the Utah Supreme Court published an exhaustive opinion analyzing the status of the law in this area and held that hypnotically enhanced testimony, as well as testimony regarding anything first recalled from the time of a hypnotic session forward, is inadmissible as evidence.

In *Rock v. Arkansas*, 483 U.S. 44, 107 S.Ct. 2704, 97 L.Ed.2d 37 (1987), the U.S. Supreme Court held that excluding hypnotically enhanced testimony, when applied to prevent an accused from testifying to his or her own posthypnotic recall, violated her constitutional right to testify on her own behalf. Accordingly, the position of the majority of courts to exclude all hypnotically induced testimony should not prevent an accused from testifying to his or her own posthypnotic recall. Recently some state and federal courts have allowed hypnotically enhanced testimony, but only after first conducting a determination of reliability.

## Polygraph Evidence

Known in the vernacular as a lie detector, a polygraph records a subject's respiration, blood pressure, and heartbeat as the subject is questioned by an examiner. The examiner poses certain questions and records the subject's responses. The premise of the polygraph is that deception is accompanied by stress that is manifested in increased respiration, pulse, and blood pressure. The use of a polygraph is controversial. Polygraph operators argue that a properly administered polygraph test is effective in detecting deception, and they cite impressive figures attesting to the accuracy of results. However, some critics argue that an individual can so control physiological responses as to distort the findings.

**polygraph evidence**
Results of lie detector tests (generally inadmissible into evidence).

Historically, federal and state courts have declined to admit **polygraph evidence.** As late as 1989, the Minnesota Supreme Court held that the results of polygraph tests, as well as any direct or indirect references to the taking of or refusal to take such tests, are inadmissible. *State v. Fenney*, 448 N.W.2d 54 (Minn. 1989). Most state courts agree and hold that the reliability of polygraph testing has not been scientifically demonstrated to such a degree of certainty as to permit its use in evidence. However, some courts allow the results of polygraph testing to be admitted in court on stipulation of the prosecution and the defense. See, e.g., *State v. Souel*, 372 N.E.2d 1318 (Ohio 1978); *State v. Valdez*, 371 P.2d 894 (Ariz. 1962). Other state supreme courts have held that polygraph evidence is not admissible in a criminal trial even when the parties stipulate to its admissibility. See, e.g., *People v. Baynes*, 430 N.E.2d 1070 (Ill. 1981).

The prognosis for the use of polygraph evidence remains uncertain. Advocates of polygraph evidence were heartened in 1989 when the Eleventh Circuit Court of Appeals observed that polygraph testing has gained increasingly widespread acceptance as a useful and reliable scientific tool: "We agree with those courts which have found that a per se rule disallowing polygraph evidence is no longer warranted." *United States v. Piccinonna*, 885 F.2d 1529, 1535 (11th Cir. 1989). But on March 31, 1998, the U.S. Supreme Court upheld a ban on the use of polygraph evidence in military courts. *United States v. Scheffer*, 523 U.S. 303, 118 S.Ct. 1261, 140 L.Ed.2d 413 (1998). A military appeals court had ruled that an airman should not have been barred from introducing lie-detector evidence during his court-martial on charges of using drugs and writing bad checks. In reversing that decision, the Court, in an opinion by Justice Clarence Thomas, observed that there was no consensus that such evidence is reliable and ruled that the military ban on the use of such evidence did not unconstitutionally abridge the airman's right to present a defense. However, four of the justices in the court's eight-member majority recognized that in some future case, the polygraph test might be so crucial that its results should be allowed.

## Battered Woman Syndrome

Expert testimony concerning the battered woman syndrome has gained substantial scientific acceptance, and in the past several years such testimony has been received in many courts in cases where women claim to have acted in self-defense. In 1989 the Ohio Supreme Court receded from its 1981 decision declaring such evidence inadmissible. The court took a fresh look at the literature published in this area since 1981 and said that "expert testimony on the battered woman syndrome would help dispel the ordinary lay person's perception that a woman in a battering relationship is free to leave at any time. Popular misconceptions about battered women should be put to rest, including beliefs that the women are masochistic." *State v. Koss*,

551 N.E.2d 970, 971 (Ohio 1990). To some extent, a woman's reliance on evidence of the battered woman syndrome depends on whether state law imposes a duty to retreat before defending oneself with deadly force.

On May 15, 2006, the Supreme Court of New Jersey held that "[i]t is beyond debate that battered women's syndrome has gained general acceptance as a scientific doctrine within the professional community." Recognizing that the ramifications of a battering relationship are beyond the ken of the average juror, the court noted that expert testimony is admissible "because it has been determined to be useful in explaining conduct exhibited by battered women toward their abusers." *State v. Townsend*, 897 A.2d 316, 327 (N. J. 2006).

## DNA Evidence

**DNA testing** Laboratory tests that compare DNA molecules extracted from a suspect's specimen with DNA molecules extracted from specimens found at a crime scene to determine whether the samples match.

Since its introduction in the late 1980s, **DNA testing** has had a profound impact on law enforcement and criminal procedure. DNA is an abbreviation of deoxyribonucleic acid, the chemical that carries an individual's genetic information. DNA is extracted from a biological specimen (e.g., white blood cells, semen, body hair, or tissue). Through sophisticated testing results, DNA printing tests compare DNA molecules extracted from a suspect's specimen with DNA molecules extracted from specimens found at a crime scene to determine whether the samples match. Scientists and law enforcement officers attempt to develop what a layperson might call "genetic fingerprints."

In one of the first uses of DNA evidence in a criminal trial in the United States, Tommy Lee Andrews was convicted of rape by a Florida court in 1987 after his DNA was matched to that of semen traces obtained from the victim's body. *Andrews v. State*, 533 So.2d 841, 842–843 (Fla. App. 1989). Since then the use of DNA printing has proliferated, especially in rape and homicide cases.

When it was introduced, DNA profiling was widely heralded by prosecutors. Defense counsel usually accepted the validity of the evidence without presenting their own experts to challenge it. Courts, too, were extremely impressed with this new form of evidence. One federal court referred to the reliability and accuracy of DNA profiling as justifying "an aura of amazement." See *United States v. Jakobetz*, 747 F. Supp. 250, 258 (D. Vt. 1990). During the 1990s, defense counsel began to challenge DNA evidence principally on the basis of the test results. Courts became increasingly concerned over the issue of reliability of test results due to documented instances of false positive and false negative entries by DNA laboratories. See, e.g., *State v. Cauthron*, 846 P.2d 502 (Wash. 1993); *People v. Barney*, 10 Cal.Rptr.2d 731 (Cal. App. 1992).

Introduction of DNA evidence must satisfy the tests for scientific evidence. As previously noted, federal and several state courts follow *Daubert v. Merrell Dow Pharmaceuticals, Inc.*, supra, where the trial judge assesses whether the reasoning or methodology underlying an expert's testimony is scientifically valid and can be applied to the facts in issue. Many state courts continue to follow the *Frye* "general acceptance test." Irrespective of the test courts follow for admission of DNA evidence, the trend has been to take a more rigorous approach.

In *Turner v. State*, 746 So.2d 355 (Ala. 1998), the Alabama Supreme Court stated that although the *Frye* test remains the standard of admissibility for scientific evidence generally, trial courts must follow additional specific requirements in determining the admissibility of DNA evidence. The court noted that evidence concerning the use of genetic markers contained in or derived from DNA for identification purposes is admissible provided "the trial court shall be satisfied that the expert testimony or evidence meets the criteria for admissibility as set forth by the U.S. Supreme Court in *Daubert v. Merrell Dow Pharmaceuticals, Inc.*" *Id.* at 360. The court cautioned, "Trial courts should use the flexible *Daubert* analysis in making the 'reliability' (scientific validity) assessment. In making that assessment, the courts should employ the following factors: (1) testing; (2) peer review; (3) rate of error; and (4) general acceptance admissibility standard established in *Daubert.*" *Id.* at 361.

The Florida Supreme Court continues to follow the *Frye* standard for admissibility of scientific evidence but now requires proof of a two-step DNA testing process.

> The first step relies on principles of molecular biology and chemistry to determine that two DNA samples match, while a second statistical step is needed to give significance to the match. The second step relies on principles of statistics and population genetics, and the calculation techniques used in determining and reporting DNA population frequencies must also satisfy the *Frye* test. *Brim v. State*, 695 So.2d 268, 269 (Fla. 1997).

In January 2005, the Supreme Judicial Court of Massachusetts, citing recent judicial authorities, explained that

> A determination of the reliability of the [DNA] testing process entails a fact-based inquiry, including questions of credibility. . . The analysis calls on a judge to determine whether testing was properly performed. . . and whether an expert's conclusions based on clinical experience and observations were sufficiently reliable. The judge's decision under the reliability prong is reviewed under the abuse of discretion standard. *Commonwealth v. Gaynor*, 820 N.E.2d 233, 250 (Mass. 2005).

Although courts' requirements for the introduction of DNA evidence vary, no court has rejected DNA evidence on the ground that it is invalid from a scientific standpoint. But the admissibility of DNA evidence must satisfy the requirements for courts to receive scientific evidence. One current legal issue concerns the extent to which defense attorneys are entitled to discover the underlying data necessary to challenge the reliability of methods used in gathering, testing, and processing DNA evidence.

## "Your Honor, I Object"

Anyone who has observed a criminal trial, or even a television drama depicting one, is familiar with the advocates frequently addressing the court: "Your honor, I object." To this, the objecting lawyer might add "on the ground that the testimony is irrelevant." This is called a **general objection**. Or the lawyer might make a **specific objection** and add "because the testimony sought would be hearsay," "because the answer calls for an opinion of the witness which the witness is not qualified to give," or another specific reason. There are numerous other grounds for specific objections. We consider some of the more common objections in the following sections.

### On the Ground of Hearsay

**Hearsay evidence** refers to an oral or written statement by a person other than the one testifying in court. The general rule is often stated as follows: A witness may not testify as to a statement made by another if that statement is offered as proof of the matter asserted. Thus, a witness who testifies, "I know the defendant was home

**general objection** An objection raised against a witness's testimony or introduction of evidence when the objecting party does not recite a specific ground for the objection.

**specific objection** Counsel's objection to a question posed to a witness by opposing trial counsel where a specific reason is given for the objection—for example, that the question calls for hearsay evidence.

**hearsay evidence** Testimony by a witness as to facts the witness has heard from others that is offered in evidence at a trial or hearing to prove the truth of the matter asserted.

on the night of the offense because my sister told me so" would be giving hearsay testimony. The real test of hearsay is whether a lawyer can cross-examine the person responsible for the contents of a statement.

The hearsay rule has many exceptions. Sometimes a hearsay statement is admissible to prove something other than the truth of the statement itself. Spontaneous or excited utterances, a person's dying declaration, evidence of a person's reputation, matters contained in old family records, and certain business and public records are among the most common exceptions recognized by courts. Likewise, a defendant's out-of-court statement generally may be used if it is an admission, confession, or some other statement against the defendant's interest. But the use of hearsay evidence in criminal trials presents some unique constitutional issues. When a hearsay declarant is not present for cross-examination, the declarant's statement can be admitted in evidence if it bears what courts refer to as "adequate indicia of reliability." Courts have usually taken the view that the Confrontation Clause of the Sixth Amendment to the U.S. Constitution is met as long as the court found the hearsay statements reliable even though the defendant had no opportunity to cross-examine the declarant. This view was espoused by the U.S. Supreme Court in *Ohio v. Roberts*, 448 U.S. 56, 100 S.Ct. 2531, 65 L.Ed.2d 597 (1980). But in *Crawford v. Washington*, 541 U.S. 36, 124 S.Ct. 1354, 158 L.Ed.2d 177 (2004), the Court overturned *Ohio v. Roberts* and effectively barred out-of-court testimonial statements by a witness unless the witness is unavailable and the defendant has had a prior opportunity to cross-examine the witness.

The Court's *Crawford* decision left unanswered the precise meaning of *testimonial statements*, thereby creating considerable uncertainty. On June 19, 2006, in another opinion by Justice Scalia, the Supreme Court attempted to clarify its holding in *Crawford*. The Court in *Davis v. Washington*, 547 U.S. 813, 126 S.Ct. 2266, 165 L.Ed.2d 224 (2006), held that statements in response to a 911 operator are nontestimonial unless the circumstances objectively indicate that there is no such emergency. The Court went on to explain that if interrogation is intended primarily to "establish or prove past events," the resulting statements are testimonial and subject to the requirements of the Confrontation Clause. Confrontation issues frequently arise regarding out-of-court statements in cases involving charges of sexual abuse of children, and the dichotomy between testimonial and nontestimonial will be the subject of further litigation in the lower courts.

## JURISPRUDENCE

*Crawford v. Washington*, 541 U.S. 36, 124 S.Ct. 1354, 158 L.Ed.2d 177 (2004)

In 1999, Michael D. Crawford was charged with assault and attempted murder for the alleged stabbing of Kenneth Lee. Sylvia Crawford, the defendant's wife, witnessed the incident. In a tape-recorded statement to a police officer, she indicated that Crawford's actions were not in self-defense. Under the state's marital privilege, Ms. Crawford was not permitted to testify against her husband. When the State sought to introduce Ms. Crawford's recorded statement to the police as an exception to the hearsay rule, the defendant objected on the ground that admitting her statement would violate his constitutional right to confront witnesses against him. Eventually this issue reached the Supreme Court. In an opinion by Justice Antonin Scalia, the Court held that admission of Ms. Crawford's out-of-court recorded statement to police officers regarding the incident violated the Confrontation Clause, which provides that "[i]n all criminal prosecutions, the accused shall enjoy the right . . . to be confronted with the witnesses against him."

**best evidence** Primary evidence used to prove a fact—usually an original written document that evidences a communication or transaction.

### On the Ground of the Best Evidence Rule

Ordinarily, the **best evidence** of a transaction must be offered in court. This rule applies to writings and means that an original document must be offered unless the party who offers a copy can present a plausible explanation of why the original is not available. For example, historically the original check allegedly forged by the defendant had to be produced rather than a photocopy of it. But the Federal Check Clearing for the 21st Century Act, PL 108-100 (Check 21 Law) became effective on October 28, 2004. Among its many provisions, the act provides that a substitute check is the legal equivalent of the original check.

### On the Ground that the Question Calls for an Opinion from the Witness

A lay witness is supposed to testify regarding facts of which he or she has personal knowledge. In addition, lay witnesses are generally permitted to testify about matters perceived through their physical senses and matters that are within the common knowledge of most people, such as the speed of a vehicle, sizes, distances, or the appearance of a person. They cannot give opinions on matters beyond the common experience and understanding of laypersons. To illustrate, a driver can give an estimate of the speed of a vehicle he or she observed traveling on the street, but a witness must be qualified as an expert to be permitted to testify as to the speed of a car based on observation of the car's skid marks on the pavement. Such an opinion must generally be based on facts perceived by the witness and not on hearsay statements. Rule 701 of the Federal Rules of Evidence limits lay witnesses to testifying to those opinions rationally based on the perception of the witness and helpful to an understanding of the testimony or determination of a fact in issue. States have similar rules of evidence.

**opinion evidence** Testimony in which the witness expresses an opinion, as distinct from expressing knowledge of specific facts.

A trial judge has considerable discretion to determine whether to admit **opinion evidence** from a lay witness. Although it is difficult to formulate precise rules, two illustrations shed light on the views of appellate courts. In *State v. Anderson*, 390 So.2d 878 (La. 1980), the Louisiana Supreme Court held that it was an error for the trial court to have allowed a police detective to give his opinion regarding the reasons he received an anonymous call in a homicide case; however, the court found the error harmless under the circumstances of the case. In *State v. Lagasse*, 410 A.2d 537 (Me. 1980), the court held that a lay witness's opinion testimony that a girl "looked like she had been slapped" was admissible.

## Privileged Communications

**privileges** Rights extended to persons by virtue of law—for example, the right accorded to a spouse to not be required to testify against the other spouse.

The rules of evidence also recognize certain **privileges** that limit testifying. Privileges raise difficult issues by requiring the law, in the search for truth, to choose between protecting a person's confidentiality and allowing testimony that can result in full disclosure of all relevant evidence.

At common law, individuals who were in certain close relationships were privileged not to testify about certain matters. Today, statutes, court rules of evidence, and judicial decisions protect parties in certain relationships from being required to testify. These protections are known as privileges, and a person who asserts a privilege must establish the existence of the required relationship. We discuss the most common evidentiary privileges, which protect communications between attorney and client, husband and wife, and clergy and penitent.

**attorney–client privilege** The right of a person (client) not to testify about matters discussed in confidence with an attorney in the course of the attorney's representation.

### Attorney-Client Privilege

The **attorney-client privilege** can be claimed either by the client or by the attorney on behalf of the client regarding communications between them in the course of the attorney's legal representation. The privilege belongs to the client, and if the client waives that privilege, the attorney can be required to disclose the communication. *Hunt v. Blackburn*, 128 U.S. 464, 9 S.Ct. 125, 32 L.Ed. 488 (1888). Several state supreme courts have ruled that the privilege survives the client's death. There was doubt as to whether this prevailed at the federal level; however, in a 1998 case involving activities of the Independent Counsel Kenneth Starr, the U.S. Supreme Court in a 7–2 decision ruled that the attorney-client privilege does survive the client's death. *Swidler & Berlin v. United States*, 524 U.S. 399, 118 S.Ct. 2081, 1421 L.Ed.2d 379 (1998).

In 2003 the North Carolina Supreme Court recognized an exception to the principle that attorney-client privilege survives the client's death. The court held that in the context of a pretrial criminal investigation, if a trial court "determines that some or all of the communications between a client and an attorney do not relate to a matter that affected the client at the time the statements were made, about which the attorney was professionally consulted . . . , such communications are not privileged and may be disclosed." *In re Death of Eric Miller*, 565 S.E.2d 663 (N.C. 2003).

### Marital Privilege

**marital privilege** The privilege of married persons not to be compelled to testify against each other.

A husband and wife enjoy a privilege as to confidential communications between them during their marriage. This **marital privilege** emanates from the common law but has been codified by statutes and court rules in most jurisdictions. The privilege is based on the policy of promoting and preserving domestic harmony and the repugnance of convicting one person through the testimony of another who shares intimate secrets of domestic life. Either spouse may assert the privilege to avoid disclosing privileged matters; either may assert it to prevent the other spouse from testifying about privileged matters. Federal and state courts recognize the privilege, although the ramifications of it vary somewhat in different jurisdictions. The privilege does not preclude a spouse from testifying as to observations of the other's criminal activities and generally does not apply where one spouse is charged with a crime against the other or against a child of either.

A number of appellate court decisions recognize that the marital privilege survives the termination of a marriage by death or divorce. Some states have enacted statutes to so provide. See, for example, § 57-3-4 of the West Virginia Code, which states:

> Neither husband nor wife shall, without the consent of the other, be examined in any case as to any confidential communication made by one to the other while married, nor shall either be permitted, without such consent, to reveal in testimony after the marriage relation ceases any such communication made while the marriage existed.

The spousal privilege can apply to confidential communications between parties to a valid common-law marriage where such marriage is recognized by law, but numerous appellate courts have held that the privilege does not extend to unmarried cohabitants. See, e.g., *People v. Delph*, 156 Cal.Rptr. (Cal. App. 1979). But under Vermont's civil union law, which became effective July 1, 2000, same-sex couples registered under the law have the benefit of "laws relating to immunity from compelled testimony and the marital communication privilege." 15 Vt. Stat. Ann. § 1204(e)(15).

### Clergy-Penitent Privilege

**clergy–penitent privilege** The exemption of a clergyperson and a penitent from disclosing communications made in confidence by the penitent.

Generally priests, ministers, and rabbis are prohibited from testifying about matters related to them by the penitent in confidence. This is known as the **clergy-penitent privilege**, and the clergyperson can assert the privilege on behalf of the penitent.

This privilege is rooted in the English common law but is recognized by federal statute and by statutes in all fifty states. It is not based on the Religion Clauses of the First Amendment. In *Commonwealth v. Kane*, 445 N.E.2d 598 (Mass. 1983), the Massachusetts Supreme Judicial Court held that the privilege could be asserted only by the defendant and that a cleric may not refuse to answer questions where the defendant has waived the privilege. In that case, a defendant maintained that he had confessed nothing that was incriminating and wanted his priest to corroborate that position. The priest refused and was held in contempt by the trial court.

### Other Privileges

Some jurisdictions also recognize testimonial privileges between a physician and a patient, between a psychotherapist and a patient, and between an accountant and a client. These expand the common-law concept of testimonial privilege, so the statutes and judicial decisions of a particular jurisdiction must be consulted.

The common law did not provide any testimonial privilege for confidential communications between a parent and a child, and most courts have rejected such a privilege. In a few states the legislature has provided that a parent or the parent's minor child may not be examined as to any communication made in confidence by the minor to the minor's parent. See, e.g., Minn. Stat. Ann. § 595.02.

# The Trial Process

The trial is the centerpiece of the criminal justice system, and in American courts the trial judge is the person most responsible for ensuring that the system operates in a fair, efficient, and impartial manner. Trial judges come into office through election or appointment. Ideally, they are selected because of their scholarship, integrity, and the patience and compassion the public associates with the fair and impartial administration of justice. To those appearing before the court and to the jurors and court personnel, the black-robed judge stands as a symbol of justice. In previous chapters, we have pointed out that judges perform numerous functions in the pretrial phases of the criminal justice system, but the most visible aspects of the judge's work are presiding at trials and, when convictions result, setting punishments.

During a trial, the judge serves as an umpire in many respects. The judge rules on the questions that may be asked of potential jurors, determines whether witnesses are competent to testify, controls the scope of interrogation of lay and expert witnesses, and instructs the jury on the law applicable to the particular case. The judge also determines all important judicial and administrative matters concerning the trial. Trial judges are held accountable by appellate courts sitting to review judgments and sentences and to correct harmful errors. Yet in numerous administrative and procedural areas (e.g., whether to grant a postponement of a trial or to limit the number of expert witnesses), a judge's actions are discretionary, and appellate review in such areas is limited to determining whether the trial judge abused that discretion. "In discharging his responsibilities, the trial judge may properly caution, correct, advise, admonish, and, to a certain extent, criticize counsel during the case, provided it is done in such manner as not to subject counsel to contempt or ridicule, or to prejudice the accused in the minds of the jurors." *M.T. v. State*, 677 So.2d 1223, 1229 (Ala. Cr. App. 1995). Nevertheless, trial judges must be very cautious of being critical of attorneys, especially in a jury trial, because jurors place great importance on the judge's attitude. A trial judge who is critical of a defendant's attorney might hold that attorney up to ridicule in the eyes of the jury and thereby impede the fairness of the trial. In *Earl v. State*, 904 P.2d 1029 (1995), the trial judge made many derogatory remarks before the jury concerning the defense counsel's capacity as a lawyer. The appellate court reversed the defendant's conviction and remanded the case for a new trial, noting that the trial judge's comments toward the defense attorney cumulatively prejudiced the defendant's case. In *State v. Jenkins*, 445 S.E.2d 622 (N.C. App. 1994), the court reversed a defendant's convictions because the judge turned his back to the defendant and the jury during the defendant's testimony. The appellate court was concerned that the jury may have interpreted the judge's action to mean that he did not believe the defendant's testimony to be credible.

Usually, either or both sides in a criminal trial request the court to invoke the traditional rule that requires all witnesses, except the defendant, to remain outside the courtroom except when testifying. The purpose of **putting witnesses under the rule**, as lawyers commonly refer to it, is to prevent witnesses from matching narratives. Whether witnesses should be excluded from the courtroom is a matter within the sound discretion of the trial court, *Witt v. United States*, 196 F.2d 285 (9th Cir. 1952); however, the request is generally granted.

Witnesses are interrogated by counsel in the adversary system of American justice; however, it is the right, and sometimes becomes the duty, of a judge to interrogate a witness. This is another delicate area, and appellate courts have emphasized that questioning from the bench should not show bias or feeling and should not be protracted. *Commonwealth v. Hammer*, 494 A.2d 1054, 1060 (Pa. 1985).

**putting witnesses under the rule** Placing witnesses under the traditional rule that requires them to remain outside the courtroom except when testifying.

## The Opening Statements

Once the jury is in place, the trial is ready to begin. The prosecution and the defense are each allowed to make an **opening statement** outlining their respective theories of the case and the evidence to be presented. These opening statements must not be argumentative, nor may counsel make disparaging remarks against one another. Often a defense lawyer defers making an opening statement until the prosecution rests its case. Opening statements are designed to orient the jury; therefore, if the defendant elects a bench trial, they are frequently waived. If not waived, opening statements of counsel are usually very brief in bench trials. After the opening statements have been presented, the prosecution calls its first witness to take the stand.

**opening statement** A prosecutor's or defense lawyer's initial statement to the judge or jury in a trial.

## The Case for the Prosecution

Prosecutors are ever mindful that when a defendant pleads not guilty, the government must establish the defendant's guilt beyond any reasonable doubt. In presenting the government's case, the prosecuting attorney usually calls as witnesses police officers, the victim, and any other available witnesses whose testimony can support the charge against the defendant. The government's witnesses may also include experts. For example, in a homicide prosecution the prosecutor usually calls a physician; in a drug trafficking case, a chemist; in a forgery prosecution, a handwriting expert. In a DUI case the prosecution often calls the technician who performed a breath test on the defendant. A scientist who has conducted laboratory tests on DNA samples is often called to testify in homicide and sexual battery cases.

# The Right to Confrontation and Cross-Examination

The Sixth Amendment to the Constitution guarantees the defendant the right to be confronted with the witnesses who offer evidence against the defendant. This means that the defendant has the right to be present at trial, *Illinois v. Allen*, supra, and to cross-examine each witness. As explained in *California v. Green*, this right of confrontation

1. insures that the witness will give his statements under oath. . . .
2. forces the witness to submit to cross examination, the "greatest legal engine ever invented for the discovery of truth" [and]
3. permits the jury . . . to observe the demeanor of the witness . . . thus aiding the jury in assessing his credibility. 399 U.S. 149, 158, 90 S.Ct. 1930, 1935, 26 L.Ed.2d 489, 497 (1970).

**right of cross-examination** The right to question witnesses for the opposing side in a criminal trial.

The **right of cross-examination** of an adversary's witness is absolute. *Alford v. United States*, 282 U.S. 687, 51 S.Ct. 218, 75 L.Ed. 624 (1931). However, the permissible scope of cross-examination varies somewhat in different jurisdictions and is a matter largely within the discretion of the trial court. *Smith v. Illinois*, 390 U.S. 129, 88 S.Ct. 748, 19 L.Ed.2d 956 (1968). Courts generally agree that the right of cross-examination is limited to (1) questioning the witness about matters he or she testified to on direct examination; and (2) asking any questions that might tend to impeach the witness's credibility or demonstrate any bias, interest, or hostility of the witness.

**leading questions** A question that suggests an answer. Leading questions are permitted at a criminal trial on cross-examination of witnesses and in other limited instances.

The right of cross-examination is available to both the prosecutor and the defense counsel and is extremely valuable in criminal trials. Although in most instances it is objectionable for a lawyer who is examining a witness to ask **leading questions** on direct examination, the rules of evidence permit a cross-examiner to ask leading questions. When skillfully employed, cross-examination often develops facts favorable to the cross-examiner's side of the case. Frequently, a cross-examiner is successful in bringing out inconsistencies, contradictions, and any bias or hostility of the witness. A witness may also be subject to **impeachment**—that is, having his or her credibility attacked on cross-examination. A witness's credibility may be attacked in the following ways:

**impeachment** Impugning the credibility of a witness by introducing contradictory evidence or proving his or her bad character.

- Showing the witness's inability to have viewed or heard the matters the witness has testified to, or inability to recall the event testified to
- Demonstrating that the witness has made prior conflicting statements on an important point
- Showing the witness has been convicted of a crime
- Establishing that the witness bears a bad reputation for truthfulness in the community
- Showing bias, prejudice, or motive to misrepresent the facts, or that the witness has a definite interest in the result of the trial

**right of confrontation** The right to face one's accusers in a criminal case.

The defendant's **right of confrontation** guaranteeing a face-to-face meeting with witnesses appearing before the judge or jury is not absolute. It must occasionally give way to considerations of public policy and the necessities of the case. *Thomas v. People*, 803 P.2d 144 (Colo. 1990).

The constitutional right of confrontation came into sharp focus in 1988, when the Supreme Court held that a defendant's Sixth Amendment right to confront witnesses was violated in a sexual abuse case in which the trial judge, pursuant to an Iowa law, allowed a screen to be erected between the defendant and the two thirteen-year-old girls that he was accused of assaulting. The two children were situated so they could not see the defendant during their testimony. *Coy v. Iowa*, 487 U.S. 1012, 108 S.Ct. 2798, 101 L.Ed.2d 857 (1988). The Court left open the question of whether a procedure that shields a child sex abuse victim maybe constitutionally acceptable if there is an individualized finding that the witness is in need of such protection. Two years later, in *Maryland v. Craig*, 497 U.S. 836, 110 S.Ct. 3157, 111 L.Ed.2d 666 (1990), the Court held that the Confrontation Clause of the Sixth Amendment does not absolutely prohibit states from using one-way closed circuit television to receive a child's testimony in a case involving child abuse.

Since the Supreme Court's decision in *Coy*, several states have refined their **child shield statutes** affecting children who are victims of sexual abuse. These revised statutes have met with varying reactions from state appellate courts. However, one thing seems clear: to avoid the constitutional requirements of the Confrontation Clause, the prosecution must show and the trial judge must make particularized findings that a child victim of sexual abuse would suffer unreasonable and unnecessary mental or emotional harm if the child were to testify in the presence of the defendant. In view of the Supreme Court's March 8, 2004 decision in *Crawford v. Washington*, supra, requiring testimonial evidence to comport with the Sixth Amendment right of confrontation, the validity of child protective statutes may be subject to further review. Of course, *Crawford* focuses on out-of-court statements and arguably might not affect the in-court procedures addressed by child shield statutes.

It must be remembered that all evidence, whether from the prosecution or defense, must comport with the rules of evidence as previously outlined. When the prosecution rests its case, the next move is up to the defense.

> **child shield statutes** Laws that allow a screen to be placed between a child victim of sexual abuse and a defendant while the child testifies in court.

## The Defense Strategy in Moving for a Judgment of Acquittal

At the close of the prosecution's evidence, the defense counsel will frequently move the court to grant a **directed verdict** or, as it is called in federal courts and some state courts, a **judgment of acquittal**. The purpose of such a motion is to have the trial judge determine whether the evidence presented by the prosecution is legally sufficient to support a verdict of guilty. For the purpose of ruling on the motion, the trial judge must view the prosecution's evidence in the light most favorable to the government. The trial judge's authority to direct a verdict has long been recognized. *France v. United States*, 164 U.S. 676, 17 S.Ct. 219, 41 L.Ed. 595 (1897).

Should the motion be granted, the defendant is discharged. If, as in most cases, the motion is denied, defense counsel proceeds with the case on behalf of the defendant, and if additional evidence is offered, defense counsel may renew the motion at the close of the evidence. Federal appellate courts will not review the sufficiency of the evidence to support a verdict unless a motion for a judgment of acquittal was made at the close of all the evidence in the trial court. See, e.g., *Corbin v. United States*, 253 F.2d 646 (10th Cir. 1958). This principle also prevails in many state appellate courts.

> **directed verdict** A verdict rendered by a jury by direction of the presiding judge.
>
> **judgment of acquittal** In a nonjury trial, a judge's order exonerating a defendant based on a finding that the defendant is not guilty. In a case heard by a jury that finds a defendant guilty, a judge's order exonerating the defendant on the ground that the evidence was not legally sufficient to support the jury's finding of guilt.

## The Defense Case: Will the Defendant Take the Stand?

Under the Fifth Amendment, the defendant does not have to testify in a criminal case, and often defendants choose to rely simply on cross-examination of the government's witnesses in an effort to obtain an acquittal. Or the defendant may present witnesses in support of an alibi, to contradict the prosecution's witnesses, or to establish an affirmative defense.

Perhaps the major tactical decision a defendant and defense counsel must make at trial is whether the defendant will take the stand and testify on his or her behalf. The Fifth Amendment privilege against self-incrimination, which applies to the states through the Fourteenth Amendment, *Malloy v. Hogan*, 378 U.S. 1, 84 S.Ct. 1489, 12 L.Ed.2d 653 (1964), protects the defendant from being required to testify, absent a grant of immunity. Moreover, it also forbids any direct or indirect comment by the prosecution on the accused's failure to testify. *Griffin v. California*, 380 U.S. 609, 85 S.Ct. 1229, 14 L.Ed.2d 106 (1965).

When an accused chooses to testify on his or her own behalf, the prosecution may cross-examine the accused about his or her testimony with the same latitude as with any other witness. *Fitzpatrick v. United States*, 178 U.S. 304, 20 S.Ct. 944, 44 L.Ed. 1078 (1900). Moreover, even though illegally obtained evidence cannot be used to prove the government's case, in recent years it has been held that there is no federal constitutional prohibition that prevents the prosecution from using such evidence to impeach statements made by the defendant on cross-examination. *United States v. Havens*, 446 U.S. 620, 100 S.Ct. 1912, 64 L.Ed.2d 559 (1980); *Harris v. New York*, 401 U.S. 222, 91 S.Ct. 643, 28 L.Ed.2d 1 (1971). These realities must weigh heavily in a defendant's decision whether to testify, because the threat of contradiction and impeachment always exists in cross-examination. Regardless of whether the defendant testifies, any witnesses presented by the defendant are subject to cross-examination by the prosecution.

## The Rebuttals

**rebuttal witnesses**
Witnesses called to dispute the testimony of the opposing party's witnesses.

At the conclusion of the defendant's case, the prosecution is entitled to present **rebuttal witnesses** to dispute the testimony of the defendant's witnesses. After examination by the prosecution and cross-examination by the defense counsel, the defense may present its rebuttal witnesses. They, in turn, are subject to examination by the defense counsel and to cross-examination by the prosecutor. This usually concludes the evidentiary phase of the trial.

## Conduct of the Jury during the Trial

The traditional role of the juror has been to attentively listen to the evidence as presented by the prosecution and defense, to avoid any outside influences, and to withhold judgment until all the evidence has been presented and the jury retires to deliberate. Most trial judges today allow jurors to take notes. In recent years trial courts have increasingly allowed jurors to submit questions to witnesses.

Historically judges have been reluctant to allow jurors to question witnesses in criminal trials. One principal concern has been that the questions may be improper, yet counsel may hesitate to object to a juror's question. In *United States v. Witt*, 215 F.2d 580 (2nd Cir. 1954), the court said it was within the discretion of the trial judge to permit jurors to put questions to witnesses and receive answers. Other federal courts have allowed jurors to ask questions, but the practice has never been encouraged. In *United States v. Land*, 877 F.2d 17, 19 (8th Cir. 1989), the court noted that the practice of allowing jurors to submit questions to witnesses is "fraught with dangers which can undermine the orderly progress of the trial to verdict." Nevertheless, every federal circuit court and virtually every state appellate court that has considered this practice has permitted it. In *United States v. Richardson* , 233 F.3d 1285 (11th Cir. 2000), the U.S. Court of Appeals for the Eleventh Circuit rejected an appellant's claim that the trial judge's decision to allow jurors to submit questions to witnesses violated her right to a fair trial. The court, however, cautioned that "jurors should not be permitted to directly question a witness but rather should be required to submit their questions in writing to the trial judge, who should pose the questions to the witness in a neutral manner." 233 F.3d at 1290.

Based on the premise that allowing juror questions in criminal cases would impact juror impartiality and relieve the prosecution of its burden of proof, the Minnesota Supreme Court recently held that no court shall permit jurors to question witnesses in a criminal trial. *State v. Costello*, 646 N.W.2d 204 (Minn. 2002). During the 1990s, the Mississippi and Nebraska Supreme Courts and the Texas Court of Criminal Appeals made similar rulings prohibiting jurors from interrogating witnesses.

In *Coates v. State*, 855 So.2d 223 (Fla. App. 2003), the appellant contended that the trial court abused its discretion in allowing any jury questioning. He argued that allowing jurors to ask questions compels them to become advocates, rather than neutral finders of fact. The appellate court, however, pointed out that the trial judge instructed the jurors to write out their questions and hand them to the bailiff. Jurors were then asked to leave the courtroom while the judge ruled on any objections by attorneys. Thereafter, the jury was returned to the courtroom and the judge asked the question of the witness, with each attorney afforded an opportunity to ask follow-up questions. The court found the trial court had not abused its discretion in handling the questioning in such a controlled manner.

There is a definite trend in state courts to allow some form of questioning of witnesses by jurors. In a recent scholarly article, Jehle and Miller noted,

> Some states have implemented pilot projects and produced reports recommending juror questioning. The results of the reports influenced Hawaii, New Jersey, Colorado, Washington, and Tennessee to implement procedural rules for allowing the jury innovation. In addition, the Massachusetts and Ohio courts have ruled in favor of the practice after their states' pilot projects, although they used precedent for their reasoning and do not mention the projects in their decisions. Alayna Jehle and Monica K. Miller, Controversy in the Courtroom: Implications of Allowing Jurors to Question Witnesses. 32 *Wm. Mitchell L. Rev.* 27, 53 (2005).

In 2009 a Massachusetts appellate court reiterated that the decision whether to allow juror questioning and the manner of questioning rests in the sound discretion of the trial judge. *Commonwealth v. Reeder*, 901 N.E.2d 701 (Mass. App.).

## The Jury Instructions Conference

After all evidence has been presented in a jury trial, the trial judge customarily confers with counsel outside the presence of the jury concerning the instructions on the law that the judge will give to the jury. The prosecutor and defense counsel may be asked to present proposed instructions for the court to consider. More commonly, the trial judge announces that the court will give certain standard instructions and offers to supplement them with specific instructions to be chosen from those submitted by counsel. A defendant is entitled to have the jury instructed on the law applicable to any legitimate theory of defense that is supported by the evidence presented. See *United States v. Creamer*, 555 F.2d 612 (7th Cir. 1977). **Jury instructions** are settled in advance of closing arguments by counsel so that the prosecutor and defense counsel can present their arguments knowing how the judge will instruct the jury.

**jury instructions** A judge's explanation of the law applicable to a case being heard by a jury.

# The Closing Arguments of Counsel

closing arguments
Arguments presented
at trial by counsel at
the conclusion of the
presentation of evidence.

The Sixth Amendment guarantee of the right to assistance of counsel has been interpreted to include the right to present **closing arguments** in a criminal case, regardless of whether the case is tried before a jury or before a judge. *Herring v. New York*, 422 U.S. 853, 95 S.Ct. 2550, 45 L.Ed.2d 593 (1975). A defendant represented by counsel has no right to share the closing argument with his or her counsel, but if the defendant is pro se—that is, representing him- or herself—the court must allow the defendant to make a closing argument. *State v. Plaskonka*, 577 A.2d 729 (Conn. App. 1990). Although the constitutional guarantee accords the right of closing arguments to the defendant, by statute or rules of court the government and the defendant are each accorded the right to have counsel make closing arguments. The order of the arguments may be set by statute or court rule, but the trial judge retains control of the extent of the argument. The prosecutor usually argues first, followed by the defense counsel, with the prosecutor having an opportunity for a brief rebuttal.

Closing arguments are designed to assist the jury in recalling and evaluating the evidence and in drawing inferences therefrom. Many lawyers begin by recapitulating the evidence in the light most favorable to their client. After that, the arguments frequently become emotional, with each side entreating the jury to "do its duty" by either convicting or acquitting the defendant, arguing why the jury should by its interpretation of the evidence thereby either convict or acquit.

In closing arguments, counsel may comment on the weight of the evidence and the credibility of the witnesses, but it is improper for either the prosecutor or defense counsel to state a personal belief about the guilt or innocence of the accused. Likewise, it is improper for counsel to refer to any matters—other than those of common, everyday knowledge—that have not been introduced in evidence. Because a judge is trained in evaluating evidence, counsel in nonjury cases frequently waive their right to make closing arguments; otherwise, the arguments are generally quite brief.

Although prosecutors may use every legitimate method to obtain a conviction, a legion of appellate court opinions admonishes them to be fair and objective in their presentations to a jury. Characteristically, the Wisconsin Supreme Court observed that the prosecutor's role should be "to analyze the evidence and present facts with a reasonable interpretation to aid the jury in calmly and reasonably drawing just inferences and arriving at a just conclusion. . . ." *State v. Genova*, 8 N.W.2d 260, 263 (Wis. 1943).

Prosecutors are prohibited from making inflammatory remarks to the jury. If a prosecutor does make inflammatory remarks or statements that have no basis in the evidence or that can be interpreted as a comment on the defendant's failure to testify, the judge may admonish the prosecutor. Usually this is followed by a cautionary instruction directing the jury to disregard such remarks. If the defendant objects and the trial judge fails to take appropriate action, or if the prosecutor's remarks are so prejudicial that they cannot be erased from the minds of the jurors, the defendant may be able to obtain a mistrial or, if convicted, win a new trial from an appellate court.

Perhaps because the government cannot ordinarily appeal on the basis of improper comments by a defense counsel, the law seems to indulge a defendant in a somewhat wider latitude in jury arguments. Nevertheless, there are restraints, and sanctions for violations may take the form of an admonition by the trial judge or even disciplinary action where a defense lawyer's performance is egregious. Despite the fact that counsel must strive for acquittal of a client in our adversary system of justice, courts frequently remind defense lawyers that they, too, are officers of the court. Accordingly, they must aid in the administration of justice to the end that the lawful rights and privileges of the defendant are not violated. See, e.g., *State v. Leaks*, 10 A.2d 281 (N.J. 1940).

### Improper Argument by a Prosecutor

**CASE-IN-POINT** Defendant Larry Witted was charged with attempted murder and armed robbery. At his jury trial, the chief issue was whether the victim had correctly identified the defendant as the person who robbed him. While the victim's testimony was positive, it was uncorroborated by any other evidence. During closing arguments, the defense counsel argued that the process used to identify the defendant as the perpetrator was unduly suggestive. In rebuttal, the prosecutor implied that witnesses for the defense had perjured themselves at the request of defense counsel and that the defendant had a criminal background that the defense was hiding from the jury. Because the prosecutor's remarks were made during his rebuttal closing argument, the defense had no opportunity to challenge the inferences that were made. Witted was convicted, but the court awarded him a new trial, citing the prosecutor's misconduct during closing arguments.

*People v. Witted*, 398 N.E.2d 68 (Ill. App. 1979).

## The Judge Instructs the Jury

Typically, at the conclusion of the closing arguments the judge either reads the indictment or information or explains the charges against the defendant to the jury. This is followed by an admonition that the defendant is presumed innocent unless and until the government proves the defendant guilty of each element of the crime beyond a reasonable doubt. The judge defines the elements of any crime charged and explains any technical legal terms. Where applicable, the court generally instructs on an attempt to commit the crime charged as well. Where the jury may convict the defendant of a lesser offense, the judge must go further than merely defining the crime charged. For example, if the defendant is charged with first-degree murder, the judge must describe the lesser degrees of murder as well as manslaughter and excusable and justifiable homicide.

These instructions on the crimes may be followed by an explanation of any defenses pled by the defendant and the burden of proof, if any, on the defendant to sustain such defenses. A defendant is entitled to an instruction about any defense sustained by the evidence. At the request of the defendant, the judge usually informs the jury that it should not consider any inference of guilt because the defendant exercised the right not to testify. However, many defense lawyers prefer not to have the judge give this instruction.

The trial judge always explains to the jury that its role is to be the sole judge of the facts and advises the jury about some of the things it should consider in evaluating the credibility of the evidence presented. If expert witnesses have testified, the judge explains their role and informs the jury that it is free to accept or reject their opinions. In America, in contrast with the English practice, the trial judge generally is not permitted to summarize the evidence or express an opinion on the weight of that evidence or the credibility of the witnesses. Rule 31(c) of the Federal Rules of Criminal Procedure provides,

> The defendant may be found guilty of an offense necessarily included in the offense charged or of an attempt to commit either the offense charged or of an offense necessarily included therein if the attempt is an offense in its own right.

A defendant is entitled to have the jury instructed on any lesser included offense whenever (1) the elements of the lesser offense are a subset of elements of the charged offense and (2) the evidence at trial is such that a jury could rationally find the defendant guilty of the lesser offense yet acquit the defendant of the greater offense. *Schmuck v. United States*, 489 U.S. 705, 109 S.Ct. 1443, 103 L.Ed.2d 734 (1989).

Practices in state courts vary in the extent to which the trial judge must instruct a jury on offenses that are lesser than the offense charged against a defendant. Some courts distinguish between those offenses that are necessarily included in the offense charged and those that may be included based on the allegations of the offense charged and the evidence presented at trial. In state courts, a defendant is generally entitled to an instruction of an offense of a less serious nature than the one charged if the elements of the charged offense can constitute the lesser crime. If the evidence is such that no rational jury could conclude the lesser offense was proper, however, the trial court's refusal to give the lesser offense instruction is not necessarily considered a reversible error by most appellate courts. See, e.g., *People v. Tucker*, 542 N.E.2d 804 (Ill. App. 1989).

In a few states, juries determine sentences. In these jurisdictions, the judge must also instruct the jury on the range of sentences permitted. In most states that have the death penalty, a jury trial in a capital case is bifurcated, with the jury first determining guilt or innocence. If the jury finds the defendant guilty, a second phase ensues, during which the jury hears evidence of aggravating and mitigating circumstances and determines whether the death penalty should be imposed (see Chapter 19).

The judge's instructions are given orally, and in some instances the jury is given a copy of the instructions. The clerk furnishes the jury forms of verdicts so they may find the defendant not guilty, guilty as charged, or guilty of some degree of the offense charged or of a lesser included offense. In federal criminal trials and in most state courts, the judge explains the requirement of a unanimous verdict. In some states, the judge is required to inform the jury of the penalties that can be imposed for the offense charged. Finally, the jury is directed to retire, select one of its members as **foreperson**, and deliberate on its verdict. Usually a jury is allowed to take with it to the jury room all exhibits received in evidence.

**foreperson** The person selected by fellow jurors to chair deliberations and report the jury's verdict.

## The Jury Deliberates and Returns Its Verdict

When directed to deliberate, the jurors are escorted to their quarters by a court bailiff. In some cases, the judge orders the jury sequestered, which means the jury must remain together until it reaches its verdict. **Sequestration** often requires the bailiff to escort the jurors to a hotel and to be present with them during meals to ensure that no outside influences are brought to bear on their judgment. Once in the jury room, the jurors' first order of business is to elect a foreperson. Then they are ready to commence their deliberations.

**sequestration** Holding jurors incommunicado during trial and deliberations.

Because jury deliberations are secret, we can only speculate about the reasoning processes of jurors. However, we do know that juries usually take a preliminary vote shortly after electing a foreperson. In most cases, the jury probably arrives at its verdict without much discussion. In the famous "Monkey Trial" of John Scopes in Dayton, Tennessee, in 1925, the jury deliberated only eight minutes before convicting Scopes of unlawfully teaching the theory of evolution in his high school biology class. More recently, in the O. J. Simpson case the jury returned its verdict of not guilty after only four hours. In other instances, jurors may deliberate for hours or days, and many votes may be taken. In the murder trial of Charles Manson in 1971, the jury deliberated about forty-two hours.

In federal criminal trials, a jury verdict must be unanimous. *Andres v. United States*, 333 U.S. 740, 68 S.Ct. 880, 92 L.Ed. 1055 (1948); see also Fed. R. Crim. P. 31(a). The same is true in most states; however, a few states accept less-than-unanimous verdicts. The Supreme Court has approved nonunanimous verdicts rendered by twelve-person juries. *Johnson v. Louisiana*, 406 U.S. 356, 92 S.Ct. 1620, 32 L.Ed.2d 152 (1972); *Apodaca v. Oregon*, 406 U.S. 404, 92 S.Ct. 1628, 32 L.Ed.2d 184 (1972). But the Court has held that a conviction by a nonunanimous six-person jury in a state trial for a nonpetty offense violates the right to trial by jury guaranteed by the Sixth and Fourteenth Amendments. *Burch v. Louisiana*, 441 U.S. 130, 99 S.Ct. 1623, 60 L.Ed.2d 96 (1979).

## The Deadlocked Jury

Sometimes juries become "hung"—that is, they cannot agree on a verdict. This was illustrated in 1988, when a young man was tried in New York City for allegedly strangling a young woman in Central Park. The so-called "yuppie murder case" drew national attention, partly because the testimony revealed that the victim's death resulted from "a rough sexual encounter" between the defendant and the victim. After a twelve-week trial, a panel of eight men and four women deliberated for nine days. They then sent a note to the judge saying they had reached an impasse. At that point, in a desire to conclude the proceedings—and perhaps rather than risk another trial—the defendant entered a negotiated plea of guilty to manslaughter, a lesser offense than that charged.

> **deadlocked jury** A jury whose members cannot agree on a verdict. Often referred to as a "hung jury."

> **Allen charge** A judge's instruction to jurors who are deadlocked, encouraging them to listen to one another's arguments and reappraise their own positions in an effort to arrive at a verdict.

If a jury reports that it is a **deadlocked jury**, the trial judge can either declare a mistrial or urge the jury to make further attempts to arrive at a verdict. One tool that both federal and state trial judges sometimes employ is to give the jury a supplemental instruction called an ***Allen* charge**. The instruction takes its name from an opinion issued by the Supreme Court at the turn of the century, *Allen v. United States*, 164 U.S. 492, 17 S.Ct. 154, 41 L.Ed. 528 (1896). A number of modifications have been made to the original *Allen* charge, but the basic thrust remains to urge "that if much the larger number were for conviction, a dissenting juror should consider whether his doubt was a reasonable one. . . . If, upon the other hand, the majority were for acquittal, the minority ought to ask themselves whether they might not reasonably doubt the correctness of a judgment that was not concurred in by the majority." 164 U.S. at 501, 17 S.Ct. at 157, 41 L.Ed. at 531.

In Colorado the *Allen* charge is called "the third-degree instruction," and New Mexico courts have referred to it as the "shotgun instruction." *Leech v. People*, 146 P.2d 346, 347 (Colo. 1944); *State v. Nelson*, 321 P.2d 202, 204 (N.M. 1958).

The use of the *Allen* charge in its original form or in its many modified forms has been criticized as having a coercive effect for implying that the majority view is the correct one and for importuning the minority to change their views. In a few states, the state supreme court has banned its use. See, e.g., *State v. Randall*, 353 P.2d 1054 (Mont. 1960). Nevertheless, federal and most state courts have generally approved the use of some version of the instruction when it has been cautiously given. See, e.g., *Benscoter v. United States*, 376 F.2d 49 (10th Cir. 1967).

> **jury nullification** The fact of a jury disregarding the court's instructions and rendering a verdict on the basis of the consciences of the jurors.

> **jury pardon** An action taken by a jury, despite the quality of the evidence, acquitting a defendant or convicting the defendant of a lesser crime than charged.

## Jury Pardons

At times, juries disregard the evidence and the judge's instructions on the law and acquit a defendant or convict the defendant of a lesser offense than charged. This is referred to as **jury nullification** or as granting the defendant a **jury pardon**. Jurors, of course, take an oath to follow the law as charged by the judge and are expected to do so. *United States v. Powell*, 469 U.S. 57, 105 S.Ct. 471, 83 L.Ed.2d 461 (1984). But it is also recognized that a jury has the prerogative to exercise its judgment and bring in a verdict of not guilty or guilty of a lesser offense.

CASE-IN-POINT

### Factors Considered in Approving a Trial Court's Use of the *Allen* Charge Where the Jury Is Deadlocked

Defendant Lindel and others were charged in U.S. District Court with thirty-five counts of various crimes stemming from a marijuana importation scheme. They were convicted on several counts and then appealed. Among their points on appeal, the defendants contended that when the jury sent notes that it was hopelessly deadlocked, the trial court should have declared a mistrial instead of giving an *Allen* charge to the jury. In rejecting the defendants' challenge, the U.S. Court of Appeals for the Fifth Circuit first noted that the language in the judge's charge to the jury comported with the modified *Allen* charge

language repeatedly approved. Then the court pointed out that the trial lasted for three weeks, that the verdict was a discriminating one returning both guilty and not guilty verdicts on the various counts, that in giving the *Allen* charge the judge did not set a deadline on deliberations, and that the verdict was not returned until two days after the *Allen* charge was given. Considering these factors, the court found no abuse of discretion in the trial judge's having given the charge, and after rejecting other points raised by the defendants, the court of appeals affirmed the defendants' convictions.

*United States v. Lindel*, 881 F.2d 1313 (5th Cir. 1989).

In death penalty cases, there has been explicit recognition of the principle. For instance, in *Beck v. Alabama*, 447 U.S. 625, 100 S.Ct. 2382, 65 L.Ed.2d 392 (1980), the Supreme Court held that the death penalty may not be imposed if the jury is not permitted to consider a verdict of guilt of a lesser included noncapital offense when the evidence would have supported such a verdict. The Court explained that "the nearly universal acceptance of the rule in state and federal courts establishes the value to the defendant of this procedural safeguard." 447 U.S. at 637, 100 S.Ct. at 2389, 65 L.Ed.2d at 402.

In trials for noncapital offenses, the reality of jury nullification exists, but there is no requirement for a judge to inform the jury of that power. See, e.g., *United States v. Dougherty*, 473 F.2d 1113 (D.C. Cir. 1972). Acquittals by juries are not subject to appeal, so it is difficult to know when jury nullification occurs, but undoubtedly some defendants are acquitted or convicted of lesser offenses as a result of a jury pardon. In *United States v. Dougherty*, the court in footnote 33 cites a number of examples taken from a study undertaken at the University of Chicago Law School of the types of cases in which a jury voted to acquit because of its empathy with the defendant. The examples mentioned include sale of liquor to a minor who is a member of the armed forces and violence erupting after domestic strife.

## The Verdict

**verdict** The formal decision rendered by a jury in a civil or criminal trial.

**polling the jury** Practice in which a trial judge asks each member of the jury whether he or she supports the jury's verdict.

When a jury has concluded its deliberations, it returns to the courtroom and delivers its written **verdict**. The verdict is usually first handed to the judge, who reviews it to determine whether it is in proper form. If it is, the judge hands the verdict to the clerk or jury foreperson to be read aloud in open court. A defendant who is acquitted by a jury is immediately discharged. If a jury finds the defendant guilty, the defendant is generally taken into custody to await sentencing. In some instances, the defendant may be continued on bail, pending application for a new trial or an appeal. We discuss sentencing and appellate procedures in Chapters 19 and 20, respectively.

After a verdict has been read, the court or any party may have the jury polled individually. The clerk or judge handles **polling the jury** by asking each juror, "Is this your verdict?" or words to that effect. In most cases, each juror responds affirmatively and the jury is discharged. If, on the other hand, a juror expresses dissent from the verdict, the trial judge may either direct the jury to retire for further deliberation or discharge the jury. See *People v. Kellogg*, 397 N.E.2d 835 (Ill. 1979).

## Posttrial Motions

**motion for a new trial** A formal request made to a trial court to hold a new trial in a particular case that has already been adjudicated.

A convicted defendant may, and frequently does, file a **motion for a new trial**, alleging that errors were committed at trial. This type of motion affords the trial judge an opportunity to rectify errors by awarding the defendant a new trial. In most instances, however, it is a *pro forma* prelude to an appeal and is denied by the trial court. A defendant may also seek bail pending appeal (see Chapter 20). When the court disposes of these motions, the process moves into sentencing (see Chapter 19).

## Conclusion

Despite the relatively small percentage of criminal cases that go to trial, the criminal trial remains a vital part of the criminal justice system. Adjudications at trial set the overall tone for the administration of the criminal law in the community. Jury verdicts become "weather vanes" of the public's attitude on the enforcement of the law.

Criminal trials also have an important bearing on the reshaping of both the statutory and decisional law in light of contemporary community values. With counsel now readily available to indigent defendants to handle their appeals as well as to represent them at trial, appellate courts have the opportunity to update precedents and refine trial court procedures based on present constitutional standards.

Court procedures are slow to change, but changes are occurring and will continue into the future. Despite changes, the basic function of the criminal trial by a jury of one's peers will remain. It must because it is not only each citizen's protection against overzealous law enforcement and prosecutions; it also ensures the public that no defendant will gain preferred status by virtue of prominence or be dealt with unfairly because of lowly status.

## Chapter Summary

- Learning Objective 1
  - Trial by jury has historic roots in the English common law.
  - The Sixth Amendment to the U.S. Constitution, applicable to state criminal trials by the Fourteenth Amendment, grants a defendant the right to a speedy and public trial by an impartial jury, the right to be informed of the nature and cause of the accusation, the right to confront prosecution witnesses, the right to subpoena defense witnesses, and the right to have the assistance of counsel.
  - A defendant is entitled to an open and public trial, but not a private trial. Courts can close trials to protect rape victims, molested children, and witnesses and jurors from embarrassment or intimidation. The Supreme Court has said that closing a trial to the public is left to the trial judge's discretion on a case-by-case basis.
  - The Supreme Court has ruled that the right to a jury trial extends to cases where a defendant is subject to more than six months' imprisonment. Some states opt to be more liberal. In 1996 the Court ruled that a defendant

charged with multiple petty offenses is not entitled to a jury trial, although the possible sentences may add up to more than six months in prison. Juveniles and defendants in military tribunals do not have a right to a jury trial.

o The right to counsel in a criminal case is well established; a defendant also has the right of self-representation irrespective of the defendant's knowledge of legal procedures as long as the defendant's election is exercised voluntarily and intelligently. But in 2008, the Supreme Court held that a trial judge is not required to allow a minimally competent defendant to elect self-representation at trial.

- Learning Objective 2

  o A common-law jury consisted of twelve men. Federal courts require a twelve-member jury unless the defendant stipulates to fewer in writing. States require twelve-member juries in capital cases; most require twelve in felony prosecutions. Many use fewer in misdemeanor cases. In 1970 the Supreme Court upheld six-person juries in felony trials; three years later it said that a jury of only five was not acceptable.

  o Statutes commonly require jurors to be at least eighteen years old and registered voters. Statutes frequently exempt expectant mothers, mothers with young children, persons over seventy, physicians, dentists, attorneys, judges, teachers, elected officials, and police, fire, and emergency personnel. The trend is to limit exceptions.

  o The Jury Selection and Service Act of 1968 requires that jurors in federal courts be selected at random from a fair cross-section of the community. States have similar statutes. Where necessary to protect potential jurors and their families, courts can employ anonymous juries.

  o Those summoned to be jurors constitute the "venire." The judge excuses those with physical disabilities, close family relationships, or business conflicts. After swearing in the remaining members, prospective jurors answer questions from the court and counsel (the *voir dire*.)

  o Challenges for cause may be directed to prospective jurors concerning any matters that would disqualify them from serving. The prosecution and defense may exercise a limited number of peremptory challenges to excuse prospective jurors without stating any reason. In 1986, the Supreme Court held that the Equal Protection Clause prohibits racially-based peremptory challenges, in 1994 it prohibited gender-based peremptory challenges, and in 2000 it suggested that this rule applies to ethnicity as well.

  o After selection, the jury is sworn and is admonished not to discuss the case until instructed by the court to deliberate. Increasingly courts allow jurors to take written notes and to question witnesses.

  o An alternate juror sometimes sits with the jury but, unless substituted for a regular juror, is excused before the jury deliberates.

- Learning Objective 3

  o "Death qualification" of a jury is meant to assure that the views of prospective jurors in a capital case would not prevent them from voting for the death penalty.

  o The Supreme Court has said that death qualification is designed to obtain a jury that can properly and impartially apply the law to the facts at both the guilt and sentencing phases of a capital trial. The Court has held that removal before the guilt phase in a capital trial of prospective jurors whose opposition to the death penalty would impair or prevent performance of their duties at the sentencing phase is not unconstitutional.

- Learning Objective 4

  o Members of the media have a First Amendment right to monitor and report trials, but the trial judge must make sure that media coverage does not disrupt a trial and must take steps to ensure that the defendant receives a fair trial.
  o In order to keep the prosecutor and the defense counsel from "trying a case in the media," a judge can issue a gag order prohibiting the attorneys from talking to the press about the case. However, the U.S. Supreme Court has made it very difficult, if not impossible, for judges to extend gag orders to media members.
  o Federal Rules of Criminal Procedure prohibit photography of judicial proceedings, but cameras are now allowed in most state courts.
  o Judges exercise discretion and usually prohibit or restrict coverage of jurors and prohibit coverage of juveniles and victims of sex crimes.

- Learning Objective 5

  o A defendant has the right to be present at every critical stage of criminal proceedings; however, a defendant who disrupts proceedings or fails to comply with court standards forfeits that right.
  o Judges can control order in court by attendees (and usually defendants) by excising the power of contempt.
  o In 1970 the Supreme Court indicated that in addition to contempt, judges may have an unruly defendant removed from the courtroom or bound and gagged until the defendant agrees to proper decorum.
  o Trial judges must maintain dignity and neutrality and recognize that adverse comments toward the defense attorney can prejudice the case.
  o Lawyers must observe courtroom decorum and ethical rules. Offending lawyers may be disciplined by a bar association, found in contempt and fined, or even jailed in for egregious misconduct.

- Learning Objective 6

  o In 1970 the Supreme Court elevated to a constitutional mandate the historic rule that to convict a defendant the evidence must show the defendant guilty "beyond a reasonable doubt." The burden of proof is on the prosecution, not the defendant.
  o The Federal Rules of Evidence are in the U.S. Code. Some states have legislatively or judicially adopted codes of evidence; in others the rules must be gleaned from the decisional law.
  o Courts take "judicial notice" of commonly known facts without formal proof, but a party can offer proof to the contrary. Courts also take judicial notice of constitutions, statutes, and judicial opinions.
  o Evidentiary presumptions are devices to aid a party who has the burden of proof and are subject to refutation. Presumptions must be permissive, as conclusive presumptions violate due process of law.
  o Evidence of crimes or conduct similar to that charged against the defendant may be admitted in evidence to show motive, identity, or absence of mistake or accident, but not to prove the defendant's bad character or propensity to commit a crime.

- ○ Real evidence consists of such tangible items such as maps, blood samples, X-rays, photographs, stolen goods, fingerprints, knives, and guns. Testimonial evidence consists of sworn statements of witnesses.

- ○ Direct evidence includes eyewitness testimony; indirect evidence usually consists of circumstantial evidence—that is, attendant facts from which inferences can be drawn to establish other facts in issue.

- ○ Whether real or testimonial, direct or circumstantial, evidence must be relevant—that is, it must tend to prove or disprove a material fact in issue.

- ○ Trial lawyers make general objections on grounds that the evidence proffered is not relevant. They make specific objections on grounds that proffered evidence violates rules against hearsay testimony (there are many exceptions) or the rule that requires production of the best evidence of written transactions, or that questions call for an opinion that a lay witness is not competent to give.

- ○ In determining whether a witness is competent to testify, the trial judge considers the witness's ability to receive and recollect impressions, to understand questions, and to appreciate the moral duty to tell the truth. A very young child may or may not be competent to testify.

- ○ Evidentiary privileges limit testifying by not allowing testimony protected by the attorney-client privilege, the marital privilege, or the privilege for communications related by a penitent in confidence to a clergyperson.

- Learning Objective 7

  - ○ A witness with proper credentials can be received as an expert, may testify based on personal knowledge, and may respond to hypothetical questions that assume the existence of facts the evidence tends to establish.

  - ○ Historically federal and most state courts applied the general acceptance (*Frye*) test in determining admissibility of new scientific tests. But in 1993, the Supreme Court ruled that the federal rules of evidence supersede the *Frye* test and that admissibility of scientific evidence must be based on several factors, including whether the evidence can be tested and be subjected to peer review (the *Daubert* standard). In 1999, the Court extended its *Daubert* reliability requirement to nonscientific expert testimony.

  - ○ The majority of courts hold that hypnotically enhanced testimony is not sufficiently reliable to be admissible and that the reliability of polygraph testing has not been scientifically demonstrated to such a degree of certainty as to permit its use in evidence. However, some courts allow the results of polygraph testing admitted on stipulation of the prosecution and the defense.

  - ○ Expert testimony concerning the battered woman syndrome has gained substantial scientific acceptance, and some courts now receive such testimony when a woman claims to have acted in self-defense against a spouse or cohabitant.

  - ○ DNA is extracted from biological specimens such as white blood cells, semen, body hair, and tissue. DNA printing tests attempt to develop "genetic fingerprints" and compare DNA molecules extracted from a suspect's specimen with DNA molecules extracted from specimens found at a crime scene to determine whether the samples match. DNA evidence must satisfy the tests for scientific evidence.

- Learning Objective 8

  - ○ The trial judge exercises discretion in determining judicial and administrative matters at trial, including whether to exclude witnesses from the courtroom while other witnesses are testifying. Witnesses are interrogated by counsel, but the judge can allow narrative testimony.

- The prosecution and the defense are each allowed to make a non-argumentative opening statement outlining their theories and the evidence to be presented. (In a bench trial, counsel often waive opening statements or make only limited remarks.)
- The prosecution presents its witnesses first-typically, the victim, police officers, and other lay and expert witnesses.
- The Sixth Amendment guarantees a defendant the right to confront and cross-examine prosecution witnesses. Cross-examination is available to both the prosecutor and the defense counsel, but the trial judge regulates the scope of cross-examination, which is generally limited to matters that a witness has testified to on direct examination and questions that tend to impeach the witness's credibility.
- A witness's credibility may be attacked by showing the witness's inability to recall events; by prior conflicting statements; by showing the witness has an interest in the result of the trial; or by establishing that the witness has been convicted of a crime, bears a bad reputation for truthfulness, or is biased, prejudiced, or has motives to misrepresent the facts.
- In 1990 the Supreme Court held that the Sixth Amendment's Confrontation Clause does not absolutely prohibit states from using one-way closed circuit television to receive a child's testimony in a child abuse case, but the trial judge must make particularized findings that a child victim of sexual abuse would suffer unreasonable and unnecessary mental or emotional harm if required to testify in the defendant's presence.
- At the close of the prosecution's evidence, defense counsel frequently moves for a judgment of acquittal (directed verdict). In ruling, the trial judge views the prosecution's evidence in the light most favorable to the government. If the motion is denied, the defense must decide if the defendant will testify and be subject to cross-examination.
- The Fifth Amendment privilege against self-incrimination protects the defendant from being required to testify, absent a grant of immunity, and forbids any direct or indirect comment by the prosecution on the defendant's failure to testify.
- After the defendant's case has been presented, the prosecution and defense may present rebuttal witnesses.
- Jurors are directed to withhold judgment until all the evidence has been presented and the jury retires to deliberate. Most trial judges now allow jurors to take notes, and in recent years courts have increasingly allowed jurors to submit questions to witnesses.

- Learning Objective 9

  - At the conclusion of a jury trial, the judge confers with counsel outside the presence of the jury and formulates the instructions to be given to the jury.
  - A defendant is entitled to have the jury instructed on the law applicable to any legitimate theory of defense supported by the evidence.
  - The prosecution and defense are each afforded the right to closing arguments and may comment on the weight of the evidence and credibility of the witnesses. However, neither may state a personal belief about the defendant's guilt or innocence or refer to matters not in evidence, except matters of common knowledge. (In nonjury cases, counsel frequently waive their right to make closing arguments).

- ○ If the trial judge fails to take appropriate action when the prosecutor makes improper remarks, or if the prosecutor's remarks are too prejudicial to be erased from the minds of the jurors, the defendant may be able to obtain a mistrial or, if convicted, a new trial.
- ○ After closing arguments, the judge reads the charges against the defendant to the jury and admonishes the jury that the defendant is presumed innocent unless and until the prosecution proves the defendant guilty of each element of the crime beyond a reasonable doubt. The judge defines the elements of any crime charged and any lesser offenses and, where applicable, instructs on an attempt to commit any crime charged. A defendant is entitled to have the jury instructed on any lesser included offense when the jury could rationally find the defendant guilty of the lesser offense.
- ○ The trial judge is not permitted to summarize the evidence or express an opinion on the weight of the evidence or the credibility of the witnesses.

- • Learning Objective 10

  - ○ After being instructed by the judge, the members of the jury retire to the jury room, select one of their members as foreperson, and deliberate on its verdict.
  - ○ Usually a jury is allowed to take with it to the jury room all exhibits received in evidence.
  - ○ In some cases, the judge orders the jury sequestered until it reaches its verdict.
  - ○ In federal (and most state) criminal trials, a jury verdict must be unanimous. A few states accept less-than-unanimous verdicts. The Supreme Court has approved nonunanimous verdicts by twelve-person juries, but has held that a conviction by a nonunanimous six-person jury in a state trial for a nonpetty offense violates the Sixth Amendment.
  - ○ If the jury is deadlocked, the trial judge can either declare a mistrial or urge the jury to make further attempts to arrive at a verdict by giving a supplemental instruction (*Allen* charge).
  - ○ A jury nullification or jury pardon occurs when a jury disregards the evidence and the judge's instructions and acquits a defendant or convicts the defendant of a lesser offense.
  - ○ The court or any party may have the jury polled individually, asking each juror, "Is this your verdict?" If any juror expresses dissent from the verdict, the trial judge may either direct the jury to retire for further deliberation or discharge the jury.
  - ○ The defendant may be continued on bail, pending application for a new trial or an appeal. A motion for a new trial affords the trial judge an opportunity to rectify errors by awarding the defendant a new trial, but in most instances, it is a *pro forma* prelude to an appeal and is denied.

## Key Terms

| | |
|---|---|
| *Allen* charge | circumstantial evidence |
| attorney–client privilege | clergy–penitent privilege |
| bench trial | closing arguments |
| best evidence | competent to testify |
| challenges for cause | deadlocked jury |
| child shield statutes | death qualification of a jury |

direct evidence

directed verdict

DNA testing

evidentiary presumptions

eyewitness testimony

forensic experts

foreperson

gag order

gender-based peremptory challenges

general acceptance test

general objection

hearsay evidence

hypnotically enhanced testimony

hypothetical questions

impeachment

indirect evidence

judgment of acquittal

judicial notice

jury instructions

jury nullification

jury pardon

jury trial

leading questions

marital privilege

motion for a new trial

open public trials

opening statement

opinion evidence

peremptory challenges

polling the jury

polygraph evidence

power of contempt

privileges

proof beyond a reasonable doubt

putting witnesses under the rule

racially based peremptory
    challenges

real evidence

rebuttal witnesses

right of confrontation

right of cross-examination

scientific evidence

sequestration

similar fact evidence

specific objection

standby counsel

testimonial evidence

venire

verdict

*voir dire*

## Questions for Thought and Discussion

1. Jurors are generally selected from among those citizens who have registered to vote or who have registered motor vehicles. Do these methods produce juries drawn from a "representative cross-section of the community"? Can you suggest a better way of selecting jurors?

2. In England, the *voir dire* process is conducted by the trial judge and is extremely limited. Do you think the American system of criminal justice would have more credibility if *voir dire* were conducted exclusively by the judge, with only challenges for cause permitted? Explain your view.

3. What factors do you think a defense attorney considers in deciding whether to advise a client to testify on his or her own behalf at trial?

4. In 1965 Justice Tom Clark, writing for the Supreme Court in *Estes v. Texas*, observed that "[t]rial by television is . . . foreign to our system." Evaluate Justice Clark's statement in view of contemporary attitudes toward communications technology.

5. Many rules of evidence applied in jury trials are derived from the early common law, when jurors were largely uneducated. These rules were designed to prevent jurors from hearing evidence that might prejudice their judgment about the

case. Given the educational standards in the United States, should these rules be made less restrictive regarding evidence that can be presented in court? What constitutional problems would arise if hearsay evidence were allowed to be presented against a defendant?

6. What testimonial privileges are available to witnesses in your state? What is the rationale for each?

7. Do you think a trial judge should be allowed to summarize the evidence for the jury's benefit before the jurors retire to deliberate? What advantages and disadvantages can you see in such a practice? Would it be constitutional?

8. In some jurisdictions, a judge instructs the jury regarding its general duties and responsibilities at the beginning of the trial rather than waiting until the evidence has been presented. Do you favor this approach? Why or why not?

9. Do you think that the trial judge should inform a jury that it has the power to issue a jury pardon despite the evidence of the defendant's guilt when the jury feels that in "good conscience" the defendant should not be convicted of the crime charged or any lesser crime supported by the evidence at trial? Give reasons for your view.

10. The Supreme Court has said that state criminal trial juries need not observe the unanimity principle that prevails in the federal courts. Could it not be argued that the reasonable doubt standard necessarily entails the unanimity principle, as the doubt of one juror is sufficient to suggest a reasonable doubt about the guilt of the accused?

## Problems for Discussion and Solution

1. A defendant is tried before a jury on a DWI charge. At the conclusion of the trial the judge instructs the jury: "If you find from the evidence that the defendant had a blood-alcohol content of .10, you must presume she was intoxicated." On what basis should the defendant's attorney object to this instruction?

2. A defendant is being tried for first-degree murder. The prosecutor presents an eyewitness to the victim's being shot. After asking the witness some preliminary questions, the prosecutor begins a question with "When the defendant shot and killed the victim . . ." Should the defense attorney pose an objection to this question? On what ground?

3. In response to the prosecutor's questions, a lay witness who is a high school graduate testifies as follows: "I measured the defendant's skid marks, and I believe he was driving at least sixty-five miles per hour." "In my opinion, anyone who drinks two beers becomes intoxicated." "When I saw the defendant right after the accident, his face appeared flushed and he staggered as he walked." "My sister told me that the defendant did a lot of drinking at the nearby bar." What, if any, objections should the defense make to each one of the witness's statements?

4. Luke Lumberjack is being tried for raping a woman he has known for a year. The state's evidence disclosed that Lumberjack, age twenty-three, had spent an evening with the female complainant, age twenty-one. Afterward, at his invitation, they went to his apartment and had a few beers. The complainant testified that Lumberjack, a large, husky male, forced her to have sex with him, despite her stated unwillingness. During cross-examination, the complainant admitted having once before had a consensual sexual relationship with the defendant. During the state's closing argument, in referring to the defendant, the prosecutor told the jury, "This big hunk of cruelty is an animal, one who

must be put away to protect the young women of this community. It's important to do your duty by convicting him and send a message to the community." Defense counsel objected on the ground that the prosecutor's comments were inflammatory, prejudicial, and unfair. He requested that the trial judge strike the prosecutor's comments, inform the jury that they should be disregarded, and admonish the prosecutor for having made such statements. How should the trial judge rule?

5. Lawrence Liverless is being tried before a jury for armed robbery and murder of a convenience store clerk. The indictment alleges that Liverless shot and killed the clerk before prying open the cash register and stealing the $451 contained therein. Because the video surveillance camera was not working at the time of the robbery, the prosecution is relying heavily on the testimony of Officer Dusty Broome, who arrived at the scene of the robbery in response to a silent alarm triggered by the convenience store clerk before he was fatally shot. Officer Broome testified that he did not see the perpetrator, but that before he died the clerk told him that the robber had a tattoo of a dragon on his arm. The defendant, Liverless, has a large tattoo of a dragon on his right arm. On what ground might the defense object to this testimony? How should the judge rule on the objection? If the judge upholds the objection, does this constitute a basis for declaring a mistrial?

## CHAPTER 19

# Sentencing and Punishment

## JURISPRUDENCE

*Kansas v. Hendricks* (1997)

*Furman v. Georgia* (1972)

*Gregg v. Georgia* (1976)

*Ford v. Wainwright* (1986)

*Payne v. Tennessee* (1991)

*Bearden v. Georgia* (1983)

*Cunningham v. California* (2007)

*Ewing v. California* (2003)

*Apprendi v. New Jersey* (2000)

## LEARNING OBJECTIVES

After reading this chapter, you should be able to explain

1. the historical antecedents and philosophical underpinnings of the forms of criminal punishment used today

2. how and why criminal penalties are controlled by statutes as well as constitutional provisions

3. how and why judges grant and revoke probation in lieu of incarceration

4. why courts have allowed violent sexual predators who have completed their prison terms to be confined via civil commitment

5. how the death penalty has evolved and why it remains controversial

6. how the sentencing process works and why sentencing in capital cases is unique

7. the different statutory approaches to incarceration

8. why the federal government and some states have adopted sentencing guidelines

9. what constitutional rights are retained by people in prison

10. what rights are afforded to victims of crimes

## CHAPTER OPENING VIGNETTE

In November 1999, 14-year-old Kuntrell Jackson and two other teenage boys decided to commit a robbery at a video store in Arkansas. When Jackson learned that one of the boys was carrying a concealed firearm, he remained outside the store while the other two went inside, confronted the clerk and demanded money. Jackson then entered the store and said something, though what he said was in dispute at trial. The defense claimed that Jackson said to his friends, "I thought you all was playin'." The prosecution claimed that Jackson told the clerk that "[w]e ain't playin'." In any event, when the clerk refused to give up the money, one of the other teenagers shot and killed her. The three then fled the scene empty-handed. Jackson was tried as an adult, convicted of aggravated robbery and felony murder, and sentenced to life in prison without possibility of parole in accordance with Arkansas law. In reviewing the case, the U.S. Supreme Court struck down the law under which Jackson was sentenced. The Court also struck down a similar Alabama statute. Speaking for the Court, Justice Elena Kagan opined that "by requiring that all children convicted of homicide receive lifetime incarceration without possibility of parole, regardless of their age and age-related characteristics and the nature of their crimes, the mandatory sentencing schemes before us violate [the] principle of proportionality, and so the Eighth Amendment's ban on cruel and unusual punishment." *Miller v. Alabama*, 567 U.S. ___, 132 S.Ct. 2455, 183 L.Ed.2d 407 (2012). As you will see throughout this chapter, The Cruel and Unusual Punishments Clause of the Eighth Amendment figures prominently in the law affecting sentencing and punishment.

## Introduction

**retribution** Something demanded as payment or revenge from one who has committed a criminal offense; the theory of punishment that stresses just deserts.

The concept of criminal punishment is an ancient one. The Code of Hammurabi, promulgated in Babylonia circa 1800 b.c., contained a detailed schedule of crimes and punishments and first codified the notion of "an eye for an eye." In a similar vein, the Mosaic Law mandated severe but proportionate punishment based on this principle of **retribution**.

While it is sometimes equated with legalized vengeance, the concept of retribution was a great leap forward in the evolution of criminal punishment. It replaced the

**proportionality** The degree to which a particular punishment matches the seriousness of a crime or matches the penalty other offenders have received for the same crime.

personal or familial (and often excessive) acts of vengeance that frequently followed injuries to persons or property. Moreover, retribution carried with it a sense of **proportionality**, which continues to have relevance in criminal sentencing today.

Most ancient legal systems prescribed severe punishments for those who committed the kinds of acts we now consider *mala in se*. Execution, torture, mutilation, and banishment from the community were not uncommon. But ancient legal systems also employed economic sanctions such as forfeiture of property, especially when members of the upper classes committed transgressions against members of the lower classes.

## The Common-Law Background

**capital crimes** Crime for which death is a permissible punishment.

By contemporary standards, the English common law was quite severe—the death penalty was prescribed for most felonies. In the early days of the common law, nobles who committed **capital crimes** were shown mercy by simply being beheaded. Commoners who were sentenced to death were often subjected to more grisly forms of punishment—they were "broken on the wheel" (where the condemned was strapped to a wagon wheel and his limbs broken with an iron rod), "drawn and quartered" (where the condemned, after being disemboweled, was cut into four pieces), or "burned at the stake" (where the condemned was tied to a post and burned alive). Eventually, the comparatively humane method of hanging was adopted as the principal means of execution in England.

**corporal punishment** Punishment that inflicts pain or injury on a person's body.

Persons convicted of misdemeanors were generally subjected to nonlethal **corporal punishment** such as flogging. The misdemeanant was taken into the public square, bound to the whipping post, and administered as many lashes as were prescribed by law for the offense.

**general deterrence** The theory that punishment serves to deter others from committing crimes.

In England—indeed, throughout Europe—the administration of punishment was intentionally a matter of public spectacle. The idea was that public display of painful and humiliating punishment would deter others from engaging in criminal acts. This theory, known as **general deterrence**, is still prevalent today.

During the colonization of the New World, English subjects convicted of misdemeanors were often sent to penal colonies in America to do hard labor. After the American Revolution, they were sent to Australia.

## The American Experience

In colonial America, criminal punishment followed common-law practice, although the Massachusetts Code of 1648 mandated capital punishment in cases of idolatry, witchcraft, blasphemy, sodomy, and adultery, as well as for the common-law capital crimes. At the time of the American Revolution, the death penalty was in wide use for a variety of felonies. And corporal punishment, primarily flogging, was widely used for a variety of crimes, including many misdemeanors.

The American Bill of Rights, ratified in 1791, prohibited the imposition of "cruel and unusual punishments." The framers of the Bill of Rights sought to prevent the use of torture, which had been common in Europe as late as the eighteenth century. However, they did not intend to outlaw the death penalty, nor did they intend to abolish all forms of corporal punishment.

**rehabilitation** Restoring someone or something to its former status; a justification for punishment emphasizing reform rather than retribution.

During the nineteenth century, reformers introduced the concept of the penitentiary—literally, "a place to do penance." The idea was that criminals could be reformed through isolation, Bible study, and hard labor. This gave rise to the notion of **rehabilitation**: the idea that the criminal justice system could reform criminals and reintegrate them into society. Many of the educational, occupational training, and psychological programs found in modern prisons are based on this theory.

**incarceration** Another term for imprisonment.

By the twentieth century, **incarceration** had replaced corporal punishment as the mainstay of criminal sentencing. All states, as well as the federal government, constructed prisons to house persons convicted of felonies. Even cities and counties constructed jails to confine persons convicted of misdemeanors. The **death penalty** remained in wide use for the most serious violent felonies. But it was rendered more "humane" as the gallows were replaced by the firing squad, the gas chamber, the electric chair, and, eventually, lethal injection. The death penalty remains in effect today in more than half the states, as well as in the federal system, although its use is now limited to the most aggravated cases of first-degree murder. It remains one of the most intensely controversial aspects of the American system of criminal justice.

**death penalty** Capital punishment; a sentence to death for the commission of a crime.

**incapacitation** Punishment making it impossible for an offender to reoffend.

Today the focus of criminal punishment is on the goal of **incapacitation**. Incapacitation means that offenders are prevented from committing further criminal acts. In ancient societies, banishment was sometimes used to protect the community from those whose presence was regarded as unduly threatening. Contemporary American society resorts to imprisonment or, in extreme cases, execution to rid itself of seriously threatening behavior. Although nearly everyone favors incapacitation of violent offenders, in practice incapacitation extends beyond execution or incarceration. When a state revokes a person's driver's license for driving while intoxicated, the purpose is primarily incapacitation. Similarly, some states have laws offering convicted rapists the option of taking a drug to render them incapable of committing rape. Other forms of incapacitation can be extremely controversial. For example, may a judge order a convicted child abuser to refrain from having any more children to prevent future child abuse?

Those who favor incapacitation to the exclusion of the other purposes of punishment are likely to favor harsh sentences, even for relatively minor crimes. They prefer to "lock 'em up and throw away the key." Again, we must consider the issue of proportionality: Crime control is not the only goal of the criminal justice system—dispensing justice is equally important.

## Legal Constraints on Sentencing and Punishment

There are procedural as well as substantive issues in the area of sentencing and punishment. Sharp disagreements exist regarding the roles that legislatures, judges, and corrections officials should play in determining punishments. Generally, judges are required to impose sentences that fall within the parameters of appropriate punishment specified by statute, yet within these parameters, courts exercise substantial discretion. Recent concern about sentencing disparities has resulted in a variety of measures aimed at reducing the range of judicial discretion in sentencing.

Just as judges' sentencing decisions are constrained by statutes, statutory penalties must comport with substantive and procedural requirements imposed by the federal and state constitutions. Specifically, criminal punishment is limited by the Eighth Amendment prohibition of cruel and unusual punishments, the Due Process Clauses of the Fifth and Fourteenth Amendments, and similar provisions in all fifty state constitutions. Recent judicial activity in the areas of sentencing and punishment has focused on the need for procedural regularity in sentencing and proportionality in punishment.

# Contemporary Forms of Criminal Punishment

Today the criminal law provides for a variety of criminal punishments, including monetary fines, incarceration, probation, community service, and, of course, the death penalty. Although most people agree about the propriety of punishing criminal behavior, they disagree about the legality, morality, and efficacy of specific modes of criminal punishment. The death penalty in particular remains a hotly debated issue.

## Fines

**monetary fine** A sum of money that offenders are required to pay as punishment for the commission of crimes.

By far the most common form of criminal punishment today is the **monetary fine**. Most misdemeanors carry monetary fines, especially for first offenses. Some felonies, especially serious economic crimes defined by federal law, carry heavy monetary fines as penalties. For example, offenses against federal banking laws and securities and exchange laws are punishable by fines reaching into the millions of dollars. Increasingly, drug trafficking offenders are being punished by large fines.

In many states, a court can sentence a defendant to pay a fine in addition to serving a sentence of imprisonment or probation. In New Jersey, for example, such fines may range from $500 to $200,000, depending on the nature and degree of the offense. N.J. Stat. Ann. § 2C:43-3. Fines might be appropriate devices of retribution and deterrence for economic crimes, but they hardly seem suitable as punishments for criminal acts of violence. And many have questioned the fairness and effectiveness of established minimum and maximum fines that do not consider the economic circumstances of individual defendants.

## Forfeiture of Property

**forfeiture** Sacrifice of ownership or some right (usually in property) as a penalty.

Federal law provides for **forfeiture** of the proceeds of a variety of criminal activities. See, generally, 18 U.S.C.A. §§ 981–982. More controversial are the federal law provisions allowing forfeiture of property used in illicit drug activity. Under federal law, a "conveyance," which includes aircraft, motor vehicles, and vessels, is subject to forfeiture if it is used to transport controlled substances. 21 U.S.C.A. § 881(a)(4). Real estate may be forfeited if it is used to commit or facilitate the commission of a drug-related felony. 21 U.S.C.A. § 881(a)(7). Many states have similar statutes. See, e.g., Oklahoma's Uniform Controlled Dangerous Substances Act, 63 Okl. Stat. Ann. § 2-503.

State courts dealing with forfeiture under state law generally review forfeitures under the "excessive fines" provisions of their state constitutions. See, for example, *In re King Properties*, 635 A.2d 128 (Pa. 1993), where the court found that forfeiture of a house used as a base of operations in an ongoing drug business was not excessive. Where a state constitutional provision exempts a homestead from forced sale, courts generally hold that it also prohibits civil or criminal forfeiture of homestead property. See, e.g., *Butterworth v. Caggiano*, 605 So.2d 56 (Fla. 1992). However, a federal appeals court has ruled that federal law preempts—that is, overrides—state homestead exemptions when federal crimes have been committed. *United States v. Lot 5, Fox Grove, Alachua County, Fla.*, 23 F.3d 359 (11th Cir. 1994).

Under federal and state laws, asset forfeiture may be accomplished through civil or criminal proceedings. In *Austin v. United States*, 509 U.S. 602, 113 S.Ct. 2801, 125 L.Ed.2d 488 (1993), the Supreme Court said that civil forfeiture "constitutes 'payment to a sovereign as punishment for some offense' . . . and, as such, is subject to the limitations of the Eighth Amendment's Excessive Fines Clause." 509 U.S. at 622, 113 S.Ct. at 2812, 125 L.Ed.2d at 505. However, the Court left it to state and lower federal courts to determine the tests of "excessiveness" in the context of forfeiture. In 1994 the Illinois Supreme Court said that three factors should be considered in this regard: (1) the gravity of the offense relative to the value of the forfeiture, (2) whether the property was an integral part of the illicit activity, and (3) whether illicit activity involving the property was extensive. *Waller v. 1989 Ford F350 Truck (Kusumoto)*, 642 N.E.2d 460 (Ill. 1994).

## Incarceration

Confinement is generally regarded as the only effective way to deal with violent offenders. Although some question the efficacy of the prison, regarding it as little more than a factory for producing future criminals, incarceration does protect society from dangerous offenders. Prison is an effective incapacitator; it is rarely an effective rehabilitator. In fact, serving time in prison often reinforces criminal tendencies.

Today more than 1.5 million inmates are housed in federal or state prisons. See U.S. Department of Justice, Bureau of Justice Statistics, "Correctional Population in the United States, 2010," December 2011, NCJ 236319. Although the increase in the national incarceration rate has slowed somewhat since 2004, most state prisons are operating at or just below capacity. The federal system continues to operate well above its designed capacity. This problem has led to judicial intervention in many instances, yet society appears reluctant to provide additional resources to expand prison capacity. Imprisonment is expensive, costing taxpayers roughly $20 billion per year.

As criminologists have become increasingly dissatisfied with the effects of the prison system, judges have responded by imposing limits on prison populations and scrutinizing the conditions of confinement. Meanwhile, fiscal pressures prevent legislatures from appropriating the funds necessary to construct more prisons. Accordingly, attention has shifted to alternatives to incarceration, especially for less dangerous offenders. One of the most serious criticisms of all such alternatives emphasizes the difficulty of determining who should be eligible for an alternative form of punishment. In an age of overcrowded prisons, alternative punishments carry the real possibility that truly dangerous offenders will not be sufficiently controlled.

## The Boot Camp: An Alternative to Prison?

**boot camp** An institution that provides systematic discipline in a military-like environment designed to rehabilitate an offender; employed as a sentencing alternative.

One alternative to the traditional prison setting is the **boot camp**, a program designed to employ a system of discipline much like the one the military uses to instill discipline in its recruits. Boot camps were designed to rehabilitate young, nonviolent offenders who have committed theft, burglary, forgery, and other nonviolent offenses, often brought about by their drug abuse. Although boot camps produced some short-term changes in behavior, they did little to reduce recidivism, in part because of insufficient focus on the offender's reentry into the community. In January 2006, a fourteen-year-old boy died after being roughed up by guards at a sheriff's boot camp in Panama City, Florida. The boy's death led to the dismantling of the Florida boot camp program. After a lengthy investigation, in November 2006 the state charged seven former guards and a nurse at the facility with manslaughter arising out of the incident. Although the defendants were ultimately acquitted, the incident gave more impetus to criticism of boot camps nationwide, and it now appears that the national boot camp experiment is coming to an end.

## Probation

**probation** Conditional release of a convicted criminal in lieu of incarceration.

Of the various alternatives to incarceration, **probation** is by far the most common. According to the Bureau of Justice Statistics, at the end of 2010, roughly 4.9 million adult men and women were under federal, state, or local probation or parole jurisdiction. U.S. Department of Justice, Bureau of Justice Statistics, "Correctional Population in the United States, 2010," supra.

An outgrowth of nineteenth- and twentieth-century developments in criminal justice, probation is the conditional release of a convicted offender by a trial court. If prisons have become little more than factories for producing future criminals, probation seems to be a viable alternative to prison terms, especially for nonviolent first-time offenders. The primary purpose of probation is to rehabilitate the defendant. Thus, the defendant is released under the supervision of a probation officer, who is responsible to the court for making sure that the offender abides by the **conditions of probation**.

**conditions of probation** A set of rules that must be observed by a person placed on probation.

The mandatory and discretionary conditions for probation for federal offenses are set out in 18 U.S.C.A. § 3563. By 1967 all states provided for probation, often varying in the offenses and defendants eligible. State laws generally provide for certain mandatory conditions. A sentencing judge is afforded broad discretion in formulating additional conditions of a defendant's probation. Certain conditions are relatively standard—for example, that the probationer will not commit further crimes, will avoid certain persons or places, will maintain gainful employment and support any dependents, and will not travel outside the court's jurisdiction without permission of the court or probation officer. The sentencing judge, however, can tailor additional conditions to the defendant's rehabilitation, even to the extent of imposing conditions that infringe a probationer's constitutional rights, including First Amendment rights of free speech and association, as long as those conditions are related to the goal of rehabilitation. *Malone v. United States*, 502 F.2d 554 (9th Cir. 1974); *Porth v. Templar*, 453 F.2d 330 (10th Cir. 1971).

The U.S. Supreme Court has had little to say on the subject of probation since stating in 1932 that probation conditions must serve "the ends of justice and the best interest of both the public and the defendant." *Burns v. United States*, 287 U.S. 216, 220, 53 S.Ct. 154, 156, 77 L.Ed. 266, 268 (1932). In *Higdon v. United States*, 627 F.2d 893 (9th Cir. 1980), a leading federal decision, the court noted, "The only factors which the trial judge should consider when deciding whether to grant probation are the appropriateness and attainability of rehabilitation and the need to protect the public by imposing conditions which control the probationer's activities." *Id.* at 897. The court fashioned a two-step process for reviewing conditions of probation. The court first determines whether the conditions are permissible; if so, it then looks to whether there is a reasonable relationship between the conditions imposed and the purpose of the probation.

Most probationary sentences are imposed by state courts, which frequently cite *People v. Dominguez*, 64 Cal.Rptr. 290 (Cal. App. 1967), as the standard for judging the reasonableness of conditions of probation. There the court established that a condition of probation that (1) has no relationship to the crime of which the offender was convicted, (2) relates to conduct which is not in itself criminal, and (3) requires or forbids conduct which is not reasonably related to future criminality

## Conditions of Probation

CASE-IN-POINT

In 1990 the Supreme Court of Ohio reviewed the conviction of a defendant on a charge of contributing to the delinquency of a child by furnishing alcohol to three young boys. The court focused on a single point: whether the trial court abused its discretion in imposing a condition of probation stipulating that the defendant "have no association or communication, direct or indirect, with anyone under the age of 18 years not a member of his immediate family." The court noted that while a trial judge is granted broad discretion in setting conditions of probation, that discretion is not limitless, and courts must guard against overly broad conditions that impinge upon the probationer's liberty. Nevertheless, the court found that the restriction imposed against the defendant "reasonably related to rehabilitating [the defendant] without being unduly restrictive." Citing various state and federal authorities, the court said that in setting conditions of probation, trial judges should consider whether a condition to be imposed (1) is reasonably related to rehabilitating the offender, (2) has some relationship to the crime for which the offender was convicted, and (3) relates to conduct that is criminal or reasonably related to future criminality.

*State v. Jones*, 550 N.E.2d 469 (Ohio 1990).

does not serve the ends of probation and is invalid. *Id.* at 293. In *Dominguez*, the court reasoned that a condition that the probationer not become pregnant without being married was unrelated to her offense or to future criminality and thus was invalid.

Because most probationers are grateful to receive a probationary sentence and avoid incarceration, constitutional challenges to conditions are not too common. Nevertheless, some courts that have reviewed such conditions have ruled that there are limits to probation conditions. In *Biller v. State*, 618 So.2d 734 (Fla. 1993), the Florida Supreme Court invalidated a probation order that required the probationer to refrain from using or possessing alcoholic beverages. The court pointed out that nothing in the record showed any connection between alcohol consumption and the weapons violation of which the probationer had been convicted.

In *Commonwealth v. LaFrance*, 525 N.E.2d 379 (Mass. 1988), the Supreme Judicial Court of Massachusetts invalidated a condition of probation that required the defendant to submit to a search of herself, her possessions, and any place where she may be, with or without a search warrant, on request of a probation officer. Although the court determined that condition violated the defendant's rights, the court suggested that the following condition could be substituted: "On the basis of a reasonable suspicion that a condition of the probationer's probation has been violated, a probation officer, or any law enforcement officer acting on the request of the probation office, may search the probationer, her property, her residence, and any place where she may be living, and may do so with or without a search warrant depending on the requirements of law." *Id.* at 383.

Courts tend to scrutinize conditions that restrict such fundamental rights as procreation. A Florida appellate court held that although a condition of probation prohibiting custody of children had a clear relationship to the crime of child abuse and was valid, conditions prohibiting marriage and pregnancy added nothing to decrease the possibility of further child abuse and were found to be invalid. *Rodriguez v. State*, 378 So.2d 7 (Fla. App. 1979). Three years later, the same court struck down a condition of probation requiring that the defendant "must not father any children during [the] probation period." *Burchell v. State*, 419 So.2d 358 (Fla. App. 1982). In *State v. Mosburg*, 768 P.2d 313 (Kan. App. 1989), the court held that a probation condition requiring a defendant who was convicted of endangering a child to refrain from becoming pregnant during the term of probation unduly intruded on the defendant's right to privacy. At a time when some in society equated long hair with unacceptable behavior, in *Inman v. State*, 183 S.E.2d 413 (Ga. App. 1971), a Georgia appellate court held invalid a condition of probation that required a male defendant to maintain a short haircut as not related to his rehabilitation and therefore unconstitutionally invasive of his right of self-expression.

Different factual scenarios can result in different judicial approaches and reach different conclusions. Consider the approach of the Wisconsin Supreme Court. In *State v. Oakley*, 629 N.W.2d 200 (Wis. 2001), David Oakley, the father of nine children, pled no contest to intentionally refusing to provide child support. The trial judge placed him on probation to enable him to make meaningful payments of support that would not be possible if he was incarcerated. As a condition of Oakley's probation, the judge stipulated, "Oakley cannot father any additional children unless he can demonstrate that he has the financial ability to support them, and that he is supporting the children he has." *Id.* at 203. In rejecting his challenge based on his constitutional right to procreate, the court pointed out that Wisconsin law grants judges broad discretion in fashioning probation conditions and concluded, "[B]ecause Oakley can satisfy this condition by not intentionally refusing to support his current nine children and any future children required by the law, we find that the condition is narrowly tailored to serve the State's compelling interest of having parents support their children." *Id.* at 212.

Conditions of probation imposed on offenders convicted of child pornography offenses have included some innovative approaches. In *United States v. Zinn*, 321 F.3d 1084 (11th Cir. 2003), the court ruled that it was not an abuse of discretion for the district court to require the defendant to submit to polygraph testing reasonably related to his child pornography offense and his personal history.

In imposing conditions of probation, other courts have noted the strong link between child pornographers and their use of the Internet, and the need to protect children from sex offenders. For example, in *United States v. Rearden*, 349 F.3d 608, 620 (9th Cir. 2003), the defendant was convicted of shipping child pornography (over the Internet) in violation of 18 U.S.C.A. § 2253(a)(1)(A). The appellate court said the district court did not err in imposing conditions of supervised release that prohibited him from possessing or using a computer with Internet access without prior approval of his probation officer.

In *State v. Ehli*, 681 N.W.2d 808 (N.D. 2004), the defendant pleaded guilty to sexual abuse of a young child. He had used pornography from the Internet to "instruct" the child on certain adult sexual acts. The state supreme court rejected the defendant's challenge to the suspended part of his sentence that included conditions of probation that prohibited him from having access to the Internet.

In *People v. Harrisson*, 134 Cal.App.4th 637 (2005), the defendant pleaded no contest to possession of child pornography after having used his computer to send pornographic images to an undercover police officer. The court rejected his contention that the probationary part of his sentence that prohibited him access to the Internet violated his constitutional rights.

**community service** A sentence or condition of probation requiring that the criminal perform some specific service to the community for some specified period of time.

## Community Service

Another alternative to incarceration, **community service**, is growing in popularity. Community service refers to sentences whereby offenders are required to perform a specified number of hours of service to the community doing specified tasks. Often, community service is required as one of several conditions of probation.

Community service has the virtues of keeping the offender out of the undesirable prison environment and exacting a penalty that is useful to the community. Ideally, it seems like an excellent way to instill in the offender a sense of responsibility to the community for having committed criminal actions, but community service also has its drawbacks. It is difficult for the community to reap any real benefit without providing a degree of training to and supervision of the offender. Training and supervision can be costly and can, in many instances, exceed the value of the community service to be performed.

## Community Control

**community control** A sentence imposed on a person found guilty of a crime that requires that the offender be placed in an individualized program of noninstitutional confinement.

**house arrest** A sentencing alternative to incarceration where the offender is allowed to leave home only for employment and approved community service activities.

Another alternative to incarceration is **community control**, a neologism for an ancient practice known as **house arrest**. Under this alternative, an offender is allowed to leave home only for employment and approved community service activities. Increasingly, house arrest is monitored electronically by requiring persons to wear bracelets that permit officials to track their whereabouts. Community control is generally employed when incarceration is not warranted but probation is not considered sufficiently restrictive. Community control requires intensive surveillance and supervision and might not be practical in many cases. For example, consider a convicted rapist whose occupation is plumbing. To allow this offender to carry on his trade may pose a significant risk to householders. Comparable risks often militate against placing offenders under community control.

## Creative Alternatives to Confinement

Judges seeking alternatives to jail or prison have been increasingly creative recently. One judge in Houston, Texas, has been known to require offenders to clean out the police department stables as part of their "community service." Some juvenile courts require offenders to make public apologies to their victims. In a few cities, billboards have been erected bearing the names of persons convicted for driving while under the influence of intoxicating substances. Some jurisdictions even publish the names of persons who patronize prostitutes. These actions are intended to shame offenders by drawing public attention to their misconduct. In seventeenth-century Massachusetts, women found guilty of adultery were required to wear a scarlet "A." The idea that offenders need to experience shame appears to be making a comeback.

In 1987 a convicted child molester was sentenced by an Oregon court to five years' probation on the condition that he display on his front door and automobile a warning sign: "Dangerous Sex Offender: No Children Allowed." Although the unusual sentence drew praise from prosecutors and many citizens' groups, civil libertarians objected.

One county judge in Sarasota, Florida, made national news in 1986 by requiring that DWI offenders—as a condition of probation—place bumper stickers on their cars to alert the driving public to their convictions. On appeal, the practice was upheld against an Eighth Amendment attack. As the appellate court said, "The mere requirement that a defendant display a 'scarlet letter' as part of his punishment is not necessarily offensive to the Constitution." *Goldschmitt v. State*, 490 So.2d 123, 125 (Fla. App. 1986). On the other hand, the New York Court of Appeals invalidated a condition of probation that ordered the defendant to attach a "Convicted DWI" sign

---

**JURISPRUDENCE**

*Kansas v. Hendricks*, 521 U.S. 346, 117 S.Ct. 2072, 138 L.Ed.2d 501 (1997)

Leroy Hendricks, an inmate with a history of sexually molesting children, was scheduled for release from prison soon after the Sexually Violent Predator Act became effective. The state invoked the act to commit him to custody. After hearing testimony, which included Hendricks's own testimony that when he gets "stressed" he continues to be unable to control his sexual desires for children, a jury determined that he was a sexually violent predator. The court ordered him confined. On appeal, the Kansas Supreme Court invalidated the act, and the State of Kansas sought review in the U.S. Supreme Court. In a 5–4 decision, the U.S. Supreme Court held that the act does not offend the constitutional prohibitions against *ex post facto* laws and double jeopardy because it does not criminalize conduct that was legal before its enactment and because it does not constitute punishment. Writing for the majority, Justice Clarence Thomas stated that "[t]he State may take measures to restrict the freedom of the dangerously mentally ill. This is a legitimate nonpunitive governmental objective." Dissenting justices argued that the act was not simply an effort to commit Hendricks civilly but rather an effort to inflict further punishment upon him for crimes committed prior to enactment of the act.

---

to the license plate of any car driven by the defendant on the ground that it bore no relationship to the goal of rehabilitation. *People v. Letterlough*, 655 N.E.2d 146 (N.Y. 1995). Obviously, there is room for judicial disagreement on such matters.

## Civil Commitment of Violent Sexual Predators

In 1994 Kansas enacted the Sexually Violent Predator Act. The act establishes procedures for the civil commitment of persons who, because of mental abnormality or personality disorder, are likely to engage in "predatory acts of sexual violence." The Act allows for the continued confinement of sexual predators who already have completed their prison sentences. In 1997 the U.S. Supreme Court upheld this statute against the arguments that it represented "double jeopardy" and amounted to an "*ex post facto* law." *Kansas v. Hendricks*, 521 U.S. 346, 117 S.Ct. 2072, 138 L.Ed.2d 501 (1997).

A similar federal statute enacted in 2006, codified at 18 U.S.C. §4248, permits a federal district court to order the continued confinement of sexually violent offenders who have completed their prison sentences. In 2010 the Supreme Court upheld this statute against a challenge based on the argument that Congress had exceeded its implied powers under the Necessary and Proper Clause of Article I, Section 8 of the U.S. Constitution. Writing for the Court, Justice Stephen Breyer concluded that "the statute is a 'necessary and proper' means of exercising the federal authority that permits Congress to create federal criminal laws, to punish their violation, to imprison violators, to provide appropriately for those imprisoned, and to maintain the security of those who are not imprisoned but who may be affected by the federal imprisonment of others." *United States v. Comstock*, 560 U.S. ___, ___, 130 S.Ct. 1949, 1965, 176 L.Ed.2d 878, 899 (2010).

## The Death Penalty

The death penalty remains the single most controversial issue in the realm of criminal punishment. Although the death penalty has deep roots in religious and legal traditions, the twentieth century witnessed widespread abolition of capital punishment. At present, the United States is the only Western democracy that retains the death penalty. Thirty-eight states currently authorize capital punishment for first-degree murder or other types of aggravated homicide.

## Historical Background

**capital punishment** The death penalty.

The framers of the Bill of Rights did not intend for the Cruel and Unusual Punishments Clause of the Eighth Amendment to abolish the death penalty. The Bill of Rights assumes the existence of **capital punishment**. Indeed, the Fifth Amendment refers specifically to "capital" crimes and the deprivation of life. A reform movement in the nineteenth century succeeded in limiting public executions and reducing the range of capital offenses. The movement to eliminate the death penalty achieved its first victory in 1847, when Michigan abolished capital punishment. This movement grew steadily throughout the twentieth century. By the 1960s, it appeared that the death penalty was on the way out. Public opinion no longer favored it; many states abolished it. In those that did not, the courts began to impose restrictions on its use. In 1967 two persons were executed in the United States. Ten years passed before another person was put to death. When the Supreme Court declared Georgia's death penalty law unconstitutional in *Furman v. Georgia*, 408 U.S. 238, 92 S.Ct. 2726, 33 L.Ed.2d 346 (1972), some observers thought it signaled the abolition of the death penalty in America.

## Revival of the Death Penalty

The Supreme Court's 1972 decision striking down the Georgia death penalty concentrated on the virtually unlimited discretion the state placed in trial juries empowered to impose death sentences. According to Justice Potter Stewart's concurring opinion in *Furman*, Georgia's administration of the death penalty was unpredictable to the point of being "freakishly imposed." 408 U.S. 238, 310, 92 S.Ct. 2726, 2763, 33 L.Ed.2d 346, 390 (1972). In the wake of the *Furman* decision, Georgia and most other states revised their death penalty laws to address the concerns raised by the Court.

---

### JURISPRUDENCE

*Furman v. Georgia*, 408 U.S. 238, 92 S.Ct. 2726, 33 L.Ed.2d 346 (1972)

In this landmark decision the Supreme Court invalidated Georgia's death penalty statute. The decision represents three death penalty cases that were consolidated on appeal. All three defendants were African-American. One of them was convicted for murder; two were found guilty of rape. All three were sentenced to death by juries in Georgia. In a 5-4 decision, the Supreme Court struck down Georgia's death penalty. There was, however, only a brief *per curiam* opinion announcing the judgment of the Court. For the majority's rationale, one has to look at five separate concurring opinions. Only two of the five justices—Brennan and Marshall—held that the death penalty itself was cruel and unusual punishment, given the "evolving standards of decency." Of the five justices who voted to invalidate the death penalty, Justice Stewart's opinion seems to have been the most influential. For Stewart the problem with the death penalty was not the punishment itself but the manner in which it was being administered. Trial juries were being left with virtually unfettered discretion in deciding when to impose capital punishment. The result, according to Stewart, was that the death penalty was "wantonly and . . . freakishly imposed."

**bifurcated trial** A capital trial with separate phases for determining guilt and punishment.

Under the revised Georgia statute, a **bifurcated trial** is held in cases where the state seeks the death penalty. In the first stage, guilt is determined according to the usual procedures, rules of evidence, and standard of proof. If the jury finds the defendant guilty, the same jury considers the appropriateness of the death sentence in a separate proceeding where additional evidence is received to determine aggravation or mitigation of the punishment. To impose the death penalty, the jury must find at least one of several **aggravating factors** specified in the statute. The purpose of requiring aggravating factors before imposing the death penalty is to narrow the range of offenders and persons eligible for capital punishment and make the imposition of the death penalty more predictable.

**aggravating factors** Factors attending the commission of a crime that make the crime or its consequences worse.

Under Georgia law, the specific aggravating factors to be considered by the jury are whether

1. The offense . . . was committed by a person with a prior record of conviction for a capital felony;
2. The offense . . . was committed while the offender was engaged in . . . another capital felony or aggravated battery, or the offense of murder was committed while the offender was engaged in the commission of burglary or arson in the first degree;
3. The offender . . . knowingly created a great risk of death to more than one person in a public place by means of a weapon or device which would normally be hazardous to the lives of more than one person;
4. The offender committed the offense of murder for himself or another for the purpose of receiving money or any other thing of monetary value;
5. The murder of a judicial officer, former judicial officer, a district attorney or solicitor-general, or former district attorney, solicitor or solicitor-general was committed during or because of the exercise of his or her official duties;
6. The offender caused or directed another to commit murder or committed murder as an agent or employee of another person;
7. The offense . . . was outrageously or wantonly vile, horrible or inhuman in that it involved torture, depravity of mind or an aggravated battery to the victim;
8. The offense of murder was committed against any peace officer, corrections employee, or fireman while engaged in the performance of his official duties;
9. The offense of murder was committed by a person in, or who has escaped from, the lawful custody of a peace officer or place of lawful confinement; or
10. The murder was committed for the purpose of avoiding, interfering with, or preventing a lawful arrest or custody in a place of lawful confinement, of himself or another; or
11. The offense of murder, rape, or kidnapping was committed by a person previously convicted of rape, aggravated sodomy, aggravated child molestation, or aggravated sexual battery.

Official Ga. Code Ann. § 17-10-30(b).

To hand down a death sentence, a Georgia jury must find that at least one of these aggravating circumstances was present in the crime. The jury must then weigh the aggravating factors against any **mitigating factors** presented by the defense. See Official Ga. Code Ann. § 17-10-31. Should the jury make this finding and opt for the death penalty, the statute provides for automatic appeal to the state supreme court.

**mitigating factors** Circumstances or factors that tend to lessen culpability.

*Gregg v. Georgia*, 428 U.S. 153, 96 S.Ct. 2909, 49 L.Ed.2d 859 (1976)

Troy Gregg, was convicted of armed robbery and murder and was sentenced to death. In accordance with Georgia's death penalty law revised after *Furman v. Georgia*, the trial was conducted in two stages, a guilt stage and a sentencing stage. For the jury to impose the death penalty, it has to find at least one of several statutorily prescribed aggravating factors. Automatic appeal to the state supreme court is also provided. The appellate review must consider not only the procedural regularity of the trial, but whether the evidence supports the finding of the aggravating factor and whether

the death sentence is disproportionate to the penalty imposed in similar cases. The Court had little difficulty upholding the new Georgia statute, with only Justices Brennan and Marshall dissenting. Justice Stewart's opinion announcing the judgment stated: "The new Georgia sentencing procedures . . . focus the jury's attention on the particularized nature of the crime and the particularized characteristics of the individual defendant. . . . In this way the jury's discretion is channeled. No longer can a jury wantonly and freakishly impose the death sentence, it is always circumscribed by the legislative guidelines." Thus, after a hiatus of four years, the death penalty was reinstated.

That court is required to consider

1. Whether the sentence of death was imposed under the influence of passion, prejudice or any other arbitrary factor; and
2. Whether . . . the evidence supports the jury's or judge's finding of a statutory aggravating circumstance . . .; and
3. Whether the sentence of death is excessive or disproportionate to the penalty imposed in similar cases, considering both the crime and the defendant.

Official Code Ga. Ann. § 17-10-35(c).

In *Gregg v. Georgia*, 428 U.S. 153, 96 S.Ct. 2909, 49 L.Ed.2d 859 (1976), the Supreme Court upheld Georgia's revised death penalty statute by a vote of 7–2. Apparently, the Court was satisfied that this scheme had sufficiently addressed the evils identified in *Furman*. Thirty-eight states now have death penalty statutes modeled along the lines of the law upheld in *Gregg*.

Shortly after the death penalty was effectively reinstated by the Supreme Court's *Gregg* decision, executions in the United States began anew. On January 17, 1977, the state of Utah executed convicted murderer Gary Gilmore by firing squad. Between the date of the Gilmore execution and the end of 2005, a total of 1,004 prisoners were executed in the United States. At the end of 2005, there were 3,254 persons under sentence of death in thirty-eight jurisdictions (thirty-six states, the U.S. military, and the federal government). U.S. Department of Justice, Bureau of Justice Statistics, *Capital Punishment 2005*, December 2006, NCJ 21508.

## The Federal Death Penalty

In August 1997, Timothy McVeigh was sentenced to death by lethal injection for his role in the bombing of the federal office building in Oklahoma City in 1995. In his federal trial, McVeigh was convicted of twenty-eight counts of murder of a federal law enforcement agent on active duty. See 18 U.S.C.A. § 1114. Under federal law, executions are carried out in the state where the defendant was sentenced unless that state has no death penalty, in which case the prisoner is transferred to another state for execution. 18 U.S.C.A. § 3596. McVeigh was executed at the federal prison in Terre Haute, Indiana, in June 2001. Prior to the McVeigh execution, the federal government had not put anyone to death since 1963.

The Anti-Drug Abuse Act of 1988, 21 U.S.C.A. § 848(e), allows the death penalty for so-called "drug kingpins" who control "continuing criminal enterprises" whose members intentionally kill or procure others to kill in furtherance of the enterprise. In 1993 Juan Raul Garza was sentenced to death under this statute for three murders committed as head of a Texas-based drug trafficking organization. The conviction and sentence were affirmed by the U.S. Court of Appeals for the Fifth Circuit. *United States v. Flores & Garza*, 63 F.3d 1342 (5th Cir. 1995). A federal district judge set Garza's execution for August 5, 2000, but in July of that year President Bill Clinton ordered the execution delayed to allow Garza to request executive clemency under new rules promulgated by the Justice Department. After President George W. Bush denied his plea for clemency, Garza was finally put to death in June 2001.

**Federal Death Penalty Act (FDPA)** Federal legislation that (1) lists the mitigating and aggravating factors affecting a decision of whether to impose the death penalty and (2) provides for a special hearing to determine whether a sentence of death is justified in a particular federal case.

In 1994, Congress enacted the **Federal Death Penalty Act (FDPA)**, 18 U.S.C.A. §§ 3591 *et seq.* Section 3592 lists the mitigating and aggravating factors affecting a decision of whether to impose the death penalty. Section 3593 provides for a special hearing to determine whether a sentence of death is justified in a particular case. The FDPA dramatically increased the number of federal crimes eligible for the death penalty. Capital punishment is now authorized for dozens of federal crimes, including nonhomicidal offenses such as treason and large-scale drug trafficking. It remains to be seen whether the federal courts will permit the death penalty for nonhomicidal crimes. In *Coker v. Georgia*, 433 U.S. 584, 97 S.Ct. 2861, 53 L.Ed.2d 982 (1977), the Supreme Court prohibited capital punishment for the crime of rape. *Coker* suggests that the death penalty is an inappropriate punishment for any crime that does not involve the taking of a human life.

## Death, Deterrence, Retribution, and Incapacitation

One of the most intense battles among academicians in the field of criminal justice has been waged over the alleged deterrent value of the death penalty. At this point, the evidence appears to be mixed, making firm conclusions impossible. Whatever the possible deterrent value of the death penalty, its actual deterrent effect is reduced by the years of delay between sentencing and execution. Obviously, the death penalty has no value as a means of rehabilitation. Therefore, if the death penalty is to be justified, it must be primarily on grounds of retribution and incapacitation. Supporters of the death penalty argue, perhaps ironically, that the value of human life is underscored by imposing the severest of sanctions on those who commit murder. Certainly the death penalty is proportionate to the crime of murder. Indeed, the Supreme Court has made it clear that murder is the only crime for which the death penalty is permissible. *Coker v. Georgia*, supra.

Advocates of capital punishment also stress the incapacitation of the offender, and it is difficult to argue that death is not a complete incapacitator. But are retribution and incapacitation sufficient justifications for the death penalty?

## Is the Death Penalty Racially Discriminatory?

Whether the Court achieved the evenhandedness in the administration of capital punishment it sought through its decisions in *Furman* and *Gregg* is questionable. Critics have long charged that the death penalty is racially discriminatory. During the 1970s, criminologist David Baldus collected data on more than 1,000 murder cases in Georgia and found significant disparities in the imposition of the death penalty based primarily on the race of the murder victims and, to a lesser extent, on the race of the defendants. The data reveal that blacks who killed whites were more than seven times more likely to receive the death sentence than were whites who killed blacks.

In April 1987, the Supreme Court reviewed the death sentence of a black man convicted of killing a white police officer in Georgia. The Court refused to accept statistical evidence derived from the Baldus study as a basis for reversing the death sentence. In the Court's view, even if there is statistical evidence of race discrimination, a defendant sentenced to death cannot prevail on appeal unless the defendant can show that the death sentence was imposed because of race discrimination in this case. *McCleskey v. Kemp*, 481 U.S. 279, 107 S.Ct. 1756, 95 L.Ed.2d 262 (1987). Obviously, this would be difficult, although certainly not impossible, for a defendant to demonstrate.

In a 1990 report, the U.S. General Accounting Office concluded that available research demonstrated "a pattern of evidence indicating racial disparities in the charging, sentencing, and imposition of the death penalty." Similarly, in 1994 the U.S. House of Representatives Subcommittee on Civil and Constitutional Rights concluded that members of racial minorities were being disproportionately prosecuted under the federal death penalty law. According to the Death Penalty Information Center, of the 133 defendants authorized for death penalty prosecution from 1988 to 1998, 76 percent were members of racial minorities. Of the 3,254 death row inmates in the United States at the end of 2005, 42 percent were African American. U.S. Department of Justice, Bureau of Justice Statistics, *Capital Punishment 2005*, December 2006, NCJ 215083. Certainly these statistics provide a basis for concern about the fairness with which the death penalty has been administered in this country.

## Capital Punishment of Juvenile Offenders

One very difficult issue that the Supreme Court faced during the 1980s was whether, and under what circumstances, a juvenile may be executed when convicted of a capital crime. The Court responded in three decisions. In *Thompson v. Oklahoma*, 487 U.S. 815, 108 S.Ct. 2687, 101 L.Ed.2d 702 (1988), the Court ruled in a 6–3 decision that the Constitution forbids executing a juvenile who was fifteen years of age or younger at the time of commission of a capital crime. The following year, in *Stanford v. Kentucky*, 492 U.S. 361, 109 S.Ct. 2969, 106 L.Ed.2d 306 (1989), the Supreme Court split 5–4 in holding that a juvenile sixteen or older at the time of the crime may be sentenced to death.

Concurring in *Stanford*, Justice Sandra Day O'Connor commented that "it is sufficiently clear that no national consensus forbids the imposition of capital punishment on 16- or 17-year-old capital murderers." 492 U.S. at 381, 109 S.Ct. at 2981, 106 L.Ed.2d at 325. In both *Thompson* and *Stanford*, the Court referred to "evolving standards of decency" as the proper test for judging the constitutionality of whether a juvenile may be executed. Applying that test, the Court in *Roper v. Simmons*, 543 U.S. 551, 125 S.Ct. 1183, 161 L.Ed.2d 1 (2005), forbade the execution of anyone who was under eighteen at the time of their offense.

Writing for the Court in *Roper*, Justice Anthony Kennedy noted the decreasing frequency with which juvenile offenders were being sentenced to death as evidence of an emerging national consensus against capital punishment for juveniles. At the time of the *Roper* decision, only twenty states still allowed juveniles to be executed, and since 1995 only three states (Oklahoma, Texas, and Virginia) had actually executed inmates for crimes committed as juveniles. In any event, the Supreme Court's decision in *Roper* effectively ended the execution of juveniles in the United States.

## Execution of Prisoners Who Have Become Insane

The rate of mental illness is abnormally high among prisoners and especially high among those on death row. Should a death row inmate whose mental illness has become so severe as to meet the legal definition of insanity be put to death? For those who view capital punishment solely as a means of incapacitation, analogous to "putting down" a rabid dog, the mental health of the prisoner to be executed makes little difference. But in *Ford v. Wainwright*, 477 U.S. 399, 106 S.Ct. 2595, 91 L.Ed.2d 335 (1986), the Supreme Court held that the Constitution forbids the execution of someone who is legally insane. Writing for a plurality of justices, Justice Thurgood Marshall declared that "[i]t is no less abhorrent today than it has been for centuries to exact in penance the life of one whose mental illness prevents him from comprehending the reasons for the penalty or its implications." 477 U.S. at 417, 106 S.Ct. at 2606, 91 L.Ed.2d at 351. In 2007, the Court ruled that once a prisoner makes a preliminary showing that his current mental state would bar his execution, he is entitled to a hearing to determine his condition. *Panetti v. Quarterman*, 551 U.S. 930, 127 S.Ct. 2842, 168 L.Ed.2d 662 (2007). Today it is not uncommon for executions to be delayed pending the outcome of such hearings.

## Execution of Mentally Retarded Persons

Like mental illness, mental retardation is unusually prevalent among people who commit the sorts of grisly murders that lead to sentences of capital punishment. In *Penry v. Lynaugh*, 492 U.S. 302, 109 S.Ct. 2934, 106 L.Ed.2d 256 (1989), the U.S. Supreme Court held that execution of a mentally retarded prisoner does not

### JURISPRUDENCE

*Ford v. Wainwright*, 477 U.S. 399, 106 S.Ct. 2595, 91 L.Ed.2d 335 (1986)

In 1974 Alvin Ford was convicted of murder and sentenced to death by a Florida court. There was no indication that he was mentally incompetent at the time of the trial. However, while in prison awaiting execution, Ford began to exhibit profound changes in behavior and to experience bizarre delusions. In 1983 a prison psychiatrist diagnosed Ford as suffering from a severe and uncontrollable mental disease closely resembling paranoid schizophrenia. Ford's attorney then invoked procedures under Florida law governing the determination of competency of a condemned prisoner. A panel of psychiatrists examined Ford, and although they differed in their specific diagnoses, all agreed that Ford was not insane under Florida law.

On April 30, 1984, Governor Bob Graham signed Ford's death warrant. Ford's attorney then filed a petition for habeas corpus in the U.S. District Court, seeking an evidentiary hearing on his client's sanity. The district court denied relief, and the court of appeals affirmed. The U.S. Supreme Court agreed to review the case to resolve the issue of whether the Eighth Amendment prohibits the execution of a person who is insane. On June 26, 1986, the Supreme Court announced its decision in *Ford v. Wainwright* holding that the Eighth Amendment bars the execution of a person who is insane. The Court also held that Florida's procedures for determining the sanity of a death row prisoner violated due process standards. The Court ruled that Ford was entitled to a *de novo* evidentiary hearing in the district court on the question of his competence to be executed.

necessarily violate the Cruel and Unusual Punishments Clause. However, the Court held that juries must be allowed to consider evidence of mental retardation as a mitigating factor in the sentencing phase of a capital trial. By 2001 eighteen of the thirty-eight states that allowed the death penalty had, either by statute or judicial decision, outlawed the execution of retarded prisoners. In *Atkins v. Virginia*, 536 U.S. 304, 122 S.Ct. 2242, 153 L.Ed.2d 335 (2002), the U.S. Supreme Court reconsidered the issue and held that there was a sufficient national consensus for the Court to prohibit the execution of mentally retarded persons via the Eighth Amendment. Writing for a majority of six justices, Justice John Paul Stevens concluded that

> mentally retarded persons who meet the law's requirements for criminal responsibility should be tried and punished when they commit crimes. Because of their disabilities in areas of reasoning, judgment and control of their impulses, however, they do not act with the level of moral culpability that characterizes the most serious adult criminal conduct. 536 U.S. at 306, 122 S.Ct. at 2244, 153 L.Ed.2d at 341.

Writing for the three dissenters, Justice Antonin Scalia argued that the decision had "no support in the text or history of the Eighth Amendment." Justice Scalia accused the majority of making policy rather than law, saying, "Seldom has an opinion of this Court rested so obviously upon nothing but the personal views of its members." 536 U.S. at 338, 122 S.Ct. at 2259, 153 L.Ed.2d at 363.

## Should Child Rapists Be Subject to the Death Penalty?

We noted that in *Coker v. Georgia*, supra, the Supreme Court said that capital punishment is disproportionate to the crime of rape. In *Kennedy v. Louisiana*, 554 U.S. 407, 128 S.Ct. 2641, 171 L.Ed.2d 525 (2008), the Court continued to narrow the scope of offenses for which the death penalty may be given by striking down a state law allowing child rapists to be sentenced to death. Writing for a sharply divided bench, Justice Anthony Kennedy held that the Eighth Amendment "bars [imposing] the death penalty for the rape of a child where the crime did not result, and was not intended to result, in death of the victim." 554 U.S. at 413, 128 S.Ct. at 2646, 171 L.Ed.2d at 534. Citing "a consensus against the death penalty for child rape," Kennedy observed that "[d]ifficulties in administering the penalty to ensure against its arbitrary and capricious application require adherence to a rule reserving its use, at this stage of evolving standards and in cases of crimes against individuals, for crimes that take the life of the victim." 554 U.S. at 446-447, 128 S.Ct. at 2665, 171 L.Ed.2d at 555. Joined by three of his colleagues, Justice Samuel Alito dissented vigorously, arguing that

> (1) This holding is not supported by the original meaning of the Eighth Amendment; (2) neither *Coker* nor any other prior precedent commands this result; (3) there are no reliable "objective indicia" of a "national consensus" in support of the Court's position; (4) sustaining the constitutionality of the state law before us would not "extend" or "expand" the death penalty; (5) this Court has previously rejected the proposition that the Eighth Amendment is a one-way ratchet that prohibits legislatures from adopting new capital punishment statutes to meet new problems; (6) the worst child rapists exhibit the epitome of moral depravity; and (7) child rape inflicts grievous injury on victims and on society in general. 554 U.S. at 469, 128 S.Ct. at 2677, 171 L.Ed.2d at 569.

## Methods of Execution

Until recently, there were five methods of execution in the United States: the electric chair, the gas chamber, the firing squad, hanging, and lethal injection. As a result of litigation invoking the Cruel and Unusual Punishments Clause, as well as changes in state laws, lethal injection has now become the standard means of execution.

Although lethal injection is hailed by many as a more humane alternative to the electric chair and the gas chamber, death penalty opponents are now attacking lethal injection as cruel and unusual punishment. In particular, they claim that the paralyzing agent used as part of the lethal combination of drugs masks the pain and suffering of the person being executed.

In *Baze v. Rees*, 553 U.S. 35, 128 S.Ct. 1520, 170 L.Ed.2d 420 (2008), the Supreme Court upheld Kentucky's protocol for lethal injection, a protocol used by most states that employ lethal injection to administer the death penalty. Had that decision gone the other way, it might well have signaled the demise of the death penalty in America. Despite the Court's decision in *Baze v. Rees*, litigation over lethal injection continues, as lawyers for death row inmates continue to challenge protocols that differ somewhat from Kentucky's.

Critics of lethal injection also point to cases where technicians have struggled to find veins, thus subjecting the condemned inmates to unnecessary stress and discomfort. In one noteworthy case in 2006, the execution of Angel Díaz in Florida was botched when the needle missed the vein. An additional injection was required and it took more than a half hour for Díaz to die. Of course, defenders of the death penalty tend to dismiss such concerns. For most of them, the fact that capital punishment entails stress and pain is not a serious problem.

# The Sentencing Stage of the Criminal Process

**presentence investigation** An investigation held to aid the court in determining the appropriate punishment before sentencing a convicted criminal.

Every jurisdiction requires that criminal sentences for adults be imposed in open court, although in many instances juvenile offenders may be sentenced *in camera*. In misdemeanor cases, sentencing usually occurs immediately on conviction. In felony cases, where penalties are greater, sentencing may be postponed to allow the court to conduct a **presentence investigation**.

## The Presentence Report

**presentence report** A report containing the results of a presentence investigation.

In many states, as well as in the federal system, the court is required to order a **presentence report** when the offender to be sentenced is a first offender or is under a certain age. In other state jurisdictions, the sentencing judge is accorded discretion in this area. For example, rule 702 of the Pennsylvania Rules of Criminal Procedure provides as follows:

A. Presentence Investigation Report.

1. The sentencing judge may, in the judge's discretion, order a presentence investigation report in any case.

2. The sentencing judge shall place on the record the reasons for dispensing with the presentence investigation report if the judge fails to order a presentence report in any of the following instances:

(a) when incarceration for one year or more is a possible disposition under the applicable sentencing statutes; or

(b) when the defendant is less than twenty-one years old at the time of conviction or entry of a plea of guilty; or

(c) when a defendant is a first offender in that he or she has not heretofore been sentenced as an adult.

3. The presentence investigation report shall include information regarding the circumstances of the offense and the character of the defendant sufficient to assist the judge in determining sentence.

4. The presentence investigation report shall also include a victim impact statement as provided by law.

Rule 703 makes the reports confidential and available only to the sentencing judge, counsel for the state and the defense, and experts appointed by the court to assist the court in sentencing.

In some states, statutes, court rules, or judicial interpretations mandate that courts release a presentence report to the defendant or defendant's counsel, usually allowing some exemptions for sensitive material. In other states, courts have ruled that this is a matter within the discretion of the sentencing judge. In some instances, courts will reveal factual material such as police reports but decline to disclose statements made in confidence to investigators. Often the judicial interpretation depends on the language of the statute or court rule. The Supreme Court requires the release of presentence reports to defendants who may be sentenced to death.

The presentence report sets forth the defendant's history of delinquency or criminality, medical history, family background, economic status, education, employment history, and other information. Much of this information is obtained by probation officers, who interview individuals such as the defendant's family members, friends, and employers. In addition, most jurisdictions allow courts to order physical or mental examinations of defendants. This information can be very useful to a judge who must determine a sentence that is at once fair, humane, and meaningful.

## The Sentencing Hearing

**sentencing hearing** A hearing held by a trial court before the sentence is pronounced.

After the presentence report is completed, a **sentencing hearing** is held. At this hearing, the court considers the evidence received at trial, the presentence report, any evidence offered by either party in aggravation or mitigation of sentence, and any statement the defendant wishes to make. In addition, most jurisdictions require judges to hear arguments concerning various sentencing alternatives. Sentencing is a critical stage of the criminal process, and counsel must be supplied to indigent defendants. *Mempa v. Rhay*, 389 U.S. 128, 88 S.Ct. 254, 19 L.Ed.2d 336 (1967).

## Pronouncement of Sentence

**pronouncement of sentence** Formal announcement of a criminal punishment by a trial judge.

After the judge has digested the sentencing report, heard arguments from counsel and the defendant's statement, and considered the relevant provisions of law, the sentence is pronounced in open court. The **pronouncement of sentence** is the stage when the trial court imposes a penalty on a defendant for the offense of which the defendant has been adjudged guilty. Sentences are usually pronounced by the judge who presided at the defendant's trial or the entry of plea. In misdemeanor cases, sentencing often occurs immediately after the entry of a plea or a finding of guilty by the judge or jury. In felony cases, the pronouncement is often delayed until the court has received a presentence investigation report or until the prosecutor and defense counsel have had an opportunity to prepare a presentation. The procedure at the pronouncement stage is generally outlined in the criminal procedure rules of each jurisdiction. See, e.g., Rule 704 of the Pennsylvania Rules of Criminal Procedure.

The rules of evidence are relaxed during a sentencing proceeding. Traditionally, a defendant has been afforded an opportunity to make a statement on his or her own behalf, a procedure often referred to as the **right of allocution**. Generally, special rules govern the sentencing of a defendant who is insane, and often sentencing must be deferred for a female defendant who is pregnant.

**right of allocution** The right of a criminal defendant to make a statement on his or her own behalf before the sentence is pronounced.

## Suspended Sentences and Credit for Time Served

When the trial court sentences a defendant to incarceration, it generally allows the defendant credit against any term of incarceration for all time spent in custody as a result of the charge for which the sentence is imposed. In most instances where defendants are convicted of **noncapital crimes**, courts are authorized to suspend the imposition of the sentence and place defendants on probation or under community control for some determinate period. Statutes often require courts to impose certain conditions (similar to probation conditions) on a defendant whose sentence is suspended. See, e.g., N.J. Stat. Ann. § 2C:45–1. Of course, if the defendant violates conditions set by the court, the original sentence may be imposed. A **suspended sentence** is most often used for first offenses or nonviolent offenses. Authority to suspend a felony conviction is generally limited to a first conviction. See, e.g., La. C. Cr. P. Art. 83.

**noncapital crimes** Crimes that do not carry the ultimate penalty, whether death or life in prison with no possibility of parole.

**suspended sentence** Trial court's decision to place a defendant on probation or under community control instead of imposing an announced sentence on the condition that the original sentence may be imposed if the defendant violates the conditions of the suspended sentence.

## Concurrent and Consecutive Sentences

A defendant who is convicted of multiple crimes must be given separate sentences for each offense. These sentences may run consecutively or concurrently, usually at the discretion of the sentencing judge. See, e.g., Pa. R. Crim. P. 705. **Concurrent sentencing** in a given case may simply reflect the court's view that **consecutive sentencing** would result in a punishment that is too harsh for the crime. In *Oregon v. Ice*, 555 U.S. 160, 129 S.Ct. 711, 172 L.Ed.2d 517 (2009), Justice Ruth Bader Ginsburg observed:

**concurrent sentencing** The practice by which a trial court imposes separate sentences to be served at the same time.

**consecutive sentencing** The practice by which a trial court imposes a sentence or sentences to be served following completion of a prior sentence or sentences.

> Most States continue the common-law tradition: They entrust to judges' unfettered discretion the decision whether sentences for discrete offenses shall be served consecutively or concurrently. In some States, sentences for multiple offenses are presumed to run consecutively, but sentencing judges may order concurrent sentences upon finding cause therefor. Other States, including Oregon, constrain judges' discretion by requiring them to find certain facts before imposing consecutive, rather than concurrent, sentences. 555 U.S. at 163–164, 129 S.Ct. at 714, 172 L.Ed.2d at 522.

## Sentencing in Capital Cases

In those cases where the prosecution is permitted by law to seek the death penalty, the sentencing procedure is considerably more complex. As we noted in the discussion of the death penalty, a bifurcated trial is employed. Following the conviction for a capital crime, the jury hears testimony in aggravation or mitigation of the sentence. For the jury to hand down the death penalty, it must find beyond a reasonable doubt that the aggravating factors outweigh the mitigating ones. The aggravating factors are specified by law; the mitigating factors are those characteristics of the defendant or the crime that suggest that leniency might be appropriate. Quite often the defense attorney will put the defendant's relatives on the stand to testify about the defendant's redeeming qualities or to generally plead for mercy.

## Victim Impact Evidence

**victim impact evidence**
Evidence relating to the physical, economic, and psychological impact that a crime has on the victim or victim's family.

**victim impact statement**
Statement read into the record during the sentencing phase of a criminal trial to inform the court about the impact of the crime on the victim or victim's family.

Prosecutors counter emotional pleas on the defendant's behalf by presenting **victim impact evidence**. This evidence takes the form of testimony addressing the impact of the murder on the victim and the victim's family, including the physical, economic, and psychological effects of the crime. For example, the victim's surviving spouse might be called to testify to the toll the homicide has taken on the family. Needless to say, such testimony is often fraught with emotion and can have a powerful impact on the jury.

In 1987 the U.S. Supreme Court struck down a Maryland statute requiring that a **victim impact statement** be considered during the penalty phase of capital cases. *Booth v. Maryland*, 482 U.S. 496, 107 S.Ct. 2529, 96 L.Ed.2d 440 (1987). The Court said that such statements raised the real possibility that death sentences would be based on irrelevant considerations. Four years later, however, in *Payne v. Tennessee*, 501 U.S. 808, 111 S.Ct. 2597, 115 L.Ed.2d 720 (1991), the Court overruled its decision in *Booth*. According to Chief Justice William Rehnquist, who wrote the majority opinion in *Payne*, the *Booth* decision "deprives the State of the full moral force of its evidence and may prevent the jury from having before it all the information necessary to determine the proper punishment for a first-degree murder." 501 U.S. at 825, 111 S.Ct. at 2608, 115 L.Ed.2d at 735. Notwithstanding the Supreme Court's

### JURISPRUDENCE

*Payne v. Tennessee*, 501 U.S. 808, 111 S.Ct. 2597, 115 L.Ed.2d 720 (1991)

After drinking beer and injecting cocaine, Pervis Tyrone Payne entered an apartment occupied by twenty-eight-year-old Charisse Christopher, her two-year-old daughter Lacie, and her three-year-old son Nicholas. After Chrissie resisted Payne's sexual advances, Payne became enraged and repeatedly stabbed the woman and her two children with a kitchen knife. Only the three-year old boy survived the attack. Payne was convicted by a jury on two counts of first-degree murder and one count of assault with intent to commit murder in the first degree. During the penalty phase of Payne's trial, the State presented the testimony of the mother of one of the victims. In his closing argument to the jury, the prosecutor commented at some length on this "victim impact evidence." Payne was sentenced to death for each of the murders and to thirty years in prison for the assault. The Tennessee Supreme Court upheld Payne's convictions and sentence. On certiorari, the U.S. Supreme Court, splitting 6–3, affirmed the judgment, thereby receding from its holdings in prior cases. Writing for the Court, Chief Justice Rehnquist opined that the "State may legitimately conclude that evidence about the victim and about the impact of the murder on the victim's family is relevant to the jury's decision as to whether or not the death penalty should be imposed." Dissenting, Justice John Paul Stevens observed, "Until today our capital punishment jurisprudence has required that any decision to impose the death penalty be based solely on evidence that tends to inform the jury about the character of the offense and the character of the defendant. Evidence that serves no purpose other than to appeal to the sympathies or emotions of the jurors has never been considered admissible."

decision in *Payne v. Tennessee*, appellate courts may still find that a particular victim impact statement has impermissibly injected too much emotionalism into the jury's sentencing deliberations.

## What Are Juries Entitled to Know about the Defendant?

In 1994 the Supreme Court also decided two important cases dealing with the information that juries may consider in deciding whether to impose the death penalty. In *Romano v. Oklahoma*, 512 U.S. 1, 114 S.Ct. 2004, 129 L.Ed.2d 1 (1994), the Court held that neither the Eighth Amendment nor the Due Process Clause of the Fourteenth Amendment prohibits capital-sentencing juries from being informed that the defendant is already under sentence of death for another crime. Petitioner John Romano had already been sentenced to death for robbing and murdering one man when he was tried for another robbery-murder. During the sentencing phase, the prosecution sought to introduce evidence of the former crime and sentence. Romano's attorney objected, claiming that the jury knowledge of the previous death sentence would diminish its sense of responsibility in imposing another death sentence. The trial judge overruled the objection, and Romano was sentenced to death. Writing for the Supreme Court, Chief Justice Rehnquist observed that although the prior death sentence was irrelevant, the Constitution "does not establish a federal code of evidence to supersede state evidentiary rules in capital sentencing proceedings." 512 U.S. at 12, 114 S.Ct. at 2011, 129 L.Ed.2d at 13.

Chief Justice Rehnquist's observation in *Romano* notwithstanding, the Court in *Simmons v. South Carolina*, 512 U.S. 154, 114 S.Ct. 2187, 129 L.Ed.2d 133 (1994), held that defendants facing the death penalty have a right to tell juries if the only alternative to a death sentence is life imprisonment without the possibility of parole. Jonathan Simmons was convicted of murdering a seventy-nine-year-old woman in her home. Because Simmons had been convicted twice before of sexually assaulting elderly women, South Carolina law provided that he would be ineligible for parole if sentenced to prison. Over defense counsel's objection, the trial judge granted the prosecution's motion to exclude any mention of parole during the trial. During the sentencing phase, the court denied the defense counsel's request to explain to the jury that a life sentence carried no possibility of parole. Finally, during deliberations the judge told the jury not to consider whether Simmons could be paroled if he was sentenced to life imprisonment. Simmons was sentenced to death. The Supreme Court remanded the case for resentencing, saying that the trial judge's refusal to provide the requested instruction constituted a denial of due process. In dissent, Justice Scalia accused the Court of trying to impose "Federal Rules of Death Penalty Evidence" on the states. 512 U.S. at 185, 114 S.Ct. at 2205, 129 L.Ed.2d at 156.

## The Role of the Judge in Capital Sentencing

States vary as to the role of the trial judge in determining death sentences. Under the capital sentencing procedures in Georgia, where the jury finds at least one statutory aggravating circumstance and recommends the death penalty, the trial judge must sentence the defendant to death. Official Ga. Code Ann. § 17-10-31. In other states, a different method is employed. For example, in Florida the trial court decides whether to accept a jury's recommendation of death or life imprisonment. See *Spaziano v. Florida*, 468 U.S. 447, 104 S.Ct. 3154, 82 L.Ed.2d 340 (1984). Where a jury recommends life imprisonment and the trial court overrides that recommendation and imposes the death penalty, the decision is carefully scrutinized by the Florida Supreme Court. For the trial court's override to be sustained, the life imprisonment recommendation by the jury must have been unreasonable. If the supreme court's review finds there was a reasonable basis for the jury's recommendation, it reverses the court's imposition of the death penalty and remands the case for a sentence as recommended by the jury. *Buford v. State*, 570 So.2d 923 (Fla. 1990).

## What Happens When a Capital Jury Is Deadlocked on the Sentence?

When the jury in a capital case cannot agree on the appropriate sentence, sentencing normally reverts to the judge. As we have seen, in some jurisdictions, the judge is barred from imposing the death penalty without a jury recommendation. In such instances, the judge must sentence the defendant to any lesser sentence authorized by law. The judge is not required to instruct the jury with regard to the consequences of deadlock, however. *Jones v. United States*, 527 U.S. 373, 119 S.Ct. 2090, 144 L.Ed.2d 370 (1999).

# Granting and Revoking Probation

Probation is a sentencing option in the federal courts and in most state courts. Under federal law, a defendant who has been found guilty of an offense may be sentenced to a term of probation unless (1) the offense is a felony where the maximum term of imprisonment authorized is twenty-five years or more, life imprisonment, or death; (2) the offense is one for which probation has been expressly precluded; or (3) the defendant is sentenced at the same time to a term of imprisonment for the same or a different offense. A defendant who has been convicted for the first time of a domestic violence crime must be sentenced to a term of probation if not sentenced to a term of imprisonment. 18 U.S.C.A. § 3561. Probation terms for a felony must not be less than one nor more than five years and for a misdemeanor not more than five years. 18 U.S.C.A. § 3561. Certain conditions of probation are mandatory, and others are discretionary with the federal judge who imposes probation. 18 U.S.C.A. § 3563.

In most states, the term of probation is limited to the maximum statutory term of confinement for the particular offense. As in federal cases, probation is subject to mandatory and special conditions. Probation is often combined with a fine, restitution to the victim, or a short term of incarceration to give the probationer "a taste of jail." Because the procedures in state courts vary widely, it is difficult to generalize; however, it is important for the probationer to receive a written order incorporating the terms of probation and outlining his or her responsibilities to the probation officer and the court. Courts must guard against imposing vague conditions of probation or delegating overly broad authority to probation officers.

## Revocation of Probation

In every jurisdiction, the commission of a felony while on probation is grounds for revocation. In many jurisdictions, certain misdemeanors likewise qualify as grounds for revocation. In addition, the violation of any substantive condition of probation is grounds for revocation. Typically, a probation officer is vested with broad discretion in determining when to seek revocation of probation.

In August 2006, the South Carolina Supreme Court upheld revocation of probation where the probationer violated a condition "that probationer not associate with people who had criminal records." The court found the condition was not so overly broad that it violated due process. The court, however, explained that the evidence must show that the probationer knew about the person's criminal record during the period of association before the condition may be applied to revoke probation. *State v. Allen*, 634 S.E.2d 653 (S.C. 2006).

A probationer facing the loss of freedom is entitled to a fair hearing. At this hearing the probationer has the right to call favorable witnesses, to confront hostile witnesses, and to be represented by counsel. *Gagnon v. Scarpelli*, 411 U.S. 778, 93 S.Ct. 1756, 36 L.Ed.2d 656 (1973). In *Gagnon*, the Supreme Court said that indigent probationers may have a constitutional right to have counsel appointed at revocation hearings, depending on the complexity of the issues involved, and that if counsel is not provided, the judge must state the reason. In practice, counsel is usually provided. There is a statutory right to appointment of counsel for those financially unable to obtain counsel in federal probation revocation proceedings. 18 U.S.C.A. § 3006A.

The Federal Rules of Criminal Procedure require a two-step process before probation can be revoked: a preliminary hearing to determine if there is probable cause to believe that a violation occurred and, if so, a revocation hearing. Fed. R. Crim. P. 32.1(b).

The rules of evidence applicable at criminal trials are relaxed at probation revocation hearings. For example, in federal courts hearsay evidence may be received over a probationer's objection because a probation revocation hearing is not a criminal trial. *United States v. Miller*, 514 F.2d 41 (9th Cir. 1975). In most state courts, "reliable" hearsay evidence is admissible in probation revocation proceedings. This most commonly applies to laboratory reports and other documentation. Nevertheless, a legion of state appellate court decisions hold that probation cannot be revoked solely on the basis of hearsay evidence. See *Turner v. State*, 293 So.2d 771 (Fla. App. 1974). Thus, an appellate court found insufficient evidence that a defendant violated a condition of his probation prohibiting changing residence without permission where the only evidence of violation was hearsay testimony from the defendant's probation officer that the probationer's mother stated that she did not know where he was. *Cito v. State*, 721 So.2d 1192 (Fla. App. 1998). Some state courts hold hearsay evidence to be inadmissible in probation revocation proceedings. See, for example, *Wolcott v. State*, 604 S.E.2d 478 (Ga. 2004), where the Georgia Supreme Court held that hearsay evidence is inadmissible but found it harmless in the particular case because it was cumulative to other admissible evidence that established that the defendant had committed an offense that constituted a probation violation.

As noted, a large number of state appellate court decisions make it clear that hearsay evidence alone is not sufficient to revoke probation. See *Nadeau v. State*, 920 So.2d 206 (Fla. App. 2006). Most revocation cases do not reach the highest state courts, but in 1993 the Tennessee Supreme Court held that probation could not be revoked based solely on a lab test indicating that the probationer had used illicit drugs where the technician who performed the drug test was not available to be cross-examined at the revocation hearing. *State v. Wade*, 863 S.W.2d 406 (Tenn. 1993).

**JURISPRUDENCE**

*Bearden v. Georgia*, 461 U.S. 660, 103 S.Ct. 2064, 76 L.Ed.2d 221 (1983)

Danny Bearden pleaded guilty to charges of burglary and theft. Pursuant to Georgia's First Offenders Act, Official Code Ga. Ann. § 27-2727 *et seq.*, current version at § 42-8-60, he was placed on three years' probation and was required to pay a $500 fine and make restitution of $250. After making some payments, Bearden was laid off from work and became unable to continue making payments. As a result, the trial court revoked his probation and sentenced him to serve the remaining portion of his term of probation in prison. The U.S. Supreme Court reversed the revocation of probation because the trial court had made no finding that Bearden was responsible for his failure to make the required payments. Nevertheless, the Court said, "If the probationer willfully refused to pay or failed to make sufficient bona fide efforts legally to acquire the resources to pay, the court may revoke probation."

Courts have frequently articulated that the standard to be applied at revocation hearings is not "reasonable doubt" or "preponderance of evidence," but whether from the evidence presented the court is reasonably satisfied of the probationer's violation. Nor is there any requirement that a probationer be granted a jury trial in revocation proceedings, even when those proceedings are predicated on a violation of a criminal law. *United States v. Czajak*, 909 F.2d 20 (1st Cir. 1990). Often a court will modify rather than revoke a defendant's probation, but if the court does revoke probation, statutory and decisional law generally permit it to sentence the defendant to any term that would have been appropriate for the underlying offense. And although a probationer may not be sentenced on revocation for the conduct that constituted the probation violation, it is proper for the trial court to consider the probationer's conduct while on probation to assess a potential for rehabilitation. See, e.g., *People v. Vilces*, 542 N.E.2d 1269 (Ill. App. 1989).

The violation of any valid substantive condition is grounds for revocation of probation, but in practice courts may hold that a minor or technical violation, such as a probationer's being a day late in filing a monthly report, is not sufficient for a court to revoke probation.

# Statutory Approaches to Incarceration

Once it has been determined that a defendant is to be incarcerated, several variations of the type and extent of the defendant's sentence may be available. The legislative trend has been to limit judicial discretion in imposing incarceration by statutorily providing whether the defendant is subject to an indeterminate or determinate sentence and whether a minimum mandatory term is to be imposed. In recent years, in an attempt to cope with the problem of recidivism, legislatures have enacted laws providing for enhanced terms of incarceration.

## Indeterminate Sentencing

For much of the twentieth century, legislatures commonly allowed judges to sentence criminals to imprisonment for indeterminate periods. This was designed to assist corrections officials in rehabilitating offenders. Officials were permitted to hold a criminal in custody until they determined that he or she was rehabilitated. Under this system, release from prison took the form of parole. Abuses of the system, combined

**indeterminate sentencing** Form of criminal sentencing where criminals are sentenced to prison for indeterminate periods until corrections officials determine that rehabilitation has been accomplished.

with the decline of popular support for rehabilitation, have led most jurisdictions to abandon the concept of **indeterminate sentencing**.

Notwithstanding the trend away from indeterminate sentencing, a number of state laws retain indeterminate sentencing for youthful offenders. For example, New Jersey law specifies the following:

> Any person who, at time of sentencing, is less than 16 years of age and who has been convicted of a crime may be sentenced to an indeterminate term at the Youth Correctional Institution Complex, . . . in the case of men, and to the Correctional Institute for Women, . . . in the case of women, instead of the sentences otherwise authorized by the code. N.J. Stat. Ann. § 2C:43-5.

In *State v. Styker*, 619 A.2d 1016 (N.J. Super. 1993), the court pointed out that while the youthful offender law offers the benefits of rehabilitation in certain instances, "its application is now merely an option, the exercise of which is reserved solely for those limited cases where the sentencing court, in its sound discretion, deems it to be appropriate." *Id.* at 1024.

## Definite and Determinate Sentencing

**definite sentencing** Legislatively determined sentencing with no discretion given to judges or corrections officials to individualize punishment.

**determinate sentencing** The process of sentencing whereby the judge sets a fixed term of years within statutory parameters and the offender must serve that term without possibility of early release.

At the opposite extreme from indeterminate sentencing is **definite sentencing**. The concept here is to eliminate discretion and ensure that offenders who commit the same crimes are punished equally. The definite sentence is set by the legislature, with no lee-way for judges or corrections officials to individualize punishment. Under **determinate sentencing**, a variation of the definite sentence, the judge sets a fixed term of years within statutory parameters, and the offender is required to serve that term without the possibility of early release. Although the sentence is for a fixed term, these laws often allow the trial court to increase the term if it finds one or more aggravating circumstances.

## Indefinite Sentencing

**indefinite sentencing** Form of criminal sentencing whereby a judge imposes a term of incarceration within statutory parameters and corrections officials determine actual time served through parole or other means.

The most common statutory approach to sentencing is referred to as **indefinite sentencing**. Here, there is judicial discretion to impose sentences within a range of prescribed minimum and maximum penalties for specific offenses. What distinguishes indefinite from determinate sentencing is that indefinite sentencing allows early release from prison on parole. This example of a statute that permits indefinite sentencing is drawn from the New Jersey Code:

> Except as otherwise provided, a person who has been convicted of a crime may be sentenced to imprisonment, as follows: (1) In the case of a crime of the first degree, for a specific term of years which shall be fixed by the court and shall be between 10 years and 20 years; (2) In the case of a crime of the second degree, for a specific term of years which shall be fixed by the court and shall be between 5 years and 10 years; (3) In the case of a crime of the third degree, for a specific term of years which shall be fixed by the court and shall be between 3 years and 5 years; (4) In the case of a crime of the fourth degree, for a specific term which shall be fixed by the court and shall not exceed 18 months. N.J. Stat. Ann. § 2C:43-6(a).

Except for certain offenses where a mandatory minimum sentence applies, New Jersey judges retain discretion to impose probation, fines, or other alternatives to incarceration. N.J. Stat. Ann. § 2C:43-2. If the judge opts for imprisonment, the judge's discretion is channeled as indicated earlier. The New Jersey scheme qualifies as indefinite sentencing because in most cases the law allows offenders to be released on parole before the completion of their prison terms.

*Cunningham v. California*, 549 U.S. 270, 127 S.Ct. 856, 166 L.Ed.2d 856 (2007)

John Cunningham was tried by jury and convicted in a California court of continuous sexual abuse of a child under the age of fourteen. The jury found him guilty but made no factual findings. The California determinate sentencing law required the trial court to sentence Cunningham to twelve years unless it found one or more additional facts in aggravation. The trial court found several aggravating factors and sentenced Cunningham to an additional four years' imprisonment. The sentence was affirmed by the state courts.

The U.S. Supreme Court granted review and on January 22, 2007, held that California's determinate sentencing law, which authorized a judge, not a jury, to find facts exposing a convicted defendant to an elevated sentence, violated a defendant's right to trial by jury. Writing for a 6–3 majority, Justice Ruth Bader Ginsburg observed that the jury's verdict alone limited the permissible sentence to twelve years and that by sentencing Cunningham to an additional four years based on the trial court's fact finding, the trial court deprived him of his right to a jury trial under the Sixth Amendment.

## Mandatory Minimum Sentencing

Mandatory sentences result from legislative mandates that offenders who commit certain crimes must be sentenced to prison terms for minimum periods. Under mandatory minimum sentencing, judges have no option to place offenders on probation. Most often, mandatory sentences are required for violent crimes, especially those involving the use of firearms. For example, Iowa law mandates that persons who use firearms in the commission of "forcible felonies" must be sentenced to a five-year minimum prison term with no eligibility for parole until the person has served the minimum sentence of confinement. Iowa Code Ann. § 902.7.

As a result of the "war on drugs" launched in the 1980s, federal law now mandates minimum prison terms for serious drug crimes prosecuted in federal courts. For example, a person charged with possession with the intent to distribute more than five kilograms of cocaine is subject to a mandatory minimum sentence of ten years in prison. See 21 U.S.C.A. § 841(b)(1)(A). In *Melendez v. United States*, 518 U.S. 120, 116 S.Ct. 2057, 135 L.Ed.2d 427 (1996), the U.S. Supreme Court made it clear in a unanimous decision that federal courts have no authority to impose lesser sentences than those mandated by Congress unless prosecutors specifically request such departures. This, of course, provides federal prosecutors substantial leverage in persuading defendants to provide evidence against other suspects, which is particularly useful in prosecuting drug distribution conspiracies.

Mandatory minimum sentences for federal drug crimes have contributed to prison overcrowding. Moreover, a difference in how the law treated crack and powder cocaine contributed to the racial imbalance in the federal prisons. Under the Anti-Drug Abuse Act of 1986, 21 U.S.C.A. §841, possession of "crack" cocaine was subject to the same prison term as one hundred times more powder cocaine. Because crack tends to be used more among African-Americans and powder tends to be favored by white users, African-Americans were being punished much more severely for essentially the same offense. A chorus of criticism of this policy led to the enactment of the Fair Sentencing Act of 2010, Pub. L. 111-220. The new law reduced the ratio between powder and crack cocaine from 100:1 to 18:1. It also eliminated the mandatory five-year minimum sentence that formerly applied to the simple possession of crack cocaine.

## Habitual Offender Statutes

In an effort to incapacitate habitual offenders, the laws of many states require automatic increased penalties for persons convicted of repeated felonies. For example, an Iowa law states,

> An habitual offender is any person convicted of a class "C" or a class "D" felony, who has twice before been convicted of any felony in a court of this or any other state, or of the United States. An offense is a felony if, by the law under which the person was convicted, it is so classified at the time of the person's conviction. A person sentenced as an habitual offender shall not be eligible for parole until he or she has served the minimum sentence of confinement of three years. Iowa Code Ann. § 902.8.

Most courts hold that habitual offender status is not established if a defendant committed the present offense before having been convicted of a prior offense. Courts have struggled with the issue of whether multiple convictions entered on one day are to be treated as separate or as one conviction, but they usually treat these multiple convictions as one irrespective of whether they arise from one or multiple criminal transactions.

In *Rummel v. Estelle*, 445 U.S. 263, 100 S.Ct. 1133, 63 L.Ed.2d 382 (1980), the U.S. Supreme Court upheld a life sentence imposed under the Texas habitual offender statute mandating life terms for persons convicted of three felonies. Rummel was convicted of obtaining $120.75 under false pretenses after previously being convicted of the fraudulent use of a credit card to obtain $80.00 worth of goods and passing a forged check for $28.36. After his third felony conviction, Rummel was sentenced to life imprisonment.

In *Solem v. Helm*, 463 U.S. 277, 103 S.Ct. 3001, 77 L.Ed.2d 637 (1983), the Court vacated a life sentence without parole under a South Dakota **habitual offender statute**. Because the defendant's convictions involved nonviolent felonies, the Court found the life sentence to be "significantly disproportionate" and thus invalid under the Eighth Amendment.

## "Three Strikes and You're Out"

A variation on the habitual offender law is known colloquially as **three strikes and you're out**. In 1994 California voters overwhelmingly approved a ballot initiative under which persons convicted of a third violent or "serious" felony would be incarcerated for twenty-five years to life. Prosecutors immediately availed themselves of this new weapon, but in many instances the new law led to controversial results. In one well-known case, a man received twenty-five years to life after being convicted of robbery stemming from an incident where he stole a slice of pizza. *People v. Romero*, 917 P.2d 628 (Cal. 1996). In reversing the sentence, the California Supreme Court said that judges must retain the power to set sentences in furtherance of justice.

The 1994 Federal Crime Bill provided for mandatory life sentences for persons convicted in federal court of a "serious violent felony" after having been previously convicted, in federal or state court, of two "serious violent felonies" or "one or more serious violent felonies and one or more serious drug offenses; and each serious violent felony or serious drug offense used as a basis for sentencing under this subsection, other than the first, was committed after the defendant's conviction of the preceding serious violent felony or serious drug offense." 18 U.S.C.A. § 3559. Currently, the federal government and most states have some form of habitual

**habitual offender statute** A law that imposes an additional punishment on a criminal who has previously been convicted of crimes.

**three strikes and you're out** Popular term for a statute that provides for mandatory life imprisonment for a convicted felon who has been previously convicted of two or more serious felonies.

**JURISPRUDENCE**

*Ewing v. California*, 538 U.S. 11, 123 S.Ct. 1179, 155 L.Ed.2d 108 (2003)

Gary Ewing was convicted of grand theft for stealing several golf clubs worth nearly $1,000. In 2000, when Ewing committed this crime, he was on parole after having served six years in prison for robbery and burglary committed in the fall of 1993. Aptly described by the Supreme Court as "no stranger to the criminal justice system," Ewing had previously been convicted of grand theft auto (1988), petit theft (1990), battery (1992), burglary (January 1993), possession of drug paraphernalia (February 1993), appropriating lost property (July 1993), and unlawful possession of a firearm and trespassing (September 1993). After being convicted of grand theft for stealing the golf clubs, Ewing was sentenced under the three-strikes law to twenty-five years to life. In a 5–4 decision, the

Supreme Court upheld Ewing's sentence and the three-strikes statute on which it was based. However, the Court failed to produce a majority opinion. Writing for a plurality of three justices, Justice O'Connor concluded that Ewing's sentence was constitutionally permissible as it was not "grossly disproportionate" to his offenses. The remaining members of the majority, Justices Thomas and Scalia, rejected the approach taken by Justice O'Connor. In their view, the Eighth Amendment "was aimed at excluding only certain *modes* of punishment, and was not a 'guarantee against disproportionate sentences.'" Writing for the four dissenters, Justice Stephen Breyer concluded that Ewing's sentence was "grossly disproportionate" inasmuch as it was "2 to 3 times the length of sentences that other jurisdictions would impose in similar circumstances."

offender or "three-strikes" statute. In most states, prosecutions under these statutes are relatively infrequent. In 2003 the U.S. Supreme Court upheld California's three-strikes law against constitutional challenges based on the Eighth Amendment's Cruel and Unusual Punishments Clause. *Ewing v. California*, 538 U.S. 11, 123 S.Ct. 1179, 155 L.Ed.2d 108 (2003); *Lockyer v. Andrade*, 538 U.S. 63, 123 S.Ct. 1166, 155 L.Ed.2d 144 (2003).

## Truth in Sentencing

**truth in sentencing** Laws requiring that people sentenced to prison serve a specified proportion of their sentences.

**Federal Sentencing Reform Act of 1984** A federal act directing the promulgation of sentencing guidelines.

**good-time credit** Credit toward early release from prison based on good behavior during confinement.

**Truth in sentencing** refers to a movement that began in the 1980s to close the gap between the sentences imposed by courts and the time actually served in prison. Prior to the enactment of truth-in-sentencing laws, the average prisoner served less than half the sentence in prison before being paroled. The **Federal Sentencing Reform Act of 1984** dramatically toughened federal sentencing policies by abolishing parole, ending **good-time credit** (time off for good behavior in prison), and prohibiting judges from imposing suspended sentences. Of course, these reforms applied only to the federal justice system. In 1994 Congress provided a strong financial incentive to the states to change their sentencing laws. The Violent Crime Control and Law Enforcement Act of 1994 provided federal grants to states that conform to the federal truth-in-sentencing guideline, which mandates actual confinement for at least 85 percent of the court-imposed prison sentence. By 2001, more than two-thirds of the states had adopted truth-in-sentencing laws to comply with the federal guideline. Since then, budgetary pressures have led some states to repeal or liberalize these laws.

## Penalty Enhancement

Another approach to sentencing that has gained popularity in recent years is enhancing or extending penalties based on characteristics of the crime or the victim. For example, in an effort to strengthen law enforcement in the war on drugs, the Violent

Crime Control and Law Enforcement Act of 1994 included several provisions for enhanced penalties. Drug trafficking in prisons and "drug-free" zones, and illegal drug use in or smuggling drugs into federal prisons, are now subject to enhanced penalties. See 42 U.S.C.A. §§ 14051, 14052.

## Enhanced Penalties for Hate Crimes

Throughout the United States, recent years have seen growing concern over "hate crimes," crimes where victims are targeted on the basis of race, gender, or other characteristics. The federal government and many states currently have laws increasing the severity of punishment in hate crime cases. In 1993 the U.S. Supreme Court upheld a Wisconsin statute of this type. *Wisconsin v. Mitchell,* 508 U.S. 476, 113 S. Ct. 2194, 124 L.Ed.2d 436 (1993). Stressing that the statute was aimed at conduct rather than belief, the Court held that increasing punishment because the defendant targeted the victim on the basis of his race does not infringe the defendant's freedom of conscience as protected by the First Amendment.

**penalty enhancement statutes** Sentencing laws that provide for increased penalties when certain conditions were present in crimes—for example, the racial motivations of the perpetrator.

Typically, **penalty enhancement statutes** require that a judge find by a preponderance of the evidence that a crime was racially motivated before applying penalty enhancement during sentencing. In a decision with far-reaching implications, the U.S. Supreme Court in June 2000 ruled that any fact that increases criminal punishment beyond the statutory maximum (other than a prior conviction) must be submitted to a jury and proved beyond a reasonable doubt. *Apprendi v. New Jersey,* 530 U.S. 466, 120 S.Ct. 2348, 147 L.Ed.2d 435 (2000). This 5–4 decision raises questions about numerous statutory sentencing schemes under which particular sentencing determinations are based on facts found by judges during sentencing rather than by juries as part of the trial. In a later 5–4 decision, *Oregon v. Ice,* 555 U.S. 160, 129 S.Ct. 711, 172 L.Ed.2d 517 (2009), the Court, in an opinion by Justice Ginsburg, ruled that the Sixth Amendment, as construed in *Apprendi,* does not prohibit judges

## JURISPRUDENCE

*Apprendi v. New Jersey,* 530 U.S. 466, 120 S.Ct. 2348, 147 L.Ed.2d 435 (2000)

Charles Apprendi fired several gunshots into a house occupied by an African-American family and also made a statement that he did not want that family in his neighborhood. Apprendi was charged with second-degree possession of a firearm for an unlawful purpose. After Apprendi pleaded guilty, the prosecutor filed a motion to enhance the sentence, due to race being an underlying motivation of the offense. The trial court found that the shooting was racially motivated and sentenced Apprendi to twelve years in prison on the firearms charge. Apprendi appealed the sentence on the grounds that the Due Process Clause of the Fourteenth Amendment requires that a finding used to enhance a penalty must be proved to a jury beyond a reasonable doubt. The

state appellate courts affirmed the sentence holding that a judge's finding based on a preponderance of the evidence was sufficient for penalty enhancement. The U.S. Supreme Court reversed, holding that the Constitution "requires that any fact that increases the penalty for a crime beyond the prescribed statutory maximum, other than the fact of a prior conviction, must be submitted to a jury and proved beyond a reasonable doubt." Justice Stevens, speaking for the majority, stated that the "Fourteenth Amendment right to due process and the Sixth Amendment right to trial by jury, taken together, entitle a criminal defendant to a jury determination that he is guilty of every element of the crime with which he is charged, beyond a reasonable doubt." As a result, Apprendi's sentence was overturned and the case remanded for further proceedings.

from finding facts necessary to the imposition of consecutive, rather than concurrent, sentences for multiple offenses. Writing for four dissenting justices, Justice Scalia argued that to permit judges to increase the presumed sentence based on facts found by the judge rather than a jury violates the Sixth Amendment as interpreted in *Apprendi*.

## Sentencing Guidelines

**sentencing guidelines**
Legislative guidelines mandating that sentencing conform to guidelines absent a compelling reason for departing from them.

Facing considerable criticism of judicial discretion, which often resulted in great disparities in sentences, Congress and a number of state legislatures adopted **sentencing guidelines**. Some states have adopted voluntary guidelines; others have mandated that sentencing conform to guidelines absent a compelling reason for departing from them.

### The Sentencing Reform Act of 1984

**United States Sentencing Commission** A federal body that proposes guideline sentences for defendants convicted of federal crimes.

The federal guidelines came into being with the enactment of the Sentencing Reform Act of 1984, now codified at 18 U.S.C.A. §§ 3551 *et seq.* 28 U.S.C.A. §§ 991–998. The new act applies to all crimes committed after November 1, 1987. Its stated purpose was "to establish sentencing policies and practices for the federal criminal justice system that will assure the ends of justice by promulgating detailed guidelines prescribing the appropriate sentences for offenders convicted of federal crimes." To accomplish this, the act created the **United States Sentencing Commission** to establish sentencing guidelines. The commission promulgated guidelines that drastically reduced the discretion of federal judges by establishing a narrow sentencing range, with the requirement that judges who depart from these ranges state in writing their reasons for doing so. In addition, the new act provides for appellate review for sentences and abolishes the U.S. Parole Commission.

In *United States v. Scroggins*, 880 F.2d 1204 (11th Cir. 1989), the Eleventh Circuit Court of Appeals discussed the mechanics of sentencing under the new federal guidelines:

> [T]he district court begins the guidelines sentencing process by determining the circumstances of the defendant's offense conduct, the defendant's criminal history, and any other facts deemed relevant by the guidelines. The court then proceeds to assess the severity of the defendant's offense by applying the guidelines to the facts and circumstances of the defendant's offense conduct. . . . This process yields a numeric "total offense level" that consists of three elements: a "base offense level," which reflects the seriousness of the average offense sentenced under that particular guideline; "specific offense characteristics," which increase or decrease the base offense level in light of various factors considered relevant to the defendant's offense conduct; and "adjustments," which increase or decrease the offense level in light of certain factors considered generally relevant for sentencing purposes. The resulting total offense level can range from 1 (least serious) to 43 (most serious).
>
> Having determined the total offense level, the court next surveys the criminal history of the offender. . . . This inquiry places the defendant within a "criminal history category" that evaluates the need to increase his sentence incrementally to deter him from further criminal activity. By correlating the offense level with the offender's criminal history category on the sentencing table developed by the Sentencing Commission, the court then identifies the "guideline range" for the offender's sentence. . . . In general, the district court must sentence the offender within this range.

### Departure from the Guidelines

The sentences prescribed by the guidelines were not intended to be absolute. The sentencing court is permitted to depart from the guidelines if it "finds that there exists an aggravating or mitigating circumstance of a kind, or to a degree, not adequately taken into consideration . . . in formulating the guidelines that should result in a sentence different from that described." *United States v. Aguilar-Pena*, 887 F.2d 347, 349 (1st Cir. 1989). Of course, it is impermissible to depart from the guidelines on the basis of the defendant's race, sex, national origin, religion, or socioeconomic status. *United States v. Burch*, 873 F.2d 765 (5th Cir. 1989). Other factors not ordinarily deemed relevant in determining whether to depart include the defendant's age, education, mental and physical condition, employment history, and family and community ties. *United States v. Lira-Barraza*, 897 F.2d 981 (9th Cir. 1990), n.5.

In *Nichols v. United States*, 511 U.S. 738, 114 S.Ct. 1921, 128 L.Ed.2d 745 (1994), the Supreme Court overruled precedent and held that a prior misdemeanor conviction in which the defendant was not represented by counsel could form the basis for a two-year sentence enhancement under the federal sentencing guidelines. Acting without counsel, Kenneth Nichols pleaded no contest to a DUI charge in 1983. In 1990, then represented by counsel, Nichols was convicted of a federal drug conspiracy offense. The judge gave Nichols an enhanced sentence based on the prior DUI conviction. The Supreme Court upheld the enhanced sentence, saying that the sentencing process is a broad inquiry that may bring in information regarding the defendant's past misconduct even if it had not resulted in a criminal conviction. The Court thus went well beyond the facts of the case to permit federal judges broad discretion in handing down enhanced sentences under the sentencing guidelines. Critics of the Court's decision in *Nichols* pointed out that the reason the guidelines were adopted was to reduce judicial discretion in sentencing.

*Blakely v. Washington*, 542 U.S. 296, 124 S.Ct. 2531, 159 L.Ed.2d 403 (2004), involved a challenge to the Washington sentencing guidelines, which, like the federal guidelines, permitted the trial court to enhance a defendant's sentence based on facts that were not found by a jury. The Supreme Court held that the state trial court's sentencing of a defendant to a prison term above the statutory maximum of the standard range for his offense, on the basis of the sentencing judge's finding that the defendant acted with deliberate cruelty, violated the defendant's Sixth Amendment right to a trial by jury.

Although Congress intended the federal sentencing guidelines to be mandatory, the U.S. Supreme Court's decision in *United States v. Booker*, 543 U.S. 220, 125 S.Ct. 738, 160 L.Ed.2d 621 (2005), effectively relegated the guidelines to an advisory position. Relying on its 2000 decisions in *Apprendi v. New Jersey*, supra, and its 2004 decision in *Blakely v. Washington*, supra, the Court in *Booker* held that as originally constituted, the guidelines violated the Sixth Amendment right to trial by jury inasmuch as they authorized judges to increase sentences based on factual determinations not made by juries. Rather than invalidate the guidelines altogether, the *Booker* Court chose to strike down the provisions making them mandatory.

In *Booker* the Court held that "[a]ny fact (other than a prior conviction) which is necessary to support a sentence exceeding the maximum authorized by the facts established by a plea of guilty or a jury verdict must be admitted by the defendant or proved to a jury beyond a reasonable doubt." *Booker,* 523 U.S. at 244, 125 S.Ct. at 756, 160 L.Ed.2d at 650. After *Booker* a district court's authority to determine sentencing factors by a preponderance of the evidence endures and does not violate the Due Process Clause of the Fifth Amendment. *United States v. Vaughn*, 430 F.3d

518 (2d Cir. 2005). *Booker,* however, forbids use of a judge's finding of fact, based on a preponderance of the evidence, to increase a defendant's maximum or mandatory punishment. Thus in *United States v. Mickens,* 453 F.3d 668, 673 (6th Cir. 2006), the court explained that post-*Booker,* the district court retains the ability to make findings of fact based on a preponderance of evidence as long as the court appreciates that the guidelines are advisory, not binding.

In the wake of *Booker,* federal judges are not required to use the sentencing guidelines, but many still do use them on an "advisory" basis. Many cases from the lower federal courts reflected uncertainty with respect to application of the sentencing guidelines. The Supreme Court recognized this and in *Rita v. United States,* 551 U.S. 338, 127 S.Ct. 2456, 168 L.Ed.2d 203 (2007), it held that federal appeals courts hearing challenges of a defendant's sentence may presume that a sentence imposed within properly calculated sentencing guidelines is reasonable.

### The State Experience

States have experimented with sentencing guidelines with varying results. Minnesota, which in 1970 was the first state to adopt presumptive sentencing guidelines, has a relatively simple system that has proven to be workable, although it has resulted in a higher incarceration rate. Washington's sentencing guidelines worked reasonably well until the state legislature began to mandate increased penalties overall as well as harsher minimum sentences for particular crimes. This has necessitated that the guidelines be revised. In Tennessee, the commission that established sentencing guidelines was terminated, although the guidelines themselves remain in effect. In Wisconsin, one of the early states to adopt sentencing guidelines, the sentencing commission as well as the guidelines it promulgated have been abolished by the state legislature because of political forces and fiscal pressures.

In 1990 the North Carolina legislature created the Sentencing and Policy Advisory Commission to study and repair a system of sentencing that had become dysfunctional. Due to prison overcrowding, felons were being paroled to the point that the system had become a revolving door. Thus, sentencing guidelines in North Carolina originated not so much from concern for sentencing disparity but from a desire to rationalize a system that had become chaotic. The commission followed the example of states such as Washington and Minnesota in adopting a simplified model of sentencing guidelines. Whereas the federal sentencing guidelines contain forty-three levels of felony offenses, the North Carolina guidelines contain ten levels. Thus far, the system seems to have worked reasonably well. However, it should be noted that North Carolina has eased pressure on the prison system by adopting intermediate measures such as house arrest and electronic monitoring for less serious offenders.

There is still considerable uncertainty about the efficacy of sentencing guidelines. There is evidence that they have reduced sentencing disparities, but they clearly have not eliminated this problem altogether. There is also concern that sentencing guidelines have generally promoted higher incarceration rates and have thus contributed to the problem of prison overcrowding. It is fair to say that to be successful, sentencing guidelines must be accompanied by policies designed to effectively manage prison populations.

Finally, state sentencing guidelines must now be viewed in the wake of the U.S. Supreme Court's decision in *Blakely v. Washington,* supra. There the Court held that the State of Washington's sentencing guidelines violated the defendant's Sixth Amendment right to trial by jury to the extent that they allowed a judge to enhance a defendant's criminal sentences beyond the statutory maximum based on facts other than those decided by a jury or confessed to by a defendant.

# The Rights of Prisoners

**minimum security facilities** Prisons and jails that offer inmates the most freedom of movement within the least secure environment.

**maximum security prisons** Prisons designed to minimize the movement and maximize the surveillance and control of inmates.

Contrary to popular mythology, America's prisons are not country clubs. Although some **minimum security facilities** (like the military base where the Watergate conspirators were confined) are reasonably comfortable, **maximum security prisons** are another story. They are sometimes unsanitary; they are almost all overcrowded. All are violent, dangerous places to live.

The federal courts have made it clear that the Eighth Amendment's prohibition of cruel and unusual punishments imposes obligations on prison administrators to maintain certain standards of confinement. A sizable number of state prison systems have been or are currently under court orders to improve conditions of confinement or reduce overcrowding. Recently, some state courts have begun to focus their attention on the deplorable conditions existing in many city and county jails.

Historically, courts were quite unreceptive to claims brought by prisoners. They essentially adopted a "hands-off" policy, allowing prison officials free rein. In the late 1960s, that began to change as federal and state tribunals examined prison conditions and policies. As the courts signaled their willingness to scrutinize the prisons, litigation in this area mushroomed.

**conditions of confinement** The conditions under which inmates are held in jails and prisons. These conditions are subject to challenge under the Eighth Amendment's Cruel and Unusual Punishments Clause.

In one dramatic case involving prison conditions, Federal District Judge Frank M. Johnson, Jr., found that the **conditions of confinement** in the Alabama system were barbarous and inhumane, thus violating the Eighth Amendment. Judge Johnson issued a detailed set of requirements to remedy the situation and appointed a special committee to oversee implementation of the order. Moreover, he threatened to close down the prison system unless his requirements were met. *Pugh v. Locke*, 406 F. Supp. 318 (M.D. Ala. 1976), aff'd sub nom. *Newman v. Alabama*, 559 F.2d 283 (5th Cir. 1977).

Perhaps the most notorious story of prison conditions is that of the Arkansas prison system, which was scrutinized in a series of federal lawsuits beginning in 1969 with *Holt v. Sarver*, 309 F. Supp. 362 (E.D. Ark. 1970), aff'd, 442 F.2d 304 (8th Cir. 1971). The most egregious conditions occurred at prison farms run largely by "trusties," senior prisoners entrusted with the job of controlling their fellow inmates. It should be noted that the trusty system is widely condemned by penologists. Under the Arkansas system, trusties smuggled in weapons, liquor, and drugs and sold them to the other inmates. Trusties hoarded food purchased with taxpayers' money and forced the other inmates to pay for their meals. Violence and even torture were commonly used by the trusties in maintaining their grip over the other prisoners. Medical care was almost totally lacking, and conditions of sanitation were miserable. Some prisoners were held in punitive isolation cells for months at a time. Overall, the penal farms were characterized by pervasive filth, disease, and violence.

In a series of decisions handed down during the 1970s, the federal district court issued detailed orders aimed at remedying the conditions in the Arkansas prison system. Especially controversial was an order placing a maximum limit of thirty days on the use of punitive isolation. The Supreme Court had little difficulty upholding this measure on appeal. *Hutto v. Finney*, 437 U.S. 678, 98 S.Ct. 2565, 57 L.Ed.2d 522 (1978).

As currently interpreted, the Eighth Amendment requires that prisoners must be provided with reasonably adequate food, clothing, shelter, medical care, and sanitation. There must also be a reasonable assurance of their personal safety. Nevertheless, the Eighth Amendment does not require that prisoners be furnished everything they deem essential to their physical or psychological well-being. *Newman v. Alabama*, supra. Air conditioning, television, weightlifting equipment, and other nonessential items can be provided or removed at the discretion of prison authorities.

In 1992 the Supreme Court held that a prisoner who is beaten maliciously by guards may bring a civil action for damages based on a claim of cruel and unusual punishment, even if the prisoner does not suffer "significant injuries." *Hudson v. McMillian*, 503 U.S. 1, 112 S.Ct. 995, 117 L.Ed.2d 156 (1992). During the 1990s, prisoners began litigating the question of whether being subjected to environmental tobacco smoke (ETS) amounts to a violation of a prisoner's right to be free from cruel and unusual punishment under the Eighth Amendment. Lower federal courts recognized that the government has a duty to provide a safe environment for those incarcerated in its institutions but had disagreed as to whether exposure to ETS in a penitentiary setting constituted cruel and unusual punishment.

In 1993, the Supreme Court in *Helling v. McKinney*, 509 U.S. 25, 113 S.Ct. 2475, 125 L.Ed.2d 22, squarely faced the issue of whether the health risk posed by involuntary exposure of a prison inmate to ETS can be the basis of a claim for relief under the Eighth Amendment. In its landmark decision, the Court held that a prisoner who alleged that the prison system had, with "deliberate indifference," exposed him to levels of environmental tobacco smoke that posed an unreasonable risk of serious damage to his future health stated an actionable claim under the Eighth Amendment against his custodians.

## The Overcrowding Issue

Much of the current litigation challenging conditions of criminal confinement focuses on the problem of prison overcrowding. During the 1980s, the prison population in the United States nearly doubled. Rising crime rates and an increasingly punitive posture adopted by legislatures and courts, combined with fiscal stress, led to an overcrowding crisis in many prison systems. As mandatory sentence laws and sentencing guidelines have required judges to imprison larger numbers of convicted criminals, the number of prisoners has far outstripped the capacity of prisons in the United States. Today most state prisons are filled well beyond design capacity.

Throughout the 1980s, litigation in the federal courts by prisoners increased dramatically. Although the Supreme Court has said that "the Constitution does not mandate comfortable prisons," *Rhodes v. Chapman*, 452 U.S. 337, 101 S.Ct. 2392, 69 L.Ed.2d 59 (1981), lower federal courts have intervened to limit the number of inmates who can be housed in some prisons. The public is relatively unconcerned about prison overcrowding, but prison officials often welcome judicial intervention. Prison overcrowding makes it considerably more difficult to control inmate populations.

## The Problem of Prison Rape

One of the most serious problems that a prison inmate can encounter is rape by a fellow inmate. Prison officials have not succeeded in eliminating this brutal aspect of prison life. Smaller, weaker inmates, especially those not aligned with a particular gang, are the most vulnerable to such attack. In recent years the problem has gained national attention, and in July 2003 Congress enacted the Prison Rape Reduction Act. The new act created a commission to examine all issues relating to the problem and requires the Department of Justice to provide assistance to federal, state, and local officials. It envisions the development of national standards applicable to the federal prisons with provisions for grants to encourage the states and local authorities to adopt such standards.

# Other Rights of Prisoners

**constitutional rights of prison inmates** Under modern interpretation of the federal and state constitutions, prisoners retain those constitutional rights that are not inconsistent with the fact that they are confined in a secure environment.

In addition to Eighth Amendment challenges to prison conditions, numerous lawsuits have sought to persuade the courts to recognize other **constitutional rights of prison inmates**. Traditionally, convicted felons were viewed as having forfeited most, if not all, of their constitutional rights. Thus, even reform-minded judges have been cautious in this area. For the most part they have deferred to prison officials, stressing the traditional view that "lawful incarceration brings about the necessary withdrawal or limitation of many privileges and rights, a retraction justified by the considerations underlying our penal system." *Price v. Johnston*, 334 U.S. 266, 285, 68 S.Ct. 1049, 92 L.Ed. 1356, 1369 (1948). Nevertheless, certain constitutional rights have been recognized. The Supreme Court has held that a prison inmate retains those First Amendment rights "that are not inconsistent with his status as a prisoner or with the legitimate penological objectives of the corrections system." *Pell v. Procunier*, 417 U.S. 817, 822, 94 S.Ct. 2800, 2804, 41 L.Ed.2d 495, 501 (1974).

For example, consider rights arising under the free exercise of religion clause of the First Amendment. Courts are generally receptive to prisoners' rights to possess Bibles, prayer books, and other religious materials, as well as inmates' rights to be visited by the clergy. On the other hand, courts have generally upheld restrictions on religious exercises if they disrupt prison order or routine. See, e.g., *O'Lone v. Estate of Shabazz*, 482 U.S. 342, 107 S.Ct. 2400, 96 L.Ed.2d 282 (1987). If prison officials allow inmates who belong to mainstream religious denominations to attend worship services, however, then members of other religious sects must be given a reasonable opportunity to exercise their religious beliefs as well. *Cruz v. Beto*, 405 U.S. 319, 92 S.Ct. 1079, 31 L.Ed.2d 263 (1972).

One of the most firmly established rights of prisoners is the right of access to the courts. The Supreme Court made it clear decades ago that prison officials may not deny inmates access to the courts or penalize them for using that access. *Ex parte Hull*, 312 U.S. 546, 61 S.Ct. 640, 85 L.Ed. 1034 (1941). Similarly, courts have held that indigent inmates must be furnished writing materials and notary services to assist in filing petitions and seeking writs from courts. Courts have generally upheld the right of prisoners to meet with counsel in privacy and, in the absence of other forms of legal assistance, to have access to law libraries. See *Bounds v. Smith*, 430 U.S. 817, 97 S.Ct. 1491, 52 L.Ed.2d 72 (1977).

The courts have also recognized that prisoners are entitled to limited rights of expression. For example, prisoners retain a limited right to communicate with the outside world via the mails, although prison officials may limit and censor the mail prisoners send and receive, provided there is no interference with attorney–client relationships. *Lee v. Tahash*, 352 F.2d 970 (8th Cir. 1965).

Prison officials also have broad latitude to restrict visitation privileges if there is reason to believe that an inmate is receiving contraband smuggled into the prison by visitors. *Kentucky Department of Corrections v. Thompson*, 490 U.S. 454, 109 S.Ct. 1904, 104 L.Ed.2d 506 (1989). Likewise, prison regulations impinging on inmates' interests in free assembly and association have been consistently upheld. See, for example, *Jones v. North Carolina Prisoners' Labor Union, Inc.*, 433 U.S. 119, 97 S.Ct. 2532, 53 L.Ed.2d 629 (1977), where the Supreme Court refused to extend First Amendment protection to an effort to organize a labor union among prisoners. Obviously, prison is by definition antithetical to the ideas of freedom of assembly and freedom of association. Congress enacted the Ensign Amendment as part of the Omnibus Consolidated Appropriations Act of 1997. Pub. L. No. 104-208, § 614, 109

Stat. 3009-66 (1996). The Ensign Amendment prohibits prisons from using federal funds to distribute any information or material that is sexually explicit or features nudity. The law exempts any nudity featured for purposes of medical, educational, or anthropological content.

## Prison Disciplinary Measures

**prison disciplinary measures** Steps taken by prison officials to punish prisoners for misconduct, largely accomplished by removing good-time credits that prisoners earn for exemplary behavior in prison.

**punitive isolation** Solitary confinement of a person who is incarcerated.

The federal courts have imposed limits on **prison disciplinary measures** such as corporal punishment and the extended use of **punitive isolation**. Today, at least in most state prisons, discipline is largely accomplished by granting and removing good-time credit—that is, early release for good behavior. If officials pursue this policy, then due process demands that certain procedural requirements be observed before good time credit is removed for disciplinary purposes. Specifically, there must be written notice of the disciplinary action, and the inmate has the right to an administrative hearing with a written record. The inmate must be accorded the right to produce evidence refuting the charges of misconduct and may even call witnesses on his or her behalf. *Wolff v. McDonnell*, 418 U.S. 539, 94 S.Ct. 2963, 41 L.Ed.2d 935 (1974). These rights have not been extended to allow an inmate to have counsel present at such a hearing. *Baxter v. Palmigiano*, 425 U.S. 308, 96 S.Ct. 1551, 47 L.Ed.2d 810 (1976).

## Parole and Its Revocation

**parole** Conditional release from jail or prison of a person who has served part of his or her sentence.

**parole revocation hearings** Administrative hearings held for the purpose of determining whether an offender's parole should be revoked.

Historically, the federal government and most states provided for early release from prison on **parole** for those inmates who could demonstrate to the parole board's satisfaction their willingness to conform their conduct to the requirements of the law. In recent years, parole has been abolished or restricted greatly in many jurisdictions. This generally corresponds to the "truth-in-sentencing" movement described above. Naturally, there are also provisions by which parole can be revoked if the offender violates the conditions of release. As with internal prison disciplinary actions, the revocation of parole is affected by due process considerations. Essentially, before parole can be revoked, the parolee has the right to a hearing within a reasonable time after being retaken into custody. *Morrissey v. Brewer*, 408 U.S. 471, 92 S.Ct. 2593, 33 L.Ed.2d 484 (1972). However, the Supreme Court has stressed the informality of this hearing, saying that "the process should be flexible enough to consider evidence including letters, affidavits, and other material that would not be admissible in an adversary criminal trial." 408 U.S. at 489, 92 S.Ct. at 2604, 33 L.Ed.2d at 499. In practice, courts generally admit any relevant evidence that is not privileged, but as previously pointed out in respect to revocation of probation, courts generally do not allow revocation of parole based solely on hearsay evidence. See, e.g., *Grello v. Commonwealth*, 477 A.2d 45 (Pa. Cmwlth. 1984). A year after its decision in *Morrissey v. Brewer*, the Supreme Court held that the right to counsel may apply to **parole revocation hearings**, depending on the complexity of the issues involved. *Gagnon v. Scarpelli*, supra.

## The Rights of Crime Victims

Although crime is by definition an injury to society as a whole, we must not forget that most serious crimes injure individual victims, often quite severely. The injury may transcend physical or economic injury to include emotional hardship. During the 1960s the dominant concern of the criminal law was for the rights of the accused.

**victims' rights** Refers to the various rights possessed by victims of crimes.

In the 1990s the trend was to recognize the rights of crime victims. Most states have adopted constitutional amendments specifically recognizing **victims' rights**, while others have adopted statutes along these lines. See, e.g., West's Ann. Cal. Penal Code § 679 *et seq*. During the 1990s a proposal to add a victims' rights amendment to the U.S. Constitution surfaced in Congress. Although that measure did not pass, it provided the impetus for Congress to enact legislation in this area.

**Crime Victims' Rights Act (CVRA)** Federal legislation that provides eight basic rights for crime victims where crimes are prosecuted in the federal system.

In 2004 Congress enacted the **Crimes Victims' Rights Act (CVRA)**. Title 18 U.S.C.A. 3771 provides eight basic rights:

**Crime victims' rights.**

(a) A crime victim has the following rights:

(1) The right to be reasonably protected from the accused.

(2) The right to reasonable, accurate, and timely notice of any public court proceeding, or any parole proceeding, involving the crime or of any release or escape of the accused.

(3) The right not to be excluded from any such public court proceeding, unless the court, after receiving clear and convincing evidence, determines that testimony by the victim would be materially altered if the victim heard other testimony at that proceeding.

(4) The right to be reasonably heard at any public proceeding in the district court involving release, plea, sentencing, or any parole proceeding.

(5) The reasonable right to confer with the attorney for the Government in the case.

(6) The right to full and timely restitution as provided in law.

(7) The right to proceedings free from unreasonable delay.

(8) The right to be treated with fairness and with respect for the victim's dignity and privacy.

18 U.S.C.A. 3771(b) provides that "the court shall ensure that the crime victim is afforded the rights described in subsection (a)."

The federal Crime Victims' Rights Act has become an important component in the federal criminal justice system. It not only assists victims of federal crimes, but it also provides an impetus to states to update their victims' rights laws. Most crimes are prosecuted under state laws and each state has now adopted constitutional amendments or has enacted laws providing crime victims with rights in the criminal justice process. The National Crime Victims Law Institute, organized in 1997, is a "national resource for crime victim lawyers and victims to support the assertion and enforcement of victims' rights in criminal and civil processes." Its website, www.ncvli.org, includes a wealth of information on rights of crime victims, including a listing of victims' rights laws in each state.

## The Uniform Victims of Crime Act

**Uniform Victims of Crime Act (UVCA)** A law proposed by the Uniform Law Commission designed to provide uniform rights and procedures concerning crime victims.

The **Uniform Victims of Crime Act (UVCA)** is an attempt to lend uniformity to the patchwork of victims' rights laws that now exists at the state level. The UVCA was developed by the Uniform Law Commission, a voluntary association representing the legal profession. Like the Model Penal Code developed by the American Law Institute, the UVCA has no status as law unless and until it is adopted by a state legislature. Under the UVCA, prosecutors or court personnel must notify victims of their rights under the act, as well as the times of any court proceedings involving the person or persons who allegedly victimized them. A crime victim has the right to be present at any court proceeding that the defendant has the right to attend. If the defendant is convicted, the victim has the right to make an impact statement during the sentencing hearing and assert an opinion as to the proper sentence. Finally, the UVCA provides for victims to be compensated by the state, up to $25,000, for any physical or emotional injuries suffered as the result of the victimization. However, this amount may be denied or reduced if the victim receives compensation through insurance or restitution from the defendant.

## Restitution

**restitution** The act of compensating someone for losses suffered.

**Restitution** is a time-honored means of protecting the interests of crime victims. Restitution refers to "the return of a sum of money, an object, or the value of an object that the defendant wrongfully obtained in the course of committing the crime." *State v. Stalheim*, 552 P.2d 829, 832 (Or. 1976). Although restitution was practiced under the early common law, it was eventually abandoned as a remedy in criminal cases in favor of fines payable to the Crown. In modern America, however, restitution is making a comeback in the criminal law. Several states have enacted laws allowing trial courts to require restitution as a condition of probation in lieu of sentencing offenders to prison. In states that have adopted restitution laws, courts have held that (1) restitution is not necessarily incompatible with incarceration, *State v. Murray*, 621 P.2d 334 (Hawaii 1980); (2) restitution may be ordered for damages caused by the defendant during a criminal episode, irrespective of whether the loss is directly related to a specific conviction, *People v. Gallagher*, 223 N.W.2d 92 (Mich. App. 1974); and (3) a defendant may be ordered to pay restitution to a party other than the victim, *Shenah v. Henderson*, 476 P.2d 854 (Ariz. 1970).

Restitution is not practical in many criminal cases. Many offenders are not suited to probation, and even among those who are, there is no guarantee that they will be able to make payments to the victim. Recognizing this problem, several states have established victims' compensation commissions. For example, the Florida Crimes Compensation Act of 1977 makes victims and certain relatives eligible for compensation from a state commission where a crime results in injuries and is reported within seventy-two hours. Awards are limited to meeting the victims' actual needs. West's Fla. Stat. Ann. §§ 960.001-960.298.

## Conclusion

The various forms of punishment meted out to convicted criminals rest on differing assumptions about crime and human nature. These assumptions lead to differing philosophies of punishment that stress retribution, deterrence, incapacitation, or rehabilitation. A great debate continues regarding both the propriety of these goals and the efficacy of the measures designed to achieve them. In particular, the deterrent value of the death penalty and the rehabilitative value of incarceration have been seriously questioned.

Courts of law tend to avoid the philosophical, theoretical, and empirical questions that surround the various forms of criminal punishment. Rather, they focus on the substantive and procedural limitations that the federal and state constitutions impose on the criminal justice system. In so doing, they tend to reflect the dominant values of the society.

# Chapter Summary

- Learning Objective 1

  - Early forms of criminal punishment were based on the concept of retribution, which carried a sense of proportionality. Colonial America followed the English common law, which prescribed the death penalty for most felonies and corporal punishment for misdemeanors.

  - Nineteenth-century reforms introduced the penitentiary and the concept of rehabilitation. By the twentieth century, incarceration had replaced corporal punishment, and state and the federal governments housed convicted felons in prisons.

  - In contemporary America incarceration is imposed for most serious offenses, although the death penalty remains in effect in more than half the states for aggravated cases of murder.

  - With federal and state prisons at or in excess of capacity, attention has shifted to alternative forms of punishment.

- Learning Objective 2

  - Congress provides for penalties for persons convicted of violating federal laws. State legislatures do likewise for state offenders. Sentences meted out by courts must comport with these statutory provisions.

  - The Eighth Amendment to the U.S. Constitution, ratified in 1791, prohibits "cruel and unusual punishments." The Supreme Court has said that the Amendment applies to the states and must draw its meaning from "evolving standards of decency."

  - The process by which offenders are sentenced and punishments carried out must also comport with the Due Process Clauses of the Fifth and Fourteenth Amendments, and with similar provisions in all fifty state constitutions.

- Learning Objective 3

  - Where judges consider it appropriate, they increasingly grant probation for nonviolent first-time offenders. Probation is the conditional release of a convicted offender under the supervision of a probation officer.

  - Statutes prescribe certain mandatory conditions on the probationer's activities and judges impose additional conditions that have a relationship to the defendant's offense.

  - Courts have held that probation conditions may infringe a probationer's constitutional rights, including First Amendment rights of free speech and association, as long as the conditions are related to the goal of rehabilitation. Appellate courts have invalidated conditions that restrict such fundamental rights as marriage, procreation, and the right of self-expression, but have upheld conditions restricting a probationer's use of the Internet by a defendant convicted of sexual and child abuse offenses.

  - Community service is sometimes imposed as a condition of probation.

  - Courts increasingly impose community control (house arrest), where an offender is allowed to leave home only for employment and approved community service activities. House arrest is often monitored by requiring persons to wear bracelets that permit officials to track their whereabouts. Some courts have imposed forms of creative punishment, for example, bumper stickers and signs indicating a person's status as an offender.

- Learning Objective 4

  o In 1997 the U.S. Supreme Court, in a 5–4 decision, upheld the constitutionality of a Kansas law that establishes procedures for the civil commitment of persons who, due to a "mental abnormality" or a "personality disorder," are likely to engage in "predatory acts of sexual violence."

  o In 2010 the Supreme Court upheld the federal statute that allows for civil commitment of violent sexual predators who have completed their prison sentences.

- Learning Objective 5

  o By the 1960s many states had abolished the death penalty. In 1972 the Supreme Court declared Georgia's death penalty law unconstitutional because it allowed juries virtually unlimited discretion. Georgia revised its laws to make the death penalty more predictable. In 1976 the Court upheld Georgia's revised death penalty statute. Thirty-eight states with death penalty laws have modeled their statutes along the lines of the revised Georgia statute.

  o Federal crimes subject to the death penalty now include dozens of nonhomicidal offenses including treason and large-scale drug trafficking. It remains to be seen whether the federal courts will permit the death penalty for nonhomicidal crimes.

  o Since the 1980s the Supreme Court has rendered several significant decisions in appeals involving the death penalty: In 1986, the Court held that the Eighth Amendment bars the execution of a person who is insane. In 1989 it said that execution of a mentally retarded prisoner does not necessarily violate the Eighth Amendment. In 2002 the Court ruled that there was a sufficient national consensus to prohibit execution of mentally retarded persons. And in 2005 the Court prohibited execution of anyone who was under eighteen at the time of their offense.

  o In the modern era executions have been carried out using the electric chair, the gas chamber, the firing squad, hanging, and lethal injection. In 2008, the U.S. Supreme Court upheld Kentucky's protocol for lethal injection, which is used by most states that employ lethal injection to administer the death penalty.

- Learning Objective 6

  o Every jurisdiction requires that adults be sentenced in open court; in many instances juvenile offenders are sentenced *in camera*. For misdemeanors, sentencing usually occurs immediately on conviction. In felony cases, sentencing may be postponed to allow for a presentence investigation (PSI).

  o Sentencing is a critical stage of the criminal process, and counsel must be supplied to indigent defendants.

  o At the sentencing hearing, the court considers the evidence received at trial, any presentence report, evidence offered by the prosecution and defense relevant to sentencing, and any statement the defendant wishes to make.

  o Upon pronouncement of the sentence, a defendant to be incarcerated is given credit for time served since arrest. A defendant convicted of multiple crimes must be given separate sentences for each offense. Sentences may run consecutively or concurrently, usually at the discretion of the judge.

  o Where the prosecution seeks the death penalty, the jury hears the evidence of mitigating and aggravating circumstances. To hand down a death sentence, the jury must find beyond a reasonable doubt that the aggravating factors outweigh the mitigating ones.

- ○ In 1991, receding from its previous position, the Supreme Court ruled that the prosecution may submit a victim impact statement to be considered by a jury in determining whether to impose the death penalty.
- ○ In 1994 the Court held that defendants facing the death penalty have a right to tell juries if the only alternative to a death sentence is life imprisonment without the possibility of parole.

- • Learning Objective 7

  - ○ Formerly, legislatures commonly allowed judges to sentence criminals to imprisonment for indeterminate periods—that is, until corrections officials decided the convict was sufficiently rehabilitated. Abuses of the system, combined with the decline of popular support for rehabilitation, have led most jurisdictions to abandon the concept of indeterminate sentencing.
  - ○ Under determinate sentencing, the judge sets a fixed term of years within statutory parameters, and the offender is required to serve that term without the possibility of early release.
  - ○ Many states now require mandatory minimum sentences for violent crimes and offenses involving firearms. Federal law now mandates minimum prison terms for serious drug crimes prosecuted in federal courts.
  - ○ In many states, "habitual offender" laws require increased penalties for persons convicted of repeated felonies. Currently, the federal government and most states have some form of habitual offender or "three-strikes-and-you're-out" statute. In most states, prosecutions under the "three-strikes" statutes are infrequent. In 2003 the Supreme Court upheld California's three-strikes law against a constitutional challenge based on the Eighth Amendment's Cruel and Unusual Punishments Clause.
  - ○ Truth in sentencing refers to movement seeking to close the gap between the sentences imposed and time actually served in prison. By 2001 more than two-thirds of the states had adopted "truth-in-sentencing" laws. Since then budgetary pressures and prison overcrowding have caused some states to repeal or liberalize these laws.

- • Learning Objective 8

  - ○ To eliminate the disparities in sentencing, Congress and a number of states adopted sentencing guidelines; some mandatory, others advisory. The federal guidelines resulted from the Sentencing Reform Act of 1984. State sentencing guidelines came about before and after that date.
  - ○ The guidelines provide a matrix of various factors to be considered in setting a defendant's sentence. Courts have leeway to depart from the guidelines for exceptional reasons. The guidelines have reduced, but not eliminated, unwarranted sentencing disparities. They have increased rates of incarceration, thereby contributing to the overcrowding in prisons.
  - ○ In 2004 the Supreme Court held that a state trial court's sentencing of a defendant to a prison term above the statutory maximum on the basis of the judge's finding that the defendant acted with deliberate cruelty violated the defendant's Sixth Amendment right to a trial by jury.
  - ○ Although Congress intended the federal sentencing guidelines to be mandatory, in 2005 the Supreme Court effectively relegated the guidelines to an advisory position.

- Learning Objective 9

  - Historically, courts allowed prison officials free rein in running prisons and dealing with prisoners. In the late 1960s, as federal and state tribunals examined prison conditions and policies, litigation mushroomed.
  - As currently interpreted, the Eighth Amendment requires that prisoners must be provided with reasonably adequate food, clothing, shelter, medical care, sanitation, and a reasonable assurance of their personal safety. Nevertheless, the Eighth Amendment does not require that prisoners be furnished everything they deem essential to their physical or psychological well-being.
  - Although the Supreme Court has said that "the Constitution does not mandate comfortable prisons," lower federal courts have intervened to limit the number of inmates who can be housed in some prisons.
  - The Supreme Court has held that a prison inmate retains those First Amendment rights "that are not inconsistent with his status as a prisoner or with the legitimate penological objectives of the corrections system." Courts say that prisoners may possess Bibles, prayer books, and other religious materials, and be visited by the clergy. On the other hand, courts have generally upheld restrictions on religious exercises that disrupt the prison routine.
  - Prisoners retain a limited right to communicate via the mails, although prison officials may limit and censor the mail prisoners send and receive, provided there is no interference with attorney–client relationships.
  - Prison officials also have broad latitude to restrict the visitation privileges of an inmate who is receiving contraband smuggled into the prison by visitors.
  - Courts have consistently upheld prison regulations restricting free assembly and association.
  - The Supreme Court has long held that prison officials may not deny inmates access to the courts or penalize them for using courts. More recently courts have held that inmates must be furnished writing materials and notary services to assist them in filing petitions and seeking writs from courts. Courts have generally upheld the right of prisoners to meet with counsel in private and, in absence of other forms of legal assistance, to have access to law libraries.
  - Courts have said that there must be written notice of disciplinary actions, and that an inmate has the right to an administrative hearing with a written record and the right to produce evidence refuting the charges of misconduct, and may even call witnesses on his or her behalf. Likewise, revocation of parole is subject to minimal due process considerations.

- Learning Objective 10

  - The Uniform Victims of Crime Act (UVCA) provides for notification to victims of court proceedings involving the persons who allegedly victimized them, and the right to be present at any court proceeding that the defendant has the right to attend. If the defendant is convicted, the victim has the right to make an impact statement during the sentencing hearing and assert an opinion as to the proper sentence. Finally, the Uniform Act recognizes that many offenders are not suited to probation, and even among those who are, there is no guarantee they will be able to make restitution to the victim and certain relatives.

    o  Where a crime results in injuries and is promptly reported, UVCA provides for victims to be compensated by the state for any physical or emotional injuries suffered as the result of the victimization and provides for funding to state agencies that have established compensation programs to reimburse crime victims.

    o  In 2004 Congress enacted the Federal Crimes Victims Act, which provides eight basic rights to crime victims where crimes are prosecuted in the federal system. Importantly, the Act stipulates that the court shall ensure that crime victims are afforded these rights.

## Key Terms

aggravating factors

bifurcated trial

boot camp

capital crimes

capital punishment

community control

community service

concurrent sentencing

conditions of confinement

conditions of probation

consecutive sentencing

constitutional rights of prison inmates

corporal punishment

Crime Victims' Rights Act (CVRA)

death penalty

definite sentencing

determinate sentencing

Federal Death Penalty Act (FDPA)

Federal Sentencing Reform Act of 1984

forfeiture

general deterrence

good-time credit

habitual offender statute

house arrest

incapacitation

incarceration

indefinite sentencing

indeterminate sentencing

maximum security prisons

minimum security facilities

mitigating factors

monetary fine

noncapital crimes

parole

parole revocation hearings

penalty enhancement statutes

presentence investigation

presentence report

prison disciplinary measures

probation

pronouncement of sentence

proportionality

punitive isolation

rehabilitation

restitution

retribution

right of allocution

sentencing guidelines

sentencing hearing

suspended sentence

three strikes and you're out

truth in sentencing

Uniform Victims of Crime Act (UVCA)

United States Sentencing Commission

victim impact evidence

victim impact statement

victims' rights

## Questions for Thought and Discussion

1. Why have the courts generally viewed corporal punishment as "cruel and unusual" yet been unwilling to take the same view of capital punishment?

2. How could a prisoner on death row establish that his or her death sentence was the result of racial discrimination?

3. Does your state impose the death penalty? If so, what does the state law provide with respect to juries considering aggravating and mitigating factors? Do you think your state's law governing the death penalty should be amended? If so, explain why and how.

4. What alternatives to imprisonment exist to deal with violent criminals who are repeat offenders? What alternatives, if any, would you propose? What legal problems are implicit in these alternatives to incarceration?

5. Discuss the pros and cons of mandatory sentences. Do mandatory sentences remove discretion from the sentencing judge and vest discretion in the prosecutor, who may elect to charge a defendant with a lesser offense to avoid imposition of a mandatory sentence?

6. Suppose you were a probation officer and a judge asked you to recommend probation conditions for a first-time offender convicted of the sale and possession of cocaine. What specific conditions would you propose?

7. Should a defendant always be permitted to view the contents of a presentence report? What are the arguments for and against this?

8. In August of 2003, Justice Anthony Kennedy made a speech in which he strongly criticized mandatory sentencing laws. Do you agree or disagree with Justice Kennedy? Why?

9. What implications do the U.S. Supreme Court's decisions in *Apprendi v. New Jersey* (2000), *Blakely v. Washington* (2004), and *United States v. Booker* (2005) have for future use of sentencing guidelines?

10. What is the rationale for granting only minimal due process rights to parolees and probationers and to prisoners in disciplinary proceedings?

11. To what extent have the legal rights of prisoners been expanded since the 1960s? Have the courts been unduly solicitous in entertaining lawsuits brought by prison inmates?

12. Do you think that the introduction of a victim impact statement during the sentencing phase of a capital trial is appropriate, or do you think it might inject too much emotionalism into the process?

13. Should the government be permitted to require continued custodial supervision of sexual predators who have served their sentence for sexual abuse of children? Support your views.

14. What are the merits of granting or denying "good-time credit" to prisoners?

## Problems for Discussion and Solution

1. Inmate Jay Leburd has brought suit in federal court challenging the conditions of his confinement in the Intensive Management Unit (IMU) of a maximum security state prison. Specifically, Leburd argues that the lack of any opportunity for outdoor exercise, total lack of reading materials, and absence of radio and television amount to "cruel and unusual punishment" in violation of the Eighth Amendment. Responding to the suit, the state prison system has conceded that the conditions in the IMU are "substantially as described by plaintiff."

Nevertheless, the state has asked the court to dismiss the suit on the ground that "the Eighth Amendment does not guarantee fresh air and sunshine to inmates in solitary confinement, nor does it require that they be entertained." What is the federal judge likely to do? What do you think the judge should do?

2. In 1987 Douglas Deville was convicted in a state court for felonious possession of cocaine. He received probation for that offense. Three years later, Deville was found guilty of another drug-related felony in the same state. For that offense, he served five years in state prison. Three months after being released from prison, Deville was arrested for possession of 100 grams of cocaine base and 400 grams of marijuana. This time the case was prosecuted in federal court, where Deville was convicted of felony possession with intent to distribute. Because this was his third drug-related felony, Deville was sentenced to life imprisonment without parole under 21 U.S.C.A. § 841(b)(1)(A) (1994). On appeal, Deville claims that this sentence is "utterly disproportionate to his offense" and that, accordingly, it constitutes a violation of the Eighth Amendment's Cruel and Unusual Punishments Clause. Deville is relying on the U.S. Supreme Court's opinion in *Solem v. Helm* (1983). Does Deville have a case? Is he likely to prevail? In your opinion, is Deville's sentence fair and just? Is it constitutional?

3. Megan Mortensen was convicted of kidnapping and first-degree murder stemming from an incident in which she and her boyfriend, Vigo Stern, kidnapped, tortured, and killed an off-duty police officer. In a separate trial, Stern has been found guilty of the same offenses and sentenced to death by lethal injection. Upon what additional facts would a jury be likely to sentence Megan to death? Upon what facts would the jury be likely to choose a lesser punishment? If you were representing Megan in this case, what would you want to know about her beyond the facts of the case?

# CHAPTER 20

# Appeal and Postconviction Relief

## CHAPTER OUTLINE

## JURISPRUDENCE

*Chapman v. California* (1967)

*Douglas v. California* (1963)

*Felker v. Turpin* (1996)

*O'Sullivan v. Boerckel* (1999)

*Wiggins v. Smith* (2003)

## LEARNING OBJECTIVES

After reading this chapter, you should be able to explain

1. the different mechanisms by which appellate courts review criminal convictions and sentences

2. what defendants may challenge on appeal and the limited circumstances under which the prosecution can appeal

3. the error correction and lawmaking functions of appellate courts

4. the circumstances under which persons appealing their convictions may obtain pretrial release while their appeals are being adjudicated

5. the extent to which indigent persons convicted of crimes are entitled to representation at public expense to pursue appeals

6. the procedural steps followed by appellate courts in reviewing criminal cases

7. how and why the writ of habeas corpus is an important component of the modern appeals process

8. how states have adopted postconviction remedies that do not rely on habeas corpus

9. why DNA evidence can play an important role in postconviction relief

10. the nonjudicial remedies available to persons convicted of crimes

# CHAPTER OPENING VIGNETTE

In the overwhelming majority of criminal cases there is no appeal. This is because most defendants are induced to plead guilty and in so doing bring closure to the judicial process. Death penalty cases are different. Most states that retain the death penalty provide for automatic appeals of death sentences. Many death penalty cases also involve some form of postconviction relief after the ordinary appeals process has concluded. Contemporary death penalty cases often highlight the complex character of modern judicial federalism. For example, consider the case of Robert Glen Coe.

In 1979, eight-year-old Cary Ann Medlin was abducted a few blocks from her home in Greenfield, Tennessee. Her body was found in a field the next day; she had been raped and stabbed to death. Three days later police arrested twenty-three-year-old Robert Glen Coe as he prepared to board a bus for Georgia. In 1981, Coe was sentenced to death for first-degree murder and given life sentences for aggravated rape and aggravated kidnapping. In 1983 the Tennessee Supreme Court affirmed Coe's conviction and sentence. The following year, the U.S. Supreme Court denied Coe's petition for discretionary review. Coe then filed a petition for postconviction relief in the state court where he had been tried, arguing that he had been denied a fair trial because his lawyers had not put on an adequate defense. In 1986, that petition was denied and the denial was affirmed by a state appellate court. Coe then filed a petition for habeas corpus in federal district court. In 1989 that petition was denied on the grounds that Coe had failed to exhaust his remedies in the state courts. Coe then filed a second petition for postconviction relief in the state courts. That petition was denied, the denial affirmed on appeal, and review denied by the state supreme court. Coe then returned to federal court with a second petition for habeas corpus. In 1996, a federal district court judge overturned Coe's conviction and sentence on the basis of improper jury instructions and other errors in his trial. Two years later, a three-judge panel of the U.S. Circuit Court of Appeals for the Sixth Circuit reversed that ruling and reinstated Coe's conviction and sentence. The following year, the Sixth Circuit denied Coe's petition to have the case reconsidered by a full bench. The U.S. Supreme Court denied review. While Coe's second federal habeas petition was being litigated, his third petition for postconviction relief was being considered, and ultimately was denied, by the Tennessee courts. In early 2000, Coe made his last effort to avoid execution by asking the state trial court to find him mentally incompetent. When that failed, Coe's case was reviewed once more by the Tennessee Supreme Court, which approved his execution. Coe was put to death by lethal injection in April of 2000, more than twenty years after the murder of Cary Ann Medlin.

# Introduction

**trial *de novo*** "New trial." Refers to trial court review of convictions for minor offenses by courts of limited jurisdiction by conducting a new trial instead of merely reviewing the record of the initial trial.

**appeal of right** An appeal that a defendant is entitled to make as a matter of law.

**discretionary review** Form of appellate court review of lower court decisions that is not mandatory but occurs at the discretion of the appellate court.

**postconviction relief** Term applied to various mechanisms a defendant may use to challenge a conviction after other routes of appeal have been exhausted.

**writ of habeas corpus** "You have the body." A judicial writ requiring that a party be brought before a court. The primary function of habeas corpus is to release a person from unlawful confinement.

**error correction** The function of appellate courts in reviewing routine appeals and correcting the errors of trial courts.

Society's commitment to standards of fairness and procedural regularity is reflected in the opportunities that exist for defendants in criminal cases to seek judicial review of adverse court decisions. These opportunities have increased in recent decades, largely through judicial interpretation of various constitutional and statutory provisions.

Forms of review in criminal cases include **trial *de novo***, **appeal of right**, **discretionary review**, and **postconviction relief**. Trial *de novo* occurs when a trial court of general jurisdiction reviews a conviction rendered by a court of limited jurisdiction. Appeal of right, the most common form of appeal, refers to an appellate court's review of a criminal conviction rendered by a trial court of general jurisdiction. A defendant whose conviction is affirmed on appeal may seek further review by a higher court by petitioning for discretionary review. Finally, a defendant confined to prison may seek additional review of his or her conviction or sentence by applying for a **writ of habeas corpus** or seeking another form of postconviction relief. The writ of habeas corpus allows a court of competent jurisdiction to review the legality of a prisoner's confinement. This device permits prisoners to raise a variety of legal issues in attacking their convictions and sentences. Each mechanism plays an important part in determining cases that move beyond the trial stage of the criminal process. In addition to correcting errors made by lower courts, appeals allow higher courts to refine and standardize both the substantive and procedural law.

## Error Correction and Lawmaking Functions of Appellate Courts

Appellate courts perform dual functions in the criminal process: **error correction** and **lawmaking**. Most criminal appeals are reviewed by intermediate federal or state appellate courts, although in the less populous states, routine appeals are handled by the highest court of the state (see Figure 20.1). In these routine appeals, the primary function of appellate courts is correcting errors made by trial courts. Appellate review is designed to ensure that substantive justice has been accomplished under constitutional standards of due process of law. Because of gaps in the statutory law and the inevitable need to interpret both statutory and constitutional provisions, appellate courts in effect must "make law." This lawmaking function is more characteristic of the highest levels of courts than of intermediate appellate tribunals.

| | |
|---|---|
| **Florida Supreme Court** | The highest appellate court in the state, consisting of seven justices. Hears appeals from circuit courts where the death penalty has been imposed. May also review some decisions of the district courts of appeal. |
| ↑ | |
| **5 District Courts of Appeal** | The primary appellate courts. Hear appeals from circuit courts. Cases are decided by panels of three judges, and decisions are final in the great majority of cases. |
| ↑ | |
| **20 Circuit Courts** | The major trial courts. Conduct criminal trials by bench and jury. Convictions and sentences (other than where death penalty is imposed) may be appealed to the district courts of appeal. |
| ↑ | |
| **67 County Courts** | The minor trial courts. Conduct bench and jury trials in misdemeanor cases. Convictions and sentences may be appealed to the circuit courts. |

**FIGURE 20.1** Criminal Appeals in the Florida Court System.
Source: West's Fla. Stat. Ann. Const. Art. V. §§ 1–6; West's Fla. Stat. Ann. chs. 26, 34, 35.

## The Common-Law Background

**lawmaking** One of the principal functions of an appellate court; often referred to as the law development function.

Before the eighteenth century, there was no common-law right to appeal from a criminal conviction. On rare occasions, the Crown issued a writ of error to require a new trial, but there was no appeal in the modern sense. Indeed, the term "appeal" at common law had a very different usage from ours. At common law, appeal referred to an effort by a person convicted of treason to obtain a pardon from the Crown by accusing others of being accomplices to the treasonable act.

**writ of error** A writ issued by an appellate court for the purpose of correcting an error revealed in the record of a lower court proceeding.

In a landmark decision, the Court of King's Bench ruled in 1705 that a **writ of error** had to be issued where a person convicted of a misdemeanor made proper application for the writ. *Paty's Case*, 91 Eng. Rep. 431 (K.B. 1705). In cases of felony and treason, the writ of error continued to be discretionary, although after 1700 the courts became more liberal in their issuance of the writ. The writ of error was finally abolished when Parliament enacted the Criminal Appeal Act of 1907, giving defendants the right to appeal their convictions.

## Appeal of Right

The federal constitution makes no mention of the right to appeal from a criminal conviction, although some might argue that the right to appeal is implicit in the Due Process Clauses of the Fifth and Fourteenth Amendments. In 1894 the U.S. Supreme Court held that the federal constitution provides no right to appeal from a criminal conviction. *McKane v. Durston*, 153 U.S. 684, 14 S.Ct. 913, 38 L.Ed. 867 (1894). Referring to the 1894 decision, Justice (later Chief Justice) Rehnquist observed that "[w]hile no one would agree that the State may simply dispense with the trial stage of proceedings without a criminal defendant's consent, it is clear that the State need not provide any appeal at all." *Ross v. Moffitt*, 417 U.S. 600, 611, 94 S.Ct. 2437, 2444, 41 L.Ed.2d 341, 351 (1974). Given the recent expansion of the concept of due process, the Court might reconsider this holding but for the fact that federal and state statutes now allow criminal defendants to appeal their convictions and seek other forms of postconviction relief. Defendants convicted after entering a plea of not guilty are entitled under federal and state law to one appeal as a matter of right.

Appeals of right in federal criminal cases are heard by U.S. Courts of Appeals (circuit courts). State criminal appeals are heard by state supreme courts, by intermediate appellate courts, and—in Alabama, Oklahoma, Tennessee, and Texas—by specialized appellate courts that hear only criminal appeals. Beyond these appeals of right, opportunities exist for defendants to have their cases reviewed by the highest state courts and the U.S. Supreme Court, which may review convictions by issuing **writs of certiorari**.

Most states that allow the death penalty provide for automatic appeals of death sentences to their highest court. In such cases the defendant does not have to file an appeal; the process begins automatically.

A party who takes an appeal of right is called the **appellant**; the party against whom the appeal is taken is the **appellee**. A party who seeks further review is referred to as the **petitioner**; the other party is designated the **respondent**.

## What Defendants May Challenge on Appeal

In a direct appeal from a criminal conviction, a defendant may challenge any act of the trial court objected to by the defendant during the pretrial, trial, or posttrial phases of the defendant's case. Irrespective of whether an objection was made in the trial court, a defendant may challenge the trial court's jurisdiction and those trial court actions or rulings considered to be **fundamental errors**. Appellate courts take different approaches to how serious an error must be to be classified as fundamental. Essentially, the courts will deem an error to be fundamental if it undermines confidence in the integrity of the criminal proceeding. When the defendant has been convicted of a capital crime, courts are more liberal in reviewing errors first challenged at the appellate stage. Indeed, the U.S. Supreme Court has said that those fundamental errors not specifically challenged by the appellant should be corrected when a person's life is at stake. *Fisher v. United States*, 328 U.S. 463, 66 S.Ct. 1318, 90 L.Ed. 1382 (1946).

In practice, a defendant usually raises one to six major points on appeal as a basis for reversal of the trial court's judgment or sentence. Often these points are referred to as **assignments of error**. The most common assignments of error on direct appeal are claims that the trial court erred in its ruling in one or more of the following areas:

1. pretrial violations of the defendant's rights, particularly those rights guaranteed by the Fourth, Fifth, and Sixth Amendments to the federal constitution
2. procedural matters, especially trial court rulings admitting or excluding evidence
3. irregularities in the impaneling or conduct of the jury
4. failure to give jury instructions requested by the defendant, or giving instructions objected to by the defendant
5. prosecutorial misconduct such as improper remarks or arguments
6. sufficiency of the evidence to support a finding of the defendant's guilt beyond a reasonable doubt

---

**writs of certiorari** Order issued by an appellate court to grant discretionary review of a case decided by a lower court.

**appellant** The party that takes an appeal to a higher court.

**appellee** The party against whom an appeal is taken.

**petitioner** A party who brings a petition before a court of law.

**respondent** A party asked to respond to a lawsuit or writ.

**fundamental errors** Errors in a judicial proceeding that adversely affect the substantial rights of the accused.

**assignments of error** A written presentation to an appellate court identifying the points that the appellant claims constitute errors made by the lower tribunal.

7. interpretations of statutes or ordinances
8. the legality and, in some jurisdictions, the reasonableness of the sentence imposed
9. jury selection, deliberation, and misconduct
10. the voluntariness of a guilty plea

## The Doctrine of Harmless Error

Although appellate review is designed to correct errors that occur before, during, or after trial, not all errors necessitate reversal. To obtain reversal of a judgment, the appellant must generally show that some prejudice resulted from the error and that the outcome of the trial or the sentence imposed would probably have been different in the absence of the error. Although specific standards vary among jurisdictions, all appellate courts operate on the principle that reversal is required only when substantial, as distinct from merely technical, errors are found in the record. This approach is illustrated by a provision of the California constitution that permits reversal on appeal only to prevent a **miscarriage of justice**. The California Supreme Court has interpreted this standard as follows: [A] "miscarriage of justice" should be declared only when the court, after an examination of the entire cause, including the evidence, is of the opinion that it is reasonably probable that a result more favorable to the appealing party would have been reached in the absence of the error. *People v. Watson*, 299 P.2d 243, 254 (Cal. 1956).

> **miscarriage of justice** Decision of a court that is inconsistent with the substantial rights of a party to a case.

Appellate courts frequently find that technical errors cited by appellants are harmless and do not merit a reversal; however, the U.S. Supreme Court has imposed a strict standard on the finding of harmless error. Where an error at trial involves provisions of the federal constitution, the Supreme Court has said that appellate courts must find beyond a reasonable doubt that the error was harmless if they are to affirm the trial court. *Chapman v. California*, 386 U.S. 18, 87 S.Ct. 824, 17 L.Ed.2d 705 (1967).

> **doctrine of harmless error** An error that does not affect a party's substantive rights or the case's outcome.

The **doctrine of harmless error** is subject to certain qualifications. For example, appellate courts generally do not consider each error at trial in isolation. Rather,

---

**JURISPRUDENCE**

*Chapman v. California*, 386 U.S. 18, 87 S.Ct. 824, 17 L.Ed.2d 705 (1967)

Ruth Elizabeth Chapman and Thomas LeRoy Teale were convicted of robbery, kidnapping and murder. Chapman was sentenced to life in prison; Teale received a death sentence. Neither Chapman nor Teale testified at their trials. California law at that time allowed the prosecutor to comment on a defendant's decision not to testify. When Chapman refused to testify at her trial, the prosecutor commented extensively on that fact to the jury. The judge presiding over the trial informed members of the jury that they were free to draw their own conclusions from Chapman's decision not to take the stand. After Chapman's trial, but prior to her appeal, the U.S. Supreme Court

invalidated the law allowing prosecutors to comment on a defendant's decision not to testify. Nevertheless, the California Supreme Court upheld Chapman's conviction on the basis of the harmless error doctrine. The U.S. Supreme Court reversed Chapman's conviction. The Court, speaking through Justice Black, held in order for an error to be harmless, the state "must be able to demonstrate beyond a reasonable doubt" that the error was in fact harmless. In this particular case, the Court held that the state was unable to establish beyond a reasonable doubt that the prosecutor's "repetitive comments to the jury, and the trial court's instruction . . . did not contribute to the convictions." As a result, Chapman's conviction was vacated and the case was remanded for a new trial.

they often consider the cumulative effect of a series of errors. Thus, an appellant might secure reversal of a conviction where the trial was replete with error, even though each particular error might be considered harmless by itself.

## When an Appeal May Be Taken by a Defendant

Generally, only a defendant who has pled not guilty has the right to appeal, and that appeal must wait until the defendant has been convicted and sentenced. However, there are some instances in which courts permit other appeals by defendants. For example, an order modifying or revoking probation is usually appealable.

Typically, a defendant who pleads guilty may raise on appeal only those issues relating to the trial court jurisdiction, the voluntariness of the guilty plea, and the legality of the sentence imposed. Even then, an appellate court may refuse to review these aspects of a case, other than the issue of jurisdiction, unless the trial court has refused the defendant's request to withdraw the plea of guilty.

Federal Rule of Criminal Procedure 11(a)(2) provides, "With the consent of the court and the government, a defendant may enter a conditional plea of guilty or *nolo contendere*, reserving in writing the right to have an appellate court review an adverse determination of a specified pretrial motion. A defendant who prevails on appeal may then withdraw the plea."

Some state jurisdictions also permit a defendant to plead *nolo contendere* or guilty and reserve the right to appeal a specific ruling of the trial court. See, for example, Fla. Stat. § 924.051. Defendants who unsuccessfully employ a constitutional defense frequently rely on this procedure. For instance, a defendant may file a pretrial motion to suppress certain evidence on the ground that it was obtained in violation of the Fourth Amendment, or a motion challenging the legal sufficiency of the charging document or constitutionality of a controlling statute. If the trial judge denies the motion, the defendant can plead *nolo contendere*, reserving the right to appeal that specific point of law. Generally the point reserved must be one that would be dispositive of the appeal.

## Appeals by the Prosecution

Early rulings by American state courts uniformly denied state governments the right to appeal acquittals of criminal defendants. The U.S. Supreme Court adopted this position in 1892, when it ruled that the federal government had no right to appeal an acquittal. *United States v. Sanges*, 144 U.S. 310, 12 S.Ct. 609, 36 L.Ed. 445 (1892). This prohibition is sensible inasmuch as the Double Jeopardy Clause of the Fifth Amendment (applicable to the states through the Fourteenth Amendment) prohibits a defendant who has been acquitted from being tried again for the same offense.

Texas law makes the following provisions regarding the prosecution's right to appeal:

(a) The state is entitled to appeal an order of a court in a criminal case if the order:

    (1) dismisses an indictment, information, or complaint or any portion of an indictment, information, or complaint;

    (2) arrests or modifies a judgment;

    (3) grants a new trial;

    (4) sustains a claim of former jeopardy;

    (5) grants a motion to suppress evidence, a confession, or an admission, if jeopardy has not attached in the case and if the prosecuting attorney certifies to

the trial court that the appeal is not taken for the purpose of delay and that the evidence, confession, or admission is of substantial importance in the case;

(6) is issued under Chapter 64 [refers to orders concerning DNA testing].

(b) The state is entitled to appeal a sentence in a case on the ground that the sentence is illegal.

(c) The state is entitled to appeal a ruling on a question of law if the defendant is convicted in the case and appeals the judgment. . . .

(d) The state is entitled to appeal an order granting relief to an applicant for a writ of habeas corpus. . . .

Vernon's Tex. Code Crim. Proc. Art. 44.01.

Either by statute or rule of court, most states afford similar opportunities for appeals by the prosecution. Similarly, 18 U.S.C.A. § 3731 permits the federal government to appeal an order of a federal district court (a) dismissing an indictment, (b) granting a new trial after judgment or verdict, (c) releasing a defendant before trial or after conviction, or (d) suppressing evidence or requiring the return of seized property before the time that the defendant is put in jeopardy. Both the government and the defendant have the right to appeal from a sentence imposed in violation of law, one that results from an erroneous application of a sentencing guideline, or one that is imposed by the court in violation of the terms of a plea agreement. Appeals by the prosecution from sentencing require prior approval by the office of the Attorney General or Solicitor General. 18 U.S.C.A. §§ 3742(a) and (b).

The constitutional proscription of double jeopardy does not prevent appeals by the prosecutor of pretrial orders because jeopardy does not apply before the impaneling of a jury or the taking of evidence in a nonjury trial. *Crist v. Bretz*, 437 U.S. 28, 98 S.Ct. 2156, 57 L.Ed.2d 24 (1978); *Serfass v. United States*, 420 U.S. 377, 95 S.Ct. 1055, 43 L.Ed.2d 265 (1975).

## Trial *de Novo* in Minor Misdemeanor Cases

Most criminal appeals are heard "on the record." This means that the appellate court is asked to scrutinize the official record of the pretrial, trial, and posttrial proceedings for procedural errors that would require reversal of the judgment. Many misdemeanor cases are tried in local courts that are not courts of record; therefore, no record of the proceedings is available for review. Most of these involve summary justice. Trial is before a judge or magistrate without a jury in what is commonly called a bench trial. Counsel is rarely present, and frequently the only witnesses for the prosecution are police officers. The defendant may or may not choose to testify. Yet persons convicted of misdemeanors are generally entitled to an appeal by law. Where no record has been made of the proceedings, a trial *de novo* (literally, a "new trial") is held in a trial court of superior jurisdiction. In many instances, persons convicted at trial *de novo* may take an appeal to a higher court, but further review of such cases is generally discretionary.

## Discretionary Review

A defendant whose conviction has been sustained by an intermediate appellate court may petition a court of last resort for discretionary review. In the U.S. Supreme Court and most state supreme courts, discretionary review occurs through the grant of a writ of certiorari. Rule 13 of the Rules of the U.S. Supreme Court states that a "petition for a writ of certiorari . . . shall be in time when it is filed . . . within 90 days after the entry of the judgment" of the lower court. The highest court in each state (usually the state supreme court) may entertain petitions if they are filed within the time prescribed by the court's rules, usually thirty days after the intermediate appellate court enters its decision.

"Cert petitions," as they are commonly called, are granted at the discretion of the reviewing court. In deciding whether to exercise its discretion, the U.S. Supreme Court evaluates whether a **substantial federal question** is involved. If so, the Court is then interested in whether the petitioner has exhausted all other remedies available. In deciding whether to grant certiorari, the Court follows the **rule of four**, meaning that at least four of the nine justices must vote to place a case on the docket.

In determining whether to grant review, the high state appellate tribunals usually have unlimited discretion. The U.S. Supreme Court's rule of four serves as a model for some state supreme courts; however, others are guided by formal or informal rules in determining whether to "grant cert." Among the criteria frequently employed are whether the intermediate appellate court's decision conflicts with a decision of another intermediate court or the supreme court, is without authoritative precedent, or departs from the essential requirements of the law.

**substantial federal question** A significant legal question pertaining to the U.S. Constitution or a federal statute, treaty, regulation, or judicial interpretation of any of the foregoing.

**rule of four** U.S. Supreme Court rule whereby the Court grants certiorari only on the agreement of at least four justices.

## The Appellate Process

To the layperson, the jurisdictional requirements and procedures of appellate courts appear complex. Although these procedures vary in detail, they essentially follow the same basic path. In some instances the defendant must file a motion for a new trial before making an appeal. This is often *a pro forma* measure, but it affords the trial judge an opportunity to review the defendant's claim of error and award a new trial if necessary.

### Release of Defendant on Bail Pending Appeal

Federal and state statutes and rules of court usually specify criteria for the release of a convicted defendant pending appeal. Admission to bail after conviction is not a matter of right, but instead is at the discretion of the trial court. A defendant wanting to appeal is not aided by a presumption in favor of release on bail. Principally, the trial judge attempts to determine whether an appeal is taken in good faith and whether it presents a debatable point of law for appellate review. An appeal must not be frivolous or taken for the purpose of delay. *Birge v. State*, 230 S.E.2d 895 (Ga. 1976).

Trial judges typically consider several factors in exercising their discretion to grant or deny bail pending appeal. Among those factors are the defendant's habits and respect for the law, family and community ties, and the severity of punishment imposed. If the term of imprisonment imposed is relatively short, the court may also consider whether the denial of bail would render the defendant's right to appeal meaningless. Rules of criminal procedure generally provide for prompt appellate review of a decision denying bail to a convicted defendant or setting that bail unreasonably high. Absent such procedures, a defendant may seek a writ of habeas corpus.

If the state takes an appeal, the defendant is often released on personal recognizance during the **pendency of the appeal**—that is, while the appeal is being decided. Most states provide for the release of defendants pending an appeal by the prosecution. In Illinois, for example, "a defendant shall not be held in jail or to bail during the pendency of an appeal by the State . . . unless there are compelling reasons for his continued detention or being held to bail." Ill. Sup. Ct. Rule 604(a)(3).

**pendency of the appeal** The period after an appeal is filed but before the appeal is adjudicated.

# Release of the Defendant in Federal Appeals

Under the Federal Bail Reform Act of 1966 (repealed in 1984), the defendant in a federal court was entitled to bail unless there was "reason to believe that no one or more conditions of release will reasonably assure that the person will not flee, or pose a danger to any other person or any other community." The **Bail Reform Act of 1984**, 18 U.S.C.A. §§ 3141–3150, reversed that presumption of entitlement and allows federal judges to detain a criminal defendant without bail if the defendant poses a special threat to community safety or a high risk of flight.

Under the Bail Reform Act, the defendant has the burden of proving an entitlement to bail based on criteria specified in the law. Before granting bail pending appeal, the court must find:

1. that the defendant is not likely to flee or pose a danger to the safety of any other person or the community if released;
2. that the appeal is not for the purpose of delay;
3. that the appeal raises a substantial question of law or fact; and
4. that if that substantial question is determined favorably to defendant on appeal, that decision is likely to result in reversal or an order for a new trial of all counts on which imprisonment has been imposed. *United States v. Miller*, 753 F.2d 19, 24 (3rd Cir. 1985).

In an earlier topic, we pointed out that the federal government can take an appeal from certain pretrial orders under 18 U.S.C.A. § 3731 or from sentencing or plea agreement violations under 18 U.S.C.A. § 3742(b). Where an appeal is taken under § 3731, the Bail Reform Act ordinarily governs release of the defendant pending the appeal. If the government's appeal is taken under § 3742 and the defendant has been sentenced to imprisonment, the defendant is ordinarily not released pending the appeal.

# Right to Counsel on Appeal

As we pointed out in Chapter 17, the U.S. Supreme Court has interpreted the Constitution to require that indigent defendants be furnished assistance of counsel in criminal prosecutions. To what extent does the Constitution require the appointment of counsel for indigent defendants who appeal their convictions to higher courts? In *Douglas v. California*, 372 U.S. 353, 83 S.Ct. 814, 9 L.Ed.2d 811 (1963), the Supreme Court said that states must provide counsel to indigent persons convicted of felonies who exercise their statutory right to appeal. In *Ross v. Moffitt*, 417 U.S. 600, 94 S.Ct. 2437, 41 L.Ed.2d 341 (1974), however, the Supreme Court held that a state's failure to provide counsel to an indigent defendant seeking discretionary review in the state and federal supreme courts did not violate due process or equal protection. Thus, the government must provide counsel as a matter of course when defendants have a statutory right to be heard in an appellate court. At later stages of the appeals process, there is no such requirement.

The Supreme Court's decision in *Douglas v. California* produced a tremendous increase in appellate caseloads. Providing counsel at public expense aggravated the problem of **frivolous appeals** (that is, appeals lacking any arguable basis for reversal). In such cases, appointed counsel often attempt to withdraw.

In *Anders v. California*, 386 U.S. 738, 87 S.Ct. 1396, 18 L.Ed.2d 493 (1967), the Supreme Court invalidated a state rule that allowed appointed counsel to withdraw by merely stating that an appeal had no merit. Reasoning that the right to counsel

**Bail Reform Act of 1984** An act that provides that a defendant charged with a federal crime may be denied bail if the prosecution can show that the defendant poses a threat to public safety.

**frivolous appeals** Appeals wholly lacking in legal merit.

**Steps in the Appellate Process**

Usually the appellate process in a criminal appeal will take between nine and twelve months, depending on whether counsel must seek extensions of permitted times for record preparation and briefing, whether the case is orally argued, and the court's caseload. The following describes the usual steps in a direct appeal of right to a state or federal appellate court.

1. **Filing a notice of appeal by appellant**, usually with the clerk of a lower court, with a copy served on the opposing party.

2. **Filing a record of lower court proceedings**, and, where there has been a trial, evidentiary exhibits, transcript of trial testimony, and the judge's instructions to the jury. Although this is a function of the court reporter and clerk of the lower court, the appellant is responsible for ensuring that the record is properly completed and filed in the appellate court.

3. **Filing by the appellant of an initial brief** raising the issues to be argued, supported by citations to the record on appeal and relevant constitutional provisions, statutes, and judicial decisions.

4. **Filing of motions** by the appellant (and sometimes the appellee) seeking interim forms of relief such as bail reductions, stay orders, extensions of time requirements for filing briefs, continuances of oral arguments, supplementing the record on appeal, striking sections of briefs, and so forth.

5. **Rulings** by the appellate court on motions.

6. **Filing by the appellant of an application for oral argument,** if desired.

7. **Filing by the appellee of an answer brief** refuting the appellant's arguments, likewise supported by citations to the record on appeal and relevant constitutional provisions, statutes, and judicial decisions.

8. **Filing by the appellee of an application for oral argument,** if desired and if not already requested by the appellant.

9. **Filing by the appellant of a brief in reply** to the appellee's answer brief.

10. **Review of the record and briefs by the judges** who are assigned to hear and decide the appeal.

11. **Oral argument by counsel**, where requested by counsel and granted by the court.

12. **Conference of judges** assigned to decide the case, often resulting in a tentative decision and assignment of a judge to prepare the court's decision.

13. **Additional research** by the appellate court's staff attorneys, where necessary.

14. **Drafting of proposed decision** by the assigned judge and circulation of it to remaining judges who have participated in the case, followed by their agreement with the proposed decision or by their offering a dissenting or concurring opinion.

15. **Issuance of the court's decision** by the clerk of the appellate court and circulation of that decision to counsel for the parties.

16. **Motion by the losing party for a rehearing** or issuance of a clarifying decision, usually based on an allegation of the court's having overlooked some significant fact or point of law, followed by the court's ruling on the motion.

17. **Motion for *en banc* rehearing**, assuming the case was heard by fewer than all judges on the court.

18. **Ruling on motion for *en banc* review**. If granted, the court proceeds to rehear the case *en banc* and issues a decision by all judges who participate.

19. **Issuance of mandate.** After time for motions for rehearing to be filed, and, if granted, disposed of, the appellate court issues a mandate commanding the court's decision be followed. This is served on counsel and filed in the lower court.

© *Cengage Learning*

meant the right to have an effective advocate on appeal, the Court held that appointed counsel could withdraw only after submitting a brief claiming that the appeal was wholly frivolous and referring to any arguable issues. Recently, California developed a new procedure for handling criminal appeals by indigents. An appointed attorney may now write a "no-merit brief" summarizing the procedural and factual history of the case. The court orders a briefing by counsel only if it finds arguable

## JURISPRUDENCE

*Douglas v. California*, 372 U.S. 353, 83 S.Ct. 814, 9 L.Ed.2d 811 (1963)

William Douglas and his codefendant, Bennie Will Meyes, were tried jointly and convicted on thirteen various felonies. At trial they were represented by the public defender's office. Douglas requested appointed counsel for his appeal by right to the state appellate court. The trial court, in accordance with the relevant state rule of criminal procedure, reviewed the record and concluded that the appointment of counsel would neither serve

Douglas's interests nor be "helpful to the appellate court." As a result, Douglas's appeal was heard without the assistance of counsel and his conviction was affirmed. The U.S. Supreme Court held that "where the merits of the one and only appeal an indigent has as of right [are] decided without [the] benefit of counsel in a state criminal case, there has been a discrimination between the rich and the poor which violates the Fourteenth Amendment." As a result, the judgment was vacated and the case remanded to the lower court.

issues. Therefore, before rejecting the appeal, both counsel and the court have to find the appeal lacking in arguable issues. In January 2000, in *Smith v. Robbins*, 528 U.S. 259, 120 S.Ct. 746, 145 L.Ed.2d 756, the U.S. Supreme Court ruled that such "no-merit brief" procedure satisfies the requirements of *Anders v. California*. The basic *Anders* approach is followed in most jurisdictions, and when an appellate court accepts an **Anders brief**, it usually notifies the defendant of the appointed counsel's withdrawal and permits the defendant to file a memorandum pointing to any claim of error. With the proliferation of criminal appeals by indigent defendants, the *Anders* brief has become a commonplace element of appellate procedure.

**Anders brief** A law brief submitted to an appellate court by publicly appointed defense counsel in which counsel explains that the defendant's appeal is nonmeritorious and requests release from further representation of the defendant.

## Self-Representation on Appeal

In Chapter 17 we pointed out that it is incumbent on a trial judge to allow self-representation by a defendant who voluntarily and intelligently elects to proceed in the trial court without counsel. *Faretta v. California*, 422 U.S. 806, 95 S.Ct. 2525, 45 L.Ed.2d 562 (1975). We also pointed out in Chapter 18 that in 2008 the Supreme Court held that a trial judge is not required to allow a minimally competent defendant to elect self-representation at trial. *Indiana v. Edwards*, 554 U.S. 164, 128 S.Ct. 2379, 171 L.Ed.2d 345 (2008).

Many appellate courts allow convicted defendants to file *pro se* petitions for habeas corpus but generally do not allow defendants to handle direct appeals on a *pro se* basis. After Salvador Martinez represented himself before a trial court, the California courts denied him the right to represent himself before the California Court of Appeal. He obtained review in the U.S. Supreme Court, and on January 12, 2000, the Court upheld California's denial of his right to handle his appeal without counsel. The Court observed that although the Sixth Amendment to the Constitution provides a basis for self-representation at the trial level, it does not include any right to appeal. The Court pointed to significant differences between the trial and appellate stages of a criminal proceeding and emphasized the need for a defendant to have counsel when attempting to overturn a criminal conviction. The Court recognized that states are free to determine whether to allow a defendant to proceed in an appellate court without counsel; nevertheless, it held that a criminal defendant does not have the right under the U.S. Constitution to elect self-representation on a direct appeal from a judgment of conviction. *Martinez v. California Court of Appeal*, 528 U.S. 152, 120 S.Ct. 684, 145 L.Ed.2d 597 (2000).

## Filing the Appeal

Once the appellant has determined the correct forum for an appeal or a petition for discretionary review, the process is governed by federal or state rules of appellate procedure. The notice of appeal or petition for review must be filed in the appropriate court within a specified period of time. The time requirement tends to be strictly enforced because this notice or petition confers jurisdiction on the appellate court to act on the case.

**Federal Rules of Appellate Procedure** Rules of procedure governing the practice of law before the U.S. courts of appeals.

Rule 4(b) of the **Federal Rules of Appellate Procedure** provides that an appeal by a defendant from a judgment and sentence in a federal district court must be filed within ten days after the entry of the judgment or the filing of the government's notice of appeal. Under certain circumstances the time period may be extended, but the extension cannot exceed an additional thirty days. If a defendant makes a timely motion for judgment of acquittal for a new trial or for arrest of a judgment, then the **notice of appeal** must be filed within ten days after the trial court enters an order disposing of such motion(s). When an appeal by the government is authorized by statute, the notice of appeal must be filed within thirty days after the entry of judgment.

**notice of appeal** Document filed notifying an appellate court of an appeal from a judgment of a lower court.

In state courts, an aggrieved party usually has thirty days after entry of judgment and sentence to file an appeal. For example, Maryland requires that the notice of appeal must be filed within thirty days after the trial court has entered its judgment or denied a motion for a new trial. Md. Rules, Rule 8-202(a)(b). The filing of a notice of appeal must be accompanied by the payment of a required filing fee, unless the appellant is represented by the public defender's office or other counsel assigned by any other legal services organization that accepts as clients only those persons meeting the financial eligibility criteria established by the Federal Legal Services Corporation or other appropriate governmental agency. Md. Rules, Rule 8-201(b).

## Motions

During the early stages of the appellate process, counsel for both parties frequently file motions in the appellate court. Some motions address substantive issues—for example, a motion asserting legal grounds to dismiss the appeal. More commonly, counsel use motions to draw the court's immediate attention to procedural matters outside the routine of the appellate process. For example, counsel may request additional time to meet deadlines for filing petitions and briefs. Occasionally, counsel will move for expedited consideration of an appeal. By appropriate motions, separate appeals may be consolidated and multiple appeals may be severed. Ordinarily, filing an appeal does not stay the judgment or sentence. However, on a showing of good cause, an appellate court may stay a judgment or sentence pending resolution of the appeal.

After a notice of appeal or a petition for discretionary review has been filed, a series of procedural steps are set in motion. It is incumbent on the appellant or petitioner to have the clerk of the trial court forward to the appellate tribunal certified copies of pertinent records and transcripts of testimony relevant to the issues to be raised on appeal. Beyond this, procedures vary somewhat, depending largely on whether the appeal is one of right or whether the defendant is seeking discretionary relief.

## Submission of Briefs by Counsel

**brief** A document filed by a party to a lawsuit to convince the court of the merits of that party's case.

In an appeal of right, the appellant files a **brief** summarizing the legal posture and the factual background of the case in the lower tribunal, the issues on appeal, and the legal authorities that support a reversal of the trial court's rulings. Briefs are the principal instruments used to persuade the appellate court to reverse, affirm, or modify the decision being appealed. They are usually heavily laden with citations to constitutional provisions, statutes, and court decisions regarded as persuasive by the advocates. The extent of background information contained in the briefs depends on the points to be presented to the appellate court. The appellee is permitted to respond to the appellant's contentions by filing an **answer brief**, and the appellant is usually permitted a **reply brief**. The whole process resembles the order of a classroom debate, where the affirmative presents its case, followed by the negative, and then by a rebuttal by the affirmative.

> **answer brief** The appellee's written response to the appellant's law brief filed in an appellate court.
>
> **reply brief** A brief submitted by an appellant in response to an appellee's answer brief.

Where a petitioner seeks discretionary review, the appellate court must first decide whether to accept or deny the request to take jurisdiction. If the court determines to proceed on the petition, it will order all affected parties to furnish the court a written response. As in an appeal of right, often the petitioner is permitted to file a reply to that response. The petition and response may be supplemented by such briefs as the court requires.

The format and submission of briefs must adhere closely to the requirements of the particular jurisdiction. Counsel must always furnish copies of briefs and other materials to their adversaries.

## Oral Argument

> **oral argument** Verbal presentation made to an appellate court in an attempt to persuade the court to affirm, reverse, or modify a lower court decision.

After briefs have been submitted and reviewed by the appellate court, an **oral argument** may be held where counsel for both parties appear. Typically, appellate courts conduct oral arguments in about half the cases they decide. (In the federal courts, the rate may be closer to 25 percent.) During oral arguments, counsel for both parties summarize their positions orally and then respond to questions from the bench. The trend is for oral argument to be less structured and more of a dialogue between court and counsel.

The appellate rules of courts in many jurisdictions set out the time allowed for oral argument. For example, as Rule 24 of the Rhode Island Rules of Appellate Procedure stipulates, "Counsel on each side will be allowed a period not in excess of thirty minutes for presentation of argument, and a period not in excess of ten minutes will be allowed for the moving party for reply." Rule 28 of the U.S. Supreme Court provides, "Oral argument should emphasize and clarify the written arguments in the briefs on the merits. Counsel should assume that all Justices have read the briefs before oral argument." It further states, "Unless the Court directs otherwise, each side is allowed one-half hour for argument." Rule 34(d) of the U.S. Court of Appeals for the Fourth Circuit allows either fifteen or twenty minutes, depending on the type of appeal. Rather than stipulating a specific time, rules in some federal and state jurisdictions provide that the appellate court will specify the times for oral argument on the court calendar. Most state appellate courts allow twenty or thirty minutes for oral argument, but the court always reserves the right to shorten or lengthen the time allocated.

## The Judicial Conference

> **judicial conference** A meeting of judges to deliberate on the disposition of a case.

Appellate judges customarily confer about the disposition of appeals. The **judicial conference** is regarded as an essential part of the collegial process that distinguishes the appellate role from that of the trial court. If there has been oral argument, it is common for the panel of judges that heard the case to confer shortly thereafter. At that time the panel frequently attempts to determine the disposition of the appeal but, in some instances, finds it necessary to further canvass the record or call on counsel or the court's own staff lawyers for additional legal research. Where there has been no oral argument, the panel of judges assigned to the case usually confers after each judge has reviewed the briefs, pertinent records, and results of any research assignments given to the court's legal staff.

## Judgment of the Court

Essentially, an appellate court has three options in addressing a case before it. First, it may dismiss the appeal. This is uncommon in appeals of right unless the appeal is untimely. Dismissal is more common in cases of discretionary review. For example, the U.S. Supreme Court will sometimes dismiss a petition for certiorari as having been improvidently granted even after the case has been fully argued. When an appeal or cert petition is dismissed, the judgment of the lower court remains undisturbed. The second option of the appellate court is to **affirm** the decision being reviewed, which preserves the judgment of the lower court. The third option is to **reverse** the judgment of the lower court. A reversal is usually accompanied by an order to **remand** the case to the lower court for further proceedings consistent with the higher court's opinion. In the criminal context, this may mean the defendant receives a new trial or new sentencing hearing. When a court of last resort remands a case to an intermediate appellate court, the latter must reconsider the case based on the higher court's decision.

## Appellate Court Opinions

After an appellate court has arrived at a decision, the court will issue an opinion announcing its decision. Some opinions simply announce the court's decision; others are quite lengthy in considering the arguments of counsel and articulating the reasons for the court's decision. Opinions are generally prepared by an individual judge or justice. If responsibility for the preparation of an opinion has not been previously given to one judge, that responsibility is usually assigned at conference by the senior judge or the senior judge voting with the majority of the panel.

There are two basic types of appellate court opinions: *per curiam* and signed. A ***per curiam* opinion** represents the appellate court as a whole; it is not attributed to any individual judge or group of judges on the court. More commonly the decision of the appellate court is announced in an **opinion of the court** authored by one judge and joined by other judges constituting a majority. A judge who disagrees with the decision of the court may write a **dissenting opinion**. A judge who agrees with the court's decision but wants to address or emphasize certain arguments not addressed or emphasized in the opinion of the court may write a separate **concurring opinion**. Sometimes, a separate opinion is listed as **concurring in the judgment** only, meaning that it supports the decision of the court but for reasons other than those articulated in the court's opinion.

## Publication of Appellate Decisions

Most decisions of appellate courts in America are published in books known as **reporters**. The publication of appellate decisions plays an important role in developing the law because judges and lawyers regularly consult the case reporters for

---

**affirm** To uphold, ratify, or approve.

**reverse** To set aside a decision on appeal.

**remand** To send back, usually with instructions.

***per curiam* opinion** An opinion rendered "by the court," as distinct from one attributed to one or more judges.

**opinion of the court** The opinion expressing the judgment and reasoning of the court, representing the views of at least a majority of the judges participating in a decision.

**dissenting opinion** An opinion rendered by a judge disavowing or disagreeing with the decision of a collegial court.

**concurring opinion** An opinion handed down by a judge that supports the judgment of the court but often does so through different reasoning.

**concurring in the judgment** Issuance of an opinion by a judge or justice that agrees with the judgment of an appellate court without agreeing with the court's reasoning process.

**reporters** Books containing judicial decisions and accompanying opinions.

guidance in pending cases. Today, it is common for appellate opinions to become immediately available via the Internet. The U.S. Supreme Court, each of the federal circuits, and most state appellate courts maintain websites from which opinions are downloadable at no cost. (Access to published opinions, through both electronic and traditional means, is discussed in some detail in Appendix A.)

## Motions for Rehearing

**motion for rehearing** A formal request made to a court of law to convene another hearing in a case in which the court has already ruled.

**en banc rehearing** A hearing in an appellate court in which all or a substantial number of the judges assigned to that court participate.

Rules of appellate procedure uniformly permit the filing of a motion asking the appellate court to reconsider its decision in a given case. A **motion for rehearing** is designed to address some misstatement of material fact in the court's opinion or to direct the court's attention to an overlooked or misapprehended proposition of law. In the U.S. Courts of Appeals and in many state appellate courts, where cases are decided by panels of judges, a party may request that all judges (or a majority of the judges in appellate courts consisting of a large number of judges) of the court participate in an ***en banc* rehearing**. The likelihood of an appellate court's granting a motion for *en banc* rehearing is greater when there are conflicting opinions between or among panels of judges within the court. Appellate courts view many motions for rehearing as little more than attempts by dissatisfied parties to have another chance to persuade the court of their position. Accordingly, motions for rehearing are seldom granted.

## Postconviction Relief

Normally, an appeal of a lower court decision must be made in a timely manner, usually within thirty days after that court's judgment or sentence. Petitions for certiorari (or other forms of discretionary review) are also subject to time limits. Yet incarcerated criminals may seek review of their convictions long after their rights to appeal have been exhausted or expired by means of a mechanism known as the writ of habeas corpus. It is available in the federal courts and in all fifty state judicial systems.

"Habeas corpus" is a Latin term meaning "you have the body." In law, it refers to a writ issued by a court to a person who is holding another in custody, requiring that the former show cause for holding the latter. Habeas corpus has roots deep in the common law. Blackstone called it "the most celebrated writ in the English law." 3 W. Blackstone, *Commentaries* 129. The framers of the American Constitution explicitly recognized habeas corpus as a fundamental right of citizens by declaring that "[t]he Privilege of the Writ of Habeas Corpus shall not be suspended unless when in Cases of Rebellion or Invasion the public Safety may require it." U.S. Const., Art. 1, Sec. 9. Only once in our history, during the Civil War, was the writ of habeas corpus suspended throughout the federal courts. This was accomplished via an executive order issued by President Lincoln in November 1862 and a subsequent act of Congress in March 1863. After hostilities had ceased, this thoroughgoing suspension of habeas corpus was declared unconstitutional by the Supreme Court. *Ex parte Milligan*, 71 U.S. (4 Wall.) 2, 18 L.Ed. 281 (1866).

**federal habeas corpus review** Review of a state criminal trial by a federal district court on a writ of habeas corpus after the defendant has been convicted, has been incarcerated, and has exhausted appellate remedies in the state courts.

## Challenging State Court Convictions in Federal Court

The U.S. Supreme Court can review only a minute proportion of the thousands of petitions for certiorari through which persons convicted in state courts challenge their convictions on federal constitutional grounds. In recent decades, **federal habeas corpus review** of state criminal convictions has become a common form of appellate procedure. It has also greatly multiplied the opportunities for persons convicted of state offenses to obtain relief. Consequently, it has become the focus of considerable controversy.

The Judiciary Act of 1789, 1 Stat. 82 (1789), recognized the power of federal courts to issue writs of habeas corpus for federal prisoners only. In 1867 federal law was amended, 14 Stat. 385, 386, to allow federal courts to entertain habeas corpus petitions from state prisoners who allege that their incarceration violates provisions of the U.S. Constitution or federal statutes or treaties. The federal law on habeas corpus currently provides the following:

> The Supreme Court, a Justice thereof, a circuit judge, or a district court shall entertain an application for a writ of habeas corpus in behalf of a person in custody pursuant to the judgment of a State court only on the ground that he is in custody in violation of the Constitution or laws or treaties of the United States. 28 U.S.C.A. § 2254(a).

Before the twentieth century, the federal habeas corpus jurisdiction was seldom used to review state criminal convictions. When habeas corpus was granted, it was merely to ascertain that the state trial court had jurisdiction over the person being tried. In *Frank v. Mangum*, 237 U.S. 309, 35 S.Ct. 582, 59 L.Ed. 969 (1915), the Supreme Court broadened federal habeas corpus review to ensure that states supplied some "corrective process" whereby criminal defendants could seek to vindicate their federal constitutional rights. In 1953 the Court held that federal courts could use habeas corpus review to readjudicate federal constitutional issues that had been addressed in state court proceedings. *Brown v. Allen*, 344 U.S. 443, 73 S.Ct. 397, 97 L.Ed. 469 (1953).

Federal law had long provided that federal habeas corpus relief was available only to state prisoners who had exhausted all available remedies in the state courts. In 1963 the Supreme Court under Chief Justice Earl Warren held that a state prisoner did not have to take a direct appeal to the state supreme court to seek federal habeas corpus review. Nor was the prisoner barred from raising constitutional issues in federal court merely because the issues had not been raised on direct appeal in state courts. *Fay v. Noia*, 372 U.S. 391, 83 S.Ct. 822, 9 L.Ed.2d 837 (1963). The Warren Court also held that a petitioner could challenge a state conviction despite a failure to develop a material fact in state proceedings unless it was determined that the petitioner deliberately bypassed the opportunity to develop the fact in the state courts. *Townsend v. Sain*, 372 U.S. 293, 83 S.Ct. 745, 9 L.Ed.2d 770 (1963).

The Warren Court's efforts to broaden the availability of federal habeas corpus review coincided with its expansion of the constitutional rights of the accused. No doubt, the Court was initially reluctant to depend on state courts to implement these expanded rights, so it broadened the power of the federal district courts to review state criminal convictions. This resulted in numerous state convictions being overturned by the federal courts, often on Fourth or Fifth Amendment grounds. Indeed, many observers came to see state criminal trials merely as precursors to inevitable federal intervention.

## The Supreme Court Restricts Access to Federal Habeas Corpus

Growing criticism of federal court intervention, coupled with the increasing professionalism of the state judiciaries, led the Supreme Court to restrict access to federal habeas corpus relief during the 1970s, '80s, and '90s. The following are synopses of the most significant decisions of that period:

- *Stone v. Powell*, 428 U.S. 465, 96 S.Ct. 3037, 49 L.Ed.2d 1067 (1976). The Court held that state prisoners could not use federal habeas corpus hearings to challenge searches and seizures where they had been provided an opportunity for full and fair litigation of a Fourth Amendment claim in the state courts.

- *Engle v. Isaac*, 456 U.S. 107, 102 S.Ct. 1558, 71 L.Ed.2d 783 (1982). The Court refused to allow a state prisoner to use federal habeas corpus to challenge a questionable jury instruction to which he had failed to object during trial.

- *McCleskey v. Zant*, 499 U.S. 467, 111 S.Ct. 1454, 113 L.Ed.2d 517 (1991). The Court said that a death row inmate abused the writ of habeas corpus when he filed a second federal habeas corpus petition. The Court held that a state need not prove that a petitioner deliberately abandoned a constitutional claim in his or her first habeas corpus petition for the petitioner to be barred from raising the claim in a subsequent petition.

- *Keeney v. Tamayo-Reyes*, 504 U.S. 1, 112 S.Ct. 1715, 118 L.Ed.2d 318 (1992). The Court overturned precedent (*Townsend v. Sain*, supra) and held that a petitioner's failure to develop a claim in state court proceedings should be excused only if he or she can show that a fundamental miscarriage of justice would result from failure to hold a federal evidentiary hearing.

- *Brecht v. Abrahamson*, 507 U.S. 619, 113 S.Ct. 1710, 123 L.Ed.2d 353 (1993). The Court ruled that federal district courts may not overturn state convictions unless the petitioner can show "actual prejudice" from the errors cited in the habeas corpus petition. Previously, the state carried the burden of proving beyond a reasonable doubt that any constitutional error committed during or before trial was "harmless"—that is, not prejudicial to the defendant. *Brecht v. Abrahamson* had the effect of shifting the burden of proof from the state to the petitioner in a federal habeas corpus hearing.

The Supreme Court's decisions in *McCleskey v. Zant*, *Engle v. Isaac*, *Keeney v. Tamayo-Reyes* and *Brecht v. Abrahamson* came when many in Congress were calling for legislative restrictions on federal habeas corpus. Both the Supreme Court and Congress were responding to a widespread perception that state prisoners were being afforded excessive opportunities to challenge their convictions in federal courts. Indeed, some commentators questioned the need for federal postconviction review of state criminal cases altogether.

## Congress Modifies the Federal Habeas Corpus Procedure

On April 24, 1996, President Clinton signed into law the Antiterrorism and Effective Death Penalty Act of 1996. One provision of this statute curtails second habeas corpus petitions by state prisoners who have already filed such petitions in federal court. Under the new statute, any second or subsequent habeas petition must meet a particularly high standard and must pass through a gatekeeping function exercised by the U.S. Courts of Appeals. The grant or denial of an authorization by a court of appeals for an inmate to file a second or successive petition for habeas corpus in the district court is not appealable and is not subject to a petition for rehearing or for a writ of certiorari. 28 U.S.C.A. § 2244(b)(3).

In *Felker v. Turpin*, 518 U.S. 651, 116 S.Ct. 2333, 135 L.Ed.2d 827 (1996), an inmate awaiting execution in Georgia challenged the constitutionality of this provision, posing two constitutional objections: (1) that the new law amounted to an unconstitutional "suspension" of the writ of habeas corpus, and (2) that the prohibition against Supreme Court review of a circuit court's denial of permission to file a subsequent habeas petition is an unconstitutional interference with the Supreme Court's

**JURISPRUDENCE**

*Felker v. Turpin*, 518 U.S. 651, 116 S.Ct. 2333, 135 L.Ed.2d 827 (1996)

Ellis Wayne Felker was convicted of murder and sentenced to death in a Georgia state court. Felker appealed his conviction on a direct appeal, but was denied relief. Felker also sought and was denied relief in a federal habeas corpus proceeding. While Felker was awaiting execution, the Antiterrorism and Effective Death Penalty Act of 1996 was signed into law. The act requires "dismissal of a claim presented in a state prisoner's second or successive federal habeas application if the claim was also presented in a prior application." The Act also compels "dismissal of a claim that was not presented in a prior federal application, unless certain conditions apply. The Act also functions as a "gatekeeping mechanism, whereby the prospective applicant files in the court of appeals a motion for leave to file a second or successive habeas application in the district court, and a three-judge panel determines whether the application makes a prima facie showing that it satisfies" the Act's requirements.

Lastly, the Act declares that a panel's grant or denial of authorization to file "shall not be appealable and shall not be the subject of a petition for . . . writ of certiorari." As a result of these provisions, Felker filed a motion in a federal appeals court for leave to file a second federal habeas petition," which was denied based on the premise that "the grounds raised had not been presented in his first petition." After the appellate court's denial, Felker filed a petition before the Supreme Court for a writ of habeas corpus and certiorari. The Supreme Court held that the Act "does not violate the Constitution's Suspension Clause, which provides that '[t]he Privilege of the Writ of Habeas Corpus shall not be suspended'." The Court held that "the new restrictions on successive habeas petitions constituted a modified res judicata rule, a restraint on what is called . . . 'abuse of the writ'." Because Felker did not comply with the Act's requirements nor did he show "exceptional circumstances" in "justifying the issuance of the writ" of habeas corpus, the Court denied Felker's petition.

jurisdiction as defined in Article III of the Constitution. In a unanimous decision rendered less than one month after the case was argued, the Supreme Court rejected these challenges and upheld the statute. In a "saving construction" of the statute, the Court interpreted the law in such a way as to preserve the right of state prisoners to file habeas corpus petitions directly in the Supreme Court. However, the Court stated that it would exercise this jurisdiction only in "exceptional circumstances."

## Claims of Actual Innocence

In *Herrera v. Collins*, 506 U.S. 390, 113 S.Ct. 853, 122 L.Ed.2d 203 (1993), the Supreme Court held that a belated claim of innocence does not entitle a state prisoner on death row to a federal district court hearing before being executed. But two years later, in *Schlup v. Delo*, 513 U.S. 298, 115 S.Ct. 851, 130 L.Ed.2d 808 (1995), the Court mitigated somewhat the harshness of *Herrera v. Collins. In Schlup* the Court held that where claims of actual innocence are coupled with assertions of constitutional violations, in order to prevent a miscarriage of justice a federal court may grant habeas corpus relief that would normally be procedurally barred.

## Assistance of Counsel in Federal Habeas Corpus Cases

As we have seen, there is no federal constitutional right to counsel beyond the appeal of right. Congress has provided for representation of federal prisoners seeking habeas corpus relief in federal court, see 18 U.S.C.A. § 3006A, but has not provided for counsel for state prisoners seeking federal habeas corpus review. Representation

---

### JURISPRUDENCE

*O'Sullivan v. Boerckel,* 526 U.S. 838, 119 S.Ct. 1728, 144 L.Ed.2d 1 (1999)

Darren Boerckel was convicted in an Illinois court of rape, burglary, and aggravated battery. The Illinois Appellate Court affirmed the conviction, and the Illinois Supreme Court denied Boerckel's petition for discretionary review. Boerckel then initiated a federal habeas corpus action in which he raised six federal constitutional claims. The federal district court denied the petition, finding that Boerckel had "procedurally defaulted" his first three claims by failing to include them in his petition for discretionary review to the

Illinois Supreme Court. On appeal, the Seventh Circuit reversed, holding that filing for discretionary review by the state's highest court is not necessary to exhaust one's state court remedies for purposes of the federal habeas corpus statute. Reviewing the case on certiorari, the Supreme Court reversed again, holding that a state prisoner must present his claims to a state supreme court in a petition for discretionary review when such review is part of the State's "ordinary appellate review procedure." Failure to do so constitutes procedural default and precludes these issues from being raised on federal habeas corpus review.

---

in such cases is sometimes provided *pro bono* by groups such as the American Civil Liberties Union or the Legal Aid Society. In some instances, prisoners write their own petitions for federal habeas corpus review or get fellow inmates to do this for them.

## Ineffective Counsel as a Basis for Postconviction Relief

The Supreme Court has recognized that the right to counsel means little unless counsel provides a defendant with effective representation. *McMann v. Richardson,* 397 U.S. 759, 90 S.Ct. 1441, 25 L.Ed.2d 763 (1970). Failure of counsel, whether appointed or retained, to be an effective advocate for the defendant constitutes a basis to award a defendant a new trial. *Cuyler v. Sullivan,* 446 U.S. 335, 100 S.Ct. 1708, 64 L.Ed.2d 333 (1980). Some examples of ineffective representation where relief might well be afforded include failure of counsel to present evidence favorable to the accused, failure to challenge the admissibility of evidence presented by the prosecution, and failure to challenge prosecutorial misconduct.

**ineffective assistance of counsel** Deficient performance by a lawyer representing a defendant that results in serious errors that prejudice the right of a defendant to a fair trial.

The requirement to furnish counsel to indigent defendants has probably contributed to a rise in claims of **ineffective assistance of counsel**. Indigent defendants are sometimes distrustful of public defenders and other appointed counsel. If convicted, these defendants may be more likely to feel that their representation was ineffective compared with that provided by privately retained attorneys.

A defendant's claim of error or deficiency in counsel's performance is rarely challenged in the trial court, so it is not generally subject to being raised on direct appeal. But in some instances where the record of the trial shows on its face that counsel was ineffective, an appellate court will consider the issue on direct appeal. For example, in *Eure v. State,* 764 So.2d 798 (Fla. App. 2000), on a direct appeal from the defendant's conviction for possession and sale of cocaine, a Florida appellate court reversed the defendant's conviction because it found the defendant's counsel was ineffective for failing to object to a series of improper arguments by the prosecutor.

In *Strickland v. Washington,* 466 U.S. 668, 104 S.Ct. 2052, 80 L.Ed.2d 674 (1984), the Supreme Court articulated a uniform constitutional standard for determining the issue of ineffective counsel:

> First, the defendant must show that counsel's performance was deficient. This requires showing that counsel made errors so serious that counsel was not functioning

as the "counsel" guaranteed the defendant by the Sixth Amendment. Second, the defendant must show that the deficient performance prejudiced the defense. This requires showing that counsel's errors were so serious as to deprive the defendant of a fair trial, a trial whose result is reliable. Unless a defendant makes both showings, it cannot be said that the conviction . . . resulted from a breakdown in the adversary process that renders the result unreliable. 466 U.S. at 687, 104 S.Ct. at 2063, 80 L.Ed.2d at 693.

The standard announced in *Strickland v. Washington* has been criticized by numerous commentators as being too lax. Only twice since 1984 has the Supreme Court upheld a claim of ineffective assistance on the basis of the *Strickland* test. In the first of these decisions, *Williams v. Taylor*, 529 U.S. 362, 120 S.Ct. 1495, 146 L.Ed.2d 389 (2000), the Court upheld a lower court determination that the attorneys representing Terry Williams in a capital murder case failed to provide effective assistance during the sentencing phase and that it was reasonably probable that Williams would not have received the death penalty if his attorneys had presented and fully explained to the jury all of the available evidence pertaining to mitigating factors. More recently, in *Wiggins v. Smith*, 539 U.S. 510, 123 S.Ct. 2527,156 L.Ed.2d 471 (2003), the Court noted that the failure of the assistant public defenders to discover and present powerful mitigating evidence in the sentencing phase of a capital murder trial

## JURISPRUDENCE

*Wiggins v. Smith,* 539 U.S. 510, 123 S.Ct. 2527,156 L.Ed.2d 471 (2003)

Kevin Wiggins was convicted of capital murder and sentenced to death in a Maryland court. At the sentencing phase, Wiggins's public defender stated in his opening statement that the jury would hear evidence regarding Wiggins's "difficult life," but no evidence was actually submitted to the jury for their consideration. The only mitigating evidence presented at sentencing was that Wiggins had no prior criminal history. At a subsequent postconviction relief hearing, Wiggins's new counsel argued "that his trial counsel had rendered ineffective assistance by failing to investigate and present mitigating evidence of his dysfunctional background." Expert testimony revealed "the severe physical and sexual abuse [Wiggins] had suffered at the hands of his mother and while under the care of a series of foster parents." Trial counsel testified at the hearing that while funds were available for such expert testimony, "he did not remember retaining a forensic social worker to prepare a social history before sentencing." The trial court denied Wiggins's petition for postconviction relief, and the state court of appeals affirmed. However, the U.S. District Court "granted Wiggins relief on his federal habeas petition, holding

that the Maryland court's rejection of his ineffective assistance claim involved an unreasonable application of clearly established federal law." The Fourth Circuit Court of Appeals reversed. The Supreme Court agreed with the District Court, holding, "The performance of Wiggins'[s] attorney at sentencing violated his Sixth Amendment right to effective assistance of counsel." In writing for the majority, Justice O'Connor noted that Wiggins's trial counsel failed to conduct "a reasonable investigation," which "fell short of the professional standards." Also, Justice O'Connor observed that "in light of the facts counsel discovered in the DSS records concerning Wiggins's alcoholic mother and his problems in foster care, counsel's decision to cease investigating when he did was unreasonable." O'Connor wrote that "Any reasonably competent attorney would have realized that pursuing such leads was necessary to making an informed choice among possible defenses, particularly given the apparent absence of aggravating factors from Wiggins's background." As a result of the inadequate representation at sentencing, the Court held "counsel's failures prejudiced Wiggins's defense." Given, Wiggins's sufficiently satisfied the two-prong test in *Strickland*, the Court reversed the death sentence and remanded the case for further proceedings.

was constitutionally deficient. Writing for a majority of five justices, Justice Sandra Day O'Connor noted, "Had the jury been able to place petitioner's excruciating life history on the mitigating side of the scale, there is a reasonable probability that at least one juror would have struck a different balance." 539 U.S. at 536, 123 S.Ct. at 2543, 156 L.Ed.2d at 495.

The Court's decisions in the *Williams* and *Wiggins* cases suggest the Court's willingness to scrutinize the performance of counsel at sentencing as well as the trial stage in cases where defendants' lives are at stake.

## Collateral Attack in State Court

At one time federal habeas corpus review was the only real means of postconviction relief available to state prisoners who had exhausted their appeals of right in the state courts. Today, most states have statutes or court rules that permit state prisoners, under appropriate circumstances, to challenge illegal convictions or sentences even after their ordinary appeals have been exhausted. These procedures, known as **collateral attack** or postconviction relief, provide for state-level judicial review of judgments and sentences imposed in violation of the federal or state constitutions. As access to federal habeas corpus relief has been constricted by Congress and the Supreme Court, these state-level mechanisms take on even greater importance.

North Carolina statutes that provide opportunities for collateral relief to convicted defendants appear typical of the grounds for postconviction relief available to defendants convicted in state courts. The grounds that a defendant may assert by a motion for collateral relief include the following:

- The trial court lacked jurisdiction over the defendant.
- The defendant's conviction was obtained in violation of the U.S. or North Carolina constitutions.
- A significant change has occurred in the law applied in the proceedings leading to the defendant's conviction or sentence, and such changed law must be applied retroactively.
- The defendant's sentence is illegal; or the defendant is entitled to release for having fully served the sentence imposed.

In addition, within a reasonable time after discovery, a defendant may assert that evidence is available that was unknown or unavailable to the defendant at trial and that has a direct and material bearing on the defendant's eligibility for the death penalty or the defendant's guilt or innocence. West's N.C.G.S.A. § 15A-1415. This is particularly significant in light of the Supreme Court's decision in *Herrera v. Collins*, supra, that federal habeas corpus review is not the proper mechanism for litigation of belated claims of actual innocence brought by persons convicted in state courts. The other states have similar provisions for postconviction relief.

## DNA Evidence as a Basis for Postconviction Relief

As we pointed out in Chapter 18, the introduction of DNA testing has had an enormous impact on criminal trials, especially in rape and homicide prosecutions. But DNA evidence is not only useful to prosecutors seeking convictions, it is also extremely valuable as a mean of proving the actual innocence of persons who were convicted of rape or homicide on the basis of eyewitness testimony or circumstantial evidence. According to research conducted by the Innocence Project, there have been more than 180 DNA exonerations in the United States since the first one in

**collateral attack** The attempt to defeat the outcome of a judicial proceeding by challenging it in a different proceeding or court.

1989. Fourteen of these exonerees were death-row inmates wrongly convicted of murder. See www.innocenceproject.org/docs/DNAExonerationFacts_WEB.pdf.

Most states now recognize newly discovered evidence as a basis for postconviction relief. In the case of DNA evidence, though, testing of genetic material is required before such evidence can be obtained. In most cases, a convicted person needs to gain access to evidence through a sort of postconviction discovery process. Yet many jurisdictions have not established standards or procedures to govern such discovery. In some states, courts have formulated standards and procedures based on norms of due process and expressed through judicial opinions. In other states, prisoners seeking to demonstrate their innocence on the basis of DNA evidence must apply for executive clemency. A few states now have statutes addressing this problem. For example, New York law provides that

> in cases of convictions . . . where the defendant's motion requests the performance of a forensic DNA test on specified evidence, and upon the court's determination that any evidence containing deoxyribonucleic acid (DNA) was secured in connection with the trial resulting in the judgment, the court shall grant the application for forensic DNA testing of such evidence upon its determination that if a DNA test had been conducted on such evidence, and if the results had been admitted in the trial resulting in the judgment, there exists a reasonable probability that the verdict would have been more favorable to the defendant. McKinney's N.Y. Crim. Proc. Law § 440.30 (1-a)(a).

Unlike New York, some states, through legislation or rules of court, impose time limits on applications for postconviction DNA testing. Florida Rule of Criminal Procedure 3.853 originally imposed a deadline, but, after several extensions the Supreme Court of Florida, in 2007, revised Rule 3.853 to provide: "The motion for postconviction DNA testing may be filed or considered at any time following the date that the judgment and sentence in the case becomes final." *Amendments to Florida Rules of Criminal Procedure, 953 So.2d 513* (Fla. 2007). Likewise the requirements for seeking DNA testing are different under various state statutes and rules of court. Florida Rule of Criminal Procedure 3.853(b), as recently amended, requires that a motion for postconviction DNA testing must be under oath and must include:

1. a statement of the facts relied on in support of the motion, including a description of the physical evidence containing DNA to be tested and, if known, the present location or last known location of the evidence and how it originally was obtained;
2. a statement that the evidence was not tested previously for DNA, or a statement that the results of previous DNA testing were inconclusive and that subsequent scientific developments in DNA testing techniques likely would produce a definitive result establishing that the movant is not the person who committed the crime;
3. a statement that the movant is innocent and how the DNA testing requested by the motion will exonerate the movant of the crime for which the movant was sentenced, or a statement of how the DNA testing will mitigate the sentence received by the movant for that crime;
4. a statement that identification of the movant is a genuinely disputed issue in the case and why it is an issue, or an explanation of how the DNA evidence would either exonerate the defendant or mitigate the sentence that the movant received;
5. a statement of any other facts relevant to the motion; and
6. a certificate that a copy of the motion has been served on the prosecuting authority.

Advocates of expanding prisoners' access to postconviction relief based on DNA evidence believe that prosecutors should be required to maintain biological evidence used to secure a conviction as long as that person is incarcerated. They also argue that statutes of limitations on convicted persons seeking postconviction relief should be abolished (as Florida recently did) and that funding should be provided so that prisoners seeking postconviction relief can have adequate legal representation throughout the process.

Exonerations of convicted persons, especially those on death row, based on DNA testing have received enormous media coverage and have shocked the conscience of the public. While prosecutors often resist efforts to undo convictions through DNA testing, there is growing public sentiment that the need for finality in the judicial process must give way to the search for truth when such powerful scientific means of seeking the truth are now available.

### The U.S. Supreme Court Grants Relief Based On Newly Discovered DNA Evidence

In *House v. Bell*, 547 U.S. 518, 126 S.Ct. 2064, 165 L.Ed.2d 1 (2006), a case reminiscent of *Schlup v. Delo*, supra, the Supreme Court, in a 5–3 decision, granted Paul Gregory House, a Tennessee death row inmate, a hearing in federal district court to litigate a procedurally defaulted claim of ineffective assistance of counsel on the basis on newly discovered DNA evidence. Writing for the majority, Justice Kennedy summed up the case as follows:

> This is not a case of conclusive exoneration. Some aspects of the State's evidence . . . still support an inference of guilt. Yet the central forensic proof connecting House to the crime . . . has been called into question, and House has put forward substantial evidence pointing to a different suspect. Accordingly, and although the issue is close, we conclude that this is the rare case where—had the jury heard all the conflicting testimony—it is more likely than not that no reasonable juror viewing the record as a whole would lack reasonable doubt. 547 U.S. at 553, 126 S.Ct. at 2086, 165 L.Ed.2d at 63.

By allowing appeals based on newly discovered DNA and other technological developments, courts risk more extended processes with attendant delays and costs. But the risk of affirming convictions based on evidence that is proven to be

**CASE-IN-POINT**

### DNA Evidence Used to Exonerate a Man Falsely Convicted of Rape

In 1983, Bernard Webster was convicted of rape and sentenced to thirty years in prison by a Maryland court after a schoolteacher identified him as the man who sexually assaulted her in her apartment. Twenty years later, Webster was exonerated after DNA testing was performed on semen residues that had been obtained from the victim shortly after the rape occurred in 1982. In proving his innocence, Webster took advantage of a Maryland statute enacted in 2001 that requires judges to order DNA testing pursuant to motions for postconviction relief in murder and rape cases where there is "reasonable probability" that testing will produce evidence of actual innocence. In securing postconviction relief, Webster was aided by the Innocence Project, a *pro bono* group dedicated to assisting persons who were wrongfully convicted of crimes. According to a study conducted by the Center for Wrongful Convictions at Northwestern University, false identification by eyewitnesses is a leading cause of wrongful convictions.

*© Cengage Learning*

scientifically unreliable forcefully argues for expansion of the appellate process to accommodate such developments. This is an issue that legislative bodies and courts are now facing as new technologies are being developed and convicted defendants seek the right to ask expansion of the appellate process.

# Nonjudicial Remedies Available to Persons Convicted of Crimes

**clemency** A grant of mercy by an executive official commuting a sentence or pardoning a criminal.

Under the English common law, appeal to the Crown predated appeal to higher courts as the remedy for an unjust conviction or unreasonable sentence. In addition, because a crime was viewed as an offense against the Crown, the monarch possessed the authority to forgive the wrongdoer or grant **clemency**. In contemporary America, the appeal to executive authority remains as a carryover from the common law and as a supplement to judicial review.

## Presidential Pardons

**pardon** An executive action that mitigates or sets aside punishment for a crime.

Article II, Section 2, Clause 1 of the U.S. Constitution states that the president "shall have Power to grant Reprieves and Pardons for Offences against the United States, except in Cases of Impeachment." This broad power includes the right to commute sentences, remit fines and penalties, and even grant conditional pardons. Indeed, the presidential **pardon** may be issued before conviction, as was amply demonstrated in 1974, when President Gerald Ford pardoned former president Richard Nixon for his role in the Watergate scandal. It was demonstrated again in December 1992, when President George H. W. Bush granted a pardon to Caspar Weinberger, the former Secretary of Defense, and five others who allegedly were involved in the much-publicized controversy concerning the trading of arms for hostages. These pardons were politically controversial, but there was no question as to their legality.

Equally if not more controversial was President Clinton's last-minute pardon of Marc Rich, a fugitive from a 1983 indictment for federal income tax evasion. The Rich pardon, which was given without the normal consultation with the Department of Justice, prompted congressional hearings and an investigation by federal prosecutors. Investigators looked into the possibility that Rich purchased a presidential pardon by passing money through his former wife, who made large contributions both to the Clinton presidential library foundation and to Hillary Clinton's 2000 Senate campaign.

The Supreme Court has said that "[t]he plain purpose of the broad power conferred . . . was to allow . . . the President to 'forgive' the convicted person in part or entirely, to reduce a penalty in terms of a specified number of years, or to alter it with conditions which are in themselves constitutionally unobjectionable." *Schick v. Reed*, 419 U.S. 256, 266, 95 S.Ct. 379, 385, 42 L.Ed.2d 430, 438–439 (1974). Therefore, a full presidential pardon totally restores any civil rights the recipient may have lost as a result of conviction. In effect, the full pardon makes an individual as innocent as if the crime had never been committed. *Ex parte Garland*, 71 U.S. (4 Wall.) 333, 18 L.Ed. 366 (1866).

## Clemency at the State Level

Either by constitutional or statutory provisions, executive authorities in all fifty states are likewise granted broad powers to pardon and commute sentences of persons convicted of violations of state criminal law. In many states, the pardoning power is vested exclusively in the governor. In a few states, the governor is limited to granting pardons approved by a state commission. In some states, the pardoning power is vested entirely in a state commission.

In recent years, a number of state prisoners convicted of rape and murder have sought executive clemency based on DNA testing that shows their innocence. Increasingly, such claims are handled judicially through motions for postconviction relief, as courts and legislatures recognize the need to allow persons who claim to have been wrongfully convicted of crimes to prove their innocence through DNA testing.

One of the most dramatic uses of executive clemency in American history took place in January 2003, when Governor George Ryan commuted the death sentences of 156 inmates awaiting execution in Illinois. All but three of the inmates had their sentences commuted to life in prison without the possibility of parole; the other three were given life sentences with the possibility of seeking parole. Governor Ryan's dramatic and controversial order came three years after he announced a moratorium on the death penalty in Illinois and appointed a commission to study the issue. After receiving the commission's report, which identified various problems with trials, sentencing, and the appeals process, Governor Ryan concluded that the system was "haunted by the demon of error, error in determining guilt, and error in determining who among the guilty deserves to die."

## Conclusion

Under the early English common law, the right to appeal was nonexistent. Eventually, through court decisions and statutes, defendants gained the right to appeal criminal convictions. In America, federal and state statutes guarantee at least one appeal of right to defendants who are convicted after entering a plea of not guilty. Beyond these appeals of right, defendants may seek review from higher courts by filing petitions for certiorari or discretionary review. Finally, the historic writ of habeas corpus provides prisoners with an avenue to seek postconviction relief in state and federal tribunals. In many states, postconviction relief has become structured under criteria specified by statute or rules of court. One of the most common issues raised on postconviction review is whether a defendant received the effective assistance of counsel at trial. Perhaps the most dramatic recent development in appellate processes has been acceptance of DNA evidence as proof of innocence of persons convicted of rape and homicide crimes on the basis of eyewitness testimony or circumstantial evidence.

There is considerable criticism today of the delays caused by the seemingly inexhaustible routes of appellate review of some cases, but the public is generally unaware of the thousands of appeals that are resolved in a timely manner. In America, where criminal law and procedure are guided by due process values as well as by society's need for crime control, delays in appellate processes must be weighed against society's deep and historic commitment to fundamental fairness.

## Chapter Summary

- Learning Objective 1
    - Until Parliament enacted the Criminal Appeal Act of 1907, the English common law afforded defendants limited review of criminal convictions.
    - In America, review includes trial *de novo*, appeal of right, discretionary review, and postconviction relief. Trial *de novo* occurs when a trial court of general jurisdiction reviews a conviction by a court of limited jurisdiction.

o Appeal of right refers to an appellate court's review of a criminal conviction from a trial court of general jurisdiction. Appeals of right in federal criminal cases are heard by U.S. Courts of Appeals (circuit courts). Intermediate state appellate courts hear most appeals of right, although in less populous states, the highest court of the state handles routine appeals. In four states, special appellate courts hear only criminal appeals.

o A defendant whose conviction has been sustained by an intermediate appellate court may petition a court of last resort for a writ of certiorari (discretionary review). The U.S. Supreme Court may review federal and state criminal cases involving federal issues by exercising its certiorari jurisdiction.

o A defendant in prison may seek additional review of a conviction or sentence by applying for a writ of habeas corpus or another form of postconviction relief.

- Learning Objective 2

o On appeal, a defendant may challenge trial court rulings objected to during pretrial, trial, or posttrial phases. Irrespective of an objection, a defendant may challenge the trial court's jurisdiction and any fundamental errors.

o A defendant usually raises from one to six major assignments of error or points as a basis to secure a reversal of the trial court's judgment or sentence.

o Typically, a defendant who pleads guilty may raise on appeal only issues relating to the trial court's jurisdiction, voluntariness of the guilty plea, and legality of the sentence. Even then, an appellate court may refuse to review other than jurisdictional issues unless the trial court has denied the defendant's request to withdraw a plea of guilty.

o The Federal Rules of Criminal Procedure allow defendants to enter conditional pleas of guilty or *nolo contendere*, reserving in writing the right to have an appellate court review an adverse determination of a specified pretrial motion. Some states have similar provisions.

o Most states provide automatic appeals of death sentences to their highest court.

o The federal government has no right to appeal a defendant's acquittal but may appeal dismissal of an indictment, granting a defendant a new trial, releasing a defendant before trial or after conviction, or orders suppressing evidence before the defendant is put in jeopardy. States, in general, limit appeals by the prosecution to similar grounds.

- Learning Objective 3

o The primary function of appellate courts is to correct trial court errors. Appellate courts (especially the highest state courts and the U.S. Supreme Court) not only interpret statutory and constitutional provisions, they "fill in gaps" in the law, and effectively "make law."

o Most criminal appeals are heard "on the record," which appellate courts scrutinize for procedural errors of trial courts. Appellate courts frequently find technical errors to be harmless; however, in 1967 the U.S. Supreme Court ruled that where an error involves provisions of the federal constitution, before affirming a trial court judgment, an appellate court must find beyond a reasonable doubt that the error was harmless.

- Learning Objective 4

o The Bail Reform Act of 1984 allows federal judges to detain a criminal defendant without bail if the defendant poses a special threat to community safety or a high risk of flight. A defendant who appeals a conviction has the burden of proving an entitlement to bail based on criteria specified in the law. The Act also governs release pending appeal by the government.

○ In an appeal from a state court conviction, the trial court usually determines whether a defendant can be released by considering the defendant's family and community ties and whether the appeal is taken in good faith and presents a debatable point of law. If the state appeals, the defendant is usually released on personal recognizance.

- Learning Objective 5

   ○ In 1963 the Supreme Court held that an indigent defendant is entitled to be furnished counsel to pursue an appeal of right; in 1974 the Court ruled that there is no requirement to furnish counsel to assist an indigent defendant who seeks further discretionary review.

   ○ In 1967 the Court ruled that appointed counsel who finds no merit to a defendant's appeal may withdraw from representation, but only after submitting a brief claiming that the appeal was wholly frivolous and referring to any arguable issues.

- Learning Objective 6

   ○ Filing a notice of appeal invokes requirements for the appellant to file pertinent lower court records and briefs on the law. The appellee has the right to respond.

   ○ Briefs of counsel are the principal instruments used to persuade the appellate court to reverse, affirm, or modify the decision being appealed.

   ○ In some appeals, courts hear oral arguments by counsel, but appellate court decisions are made in private conferences.

   ○ Once judges arrive at a decision, the appellate court releases its opinion. A *per curiam* opinion represents the appellate court as a whole; more commonly an opinion is authored by one judge and joined by other judges.

   ○ A judge who disagrees with the court's decision may write a dissenting opinion.

   ○ A judge who agrees with the court's decision but wants to write on issues not addressed or emphasized in the court's opinion may write a separate concurring opinion, or may simply concur in the court's judgment.

   ○ Most appellate court decisions are published in books known as reporters. Published appellate opinions play an important role in developing the law, as judges and lawyers regularly consult the reporters for guidance in pending cases.

   ○ After the court issues its decision, counsel may seek a rehearing or rehearing *en banc*.

- Learning Objective 7

   ○ Long after the right to appeal has expired or appeals have been exhausted, a prisoner may seek a writ of habeas corpus. The U.S. Constitution declares that "[t]he Privilege of the Writ of Habeas Corpus shall not be suspended unless when in Cases of Rebellion or Invasion the public Safety may require it." U.S. Const., Art. 1, Sec. 9.

   ○ Before the twentieth century, the federal habeas corpus jurisdiction was seldom used to review state criminal convictions except to ascertain that the state trial court had jurisdiction over the person being tried. In 1915 the

Supreme Court broadened issuance of the writ to ensure that states supplied some "corrective process" whereby criminal defendants could seek to vindicate their federal constitutional rights.

o During the 1960s under Chief Justice Earl Warren, the Supreme Court greatly broadened federal habeas corpus to allow a state prisoner to seek the writ without having first taken a direct appeal in state courts. Criticism of federal court intervention, coupled with the increasing professionalism of the state judiciaries, led the Supreme Court to restrict access to federal habeas corpus relief during the 1970s, 80s and 90s.

o The Antiterrorism and Effective Death Penalty Act of 1996 curtailed second habeas corpus petitions by state prisoners who have already filed such petitions in federal court. The Supreme Court unanimously rejected constitutional challenges to the Act.

- Learning Objective 8

  o Today, most states have statutes or court rules that permit state prisoners, under appropriate circumstances, to challenge illegal convictions or sentences even after their ordinary appeals have been exhausted. These procedures, known as collateral or postconviction relief, provide opportunities for prisoners to seek state-level judicial review of judgments and sentences allegedly issued in violation of federal or state constitutions.

  o States recognize claims of ineffective counsel and newly discovered evidence as a basis for postconviction relief. In 1984, the Supreme Court articulated a uniform constitutional standard for determining the issue of ineffective counsel that requires a defendant to show that counsel's performance was deficient and that such deficiency prejudiced the defense.

- Learning Objective 9

  o In 2006 the Supreme Court granted a death row inmate a hearing in federal district court to litigate a procedurally defaulted claim of the ineffective assistance of counsel on the basis on newly discovered DNA evidence. Since then, state legislatures and courts have recognized that DNA evidence may establish the innocence of defendants convicted of rape and homicidal crimes on the basis of eyewitness testimony.

  o In most cases, a convicted person needs to gain access to DNA evidence through a postconviction discovery process.

- Learning Objective 10

  o Article II, Section 2, Clause 1 of the U.S. Constitution states that the president "shall have Power to grant Reprieves and Pardons for Offences against the United States, except in Cases of Impeachment." This broad power includes the right to commute sentences, remit fines and penalties, and even grant conditional pardons. In effect, the full pardon makes an individual as innocent as if the crime had never been committed.

  o Either by constitutional or statutory provisions, executive authorities in all fifty states are granted broad powers to pardon and commute sentences of persons convicted of violations of state criminal laws.

  o In many states, the pardoning power is vested exclusively in the governor. In a few, the governor is limited to granting pardons approved by a state commission. In some states, the pardoning power is vested entirely in a state commission.

## Key Terms

| | |
|---|---|
| affirm | judicial conference |
| *Anders* brief | lawmaking |
| answer brief | miscarriage of justice |
| appeal of right | motion for rehearing |
| appellant | notice of appeal |
| appellee | opinion of the court |
| assignments of error | oral argument |
| Bail Reform Act of 1984 | pardon |
| brief | pendency of the appeal |
| clemency | *per curiam* opinion |
| collateral attack | petitioner |
| concurring in the judgment | postconviction relief |
| concurring opinion | remand |
| discretionary review | reply brief |
| dissenting opinion | reporters |
| doctrine of harmless error | respondent |
| *en banc* rehearing | reverse |
| error correction | rule of four |
| federal habeas corpus review | substantial federal question |
| Federal Rules of Appellate Procedure | trial *de novo* |
| frivolous appeals | writ of error |
| fundamental errors | writ of habeas corpus |
| ineffective assistance of counsel | writs of certiorari |

## Questions for Thought and Discussion

1. What court or courts in your state have jurisdiction to hear appeals from felony convictions? What changes, if any, would you propose for your state's system of appellate courts?

2. Is the right to appeal a necessary concomitant of due process of law? In the absence of statutory rights to appeal, would the current Supreme Court find a constitutional right to appeal implicit in the due process requirements of the Constitution?

3. What new or revised procedures would expedite the resolution of criminal appeals? Would such procedures detract from the fair and deliberative review essential to determine whether the decision of the trial court in a criminal case was arrived at fairly and accurately?

4. In addition to determining whether a sentence imposed on a convicted defendant is within the statutory bounds, do you think an appellate court is an appropriate forum to reconsider the reasonableness of the sentence imposed by the trial court?

5. How has the "nationalization" of the criminal law that occurred through decisions of the U.S. Supreme Court during the 1960s and 1970s affected the appellate process?

6. The U.S. Supreme Court has recognized a constitutional right to represent one-self in a criminal trial. Could a person who insisted on self-representation at trial later challenge his or her conviction by claiming ineffective assistance of counsel?

7. Where a defendant has had an opportunity for a full and fair review of his or her trial through an appeal, what justifies the availability of additional avenues of review through collateral attack?

8. After studying briefs submitted by counsel and hearing oral arguments in a proceeding open to the public, appellate judges retire to privately discuss and decide the merits of criminal appeals. Should these deliberations be open to the public? Why or why not?

9. In a substantial number of criminal appeals, some state appellate courts routinely issue decisions merely stating "Judgment Affirmed." When an appellate court rejects a defendant's issues on appeal, should it be required to issue an opinion justifying its decision? In discussing this issue, consider whether such a requirement would (a) require greatly increasing the number of judges and support staff and the additional costs thereof, or (b) detract from the court's ability to direct its efforts to writing opinions on novel questions of law.

10. Do you think the ability of a convicted defendant to secure DNA testing rises to an issue of due process of law? Should there be a statute of limitations on a defendant raising the issue? Does Congress have a role to play in providing a standardized process throughout the country? Should the process be governed by federal statute, or should state legislatures and courts be left free to develop their own procedures?

## Problems for Discussion and Solution

1. John Dunnit was convicted of aggravated sexual battery and was sentenced to state prison. After exhausting his appellate remedies in the state courts, Dunnit filed a federal habeas corpus application, which was denied. Dunnit challenged the denial in an appeal to the federal circuit court and was again denied relief. Dunnit filed a second federal habeas corpus petition after President Clinton signed the Antiterrorism and Effective Death Penalty Act of 1996 amending the federal habeas corpus statute. How does this new law affect Dunnit's case? Is Dunnit's second application for a writ of habeas corpus affected by recent Supreme Court decisions mentioned in this chapter?

2. Culp Able was convicted of murder in state court. Central to the state's case was a confession that Able uttered before being given his *Miranda* warnings. The trial judge received the confession in evidence over the defendant's objection, and Able was convicted. On appeal, the intermediate state appellate court and later the state supreme court considered and rejected Able's challenge to the admissibility of the confession. Then Able filed an application for federal habeas corpus relief, citing only the alleged *Miranda* violation as a basis for the reversal of his conviction. Relying on *Stone v. Powell* (1976), the state argues that the petition should be dismissed because Able was afforded "a full and fair opportunity to litigate his Fifth Amendment claim in the state courts." If you were the federal district judge, how would you rule? Should Able get his day in federal court?

3. Imagine that Congress adopted a statute requiring all state and federal courts to consider belated claims of innocence based on newly discovered physical evidence, regardless of the amount of time that has elapsed since conviction. Boris Bonanza, who is currently on death row in the state of Cornucopia, was

convicted of first-degree murder seventeen years ago. The victim in the case, Sheila Softmore, had been stabbed repeatedly with a knife. Bonanza was found on the scene, his clothes stained with blood. A bloody kitchen knife was found on the floor nearby. At trial Bonanza claimed that he was innocent and that the blood found on his clothes were not from the victim, but from the real killer, whom he had stabbed after wrestling the knife from him. According to the statement Bonanza gave police, Bonanza arrived on the scene too late to save Softmore and the real killer fled after being stabbed. The crime lab determined that the blood on Bonanza's shirt was the same type as the victim's, O-positive, but no DNA test was performed. The state of Cornucopia has a statute of limitations on the use of newly discovered physical evidence to support belated claims of evidence, and the statute has already tolled in Bonanza's case. In a petition for postconviction relief, Bonanza's attorney is arguing that under the new federal statute, Bonanza is entitled to a DNA comparison between blood residue on his shirt, which remains in storage at the crime lab, and the victim, whose body would have to be exhumed to make the comparison. How might the assistant state attorney general, who is arguing against the petition, argue the state's case? If you were the judge, how would you be inclined to rule? What additional information would you need to make a ruling?

# APPENDIX A

# Access to the Law through Legal Research

## The Nature of Legal Research

Successful legal research requires a systematic method of finding the law applicable to a particular problem or set of facts. Before beginning research, it is helpful, if not essential, for the criminal justice professional or student to have a basic understanding of the law and the legal system.

After assembling the relevant facts and completing a preliminary analysis of the problem, the researcher must find the applicable constitutional and statutory materials and then search for authoritative interpretations of the law. Interpretations are usually found in appellate court decisions construing the particular constitutional provision or statute in analogous situations. These judicial decisions are referred to as cases in point. Legislative and judicial sources of the law are referred to as primary sources because they are authoritative.

A variety of other legal materials, called secondary sources, are available to the researcher. These consist of legal encyclopedias, textbooks by scholars and practitioners, law reviews published by law schools, and journals and periodicals published by various legal organizations. These secondary sources are extremely helpful to the researcher, especially to one unfamiliar with the law in a given area.

### Getting Started in Legal Research

Once you become knowledgeable about the sources of the law and the process of its development by courts and you develop the skill of analyzing a problem, you can get started in legal research. Here is a suggestion that can help. If you attend a college at or near a law school, a law librarian might help you in the use of law books or electronic sources. Or you might get assistance from law students, as they usually take a course in legal research in their first year. If you are working from home, do not overlook the fact that in many communities, local governments, courthouses, and bar associations have established law libraries that are usually available to the public; some of these may even offer the free use of legal research databases and other electronic sources.

Legal research has changed rapidly due to the Internet, and more information is becoming available online every day. But before undertaking online research, it is essential that the legal researcher become knowledgeable about the sources that are the traditional professional tools for legal research, when books are the best sources to use, and when to go online instead.

# Primary Legal Sources

Federal and state constitutions are often the beginning points in legal research in the criminal justice area because they provide the framework for our government and guarantee certain basic rights to the accused. As explained in this text, the rights of an accused are protected by several provisions of the federal constitution and the Bill of Rights. Most state constitutions afford criminal defendants similar protections. Thus, a person concerned about the legality of an arrest, search, or seizure would examine the relevant federal and state constitutional provisions and then seek to determine how the courts have construed the law in analogous situations.

Federal offenses are defined in statutes enacted by the U.S. Congress, and state offenses are defined in statutes enacted by state legislatures. Federal statutes (in sequence of their adoption) are published annually in the *United States Statutes at Large*. Most states have similar volumes, called session laws, which incorporate the laws enacted during a given session of the legislature. These federal and state laws are initially compiled in sequence of their adoption and are generally consulted to find the history of a law. Later they are merged into legal codes that systematically arrange the statutes by subject and provide an index. Of far greater assistance to the criminal justice researcher are commercially prepared versions of these codes that classify all federal and state laws of a general and permanent nature by subject and include reference materials and exhaustive indexes. These volumes are kept current by periodic supplements and revised volumes.

## The United States Code Annotated

One popular compilation of the federal law widely used by lawyers, judges, and criminal justice professionals is the *United States Code Annotated*. The "U.S.C.A.," as it is known, is published by Thomson/West. The U.S.C.A. consists of fifty separate titles that conform to the text of the Official Code of the Laws of the United States (the official name for the U.S. Code). For instance, Title 18 is titled "Crimes and Criminal Procedure" and is of particular interest to the criminal justice researcher. Each statute in the U.S.C.A. is followed by a series of annotations consisting of court decisions interpreting the particular statute, along with historical notes, cross-references, and other editorial features. The U.S.C.A. also has a General Index, printed annually, that will guide the researcher to a particular title and section number by subject. If the researcher knows only the popular name of a federal statute, the corresponding U.S. Code title and section number can be found in the Popular Name Table. The U.S.C.A. is kept up to date by the use of "pocket parts," annual updates with the latest laws and amendments, which are slipped into the back pockets of the individual volumes so that the researcher can easily find the latest versions of the laws.

## Annotated State Codes

Most states have annotated statutes published by either the state or a private publisher. For example, West's *Annotated California Codes* follows the same general format as the U.S.C.A. Annotated statutes are popular aids to legal research and can save the researcher valuable time in locating cases in point. They are especially effective tools for locating interpretations of criminal statutes.

## The National Reporter System

Volumes containing appellate court decisions are referred to as reporters. The National Reporter System, by Thomson/West, includes decisions from the U.S. Supreme Court, the lower federal courts, and the state appellate courts. Reported cases are available in bound volumes and online through Westlaw and various Internet sites.

Decisions of the U.S. Supreme Court are officially published in the *United States Reports* (abbreviated U.S.). Two private organizations also report these decisions in hardcover volumes. The *Supreme Court Reporter* (abbreviated S.Ct.) is published by Thomson/West, and *Lawyers Edition,* now in its second series (abbreviated L.Ed.2d), is published by West/Lawyers Cooperative. Although the three reporters have somewhat different editorial features, the actual opinions of the Supreme Court are reproduced identically in all three reporters.

References to judicial decisions found in the reporters are called citations. U.S. Supreme Court decisions are often cited to all three publications—for example, *Miranda v. Arizona,* 384 U.S. 436, 86 S.Ct. 1602, 16 L.Ed.2d 694 (1966). For each of these publications, the citation tells you exactly where the case is published. For example, "384 U.S. 436" means that the *Miranda* case is in volume 384 of the United States Reports on page 436.

Since 1889, the decisions of the U.S. courts of appeals have been published in *West's Federal Reporter,* now in its third series (abbreviated F.3d). Decisions of federal district (trial) courts are published in *West's Federal Supplement,* which is now in its second series (abbreviated F. Supp. 2d). A citation to a case in *Federal Reporter* will read, for example, *Newman v. United States,* 817 F.2d 635 (10th Cir. 1987). This refers to a 1987 case reported in volume 817, page 635 of the *Federal Reporter,* second series, decided by the United States Court of Appeals for the Tenth Circuit. A citation to *United States v. Klopfenstine,* 673 F. Supp. 356 (W.D. Mo. 1987), refers to a 1987 federal district court decision from the Western District of Missouri, reported in volume 673, page 356 of the *Federal Supplement.*

Additional federal reporters publish the decisions from other federal courts (e.g., bankruptcy and military appeals), but the federal reporters referred to earlier are those most frequently used by criminal justice professionals.

## The Regional Reporters

The decisions of the highest state courts (usually but not always called supreme courts) and the decisions of other state appellate courts (usually referred to as intermediate appellate courts) are found in seven regional reporters, West's *California Reporter,* and the *New York Supplement.* Regional reporters, with their abbreviations in parentheses, include decisions from the following states:

- *Atlantic Reporter* (A. and A.2d): Maine, Vermont, New Hampshire, Connecticut, Rhode Island, Pennsylvania, New Jersey, Maryland, Delaware, and the District of Columbia
- *North Eastern Reporter* (N.E. and N.E.2d): Illinois, Indiana, Massachusetts, New York (court of last resort only—other New York appellate courts have their opinions in the New York Supplement), and Ohio
- *North Western Reporter* (N.W. and N.W.2d): North Dakota, South Dakota, Nebraska, Minnesota, Iowa, Michigan, and Wisconsin
- *Pacific Reporter* (P., P.2d and P.3d): Washington, Oregon, California, Montana, Idaho, Nevada, Utah, Arizona, Wyoming, Colorado, New Mexico, Kansas, Oklahoma, Alaska, and Hawaii

- *Southern Reporter* (So., So.2d and So.3d): Florida, Alabama, Mississippi, and Louisiana
- *South Eastern Reporter* (S.E. and S.E.2d): Virginia, West Virginia, North Carolina, South Carolina, and Georgia
- *South Western Reporter* (S.W., S.W.2d and S.W.3d): Texas, Missouri, Arkansas, Kentucky, and Tennessee

For many states (in addition to New York and California), West publishes separate volumes reporting the decisions as they appear in the regional reporters. *Pennsylvania Reporter* and *Texas Cases* are examples of this.

The following examples of citation forms appear in some of the regional reporters:

- *State v. Hogan*, 480 So.2d 288 (La. 1985). This refers to a 1985 decision of the Louisiana Supreme Court found in volume 480, page 288 of the *Southern Reporter*, second series.
- *State v. Nungesser*, 269 N.W.2d 449 (Iowa 1978). This refers to a 1978 decision of the Iowa Supreme Court found in volume 269, page 449 of the *North Western Reporter*, second series.
- *Henry v. State*, 567 S.W.2d 7 (Tex. Cr. App. 1978). This refers to a 1978 decision of the Texas Court of Criminal Appeals found in volume 567, page 7 of the *South Western Reporter*, second series.

## Syllabi, Headnotes, and Key Numbers

The National Reporter System and the regional reporters contain not only the official text of each reported decision but also a brief summary of the decision, called the syllabus, and one or more topically indexed "headnotes." These headnotes briefly describe the principles of law expounded by the court and are indexed by a series of topic "key numbers." West assigns these key numbers to specific points of decisional law. For instance, decisions dealing with first-degree murder are classified under the topic "homicide" and a key number is assigned for each particular aspect of that crime. Thus, a homicide case dealing with the intent requirement in first-degree murder may be classified as "Homicide 9—Intent and design to effect death." Using this key number system, a researcher can locate headnotes of various appellate decisions on this aspect of homicide and is, in turn, led to other relevant cases.

In addition, each of these volumes contains a table of statutes construed in the cases reported in that volume, with reference also to the American Bar Association's *Standards for Criminal Justice*.

### United States Law Week

*United States Law Week*, published by the Bureau of National Affairs, Inc., Washington, D.C., presents a weekly survey of American law. *Law Week* includes all the latest decisions from the U.S. Supreme Court as well as significant current decisions from other federal and state courts.

### Criminal Law Reporter

Also published by the Bureau of National Affairs, Inc., the weekly *Criminal Law Reporter* reviews contemporary developments in the criminal law. It is an excellent source of commentaries on current state and federal court decisions in the criminal law area.

## Digests

Digests are tools that enable the researcher to locate cases in point through topics and key numbers. By finding a particular topic and key number and looking it up in the pertinent digest, the researcher can locate other cases on the narrow point of law covered by that key number. West publishes the *Decennial Digests*, which topically index all the appellate court decisions from the state and federal courts. The *Decennial Digests* are kept current by a set called the *General Digests* so that the researcher can always find the latest cases.

A series of federal digests contains key number headnotes for decisions of the federal courts. The current series published by West is *Federal Practice Digest 4th*. In addition, separate digests are published for some states as well as for the Atlantic, North Western, Pacific, and South Eastern reporters.

The index at the beginning of each topic identifies the various points of law by numerically arranged key numbers. In addition to the basic topic of criminal law, many topics in the field of criminal law are listed by specific crimes (such as homicide, forgery, and bribery). Procedural topics such as arrest and search and seizure are also included. The digests contain a descriptive word index and a table of cases sorted by name, listing the key numbers corresponding to the decisions. Thus, the researcher can find, by key number, topics that relate to the principles set out in the headnotes prepared for each judicial decision. A researcher who locates a topic and key number has access to all reported decisions on this point of law.

### Shepard's Citations

*Shepard's Citations* is a series that provides the judicial history of cases by reference to the volume and page number of the cases in the particular reporters. Because the law is constantly changing and new laws and decisions come out all the time, it is essential that a researcher keep up to date and know if there are new cases or what might have happened to a case the researcher has found. By using the symbols explained in *Shepard's Citations*, the researcher can determine whether a particular decision has been affirmed, followed, distinguished, modified, or reversed by subsequent court decisions. Most attorneys "Shepardize" the cases they cite in their law briefs to support various principles of law. There is a separate set of *Shepard's Citations* for the U.S. Supreme Court reports, for the federal appellate and district courts, for each regional reporter, and for each state that has an official reporter. *Shepard's* can also be found on Lexis.

## KeyCite

Another source that is used for updating a case history, and locating cases that refer to it, is KeyCite, available online as part of Westlaw. Like *Shepard's* (both print and computer versions), KeyCite gives the history of a case and subsequent cases that have cited it. Among other useful features that KeyCite has is a ranking system for the later cases, which shows which cases have discussed or explained the original one in detail and which give a mere mention of the case. This is of great help to the researcher who might otherwise be faced with a long list of cases to read and no way to differentiate their value.

## Secondary Sources

Legal authorities other than constitutions, statutes, ordinances, regulations, and court decisions are called secondary sources. Secondary sources explain the law and provide background and analysis of it. They help you understand the law and its applications and also will help you locate even more authorities, such as other cases and statutes.

A basic necessity for any legal researcher's work is a good law dictionary. Several are published, and *Black's Law Dictionary* (9th ed.), published by Thomson/West, is one of the best known. *Black's* is available both in print and on Westlaw.

## Legal Encyclopedias

Beyond dictionaries, the most commonly used secondary legal authorities are legal encyclopedias. These are arranged alphabetically by subject and are used much like any standard encyclopedia.

There are two principal national encyclopedias of the law: *Corpus Juris Secundum* (C.J.S.), published by West, and *American Jurisprudence,* second edition (Am.Jur.2d), published by West /Lawyers Cooperative. Appellate courts frequently include citations to these encyclopedias, as well as to cases in the reporters, to document the rules and interpretations contained in their opinions.

Each of these encyclopedias is an excellent set of reference books; one significant difference is that *Corpus Juris Secundum* cites more court decisions, whereas *American Jurisprudence 2d* limits footnote references to the leading cases pertinent to the principles of law in the text. *Corpus Juris Secundum* includes valuable cross-references to West topic key numbers and other secondary sources, including forms. *American Jurisprudence 2d* includes valuable footnote references to another of the company's publications, *American Law Reports*, now in its sixth series. These volumes (cited as A.L.R.) include annotations to the decisional law on selected topics. For example, a 1987 annotation from A.L.R. entitled "Snowmobile Operation as D.W.I. or D.U.I." appears in 56 A.L.R.4th 1092. Both *Corpus Juris Secundum* and *American Jurisprudence 2d* are supplemented annually by cumulative pocket parts and are exceptionally well indexed. They serve as an excellent starting point for a researcher because they provide a general overview of topics. A general index for each set is published annually, and researchers should use this first to find their specific subjects and section numbers.

For example, a person researching the defenses available to a defendant charged with forgery would find a good discussion of the law in this area in either of these encyclopedias. A citation to the text on defenses to forgery found in *Corpus Juris Secundum* would read as follows: 37 C.J.S. Forgery § 41; in *American Jurisprudence 2d* it would read like this: 36 Am.Jur.2d Forgery § 42. In addition to these major national encyclopedias, some states have encyclopedias for the jurisprudence of their state—for example, *Pennsylvania Law Encyclopedia* and *Texas Jurisprudence.* Like the volumes of *Corpus Juris Secundum* and *American Jurisprudence 2d,* most encyclopedias of state law are annually supplemented with cumulative pocket parts.

## Textbooks

Textbooks and other treatises on legal subjects often read much like encyclopedias; however, most address specific subjects in greater depth. One of the better-known textbooks is LaFave and Scott, *Criminal Law*, published by Thomson/West.

## Law Reviews, Journals and Professional Publications

Most leading law schools publish law reviews that contain articles, commentaries, and notes by academics, judges, lawyers, and law students who exhaustively research topics. Law review articles can be excellent sources of in-depth analysis and background information on specific legal topics. A citation for a law review article in the criminal justice field, "Consequences of Refusing Consent to a Search and Seizure," 75 S. Cal. L. Rev. 901 (2002), refers to a scholarly article published in volume 75 at page 901 of the *Southern California Law Review*.

An example of a professional publication is the *Criminal Law Bulletin*, published bimonthly by Warren, Gorham & Lamont of Boston. It contains many valuable articles of contemporary interest. For instance, "Probable Cause and the Fourth Amendment" was published in the September 2003 issue. The American Bar Association and most state bar associations publish numerous professional articles in their journals and reports. Some of these present contemporary views on the administration of justice; often they talk more about how the law is actually applied, not just the theory behind it that law review articles sometimes focus on.

The *Index to Legal Periodicals*, published by H. W. Wilson Company of the Bronx, New York, indexes articles from leading legal publications by subject and author. Another index for legal articles is the *Current Law Index*, published by Gale/Cengage in cooperation with the American Association of Law Libraries. These valuable research tools are found in many law libraries and are kept current by periodic supplements. Many college and law school libraries also have these available online. Periodicals published by law schools, bar associations, and other professional organizations can be valuable both in doing research and in gaining a perspective on many contemporary problems in the criminal justice field. The federal government also publishes numerous studies of value to the criminal justice professional and student.

## Words and Phrases

*Words and Phrases*, another West publication, consists of numerous volumes alphabetically arranged in dictionary form. Hundreds of thousands of legal terms are defined with citations to appellate court decisions. The volumes are kept current by annual pocket part supplements.

# Computerized Legal Research

Increasingly, legal research is being done electronically using computerized legal databases such as Westlaw. Westlaw operates from a central computer system at the West headquarters in St. Paul, Minnesota, and has databases for state and federal statutes, appellate decisions, attorney general opinions, and certain legal periodicals. For example, the law review article referred to earlier, "Consequences of Refusing Consent to a Search and Seizure," 75 S. Cal. L. Rev. 901 (2002), is available on Westlaw in the ScALR database and can be quickly retrieved by typing the citation—75 S. Cal. L. Rev. 901—into the "find this document" box on the welcome page. Subscribers can access Westlaw through the Internet. Westlaw users enter queries into the system to begin research, using connectors recognized by the system. A properly formulated query pinpoints the legal issue to be researched and instructs Westlaw to retrieve all data relevant to the query.

Westlaw also has a searching method that uses natural language, which allows queries to be entered in plain English without special terms or connectors. The statutes, cases, and other research results found on Westlaw can be printed, downloaded, or e-mailed. One of the most useful features of Westlaw is the ability to check the history of cases using KeyCite. When the researcher needs to update a large number of cases, Westlaw can save a tremendous amount of time and substantially reduce the possibility of error.

Westlaw is constantly adding new features and new types of materials, such as court documents and practice guides. Westlaw provides tutorials on how to use its new features when they are added.

Lexis is an excellent competing system. As with Westlaw, researchers can use Lexis to find cases and statutes, search for items either by forming queries or using natural language, and find cases by typing in their citations. Unlike Westlaw, which has KeyCite to check citation history, Lexis has an electronic version of *Shepard's* to check cites. It is a bit easier to use and more up-to-date than the printed *Shepard's* volumes. Lexis also has tutorials available to help you find out about new features or ways to search.

## Legal Research Using the Internet

The phenomenal growth of the Internet makes it impossible to firmly state what legal sources or sites currently are available because new things are being added constantly. The federal and state governments are among those rapidly adding data to the Internet, and for that reason a person looking for government information, or statutes and codes, is likely to find it on the Internet. Among the best ways to search for legal information is to use a comprehensive legal site such as ALSO!—American Law Sources On-line (www.lawsource.com)—which has a detailed listing of law websites for each state and for federal sources. ALSO! provides links to official sites such as those of government agencies, courts, and codes as well as other helpful sites such as state bar associations and legal aid groups. Another major site is Findlaw (www.findlaw.com), which uses categories to neatly divide legal information so that a user can search for the appropriate category and then find the information available on that topic or issue. Among Findlaw's categories are state law (further divided into categories for each individual state) and international law (indeed, the Internet is currently the best source for locating law from other countries). Another excellent source for federal information is Thomas (thomas.loc.gov), the Library of Congress website, which contains pending bills, federal laws, and links to other federal sites.

Findlaw's Supreme Court category offers U.S. Supreme Court opinions dating back to 1893 in a searchable format. In addition, the Legal Information Institute (LII) at Cornell University (www.law.cornell.edu/supct/) offers downloadable Supreme Court opinions. The LII archive now contains all opinions of the Court issued since May 1990 as well as hundreds of the most important historical decisions of the Court. The Supreme Court itself now has its own website, useful for finding information about pending or recently decided cases, at www.supremecourtus.gov.

More and more lower courts, both at the federal and state levels, are putting up their own websites, and often very recently decided cases can be found on them. ALSO! is a good place to begin in trying to locate these sites, as its listing for each state includes links to courts of that state. (The researcher may notice that many states have websites that cover all of their courts; for example, www.flcourts.org, the Florida courts website, has links to extensive information from all Florida appellate courts and many of the trial-level courts, too.) Findlaw also can help the researcher find the statutes, court decisions, and court rules of most states, almost all of which are now on the Internet. Regular search engines such as Google and Yahoo can be very helpful in locating court sites and other legal information. When using one of these search engines to locate a particular court decision, it is important to be very specific. One might try a docket number or an obscure or unique term that is found in the case. Most search engines also have advanced search features that let a researcher narrow the search to a particular web domain (e.g., only government web sites), or format (such as .pdf files), or date. These can be extremely helpful to use.

One of the most helpful sites for finding case law and even secondary sources on the internet is Google Scholar (scholar.google.com). By going to this and clicking on "legal opinions," the researcher can then do a search for federal and state cases; using the advanced search features, the researcher can specify what courts or dates to look through. While Google Scholar does not offer the wide variety of searching methods that are available on Westlaw, it is a free resource to use when looking for cases.

Although the Internet is convenient and low in cost, there are limitations to consider in doing research there. The Internet is a solid source for finding up-to-date information, such as current state statutes and some recent court decisions; it is also a good source for finding factual material, such as statistics and background information. Because most legal research involves finding more than just the latest cases and laws, however, a researcher may need to use other print or computer resources in addition to the Internet. When that is the case, the researcher will need to fall back on traditional methods of research.

# How to Research a Specific Point of Law

The following example demonstrates how a legal researcher might employ the research tools discussed earlier to find the law applicable to a given set of facts. Consider this hypothetical scenario:

> Mary Jones, a student at a Florida college, filed a complaint accusing Jay Grabbo of taking her purse while she was walking across campus on the afternoon of November 20, 2008. In her statement to the police, Jones was vague on whether Grabbo had used any force in taking the purse and whether she had offered any resistance. She stated that she had recently purchased the purse for $49 and that it contained $22 in cash plus a few loose coins and personal articles of little value. Further inquiry by the police revealed that Grabbo was unarmed.

A researcher who needs to gain a general background on the offense of robbery and how it differs from theft can profitably consult one of the legal encyclopedias mentioned earlier. Someone with a general knowledge of criminal offenses might still need to review the offense of robbery from the standpoint of state law. If so, *Florida Jurisprudence 2d* or some similar text should be consulted.

Given a general knowledge of the crimes of theft and robbery, a likely starting point would be the state statutes. In this instance, reference could be made to the official Florida Statutes. But from a research standpoint, it might be more productive to locate the statutes proscribing theft and robbery in the index to *West's Florida Statutes Annotated* and review the statutes and pertinent annotations in both the principal volume and the pocket part. The researcher would quickly find the offense of theft defined in § 812.014 and the offense of robbery defined in § 812.13.

Research of the statutory law would disclose that under Florida law, the theft of Jones's purse would be petit theft in the second degree if the total value was less than $100. West's Fla. Stat. Ann. § 812.014. This offense is a misdemeanor for which the maximum penalty is sixty days in jail and a $500 fine. West's Fla. Stat. Ann. § 775.082 and § 775.083. Unarmed robbery, on the other hand, is defined in West's Fla. Stat. Ann. § 812.13(1) as the taking of money or other property which may be the subject of larceny from the person or custody of another, with intent to either permanently or temporarily deprive the person or the owner of the money or other property, when in the course of the taking there is the use of force, violence, assault, or putting in fear.

If in the course of committing the robbery the offender carried no firearm, deadly weapon, or other weapon, then the robbery is a felony of the second degree, punishable by fifteen years' imprisonment and a maximum fine of $10,000 as provided in §§ 775.082, 775.083, or 775.084. (The latter statute refers to sentences for habitual offenders.) Therefore, it becomes very important to determine whether Grabbo should be charged with petit theft or robbery.

The researcher would then proceed to references noted under the topics of "force" and "resistance" that follow the text of the robbery statute. The annotated statutes would identify pertinent Florida appellate decisions on these points. For example, the researcher would find a note to *Mims v. State,* 342 So.2d 116 (Fla. App. 1977), indicating that purse snatching is not robbery if no more force is used than is necessary to physically remove the property from a person who does not resist. If the victim does resist and that resistance is overcome by the force of the perpetrator, however, the crime of robbery is complete. Another reference points the researcher to *Goldsmith v. State,* 573 So.2d 445 (Fla. App. 1991), which held that the slight force used in snatching a $10 bill from a person's hand without touching the person was insufficient to constitute robbery and instead constituted petit theft. Additional decisions refer to these and related points of law. For example, *Robinson v. State,* 680 So.2d 481 (Fla. App. 1999), indicates that while a stealthful taking may be petit theft, the force required to take someone's purse can make the offense robbery.

A further check into *West's Florida Statutes Annotated* reveals that the legislature enacted a new statute called "Robbery by Sudden Snatching" effective October 1, 1999. The new statute has been indexed as § 812.131 and provides,

(1) "Robbery by sudden snatching" means the taking of money or other property from the victim's person, with intent to permanently or temporarily deprive the victim or the owner of the money or other property, when, in the course of the taking, the victim was or became aware of the taking. In order to satisfy this definition, it is not necessary to show that:

(a) The offender used any amount of force beyond that effort necessary to obtain possession of the money or other property; or

(b) There was any resistance offered by the victim to the offender or that there was injury to the victim's person.

This offense is a third-degree felony, punishable by a maximum of five years' imprisonment and a fine of $5,000. West's Fla. Stat. Ann. § 775.082 and § 775.083.

Annotations to Fla. Stat. § 775.082 reveal that in *Brown v. State,* 848 So.2d 361 (Fla. App. 2003), the court reversed a defendant's conviction for robbery by sudden snatching where the victim herself was unaware of the snatching of her purse at the time it was taken. The court noted that the offense requires that property be taken from the victim's actual, physical possession, and that because the evidence at the defendant's trial revealed that the victim was unaware of the snatching until after it had been accomplished, the defendant should be acquitted of the charge of robbery by sudden snatching.

In *Walker v. State,* 933 So.2d 1236 (Fla. App. 2006), the appellate court agreed with *Brown v. State* and reversed a defendant's conviction because the State failed to prove beyond a reasonable doubt that the victim knew that her property was being taken during the course of the taking. Finally, on April 18, 2008, in *Walls v. State*, 977 So.2d 802 (Fla. App. 2008), the court of appeals found that because the state presented no testimony or other evidence indicating that the defendant took the purse by snatching it from the victim's person, the court correctly reduced the defendant's conviction to petit theft.

After locating these and other pertinent references, the researcher should go to the *Southern Reporter 2d* and *3d* to read the located cases. After concluding the search, the researcher should "Shepardize" or "KeyCite" the decisions to determine whether they have been subsequently commented on, distinguished, or even reversed.

In view of the newer statute and the recent appellate court interpretation, before arriving at a conclusion, the researcher will likely need additional information from the victim as to her awareness of Grabbo's taking her purse and what, if any, force was involved. If the research is undertaken for the prosecutors or the police, they can determine whether any further factual investigation is necessary. They can then decide the charge to place against Grabbo and the proof required to sustain that charge. On the other hand, if the research is undertaken for a defense attorney, once charges are placed against the accused the defense attorney can obtain more precise information from the victim's testimony through discovery procedures. That, along with the results of the legal research, would assist counsel in advising Grabbo, assuming he is charged with a crime, on how to plead and what defenses may be available.

The steps outlined here are basic and are designed to illustrate rudimentary principles of gaining access to the criminal law on a particular subject. As previously indicated, another method might involve using digests with the key number system of research. Moreover, there will often be issues of interest still undecided by courts in a particular state. If so, then research into the statutes and court decisions of other states may be undertaken. The methodology and level of research pursued will often depend on the researcher's objectives, knowledge of the subject, and experience in conducting legal research.

# Conclusion

Understanding how to gain access to the primary and secondary sources of the criminal law is tremendously important. The ability to assemble relevant facts, analyze a problem, and conduct a systematic search for applicable authoritative statements of constitutional, statutory, and decisional law is a skill to be acquired by both the criminal justice student and the working professional. Professionally trained lawyers, who must make the critical judgments concerning the prosecution and defense of criminal actions, increasingly assign basic legal research to paralegals and criminal justice personnel. The ability to access the law through traditional as well as computerized methods will assist the student and professional in becoming better acquainted with the dynamics of the criminal law. Moreover, the honing of such skill will enhance a person's ability to carry out specific research assignments and to support his or her recommendations with relevant legal authorities.

# The Constitution of the United States of America

We the People of the United States, in Order to form a more perfect Union, establish Justice, insure domestic Tranquility, provide for the common defense, promote the general Welfare, and secure the Blessings of Liberty to ourselves and our Posterity, do ordain and establish this Constitution for the United States of America.

## Article I

**Section 1.** All legislative Powers herein granted shall be vested in a Congress of the United States, which shall consist of a Senate and House of Representatives.

**Section 2.** (1) The House of Representatives shall be composed of Members chosen every second Year by the People of the several States, and the Electors in each State shall have the Qualifications requisite for Electors of the most numerous Branch of the State Legislature.

(2) No Person shall be a Representative who shall not have attained to the age of twenty-five Years, and been seven Years a Citizen of the United States, and who shall not, when elected, be an Inhabitant of that State in which he shall be chosen.

(3) Representatives and direct Taxes shall be apportioned among the several States which may be included within this Union, according to their respective Numbers, which shall be determined by adding to the whole Number of free Persons, including those bound to Service for a Term of Years, and excluding Indians not taxed, three fifths of all other Persons. The actual Enumeration shall be made within three Years after the first Meeting of the Congress of the United States, and within every subsequent Term of ten Years, in such Manner as they shall by Law direct. The Number of Representatives shall not exceed one for every thirty Thousand, but each State shall have at Least one Representative; and until such enumeration shall be made, the State of New Hampshire shall be entitled to choose three, Massachusetts eight, Rhode Island and Providence Plantations one, Connecticut five, New York six, New Jersey four, Pennsylvania eight, Delaware one, Maryland six, Virginia ten, North Carolina five, South Carolina five, and Georgia three.

(4) When vacancies happen in the Representation from any State, the Executive Authority thereof shall issue Writs of Election to fill such Vacancies.

(5) The House of Representatives shall choose their Speaker and other Officers; and shall have the sole Power of Impeachment.

**Section 3.** (1) The Senate of the United States shall be composed of two Senators from each State, chosen by the Legislature thereof, for six Years; and each Senator shall have one Vote.

(2) Immediately after they shall be assembled in Consequence of the first Election, they shall be divided as equally as may be into three Classes. The Seats of the Senators of the first Class shall be vacated at the Expiration of the second Year, of the second Class at the Expiration of the fourth Year, and of the third Class at the Expiration of the sixth Year, so that one third may be chosen every second Year; and if Vacancies happen by Resignation, or otherwise, during the Recess of the Legislature of any State, the Executive thereof may make temporary Appointments until the next Meeting of the Legislature, which shall then fill such Vacancies.

(3) No Person shall be a Senator who shall not have attained, to the Age of thirty Years, and been nine Years a Citizen of the United States, and who shall not, when elected, be an Inhabitant of that State for which he shall be chosen.

(4) The Vice President of the United States shall be President of the Senate, but shall have no Vote, unless they be equally divided.

(5) The Senate shall choose their other Officers, and also a President pro tempore, in the Absence of the Vice President, or when he shall exercise the Office of the President of the United States.

(6) The Senate shall have the sole Power to try all Impeachments. When sitting for that Purpose, they shall be on Oath or Affirmation. When the President of the United States is tried, the Chief Justice shall preside: And no Person shall be convicted without the Concurrence of two thirds of the Members present.

(7) Judgment in Cases of Impeachment shall not extend further than to removal from Office, and disqualification to hold and enjoy any Office of honor, Trust or Profit under the United States: but the Party convicted shall nevertheless be liable and subject to Indictment, Trial, Judgment and Punishment, according to Law.

**Section 4.** (1) The Times, Places and Manner of holding Elections for Senators and Representatives, shall be prescribed in each State by the Legislature thereof; but the Congress may at any time by Law make or alter such Regulations, except as to the Places of choosing Senators.

(2) The Congress shall assemble at least once in every Year, and such Meeting shall be on the first Monday in December, unless they shall by Law appoint a different Day.

**Section 5.** (1) Each House shall be the Judge of the Elections, Returns and Qualifications of its own Members, and a Majority of each shall constitute a Quorum to do Business; but a smaller Number may adjourn from day to day, and may be authorized to compel the Attendance of absent Members, in such Manner, and under such Penalties as each House may provide.

(2) Each House may determine the Rules of its Proceedings, punish its Members for disorderly Behavior, and, with the Concurrence of two thirds, expel a Member.

(3) Each House shall keep a Journal of its Proceedings, and from time to time publish the same, excepting such Parts as may in their Judgment require Secrecy; and the Yeas and Nays of the Members of either House on any question shall, at the Desire of one fifth of those Present, be entered on the Journal.

(4) Neither House, during the Session of Congress, shall, without the Consent of the other, adjourn for more than three days, nor to any other Place than that in which the two Houses shall be sitting.

**Section 6.** (1) The Senators and Representatives shall receive a Compensation for their Services, to be ascertained by Law, and paid out of the Treasury of the United States. They shall in all Cases, except Treason, Felony and Breach of the Peace, be privileged from Arrest during their Attendance at the Session of their respective Houses, and in going to and returning from the same; and for any Speech or Debate in either House, they shall not be questioned in any other Place.

(2) No Senator or Representative shall, during the Time for which he was elected, be appointed to any civil Office under the Authority of the United States, which shall have been created, or the Emoluments whereof shall have been increased during such time; and no Person holding any Office under the United States, shall be a Member of either House during his Continuance in Office.

**Section 7.** (1) All Bills for raising Revenue shall originate in the House of Representatives; but the Senate may propose or concur with Amendments as on other Bills.

(2) Every Bill which shall have passed the House of Representatives and the Senate, shall, before it become a Law, be presented to the President of the United States; If he approve he shall sign it, but if not he shall return it, with his Objections to that House in which it shall have originated, who shall enter the Objections at large on their Journal, and proceed to reconsider it. If after such Reconsideration two thirds of that House shall agree to pass the Bill, it shall be sent, together with the Objections, to the other House, by which it shall likewise be reconsidered, and if approved by two thirds of that House, it shall become a Law. But in all such Cases the Votes of both Houses shall be determined by Yeas and Nays, and the Names of the Persons voting for and against the Bill shall be entered on the Journal of each House respectively. If any Bill shall not be returned by the President within ten Days (Sunday excepted) after it shall have been presented to him, the Same shall be a Law, in like Manner as if he had signed it, unless the Congress by their Adjournment prevent its Return, in which Case it shall not be a Law.

(3) Every Order, Resolution, or Vote to which the Concurrence of the Senate and House of Representatives may be necessary (except on a question of Adjournment) shall be presented to the President of the United States; and before the Same shall take Effect, shall be approved by him, or being disapproved by him, shall be repassed by two thirds of the Senate and House of Representatives, according to the Rules and Limitations prescribed in the Case of a Bill.

**Section 8.** (1) The Congress shall have Power To lay and collect Taxes, Duties, Imposts and Excises, to pay the Debts and provide for the common Defense and general Welfare of the United States; but all Duties, Imposts and Excises shall be uniform throughout the United States;

(2) To borrow Money on the credit of the United States;

(3) To regulate Commerce with foreign Nations, and among the several States, and with the Indian Tribes;

(4) To establish an uniform Rule of Naturalization, and uniform Laws on the subject of Bankruptcies throughout the United States;

(5) To coin Money, regulate the Value thereof, and of foreign Coin, and to fix the Standard of Weights and Measures;

(6) To provide for the Punishment of counterfeiting the Securities and current Coin of the United States;

(7) To establish Post Offices and post Roads;

(8) To promote the Progress of Science and useful Arts, by securing for limited Times to Authors and Inventors the exclusive Right to their respective Writings and Discoveries;

(9) To constitute Tribunals inferior to the supreme Court;

(10) To define and punish Piracies and Felonies committed on the high Seas, and Offenses against the Law of Nations;

(11) To declare War, grant Letters of Marque and Reprisal, and make Rules concerning Captures on Land and Water;

(12) To raise and support Armies, but no Appropriation of Money to that Use shall be for a longer Term than two Years;

(13) To provide and maintain a Navy;

(14) To make Rules for the Government and Regulation of the land and naval Forces;

(15) To provide for calling forth the Militia to execute the Laws of the Union, suppress Insurrections and repel Invasions;

(16) To provide for organizing, arming, and disciplining, the Militia, and for governing such Part of them as may be employed in the Service of the United States, reserving to the States respectively, the Appointment of the Officers, and the Authority of training the Militia according to the discipline prescribed by Congress;

(17) To exercise exclusive Legislation in all Cases whatsoever, over such District (not exceeding ten Miles square) as may, by Cession of particular States, and the Acceptance of Congress, become the Seat of the Government of the United States, and to exercise like Authority over all Places purchased by the Consent of the Legislature of the State in which the Same shall be, for the Erection of Forts, Magazines, Arsenals, dock-Yards, and other needful Buildings;—And

(18) To make all Laws which shall be necessary and proper for carrying into Execution the foregoing Powers, and all other Powers vested by this Constitution in the Government of the United States, or in any Department or Officer thereof.

**Section 9.** (1) The Migration or Importation of such Persons as any of the States now existing shall think proper to admit, shall not be prohibited by the Congress prior to the Year one thousand eight hundred and eight, but a Tax or Duty may be imposed on such Importation, not exceeding ten dollars for each Person.

(2) The Privilege of the Writ of Habeas Corpus shall not be suspended unless when in Cases of Rebellion or Invasion the public Safety may require it.

(3) No Bill of Attainder or ex post facto Law shall be passed.

(4) No Capitation, or other direct, Tax shall be laid, unless in Proportion to the Census or Enumeration herein before directed to be taken.

(5) No Tax or Duty shall be laid on Articles exported from any State.

(6) No Preference shall be given by any Regulation of Commerce or Revenue to the Ports of one State over those of another; nor shall Vessels bound to, or from, one State, be obliged to enter, clear or pay Duties in another.

(7) No Money shall be drawn from the Treasury, but in Consequence of -Appropriations made by Law; and a regular Statement and Account of the Receipts and Expenditures of all public Money shall be published from time to time.

(8) No Title of Nobility shall be granted by the United States: And no Person holding any Office of Profit or Trust under them, shall, without the Consent of the Congress, accept of any present, Emolument, Office, or Title, of any kind whatever, from any King, Prince or foreign State.

**Section 10.** (1) No State shall enter into any Treaty, Alliance, or Confederation; grant Letters of Marque and Reprisal; coin Money; emit Bills of Credit; make any Thing but gold and silver Coin a Tender in Payment of Debts; pass any Bill of Attainder, expost facto Law, or Law impairing the Obligation of Contracts, or grant any Title of Nobility.

(2) No State shall, without the Consent of Congress, lay any Imposts or Duties on Imports or Exports, except what may be absolutely necessary for executing its inspection Laws: and the net Produce of all Duties and Imposts, laid by any State on Imports or Exports, shall be for the Use of the Treasury of the United States; and all such Laws shall be subject to the Revision and Control of the Congress.

(3) No State shall, without the Consent of Congress, lay any Duty of Tonnage, keep Troops, or Ships of War in time of Peace, enter into any Agreement or Compact with another State, or with a foreign Power, or engage in War, unless actually invaded, or in such imminent Danger as will not admit of Delay.

# Article II

**Section 1.** (1) The executive Power shall be vested in a President of the United States of America. He shall hold his Office during the Term of four Years, and, together with the Vice President, chosen for the same Term, be elected, as follows:

(2) Each State shall appoint, in such Manner as the Legislature thereof may direct, a Number of Electors, equal to the whole Number of Senators and Representatives to which the State may be entitled in the Congress: but no Senator or Representative, or Person holding an Office of Trust or Profit under the United States, shall be appointed an Elector.

The Electors shall meet in their respective States, and vote by Ballot for two Persons, of whom one at least shall not be an Inhabitant of the same State with themselves. And they shall make a List of all the Persons voted for, and of the Number of Votes for each; which List they shall sign and certify, and transmit sealed to the Seat of the Government of the United States, directed to the President of the Senate. The President of the Senate shall, in the presence of the Senate and House of Representatives, open all the Certificates, and the Votes shall then be counted. The Person having the greatest Number of Votes shall be the President, if such Number be a Majority of the whole Number of Electors appointed; and if there be more than one who have such Majority, and have an equal Number of Votes, then the House of Representatives shall immediately choose by Ballot one of them for President; and if no Person have a Majority, then from the five highest on the List the said House shall in like Manner choose the President. But in choosing the President, the Votes shall be taken by States, the Representation from each State having one Vote; a quorum for this Purpose shall consist of a Member or Members from two thirds of the States, and a Majority of all the States shall be necessary to a Choice. In every Case, after the Choice of the President, the Person having the greatest Number of Votes of the Electors shall be the Vice President. But if there should remain two or more who have equal Votes, the Senate shall choose from them by Ballot the Vice President.

(3) The Congress may determine the Time of choosing the Electors, and the Day on which they shall give their Votes; which Day shall be the same throughout the United States.

(4) No Person except a natural born Citizen, or a Citizen of the United States, at the time of the Adoption of this Constitution, shall be eligible to the Office of President; neither shall any Person be eligible to that Office who shall not have attained to the Age of thirty five Years, and been fourteen Years a Resident within the United States.

(5) In Case of the Removal of the President from Office, or of his Death, Resignation, or Inability to discharge the Powers and Duties of the said Office, the Same shall devolve on the Vice President, and the Congress may by Law provide for the Case of Removal, Death, Resignation or Inability, both of the President and Vice President, declaring what Officer shall then act as President, and such Officer shall act accordingly, until the Disability be removed, or a President shall be elected.

(6) The President shall, at stated Times, receive for his Services, a Compensation, which shall neither be increased nor diminished during the Period for which he shall have been elected, and he shall not receive within that Period any other Emolument from the United States, or any of them.

(7) Before he enter on the Execution of his Office, he shall take the following Oath or Affirmation:—"I do solemnly swear (or affirm) that I will faithfully execute the Office of President of the United States, and will to the best of my Ability, preserve, protect and defend the Constitution of the United States."

**Section 2.** (1) The President shall be Commander in Chief of the Army and Navy of the United States, and of the Militia of the several States, when called into the actual Service of the United States; he may require the Opinion, in writing, of the principal Officer in each of the executive Departments, upon any Subject relating to the Duties of their respective Offices, and he shall have Power to grant Reprieves and Pardons for Offenses against the United States, except in Cases of Impeachment.

(2) He shall have Power, by and with the Advice and Consent of the Senate, to make Treaties, provided two thirds of the Senators present concur; and he shall nominate, and by and with the Advice and Consent of the Senate, shall appoint -Ambassadors, other public Ministers and Consuls, Judges of the supreme Court, and all other Officers of the United States, whose Appointments are not herein otherwise provided for, and which shall be established by Law: but the Congress may by Law vest the Appointment of such inferior Officers, as they think proper, in the President alone, in the Courts of Law, or in the Heads of Departments.

(3) The President shall have Power to fill up all Vacancies that may happen during the Recess of the Senate, by granting Commissions which shall expire at the End of their next Session.

**Section 3.** He shall from time to time give to the Congress Information of the State of the Union, and recommend to their Consideration such Measures as he shall judge necessary and expedient; he may, on extraordinary Occasions, convene both Houses, or either of them, and in Case of Disagreement between them, with Respect to the Time of Adjournment, he may adjourn them to such Time as he shall think proper; he shall receive Ambassadors and other public Ministers; he shall take Care that the Laws be faithfully executed, and shall Commission all the Officers of the United States.

**Section 4.** The President, Vice President and all Civil Officers of the United States, shall be removed from Office on Impeachment for, and Conviction of, Treason, Bribery, or other high Crimes and Misdemeanors.

# Article III

**Section 1.** The judicial Power of the United States, shall be vested in one supreme Court, and in such inferior Courts as the Congress may from time to time ordain and establish. The Judges, both of the supreme and inferior Courts, shall hold their Offices during good Behavior, and shall, at stated Times, receive for their Services, a Compensation, which shall not be diminished during their Continuance in Office.

**Section 2.** (1) The judicial Power shall extend to all Cases, in Law and Equity, arising under this Constitution, the Laws of the United States, and Treaties made, or which shall be made, under their Authority;—to all Cases affecting Ambassadors, other public Ministers and Consuls;—to all Cases of admiralty and maritime Jurisdiction;—to Controversies to which the United States shall be a party;—to Controversies between two or more States;—between a State and Citizens of another State;—between Citizens of different States;—between Citizens of the same State claiming Lands under Grants of different States, and between a State, or the Citizens thereof, and foreign States, Citizens or Subjects.

(2) In all Cases affecting Ambassadors, other public Ministers and Consuls, and those in which a State shall be Party, the supreme Court shall have original Jurisdiction. In all the other Cases before mentioned, the supreme Court shall have appellate Jurisdiction, both as to Law and Fact, with such Exceptions, and under such Regulations as the Congress shall make.

(3) The Trial of all Crimes, except in Cases of Impeachment, shall be by Jury; and such Trial shall be held in the State where the said Crimes shall have been committed; but when not committed within any State, the Trial shall be at such Place or Places as the Congress may by Law have directed.

**Section 3.** (1) Treason against the United States, shall consist only in levying War against them, or in adhering to their Enemies, giving them Aid and Comfort. No Person shall be convicted of Treason unless on the Testimony of two Witnesses to the same overt Act, or on Confession in open Court.

(2) The Congress shall have Power to declare the Punishment of Treason, but no Attainder of Treason shall work Corruption of Blood, or Forfeiture except during the Life of the Person attainted.

# Article IV

**Section 1.** Full Faith and Credit shall be given in each State to the public Acts, Records, and judicial Proceedings of every other State. And the Congress may by general Laws prescribe the Manner in which such Acts, Records and Proceedings shall be proved, and the Effect thereof.

**Section 2.** (1) The Citizens of each State shall be entitled to all privileges and -Immunities of Citizens in the several States.

(2) A Person charged in any State with Treason, Felony, or other Crime, who shall flee from Justice, and be found in another State, shall on Demand of the executive Authority of the State from which he fled, be delivered up, to be removed to the State having Jurisdiction of the Crime.

(3) No Person held to Service of Labor in one State, under the Laws thereof, escaping into another, shall, in Consequence of any Law or Regulation therein, be discharged from such Service or Labor, but shall be delivered up on Claim of the Party to whom such Service or Labor may be due.

**Section 3.** (1) New States may be admitted by the Congress into this Union; but no new State shall be formed or erected within the Jurisdiction of any other State; nor any State be formed by the Junction of two or more States, or Parts of States, without the Consent of the Legislatures of the States concerned as well as of the Congress.

(2) The Congress shall have power to dispose of and make all needful Rules and Regulations respecting the Territory or other Property belonging to the United States; and nothing in this Constitution shall be so construed as to Prejudice any Claims of the United States, or of any particular State.

**Section 4.** The United States shall guarantee to every State in this Union a Republican Form of Government, and shall protect each of them against Invasion; and on Application of the Legislature, or of the Executive (when the Legislature cannot be convened) against domestic Violence.

# Article V

The Congress, whenever two thirds of both Houses shall deem it necessary, shall propose Amendments to this Constitution, or, on the Application of the Legislatures of two thirds of the several States, shall call a Convention for proposing Amendments, which, in either Case, shall be valid to all Intents and Purposes, as Part of this Constitution, when ratified by the Legislatures of three fourths of the several States, or by Conventions in three fourths thereof, as the one or the other Mode of Ratification may be proposed by the Congress; Provided that no Amendment which may be made prior to the Year One thousand eight hundred and eight shall in any Manner affect the first and fourth Clauses in the Ninth Section of the first Article; and that no State, without its Consent, shall be deprived of its equal Suffrage in the Senate.

# Article VI

(1) All Debts contracted and Engagements entered into, before the Adoption of this Constitution, shall be as valid against the United States under this Constitution, as under the Confederation.

(2) This Constitution, and the Laws of the United States which shall be made in Pursuance thereof; and all Treaties made, or which shall be made, under the Authority of the United States, shall be the supreme Law of the Land; and the Judges in -every State shall be bound thereby, any Thing in the Constitution or Laws of any State to the Contrary notwithstanding.

(3) The Senators and Representatives before mentioned, and the Members of the several State Legislatures, and all executive and judicial Officers, both of the United States and of the several States, shall be bound by Oath or Affirmation, to support this Constitution; but no religious Test shall ever be required as a Qualification to any Office or public Trust under the United States.

# Article VII

The Ratification of the Conventions of nine States, shall be sufficient for the Establishment of this Constitution between the States so ratifying the Same.

Articles in Addition to, and Amendment of, the Constitution of the United States of America, Proposed by Congress, and Ratified by the -Several States, Pursuant to the Fifth Article of the Original Constitution

# Amendment I (1791)

Congress shall make no law respecting an establishment of religion, or prohibiting the free exercise thereof; or abridging the freedom of speech, or of the press; or the right of the people peaceably to assemble, and to petition the Government for a -redress of grievances.

# Amendment II (1791)

A well regulated Militia, being necessary to the security of a free state, the right of the people to keep and bear Arms, shall not be infringed.

# Amendment III (1791)

No Soldier shall, in time of peace be quartered in any house, without the consent of the Owner, nor in time of war, but in a manner to be prescribed by law.

# Amendment IV (1791)

The right of the people to be secure in their persons, houses, papers, and effects, against unreasonable searches and seizures, shall not be violated, and no Warrants shall issue, but upon probable cause, supported by Oath or affirmation, and particularly describing the place to be searched, and the persons or things to be seized.

## Amendment V (1791)

No person shall be held to answer for a capital, or otherwise infamous crime, unless on a presentment or indictment of a Grand Jury, except in cases arising in the land or naval forces, or in the Militia, when in actual service in time of War or public danger; nor shall any person be subject for the same offence to be twice put in jeopardy of life or limb; nor shall be compelled in any criminal case to be a witness against himself, nor be deprived of life, liberty, or property, without due process of law; nor shall private property be taken for public use, without just compensation.

## Amendment VI (1791)

In all criminal prosecutions, the accused shall enjoy the right to a speedy and public trial, by an impartial jury of the State and district wherein the crime shall have been committed, which district shall have been previously ascertained by law, and to be informed of the nature and cause of the accusation; to be confronted with the witnesses against him; to have compulsory process for obtaining witnesses in his favor, and to have the Assistance of Counsel for his defense.

## Amendment VII (1791)

In Suits at common law, where the value in controversy shall exceed twenty dollars, the right of trial by jury shall be preserved, and no fact tried by a jury, shall be otherwise re-examined in any Court of the United States, than according to the rules of the common law.

## Amendment VIII (1791)

Excessive bail shall not be required, nor excessive fines imposed, nor cruel and unusual punishments inflicted.

## Amendment IX (1791)

The enumeration in the Constitution, of certain rights, shall not be construed to deny or disparage others retained by the people.

## Amendment X (1791)

The powers not delegated to the United States by the Constitution, nor prohibited by it to the States, are reserved to the States respectively, or to the people.

## Amendment XI (1798)

The Judicial power of the United States shall not be construed to extend to any suit in law or equity, commenced or prosecuted against one of the United States by Citizens of another State, or by Citizens or Subjects of any Foreign State.

# Amendment XII (1804)

The Electors shall meet in their respective states and vote by ballot for President and Vice-President, one of whom, at least, shall not be an inhabitant of the same state with themselves; they shall name in their ballots the person voted for as President, and in distinct ballots the person voted for as Vice-President, and they shall make distinct lists of all persons voted for as President, and of all persons voted for as Vice-President, and of the number of votes for each, which lists they shall sign and certify, and transmit sealed to the seat of the government of the United States, directed to the President of the Senate;—The President of the Senate shall, in the presence of the Senate and House of Representatives, open all the certificates and the votes shall then be counted;—The person having the greatest number of votes for President, shall be the President, if such number be a majority of the whole number of Electors appointed; and if no person have such majority, then from the persons having the highest numbers not exceeding three on the list of those voted for as President, the House of Representatives shall choose immediately, by ballot, the President. But in choosing the President, the votes shall be taken by states, the representation from each state having one vote; a quorum for this purpose shall consist of a member or members from two-thirds of the states, and a majority of all the states shall be necessary to a choice. And if the House of Representatives shall not choose a President whenever the right of choice shall devolve upon them, before the fourth day of March next following, then the Vice-President shall act as President, as in the case of the death or other constitutional disability of the President—The person having the greatest number of votes as Vice-President, shall be the Vice-President, if such number be a majority of the whole number of Electors appointed, and if no person have a majority, then from the two highest numbers on the list, the Senate shall choose the Vice-President; A quorum for the purpose shall consist of two-thirds of the whole number of Senators, and a majority of the whole number shall be necessary to a choice. But no person constitutionally ineligible to the office of President shall be eligible to that of Vice-President of the United States.

# Amendment XIII (1865)

**Section 1.** Neither slavery nor involuntary servitude, except as a punishment for crime whereof the party shall have been duly convicted, shall exist within the United States, or any place subject to their jurisdiction.
**Section 2.** Congress shall have power to enforce this article by appropriate legislation.

# Amendment XIV (1868)

**Section 1.** All persons born or naturalized in the United States and subject to the jurisdiction thereof, are citizens of the United States and of the State wherein they reside. No State shall make or enforce any law which shall abridge the privileges or immunities of citizens of the United States; nor shall any State deprive any person of life, liberty, or property, without due process of law; nor deny to any person within its jurisdiction the equal protection of the laws.
**Section 2.** Representatives shall be apportioned among the several States according to their respective numbers, counting the whole number of persons in each State, excluding Indians not taxed. But when the right to vote at any election

for the choice of electors for President and Vice-President of the United States, Representatives in Congress, the Executive and Judicial officers of a State, or the members of the Legislature thereof, is denied to any of the male inhabitants of such State, being twenty-one years of age, and citizens of the United States, or in any way abridged, except for participation in rebellion, or other crime, the basis of representation therein shall be reduced in the proportion which the number of such male citizens shall bear to the whole number of male citizens twenty-one years of age in such State.

**Section 3.** No person shall be a Senator or Representative in Congress, or elector of President and Vice-President, or hold any office, civil or military, under the United States, or under any State, who, having previously taken an oath, as a member of Congress, or as an officer of the United States, or as a member of any State legislature, or as an executive or judicial officer of any State, to support the Constitution of the United States, shall have engaged in insurrection or rebellion against the same, or given aid or comfort to the enemies thereof. But Congress may by a vote of two-thirds of each House, remove such disability.

**Section 4.** The validity of the public debt of the United States, authorized by law, including debts incurred for payment of pensions and bounties for services in suppressing insurrection or rebellion, shall not be questioned. But neither the United States nor any State shall assume or pay any debt or obligation incurred in aid of insurrection or rebellion against the United States, or any claim for the loss or emancipation of any slave; but all such debts, obligations and claims shall be held illegal and void.

**Section 5.** The Congress shall have power to enforce, by appropriate legislation, the provisions of this article.

# Amendment XV (1870)

**Section 1.** The right of citizens of the United States to vote shall not be denied or abridged by the United States or by any State on account of race, color, or previous condition of servitude.

**Section 2.** The Congress shall have power to enforce this article by appropriate legislation.

# Amendment XVI (1913)

The Congress shall have power to lay and collect taxes on incomes, from whatever source derived, without apportionment among the several States, and without regard to any census or enumeration.

# Amendment XVII (1913)

The Senate of the United States shall be composed of two Senators from each State, elected by the people thereof, for six years; and each Senator shall have one vote. The electors in each State shall have the qualifications requisite for electors of the most numerous branch of the State legislatures.

When vacancies happen in the representation of any State in the Senate, the executive authority of such State shall issue writs of election to fill such vacancies: Provided That the legislature of any State may empower the executive thereof to make temporary appointments until the people fill the vacancies by election as the legislature may direct.

This amendment shall not be so construed as to affect the election or term of any Senator chosen before it becomes valid as part of the Constitution.

# Amendment XVIII (1919)

**Section 1.** After one year from the ratification of this article the manufacture, sale, or transportation of intoxicating liquors within, the importation thereof into, or the exportation thereof from the United States and all territory subject to the jurisdiction thereof for beverage purposes is hereby prohibited.

**Section 2.** The Congress and the several States shall have concurrent power to -enforce this article by appropriate legislation.

**Section 3.** This article shall be inoperative unless it shall have been ratified as an amendment to the Constitution by the legislatures of the several States, as provided in the Constitution, within seven years from the date of the submission hereof to the States by the Congress.

# Amendment XIX (1920)

The right of citizens of the United States to vote shall not be denied or abridged by the United States or by any State on account of sex.

Congress shall have power to enforce this article by appropriate legislation.

# Amendment XX (1933)

**Section 1.** The terms of the President and Vice President shall end at noon on the 20th day of January, and the terms of Senators and Representatives at noon on the 3rd day of January, of the years in which such terms would have ended if this -article had not been ratified; and the terms of their successors shall then begin.

**Section 2.** The Congress shall assemble at least once in every year, and such meeting shall begin at noon on the 3rd day of January, unless they shall by law appoint a different day.

**Section 3.** If, at the time fixed for the beginning of the term of the President, the President elect shall have died, the Vice President elect shall become President. If a President shall not have been chosen before the time fixed for the beginning of his term, or if the President elect shall have failed to qualify, then the Vice President elect shall act as President until a President shall have qualified; and the Congress may by law provide for the case wherein neither a President elect nor a Vice President elect shall have qualified, declaring who shall then act as President, or the manner in which one who is to act shall be selected, and such person shall act accordingly until a President or Vice President shall have qualified.

**Section 4.** The Congress may by law provide for the case of the death of any of the persons from whom the House of Representatives may choose a President whenever the right of choice shall have devolved upon them, and for the case of the death of any of the persons from whom the Senate may choose a Vice President whenever the right of choice shall have devolved upon them.

**Section 5.** Sections 1 and 2 shall take effect on the 15th day of October following the ratification of this article.

**Section 6.** This article shall be inoperative unless it shall have been ratified as an amendment to the Constitution by the legislatures of three-fourths of the several States within seven years from the date of its submission.

# Amendment XXI (1933)

**Section 1.** The eighteenth article of amendment to the Constitution of the United States is hereby repealed.

**Section 2.** The transportation or importation into any State, Territory or possession of the United States for delivery or use therein of intoxicating liquors, in violation of the laws thereof, is hereby prohibited.

**Section 3.** This article shall be inoperative unless it shall have been ratified as an amendment to the Constitution by conventions in the several States, as provided in the Constitution, within seven years from the date of the submission hereof to the States by the Congress.

# Amendment XXII (1951)

**Section 1.** No person shall be elected to the office of the President more than twice, and no person who has held the office of President, or acted as President, for more than two years of a term to which some other person was elected President shall be elected to the office of the President more than once. But this Article shall not -apply to any person holding the office of President when this Article was proposed by the Congress, and shall not prevent any person who may be holding the office of President, or acting as President, during the term within which this Article becomes operative from holding the office of President or acting as President during the remainder of such term.

**Section 2.** This Article shall be inoperative unless it shall have been ratified as an amendment to the Constitution by the legislatures of three-fourths of the several States within seven years from the date of its submission to the States by the Congress.

# Amendment XXIII (1961)

**Section 1.** The District constituting the seat of Government of the United States shall appoint in such manner as the Congress may direct:

A number of electors of President and Vice President equal to the whole number of Senators and Representatives in Congress to which the District would be entitled if it were a State, but in no event more than the least populous State; they shall be in addition to those appointed by the States, but they shall be considered, for the purposes of the election of President and Vice President, to be electors appointed by a State; and they shall meet in the District and perform such duties as provided by the twelfth article of amendment.

**Section 2.** The Congress shall have power to enforce this article by appropriate legislation.

# Amendment XXIV (1964)

**Section 1.** The right of citizens of the United States to vote in any primary or other election for President or Vice President, for electors for President or Vice President, or for Senator or Representative in Congress, shall not be denied or abridged by the United States or any State by reason of failure to pay any poll tax or other tax.

**Section 2.** The Congress shall have power to enforce this article by appropriate legislation.

# Amendment XXV (1967)

**Section 1.** In case of the removal of the President from office or of his death or resignation, the Vice President shall become President.

**Section 2.** Whenever there is a vacancy in the office of the Vice President, the President shall nominate a Vice President who shall take office upon confirmation by a majority vote of both Houses of Congress.

**Section 3.** Whenever the President transmits to the President pro tempore of the Senate and the Speaker of the House of Representatives his written declaration that he is unable to discharge the powers and duties of his office, and until he transmits to them a written declaration to the contrary, such powers and duties shall be discharged by the Vice President as Acting President.

**Section 4.** Whenever the Vice President and a majority of either the principal officers of the executive departments or of such other body as Congress may by law provide, transmit to the President pro tempore of the Senate and the Speaker of the House of Representatives their written declaration that the President is unable to discharge the powers and duties of his office, the Vice President shall immediately assume the powers and duties of the office as Acting President.

Thereafter, when the President transmits to the President pro tempore of the Senate and the Speaker of the House of Representatives his written declaration that no inability exists, he shall resume the powers and duties of his office unless the Vice President and a majority of either the principal officers of the executive department or of such other body as Congress may by law provide, transmit within four days to the President pro tempore of the Senate and the Speaker of the House of Representatives their written declaration that the President is unable to discharge the powers and duties of his office. Thereupon Congress shall decide the issue, assembling within forty-eight hours for that purpose if not in session. If the Congress, within twenty-one days after receipt of the latter written declaration, or, if Congress is not in session, within twenty-one days after Congress is required to assemble, determines by two-thirds vote of both Houses that the President is unable to discharge the powers and duties of his office, the Vice President shall continue to discharge the same as Acting President; otherwise, the President shall resume the powers and duties of his office.

# Amendment XXVI (1971)

**Section** The right of citizens of the United States, who are eighteen years of age or older, to vote shall not be denied or abridged by the United States or by any State on account of age.

**Section 2.** The Congress shall have power to enforce this article by appropriate legislation.

# Amendment XXVII (1992)

No law, varying the compensation for the services of the Senators and Representatives, shall take effect, until an election of Representatives shall have intervened.

# Glossary

**abandoned property** Property over which the former owner has relinquished any claim of ownership.

**abortion** The intentional termination of a pregnancy.

**abuse of the elderly** Infliction of physical or mental harm on elderly persons.

**access device fraud** The crime of knowingly producing, using, or trafficking in counterfeit credit cards, personal identification numbers, access codes, account numbers, etc. with the intent to fraudulently obtain money, goods or services.

**access devices** Cards, plates, codes, electronic serial numbers, mobile identification numbers, personal identification numbers, and telecommunications services, equipment, or instrument identifiers or other means that can be used to obtain goods or services.

**accessory after the fact** A person who, with knowledge that a crime has been committed, conceals or protects the offender.

**accessory before the fact** A person who aids or assists another in commission of an offense.

**accomplice** A person who voluntarily unites with another in commission of an offense.

**act of omission** The failure to perform an act required by law.

**actual imprisonment standard** The standard governing the applicability of the federal constitutional right of an indigent person to have counsel appointed in a misdemeanor case. For the right to be violated, the indigent defendant must actually be sentenced to jail or prison after having been tried without appointed counsel.

**actual possession** Possession of something with the possessor having immediate control.

**actus reus** A "wrongful act" that, combined with other necessary elements of crime, constitutes criminal liability.

**administrative searches** Searches of premises by administrative agency official to determine compliance with regulations.

**administrative-type acts** Ministerial acts performed by executive officers in carrying out duties assigned by law.

**adultery** Voluntary sexual intercourse where at least one of the parties is married to someone other than the sexual partner.

**affiant** A person who makes an affidavit.

**affidavit** A written document attesting to specific facts of which the affiant has knowledge, and sworn to or affirmed by the affiant.

**affirm** To uphold, ratify, or approve.

**affirmative defense** Defense to a criminal charge where the defendant bears the burden of proof. Examples include automatism, intoxication, coercion, and duress.

**aggravated assault** An assault committed with a dangerous weapon or with intent to commit a felony.

**aggravated battery** A battery committed by use of an instrument designed to inflict great bodily harm on the victim.

**aggravated robbery** A robbery committed by a person armed with a dangerous weapon.

**aggravating factors** Factors attending the commission of a crime that make the crime or its consequences worse.

**aiding and abetting** Assisting in or otherwise facilitating the commission of a crime.

**Alford plea** A plea of guilty with a protestation of innocence.

**ALI standard** A test proposed by American Law Institute to determine if a defendant is legally insane. See substantial capacity test.

**alibi** Defense to a criminal charge that places the defendant at some place other than the scene of the crime at the time the crime occurred.

**Allen charge** A judge's instruction to jurors who are deadlocked, encouraging them to listen to one another's arguments and reappraise their own positions in an effort to arrive at a verdict.

**Anders brief** A law brief submitted to an appellate court by publicly appointed defense counsel in which counsel explains that the defendant's appeal is nonmeritorious and requests release from further representation of the defendant.

**answer brief** The appellee's written response to the appellant's law brief filed in an appellate court.

**anticipatory search warrant** A search warrant issued based on an affidavit that at a future time evidence of a crime will be at a specific place.

**antismoking laws** Statutes or ordinances prohibiting or restricting smoking in all or specified public places.

**Antiterrorism and Effective Death Penalty Act of 1996** A federal statute designed to effectuate reforms in administration of the death penalty by curtailing successive petitions for habeas corpus by prisoners sentenced to death.

**antitrust violations** Violations of laws designed to protect the public from price fixing, price discrimination, and monopolistic practices in trade and commerce.

**appeal of right** An appeal that a defendant is entitled to make as a matter of law.

**appellant** A party that takes an appeal to a higher court.

**appellate courts** Judicial tribunals that review decisions from lower tribunals.

**appellee** A party against whom an appeal is taken.

**arraignment** An appearance before a court of law for the purpose of pleading to a criminal charge.

**arrest** To take someone into custody or otherwise deprive that person of freedom of movement.

**arrest warrant** A document issued by a magistrate or judge directing that a named person be taken into custody for allegedly having committed an offense.

**arson** The crime of intentionally burning someone else's house or building—now commonly extended to other property as well.

**asportation** The carrying away of something: in kidnapping, the carrying away of the victim; in larceny, the carrying away of the victim's property.

**assault** The attempt or threat to inflict bodily injury upon another person.

**assignments of error** A written presentation to an appellate court identifying the points that the appellant claims constitute errors made by the lower tribunal.

**assisted suicide** An offense (in some jurisdictions) of aiding or assisting a person to take his or her life.

**attempt** An intent to commit a crime coupled with an act taken toward committing the offense.

**Attorney General** The highest legal officer of a state or of the United States.

**attorney-client privilege** The right of a person (client) not to testify about matters discussed in confidence with an attorney in the course of the attorney's representation.

**automatism** The condition under which a person performs a set of actions during a state of unconsciousness.

**automobile exception** Exception to the Fourth Amendment warrant requirement. The exception allows the warrantless search of a vehicle by police who have probable cause to search but because of exigent circumstances are unable to secure a warrant.

**bail bond** Sum of money posted to ensure a defendant's subsequent appearance in court.

**Bail Reform Act of 1984** See Federal Bail Reform Act of 1984.

**bankruptcy fraud** Dishonest or deceitful acts committed by one who seeks relief under laws designed to protect honest debtors from their creditors.

**battered child syndrome** A group of symptoms typically manifested by a child who has suffered continued physical or mental abuse, often from a parent or person having custody of the child.

**battered woman syndrome** A group of symptoms typically manifested by a woman who has suffered continued physical or mental abuse, usually from a male with whom she lives.

**battery** The unlawful use of force against another person that entails some injury or offensive touching.

**bench trial** A trial held before a judge without a jury present.

**best evidence** Primary evidence used to prove a fact—usually an original written document that evidences a communication or transaction.

**beyond a reasonable doubt** The standard of proof that is constitutionally required to be introduced before a defendant can be found guilty of a crime or before a juvenile can be adjudicated as a delinquent.

**bid rigging** An illegal manipulation in submitting bids to obtain a contract, usually from a public body.

**bifurcated trial** A capital trial with separate phases for determining guilt and punishment.

**bigamy** The crime of being married to more than one person at the same time.

**bill of attainder** A legislative act imposing punishment without trial upon persons deemed guilty of treason or felonies (prohibited by the U.S. Constitution).

**Bill of Rights** A written enumeration of basic rights, usually annexed to a written constitution—for example, the first ten amendments to the U.S. Constitution.

**blackmail** Extortion of money, property, or services from a person by threatening to expose embarrassing or harmful information about that person.

**Blackstone's *Commentaries*** A massive treatise on the English common law published in 1769 by Sir William Blackstone, a professor at Oxford University. In America, Blackstone's *Commentaries* became something of a legal bible.

**_Blockburger_ test** A test applied by courts to determine if the charges against a defendant would constitute a violation of the constitutional prohibition against double jeopardy—that is, being tried twice for the same offense. The *Blockburger* test holds that it is not double jeopardy for a defendant to be tried for two offenses if each offense includes an element that the other offense does not.

**boot camp** An institution that provides systematic discipline in a military-like environment designed to rehabilitate an offender; employed as a sentencing alternative.

**bootlegging** The crime of knowingly trafficking in counterfeit labels affixed or designed to be affixed to copies of musical recordings, computer programs, motion pictures, etc.

**border search** A search of persons entering the borders of the United States.

**bounty hunter** A person paid a fee or commission to capture a defendant who has fled a jurisdiction to escape punishment.

**Brady Bill** Legislation passed by Congress in 1993 requiring a five-day waiting period before the purchase of a handgun, during which time a background check is conducted of the buyer.

**brain death** The cessation of activity of the central nervous system.

**breach of contract** The violation of a provision in a legally enforceable agreement that gives the damaged party the right to recourse in a court of law.

**breach of the peace** The crime of disturbing the public tranquility and order; a generic term encompassing disorderly conduct, riot, etc.

**breaking** See breaking and entering.

**breaking and entering** Forceful, unlawful entry into a building or conveyance.

**breathalyzer** A device that detects the amount of alcohol in a sample of a person's breath.

**bribery** The crime of offering, giving, requesting, soliciting, or receiving something of value to influence a decision of a public official.

**brief** A document filed by a party to a lawsuit to convince the court of the merits of that party's case.

**burden of production of evidence** The obligation of a party to produce some evidence in support of a proposition asserted.

**burden of proof** The duty of a party to introduce evidence to sustain a fact or proposition.

**canons of construction** Rules governing the judicial interpretation of constitutions, statutes, and other written instruments.

**capias** "That you take." A general term for various court orders requiring that some named person be taken into custody.

**capital crime** A crime for which death is a permissible punishment.

**capital punishment** The death penalty.

**carjacking** Taking a motor vehicle from someone by force and violence or by intimidation.

**carnal knowledge** Sexual intercourse.

**castle doctrine** "A man's home is his castle." At common law, the right to use whatever force is necessary to protect one's dwelling and its inhabitants from an unlawful entry or attack.

**causation** An act that produces an event or an effect.

**cert petition** A petition to a higher court asking the court to review a lower court decision.

**certiorari** Writ issued by an appellate court to grant discretionary review of a case decided by a lower court.

**challenge for cause** Objection to a prospective juror on some specified ground (for example, a close relationship to a party in the case).

**change of venue** The removal of a legal proceeding, usually a trial, to a new location.

**child abuse** Actions that physically, mentally, or morally endanger the welfare of a child.

**child pornography** Material depicting persons under the age of legal majority in sexual poses or acts.

**child shield statutes** Laws that allow a screen to be placed between a child victim of sexual abuse and a defendant while the child testifies in court.

**child snatching** Action by one parent in deliberately retaining or concealing a child from the other parent.

**churning** Making purchases and sales of securities in a client's account simply to generate commissions for the broker.

**circumstantial evidence** Indirect evidence from which the existence of certain facts may be inferred.

**citation** (1) A summons to appear in court, often used in traffic violations. (2) A reference to a statute or court decision, often designating a publication where the law or decision appears.

**cite and release statutes** Laws permitting or requiring police officers to issue citations instead of making arrests for traffic violations or other minor misdemeanors or infractions.

**citizen's arrest** An arrest made by a person who is not a law enforcement officer.

**civil action** A lawsuit brought to enforce private rights and to remedy violations thereof.

**civil contempt** Being held in contempt of court pending the performance of some court-ordered act.

**civil forfeiture** Taking of property used in or obtained through unlawful activity pursuant to a civil proceeding in which the property itself is named as the defendant.

**civil infractions** Noncriminal violation of a law, often referring to minor traffic violations.

**civil rights** Rights protected by the federal and state constitutions and statutes. The term is often used to denote the right to be free from unlawful discrimination.

**Clean Air Act** A federal statute designed to deter polluters and thereby enhance the quality of the air.

**Clean Water Act** A federal statute designed to deter polluters and thereby enhance the quality of bodies of public water.

**clear and convincing evidence standard** An evidentiary standard that is higher than the standard of "preponderance of the evidence" applied in civil cases but lower than the standard of "beyond a reasonable doubt" applied in criminal cases. For example, under the new federal standard for the affirmative defense of insanity, the defendant must establish the defense of insanity by "clear and convincing evidence."

**clear and present danger doctrine** In constitutional law, the doctrine that the First Amendment does not protect those forms of expression that pose a "clear and present danger" of bringing about some substantive evil that government has a right to prevent.

**clemency** A grant of mercy by an executive official commuting a sentence or pardoning a criminal.

**clergy-penitent privilege** The exemption of a clergy-person and a penitent from disclosing communications made in confidence by the penitent.

**closing arguments** Arguments presented at trial by counsel at the conclusion of the presentation of evidence.

**coerced confession** A confession or other incriminating statements obtained from a suspect by police through force, violence, threats, intimidation, or undue psychological pressure.

**collateral attack** The attempt to defeat the outcome of a judicial proceeding by challenging it in a different proceeding or court.

**commercial bribery** Offering, soliciting, or accepting a benefit or consideration in respect to a business or professional matter in violation of a person's duty of fidelity.

**common-law rape** Sexual intercourse by a male with a female, other than his wife, by force and against the will of the female.

**community control** A sentence imposed on a person found guilty of a crime that requires that the offender be placed in an individualized program of noninstitutional confinement.

**community policing** Style of police work that stresses development of close ties between police officers and the communities they serve.

**community service** A sentence requiring that the criminal perform some specific service to the community for some specified period of time.

**compelling government interest** A government interest sufficiently strong that it overrides the fundamental rights of persons adversely affected by government action or policy.

**competent to testify** A person who has the legal capacity to offer evidence under oath in court.

**compounding a crime** The acceptance of money or something else of value in exchange for an agreement not to prosecute a person for committing a crime.

**Comprehensive Environmental Response, Compensation, and Liability Act** Federal statute commonly known as the Superfund Law. Its purpose is to finance cleanup and provide for civil suits by citizens. The act also imposes reporting requirements for the collection and disposal of solid wastes.

**compulsory process** See subpoena.

**computer fraud** An offense consisting of obtaining property or services by false pretenses through use of a computer or computer network.

**Computer Fraud and Abuse Act** Federal law criminalizing fraud and related activity in connection with computers.

**computer trespass** An offense consisting of the unauthorized copying, alteration, or removal of computer data, programs, or software.

**concealed weapon** A weapon carried on or about a person in such a manner as to hide it from the ordinary sight of another person.

**concurrent sentencing** The practice in which a trial court imposes separate sentences to be served at the same time.

**concurring in the judgment** An opinion by a judge or justice agreeing with the judgment of an appellate court without agreeing with the court's reasoning process.

**concurring opinion** Opinion handed down by a judge that supports the judgment of the court but often through different reasoning.

**conditions of confinement** The conditions under which inmates are held in jails and prisons. These conditions are subject to challenge under the Eighth Amendment's Cruel and Unusual Punishments Clause.

**conditions of probation** A set of rules that must be observed by a person placed on probation.

**confidential informant (CI)** An informant known to the police but whose identity is held in confidence.

**consanguinity** Kinship; the state of being related by blood.

**consecutive sentencing** The practice in which a trial court imposes a sentence or sentences to be served following completion of a prior sentence or sentences.

**consent** Voluntarily yielding to the will or desire of another person.

**consent to a search** The act of a person voluntarily permitting police to conduct a search of person or property.

**consideration, prize, and chance** The legal elements that constitute gambling under most statutes that make it an offense to gamble.

**conspiracy** The crime of two or more persons' agreeing or planning to commit a crime. The crime of conspiracy is distinct from the crime contemplated by the conspirators (the target crime).

**constitutional right of privacy** See privacy, constitutional right of.

**constitutional rights of prison inmates** Under modern interpretation of the federal and state constitutions, prisoners retain those constitutional rights that are not inconsistent with the fact that they are confined in a secure environment.

**constitutional supremacy** The doctrine that the Constitution is the supreme law of the land and that all actions and policies of government must be consistent with it.

**constructive intent** Intent inferred by law as a result of circumstances surrounding a party's actions.

**constructive possession** Being in the position to effectively control something, even if it is not actually in one's possession.

**contemnor** A person found to be in contempt of court.

**continuance** Delay of a judicial proceeding on the motion of one of the parties.

**contraband** Any property that is inherently illegal to produce or possess.

**contractual immunity** A grant by a prosecutor with approval of a court that makes a witness immune from prosecution in exchange for the witness's testimony.

**controlled substance** A drug designated by law as contraband.

**Controlled Substances Act** A federal law listing controlled substances according to their potential for abuse. States have similar statutes.

**copyright** A form of legal protection provided to the authors of original literary, musical, artistic, and architectural works as well as videos and computer software and databases.

**corporal punishment** Punishment that inflicts pain or injury to a person's body.

**corporate defendants** Corporations charged with criminal offenses.

**corpus delicti** "The body of the crime." The material thing upon which a crime has been committed (for example, a burned-out building in a case of arson).

**corrections system** The system of prisons, jails, and other penal and correctional institutions.

**counterfeiting** Making an imitation of something with the intent to deceive—for example, the offense of making imitations of U.S. coins and currency.

**court-martial** A military tribunal convened by a commander of a military unit to try a person subject to the Uniform Code of Military Justice who is accused of violating a provision of that code.

**Court of Appeals for the Armed Forces** The court (formerly known as the Court of Military Appeals) consisting of five civilian judges that reviews sentences affecting a general or flag officer or imposing the death penalty and that reviews cases certified for review by the judge advocate general of a branch of service. May grant review of convictions and sentences on petitions by service members.

**courts of general jurisdiction** Courts that conduct trials in felony and major misdemeanor cases. Also refers to courts that have jurisdiction to hear civil as well as criminal cases.

**courts of limited jurisdiction** Courts that handle pretrial matters and conduct trials in minor misdemeanor cases.

**crime syndicates** An association or group of people that carries out organized crime activities.

**criminal contempt** Punishment imposed by a judge against a person who violates a court order or otherwise intentionally interferes with the administration of the court.

**criminal forfeiture** Government confiscation of private property obtained through or otherwise involved in criminal activity pursuant to a criminal conviction of the owner of said property.

**criminal negligence** Conduct involving the reckless and flagrant disregard of the life or safety of another.

**criminal procedure** The rules of law governing the procedures by which crimes are investigated, prosecuted, adjudicated, and punished.

**criminal responsibility** Refers to the set of doctrines under which individuals are held accountable for criminal conduct.

**criminal trial** A trial in a court of law to determine the guilt or innocence of a person charged with a crime.

**critical pretrial stages** Significant procedural steps that occur before a criminal trial. A defendant has the right to counsel at these critical stages.

**cruel and unusual punishment** Punishment that shocks the moral conscience of the community—for example, torturing or physically beating a prisoner.

**curfew ordinances** Ordinances typically requiring minors to be off the streets by a certain time of night.

**curtilage** At common law, the enclosed space surrounding a dwelling house; in modern codes, this space has been extended to encompass other types of buildings.

**deadlocked jury** A jury whose members cannot agree on a verdict. Often referred to as a "hung jury."

**deadly force** The degree of force that may result in the death of the person against whom the force is applied.

**death penalty** Capital punishment; a sentence to death for the commission of a crime.

**death-qualified jury** A trial jury composed of people who do not entertain scruples against imposing a death sentence.

**decisional law** Law declared by appellate courts in their written decisions and opinions.

**decriminalization of routine traffic offenses** The recent trend toward treating minor motor vehicle offenses—for example, speeding—as civil infractions rather than crimes.

**defense attorney** A lawyer who represents defendants in criminal cases.

**defense of habitation and other property** The right of a defendant charged with an offense to assert that he or she used reasonable force to protect his or her home or property.

**defense of others** The defense asserted by one who claims the right to use reasonable force to prevent the commission of a felony against another person.

**definite sentencing** Legislatively determined sentencing with no discretion given to judges or corrections officials to individualize punishment.

**Department of Justice** The department within the executive branch of the federal government that is headed by the Attorney General and staffed by U.S. Attorneys.

**deposition** The recorded sworn testimony of a witness; not given in open court.

**depraved mind or heart** A serious moral deficiency; a high level of malice often linked to second-degree murder.

**derivative evidence** Evidence that is derived from or obtained only as a result of other evidence.

**determinate sentencing** The process of sentencing whereby the judge sets a fixed term of years within statutory parameters and the offender must serve that term without possibility of early release.

**diminished capacity** See substantial capacity test.

**diplomatic immunity** A privilege to be free from arrest and prosecution granted under international law to diplomats, their staffs, and their household members.

**direct contempt** An obstructive or insulting act committed by a person in the immediate presence of the court.

**direct evidence** Evidence that applies directly to proof of a fact or proposition. For example, a witness who testifies to having seen an act done or heard a statement made is giving direct evidence.

**directed verdict** A verdict rendered by a jury by direction of the presiding judge.

**discretionary review** Form of appellate court review of lower court decisions that is not mandatory but occurs at the discretion of the appellate court. See also certiorari.

**disorderly conduct** Illegal behavior that disturbs the public peace or order.

**disorderly intoxication** An offense consisting of misbehavior by a person who is drunk that results in disturbing the public peace or safety.

**dispositive motion** A motion made to a court where the ruling on the motion will determine the outcome of the case.

**dissenting opinion** An opinion rendered by a judge disavowing or disagreeing with the decision of a collegial court.

**DNA testing** Laboratory tests that compare DNA molecules extracted from a suspect's specimen with DNA molecules extracted from specimens found at a crime scene to determine whether the samples match.

**doctrine of harmless error** See harmless error, doctrine of.

**doctrine of incorporation** See incorporation, doctrine of.

**doctrine of overbreadth** See overbreadth, doctrine of.

**doctrine of transferred intent** See transferred intent, doctrine of.

**double jeopardy** The condition of being tried twice for the same criminal offense.

**driving under the influence (DUI)** The crime of driving under the influence of alcohol or drugs.

**driving while intoxicated (DWI)** The crime of driving while intoxicated by alcohol or drugs.

**driving with an unlawful blood-alcohol level (DUBAL)** The offense of operating a motor vehicle while one's blood-alcohol level is higher than allowed by law.

**drug courier profiles** Sets of characteristics thought to typify people engaged in drug smuggling.

**drug court** A specialized court or division of a court designed to deal specifically with defendants charged with violating laws proscribing the possession and use of controlled substances. Drug courts emphasize rehabilitation of offenders.

**drug paraphernalia** Items closely associated with the use of illegal drugs.

**drug-testing** Procedures, usually involving urinalysis, designed to test for the presence of illegal drugs in the body.

**Due Process Clause** The clause of the Fifth Amendment to the U.S. Constitution that prohibits the federal government from depriving persons within its jurisdiction of life, liberty, or property without due process of law. A similar provision in the Fourteenth Amendment imposes the same prohibition on state governments.

**due process of law** Procedural and substantive rights of citizens against government actions that threaten the denial of life, liberty, or property.

**duress** The use of illegal confinement or threats of harm to coerce someone to do something he or she would not do otherwise.

***Durham* test** A test for determining insanity developed by the U.S. Court of Appeals for the District of Columbia Circuit in the case of *Durham v. United States* (1954). Under this test, a person is not criminally responsible for an unlawful act if it was the product of a mental disease or defect.

**electronic eavesdropping** Covert listening to or recording of a person's conversations by electronic means.

**embezzlement** The crime of using a position of trust or authority to transfer or convert the money or property of another to oneself.

**emergency search** A search by law enforcement officers in response to an emergency. In such an instance, police can seize evidence in plain view despite not having a search warrant.

***en banc* hearing** A hearing in an appellate court in which all or a majority of the judges participate.

***en banc* rehearing** A rehearing in an appellate court in which all or a majority of the judges participate.

**Endangered Species Act** A 1973 act of Congress designed to conserve ecosystems by preserving wildlife, fish, and plants. The act imposes criminal penalties against any person who knowingly violates regulations issued under the act.

**endangering the welfare of a child** Knowingly acting in a manner likely to be injurious to the physical, mental, or moral welfare of a child.

**English common law** The body of decisional law based largely on custom as declared by English judges after the Norman Conquest of 1066. See also *stare decisis*.

**enterprise** An individual, partnership, corporation, association, or other legal entity; a union or group of individuals although not a legal entity.

**entrapment** The act of government agents in inducing someone to commit a crime that the person would not otherwise be disposed to commit.

**enumerated powers** Powers explicitly granted to governments by their constitutions.

**environmental crime** A violation of a criminal provision of an environmental statute such as the Clean Water Act.

**Environmental Protection Agency** Agency within the executive branch of the national government with principal responsibility for the enforcement of environmental laws, promulgation of environmental regulations, and administration of environmental programs.

**equal protection of the laws** Constitutional requirement that the government afford the same legal protection to all persons.

**error correction** The function of appellate courts in reviewing routine appeals and correcting the errors of trial courts.

**escape** Unlawfully fleeing to avoid arrest or confinement.

**espionage** The crime of turning over state secrets to a foreign government.

**evanescent evidence** Evidence that tends to disappear or be destroyed. Often, police seek to justify a warrantless search on the ground that destruction of the evidence is imminent.

**evidentiary presumption** Establishment of one fact allows inference of another fact or circumstance.

***ex post facto* law** A retroactive law that criminalizes actions that were legal at the time they were taken or increases punishment for a criminal act after it was committed.

**excessive bail** Where a court requires a defendant to post an unreasonably large amount or imposes unreasonable conditions as a prerequisite for a defendant to be released before trial. The Eighth Amendment to the U.S. Constitution prohibits courts from requiring "excessive bail."

**excessive noise** Unnecessarily loud sounds that interfere with the public peace and endanger the public peace, health, and welfare; sounds emitted that exceed the levels permitted by law or ordinance.

**exclusionary rule** Judicial doctrine forbidding the use of evidence in a criminal trial where the evidence was obtained in violation of the defendant's constitutional rights.

**exculpatory evidence** That which exonerates or tends to exonerate a person from fault or guilt.

**excusable homicide** A death caused by accident or misfortune.

**exigent circumstances** Unforeseen situations that demand unusual or immediate action.

**extortion** The crime of obtaining money or property by threats of force or the inducement of fear.

**extradition** The surrender of a person by one jurisdiction to another for the purpose of criminal prosecution.

**eyewitness testimony** Testimony given by a person based on personal observation of an event.

**factual basis** When a defendant pleads guilty to an offense the court requires a recitation of facts (usually by counsel) to establish that proof is available to show the defendant's guilt of the elements of the offense.

**factual impossibility** That which is in fact impossible to achieve.

**fair hearing** A hearing in which both parties have a reasonable opportunity to be heard—to present evidence and make arguments. A fundamental element of due process of law.

**fair notice** The requirement, stemming from due process, that government provide adequate notice to a person before it deprives that person of life, liberty, or property.

**false arrest** The tort or crime of unlawfully restraining a person.

**False Claims Act** A federal statute that makes it unlawful for a person to knowingly present a false or fraudulent claim to the U.S. government.

**false imprisonment** See false arrest.

**false pretenses** The crime of obtaining money or property through misrepresentation.

**False Statements Act** A federal statute making it a crime for a person to knowingly make a false and material statement to a U.S. government agency to obtain a government benefit or in connection with performing work for the government.

**Federal Anti-Riot Act** A federal law enacted in 1968 making it a crime to travel or use interstate or foreign commerce facilities in connection with inciting, participating in, or aiding acts of violence.

**Federal Bail Reform Act of 1984** An act that provides that a defendant charged with a federal crime may be denied bail if the prosecution can show that the defendant poses a threat to public safety.

**Federal Bureau of Investigation (FBI)** The primary federal agency charged with investigating violations of federal criminal laws.

**Federal Gun Control Act** This 1968 statute prohibits firearms dealers from transferring handguns to people who are younger than twenty-one, nonresidents of the dealer's state, and those who are otherwise prohibited by state or local laws from purchasing or possessing firearms. It also forbids possession of a firearm by, and transfer of a firearm to, people in a number of categories, including convicted felons, users of controlled substances, those adjudicated as incompetent or committed to mental institutions, illegal aliens, those dishonorably discharged from the military, those who have renounced their citizenship, and fugitives from justice.

**federal habeas corpus review** Review of a state criminal trial by a federal district court on a writ of habeas corpus after the defendant has been convicted, has been incarcerated, and has exhausted appellate remedies in the state courts.

**Federal Rules of Appellate Procedure** Rules of procedure governing the practice of law before the U.S. courts of appeals.

**Federal Sentencing Reform Act of 1984** A federal act directing the promulgation of sentencing guidelines.

**federalism** The constitutional distribution of government power and responsibility between the national government and the states.

**felony** A serious crime for which a person may be imprisoned for more than one year.

**felony murder** A homicide committed during the course of committing another felony other than murder (for

example, armed robbery). The felonious act substitutes for the malice aforethought ordinarily required in murder.

**field sobriety test** A test administered by police to people suspected of driving while intoxicated. Usually consists of requiring the suspect to demonstrate the ability to perform such physical acts as touching one's finger to one's nose or walking backward.

**fighting words** Utterances that are inherently likely to provoke a violent response from the audience.

**fines** See monetary fines.

**First Amendment** Article of the Bill of Rights recognizing the freedoms of religion, speech, press and assembly as well as the right to petition government for a redress of grievances.

**first-degree murder** The highest degree of unlawful homicide, usually defined as "an unlawful act committed with the premeditated intent to take the life of a human being."

**force** The element of compulsion in such crimes against persons as rape and robbery.

**forcible rape** Sexual intercourse by force and against the will of the victim.

**forensic evidence** Evidence obtained through scientific techniques of analyzing physical evidence.

**forensic experts** Persons qualified in the application of scientific knowledge to legal principles, usually applied to those who participate in discourse or who testify in court.

**foreperson** The person selected by fellow jurors to chair deliberations and report the jury's verdict.

**forfeiture** Sacrifice of ownership or some right (usually property) as a penalty.

**forgery** The crime of making a false written instrument or materially altering a written instrument (such as a check, promissory note, or college transcript) with the intent to defraud.

**fornication** Sexual intercourse between unmarried persons; an offense in some jurisdictions.

**Fourteenth Amendment** Amendment to the U.S. Constitution ratified after the Civil War in 1868. Prohibits states from denying due process and equal protection of law to persons within their jurisdictions and provides Congress legislative power to enforce these prohibitions.

***Franks* hearing** A pretrial proceeding that allows a defendant to challenge the veracity of an affiant's statements in the affidavit that supports the issuance of a search warrant.

**freedom of expression** The right of the individual to express thoughts and feelings through speech, writing, and other media of expression; protected by the First Amendment to the U.S. Constitution.

**freedom of religion** The First Amendment right to the free exercise of one's religion.

**frivolous appeals** Appeals wholly lacking in legal merit.

**fruit of the poisonous tree doctrine** A doctrine based on the judicial interpretation of the Fourth Amendment that holds that evidence derived from other, illegally seized evidence cannot be used by the prosecution.

**Frye test** See general acceptance test.

**fundamental constitutional rights** Those constitutional rights that have been declared to be fundamental by the courts. Include First Amendment freedoms, the right to vote, and the right to privacy.

**fundamental error** An error in a judicial proceeding that adversely affects the substantial rights of the accused.

**fundamental rights** See fundamental constitutional rights.

**gambling** Operating or playing a game for money in the expectation of gaining more than the amount played.

**gender-based peremptory challenges** A challenge to a prospective juror's competency to serve based solely on the prospective juror's gender.

**gender-neutral offense** A crime that may be committed by members of either sex against members of either sex.

**general acceptance test** Also known as the *Frye* test, this test is used by many state courts to determine whether to admit expert testimony in scientific matters. It must be established that the scientific principle from which the expert's deduction is made has gained general acceptance in its field.

**general deterrence** The theory that punishment serves to deter others from committing crimes.

**general intent** The state of mind to do something prohibited by law without necessarily intending to accomplish the harm that results from the illegal act.

**general objection** An objection raised against a witness's testimony or introduction of evidence when the objecting party does not recite a specific ground for the objection.

**general warrant** A search or arrest warrant that is not particular as to the person to be arrested, place to be searched, or property to be seized.

**general-intent statutes** Statutes defining crimes that require only general intent, as distinct from specific intent, on the part of the violator.

**good-faith exception** An exception to the exclusionary rule (which bars the use of evidence obtained by a search warrant found to be invalid). The exception allows use of the evidence if the police relied in good faith on the search warrant, even though the warrant is subsequently held to be invalid.

**good time credit** Credit toward early release from prison based on good behavior during confinement (often referred to as gain time).

**grand jury** A group of citizens convened either to conduct an investigation or to determine whether there is sufficient evidence to warrant the prosecution of an accused.

**grand theft** Theft of a sufficient value of property to make the crime a felony.

**guilty but mentally ill** A form of verdict that may be rendered in some states where the jury finds that the defendant's mental illness does not deprive the defendant of substantial capacity sufficient to satisfy the insanity test but warrants the defendant's treatment in addition to incarceration.

**gun control laws** Laws regulating the manufacture, importation, sale, distribution, possession, or use of firearms.

**Gun-Free School Zones Act** Federal statute making it a crime "for any individual knowingly to possess a firearm at a place that the individual knows, or has reasonable cause to believe, is a school zone." This law was declared unconstitutional by the U.S. Supreme Court in *United States v. Lopez* (1995).

**habeas corpus** "You have the body." A judicial writ requiring that a party be brought before a court. The primary function of habeas corpus is to release a person from unlawful confinement.

**habitual offender statute** A law that imposes an additional punishment on a criminal who has previously been convicted of crimes.

**Hale's Rule** English common law credited to Sir Matthew Hale, Lord Chief Justice in the seventeenth century, holding that a husband could not be charged with the rape of his wife.

**handwriting exemplar** A sample of a suspect's handwriting.

**hard-core pornography** Material that is extremely graphic in its depiction of sexual conduct.

**hate crimes** Crimes in which the victim is selected on the basis of race, religion, sexual orientation, or ethnicity.

**hate speech** Offensive speech directed at members of racial, religious, sexual, or ethnic minorities.

**hearsay evidence** Testimony by a witness as to facts the witness has heard from others that is offered in evidence at a trial or hearing to prove the truth of the matter asserted.

**heat of passion** A violent and uncontrollable rage resulting from a provocation that would cause such a response by a reasonable person—for example, a person who views his or her spouse in the act of committing adultery.

**Hobbs Act** A 1946 act of Congress authorizing criminal penalties for whoever in any way or degree obstructs, delays, or affects commerce or the movement of any article or commodity in commerce, by robbery or extortion or attempts or conspires so to do, or commits or threatens physical violence to any person or property in furtherance of a plan or purpose to do anything in violation of this section.

**homicide** The killing of a human being.

**hostage taking** The act in which the perpetrator of a robbery or some other crime forcibly detains innocent bystanders.

**hot pursuit** (1) The right of police to cross jurisdictional lines to apprehend a suspect or criminal; (2) the Fourth Amendment doctrine allowing warrantless searches and arrests where police pursue a fleeing suspect into a protected area.

**house arrest** A sentencing alternative to incarceration where the offender is allowed to leave home only for employment and approved community service activities.

**human trafficking** The illegal trade in human beings for the purpose of migration, labor, or commercial sexual exploitation.

**hypnotically induced testimony** Testimony offered by a witness whose memory has been refreshed through hypnosis.

**hypothetical question** A question based on an assumed set of facts. Hypothetical questions may be asked of expert witnesses in criminal trials.

**identification procedures** Scientific and nonscientific procedures employed by police to assist in the identification of suspects.

**identity theft** The crime of using someone else's personal information—such as their name, Social Security number, or credit card number—without their permission to commit fraud or other crimes.

**immigration offenses** Violations of criminal provisions of the Immigration and Nationality Act, a federal law that relates to immigration.

**imminent lawless action** Unlawful conduct that is about to take place and that is inevitable unless there is intervention by the authorities.

**immunity** Exemption from civil suit or prosecution. See also use immunity and transactional immunity.

**impeachment** (1) A legislative act bringing a charge against a public official that, if proven in a legislative trial, will cause his or her removal from public office; (2) impugning the credibility of a witness by introducing contradictory evidence or proving his or her bad character.

**implied consent** An agreement or acquiescence manifested by a person's actions or inaction.

**implied consent statutes** Laws providing that by accepting a license, a driver arrested for a traffic offense consents to urine, blood, and breath tests to determine blood-alcohol content.

**implied exception** An exclusion that can reasonably be inferred or assumed based on the purpose and intent of an ordinance, statute, or contract.

**implied powers** Powers not expressly granted to government by a constitution but fairly implied by the document.

**impotency** Lacking in power; in reference to a male, the inability to copulate.

**in camera** In a judge's chambers.

**incapacitation** Punishment making it impossible for an offender to reoffend.

**incarceration** Imprisonment.

**incest** Sexual intercourse with a close blood relative or, in some cases, a person related by affinity.

**inchoate offenses** Offenses preparatory to committing other crimes. Inchoate offenses include attempt, conspiracy, and solicitation.

**inciting a riot** The crime of instigating or provoking a riot.

**incorporation, doctrine of** The doctrine under which provisions of the Bill of Rights are held to be incorporated within the Due Process Clause of the Fourteenth Amendment and are thereby made applicable to actions of the state and local governments.

**incriminating statements** Statements typically made to police that increase the likelihood that one will be found guilty of a crime.

**indecent exposure** The intentional exposure in public of private areas of a person's body.

**indefinite sentencing** Form of criminal sentencing whereby a judge imposes a term of incarceration within statutory parameters and corrections officials determine actual time served through parole or other means.

**independent counsel** A special prosecutor appointed to investigate and, if warranted, prosecute official misconduct.

**independent source doctrine** The doctrine that permits evidence to be admitted at trial as long as it was obtained independently from illegally obtained evidence.

**indeterminate sentencing** Form of criminal sentencing where criminals are sentenced to prison for indeterminate periods until corrections officials determine that rehabilitation has been accomplished.

**indictment** A formal document handed down by a grand jury accusing one or more persons of the commission of a crime or crimes.

**indigency** Poverty.

**indigent defendants** Defendants who cannot afford to retain private legal counsel and are therefore entitled to be represented by a public defender or a court-appointed lawyer.

**indirect contempt** An act committed outside the presence of the court that insults the court or obstructs a judicial proceeding.

**indirect evidence** Inferences and presumptions that are probative of various facts in issue.

**ineffective assistance of counsel** Deficient performance by a lawyer representing a defendant that results in serious errors that prejudice the right of a defendant to a fair trial.

**inevitable discovery doctrine** The doctrine that holds that evidence derived from inadmissible evidence is admissible if it inevitably would have been discovered independently by lawful means.

**infancy** The condition of being below the age of legal majority.

**information** A document filed by a prosecutor under oath charging one or more persons with commission of a crime.

**initial appearance** After arrest, the first appearance of the accused before a judge or magistrate where the charges against a defendant are read and the defendant is advised of his or her constitutional rights. Sometimes referred to as the "first appearance."

**insanity** A degree of mental illness that negates the legal capacity or responsibility of the affected person.

**Insanity Defense Reform Act of 1984** An act of Congress that specifies that insanity is an affirmative defense to a prosecution under a federal statute and details the requirements for establishing such a defense.

**insider trading** Transactions in securities by a person who operates inside a corporation and, by using material nonpublic information, trades to his or her advantage without first disclosing that information to the public.

**insufficient evidence** Evidence that falls short of establishing what is required by law, usually referring to evidence that does not legally establish an offense or a defense.

**intellectual property** Products of the human intellect, such as inventions, plays, stories, films, music and trade secrets.

**intent to deprive** The willful design to take goods or services from another without permission or authority of law.

**intentionally** Willfully; with a mental purpose to act.

**intermediate appellate courts** Judicial tribunals consisting of three or more judges that review decisions of trial courts but that are subordinate to the final appellate tribunals.

**interrogation** Questioning of a suspect by police or questioning of a witness by counsel.

**interstate commerce** Economic activity between or among states or affecting more than one state.

**intoxication** Condition in which a person has impaired physical or mental capacities due to the ingestion of drugs or alcohol.

**inventory search** An exception to the warrant requirement that allows police who legally impound a vehicle to conduct a routine inventory of the contents of the vehicle.

**investigatory detention** Brief detention of suspects by a police officer who has reasonable suspicion that criminal activity is afoot. See also stop-and-frisk.

**involuntary intoxication** Intoxication that is not the result of a person's intentional ingestion of an intoxicating substance. A person may become involuntarily intoxicated through the trickery or fraud of another person or through the inadvertent ingestion of medicine.

**involuntary manslaughter** The unintentional killing of another person as the result of gross or wanton negligence.

**irresistible impulse** A desire that cannot be resisted due to impairment of the will by mental disease.

***Jencks* Act** The common name for a federal statute that permits a defendant to review a witness's prior written or recorded statement, but only after the witness has testified on direct examination for the government.

**joinder and severance of parties** The uniting or severing of two or more parties charged with a crime or crimes.

**joinder of offenses** The uniting of different charges or counts alleged in an information or indictment into one case for trial.

**judgment of acquittal** In a nonjury trial, a judge's order exonerating a defendant based on a finding that the defendant is not guilty. In a case heard by a jury finding a defendant guilty, a judge's order exonerating a defendant on the ground that the evidence was not legally sufficient to support the jury's finding of guilt.

**judicial conference** A meeting of judges to deliberate on the disposition of a case.

**judicial notice** The act of a court recognizing, without proof, the existence of certain facts that are commonly known. Such facts are often brought to the court's attention through the use of a calendar or almanac.

**judicial review** The power of courts of law to review governmental acts and declare them null and void if they are found to be unconstitutional.

**jurisdiction** The authority of a court to hear and decide certain categories of legal disputes. Jurisdiction relates to the authority of a court over the person, subject matter, and geographical area.

**jury** A group of citizens convened for the purpose of deciding factual questions relevant to a civil or criminal case.

**jury instructions** A judge's explanation of the law applicable to a case being heard by a jury.

**jury nullification** The fact of a jury disregarding the court's instructions and rendering a verdict on the basis of the consciences of the jurors.

**jury pardon** An action taken by a jury, despite the quality of the evidence, acquitting a defendant or convicting the defendant of a lesser crime than charged.

**jury trial** A judicial proceeding to determine a defendant's guilt or innocence conducted before a body of people sworn to render a verdict based on the law and the evidence presented.

**justifiable homicide** Killing another in self-defense or defense of others when there is serious danger of death or great bodily harm to self or others or when authorized by law.

**justifiable use of force** The necessary and reasonable use of force by a person in self-defense, defense of another, or defense of property.

**juvenile court** A judicial tribunal having jurisdiction over minors defined as juveniles who are alleged to be status offenders or to have committed acts of delinquency.

**juvenile delinquency** Actions of a juvenile in violation of the criminal law.

**kidnapping** The forcible abduction and carrying away of a person against that person's will.

**kidnapping for ransom** The offense of unlawfully taking and confining a person until a specified payment is made to the offender.

**knock-and-announce rule** The provision under federal and most state laws that requires a law enforcement officer to first knock and announce his or her presence and purpose before entering a person's home to serve a search or arrest warrant.

**knowingly** Consciously, i.e., with knowledge.

**larceny** At common law, the unlawful taking of property with the intent of permanently depriving the owner of same.

**lawmaking function** One of the principal functions of an appellate court, often referred to as the law development function.

**leading questions** A question that suggests an answer. Leading questions are permitted at a criminal trial on cross-examination of witnesses and in other limited instances.

**legal impossibility** A defense allowed in some jurisdictions when, although the defendant intended to commit a crime, it was impossible to do so because the completed act is not a crime.

**legislative intent** The purpose the legislature sought to achieve in enacting a particular provision of law.

**legislature** An elected lawmaking body such as the Congress of the United States or a state assembly.

**lewd and lascivious conduct** Indecent exposure of a person's private parts in public; indecent touching or fondling of a child.

**lineup** A police identification procedure where a suspect is included in a group with other persons and the group is exhibited to a victim.

**littering** The crime of disposing of garbage along a public street or road.

**loan sharking** The practice of lending money at illegal rates of interest.

**loitering** Standing around idly; "hanging out."

**lottery** A drawing in which prizes are distributed to winners selected by lot from among those who have participated by paying a consideration.

**_M'Naghten_ Rule** Under this rule, for a defendant to be found not guilty by reason of insanity, it must be clearly proved that, at the time of committing the act, the defendant was suffering such a defect of reason, from disease of the mind, as not to know the nature and quality of the act he was doing; or, if he did know it, that he did not know what he was doing was wrong.

**mail fraud** A scheme devised or intended to defraud or to obtain money or property by fraudulent means, or the use or causing to use the mails in furtherance of the fraudulent scheme.

**_mala in se_** "Evil in itself."

**_mala in se_ offenses** Crimes such as murder that are universally condemned.

**_mala prohibita_** "Prohibited evil."

**_mala prohibita_ offenses** Crimes that are wrong because the law declares them to be wrong.

**malice aforethought** The mental predetermination to commit an illegal act.

**malicious mischief** The crime of willful destruction of the personal property of another.

**mandatory child restraint laws** Laws requiring that children below a specified age be restrained by approved safety devices when riding in automobiles.

**mandatory minimum sentence** A sentence in which the minimum duration of incarceration is specified by law.

**mandatory seat belt laws** Laws requiring automobile drivers and passengers to wear seat belts.

**manifest necessity** That which is clearly or obviously necessary or essential.

**manslaughter** The crime of unlawfully killing another person without malice.

**marital exception** The traditional common-law principle that a husband could not be guilty of raping his wife.

**marital privilege** The privilege of married persons not to be compelled to testify against each other.

**maximum security prisons** Prisons designed to minimize the movement and maximize the surveillance and control of inmates.

**mayhem** At common law, the crime of injuring someone so as to render that person less able to fight.

**Megan's law** Name applied to statutes that require convicted sex offenders, upon release from prison, to register with local law enforcement agencies (named in memory of Megan Kanka, who died in 1994 at the hands of a released offender).

**_mens rea_** "Guilty mind"; criminal intent.

**Migratory Bird Conservation Act** Act of Congress protecting certain species of migratory birds from hunting within the United States and its territories.

**minimum security facilities** Prisons and jails that offer inmates the most freedom of movement within the least secure environment.

***Miranda* warning** Based on the Supreme Court's decision in *Miranda v. Arizona* (1966), this warning is given by police to individuals who are taken into custody before they are interrogated. The warning informs persons in custody that they have the right to remain silent and to have a lawyer present during questioning, and that anything they say can and will be used against them in a court of law.

**miscarriage of justice** Decision of a court that is inconsistent with the substantial rights of a party to a case.

**misdemeanor** A minor offense usually punishable by fine or imprisonment for less than one year.

**misprision of felony** The crime of concealing a felony committed by another.

**misrepresentation** An untrue statement of fact made to induce action.

**mistake of law** An erroneous opinion of legal principles applied to a set of facts.

**mitigating factors** Circumstances or factors that tend to lessen culpability.

**Model Penal Code (MPC)** Published by the American Law Institute (ALI), the MPC consists of general provisions concerning criminal liability, sentences, defenses, and definitions of specific crimes. The MPC is not law; rather, it is designed to serve as a model code of criminal law for all states.

**monetary fines** Sums of money that offenders are required to pay as punishment for the commission of crimes.

**money laundering** The offense of disguising illegal income to make it appear legitimate.

**motion for a new trial** A formal request made to a trial court to hold a new trial in a particular case that has already been adjudicated.

**motion for rehearing** A formal request made to a court of law to convene another hearing in a case in which the court has already ruled.

**motion to dismiss** A formal request to a trial court to dismiss the criminal charges against the defendant.

**motive** A person's conscious reason for acting.

**motor vehicle offenses** Minor crimes or infractions involving the operation of motor vehicles; see rules of the road.

**motor vehicle violations** See motor vehicle offenses.

**necessity** A condition that compels or requires a certain course of action.

**negative defense** Any criminal defense not required to be specifically pled.

**no bill** "Not found"; conclusion of a grand jury that declines to return an indictment.

**no contest plea** (Also called a plea of *nolo contendere*). A defendant's plea to a criminal charge that, although it is not an admission of guilt, generally has the same effect as a plea of guilty. A no contest plea is usually not admissible in evidence in a subsequent civil suit.

**noise ordinances** Local laws restricting the making of noise.

***nolle prosequi*** A formal entry by a prosecutor who declines to proceed further in the prosecution of an offense; commonly called a *nol pros*.

***nolo contendere*** See no contest plea.

**noncapital crimes** Crimes that do not carry the ultimate penalty, whether death or life in prison with no possibility of parole.

**nondeadly force** Force that does not result in death.

**not guilty by reason of insanity** A plea that admits criminal conduct but raises the insanity defense.

**notice of appeal** Document filed notifying an appellate court of an appeal from a judgment of a lower court.

**novel and innovative defenses** New defenses based on heretofore unaccepted principles of criminal responsibility.

**nuisance** An unlawful or unreasonable use of a person's property that results in an injury to another or to the public.

***nullen crimen, nulla poena, sine lege*** "There is no crime, there is no punishment, without law." Refers to the doctrine that one cannot be found guilty of a crime unless there is a violation of an existing provision of law defining the applicable criminal conduct.

**numbers racket** A common form of illegal gambling in which one places a bet on a number with the hope that it will correspond to a preselected number.

**objective test** A legal test based on external circumstances rather than the perceptions or intentions of an individual actor.

**objective test for the use of deadly force** Under this test, the judge or jury places themselves in the shoes of a hypothetical reasonable and prudent person to determine whether a defendant's use of deadly force was permissible.

**objective test of entrapment** Under this approach to determining whether police engaged in entrapment, a court inquires whether the police methods were so improper that they were likely to induce or ensnare a reasonable person into committing a crime.

**obscenity** Explicit sexual material that is patently offensive, appeals to a prurient or unnatural interest in sex, and lacks serious scientific, artistic, or literary content.

**obstruction of justice** The crime of impeding or preventing law enforcement or the administration of justice.

**one year and a day rule** A common-law rule that to convict a defendant of homicide, not more than a year and a day can intervene from the defendant's criminal act to the death of the victim.

**open fields doctrine** The doctrine that the Fourth Amendment does not apply to the open fields around a home, even if these open fields are private property.

**open public trial** A trial that is held in public and is open to spectators.

**opening statement** A prosecutor's or defense lawyer's initial statement to the judge or jury in a trial.

**opinion evidence** Testimony in which the witness expresses an opinion, as distinct from expressing knowledge of specific facts.

**opinion of the court** The opinion expressing the views of the majority of judges participating in a judicial decision.

**oral argument** Verbal presentation made to an appellate court in an attempt to persuade the court to affirm, reverse, or modify a lower court decision.

**order maintenance** The police officer's function of keeping the peace, as distinct from enforcement of the law.

**ordinance** An enactment of a local governing body such as a city council or commission.

**organized crime** Syndicates involved in racketeering and other criminal activities.

**Organized Crime Control Act of 1970** Federal law dealing with organized crime. Title IX of the act is entitled "Racketeer Influenced and Corrupt Organizations" and is commonly referred to by the acronym RICO.

**overbreadth, doctrine of** Doctrine enabling a person to make a facial challenge to a law on the ground that the law might be applied in the future against activities protected by the First Amendment.

**overt act** A visible act by an individual.

**panhandling** Begging for money in public.

**pardon** An executive action that mitigates or sets aside punishment for a crime.

*parens patriae* "The parent of the country." Refers to the role of the state as the guardian of minors or other legally disabled persons.

**Parental Kidnapping Prevention Act (PKPA)** A federal act adopted in 1980 designed to prevent jurisdictional conflicts over child custody matters. The primary goal of the statute is to reduce any incentive for parental child snatching.

**parole** Conditional release from jail or prison of a person who has served part of his or her sentence.

**parole revocation hearing** An administrative hearing held for the purpose of determining whether an offender's parole should be revoked.

**partial birth abortion** A method of abortion in which the fetus is partially delivered before its life is terminated and it is removed from the mother's body.

**pat-down search** A manual search by a police officer of the exterior of a suspect's outer garments.

**patent** A government grant of the right to exclude others from producing or using a discovery or invention for a certain period of time.

**patently offensive** That which is obviously offensive or disgusting.

**pattern of racketeering** To obtain a conviction under the federal RICO statute, the government must establish the defendant's involvement in a "pattern of racketeering" that requires proof of at least two predicate acts of racketeering having occurred within a period of ten years, excluding any period of imprisonment.

**pen register** Device that enables law enforcement to obtain the numbers that have been dialed by use of a specific telephone instrument.

**penalty enhancement statutes** Sentencing laws that provide for increased penalties when certain conditions were present in crimes—for example, the racial motivations of the perpetrator.

**pendency of the appeal** The period after an appeal is filed but before the appeal is adjudicated.

**penitentiary** Prison.

*per curiam* **opinion** An opinion rendered "by the court" as distinct from one attributed to one or more judges.

**peremptory challenge** An objection to the selection of a prospective juror in which the attorney making the challenge is not required to state the reason for the objection.

**perjury** The crime of making a material false statement under oath.

**perjury by contradictory statements** Commission of the offense of perjury by a witness who makes conflicting statements under oath.

**petit (trial) jury** A trial jury, usually composed of either six or twelve persons.

**petit theft** Minor form of larceny; theft of property of sufficiently small value that the offense is classified as a misdemeanor.

**petitioner** A person who brings a petition before a court of law.

**petty (petit) offenses** Minor crimes for which fines or short jail terms are the only prescribed modes of punishment.

**photo pack** A collection of "mug shots" to be exhibited to a victim or witness in an attempt to identify the perpetrator of a crime.

*Pinkerton* **Rule** Rule enunciated by the Supreme Court in *Pinkerton v. United States* (1946) holding that a member of a conspiracy is liable for all offenses committed in furtherance of the conspiracy.

**plain meaning rule**  The judicial doctrine holding that if the meaning of a text is plain, a court may not interpret it but must simply apply it as written.

**plain view**  Readily visible to the naked eye.

**plain view doctrine**  The Fourth Amendment doctrine under which a police officer may seize evidence of a crime that is readily visible to the officer's naked eye as long as the officer is legally in the place where the evidence becomes visible.

**plea bargain**  An agreement between a defendant and a prosecutor whereby the defendant agrees to plead guilty in exchange for some concession (such as a reduction in the number of charges brought).

**plea of guilty**  A formal answer to a criminal charge in which the accused acknowledges guilt and waives the right to trial.

**plea of not guilty**  A formal answer to a criminal charge in which the accused denies guilt and thus exercises the right to a trial.

**poaching**  Taking of game illegally, either by hunting protected species, hunting out of season, hunting in areas in which hunting is prohibited, or violating restrictions as to the number or size of animals that may be taken.

**point source**  Any discernible, confined and discrete conveyance from which pollutants are or may be discharged.

**police deception**  Intentional deception by police in order to elicit incriminating statements from a suspect.

**police departments**  Organizations established by municipalities and sometimes states whose function is to enforce the criminal laws within their respective jurisdictions.

**police power**  The power of government to legislate to protect public health, safety, welfare, and morality.

**polling the jury**  Practice in which a trial judge asks each member of the jury whether he or she supports the jury's verdict.

**polygraph evidence**  Results of lie detector tests (generally inadmissible into evidence).

**pornography**  Material that appeals to the sexual impulse or appetite.

**possession**  The actual or constructive control or occupancy of real or personal property. See also actual possession; constructive possession.

**possession of burglar's tools**  The knowing control of instruments, machines, or substances designed to enable one to forcefully break into buildings or vaults in order to carry out the intent to steal or destroy property.

**postconviction relief**  Term applied to various mechanisms a defendant may use to challenge a conviction after other routes of appeal have been exhausted.

**power of contempt**  The authority of a court of law to punish someone who insults the court or flouts its authority.

**predicate acts**  Prior acts of racketeering used to demonstrate a pattern of racketeering in a RICO prosecution.

**preliminary hearing**  A hearing held to determine whether there is sufficient evidence to hold an accused for trial.

**premeditation**  Deliberate decision or plan to commit a crime.

**preparatory conduct**  Actions taken to prepare to commit a crime.

**preponderance of the evidence**  Evidence that has greater weight than countervailing evidence.

**presentence investigation**  An investigation held to aid the court in determining the appropriate punishment before sentencing a convicted criminal.

**presentence report**  A report containing the results of a presentence investigation.

**presumption of innocence**  In a criminal trial, the accused is presumed innocent until proven guilty.

**pretextual stop**  An incident in which police stop a suspicious vehicle on the pretext of a motor vehicle infraction.

**pretrial detention**  Holding a defendant in jail pending trial.

**pretrial discovery**  The process by which the defense and prosecution interrogate witnesses for the opposing party and gain access to the evidence possessed by the opposing party prior to trial.

**pretrial diversion program**  A program in which a first-time offender is afforded the opportunity to avoid criminal prosecution by participating in some specified treatment, counseling, or community service.

**pretrial motion**  A request for a ruling or an order before the commencement of a trial.

**pretrial release**  Release of a defendant on bail or personal recognizance pending adjudication of criminal charges.

**price fixing**  Sellers unlawfully entering into agreements as to the price of products or services.

**primary offense**  A motor vehicle offense that in and of itself justifies police stopping and citing or arresting a motorist.

**principal**  A perpetrator of or an aider and abettor in the commission of a crime (as distinguished from an accessory).

**principals**  People whose conduct involves direct participation in a crime.

**principle of legality**  The principle that there can be no crime or punishment in the absence of law.

**prison disciplinary measures** Steps taken by prison officials to punish prisoners for misconduct, largely accomplished by removing good-time credits that prisoners earn for exemplary behavior in prison.

**privacy, constitutional right of** Implied constitutional right allowing individuals to be free of government interference in intimate activities, especially those involving sex and reproduction.

**privacy, reasonable expectations of** Doctrine holding that the Fourth Amendment protects persons from official intrusions as long as they have a subjective expectation of privacy that society is prepared to accept.

**privileges** Rights extended to persons by virtue of law—for example, the right accorded to a spouse in not being required to testify against the other spouse.

**pro se defense** Representing oneself in a criminal case.

**probable cause** A reasonable ground for belief in certain alleged facts.

**probation** Conditional release of a convicted criminal in lieu of incarceration.

**procedural criminal law** The branch of the criminal law that deals with the processes by which crimes are investigated, prosecuted, and punished.

**profanity** Irreverence toward sacred things; foul language.

**pronouncement of sentence** Formal announcement of a criminal punishment by a trial judge.

**proof beyond a reasonable doubt** The standard of proof in a criminal trial or a juvenile delinquency hearing.

**proportionality** The degree to which a particular punishment matches the seriousness of a crime or matches the penalty other offenders have received for the same crime.

**prosecutor** A public official empowered to initiate criminal charges and conduct prosecutions.

**prosecutor's information** An accusatorial document filed under oath by a prosecutor charging a person with one or more violations of the criminal law; similar to an indictment issued by a grand jury.

**prosecutorial discretion** The leeway afforded to prosecutors in deciding whether or not to bring charges and to engage in plea bargaining.

**prosecutorial immunity** A prosecutor's legal shield against civil suits stemming from his or her official actions.

**prostitution** The practice of selling sexual favors.

**provocation** Refers to conduct that prompts another person to react through criminal conduct.

**proximate cause** The cause that is nearest to a given effect in a causal relationship.

**prurient interest** An excessive or unnatural interest in sex.

**public defender** An attorney responsible for defending indigent persons charged with crimes.

**public drunkenness** The offense of appearing in public while intoxicated.

**public forum** A public space generally acknowledged as appropriate for public assemblies or expressions of views.

**public health** Refers to services designed to protect society from diseases and toxins.

**public indecency** Vulgar, lewd, immoral, or obscene acts committed in public that are defined as offensive by law in accordance with constitutional standards.

**public safety exception** Exception to the requirement that police officers promptly inform suspects taken into custody of their rights to remain silent and have an attorney present during questioning. Under the public safety exception, police may ask suspects questions motivated by a desire to protect public safety without jeopardizing the admissibility of suspects' answers to those questions or subsequent statements.

**punitive isolation** Solitary confinement of a person who is incarcerated.

**Pure Food, Drug, and Cosmetic Act** Federal law that prohibits traffic in food, drugs, and cosmetics prepared or handled under unsanitary circumstances or under conditions that render them injurious to health.

**putting witnesses under the rule** Placing witnesses under the traditional rule that requires them to remain outside the courtroom except when testifying.

**Quiet Communities Act** Federal law enacted in 1978 to protect the environment against noise pollution.

**racial profiling** Practice of singling out members of minority groups by law enforcement officers.

**racially based peremptory challenges** Peremptory challenges to prospective jurors that are based solely on racial animus or racial stereotypes.

**Racketeer Influenced and Corrupt Organizations (RICO)** A federal law enacted in 1970 imposing civil and criminal liability where two or more acts of racketeering show a pattern of criminal activity carried on by an enterprise. (Many states now have adopted RICO laws.)

**rape shield law** A law that protects the identity of a rape victim or prevents disclosure of a victim's sexual history.

**rape trauma syndrome** A recurring pattern of physical and emotional symptoms experienced by rape victims.

**rational basis test** The judicial requirement that legislation must be rationally related to a legitimate government objective in order to survive constitutional challenge.

**real evidence** Refers to maps, blood samples, X-rays, photographs, stolen goods, fingerprints, knives, guns, and other tangible items introduced into evidence.

**reasonable doubt standard** Standard used by a judge or jury to determine whether criminal charges against a defendant have been proven. The Supreme Court's decision, *In re Winship* (1970), adopted this historic standard by ruling that the Fourteenth Amendment requires the prosecution to establish the elements of a criminal charge beyond a reasonable doubt.

**reasonable expectation of privacy** A person's expectations of privacy that society is prepared to recognize as reasonable and legitimate.

**reasonable force** The maximum degree of force that is necessary to accomplish a lawful purpose.

**reasonable suspicion** A police officer's belief based on all relevant circumstances that criminal activity is afoot.

**rebuttal witnesses** Witnesses called to dispute the testimony of the opposing party's witnesses.

**recantation** The withdrawal or repudiation of previous statements. In some instances, a person who has lied under oath is permitted to recant to avoid being charged with perjury.

**receiving stolen property** Knowingly receiving possession and control of personal property belonging to another with the intent to permanently deprive the owner of possession of such property.

**recklessly** Without regard to consequences.

**redaction** Editing out portions of a transcript in order to maintain secrecy of someone's identity or other information.

**regulatory offenses** Strict-liability criminal offenses dealing with public health and the environment.

**rehabilitation** Restoring someone or something to its former status; a justification for punishment emphasizing reform rather than retribution.

**release on personal recognizance** Pretrial release of a defendant based solely on the defendant's promise to appear for future court dates.

**remand** To send back, usually with instructions.

**reply brief** A brief submitted by an appellant in response to an appellee's answer brief.

**reporters** Books containing judicial decisions and accompanying opinions.

**request for information or identification** A police-citizen encounter in which the police officer requests the citizen to provide identification or provide certain information.

**resisting arrest** The crime of obstructing or opposing a police officer making an arrest.

**Resource Conservation and Recovery Act (RCRA)** Enacted in 1976, RCRA is the major federal law dealing with the transportation, storage, and disposal of hazardous waste.

**respondent** A person asked to respond to a lawsuit or writ.

**responsible corporate officer** A person holding a supervisory position in an organization who may be subject to criminal liability for regulatory offenses committed by subordinates.

**restitution** The act of compensating someone for losses suffered.

**retreat rule** The common-law requirement that a person being attacked "retreat to the wall" before using deadly force in self-defense.

**retribution** Something demanded as payment or revenge from one who has committed a criminal offense; the theory of punishment that stresses just deserts.

**retroactive** Having an effect on things or actions in the past.

**reverse** To set aside a decision on appeal.

**RICO** See Racketeer Influenced and Corrupt Organizations.

**right from wrong test** See *M'Naghten* Rule.

**right of allocution** The right of a criminal defendant to make a statement on his or her own behalf before the sentence is pronounced.

**right of confrontation** The right to face one's accusers in a criminal case.

**right of cross-examination** The right to question witnesses for the opposing side in a criminal trial.

**right of privacy** Constitutional right to engage in intimate personal conduct or make fundamental life decisions without interference by the government.

**right to a speedy trial** Constitutional right to have an open public trial conducted without unreasonable delay.

**right to counsel** (1) The right to retain an attorney to represent oneself in court; (2) the right of an indigent person to have an attorney provided at public expense.

**right to die** Controversial "right" to terminate one's own life under certain circumstances.

**right to keep and bear arms** Right to possess certain weapons, protected against federal infringement by the Second Amendment to the U.S. Constitution.

**right to refuse medical treatment** The right of a patient—or patient's surrogate in some instances—to refuse to allow doctors to administer medical treatment.

**riot** A public disturbance involving acts of violence, usually by three or more persons.

**Rivers and Harbors Act** An 1899 act of Congress making it a misdemeanor to discharge refuse into the navigable waters of the United States.

**roadblocks** Barriers set up by police to stop motorists.

**robbery** The crime of taking money or property from a person against that person's will by means of force or intimidation.

**rout** At common law, a disturbance of the peace similar to a riot but without carrying out the intended purpose.

**rule of four** U.S. Supreme Court rule whereby the Court grants certiorari only on the agreement of at least four justices.

**rule of law** The idea that law, not the discretion of officials, should govern public affairs.

**rules of evidence** Legal rules governing the admissibility of evidence at trial.

**rules of procedure** Rules promulgated by courts of law under constitutional or statutory authority governing procedures for trials and other judicial proceedings.

**rules of statutory interpretation** Rules developed by courts to determine the meaning of legislative acts.

**rules of the road** Rules for the operation of motor vehicles on the public streets.

**sabotage** The crime of infiltrating and destroying a nation's war-making capabilities.

**same elements test** Test that bars separate punishment for offenses that have the same elements or for one offense that includes or is included in another offense.

**same evidence test** A test applicable to the Double Jeopardy Clause of the Fifth Amendment. If to establish an essential element of an offense charged the government will prove conduct that constitutes an offense for which the defendant has already been prosecuted, a second prosecution is barred.

**scientific evidence** Evidence obtained through scientific and technological innovations.

**scope of an agent's authority** In white-collar crime cases, the scope of an agent's authority depends on whether the commission of the offense was authorized, requested, commanded, performed, or recklessly tolerated by the board of directors or by a high managerial agent acting in behalf of the corporation within the scope of his or her office or employment.

**search** Inspection; attempt to locate a particular person or object.

**search incident to a lawful arrest** Search of a person placed under arrest and the area within the arrestee's grasp and control.

**secondary offense** An offense that does not in and of itself justify police stopping and citing a motorist. Police can issue a citation for a secondary offense only if they have stopped a driver for a primary offense.

**second-degree murder** Typically refers to a killing perpetrated by any act imminently dangerous to another and evincing a depraved mind regardless of human life, although without any premeditated design to effect the death of any particular individual.

**Securities and Exchange Act** The 1934 act of Congress regulating the sale of securities in interstate commerce.

**sedition** The crime of advocating or working toward the violent overthrow of one's own government.

**seduction** The crime of inducing a woman to have sexual intercourse outside of wedlock on the promise of marriage.

**seizure** Action of police in taking possession or control of property or persons.

**selective prosecution** Singling out defendants for prosecution on the basis of race, religion, or other impermissible classifications.

**self-defense** The protection of one's person against an attack.

**self-representation** See *pro se* defense.

**sentencing guidelines** Legislative guidelines mandating that sentencing conform to guidelines absent a compelling reason for departing from them.

**sentencing hearing** A hearing held by a trial court before the sentence is pronounced.

**separation of powers** Constitutional assignment of legislative, executive, and judicial powers to different branches of government.

**sequestration** Holding jurors incommunicado during trial and deliberations.

**session laws** Collection of laws enacted during a particular legislative session.

**severance of charges** Conducting multiple trials for multiple charges, as distinct from joinder, which refers to trying all charged offenses at once. Where two or more related offenses are charged in a single indictment or information, the trial judge often grants a severance of the charges on the motion of either the defense or the prosecution.

**sexual contact** The intentional touching of the victim's intimate parts or the intentional touching of the clothing covering the immediate area of the victim's intimate parts, if that intentional touching can reasonably be construed as being for the purpose of sexual arousal or gratification.

**sexual penetration** Sexual intercourse, cunnilingus, fellatio, anal intercourse, or any other intrusion, however slight, of any part of a person's body or by any object into the genital or anal openings of another person's body.

**sheriff** The chief law enforcement officer of the county.

**Sherman Antitrust Act** A federal statute prohibiting any contract, combination, or conspiracy in restraint of trade. The act is designed to protect and preserve a system of free and open competition. Its scope is broad and reaches individuals and entities in profit and nonprofit activities as well as local governments and educational institutions.

**showup** An event in which a crime victim is taken to see a suspect to make an identification.

**similar fact evidence** Refers to evidence of facts similar to the facts in the crime charged. The test of admissibility is whether such evidence is relevant and has a probative value in establishing a material issue. Under some limited circumstances, evidence of other crimes or conduct similar to that charged against the defendant may be admitted in evidence in a criminal prosecution.

**simple kidnapping** The abduction of another person without a demand for ransom.

**skip tracer** A person who tracks down alleged offenders who have fled to avoid prosecution. Also known as bounty hunter.

**sobriety checkpoints** Roadblocks set up for the purpose of administering field sobriety tests to motorists who appear to be intoxicated.

**sodomy** Oral or anal sex between persons or sex between a person and an animal, the latter commonly referred to as bestiality.

**solicitation** The inchoate offense of requesting or encouraging someone to engage in illegal conduct.

**special agents** Officers of the Federal Bureau of Investigation with the power to make arrests and use force in the enforcement of federal law.

**specific intent** The mental purpose to accomplish a specific act prohibited by law.

**specific-intent statute** A statute defining criminal conduct in which the offender must harbor a specific intent to accomplish a prohibited result.

**specific objection** Counsel's objection to a question posed to a witness by opposing trial counsel where a specific reason is given for the objection—for example, that the question calls for hearsay evidence.

**speedy and public trial** An open and public criminal trial held without unreasonable delay.

**Speedy Trial Act of 1974** This federal statute provides specific time limits for pretrial and trial procedures in the federal courts. For example, an indictment must be filed within thirty days of arrest, and trial must commence within seventy days after the indictment.

**sports bribery** Offering anything of value to a participant or official in an amateur or professional athletic contest to vary his or her performance.

**spousal abuse** Physical, emotional, or sexual abuse of one's husband or wife.

**stalking** Following or placing a person under surveillance and threatening that person with bodily harm, sexual assault, confinement, or restraint, or placing that person in reasonable fear of bodily harm, sexual assault, confinement, or restraint.

**standby counsel** An attorney appointed to assist an indigent defendant who elects to represent himself or herself at trial.

**standing** The right to initiate a legal action or challenge based on the fact that one has suffered or is likely to suffer a real and substantial injury.

***stare decisis*** The doctrine of deciding cases based on precedent.

**state supreme court** The highest appellate court of a state.

**state's attorney** A state prosecutor.

**status** One's condition or situation.

**status offenses** Noncriminal conduct on the part of juveniles that may subject juveniles to the authority of a juvenile court.

**statute** A generally applicable law enacted by a legislature.

**statute of limitations** A law proscribing prosecutions for specific crimes after specified periods of time.

**statutory rape** The strict liability offense of having sexual intercourse with a minor, irrespective of the minor's consent.

**stop-and-frisk** An encounter between a police officer and a suspect during which the latter is temporarily detained and subjected to a pat-down search for weapons.

**strict judicial scrutiny** Judicial review of government action or policy in which the ordinary presumption of constitutionality is reversed. This standard is applied in review of laws and involving suspect classifications, for example, race and voting rights.

**strict liability** Criminal responsibility based solely on the commission of a prohibited act.

**strict liability offenses** Offenses that do not require proof of the defendant's intent.

**strip searches** Searches of suspects' or prisoners' private parts.

**structuring** Engaging in multiple smaller transactions to avoid currency reporting requirements.

**subjective standard of reasonableness** A test used by courts to determine whether it was appropriate for a defendant to use deadly force in self-defense. Under this approach, the jury is asked to place itself in the shoes of the defendant.

**subjective test of entrapment** Whether the defendant's criminal intent originated in the mind of the police officer or the defendant was predisposed to commit the offense.

**subornation of perjury** The crime of procuring someone to lie under oath.

**subpoena** A judicial order to appear at a certain place and time to give testimony.

**substantial capacity test** The doctrine that a person is not responsible for criminal conduct if at the time of such conduct, as a result of mental disease or defect, the person lacks substantial capacity either to appreciate the wrongfulness of his or her conduct or to conform his or her conduct to the requirements of the law.

**substantial federal question** A significant legal question pertaining to the U.S. Constitution, a federal statute, treaty, regulation, or judicial interpretation of any of the foregoing.

**substantial step** A significant step toward completion of an intended result.

**substantive criminal law** That branch of the criminal law that defines criminal offenses and defenses and specifies criminal punishments.

**suicide** The intentional taking of a person's own life.

**suppression doctrine** See exclusionary rule.

**suppression of evidence** See exclusionary rule.

**surety bond** A sum of money or property that is posted or guaranteed by a party, usually an insurer, to ensure the future court appearance of another person.

**suspended sentence** Trial court's decision to place a defendant on probation or under community control instead of imposing an announced sentence on the condition that the original sentence may be imposed if the defendant violates the conditions of the suspended sentence.

**sworn officers** Law enforcement officers sworn to uphold the Constitution and laws of the United States and of their own states.

**symbolic speech** Expression by symbols, gestures, and so forth.

**tangible property** Property that has physical form, substance, and value in itself.

**target crime** A crime that is the object of a conspiracy. For example, in conspiracy to traffic in illegal drugs, the offense of trafficking in illegal drugs is the target crime.

**tax fraud** False or deceptive conduct performed with the intent of violating revenue laws, especially the Internal Revenue Code.

**terrorism** Crime of inflicting terror on a population through the indiscriminate killing of people and destruction of property, often done with explosive devices.

**Terry-stop** See stop-and-frisk.

**testimonial evidence** Evidence received by a court from witnesses who have testified under oath.

**texting while driving** The offense of using a cell phone or other handheld device to send text messages or emails while operating a motor vehicle.

**theft of computer services** Stealing software, data, computer access codes, computer time, and so on.

**third-party consent** Consent, usually to a search, given by a person on behalf of another—for example, a college roommate who allows the police to search his or her roommate's effects.

**three strikes and you're out** Popular term for a statute that provides for mandatory life imprisonment for a convicted felon who has been previously convicted of two or more serious felonies.

**three strikes laws** Statutes that provide for mandatory life imprisonment for a convicted felon who has been previously convicted of two or more serious felonies.

**time, place, and manner regulations** Government limitations on the time, place, and manner of expressive activities.

**tolling** Ceasing. For example, one who conceals himself or herself from the authorities generally causes a tolling of the statutes of limitation on the prosecution of a crime.

**tort** A wrong or injury other than a breach of contract for which the remedy is a civil suit for damages.

**totality of circumstances** Circumstances considered in the aggregate as opposed to individually.

**Toxic Substances Control Act** A federal statute authorizing the Environmental Protection Agency to prohibit the manufacture, distribution, or use of chemicals that present unreasonable risks to the environment and to regulate the disposal of such chemicals.

**trade secret** A formula, pattern, physical device, idea, process, compilation of information, or other information that provides a business with a competitive advantage.

**trademark** A distinctive word, phrase, or graphic symbol used to distinguish a commercial product.

**trademark counterfeiting** The offense of using a registered trademark to falsely market a product or service.

**traffic citation** A summons to appear in court to answer an allegation of a motor vehicle violation such as speeding.

**traffic court** Court of limited jurisdiction whose main function is the adjudication of traffic offenses and other minor misdemeanors.

**transactional immunity** A grant of immunity applying to offenses that a witness's testimony relates to.

**trap and trace device** Device that captures incoming electronic impulses that identify the originating number of a device from which an electronic communication was transmitted.

**treason** The crime of making war against one's own government or giving aid and comfort to its enemies.

**treatment programs** Programs designed to rehabilitate an offender.

**trial courts** Judicial tribunals usually presided over by one judge who conducts proceedings and trials in civil and criminal cases with or without a jury.

**trial de novo** "A new trial." Refers to trial court review of convictions for minor offenses by courts of limited jurisdiction by conducting a new trial instead of merely reviewing the record of the initial trial.

**true bill** An indictment handed down by a grand jury.

**truth in sentencing laws** Laws requiring that people sentenced to prison serve a specified proportion of their sentences.

**two-witness rule** A requirement that to prove a defendant guilty of perjury, the prosecution must prove the falsity of the defendant's statements either by two witnesses or by one witness and corroborating documents or circumstances.

**ultra vires** Beyond the scope of a prescribed authority.

**unconstitutional as applied** Declaration by a court of law that a statute is invalid insofar as it is enforced in some particular context.

**unconstitutional per se** A statute that is unconstitutional under any given circumstances.

**Uniform Child Custody Jurisdiction Act (UCCJA)** A law in force in all fifty states that generally continues jurisdiction for custody of children in the home or resident state of the child.

**Uniform Code of Military Justice (UCMJ)** A code of laws enacted by Congress that governs military service personnel and defines the procedural and evidentiary requirements in military law and the substantive criminal offenses and punishments.

**Uniform Victims of Crime Act** A law proposed by the Uniform Law Commission designed to provide uniform rights and procedures concerning crime victims.

**United States Code Annotated (U.S.C.A.)** An annotated version of the United States Code.

**U.S. Attorneys** Attorneys appointed by the president with consent of the U.S. Senate to prosecute federal crimes in a specific geographical area of the United States.

**U.S. Code** The comprehensive and systematic collection of federal laws currently in effect.

**U.S. Congress** The national legislature of the United States.

**U.S. Court of Appeals for the Armed Forces** See Court of Appeals for the Armed Forces. A court composed of civilian judges for review of court-martial convictions from the various branches of the military forces.

**U.S. Courts of Appeals** The twelve intermediate appellate courts of appeals in the federal system that sit in specified geographical areas of the United States and in which panels of appellate judges hear appeals in civil and criminal cases, primarily from the U.S. District Courts.

**U.S. District Courts** The principal trial courts in the federal system that sit in ninety-four districts. Usually, one judge hears proceedings and trials in civil and criminal cases.

**U.S. Marshals** Service Law enforcement officers of the U.S. Department of Justice who are responsible for enforcing federal laws, enforcing federal court decisions, and effecting the transfer of federal prisoners.

**U.S. Sentencing Commission** A federal body that proposes guideline sentences for defendants convicted of federal crimes.

**U.S. Supreme Court** The highest court in the United States, consisting of nine justices, that has jurisdiction to review, by appeal or writ of certiorari, the decisions of lower federal courts and many decisions of the highest courts of each state.

**unlawful assembly** A group of individuals, usually five or more, assembled to commit an unlawful act or to commit a lawful act in an unlawful manner.

**USA PATRIOT Act** Controversial act of Congress enacted in 2001 to strengthen the federal government's efforts to combat terrorism.

**use immunity** A grant of immunity that forbids prosecutors from using immunized testimony as evidence in criminal prosecutions.

**uttering a forged instrument** The crime of passing a false or worthless instrument, such as a check, with the intent to defraud or injure the recipient.

**vagrancy** The common-law offense of going about without any visible means of support.

**vagueness doctrine** Doctrine of constitutional law holding unconstitutional (as a violation of due process) legislation that fails to clearly inform the person what is required or proscribed.

**vandalism** The willful destruction of the property of another person.

**vehicular homicide** Homicide resulting from the unlawful and negligent operation of a motor vehicle.

**venire** The group of citizens from whom a jury is chosen in a given case.

**venue** The location of a trial or hearing.

**verdict** The formal decision rendered by a jury in a civil or criminal trial.

**vice** Conduct widely considered immoral such as prostitution, gambling, and drug abuse.

**victim** A person who is the object of a crime or tort.

**victim impact evidence** Evidence relating to the physical, economic, and psychological impact that a crime has on the victim or victim's family.

**victim impact statement** Statement read into the record during the sentencing phase of a criminal trial to inform the court about the impact of the crime on the victim or victim's family.

**victims' rights** Refers to the various rights possessed by victims of crimes. See Uniform Victims of Crime Act.

**Violent Crime Control and Law Enforcement Act of 1994** Known generally as the Crime Bill or the Violent Crime Act, this federal statute dramatically increased the number of federal crimes eligible for the death penalty, authorized federal grants for drug court programs that include court-supervised drug treatment, and created the offense of interstate domestic violence.

**voice exemplar** A sample of a person's voice, usually taken by police for the purpose of identifying a suspect.

**void for vagueness** See vagueness doctrine.

*voir dire* "To speak the truth." The process by which prospective jurors are questioned by counsel and/or the court before being selected to serve on a jury.

**voluntariness of a confession** The quality of a confession having been freely given.

**voluntary intoxication** The state of becoming drunk or intoxicated of one's own free will.

**voluntary manslaughter** The intentional killing of a human without malice or premeditation and usually occurring during a sudden quarrel or in the heat of passion.

**voyeurism** The practice of seeking sexual gratification by observing the naked bodies or sexual acts of others, usually from a hidden vantage point.

**waiver of *Miranda* rights** A known relinquishment of the right to remain silent and/or have counsel present during police interrogation.

**warrant** A judicial writ or order directed to a law enforcement officer authorizing the doing of a specified act, such as an arrest or a search.

**warrantless arrest** An arrest made by police who do not possess an arrest warrant.

**warrantless searches** Searches made by police who do not possess search warrants.

**weapons of mass destruction** Weapons designed to kill large numbers of people and/or damage extensive areas. Includes nuclear, radiological, biological, and chemical weapons.

**weapons offenses** Violations of laws restricting or prohibiting the manufacture, sale, transfer, possession, or use of certain firearms.

**weight of the evidence** The balance or preponderance of the evidence. Weight of the evidence is to be distinguished from "legal sufficiency of the evidence," which is the concern of an appellate court.

**well-regulated Militia** This phrase, from the Second Amendment to the U.S. Constitution, refers to a citizen army subject to government regulations. In the early history of the United States, the militia was the set of able-bodied men who could be pressed into military service by the governor of the state. The National Guard is the modern counterpart.

**Wharton's Rule** Named after Francis Wharton, a well-known commentator on criminal law, this rule holds that two people cannot conspire to commit a crime such as adultery, incest, or bigamy inasmuch as these offenses involve only two participants.

**white-collar crimes** Economic offenses characterized by deception or abuse of trust and often involving the use of computers or other modern technologies.

**wire fraud** A fraudulent scheme that uses interstate television, radio, or wire communications.

**wiretap order** A court order permitting electronic surveillance for a limited period.

**wiretapping** The use of highly sensitive electronic devices designed to intercept electronic communications.

**worthless check statutes** Laws making it an offense to knowingly pass a worthless check.

**writ** An order issued by a court of law requiring the performance of some specific act.

**writ of certiorari** See certiorari.

**writ of error** A writ issued by an appellate court for the purpose of correcting an error revealed in the record of a lower court proceeding.

**writ of habeas corpus** See habeas corpus.

**zoning ordinance** A local law regulating the use of land.

# Case Index

# Subject Index